Helen Kate Rogers Furness

A Concordance to Shakespeare's Poems
An Index to Every Word Contained

ISBN/EAN: 9783337063689

Printed in Europe, USA, Canada, Australia, Japan

Cover: Foto ©Thomas Meinert / pixelio.de

More available books at **www.hansebooks.com**

A

CONCORDANCE

TO

SHAKESPEARE'S POEMS:

AN INDEX

TO EVERY WORD THEREIN CONTAINED

BY

MRS HORACE HOWARD FURNESS

'—— TO YOUR AUDIT COMES
THEIR DISTRACT PARCELS IN COMBINED SUMS.'

[*SECOND EDITION*]

PHILADELPHIA
J. B. LIPPINCOTT COMPANY
LONDON: 15 RUSSELL STREET, COVENT GARDEN

PREFACE

As it is impossible to limit the purposes for which the language of Shakespeare may be studied, or to say that the time will not come, if it has not already, when his use of every part of speech, down to the humblest conjunction, will be criticised with as much nicety as has been bestowed upon Greek and Latin authors, it seems to me that, in the selection of words to be recorded, no discretionary powers should be granted to the 'harmless drudge' compiling a Concordance. Within a year or two a German scholar has published a pamphlet of some fifty pages on Shakespeare's use of the auxiliary verb *to do*, and ABBOTT's *Grammar* shows with what success the study of Shakespeare's language in its minutest particulars may be pursued. I have therefore cited in the following pages every word in his Poems.

I would not have it thought that any imperfection is hereby imputed to Mrs CLARKE's invaluable Concordance of the Dramas. The bulk of that work was a sufficient bar to the plan I have been enabled to follow in the lesser task which was before me.

Having adopted the rule of recording every word, I thought it a needless expenditure of space to insert in every instance the entire line in which a word occurs. I have given the clause in which the word stands and the number of the line, and then, that nothing may be wanting to the convenience of the student, the Poems themselves are reprinted at the end. If in any case the citations appear meagre, the original is instantly accessible.

Compound words, such as *seal-manual*, are entered under each word; but not compounds without a hyphen, such as *eyelid;* nor words not separated by a hyphen from their prefixes.

Such words as *'stonished*, *'mongst*, etc. are given under their unabbreviated forms also.

Where the same word has two or more meanings, such as *lie*, *light*, *wish*, etc., an Italic catchword indicates the change from one sense to another. I have not thus subdivided words when there were less than half a dozen instances of the word; nor have I thought it necessary to indicate purely grammatical distinctions. Such an attempt seems not properly to belong to a mere Verbal Index, and would, moreover, to be thorough, demand a familiarity with Shakespeare's use of language to which I can lay no claim.

I have not placed under a separate catchword the third person singular of verbs, lest I should be introducing subdivisions that would not compensate for the confusion that might arise, especially where there is a difference of spelling; and for the same reason I have not separated the singulars and plurals.

Where *and* is used as a copula of two nouns, both nouns are given.

I have followed the text of the Cambridge Edition, with the exception of some trifling deviations in punctuation.

As the pages are stereotyped, corrections can be made at any time of misprints, against which it seems that no human vigilance can guard, and I shall be grateful to the kindness that will notify me of them.

My special thanks are gladly given to Mr W. A. WHEELER, of *The Boston Public Library*, for the handsome way in which he placed at my disposal his MS. Concordance of these Poems. As my work was well advanced when his offer came, I have not availed myself of his kindness, yet it is none the less felt. The motto on the title-page is his witty suggestion.

H. K. F.

A

CONCORDANCE

TO

SHAKESPEARE'S POEMS

A

A—like a bold-faced suitor	*V A*	....	6
more lovely than a man	"	....	9
A thousand honey secrets	"	....	16
A summer's day will seem	"	....	23
to do a goddess good	"	....	28
in a dull disdain	"	....	33
on a ragged bough	"	....	37
murders with a kiss	"	....	54
as on a prey	"	....	63
how a bird lies tangled in a net	"	....	67
Rain added to a river	"	....	71
For to a pretty ear	"	....	74
with a more delight	"	....	78
Like a dive-dapper peering through a wave	"	....	86
but a kiss I beg	"	....	96
in a red-rose chain	"	....	110
like a fairy, trip	"	....	146
Like a nymph, with long	"	....	147
a spirit all compact of fire	"	....	149
with a lazy spright	"	....	181
and with a heavy, dark	"	....	182
made a shadow for thee	"	....	191
Art thou a woman's son	"	....	201
borne so hard a mind	"	....	203
Thing like a man	"	....	214
of a man's complexion	"	....	215
Doth provoke a pause	"	....	218
infold him like a band	"	....	225
I'll be a park	"	....	231
I am such a park	"	....	239
though a thousand bark	"	....	240
appears a pretty dimple	"	....	242
in a tomb so simple	"	....	244
needs a second striking	"	....	250
To love a cheek that smiles	"	....	252
from forth a copse	"	....	259
A breeding jennet	"	....	260
tied unto a tree	"	....	263
As from a furnace	"	....	274
Look, when a painter	"	....	289
a well-proportion'd steed	"	....	290
excel a common one	"	....	293
Look, what a horse should have	"	....	299
Save a proud rider on so proud a back	"	....	300
Stirring of a feather	"	....	302
To bid the wind a base	"	....	303

A

A—like a melancholy malcontent	*V A*	....	313
like a falling plume	"	....	314
Even as a dying coal	"	....	338
O, what a sight it was	"	....	343
like a lowly lover	"	....	350
O, what a war of looks	"	....	355
A lily prison'd in a gaol of snow	"	....	362
So white a friend engirts so white a foe	"	....	364
And I a man	"	....	369
Affection is a coal	"	....	387
How like a jade he stood	"	....	391
a leathern rein	"	....	392
a whiter hue than white	"	....	398
Unless it be a boar	"	....	410
it is a life in death	"	....	413
and all but with a breath	"	....	414
'Who wears a garment	"	....	415
where a heart is hard	"	....	426
'hast thou a tongue	"	....	427
Like a red morn	"	....	453
deadly bullet of a gun	"	....	461
A smile recures the wounding of a frown	"	....	465
'A thousand kisses buys	"	....	517
Such a trouble	"	....	522
you shall have a kiss	"	....	536
his neck, a sweet embrace	"	....	539
a desperate courage	"	....	556
Like a wild bird	"	....	560
like a pale-faced coward	"	....	569
not repel a lover	"	....	573
Whereat a sudden pale	"	....	589
deserved a greater fee	"	....	609
A churlish swine to gore	"	....	616
Like to a mortal butcher	"	....	618
he hath a battle set	"	....	619
And in a peaceful hour	"	....	652
with a thousand doubles	"	....	682
Are like a labyrinth	"	....	684
among a flock of sheep	"	....	685
with a herd of deer	"	....	689
far off upon a hill	"	....	697
and hear a little more	"	....	709
rob thee of a kiss	"	....	723
Steal a kiss, and die forsworn	"	....	726
but a swallowing grave	"	....	757
So fair a hope is slain	"	....	762

1

A—A mischief worse	V A	764
A false sound enter there	"	780
like a glutton dies	"	803
how a bright star	"	815
a late-embarked friend	"	818
dropp'd a precious jewel	"	824
begins a wailing note	"	835
a woeful ditty	"	836
There lives a son	"	863
hasteth to a myrtle grove	"	865
Like a milch doe	"	875
hounds are at a bay	"	877
in a trembling ecstasy	"	895
'tis a causeless fantasy	"	897
A second fear through all	"	903
A thousand spleens bear her a thousand ways	"	907
of a drunken brain	"	910
in a brake she finds a hound	"	913
bid thee crop a weed, thou pluck'st a flower	"	946
may a heavy groan	"	950
like a stormy day	"	965
A nurse's song ne'er pleased	"	974
felt a kind of fear	"	998
'how much a fool was I	"	1015
a weak and silly mind	"	1016
a merry horn	"	1025
Who, like a king	"	1043
gives a deadly groan	"	1044
looketh for a grave	"	1106
But by a kiss	"	1114
in his ears a heavy tale	"	1125
A thousand times	"	1130
in a breathing while	"	1142
the old become a child	"	1152
melted like a vapour	"	1166
A purple flower sprung up	"	1168
a more sweet-smelling sire	"	1178
to such a peerless dame	R L	21
enjoy'd but of a few	"	22
from a world of harms	"	28
proud issue of a king	"	37
of so rich a thing	"	39
in so false a foe	"	77
to find a stranger just	"	159
on a flint he softly smiteth	"	176
Whereat a waxen torch	"	178
to so pure a shrine	"	194
A martial man to be	"	200
a true respect should have	"	201
A dream, a breath, a froth of fleeting	"	212
a minute's mirth to wail a week	"	213
to get a toy	"	214
and in a desperate rage	"	219
with so black a deed	"	226
Who fears a sentence	"	244
Shall by a painted cloth	"	245
Which in a moment	"	250
like a virtuous deed	"	252
with so sweet a cheer	"	264
That now he vows a league	"	287
Unto a view so false	"	292
But with a pure appeal	"	293
Who with a lingering stay	"	328
To add a more rejoicing	"	332
Which with a yielding latch	"	339
Rushing from forth a cloud	"	373
A—with a greater light	R L	375
of a lawful kiss	"	387
Where like a virtuous monument	"	391
A pair of maiden worlds	"	408
like a foul usurper	"	412
Unto a greater uproar	"	427
such a dignity	"	437
in a thousand fears	"	456
Like to a new-kill'd bird	"	457
First, like a trumpet	"	470
To sound a parley	"	471
guarded with a sting	"	493
Which, like a falcon	"	506
is as a thought unacted	"	527
A little harm done to a great good	"	528
In a pure compound	"	531
Worse than a slavish wipe	"	537
Here with a cockatrice' dead-killing eye	"	540
and makes a pause	"	541
Like a white hind	"	543
Pleads, in a wilderness	"	544
But when a black-faced cloud	"	547
A swallowing gulf	"	557
a poor unseasonable doe	"	581
Myself a weakling	"	584
like a troubled ocean	"	589
than a stone thou art	"	593
a god, a king	"	601
once thou art a king	"	606
but a bawd	"	623
From a pure heart	"	625
how vile a spectacle	"	631
pay a daily debt	"	649
'a sea, a sovereign king	"	652
Thy sea within a puddle	"	657
so pure a bed	"	684
lost a dearer thing	"	687
force a further strife	"	689
Till, like a jade	"	707
Like to a bankrupt	"	711
A captive victor	"	730
of a guilty mind	"	735
He like a thievish dog	"	736
She like a wearied lamb	"	737
a heavy convertite	"	743
remains a hopeless cast-away	"	744
with a cunning brow	"	749
so pure a mind	"	761
be made a theme	"	822
a drone-like bee	"	836
a wandering wasp	"	839
in such a devil	"	847
to a public fast	"	891
to a ragged name	"	892
A thousand crosses	"	912
Sin ne'er gives a fee	"	913
of a lawful bed	"	938
the child a man, the man a child	"	954
a thousand thousand friends	"	963
a hideous shapeless devil	"	973
to live a loathed slave	"	984
a beggar's orts to crave	"	985
deathsman to so base a slave	"	1001
coming from a king	"	1002
force not argument a straw	"	1021
to end a hapless life	"	1045
seek a knife	"	1047
I was a loyal wife	"	1048

A—A badge of fame	R L	....	1054
A dying life	"	....	1055
a mountain spring that feeds a dale	"	....	1077
testy as a child	"	....	1094
in a sea of care	"	....	1100
like a gentle flood	"	....	1118
A woeful hostess	"	....	1125
will strain a tear	"	....	1131
And whiles against a thorn	"	....	1135
Will fix a sharp knife	"	....	1138
with a winding maze	"	....	1151
tries a merciless conclusion	"	....	1160
and sorts a sad look	"	....	1221
like a melting eye	"	....	1227
Who in a salt-waved ocean	"	....	1231
A pretty while	"	....	1233
semblance of a devil	"	....	1246
like a goodly champaign plain	"	....	1247
in a rough-grown grove	"	....	1249
abuse a body dead	"	....	1267
Till after a deep groan	"	....	1276
may be call'd a hell	"	....	1287
A letter to my lord	"	....	1293
a press of people at a door	"	....	1301
a part of woe	"	....	1327
'Tis but a part	"	....	1328
with a steadfast eye	"	....	1339
have a true respect	"	....	1347
a little while doth stay	"	....	1364
where hangs a piece	"	....	1366
A thousand lamentable objects	"	....	1373
a dry drop seem'd a weeping tear	"	....	1375
About him were a press	"	....	1408
A hand, a foot, a face, a leg, a head	"	....	1427
a kind of heavy fear	"	....	1435
To find a face	"	....	1444
in a body dead	"	....	1456
and not a tongue	"	....	1463
without a sound	"	....	1464
To plague a private sin	"	....	1484
like a heavy-hanging bell	"	....	1493
she sees a wretched image	"	....	1501
A brow unbent	"	....	1509
But, like a constant	"	....	1513
He entertain'd a show	"	....	1514
Into so bright a day	"	....	1518
a form lodged not a mind	"	....	1530
lurk in such a look	"	....	1535
a face should bear a wicked	"	....	1540
tear he falls a Trojan bleeds	"	....	1551
old acquaintance in a trance	"	....	1595
A stranger came	"	....	1620
A creeping creature with a flaming	"	....	1627
with so strong a fear	"	....	1647
his sorrows make a saw	"	....	1672
'tis a meritorious fair design	"	....	1692
While with a joyless smile	"	....	1711
Here with a sigh	"	....	1716
A harmful knife	"	....	1724
Who, like a late sack'd island	"	....	1740
a watery rigol goes	"	....	1745
Shows me a bare-boned death	"	....	1761
starts Collatine as from a dream	"	....	1772
to die with her a space	"	....	1776
Have served a dumb arrest	"	....	1780
self, supposed a fool	"	....	1819
to give thyself a blow.	"	....	1823
Making a famine	Son	1	7
WL. be a tatter'd weed	"	2	4
A—So great a sum of sums	Son	4	8
A liquid prisoner	"	5	10
unless thou get a son	"	7	11
to wet a widow's eye.	"	9	1
like a makeless wife	"	9	4
so fair a house fall	"	13	9
You had a father	"	13	11
but a little moment	"	15	2
do not you a mightier way	"	16	1
it is but as a tomb	"	17	3
be term'd a poet's rage	"	17	11
thee to a summer's day	"	18	1
all too short a date	"	18	4
A woman's face	"	20	1
A woman's gentle heart	"	20	3
A man in hue	"	20	7
And for a woman wert thou	"	20	9
Stirr'd by a painted beauty	"	21	2
Making a complement	"	21	5
For at a frown	"	23	8
After a thousand victories	"	25	10
a journey in my head	"	27	3
Intend a zealous	"	27	6
Which, like a jewel hung	"	27	11
many a thing I sought	"	30	3
of many a vanished sight	"	30	8
How many a holy	"	31	5
A dearer birth than this	"	32	11
Full many a glorious morning	"	33	1
such a beauteous day	"	34	1
such a salve can speak	"	34	7
a lawful plea commence	"	35	11
lives a separable spite	"	36	6
As a decrepit father	"	37	1
And by a part of all	"	37	12
O absence, what a torment	"	39	9
it is a greater grief	"	40	11
to break a twofold truth	"	41	12
A loss in love	"	42	4
are at a mortal war	"	46	1
A closet never pierced	"	46	6
A quest of thoughts	"	46	10
and heart a league is took	"	47	1
is famish'd for a look	"	47	3
doth share a part	"	47	8
thievish for a prize	"	48	14
he answers with a groan	"	50	11
have full as deep a dye	"	54	5
with a perpetual dullness	"	56	8
But, like a sad slave	"	57	11
So true a fool	"	57	13
burthen of a former child	"	59	4
with a backward look	"	59	5
For such a time	"	63	9
This thought is as a death	"	64	13
shall beauty hold a plea	"	65	3
no stronger than a flower	"	65	4
desert a beggar born	"	66	2
on a living brow	"	68	4
To live a second life	"	68	7
And him as for a map	"	68	13
A crow that flies	"	70	4
a pure unstained prime	"	70	8
conquest of a wretch's knife	"	74	11
As twixt a miser and his wealth	"	75	4
clean starved for a look	"	75	10
invention in a noted weed	"	76	6
To take a new acquaintance	"	77	12
grace a double majesty	"	78	8

A—travail of a worthier pen	*Son*	79	6
knowing a better spirit doth use	"	80	2
I am a worthless boat	"	80	11
but a common grave	"	81	7
a limit past my praise	"	82	6
tender of a poet's debt	"	83	4
How far a modern quill	"	83	7
and bring a tomb	"	83	12
And such a counterpart	"	84	11
beauteous blessings add a curse	"	84	13
Above a mortal pitch	"	86	6
as a dream doth flatter	"	87	13
In sleep a king	"	87	14
I can set down a story	"	88	6
will be a gainer too	"	88	9
To set a form	"	89	6
of a conquer'd woe	"	90	6
a windy night a rainy morrow	"	90	7
out a purposed overthrow	"	90	8
a joy above the rest	"	91	6
I see a better state	"	92	7
O, what a happy title	"	92	11
Like a deceived husband	"	93	2
Which, like a canker	"	95	2
but in a kind of praise	"	95	7
O, what a mansion	"	95	9
finger of a throned queen	"	96	5
If like a lamb	"	96	10
How like a winter	"	97	1
'tis with so dull a cheer	"	97	13
Hath put a spirit	"	98	3
A third nor red nor white	"	99	10
A vengeful canker eat him up	"	99	13
be a satire to decay	"	100	11
outlive a gilded tomb	"	101	11
a scope to show her pride	"	103	2
and there appears a face	"	103	6
like a dial-hand	"	104	9
in a wondrous excellence	"	105	6
Even such a beauty	"	106	8
forfeit to a confined doom	"	107	4
a motley to the view	"	110	2
A god in love	"	110	12
my name receives a brand	"	111	5
like a willing patient	"	111	9
had a perfect best	"	114	7
Love is a babe	"	115	13
found a kind of meetness	"	118	7
medicine a healthful state	"	118	11
you've pass'd a hell of time	"	120	6
And I, a tyrant	"	120	7
now becomes a fee	"	120	13
dressings of a former sight	"	123	4
Hence, thou suborn'd informer! a true soul	"	125	13
with a bastard shame	"	127	4
with a false esteem	"	127	12
in a waste of shame	"	129	1
as a swallow'd bait	"	129	7
A bliss in proof, and proved, a very woe	"	129	11
Before a joy proposed, behind, a dream	"	129	12
a far more pleasing sound	"	130	10
never saw a goddess go	"	130	11
A thousand groans	"	131	10
A torment thrice threefold	"	133	8
And sue a friend	"	134	11
Among a number	"	136	8
A—a something sweet to thee	*Son*	136	12
think that a several plot	"	137	9
upon so foul a face	"	137	12
a thousand errors note	"	141	2
the likeness of a man	"	141	11
as a careful housewife	"	143	1
is a man right fair	"	144	3
a woman colour'd ill	"	144	4
my saint to be a devil	"	144	7
who, like a fiend	"	145	11
having so short a lease	"	146	5
My love is as a fever	"	147	1
so foul a lie	"	152	14
A maid of Dian's this	"	153	2
In a cold valley-fountain	"	153	4
A dateless lively heat	"	153	6
And grew a seething bath	"	153	7
maladies a sovereign cure	"	153	8
a sad distemper'd guest	"	153	12
by a virgin hand disarm'd	"	154	8
quench in a cool well	"	154	9
a bath and healthful remedy	"	154	11
From off a hill whose concave	*L C*	.....	1
A plaintful story from a sistering	"	.....	2
espied a fickle maid	"	.....	5
a platted hive of straw	"	.....	8
The carcass of a beauty	"	.....	11
a careless hand of pride	"	.....	30
A thousand favours from a maund	"	.....	36
she in a river threw	"	.....	38
had she many a one	"	.....	43
Crack'd many a ring	"	.....	45
A reverend man that grazed	"	.....	57
Sometime a blusterer	"	.....	58
injury of many a blasting	"	.....	72
have been a spreading flower	"	.....	75
A youthful suit	"	.....	79
Love lack'd a dwelling ,	"	.....	82
was he such a storm	"	.....	101
falseness in a pride of truth	"	.....	105
And controversy hence a question	"	.....	110
The one a palate hath	"	.....	167
from many a several fair	"	.....	206
was sent me from a nun	"	.....	232
to charm a sacred nun	"	.....	260
a river running from a fount	"	.....	283
what a hell of witchcraft	"	.....	288
a plenitude of subtle matter	"	.....	302
That not a heart which	"	.....	309
the garment of a Grace	"	.....	316
Which, like a cherubin	"	.....	319
do again for such a sake	"	.....	322
pervert a reconciled maid	"	.....	329
is a soothing tongue	*P P*	1	11
angel is a man right fair	"	2	3
a woman colour'd ill	"	2	4
my saint to be a devil	"	2	7
A woman I forswore	"	3	5
Thou being a goddess	"	3	6
thou a heavenly love	"	3	7
and breath a vapour is	"	3	9
to win a paradise	"	3	14
sitting by a brook	"	4	1
with many a lovely look	"	4	3
A longing tarriance	"	6	4
osier growing by a brook	"	6	5
A brook where Adon used	"	6	6
'why was not I a flood	"	6	14
Mild as a dove	"	7	2

| A | 5 | ACCIDENT |

Entry	Ref	Page	Line
A—A lily pale, with damask	P P	7	5
Was this a lover or a lecher	"	7	17
a youngster proud and wild	"	9	4
upon a steep-up hill	"	9	5
'did I see a fair sweet youth	"	9	9
deep-wounded with a boar	"	9	10
a spectacle of ruth	"	9	11
a green plum that hangs upon a tree	"	10	5
under a myrtle shade	"	11	2
Beauty is but a vain	"	13	1
A shining gloss	"	13	2
A flower that dies	"	13	3
A brittle glass that's broken	"	13	4
A doubtful good, a gloss, a glass, a flower	"	13	5
daff'd me to a cabin	"	14	3
'Wander,' a word for shadows	"	14	11
each minute seems a moon	"	15	15
It was a lording's daughter	"	16	1
alas, it was a spite	"	16	7
Which by a gift of learning	"	16	14
On a day, alack the day	"	17	1
Spied a blossom passing fair	"	17	3
so apt to pluck a sweet	"	17	14
There a nay is placed	"	18	12
Like a thousand vanquish'd men	"	18	36
For a sweet content	"	18	51
A cripple soon can find a halt	"	19	10
A woman's nay doth stand	"	19	42
make thee a bed of roses	"	20	9
With a thousand fragrant	"	20	10
A cap of flowers and a kirtle	"	20	11
A belt of straw and ivy buds	"	20	13
it fell upon a day	"	21	1
Sitting in a pleasant shade	"	21	3
Which a grove of myrtles made	"	21	4
her breast up-till a thorn	"	21	10
but he were a king	"	21	42
He with thee doth bear a part	"	21	56
In a mutual flame	P T		24
But in them it were a wonder	"		32
How true a twain	"		45
For these dead birds sigh a prayer	"		67
Abate—Air and water do	V A		654
Abettor—Thou foul . . .	R L		886
Abhor—why dost .... me	V A		138
humanity abhor the deed	R L		195
to whom I pray abhor this fact	"		349
what others do abhor	Son	150	11
shouldst not abhor my state	"	150	12
Age, I do abhor thee	P P	12	9
Abide—			
With patience must my will	R L		486
huge fires abide	"		647
still doth red abide	"		1749
from far where I abide	Son	27	5
wherever I abide	"	45	2
in his fair parts she did abide	L C		83
A-billing—doves that sit	V A		366
Able—that .... spirit affords	Son	85	7
Abomination—see his own	R L		704
of incest, that abomination	"		921
suffer these abominations	"		1832
About—goeth .... to take him	V A		319
some twine about her thigh	"		873
about he walks	R L		367
a foul usurper went about	"		412
Knit poisonous clouds about his golden head	"		777
About— .... him were a press	R L		1406
throws her eyes about the painting round	"		1399
about her tear-distained eye	"		1586
About the mourning	"		1744
governs me to go about	Son	113	2
Above—Sweet .... compare	V A		8
Above a mortal pitch	Son	86	6
a joy above the rest	"	91	6
but, by all above	"	110	6
above that idle rank	"	122	8
above them hover'd	L C		319
Abridgement—This brief ...	R L		1198
Abroad—which .... they find	L C		137
offences that abroad you see	"		183
Absence—O ...., what a torment	Son	39	9
the bitterness of absence	"	57	7
absence of your liberty	"	58	6
hath my absence been	"	97	1
Though absence seem'd	"	109	2
makes her absence valiant	L C		245
Absent— .... from thy heart	Son	41	2
These present-absent with swift motion slide	"	45	4
Be absent from thy walks	"	89	9
have I been absent	"	98	1
Absolute—perfection is so	R L		853
Absolution—is clear'd with	"		354
Abstaining—			
hopes persuade him to	"		130
Abundance—where .... lies	Son	1	7
whose strength's abundance	"	23	4
That I in thy abundance	"	37	11
And in abundance addeth	"	135	10
Abundant—Yet this .... issue	"	97	9
Abuse—			
themselves are growth's	V A		16
lawd to lust's abuse	"		792
remorse in poor abuses	R L		269
this false night's abuses	"		1075
With men's abuses	"		1259
her own gross abuse	"		1315
stain'd with this abuse	"		1655
At my abuses reckon up	Son	121	10
through my unkind abuse	"	134	12
Abuse—do presently abuse it	R L		864
abuse a body dead	"		1267
why dust thou abuse	Son	4	5
even so doth she abuse me	"	42	7
Abused—			
some shape in Sinon's was	R L		1529
in thee it is abused	Son	82	14
Abusing—wail the .... of his time	R L		994
Abysm—In so profound	Son	112	9
Accent—so her .... breaks	R L		566
many accents and delays	"		1719
In other accents do this praise	Son	69	7
Acceptable—			
What .... audit can'st thou	"	4	12
Acceptance—no fair .... shine	"	135	8
Their kind acceptance	L C		207
Accessary—An .... by thine inclination	"		922
To accessary yieldings but still pure	"		1658
That I an accessary	Son	35	13
Accident—			
Time, whose million'd	"	115	5
builded far from accident	"	124	5
The accident which brought me	L C		247

Accidental—.... things of trial	*R L*	326	Addition—And by	*Son*	20	11
Accomplished—.... in himself	*L C*	116	making addition thus	"	135	4
Accomplishment—Who this	*R L*	716	came for additions	*L C*		118
Accorded—this double voice	*L C*	3	Addressed—.... to answer	*R L*		1606
Account—			Adieu—and, ere he says, ...	*V A*		537
The sad .... of forebemoaned	*Son*	30	11	bid your servant once adieu	*Son*	57	8
the account of hours to crave	"	54	3	Adjunct—Though death be	*R L*		133
no truth of such account	"	62	6	bath his adjunct pleasure	*Son*	91	5
Though in thy store's account	"	136	10	To keep an adjunct	"	122	13
Accounted—shall be ... evil	*R L*		1245	Admiration—than .... he admired	*R L*		418
Across—and wretched arms	"		1662	Admire—and therefore we	*Son*	123	5
Accumulate—			I thy parts admire	*P P*	5	10
on just proof surmise	*Son*	117	10	Admired—To be .... of lewd	"		392
Accurst—the more am I	*V A*		1120	than admiration be admired	"		418
Accuse—.... me thus	*Son*	117	1	style admired everywhere	*Son*	84	12
breach do I accuse thee	"	152	5	Admiring—have given .... praise	"	59	14
Accusing—Without .... you	"	58	8	Admit—His ear her prayers admits	*R L*		558
Ache—whose swelling dugs do	*V A*		875	admit impediments	*Son*	116	2
make the wound ache more	*R L*		1116	Admitted—is .... there	"	136	3
Achieve—advantage should	*Son*	67	3	Ado—			
Achilles—That for .... image	*R L*		1424	With much .... the cold fault	*V A*		694
Acknowledge—evermore .... thee	*Son*	36	9	Adon—'Nay, then,' quoth	"		769
Acquaintance—old .... in a trance	*R L*		1595	'behold two Adons dead	"		1070
To take a new acquaintance	*Son*	77	12	Adon used to cool his spleen	*P P*	6	6
I will acquaintance strangle	"	89	8	For Adon's sake	"	9	4
of our old acquaintance tell	"	89	12	Adonis—Rose-cheek'd ... hied him	*V A*		3
Acquainted—but not	"	20	3	in her arms Adonis lies	"		68
being best acquainted	"	88	5	Wishing Adonis had	"		179
Acquit—.... my forced offence	*R L*		1071	and now Adonis	"		181
acquit me from this chance	"		1706	At this Adonis smiles	"		241
Act—had his .... made plain	*V A*		359	Adonis' trampling courser	"		261
O, impious act including all foul	*R L*		199	and left Adonis there	"		322
assist me in the act	"		350	down Adonis sits	"		325
The loathsome act of lust	"		1636	Because Adonis' heart	"		378
this act will be	"		1637	it is Adonis' voice	"		978
with the foul act dispense	"		1704	Adonis lives, and Death	"		992
For his foul act	"		1824	that Adonis is alive	"		1009
In act thy bed-vow broke	*Son*	152	3	But when Adonis lived	"		1085
Act—I did but act	*V A*		1006	then would Adonis weep	"		1090
on his did act the seizure	*P P*	11	10	thus was Adonis slain	"		1111
Action—			to her Adonis' breath	"		1172
till .... might become them better	*R L*		1323	Describe Adonis	*Son*	53	5
such sober action with his hand	"		1403	With young Adonis	*P P*	4	2
they such odd action yield	"		1433	tarriance for Adonis made	"	6	4
Whose action is no stronger	*Son*	65	4	Anon Adonis comes	"	9	6
Is lust in action; and till action, lust	"	129	2	Venus with young Adonis	"	11	1
Active—To see his .... child	"	37	2	she clipp'd Adonis in her arms	"	11	6
Actor—From vassal actors	*R L*		608	Adore—the capitol that we	*R L*		1835
As an imperfect actor	*Son*	23	1	adore his beauty still	*Son*	7	7
Acture—with .... they may be	*L C*		185	youth, I do adore thee	*P P*	12	9
Add—Now she adds honours	*V A*		994	Adored—.... by this devil	*R L*		85
To add a more rejoicing	*R L*		332	Adorn—open to .... the day	"		399
her oratory adds more grace	"		564	A-doting—			
Add to his flow	"		651	as she wrought thee, fell	*Son*	20	10
add the rank smell	*Son*	69	12	Adulterate—			
blessings add a curse	"	84	13	The .... death of Lucrece	*R L*		1645
add something more	"	85	10	false adulterate eyes	*Son*	121	5
'Will' add to thy 'Will'	"	135	11	his foul adulterate heart	*L C*		175
Added—Rain .... to a river	*V A*		71	Advance—			
Have added feathers	*Son*	78	7	low declined honour to	*R L*		1705
my added praise beside	"	103	4	all my art, and dost advance	*Son*	78	13
minutes added to the hours	*P P*	15	14	O, then advance of yours	*L C*		227
Adder—one that spies an	*V A*		878	Advantage—let not .... slip	*V A*		129
The adder hisses	*R L*		871	to take advantage	"		405
that my adder's sense	*Son*	112	10	Advantage on the kingdom	*Son*	64	6
Addeth— ... to his store	"	135	10	advantage should achieve	"	67	3
Addict—be .... to vice	*P P*	21	43	this advantage found	"	153	2
Adding—By .... one thing to my purpose	*Son*	20	12	For this advantage still	*L C*		123
				Advantage—groan advantage thee	*V A*		950

Adverse—		
Thy .... party is thy advocate	Son 35	10
Advice— .... is sporting while infection breeds	R L	907
swallow up his sound advice	"	1409
advice is often seen	L C	160
Advised—O, be ....; thou know'st	V A	615
sworn to this advised doom	R L	1849
by advised respects	Son 49	4
Advisedly— .... she marketh	V A	457
thus speaks advisedly	R L	180
she advisedly perused	"	1527
and arm his long-hid wits advisedly	"	1816
Advocate—adverse party is thy	Son 35	10
Æma—As smoke from	R L	1042
Afar—may read the mot	"	830
chase thee afar behind	Son 143	10
Afeard—And wast .... to scratch	R L	1035
Affable—That .... familiar ghost	Son 86	9
Affairs—His honour, his	R L	45
or your affairs suppose	Son 57	10
To stand in thy affairs	" 151	12
Affected—to thine own face	V A	157
Affectedly—silk feat and	L C	48
Affection— .... is a coal	V A	387
Affection faints not	"	569
himself Affection's sentinel	"	650
Affection is my captain	R L	271
affection's course control	"	500
wrong thy true affection so	"	1060
Made old offences of affections new	Son 110	4
And nice affections wavering stood	L C	97
Throw my affections in his charmed power	"	146
my affection put to the smallest teen	"	192
trophies of affections hot	"	218
Afflict— .... him in his bed	R L	973
Afflicted— .... fancy fastly drew	L C	61
Afford—too much talk	R L	1106
next vouchsafe t' afford	"	1305
in thy cheek: he can afford	Son 79	11
that able spirit affords	" 85	7
which wondrous scope affords	" 105	12
Afloat—will hold me up	" 80	9
Afraid—that they are	V A	898
of my holy vows afraid	L C	179
but seems afraid	P P 18	30
Afresh—And weep	Son 30	7
Affright—his lewd eyes	R L	971
to affright mine eye	"	1138
After—like sunshine .... rain	V A	799
tempest after sun	"	800
Which after him she darts	"	817
And would say after her	"	852
Long after fearing	"	1036
after supper long he questioned	R L	122
Till after a deep groan	"	1276
old Priam after slew	"	1522
after many accents and delays	"	1719
after yourself's decease	Son 13	7
After a thousand victories imitated after you	" 25	10
	" 53	6
after I am gone	" 71	14
After my death, dear love	" 72	3
As after sunset fadeth	" 73	6
after their lord's decease	" 97	8
Drawn after you, you pattern	" 98	12
after that which flies	" 143	9
after new love bearing	" 152	4

After-loss—drop in for an	Son 90	4
Afterwards—should .... burn clearer	" 115	4
Again—them dry ...., she seeks	V A	52
to kiss? then wink again	"	121
I'll give it thee again	"	209
and forth again	"	273
never lost again	"	408
breatheth life in her again	*	474
kill me once again	"	499
'you will fall again	"	709
she untreads again	"	908
And, sighing it again	"	930
opens them again	"	960
make them wet again	"	966
chaos comes again	"	1020
creep forth again	"	1036
wound the heart with looks again	"	1042
whet his teeth at him again	"	1113
return again in haste	R L	321
Then Collatine again, by Lucrece	"	381
what he would lose again	"	688
should not peep again	"	788
till he return again	"	1339
Retire again, till meeting	"	1441
his breath drinks up again	"	1666
fountain clears itself again	"	1707
Lucrece, live again and see	"	1770
He doth again repeat	"	1848
Yourself again, after yourself's	Son 13	7
not to give back again	" 22	14
come back again, assured	" 45	11
I send them back again	" 45	14
To-morrow see again	" 56	7
Spending again what is	" 76	12
and pays it thee again	" 79	8
back again is swerving	" 87	8
Comes home again, on better judgment	" 87	12
I return again •	" 109	6
He again desires her	L C	66
do again for such a sake	"	322
Would yet again betray	"	328
and come again to-morrow	P P 14	5
again to make me wander	" 14	10
Against—strive .... the stream	V A	772
'gainst venom'd sores	"	916
Against the welkin volleys out	"	921
Against the golden splendour	R L	25
Against love's fire fear's frost bath	"	355
against long-living laud	"	622
For now against himself	"	717
Against the unseen secrecy	"	765
against proportion'd course	"	774
against himself to rave	"	982
And whiles against a thorn	"	1135
well, against my heart	"	1137
against the wither'd flower	"	1254
against my heart he set	"	1640
That 'gainst thyself thou stick'st	Son 10	6
Nothing 'gainst Time's scythe	" 12	13
Against this coming end	" 13	3
Against the stormy gusts	" 13	11
'gainst myself a lawful plea commence	" 35	11
stand against thy sight	" 38	6
Against that time, if ever	" 49	1
Against that time when thou	" 49	5
Against that time do I	" 49	9
against myself uprear	" 49	11

Entry	Ref		
Against—'Gainst death and all-oblivious enmity	Son	53	9
eclipses 'gainst his glory fight	"	60	7
Against my love shall be	"	63	1
Against confounding age's cruel knife	"	63	10
Against the wreckful siege	"	65	6
which shake against the cold	"	73	3
against myself I'll fight	"	88	3
Against thy reasons	"	89	4
against myself I'll vow	"	89	13
Potions of eisel 'gainst my strong infection	"	111	10
When I against myself	"	149	2
against the thing they see	"	152	12
To swear against the truth	"	152	14
Against strange maladies	"	153	8
examples 'gainst her own content	L C		157
'gainst rule, 'gainst sense, 'gainst shame	"		271
that you make 'gainst mine	"		277
Against the thing he sought	"		313
'Gainst whom the world	P P	3	2
Age—Thy mark is feeble	V A		941
Teaching decrepit age	"		1148
the golden age to gild	R L		60
ease in waning age	"		142
wait on wrinkled age	"		275
be seeded in thine age	"		603
minute in an age	"		962
of the worn-out age	"		1350
my old age new born	"		1759
of thine age shalt see	Son	3	11
youth in his middle age	"	7	6
Like feeble age, he reeleth	"	7	10
age and cold decay	"	11	6
The age to come would say	"	17	7
yellowed with their age	"	17	9
grown with this growing age	"	32	10
Painting my age with beauty	"	62	14
to age's steepy night	"	63	5
Against confounding age's	"	63	10
of outworn buried age	"	64	2
Doubting the filching age	"	75	6
And to be praised of ages	"	101	12
hear this, thou age unbred	"	104	13
olives of endless age	"	107	8
dust and injury of age	"	108	10
In the old age	"	127	1
And age in love	"	138	12
through lattice of scar'd age	L C		14
And, privileged by age	"		62
In the charity of age	"		70
Not age, but sorrow	"		74
And age, in love	P P	1	12
Crabbed age and youth	"	12	1
age is full of care	"	12	2
age like winter weather	"	12	3
age like winter bare	"	12	4
age's breath is short	"	12	5
age is lame	"	12	6
age is weak and cold	"	12	7
and age is tame	"	12	8
Age, I do abhor thee	"	12	9
Age, I do defy thee	"	12	11
Wher. time with age	"	19	46
Aged—The .... man that coffers	R L		855
of time in aged things	"		941
Agent—His other agents aim	V A		400
Aggravate—to .... thy store	Son	146	10
Agree—with his proud sight agrees	V A		288
his mood with nought agrees	R L		1095
and sweet poetry agree	P P	8	1
Agreeing—with his gust is 'greeing	Son	114	11
Ague—agues pale and faint	V A		739
Ah—....! if thou issueless	Son	9	3
Ah, but those tears	"	34	13
But, ah, thought kills me	"	44	9
Ah, wherefore with infection	"	67	1
Ah, do not, when my heart	"	90	5
Ah, yet doth beauty	"	104	9
ah, my love well knows	"	139	9
But, ah, whoever shunn'd	L C		155
ah, fool too froward	P P	4	14
Ah, that I had my lady	"	11	13
Ah, neither be my share	"	14	1
Ah, thought I, thou mourn'st	"	21	19
Aid—by whose swift	V A		1190
keep them from thy aid	R L		912
began to promise aid	"		1696
In his poor heart's aid	"		1784
did call upon thy aid	Son	79	1
Giving him aid, my verse	"	86	8
All aid, themselves made fairer	L C		117
Aidance—the .... of the tongue	V A		330
Aim—His other agents	"		400
Mistakes that aim, and cleaves	"		942
The aim of all	R L		141
And in this aim	"		143
End thy ill aim	"		579
of his all-hurting aim	L C		310
Air—moisture, ... of grace	V A		64
His nostrils drink the air	"		273
As air and water	"		654
ravish the morning air	R L		778
that in air consumes	"		1042
The dispersed air	"		1805
That heaven's air	Son	21	8
fix'd in heaven's air	"	21	12
slight air and purging fire	"	45	1
in heaven's sweetest air	"	70	4
in the wanton air	P P	17	4
'Air,' quoth he	"	17	9
Air, would I might	"	17	10
Airy—the .... scale of praise	L C		226
Ajax—In .... and Ulysses	R L		1394
In Ajax' eyes blunt rage	"		1398
Alabaster—In an .... band	V A		363
her alabaster skin	R L		419
Alack—'....', what were it	"		1156
But, out, alack! he was	Son	33	11
meditation! where, alack	"	65	9
Alack, what poverty	"	103	1
alack, too timely shaded	P P	10	3
On a day, alack the day	"	17	1
Vow, alack! for youth unmeet	"	17	13
Alarm—To love's alarms	V A		424
Gives false alarms	"		651
rash alarm to know	R L		473
Alarum—Anon their loud alarums	V A		700
heart, alarum striking	R L		433
Alas—'....', he nought esteems	V A		631
'Alas, poor world'	"		1075
Alas, how many bear	R L		832
From that, alas, thy Lucrece	"		1624
Alas, 'tis true I have gone	Son	110	1
Alas, why, fearing	"	115	9
alas, it was a spite	P P	16	7

ALAS   9   ALL

Entry	Source	Line		Entry	Source	Line	
Alas—...., she could not help it	P P	16	12	All—they .... rate his ill	R L	.....	304
But, alas! my hand	"	17	11	But all these poor forbiddings	"	.....	323
Alchemy—with heavenly	Son	33	4	heart of all her land	"	.....	439
taught it this alchemy	"	114	4	with all my might	"	.....	488
Alien—As every .... pen	"	78	3	All this beforehand	"	.....	494
Alight—to .... thy steed	V A	.....	13	all the power of both	"	.....	572
Alike—Since all .... my songs	Son	105	3	'All which together	"	.....	589
Alive—still is left	V A	.....	174	To all the host	"	.....	598
that Adonis is alive	"	.....	1009	all that brood to kill	"	.....	627
What face remains alive	"	.....	1076	If all these petty ills	"	.....	656
faltering feeble souls alive	R L	.....	1768	Feeble Desire, all recreant	"	.....	710
of yours alive that time	Son	17	13	That all the faults	"	.....	804
nor I to none alive	"	112	7	all sins past and all that are	"	.....	923
None alive will pity me	P P	21	28	Thou nursest all and murder'st all	"	.....	929
All—Stain to .... nymphs	V A	.....	9	My tongue shall utter all	"	.....	1076
devouring all in haste	"	.....	57	to all fair eyes	"	.....	1083
making her cheeks all wet	"	.....	83	And to herself all sorrow	"	.....	1192
all compact of fire	"	.....	149	And all my fame	"	.....	1203
All swoln with chafing	"	.....	325	all the little worms	"	.....	1248
For all askance he holds	"	.....	342	through all her body spread	"	.....	1266
And all this dumb play	"	.....	379	smeared all with dust	"	.....	1381
All whole as thine	"	.....	370	his beard all silver white	"	.....	1405
For all my mind	"	.....	383	All jointly listening	"	.....	1410
And all but with a breath	"	.....	414	all boll'n and red	"	.....	1417
And all amazed brake off	"	.....	469	where all distress is still'd	"	.....	1444
and all the earth	"	.....	484	all distress and dolour dwelled	"	.....	1446
borrow'd all their shine	"	.....	488	Of all the Greeks	"	.....	1470
she takes all she can, not all she listeth	"	.....	564	Here, all enraged	"	.....	1562
and picks them all	"	.....	576	Which all this time	"	.....	1576
All is imaginary	"	.....	597	To tell them all	"	.....	1617
But all in vain	"	.....	607	all the task it hath to say	"	.....	1618
all the world amazes	"	.....	634	unless I took all patiently	"	.....	1641
all stain'd with gore	"	.....	664	Comes all too late	"	.....	1686
desire sees best of all	"	.....	720	they all at once began	"	.....	1709
And all is but to rob	"	.....	723	and all his lordly crew	"	.....	1731
of all these maladies	"	.....	745	all the beauty of my glass	"	.....	1763
And all in vain	"	.....	772	By all our country rights	"	.....	1838
Love is all truth	"	.....	804	where all thy beauty lies	Son	2	5
That all the neighbor caves	"	.....	830	Where all the treasure	"	2	6
they answer all	"	.....	851	Who, all in one	"	8	12
patron of all night	"	.....	860	If all were minded so	"	11	7
And all in haste	"	.....	870	sable curls all silver'd o'er	"	12	4
all strain courtesy	"	.....	888	all girded up in sheaves	"	12	7
her senses all dismay'd	"	.....	896	And all in war with Time	"	15	13
bepainted all with red	"	.....	901	number all your graces	"	17	6
through all her sinews	"	.....	903	hath all too short a date	"	18	4
nought at all respecting	"	.....	911	and all her fading sweets	"	19	7
In hand with all things, nought at all affecting	"	.....	912	all 'hues' in his controlling	"	20	7
all other eyes to see	"	.....	952	and all things rare	"	21	7
All entertain'd each passion	"	.....	969	For all that beauty	"	22	5
Join they all together	"	.....	971	And all the rest forgot	"	25	12
called him all to nought	"	.....	993	all naked, will bestow it	"	26	8
of all mortal things	"	.....	996	I all alone beweep	"	29	2
And there all smother'd	"	.....	1035	All losses are restored	"	30	14
That all love's pleasure	"	.....	1140	endeared with all hearts	"	31	1
to all discontents	"	.....	1161	and all love's loving parts	"	31	3
all in post	R L	.....	1	And all those friends	"	31	4
Neglected all with swift intent	"	.....	46	who all their parts	"	31	11
Which, having all, all could not satisfy	"	.....	96	thou, all they, hast all the all of me	"	31	14
The aim of all	"	.....	141	ransom all ill deeds	"	34	14
That one for all or all for one	"	.....	144	All men make faults and	"	35	5
the death of all, and all together	"	.....	147	Take all my comfort	"	37	4
all for want of wit	"	.....	153	these all, or all or more	"	37	6
including all foul harms	"	.....	199	of all thy glory live	"	37	12
All pure effects	"	.....	251	art all the better part of me	"	39	2
All orators are dumb	"	.....	268	Take all my loves, my love, yea take them all	"	40	1
				all mine was thine	"	40	4
				steal thee all my poverty	"	40	10

Phrase	Ref	#	#
All—in whom .... ill well shows	Son	40	13
It is not all my grief	"	42	1
For all the day they view	"	43	2
All days are nights to see	"	43	13
all tenants to the heart	"	46	10
all art of beauty set	"	53	7
In all external grace	"	53	13
eyes of all posterity	"	55	11
time at all to spend	"	57	3
In sequent toil all forwards do	"	60	4
with others all too near	"	61	14
possesseth all mine eye	"	62	1
all my soul and all my every part	"	62	2
As I all other in all worths surmount	"	62	8
And all those beauties	"	63	6
Tired with all these for restful	"	66	1
Tired with all these from these	"	66	13
Without all ornament itself and true	"	68	10
All tongues the voice of souls	"	69	3
seals up all in rest	"	73	8
Without all hail shall carry	"	74	2
Sometime all full with feasting	"	75	9
on all, or all away	"	75	14
I still all one, ever the same	"	76	5
So all my best is dressing	"	76	11
Thou art all my art	"	78	13
had all thy gentle grace	"	79	2
spends all his might	"	80	3
to all the world must die	"	81	6
When all the breathers of this world	"	81	12
by all the Muses filed	"	85	4
of all too precious you	"	86	2
bonds in thee are all determinate	"	87	4
bending all my loving thoughts	"	88	10
myself will bear all wrong	"	88	14
All these I better in one general best	"	91	8
of all men's pride I boast	"	91	12
All this away and me	"	91	14
And all things turn	"	93	12
strength of all thy state	"	96	12
dressed in all his trim	"	98	2
you pattern of all those	"	98	12
of all his growth	"	99	12
gives thee all thy might	"	100	2
argument, all bare is of more	"	103	3
since all alike my songs	"	105	3
is all my argument	"	105	9
so all their praises	"	106	9
all you prefiguring	"	106	10
All frailties that besiege all kinds of love	"	109	10
nothing all thy sum of good	"	109	12
in it thou art my all	"	109	14
but, by all above	"	110	6
Now all is done	"	110	9
You are my all the world	"	112	5
I throw all care	"	112	9
That all the world besides	"	112	14
That I have scanted all	"	117	1
Whereto all bonds	"	117	4
to all the winds	"	117	7
All men are bad	"	121	14
Beyond all date even to eternity	"	122	4
But all alone stands hugely	"	124	11
Lose and more	"	125	6
All this the world well knows	"	129	13
All—And .... they foul that	Son	132	14
and all that is in me	"	133	14
put'st forth all to use	"	134	10
The sea, all water	"	135	9
Think all but one	"	135	14
where all men ride	"	137	6
makes all swift dispatch	"	143	3
not so true as all men's	"	148	8
Am of myself all tyrant	"	149	2
When all my best	"	149	11
thy worst all best exceeds	"	150	8
all my vows are oaths	"	152	7
And all my honest faith	"	152	8
scythed all that youth begun	L C		12
Nor youth all quit	"	....	13
In clamours of all size	"	....	21
but were all graced by him	"	....	42
stuck over all his face	"	....	81
All aids, themselves	"	....	117
but where all graced by him	"	....	119
All kind of arguments	"	....	121
All replication prompt	"	....	122
Catching all passions	"	....	126
gave him all my flower	"	....	147
All my offences that abroad	"	....	183
Lo, all these trophies	"	....	218
Take all these similes	"	....	227
And now, to tempt all	"	....	232
Have emptied all their fountains	"	....	243
pour your ocean all among	"	....	256
your victory us all congest	"	....	258
All vows and consecrations	"	....	263
art all, and all things	"	....	266
The aloes of all forces	"	....	273
Now all these hearts	"	....	274
All melting; though our drops	"	....	300
all strange forms receives	"	....	303
O, all that borrow'd motion	"	....	327
cures all disgrace in me	P P	3	8
Where all those pleasures	"	5	6
All ignorant that soul that	"	5	9
all in love forlorn	"	6	3
all her pure protestings	"	7	11
and all were jestings	"	7	12
As passing all conceit	"	8	8
and left her all alone	"	9	14
All unseen 'gan passage find	"	17	6
All is amiss	"	18	4
All my merry jigs	"	18	9
All my lady's love is lost	"	18	10
Wrought all my loss	"	18	14
All fears scorn I	"	18	20
All help needing	"	18	24
Plays not at all	"	18	30
Flocks all sleeping	"	18	42
All our pleasure known	"	18	43
All our merry meetings	"	18	46
All our evening sport	"	18	47
All our love is lost	"	18	48
cause of all my moan	"	18	51
frame all thy ways	"	19	25
all the joys in bed	"	19	47
all the pleasures prove	"	20	2
all the craggy mountains	"	20	4
all with leaves of myrtle	"	20	12
as all forlorn	"	21	9
All thy friends are	"	21	24
All thy fellow birds	"	21	25
Grace in all simplicity	P T	....	54

Allayed—by feeding is	Son	56	3
All-eating—Were an .... shame	"	2	8
Allege—I can .... no cause	"	49	14
All-hiding—thy black .... cloak	R L	....	801
All-hurting—of his .... aim	L C	....	310
All-oblivious—and .... enmity	Son	55	9
Allotted—reproach to him	R L	....	824
Allow—did his words	"	....	1845
untainted do allow	Son	19	11
my bad, my good allow	"	112	4
All-too-timeless—his .... speed	R L	....	44
All-triumphant—			
With .... splendour	Son	33	10
Allure—favours to .... his eye	P P	4	6
Almighty—by high .... Jove	R L	....	568
Almost—Is .... choked	"	....	282
almost hid behind	"	....	1413
myself almost despising	Son	29	9
doth almost tell my name	"	76	7
And almost thence my nature	"	111	6
Alms—that by .... doth live	R L	....	986
Aloe—The aloes of all forces	L C	....	273
Aloft—			
shakes .... his Roman blade	R L	....	505
ignorance aloft to fly	Son	78	6
Alone—but the eye	V A	....	213
leave me here alone	"	....	382
while now it sleeps alone	"	....	786
But I alone alone must sit	R L	....	795
alone committed, light alone	"	....	1480
traffic with thyself alone	Son	4	9
I all alone beweep my outcast state	"	29	2
now is thine alone	"	31	12
by me be borne alone	"	36	4
which thou deservest alone	"	39	8
then she loves but me alone	"	42	14
being made of four, with two alone	"	45	7
I leave my love alone	"	66	14
Then thou alone kingdoms of hearts shouldst owe	"	70	14
to be with you alone	"	75	7
Whilst I alone did call upon thy aid	"	79	1
My verse alone had all thy gentle grace	"	79	2
Than this rich praise that you alone are you	"	84	2
Wretched in this alone	"	91	13
have often lived alone	"	105	13
But all alone stands hugely politic	"	124	11
Although I swear it to myself alone	"	131	8
Is 't not enough to torture me alone	"	133	3
To any sensual feast with thee alone	"	141	8
and left her all alone	P P	0	14
Must live alone	"	18	53
Save the nightingale alone	"	21	8
Along—So soon was she .... as he was down	V A	....	43
the lion walk'd along	"	....	1093
Aloof—from judgement stand	L C	....	168
Aloud—snorts and neighs	V A	....	262
dogs exclaim aloud	"	....	886
Already—to those .... spent	R L	....	1359
what is already spent	Son	76	12
Altar—Over my altars hath he hung	V A	....	103
Since I their altar	L C	....	224
Alter—but .... not his taste	R L	....	651
and alter their contents	"	....	948
Which though it alter not love's sole effect	Son	36	7
Alter—Which alters when it alteration finds	Son	116	3
Love alters not with his brief hours	"	116	11
Alteration—when it .... finds	"	116	3
Alter'd—though alter'd new	"	93	3
'I hate' she alter'd with an end	"	145	9
Altering—to the course of .... things	"	115	8
Although—, ... he mount her	V A	....	598
Although our undivided loves are one	Son	36	2
Although thou steal thee	"	40	10
although my foot did stand	"	44	5
although to-day thou fill	"	56	5
although their eyes were kind	"	69	11
Although in me each part	"	81	4
although his height be taken	"	116	8
Although I swear it to myself alone	"	131	8
Although she knows my days	"	138	6
Although I know my years	P P	1	6
Altogether—or .... balk	R L	....	696
Always—doth .... fresh remain	V A	....	801
I always write of you	Son	76	9
Serve always with assured trust	P P	19	31
Am—What .... I that thou	V A	....	205
I am such a park	"	....	239
thou wert as I am	"	....	369
I am bereft him so	"	....	384
O, where am I	"	....	493
'I am,' quoth he	"	....	718
more am I accurst	"	....	1120
Under that colour am I come	R L	....	481
Yet am I guilty	"	....	841
So am I now	"	....	1049
I am the mistress of my fate	"	....	1069
shall not persuade me I am old	Son	22	1
I that love and am beloved	"	25	13
That am debarr'd the benefit	"	28	2
then I am not lame	"	37	9
I in thy abundance am sufficed	"	37	11
When I am sometime absent	"	41	2
I am not thought	"	44	9
And I am still with them	"	47	12
So am I as the rich	"	52	1
I am to wait though waiting so	"	58	13
O, sure I am the wits of former days	"	59	13
my love shall be as I am now	"	63	1
mourn for me when I am dead	"	71	1
Give warning to the world that I am fled	"	71	3
I perhaps compounded am with clay	"	71	10
after I am gone	"	71	14
For I am shamed	"	72	13
I am a worthless boat	"	80	11
When I in earth am rotten	"	81	2
wherein I am attainted	"	88	7
To whom I am confined	"	110	12
No, I am that I am	"	121	9
I am forsaken	"	133	7
Perforce am thine	"	133	14
And I myself am mortgaged	"	134	2
And yet am I not free	"	134	14
More than enough am I that vex thee still	"	135	3
And wherefore say not I that I am old	"	138	10
but since I am near slain	"	139	13
Past cure I am	"	147	9
Am of myself, all tyrant	"	149	4

Am—thou lovest, and I .... blind	Son	149	14
thou know'st I am forsworn	"	152	1
I am perjured most	"	152	6
tell your judgement I am old	L C		73
say not I that I am old	P P	1	10
in deep delight am chiefly drown'd	"	8	11
Amain—Venus makes .... unto him V A			5
Amaze—all the world amazes	"		634
to amaze his foes	"		684
Amazed—And all	"		469
amazed, as one that unaware	"		823
poor people are amazed	"		925
She, much amazed	R L		446
make him more amazed	"		1356
Amazedly— .... in her sad face	"		1591
Amazeth—and women's souls	Son	20	8
Ambassage—this written	"	26	3
Amber—			
Of ...., crystal, and of beaded jet	L C		37
With coral clasps and amber studs	P P	20	14
Ambition—Yet their	R L		68
in Tarquin new ambition bred	"		411
Ambitious—			
And this .... foul infirmity	"		150
Ambush—Or lain in	"		233
the ambush of young days	Son	70	9
Amen—still cry 'Amen	"	85	6
Amend—return to make amends	R L		961
what shall be thy amends	Son	101	1
sickly radiance do amend	L C		214
Amended—that cannot be	R L		578
Amending—can give the fault	"		1614
Amid—			
famish them .... their plenty	V A		20
Amiss—salving thy	Son	35	7
for invention, bear amiss	"	59	3
urge not my amiss	"	151	3
All is amiss	P P	18	4
Among— .... a flock of sheep	V A		685
among the wastes of time	Son	12	10
Weeds among flowers	"	124	4
Among a number	"	136	8
Among the many	L C		190
pour your ocean all among	"		256
Amongst—'Mongst our mourners			
shalt thou go	P T		20
Amorous—and his .... spoil	L C		154
Amorously—metal .... impleach'd	"		205
Amplify—sonnets that did	"		209
An— .... hour but short	V A		23
Even as an empty cage	"		55
An oven that is stopp'd	"		331
in an alabaster band	"		363
like an earthquake	"		648
an angry-chafing boar	"		662
an image like thyself	"		664
suck'd an earthly mother	"		863
one that spies an adder	"		878
cleaves an infant's heart	"		942
an orient drop beside	"		981
one minute in an hour	"		1187
An expired date	R L		26
men without an orator	"		30
And be an eye-sore	"		205
bear an ever-during blame	"		224
or an old man's saw	"		244
Show'd like an April daisy	"		395
batter such an ivory wall	"		464
Only he hath an eye	"		496
An—enters at .... iron gate	R L		595
When wilt thou sort an hour	"		899
An accessary by thine	"		922
One poor retiring minute in an age	"		962
would such an office have	"		1000
with an infringed oath	"		1061
Like an unpractised swimmer	"		1098
These means as frets upon an instrument	"		1140
an eager combat fight	"		1298
Griped in an armed hand	"		1425
An humble gait, calm looks	"		1508
As through an arch	"		1667
Were an all-eating shame	Son	2	8
Look, what an unthrift	"	9	9
in the world an end	"	9	11
metre of an antique song	"	17	12
An eye more bright	"	20	5
As an unperfect actor	"	23	1
Then can I drown an eye	"	30	5
That I an accessary needs must be	"	35	13
proud as an enjoyer	"	75	5
And do not come in for an after-loss	"	90	4
thy name blesses an ill report	"	95	8
as an idol show	"	105	2
to try an older friend	"	110	11
it is an ever-fixed mark	"	116	5
To keep an adjunct	"	122	13
she alter'd with an end	"	145	9
but an art of craft	L C		295
To break an oath	P P	3	14
with such an earthly tongue	"	5	14
Under an osier	"	6	5
dead within an hour	"	13	6
Till looking on an Englishman	"	16	3
Juno but an Ethiope were	"	17	16
with an outward show	"	19	38
Anatomized—			
In her the painter had . ..	R L		1450
Anchored—He anchor'd in the bay	Son	137	6
Ancient—			
from .... ravens' wings	R L		949
And— .... like a bold-faced suitor	V A		6
more white and red	"		10
And rein his proud head	"		14
Here come and sit	"		17
And being set I'll smother	"		18
And yet not cloy	"		19
Making them red and pale	"		21
of pith and livelihood	"		26
And, trembling in her passion	"		27
Who blush'd and pouted	"		33
red and hot as coals	"		35
stalled up, and even now	"		39
And govern'd him	"		42
on their elbows and their hips	"		44
And 'gins to chide	"		46
And kissing speaks	"		47
sighs and golden hairs	"		51
fan and blow them dry	"		52
feathers, flesh and bone	"		56
And where she rends	"		60
and breatheth in her face	"		62
And calls it heavenly	"		64
shame and awed resistance	"		69
and prettily entreats	"		73
he lours and frets	"		75
shame and anger ashy-pale	"		76
and being white	"		77

And—And by her fair	V A	80	And—.... there he stares	V A	301
And one sweet kiss	"	81	And whether he ran	"	304
and turns his lips	"	90	through his mane and tail	"	305
stern and direful god of war	"	98	and neighs unto her	"	307
my captive and my slave	"	101	and scorns the heat	"	311
And begg'd for that	"	102	and bites the poor flies	"	316
And for my sake hath learn'd to sport and dance	"	105	and his fury was assuaged	"	318
			and left Adonis there	"	322
dally, smile, and jest	"	106	boisterous and unruly	"	326
drum and ensign red	"	107	And now the happy season	"	327
And I will wink	"	122	and begins to glow	"	337
Rot and consume themselves	"	132	And with his bonnet	"	339
despised, rheumatic, and cold	"	135	How white and red	"	346
lean and lacking juice	"	136	pale, and by and by	"	347
Mine eyes are grey, and bright, and quick in turning	"	140	And like a lowly lover	"	350
			And all this dumb play	"	359
flesh is soft and plump	"	142	wilful and unwilling	"	365
And yet no footing seen	"	148	and I a man	"	369
light and will aspire	"	150	and thou shalt have it	"	374
sweet boy, and may it be	"	155	And being steel'd	"	376
and complain on theft	"	160	let go and let me go	"	379
And died to kiss	"	162	And 'tis your fault	"	381
and sappy plants to bear	"	165	and leave me here alone	"	382
and beauty breedeth	"	167	And learn of him	"	404
And so, in spite of death	"	173	And once made perfect	"	408
And Titan, tired	"	177	and then I chase it	"	410
and by Venus' side	"	180	and I will not owe it	"	411
And now Adonis	"	181	That laughs, and weeps, and all but with a breath	"	414
And with a heavy	"	182			
young, and so unkind	"	187	shapeless and unfinish'd	"	415
And, lo, I lie between that sun and thee	"	194	colt that's back'd and burden'd	"	419
			and never waxeth strong	"	420
And were I not immortal	"	197	And leave this idle theme	"	422
this heavenly and earthly sun	"	198	And heart's deep-sore wounding	"	432
and canst not feel	"	201	inward beauty and invisible	"	434
And one for interest	"	210	And that I could not	"	440
cold and senseless stone	"	211	And nothing but the very	"	441
image dull and dead	"	212	Being nurse and feeder	"	446
And swelling passion	"	218	And bid Suspicion	"	448
Red cheeks and fiery eyes	"	219	Gusts and foul flaws to herdmen and to herds	"	456
And now she weeps, and now she fain	"	221			
			and at his look	"	463
And now her sobs	"	222	And love by looks	"	464
and then his hand	"	223	And all amazed brake off	"	469
And when from thence	"	227	and she, by her good will	"	479
and thou shalt be my deer	"	231	and all the earth	"	484
and if those hills be dry	"	233	And as the bright sun	"	485
bottom-grass and high delightful plain	"	236	and life was death's annoy	"	497
			and death was lively joy	"	498
obscure and rough	"	237	and such disdain	"	501
tempest and from rain	"	238	And these mine eyes	"	502
and there he could not die	"	246	And as they last	"	507
And from her twining arms	"	256	thou wilt buy, and pay, and use good dealing	"	514
and hasteth to his horse	"	258			
lusty, young, and proud	"	260	And pay them at thy leisure	"	518
And forth she rushes, snorts and neighs aloud	"	262	and quickly gone	"	520
			And coal-black clouds	"	533
and to her straight	"	264	and bid good night	"	534
And now his woven girths	"	266	and so say you	"	535
and forth again	"	273	and ere he says 'Adieu	"	537
courage and his high desire	"	276	and backward drew	"	541
majesty and modest pride	"	278	and glutton-like she feeds	"	548
curvets and leaps	"	279	And having felt	"	553
And this I do	"	281	Her face doth reek and smoke	"	555
and nothing else he sees	"	287	And careless lust	"	556
colour, pace, and bone	"	294	and honour's wrack	"	558
fetlocks shag and long	"	295	Hot, faint, and weary	"	559
small head and nostrils wide	"	296	and now no more resisteth	"	563
straight legs and passing strong	"	297	And yields at last	"	566

And—Foul words .... frowns	V A	.....	573	And—.... shining star doth borrow V A 861
and picks them all at last	"	.....	576	and yet she hears " 867
and look well to her heart	"	.....	580	and for his horn " 868
And on his neck	"	.....	592	And all in haste " 870
and to lack her joy	"	.....	600	And as she runs " 871
and pine the maw	"	.....	602	make him shake and shudder " 880
and yet she is not loved	"	.....	610	and her spirit confounds " 882
And whom he strikes	"	.....	624	doubt and bloodless fear " 891
and embracing bushes	"	.....	629	and dare not stay " 894
sweet lips and crystal eyne	"	.....	633	And childish error " 898
and my joints did tremble	"	.....	642	And with that word " 900
and fell I not downright	"	.....	645	Like milk and blood " 902
beats, and takes no rest	"	.....	647	and now she will " 903
And in a peaceful hour	"	.....	652	And asks the weary " 914
air and water do abate	"	.....	654	And there another " 915
and whispers in mine ear	"	.....	659	And here she meets " 917
And more than so	"	.....	661	and he replies with howling " 918
with grief and hang the head	"	.....	666	mourner, black and grim " 920
And fear doth teach it	"	.....	670	Another and another answer " 922
And on thy well-breath'd horse	"	.....	678	signs and prodigies " 926
And when thou hast	"	.....	679	And, sighing it again " 930
and with what care	"	.....	681	stifle beauty and to steal " 934
He cranks and crosses	"	.....	682	breath and beauty set " 935
And sometime where	"	.....	687	and cleaves an infant's heart " 942
And sometime sorteth	"	.....	689	And, hearing him " 944
And now his grief	"	.....	701	And not Death's ebon dart " 948
Turn, and return	"	.....	704	And with his strong course opens " 960
And being low	"	.....	708	how her eyes and tears did lend and
and hear a little more	"	.....	709	borrow " 961
this to that and so to so	"	.....	713	and flatters her it is " 978
and then the story aptly ends	"	.....	716	and yet too credulous " 986
And now 'tis dark, and going I shall				Thy weal and woe " 987
fall	"	.....	719	Despair, and hope " 988
And all is but to rob	"	.....	723	Adonis lives, and Death " 992
cloudy and forlorn	"	.....	725	and grave for kings " 995
Steal a kiss, and die forsworn	"	.....	726	and never woman yet " 1007
and her by night	"	.....	732	And that his beauty " 1011
And therefore hath she	"	.....	733	Statues, tombs and stories " 1013
And pure perfection	"	.....	736	his triumphs and his glories " 1014
and much misery	"	.....	738	a weak and silly mind " 1016
agues pale and faint	"	.....	739	lives and must not die " 1017
and frenzies wood	"	.....	740	And beauty dead " 1020
grief and damn'd despair	"	.....	743	And in her haste " 1029
And not the least	"	.....	745	And there all smother'd " 1035
hue and qualities	"	.....	747	their office and their light " 1039
wasted, thaw'd, and done	"	.....	749	and never wound the heart " 1042
and self-loving nuns	"	.....	752	and being open'd " 1051
And barren dearth of daughters				and seem'd with him " 1056
and of sons	"	.....	754	And then she reprehends " 1063
And all in vain	"	.....	772	And yet,' quoth she " 1070
like you worse and worse	"	.....	774	colours fresh and trim " 1079
And every tongue	"	.....	776	lived and died with him " 1080
And will not let	"	.....	780	and the wind doth hiss you " 1084
And then my little heart	"	.....	783	Sun and sharp air " 1085
stains and soon bereaves	"	.....	797	And therefore would he " 1087
And homeward through the dark	"	.....	813	and, being gone " 1089
merciless and pitchy night	"	.....	821	And straight, in pity " 1091
and now she beats	"	.....	829	and gently hear him " 1096
and twenty times ' Woe, woe	"	.....	833	And never fright " 1098
And twenty echoes	"	.....	834	and ripe-red cherries " 1103
And sings extemporally	"	.....	836	grim, and urchin-snouted " 1105
and old men dote	"	.....	837	kiss him and hath kill'd " 1110
And still the choir	"	.....	840	And nuzzling in his flank " 1115
and outwore the night	"	.....	841	is dead, and never " 1119
and are never done	"	.....	846	And stains her face " 1122
And would say after her	"	.....	852	and they are pale " 1123
And wakes the morning	"	.....	853	and that is cold " 1124
cedar tops and hills	"	.....	858	and now no more " 1130
and patron of all light	"	.....	869	And every beauty " 1132

And—false .... full of fraud	*V A*	1141
Bud, and be blasted	"	1142
and the top o'erstraw'd	"	1143
and teach the fool	"	1146
and too full of riot	"	1147
raging-mad and silly-mild	"	1151
merciful and too severe	"	1153
And most deceiving	"	1156
war and dire events	"	1159
And set dissension 'twixt the son and sire	"	1160
subject and servile	"	1161
And in his blood	"	1167
pale cheeks and the blood	"	1169
And says, within her bosom	"	1173
and in the breach appears	"	1175
And so 'tis thine	"	1181
and 'tis thy right	"	1184
rock thee day and night	"	1186
And yokes her silver doves	"	1190
and not be seen	"	1191
And to Collatium	*R L*	4
And girdle with embracing	"	6
unmatched red and white	"	11
And, if possess'd, as soon decay'd and done	"	23
Honour and beauty	"	27
blasts, and ne'er grows old	"	49
beauty and virtue strived	"	52
cheeks, and call'd it then	"	61
beauty's red and virtue's white	"	65
war of lilies and of roses	"	71
And reverend welcome	"	90
And decks with praises	"	108
arms and wreaths of victory	"	110
And wordless so greets heaven	"	112
Mother of dread and fear	"	117
And in her vaulty prison	"	119
and wore out the night	"	123
And every one to rest	"	125
Save thieves and cares and troubled minds	"	126
And when great treasure	"	132
They scatter and unloose it	"	136
And so, by hoping more	"	137
surfeit, and such griefs	"	139
wealth and ease	"	142
And in this aim	"	143
and oft that wealth	"	146
death of all, and all	"	147
And this ambitious	"	150
and, all for want of wit	"	153
And for himself	"	157
and wretched hateful days	"	161
and wolves' death-boding cries	"	165
are dead and still	"	167
While lust and murder wakes to stain and kill	"	168
And now this lustful lord	"	169
between desire and dread	"	171
And to the flame	"	180
and in his inward mind	"	185
And justly thus controls	"	189
and lend it not	"	190
And die, unhallow'd thoughts	"	192
That spots and stains	"	196
and to shining arms	"	197
And be an eye-sore	"	205
and hold it for no sin	"	209
And—.... in a desperate rage	*R L*	219
And extreme fear	"	230
The shame and fault	"	238
but denial and reproving	"	242
conscience and hot-burning will	"	247
And with good thoughts	"	248
doth confound and kill	"	250
and doth so far proceed	"	251
And gazed for tidings	"	254
'And how her hand	"	260
and then it faster rock'd	"	262
and he leadeth	"	271
And when his gaudy banner	"	272
and will not be dismay'd	"	273
Respect and reason	"	275
Sad pause and deep regard	"	277
and beats these from the stage	"	278
and full of fond mistrust	"	284
and now invasion	"	287
And in the self-same seat	"	289
And therein heartens up	"	295
And as their captain	"	298
between her chamber and his will	"	302
little vents and crannies	"	310
And blows the smoke	"	312
And being lighted	"	316
And griping it	"	319
And give the suscaped birds	"	333
shelves and sands	"	335
and with no more	"	339
And they would stand	"	347
Then Love and Fortune	"	351
and misty night	"	356
And with his knee	"	359
And gazeth on	"	366
fair and fiery-pointed sun	"	372
and keep themselves enclosed	"	378
And holy-thoughted Lucrece	"	384
And canopied in darkness	"	398
And death's dim look	"	403
and death in life	"	406
And him by oath	"	410
And in his will	"	417
And they, like straggling slaves	"	428
bloody death and ravishment	"	430
and bids them	"	434
destitute and pale	"	441
their dear governess and lady	"	443
And fright her	"	445
dimm'd and controll'd	"	448
Wrapp'd and confounded	"	456
rise up and fall	"	466
more rage and lesser pity	"	468
To make the breach and enter	"	469
And the red rose	"	479
plead for me and tell	"	480
reproof and reason	"	489
is deaf and hears no heedful friends	"	495
And dotes on what he looks	"	497
disdain and deadly enmity	"	503
And in thy dead arms	"	517
and thou, the author	"	523
And sung by children	"	525
and thy children's sake	"	533
and makes a pause	"	541
And moody Pluto winks	"	553
And midst the sentence	"	566
and sweet friendship's oath	"	569
human law and common troth	"	571

And—			And—		
By heaven .... earth, ... all the power	R L	572	nursest all .... murder'st all	R L	929
and stoop to honour	"	574	and enchained me	"	934
rocky and wreck-threatening	"	590	and bring truth to light	"	940
and be compassionate	"	594	and sentinel the night	"	942
and if the same	"	600	And smear with dust	"	945
'And wilt thou be	"	617	and alter their contents	"	948
And makest fair reputation	"	623	and cherish springs	"	950
and thou didst teach the way	"	630	And turn the giddy round	"	952
and flattering thoughts retire	"	641	unicorn and lion wild	"	956
And wipe the dim mist	"	643	And waste huge stones	"	959
see thy state and pity mine	"	644	prevent this storm and shun	"	966
And with the wind	"	648	And the dire thought	"	972
And, lo, then falls	"	653	And let mild women	"	979
And not the puddle	"	658	And time to see	"	980
and thou their slave	"	659	And merry fools to mock	"	989
and they thy fouler grave	"	661	and how swift and short	"	991
For light and lust	"	674	and his time of sport	"	992
And he hath won	"	688	And ever let his unrecalling crime	"	993
And Lust, the thief,	"	693	good and bad	"	995
And then with lank and lean	"	708	And unperceived fly	"	1010
knit brow and strengthless pace	"	709	at Tarquin and uncheerful Night	"	1024
poor and meek	"	710	And wast afeard to scratch	"	1035
and when that decays	"	713	kill both thyself and her	"	1036
And by their mortal fault	"	724	'I live, and seek in vain	"	1044
and made her thrall	"	725	And therefore now I need not fear	"	1052
death and pain	"	726	And with my trespass	"	1070
And he the burthen	"	735	And solemn night with slow sad gait	"	1081
He scowls, and hates himself	"	738	And therefore still	"	1085
He runs, and chides	"	742	And seems to point her out	"	1087
And my true eyes	"	748	fond and testy	"	1094
And therefore would they	"	752	And to herself	"	1102
And grave, like water that doth eat	"	755	And as one shifts	"	1104
against repose and rest	"	757	her grief is dumb and hath no words	"	1105
And bids her eyes	"	758	'tis mad and too much talk affords	"	1106
And bids it leap	"	760	And in my hearing be you mute and dumb	"	1123
Dim register and notary	"	765			
tragedies and murders	"	766	And with deep groans	"	1132
treason and the ravisher	"	770	And whiles against a thorn	"	1135
vaporous and foggy Night	"	771	fall and die	"	1139
And let thy misty vapours	"	782	'And for, poor bird, thou sing'st not	"	1142
and make perpetual night	"	784	and then we will unfold	"	1146
And fellowship in woe	"	790	and death reproach's debtor	"	1155
and hang their heads	"	793	and be nurse to none	"	1162
and hide their infamy	"	794	for heaven and Collatine	"	1166
must sit and pine	"	795	and his sap decay	"	1168
And fright her crying babe	"	814	And as his due	"	1183
And undeserved reproach	"	824	And, for my sake	"	1197
And Tarquin's eye	"	830	My soul and body to the skies and ground	"	1199
and I, a drone-like bee	"	836			
But robb'd and ransack'd	"	838	And all my fame	"	1203
And suck'd the honey	"	840	live and think no shame	"	1204
And talk'd of virtue	"	846	both die and both shall victors be	"	1211
cramps and gouts and painful fits	"	856	And wiped the brinish pearl	"	1213
And scarce hath eyes	"	857	And sorts a sad look	"	1221
and useless barns	"	859	And then they drown	"	1239
And leaves it to be master'd	"	863	And therefore are they form'd	"	1241
and they too strong	"	865	and shame that might ensue	"	1263
And in thy shady cell	"	881	And who cannot	"	1267
and displacest haud	"	887	and there she stay'd	"	1275
And bring him where his suit	"	898	And ere I rose	"	1281
Wrath, envy, treason, rape, and murder's rages	"	909	And that deep torture	"	1287
			paper, ink, and pen	"	1289
Truth and Virtue	"	911	ready by and by to bear	"	1292
and thou art well appaid	"	914	and it will soon be writ	"	1295
murder and of theft	"	918	and she prepares to write	"	1296
perjury and subornation	"	919	Conceit and grief	"	1298
forgery and shift	"	920	this blunt and ill	"	1300
all sins past and all that are	"	923	come and visit me	"	1307

AND   17   AND

	R L	
And—the life .... feeling	"	1317
When sighs and groans and tears	"	1319
And sorrow ebbs	"	1330
and on it writ	"	1331
and she delivers it	"	1333
but dull and slow	"	1336
And blushing on her	"	1339
life and bold audacity	"	1346
And blushing with him	"	1355
And yet the duteous vassal	"	1360
to weep and groan	"	1362
And dying eyes	"	1378
and smeared all with dust	"	1381
And from the towers of Troy	"	1382
grace and majesty	"	1387
quick bearing and dexterity	"	1389
And here and there	"	1390
quake and tremble	"	1393
In Ajax and Ulysses	"	1394
blunt rage and rigour roll'd	"	1398
regard and smiling government	"	1400
Wagg'd up and down and from his lips	"	1406
all bull'n and red	"	1417
to pelt and swear	"	1418
And in their rage	"	1419
And from the walls	"	1429
And to their hope	"	1433
And from the strand	"	1436
and their ranks began	"	1439
the galled shore, and than	"	1440
They join and shoot	"	1442
all distress and dolour	"	1446
and grim care's reign	"	1451
with chaps and wrinkles	"	1452
And shapes her sorrow	"	1458
And bitter words	"	1460
And therefore Lucrece	"	1462
and not a tongue	"	1463
And drop sweet balm	"	1466
And rail on Pyrrhus	"	1467
And with my tears	"	1468
And with my knife	"	1469
And here in Troy	"	1476
dame and daughter die	"	1477
And friend to friend	"	1488
And one man's lust	"	1489
and not with fire	"	1491
and colour'd sorrow	"	1497
and she their looks	"	1498
And who she finds forlorn	"	1500
To hide deceit and give	"	1507
a constant and confirmed devil	"	1513
And therein so ensconced	"	1515
craft and perjury	"	1517
And little stars	"	1525
And chid the painter	"	1528
And still on him she gazed, and gazing still	"	1531
And from her tongue	"	1537
And turn'd it thus	"	1539
so weary and so mild	"	1542
and yet not wise	"	1550
And in that cold	"	1557
and make them bold	"	1559
Thus ebbs and flows	"	1569
And time doth weary time	"	1570
and then she longs	"	1571
And both she thinks	"	1572

	R L	
And—And they that watch	"	1575
his lord and other company	"	1584
And round about	"	1586
look'd red and raw	"	1592
And thus begins	"	1598
And tell thy grief	"	1603
Collatine and his consorted lords	"	1609
And now this pale swan	"	1611
And my laments	"	1616
and on that pillow lay	"	1620
And what wrong else	"	1622
And softly cried	"	1628
And entertain my love	"	1629
On thee and thine	"	1630
and then I'll slaughter thee	"	1634
And swear I found you	"	1635
and so did kill	"	1636
and thy perpetual infamy	"	1638
to start and cry	"	1639
And then against my heart	"	1640
And never be forgot	"	1644
Lucrece and her groom	"	1645
And far the weaker	"	1647
And when the judge is robb'd	"	1652
Immaculate and spotless	"	1656
head declined and voice damm'd up	"	1661
sad-set eyes and wretched arms	"	1662
and back the same grief	"	1673
And his untimely frenzy	"	1675
And for my sake	"	1681
And why not I	"	1708
many accents and delays	"	1719
sick and short assays	"	1720
and through her wounds	"	1728
and all his lordly crew	"	1731
And from the purple fountain	"	1734
and, as it left the place	"	1735
And bubbling from her breast	"	1737
Bare and unpeopled	"	1741
pure and red remain'd	"	1742
And some look'd black, and that false Tarquin	"	1743
the mourning and congealed face	"	1744
And ever since	"	1747
And blood untainted	"	1749
and they none of ours	"	1757
dim and old	"	1760
And shiver'd all the beauty	"	1763
and last no longer	"	1765
And leave the faltering feeble souls	"	1768
live again and see	"	1770
and not thy father thee	"	1771
And bids Lucretius	"	1773
And then in key-cold Lucrece	"	1774
He falls, and bathes	"	1775
And counterfeits to die	"	1776
And live to be revenged	"	1778
it rains, and busy winds	"	1790
Then son and father	"	1791
And only must be wail'd	"	1799
too early and too late	"	1801
I owed her and 'tis mine	"	1803
'My daughter' and 'my wife	"	1804
'my daughter' and 'my wife	"	1805
in state and pride	"	1809
and uttering foolish things	"	1813
And arm'd his long-hid wits	"	1816
and help to bear thy part	"	1830
And by this chaste blood	"	1836

2

And—And by chaste Lucrece	*R. L*	 1639	And—And do whate'er thou wilt	*Son*	19	6
and by this bloody knife	"	 1840	world and all her fading sweets	"	19	7
And kiss'd the fatal knife	"	 1843	men's eyes and women's souls	"	20	8
And to his protestation	"	 1844	And for a woman wert thou first			
And that deep vow	"	 1847	created	"	20	9
and that they swore	"	 1848	And by addition me of thee defeated	"	20	11
And so to publish	"	 1852	love, and thy love's use	"	20	14
And only herald to the gaudy	*Son*	1	10	And every fair with his fair	"	21	4
and tender churl, makest waste	"	1	12	with sun and moon, with earth and			
by the grave and thee	"	1	14	seas	"	21	6
and dig deep trenches	"	2	2	flowers, and all things rare	"	21	7
Shame and thriftless praise	"	2	8	And then believe me	"	21	10
and make my old excuse	"	2	11	youth and thou are of one date	"	22	2
and see thy blood warm	"	2	14	And in mine own	"	23	7
Look in thy glass and tell the face	"	3	1	And dumb presages	"	23	10
thy mother's glass and she in thee	"	3	9	love, and look for recompense	"	23	11
Die single, and thine image dies	"	3	14	play'd the painter and hath stell'd	"	24	1
And being frank, she lends	"	4	4	And perspective it is best painters'			
And that unfair which fairly	"	5	4	art	"	24	4
hideous winter and confounds him	"	5	6	drawn thy shape and thine for me	"	24	10
frost and lusty leaves	"	5	7	honour and proud titles	"	25	2
Beauty o'ersnow'd and bareness	"	5	8	And in themselves	."	25	7
death's conquest and make worms	"	6	14	And all the rest forgot	"	25	12
And having climb'd the steep-up	"	7	5	love and am beloved	"	25	13
low tract, and look another way	"	7	12	And puts apparel	"	26	11
sire and child and happy mother	"	8	11	And keep my drooping eye-lids	"	27	7
will be widow and still weep	"	9	5	beauteous and her old face new	"	27	12
And kept unused, the user	"	9	12	For thee and for myself	"	27	14
presence is gracious and kind	"	10	11	But day by night, and night by day	"	28	4
And that fresh blood	"	11	3	And each, though enemies	"	28	5
wisdom, beauty, and increase	"	11	5	And dost him grace	"	28	10
folly, age, and cold decay	"	11	6	And night doth nightly make	"	28	14
And threescore year would make	"	11	8	fortune and men's eyes	"	29	1
Harsh, featureless, and rude	"	11	10	And trouble deaf heaven	"	29	3
for her seal, and meant thereby	"	11	13	And look upon myself and curse	"	29	4
And see the brave day	"	12	2	this man's art and that man's scope	"	29	7
And sable curls all silver'd o'er	"	12	4	thee, and then my state	"	29	10
And summer's green all girded up	"	12	7	And with old woes new wail	"	30	4
White and bristly beard	"	12	8	And weep afresh	"	30	7
Since sweets and beauties do	"	12	11	And moan the expense	"	30	8
And die as fast as they see	"	12	12	And heavily from woe to woe	"	30	10
And nothing 'gainst time's scythe	"	12	13	restored and sorrows end	"	30	14
And your sweet semblance	"			And there reigns love and all love's	"	31	3
And barren rage of death's eternal	"	13	12	And all those friends	"	31	4
And yet methinks I have	"	14	2	holy and obsequious	"	31	5
his thunder, rain, and wind	"	14	6	And thou, all they	"	31	14
And, constant stars, in them I read	"	14	10	And shalt by fortune	"	32	3
As truth and beauty shall together				And though they be outstripp'd	"	32	6
thrive	"	14	11	died, and poets better prove	"	32	13
truth's and beauty's doom and date	"	14	14	And from the forlorn world	"	33	7
Cheered and check'd even by	"	15	6	And make me travel	"	34	2
And wear their brave state	"	15	8	wound and cures not	"	34	8
And all in war with Time	"	15	13	And they are rich and ransom all	"	34	14
And fortify yourself in your decay	"	16	3	thorns, and silver fountains mud	"	35	2
And many maiden gardens	"	16	6	Clouds and eclipses stain both moon			
And you must live, drawn	"	16	14	and sun	"	35	3
Which hides your life and shows not	"	17	4	And loathsome canker	"	35	4
And in fresh numbers	"	17	6	faults, and even I	"	35	5
And your true rights	"	17	11	And 'gainst myself	"	35	11
And stretched metre	"	17	12	my love and hate	"	35	12
live twice, in it and in my rhyme	"	17	14	worth and truth	"	37	4
lovely and more temperate	"	18	2	And by a part	"	37	12
And summer's lease hath all	"	18	4	And he that calls on thee	"	38	11
And often is his gold complexion	"	18	6	And what is 't but mine own	"	39	4
And every fair from fair	"	18	7	And our dear love	"	39	6
So long lives this, and this gives life	"	18	14	Which time and thoughts so sweetly	"	39	12
And make the earth devour	"	19	2	And that thou teachest	"	39	13
And burn the long-lived phœnix	"	19	4	And yet, love knows	"	40	11
Make glad and sorry seasons	"	19	5	Thy beauty and thy years	"	41	3

And—Gentle thou art, ... therefore	Son	41	5	And—And brass, eternal slave	Son	64	4
And when a woman woos	"	41	7	And the firm soil	"	64	7
And chide thy beauty and thy straying youth	"	41	10	loss and loss with store	"	64	8
				come and take my love away	"	64	12
And yet it may be	"	42	2	And needy nothing trimm'd	"	66	3
And for my sake	"	42	7	And purest faith unhappily forsworn	"	66	4
And losing her	"	42	10				
Both find each other, and I lose both	"	42	11	And gilded honour shamefully misplaced	"	66	5
And both for my sake	"	42	12				
my friend and I are one	"	42	13	And maiden virtue rudely strumpeted	"	66	6
And, darkly bright	"	43	4				
And night's bright days	"	43	14	And right perfection wrongfully disgraced	"	66	7
both sea and land	"	44	7				
earth and water wrought	"	44	11	And strength by limping sway disabled	"	66	8
slight air and purging fire	"	45	1				
again, and straight grow sad	"	45	14	And art made tongue-tied	"	66	9
Mine eye and heart	"	46	1	And folly, doctor-like, controlling skill	"	66	10
And says in him	"	46	8				
And by their verdict	"	46	11	And simple truth miscall'd	"	66	11
moiety and the dear heart's part	"	46	12	And captive good attending	"	66	12
And my heart's right	"	46	14	And with his presence	"	67	2
Betwixt eye and heart	"	47	1	And lace itself	"	67	4
And each doth good turns	"	47	2	And steal dead seeing	"	67	6
And to the painted banquet	"	47	6	And, proud of many	"	67	12
And in his thoughts	"	47	8	beauty lived and died	"	68	2
And I am still with them and they with me	"	47	12	itself and true	"	68	10
				And him as for a map	"	68	13
heart's and eye's delight	"	47	14	And that, in guess	"	69	10
dearest and mine only care	"	48	7	And thou present'st	"	70	8
may'st come and part	"	48	12	And mock you with me	"	71	11
And even thence	"	48	13	And hang more praise	"	72	7
And scarcely greet me	"	49	6	And live no more	"	72	12
And this my hand	"	49	11	And so should you	"	72	14
that ease and that repose	"	50	3	by and by black night	"	73	7
lies onward, and my joy behind	"	50	14	And that is this, and this with thee	"	74	14
run and give him leave	"	51	14	And for the peace	"	75	3
feasts solemn and so rare	"	52	5	miser and his wealth	"	75	4
And you, but one, can every shadow	"	53	4	enjoyer, and anon	"	75	5
Adonis, and the counterfeit	"	53	5	And by and by	"	75	10
And you in Grecian tires	"	53	8	pine and surfeit	"	75	13
spring and foison of the year	"	53	9	methods and to compounds strange	"	76	4
And you in every blessed shape	"	53	12	And keep invention	"	76	6
thorns, and play as wantonly	"	54	7	birth and where they did proceed	"	76	8
unwoo'd and unrespected fade	"	54	10	And you and love	"	76	10
And so of you, beauteous and lovely youth	"	54	13	daily new and old	"	76	13
				And of this book	"	77	4
And broils root out	"	55	6	blanks, and thou shalt find	"	77	10
death and all-oblivious enmity	"	55	9	thee and much enrich thy book	"	77	14
You live in this and dwell	"	55	14	And found such fair	"	78	2
see again, and do not kill	"	56	7	And under thee	"	78	4
the hours and times	"	57	2	And heavy ignorance	"	78	6
stay and think of nought	"	57	11	And given grace	"	78	8
And patience, tame to sufferance	"	58	7	thine and born of thee	"	78	10
And Time that gave doth now	"	60	8	And arts with thy sweet graces	"	78	12
And delves the parallels	"	60	10	art, and dost advance	"	78	13
And nothing stands but for his scythe	"	60	12	And my sick Muse	"	79	4
				He robs thee of, and pays it thee	"	79	8
And yet to times in hope my verse	"	60	13	and he stole that word	"	79	9
shames and idle hours	"	61	7	And found it in thy cheek	"	79	11
scope and tenour	"	61	8	And in the praise	"	80	3
And all my soul and all my every	"	62	2	building and of goodly pride	"	80	12
And for this sin	"	62	3	thrive and I be cast away	"	80	13
And for myself mine own worth	"	62	7	And tongues to be	"	81	11
Beated and chopp'd	"	62	10	And therefore may'st	"	82	2
hand crush'd and o'erworn	"	63	2	And therefore art	"	82	7
drain'd his blood and fill'd his brow	"	63	3	And do so, love	"	82	9
With lines and wrinkles	"	63	4	And their gross painting	"	82	13
And all those beauties	"	63	6	And therefore to your fair	"	83	2
And they shall live, and he in them	"	63	14	And therefore have I slept	"	83	5

Phrase	Ref	No.	Line	Phrase	Ref	No.	Line
And—give life .... bring a tomb	Son	83	12	And—'Fair, kind, ... true	Son	105	13
And such a counterpart	"	84	11	And beauty making beautiful	"	106	3
And precious phrase	"	85	4	ladies dead and lovely knights	"	106	4
And, like unletter'd clerk	"	85	6	And, for they look'd	"	106	11
And to the most of praise	"	85	10	And the sad augurs	"	107	6
And like enough	"	87	2	And peace proclaims olives	"	107	8
And for that riches	"	87	6	and Death to me subscribes	"	107	10
And so my patent back again	"	87	8	dull and speechless tribes	"	107	12
And place my merit	"	88	2	And thou in this shalt find	"	107	13
And prove thee virtuous	"	88	4	crests and tombs	"	107	14
And I by this will be a gainer too	"	88	9	dust and injury of age	"	108	10
And I will comment	"	89	2	time and outward form	"	108	14
lameness, and I straight will halt	"	89	3	gone here and there	"	110	1
strangle and look strange	"	89	8	And made myself	"	110	2
and in my tongue	"	89	9	Askance and strangely	"	110	6
And haply of our old acquaintance	"	89	12	And worse essays	"	110	8
And do not drop in for an after-loss	"	90	4	pure and most most loving breast	"	110	14
And other strains of woe	"	90	13	And almost thence	"	111	6
hawks and hounds	"	91	4	and wish I were renewed	"	111	8
And every humour	"	91	5	friend, and I assure you	"	111	13
And having thee	"	91	12	Your love and pity	"	112	1
away and me most wretched make	"	91	14	and I must strive	"	112	5
And life no longer	"	92	3	my shames and praises	"	112	6
false and yet I know it not	"	92	14	To critic and to flatterer	"	112	11
Is writ in moods and frowns and wrinkles strange	"	93	8	And that which governs	"	113	2
				function and is partly blind	"	113	3
hurt and will do none	"	94	1	And that your love	"	114	4
cold and to temptation slow	"	94	4	monsters and things indigest	"	114	5
And husband nature's riches	"	94	6	And my great mind most kingly	"	114	10
lords and owners	"	94	7	And to his palate	"	114	12
only live and die	"	94	10	loves it and doth first begin	"	114	14
sweet and lovely	"	95	1	and change decrees of kings	"	115	6
And all things turn	"	95	12	tempests and is never shaken	"	116	6
youth and gentle sport	"	96	2	rosy lips and cheeks	"	116	9
grace and faults are loved of more and less	"	96	3	brief hours and weeks	"	116	11
				be error and upon me proved	"	116	13
translated and for true things	"	96	8	And given to time	"	117	6
And yet this time	"	97	5	wilfulness and errors down	"	117	9
orphans and unfather'd fruit	"	97	10	And on just proof	"	117	10
for summer and his pleasure	"	97	11	constancy and virtue	"	117	14
And, thou away, the very birds are	"	97	12	And sick of welfare	"	118	7
laugh'd and leap'd with him	"	98	4	And brought to medicine	"	118	11
In odour and in hue	"	98	6	learn, and find the lesson	"	118	13
winter still and you away	"	98	13	hopes and hopes to fears	"	119	3
And buds of marjoram	"	99	7	And ruin'd love when it is built	"	119	11
And to his robbery	"	99	11	And gain by ill	"	119	14
and straight redeem	"	100	5	And for that sorrow	"	120	2
And gives thy pen both skill and argument	"	100	8	And I, a tyrant, have no leisure	"	120	7
				And soon to you	"	120	11
And make Time's spoils	"	100	12	and yours must ransom me	"	120	14
scythe and crooked knife	"	100	14	And the just pleasure	"	121	3
Both truth and beauty	"	101	3	I am, and they that level	"	121	9
and therein dignified	"	101	4	and in their badness reign	"	121	14
And to be praised	"	101	12	as brain and heart	"	122	5
was new, and then but in the spring	"	102	5	and therefore we admire	"	123	5
And stops her pipe	"	102	8	And rather make them	"	123	7
And sweets grown common	"	102	12	Thy registers and thee	"	123	9
and there appears a face	"	103	6	records and what we see	"	123	11
Dulling my lines and doing me disgrace	"	103	8	vow, and this shall ever be	"	123	13
				thy scythe and thee	"	123	14
your graces and your gifts	"	103	12	lose all, and more	"	125	6
And more, much more	"	103	13	And take thou my oblation	"	125	10
and no pace perceived	"	104	10	waning grown and therein show'st	"	126	3
Hath motion, and mine eye	"	104	12	disgrace and wretched minutes kill	"	126	8
songs and praises be	"	105	3	And her quietus is to render thee	"	126	12
still such and ever so	"	105	4	And beauty slander'd	"	127	4
'Fair, kind, and true	"	105	9	and they mourners seem	"	127	10
'Fair, kind, and true	"	105	10	And situation with those dancing chips	"	128	10
And in this change	"	105	11				

And—.... till action, lust	Son	129	2
and no sooner had	"	129	6
pursuit, and in possession so	"	129	9
having and in quest to have	"	129	10
in proof, and proved	"	129	11
red and white	"	130	5
And in some perfumes	"	130	7
And yet by heaven	"	130	13
fairest and most precious	"	131	4
And to be sure	"	131	9
And thence this slander	"	131	14
I love, and they, as pitying me	"	132	1
on black and loving mourners	"	132	3
And truly not	"	132	5
And suit thy pity	"	132	12
And all they foul	"	132	14
my friend and me	"	133	2
And my next self	"	133	6
myself and thee	"	133	7
And yet thou wilt	"	133	13
and all that is in me	"	133	14
And I myself	"	134	2
covetous and he is kind	"	134	6
And sue a friend	"	134	11
both him and me	"	134	13
and yet am I not free	"	134	14
And 'Will' to boot and 'Will' in overplus	"	135	2
large and spacious	"	135	5
And in my will	"	135	8
And in abundance	"	135	10
and me in that one 'Will	"	135	14
And will, thy soul knows	"	136	3
and my will one	"	136	6
and love that still	"	136	13
And then thou lovest me	"	136	14
behold, and see not	"	137	2
my heart and eyes have err'd	"	137	13
And to this false plague	"	137	14
And wherefore say not I	"	138	10
And age in love	"	138	12
I lie with her and she with me	"	138	13
And in our faults	"	138	14
and slay me not by art	"	139	4
And therefore from	"	139	11
and rid my pain	"	139	14
words and words express	"	140	3
And in my madness	"	140	10
slave and vassal wretch to be	"	141	12
and thy dear virtue hate	"	142	1
And thou shalt find	"	142	4
And seal'd false bonds	"	142	7
sets down her babe and makes	"	143	3
And play the mother's part	"	143	12
turn back and my loud crying still	"	143	14
of comfort and despair	"	144	1
And would corrupt my saint	"	144	7
And whether that my angel	"	144	9
And taught it thus	"	145	8
And saved my life	"	145	14
pine within and suffer dearth	"	146	3
And let that pine	"	146	10
And Death once dead	"	146	14
and I desperate now approve	"	147	7
And frantic-mad with ever-more unrest	"	147	10
thoughts and my discourse	"	147	11
and thought thee bright	"	147	13
with watching and with tears	"	148	10

And—.... I am blind	Son	149	14
And swear that brightness	"	150	4
strength and warrantise of skill	"	150	7
hear and see just cause	"	150	10
for whose dear love I rise and fall	"	151	11
and new faith torn	"	152	3
And all my honest faith	"	152	8
And, to enlighten thee	"	152	11
laid by his brand and fell asleep	"	153	1
And his love-kindling fire	"	153	3
And grew a seething bath	"	153	7
And thither hied	"	153	12
And so the general of hot desire	"	154	7
a bath and healthful remedy	"	154	11
cure, and this by that I prove	"	154	13
And down I laid	L C		4
sorrow's wind and rain	"		7
beauty spent and done	"		11
And often reading	"		19
both high and low	"		21
and nowhere fix'd	"		27
The mind and sight distractedly	"		28
pale and pined cheek beside	"		32
And, true to bondage	"		34
crystal, and of beaded jet	"		37
tore, and gave the flood	"		41
of posied gold and bone	"		45
silk feat and affectedly	"		48
and seal'd to curious secresy	"		49
and often kiss'd, and often 'gan to tear	"		51
more black and damned here	"		54
and had let go by	"		59
And, privileged by age	"		62
grounds and motives of her woe	"		63
And comely-distant sits he	"		65
and to no love beside	"		77
and made him her place	"		82
And when in his fair parts lodged and newly deified	"		83
	"		84
And every light occasion	"		86
And nice affections	"		97
maiden-tongued he was and there- of free	"		100
May and April is to see	"		102
and often men would say	"		106
And controversy hence	"		110
gave life and grace	"		114
To appertainings and to ornament	"		115
arguments and question deep	"		121
prompt and reason strong	"		122
did wake and sleep	"		123
dialect and different skill	"		125
and sexes both enchanted	"		128
And dialogued for him	"		132
and made their wills obey	"		133
and in it put their mind	"		135
Of lands and mansions	"		138
And labouring in moe pleasures	"		139
And was my own fee-simple	"		144
art in youth and youth in art	"		145
and gave him all my flower	"		147
and his amorous spoil	"		154
Though Reason weep, and cry	"		168
And knew the patterns	"		170
and words merely but art	"		174
And bastards of his foul adulterate	"		175
And long upon these terms	"		176
And be not of my holy vows	"		179

And—And so much less of shame	L C	188	And—with horn .... hounds	P P	9	6
And reign'd, commanding	"	196	And blushing fled and left her	"	9	14
and rubies red as blood	"	198	and vaded in the spring	"	10	2
Of grief and blushes	"	200	And falls through wind	"	10	6
and the encrimson'd mood	"	201	and yet no cause I have	"	10	7
terror and dear modesty	"	202	And yet thou left'st me more	"	10	9
And, lo, behold these talents	"	204	And as he fell to her	"	11	4
And deep-brain'd sonnets	"	209	And then she clipp'd Adonis	"	11	6
worth and quality	"	210	And with her lips on his	"	11	10
'twas beautiful and hard	"	211	And as she fetched breath	"	11	11
sapphire and the opal blend	"	215	And would not take her meaning	"	11	12
Of pensived and subdued desires	"	219	To kiss and clip me	"	11	14
my origin and ender	"	222	Crabbed age and youth	"	12	1
and to your audit comes	"	230	Youth is hot and bold, age is weak			
and did thence remove	"	237	and cold	"	12	7
And makes her absence	"	245	Youth is wild and age is tame	"	12	8
And now she would	"	249	a vain and doubtful good	"	13	1
And now, to tempt all	"	252	And as goods lost	"	13	7
And mine I pour	"	256	painting, pain, and cost	"	13	12
o'er them, and you o'er me	"	257	And dall'd me to a cabin	"	14	3
vows and consecrations	"	263	and come again to-morrow	"	14	5
thou art all, and all things	"	266	sits and sings I sit and mark	"	15	5
And sweetens, in the suffering pangs	"	272	And wish her lays	"	15	6
forces, shocks, and fears	"	275	And drives away dark dreaming			
And supplicant their sighs	"	276	night	"	15	8
And credent soul to that strong-			and eyes their wished sight	"	15	10
bonded oath	"	279	and solace mix'd with sorrow	"	15	11
prefer and undertake my troth	"	280	and bade me come to-morrow	"	15	12
and chill extincture hath	"	294	and length thyself to-morrow	"	15	13
sober guards and civil fears	"	298	And deny himself for Jove	"	17	17
and mine did him restore	"	301	And stall'd the deer	"	19	2
and he takes and leaves	"	303	And when thou comest	"	19	7
and swound at tragic shows	"	308	And set thy person forth to sell	"	19	12
is both kind and tame	"	311	And then too late she will repent	"	19	15
And, veil'd in them	"	312	And twice desire, ere it be day	"	19	17
and praised cold chastity	"	315	And ban and brawl, and say thee			
naked and concealed fiend	"	317	nay	"	19	20
Who, young and simple	"	320	And to her will frame all thy ways	"	19	25
I fell and yet do question make	"	322	Spare not to spend and chiefly there	"	19	26
And new pervert a reconciled maid	"	329	castle, tower, and town	"	19	29
And wherefore say not I	P P	1	10	And in thy suit be humble true	"	19	32
And age, in love	"	1	12	wiles and guiles that women	"	19	37
I'll lie with love and love with me	"	1	13	The tricks and toys that in them	"	19	39
of comfort and despair	"	2	1	To sin and never for to saint	"	19	44
And would corrupt my saint	"	2	7	Live with me and be my love	"	20	1
And whether that my angel	"	2	9	And we will all the pleasures prove	"	20	2
and breath a vapour is	"	3	9	hills and valleys, dales and fields	"	20	3
lovely, fresh, and green	"	4	2	And all the craggy mountains yields	"	20	4
she touch'd him here and there	"	4	7	And see the shepherds feed	"	20	6
But smile and jest	"	4	12	A cap of flowers, and a kirtle	"	20	11
fair queen, and toward	"	4	13	A belt of straw and ivy buds	"	20	13
He rose and ran away	"	4	14	With coral clasps and amber studs	"	20	14
bias leaves, and makes his book	"	5	5	And if these pleasures	"	20	15
Is music and sweet fire	"	5	12	Then live with me and be my love	"	20	16
And scarce the herd	"	6	2	the world and love were young	"	20	17
and throws his mantle by	"	6	9	And truth in every shepherd's	"	20	18
And stood stark naked	"	6	10	To live with thee and be thy love	"	20	20
Brighter than glass and yet as glass	"	7	3	Beasts did leap and birds did sing	"	21	5
Softer than wax, and yet as iron	"	7	4	Trees did grow and plants did spring	"	21	6
her tears, and all were jestings	"	7	12	And there sung the dolefull'st ditty	"	21	11
and yet she foil'd the framing	"	7	15	'Tereu, Tereu!' by and by	"	21	14
and yet she fell a-turning	"	7	16	Thou and I were both beguiled	"	21	30
If music and sweet poetry agree	"	8	1	And with such-like fluttery	"	21	41
the sister and the brother	"	8	2	Herald sad and trumpet be	P T		3
'twixt thee and me	"	8	3	And thou treble-dated crow	"		17
the one and I the other	"	8	4	breath thou givest and takest	"		19
And I in deep delight	"	8	11	Love and constancy is dead	"		22
and both in thee remain	"	8	14	Phœnix and the turtle fled	"		23
a youngster proud and wild	"	9	4	Distance, and no space was seen	"		30

And—

'Twixt the turtle .... his queen	P T	.....	31
To the phoenix and the dove	"	.....	50
Co-supremes and stars of love	"	.....	51
Beauty, truth, and rarity	"	.....	53
And the turtle's loyal breast	"	.....	57
Truth and beauty buried be	"	.....	64

Anew—she doth .... begin V A 60
- enforced to seek anew Son 82 7
- when it is built anew " 119 11
- And taught it thus anew to greet " 145 8
- Press never thou to choose anew P P 19 31

Angel—The better .... is a man right fair Son 144 3
- my better angel from my side " 144 6
- my angel be turn'd fiend " 144 9
- one angel in another's hell " 144 12
- my bad angel fire my good one out " 144 11
- My better angel is a man right fair P P 2 3
- my better angel from my side " 2 6
- my angel be turn'd fiend " 2 9
- one angel in another's hell " 2 12
- my bad angel fire my good one out " 2 14

Anger—and ... ashy-pale V A 76
- for anger makes the lily pale R L 478
- anger thrusts into his hide Son 50 10
- Which, not to anger bent P P 3 12

Angry—beauty in his .... eyes V A 70
- his rider's angry stir " 283
- hides his angry brow " 339
- Who, therefore angry, seems R L 388
- angry that the eyes fly from their " 461
- would debate with angry swords " 1421
- scratch out the angry eyes " 1459
- Angry that his prescriptions Son 147 6

Angry-chafing—
- The picture of an .... boar V A 662

Annexation—
- annexations of fair gems L C 208

Annexed—But ill-annexed Opportunity R L 874
- had annex'd thy breath Son 99 11

Annoy—life was death's .... V A 497
- Tantalus' is her annoy " 599
- For mirth doth search the bottom of annoy R L 1109
- cloud-kissing Ilion with annoy " 1370
- receivest with pleasure thine annoy Son 8 4

Anon—.... he rears upright V A 279
- Anon he starts at stirring " 302
- Anon their loud alarums " 700
- Anon she hears them " 849
- Anon his beating heart R L 433
- Anon permit the basest clouds Son 33 5
- Now proud as an enjoyer, and anon " 75 5
- anon their gazes lend L C 26
- Anon he comes P P 6 9
- Anon Adonis comes " 9 6

Another—his lips .... way V A 90
- As if another chase " 696
- And there another " 913
- another sadly scowling " 917
- Another flap-mouth'd mourner " 920
- Another and another answer " 922
- Puffs forth another wind R L 313
- thy present trespass in another " 632
- The branches of another root " 823
- another straight ensues " 1104
- lean'd on another's head " 1415

Another—

- Another smother'd seems to pelt R L 1418
- to speak another word " 1642
- Another power; no flood by raining " 1677
- that face should form another Son 3 2
- to breed another thee " 6 7
- and look another way " 7 12
- sweet husband to another " 8 9
- Make thee another self " 10 13
- Another time mine eye " 47 7
- Ere beauty's dead fleece made another gay " 68 8
- no summer of another's green " 68 11
- doth give another place " 79 4
- another white despair " 99 9
- gave my heart another youth " 110 7
- One on another's neck " 131 11
- one angel in another's hell " 144 12
- one angel in another's hell P P 2 12
- One woman would another woo " 19 44

Answer—she answers him, as if V A 308
- echoes answer so " 840
- they answer all ''Tis so " 851
- Another and another answer " 922
- Tarquin answers with surmise R L 83
- to answer her but cries " 1459
- to answer his desire " 1606
- If thou could'st answer Son 2 10
- he answers with a groan " 50 11
- answer not thy show " 93 14
- Answer—that stops his .... so R L 1654
- Make answer, Muse Son 101 5

Answer'd—Answer'd their cries R L 1846
- though delay'd answer'd must be Son 126 11

Answering—
- tapsters .... every call V A 849

Anthem—Her heavy .... " 839
- Here the anthem doth commence P T 21

Antic—Quick-shifting antics R L 459
- Antickpate—in love, to .... Son 118 9

Antique—metre of an ... song " 17 12
- with thine antique pen " 19 10
- In some antique book " 59 7
- those holy antique hours " 68 9
- I see their antique pen " 106 7

Antiquity—To spoil antiquities R L 951
- Beated and chopp'd with tann'd antiquity Son 62 10
- Makes antiquity for aye his page " 108 12

Any—snow takes .... dint V A 354
- be any jot diminish'd " 417
- if any love you owe me " 523
- never relieved by any " 704
- or any thing ensuing " 1078
- As shaming any eye R L 1143
- May any terms acquit me " 1705
- deny that thou bear'st love to any Son 10 1
- As any mother's child " 21 11
- Or any of these all " 37 6
- lock'd up in any chest " 48 9
- Though you do any thing " 57 11
- I was not sick of any fear from thence " 86 12
- make me any summer's story tell " 98 7
- If time have any wrinkle graven " 100 10
- If any, be a satire to decay " 100 11
- As any she belied with false compare " 130 14
- To any sensual feast " 141 8
- Or any of my leisures L C 193

| APACE | 24 | ARE |

Apace—			
through the dark laund runs	V A	813	
downward flow'd apace	L C	284	
Appaid—thou art well	R L	914	
Appal—Appals her senses	V A	882	
Appalled—Property was thus	P T	37	
Apparel—And puts .... on my tattered loving	Son 26	11	
Apparition—At apparitions, signs	V A	926	
Appeal—Since my .... says	Son 117	13	
But with a pure appeal	R L	293	
my heaved-up hands appeal	"	638	
Appear—in each cheek appears	V A	242	
and in the breach appears	"	1175	
in his fair welkin once appear	R L	116	
yet winking there appears	"	458	
faults do seldom to themselves appear	"	633	
of Troy there would appear	"	1382	
their light joy seem'd to appear	"	1434	
As interest of the dead which now appear	Son 31	7	
your bounty doth appear	" 53	11	
doth wilfully appear	" 80	8	
though less the show appear	" 102	2	
and there appears a face	" 103	6	
began but to appear	L C	93	
Appear to him as he to me appears	"	299	
Appearance—In him thy fair .... lies	Son 46	8	
Appearing—homage to his new-appearing sight	" 7	3	
Appertaining—To appertainings and to ornament	L C	115	
Appetite—With leaden	V A	34	
edge on his keen appetite	R L	9	
Nor aught obeys but his foul appetite	"	546	
Thy edge should blunter be than appetite	Son 56	2	
Mine appetite I never more	" 110	10	
to make our appetites more keen	" 118	1	
sickly appetite to please	" 147	4	
O appetite from judgement	L C	166	
Apple—How like Eve's	Son 93	13	
Applied—being so	R L	531	
there may be aught applied	L C	68	
if I had self-applied	"	76	
Applied to cautels	"	303	
Applying—Applying this to that	V A	713	
Applying fears to hopes	Son 119	3	
applying wet to wet	L C	40	
Approach—Welcomes the warm	V A	386	
For his approach that often there	P P	68	
Approve—for my sake to .... her	Son 42	8	
slander doth but approve	" 70	5	
I desperate now approve	" 147	7	
Apology—Apologies be made	R L	31	
April—Show'd like an .... daisy	"	395	
calls back the lovely April of her prime	Son 3	10	
With April's first-born flowers	" 21	7	
When proud-pied April dress'd in	" 98	2	
Three April perfumes	" 104	7	
'twixt May and April is to see	L C	102	
Apt—As .... as new-fall'n snow	V A	354	
Youth so apt to pluck	P P 17	14	
Aptly—the story .... ends	V A	716	
to do will aptly find	L C	88	

Aptly—blushes, ... understood	L C	200	
Aptness—In either's	"	306	
Arabian—the sole .... tree	P T	2	
Arbitrator—Unprofitable sounds, weak arbitrators	R L	1017	
Arch—As through an	"	1667	
Arden—From the besieged	"	1	
At Ardea to my lord	"	1332	
Are—doves or roses	V A	10	
yet are they red	"	116	
there are but twain	"	123	
flowers that are not gather'd	"	131	
Mine eyes are grey	"	140	
Torches are made to light	"	163	
are growth's abuse	"	166	
Her words are done	"	254	
proud, as females are	"	309	
beams upon his hairless face are fix'd	"	487	
Are they not quickly	"	520	
sheep are gone to fold	"	532	
Her lips are conquerors	"	549	
are both of them extremes	"	567	
Things out of hope are compass'd oft	"	567	
Are better proof	"	626	
Are like a labyrinth	"	684	
hounds are driven to doubt	"	692	
Are on the sudden	"	749	
night-wanderers often are	"	825	
hours are long	"	842	
and are never done	"	846	
hounds are at a bay	"	877	
that they are afraid	"	898	
poor people are amazed	"	925	
are both of them extremes	"	987	
her eyes are fled	"	1037	
Her eyes are mad	"	1062	
My sighs are blown away	"	1071	
Mine eyes are turn'd to fire	"	1072	
The flowers are sweet	"	1079	
and they are pale	"	1123	
Are weakly fortress'd	R L	28	
Those that much covet are with gain so fond	"	134	
The things we are for that which	"	149	
pure thoughts are dead and still	"	167	
All orators are dumb	"	268	
Our mistress' ornaments are chaste	"	322	
Thoughts are but dreams	"	353	
But blind they are	"	378	
Are by his flaming torch	"	448	
Such shadows are the weak brain's	"	460	
Are nature's faults	"	539	
in a wilderness where are no laws	"	544	
pity-pleading eyes are sadly fix'd	"	561	
monarchs still are fear'd for love	"	611	
For princes are the glass	"	615	
O, how are they wrapp'd	"	636	
Small lights are soon blown out	"	647	
light and lust are deadly enemies	"	674	
faults which in thy reign are made	"	804	
branches of another root are rotted	"	823	
all that are to come	"	923	
and murder'st all that are	"	929	
grooms are sightless night	"	1013	
Gnats are unnoted	"	1014	
eyes that are sleeping	"	1090	
Sad souls are slain	"	1110	
Their gentle sex to weep are often willing	"	1237	

Are—And therefore.... they form'd	*R L*	1241
Poor women's faces are their own faults' books	"	1253
that they are so fulfill'd	"	1258
that down thy cheeks are raining	"	1271
My woes are tedious, though my words are brief	"	1309
Greeks that are thine enemies	"	1470
Are balls of quenchless fire	"	1554
words are now depending	"	1615
We are their offspring	"	1757
As silly jeering idiots are with kings	"	1812
she lends to those are free	*Son*	4 4
The eyes, 'fore-duteous, now converted are	"	7 11
were yourself! but, love, you are	"	13 1
youth and thou are of one date	"	22 2
Are windows to my breast	"	24 11
Let those who are in favour	"	25 1
All losses are restored	"	30 14
Ah, but those tears are pearl	"	34 13
And they are rich and ransom	"	34 14
Excusing thy sins more than thy sins are	"	35 8
our undivided loves are one	"	36 2
my friend and I are one	"	42 13
darkly bright, are bright in dark	"	43 4
All days are nights to see till I see	"	43 13
Are both with thee	"	45 2
For when these quicker elements are gone	"	45 5
Mine eye and heart are at a mortal war	"	46 1
my jewels trifles are	"	48 5
Thus far the miles are measured	"	50 4
Therefore are feasts so solemn and	"	52 5
Like stones of worth they thinly placed are	"	52 7
Blessed are you, whose worthiness	"	52 13
whereof are you made	"	53 1
And you in Grecian tires are painted new	"	53 8
Of their sweet deaths are sweetest odours made	"	54 12
where you are how happy you	"	57 12
how are our brains beguiled	"	59 2
Whether we are mended	"	59 11
Are vanishing or vanish'd	"	63 7
When rocks impregnable are not so stout	"	65 7
those holy antique hours are seen	"	68 9
So are you to my thoughts	"	75 1
sweet-season'd showers are to the	"	75 2
And you and love are still my argument	"	76 10
my gracious numbers are decayed	"	79 3
breathers of this world are dead	"	81 12
praise that you alone are you	"	84 2
That you are you	"	84 8
My bonds in thee are all	"	87 4
these particulars are not my	"	91 8
Who, moving others, are themselves as stone	"	94 3
They are the lords and owners	"	94 7
Both grace and faults are loved	"	95 3
So are those errors that in thee are seen	"	96 7
the very birds are mute	"	97 12
I saw you fresh which yet are green	"	104 8
Are—praises.... but prophecies	*Son*	106 9
crests and tombs of brass are spent	"	107 11
You are my all the world	"	112 5
To critic and to flatterer stopped are	"	112 11
You are so strongly in my purpose	"	112 13
That all the world beside methinks are dead	"	112 14
Or on my frailties why are frailer spies	"	121 7
All men are bad	"	121 14
Thy gift, thy tables are within	"	122 1
To me are nothing novel	"	123 3
They are but dressings	"	123 4
Our dates are brief	"	123 5
my mistress' eyes are raven black	"	127 9
saucy jacks so happy are in this	"	128 13
my mistress' eyes are nothing like the sun	"	130 1
her breasts are dun	"	130 3
are they now transferred	"	137 14
my days are past the best	"	138 6
Nor are mine ears	"	141 5
prescriptions are not kept	"	147 6
and my discourse as madmen's are	"	147 11
my vows are oaths	"	152 7
their poor balls are tied	*L C*	24
Are errors of the blood	"	181
How mighty then you are	"	253
all things else are thine	"	266
what are precepts worth	"	267
Love's arms are peace	"	271
goods lost are seld or never found	*P P*	13 7
now are minutes added	"	15 14
All my merry jigs are quite forgot	"	18 9
friends are lapp'd in lead	"	21 24
Words are easy, like the wind	"	21 33
Faithful friends are hard to find	"	21 34
These are certain signs to know	"	21 57
That are either true or fair	*P T*	66
Aright—what they see....	*Son*	148 4
Arise—What following sorrow may on this arise	*R L*	186
quoth he, 'arise	"	1818
so, till the judgement that yourself arise	*Son*	55 13
Ariseth—		
The sun.... in his majesty	*V A*	856
Arising—at break of day....	*Son*	29 11
Argued—Argued by beauty's red	*R L*	65
Argument—I force not.... a straw	"	1021
Thine own sweet argument	*Son*	38 3
And you and love are still my argument	"	76 10
I grant, sweet love, thy lovely argument	"	79 5
both skill and argument	"	100 8
The argument, all bare, is of more worth	"	103 3
is all my argument	"	105 9
All kind of arguments	*L C*	121
could not hold argument	*P P*	3 2
Arm—Over one.... the lusty	*V A*	31
fasten'd in her arms	"	68
my arms his field	"	108
her arms infold him	"	225
in her arms be bound	"	226
twining arms doth urge	"	256
Her arms do lend	"	539
yoking arms she throws	"	592

Arm—those fair arms which bound	V A	.....	812
Honour and beauty in the owner's arms	R L		27
With bruised arms and wreaths	"	.....	110
Throwing his mantle rudely o'er his arm	"	.....	170
knighthood and to shining arms	"	.....	197
And in thy dead arms	"	.....	517
To cross their arms	"	.....	793
and wretched arms across	"	.....	1662
with revengeful arms	"	.....	1693
By our strong arms	"	.....	1834
Love's arms are peace	L C	.....	271
clipp'd Adonis in her arms	P P	11	6
with arms contending	"	16	13
Armed—with hairy bristles	V A	.....	625
stands armed in mine ear	"	.....	779
Griped in an armed hand	R L	.....	1425
To me came Tarquin armed	"	.....	1544
And arm'd his long-hid wits	"	.....	1816
Armour—His naked	"	.....	188
Army—To these two armies	"	.....	76
Array—In his fresh	V A	.....	483
these rebel powers that thee array	Son	146	2
Arrest—Hath served a dumb upon his tongue	R L	.....	1780
when that fell arrest	Son	74	1
Arrive—Ere he .... his weary noon-tide prick	R L	.....	781
Arrived—this false lord	"	.....	50
Arrow—Love's golden	V A	.....	947
Art—His .... with nature's	"	.....	291
In scorn of nature art gave lifeless life	R L	.....	1374
In Ajax and Ulysses, O, what art	"	.....	1394
And, constant stars, in them I read such art	Son	14	3
It is best painter's art	"	24	4
Yet eyes this cunning want to grace their art	"	24	13
Desiring this man's art	"	29	7
On Helen's cheek all art of beauty set	"	53	7
And art made tongue-tied by	"	66	9
To show false Art	"	68	14
And arts with thy sweet graces graced be	"	78	12
Which is not mix'd with seconds knows no art	"	125	11
with art's false-borrow'd face	"	127	6
slay me not by art	"	139	4
What with his art in youth, and youth in art	L C	.....	145
Thought, characters, and words merely but art	"	.....	174
but an art of craft	"	.....	295
those pleasures live that art can comprehend	P P	5	6
Thus art with arms contending	"	16	13
Art—why art thou coy	V A	.....	96
Art thou ashamed	"	.....	121
thou art bound to breed	"	.....	171
thou thyself art dead	"	.....	172
Art thou obdurate	"	.....	199
Art thou a woman's son	"	.....	201
Thou art no man	"	.....	215
thyself art made away	"	.....	763
thou art so full	"	.....	1021
Since thou art dead	"	.....	1135
Art—Thou .... the next	V A	.....	1184
Thyself art mighty	R L	.....	583
harder than a stone thou art	"	.....	593
Thou art not what thou seem'st	"	.....	600
Thou seem'st not what thou art	"	.....	601
when once thou art a king	"	.....	6
'Thou art,' quoth she, 'a sea	"	.....	652
Since thou art guilty	"	.....	772
and thou art well appaid	"	.....	914
Guilty thou art of murder	"	.....	918
thou art doting father	"	.....	1064
Priam, why art thou old	"	.....	1550
Why art thou thus attired	"	.....	1601
Thou that art now the world's	Son	1	9
when thou art old	"	2	13
Thou art thy mother's glass	"	3	9
happier than thou art	"	6	9
for thou art much too fair	"	6	13
Who for thyself art so unprovident	"	10	2
thou art beloved of many	"	10	3
thou art so possess'd	"	10	5
Thou art more lovely	"	18	2
elder than thou art	"	22	8
thou art bright	"	28	9
Thou art the grave	"	31	9
When thou art all the better part	"	39	2
temptation follows where thou art	"	41	4
Gentle thou art	"	41	5
Beauteous thou art	"	41	6
Where thou art forced to break	"	41	12
when thou art gone	"	44	10
Thyself away art present still	"	47	10
Art left the prey	"	48	8
Save where thou art not, though I feel thou art	"	48	10
From where thou art	"	51	3
That thou art blamed	"	70	1
But thou art all my art and dost advance	"	78	13
Thou art as fair	"	82	5
And therefore art enforced to seek	"	82	7
thou art too dear	"	87	1
though thou art forsworn	"	88	4
thou art assured mine	"	92	2
I live supposing thou art true	"	93	1
Where art thou, Muse, that thou	"	100	1
thou art my all	"	109	14
Thou art as tyrannous, so as thou art	"	131	1
Thou art the fairest	"	131	4
In nothing art thou black	"	131	13
For thou art covetous	"	134	6
Be wise as thou art cruel	"	140	1
Who art as black as hell	"	147	14
But thou art twice forsworn	"	152	2
For thou art all, and all things	L C	.....	266
Celestial thou art	P P	5	13
As—Even .... the sun	V A	.....	1
Ten kisses short as one, one long as twenty	"	.....	22
red and hot as coals	"	.....	35
him, as she would be thrust	"	.....	41
along as he was down	"	.....	43
Even as an empty eagle	"	.....	55
steam as on a prey	"	.....	63
ducks as quickly in	"	.....	87
woo'd as I entreat thee now	"	.....	97
thine own as well as mine	"	.....	117
My beauty as the spring	"	.....	141

AS 27 AS

As—flinty, hard .... steel	V A	 199	As—First red .... roses	R L	 258
Smiles as in disdain	"	 241	Then white as lawn	"	 259
As from a furnace	"	 274	had Narcissus seen her as she stood	"	 265
as if he told the steps	"	 277	As corn o'ergrown by weeds	"	 281
As who should say	"	 280	Both which, as servitors to the un-		
As if the dead	"	 292	just	"	 285
She answers him as if	"	 308	That eye which him beholds as		
proud, as females are	"	 309	more divine	"	 291
As they were mad	"	 323	as minutes fill up hours	"	 297
as desperate in his suit	"	 336	And as their captain	"	 298
Even as a dying coal	"	 338	But, as they open	"	 301
as lightning from the sky	"	 348	As each unwilling portal	"	 309
before him as he sat	"	 349	As who should say	"	 320
as apt as new-fall'n snow	"	 354	Or as those bars which stop	"	 327
eyes as they had not seen them	"	 357	As if the heavens should counte-		
thou wert as I am	"	 369	nance his sin	"	 343
all whole as thine	"	 370	Look, as the fair and fiery-pointed		
Thy palfrey, as he should	"	 385	sun	"	 372
my love to thee be still as much	"	 442	As if between them twain	"	 403
Even as the wind is hush'd	"	 458	As the grim lion	"	 421
Or as the wolf doth grin	"	 459	as proud of such a dignity	"	 437
Or as the berry breaks	"	 460	Whose ranks of blue veins as his		
lies as she were slain	"	 473	hand did scale	"	 440
And as the bright sun	"	 485	Imagine her as one in dead of night	"	 449
As if from thence	"	 488	But as reproof and reason beat it		
And as they last	"	 507	dead	"	 489
as the fleet-foot roe	"	 561	as fowl hear falcon's bells	"	 511
Even as poor birds	"	 601	A fault unknown is as a thought		
As those poor birds	"	 604	unacted	"	 527
assay'd as much as	"	 608	With such black payment as thou		
As fearful of him	"	 630	hast pretended	"	 576
beauties as he roots the mead	"	 636	Look as the full-fed hound	"	 694
As air and water do abate	"	 654	Were Tarquin Night as he is but		
As if another chase	"	 696	Night's child	"	 785
As burning fevers	"	 739	As palmers' chat makes short their		
As mountain snow	"	 750	pilgrimage	"	 791
As caterpillars do	"	 798	That is as clear from this attaint	"	 825
she darts, as one on shore	"	 817	As I, ere this, was pure to Collatine	"	 826
amazed, as one	"	 823	hours wait on them as their pages	"	 910
'stonish'd as night wanderers	"	 825	As well to hear as grant what he		
as seeming troubled	"	 839	hath said	"	 913
as thou dost lend	"	 864	As slanderous death's-man to so		
And as she runs	"	 871	base a slave	"	 1001
bleeding as they go	"	 924	As smoke from Ætna that in air		
as one full of despair	"	 953	consumes	"	 1042
As striving who	"	 968	As from a mountain spring that		
As scorning it should pass	"	 982	feeds	"	 1077
When as I met the boar	"	 999	testy as a child	"	 1094
As one with treasure	"	 1022	And as one shifts another straight		
As falcons to the lure	"	 1027	ensues	"	 1104
as murdered with the view	"	 1031	As the dank earth weeps	"	 1130
Or, as the snail	"	 1033	These means, as frets upon an in-		
As when the wind	"	 1046	strument	"	 1140
As if they heard	"	 1126	As shaming any eye	"	 1143
As dry combustious matter	"	 1162	As the poor frighted deer	"	 1149
know, it is as good	"	 1181	And as his due	"	 1183
my breast as in his blood	"	 1182	As winter meads when sun doth	"	 1218
mortal stars, as bright as heaven's			But as the earth doth weep	"	 1226
beauties	R L	 13	are they form'd as marble will	"	 1241
as soon decay'd and done	"	 23	as in a rough-grown grove	"	 1249
As is the morning's silver-melting			to hie as fast	"	 1331
dew	"	 24	As lagging fowls before the north-		
As one of which doth	"	 127	ern blast	"	 1335
As life for honour in fell battle's			as knowing Tarquin's lust	"	 1354
rage	"	 145	As heaven, it seem'd	"	 1372
As from this cold flint I enforced			As 'twere encouraging	"	 1402
this fire	"	 181	As if some mermaid	"	 1411
As in revenge or quittal	"	 236	As, but for loss of Nestor's golden		
But as he is my kinsman	"	 237	words	"	 1420

As—For even .... subtle Sinon here is painted	R L	1541	As—This thought is .... a death	Son	64	13
As if with grief or travail	"	1543	As to behold desert a beggar-born	"	66	2
as Priam did him cherish	"	1546	lived and died as flowers do now	"	68	2
wretched as he is he strives in vain	"	1655	And him as for a map doth Nature store	"	68	13
As through an arch the violent roaring tide	"	1667	even so as foes commend	"	69	4
As bound in knighthood to her imposition	"	1697	Do not so much as my poor name rehearse	"	71	11
as if her heart would break	"	1716	As after sunset fadeth in the west	"	73	6
and, as it left the place	"	1735	As the death-bed whereon it must expire	"	73	11
as pitying Lucrece' woes	"	1747	So are you to my thoughts as food to life	"	75	1
starts Collatine as from a dream	"	1772	Or as sweet-season'd showers	"	75	2
as if the name he tore	"	1787	As 'twixt a miser and his wealth	"	75	4
As silly-jeering idiots are with kings	"	1812	Now proud as an enjoyer	"	75	5
But as the riper should by time decease	Son	1	3	For as the sun is daily new and old	"	76	13
Be, as thy presence is, gracious	"	10	11	so oft as thou wilt look	"	77	13
As fast as thou shalt wane	"	11	1	As every alien pen hath got	"	78	3
And die as fast as they see others grow	"	12	12	As high as learning my rude ignorance	"	78	14
As truth and beauty shall together thrive	"	14	11	your worth wide as the ocean is	"	80	5
When I perceive that men as plants increase	"	15	5	The humble as the proudest sail	"	80	6
As he takes from you	"	15	14	Thou art as fair in knowledge as in hue	"	82	5
It is but as a tomb	"	17	3	As victors, of my silence cannot boast	"	86	11
So long as men can breathe	"	18	13	as a dream doth flatter	"	87	13
Make glad and sorry seasons as thou fleet'st	"	19	5	As I'll myself disgrace	"	89	7
With shifting change as is false women's fashion	"	20	4	are themselves as stone	"	94	3
Nature as she wrought thee	"	20	10	As on the finger of a throned queen	"	96	5
So is it not with me as with that Muse	"	21	1	As thou being mine mine is thy good report	"	96	14
my love is as fair	"	21	10	As with your shadow I with these	"	98	14
As any mother's child	"	21	11	seem long hence as he shows now	"	101	14
As those gold candles	"	21	12	As Philomel in summer's front	"	102	7
So long as youth and thou are of one date	"	22	2	For as you were when first	"	104	2
live as thine in me	"	22	7	Nor my beloved as an idol show	"	105	2
As I, not for myself, but for thee will	"	22	10	such a beauty as you master now	"	106	8
As tender nurse her babe	"	22	12	Supposed as forfeit to a confined doom	"	107	4
As an unperfect actor	"	23	1	Even as when first I hallow'd	"	108	8
But as the marigold at the sun's eye	"	25	6	As easy might I from myself depart	"	109	3
wit so poor as mine	"	26	5	As from my soul which in thy breast	"	109	4
pay as if not paid before	"	30	12	such cherubins as your sweet self resemble	"	114	6
As interest of the dead	"	31	7	As fast as objects to his beams assemble	"	114	8
As thou being mine	"	36	14	Like as, to make our appetites	"	118	1
As a decrepit father takes delight	"	37	1	As, to prevent our maladies	"	118	3
As soon as think the place where he would be	"	44	8	from limbecks foul as hell within	"	119	2
As thus; mine eye's due	"	46	13	As I by yours you've pass'd	"	120	6
When as thy love hath cast his utmost sum	"	49	3	And soon to you as you to me	"	120	11
As if by some instinct	"	50	7	so long as brain and heart	"	122	5
So am I as the rich	"	52	1	As subject to Time's love	"	124	3
keeps you as my chest	"	52	9	Thy lover's withering as thy sweet self	"	126	4
Or as the wardrobe	"	52	10	As thou goest onwards still will pluck	"	126	6
as your bounty doth appear	"	53	11	hated as a swallow'd bait	"	129	7
The canker-blooms have full as deep a dye	"	54	5	I think my love as rare	"	130	13
As the perfumed tincture	"	54	6	As any she belied with false compare	"	130	14
and play as wantonly	"	54	7	Thou art as tyrannous so as thou art	"	131	1
Like as the waves make toward	"	60	1	As those whose beauties proudly make	"	131	2
no face so gracious is as mine	"	62	5	this slander, as I think, proceeds	"	131	14
As I all other in all worths surmount	"	62	8	and they, as pitying me	"	132	1
my love shall be, as I am now	"	63	1	As those two mourning eyes	"	132	9

AS   29   AT

As—then .... well beseem thy heart	*Son*	132	10
that him as fast doth bind	"	134	8
Be wise as thou art cruel	"	140	1
As testy sick men when their death	"	140	7
false bonds of love as oft as mine	"	142	7
I love thee as thou lovest those	"	142	9
thine eyes woo as mine importune	"	142	10
as a careful housewife	"	143	1
That follow'd it as gentle day	"	145	10
My love is as a fever	"	147	1
My thoughts and my discourse as madmen's are	"	147	11
Who art as black as hell, as dark as night	"	147	14
so true as all men's	"	148	8
As his triumphant prize	"	151	10
As often shrieking	*L C*		20
As they did battery	"		23
hours, observed as they flew	"		60
I might as yet have been	"		75
If best were as it was	"		98
His qualities were beauteous as his form	"		99
As oft 'twixt May and April	"		102
as some my equals did	"		148
heart so much as warmed	"		191
rubies red as blood	"		198
As compound love to physic your cold breast	"		259
Appear to him as he to me appears	"		299
as it best deceives	"		306
Such looks as none could look	*P P*	4	4
Celestial as thou art	"	5	13
wistly as this queen on him	"	6	12
but not so fair as fickle	"	7	1
Mild as a dove	"	7	2
and yet, as glass is, brittle	"	7	3
and yet as iron rusty	"	7	4
as straw with fire flameth	"	7	13
as soon as straw out-burneth	"	7	14
As they must needs	"	8	2
As passing all conceit	"	8	8
When as himself to singing	"	8	12
god of both, as poets feign	"	8	13
And as he fell to her	"	11	4
As if the boy should use	"	11	8
And as she fetched breath	"	11	11
And as goods lost are sold or never	"	13	7
As vaded gloss no rubbing	"	13	8
As flowers dead lie wither'd	"	13	9
As broken glass no cement	"	13	10
As take the pain	"	14	12
as well as well might be	"	16	2
When as thine eye hath chose	"	19	1
As well as fancy	"	19	4
Had women been so strong as men	"	19	23
As it fell upon a day	"	21	1
poor bird, as all forlorn	"	21	9
Whilst as fickle Fortune smiled	"	21	29
So they loved, as love in twain	*P T*		25
As chorus to their tragic scene	"		52
A-shaking—sets every joint	*R L*		452
Ashamed—Art thou .... to kiss	*V A*		121
Like stars ashamed of day	"		1032
Ashes—So of shame's .... shall my fame be bred	*R L*		1188
That on the ashes of his youth	*Son*	73	10
Ashy—			
gleam'd forth their .... lights	*R L*		1378

Ashy-pale—and anger	*V A*		76
Nor ashy-pale the fear	*R L*		1512
Aside—			
sees the lurking serpent steps	"		362
do I not glance aside	*Son*	76	3
to glance thine eye aside	"	139	6
Ask—And asks the weary caitiff	*V A*		911
To ask the spotted princess	*R L*		721
But durst not ask of her audaciously	"		1223
to ask her how she fares	"		1594
Askance—all .... he holds her	*V A*		342
That from their own misdeeds askance their eyes	*R L*		637
Askance and strangely	*Son*	110	6
Asked—Then being ask'd where all thy beauty lies	"	2	5
Ask'd their own wills and made their wills obey	*L C*		133
Asleep—and fell	*Son*	153	1
Love-god lying once asleep	"	154	1
Aspect—With pure aspects did him peculiar duties	*R L*		14
Whose grim aspect sets every joint a-shaking	"		452
graciously with fair aspect	*Son*	26	10
Aspire—but light and will	*V A*		150
in pale embers hid lurks to aspire	*R L*		5
Aspiring—			
the .... mountains hiding	"		548
Assail—such passion her assails	"		1562
when they to assail begun	*L C*		262
Assailed—When shame assail'd	*R L*		63
Assail'd by night with circumstances	"		1262
therefore to be assailed	*Son*	41	6
Either not assail'd or victor	"	70	10
Assault—by strong .... it is bereft	*R L*		835
Assay—sick and short assays	"		1720
she must herself assay	*L C*		156
Assayed—She hath assay'd as much	*V A*		608
Assemble—objects to his beams	*Son*	114	8
Assigned—theirs in thought assign'd	*L C*		138
Assist—they then .... me in the act	*R L*		330
Assistance—fair .... in my verse	*Son*	78	2
Assuage—love's fire doth	*V A*		334
woe doth woe assuage	*R L*		790
suffering ecstasy assuage	*L C*		69
Assumed—his fury was	*V A*		318
Assure—I would .... thee	"		371
dear friend, and I assure ye	*Son*	111	13
Assured—come back again	"	45	11
thou art assured mine	"	92	2
now crown themselves assured	"	107	7
grew to faults assured	"	118	10
always with assured trust	*P P*	19	31
Astonished—			
'stonish'd as night wanderers	*V A*		825
astonish'd with this deadly deed	*R L*		1730
my verse astonished	*Son*	86	8
Astronomy—methinks I have	"	14	2
Asunder—girths he breaks	*V A*		266
Hearts remote, yet not asunder	*P T*		23
At—with herself .... strife	*V A*		11
stone at rain relenteth	"		200
At this Adonis smiles	"		241
Struck dead at first	"		250
that smiles at thee	"		252
workmanship at strife	"		291
Anon he starts at stirring	"		302

Entry	Source	Line
At—Spurns ... his love	V A	311
other agents aim at like delights	"	400
And at his look	"	463
at thy leisure, one by one	"	518
And yields at last	"	566
picks them all at last	"	576
trembles at his tale	"	591
having thee at vantage	"	635
Knocks at my heart	"	659
tremble at the imagination	"	668
at the timorous flying hare	"	674
Or at the fox	"	675
Or at the roe	"	676
hounds are at a bay	"	877
nought at all respecting	"	911
nought at all effecting	"	912
At apparitions, signs	"	924
at these sad signs	"	929
thou should'st strike at it	"	938
at random dost thou hit	"	940
at him should have fled	"	947
Even at this word	"	1025
So, at his bloody view	"	1037
melt at nine eyes' red fire	"	1073
whet his teeth at him again	"	1113
at such high-proud rate	R L	19
When at Collatium this proud lord arrived	"	50
ere rich at home he lands	"	336
Lies at the mercy of his mortal sting	"	364
blush at her own disgrace	"	479
hang their heads at this disdain	"	521
Beat at thy rocky and wreck-threatening heart	"	590
Melt at my tears	"	594
enters at an iron gate	"	595
wither at the cedar's root	"	665
May set at noon	"	784
that spurn'st at right, at law, at reason	"	880
to mock at him	"	989
At his own shadow	"	997
I rail at Opportunity	"	1023
At Time, at Tarquin	"	1024
I spurn at my confirm'd despite	"	1026
why quiver'st thou at this decree	"	1030
at least I give	"	1053
Nor shall he smile at thee	"	1065
Nor laugh with his companions at thy state	"	1066
grieves most at that would do it good	"	1117
weeps at thy languishment	"	1130
So I at each sad strain	"	1131
frighted deer that stands at gaze	"	1149
to guess at others' smarts	"	1238
a press of people at a door	"	1301
At last she thus begins	"	1363
At Ardea to my lord	"	1332
At last she calls to mind	"	1366
shoot their foam at Simols' banks	"	1442
At last she sees a wretched image	"	1501
At last she smilingly with this gives o'er	"	1567
At last he takes her	"	1597
At length address'd	"	1606
Or, at the least	"	1654
At this request, with noble disposition	"	1695
all at once began to say	"	1709
At—blushing .... that which is so putrified	R L	1750
At last it rains, and busy winds give	"	1790
Who, wondering at him	"	1845
to thyself at least kind-hearted prove	Son	10 12
at height decrease	"	15 7
as the marigold at the sun's eye	"	25 6
at a frown they in their glory die	"	25 8
to the lark at break of day arising	"	29 11
sings hymns at heaven's gate	"	29 12
grieve at grievances foregone	"	30 9
No more be grieved at that which	"	35 1
are at a mortal war	"	46 1
From whence at pleasure	"	48 12
no precious time at all to spend	"	57 3
Or at your hand the account of hours to crave	"	58 3
being at your beck	"	58 5
Since mind at first in character	"	59 8
At first the very worst	"	90 12
wonder at the lily's white	"	98 9
shoot not at me	"	117 12
Grows fairer than at first	"	119 12
At my abuses reckon up their own	"	121 10
Or, at the least so long as brain	"	122 5
Not wondering at the present	"	123 10
At such who, not born fair	"	127 11
At the wood's boldness	"	128 8
At random from the truth	"	147 12
But rising at thy ruin	"	151 9
But at my mistress' eye Love's brand new-fired	"	153 9
To every place at once	L C	27
To blush at speeches rank, to weep at woes	"	307
swound at tragic shows	"	308
jest at every gentle offer	P P	4 12
I had my lady at this bay	"	11 13
Yet at my parting	"	14 7
to jest at my exile	"	14 9
Plays not at all	"	18 30
will yield at length	"	19 21
They have at commandment	"	21 46
Attaint—sickness, whose	V A	741
from this attaint of mine	R L	825
poison thee with my attaint	"	1072
mayst without attaint or look	Son	82 2
age shall them attaint	P P	19 46
Attainted—wherein I am	Son	88 7
Attempt—		
I see crosses my .... will bring	R L	491
Attend—hereafter shall	V A	1136
these lets attend the time	R L	330
tie the hearers to attend each line	"	818
The post attends, and she delivers it	"	1333
thy Lucrece now attend me	"	1682
I must attend time's leisure	Son	44 12
to attend this double voice	L C	3
Attended—to your wanton talk	V A	809
too early I attended	L C	78
Attendeth—Which speechless woe of his poor she	R L	1674
Attending—Attending on his golden pilgrimage	Son	7 8
captive good attending captain ill	"	66 12
Attention—that it beguiled	R L	1404
With sad attention	"	1610
Attired—.... in discontent	"	1601

Attorney—heart's .... once is mute	V A	335
A-turning—and yet she fell	P P	7	16
Her fancy fell a-turning	"	16	4
A-twain—breaking rings	L C		6
Audaciously—ask of her	R L		1223
Audacity—life and bold	"		1346
Audience—End without	V A		846
Lending soft audience	L C		278
Audit—What acceptable .... canst thou leave	Son	4	12
Call'd to that audit by advised respects	"	49	4
Her audit, though delay'd, answer'd must be	"	126	11
and to your audit comes	L C		230
Aught—Nor .... obeys	R L		546
if aught in me	Son	38	5
Were 't aught to me	"	125	1
there may be aught applied	L C		68
Augmenting—nothing by .... it	R L		154
Augur—And the sad augurs mock their own presage	Son	107	6
Augur of the fever's end	P T		7
Auspicious—stand .... to the hour	R L		347
Author—.... of thy slander	V A		1006
author of their obloquy	R L		523
the authors of their ill	"		1244
Authority—.... for sin	"		620
tongue-tied by authority	Son	66	9
Authorized—with his .... youth	L C		104
Authorizing—.... thy trespass	Son	35	6
Autumn—The teeming .... big with rich increase	"	97	6
to yellow autumn turn'd	"	104	5
Avail—it small avails my mood	R L		1273
Avaunt—childish fear	"		274
Awake—Awake, thou Roman dame	"		1628
Awakes my heart	Son	47	14
keeps mine eye awake	"	61	10
Awaketh—frenzy thus	R L		1675
Award—That she that makes me sin awards me pain	Son	141	14
Away—her object will	V A		255
Away he springs	"		258
thyself art made away	"		763
now I will away	"		807
away she flies	"		1027
My sighs are blown away	"		1071
away she hies	"		1189
away by brain-sick rude desire	R L		175
the roses took away	"		239
Away he steals	"		283
can be wiped away	"		608
Bearing away the wound	"		731
remains a hopeless cast-away	"		744
fly with the filth away	"		1010
the treasure stol'n away	"		1056
her bark being peel'd away	"		1169
was Tarquin gone away	"		1284
The grief away that stops	"		1664
with a joyless smile she turns away	"		1711
do not take away	"		1796
would make the world away	Son	11	8
To give away yourself	"	16	13
Thyself away art present	"	47	10
Stealing away the treasure	"	63	8
and take my love away	"	64	12
The right of sepulchres, were shorn away	"	68	6
Away—black night doth take	Son	73	7
shall carry me away	"	74	2
on all, or all away	"	75	14
and I be cast away	"	80	13
All this away and me	"	91	14
to steal thyself away	"	92	1
might'st thou lead away	"	96	11
And, thou away, the very birds	"	97	12
winter still, and you away	"	98	13
feather'd creatures broke away	"	143	2
to hell is flown away	"	145	12
'I hate' from hate away she threw	"	145	13
He rose and ran away	P P	4	14
away he skips	"	11	11
till I run away	"	11	14
that kept my rest away	"	14	2
And drives away	"	15	8
did bear the maid away	"	16	14
with scorn she put away	"	19	18
Awe—be kept in	R L		245
Awed—
.... resistance made him fret	V A		69
Awhile—Counsel may stop	L C		139
A-work—So Lucrece set	R L		1496
Ay—'Ay me,' quoth Venus	V A		187
'Ay me,' she cries	"		833
ay, if the fact be known	R L		239
Ay me! the bark	"		1167
Ay me! but yet thou might'st	Son	41	9
Ay, fill it full with wills	"	136	6
ay, dieted in grace	L C		261
Ay me! I fell	"		321
Aye—antiquity for .... his page	Son	108	12
Azure—Her .... veins	R L		419
Babe—ne'er pleased her .... so well	V A		974
fright her crying babe with Tarquin's name	R L		814
Who, having two sweet babes	"		1161
nurse her babe from faring ill	Son	22	12
Love is a babe	"	115	13
Sets down her babe	"	143	3
Whilst I thy babe chase thee	"	143	10
Back—on so proud a	V A		300
his back, his breast	"		396
she on her back	"		594
On his bow-back	"		619
on his back doth lie	"		663
upon her back	"		814
Then fell she on her back	P P	4	13
Back—beating reason	V A		557
But back retires	"		906
I could not put him back	R L		843
would'st thou one hour come back	"		965
bears back all boll'n and red	"		1417
mindful messenger come back	"		1583
Back to the strait	"		1670
and back the same grief draw	"		1673
Held back his sorrow's tide	"		1789
Calls back the lovely April	Son	3	10
not to give back again	"	22	14
now come back again assured	"	45	11
I send them back again	"	45	11
can hold his swift foot back	"	65	11
And so my patent back again is swerving	"	87	8
still will pluck thee back	"	126	6
turn back to me	"	143	11
If thou turn back	"	143	14

Back—Nymphs .... peeping	P P	18	43
though she put thee back	"	19	36
Back'd—The colt that's back'd and burden'd	V A	.....	419
My will is back'd with resolution	R L	.....	352
Back'st—Thou .... reproach	"	.....	622
Backward—			
Backward she push'd him	V A	.....	41
and backward drew	"	.....	541
Shrinks backward in his shelly cave	"	.....	1034
O, that record could with a backward look	Son	59	5
Bad—Being so ...., such numbers seek for thee	R L	.....	896
that to bad debtors lends	"	.....	964
O Time, thou tutor both to good and bad	"	.....	995
before these last so bad	Son	67	14
So you o'er-green my bad, my good allow	"	112	4
Creating every bad a perfect best	"	114	7
count bad what I think good	"	121	8
All men are bad and in their badness reign	"	121	14
world is grown so bad	"	140	11
Till my bad angel fire my good one out	"	144	14
Till my bad angel fire my good one out	P P	2	14
Bad in the best	"	7	18
Bade—She .... love last	"	7	16
She bade good night	"	14	2
bade me come to-morrow	"	15	12
Badge—A .... of fame	R L	.....	1054
But heavy tears badges of either's woe	Son	44	14
Badness—In their .... reign	"	121	14
Ball—That blow did .... it	R L	.....	1725
Without all ball	Son	74	2
let my poor heart ball	"	133	10
Bait—			
She touch'd no unknown baits	R L	.....	103
as a swallow'd bait	Son	129	7
would not touch the bait	P P	4	11
Balk—Make slow pursuit, or altogether	R L	.....	696
Ball—Are balls of quenchless fire	"	.....	1554
their poor balls are tied	L C	.....	24
Balm—in her passion calls it	V A	.....	27
And drop sweet balm	R L	.....	1466
Balmy—of this most .... time	Son	107	9
Ban—And bitter words to .... her cruel foes	R L	.....	1460
And ban and brawl	P P	19	20
Band—			
her arms infold him like a	V A	.....	225
Or ivory in an alabaster band	"	.....	363
news from the warlike band	R L	.....	255
Bane—			
my body's .... would cure thee	V A	.....	372
Banish—Everything did .... moan	P P	21	7
Banish'd—			
the plague is .... by thy breath	V A	.....	510
Banishment—			
Tarquin's everlasting banishment	R L	.....	1855
Bank—force it overflow the	V A	.....	72
this primrose bank whereon I lie	"	.....	151
the bounding banks o'erflows	R L	.....	1119
Bank—To Simois' reedy banks	R L	.....	1437
Shoot their foam at Simois' banks	"	.....	1442
Come daily to the banks	Son	56	11
Bankrupt—But blessed	V A	.....	466
bankrupt in this poor-rich gain	R L	.....	140
Like to a bankrupt beggar	"	.....	711
now Nature bankrupt is	Son	67	9
Banner—			
when his gaudy .... is display'd	R L	.....	272
Banning—Banning his boisterous unruly beast	V A	.....	326
Banquet—But, O, what	"	.....	445
to the painted banquet bids	Son	47	6
Bar—Or as those bars which stop the hourly dial	R L	.....	327
Whilst I whom fortune of such triumph bars	Son	25	3
thy picture's sight would bar	"	46	3
under truest bars to thrust	"	48	2
Bare—			
What .... excuses makest thou	V A	.....	188
On her bare breast	R L	.....	439
Bare and unpeopled	"	.....	1741
May make seem bare	Son	26	6
Uttering bare truth	"	69	4
Bare ruin'd choirs where late the	"	73	4
The argument all bare	"	103	3
Whose bare out-bragg'd the web	L C	.....	95
age like winter bare	P P	12	4
Bare-boned—Shows me a .... death	R L	.....	1761
Bareness—and .... everywhere	Son	5	8
December's bareness everywhere	"	97	4
Bargain—			
What bargains may I make	V A	.....	512
Bark—though a thousand	"	.....	240
the bark peel'd from the lofty pine	R L	.....	1167
her bark being peel'd away	"	.....	1169
My saucy bark, inferior far to his	Son	80	7
to every wandering bark	"	116	7
Barketh—			
wolf doth grin before he	V A	.....	459
Barn—And useless barns the harvest of his wits	R L	.....	859
Barr'd—When it is	V A	.....	330
to be barr'd of rest	"	.....	784
barr'd him from the blessed thing	R L	.....	340
Barren—			
...., lean, and lacking juice	V A	.....	136
barren dearth of daughters	"	.....	754
his barren skill to show	R L	.....	81
trees I see barren of leaves	Son	12	5
barren rage of death's eternal cold	"	13	12
than my barren rhyme	"	16	4
so barren of new pride	"	76	1
The barren tender of a poet's debt	"	83	4
Barrenly—featureless and rude, ... perish	"	11	10
Base—To bid the wind a	V A	.....	303
Or laid great bases for eternity	Son	125	3
Base—Throwing the base thong	V A	.....	395
Hiding base sin in plaits of majesty	R L	.....	93
digression is so vile, so base	"	.....	202
Thou nobly base, they basely dignified	"	.....	660
to the base shrub's foot	"	.....	664
Unto the base bed	"	.....	671
Base watch of woes	"	.....	928
For who so base would such an office have	"	.....	1000

Base—deathsman to so.... a slave	R L	1001	
to let base clouds o'ertake me	Son	34	3
Too base of thee to be remembered	"	74	12
with base infection meet	"	94	11
to lend base subjects light	"	100	4
to base touches prone	"	141	6
Basely—They.... fly, and dare not	V A	894	
they basely dignified	R L	660	
Basely with gold	"	1068	
Baser—The baser is he, coming from a king	"	1002	
Basest—Anon permit the.... clouds to ride	Son	33	5
The basest weed outbraves his dignity	"	94	12
The basest jewel will be well esteem'd	"	96	6
Bashful—He burns with.... shame	V A	49	
with bashful innocence doth hie	R L	1341	
Bastard—This.... graff shall never come to growth	"	1062	
Before these bastard signs	Son	68	3
Fortune's bastard be unfather'd	"	124	2
slander'd with a bastard shame	"	127	4
bastards of his foul adulterate heart	L C	175	
Bastardy—Thy issue blurr'd with nameless....	R L	522	
Bat—upon his grained....	L C	64	
Bate-breeding—this.... spy	V A	655	
Bateless—This.... edge on his keen appetite	R L	9	
Bath—And grew a seething....	Son	153	7
the help of bath desired	"	153	11
the bath for my help lies	"	153	13
Growing a bath and healthful remedy	"	154	11
Bathe—She bathes in water	V A	94	
The crow may bathe his coal-black wings in mire	R L	1009	
bathes the pale fear	"	1775	
Bathed—.... she in her fluxive eyes	L C	50	
Batter—Rude ram, to.... such an ivory wall	R L	464	
Batter'd—His batter'd shield	V A	104	
Have batter'd down her consecrated wall	R L	723	
Her mansion batter'd by the enemy	"	1171	
Battering—siege of.... days	Son	65	6
Battery—they make no....	V A	426	
As they did battery	L C	23	
To leave the battery	"	277	
Battle—in.... ne'er did bow	V A	99	
he hath a battle set	"	619	
in fell battle's rage	R L	145	
to imitate the battle sought	"	1438	
The scars of battle	L C	244	
Bawd—the.... to lust's abuse	V A	792	
fair reputation but a bawd	R L	623	
Blind muffled bawd	"	768	
thou notorious bawd	"	886	
Bay—the hounds are at a....	V A	877	
Be anchor'd in the bay where all men ride	Son	137	6
Ah, that I had my lady at this bay	P P	11	13
Be—she would.... thrust	V A	41	
Till either gorge be stuff'd or prey be gone	"	58	
O, be not proud	"	113	
mine be not so fair	"	116	

Be—shall.... thine own	V A	117	
Be bold to play	"	124	
mayst thou well be tasted	"	128	
sweet boy, and may it be	"	155	
be of thyself rejected	"	159	
with thy increase be fed	"	170	
makest thou to be gone	"	188	
or else be mute	"	208	
in her arms be bound	"	226	
Struggles to be gone	"	227	
I'll be a park, and thou shalt be my deer	"	231	
if those hills be dry	"	238	
Then be my deer	"	239	
He might be buried	"	244	
by pleading may be blest	"	328	
sorrow may be said	"	333	
coal that must be cool'd	"	387	
Though thy horse be gone	"	390	
dares not be so bold	"	401	
Unless it be a boar	"	410	
be any jot diminish'd	"	417	
should I be in love	"	438	
my love to thee be still	"	442	
still to be sealing	"	512	
can be well contented	"	513	
good queen, it will not be	"	607	
much as may be proved	"	608	
O, be advised	"	615	
cannot be easily harm'd	"	627	
be ruled by me	"	673	
may be compared well	"	701	
nature be condemn'd of treason	"	729	
Be prodigal: the lamp	"	755	
to be barr'd of rest	"	784	
ere summer half be done	"	802	
to be so curst	"	887	
If he be dead,—O no, it cannot be	"	937	
Be wreak'd on him	"	1004	
To be of such a weak	"	1010	
where no breach should be	"	1066	
The tiger would be tame	"	1096	
should yet be light	"	1134	
shall be waited on	"	1137	
It shall be fickle	"	1141	
Bud, and be blasted	"	1142	
It shall be sparing	"	1147	
it shall be raging-mad	"	1151	
It shall be merciful	"	1155	
Perverse it shall be	"	1157	
shall be cause of war	"	1159	
There shall not be	"	1187	
and not be seen	"	1194	
kings might be espoused to more fame	R L	20	
What needeth then apologies be made	"	31	
by our ears our hearts oft tainted be	"	38	
between them both it should be kill'd	"	74	
Though death be adjunct	"	133	
So that in venturing ill we leave to be	"	148	
if there be no self-trust	"	158	
Which must be lode-star to his lustful eye	"	179	
A martial man to be soft fancy's slave	"	200	

Be—And .... an eye-sore in my golden coat	R L	.....	205	Be—No more than wax shall .... accounted evil	R L	 1245
Would with the sceptre straight be strucken down	"	.....	217	O, let it not be hild	"	 1257
Will not my tongue be mute	"	.....	227	if your maid may be so bold	"	 1282
if the fact be known	"	.....	239	if it should be told	"	 1284
Shall by a painted cloth be kept in awe	"	.....	245	that deep torture may be call'd a hell	"	 1287
The coward fights, and will not be dismayed	"	.....	273	Bid thou be ready	"	 1292
Love and Fortune be my gods	"	.....	351	and it will soon be writ	"	 1295
till their effects be tried	"	.....	353	the whole to be imagined	"	 1428
ere traitors be espied	"	.....	361	Let guiltless souls be freed from guilty woe	"	 1482
To be admired of lewd unhallow'd eyes	"	.....	392	'It cannot be,' quoth she	"	 1534
The blemish that will never be forgot	"	.....	536	It cannot be she in that sense forsook	"	 1538
				It cannot be, I find	"	 1539
Mar not the thing that cannot be amended	"	.....	578	his wounds will not be sore	"	 1568
				Though woe be heavy	"	 1574
End thy ill aim before thy shoot be ended	"	.....	579	And my laments would be drawn out too long	"	 1616
Be moved with my tears	"	.....	588	then be this all the task	"	 1618
and be compassionate	"	.....	594	And what wrong else may be imagined	"	 1622
How will thy shame be seeded in thine age	"	.....	603	By foul enforcement might be done to me	"	 1623
O, be remember'd	"	.....	607	this act will be	"	 1637
From vassal actors can be wiped away	"	.....	608	And never be forgot	"	 1644
Then kings' misdeeds cannot be hid in clay	"	.....	609	Though my gross blood be stain'd with this abuse	"	 1655
				Be suddenly revenged on my foe	"	 1683
wilt thou be the school	"	.....	617	How may this forced stain be wiped from me	"	 1701
Wilt thou be glass	"	.....	619			
So shall these slaves be king	"	.....	639	If they surcease to be	"	 1766
to be thy partner in this shameful doom	"	.....	672	And live to be revenged	"	 1778
				And only must be wail'd by Collatine	"	 1799
would they still in darkness be	"	.....	752			
bids her eyes hereafter still be blind	"	.....	758	else this glutton be	Son	1 13
May likewise be sepulchred	"	.....	805	Will be a tatter'd weed	"	2 4
dear love be kept unspotted	"	.....	821	this were to be new made	"	2 13
If that be made a theme	"	.....	822	Or who is he so fond will be the tomb	"	3 7
Or kings be breakers	"	.....	852	remember'd not to be	"	3 13
And leaves it to be master'd by his young	"	.....	863	when nature calls thee to be gone	"	4 11
				beauty must be tomb'd with thee	"	4 13
'When wilt thou be the humble suppliant's friend	"	.....	897	Which, us'd, lives th' executor to be	"	4 14
				ere thou be distill'd	"	6 2
his suit may be obtain'd	"	.....	898	ere it be self-kill'd	"	6 4
Be guilty of my death	"	.....	931	Or ten times happier be it ten for one	"	6 8
To trembling clients be you mediators	"	.....	1020	'Be not self-will'd	"	6 13
by Tarquin's falchion to be slain	"	.....	1046	To be death's conquest	"	6 14
O no, that cannot be	"	.....	1049	The world will be thy widow	"	9 5
still in night would cloister'd be	"	.....	1085	Which to repair should be thy chief desire	"	10 8
be you mute and dumb	"	.....	1123			
Will slay the other and be nurse to none	"	.....	1162	Shall hate be fairer lodged	"	10 10
				Be, as thy presence is	"	10 11
let it not be call'd impiety	"	.....	1174	Be scorn'd, like old men	"	17 10
Which by him tainted shall for him be spent	"	.....	1182	Mine be thy love	"	20 14
				How can I then be older	"	22 8
shall my fame be bred	"	.....	1188	be of thyself so wary	"	22 9
My resolution, love, shall be thy boast	"	.....	1193	let my books be then the eloquence	"	23 9
				Where I may not remove nor be removed	"	25 14
thou revenged may'st be	"	.....	1194			
How Tarquin must be used	"	.....	1195	though they be outstripp'd by every pen	"	32 6
mine honor be the knife's	"	.....	1201			
My shame be his that did my fame confound	"	.....	1202	No more be grieved at that	"	35 1
				That I an accessary needs must be	"	35 13
fame that lives disbursed be	"	.....	1203	Let me confess that we two must be twain	"	36 1
'So be it	"	.....	1209			
both shall victors be	"	.....	1211	by me be borne alone	"	36 4

Be—Be thou the tenth Muse	Son	38	9	Be—mine eye may ... deceived	Son	104	12
The pain be mine, but thine shall be the praise	"	38	14	Let not my love be call'd idolatry	"	105	1
But yet be blamed	"	40	7	Since all alike my songs and praises be	"	105	3
yet we must not be foes	"	40	14	That it could so preposterously be stain'd	"	109	11
Gentle thou art, and therefore to be won	"	41	5	If it be poison'd	"	111	13
Beauteous thou art, therefore to be assailed	"	41	6	although his height be taken	"	116	8
				If this be error	"	116	13
yet it may be said	"	42	2	To be diseased	"	118	8
mine eyes be blessed made	"	43	9	would by ill be cured	"	118	12
I would be brought	"	44	3	'Tis better to be vile	"	121	1
the place where he would be	"	44	8	When not to be receives reproach	"	121	2
Until life's composition be recured	"	45	9	I may be straight though they themselves be bevel	"	121	11
thence thou wilt be stol'n	"	48	13				
be it not said	"	56	1	my deeds must not be shown	"	121	12
Thy edge should blunter be than appetite	"	56	2	thy record never can be miss'd	"	122	8
				and this shall ever be	"	123	13
So, love, be thou	"	56	5	I will be true	"	123	14
Let this sad interim like the ocean be	"	56	9	It might be for Fortune's bastard be unfather'd	"	124	2
more blest may be the view	"	56	12				
Where you may be	"	57	10	let me be obsequious	"	125	9
Be where you list	"	58	9	Her audit, though delay'd, answer'd must be	"	126	11
though waiting so be hell	"	58	13				
be it ill or well	"	58	14	To be so tickled	"	128	9
If there be nothing new	"	59	1	If snow be white	"	130	3
Or whether revolution be the same	"	59	12	If hairs be wires	"	130	4
my slumbers should be broken	"	61	3	I dare not be so bold	"	131	7
Against my love shall be	"	63	1	And to be sure	"	131	9
shall in these black lines be seen	"	63	13	and loving mourners be	"	132	3
from thence would I be gone	"	66	13	my sweet'st friend must be	"	133	4
That thou art blamed shall not be thy defect	"	70	1	thus to be cross'd	"	133	8
				let my heart be his guard	"	133	11
So thou be good	"	70	5	to be my comfort still	"	134	4
Yet thus thy praise cannot be so thy praise	"	70	11	nor he will not be free	"	134	5
				Though in thy stores' account I one must be	"	136	10
That I in your sweet thoughts would be forgot	"	71	7	Yet what the best is take the worst to be	"	137	4
My name be buried	"	72	11				
But be contented	"	74	1	Be anchor'd in the bay	"	137	6
Too base of thee to be remembered	"	74	12	by lies we flatter'd be	"	138	14
to be with you alone	"	75	7	Be wise as thou art cruel	"	140	1
or must from you be took	"	75	12	As testy sick men, when their deaths be near	"	140	7
Yet be most proud	"	78	9				
with thy sweet graces graced be	"	78	12	by mad ears believed be	"	140	12
and I be cast away	"	80	13	That I may not be so	"	140	13
each part will be forgotten	"	81	4	desire to be invited	"	141	7
Your monument shall be my gentle verse	"	81	9	and vassal wretch to be	"	141	12
				Be it lawful I love thee	"	142	9
And tongues to be your being shall rehearse	"	81	11	Thy pity may deserve to pitied be	"	142	12
				By self-example mayst thou be denied	"	142	14
And their gross painting might be better used	"	82	13				
				kiss me, be kind	"	143	12
Which shall be most my glory	"	83	10	would corrupt my saint to be a devil	"	144	7
When thou shalt be disposed	"	88	1	whether that my angel be turn'd fiend	"	144	9
And I by this will be a gainer too	"	88	9				
Be absent from thy walks	"	89	9	Within be fed, without be rich no more	"	146	12
Of more delight than hawks or horses be	"	91	11				
				If that be fair	"	148	5
Thou mayst be false	"	92	14	If it be not, then love doth well denote	"	148	7
Whate'er thy thoughts or thy heart's workings be	"	93	11				
				to be beloved of thee	"	148	9
The basest jewel will be well esteem'd	"	96	6	O, how can Love's eye be true	"	150	14
				thy poor drudge to be	"	151	11
If any, be a satire to decay	"	100	11	If that from him there may be aught applied	L. C.		68
what shall be thy amends	"	101	1				
wilt thou be dumb	"	101	9	unruly though they be		....	106
And to be praised of ages yet to be	"	101	12	To be forbod the sweets	"	....	164
you never can be old	"	104	1	And be not of my holy vows afraid	"	....	179

Be—with acture they may	L C	....	185
these, of force, must your oblations be	"	....	223
Not to be tempted, would she be immured	"	....	251
Who, young and simple, would not be so lover'd	"	....	320
Although I know my years be past the best	P P	1	6
our faults in love thus smother'd be	"	1	14
would corrupt my saint to be a devil	"	2	7
And whether that my angel be turn'd fiend	"	2	9
If knowledge be the mark	"	5	7
Then must the love be great 'twixt thee and me	"	8	3
before the fall should be	"	10	6
Ah, neither be my share	"	14	1
'T may be, she joy'd to jest	"	14	9
'T may be again to make	"	14	10
as well as well might be	"	16	2
But one must be refused	"	16	9
That nothing could be used	"	16	10
What though her frowning brows be bent	"	19	13
twice desire, ere it be day	"	19	17
And in thy suit be humble true	"	19	32
be thou not slack	"	19	35
To teach my tongue to be so long	"	19	52
here be it said	"	19	53
Live with me and be my love	"	20	1
Then live with me and be my love	"	20	16
To live with thee and be thy love	"	20	20
Every man will be thy friend	"	21	35
But if store of crowns be scant	"	21	37
If that one be prodigal	"	21	39
If he be addict to vice	"	21	43
If to women he be bent	"	21	45
Herald sad and trumpet be	P T	....	3
Be the death-divining swan	"	....	15
Truth may seem, but cannot be	"	....	62
Truth and beauty buried be	"	....	64
Beaded—and of .... jet	L C	....	37
Beak—Tires with her	V A	....	56
Whose crooked beak	R L	....	508
Beam—Whose beams upon his hairless face	V A	....	487
Mock with thy tickling beams	R L	....	1090
to his beams assemble	Son	114	8
Bear—rough ...., or lion proud	V A	....	884
Bear—and sappy plants to bear	"	....	165
bear her a thousand ways	"	....	907
to Collatium bears the lightless fire	R L	....	4
Whose crime will bear an everduring blame	"	....	224
thou perforce must bear	"	....	612
I mean to bear thee	"	....	670
She bears the load of lust	"	....	734
how many bear such shameful blows	"	....	832
infant sorrows, bear them mild	"	....	1096
with deep groans the diapason bear	"	....	1132
let beasts bear gentle minds	"	....	1148
with greater patience bear it	"	....	1158
be ready by and by to bear	"	....	1292
From that suspicion which the world might bear her	"	....	1321
a part of woe doth bear	"	....	1327
bears back all boil'n and red	"	....	1417
Bear—signs of rage they	R L	....	1419
burning Troy doth bear	"	....	1474
such a face should bear a wicked mind	"	....	1540
that map which deep impression bears	"	....	1712
and help to bear thy part	"	....	1830
conclude to bear dead Lucrece	"	....	1050
His tender heir might bear his memory	Son	1	4
parts that thou shouldst bear	"	8	8
your sweet form should bear	"	13	8
would bear your living flowers	"	16	7
to him that bears the strong offence's cross	"	34	12
To bear love's wrong	"	40	12
The beast that bears me	"	50	5
to bear that weight in me	"	50	6
Which, laboring for invention, bear amiss	"	59	3
thy mind's imprint will bear	"	77	3
as the proudest sail doth bear	"	80	6
myself will bear all wrong	"	88	14
But bears it out even to the edge	"	116	12
One on another's neck, do witness bear	"	131	11
Bear thine eyes straight	"	140	14
reading what contents it bears	L C	....	19
What unapproved witness dost thou bear	"	....	53
In the suffering pangs it bears	"	....	272
did bear the maid away	P P	16	14
He with thee doth bear a part	"	21	56
Beard—his .... all silver white	R L	....	1405
with white and bristly beard	Son	12	8
Bearer—Of my dull	"	51	2
Bear'st—against a thorn thou ....thy part	R L	....	1135
deny that thou bear'st love to any	Son	10	1
Bearing—The .... earth with his hard hoof be wounds	V A	....	267
now press'd with bearing	"	....	430
no bearing yoke they knew	R L	....	409
Bearing away the wound	"	....	731
quick bearing and dexterity	"	....	1389
Bearing thy heart, which I will keep	Son	22	11
Bearing the wanton burthen of the prime	"	97	7
after new love bearing	"	152	4
Beast—boisterous and unruly	V A	....	326
that bloody beast	"	....	999
to the rough beast	R L	....	545
since men prove beasts, let beasts bear gentle minds	"	....	1148
The beast that bears me	Son	50	5
will my poor beast then find	"	51	5
Beasts did leap	P P	21	5
Ruthless beasts they will not cheer thee	"	21	22
Beat—beats, and takes no rest	V A	....	647
now she beats her heart	"	....	829
beats these from the stage	R L	....	278
reproof and reason beat it dead	"	....	489
Beat at thy rocky and wreck-threatening heart	"	....	590
The golden bullet beats it down	P P	19	30
Beated—Beated and chopp'd	Son	62	10
Beaten—Beaten away by brain-sick rude desire	R L	....	175

Beaten—quite .... from her breast	R L	....	1363
the rain on my storm-beaten face	Son	34	6
Beating—			
Beating his kind embracements	V A	....	312
beating reason back	"	....	557
Anon his beating heart	R L	....	433
Beating her bulk	"	....	467
beating on her breast	"	....	739
Beauteous—This .... combat	V A	....	355
The beauteous influence	"	....	802
Ne'er saw the beauteous livery	"	....	1107
possession of his beauteous mate	R L	....	18
Then, beauteous niggard	Son	4	5
Seeking that beauteous roof	"	10	7
Makes black night beauteous	"	27	12
promise such a beauteous day	"	34	1
Beauteous thou art, therefore to be assailed	"	41	6
doth beauty beauteous seem	"	54	1
beauteous and lovely youth	"	54	13
You to your beauteous blessings	"	84	13
Three beauteous springs	"	104	5
beauteous as his form	L C	....	99
Beautiful—making .... old rhyme	Son	106	3
why 'twas beautiful and hard	L C	....	211
Beautify—themselves so	R L	....	401
Beauty—Which bred more	V A	....	79
there thy beauty lies	"	....	119
Beauty within itself	"	....	130
My beauty as the spring	"	....	141
fresh beauty for the use	"	....	164
beauty breedeth beauty	"	....	167
That inward beauty	"	....	434
Were beauty under twenty	"	....	575
Would root these beauties	"	....	636
Beauty hath nought to do	"	....	638
To mingle beauty	"	....	735
brings beauty under	"	....	746
Upon fresh beauty	"	....	796
To stifle beauty and to steal	"	....	934
his breath and beauty set	"	....	935
Seeing his beauty	"	....	938
beauty may the better thrive	"	....	1011
with him is beauty slain	"	....	1019
And, beauty dead	"	....	1020
But true-sweet beauty	"	....	1080
every beauty robb'd	"	....	1132
as bright as heaven's beauties	R L	....	13
Honour and beauty	"	....	27
Beauty itself doth of itself	"	....	29
beauty and virtue strived	"	....	52
beauty would blush for shame	"	....	54
When beauty boasted blushes	"	....	55
But beauty, in that white intituled	"	....	57
virtue claims from beauty beauty's red	"	....	59
Argued by beauty's red	"	....	65
In that high task hath done her beauty wrong	"	....	80
All orators are dumb when beauty pleadeth	"	....	268
beauty my prize	"	....	279
Thy beauty hath ensnared thee	"	....	483
By thy bright beauty	"	....	490
an eye to gaze on beauty	"	....	496
Time's ruin, beauty's wreck	"	....	1451
her beauty I may tear	"	....	1472
That my poor beauty had purloin'd his eyes	"	....	1651

Beauty—			
shiver'd all the ... of my glass	R L	....	1764
That thereby beauty's rose might never die	Son	1	2
dig deep trenches in thy beauty's field	"	2	2
being ask'd where all thy beauty lies	"	2	5
how much more praise deserved thy beauty's use	"	2	9
Proving his beauty by succession thine	"	2	12
Upon thyself thy beauty's legacy	"	4	2
Thy unused beauty must be tomb'd with thee	"	4	13
Beauty o'ersnow'd and bareness every where	"	5	8
Beauty's effect with beauty were bereft	"	5	11
With beauty's treasure, ere it be	"	6	4
mortal looks adore his beauty still	"	7	7
But beauty's waste hath in the world an end	"	9	11
That beauty still may live	"	10	13
wisdom, beauty, and increase	"	11	5
of thy beauty do I question make	"	12	9
Since sweets and beauties do themselves forsake	"	12	11
that beauty which you hold in lease	"	13	5
As truth and beauty shall together thrive	"	14	11
Thy end is truth's and beauty's doom	"	14	14
If I could write the beauty of your eyes	"	17	5
For beauty's pattern to succeeding men	"	19	12
Stirr'd by a painted beauty	"	21	2
For all that beauty that doth cover thee	"	22	5
Thy beauty's form in table of my heart	"	24	2
For whether beauty, birth, or wealth	"	37	5
Thy beauty and thy years full well befits	"	41	3
And chide thy beauty	"	41	10
Hers, by thy beauty tempting her to thee	"	41	13
Thine, by thy beauty being false to me	"	41	14
On Helen's cheek all art of beauty set	"	53	7
doth shadow of your beauty show	"	53	10
O, how much more doth beauty beauteous seem	"	54	1
delves the parallels in beauty's brow	"	60	10
Painting my age with beauty of thy days	"	62	14
all those beauties whereof now he's king	"	63	6
My sweet love's beauty	"	63	12
His beauty shall in these black lines	"	63	13
How with this rage shall beauty hold a plea	"	65	3
who his spoil of beauty can forbid	"	65	12
Why should poor beauty indirectly seek	"	67	7
When beauty lived and died	"	68	2

Beauty—Ere beauty's dead fleece made another gay	*Son* 68	8
to dress his beauty new	" 68	12
To show false art what beauty was of yore	" 68	14
They look into the beauty of thy mind	" 69	9
The ornament of beauty is suspect	" 70	3
Thy glass will show thee how thy beauties wear	" 77	1
beauty doth he give	" 79	10
I impair not beauty being mute	" 83	11
like Eve's apple doth thy beauty grow	" 93	13
Doth spot the beauty of thy budding name	" 95	3
Where beauty's veil doth cover every blot	" 95	11
thy neglect of truth in beauty died	" 101	2
Both truth and beauty on my love depends	" 101	3
Beauty no pencil, beauty's truth to lay	" 101	7
Such seems your beauty still	" 104	3
yet doth beauty, like a dial-hand	" 104	9
Ere you were born was beauty's summer dead	" 104	14
beauty making beautiful old rhyme	" 106	3
in the blazon of sweet beauty's best	" 106	5
Even such a beauty as you master now	" 106	8
Tan sacred beauty	" 115	7
it bore not beauty's name	" 127	2
now is black beauty's successive heir	" 127	3
And beauty slander'd with a bastard shame	" 127	4
Sweet beauty hath no name	" 127	7
who not born fair, no beauty lack	" 127	11
every tongue says beauty should look so	" 127	14
those whose beauties proudly make them cruel	" 131	2
will I swear beauty herself is black	" 132	13
The statue of thy beauty thou wilt take	" 134	9
They know what beauty is	" 137	3
The carcass of a beauty	*L C*	11
Some beauty peep'd through lattice of sear'd age	"	14
Such looks as none could look but beauty's queen	*P P* 4	4
If not to beauty vowed	" 5	2
Beauty is but a vain and doubtful good	" 13	1
So beauty blemish'd once 's forever lost	" 13	11
Beauty, truth, and rarity	*P T*	53
Beauty brag, but 'tis not she	"	63
Truth and beauty buried be	"	64
Became—		
the horse by him .... his deed	*L C*	111
Because—Because Adonis' heart hath made mine hard	*V A*	378
Because the cry remaineth	"	885
because he would not fear him	"	1094
because it is his own	*R L*	35
because thou know'st I love her	*Son* 42	6
because he needs no praise	" 101	9
Because I would not dull you	" 102	14
Because—		
Because thou lovest the one	*P P* 8	4
Bechance—Let there .... him pitiful mischances	*R L*	976
Beck—being at your	*Son* 58	5
Become—		
who should best .... her grief	*V A*	968
the old become a child	"	1152
With words, till action might become them better	*R L*	1323
Become the public plague	"	1479
your trespass now becomes a fee	*Son* 120	13
Better becomes the gray cheeks of the east	" 132	6
As those two mourning eyes become thy face	" 132	9
Becoming—.... of their woe	" 127	13
this becoming of things ill	" 150	5
Bed—his tent my	*V A*	108
in her naked bed	"	397
from their dark beds	"	1030
Here was thy father's bed	"	1183
is Tarquin brought unto his bed	*R L*	120
this lustful lord leap'd from his bed	"	169
The Roman lord marcheth to Lucrece' bed	"	301
on her yet unstained bed	"	366
In his clear bed	"	382
Without the bed her other fair hand was	"	393
For in thy bed I purpose to destroy thee	"	514
That to his borrow'd bed he make retire	"	573
the base bed of some rascal groom	"	671
lust should stain so pure a bed	"	684
yet ere he go to bed	"	776
Not spend the dowry of a lawful bed	"	938
Afflict him in his bed	"	975
in the interest of thy bed	"	1619
I haste me to my bed	*Son* 27	1
As the death-bed whereon it must expire	" 73	11
Robb'd others' beds' revenues	" 142	8
Were kisses all the joys in bed	*P P* 19	47
There will I make thee a bed of roses	" 20	9
Bedabbled—		
the dew-bedabbled wretch	*V A*	703
Bedchamber—In his	"	784
Bedrid—Afflict him in his bed with .... groans	*R L*	975
Bed-row—In act thy .... broke	*Son* 152	3
Bee—and I a drone-like	*R L*	836
the honey which thy chaste bee kept	"	840
The old bees die	"	1769
Been—I have .... woo'd	*V A*	97
Yet hath he been my captive	"	101
Thou hadst been gone	"	613
Had I been tooth'd	"	1117
For it had been dishonour	*R L*	814
Troy had been bright with fame	"	1491
Hath been before	*Son* 59	2
like a winter hath my absence been	" 97	1
From you have I been absent	" 98	1
I have frequent been with unknown	" 117	5
mine eyes out of their spheres been fitted	" 119	7

Been—Her pretty looks have mine enemies	Son	139	10
I might as yet have been a spreading flower	L C		75
For feasts of love I have been call'd unto	"		181
that often there had been	P P	6	8
Had women been so strong as men	"	19	23
Befallen—Hath thee....	R L		1599
Befit—Thy beauty and thy years full well befits	Son	41	3
Before—Being mad....	V A		249
she just before him	"		319
before one leaf put forth	"		416
I had my load before	"		430
before it raineth	"		458
before he barketh	"		459
before it staineth	"		460
Before I know myself	"		525
For he the night before	R L		15
And die, unhallow'd thoughts, before you blot	"		192
End thy ill aim before thy shoot be ended	"		579
Thy vices bud before thy spring	"		604
far poorer than before	"		693
which shall go before	"		1302
As lagging fowls before the northern blast	"		1335
Before the which is drawn	"		1368
which Brutus made before	"		1847
The eyes, 'fore duteous	Son	7	11
in youth before my sight	"	15	10
as if not paid before	"	30	12
more than thou hadst before	"	40	2
before thou hadst this more	"	40	4
Hath been before, how are our	"	59	2
with that which goes before	"	60	3
before these last so bad	"	67	14
Before these bastard signs	"	68	3
Before the golden tresses	"	68	5
holds his rank before	"	85	12
To mar the subject that before was well	"	103	10
Those lines that I before have writ	"	115	1
that we before have heard	"	123	8
Before a joy proposed; behind a dream	"	129	12
that which flies before her face	"	143	7
before the fall should be	P P	10	6
They that fawn'd on him before	"	21	49
Beforehand—			
All this.... counsel comprehends	R L		494
Befriend—			
once unkind befriends me now	Son	120	1
Beg—'Tis but a kiss I beg	V A		96
I'll beg her love	R L		241
but where excess begs all	L C		42
Began—than myself, thus she....	V A		7
'O pity,' 'gan she cry	"		95
queen began to sweat	"		175
of her thoughts began	"		367
began to turn their tide	"		979
with swelling drops 'gan wet	R L		1228
and their ranks began	"		1439
the strumpet that began this stir	"		1471
Each present lord began to promise aid	"		1696
they all at once began to say	"		1709

Began—...., to clothe his wit	R L		1809
and often 'gan to tear	L C		51
His phoenix down began but to appear	"		93
till thus he 'gan besiege me	"		177
shade began to woo him	P P	11	2
All unseen 'gan passage find	"	17	6
Beget—use more gold begets	V A		768
or begets him hate	R L		1005
Beggar—Or what fond....	"		216
Like to a bankrupt beggar wails	"		711
a beggar's orts to crave	"		985
As to behold desert a beggar born	Son	66	2
Beggar'd—.... of blood to blush	"	67	10
Begg'd—And .... for that	V A		102
Begin—suitor 'gins to woo him	"		6
she begins to prove	"		49
And 'gins to chide	"		46
she doth anew begin	"		60
and begins to glow	"		337
she begins to forage	"		554
begins a wailing note	"		845
to pray he doth begin	R L		342
doth his tongue begin	"		470
That twice she doth begin ere once	"		567
At last she thus begins	"		1303
And thus begins	"		1598
Begins the sad dirge	"		1612
I did begin to start	"		1639
From his lips new-waxen pale begins to blow	"		1663
Begins to talk	"		1783
Then begins a journey	Son	27	3
when first it 'gins to bud	P P	13	3
That mine eye loves it and doth first begin	"	114	11
Beginning—Find sweet....	V A		1136
Begot—Thou wast....	"		168
Beguile—the truest sight....	"		1144
Thou dost beguile the world	Son	3	4
Beguiled—To mock the subtle in themselves....	R L		957
That it beguiled attention	"		1404
Tarquin armed; so beguiled	"		1544
how are our brains beguiled	Son	59	2
Thou and I were both beguiled	P P	21	30
Beguiling—			
Such time-beguiling sport	V A		24
of his foul beguiling	L C		170
Begrimed—Begrimed with sweat	R L		1381
Begun—ere his words....	V A		462
stories, oftentimes begun	"		845
cancell'd ere well begun	R L		26
the curtain drawn, his eyes begun	"		374
all that youth began	L C		12
when they to assail begun	"		262
Behaviour—Her sad.... feeds	R L		556
From thy behaviour	Son	79	10
Beheld—,.... his shadow	V A		1099
where herself herself beheld	"		1129
What he beheld	R L		416
beheld some ghastly sprite	"		451
despairing Hecuba beheld	"		1447
Behest—breakers of their own behests	"		852
Behind—Behind some hedge	V A		1094
the load of lust he left behind	R L		734
The scalps of many, almost hid behind	"		1413
an armed hand; himself behind	"		1425

Behind—
no form of thee hast left.... *Son* 9 6
grief lies onward, and my joy behind " 50 14
behind, a dream " 129 12
I thy babe chase thee afar behind " 143 10
Behold—Who doth the world so gloriously.... *V A* 857
behold two Adons dead " 1070
That eye which him beholds as more divine, *R L* 291
this tumult to behold " 447
she never may behold the day " 746
which they themselves behold " 751
Let not the jealous Day behold that face " 800
And scarce hath eyes his treasure to behold " 857
any eye should thee behold " 1143
The heavy motion that it doth behold " 1326
every eye beholds their blame " 1343
You might behold " 1388
Of physiognomy might one behold " 1395
the eye that doth behold his haste " 1668
that beholds her bleed " 1732
I often did behold " 1758
When I behold the violet *Son* 12 3
in thee time's furrows I behold " 22 3
As to behold desert a beggar born " 66 2
That time of year thou mayst in me behold " 73 1
now behold these present days " 106 13
Yet, in good faith, some say that thee behold " 131 5
That they behold, and see not " 137 2
though it in me you behold *L C* 71
behold these talents " 204
Beholding—that place .... food *R L* 1115
her sad-beholding husband saw " 1590
Behoof—
harms that preach in our .... *L C* 165
Being—.... set, I'll smother *V A* 18
Being wasted in such " 24
Being so enraged " 29
Being red, she loves him best; and being white " 77
Who being look'd on " 87
Being judge in love " 220
Being mad before " 249
being tied unto a tree " 263
Being proud, as females are " 309
And being steel'd " 376
the weather being cold " 402
burden'd being young " 419
Being nurse and feeder " 446
Or being early pluck'd " 528
bird being tamed " 560
Like lawn being spread " 590
Being moved, he strikes " 623
Being ireful, on the lion " 628
fresh flowers being shed " 665
with others being mingled " 691
And being low " 708
milk and blood being mingled " 902
Being prison'd in her eye " 980
For he being dead " 1019
horns being hit " 1033
And being open'd " 1051

Being—the brain .... troubled *V A* 1068
and, being gone " 1089
That, thou being dead " 1134
The sovereignty of either being so great *R L* 69
He makes excuses for his being there " 114
The guilt being great " 229
her hand in my hand being lock'd " 260
And being lighted " 316
The curtains being close " 367
To wink, being blinded " 375
being so applied " 511
The flesh being proud " 712
Being so bad, such numbers seek for thee " 896
The moon being clouded " 1007
Who, being stopp'd " 1119
her bark being peel'd away " 1169
the other being dead " 1187
doth weep, the sun being set " 1226
sorrow ebbs being blown with " 1330
His nose being shadow'd " 1416
Here one being throng'd " 1417
Being from the feeling of her own grief brought " 1578
recall'd in rage, being past " 1671
Being constrain'd with dreadful circumstance " 1703
Which being done " 1833
Then being ask'd *Son* 2 5
And being frank she lends " 4 4
Whose speechless song, being many, seeming one " 8 13
As thou being mine " 36 14
Thine by thy beauty being false to me " 41 14
My life, being made of four " 45 7
speed being made from thee " 50 8
desire, of perfect'st love being made " 51 10
Being bad, to triumph, being lack'd, to hope " 52 14
winter, which, being full of care " 56 13
Being your slave " 57 1
Being your vassal " 58 4
being at your back " 58 5
wherewith being crown'd " 60 6
being woo'd of time " 70 6
or victor being charged " 70 10
my body being dead " 74 10
Or, being wreck'd " 80 11
tongues to be your being shall rehearse " 81 11
you yourself, being extant " 83 6
my glory, being dumb " 83 10
beauty being mute " 83 11
being fond on praise " 84 14
being best acquainted " 88 5
As thou being mine " 96 14
my mind, being crown'd with you " 114 1
Even so, being full of your ne'ercloying sweetness " 118 5
When not to be receives reproach of being " 121 2
for I, being pent in thee " 133 13
so thou, being rich in 'Will " 135 11
But being both from me " 144 11
he again desires her, being sat *L C* 66
nor being desired yielded " 149

Being—you o'er me .... strong	L C	257		Bequeath—thou didst .... to me	P P	19	12
For being both to me	P P	2	11	Bequeathed—unto the clouds	R L		1727
Thou being a goddess	"	3	6	Bequest—			
Thy grace being gain'd	"	3	8	Nature's .... gives nothing	Son	4	3
Beldam—				Bereave—stains and soon bereaves	V A		797
To show the .... daughters	R L		953	Rushing from forth a cloud be-			
shapes her sorrow to the beldam's				reaves our sight	R L		373
woes	"		1458	Bereft—I am .... him so	V A		381
Belied—the picture was	"		1533	sense of feeling were bereft me	"		439
As any she belied with false com-				From me by strong assault it is			
pare	Son	130	14	bereft	R L		835
not be so, nor thou belied	"	140	13	Beauty's effect with beauty were			
Believe—Not to ...., and yet	V A		986	bereft	Son	5	11
Who will believe my verse	Son	17	1	Berry—Or as the .... breaks	V A		460
And then believe me	"	21	10	that helpless berries saw	"		604
Never believe though in my nature	"	109	9	they him with berries	"		1104
I do believe him	"	138	2	Beseech—I heartily .... thee	"		404
I do believe her	P P	1	2	Beseech'd—			
Believed—by mad ears .... be	Son	140	12	acceptance weepingly beseech'd	L C		207
Believed her eyes when they to as-				Beseecher—no fair beseechers kill	Son	135	13
sail	L C		262	Beseem—			
Believing—.... she is dead	V A		467	deep regard beseems the sage	R L		277
O hard-believing love	"		985	as well beseem thy heart	Son	132	10
Bell—that hears the passing-bell	"		702	Beset—she is dreadfully	R L		444
as fowl hear falcon's bells	R L		511	Beshrew—Beshrew that heart	Son	133	1
like a heavy-hanging bell	"		1493	Beside—falls an orient drop	V A		981
the surly sullen bell	Son	71	2	my added praise beside	Son	103	4
My wether's bell rings doleful knell	P P	18	28	her pale and pined cheek beside	L C		32
Belly—He on her .... falls	V A		594	and to no love beside	"		77
Belong—				Besides—...., his soul's fair temple	R L		719
danger to resistance did	R L		1265	Besides, of weariness he did com-			
belongs to love's fine wit	Son	23	14	plain him	"		845
to you it doth belong	"	58	11	Besides, the life and feeling	"		1317
to thee I so belong	"	88	13	Who with his fear is put besides			
better state to me belongs	"	92	7	his part	Son	23	2
bosoms that to me belong	L C		254	all the world besides methinks are			
Beloved—				dead	"	112	14
Where her .... Collatinus lies	R L		256	Besiege—When forty winters shall			
thou art beloved of many	Son	10	3	.... thy brow	Son	2	1
that love and am beloved	"	25	13	besiege all kinds of blood	"	109	10
Thy sweet beloved name	"	89	10	Till thus he 'gan besiege me	L C		177
Nor my beloved as an idol shew	"	105	2	Besieged—From the .... Ardea	R L		1
I to be beloved of thee	"	150	14	the walls of strong-besieged Troy	"		1429
Below—to the ground	V A		923	Besmeared—			
Coucheth the fowl below with his				besmear'd with sluttish time	Son	55	4
wings' shade	R L		507	Best—red, she loves him	V A		77
Belt—A .... of straw and ivy buds	P P	20	13	Her best is better'd	"		78
Bemoaned—fore-bemoaned moan	Son	30	11	But then woos best	"		570
Bend—He bends her fingers	V A		476	desire sees best of all	"		720
woodman that doth bend his bow	R L		580	Since her best work	"		954
Or bends with the remover	Son	116	4	best become her grief	"		968
Bending—from his .... crest	V A		395	But none is best	"		971
bending all my loving thoughts	Son	88	10	They that love best	"		1164
Within his bending sickle's com-				Grief best is pleased with grief's			
pass come	"	116	10	society	R L		1111
Benefit—the .... of rest	"	28	2	shall fit the trespass best	"		1613
O benefit of ill	"	119	9	Look, whom she best endow'd	Son	11	11
Bent—butcher, ... to kill	V A		618	perspective it is best painter's art	"	24	4
The world is bent my deeds to cross	Son	90	2	what is best, that best I wish in thee	"	37	13
whose busy care is bent	"	143	6	then do mine eyes best see	"	43	1
Which, not to anger bent	P P	5	12	Thou, best of dearest	"	48	7
What though her frowning brows				Shall Time's best jewel	"	65	10
be bent	"	19	13	best to be with you alone	"	75	7
If to women be be bent	"	21	45	So all my best is dressing old words			
Bepainted—.... all with red	V A		901	new	"	76	11
Bequeath—.... not to their lot	R L		534	being best acquainted	"	88	5
to Tarquin I'll bequeath	"		1181	I better in one general best	"	91	8
I'll bequeath unto the knife	"		1184	But best is best, if never intermix'd	"	101	8
shall I bequeath to thee	"		1192	of sweet beauty's best	"	106	5

Best—proved thee my best of love	Son	110	8	Bettering—		
next my heaven the best	"	110	13	stamp of the time-bettering days	Son 82	8
Creating every bad a perfect best	"	114	7	Betumbled—from her .... couch	R L	1037
Now I love you best	"	115	10	Between—And, lo, I lie between that		
Yet what the best is	"	137	4	sun and thee	V A	194
my days are past the best	"	138	6	Between this heavenly and earthly		
O, love's best habit	"	138	11	sun	"	198
When all my best doth worship	"	149	11	a war of looks was then between		
thy worst all best exceeds	"	150	8	them	"	355
If best were as it was, or best				lest between them both it should	R L	74
without	L C	.....	98	between desire and dread	"	171
as it best deceives	"	.....	306	'Tween frozen conscience and hot-		
my years be past the best	P P	1	6	burning will	"	247
O, love's best habit	"	1	11	between her chamber and his will	"	302
Bad in the best	"	7	18	Between whose hills	"	390
Bestow—all naked, will bestow it	Son	26	8	As if between them twain	"	405
in more pleasures to bestow them	L C	.....	139	Between each kiss	P P 7	8
Bestow'd—The kiss I gave you is be-				So between them love did shine	P'T	33
stow'd in vain	V A	.....	771	Betwixt—		
O, that sad breath his spongy lungs				'Twixt crimson shame and anger	V A	76
bestow'd	L C	.....	326	'twixt the sun and sire	"	1160
Bestow'st—which youngly thou....	Son	11	3	Betwixt mine eye and heart	Son 47	1
Betake—every one to rest themselves				As 'twixt a miser and his wealth	" 75	4
betake	R L	.....	125	As oft 'twixt May and April	L C	102
oft betake him to retire	"	.....	175	must the love be great 'twixt thee		
to singing he betakes	P P	8	12	and me	P P 8	3
Bethinking—with false .... grieves	V A	.....	1024	Bevel—		
Betoken'd—that ever yet betoken'd	"	.....	453	though they themselves be bevel	Son 121	11
Betray—himself confounds, betrays	R L	.....	160	Bewailed—Lest my bewailed guilt	" 36	10
to betray my life	"	.....	233	Beware—Hadst thou but bid beware	V A	943
thine eyes betray thee unto mine	"	.....	483	Beweep—beweep my outcast state	Son 29	2
might the stern wolf betray	Son	96	3	Bewitch'd—bewitch'd with lust's foul		
betraying me, I do betray	"	151	5	charm	R L	173
betray the fore-betray'd	L C	.....	328	Consents bewitch'd, ere he desire	L C	131
Betray'd—Betray'd the hours	R L	.....	933	Bewitching—Bewitching like the		
Betraying—.... me, I do betray	Son	151	5	wanton mermaid's song	V A	777
Better—Are better proof	V A	.....	626	Bewray'd—the hateful foe bewray'd	R L	1698
his beauty may the better thrive	"	.....	1011	To hear her secrets so bewray'd	P P 19	54
While thou on Tereus descant'st				Beyond—Devise extremes beyond ex-		
better skill	R L	.....	1134	tremity	R L	969
which of the twain were better	"	.....	1154	Beyond all date	Son 122	4
the better so to clear her	"	.....	1320	Bias—Study his bias leaves	P P 5	5
might become them better	"	.....	1323	Bid—Bid us discourse	V A	145
in ranks of better equipage	Son	32	12	To bid the wind a base	"	303
and poets better prove	"	32	13	And bid Suspicion	"	448
all the better part of me	"	39	2	and bid good night	"	534
or whether better they	"	59	11	Bids him farewell	"	580
the better part of me	"	74	8	bid them leave quaking, bids them		
Knowing a better spirit	"	80	2	fear no more	"	899
might be better used	"	82	13	thou but bid beware	"	943
on better judgement making	"	87	12	They bid thee crop	"	946
these I better in one general best	"	91	8	bids her rejoice	"	977
Thy love is better	"	91	9	Who bids them still	"	1041
I see a better state	"	92	7	and bids them do their liking	R L	434
That did not better for my life pro-				And bids her eyes hereafter still be		
vide	"	111	3	blind	"	758
That better is by evil still made				bids it leap from thence	"	760
better	"	119	10	bid fair Lucrece speak	"	1268
'Tis better to be vile than vile es-				Bid thou be ready	"	1292
teemed	"	121	1	Bid him with speed	"	1294
Better becomes the grey cheeks	"	132	6	And bids Lucretius give	"	1773
teach thee wit, better it were	"	140	5	shame bids him possess his breath	"	1777
The better angel is a man right fair	"	144	3	to the painted banquet bids my		
Tempteth my better angel	"	144	6	heart	Son 47	6
My better angel is a man right fair	P P	2	3	bid your servant once adieu	" 57	8
Tempteth my better angel	"	2	6	Bidding—Bidding them find their		
Better'd—Her best is better'd	V A	.....	78	sepulchres	L C	46
Then better'd that the world	Son	75	8	Bide—		
Bettering—with the .... of the time	"	32	5	tame to sufferance, bide each check	Son 53	7

Bide—
 my o'er-press'd defence can bide *Son* 139   8
 Some in her threaden fillet still did
  bide *L C* 33
Biding—
 pitchy vapours from their biding *R L* 550
Bier—Borne on the bier with white *Son* 12   8
Big—
 autumn, big with rich increase " 97   6
 Big discontent so breaking *L C* 56
Bill—That some would sing, some
  other in their bills *V A* 1102
Billing—doves that sit a-billing " 366
Bin—I their father had not bin *R L* 210
Bind—
 bond that him as fast doth bind *Son* 134   8
Bird—Look how a bird lies *V A* 67
 woe unto the birds " 455
 birds to their nest " 532
 Like a wild bird " 560
 Even as poor birds " 601
 birds that helpless berries saw " 604
 the birds such pleasure " 1101
 Birds never limed *R L* 88
 give the snaped birds more cause
  to sing " 333
 like to a new-kill'd bird " 457
 where the sweet birds sing " 871
 The little birds that tune " 1107
 'You mocking birds,' quoth she " 1121
 And for, poor bird, thou sing'st " 1142
 choirs, where late the sweet birds
  sang *Son* 73   4
 The very birds are mute " 97 12
 Yet nor the lays of birds " 98   5
 Of bird, of flower, or shape " 113   6
 Sweet birds sing not *P P* 18 38
 Melodious birds sing madrigals " 20   8
 and birds did sing " 21   5
 She, poor bird, as all forlorn " 21   9
 All thy fellow birds do sing " 21 25
 Even so, poor bird, like thee " 21 27
 Let the bird of loudest lay *P T*   1
 For these dead birds sigh a prayer " 67
Birth—A dearer birth than this *Son* 32 11
 birth, or wealth, or wit " 37   5
 Showing their birth " 76   8
 Some glory in their birth " 91   1
 better than high birth to me " 91   9
Birth-hour—or birth-hour's blot *R L* 537
Bit—The iron bit he crusheth *V A* 269
Bite—and bites the poor flies " 316
Bitter—to bitter wormwood taste *R L* 893
 And bitter words to ban " 1460
 that I will bitter think *Son* 111 11
 To bitter sauces did I frame my
  feeding " 118   6
Bitterness—Nor think the bitterness
  of absence sour " 57   7
 No bitterness that I will " 111 11
Blab—Never can blab *V A* 126
Black—And coal-black clouds " 533
 mourner, black and grim " 920
 black chaos comes again " 1020
 with so black a deed *R L* 226
 With such black payment " 576
 Black lust, dishonour, shame " 654
 Black stage for tragedies and mur-
  ders fell " 766

Black—Through Night's black bo-
 som should not peep again *R L* 788
 underneath thy black all-hiding
  cloak " 801
 bathe his coal-black wings " 1009
 changed to black in every vein " 1454
 Lucrece clad in mourning black " 1585
 And some look'd black " 1713
 Of that black blood " 1745
 Makes black night beauteous *Son* 27 12
 In these black lines be seen " 63 13
 That in black ink my love may still
  shine bright " 65 14
 black night doth take away " 73   7
 black was not counted fair " 127   1
 But now is black beauty's successive
  heir " 127   3
 my mistress' eyes are raven black " 127   9
 black wires grow on her head " 130   4
 Thy black is fairest " 131 12
 In nothing art thou black " 131 13
 Have put on black, and loving
  mourners be " 132   3
 beauty herself is black " 132 13
 Who art as black as hell " 147 14
 more black and damned here *L C* 54
 In black mourn I *P P* 18 19
Blackest—The .... sin is clear'd *R L* 354
Black-faced—by this .... night *V A* 773
 but when a black-faced cloud *R L* 547
 such black-faced storms " 1518
Blade—
 he shakes aloft his Roman blade " 505
Blame—blames her miss *V A* 53
 blotting it with blame " 796
 Death is not to blame " 992
 bear an ever-during blame *R L* 224
 warrant for blame " 620
 nurse of blame " 767
 Is worthy blame " 1257
 those proud lords to blame " 1259
 The more to blame my sluggard
  negligence " 1278
 every eye beholds their blame " 1343
 I cannot blame thee *Son* 40   6
 Not blame your pleasure " 58 11
 O, blame me not " 103   5
 bloody, full of blame " 129   3
 Let reason rule things worthy
  blame *P P* 19   3
Blamed—But yet be blamed *Son* 40   7
 That thou art blamed " 70   1
Blank—Commit to these waste blanks " 77 10
Blast—Thy hasty spring still blasts *R L* 49
 Unruly blasts wait " 869
 before the northern blast " 1335
Blasted—Bud, and be blasted *V A* 1142
Blasting—of many a blasting hour *L C* 72
Blaze—fiery eyes blaze forth her
  wrong *V A* 219
Blazed—red fires in both their faces
  blazed *R L* 1353
Blazon—In the blazon of sweet beau-
  ty's best *Son* 106   5
Blazon'd—With wit well blazon'd *L C* 217
Bleed—make my faint heart bleed *V A* 669
 seem'd with him to bleed " 1056
 my false heart bleed *R L* 228
 every tear he falls a Trojan bleeds " 1551

Entry	Work	Line
Bleed—that beholds her bleed	R L	1732
by whom thy fair wife bleeds	"	1824
Bleeding—bleeding as they go	V A	924
bleeding under Pyrrhus' proud foot	R L	1440
key-cold Lucrece' bleeding stream	"	1774
To shew her bleeding body	"	1851
Of proofs new-bleeding	L C	153
with bleeding groans they pine	"	275
Heart is bleeding	P P	18, 23
Blemish—The blemish that will never be forgot	R L	536
spied in her some blemish	"	1358
Blemish'd—If in this blemish'd fort	"	1175
So beauty blemish'd once 's for ever lost	P P	13, 11
Blench—These blenches gave my heart	Son	110, 7
Blend—sapphire and the opal blend	L C	215
Bless—and never did he bless	V A	1119
Naming thy name blesses an ill report	Son	95, 8
Blessed—But blessed bankrupt	V A	466
from the blessed thing he sought	R L	340
this blessed league to kill	"	383
To hold their cursed-blessed fortune	"	866
With means more blessed than my barren rhyme	Son	16, 4
mine eyes be blessed made	"	43, 9
the rich, whose blessed key	"	52, 1
Blessed are you whose worthiness	"	52, 13
In every blessed shape we know	"	53, 12
It hath thought itself so blessed never	"	119, 6
upon that blessed wood	"	128, 2
Blessed-fair—But what's so....	"	92, 13
Blessing—blessing every book	"	82, 4
to your beauteous blessings add a curse	"	84, 13
Blest—by pleading may be blest	V A	328
more blest than living lips	Son	52, 11
more blest may be the view	"	56, 12
some special instant special blest	"	128, 12
Blind—But blind they are, and keep themselves	R L	378
in blind concealing night	"	675
her eyes hereafter still be blind	"	758
Blind, muffled bawd	"	768
The poor, lame, blind	"	902
which the blind do see	Son	27, 8
and is partly blind	"	113, 3
Swear to thy blind soul	"	136, 2
Thou blind fool, Love	"	137, 1
with tears thou keep'st me blind	"	148, 13
thou lovest, and I am blind	"	149, 14
Blinded—.... with a greater light	R L	375
Blindfold—With blindfold fury	V A	554
Blindness—gave eyes to blindness	Son	152, 11
Bliss—to want his bliss	R L	389
A bliss in proof	Son	129, 11
Blood—her blood doth boil	V A	555
Whose blood upon	"	645
heating of the blood	"	742
Like milk and blood	"	902
But stole his blood	"	1056
his congealed blood	"	1122
his blood, that on the ground	"	1167
pale cheeks and the blood	"	1169
in my breast as in his blood	"	1182
Blood—		
Thou art the next of blood	R L	1184
to stain the ocean of thy blood	"	655
such wretched blood should spill	"	999
my foul-defiled blood	"	1029
My stained blood to Tarquin	"	1181
My blood shall wash	"	1207
Ere she with blood had stain'd	"	1316
the blood his checks replenish	"	1357
The red blood reek'd	"	1377
To Simois' reedy banks the red blood ran	"	1437
Her blue blood changed	"	1454
Though my gross blood	"	1655
Her blood in poor revenge	"	1736
that the crimson blood	"	1738
Some of her blood still pure and red remain'd	"	1742
of that black blood	"	1743
Corrupted blood some watery token shows	"	1748
And blood untainted	"	1749
blood so unjustly stain'd	"	1836
And see thy blood warm	Son	2, 14
And that fresh blood	"	11, 3
burn the long-lived phoenix in her blood	"	19, 4
When hours have drain'd his blood	"	63, 3
Beggar'd of blood to blush through lively veins	"	67, 10
Where checks need blood	"	82, 14
besiege all kinds of blood	"	109, 10
to my sportive blood	"	121, 6
sadly penn'd in blood	L C	47
O false blood, thou register of lies	"	52
satisfaction to our blood	"	162
Are errors of the blood	"	184
and rubies red as blood	"	198
Bloodless—by doubt and .... fear	V A	891
takes her by the bloodless hand	R L	1597
In bloodless white	L C	201
Bloody—the boar, that .... beast	V A	999
So, at his bloody view	"	1037
In bloody death	R L	430
Here friend by friend in bloody channel lies	"	1487
My bloody judge forbade	"	1648
and by this bloody knife	"	1840
upon this bloody tyrant, Time	Son	16, 2
The bloody spur cannot provoke him on	"	50, 9
bloody, full of blame	"	129, 3
vanquish'd men in bloody fight	P P	18, 36
Bloom—The canker-blooms have full as deep	Son	54, 5
Blossom—made the blossoms dote	L C	235
Spied a blossom passing fair	P P	17, 3
Blot—when they blot the sky	V A	184
die, unhallow'd thoughts, before you blot	R L	192
a slavish wipe or birth-hour's blot	"	537
To blot old books and alter their contents	"	948
To shun this blot she would not blot the letter	"	1322
Or blot with hell-born sin	"	1519
when clouds do blot the heaven	Son	28, 10
So shall those blots that do with me remain	"	36, 3

Blot—But what's so blessed-fair that fears no blot	*Son*	92	13
beauty's veil doth cover every blot	"	93	11
Blotted—What wit sets down is blotted straight with will	*R L*		1299
Blotting—blotting it with blame	*V A*		796
Blow—bear such shameful blows	*R L*		832
that blow did bail it	"		1725
to give thyself a blow	"		1823
Under the blow of thralled discontent	*Son*	124	7
Blow—To fan and blow them dry	*V A*		52
wind would blow it off	"		1089
And blows the smoke	*R L*		312
blows these pitchy vapours	"		550
From lips new-waxen pale begins to blow	"		1663
till it blow up rain	"		1788
thy cheeks may blow	*P P*	17	9
Blow'st—Thou blow'st the fire	*R L*		884
Blown—The tempting tune is....	*V A*		778
Their light blown out	"		826
My sighs are blown away	"		1071
Small lights are soon blown out	*R L*		647
sorrow ebbs, being blown with wind of words	"		1330
Blue—Her two blue windows	*V A*		482
globes circled with blue	*R L*		407
Whose ranks of blue veins	"		440
Her blue blood changed	"		1454
Blue circles stream'd like rainbows	"		1587
Blue-vein'd—These.... violets	*V A*		125
Blunt—But the blunt boar	"		884
this blunt and ill	*R L*		1300
blunt rage and rigour roll'd	"		1398
with the blunt swain he goes	"		1504
Devouring Time, blunt thou the lion's paws	*Son*	19	1
That over-goes my blunt invention quite	"	103	7
blunt the sharp'st intents	"	115	7
Blunter—Thy edge should blunter be than appetite	"	56	2
Blunting—For.... the fine point	"	52	4
By blunting us to make our wits more keen	*L C*		161
Blur—This blur to youth	*R L*		222
Blurr'd—Thy issue blurr'd with nameless bastardy	"		52
Blush—			
Forgetting shame's pure blush	*V A*		558
beauty would blush for shame	*R L*		54
when beauty boasted blushes	"		55
the red rose blush at her own disgrace	"		479
I have no one to blush with me	"		792
to blush through lively veins	*Son*	67	10
Of grief and blushes	*L C*		200
Of burning blushes	"		304
To blush at speeches rank	"		307
Yet will she blush	*P P*	19	53
Blush'd—Who blush'd and pouted	*V A*		33
he blush'd to see her shame	*R L*		1344
She thought he blush'd	"		1354
Blushing—spread upon the.... rose	*V A*		590
when, lo, the blushing morrow	*R L*		1082
And blushing on her	"		1339
And blushing with him	"		1355
That blushing red	"		1511
Blushing—Blushing at that	*R L*		1750
One blushing shame	*Son*	99	9
by thee blushing stand	"	128	8
And blushing fled	*P P*	9	14
Blusterer—Sometime a blusterer	*L C*		58
Blustering—stormy,.... weather	*R L*		115
Boar—Unless it be a boar	*V A*		410
To hunt the boar	"		588
'The boar!' quoth she	"		589
wouldst hunt the boar	"		614
thou didst name the boar	"		641
an angry-chafing boar	"		662
with the boar to-morrow	"		672
the hunting of the boar	"		711
But the blunt boar	"		884
spied the hunted boar	"		900
to rate the boar	"		905
the boar, that bloody beast	"		999
the boar provoked	"		1003
The foul boar's conquest	"		1030
that the boar had trench'd	"		1052
urchin-snouted boar	"		1105
He ran upon the boar	"		1112
deep-wounded with a boar	*P P*	9	10
Boast—Perchance his boast	*R L*		36
My resolution, love, shall be thy boast	"		1193
In that my boast is true	*L C*		246
Boast—What canst thou boast	*V A*		1077
He shall not boast	*R L*		1064
and proud titles boast	*Son*	25	2
to boast how I do love thee	"	26	13
As victors of my silence cannot boast	"	86	11
of all men's pride I boast	"	91	12
Time, thou shalt not boast	"	123	1
Boasted—When beauty.... blushes	*R L*		55
Boast—I am a worthless boat	*Son*	80	11
Boding—My boding heart pants	*V A*		647
wolves' death-boding cries	*R L*		165
Body—			
my body's bane would cure thee	*V A*		372
What is thy body but a swallowing grave	"		757
The strongest body shall it make most weak	"		1145
But with my body	*R L*		1137
My body or my soul	"		1163
That wounds my body	"		1185
My soul and body	"		1199
through all her body spread	"		1266
cannot abuse a body dead	"		1267
imprison'd in a body dead	"		1456
Her body's stain	"		1710
Himself on her self-slaughter'd body threw	"		1733
Circles her body in on every side	"		1739
To show her bleeding body	"		1851
My body is the frame	*Son*	24	3
when body's works expired	"	27	4
My name be buried where my body is	"	72	11
my body being dead	"	74	10
some in their body's force	"	91	2
is this thy body's end	"	146	8
to my gross body's treason	"	151	6
My soul doth tell my body	"	151	7
Boil—her blood doth boil	*V A*		555
Boisterous—.... and unruly beast	"		326
Bold—Be bold to play	"		124
dares not be so bold	"		401

BOLD 46 BOTH

Bold—			
with bold, stern looks	R L	....	1252
if your maid may be so bold	"	....	1282
life and bold audacity	"	....	1346
bold Hector, march'd to field	"	....	1430
to flatter fools and make them bold	"	....	1359
to give them from me was I bold	Son	122	11
I dare not be so bold	"	131	7
Youth is hot and bold	P P	12	7
Bold-faced—like a bold-faced suitor	V A	....	6
Boldness—At the wood's boldness	Son	128	8
Boll'n—one being throng'd bears back, all boll'n and red	R L	....	1417
Bond—unloose it from their bond	"	....	136
My bonds in thee	Son	87	4
Whereto all bonds do tie me	"	117	4
Under that bond	"	134	8
seal'd false bonds of love	"	142	7
vow, bond, nor space	L C	....	264
to that strong-bonded oath	"	....	279
Bondage—			
He held such petty .... in disdain	V A	....	394
And, true to bondage	L C	....	34
Bone—on feathers, flesh, and bone	V A	....	56
colour, pace, and bone	"	....	294
Shall curse my bones	R L	....	209
my bones with dust shall cover	Son	32	2
a ring of posied gold and bone	L C	....	45
Boned—			
Shows me a bare-boned death	R L	....	1761
Bonnet—And with his bonnet	V A	....	339
Bonnet nor veil henceforth no creature wear	"	....	1081
he put his bonnet on	"	....	1087
Book—margents of such books	R L	....	102
the school, the book	"	....	615
To blot old books and alter their contents	"	....	948
To cipher what is writ in learned books	"	....	811
women's faces are their own faults' books	"	....	1253
O, let my books be then the eloquence	Son	23	9
Is from the book of honour razed	"	25	11
In some antique book	"	59	7
And of this book this learning	"	77	4
and much enrich thy book	"	77	14
blessing every book	"	82	4
makes his book thine eyes	P P	5	5
Book—Book both my wilfulness and errors down	Son	117	9
Boot—And 'Will' to boot	"	135	2
Bootless—			
this idle theme, this bootless chat	V A	....	422
trouble deaf heaven with my bootless cries	Son	29	3
Bore—I bore the canopy	"	125	1
it bore not beauty's name	"	127	2
our drops this difference bore	L C	....	300
Born—mine honour is new-born	R L	....	1190
or blot with hell-born sin	"	....	1519
my old age new born	"	....	1759
With April's first-born flowers	Son	21	7
As to behold desert a beggar born	"	66	2
Before these bastard signs of fair were born	"	68	3
is thine and born of thee	"	78	10
Ere you were born	"	104	14
born to our desire	"	123	7
Born—who, not born fair	Son	127	11
conscience is born of love	"	151	2
Borne—borne so hard a mind	V A	....	203
Borne by the trustless wings	R L	....	2
Borne on the bier with white and by me be borne alone	Son	12	8
	"	36	4
Borrow—'Tis much to borrow	V A	....	411
shining star doth borrow	"	....	861
tears did lend and borrow	"	....	961
eyes that light will borrow	R L	....	1083
she their looks doth borrow	"	....	1498
good day, of night now borrow	P P	13	17
Borrow'd—			
they borrow'd all their shine	V A	....	488
That to his borrow'd bed he make retire	R L	....	573
To see those borrow'd tears	"	....	1549
with art's false borrow'd face	Son	127	6
Which borrow'd from this holy fire of love	"	153	5
O, all that borrow'd motion	L C	....	327
Bosom—From his soft bosom	V A	....	81
Within my bosom	"	....	646
of her bosom dropp'd	"	....	958
within her bosom	"	....	1173
Through Night's black bosom	R L	....	788
But they whose guilt within their bosoms lie	"	....	1342
in that bosom sits	Son	9	13
Which in my bosom's shop	"	24	7
Thy bosom is endeared	"	31	1
salve which wounded bosoms fits	"	120	12
In thy steel bosom's ward	"	133	9
he did in the general bosom reign	L C	....	127
The broken bosoms that to me belong	"	....	254
Both—Both favour, savour	V A	....	747
mingled both together	"	....	902
Both crystals, where they	"	....	963
both of them extremes	"	....	987
Could rule them both	"	....	1008
They both would strive	"	....	1092
Which of them both	R L	....	53
lost between them both	"	....	74
Both which, as servitors	"	....	285
and all the power of both	"	....	572
tutor both to good and bad	"	....	995
Kill both thyself and her	"	....	1036
both were kept for heaven	"	....	1166
Thou dead, both die, and both shall victors be	"	....	1211
In both their faces blazed	"	....	1353
And both she thinks too long	"	....	1572
Both stood, like old acquaintance	"	....	1593
stain both moon and sun	Son	35	3
Both find each other, and I lose both twain	"	42	11
And both for my sake	"	42	12
can jump both sea and land	"	44	7
Are both with thee	"	45	2
Than both your poets	"	83	14
Both grace and faults	"	96	3
had stol'n of both	"	99	10
both skill and argument	"	100	8
Both truth and beauty	"	101	3
Book both my wilfulness and errors down	"	117	9
Thy registers and thee I both defy	"	123	9
thou hast both him and me	"	134	13

Both—On both sides thus is simple				Boy—sweet boy, ere this	V A 613	
truth suppress'd	Son	138	8	By this the boy	" 1165	
But being both from me, both to				Nothing, sweet boy	Son 108	5
each friend	"	144	11	O thou, my lovely boy	" 126	1
of all sizes both high and low	L C		21	The boy for trial	" 153	10
and sexes both enchanted	"		128	Forbade the boy	P P 9	8
Both fire from hence	"		294	As if the boy should use	" 11	8
nature is both kind and tame	"		311	Brag—brag not of thy might	V A 113	
both to me, both to each friend	P P	2	11	Nor shall Death brag	Son 18	11
One god is god of both	"	8	13	Beauty brag, but 'tis not she	P T 63	
One knight loves both, and both in				Bragg'd—When virtue bragg'd	R L 54	
thee remain	"	8	14	Whose bare out-bragg'd the web	L C 95	
to turn them both to gain	"	16	10	Braided—his .... hanging mane	V A 271	
Thou and I were both beguiled	"	21	30	braided in loose negligence	L C 35	
Bottom—				Brain—		
the bottom poison, and the top	V A		1143	proceedings of a drunken brain	V A 910	
search the bottom of annoy	R L		1109	disposing of her troubled brain	" 1040	
Bottom-grass—Sweet bottom-grass	V A		236	the brain being troubled	" 1068	
Bottomless—				the weak brain's forgeries	R L 460	
O, deeper sin than .... conceit	R L		701	how are our brains beguiled	Son 59	2
Bough—on a ragged bough	V A		37	deliver'd from thy brain	" 77	11
Upon those boughs	Son	73	3	In my brain inhearse	" 86	3
music burthens every bough	"	102	11	What's in the brain	" 108	1
Bought—thy interest was not	R L		1067	thy tables are within my brain	" 122	1
Bounced—He, spying her, ... in	P P	6	13	so long as brain and heart	" 122	5
Bound—The sea hath bounds	V A		389	Brain'd—And deep-brain'd sonnets	L C 209	
What rounds, what bounds	L C		109	Brain-sick—by .... rude desire	R L 175	
Bound—thou art bound to breed	V A		171	Brake—brakes obscure and rough	V A 237	
in her arms be bound	"		226	brake off his late intent	" 469	
be neighs, he bounds	"		265	fawn hid in some brake	" 876	
bound him to her breast	"		812	Here kennel'd in a brake	" 913	
a wretched image bound	R L		1501	Here in these brakes	P P 9	10
As bound in knighthood	"		1697	Bramble—The thorny brambles	V A 629	
bound to stay your leisure	Son	58	4	Branch—		
Bound for the prize	"	86	2	the branches of another root	R L 823	
Boundeth—Yet in the eddy	R L		1669	Brand—my name receives a brand	Son 111	5
Bounding—the .... banks o'erflows	"		1119	Cupid laid by his brand	" 153	1
Boundless—				Love's brand new-fired	" 153	9
there falls into thy boundless flood	"		653	his heart-inflaming brand	" 154	2
nor earth, nor boundless sea	Son	65	1	This brand she quenched	" 154	9
Bounteous—				Brand—Brand not my forehead	R L 1091	
The bounteous largess given thee	"	4	6	Brass—And brass eternal slave to		
which bounteous gift	"	11	12	mortal rage	Son 64	4
Bountiful—				Since brass, nor stone	" 65	1
Bountiful they will him call	P P	21	40	tombs of brass are spent	" 107	14
Bounty—shouldst in bounty cherish	Son	11	12	Unless my nerves were brass	" 120	4
as your bounty doth appear	"	53	11	Brave—When their brave hope	R L 1430	
that lets not bounty fall	L C		41	And see the brave day	Son 12	2
Bow—to the saddle-bow	V A		14	Save breed, to brave him	" 12	14
by Cupid's bow she doth protest	"		581	And wear their brave state	" 15	8
that doth bend his bow	R L		580	weed out-braves his dignity	" 94	12
Bow—in battle ne'er did bow	V A		99	Youth like summer brave	P P 12	4
joints forget to bow	"		1061	Bravery—Hiding thy bravery	Son 34	4
She bows her head	"		1171	Braving—Braving compare, disdain-		
to the ground their knees they bow	R L		1846	fully did sting	R L 40	
make me bow	Son	90	3	Brawl—And ban and brawl	P P 19	20
under my transgression bow	"	120	3	Brawny—his brawny sides	V A 625	
Bow-back—On his bow-back	V A		619	Breach—where no breach should be	" 1066	
Bowed—to thee like osiers bowed	P P	5	4	In the breach appears	" 1175	
As heaven, it seem'd, to kiss the				To make the breach	R L 469	
turrets bow'd	R L		1372	The impious breach	" 809	
Bower—hath no name, no holy	Son	127	7	why of two oaths' breach	Son 152	5
Boy—was the tender boy	V A		32	Break—her intendments break	V A 222	
cry, flint-hearted boy	"		95	girths he breaks asunder	" 266	
Is love so light, sweet boy	"		155	The client breaks	" 336	
to the wayward boy	"		344	the berry breaks before	" 460	
excuse thy courser, gentle boy	"		403	love breaks through	" 576	
silly boy, believing she is dead	"		467	breaks the silver rain	" 959	
'sweet boy,' she says	"		583	breaks ope her lock'd-up eyes	R L 446	

Break—so her accent breaks	R L	566
or break their hearts	"	1239
on what occasion break	"	1270
stirring ere the break of day	"	1280
to break upon the galled shore	"	1440
as if her heart would break	"	1716
at break of day arising	Son 29	11
through the cloud thou break	" 34	5
to break a twofold truth	" 41	12
When I break twenty	" 152	6
would not break from thence	L C	34
Feeling it break	"	275
To break an oath	P P 3	14
Breaker—Or kings be breakers	R L	852
Breaketh—Breaketh his rein	V A	264
breaketh from the sweet embrace	"	811
She wildly breaketh	"	874
Breaking—breaking rings a-twain	L C	6
so breaking their contents	"	56
Breast—Broad breast, full eye	V A	296
his back, his breast	"	396
incaged in his breast	"	582
shakes thee on my breast	"	648
closure of my breast	"	782
bound him to her breast	"	812
from whose silver breast	"	855
in my breast as in his blood	"	1182
here in my breast	"	1183
her breasts, like ivory globes	R L	407
On her bare breast	"	439
remains upon her breast	"	463
by beating on her breast	"	759
lurk in gentle breasts	"	851
hollow-swelling feather'd breasts	"	1122
beaten from her breast	"	1563
she sheathed in her harmless breast	"	1723
And bubbling from her breast	"	1737
he struck his hand upon his breast	"	1642
Which in thy breast doth live	Son 22	7
of my speaking breast	" 23	10
Are windows to my breast	" 24	11
Within the gentle closure of my breast	" 48	11
which in thy breast doth lie	" 109	4
and most most loving breast	" 110	14
then her breasts are dun	" 130	3
needs would touch my breast	" 153	10
to physic your cold breast	L C	259
What breast so cold	"	292
Lean'd her breast up-till a thorn	P P 21	10
And the turtle's loyal breast	P T	57
Breath—I'll sigh celestial breath	V A	189
all but with a breath	"	414
Comes breath perfumed	"	444
his breath breatheth	"	474
Banish'd by thy breath	"	510
draws up her breath	"	929
to steal his breath	"	934
his breath and beauty set	"	935
to her Adonis' breath	"	1172
A dream, a breath	R L	212
play'd with her breath	"	400
unwholesome breaths make sick	"	779
for passage of her breath	"	1040
made my stop my breath	"	1180
Thin winding breath	"	1407
his breath drinks up again	"	1666
bids him possess his breath	"	1777
When summer's breath	Son 54	8
Breath—summer's honey breath	Son 65	5
Where breath most breathes	" 81	14
Then others for the breath of words respect	" 85	13
If not from my love's breath	" 99	3
had annex'd thy breath	" 99	11
Than in the breath	" 130	8
O, that sad breath	L C	326
My vow was breath, and breath a vapour is	P P 3	9
as she fetched breath	" 11	11
age's breath is short	" 12	5
Wish'd himself the heaven's breath	" 17	8
With the breath thou givest and takest	P T	19
Breathe—		
breathes she forth her spite	R L	762
What he breathes out	"	1666
So long as men can breathe	Son 18	13
While thou dost breathe	" 38	2
Where breath most breathes	" 81	14
When winds breathe sweet	L C	103
Breath'd—		
on thy well-breath'd horse	V A	678
Lust-breathed Tarquin leaves	R L	3
Breathed forth the sound	"	1726
prison where it breathed	Son 145	2
Breather—When all the breathers	" 81	12
Breatheth—breatheth in her face	V A	62
his breath breatheth life in her	"	474
Breathing—Untimely breathings	R L	1720
Breathing-while—in a	V A	1142
Breathless—Till .... be disjoin'd	V A	541
Bred—Which bred more beauty	"	70
but of no woman bred	"	214
than civil home-bred strife	"	764
in Tarquin new ambition bred	R L	411
By thy bright beauty was it newly bred	"	490
errors by opinion bred	"	937
shall my fame be bred	"	1188
conceit of love there bred	Son 108	13
strongly in my purpose bred	" 112	13
Breed—thou art bound to breed	V A	171
breeds by heating of the blood	"	742
would breed a scarcity	"	753
what sorrow I shall breed	R L	499
joy breeds months of pain	"	690
What virtue breeds	"	872
while infection breeds	"	907
breeds the fat earth's store	"	1837
That's for thyself to breed another thee	Son 6	7
Save breed to brave him	" 12	14
which public manners breeds	" 111	4
My ewes breed not	P P 18	2
Breeder—Of the fair breeder	V A	282
unback'd breeder, full of fear	"	320
Breedeth—beauty breedeth beauty	"	167
breedeth love by smelling	"	444
Breeding—A breeding jennet	"	260
this hate-breeding spy	"	655
Bribed—hath she .... the Destinies	"	733
Bridle—The studded brikle	"	37
Brief—This brief abridgement	R L	1198
though my words are brief	"	1309
Nor can I fortune to brief minutes tell	Son 14	5
with his brief hours and weeks	" 116	11

Brief—Our dates are brief	*Son*	123	5
In brief the grounds and motives of her woe	*L C*		63
Brier—Each envious brier	*V A*		705
Bright—grey, and bright, and quick	"		140
And as the bright sun	"		485
a bright star shooteth	"		815
that makes him bright	"		862
as bright as heaven's beauties	*R L*		13
that she reflects so bright	"		376
By thy bright beauty	"		490
pearl from her bright eyes	"		1213
their youthful sons bright weapons wield	"		1432
Like bright things stain'd	"		1435
Troy had been bright	"		1491
Into so bright a day	"		1518
to thine own bright eyes	*Son*	1	5
An eye more bright	"	20	5
though not so bright	"	21	11
to please him thou art bright	"	28	9
darkly bright are bright in dark	"	43	4
shadows doth make bright	"	43	5
And nights bright days	"	43	14
you shall shine more bright	"	55	3
my love may still shine bright	"	65	14
and thought thee bright	"	147	13
Bright orient pearl	*P P*	10	3
Brighter—Brighter than glass	"	7	3
Brightness—And swear that brightness doth not grace	*Son*	150	4
Brim—Under whose brim	*V A*		1088
on the brook's green brim	*P P*	6	10
Brine—with showers of silver brine	*R L*		796
the silken figures in the brine	*L C*		17
Bring—sometime false doth bring	*V A*		658
brings beauty under	"		746
Would bring him mulberries	"		1103
my attempt will bring	*R L*		491
And bring him where his suit	"		898
and bring truth to light	"		940
Brings home his lord	"		1584
thy sweet love remember'd such wealth brings	*Son*	29	13
For to thy sensual fault I bring in sense	"	35	9
let him bring forth	"	38	11
to mine own self-bring	"	39	3
Can bring him to his sweet up-locked treasure	"	52	2
by that which I bring forth	"	72	13
give life and bring a tomb	"	83	12
my Muse brings forth	"	103	1
bring water for my stain	"	109	8
Bring me within the level	"	117	11
Green plants bring not	*P P*	18	39
Brinish—And wiped the .... pearl	*R L*		1213
With brinish current	*L C*		284
Bristle—with hairy bristles armed	*V A*		625
Bristly—Of bristly pikes	"		620
with white and bristly beard	*Son*	12	8
Brittle—yet, as glass is, brittle	*P P*	7	3
A brittle glass that's broken	"	13	4
Broad—Broad breast, full eye	*V A*		296
broad buttock, tender hide	"		298
On your broad main	*Son*	80	8
Broil—And broils root out	"	55	6
Broke—feather'd creatures .... away	"	143	2
In act thy bed-vow broke	"	152	3

Broke—Vows for thee broke	*P P*	3	4
If by me broke	"	3	13
Broken—with lustful language	*V A*		47
Poor broken glass	*R L*		1758
my slumbers should be broken	*Son*	61	3
The broken bosoms	*L C*		254
If broken, then it is no fault	*P P*	3	12
that's broken presently	"	13	4
broken dead within an hour	"	13	6
As broken glass no cement can redress	"	13	10
Broker—			
were ever brokers to defiling	*L C*		173
Brood—all that brood to kill	*R L*		627
devour her own sweet brood	*Son*	19	2
Brook—his shadow in the brook	*V A*		162
his shadow in the brook	"		1099
sitting by a brook	*P P*	4	1
growing by a brook	"	6	5
A brook where Adon	"	6	6
on the brook's green brim	"	6	10
Brook—brooks not merry guests	*R L*		1125
Brother—death-worthy in thy....	"		635
the sister and the brother	*P P*	8	2
Brought—			
She had not brought forth thee	*V A*		204
brought unto his bed	*R L*		120
fault brought in subjection	"		724
of her own grief brought	"		1578
than his love had brought	*Son*	32	11
I would be brought	"	44	3
And brought to medicine	"	118	11
which brought me to her eye	*L C*		247
Brow—Even so she kiss'd his brow	*V A*		59
one wrinkle in my brow	"		139
His louring brows	"		183
hides his angry brow	"		339
with his brows repine	"		490
With heavy eye, knit brow	*R L*		709
with a cunning brow	"		749
To mask their brows	"		794
character'd in my brow	"		807
A brow unbent	"		1509
shall besiege thy brow	*Son*	2	1
my love's fair brow	"	19	9
splendour on my brow	"	33	10
delves the parallels in beauty's brow	"	60	10
drain'd his blood and fill'd his brow	"	63	3
inhabit on a living brow	"	68	4
of lip, of eye, of brow	"	106	6
stamp'd upon my brow	"	112	2
her frowning brows be bent	*P P*	19	13
Browny—His browny locks did hang	*L C*		85
Bruised—			
With bruised arms and wreaths	*R L*		110
Brutus—from the purple fountain Brutus drew	"		1734
Brutus, who pluck'd the knife	"		1807
which Brutus made before	"		1847
Bubbling—And .... from her breast	"		1737
Bud—Who plucks the bud	*V A*		416
intrude the maiden bud	*R L*		848
Within thine own bud	*Son*	1	11
the darling buds of May	"	18	3
loathsome canker lives in sweetest bud	"	35	4
their masked buds disclose	"	54	8
For canker vice the sweetest buds doth love	"	70	7

4

BUD   50   BUT

Bud—And buds of marjoram	Son	99	7
Pluck'd in the bud	P P	10	2
A belt of straw and ivy buds	"	20	13
Bud—Bud, and be blasted	V A	....	1142
bud before thy spring	R L	....	604
when first it 'gins to bud	P P	13	3
Budding—of thy budding name	Son	95	3
Bulk—beating her bulk	R L	....	467
Bullet—deadly bullet of a gun	V A	....	461
The golden bullet beats it down	P P	19	30
Bulwarks—			
for me many bulwarks builded	L C	....	152
Builded—builded far from accident	Son	124	5
for me many bulwarks builded	L C	....	152
Building—			
To ruinate proud buildings	R L	....	944
He of tall building	Son	80	12
Built—Though weak-built hopes persuade	R L	....	130
Of rich-built Ilion	"	....	1324
when it is built anew	Son	119	11
built up with newer might	"	123	2
Burden'd—			
back'd and burden'd being young	V A	....	419
Burden-wise—For .... I'll hum	R L	....	1133
Buried—He might be buried	V A	....	244
their pride lies buried	Son	25	7
which I thought buried	"	31	4
where buried love doth live	"	31	9
cost of outworn buried age	"	64	2
My name be buried	"	72	11
Truth and beauty buried be	P T	....	64
Buriest—Within thine own bud buriest content	Son	1	11
Burn—			
He burns with bashful shame	V A	....	49
her fire must burn	"	....	94
The sun doth burn my face	"	....	186
If they burn too	"	....	192
lamp that burns by night	"	....	755
Do burn themselves	"	....	810
Fair torch, burn out thy light	R L	....	190
To burn the guiltless casket	"	....	1057
quench Troy that burns so long	"	....	1468
fire to burn thy city	"	....	1554
to burn his Troy with water	"	....	1561
burn the long-lived phœnix	Son	19	4
war's quick fire shall burn	"	55	7
full flame should afterwards burn clearer	"	115	4
Burn'd—in three hot Junes burn'd	"	104	7
When he most burn'd	L C	....	314
She burn'd with love	P P	7	13
She burn'd out love	"	7	14
Burneth—the fire that burneth me	V A	....	196
Burneth more hotly	"	....	332
fire that burneth here	R L	....	1475
as soon as straw out-burneth	P P	7	14
Burning—			
maiden burning of his cheeks	V A	....	50
my marrow burning	"	....	142
With burning eye	"	....	178
As burning fevers	"	....	739
conscience and hot-burning will	R L	....	247
cheers up his burning eye	"	....	435
burning Troy doth bear	"	....	1474
Lifts up his burning head	Son	7	2
that burning lungs did raise	L C	....	228
Of burning blushes	"	....	304

Burnish'd—hills seem .... gold	V A	....	858
Burnt—two lamps, burnt out, in darkness lie	"	....	1128
burnt out in tedious nights	R L	....	1379
burnt the shining glory	"	....	1523
Burthen—			
be the burthen of a guilty mind	"	....	735
burthen of mine own love's might	Son	23	8
The second burthen of a former child	"	59	4
wanton burthen of the prime	"	97	7
wild music burthens every bough	"	102	11
Bury—to bury that posterity	V A	....	758
Burying—			
Burying in Lucrece' wound	R L	....	1810
Bush—			
brambles and embracing bushes	V A	....	629
the bushes in the way	"	....	871
no secret bushes fear	R L	....	88
shape every bush a hideous shapeless devil	"	....	973
Busy—my thought, my busy care	V A	....	383
Busy yourselves in skill-contending schools	R L	....	1018
busy winds give o'er	"	....	1790
whose busy care is bent	Son	143	6
But—but love be laugh'd to scorn	V A	....	4
But rather famish	"	....	20
seem an hour but short	"	....	23
but frosty in desire	"	....	36
but soon she stops	"	....	46
but never to obey	"	....	61
cannot choose but love	"	....	79
But when her lips	"	....	89
But help she cannot get	"	....	93
'Tis but a kiss I beg	"	....	96
Touch but my lips	"	....	115
there are but twain	"	....	123
But having no defects	"	....	138
but light, and will aspire	"	....	150
shines but warm	"	....	193
but died unkind	"	....	204
but speak fair words	"	....	208
but the eye alone	"	....	213
but of no woman bred	"	....	214
But, lo, from forth	"	....	259
But when the heart's attorney	"	....	335
But now her cheek	"	....	347
but my body's bane	"	....	372
but deep desire hath none	"	....	389
But when he saw	"	....	393
But, when his glutton	"	....	399
the lesson is but plain	"	....	407
love but to disgrace it	"	....	412
all but with a breath	"	....	414
Had I no eyes but ears	"	....	433
that were but sensible	"	....	436
nothing but the very smell	"	....	441
But, O, what banquet	"	....	445
But blessed bankrupt	"	....	466
But hers, which through	"	....	491
But now I lived	"	....	497
But now I died	"	....	498
But for thy piteous lips	"	....	504
but the ungrown fry	"	....	526
but dissolves with tempering	"	....	565
But then woos best	"	....	570
But all in vain	"	....	607
But that thou told'st me	"	....	614

But—But having thee at vantage	V A	635
But like an earthquake	"	648
But if thou needs wilt hunt	"	673
But if thou fall	"	721
all is but to rob thee	"	723
But in one minute's fight	"	746
thy body but a swallowing grave	"	757
But gold that's put to use	"	768
But soundly sleeps	"	786
but your device in love	"	789
But Lust's effect	"	800
but more I dare not say	"	805
But idle sounds	"	848
But the blunt boar	"	884
But back retires	"	906
But hatefully at random	"	940
but thy false dart	"	941
thou but bid beware	"	943
But through the flood-gates	"	959
But like a stormy day	"	965
But none is best	"	971
Who is but drunken	"	984
I did but jest	"	997
but is still severe	"	1000
I did but act	"	1006
was but late forlorn	"	1026
But stole his blood	"	1056
But true-sweet beauty	"	1080
But when Adonis lived	"	1085
But this foul, grim	"	1105
But by a kiss	"	1114
But he is dead	"	1119
but unsavoury end	"	1138
but high or low	"	1139
but know, it is as good	"	1181
But king nor peer	R L	21
O happiness, enjoy'd but of a few	"	22
But some untimely thought	"	43
But beauty, in that white intituled	"	57
But, poorly rich	"	97
But she, that never coped	"	99
they have but less	"	137
Is but to surfeit	"	139
Is but to nurse the life	"	141
No noise but owls' and wolves' death-boding cries	"	165
But honest fear, bewitch'd	"	173
Or what fond beggar, but to touch the crown	"	216
But coward-like with trembling	"	231
But as he is my kinsman	"	237
but she is not her own	"	241
The worst is but denial	"	242
But with a pure appeal	"	283
But, as they open, they all rate	"	304
But his hot heart, which	"	314
But all these poor forbiddings	"	323
But in the midst of his unfruitful prayer	"	341
Thoughts are but dreams	"	353
But she, sound sleeping	"	363
But blind they are	"	378
But they must ope	"	383
But that life lived in death	"	406
but mightily he noted	"	411
but strongly he desired	"	415
but she, in worser taking	"	453
But she with vehement prayers	"	475
But as reproof and reason	"	489
But—But will is deaf	R L	495
But nothing can perfection's course control	"	500
But if thou yield	"	526
but his foul appetite	"	546
But when a black-faced cloud	"	547
he doth but dally	"	554
but his heart granteth	"	558
But happy monarchs still are fear'd	"	611
If but for fear of this	"	614
fair reputation but a bawd	"	623
Think but how vile	"	631
but swells the higher by this let	"	649
but alter not his taste	"	651
But low shrubs wither	"	665
But she hath lost	"	687
But her foresight could not forestall	"	728
but that every eye can see	"	750
as he is but Night's child	"	785
But I alone alone must sit	"	795
but he that gives	"	833
But robb'd and ransack'd	"	838
But no perfection is so absolute	"	853
But like still-pining Tantalus	"	858
But torment that it cannot cure	"	861
But ill-annexed Opportunity	"	874
But they ne'er meet with Opportunity	"	903
but Sin ne'er gives a fee	"	913
but he was stay'd by thee	"	917
but pity not his moans	"	977
But little stars may hide them	"	1008
But if the like the snow-white swan desire	"	1011
But eagles gazed upon	"	1015
But if I live	"	1035
But this no slaughterhouse	"	1039
But when I fear'd	"	1048
But thou shalt know	"	1067
but stol'n from forth thy gate	"	1068
But cloudy Lucrece	"	1084
No object but her passion's strength	"	1103
But with my body	"	1157
but stoutly say, 'So be it	"	1209
But durst not ask of her	"	1223
But as the earth doth weep	"	1226
No cause, but company	"	1236
But chide rough winter	"	1255
Not that devour'd, but that which doth devour	"	1256
But tell me, girl, when went	"	1275
'But, lady, if your maid	"	1282
but not her grief's true quality	"	1313
'Tis but a part of sorrow	"	1328
but dull and slow she deems	"	1336
But they whose guilt	"	1342
but do it leisurely	"	1349
but laid no words to gage	"	1351
But long she thinks	"	1359
But the mild glance	"	1399
listening, but with several graces	"	1410
As, but for loss	"	1420
But none where all distress	"	1446
Who nothing wants to answer her but cries	"	1459
red nor pale, but mingled so	"	1511
But, like a constant and confirmed devil	"	1513
But Tarquin's shape came	"	1536

Phrase	Source		
But—But such a face should bear	R L	....	1540
honesty, but yet defiled	"	....	1545
But now the mindful messenger	"	....	1583
yieldings, but still pure	"	....	1656
But, wretched as he is	"	....	1665
But, ere I name him	"	....	1688
But she, that yet her sad task	"	....	1699
But more than ' he	"	....	1718
But now that fair fresh mirror	"	....	1760
but through his lips do throng	"	....	1783
But through his teeth	"	....	1787
But now he throws that shallow habit by	"	....	1814
But kneel with me and help	"	....	1830
But as the riper should by time decease	Son	1	3
But thou, contracted to thine own	"	1	5
But if thou live	"	3	13
gives nothing, but doth lend	"	4	3
But flowers distill'd	"	5	13
Leese but their show	"	5	14
But when from highmost pitch	"	7	9
They do but sweetly chide thee	"	8	7
Shifts but his place	"	9	10
But beauty's waste hath in the world	"	9	11
But that thou none lovest	"	10	4
but, love, you are	"	13	1
O, none but unthrifts	"	13	13
But not to tell	"	14	3
But from thine eyes	"	14	9
but a little moment	"	15	2
presenteth nought but shows	"	15	3
But wherefore do not you	"	16	1
it is but as a tomb	"	17	3
But were some child of yours	"	17	13
But thy eternal summer	"	18	9
But I forbid thee	"	19	8
but not acquainted	"	20	3
But since she prick'd me out	"	20	13
true in love, but truly write	"	21	9
But when in thee	"	22	3
Is but the seemly raiment	"	22	6
but for thee will	"	22	10
They draw but what they see	"	24	14
But as the marigold	"	25	6
But that I hope	"	26	7
But then begins a journey	"	27	3
But day by night	"	28	4
But day doth daily draw	"	28	13
But if the while I think on thee	"	30	13
But things removed	"	31	8
but this loving thought	"	32	9
But since he died	"	32	13
But, out, alack, he was but one hour mine	"	33	11
sorrow lends but weak relief	"	34	11
Ah, but those tears are pearl	"	34	13
there is but one respect	"	36	5
But do not so	"	36	13
but thine shall be the praise	"	38	14
what is't but mine own	"	39	4
But yet be blamed	"	40	7
but yet thou might'st my seat	"	41	9
But here's the joy	"	42	13
then she loves but me alone	"	42	14
But when I sleep	"	43	8
But, ah, thought kills me	"	44	9
But that, so much of earth	"	44	11
But heavy tears, badges of	"	44	14
But—Who even but now come back again	Son	45	11
but then no longer glad	"	45	13
But the defendant doth that plea deny	"	46	7
But thou, to whom my jewels	"	48	5
swift extremity can seem but slow	"	51	6
But love, for love	"	51	12
And you, but one	"	53	4
But you like none	"	53	14
but fairer we it deem	"	54	3
But, for their virtue	"	54	9
But you shall shine more bright	"	55	3
Which but to-day	"	56	3
what should I do but tend	"	57	1
But, like a sad slave	"	57	11
but that which is	"	59	1
stands but for his scythe to mow	"	60	12
But when my glass	"	62	9
But weep to have	"	64	14
But sad mortality	"	65	2
but Time decays	"	65	8
no exchequer now but his	"	67	11
But those same tongues	"	69	6
But why thy odour	"	69	13
slander doth but approve	"	70	5
But let your love	"	71	12
But be contented	"	74	1
The earth can have but earth	"	74	7
thou hast but lost the dregs of life	"	74	9
thou dost but mend the style	"	78	11
But thou art all my art	"	78	13
But now my gracious numbers	"	79	3
No praise to thee but what in thee doth live	"	79	12
But since your worth	"	80	5
can yield me but a common grave	"	81	7
But he that writes of you	"	84	7
Let him but copy	"	84	9
But that is in my thought	"	85	11
But when your countenance	"	86	13
but by thy granting	"	87	5
but waking no such matter	"	87	14
But in the onset come	"	90	11
But these particulars	"	91	7
But do thy worst	"	92	1
But what's so blessed-fair	"	92	13
But heaven in thy creation	"	93	9
nothing thence but sweetness tell	"	93	12
Others but stewards	"	94	8
But if that flower	"	94	11
but in a kind of praise	"	95	7
But do not so	"	96	13
But hope of orphans	"	97	10
They were but sweet, but figures of delight	"	98	11
But, for his theft	"	99	12
But sweet or colour	"	99	15
But best is best	"	101	8
then but in the spring	"	102	5
But that wild music	"	102	11
their praises are but prophecies	"	106	9
they look'd but with divining eyes	"	106	11
but lack tongues to praise	"	106	14
but yet, like prayers divine	"	108	5
But makes antiquity	"	108	12
but, by all above	"	110	6
but effectually is out	"	113	4
But reckoning Time	"	115	5

But—But bears it out	Son	116	12	But—Beauty is but a vain	P P	13	1
But shoot not at me	"	117	12	take the pain but cannot pluck the			
But thence I learn	"	118	13	pelf	"	14	12
But that your trespass	"	120	13	But now are minutes	"	15	14
but by others' seeing	"	121	4	But one must be refused	"	16	9
They are but dressings	"	123	4	But, alas! my hand hath sworn	"	17	11
love were but the child of state	"	124	1	Juno but an Ethiope were	"	17	16
But all alone stands	"	124	11	Plays not at all, but seems afraid	"	18	30
poor but free	"	125	10	But plainly say thou lovest	"	19	11
But mutual render	"	125	12	But, soft! enough	"	19	49
She may detain, but not still keep,				But if store of crowns be scant	"	21	37
her treasure	"	126	10	Pity but he were a king	"	21	42
But now is black	"	127	3	But if Fortune once do frown	"	21	47
but is profaned	"	127	8	But thou shrieking harbinger	P T	.....	5
but despised straight	"	129	5	Had the essence but in one	"	.....	26
But no such roses	"	130	6	But in them it were a wonder	"	.....	32
but thinking on thy face	"	131	10	Truth may seem, but cannot be	"	.....	62
But slave to slavery	"	133	4	Beauty brag, but 'tis not she	"	.....	63
But then my friend's heart	"	133	10	Butcher—Like to a mortal butcher	V A	.....	618
But thou wilt not	"	134	5	Butcher-sire—Or .... that reaves	"	.....	766
He learn'd but surety-like	"	134	7	Buttock—broad buttock, tender hide	"	.....	298
Think all but one	"	135	14	to his melting buttock lent	"	.....	315
Make but my name thy love	"	136	13	Buy—So thou wilt buy	"	.....	514
But wherefore says she not	"	138	9	buys my heart from me	"	.....	517
but with thy tongue	"	139	3	Who buys a minute's mirth	R L	.....	213
but in my sight	"	139	5	They buy thy help	"	.....	913
but since I am near slain	"	139	13	Buy terms divine	"	146	11
No news but health	"	140	8	By—eagle, sharp by fast	V A	.....	55
But 'tis my heart that loves	"	141	3	by her fair immortal hand	"	.....	80
But my five wits	"	141	9	by the stern and direful	"	.....	98
O, but with mine	"	142	3	By law of nature	"	.....	171
But if thou catch thy hope	"	143	11	By this, the love-sick queen	"	.....	175
But being both from me	"	144	11	and by Venus' side	"	.....	180
but live in doubt	"	144	13	even by their own direction	"	.....	216
But when she saw	"	145	4	copse that neighbours by	"	.....	259
But, love, hate on	"	149	13	that is standing by	"	.....	282
But rising at thy name	"	151	9	by pleading may be blest	"	.....	328
But thou art twice forsworn	"	152	2	and by and by	"	.....	347
But why of two oaths' breach	"	152	5	takes him by the hand	"	.....	361
are oaths but to misuse thee	"	152	7	by touching thee	"	.....	438
But at my mistress' eye	"	153	9	breedeth love by smelling	"	.....	444
But found no cure	"	153	13	by his stealing in	"	.....	450
but in her maiden hand	"	154	4	love by looks reviveth	"	.....	464
but I, my mistress' thrall	"	154	12	that by love so thriveth	"	.....	466
but, spite of heaven's fell rage	L C	.....	13	she, by her good will	"	.....	479
but where excess begs all	"	.....	42	seen by night	"	.....	492
Not age, but sorrow	"	.....	74	banish'd by thy breath	"	.....	510
But, woe is me	"	.....	78	at thy leisure, one by one	"	.....	518
began but to appear	"	.....	93	by Cupid's bow	"	.....	581
But quickly on this side	"	.....	113	still hanging by his neck	"	.....	593
but were all graced by him	"	.....	119	Do surfeit by the eye	"	.....	602
But, ah, who ever shunn'd	"	.....	155	his danger by thy will	"	.....	639
and words merely but art	"	.....	174	be ruled by me	"	.....	673
but ne'er was harmed	"	.....	194	lives by subtlety	"	.....	675
but mine own was free	"	.....	195	By this, poor Wat	"	.....	697
but fighting outwardly	"	.....	203	trodden on by many	"	.....	707
But yield them up	"	.....	221	relieved by any	"	.....	708
But kept cold distance	"	.....	237	To shame the sun by day and her			
But, O my sweet	"	.....	239	by night	"	.....	732
But with the inundation	"	.....	290	Disorder breeds by heating	"	.....	742
but an art of craft	"	.....	295	lamp that burns by night	"	.....	755
But wherefore says my love	P P	1	9	Which by the rights	"	.....	759
but live in doubt	"	2	13	by this black-faced night	"	.....	773
but I will prove	"	3	5	catch her by the neck	"	.....	872
none could look but beauty's queen	"	4	4	By this she hears	"	.....	877
But whether unripe years	"	4	9	Who, overcome by doubt	"	.....	891
But smile and jest	"	4	12	By this, far off	"	.....	973
but not so fair as fickle	"	7	1	By their suggestion	"	.....	1044
but neither true nor trusty	"	7	2	shall I die by drops	"	.....	1074

By—When he was by	V A	1101	By—what's done by night	R L	1092
But by a kiss	"	1114	batter'd by the enemy	"	1171
takes him by the hand	"	1124	Which by him tainted	"	1182
By this the boy that by her side lay kill'd	"	1165	By whose example enforced by sympathy	"	1194
reft from her by death	"	1174	by force, by fraud or skill	"	1229
By whose swift aid	"	1190	Assail'd by night	"	1243
Borne by the trustless wings	R L	2	By that her death to do her husband wrong	"	1262
For by our ears	"	38	By this, mild patience bid fair Lucrece speak	"	1261
welcomed by the Roman dame	"	51	be ready by and by	"	1268
Argued by beauty's red	"	65	by this short schedule	"	1292
adored by this devil	"	85	when he is by to hear her	"	1312
made glorious by his manly chivalry	"	109	Shed for the slaughter'd husband by the wife	"	1318
And so, by hoping more	"	137	shadow'd by his neighbour's ear	"	1376
Make something nothing by augmenting it	"	154	Here friend by friend	"	1416
Beaten away by brain-sick rude desire	"	175	By deep surmise of others' detriment	"	1487
Shall by a painted cloth	"	245	takes her by the bloodless hand	"	1579
She took me kindly by the hand	"	253	ta'en prisoner by the foe	"	1597
As corn o'ergrown by weeds	"	281	By foul enforcement might be done	"	1608
Is almost choked by unresisted lust	"	282	no flood by raining slaketh	"	1623
flatter'd by their leader's jocund show	"	296	Knights, by their oaths	"	1677
By reprobate desire	"	300	By my excuse shall claim	"	1694
Each one by him enforced	"	303	death by time outworn	"	1715
by the light he spies	"	316	By this starts Collatine	"	1761
By their high treason	"	369	And only must be wail'd by Collatine	"	1772
by Lucrece' side	"	381	throws that shallow habit by	"	1799
him by oath they truly honoured	"	410	by whom thy fair wife bleeds	"	1814
hunger by the conquest satisfied	"	422	By our strong arms	"	1824
lust by gazing qualified	"	424	Now, by the Capitol	"	1834
for standing by her side	"	425	And by this chaste blood	"	1835
Are by his flaming torch dimm'd	"	448	By heaven's fair sun	"	1836
From forth dull sleep by dreadful fancy waking	"	450	By all our country rights	"	1837
by dumb demeanour seeks to show	"	474	And by chaste Lucrece' soul	"	1838
By thy bright beauty	"	490	and by this bloody knife		1839
And sung by children	"	525	should by time decease	Son	1840
by this dividing	"	551	To eat the world's due, by the grave and thee	"	1 3
She conjures him by high almighty Jove	"	568	Proving his beauty by succession thine	"	1 14
By knighthood, gentry	"	569	By unions married	"	2 12
By her untimely tears	"	570	Strikes each in each by mutual ordering	"	8 6
By holy human law	"	571	By children's eyes	"	8 10
By heaven and earth	"	572	By oft predict that I in heaven find	"	9 8
by him that gave it thee	"	624	check'd even by the self-same sky	"	14 8
When, pattern'd by thy fault	"	629	drawn by your own sweet skill	"	15 6
swells the higher by this let	"	646	By chance or nature's changing course	"	16 14
by heaven, I will not hear thee	"	667	And by addition me of thee defeated	"	18 8
wherein by nature they delight	"	697	By adding one thing to my purpose nothing	"	20 11
lived by foul devouring	"	700	Stirr'd by a painted beauty to his verse	"	20 12
And by their mortal fault	"	721	by day my limbs, by night my mind	"	21 2
wakes her heart by beating on her breast	"	759	not eased by night	"	27 13
by him defiled	"	787	But day by night and night by day	"	28 3
From me by strong assault	"	835	The one by toil, the other to complain	"	28 4
ransack'd by injurious theft	"	838	Which I by lacking	"	28 7
master'd by his young	"	863	And shalt by fortune	"	31 2
souls that wander by him	"	882	outstripp'd by every pen	"	32 3
he was stay'd by thee	"	917	Exceeded by the height	"	32 6
An accessary by thine inclination	"	922	by me be borne alone	"	32 8
errors by opinion bred	"	937		"	36 4
that doth live by slaughter	"	935			
that by alms doth live	"	986			
I fear'd by Tarquin's falchion	"	1046			
clear this spot by death	"	1053			
By this, lamenting Philomel	"	1079			

By—made lame by fortune's dearest spite	Son 37	3
And by a part of all thy glory	" 37	12
That by this separation I may give	" 39	7
By praising him here	" 39	14
By wilful taste of what thyself refusest	" 40	8
Hers, by thy beauty	" 41	13
Thine, by thy beauty	" 41	14
By looking on thee	" 43	10
Receiving nought by elements so slow	" 44	13
By those swift messengers	" 45	10
And by their verdict is determined	" 46	11
either by thy picture or my love	" 47	9
Call'd to that audit by advised respects	" 49	4
As if by some instinct the wretch did know	" 50	7
By new unfolding	" 52	12
By that sweet ornament	" 54	2
my verse distills your truth	" 54	14
Which but to-day by feeding is allay'd	" 56	3
by Time's fell hand defaced	" 64	1
strength by limping sway disabled	" 66	8
art made tongue-tied by authority	" 66	9
That sin by him advantage should achieve	" 67	3
By seeing farther than the eye hath shown	" 69	8
they measure by thy deeds	" 69	10
pass'd by the ambush	" 70	9
shamed by that which I bring forth	" 72	13
Which by and by black night doth take	" 73	7
Consumed with that which it was nourish'd by	" 73	12
And by and by clean starved	" 75	10
surfeit day by day	" 75	13
Thou by thy dial's shady stealth	" 77	7
by thy true-telling friend	" 82	12
phrase by all the Muses filed	" 85	4
spirit, by spirits taught	" 86	5
he nor his compeers by night	" 86	7
I hold thee but by thy granting	" 87	5
And I by this will be a gainer too	" 88	9
turn sourest by their deeds	" 94	13
but, by all above	" 110	6
bonds do tie me day by day	" 117	4
would by ill be cured	" 118	12
better is by evil still made better	" 119	10
gain by ill thrice more than I have spent	" 119	14
you were by my unkindness shaken	" 120	5
As I by yours	" 120	6
Not by our feeling, but by others' seeing	" 121	4
By their rank thoughts	" 121	12
have faculty by nature to subsist	" 122	6
Made more or less by thy continual haste	" 123	12
by paying too much rent	" 125	6
Who hast by waning grown	" 126	3
by thee blushing stand	" 128	8
And yet, by heaven, I think	" 130	13
eyes corrupt by over-partial looks	" 137	5
by lies we flatter'd be	" 138	14
slay me not by art	" 139	4

By—Mad slanderers by mad ears believed be	Son 140	12
By self-example mayst thou be denied	" 142	14
Commanded by the motion of thine eyes	" 149	12
fall by thy side	" 151	12
Cupid laid by his brand	" 153	1
Laid by his side	" 154	2
Came tripping by	" 154	4
Was sleeping by a virgin hand disarm'd	" 154	8
This brand she quenched in a cool well by	" 154	9
this by that I prove	" 154	13
Which one by one	L C	38
Of court, of city, and had let go by	"	59
And, privileged by age	"	62
sits he by her side	"	63
by nature's outwards so commended	"	89
by that cost more dear	"	96
noble by the sway	"	108
by him because his deed	"	111
Or he his manage by the well-doing steed	"	112
fairer by their place	"	117
were all graced by him	"	119
who ever shunn'd by precedent	"	155
By blunting us to make our wits more keen	"	161
By how much of me	"	189
by spirits of richest coat	"	236
'scapeth by the flight	"	241
If by me broke	P P 3	13
sitting by a brook	" 4	1
growing by a brook	" 6	5
throws his mantle by	" 6	9
kill'd too soon by death's sharp sting	" 10	4
Adonis sitting by her	" 11	1
Which by a gift of learning	" 16	14
By ringing in thy lady's ear	" 19	28
There is no heaven, by holy then	" 19	45
By shallow rivers, by whose falls	" 20	7
'Tereu, Tereu,' by and by	" 21	14
By-past—To put the by-past perils	L C	158
Cabin—keep his loathsome cabin	V A	637
Into the deep-dark cabins of her head	"	1038
to a cabin hang'd with care	P P 14	3
Cabinet—From his moist cabinet	V A	854
They, mustering to the quiet cabinet	R L	442
Caged—she would the caged cloister fly	L C	249
Caitiff—asks the weary caitiff	V A	914
Call—tapsters answering every call	"	849
Call—in her passion, calls it balm	"	27
calls it heavenly moisture	"	64
Doth call himself	"	650
'Call it not love	"	793
Even in the moment that we call them ours	R L	868
she hoarsely calls her maid	"	1211
call them not the authors	"	1241
At last she calls to mind	"	1359
The one doth call her his	"	1793
Calls back the lovely April	Son 3	10

Call—nature calls thee to be gone	Son	4	11
Thou mayst call thine	"	11	4
And he that calls on thee	"	38	11
that thou mayst true love call	"	40	3
Or call it winter	"	56	13
I alone did call upon thy aid	"	79	1
For nothing this wide universe I call	"	109	13
who calls me well or ill	"	112	3
upon your dearest love to call	"	117	3
Whereto th' inviting time our fashion calls	"	124	8
To this I witness call the fools of time	"	124	13
O, call not me to justify the wrong	"	139	1
that I do call my friend	"	149	5
No want of conscience hold it that I call	"	151	13
Bountiful they will him call	PP	21	40
Called—call'd him all to nought	VA	....	993
call'd it then their shield	RL	....	61
let it not be call'd impiety	"	....	1174
may be call'd a hell	"	....	1287
Call'd to that audit	Son	49	4
Let not my love be call'd idolatry	"	105	1
I have been call'd unto	LC	....	181
Neither two nor one was called	PT	....	40
Calm—to calm contending kings	RL	....	939
calm looks, eyes wailing still	"	....	1596
Her cloudy looks will calm ere night	PP	19	14
Came—if there be came to lie	VA	....	243
How she came stealing	"	....	344
came in her mind the while	RL	....	1536
To me came Tarquin armed	"	....	1544
A stranger came	"	....	1620
in my chamber came	"	....	1626
came evidence to swear	"	....	1650
those that came with Collatine	"	....	1689
And she a friend came debtor for my sake	Son	134	11
Came tripping by	"	154	4
Came there for cure	"	154	13
Came for additions	LC	....	115
which in his level came	"	....	309
Can—Look how he can	VA	....	79
Never can blab	"	....	126
Can thy right hand	"	....	178
sighs can never grave it	"	....	376
that can so well defend her	"	....	472
I can be well contented	"	....	513
she takes all she can	"	....	564
she can no more	"	....	577
spear's point can enter	"	....	626
For love can comment	"	....	714
can my invention make	RL	....	225
fear can neither fight nor fly	"	....	278
How can they then assist me	"	....	330
nothing can affection's course control	"	....	500
no device can take	"	....	533
From vassal actors can be wiped away	"	....	608
Can comprehend in still imagination	"	....	702
that well can thee commend	"	....	704
Ere he can see his own abomination	"	....	704
Can curb his heat	"	....	706
that every eye can see	"	....	750
no good that we can say is ours	"	....	873
Can—Thy violent vanities can never last	RL	....	894
Though men can cover crimes	"	....	1252
I thus far can dispense	"	....	1279
than I can well express	"	....	1285
'can lurk in such a look	"	....	1335
'can lurk' from 'cannot' took	"	....	1537
Ere once she can discharge	"	....	1605
no excuse can give the fault amending	"	....	1614
can see what once I was	"	....	1764
And nothing 'gainst Time's scythe can make defence	Son	12	13
Nor can I fortune to brief minutes tell	"	14	5
Can make you live	"	16	12
So long as men can breathe or eyes can see	"	18	13
How can I then be elder	"	22	5
How can I then return	"	28	1
Then can I drown an eye	"	30	5
Then can I grieve	"	30	9
of such a salve can speak	"	34	7
Nor can thy shame give physic	"	34	9
How can my Muse want subject	"	38	1
What can mine own praise	"	39	3
thought can jump both sea and land	"	44	7
I can allege no cause	"	49	14
Thus can my love	"	51	1
swift extremity can seem but slow	"	51	6
Then can no horse with my desire keep pace	"	51	9
Can bring him to his swift up-locked treasure	"	52	2
And you, but one, can every shadow lend	"	53	4
What strong hand can hold his swift foot back	"	65	11
who his spoil of beauty can forbid	"	65	12
that the thought of hearts can mend	"	69	2
in me can nothing worthy prove	"	72	4
The earth can have but earth	"	74	7
he can afford	"	79	11
The earth can yield	"	81	7
What strained touches rhetoric can lend	"	82	10
poets can in praise devise	"	83	14
which can say more	"	84	1
'if he can tell	"	84	7
I can set down a story	"	88	6
For there can live no hatred	"	93	5
that eyes can see	"	95	12
if I no more can write	"	103	5
much more than in my verse can sit	"	103	13
you never can be old	"	104	1
Can yet the lease of my true love control	"	107	3
thy record never can be missed	"	122	8
my o'erpress'd defence can bide	"	139	8
my five senses can	"	141	9
How can it? O, how can Love's eye be true	"	148	9
Those that can see thou lovest	"	149	14
that art can comprehend	PP	5	6
that well can thee commend	"	5	8
no cement can redress	"	13	10
My shepherd's pipe can sound no deal	"	18	27
A cripple soon can find a halt	"	19	10

Can—That defunctive music can	*P T*		14	**Canst**—how canst thou fulfil	*R L*	628
If what parts can so remain	"		48	yet canst not live	*S n* 4	8
Cancell'd—date, cancell'd ere well				audit canst thou leave	" 4	12
begun	*R L*		26	For thou not farther than my		
Cancell'd my fortunes	"	.....	984	thoughts canst move	" 47	11
date from cancell'd destiny	"	.....	1729	Thou canst not, love, disgrace me	" 89	9
love's long since cancell'd woe	*S n*	30	7	Thou canst not vex me	" 92	9
Candle—As those gold candles	"	21	12	Thou canst not then use rigour	" 133	12
Canker—This canker that eats up	*V A*	.....	656	Canst thou, O cruel	" 149	1
And loathsome canker lives in				**Cap**—A cap of flowers	*P P* 20	11
sweetest bud	*S n*	35	4	**Caparison**—For rich caparisons	*V A*	286
canker vice the sweetest buds doth				**Capitol**—by the Capitol that we all reverence	*R L*	1835
love	"	70	7	**Captain**—when their captain once		
a canker in the fragrant rose	"	93	2	doth yield	*V A*	893
A vengeful canker eat him up	"	99	13	Affection is my captain	*R L*	271
Canker-blooms—The canker-blooms				And as their captain	"	298
have full as deep a dye	"	54	5	captain jewels in the carcanet	*S n* 52	8
Cankering—Foul-cankering rust the				captive good attending captain ill	" 66	12
hidden treasure frets	*V A*	.....	767	**Captivate**—to captivate the eye	*V A*	281
Cannon—from discharged cannon				**Captive**—my captive and my slave	"	101
fumes	*R L*	.....	1043	The coward captive vanquished	*R L*	73
Cannot—she cannot choose but love	*V A*	.....	79	A captive victor that hath lost	"	730
help she cannot get	"	.....	93	captive good attending captain ill	*S n* 66	12
she cannot right her cause	"	.....	220	**Car**—from highmost pitch with weary		
cannot be easily harm'd	"	.....	627	car	" 7	9
that I cannot reprove	"	.....	787	**Carcanet**—captain jewels in the	" 52	8
O no, it cannot be	"	.....	957	**Carcass**—The carcass of a beauty	*L C*	11
cannot express my grief	"	.....	1019	**Care**—my thought, my busy care	*V A*	383
the thing that cannot be amended	*R L*	.....	378	and with what care	"	681
kings' misdeeds cannot be hid in				Save thieves and cares	*R L*	126
clay	"	.....	609	To whose weak ruins muster troops		
it cannot cure his pain	"	.....	861	of cares	"	720
when he cannot use it	"	.....	862	carrier of grisly care	"	926
O no, that cannot be	"	.....	1049	deep-drenched in a sea of care	"	1100
That cannot tread the way	"	.....	1152	where cares have carved some	"	1445
cannot abuse a body dead	"	.....	1267	and grim care's reign	"	1451
The repetition cannot make it less	"	.....	1285	His face, though full of cares	"	1503
The weary time she cannot enter-				kill'd with deadly cares	"	1793
tain	"	.....	1361	dearest and mine only care	*S n* 48	7
'It cannot be,' quoth she	"	.....	1534	winter, which, being full of care	" 56	13
'can lurk' from 'cannot' took	"	.....	1537	I throw all care	" 112	9
'It cannot be,' she in that sense				her whose busy care is bent	" 143	6
forsook	"	.....	1538	now reason is past care	" 147	9
'It cannot be, I find	"	.....	1539	age is full of care	*P P* 12	2
that cannot write to thee	*S n*	38	7	to a cabin hang'd with care	" 14	3
I cannot blame thee	"	40	6	**Care**—What cares he now	*V A*	283
cannot provoke him on	"	50	9	Now Nature cares not	"	953
death, which cannot choose	"	64	13	For what care I who calls me	*S n* 112	3
thy praise cannot be so thy praise	"	70	11	**Careful**—How careful was I	" 48	1
thy memory cannot retain	"	77	9	Lo, as a careful housewife	" 143	1
your memory death cannot take	"	81	3	**Careless**—careless lust stirs up	*V A*	556
of my silence cannot boast	"	86	11	a careless band of pride	*L C*	30
I cannot know thy change	"	93	6	Careless of thy sorrowing	*P P* 21	26
Cannot dispraise but in a kind of				**Carriage**—her levell'd eyes their car-		
praise	"	95	7	riage ride	*L C*	22
Crabbed age and youth cannot live				**Carrier**—carrier of grisly care	*R L*	926
together	*P P*	12	1	**Carry**—He carries thence incaged	*V A*	582
but cannot pluck the pelf	"	14	12	with speed prepare to carry it	*R L*	1294
Senseless trees they cannot hear				Without all bail shall carry me		
thee	"	21	21	away	*S n* 74	2
If thou wake, he cannot sleep	"	21	54	**Carry-tale**—This carry-tale, dissen-		
Truth may seem, but cannot be	*P T*	.....	62	tious Jealousy	*V A*	657
Canopied—And .... in darkness	*R L*	.....	398	**Carve**—O, carve not with thy hours	*S n* 19	9
Canopy—from heat did .... the herd	*S n*	12	6	**Carved**—where cares have .... some	*R L*	1445
I bore the canopy	"	125	1	carved in it with tears	"	1713
Canst—Thou canst not see	*V A*	.....	130	She carved thee for her seal	*S n* 11	13
and canst not feel	"	.....	201	**Case**—his conduct in this case	*R L*	313
What! canst thou talk	"	.....	427	beggar wails his case	"	711
what canst thou boast	"	.....	1077	my case is past the help of law	"	1022

Case—love in love's fresh case	Son	108	9
not in his case	L C		116
Casket—To burn the guiltless	R L		1057
Cast—cast into eternal sleeping	V A		951
love hath cast his utmost sum	Son	49	3
and I be cast away	"	50	13
Cast-away—a hopeless cast-away	R L		744
Castle—The strongest castle	P P	19	29
Cat—Yet foul night-waking cat	R L		554
Catch—Some catch her by the neck	V A		872
that this night-owl will catch	R L		360
holds what it doth catch	Son	113	8
housewife runs to catch	"	143	1
Cries to catch her whose busy care	"	143	6
But if thou catch thy hope	"	143	11
Catching—Jealous of catching	V A		321
Catching all passions	L C		126
Caterpillar—As caterpillars do the tender leaves	V A		798
Cattle—that grazed his cattle nigh	L C		57
Caught—caught the yielding prey	V A		547
Cause—she cannot right her cause	"		220
where is no cause of fear	"		1153
It shall be cause of war	"		1159
give the sneaped birds more cause to sing	R L		333
the cause of my untimely death	"		1178
No cause, but company	"		1236
The cause craves haste	"		1295
I can allege no cause	Son	49	14
The cause of this fair gift	"	87	7
and see just cause of hate	"	150	10
and yet no cause I have	P P	10	7
the cause of all my moan	"	18	51
Causeless—'tis a causeless fantasy	V A		897
Causer—Causer of this	P P	18	8
Cautel—Applied to cautels	L C		303
Cave—These lovely caves	V A		247
all the neighbour caves	"		830
in his shelly cave with pain	"		1034
Grim cave of death	R L		769
Cave-keeping—Cave-keeping evils	"		1250
Cavil—I cavil with mine infamy	"		1025
Thus cavils she with everything	"		1093
Cease—O time, cease thou thy course	"		1765
the times should cease	Son	11	7
Ceased—When he hath ceased	V A		919
Ceaseless—Thou ceaseless lackey	R L		967
Ceasing—.... their clamorous cry	V A		693
Cedar—The cedar stoops not	R L		664
wither at the cedar's roots	"		665
Cedar-tops—That cedar-tops and hills seem burnish'd gold	V A		858
Celestial—I'll sigh celestial breath	"		189
on his celestial face	Son	33	6
Celestial as thou art	P P	5	13
Cell—And in thy shady cell	R L		881
Cement—no cement can redress	P P	13	10
Censure—That censures falsely	Son	148	4
Centre—the .... of my sinful earth	"	146	1
Ceremony—ceremony of love's rite	"	23	6
Certain—with certain of his friends	V A		588
Her certain sorrow writ	R L		1311
dirge of her certain ending	"		1612
When I was certain	Son	115	11
These are certain signs to know	P P	21	57
Chafe—He chafes her lips	V A		477
Chafing—All swoln with chafing	"		325
of an angry-chafing boar	"		662
Chain—in a red-rose chain	V A		110
Chained—which wretchedness hath chained	R L		900
Challenge—doth .... that fair field	"		58
Chamber—The locks between her....	"		302
unto the chamber door	"		337
Into the chamber wickedly he stalks	"		365
with shining falchion in my chamber came	"		1626
Champaign—like a goodly .... plain	"		1247
Champion—Her champion mounted for the	V A		596
Chance— wondering each other's chance	R L		1596
acquit me from this chance	"		1706
By chance or nature's changing course	Son	18	8
Change—With shifting change	"	20	4
variation or quick change	"	76	2
upon desired change	"	89	6
I cannot know thy change	"	93	6
And in this change	"	105	11
Change—shall change thy good	R L		656
to change their kinds	"		1147
O, change thy thought that I may change my mind	Son	10	9
To change your day of youth	"	15	12
to change my state with kings	"	29	14
That my steel'd sense or changes right or wrong	"	112	8
and change decrees of kings	"	115	6
thou shalt not boast that I do change	"	123	1
they would change their state	"	128	9
Changed—blue blood .... to black	R L		1454
Sorrow changed to solace	P P	15	11
Changing—nature's .... course	Son	18	8
Each changing place	"	60	3
Channel—In the sweet channel	V A		958
in bloody channel lies	R L		1487
O, how the channel	L C		283
Chant—hears them chant it	V A		869
Chaos—black chaos comes again	"		1020
Vast sin-concealing chaos	R L		767
Chap—Her cheeks with chaps	"		1452
Character—at first in .... was done	Son	59	8
Reserve their character	"	85	3
that ink may character	"	108	1
it had conceited characters	L C		16
Thought characters and words merely but art	"		174
Character'd—.... in my brow	R L		807
Full character'd with lasting memory	Son	122	2
Charge—When thou shalt .... me	R L		226
Gives the hot charge	"		434
Eat up thy charge	Son	146	8
My heart doth charge the watch	P P	15	2
Charged—or victor being charged	Son	70	10
Nature hath charged me	L C		220
Charging—Charging the sour-faced groom	R L		1334
Chariot—In her light chariot	V A		1192
Charitable—no time for .... deeds	R L		908
Charity—In the charity of age	L C		70
Charm—bewitch'd with lust's foul charm	R L		173
when I might charm thee so	"		1681
to charm a sacred nun	L C		260

Charm				Cheek			
Charm—should use like loving charms		P P 11	8	Cheek—Their silver cheeks	R L		61
Charmed—charm'd the sight		R L	1404	her rosy cheek lies under	"		386
affections in his charmed power		L C	146	lank and lean discolour'd cheek	"		708
my leisures ever charmed		"	193	Upon my cheeks	"		756
Charter—your charter is so strong		Son 58	9	Poor Lucrece' cheeks	"		1217
The charter of thy worth		" 87	3	Nor why her fair cheeks	"		1225
Chary—which I will keep so chary		" 22	11	that down thy cheeks are raining	"		1271
Chase—hied him to the chase		V A	3	the blood his cheeks replenish	"		1357
As if another chase		"	696	Her cheeks with chaps	"		1452
It is no gentle chase		"	883	Cheeks neither red nor pale	"		1510
in poor revenge, held it in chase		R L	1736	O, from thy cheeks	"		1762
her neglected child holds her in chase		Son 143	5	On Helen's cheek	Son 53		7
				painting imitate his cheek	" 67		5
Chase—and then I chase it		V A	410	Thus is his cheek the map	" 68		1
To chase injustice		R L	1683	And found it in thy cheek	" 79		11
I thy babe chase thee afar behind		Son 143	16	Where cheeks need blood	" 82		14
Chased—				Which on thy soft cheek for complexion dwells	" 99		4
accomplishment so hotly chased		R L	716	though rosy lips and cheeks	" 116		9
from forth her fair streets chased		"	1834	roses see I in her cheeks	" 130		6
Chasing—roe that's tired with....		V A	561	the grey cheeks of the east	" 132		6
Chaste—Lucrece the chaste		R L	7	her pale and pined cheek beside	L C		32
Haply that name of 'chaste'		"	8	Each cheek a river	"		283
our mistress' ornaments are chaste		"	322	which in his cheek so glow'd	"		321
which thy chaste bee kept		"	849	thy cheeks may blow	P P 17		9
And by this chaste blood		"	1836	Cheek'd—Rose-cheek'd Adonis hied him	V A		3
And by chaste Lucrece' soul		"	1839				
that vow'd chaste life to keep		Son 154	3	Cheer—			
To whose sound chaste wings obey		P T	4	smiled with so sweet a cheer	R L		264
Chastest—in the chastest tears		R L	682	'tis with so dull a cheer	Son 97		13
Chastity—despite of fruitless		V A	751	she securely gives good cheer	R L		89
Pure Chastity is rifled		R L	692	Cheer—He cheers the morn	V A		481
of sweet chastity's decay		"	808	cheers up his burning eye	R L		485
my white stole of chastity		L C	297	To cheer the ploughman	"		958
and praised cold chastity		"	315	they will not cheer thee	P T 21		22
still conquer chastity		P P 4	8	Cheered—Cheered and cheek'd	Son 15		6
It was married chastity		P T	61	Cheering—cheering up her senses	V A		896
Chat—this bootless chat		V A	422	Chequer'd—chequer'd with white	"		1168
As palmers' chat makes short their pilgrimage		R L	791	Cherish—To dry the old oak's sap and cherish springs	R L		950
Cheap—sold cheap what is most dear		Son 110	3	as Priam him did cherish	"		1546
Cheater—Then gentle cheater		" 151	3	thou shouldst in bounty cherish	Son 11		12
Check—To check the tears patience, tame to sufferance, bide each check		R L	1817	Cherry— mulberries and ripe-red cherries	V A		1103
		Son 58	7	Cherubin—Such cherubins as your sweet self resemble	Son 114		6
If thy soul check thee		" 136	1	Which, like a cherubin	L C		319
Check'd—Priam check'd his son's desire		R L	1490	Chest—Some purer chest to close	R L		761
				lock'd up in any chest	Son 48		9
Sap check'd with frost		Son 5	7	time that keeps you as my chest	" 52		9
Cheered and check'd		" 15	6	from Time's chest lie hid	" 65		10
Cheek—doth she stroke his cheek		V A	45	Chid—And chid the painter	R L		1528
maiden burning of his cheeks		"	50	Chide—And 'gins to chide	V A		45
his brow, his cheek, his chin		"	59	If thou wilt chide	"		48
Wishing her cheeks were		"	63	thus chides she Death	"		932
making her cheeks all wet		"	83	if thou mean to chide	R L		484
Souring his cheeks		"	185	chides his vanish'd, loathed delight	"		742
Red cheeks and fiery eyes		"	219	But chide rough winter	"		1255
in each cheek appears		"	242	They do but sweetly chide thee	Son 8		7
a cheek that smiles		"	252	And chide thy beauty	" 41		10
now her cheek was pale		"	347	chide the world-without-end hour	" 57		5
his fair cheek feels		"	352	The forward violet thus did I chide	" 99		1
His tenderer cheek		"	353	do you with Fortune chide	" 111		1
Claps her pale cheek		"	468	Chiding—Chiding that tongue	" 145		6
strikes her on the cheeks		"	475	Chief—The field's chief flower	V A		8
Usurps her cheek		"	591	present sorrow seemeth chief	"		970
her two cheeks fair		"	957	should be thy chief desire	Son 10		8
Sighs dry her cheeks		"	966	That she hath thee, is of my wailing chief	" 42		3
Which her cheek melts		"	982				
pale cheeks and the blood		"	1109				

Chiefly—Chiefly in love whose leave exceeds	V A	568	**Circle**—Blue circles stream'd	R L		1587
			Circles her body in	"		1739
And I in deep delight am chiefly drown'd	P P	8 11	**Circled**—ivory globes.... with blue	V A		407
			Her circled eyne	"		1229
Spare not to spend, and chiefly there	" 19	26	**Circuit**—Within the circuit	"		230
Child—the old become a child	V A	1152	**Circumstance**—In such-like....	"		844
as he is but Night's child	R L	785	with circumstances strong	R L		1262
The nurse, to still her child	"	813	with dreadful circumstance	"		1703
the child a man, the man a child	"	954	**Cistern**—coral cisterns filling	"		1234
fond and testy as a child	"	1094	**Cite**—Doth cite each moving sense	P P	15	3
If in the child the father's image lies	"	1753	**Cited**—trespass cited up in rhymes	R L		524
			Citizen—May feel her heart, poor....	"		465
This fair child of mine	Son	2 10	**City**—and enter this sweet city	"		469
Resembling sire and child	"	8 11	the city to destroy	"		1369
some child of yours alive	"	17 13	fire to burn thy city	"		1554
As any mother's child	"	21 11	upon these terms, I held my city	L C		176
To see his active child	"	37 2	Of court, of city	"		59
burthen of a former child	"	59 4	**Civil**—civil home-bred strife	V A		764
were but the child of state	"	124 1	Such civil war	Son	35	12
Whilst her neglected child	"	143 5	sober guards and civil fears	L C		298
Childish—And childish error	V A	898	**Clad**—clad in mourning black	R L		1585
Then, childish fear, avaunt	R L	274	**Claim**—Then virtue claims from beauty	"		59
Such childish humour	"	1825				
Children—Nor children's tears nor mothers' groans	"	431	shall claim excuse's giving	"		1715
			possess the claim they lay	"		1794
And sung by children	"	525	**Clamorous**—Ceasing their.... cry	V A		693
and thy children's sake	"	533	**Clamour**—pens her piteous clamours in her head	R L		681
If children pre-decease progenitors	"	1756				
By children's eyes	Son	9 8	'my wife' with clamours fill'd	"		1804
Those children nursed	"	77 11	In clamours of all size	L C		21
Chill—and chill extincture hath	L C	294	**Clap**—Claps her pale cheek	V A		468
Chin—his brow, his cheek, his chin	V A	59	**Clapping**—till clapping makes it red	"		468
did he raise his chin	"	85	Clapping their proud tails	"		923
her snow-white dimpled chin	R L	420	**Clasp**—With coral clasps and amber studs	P P	20	14
peers her whiter chin	"	472				
Small show of man was yet upon his chin	L C	92	**Claw**—under the gripe's sharp claws	R L		543
			Clay—misdeeds cannot be hid in clay	"		609
Chip—with those dancing chips	Son	128 10	When I perhaps compounded am with clay	Son	71	10
Chivalry—by his manly chivalry	R L	109				
Choice—when most his choice is froward	V A	570	**Clean**—clean starved for a look	"	75	10
			Cleanly—cold fault cleanly out	V A		694
Choir—still the choir of echoes	"	840	**Cleanly-coined**—in.... excuses	R L		1073
Bare ruin'd choirs, where late	Son	73 4	**Clear**—O thou clear god	V A		860
Choke—chokes her pleading tongue	V A	217	the clear unmatched red and white	R L		11
Choked—Is almost choked	R L	282	In his clear bed	"		382
Choose—she cannot choose but love	V A	79	as clear from this attaint of mine	"		825
death, which cannot choose	Son	64 13	Those round clear pearls	"		1353
Press never thou to choose anew	P P	19 34	To the clear day	Son	43	7
Chopp'd—Heated and chopp'd	Son	62 10	The clear eye's moiety	"	46	12
Chorus—As chorus to their tragic scene	P T	52	what nature made so clear	"	84	10
			Clear wells spring not	P P	18	37
Chorus-like—.... her eyes did rain	V A	360	**Clear**—To clear this spot by death	R L		1053
Chose—for their habitation chose out thee	Son	95 10	the better so to clear her	"		1320
			fountain clears itself again	"		1707
thine eye hath chose the dame	P P	19 1	her mind untainted clears	"		1710
Chronicle—in the chronicle of wasted time	Son	106 1	sees not till heaven clears	Son	148	12
			Clear'd—sin is.... with absolution	R L		354
Churl—And tender churl	"	1 12	**Clearer**—with thy much.... light	Son	43	7
When that churl Death	"	32 2	should afterwards burn clearer	"	115	4
Then, churls, their thoughts	"	69 11	**Cleave**—cleaves an infant's heart	V A		942
Churlish—Scorning his.... drum	V A	107	**Cleft**—O cleft effect! cold modesty	L C		293
churlish, harsh in voice	"	134	**Clepe**—She clepes him king of graves	V A		995
a churlish swine to gore	"	616	**Clerk**—And like unletter'd clerk	Son	85	6
'Cide—to 'cide this title	Son	46 9	**Client**—The client breaks	V A		336
Cinder—Here enclosed in cinders lie	P T	55	To trembling clients	R L		1020
Cipher—To cipher me how fondly I did dote	R L	207	**Climb**—permit the sun to climb	"		773
			Climb'd—climb'd the steep-up heavenly hill	Son	7	5
To cipher what is writ	"	811				
Cipher'd—cipher'd either's heart	"	1396	**Clip**—to clip Elysium	V A		600

Clip—to kiss and clip me	P P	11	14
Clipp'd—And then she clipp'd Adonis "	11	6	
Cloak—To cloak offences	R L	749	
thy black all-hiding cloak	"	801	
travel forth without my cloak	Son	34	2
Clock—When I do count the clock	"	12	1
watch the clock for you	"	57	6
Cloister—the caged cloister fly	L C	249	
Cloister'd—still in night would cloister'd be	R L	1085	
Close—The coffer-lids that close his eyes	V A	1127	
The curtains being close	R L	367	
to close so pure a mind	"	761	
Closed—sleep had closed up	"	163	
Closet—Doth in her poison'd closet	"	1659	
A closet never pierced	Son	46	6
Close-tongued—With .... treason	R L	770	
Closure—into the quiet closure	V A	782	
Within the gentle closure	Son	48	11
Cloth—by a painted cloth be kept in awe	R L	245	
Clothe—Began to clothe his wit	"	1809	
Cloud—And coal-black clouds	V A	533	
with the meeting clouds contend	"	820	
Like many clouds	"	972	
To draw the cloud	R L	371	
Rushing from forth a cloud	"	373	
But when a black-faced cloud	"	547	
Knit poisonous clouds	"	777	
unto the clouds bequeathed	"	1727	
when clouds do blot the heaven	Son	28	10
the basest clouds to ride	"	33	5
The region cloud hath mask'd him	"	33	12
To let base clouds o'ertake me	"	34	3
that through the cloud thou break	"	34	5
Clouds and eclipses stain	"	35	3
Cloud-eclipsed—two suns were	R L	1224	
Clouded—clouded with his brow's repine	V A	490	
The moon being clouded	R L	1007	
Cloud-kissing—Threatening cloud-kissing Ilion	"	1370	
Cloudy—Dian cloudy and forlorn	V A	725	
No cloudy show of stormy, blustering weather	R L	115	
But cloudy Lucrece shames herself	"	1084	
Her cloudy looks will calm	P P	19	14
Cloy—yet not cloy thy lips	V A	19	
Cloy'd—That, cloy'd with much, he pineth	R L	98	
Cloying—			
of your ne'er-cloying sweetness	Son	118	5
Coal—She red and hot as coals	V A	35	
Even as a dying coal	"	338	
Affection is a coal	"	387	
To quench the coal	R L	47	
Like dying coals burnt out	"	1379	
Coal-black—And coal-black clouds	V A	533	
bathe his coal-black wings	R L	1009	
Coasteth—she coasteth to the cry	V A	870	
Coat—an eye-sore in my golden coat	R L	205	
by spirits of richest coat	L C	236	
Cock—The cock that treads them	P P	19	40
Cockatrice—a cockatrice' dead-killing eye	R L	540	
Coffer—that coffers up his gold	"	855	
Coffer-lids—She lifts the coffer-lids	V A	1127	
Coined—in cleanly-coin'd excuses	R L	1073	

Coined—tales to please me hath she coined	P P	7	9
Cold—rheumatic and cold	V A	135	
cold and senseless stone	"	211	
the weather being cold	"	402	
the cold fault cleanly out	"	694	
Which with cold terror	"	1048	
and that is cold	"	1121	
wrapp'd in repentant cold	R L	48	
from the cold stone sparks of fire	"	177	
As from this cold flint	"	181	
converts to cold disdain	"	691	
parching heat nor freezing cold	"	1145	
doth quake with cold	"	1556	
And in that cold	"	1557	
in key-cold Lucrece' bleeding stream	"	1774	
when thou feel'st it cold	Son	2	14
folly, age, and cold decay	"	11	6
of death's eternal cold	"	13	12
which shake against the cold	"	73	3
cold and to temptation slow	"	94	4
Three winters cold	"	104	3
In a cold valley-fountain	"	153	4
But kept cold distance	L C	237	
to physic your cold breast	"	259	
What breast so cold	"	292	
cold modesty, hot wrath	"	293	
and praised cold chastity	"	315	
age is weak and cold	P P	12	7
Coldly—How coldly those impediments	L C	269	
Cold-pale—With cold-pale weakness	V A	892	
Collatine—Of Collatine's fair love	R L	7	
Whom Collatine unwisely	"	10	
Or why is Collatine	"	33	
which Collatine doth owe	"	82	
Collatine's high name	"	108	
self-same seat sits Collatine	"	289	
Then Collatine again	"	381	
Tarquin wronged me, I Collatine	"	819	
For Collatine's dear love	"	821	
was pure to Collatine	"	826	
If, Collatine, thine honour	"	834	
My Collatine would else	"	916	
'well, well, dear Collatine	"	1058	
for heaven and Collatine	"	1166	
till my Collatine	"	1177	
'Thou, Collatine, shalt oversee	"	1205	
Collatine may know	"	1312	
While Collatine and his	"	1609	
those that came with Collatine	"	1689	
Stood Collatine and all	"	1731	
By this, starts Collatine	"	1772	
be wail'd by Collatine	"	1799	
'Woe, woe,' quoth Collatine	"	1802	
'Why, Collatine, is woe the cure for woe	"	1821	
Collatinus—'If Collatinus dream	"	218	
'Had Collatinus kill'd	"	232	
Where her beloved Collatinus	"	256	
in Collatinus' face	"	829	
the tears in Collatinus' eyes	"	1817	
Collatium—And to Collatium	"	4	
When at Collatium	"	50	
Colour—colour, pace, and bone	V A	294	
their colours fresh and trim	"	1079	
Of either's colour was the other queen	R L	66	

Colour—fear did make her colour rise	R L	....	257
for colour or excuses	"	....	267
Under what colour he commits this ill	"	....	476
The colour in thy face	"	....	477
Under that colour am I come	"	....	481
Her lively colour kill'd	"	....	1583
hath thy fair colour spent	"	....	1600
But sweet or colour it had stol'n	Son	99	13
Truth needs no colour, with his colour fix'd	"	101	6
Colour'd—			
with purple-colour'd face	V A	....	1
the ruby-colour'd portal	"	....	451
colour'd with his high estate	R L	....	92
pensiveness and colour'd sorrow	"	....	1497
a woman colour'd ill	Son	144	4
a woman colour'd ill	P P	2	4
Colt—The colt that's back'd	V A	....	419
Combat—This beauteous combat an eager combat fight	"	....	363
	R L	....	1298
Long was the combat doubtful	P P	16	5
Combined—parcels in .... sums	L C	....	231
Combustious—As dry .... matter	V A	....	1162
Come—Here come and sit	"	....	17
he comes in every jar	"	....	100
Comes breath perfumed	"	....	444
Come not within	"	....	639
Lust's winter comes	"	....	802
black chaos comes again	"	....	1020
Now is he come unto the chamber door	R L	....	337
am I come to scale	"	....	481
How comes it then	"	....	895
He gratis comes, and thou	"	....	914
would else have come to me	"	....	916
and all that are to come	"	....	923
wouldst thou one hour come back	"	....	965
shall never come to growth	"	....	1062
'Come, Philomel, that singst	"	....	1128
to come and visit me	"	....	1307
To this well-painted piece is Lucrece come	"	....	1443
mindful messenger come back	"	....	1583
Comes all too late	"	....	1686
so thick come in his poor heart's aid	"	....	1784
my verse in time to come	Son	17	1
The age to come would say	"	17	7
but now come back again	"	45	11
thou mayst come and part	"	48	12
if ever that time come	"	49	1
Come daily to the banks	"	56	11
Time will come and take	"	64	12
a modern quill doth come too short	"	83	7
Though words come hindmost	"	85	12
Comes home again	"	87	12
Come in the rearward	"	90	6
But in the onset come	"	90	11
dreaming on things to come	"	107	2
Thence comes it that my name	"	111	5
bending sickle's compass come	"	116	10
that I come so near	"	136	1
in her heart did mercy come	"	145	5
and to your audit comes	L C	....	230
Anon he comes, and throws	P P	6	9
Anon Adonis comes	"	9	6
and come again to-morrow	"	14	5
and bade me come to-morrow	"	15	12
Come—To this troop come thou not near	P T	....	8
Comely-distant—And .... sits he	L C	....	65
Comest—thou .... thy tale to tell	P P	19	7
Comfort—Take all my comfort	Son	37	4
Most worthy comfort	"	48	6
to be my comfort still	"	134	4
I have of comfort and despair	"	144	1
I have of comfort and despair	P P	2	1
Comfortable—No .... star did lend	R L	....	164
Comforter—Look, the world's	V A	....	529
Comforteth—.... like sunshine	"	....	799
Comfort-killing—O .... Night	R L	....	764
Coming—He sees her coming	V A	....	337
purpose of his coming hither	R L	....	113
Coming from thee	"	....	843
coming from a king	"	....	1002
Against this coming end	Son	13	3
Since, seldom coming, in the long year set	"	52	6
Command—commands mine eyes	V A	....	584
Hast thou command	R L	....	624
command thy rebel will	"	....	625
similes to your own command	L C	....	227
Commanded—Commanded by the motion	Son	149	12
Commander—on him, invisible	V A	....	1004
in great commanders	R L	....	1387
Commanding—commanding in his monarchy	L C	....	196
Commandment—They have at	P P	21	46
Commence—a lawful plea	Son	35	11
Here the anthem doth commence	P T	....	21
Commend—His eye commends the leading	R L	....	436
So, I commend me from our house	"	....	1308
even so as foes commend	Son	69	4
that tongue that well can thee commend	P P	5	8
Commended—by nature's outwards so commended	L C	....	80
Comment—For love can comment	V A	....	714
in secret influence comment	Son	15	4
While comments of your praise	"	85	2
comment upon that offence	"	89	2
making lascivious comments on thy sport	"	95	6
Commission—whose leave exceeds commission	V A	....	568
Commit—he commits this ill	R L	....	476
such murderous shame commits	Son	9	14
Those pretty wrongs that liberty commits	"	41	1
commit to these waste blanks	"	77	10
Committed—thought of his .... evil	R L	....	972
Let sin, alone committed	"	....	1480
hath my heart committed	Son	119	5
Commix'd—sight distractedly	L C	....	28
Common—excel a common one	V A	....	293
human law and common troth	R L	....	571
that thou dost common grow	Son	69	14
yield me but a common grave	"	81	7
sweets grown common	"	102	12
the wide world's common place	"	137	10
Compact—all compact of fire	V A	....	149
so compact, so kind	R L	....	1423
Compacted—The poisonous simple sometime is compacted	"	....	530
Companion—companions at thy state	"	....	1066

COMPANY 63 CONQUER

Company—slain in merry company	R L 1110	Conceit—some good conceit of thine	Son 26 7
No cause, but company	" 1236	Finding the first conceit	" 108 13
his lord and other company	" 1588	unripe years did want conceit	P P 4 9
Use his company no more	P P 21 50	whose deep conceit is such	" 8 7
Compare—sweet above compare	V A 8	As passing all conceit	" 8 8
which she compares to tears	" 1176	Conceited—the .... painter drew	R L 1371
Braving compare, disdainfully did sting	R L 40	on it had conceited characters	L C 16
		Concealed—So of concealed sorrow	V A 353
all sorrow loth compare	" 1102	of faults conceal'd	Son 88 7
Shall I compare thee	Son 18 1	the naked and concealed fiend	L C 317
a couplement of proud compare	" 21 5	Concealing—in blind .... night	R L 675
Compare them with the bettering	" 32 5	Vast sin-concealing chaos	" 767
thy trespass with compare	" 35 6	Concord—If the true concord	Son 8 5
belied with false compare	" 130 14	The wiry concord	" 128 4
O, but with mine compare	" 142 3	Concordant—Seemeth this concordant one	P T 46
Compared—may be compared well	V A 701		
Compared with loss of thee	Son 90 14	Conclude—still concludes in woe	V A 839
Comparing—Comparing it to her Adonis' breath	V A 1172	she concludes the picture	R L 1533
		They did conclude to bear	" 1850
Comparing him to that	R L 1565	Conclusion—tries a merciless	" 1160
Compass—might .... his fair fair	" 346	Condemn'd—be condemn'd of treason	V A 729
his bending sickle's compass come	Son 116 10		
Compass'd—Upon his .... crest	V A 272	The lily I condemned	Son 99 6
compass'd oft with venturing	" 567	Conduct—Extinguishing his	R L 313
Compassionate—and be	" 594	Conduit—Like ivory conduits	" 1234
Compeer—nor his compeers by night	Son 86 7	Confess—truth I must confess	V A 1001
Compelled—from this .... stain	R L 1708	like him I must confess	" 1117
Compile—of that which I compile	Son 78 9	Let me confess	Son 36 1
Compiled—of your praise, richly	" 85 2	Confess'd—So now I have confess'd	" 134 1
Complain—and complain on theft	V A 160	Confine—In whose confine immured	" 84 3
yet complain on drouth	" 544	neither sting, knot, nor confine	L C 263
host of heaven I complain me	R L 598	Confined—my verse to constancy confined	Son 105 7
of weariness he did complain him	" 845		
the other to complain	Son 28 7	forfeit to a confined doom	" 107 4
to hear her so complain	P P 21 15	to whom I am confined	" 110 12
Complained—Lucrece' soul that late complained	R L 1839	Confirmed—I spurn at my confirm'd despite	R L 1026
Complaining—counterfeit of her	" 1269	constant and confirmed devil	" 1513
weary time with her complaining	" 1570	Conflict—the fighting conflict	V A 345
Complexion—of a man's	V A 215	Confound—and her spirit confounds	" 882
is his gold complexion dimm'd	Son 18 6	doth men's minds confound	" 1048
on thy soft cheek for complexion dwells	" 99 4	himself confounds, betrays	R L 160
		doth confound and kill	" 230
that thy complexion lack	" 132 14	on her confounds his wits	" 291
Complexion'd—the swart-complexion'd night	" 28 11	that did my fame confound	" 1202
		these many lives confounds	" 1489
Composed—To this composed wonder	" 59 10	and confounds him there	Son 5 6
Composition—Until life's composition be recured	" 45 9	sweetly chide thee, who confounds	" 8 7
		doth now his gift confound	" 60 8
Compound—In a pure compound	R L 531	In other accents do this praise confound	" 69 7
and to compounds strange	Son 76 4		
With eager compounds	" 118 2	that mine ear confounds	" 128 4
For compound sweet	" 125 7	Confounded—Even so confounded	V A 827
As compound love	L C 239	confounded in a thousand fears	R L 455
Compounded—I perhaps compounded am with clay	Son 71 10	Or state itself confounded	Son 64 10
		Reason, in itself confounded	P T 41
Simple were so well compounded	P T 44	Confounding—Against .... age's	Son 63 10
Comprehend—beforehand counsel comprehends	R L 494	Confusion—with .... of their cries	R L 445
		whole is swallow'd in confusion	" 1159
comprehend in still imagination	" 702	Congealed—with his .... blood	V A 1122
pleasures live that art can comprehend	P P 5 6	mourning and congealed face	R L 1741
		Congest—Must for your victory us all congest	L C 258
Concave—whose concave womb reworded	L C 1		
		Conjure—conjures him by high almighty Jove	R L 568
Conceit—than bottomless conceit	R L 701		
Conceit and grief an eager combat fight	" 1298	Conquer—conquers where he comes	V A 100
		Which I to conquer sought	R L 488
Conceit deceitful, so compact	" 1423	my hand shall conquer thee	" 1210
the conceit of this inconstant stay	Son 15 9	still conquer chastity	P P 4 8

Conquer'd—Thy never-conquer'd fort	R L	482
in the rearward of a conquer'd woe	Son	90	6
Conqueror—Her lips are conquerors	V A	549
Conquest—.... on her fair delight	"	1030
by the conquest satisfied	R L	422
make conquest of the stronger	"	1767
To be death's conquest	Son	6	14
How to divide the conquest	"	46	2
The coward conquest of a wretch's knife	"	74	11
Conscience—'Tween frozen....	R L	247
to know what conscience is	Son	151	1
conscience is born of love	"	151	2
No want of conscience	"	151	13
Consecrate—was consecrate to thee	"	74	6
Consecrated—batter'd down her consecrated wall	R L	723
Consecration—All vows and consecrations	L C	263
Consent—plausibly did give consent	R L	1854
Do in consent shake hands	Son	28	6
Consents bewitch'd, ere he desire	L C	131
Consider—When I ... every thing	Son	15	1
Consort—consort with ugly night	V A	1041
Consorted—and his consorted lords	R L	1609
Conspirator—whispering....	"	769
Conspire—thou stick'st not to....	Son	10	6
Constancy—my verse to .... confined	"	105	7
The constancy and virtue	"	117	14
thy truth, thy constancy	"	152	10
Love and constancy is dead	P T	22
Constant—throng her constant woe	V A	967
like a constant and confirmed devil	R L	1513
And, constant stars	Son	14	10
none you, for constant heart	"	53	14
constant in a wondrous excellence	"	105	6
to thee I'll constant prove	P P	5	3
Constrain'd—constrain'd with dreadful circumstance	R L	1703
Construe—sense .... their denial	"	324
nill I construe whether	P P	14	8
Consulting—.... for foul weather	V A	972
Consume—Rot and .... themselves	"	132
that in air consumes	R L	1042
Consumed — Consumed with that which it was nourish'd by	Son	73	12
Consumest—that thou .... thyself	"	9	2
Contain—is that which it contains	"	74	13
what thy memory cannot contain	"	77	9
of me their reproach contains	L C	180
Contemn—shouldst contemn me this	V A	205
Contend—meeting clouds contend	"	820
all forwards do contend	Son	60	4
Contending—with her .... tears	V A	82
to calm contending kings	R L	930
In skill-contending schools	"	1018
Thus art with arms contending	P P	16	13
Content—Forced to content	V A	61
full of cares, yet show'd content	R L	1503
buriest thy content	Son	1	11
rebuked to my content	"	119	13
'gainst her own content	L C	137
For a sweet content	P P	18	51
Content—and alter their contents	R L	948
more bright in these contents	Son	55	3
reading what contents it bears	L C	19
Content—so breaking their contents	L C	56
Contented—I can be well contented	V A	513
With what I most enjoy contented least	Son	29	8
my well-contented day	"	32	1
But be contented	"	74	1
He is contented thy poor drudge	"	131	11
Contenting—.... but the eye alone	V A	213
Continual—with continual kissing	"	606
with their continual motion	R L	591
by thy continual haste	Son	123	12
Continuance—.... tames the one	R L	1098
Contracted—contracted to thine own bright eyes	Son	1	5
when two contracted new	"	56	10
Contradict—If thou my love's desire do contradict	R L	1631
Contrary—These contraries such unity do hold	"	1558
quite contrary I read	Son	62	11
Contrite—Her contrite sighs	R L	1727
Contrive—the herald will contrive	"	206
so to herself contrives	L C	243
Control—controls his thoughts unjust	R L	189
can affection's course control	"	500
should his use control	"	1781
control your times of pleasure	Son	58	2
lease of my true love control	"	107	3
stands least in thy control	"	125	14
Controlled—He was .... with	V A	270
truth dimm'd and controll'd	R L	448
white fleece her voice controll'd	"	678
prescience she controlled still	"	727
Controlling—Controlling what he was controlled with	V A	270
all 'hues' in his controlling	Son	20	7
folly, doctor-like, controlling skill	"	66	10
Controversy—controversy hence a question takes	L C	110
Convert—to water do convert	R L	592
desire converts to cold disdain	"	691
to store thou wouldst convert	Son	14	12
Converted—'fore duteous, now converted are	"	7	11
converted from the thing it was	"	49	7
Convertest—when thou from youth convertest	"	11	4
Convertite—departs a heavy	R L	743
Convey—I may convey this troubled soul	"	1176
Convey'd—quickly is convey'd	V A	1192
Cony—earth-delving conies keep	"	687
Cool—Shall cool the heat	"	190
Cool shadow to his melting	"	313
quench'd in a cool well by	Son	154	9
water cools not love	"	154	11
Adon used to cool his spleen	P P	6	6
Cool'd—that must be cool'd	V A	387
Cooling—Cooling his hot face	R L	682
Co-partner—co-partners in my pain	"	789
Cope—who shall cope him first	V A	888
Coped—never coped with stranger eyes	R L	99
Copesmate—copesmate of ugly Night	"	925
Copious—Their copious stories	V A	845
Copse—a copse that neighbours by	"	259
Copy—not let that copy die	Son	11	14
Let him but copy	"	84	9

Coral—that sweet coral mouth	V A	542	**Couldst**—Since thou....not defend	R L		1034
Her coral lips	R L	420	If thou couldst answer	Son	2	10
coral cisterns filling	"	1234	**Counsel**—counsel of their friends	V A		610
Coral is far more red	Son 130	2	All this beforehand counsel	R L		494
With coral clasps	P P 20	11	Counsel may stop a while	L C		159
Corn—As corn o'ergrown by weeds	R L	281	Take counsel of some wiser head	P P	19	5
Correct—to correct correction	Son 111	12	**Count**—Shall sum my count	Son	2	11
Correction—to correct correction	" 111	12	When I do count the clock	"	12	1
Correspondence—....with true sight	" 148	2	count bad what I think good	"	121	8
Corrupt—....by over-partial looks	" 137	5	thus far I count my gain	"	141	13
corrupt my saint to be a devil	" 144	7	**Counted**—black was not counted fair	"	127	1
corrupt my saint to be a devil	P P 2	7	**Countenance**—should....his sin	R L		343
Corrupted—Which once corrupted	R L	294	your countenance fill'd up his line	Son	86	13
spotted, spoil'd, corrupted	"	1172	**Counterfeit**—To the poor....	R L		1269
Corrupted blood some watery token	"	1748	And counterfeits to die	"		1776
Corrupting—Myself corrupting, salving thy amiss	Son 35	7	than your painted counterfeit	Son	16	8
			Adonis, and the counterfeit	"	53	5
Corydon—Poor Corydon	P P 18	52	**Countermand**—never....mine eye	R L		276
Cost—and oft that wealth doth cost	R L	146	**Counterpart**—such a....shall fame	Son	84	11
cost of outworn buried age	Son 64	2	**Counting**—Now counting best to be	"	75	7
prouder than garments' cost	" 91	10	Counting no old thing old	"	108	7
Why so large cost	" 146	5	**Countless**—pay this countless debt	V A		84
by that cost more dear	L C	96	**Country**—By all our country rights	R L		1838
painting, pain, and cost	P P 13	12	**Couple**—Will couple my reproach	"		816
Costly—outward walls so costly gay	Son 146	4	**Couplement**—Making a couplement	Son	21	5
Co-supreme—Co-supremes and stars of love	P T	51	**Courage**—Shows his hot courage	V A		276
			In shape, in courage	"		291
Couch—from her betumbled couch	R L	1037	stirs up a desperate courage	"		556
Coucheth—Coucheth the fowl below	"	507	courage to the coward	"		1158
Could—there he could not die	V A	246	**Courageous**—Courageous Roman, do not steep thy heart	R L		1828
that I could not see	"	440				
More I could tell	"	805	**Courageously**—Courageously to pluck him	V A		30
Could rule them both	"	1008				
he could not die	"	1060	**Course**—And with his strong course	"		940
all could not satisfy	R L	96	Holding their course	"		1193
Could pick no meaning	"	100	his course doth let	R L		328
Nor could she moralize	"	104	can affection's course control	"		500
could not stay him	"	323	against proportion'd course	"		774
What could he see	"	414	O time, cease thou thy course	"		1765
could weeping purify	"	685	nature's changing course	Son	18	8
could not forestall their will	"	724	Him in thy course	"	19	11
I could not put him back	"	843	five hundred courses of the sun	"	59	6
I could prevent this storm	"	966	to the course of altering things	"	115	8
If tears could help	"	1274	what course, what stop he makes	L C		109
itself could not mistrust	"	1516	**Courser**—the lusty courser's rein	V A		31
her poor tongue could not speak	"	1718	Adonis' trampling courser	"		261
no man could distinguish	"	1785	Let me excuse thy courser	"		403
Then what could death do	Son 6	11	**Court**—Of court, of city	L C		59
If I could write the beauty	" 17	5	her noble suit in court did shun	"		234
could with a backward look	" 59	5	Did court the lad	P P	4	3
what the old world could say	" 59	9	**Courtesy**—They all strain courtesy	V A		888
he could his looks translate	" 96	10	villain court'sies to her low	R L		1338
Could make me any	" 98	7	**Cover**—Covers the shame	"		357
yet I none could see	" 99	14	Though men can cover crimes	"		1252
it could so preposterously	" 109	11	that beauty that doth cover thee	Son	22	5
I could not love you dearer	" 115	2	my bones with dust shall cover	"	32	2
could not so much hold	" 122	9	doth cover every blot	"	95	11
Well could he ride	L C	106	**Cover'd**—The naked and concealed fiend he cover'd	L C	3	17
For further I could say	"	109				
Could 'scape the hail	"	310	**Coverlet**—On the green coverlet	R L		394
could not hold argument	P P 3	2	**Covet**—Those that much covet	"		134
none could look but beauty's queen	" 4	4	**Covetous**—For thou art covetous	Son 131		6
O never faith could hold	" 5	2	**Coward**—like a pale-faced coward	V A		569
Fare well I could not	" 14	6	Thy coward heart	"		1024
the fair'st that eye could see	" 16	3	courage to the coward	"		1158
That nothing could be used	" 16	10	The coward captive vanquished	R L		73
Alas, she could not help it	" 16	12	The coward fights	"		273
Scarce I could from tears refrain	" 21	16	Pale cowards, marching on	"		1391
Couldst—Unless thou....return	R L	961	The coward conquest	Son 74		11

5

Coward-like—.... with trembling	R L	....	231
Coy—why art thou coy	V A	....	96
to my coy disdain	"	....	112
instead of love's coy touch	R L	....	669
Cozening—Cozening the pillow	"	....	387
Crabbed—Crabbed age and youth	P P	12	1
Crack'd—Crack'd many a ring	L C	....	45
Cradle—Lo, in this hollow cradle	V A	....	1185
Craft—False-creeping craft and perjury	R L	....	1517
in his craft of will	L C	....	126
but an art of craft	"	....	295
When craft hath taught her	P P	19	22
Craggy—And all the craggy mountains yields	"	20	4
Cramp—Is plagued with cramps	R L	....	856
Crank—He cranks and crosses	V A	....	682
Cranny—vents and crannies of the place	R L	....	310
through every cranny spies	"	....	1086
Crave—what she did crave	V A	....	88
a beggar's orts to crave	R L	....	985
The cause craves haste	"	....	1293
the account of hours to crave	Son	58	3
more than I did crave	P P	10	9
I pardon crave of thee	"	10	11
Craved—I .... nothing of thee still	"	10	10
Crawl—Crawls to maturity	Son	60	6
Created—wert thou first created	"	20	9
Which eyes not yet created	"	81	10
Creating—Creating every bad a perfect best	"	114	7
Creation—From the creation	R L	....	924
But heaven in thy creation	Son	93	9
Slandering creation with a false esteem	"	127	12
Creature—Pursue these fearful creatures	V A	....	677
'Tis he, foul creature	"	....	1095
henceforth no creature wear	"	....	1081
To creatures stern sad times	R L	....	1147
these pretty creatures stand	"	....	1233
Such harmless creatures	"	....	1347
A creeping creature	"	....	1627
From fairest creatures	Son	1	1
sweet favour or deformed'st creature	"	113	10
One of her feather'd creatures	"	143	2
Fair creature kill'd too soon	P P	10	7
Credent—And credent soul	L C	....	279
Credit—I credit her false-speaking tongue	Son	138	7
credit her false-speaking tongue	P P	1	7
Credulous—and yet too credulous	V A	....	986
The credulous old Priam	R L	....	1522
Creep—fearing to creep forth	V A	....	1036
dog creeps sadly thence	R L	....	736
halt, creep, cry out for thee	"	....	902
the little worms that creep	"	....	1248
see time how slow it creeps	"	....	1575
Creep in 'twixt vows	Son	115	6
Creeping—Which drives the creeping thief	R L	....	305
False-creeping craft and perjury	"	....	1517
A creeping creature	"	....	1627
Crept—a wandering wasp hath crept	"	....	840
Crest—his uncontrolled crest	V A	....	104
Upon his compass'd crest	"	....	272
High crest, short ears	"	....	297
Crest—from his bending crest	V A	....	395
When tyrants' crests and tombs	Son	107	14
Crest-wounding—...., private scar	R L	....	828
Crew—and all his lordly crew	"	....	1731
Cried—and softly cried 'Awake	"	....	1628
Cried 'O false blood	L C	....	52
That it cried, How true a twain	P T	....	45
Cries—cries 'Fie, no more of love	V A	....	185
'Pity,' she cries	"	....	257
'For shame,' he cries	"	....	379
'Ay me!' she cries	"	....	833
owls' and wolves' death-boding cries	R L	....	165
with confusion of their cries	"	....	445
the poor lamb cries	"	....	677
Who nothing wants to answer her but cries	"	....	1459
dear daughter,' old Lucretius cries	"	....	1751
Answer'd their cries	"	....	1806
Cries to catch her	Son	143	6
Crime—Whose crime will bear	R L	....	224
art guilty of my careless crime	"	....	772
Be guilty of my death, since of my crime	"	....	931
let his unrecalling crime	"	....	993
Though men can cover crimes	"	....	1252
one most heinous crime	Son	19	8
to pardon of self-doing crime	"	58	12
how once I suffer'd in your crime	"	120	8
who have lived for crime	"	124	14
Crimeful—this cursed .... night	R L	....	970
Crimson—'Twixt crimson shame	V A	....	76
never let their crimson liveries wear	"	....	506
that the crimson blood	R L	....	1738
Cripple—A .... soon can find a halt	P P	19	10
Critic—To critic and to flatterer stopped are	Son	112	11
Crooked—crooked, churlish, harsh in voice	V A	....	134
his crooked tushes slay	"	....	624
Whose crooked beak threats	R L	....	508
crooked eclipses 'gainst his glory fight	Son	60	7
his scythe and crooked knife	"	100	14
did hang in crooked curls	L C	....	85
Crop—bid thee crop a weed	V A	....	946
she crops the stalk	"	....	1175
the ploughman with increaseful crop	R L	....	958
Cross—I see what crosses	"	....	491
A thousand crosses keep them	"	....	912
the strong offence's cross	Son	34	12
lay on me this cross	"	42	12
One silly cross	P P	18	13
Cross—He cranks and crosses	V A	....	682
To cross the curious workmanship	"	....	734
cross him with their opposite persuasion	R L	....	286
To cross their arms	"	....	793
cross Tarquin in his flight	"	....	968
is bent my deeds to cross	Son	90	2
Crossed—thus to be crossed	"	133	8
Crow—Out-stripping crows that strive	V A	....	324
The crow may bathe	R L	....	1009
A crow that flies	Son	70	4
The crow or dove	"	113	12
And thou treble-dated crow	P T	....	17

Crown—but to touch the crown	R L	216
now crown themselves assured	Son 107	7
But if store of crowns be scant	P P 21	37
Crowned—in thy parts do crowned sit	Son 37	7
wherewith being crown'd	" 69	6
with outward praise is crown'd	" 69	5
my mind being crown'd with you	" 114	1
Crowning—Crowning the present	" 115	12
Cruel—to ban her cruel foes	R L	1460
to thy sweet self too cruel	Son 1	8
despite his cruel hand	" 60	14
confounding age's cruel knife	" 63	10
rude, cruel, not to trust	" 120	4
beauties proudly make them cruel	" 131	2
thy cruel eye hath taken	" 133	5
Be wise as thou art cruel	" 140	1
Canst thou, O cruel	" 149	1
O cruel speeding	P P 18	25
Crush'd—injurious hand crush'd and o'er-worn	Son 63	2
Cry—Ceasing their clamorous cry	V A	693
she coasteth to the cry	"	870
the cry remaineth	"	885
This dismal cry	"	889
with my bootless cries	Son 29	3
Cry—'O, pity,' 'gan she cry	V A	95
doth cry 'Kill, kill!'	"	652
twenty times cry so	"	834
creep, cry out for thee	R L	902
I did begin to start and cry	"	1639
for restful death I cry	Son 66	1
still cry 'Amen	" 85	6
Where want cries some	L C	42
and cry 'It is thy last	"	168
now would she cry	P P 21	13
Crying—And fright her crying babe	R L	814
and my loud crying still	Son 143	14
Crystal—the crystal tears gave light	V A	491
sweet lips and crystal eyne	"	633
The crystal tide	"	957
Both crystals, where they view'd	"	963
Through crystal walls	R L	1251
pierced with crystal eyes	Son 46	6
Of amber, crystal	L C	37
glazed with crystal gate	"	286
Cuckoo—Or hateful cuckoos hatch	R L	849
Cunning—Which cunning love	V A	471
the cunning hounds mistake their smell	"	686
with a cunning brow	R L	749
eyes this cunning want to grace their art	Son 24	13
What need'st thou wound with cunning	" 139	7
O cunning Love	" 148	13
Cup—to his palate doth prepare the cup	" 114	12
Cupid—The which by Cupid's bow	V A	581
Cupid laid by his brand	Son 153	1
Where Cupid got new fire	" 153	11
Curb—for curb or pricking spur	V A	285
Can curb his heat	R L	706
That we must curb it	L C	164
Cure—kiss each other, for this cure	V A	505
despite of cure, remain	R L	732
is woe the cure for woe	"	1821
Past cure I am	Son 147	9
a sovereign cure	" 153	8
Cure—But found no cure	Son 153	13
Came there for cure	" 154	13
Cure—my body's bane would cure thee	V A	372
it cannot cure his pain	R L	861
heals the wound and cures not the disgrace	Son 34	8
your pity is enough to cure me	" 111	14
cures all disgrace in me	P P 3	8
Cured—though none it ever cured	R L	1581
rank of goodness would by ill be cured	Son 118	12
Careless—guilty of my ... crime	R L	772
Curious—the curious workmanship of nature	V A	734
do please these curious days	Son 38	13
seal'd to curious secrecy	L C	49
Curious-good—This is too ...	R L	1300
Curl—sable curls all silver'd o'er	Son 12	4
did hang in crooked curls	L C	85
Curled—to tear his curled hair	R L	981
Current—the current of her sorrow	"	1569
With brinish current	L C	284
Curse—The destinies will curse thee for this stroke	V A	945
Shall curse my bones	R L	209
To make him curse	"	970
Teach me to curse him	"	996
and curse my fate	Son 29	4
blessings add a curse	" 84	13
Cursed—this cursed crimeful night	R L	970
Fortune, cursed fickle dame	P P 18	15
Cursed-blessed—their ... fortune	R L	866
Curst—Finding their enemy to be so curst	V A	887
Curtain—the curtains being close	R L	367
Even so, the curtain drawn	"	374
Curtal—My curtal dog	P P 18	29
Curvets—curvets and leaps	V A	279
Cut—never cut from memory	Son 63	11
Cynthia—Cynthia for shame obscures	V A	728
Cytherea—Sweet Cytherea, sitting by a brook	P P 4	1
Cytherea, all in love forlorn	" 6	3
Daff'd—my white stole of chastity I daff'd	L C	297
daff'd me to a cabin	P P 14	3
Daily—streams that pay a daily debt	R L	649
doth daily draw my sorrows	Son 28	13
Come daily to the banks	" 56	11
the sun is daily new and old	" 76	13
Dainty—Dainties to taste	V A	164
Daisy—an April daisy on the grass	R L	395
Dale—on mountain or in dale	V A	232
mountain-spring that feeds a dale	R L	1077
hills and valleys, dales and fields	P P 20	3
Dallied—Grief dallied with, nor law nor limit knows	R L	1120
Dally—dally, smile, and jest	V A	106
he doth but dally	R L	554
Damask—with ... dye to grace her	P P 7	5
Damask'd—I have seen roses ...	Son 130	5
Dame—peer to such a peerless dame	R L	21
welcomed by the Roman dame	"	51
couldst not defend thy loyal dame	"	1034
the dame and daughter die	"	1477
Awake, thou Roman dame	"	1628

Dame—no dame hereafter living	R L	....	1714
Fortune, cursed fickle dame	P P	18	15
thine eye hath chose the dame	"	19	1
Damn'd—voice .... up with woe	R L	....	1661
Damned—imposthumes, grief, and damn'd despair	V A	....	743
more black and damned	L C	....	54
Damp—With rotten damps ravish the morning air	R L	....	778
Damsel—Unto the silly damsel	P P	16	8
Dance—learn'd to sport and dance	V A	....	105
Dance on the sands	"	....	148
Dancing—with those dancing chips	Son	128	10
Dandling—still'd with dandling	V A	....	562
Danger—or what great .... dwells	"	....	206
his danger by thy will	"	....	639
Danger deviseth shifts	"	....	690
leadeth on to danger	"	....	788
sundry dangers of his will's obtaining	R L	....	128
The dangers of his loathsome enterprise	"	....	183
Such danger to resistance	"	....	1265
Dangerous—from the ... year	V A	....	508
Dank—As the dank earth weeps	R L	....	1130
Dapper—Like a dive-dapper	V A	....	86
Dardan—from the strand of Dardan	R L	....	1436
Dare—darest not be so bold	V A	....	401
which no encounter dare	"	....	676
I dare not say	"	....	805
and dare not stay	"	....	894
She dares not look	R L	....	458
She dares not thereof make discovery	"	....	1314
Then may I dare to boast	Son	26	13
Nor dare I chide	"	57	5
Nor dare I question	"	57	9
I dare not be so bold	"	131	7
Darest—thou .... do such outrage	R L	....	605
What darest thou not	"	....	606
Daring—engirt with daring infamy	"	....	1173
Not daring trust the office	P P	13	4
Dark—heavy, dark, disliking eye	V A	....	182
'tis dark, and going I shall fall	"	....	719
Now of this dark night	"	....	727
in dark obscurity	"	....	760
thro' the dark laund	"	....	813
in the dark she lay	"	....	827
Into the deep-dark cabins	"	....	1038
from their dark beds	"	....	1050
From earth's dark womb	R L	....	549
Through the dark night he stealeth	"	....	729
dark harbour for defame	"	....	768
Some dark, deep desert	"	....	1144
in the dreadful dead of dark midnight	"	....	1625
are bright in dark	Son	43	4
what dark days seen	"	97	3
black as hell, as dark as night	"	147	14
drives away dark dreaming night	P P	15	8
Darken—To .... her whose light	R L	....	191
Darkening—Darkening thy power	Son	100	4
Darkly—And, darkly bright	"	43	4
Darkness—burnt out, in .... lies	V A	....	1128
dim darkness doth display	R L	....	118
canopied in darkness sweetly lay	"	....	398
In darkness daunts them	"	....	462
would they still in darkness be	"	....	752
Looking on darkness	Son	27	8
Darksome—in that .... prison	R L	....	379
Darling—shake the .... buds of May	Son	18	3
Dart—Thine eye darts forth	V A	....	196
she darts as one on shore	"	....	817
but thy false dart	"	....	941
not Death's ebon dart	"	....	948
night dart their injuries	Son	139	12
Dash—Some loathsome dash	R L	....	206
Date—An expired date	"	....	26
date of never-ending woes	"	....	935
date from cancell'd destiny	"	....	1729
beauty's doom and date	Son	14	14
hath all too short a date	"	18	4
youth and thou are of one date	"	22	2
to outlive long date	"	38	12
Beyond all date	"	122	4
Our dates are brief	"	123	5
Dated—And thou treble-dated crow	P T	....	17
Dateless—hid in death's .... night	Son	30	6
A dateless, lively heat	"	153	6
Daughter—dearth of daughters	V A	....	754
beldam daughters of her daughter	R L	....	953
the dame and daughter die	"	....	1477
Daughter, dear daughter	"	....	1751
for daughter or for wife	"	....	1792
'My daughter,' and 'my wife	"	....	1804
'My daughter,' and 'my wife	"	....	1806
It was a lordling's daughter	P P	16	1
Daunt—In darkness daunts them	R L	....	462
Day—A summer's day will seem	V A	....	23
So shall the day seem night	"	....	122
tired in the mid-day heat	"	....	177
My day's delight is past	"	....	380
now is turn'd to day	"	....	481
Ills day's hot task	"	....	530
sun by day, and her by night	"	....	732
melts with the mid-day sun	"	....	750
a stormy day, now wind	"	....	965
stars ashamed of day	"	....	1032
silly lamb, that day	"	....	1098
day should yet be light	"	....	1134
shall rock thee day and night	"	....	1186
in her vaulty prison stows the day	R L	....	119
and wretched, hateful days	"	....	161
open to adorn the day	"	....	399
she never may behold the day	"	....	746
'For day,' quoth she	"	....	747
the jealous Day behold that face	"	....	800
to the tell-tale Day	"	....	806
grooms are sightless night, kings glorious day	"	....	1013
Revealing day through every cranny spies	"	....	1086
day hath nought to do	"	....	1092
thou sing'st not in the day	"	....	1142
ere the break of day	"	....	1289
Into so bright a day	"	....	1518
treasure of thy lusty days	Son	2	6
he reeleth from the day	"	7	10
the brave day sunk in hideous night	"	12	2
stormy gusts of winter's day	"	13	11
To change your day of youth	"	15	12
compare thee to a summer's day	"	18	1
my days should expiate	"	22	4
Lo, thus, by day my limbs	"	27	13
When day's oppression	"	28	3
But day by night and night by day	"	28	4
I tell the day, to please him	"	28	9
But day doth daily draw	"	28	13

Day—at break of day arising	Son	29	11	Dead—Ere beauty's dead fleece	Son	68	8
survive my well-contented day	"	32	1	mourn for me when I am dead	"	71	1
promise such a beauteous day	"	34	1	my body being dead	"	74	10
do please these curious days	"	38	13	breathers of this world are dead	"	81	12
For all the day they view	"	43	2	that struck me dead	"	86	6
To the clear day	"	43	7	was beauty's summer dead	"	104	14
in the living day	"	43	10	ladies dead, and lovely knights	"	106	4
All days are nights	"	43	13	outward form would shew it dead	"	108	14
And nights bright days	"	43	14	all the world besides methinks are dead	"	112	14
the wits of former days	"	59	13
with beauty of thy days	"	62	14	Making dead wood more blest	"	128	12
wreckful siege of battering days	"	65	6	And Death once dead	"	146	14
In days long since, before these last	"	67	14	broken, dead within an hour	P P	13	6
the map of days outworn	"	68	1	As flowers dead lie wither'd	"	13	9
the ambush of young days	"	70	9	our love is lost, for Love is dead	"	18	48
the twilight of such day	"	73	5	King Pandion he is dead	"	21	23
pine and surfeit day by day	"	75	13	Love and constancy is dead	P T	.....	22
of the time-bettering days	"	82	8	For these dead birds sigh a prayer	"	.....	67
tells the story of thy days	"	95	5	Dead-killing—a cockatrice' dead-killing eye	R L	.....	540
what dark days seen	"	97	3
in growth of riper days	"	102	8	Deadly—deadly bullet of a gun	V A	.....	461
now behold these present days	"	106	13	gives a deadly groan	"	.....	1044
I must each day say o'er	"	108	6	disdain and deadly enmity	R L	.....	503
the day or night	"	113	11	light and lust are deadly enemies	"	.....	674
do tie me day by day	"	117	4	kill'd with deadly cares	"	.....	1593
my days are past the best	"	138	6	with this deadly deed	"	.....	1730
follow'd it as gentle day	"	145	10	Deaf—Or were I deaf	V A	.....	435
brightness doth not grace the day	"	150	4	But will is deaf	R L	.....	495
Hot was the day	P P	6	7	And trouble deaf heaven	Son	29	3
Pack night, peep day ; good day, of night	"	15	17	Deal—My shepherd's pipe can sound no deal	P P	18	27
was victor of the day	"	16	13	Dealing—and use good dealing	V A	.....	514
On a day, alack the day	"	17	1	Dear—were he not my dear friend	R L	.....	234
twice desire ere it be day	"	19	17	my kinsman, my dear friend	"	.....	237
As it fell upon a day	"	21	1	Where their dear governess	"	.....	443
Daylight—she doth welcome daylight	"	15	7	For Collatine's dear love	"	.....	821
Dazzleth—That dazzleth them	R L	.....	377	Well, well, dear Collatine	"	.....	1058
Dazzling—That her sight dazzling	V A	.....	1064	Dear lord of that dear jewel	"	.....	1191
Dead—thou thyself art dead	"	.....	172	my lord, my love, my dear	"	.....	1293
image dull and dead	"	.....	212	Unmask, dear dear	"	.....	1602
Struck dead at first	"	.....	250	Dear husband, in the interest	"	.....	1619
As if the dead	"	.....	292	Dear lord, thy sorrow	"	.....	1676
believing she is dead	"	.....	457	Daughter, dear daughter	"	.....	1751
If he be dead	"	.....	937	dear my love, you know	Son	13	13
to strike him dead	"	.....	948	dear repose for limbs	"	27	2
For he being dead	"	.....	1019	new wail my dear time's waste	"	30	4
And, beauty dead	"	.....	1020	I think on thee, dear friend	"	30	13
he is not dead	"	.....	1060	Hath dear religious love	"	31	6
behold two Adons dead	"	.....	1070	And our dear love	"	39	6
But he is dead	"	.....	1119	and the dear heart's part	"	46	12
That, thou being dead	"	.....	1134	for a prize so dear	"	48	14
Since thou art dead	"	.....	1135	After my death, dear love	"	72	3
the dead of night	R L	.....	162	thou art too dear for my possessing	"	87	1
pure thoughts are dead and still	"	.....	167	Take heed, dear heart	"	95	13
as one in dead of night	"	.....	449	lose their dear delight	"	102	12
and reason beat it dead	"	.....	489	my love or thy dear merit	"	108	4
And in thy dead arms	"	.....	517	sold cheap what is most dear	"	110	3
the other being dead	"	.....	1187	Pity me then, dear friend	"	111	13
My shame so dead	"	.....	1190	thy dear love to score	"	122	10
Thou dead, both die	"	.....	1211	If my dear love	"	124	1
who cannot abuse a body dead	"	.....	1267	to my dear doting heart	"	131	3
imprison'd in a body dead	"	.....	1456	Dear heart, forbear to glance	"	139	6
the dreadful dead of dark midnight	"	.....	1625	and thy dear virtue hate	"	142	1
to bear dead Lucrece thence	"	.....	1850	for whose dear love I rise and fall	"	151	14
by lacking have supposed dead	Son	31	2	by that cost more dear	L C	.....	96
As interest of the dead	"	31	7	terror and dear modesty	"	.....	202
When in dead night	"	43	11	each stone's dear nature	"	.....	210
And steal dead seeing	"	67	6	Dowland to thee is dear	P P	8	5
golden tresses of the dead	"	68	5	O yes, dear friend	"	10	11

Dearer—lost a dearer thing than life	R L	....	687
which was the dearer	"	....	1163
A dearer birth than this	Son	32	11
I could not love you dearer	"	115	2
Dearest—by fortune's dearest spite	"	37	3
Thou, best of dearest	"	48	7
your dearest love to call	"	117	3
Dearly—I loved her dearly	"	42	2
Dear-purchased—your own .... right	"	117	6
Dearth—she faint with dearth	V A	....	543
dearth of daughters	"	....	754
of dearths, or season's quality	Son	14	4
pine within and suffer dearth	"	146	3
Death—And so, in spite of death	V A	....	173
it is a life in death	"	....	413
life was death's annoy	"	....	497
death was lively joy	"	....	498
having writ on death	"	....	509
I thy death should fear	"	....	660
I prophesy thy death	"	....	671
Swear Nature's death	"	....	744
exclaims on Death	"	....	930
thus chides she Death	"	....	932
not Death's ebon dart	"	....	948
Death is not to blame	"	....	992
sweet Death, I did but jest	"	....	997
With Death she humbly	"	....	1012
To wail his death	"	....	1017
death doth my love destroy	"	....	1163
reft from her by death	"	....	1174
Though death be adjunct, there's no death	R L	....	133
The death of all	"	....	147
triumph in the map of death	"	....	402
And death's dim look	"	....	403
lived in death and death in life	"	....	406
In bloody death and ravishment	"	....	430
Wounding itself to death	"	....	466
living death and pain perpetual	"	....	726
Grim cave of death	"	....	769
Be guilty of my death	"	....	931
desperate instrument of death	"	....	1038
To clear this spot by death	"	....	1053
Till life to death acquit	"	....	1071
'Tis double death to drown in ken of shore	"	....	1114
death reproach's debtor	"	....	1155
when death takes one	"	....	1161
cause of my untimely death	"	....	1178
in my death I murder	"	....	1180
This plot of death	"	....	1212
Of present death, and shame	"	....	1263
By that her death	"	....	1264
The adulterate death of Lucrece	"	....	1645
Shows me a bare-boned death	"	....	1761
Shall rotten death make conquest	"	....	1767
to be revenged on her death	"	....	1778
the death of this true wife	"	....	1841
Then what could death do	Son	6	11
To be death's conquest	"	6	14
rage of death's eternal cold	"	13	12
Nor shall Death brag thou wander'st in his shade	"	18	11
Then look I death my days should expiate	"	22	4
hid in death's dateless night	"	30	6
When that churl Death	"	32	2
Sinks down to death	"	45	8
Of their sweet deaths	"	54	12
Death—'Gainst death and all-oblivious enmity	Son	55	9
This thought is as a death	"	64	13
for restful death I cry	"	66	1
After my death, dear love	"	72	3
Death's second self	"	73	8
your memory death cannot take	"	81	3
eat him up to death	"	99	13
and death to me subscribes	"	107	10
when their deaths be near	"	140	7
So shalt thou feed on Death	"	146	13
And Death once dead	"	146	14
Desire is death which physic did except	"	147	8
by death's sharp sting	P P	10	4
That the lover, sick to death	"	17	7
Death is now the phœnix' nest	P T	....	56
Death-bed—As the death-bed	Son	73	11
Death-boding—and wolves' death-boding cries	R L	....	165
Death-divining—Be the death-divining swan	P T	....	15
Deathsman—As slanderous	R L	....	1001
Death-worthy—seem death-worthy in thy brother	"	....	635
Debarr'd—.... the benefit of rest	Son	28	2
Debate—in his inward mind he doth debate	R L	....	185
Debate when leisure serves	"	....	1019
debate with angry swords	"	....	1421
against myself I'll vow debate	Son	89	13
Debated—debated, even in my soul	R L	....	498
Debaters—serves with dull	"	....	1019
Debateth—Time .... with Decay	Son	15	11
Debating—fear, avaunt! ...., die	R L	....	274
Debt—pay this countless debt	V A	....	84
that the debt should double	"	....	521
pays the hour his debt	R L	....	329
that pay a daily debt	"	....	649
The barren tender of a poet's debt	Son	83	4
Debtor—that to bad debtors lends	R L	....	964
and death reproach's debtor	"	....	1155
a friend came debtor for my sake	Son	134	11
Decay—with thy life's decay	R L	....	517
sweet chastity's decay	"	....	806
with decay of things	"	....	947
age and cold decay	Son	11	6
a house fall to decay	"	13	9
Time debateth with Decay	"	15	11
fortify yourself in your decay	"	16	3
itself confounded to decay	"	64	10
my love was my decay	"	80	14
a satire to decay	"	100	11
on the doubts of my decay	P P	14	4
Decay—and when that decays	R L	....	713
will wither, and his sap decay	"	....	1168
in mine own love's strength seem to decay	Son	23	7
so strong, but Time decays	"	65	8
even with my life decay	"	71	12
Decay'd—as soon decay'd and done	R L	....	23
gracious numbers are decay'd	Son	79	3
Decease—fearing my love's decease	V A	....	1002
children pre-decease progenitors	R L	....	1756
the riper should by time decease	Son	1	3
after yourself's decease	"	13	7
after their lord's decease	"	97	8
Deceased—lines of thy deceased lover	"	32	4
hang more praise upon deceased I	"	72	7

Deceit—Thou look'st not like deceit	R L	....	585
To hide deceit	"	....	1507
Saw how deceits were gilded	L C	....	172
Deceitful—Conceit...., so compact	R L	....	1423
Deceive—do not deceive me	"	....	585
thy sweet self dost deceive	Son	4	10
so sweetly doth deceive	"	39	12
as it best deceives	L C	....	306
Deceived—.... with painted grapes	V A	....	601
Like a deceived husband	Son	93	2
mine eye may be deceived	"	104	12
Deceivest—if thou thyself deceivest	"	40	7
Deceiving—the deceiving harmony	V A	....	781
And most deceiving	"	....	1156
December—old December's bareness	Son	97	4
Decide—To 'cide this title	"	46	9
Deck—And decks with praises	R L	....	108
to deck his oratory	"	....	815
Declines—fair from fair sometime declines	Son	18	7
Declined—With head declined	R L	....	1661
My low-declined honour	"	....	1705
Decrease—at height decrease	Son	15	7
Decree—quiver'st thou at this....	R L	....	1030
heaven in thy creation did decree	Son	93	9
change decrees of kings	"	115	6
Decrepit—Teaching decrepit age to tread the measures	V A	....	1148
As a decrepit father	Son	37	1
Dedicated—The dedicated words	"	82	3
Deed—Let fair humanity abhor the deed	R L	....	195
with so black a deed	"	....	226
shows like a virtuous deed	"	....	252
tears ensue the deed	"	....	502
This deed will make thee	"	....	610
time for charitable deeds	"	....	908
with deeds degenerate	"	....	1003
My life's foul deed	"	....	1208
To talk in deeds	"	....	1348
Whose deed hath made her	"	....	1566
The lechers in their deed	"	....	1637
with this deadly deed	"	....	1730
or grief help grievous deeds	"	....	1822
and ransom all ill deeds	Son	34	14
To see his active child do deeds of youth	"	37	2
into my deeds to pry	"	61	6
they measure by thy deeds	"	69	10
is bent my deeds to cross	"	90	2
turn sourest by their deeds	"	94	13
of my harmful deeds	"	111	2
my deeds must not be shown	"	121	12
save in thy deeds	"	131	13
the very refuse of thy deeds	"	150	6
by him became his deed	L C	....	111
Deem—but dull and slow she deems	R L	....	1336
but fairer we it deem	Son	54	3
Deemed—and for true things deem'd	"	96	8
which is so deemed	"	121	3
Deep—Then love's deep groans	V A	....	377
but deep desire hath none	"	....	389
Sad pause and deep regard	R L	....	277
Deep woes roll forward	"	....	1118
And with deep groans	"	....	1132
Some dark, deep desert	"	....	1144
Till after a deep groan	"	....	1276
And that deep torture	"	....	1287
Deep sounds make lesser noise	"	....	1329
Deep—show'd deep regard	R L	....	1409
By deep surmise of others' detriment	"	....	1579
which deep impression bears	"	....	1712
bail it from the deep unrest	"	....	1725
The deep vexation	"	....	1779
Wherein deep policy did him disguise	"	....	1815
And that deep vow	"	....	1847
And dig deep trenches	Son	2	2
have full as deep a dye	"	54	5
upon your soundless deep	"	80	10
praise the deep vermillion	"	98	10
For that deep wound	"	133	2
I have sworn deep oaths of thy deep kindness	"	152	9
arguments and question deep	L C	....	121
whose deep conceit is such	P P	8	7
And I in deep delight	"	8	11
Deep in the thigh	"	9	11
My sighs so deep	"	18	31
Deep-brain'd—And .... sonnets	L C	....	209
Deep-dark—Into the deep-dark cabins of her head	V A	....	1034
Deep-drenched—deep-drenched in a sea of care	R L	....	1100
Deeper—O, deeper sin	"	....	701
Deepest—My deepest sense	Son	120	10
Deep-green—The .... emerald	L C	....	213
Deeply—upon her back deeply distress'd	V A	....	814
Passion on passion deeply is redoubled	"	....	832
Deep-sore—hearts'.... wounding	"	....	432
Deep-sunken—thine own .... eyes	Son	2	7
Deep-sweet—Ear's.... music	V A	....	432
Deep-wounded—.... with a boar	P P	9	10
Deer—thou shalt be my deer	V A	....	231
Then be my deer	"	....	239
sorteth with a herd of deer	"	....	689
As the poor frighted deer	R L	....	1149
And stall'd the deer	P P	19	2
Deface—winter's ragged hand deface	Son	6	1
nor none falser to deface her	P P	7	6
Defaced—soul's fair temple is	R L	....	719
by Time's fell hand defaced	Son	64	1
Defame—dark harbour for defame	R L	....	768
minstrels tuning my defame	"	....	817
thou livest in my defame	"	....	1033
Defeat—true love that doth my rest defeat	Son	61	11
Defeated—me of thee defeated	"	20	11
Defeature—with impure defeature	V A	....	736
Defect—But having no defects	"	....	138
torments us with defect	R L	....	855
God wot, it was defect	"	....	1345
see thee frown on my defects	Son	49	2
shall not be thy defect	"	70	1
doth worship thy defect	"	149	11
Defence—'gainst Time's scythe can make defence	"	12	13
making no defence	"	89	4
my o'er-press'd defence	"	139	8
As passing all conceit needs no defence	P P	8	8
Defend—can so well defend her	V A	....	472
the growing rose defends	R L	....	492
defend thy loyal dame	"	....	1034
suppose thou dost defend me	"	....	1684

Defendant—the defendant doth that plea deny		Son	46	7		
Defiled—by him defiled		R L		787		
let forth my foul-defiled blood		"		1029		
With outward honesty, but yet defiled		"		1545		
Defiling—vows were ever brokers to defiling		L C		173		
Define—And for myself mine own worth do define		Son	62	7		
Deflower—quoth he 'I must....		R L		348		
Deformed'st—or.... creature		Son	113	10		
Defunctive—That.... music can		P T		14		
Defy—Thy registers and thee I both defy		Son	123	9		
Age, I do defy thee		P P	12	11		
Defying—Faith's defying		"	18	6		
Degenerate—with deeds degenerate		R L		1003		
Deified—new lodged and newly....		L C		84		
Deign—If thou wilt.... this favour		V A		15		
Delay—haste is mated with delays		"		909		
the glove, that did delay him		R L		325		
unhallow'd haste her words delays		"		552		
many accents and delays		"		1719		
Delay'd—Her audit, though delay'd		Son	126	11		
Delicious—His taste delicious		R L		699		
Delight—better'd with a more....		V A		78		
My day's delight is past		"		380		
aim at like delight		"		400		
on her fair delight		"		1030		
in that sky of his delight		R L		12		
shame that follows sweet delight		"		357		
her life, her world's delight		"		385		
marks thee for my earth's delight		"		487		
chides his vanish'd, loathed delight		"		742		
false slave to false delight		"		927		
sweet hours from love's delight		Son	36	8		
decrepit father takes delight		"	37	1		
to heart's and eye's delight		"	47	14		
or pursuing no delight		"	75	11		
Or more delight than hawks		"	91	11		
but figures of delight		"	98	11		
lose their dear delight		"	102	12		
is there more delight		"	130	7		
And I in deep delight		P P	8	11		
thus dissembled her delight		"	19	16		
Delight—Do I delight to die		V A		496		
others, they think, delight		"		843		
by nature they delight		R L		697		
joy delights in joy		Son	8	2		
Delights to peep		"	24	12		
stories to delight his ear		P P	4	5		
Delighted—with thy tongue's tune delighted		Son	141	5		
Delightful—and high.... plain		V A		236		
Delighting—and ravishment....		R L		430		
Deliver—and she delivers it		"		1333		
For it no form delivers to the heart		Son	113	5		
Deliver'd—deliver'd from thy brain		"	77	11		
Delve—And delves the parallels		"	60	10		
Delving—where earth-delving conies keep		V A		687		
Demand—Demand of him		L C		149		
Demeanour—he by dumb demeanour seeks to show		R L		474		
Demure—doth give...good-morrow		"		1219		
Denial—but denial and reproving		"		242		
He in the worst sense construes their denial		"		324		
Denied—mayst thou be denied		Son	142	14		
Denote—then love doth well denote		"	148	7		
Deny—If thou deny, then force		R L		513		
deny that thou bear'st love		Son	10	1		
doth that plea deny		"	46	7		
And deny himself for Jove		P P	17	17		
Denying—Love's denying		"	18	5		
Depart—that he may depart		V A		578		
He thence departs		R L		743		
if thou shouldst depart		Son	6	11		
As easy might I from myself depart		"	109	3		
Departest—from that which thou....		"	11	2		
Depend—it depends upon that love		"	92	4		
on thy humour doth depend		"	92	8		
truth and beauty on my love depends		"	101	3		
that do on mine depend		L C		274		
Depending—words are now....		R L		1615		
Deprive—to deprive dishonour'd life		"		1186		
Deprived—which thou hast here....		"		1752		
Derive—my knowledge I derive		Son	14	9		
Derived—Thou wast not to this end from me derived		R L		1755		
Descant—To descant on the doubts		P P	14	4		
Descant'st—on Tereus descant'st		R L		1134		
Descended—with slow-sad gait....		"		1081		
descended her sheaved hat		L C		31		
Descending—the heat of this descending sun		V A		190		
Describe—Describe Adonis, and the counterfeit		Son	53	5		
Descried—....in men's nativity		R L		538		
Description—I see descriptions of the fairest wights		Son	106	2		
Desert—Some deep dark desert		R L		1144		
Desert—with your most high deserts		Son	17	2		
knowledge of mine own desert		"	49	10		
As to behold desert		"	66	2		
than mine own desert		"	72	6		
your great deserts repay		"	117	2		
Where thy desert may merit praise		P P	19	27		
Deserve—Deserves the travail		Son	79	6		
may deserve to pitied be		"	142	12		
deserve not punishment		P P	3	4		
Deserved—deserved a greater fee		V A		609		
deserved thy beauty's use		Son	2	9		
Deservest—which thou....alone		"	39	8		
Deserving—where is my deserving		"	87	6		
Design—a meritorious fair design		R L		1692		
soft audience to my sweet design		L C		278		
Desire—desire doth lend her force		V A		29		
but frosty in desire		"		36		
and his high desire		"		276		
approach of sweet desire		"		386		
deep desire hath none		"		389		
or life desire		"		496		
Now quick desire		"		547		
Love in his desire		"		653		
desire sees best of all		"		720		
desire's foul nurse		"		773		
drops of hot desire		"		1074		
unto himself was his desire		"		1180		
trustless wings of false desire		R L		2		
toss'd between desire and dread		"		171		
by brain-sick rude desire		"		175		
Lucrece must I force to my desire		"		182		
or were he not my dear friend, this desire		"		234		
Desire my pilot is		"		279		

Desire—By reprobate desire	R L	300
which fond desire doth scorch	"	314
not to foul desire	"	574
His true respect will prison false desire	"	642
This hot desire	"	691
Drunken Desire must vomit	"	703
or rein his rash desire	"	706
Feeble Desire, all recreant	"	710
Desire doth fight with Grace	"	712
But if the like the snow-white swan desire	"	1011
check'd his son's desire	"	1490
to answer his desire	"	1606
If thou my love's desire do contradict	"	1631
should be thy chief desire	Son 10	8
The first my thought, the other my desire	" 45	3
with my desire keep pace	" 51	9
Therefore desire, of perfect'st love being made	" 51	10
times of your desire	" 57	2
make them born to our desire	" 123	7
Desire is death	" 147	8
And so the general of hot desire	" 154	7
Of pensive and subdued desires	L C	219
Desire—From fairest creatures we desire increase	Son 1	1
Dost thou desire my slumbers	" 61	3
nor smell, desire to be invited	" 141	7
privileged by age, desires to know	L C	62
When he again desires her	"	66
ere he desire, have granted	"	131
And twice desire ere it be day	P P 19	17
Desired—but strongly he desired	R L	415
to set a form upon desired change	Son 89	6
the help of bath desired	" 153	11
nor being desired yielded	L C	149
Desiring—Desiring this man's art	Son 29	7
Despair—grief and damn'd despair	V A	743
as one full of despair	"	955
Despair, and hope	"	988
Despair to gain doth traffic	R L	131
another white despair	Son 99	9
of comfort and despair	" 144	7
of comfort and despair	P P 2	1
Despair—of time's help to despair	R L	983
For, if I should despair	Son 140	9
Despairing—.... Hecuba beheld	R L	1447
Desperate—as desperate in his suit	V A	336
stirs up a desperate courage	"	556
theirs whose desperate hands	"	765
and in a desperate rage	R L	219
She, desperate, with her nails	"	739
some desperate instrument	"	1038
I desperate now approve	Son 147	7
Despise—looking scornfully he doth despise	R L	187
that loves what they despise	Son 141	3
thy service to despise	" 149	10
Despised—...., rheumatic, and cold	V A	135
I am not lame, poor, nor despised	Son 37	9
Time's spoils despised everywhere	" 100	12
but despised straight	" 129	5
Despising—myself almost despising	" 29	9
Despite—in high heaven's despite	V A	731
despite of fruitless chastity	"	751
boasted blushes in despite	R L	55
Despite—despite of cure remain	R L	732
at my confirm'd despite	"	1026
Despite of wrinkles	Son 3	12
despite thy wrong	" 19	13
For then despite of space	" 44	3
despite his cruel hand	" 60	14
despite thy scythe and thee	" 123	14
Who, in despite of view	" 141	4
Despitefully—despitefully I mean to bear thee	R L	670
Destined—The destined ill	L C	156
Destiny—she bribed the Destinies	V A	733
The Destinies will curse thee	"	945
date from cancell'd Destiny	R L	1729
Destitute—turrets .... and pale	"	441
Destroy—each other did destroy	V A	346
If thou destroy them not	"	760
doth my love destroy	"	1163
who will the vine destroy	R L	215
I purpose to destroy thee	"	514
the city to destroy	"	1369
the user so destroys it	Son 9	12
Detain—can no more detain him	V A	577
She may detain, but not still keep	Son 126	10
Determinate—in thee are all	" 87	4
Determination—Find no	" 13	6
Determined—by their verdict is	" 46	11
Determining—.... which way to fly	R L	1150
Detest—made herself herself detest	"	1566
Detriment—surmise of others'	"	1579
Device—but your device in love	V A	789
from them no device can take	R L	535
Lo, this device was sent me	L C	232
Devil—adored by this devil	R L	85
profaned in such a devil	"	847
a hideous, shapeless devil	"	973
the semblance of a devil	"	1246
constant and confirmed devil	"	1513
Such devils steal effects	"	1555
my saint to be a devil	Son 144	7
my saint to be a devil	P P 2	7
Devise—Devise extremes beyond extremity	R L	969
devise some virtuous lie	Son 72	5
poets can in praise devise	" 83	14
Devised—yet when they have	" 82	9
Deviseth—Danger deviseth shifts	V A	690
Devour—Devours his will	R L	700
What virtue breeds iniquity devours	"	872
but that which doth devour	"	1256
devour her own sweet brood	Son 19	2
Devour'd—Not that devour'd, but that which	R L	1256
Devouring—.... all in haste	V A	57
lived by foul devouring	R L	700
Devouring Time, blunt thou	Son 19	1
Dew—morning's silver-melting dew	R L	24
resembling dew of night	"	396
relenting dew of lamentations	"	1829
Dew-bedabbled—the .... wretch	V A	703
Dew'd—So they were dew'd	"	66
Dewy—weep like the dewy night	R L	1232
dried up the dewy morn	P P 6	1
Dexterity—quick bearing and	R L	1389
Dial—which stop the hourly dial	"	327
Thy dial how thy precious minutes	Son 77	2
by thy dial's shady stealth	" 77	7
Dialect—He had the dialect	L C	125

DIAL-HAND — DID

Entry	Ref	Line
Dial-hand—beauty like a....	Son 104	9
Dialogued—And dialogued for him	L C	132
Diamond—The diamond, why, 'twas beautiful	"	211
Dian—Make modest Dian	V A	725
A maid of Dian's	Son 153	2
Diapason—with deep groans the diapason	R L	1132
Did—did he raise his chin	V A	85
what she did crave	"	88
Never did passenger in summer's heat	"	91
in battle ne'er did bow	"	99
did hotly overlook them	"	178
so did this horse	"	293
he did not lack	"	299
each other did destroy	"	346
her eyes did rain	"	360
did honey passage yield	"	452
he did think to reprehend	"	470
love did wittily prevent	"	471
When he did frown	"	571
my joints did tremble	"	642
where did I leave	"	715
late did wonder	"	748
So did the merciless	"	821
did feed her sight	"	822
tears did lend and borrow	"	961
she did follow	"	975
I did but jest	"	997
I did but act	"	1006
he did see his face	"	1109
did not whet his teeth	"	1113
never did he bless	"	1119
Collatine unwisely did not let	R L	10
did him peculiar duties	"	14
disdainfully did sting	"	40
some untimely thought did instigate	"	43
No comfortable star did lend his light	"	164
fondly I did dote	"	207
fear did make her colour rise	"	257
her husband's welfare she did hear	"	263
the glove that did delay him	"	325
What did he note	"	415
as his hand did scale	"	440
I did entertain thee	"	596
did I entertain him	"	842
he did complain him	"	845
When Tarquin did	"	917
who did thy stock pollute	"	1063
that did my fame confound	"	1202
Such danger to resistance did belong	"	1265
did make him more amazed	"	1356
peasants did so well resemble	"	1392
from his lips did fly	"	1406
some mermaid did their ears entice	"	1411
no semblance did remain	"	1453
Lucrece swears he did her wrong	"	1462
fond Paris, did incur	"	1473
as Priam him did cherish	"	1546
So did I Tarquin, so my Troy did perish	"	1547
where you did fulfil	"	1635
act of lust, and so did kill	"	1636
I did begin to start and cry	"	1639
That blow did hail it	"	1725
I often did behold	"	1738
Did—I did give that life	R L	1800
policy did him disguise	"	1815
at him, did his words allow	"	1845
They did conclude to bear	"	1850
Romans plausibly did give consent	"	1854
Those hours that with gentle work did frame	Son 5	1
Which erst from heat did canopy the herd	"	12	6
their parts of me to thee did give	"	31	11
early morn did shine	"	33	9
my foot did stand	"	44	5
the wretch did know	"	50	7
where they did proceed	"	76	8
I alone did call upon thy aid	"	79	1
you did painting need	"	83	1
you did exceed	"	83	3
you did impute	"	83	9
That did my ripe thoughts in my brain inhearse	"	86	3
heaven in thy creation did decree	"	93	9
Nor did I wonder	"	98	9
I with these did play	"	98	14
The forward violet thus did I chide	"	99	1
on thorns did stand	"	99	8
her mournful hymn did hush the night	"	102	10
That did not better for my life provide	"	111	3
I did strive to prove	"	117	13
To bitter sauces did I frame my feeding	"	118	6
sorrow which I then did feel	"	120	2
Love's own hand did make	"	145	1
Straight in her heart did mercy come	"	145	5
which physic did except	"	147	8
fire did quickly steep	"	153	3
Oft did she heave her napkin	L C	15
As they did battery	"	23
in her threaden fillet still did bide	"	33
in his fair parts she did abide	"	83
did hang in crooked curls	"	85
did enchant the mind	"	89
Did livery falseness in a pride of truth	"	105
still did wake and sleep	"	123
did in the general bosom	"	127
that did his picture get	"	134
that did in freedom stand	"	143
Yet did I not as some my equals did	"	148
Till now did ne'er invite	"	182
that so their shame did find	"	187
sonnets that did amplify	"	209
his invised properties did tend	"	212
that burning lungs did raise	"	228
noble suit in court did shun	"	234
and did thence remove	"	237
which did no form receive	"	241
did her force subdue	"	248
his watery eyes he did dismount	"	281
and mine did him restore	"	301
did win whom he would maim	"	312
from his heart did fly	"	325
did not the heavenly rhetoric	P P	3	1
I did court the lad	"	4	3
unripe years did want conceit	"	4	9
she hotter that did look	"	6	7
did I see a fair sweet youth	"	9	9

DID 75 DISDAIN

Did—thou left'st me more than I did crave	P P	10	9
how god Mars did try her	"	11	3
her lips on his did act the seizure	"	11	10
sweetly did she smile	"	14	7
that love with love did fight	"	16	5
did bear the maid away	"	16	14
Beasts did leap, and birds did sing	"	21	5
Trees did grow, and plants did spring	"	21	6
Everything did banish moan	"	21	7
between them love did shine	P T	....	33
Didst—O, thou didst kill me	V A	....	499
thou didst name the boar	"	....	611
Didst thou not mark	"	....	643
thou didst teach the way	R L	....	630
Why didst thou promise	Son	34	1
thou didst forsake me	"	89	1
whence didst thou steal	"	93	2
thou didst bequeath to me	P P	10	12
Die—there he could not die	V A	....	246
Do I delight to die	"	....	496
and die forsworn	"	....	726
like a glutton dies	"	....	803
who lives and must not die	"	....	1017
he could not die	"	....	1060
shall I die by drops	"	....	1071
And die, unhallow'd thoughts	R L	....	192
Yea, though I die	"	....	204
with trembling terror die	"	....	231
fear, avaunt! debating, die	"	....	274
threats if he mounts he dies	"	....	508
The patient dies	"	....	991
For if I die my honour lives	"	....	1032
I need not fear to die	"	....	1052
thereon fall and die	"	....	1139
To live or die	"	....	1154
Yet die I will not	"	....	1177
Thou dead, both die	"	....	1211
the dame and daughter die	"	....	1477
here Priam dies	"	....	1485
the judge is robb'd, the prisoner dies	"	....	1652
yet let the traitor die	"	....	1686
The old bees discern	"	....	1769
Thy father die	"	....	1771
to die with her a space	"	....	1776
beauty's rose might never die	Son	1	2
Die single, and thine image dies	"	3	14
thou issueless shalt hap to die	"	9	3
Thou shouldst print more, not let that copy die	"	11	14
And die as fast as they see others grow	"	12	12
they in their glory die	"	25	8
Die to themselves	"	54	11
Save that, to die I leave my love	"	66	14
to all the world must die	"	81	6
happy to die	"	92	12
Though to itself it only live and die	"	94	10
Which die for goodness	"	124	14
A flower that dies when first	P P	13	3
Died—And died to kiss his shadow	V A	....	162
but died unkind	"	....	204
But now I died	"	....	498
lived and died with him	"	....	1080
in that darksome prison died	R L	....	579
But since he died	Son	32	13
lived and died as flowers do	"	68	2
Diest—Unlook'd on, diest unless	"	7	14
Dieted—ay, dieted in grace	L C	....	261
Difference—leaves out difference	Son	105	8
our drops this difference bore	L C	....	390
Different—Of different flowers	Son	98	6
the dialect and different skill	L C	....	125
Dig—His snout digs sepulchres	V A	....	622
And dig deep trenches	Son	2	2
Digestion—in digestion souring	R L	....	699
Dignified—they basely dignified	"	....	660
and therein dignified	Son	101	4
Dignify—so dignifies his story	"	84	8
Dignity—proud of such a dignity	R L	....	437
The bravest weed outbraves his dignity	Son	94	12
Digression—digression is so vile	R L	....	202
Dilligence—done with speedy	"	....	1853
Dim—dim darkness doth display	"	....	118
And death's dim look	"	....	403
In his dim mist	"	....	548
And wipe the dim mist	"	....	643
Dim register and notary	"	....	765
in her dim element	"	....	1588
fair fresh mirror, dim and old	"	....	1760
Diminish'd—Be any jot diminish'd	V A	....	417
Dimm'd—torch .... and controll'd	R L	....	448
is his gold complexion dimm'd	Son	18	6
Dimple—appears a pretty dimple	V A	....	242
Dimpled—her snow-white .... chin	R L	....	420
Dint—snow takes any dint	V A	....	354
Dire—The dire imagination	"	....	975
And the dire thought	R L	....	972
war and dire events	V A	....	1159
Directed—are bright in dark	Son	43	4
Direction—by their own direction	V A	....	216
Directly—yet not directly tell	Son	144	10
yet not directly tell	P P	2	10
Direful—stern and .... god of war	V A	....	98
exclaiming on the direful night	R L	....	741
Dirge—Begins the sad dirge	"	....	1612
Disabled—by limping sway disabled	Son	66	8
Disarm'd—by a virgin hand disarm'd	"	154	8
Disbursed—And all my fame that lives disbursed be	R L	....	1203
Discern—wherein it shall discern	"	....	619
Discharge—.... one word of woe	"	....	1605
Discharged—from .... cannon fumes	"	....	1043
Disciplined—Who ...., ay, dieted	L C	....	261
Discloses—their masked buds	Son	54	8
Discolour'd—and lean .... cheek	R L	....	708
Discontent—servile to all discontents	V A	....	1161
in shows of discontent	R L	....	1580
thus attired in discontent	"	....	1601
blow of thralled discontents	Son	124	7
her poor infant's discontent	"	143	8
By discontent so breaking	L C	....	56
Thy discontent thou didst bequeath	P P	10	12
Discord—Melodious discord, heavenly tune	V A	....	431
My restless discord loves no stops	R L	....	1124
Discourse—Bid me discourse	V A	....	145
My thoughts and my discourse	Son	147	11
Discovery—discovery of her way	V A	....	828
She dares not therefore make discovery	R L	....	1314
Disdain—in a dull disdain	V A	....	33
Servile to my coy disdain	"	....	112
smiles as in disdain	"	....	241
bondage in disdain	"	....	394

Disdain—and such disdain	V A	....	501
will hold thee in disdain	"	....	761
disdain and deadly enmity	R L	....	503
hang their heads at this disdain	"	....	521
converts to cold disdain	"	....	691
torments me with disdain	Son	132	2
with too much disdain	"	140	2
was wounded with disdain	P P	16	11
Disdain—dishonour to disdain him	R L	....	844
Disdain to him disdained scraps	"	....	987
disdains the tillage	Son	3	6
Disdained—eyes disdain'd the wooing	V A	....	358
disdained scraps to give	R L	....	987
Disdaineth—my love no whit	Son	33	13
Disdainfully—.... did sting	R L	....	40
Disease—longer nurseth the disease	Son	147	2
Diseased—To be diseased	"	118	8
For men diseased	"	154	12
Disgrace—love but to disgrace it	V A	....	412
disgrace me half so ill	Son	89	5
As I'll myself disgrace	"	89	7
May time disgrace	"	126	8
Disgrace—blush at her own disgrace	R L	....	479
The same disgrace which they themselves behold	"	....	751
lies martyr'd with disgrace	"	....	802
O unseen shame! invisible disgrace	"	....	827
Of her disgrace	"	....	1320
When, in disgrace with fortune	Son	29	1
to wost, with this disgrace	"	33	8
and cures not the disgrace	"	34	8
and doing me disgrace	"	103	8
if not lives in disgrace	"	127	8
cures all disgrace in me	P P	3	8
Disgraced—he stands disgraced	R L	....	718
in them doth stand disgraced	"	....	1833
perfection wrongfully disgraced	Son	66	7
Disguise—polley did him disguise	R L	....	1815
Disguised—with chaps and wrinkles were disguised	"	....	1452
Dishevell'd—with long .... hair	V A	....	147
in my dishevell'd hair	"	....	1129
Dishonour—O foul dishonour to my household's grave	"	....	198
To privilege dishonour	"	....	621
Black lust, dishonour, shame	"	....	654
For it had been dishonour	"	....	844
Dishonoured—my body so	"	....	1185
to deprive dishonour'd life	"	....	1186
Disjoin'd—till breathless he	V A	....	541
Disliking—dark, disliking eye	"	....	182
Dismal—This dismal cry	"	....	889
Dismay'd—her senses all dismay'd	"	....	896
and will not be dismay'd	R L	....	273
Dismiss—Dismiss your vows	V A	....	425
Dismount—his watery eyes he did dismount	L C	....	281
Disorder—Disorder breeds by heating	V A	....	742
Dispatch—and makes all swift	Son	113	3
Dispensation—with good thoughts makes dispensation	R L	....	248
Dispense—never will dispense	"	....	1070
I thus far can dispense	"	....	1279
with the foul act dispense	"	....	1704
with my neglect I do dispense	Son	112	12
Disperse—under thee their poesy disperse	"	78	4
Dispersed—In thy sea dispersed	R L	....	658
The dispersed air	"	....	1805
Displacest—and displacest laud	"	....	887
Display—dim darkness doth display	"	....	118
Display'd—his gaudy banner is	"	....	272
Disposed—.... to set me light	Son	88	1
Disposing—To the disposing	V A	....	1040
Disposition—with noble disposition	R L	....	1095
Dispraise—Cannot dispraise but in a kind	Son	95	7
Disputation—graceless holds he disputation	R L	....	246
made a theme for disputation	"	....	822
Holds disputation with each thing	"	....	1101
Dissemble—the boar, not to	V A	....	641
Dissembled—thus .... her delight	P P	19	16
Dissembled with an outward show	"	19	38
Dissension—And set dissension	V A	....	1160
Dissentious—Dissentious Jealousy	"	....	657
Dissolve—Would in thy palm dissolve	"	....	144
dissolves with tempering	"	....	565
Dissolved—For stones .... to water	R L	....	592
Dissolution—frost hath dissolution	"	....	355
Dissuade—.... one foolish heart	Son	141	10
Distain—silver-shining queen he would distain	R L	....	786
Distained—her tear-distained eye	"	....	1586
Distance—Injurious distance should not stop	Son	44	2
With safest distance	L C	....	151
But kept cold distance	"	....	237
Distance and no space, was seen	P T	....	30
Distant—And comely-distant sits he	L C	....	65
Distemper'd—a sad .... guest	Son	153	12
Distempering—.... gentle love	V A	....	653
Distill—by verse distills your truths	Son	54	14
Distillation—summer's distillation	"	5	9
Distill'd—But flowers distill'd	"	5	13
ere thou be distill'd	"	6	2
Distill'd from limbecks	"	119	2
Distilling—with such .... showers	V A	....	66
Distinct—Two distincts, division none	P T	....	27
Distinguish—.... what he said	R L	....	1785
Distract—Their distract parcels	L C	....	231
Distractedly—sight .... commix'd	"	....	28
Distraction—In the distraction	Son	119	8
Distress—Distress likes dumps	R L	....	1127
where all distress is stell'd	"	....	1444
distress and dolour dwell'd	"	....	1446
Distress'd—upon her back deeply distress'd	V A	....	814
her heart, poor citizen! distress'd	R L	....	465
Disturb—stealing in,.... the feast	V A	....	450
Disturb his hours of rest	R L	....	974
Disturbed—with disturbed mind	V A	....	340
From sleep disturbed	R L	....	454
Disturbing—where love reigns, disturbing Jealousy	V A	....	649
Ditty—a woeful ditty	"	....	836
welcome daylight with her ditty	P P	15	7
there sung the dolefull'st ditty	"	21	11
Dive-dapper—Like a dive-dapper	V A	....	86
Divert—Divert strong minds	Son	115	8
Diverted—Sometime diverted their poor balls	L C	....	24
Divide—from her breast it doth	R L	....	1737
How to divide the conquest	Son	46	2
with his hearing to divide	L C	....	67

Entry	Ref	Col	Line
Divided—let us divided live	Son 39		5
Dividing—their present fall by this dividing	R L		551
Divination—fear doth teach it	V. t		670
Divine—that were divine	"		730
that which is divine	R L		193
beholds, as more divine	"		291
the other made divine	"		1164
but yet like prayers divine	Son 108		5
Buy terms divine	"		146	11
Divining—look'd but with .... eyes	"	106	11
Be the death-divining swan	P T		15
Division—Two distincts, ... none	"		27
Saw division grow together	"		42
Divorce—Hateful divorce of love	V. t		932
Do—to do a goddess good	"		28
do her intendments break	"		222
this I do to captivate	"		281
hard heart do steel it	"		375
Do I delight to die	"		496
Do summon us to part	"		531
Her arms do lend	"		539
Do surfeit by the eye	"		602
to do with such foul fiends	"		638
air and water do abate	"		654
What should I do	"		667
Then do they spend	"		695
Nay, do not struggle	"		710
so do thy lips	"		724
themselves do slay	"		765
You do it for increase	"		791
As caterpillars do	"		798
Do burn themselves	"		810
Swelling dugs do ache	"		875
thoughts do seldom dream	R L		87
so then we do neglect	"		152
sparks of fire do fly	"		177
bids them do their liking	"		434
Do tell her she is dreadfully beset	"		444
do I mean to place him	"		517
do not then ensnare me	"		584
do not deceive me	"		585
stones dissolved to water do convert	"		592
put on his shape to do him shame	"		597
darest do such outrage	"		605
eyes do learn, do read, do look	"		616
Men's faults do seldom to themselves appear	"		633
do presently abuse it	"		864
have to do with thee	"		911
to do me good	"		1028
hath nought to do	"		1092
would do it good	"		1117
husband, do thou take	"		1200
to do her husband wrong	"		1264
would do me good	"		1274
do it leisurely	"		1349
These contraries such unity do hold	"		1558
If thou my love's desire do contradict	"		1631
through his lips do throng	"		1783
do not take away	"		1796
Do wounds help wounds	"		1822
do not steep thy heart	"		1828
what could death do	Son	6	11
do offend thine ear	"	8	6
They do but sweetly chide thee	"	8	7
All in one, one pleasing note do sing	"	8	12
When I do count the clock	"	12	1

Entry	Ref	Col	Line
Do—of thy beauty do I question make	Son	12	9
beauties do themselves forsake	"	12	11
from the stars do I my judgement pluck	"	14	1
wherefore do not you a mightier way	"	16	1
rough winds do shake the darling buds	"	18	3
do whate'er thou wilt	"	19	6
Him in thy course untainted do allow	"	19	11
Yet do thy worst, old Time	"	19	13
how I do love thee	"	26	13
which the blind do see	"	27	8
Do in consent shake hands	"	28	6
when clouds do blot the heaven	"	28	10
blots that do with me remain	"	36	3
my bewailed guilt should do thee shame	"	36	10
But do not so	"	36	13
To see his active child do deeds of youth	"	37	2
Entitled in thy parts do crowned sit	"	37	7
If my slight Muse do please these curious days	"	38	13
I do forgive thy robbery	"	40	9
then do mine eyes best see	"	43	1
when dreams do show thee me	"	43	14
that time do I ensconce me	"	49	9
How heavy do I journey	"	50	1
Sweet roses do not so	"	54	11
and do not kill	"	56	7
what should I do but tend	"	57	1
Nor services to do	"	57	4
Though you do any thing	"	57	14
So do our minutes hasten	"	60	2
all forwards do contend	"	60	4
shadows like to thee do mock my sight	"	61	4
for myself mine own worth do define	"	62	7
do I now fortify	"	63	9
as flowers do now	"	68	2
accents do this praise confound	"	69	7
Do not so much as my poor name rehearse	"	71	11
to do more for me	"	72	6
or none, or few, do hang	"	73	2
Thus do I pine	"	75	13
do I not glance aside	"	76	3
when I of you do write	"	80	1
And do so, love	"	82	9
For how do I hold thee	"	87	5
The injuries that to myself I do	"	88	11
should do it wrong	"	89	11
And do not drop in for	"	90	4
Ah, do not, when	"	90	5
do not leave me last	"	90	9
But do thy worst	"	92	1
what a happy title do I find	"	92	11
will do none	"	94	1
That do not do the thing they most do show	"	94	2
They rightfully do inherit	"	94	5
But do not so	"	96	13
Then do thy office	"	101	13
O, for my sake do you with Fortune chide	"	111	1

Do—with my neglect I do dispense	*Son*	112	12	**Done**—to do what's done by night	*R L* 1092
Those lines that I before have writ do lie	"	115	1	that hath done him wrong	" 1467
all bonds do tie me	"	117	4	might be done to me	" 1623
that I do change	"	123	1	done with speedy diligence	" 1853
This I do vow	"	123	13	what good turn eyes for eyes have done	*Son* 24 9
Do I envy those	"	128	5	at that which thou hast done	" 35 1
do witness bear	"	131	11	first in character was done	" 59 8
I do believe her	"	138	2	griefs have done their spite	" 90 10
Yet do not so	"	139	13	Now all is done	" 110 9
do not press	"	140	1	of a beauty spent and done	*L C* 11
I do not love thee	"	141	1	Harm have I done to them	" 198
Or, if it do, not from those lips	"	142	5	**Doom**—in this shameful doom	*R L* 672
two spirits do suggest me	"	144	2	himself he sounds this doom	" 717
Do I not think on thee	"	149	3	to the general doom	" 924
I do call my friend	"	149	5	to this advised doom	" 1849
that I do fawn upon	"	149	6	and beauty's doom and date	*Son* 14 14
do I not spend	"	149	7	out to the ending doom	" 55 12
merit do I in myself	"	149	9	forfeit to a confined doom	" 107 4
what others do abhor	"	150	11	even to the edge of doom	" 116 12
I do betray	"	151	5	in giving gentle doom	" 145 7
do I accuse thee	"	152	5	**Door**—double-lock the door	*V A* 448
sometimes they do extend	*L C*		25	The threshold grates the door	*R L* 306
What's sweet to do, to do will aptly find	"		88	The doors, the wind, the glove	" 325
their sickly radiance do amend	"	....	214	unto the chamber door	" 337
that do on mine depend	"	....	274	the door he opens wide	" 359
and yet do question make	"	....	321	a press of people at a door	" 1301
What I should do again	"	....	322	**Dost**—why dost abhor me	*V A* 138
I do believe her	*P P*	1	2	thou dost survive	" 173
two spirits do suggest me still	"	2	2	why dost thou feel it	" 373
O do not love that wrong	"	5	13	whereon thou dost lie	" 646
Age, I do abhor thee, youth, I do adore thee	"	12	9	as thou dost lend	" 864
				what dost thou mean	" 933
Age, I do defy thee	"	12	11	at random dost thou hit	" 940
All thy fellow birds do sing	"	21	25	Dost thou drink tears	" 949
If Fortune once do frown	"	21	47	If thou dost weep for grief	*R L* 1272
Doctor-like—folly, doctor-like, controlling skill	*Son*	66	19	that thou dost trembling stand	" 1599
				suppose thou dost defend me	" 1684
Doe—Like a milch doe	*V A*	....	875	Thou dost beguile the world	*Son* 3 4
a poor unseasonable doe	*R L*	....	581	why dost thou spend	" 4 1
Dog—No dog shall rouse thee	*V A*	....	240	why dost thou abuse	" 4 5
the dogs exclaim aloud	"	....	886	why dost thou use	" 4 7
He, like a thievish dog	*R L*	....	736	Thou of thyself thy sweet self dost deceive	" 4 10
My curtal dog, that wont to have play'd	*P P*	18	29	And dost him grace	" 28 10
Doing—pardon of self-doing crime	*Son*	58	12	While thou dost breathe	" 38 2
Doing thee vantage	"	88	12	thou thyself dost give invention light	" 38 8
and doing me disgrace	"	103	8	Thou dost love her	" 42 6
by the well-doing steed	*L C*		112	where thou dost stay	" 44 4
Doleful—rings out the doleful knell	*R L*		1495	thou in him dost lie	" 46 5
wether's bell rings doleful knell	*P P*	18	28	Dost thou desire	" 61 3
to see my doleful plight	"	18	33	thou dost wake elsewhere	" 61 13
Dolefull'st—sung the .... ditty	"	21	11	thou dost common grow	" 69 14
Dolour—distress and dolour dwell'd	*R L*		1446	thou dost review	" 74 5
To think their dolour	"	....	1582	thou dost but mend the style	" 78 11
Done—life were done	*V A*		197	and dost advance	" 78 13
Her words are done	"	....	254	thou thyself dost pay	" 79 14
done me double wrong	"	....	429	whom thou dost hate	" 89 14
wasted, thaw'd, and done	"	....	749	How sweet and lovely dost thou make the shame	" 95 1
ere summer half be done	"	....	802	dost thou thy sins inclose	" 95 4
and are never done	"	....	846	So dost thou too	" 101 4
hath done thee wrong	"	....	1005	What thou dost foist upon us that is old	" 123 6
as soon decay'd and done	*R L*		23	Dost hold Time's fickle glass	" 126 2
hath done her beauty wrong	"	....	80	what dost thou to mine eyes	" 137 1
That done, some worthless slave	"	....	515	If thou dost seek to have what thou dost hide	" 142 13
A little harm done	"	....	528		
'Have done,' quoth he	"	....	645		
That done, despitefully	"	....	670		

Dost—Why dost thou pine within	Son	146	3
Dost thou upon thy fading mansions spend	"	146	6
witness dost thou bear	L. C.		53
Dote—and old men dote	V. A.		837
how fondly I did dote	R. L.		207
And dotes on what he looks	"		497
Is pleased to dote	Son	141	4
whereon my false eyes dote	"	148	5
made the blossoms dote	L. C.		235
Doted—on that he firmly doted	R. L.		416
Doteth—franticly she doteth	V. A.		1059
Doth—desire doth lend her force	"		29
Now doth she stroke his cheek, now doth he frown	"		45
Doth quench the maiden	"		50
she doth anew begin	"		60
As the spring doth yearly grow	"		141
The sun doth burn my face	"		186
doth little harm	"		195
doth provoke a pause	"		218
how doth she now for wits	"		249
doth urge releasing	"		256
courser doth espy	"		261
vapours doth he send	"		274
swiftly doth forsake him	"		321
Love's fire doth assuage	"		334
as the wolf doth grin	"		459
The mellow plum doth fall	"		527
doth pitch the price	"		551
Her face doth reek and smoke, her blood doth boil	"		555
She doth protest	"		581
she doth prove	"		597
when he doth fret	"		621
Doth call himself	"		650
doth cry 'Kill, kill	"		652
Sometime false doth bring	"		658
on his back doth lie	"		663
Doth make them droop	"		666
doth make my faint heart fear doth teach it	"		669 670
alarums he doth hear	"		700
brier his weary legs doth scratch	"		705
doth always fresh remain	"		801
Who doth the world	"		857
shining star doth borrow	"		861
doth make him shake	"		880
captain once doth yield	"		886
doth labour to expel	"		976
one doth flatter thee	"		980
she doth extenuate	"		1010
humbly doth insinuate	"		1012
in shade doth sit	"		1035
doth men's minds confound	"		1048
doth so surprise	"		1049
doth she hang her head	"		1058
The sun doth scorn you, and the wind doth hiss	"		1084
death doth my love destroy	"		1163
Beauty itself doth of itself persuade	R. L.		29
doth challenge that fair field	"		58
The coward captive vanquished doth yield	"		75
that praise which Collatine doth owe	"		82
she doth express	"		111
Doth yet in his fair welkin	"		116

Doth—dim darkness doth display	R. L.		118
with life's strength doth fight	"		124
doth Tarquin lie revolving	"		127
Despair to gain doth traffic oft	"		131
oft that wealth doth cost	"		146
Doth too too oft	"		174
he doth premeditate	"		183
he doth debate	"		185
he doth despise	"		187
the fear doth still exceed	"		229
doth confound and kill	"		250
doth so far proceed	"		251
so their pride doth grow	"		298
with fond desire doth scorch	"		314
his course doth let	"		328
to pray he doth begin	"		342
o'er this sleeping soul doth Tarquin stay	"		423
heedfully doth view	"		454
doth his tongue begin	"		470
the world doth threat	"		547
some gentle gust doth get	"		549
he doth but dally	"		554
she doth begin	"		567
that doth bend his bow	"		580
then most doth tyrannize	"		676
This forced league doth force	"		689
Self-will himself doth tire	"		707
Desire doth fight with Grace	"		712
her flesh doth tear	"		739
doth open lay	"		747
water that doth eat in steel	"		755
fellowship in woe doth woe assuage	"		790
impurity doth not pollute	"		854
the tiger that doth live by slaughter	"		955
one that by alms doth live	"		986
doth me no right	"		1027
all sorrow doth compare	"		1102
For mirth doth search	"		1109
the salve doth make the wound ache more	"		1116
sun doth melt their snow	"		1218
she doth give demure good-morrow	"		1219
the earth doth weep	"		1226
that which doth devour	"		1256
that it doth behold	"		1326
a part of woe doth bear	"		1327
with bashful innocence doth hie	"		1341
a little while doth stay	"		1361
burning Troy doth bear	"		1474
sad tales doth tell	"		1496
she their looks doth borrow	"		1498
she doth lament	"		1500
doth quake with cold	"		1556
hot-burning fire doth dwell	"		1557
Sinon's tears doth flatter	"		1560
And time doth weary time	"		1570
Doth in her poison'd closet yet endure	"		1659
the eye that doth behold his haste	"		1668
and through her wound doth fly	"		1728
from her breast, it doth divide	"		1737
still doth red abide	"		1749
The one doth call her his	"		1793
in them doth stand disgraced	"		1833
He doth again repeat	"		1848
gives nothing but doth lend	Son	4	3
where every eye doth dwell	"	5	2
fairly doth excel	"	5	4

DOTH — DOVE

Entry	Work	Page	Line
Doth—Doth homage to his new-appearing sight	Son	7	3
In the world doth spend	"	9	9
for ornament doth use	"	21	3
his fair doth rehearse	"	21	4
that doth cover thee	"	22	5
Which in thy breast doth live	"	22	7
But day doth daily draw	"	28	13
And night doth nightly make	"	28	14
buried love doth live	"	31	9
Yet doth it steal sweet hours	"	36	8
that this shadow doth such substance give	"	37	10
Which time and thoughts so sweetly doth deceive	"	39	12
who doth hence remain	"	39	14
even so doth she abuse me	"	42	7
shadows doth make bright	"	43	5
sleep in sightless eyes doth stay	"	43	12
My heart doth plead	"	46	5
doth that plea deny	"	46	7
each doth good turns	"	47	2
with sighs himself doth smother	"	47	4
then my eye doth feast	"	47	5
in his thoughts of love doth share a part	"	47	8
Doth teach that case	"	50	3
same groan doth put this in my mind	"	50	13
which the robe doth hide	"	52	10
The one doth shadow	"	53	10
bounty doth appear	"	53	11
much more doth beauty	"	54	1
that sweet ornament which truth doth give	"	54	2
sweet odour which doth in it live	"	54	4
to you it doth belong	"	58	11
Time that gave doth now his gift confound	"	60	8
Time doth transfix the flourish	"	60	9
that doth my rest defeat	"	61	11
a map doth Nature store	"	68	13
world's eye doth view	"	69	1
slander doth but prove	"	70	5
vice the sweetest buds doth love	"	70	7
night doth take away	"	73	7
on the ashes of his youth doth lie	"	73	10
every word doth almost	"	76	7
sick Muse doth give	"	79	4
thy poet doth invent	"	79	7
beauty doth he give	"	79	10
what in thee doth live	"	79	12
which he doth say	"	79	13
spirit doth use your name	"	80	2
proudest sail doth bear	"	80	6
doth wilfully appear	"	80	8
he upon your soundless deep doth ride	"	80	10
modern quill doth come too short	"	83	7
what worth in you doth grow	"	83	8
penury within that pen doth dwell	"	84	5
as a dream doth flatter	"	87	13
on thy humour doth depend	"	92	8
my life on thy revolt doth lie	"	92	10
doth thy beauty grow	"	93	13
Doth spot the beauty	"	95	3
beauty's veil doth cover	"	95	11
knife ill used doth lose his edge	"	95	14
ear that doth thy lays esteem	"	100	7
Doth—owner's tongue doth publish	Son	102	4
Philomel in summer's front doth sing	"	102	7
Ah, yet doth beauty like a	"	104	9
which methinks still doth stand	"	104	11
In thy breast doth lie	"	109	4
pity doth the impression fill	"	112	1
Doth part his function	"	113	3
which it doth latch	"	113	6
holds what it doth catch	"	113	8
Or whether doth my mind	"	114	1
palate doth prepare	"	114	12
and doth first begin	"	114	14
that which still doth grow	"	115	14
what we see doth lie	"	123	11
Doth half that glory	"	132	8
mourning doth thee grace	"	132	11
bond that him as fast doth bind	"	134	8
Doth follow night	"	145	11
which doth preserve the ill	"	147	3
love doth well denote	"	148	7
my best doth worship	"	149	11
brightness doth not grace the day	"	150	4
My soul doth tell my body	"	151	7
at thy name doth point out	"	151	9
landlord which doth owe them	L C		140
that on this earth doth shine	P P	3	10
doth ravish human sense	"	8	6
My heart doth charge the watch	"	15	2
Doth cite each moving sense	"	15	3
For she doth welcome daylight	"	15	7
A woman's nay doth stand for nought	"	19	42
He with thee doth bear a part	"	21	56
the anthem doth commence	P T		21
To eternity doth rest			58
Doting—now must doting Tarquin make	R L		155
from thy doting eyne	"		643
doting father of his fruit	"		1064
Had doting Priam check'd	"		1490
as she wrought thee, fell a-doting	Son	20	10
to my dear doting heart	"	131	3
Double—done me double wrong	V A		429
that the debt should double	"		521
with a thousand doubles	"		682
'Tis double death to drown	R L		1114
given grace a double majesty	Son	78	8
Nor double penance	"	111	12
this double voice accorded	L C		3
Single nature's double name	P T		39
Doubled—each several limb is	V A		1067
Double-lock—double-lock the door	"		448
Double-vantage—	Son	88	12
Doubt—hounds are driven to doubt	V A		692
Who, overcome by doubt	"		891
I shall not know, but live in doubt	P P	2	13
on the doubts of my decay	"	14	4
I ne'er know, but live in doubt	Son	144	13
wavering stood in doubt	L C		97
Doubtful—a vain and doubtful good	P P	13	1
A doubtful good, a gloss	"	13	5
Long was the combat doubtful	"	16	5
Doubting—Doubting the filching age	Son	75	6
doubting of the rest	"	115	12
Dove—than doves or roses are	V A		10
Two strengthless doves	"		153
doves that sit a-billing	"		366
yokes her silver doves	"		1190

Dove—From Venus' doves doth challenge	R L	58
The dove sleeps fast	"	360
The crow or dove, it shapes them	Son 113	12
Mild as a dove	P P 7	2
than her milk-white dove	" 9	3
To the phœnix and the dove	P T	50
Dowland—Dowland to thee is dear	P P 8	5
Down—o'er the downs	V A	677
The stain upon his silver down	R L	1012
His phœnix down begun	L C	93
Down—along as he was down	V A	43
down Adonis sits	"	325
down she kneels	"	350
she flatly falleth down	"	463
She sinketh down	"	593
Pluck down the rich	"	1150
straight be strucken down	R L	217
batter'd down her consecrated wall	"	723
that down thy cheeks are raining	"	1271
What wit sets down	"	1299
Wagg'd up and down	"	1406
Sinks down to death	Son 45	8
I can set down a story	" 88	6
Book both my wilfulness and errors down	" 117	9
Sets down her babe	" 143	3
And down I laid	L C	4
So slides he down	"	64
weighs down the airy scale	"	226
The golden bullet beats it down	P P 19	30
Down-razed—lofty towers I see	Son 64	3
Downright—fell I not downright	V A	645
Downward—.... eye still looketh	"	1106
current downward flow'd apace	L C	284
Dowry—the dowry of a lawful bed	R L	938
Drain'd—When hours have drain'd his blood	Son 63	3
Draw—draw me through the sky	V A	153
That she will draw	"	552
draws up her breath	"	929
To draw the cloud	R L	371
Draw not thy sword	"	626
and back the same grief draw	"	1673
Nor draw no lines there	Son 19	10
They draw but what they see	" 24	14
daily draw my sorrows	" 28	13
Drawn—Even so, the curtain drawn	R L	374
is drawn the power of Greece	"	1368
would be drawn out too long	"	1616
drawn by your own sweet skill	Son 16	14
Mine eyes have drawn thy shape	" 24	10
Drawn after you, you pattern was in little drawn	L C	90
Dread—wondrous dread	V A	635
mother of dread and fear	R L	117
between desire and dread	"	171
O, this dread night	"	965
Dreadeth—the heart that shadows dreadeth	"	270
Dreadful—with dreadful prophecies	V A	928
by dreadful fancy waking	R L	450
with more dreadful sights	"	462
In the dreadful dead constrain'd with dreadful circumstance	"	1625
	"	1703
thy voice his dreadful thunder	P P 5	11
Dreadfully—she is dreadfully beset	R L	444
Dreading—.... the winter's near	Son 97	14
Dreading—Dreading my love	P P 7	10
Dream—do seldom dream on evil	R L	87
A dream, a breath	"	212
If Collatinus dream of my intent	"	218
Thoughts are but dreams	"	353
starts Collatine as from a dream	"	1772
in dreams they look on thee	Son 43	3
when dreams do show thee	" 43	14
as a dream doth flatter	" 87	13
Before, a joy proposed; behind, a dream	" 129	12
Dreaming—.... on things to come	" 107	2
dark dreaming night	P P 15	8
Dregs—but lost the dregs of life	Son 74	9
Drench'd—Or in the ocean	V A	494
that his wounds wept, was drench'd	"	1054
deep-drenched in a sea of care	R L	1100
Dress—to dress his beauty new	Son 68	12
Dress'd—dress'd in all his trim	" 98	2
Dressing—is dressing old words new	" 76	11
dressings of a former sight	" 123	4
Drew—and backward drew	V A	541
painter drew so proud	R L	1371
this mild image drew	"	1520
from the purple fountain Brutus drew	"	1734
from a maund she drew	L C	36
afflicted fancy fastly drew	"	61
Dried—Scarce had the sun dried up the dewy morn	P P 6	1
Drink—More thirst for drink	V A	92
His nostrils drink the air	"	273
Dost thou drink tears	"	949
that gave drink to thee	R L	577
his breath drinks up again	"	1666
like a willing patient I will drink	Son 111	9
Drink to the monarch's plague	" 114	2
most kingly drinks it up	" 114	10
Drive—To drive infection	V A	508
drives the creeping thief	R L	305
drives away dark dreaming night	P P 15	8
Driven—hounds are .... to doubt	V A	692
Drone-like—and I a drone-like bee	R L	836
Droop—Doth make them droop	V A	666
Drooping—keep my .... eyelids	Son 27	7
Drop—an orient drop beside	V A	981
by drops of hot desire	"	1074
Which in round drops	"	1170
should drop on them	R L	686
huge stones with little water-drops	"	959
with swelling drops 'gan wet	"	1228
Many a dry drop	"	1375
of her drops spilling	"	1236
And drop sweet balm	"	1466
His eye drops fire	"	1552
And do not drop in for an after loss	Son 90	4
Now with the drops	" 107	9
our drops this difference bore	L C	300
Dropp'd—dropp'd a precious jewel	V A	824
of her bosom dropp'd	"	958
Dropping—Green-dropping sap	"	1176
Dross—in selling hours of dross	Son 146	11
Drouth—yet complain on drouth	V A	544
Drown—labour drowns for want of skill	R L	1099
to drown in ken of shore	"	1114
And then they drown their eyes	"	1239
To drown one woe	"	1680
Then can I drown an eye	Son 30	5

Drown—nor grows with heat, nor drowns with showers		*Son*	124	12		
Drown'd—when she seemeth		*V A*		984		
never drown'd him		*R L*		266		
I in deep delight am chiefly drown'd		*P P*	8	11		
Drudge—thy poor drudge to be		*Son*	151	11		
Drug—Drugs poison him		"	118	14		
Drum—Scorning his churlish drum		*V A*		107		
Drumming—His drumming heart		*R L*		435		
Drunk—What potions have I drunk		*Son*	119	1		
Drunken—of a drunken brain		*V A*		910		
Who is but drunken		"		984		
Drunken Desire must vomit		*R L*		703		
Dry—blow them dry again		*V A*		52		
those hills be dry		"		233		
lips' rich treasure dry		"		552		
Dries up his oil		"		736		
sought still to dry		"		964		
Sighs dry her cheeks		"		966		
who first should dry		"		1092		
As dry combustious matter		"		1162		
To dry the old oak's sap		*R L*		950		
Many a dry drop		"		1375		
To dry the rain		*Son*	34	6		
Duck—ducks as quickly in		*V A*		87		
Due—And as his due writ in any testament		*R L*		1183		
To eat the world's due		*Son*	1	14		
That due of many now		"	31	12		
That due to thee		"	39	8		
mine eye's due		"	46	13		
give thee that due		"	69	3		
but earth, which is his due		"	74	7		
Dug—swelling dugs do ache		*V A*		875		
Dull—in a dull disdain		"		33		
image dull and dead		"		212		
Looks on the dull earth		"		340		
From forth dull sleep		*R L*		450		
serves with dull debaters		"		1019		
but dull and slow she seems		"		1336		
If the dull substance		*Son*	44	1		
Of my dull bearer		"	51	2		
Shall neigh,—no dull flesh		"	51	11		
'tis with so dull a cheer		"	97	13		
I would not dull you		"	102	14		
o'er dull and speechless tribes		"	107	12		
Dulling—Dulling my lines		"	103	8		
Dullness—with a perpetual dullness		"	56	8		
Dully—Plods dully on		"	50	6		
Dumb—And all this dumb play		*V A*		359		
Though I were dumb		"		406		
Strike the wise dumb		"		1146		
All orators are dumb		*R L*		268		
he by dumb demeanour		"		474		
Sometime her grief is dumb		"		1105		
be you mute and dumb		"		1123		
Hath served a dumb arrest		"		1780		
And dumb presagers		*Son*	23	10		
For who's so dumb		"	38	7		
taught the dumb on high		"	78	5		
be most my glory, being dumb		"	83	10		
Me for my dumb thoughts		"	85	14		
wilt thou be dumb		"	101	9		
Dumbly—Dumbly she passions		*V A*		1059		
Dumps—Distress likes dumps		*R L*		1127		
Dun—why then her breasts are dun		*Son*	130	3		
During—bear an ever-during blame		*R L*		224		
Durst—But durst not ask of her		"		1223		
Durst—Or durst inhabit on a living brow		*Son*	68	4		
Dust—And smear with dust		*R L*		945		
and smeared all with dust		"		1381		
my bones with dust		*Son*	32	2		
Weighs not the dust		"	108	10		
Duteous—yet the duteous vassal		*R L*		1360		
The eyes 'fore duteous		*Son*	7	11		
Duty—to get it is thy duty		*V A*		168		
did him peculiar duties		*R L*		14		
'gainst law or duty		"		497		
For fleet-wing'd duty		"		1216		
His kindled duty kindled		"		1352		
hath my duty strongly knit		*Son*	26	2		
To witness duty		"	26	4		
Duty so great		"	26	5		
In personal duty		*L C*		130		
Dwell—dwells upon my suit		*V A*		206		
within her bosom it shall dwell		"		1173		
Riot-burning fire doth dwell		*R L*		1557		
where every eye doth dwell		*Son*	5	2		
and dwell in lover's eyes		"	55	14		
with vilest worms to dwell		"	71	4		
within that pen doth dwell		"	84	5		
no more shall dwell		"	89	10		
sweet love should ever dwell		"	93	10		
for complexion dwells		"	99	4		
To dwell with him		*L C*		120		
Dwell'd—all distress and dolour dwell'd		*R L*		1446		
Dweller—Have I not seen dwellers		*Son*	125	5		
Dwelling—Love lack'd a dwelling		*L C*		82		
Dye—have full as deep a dye		*Son*	54	5		
with damask dye to grace her		*P P*	7	5		
Forth their dye		"	18	40		
Dyed—thou hast too grossly dyed		*Son*	99	5		
of truth in beauty dyed		"	101	2		
Dyer—like the dyer's hand		"	111	7		
Dying—Even as a dying coal		*V A*		338		
This dying virtue		*R L*		346		
A dying life to living infamy		"		1055		
That dying fear		"		1266		
And dying eyes		"		1378		
Like dying coals burnt out		"		1379		
there's no more dying then		*Son*	146	14		
Each—Each leaning on their elbows		*V A*		44		
in each cheek appears		"		242		
each other did destroy		"		346		
Each part in me		"		436		
they kiss each other		"		505		
Each envious brier		"		705		
Each shadow makes him stop, each murmur stay		"		706		
From whom each lamp		"		861		
numbs each feeling part		"		892		
view'd each other's sorrow		"		963		
each passion labours so		"		969		
each tributary subject		"		1043		
each part doth so surprise		"		1049		
each several limb		"		1067		
interchange each other's seat		*R L*		70		
each one by him enforced		"		303		
As each unwilling portal		"		309		
income of each precious thing		"		334		
Each in her sleep		"		404		
hearers to attend each line		"		818		
with each thing she views		"		1101		
So I at each sad strain		"		1131		

Each—Each flower moistened	R L	....	1227
each little mote will peep	"	....	1251
wondering each other's chance	"	....	1396
Each present lord began	"	....	1696
burning head, each under eye	Son	7	2
Strikes each in each	"	8	10
Pointing to each his thunder	"	14	6
And each, though enemies	"	28	5
Both find each other	"	42	11
each doth good turns now unto the other	"	47	2
Each trifle under truest bars	"	48	2
tame to sufferance, bide each check	"	58	7
Each changing place	"	60	3
each part will be forgotten	"	81	4
I must each day say o'er	"	108	6
Till each to razed oblivion	"	122	7
For since each hand	"	127	5
both to each friend	"	144	11
Each eye that saw him	L C	....	89
Each stone's dear nature	"	....	210
each several stone	"	....	216
Each cheek a river	"	....	283
both to each friend	P P	2	11
Between each kiss	"	7	8
Doth cite each moving sense	"	15	3
each minute seems a moon	"	15	15
Eager—tidings in my eager eyes	R L	....	254
an eager combat fight	"	....	1298
With eager compounds	Son	118	2
Eagle—Even as an empty eagle	V A	....	55
But eagles gazed upon	R L	....	1015
Save the eagle, feather'd king	P T	....	11
Ear—For to a pretty ear	V A	....	74
I will enchant thine ear	"	....	145
His ears up-prick'd	"	....	271
high crest, short ears	"	....	297
Ear's deep-sweet music	"	....	432
Had I no eyes but ears, my ears would love	"	....	433
neither eyes nor ears	"	....	437
whispers in mine ear	"	....	659
with listening ear	"	....	698
Yet from mine ear	"	....	778
armed in mine ear	"	....	779
Mine ears, that to your wanton talk	"	....	809
sadly in her ear	"	....	889
Shaking their scratch'd ears	"	....	924
with eye or ear	"	....	1023
She whispers in his ears	"	....	1125
From thievish ears	R L	....	35
by our ears our hearts oft tainted be	"	....	38
He stories to her ears	"	....	106
with open listening ear	"	....	283
His ear her prayer admits	"	....	358
notes to pleasing ears	"	....	1126
interprets to the ear	"	....	1325
mermaid did their ears entice	"	....	1411
shadow'd by his neighbour's ear	"	....	1416
do offend thine ear	Son	8	6
Sing to the ear that doth thy lays esteem	"	100	7
that mine ear confounds	"	128	4
by mad ears believed be	"	140	12
Nor are mine ears	"	141	5
stories to delight his ear	P P	4	5
By ringing in thy lady's ear	"	19	28
to round me on th' ear	"	19	51

Early—Or being early pluck'd	V A	....	528
Which she too early	R L	....	1801
one early morn did shine	Son	33	9
too early I attended	L C	....	78
Earnest—Her earnest eye did make him	R L	....	1356
Earth—Earth's sovereign salve	V A	....	28
Upon the earth's increase	"	....	169
Unless the earth	"	....	170
The bearing earth	"	....	267
Looks on the dull earth	"	....	340
and all the earth relieveth	"	....	484
In earth or heaven	"	....	493
fall to the earth	"	....	546
The earth, in love with thee	"	....	722
on the earth would breed	"	....	753
on earth usurp'd his name	"	....	794
earth's worm, what dost thou	"	....	933
earth's foundation shakes	"	....	1047
marks thee for my earth's delight	R L	....	487
From earth's dark womb	"	....	549
By heaven and earth	"	....	572
Seasoning the earth with showers	"	....	796
As the dank earth weeps	"	....	1130
But as the earth doth weep	"	....	1226
that breathes the fat earth's store	"	....	1837
And make the earth devour	Son	19	2
with earth and sea's rich gems	"	21	6
From sullen earth, sings hymns	"	29	12
Upon the farthest earth	"	44	6
so much of earth and water	"	44	11
nor earth nor boundless sea	"	65	1
The earth can have but earth	"	74	7
when I in earth am rotten	"	81	2
The earth can yield me	"	81	7
the centre of my sinful earth	"	146	1
To the orbed earth	L C	....	25
that on this earth doth shine	P P	3	10
Earth-delving—where earth-delving conies keep	V A	....	687
Earthly—heavenly and earthly sun	"	....	198
suck'd an earthly mother	"	....	863
This earthly saint, adored	R L	....	85
ne'er touch'd earthly faces	Son	17	8
My vow was earthly	P P	3	7
with such an earthly tongue	"	5	14
Earthquake—But like an	V A	....	648
Ease—With honour, wealth, and	R L	....	142
ease to the pained	"	....	901
Doth teach that ease	Son	50	3
with ease we prove	"	136	7
Eased—oppression is not eased by night	"	28	3
Easeth—It easeth some, though none it ever cured	R L	....	1581
Easily—cannot be easily harm'd	V A	....	627
Easing—keep him from heart-easing words	R L	....	1782
East—the grey cheeks of the east	Son	132	6
throw gazes to the east	P P	15	1
Eastern—to meet the eastern light	R L	....	773
Easy—As easy might I	Son	109	3
Words are easy, like the wind	P P	21	33
Eat—eats up Love's tender spring	V A	....	656
water that doth eat in steel	R L	....	755
To eat up errors	"	....	937
To eat the world's due	Son	1	14
canker eat him up to death	"	99	13
Eat up thy charge	"	146	8

Eater—Eater of youth, false slave	R L	....	927	Else—or else some shame supposed	R L	....	377
Eating—the marrow-eating sickness	V A	....	741	or else his quality	"	....	875
Were an all-eating shame	Son	2	8	would else have come to me	"	....	916
Ebb—And sorrow ebbs, being blown	R L	....	1330	And what wrong else may be imagined	"	....	1622
Thus ebbs and flows	"	....	1569	else lasting shame	"	....	1629
Ebon—Not Death's ebon dart	V A	....	948	Or else this glutton be	Son	1	13
Echo—spend their mouths: Echo replies	"	....	695	Or else receivest with pleasure	"	8	4
And twenty echoes	"	....	834	Or else of thee	"	14	13
still the choir of echoes	"	....	840	thou gavest it else mistaking	"	87	10
Eclipse—Clouds and eclipses stain	Son	35	3	None else to me	"	112	7
Crooked eclipses 'gainst his glory	"	60	7	and all things else are thine	L C	....	266
hath her eclipse endured	"	107	5	Elsewhere—whilst thou dost wake elsewhere	Son	61	13
Eclipsed—suns were cloud-eclipsed so	R L	....	1224	Tell me thou lovest elsewhere	"	139	5
Ecstasy—in a trembling ecstasy	V A	....	895	That they elsewhere might dart	"	139	12
her suffering ecstasy assuage	L C	....	69	Elysium—To clip Elysium	V A	....	600
Eddy—Yet in the eddy boundeth in his pride	R L	....	1669	Embarked—a late-embarked friend	"	....	818
				Embassy—In tender .... of love	Son	45	6
Edge—Thy edge should blunter be	Son	56	2	Embrace—a sweet embrace	V A	....	539
the knife ill used doth lose his edge	"	95	14	from the sweet embrace	"	....	811
even to the edge of doom	"	116	12	from their strict embrace	"	....	874
This hateless edge	R L	....	9	to embrace mine infamy	R L	....	504
Effect—The warm effects	V A	....	605	seeing thee embrace him	"	....	518
But Lust's effect	"	....	800	Embraced—the warlike god .... me	P P	11	5
robb'd of his effect	"	....	1132	Embracement—Beating his kind embracements	V A	....	312
All pure effects, and doth	R L	....	251	that lends embracements	"	....	790
till their effects be tried	"	....	353	Embracing—with her hard .... brambles and embracing bushes	"	....	539
His venom in effect	"	....	592		"	....	629
Such devils steal effects	"	....	1555	girdle with embracing flames	R L	....	6
Beauty's effect with beauty	Son	5	11	Ember—Which, in pale embers hid	"	....	5
alter not love's sole effect	"	36	7	Embroider'd—Embroider'd all with leaves	P P	20	12
my dumb thoughts, speaking in effect	"	85	14	Emerald—The deep-green emerald	L C	....	213
Effects of terror	L C	....	202	Emptied—Have emptied all their fountains	"	....	255
O cleft effect	"	....	293	Empty—Even as an empty eagle	V A	....	55
Effecting—bought at all effecting	V A	....	912	through the empty skies	"	....	1191
fell exploits effecting	R L	....	429	Emulation—Seeing such emulation	R L	....	1808
Effectually—but effectually is out	Son	113	4	Enacted—policy remains enacted	"	....	529
Eisel—Potions of eisel	"	111	10	Encamp'd—Encamp'd in hearts	L C	....	203
Either—Till either gorge be stuff'd	V A	....	58	Enchained—Cancell'd my fortunes and enchained me	R L	....	934
Of either's colour	R L	....	66	Enchant—I will enchant thine ear	V A	....	145
of either being so great	"	....	69	did enchant the mind	L C	....	89
Swelling on either side	"	....	389	Enchanted—Enchanted Tarquin answers	R L	....	83
Whose love of either	"	....	1165	and sexes both enchanted	L C	....	128
The face of either cipher'd either's heart	"	....	1396	Enchanting—round enchanting pits	V A	....	247
though enemies to either's reign	Son	28	5	Sinon, whose enchanting story	R L	....	1521
badges of either's woe	"	44	14	Encloses—his traitor eye encloses	"	....	73
So, either by thy picture	"	47	9	which their hue encloses	L C	....	287
Either not assail'd	"	70	10	Enclosed—and keep themselves	R L	....	378
In either's aptness	L C	....	306	Here enclosed in cinders lie	P T	....	55
To put in practice either	P P	16	7	Encompass'd—encompass'd with a winding maze	R L	....	1151
Either was the other's mine	P T	....	36	Encounter—for the hot encounter	V A	....	596
To themselves yet either neither	"	....	43	If thou encounter	"	....	672
That are either true or fair	"	....	66	which no encounter dare	"	....	676
Elbow—leaning on their elbows	V A	....	44	Encouraging—As 'twere encouraging the Greeks to fight	R L	....	1402
Elder—How can I then be elder	Son	22	8	Emerimson'd—and the .... mood	L C	....	201
Element—water-galls in her dim element	R L	....	1588	End—now stand on end	V A	....	272
by elements so slow	Son	44	13	but unsavoury end	"	....	1138
these quicker elements are gone	"	45	5	finds no excuse nor end	R L	....	238
Eloquence—Her modest eloquence with sighs is mixed	R L	....	563	to a great, good end	"	....	528
my books be then the eloquence	Son	23	9	my life's fair end shall free it	"	....	1208
Else—or else be mute	V A	....	208	to this end from me derived	"	....	1755
nothing else he sees	"	....	287				
For nothing else	"	....	288				
Else, suffer'd, it will set	"	....	388				

End—hath in the world an end	Son 9	11
Against this coming end	" 13	3
Thy end is truth's and beauty's doom and date	" 14	14
my weary travel's end	" 50	2
the world-without-end hour	" 57	5
our minutes hasten to their end	" 60	2
my life hath end	" 92	6
have what shall have no end	" 110	9
she alter'd with an end	" 143	9
Is this thy body's end	" 146	8
Augur of the fever's end	P T	7
End—And where she ends	V A	60
the story aptly ends	"	716
End without audience	"	816
End thy ill aim	R L	579
an hour great strifes to end	"	899
to end a hapless life	"	1045
the fatal knife, to end his vow	"	1843
losses are restored and sorrows end	Son 30	14
Endeared—Thy bosom is endeared	" 31	1
Ended—hath ended in the west	V A	530
before thy shoot be ended	R L	579
Philomel had ended	"	1079
For now my song is ended	P P 16	16
Ender—my origin and ender	L C	222
Ending—the world hath ending with thy life	V A	12
date of never-ending woes	R L	935
dirge of her certain ending	"	1012
out to the ending doom	Son 55	12
Endless—To endless date of never-ending woes	R L	935
olives of endless age	Son 107	8
Endow'd—Look, whom she best	" 11	11
Endure—their verdure still endure	V A	507
In her poison'd closet yet endure	R L	1659
lively heat, still to endure	Son 153	6
Endured—their dolour others have endured	R L	1582
hath her eclipse endured	Son 107	5
Enemy—Finding their enemy	V A	887
light and lust are deadly enemies	R L	674
batter'd by the enemy	"	1171
Greeks that are thine enemies	"	1470
Mine enemy was strong	"	1646
though enemies to either's reign	Son 28	5
have been mine enemies	" 139	10
Enfeebled—that enfeebled mine	" 86	14
Enforced—I enforced this fire	R L	181
Each one by him enforced	"	303
If not, enforced hate	"	668
enforced by sympathy	"	1228
therefore art enforced to seek anew	Son 82	7
Enforcement—By foul enforcement	R L	1623
Enfranchising—Enfranchising his mouth	V A	396
Engine—Once more the engine	"	367
Engirt—engirts so white a foe	"	364
that hath engirt his marriage	R L	221
engirt with daring infamy	"	1173
Englishman—Till looking on an Englishman	P P 16	14
Engraft—I engraft you new	Son 15	14
Engrafted—my love engrafted to this store	" 37	8
Engraven—it will live engraven in my face	R L	203
Engrossed—thou harder hast	Son 133	6
Enjoy their loves shall not enjoy	V A	1164
this night I must enjoy thee	R L	512
for still the world enjoys it	Son 9	10
With what I most enjoy	" 29	8
Enjoy'd—enjoy'd but of a few	R L	22
Enjoy'd no sooner but despised straight	Son 129	5
Enjoyer—Now proud as an enjoyer	" 75	5
Enlarged—envy evermore enlarged	" 70	12
Enlighten—And to enlighten thee	" 152	11
Enmity—disdain and deadly enmity	R L	503
death and all-oblivious enmity	Son 55	9
Enough—within this limit is relief enough	V A	235
'Tis not enough that through	Son 54	5
like enough thou know'st	" 87	2
They had not skill enough	" 106	12
your pity is enough to cure me	" 111	14
Is't not enough to torture me	" 133	3
More than enough am I	" 135	3
But soft! enough—too much	P P 19	49
Enpatron—you enpatron me	L C	224
Enraged—Being so enraged	V A	29
how he is enraged	"	317
Here, all enraged	R L	1562
Enrich—enrich the poor	V A	1150
and much enrich thy book	Son 77	14
Enrich'd—annexious of fair gems enrich'd	L C	208
Ensconce—do I ensconce me here	Son 49	9
Ensconced—so.... his secret evil	R L	1515
Ensign—churlish drum and.... red	V A	107
Ensnare—do not then ensnare me	R L	584
Ensnared—.... thee to this night	"	485
Ensue—repentant tears.... the deed	"	502
another straight ensues	"	1104
and shame that might ensue	"	1263
Ensuing—or any thing ensuing	V A	1078
Enswathed—Enswathed, and seal'd	L C	49
Enter—thy spear's point can enter	V A	626
false sound enter there	"	780
through which it enters	"	890
and enter this sweet city	R L	469
Soft pity enters at an iron gate	"	595
Enterprise—of his loathsome	"	184
Entertain—I did entertain thee	"	596
did I entertain him	"	842
The weary time she cannot entertain	"	1361
And entertain my love	"	1629
To entertain the time with thoughts of love	Son 39	11
Entertain'd—All entertain'd, each passion	V A	969
He entertain'd a show	R L	1514
Entertainment—Witness the	V A	1108
Entice—some mermaid did their ears entice	R L	1411
Quickly him they will entice	P P 21	44
Entitled—Entitled in thy parts	Son 37	7
Entomb—Entombs her outcry	R L	679
quoth she, 'your tunes entomb	"	1121
Entombed—her head entombed is entombed in men's eyes	" Son 81	390 8
Entrance—No penetrable entrance to her plaining	R L	559
Entreat—entreats, and prettily entreats	V A	73
as I entreat thee now	"	97

| ENVIOUS | 86 | EVEN |

Entry	Ref	No.
Envious—Each envious brier	V A	705
Envy—that envy of so rich a thing	R L	39
Wrath, envy, treason, rape	"	909
envy evermore enlarged	Son 70	12
Do I envy those jacks	" 128	5
Epitaph—I shall live your epitaph to make	" 81	1
Equal—weep with equal strife	R L	1791
where your equal grew	Son 84	4
as some my equals did	L C	148
Equally—Ne'er settled equally	V A	1139
Equipage—in ranks of better	Son 32	12
Ere—ere his words begun	V A	462
and, ere he says 'Adieu	"	537
sweet boy, ere this	"	613
ere summer half be done	"	802
cancell'd ere well begun	R L	26
ere rich at home he lands	"	336
works ere traitors be espied	"	361
begin ere once she speaks	"	567
Ere he can see his own	"	704
yet ere he go to bed	"	776
Ere he arrive his weary noon-tide prick	"	781
As I, ere this, was pure to Collatine	"	826
'Madam, ere I was up	"	1277
ere the break of day	"	1280
And ere I rose was Tarquin	"	1281
Ere she with blood had stain'd	"	1316
Ere once she can discharge	"	1605
But ere I name him	"	1688
ere thou be distill'd	Son 6	2
ere it be self-kill'd	" 6	4
Ere beauty's dead fleece	" 68	8
which thou must leave ere long	" 73	14
Ere you were born	" 104	14
ere that there was true needing	" 118	8
Ere long espied a fickle maid	L C	5
Consents bewitch'd, ere he desire	"	131
Her cloudy looks will calm ere night	P P 19	14
And twice desire ere it be day	" 19	17
Err—To say they err I dare not	Son 131	7
Erred—my heart and eyes have	" 137	13
Error—And childish error	V A	898
To eat up errors	R L	937
So are those errors	Son 96	7
If this be error	" 116	13
my wilfulness and errors	" 117	9
What wretched errors hath my heart committed	" 119	5
a thousand errors note	" 141	2
Are errors of the blood	L C	184
Erst—Which erst from heat	Son 12	6
Escape—'night's 'scapes doth open lay	R L	747
Could 'scape the hail	L C	310
Escaped—when my heart hath 'scaped this sorrow	Son 90	5
Escapeth—The scars of battle 'scapeth by the flight	L C	244
Espied—ere traitors be espied	R L	361
espied a fickle maid	L C	5
Espoused—might be …. to more fame	R L	26
Espy—trampling courser doth espy	V A	261
Essay—And worse essays proved th	Son 110	8
Essence—Had the … but in one	P T	26
Estate—colour'd with his high	R L	92

Entry	Ref	No.
Esteem—Alas, he nought esteems	V A	631
doth thy lays esteem	" 100	7
with a false esteem	" 127	12
Esteemed—the Romans were …. so	R L	1811
will be well esteem'd	Son 96	6
better to be vile than vile esteem'd	" 121	1
Esteeming—whose rich esteeming	" 102	3
Estimate—thou know'st thy estimate	" 87	2
Eternal—cast into eternal sleeping	V A	951
solicited the eternal powers	R L	345
of death's eternal cold	Son 13	12
But thy eternal summer	" 18	9
When in eternal lines	" 18	12
Eternal numbers to outlive	" 38	12
And brass, eternal slave	" 64	4
So that eternal love	" 108	9
spend her living in eternal love	L C	238
Eternity—sells eternity to get a toy	R L	214
Thou ceaseless lackey to eternity	"	967
thievish progress to eternity	Son 77	8
even to eternity	" 122	4
laid great bases for eternity	" 125	3
To eternity doth rest	P T	58
Ethiope—Juno but an Ethiope were	P P 17	16
Eve—How like Eve's apple	Son 93	13
Even—Even as the sun	V A	1
and even now	"	39
Even as an empty eagle	"	55
Even so she kiss'd his brow	"	59
Even by the stern	"	98
even where I list	"	154
even by their own	"	216
Even as a dying coal	"	338
Even as the wind	"	458
Even as poor birds	"	601
Even so she languisheth	"	603
Even so confounded	"	827
Even so the timorous	"	881
Even at this word	"	1025
Even there he starts	R L	348
Even so the curtain drawn	"	374
That even for anger	"	478
even in my soul	"	498
even in plenty wanteth	"	557
Even in this thought	"	729
Even in the moment	"	808
Even so the maid	"	1228
Even so this pattern	"	1350
For even as subtle Sinon	"	1541
Even so his sighs	"	1672
Even here she sheathed	"	1723
even by the self-same sky	Son 15	6
Even so my sun	" 33	9
and even I in this	" 35	5
Even for this let us divided live	" 39	5
lead me in their riot even there	" 41	11
for my sake even so doth she abuse me	" 42	7
Who even but now come back	" 45	11
And even thence thou wilt be stolen	" 48	13
Even in the eyes	" 55	11
hungry eyes even till they wink	" 56	6
Even of five hundred courses	" 59	6
even so as foes	" 69	4
your love even with my life decay	" 71	12
even in the mouths of men	" 81	14
Even such a beauty	" 106	8
Even as when first	" 108	8
Even to thy pure	" 110	14

EVEN 87 EXAMPLE

Even—Even that your pity	*Son*	111	14
Even those that said	"	115	2
bears it out even to the edge of doom	"	116	12
Even so, being full	"	118	5
Beyond all date, even to eternity	"	122	4
Even there resolved	*L C*		296
'Even thus,' quoth she	*P P*	11	5
'Even thus,' quoth she	"	11	7
'Even thus,' quoth she	"	11	9
Even so, poor bird, like thee	"	21	27
Even—or morn or weary even	*V A*		495
thou gild'st the even	*Son*	28	12
star that ushers in the even	"	132	7
Evening—All our evening sport	*P P*	18	47
Event—of war and dire events	*V A*		1159
What uncouth ill event	*R L*		1598
Ever—feast might ever last	*V A*		447
that ever yet betoken'd	"		453
that ever threat his foes	"		620
ever strive to kiss you	"		1082
Yet ever to obtain	*R L*		129
If ever man were moved	"		587
That ever modest eyes	"		683
ever let his unrecalling crime	"		993
If ever, love, thy Lucrece	"		1306
though none it ever cured	"		1384
And ever since, as pitying	"		1747
in my verse ever live young	*Son*	19	14
if ever that time come	"	49	1
watchman, ever for thy sake	"	61	12
slander's mark was ever yet the fair	"	70	2
still all one, ever the same	"	76	5
when thou wilt; if ever, now	"	90	1
sweet love should ever dwell	"	93	10
still such, and ever so	"	105	4
nor no man ever loved	"	116	14
and this shall ever be	"	123	13
that tongue that ever sweet	"	145	6
who ever shunn'd by precedent	*L C*		155
were ever brokers to defiling	"		173
to none was ever said	"		180
my leisures ever charmed	"		103
beauty blemish'd once 's for ever lost	*P P*	13	11
whose month was ever May	"	17	2
Ever-during—bear an .... blame	*R L*		224
Ever-fixed—it is an ever-fixed mark	*Son*	116	5
Everlasting—Tarquin's everlasting banishment	*R L*		1855
Evermore— .... acknowledge thee	*Son*	36	9
envy evermore enlarged	"	70	12
Frantic-mad with evermore unrest	"	147	10
Every—he comes in every jar	*V A*		100
every light impression	"		566
comment upon every woe	"		714
Every tongue more moving	"		776
unto every stranger	"		790
answering every call	"		849
every present sorrow	"		970
every beauty robb'd	"		1132
For every little grief	"		1179
And every one to rest	*R L*		125
Till every minute pays	"		329
sets every joint a-shaking	"		452
mark of every open eye	"		520
kings, like gods, should govern every thing	"		602
that every eye can see	"		750

Every—Shape every bush a hideous	*R L*		973
seek every hour to kill	"		998
gazed upon with every eye	"		1015
through every cranny spies	"		1086
with every thing she sees	"		1093
When every part a part of woe	"		1327
Imagine every eye beholds	"		1343
changed to black in every vein	"		1454
For every tear he falls	"		1551
Circles her body in on every side	"		1739
every eye doth dwell	*Son*	5	2
bareness every where	"	5	8
When every private widow	"	9	7
consider every thing	"	15	1
And every fair from fair	"	18	7
And every fair with his fair	"	21	4
outstripp'd by every pen	"	32	6
For every vulgar paper	"	38	4
prey of every vulgar thief	"	48	8
every hour survey	"	52	3
Since every one hath, every one, one shade	"	53	3
can every shadow lend	"	53	4
in every blessed shape	"	53	12
all my every part	"	62	2
That every word	"	76	7
As every alien pen	"	78	3
blessing every book	"	82	4
admired every where	"	84	12
To every hymn	"	85	7
And every humour	"	91	5
doth cover every blot	"	95	11
December's bareness every where	"	97	4
of youth in every thing	"	98	3
despised every where	"	100	12
publish every where	"	102	4
burthens every bough	"	102	11
Creating every bad	"	114	7
to every wandering bark	"	116	7
That every tongue	"	127	14
like in every part	"	132	12
To every place at once	*L C*		27
And every light occasion	"		86
jest at every gentle offer	*P P*	4	12
truth in every shepherd's tongue	"	20	18
Every thing did banish moan	"	21	7
Every one that flatters thee	"	21	31
Every man will be thy friend	"	21	35
Thus of every grief in heart	"	21	55
Every fowl of tyrant wing	*P T*		10
Evidence—lust came .... to swear	*R L*		1650
Evident—that thou none lovest is most evident	*Son*	10	4
Evil—do seldom dream on evil	*R L*		87
O, unlook'd-for evil	"		846
thought of his committed evil	"		972
shall be accounted evil	"		1245
evils that obscurely sleep	"		1250
ensconced his secret evil	"		1513
of good or evil luck	*Son*	14	3
by evil still made better	"	119	10
Unless this general evil	"	121	13
my female evil	"	144	5
my female evil	*P P*	2	5
Example—By whose example	*R L*		1194
Which should example where your equal grew	*Son*	84	4
by self-example mayst thou	"	142	14
Or forced examples	*L C*		157

Example—Of stale example	*L C*	268
Exceed—the living should exceed	*V A*	292
whose leave exceeds commission	"	568
far exceeds his barren skill	*R L*	81
the fear doth still exceed	"	229
I found you did exceed	*Son* 83	3
thy worst all best exceeds	" 150	8
Exceeded—Exceeded by the height	" 32	8
Excel—So did this horse excel	*V A*	293
which fairly doth excel	*Son* 5	4
Excell'd—wherein they late excell'd	*V A*	1131
Excellence—stewards of their	*Son* 94	8
in a wondrous excellence	" 103	6
Excellent—sweet argument, too	" 38	3
though excellent in neither	*P P* 7	18
Excelleth—whose light … thine	*R L*	191
Excelling—of thy face excelling	*V A*	443
Except—which physic did except	*Son* 147	8
Excess—the profit of excess	*R L*	138
inheritors of this excess	*Son* 146	7
but where excess begs all	*L C*	42
Exchanged—not with the time	*Son* 109	7
Exchequer—no … now but his	" 67	11
Exclaim—the dogs exclaim aloud	*V A*	686
exclaims on Death	"	930
exclaims against repose	*R L*	757
he would exclaim	*L C*	313
Exclaiming—exclaiming on the direful night	*R L*	741
Exclamation—in his pride, no	"	705
Excuse—What bare excuses	*V A*	188
O strange excuse	"	791
He makes excuses	*R L*	114
O what excuse	"	225
Might have excuse	"	235
finds no excuse nor end	"	238
for colour or excuses	"	267
in cleanly-coin'd excuses	"	1073
had stain'd her stain'd excuse	"	1316
Where no excuse can give	"	1614
to make mine own excuse	"	1653
By my excuse shall claim excuse's giving	"	1715
and make my old excuse	*Son* 2	11
O, what excuse	" 51	5
Excuse—Let me excuse thy courser	*V A*	403
thus I will excuse ye	*Son* 42	5
excuse the slow offence	" 51	1
thus shall excuse my jade	" 51	12
Excuse not silence so	" 101	10
Let me excuse thee	" 139	9
Excusing—Excusing thy sins more	" 35	8
Executest—executest the traitor's treason	*R L*	877
Executor—lives th' executor to be	*Son* 4	14
Exhale—Exhale this vapour vow	*P P* 3	11
Exhaled—their exhaled unwholesome breaths	*R L*	779
Exile—she joy'd to jest at my exile	*P P* 14	9
Exiled—for exiled majesty's repeal	*R L*	640
Expect—for that which we expect	"	149
Expected—expected of my friends	*V A*	718
Expecting—the onset still	*R L*	432
Expel—doth labour to expel	*V A*	976
Expense—And mean the expense	*Son* 30	8
husband nature's riches from expense	" 94	6
The expense of spirit	" 129	1
Experience—Experience for me	*L C*	152
Experienced—Now set thy long-experienced wit to school	*R L*	1820
Expiate—death my day should	*Son* 22	4
Expire—whereon it must expire	" 73	11
Expired—An expired date	*R L*	26
when body's works expired	*Son* 27	4
Exploit—fell exploits effecting	*R L*	429
Express—express my grief for one	*V A*	1069
with heaved-up hand she doth express	*R L*	111
than I can well express	"	1286
That may express my love	*Son* 108	4
lend me words, and words express	" 140	3
Express'd—no outward harm	*R L*	91
that more hath more express'd	*Son* 23	12
pen would have express'd	" 106	7
from the truth vainly express'd	" 147	12
Expressing—One thing expressing	" 105	8
Expressly—their manners most expressly told	*R L*	1397
Extant—being extant, well might show	*Son* 83	6
Extemporally—sings extemporally a woeful ditty	*V A*	836
Extend—sometimes they do extend	*L C*	25
their sighs to you extend	"	276
Extenuate—she doth extenuate	*V A*	1010
Extern—With my extern	*Son* 125	2
External—In all external grace	" 53	13
Extincture—and chill extincture	*L C*	294
Extinguishing—… his conduct	*R L*	313
Extreme—are both of them extremes	*V A*	987
And extreme fear can neither fight	*R L*	230
extremes beyond extremity	"	969
still urgeth such extremes	"	1337
Savage, extreme, rude	*Son* 129	4
and in quest to have, extreme	" 129	10
Extremity—extremes beyond	*R L*	969
Extremity still urgeth	"	1337
When swift extremity	*Son* 51	6
Ewe—My ewes breed not	*P P* 18	2
Eye—In his angry eyes	*V A*	70
since eyes in eyes	"	120
Mine eyes are grey	"	140
With burning eye	"	178
dark, disliking eye	"	182
Thine eye darts forth	"	196
but the eye alone	"	213
fiery eyes blaze forth	"	219
His eye, which scornfully	"	275
to captivate the eye	"	281
Broad breast, full eye	"	296
holds her in his eye	"	342
to his eyes suing	"	356
His eyes saw her eyes	"	357
Her eyes woo'd still, his eyes disdain'd	"	358
her eyes did rain	"	360
when his glutton eye	"	399
Had I no eyes	"	433
neither eyes nor ears	"	437
illumine with her eye	"	486
Thy eyes' shrewd tutor	"	500
And these mine eyes	"	503
mine eyes to watch	"	584
surfeit by the eye	"	602
His eyes, like glow-worms	"	621

EYE				EYE			
Eye—To which Love's eyes	V A	....	632	Eye—from her bright eyes	R L	....	1213
fear lurk in mine eye	"	....	641	like a melting eye	"	....	1227
presenteth to mine eye	"	....	661	And then they drown their eyes	"	....	1239
from Venus' eye	"	....	816	For then the eye	"	....	1325
Whereon with fearful eyes	"	....	927	with a steadfast eye	"	....	1339
thou hast no eyes	"	....	939	Imagine every eye	"	....	1344
eyes that taught all other eyes	"	....	952	Her earnest eye	"	....	1356
O, how her eyes	"	....	961	And dying eyes	"	....	1378
Her eyes seen in the tears, tears				The very eyes of men	"	....	1383
in her eye	"	....	962	those far-off eyes look sad	"	....	1386
prison'd in her eye	"	....	980	In Ajax' eyes	"	....	1398
with eye or ear	"	....	1023	save to the eye	"	....	1426
Which seen, her eyes	"	....	1031	with her old eyes	"	....	1448
her eyes are tied	"	....	1037	Lucrece spends her eyes	"	....	1457
once more leap her eyes	"	....	1050	scratch out the angry eyes	"	....	1469
Her eyes are mad	"	....	1062	Thy eye kindled the fire	"	....	1475
her mangling eye	"	....	1065	for trespass of thine eye	"	....	1476
oft the eye mistakes	"	....	1068	She throws her eyes about	"	....	1499
Mine eyes are turn'd	"	....	1072	calm looks, eyes waiting still	"	....	1508
mine eyes' red fire	"	....	1073	Priam wets his eyes	"	....	1548
Whose downward eye	"	....	1106	His eye drops fire	"	....	1552
that close his eyes	"	....	1127	about her tear-distained eye	"	....	1586
to wet his eyes	"	....	1179	Her eyes, though sad in tears	"	....	1592
The eyes of men	R L	....	30	beauty had purloin'd his eyes	"	....	1651
his traitor eye encloses	"	....	73	With sad-set eyes	"	....	1662
of still gazing eyes	"	....	84	Outruns the eye	"	....	1668
wonder of his eye	"	....	95	one pair of weeping eyes	"	....	1680
coped with stranger eyes	"	....	99	tears in Collatinus' eyes	"	....	1817
More than his eyes	"	....	105	thine own bright eyes	Son	1	5
closed up mortal eyes	"	....	163	own deep-sunken eyes	"	2	7
his lustful eye	"	....	179	every eye doth dwell	"	5	2
Mine eyes forego their light	"	....	228	each under eye	"	7	2
in my eager eyes	"	....	254	The eyes, 'fore duteous	"	7	11
countermand mine eye	"	....	276	to wet a widow's eye	"	9	1
That eye which looks	"	....	290	By children's eyes	"	9	8
That eye which him beholds	"	....	291	But from thine eyes	"	14	9
The eye of heaven	"	....	356	in eyes of men	"	16	12
his eyes begun	"	....	374	beauty of your eyes	"	17	5
lewd, unhallow'd eyes	"	....	392	the eye of heaven	"	18	5
Her eyes, like marigolds	"	....	397	or eyes can see	"	18	13
his wilful eye	"	....	417	An eye more bright	"	20	5
His eye, which late	"	....	426	steals men's eyes	"	20	8
cheers up his burning eye	"	....	435	To hear with eyes	"	23	14
His eye commends	"	....	436	Mine eye hath play'd	"	24	1
her lock'd-up eyes	"	....	446	with thine eyes	"	24	8
ugly in her eyes	"	....	459	what good turns eyes for eyes			
that the eyes fly	"	....	461	have done	"	24	9
For those thine eyes	"	....	483	Mine eyes have drawn thy shape	"	24	10
Only he hath an eye	"	....	496	Yet eyes this cunning	"	24	13
every open eye	"	....	520	at the sun's eye	"	25	6
cockatrice' dead-killing eye	"	....	540	fortune and men's eyes	"	29	1
Her pity-pleading eyes	"	....	561	can I drown an eye	"	30	5
Where subjects' eyes do learn	"	....	616	stol'n from mine eye	"	31	6
askance their eyes	"	....	637	with sovereign eye	"	33	2
That ever modest eyes	"	....	683	mine eyes best see	"	43	1
With heavy eye	"	....	709	to unseeing eyes	"	43	8
And my true eyes	"	....	748	mine eyes be blessed	"	43	9
every eye can see	"	....	750	on sightless eyes	"	43	12
And bids her eyes	"	....	758	Mine eye and heart	"	46	1
And Tarquin's eye	"	....	830	Mine eye my heart	"	46	3
And scarce hath eyes	"	....	857	My heart mine eye	"	46	4
his lewd eyes affright	"	....	971	with crystal eyes	"	46	6
gazed upon with every eye	"	....	1015	The clear eye's moiety	"	46	12
mine eyes, like sluices	"	....	1076	mine eye's due	"	46	13
to all fair eyes	"	....	1083	Betwixt mine eye and heart	"	47	1
O eye of eyes	"	....	1088	mine eye is famish'd	"	47	3
eyes that are sleeping	"	....	1090	my eye doth feast	"	47	5
to affright mine eye	"	....	1138	mine eye is my heart's guest	"	47	7
As charming any eye	"	....	1143	heart's and eye's delight	"	47	14

Eye—that sun, thine eye	Son	49	6
eyes of all posterity	"	55	11
and dwell in lovers' eyes	"	55	14
Thy hungry eyes	"	56	6
mine eye awake	"	61	10
possesseth all mine eye	"	62	1
world's eye doth view	"	69	1
the eye hath shown	"	69	8
their eyes were kind	"	69	11
Thine eyes, that taught	"	78	5
men's eyes shall lie	"	81	8
Which eyes not yet created	"	81	10
one of your fair eyes	"	84	13
In the eye of scorn	"	88	2
no hatred in thine eye	"	93	5
that eyes can see	"	95	12
your eye I eyed	"	104	2
eye may be deceived	"	104	12
of lip, of eye, of brow	"	106	6
with divining eyes	"	106	11
Have eyes to wonder	"	106	14
mine eye is in my mind	"	113	1
mine eye saith true	"	114	3
Mine eye well knows	"	114	11
That mine eye loves	"	114	14
mine eyes out of their sphere	"	119	7
false adulterate eyes	"	121	5
my mistress' eyes	"	127	9
Her eyes so suited	"	127	10
My mistress' eyes	"	130	1
Thine eyes I love	"	132	1
two mourning eyes	"	132	9
cruel eye hath taken	"	133	5
thou to mine eyes	"	137	1
If eyes, corrupt	"	137	5
Why of eyes' falsehood	"	137	7
Or mine eyes seeing	"	137	11
heart and eyes have erred	"	137	13
not with thine eye	"	139	3
glance thine eye aside	"	139	6
Bear thine eye straight	"	140	14
love thee with mine eyes	"	141	1
thine eyes woo	"	142	10
what eyes hath Love	"	148	1
my false eyes dote	"	148	5
Love's eye is not so true	"	148	8
can Love's eye be true	"	148	9
Lest eyes well-seeing	"	148	14
motion of thine eyes	"	149	12
gave eyes to blindness	"	152	11
mistress' eye Love's brand	"	153	9
my mistress' eyes	"	153	14
Sometimes her level'd eyes	L C	.....	22
bathed she in her fluxive eyes	"	.....	50
That maidens' eyes stuck over all his face	"	.....	81
Each eye that saw him	"	.....	89
To serve their eyes	"	.....	135
that mine eyes have seen	"	.....	190
which brought me to her eye	"	.....	247
put out Religion's eye	"	.....	250
Believed her eyes	"	.....	262
his watery eyes he did dismount	"	.....	281
the inundation of the eyes	"	.....	290
infected moisture of his eye	"	.....	323
heavenly rhetoric of thine eye	P P	3	1
favours to allure his eye	"	4	6
and makes his book thine eyes	"	5	5
Thine eye Jove's lightning seems	"	5	11
Eye—look'd on the world with glorious eye	P P	6	11
Lord, how mine eyes	"	15	1
trust the office of mine eyes	"	15	4
and eyes their wished sight	"	15	10
the fair'st that eye could see	"	16	3
When as thine eye	"	19	1
Eyeball—Look in mine eyeballs	V A	.....	119
Rolling his greedy eyeballs	R L	.....	368
Eyed—when first your eye I eyed	Son	104	2
Eyelid—She vail'd her eyelids	V A	.....	956
my drooping eyelids open wide	Son	27	7
My heavy eyelids	"	61	2
Eye-sore—And be an eye-sore	R L	.....	205
Eyne—sweet lips and crystal eyne	V A	.....	633
from my doting eyne	R L	.....	643
Her circled eyne	"	.....	1229
her napkin to her eyne	L C	.....	15
Face—with purple-colour'd face	V A	.....	1
breatheth in her face	"	.....	62
thine own face affected	"	.....	157
The sun doth burn my face	"	.....	186
of thy face excelling	"	.....	443
So is her face	"	.....	486
upon his hairless face	"	.....	487
face grows to face	"	.....	540
Her face doth reek	"	.....	555
that face of thine	"	.....	631
not mark my face	"	.....	643
My face is full of shame	"	.....	808
some kiss her face	"	.....	872
To wash the foul face	"	.....	983
His face seems twain	"	.....	1067
What face remains alive	"	.....	1076
To see his face	"	.....	1093
If he did see his face	"	.....	1109
And stains her face	"	.....	1122
Within whose face beauty and virtue strived	R L	.....	52
in Lucrece' face was seen	"	.....	64
in her fair face's field	"	.....	72
engraven in my face	"	.....	203
blows the smoke of it into his face	"	.....	312
The colour in thy face	"	.....	477
wrinkles of his face	"	.....	562
Cooling his hot face	"	.....	682
behold that face	"	.....	800
in Collatinus' face	"	.....	829
For why her face wore sorrow's livery	"	.....	1222
Poor women's faces	"	.....	1253
in both their faces blazed	"	.....	1353
triumphing in their faces	"	.....	1388
The face of either	"	.....	1396
Their face their manners most expressly told	"	.....	1397
a press of gaping faces	"	.....	1408
a face, a leg, a head	"	.....	1427
To find a face	"	.....	1444
His face, though full of cares	"	.....	1503
they view'd their faces	"	.....	1526
In his plain face	"	.....	1532
But such a face	"	.....	1540
in her sad face	"	.....	1591
The face, that map	"	.....	1712
mourning and congealed face	"	.....	1744
pale fear in his face	"	.....	1775
tell the face thou viewest	Son	3	1

Face—that face should form another	Son	3	2	Fair—this fair good-morrow	V A	859
ne'er touch'd earthly faces	"	17	8	from her two cheeks fair	"	957
face with Nature's own hand pointed	"	20	1	on her fair delight	"	1030
and her old face new	"	27	12	Having no fair to lose	"	1083
Kissing with golden face	"	33	3	to rob him of his fair	"	1086
on his celestial face	"	33	6	Of Collatine's fair love	R L	7
on my storm-beaten face	"	34	6	challenge that fair field	"	58
Methinks no face so gracious	"	62	5	in her fair face's field	"	72
husband; so love's face	"	93	2	in his fair welkin	"	116
That in thy face	"	93	10	'Fair torch, burn out thy light	"	190
owners of their faces	"	94	7	Let fair humanity abhor	"	195
my love's sweet face survey	"	100	9	foul thoughts might compass his		
and there appears a face	"	103	6	fair fair	"	346
art's false-borrow'd face	"	127	6	Look, as the fair and fiery-pointed		
Thy face hath not the power	"	131	6	sun	"	372
but thinking on thy face	"	131	10	her other fair hand was	"	393
eyes become thy face	"	132	9	From this fair throne	"	413
upon so foul a face	"	137	12	And makest fair reputation	"	623
from my face she turns	"	139	11	From their fair life	"	661
which flies before her face	"	143	7	his soul's fair temple	"	719
eyes stuck over all his face	L C		81	the supreme fair	"	780
were levell'd on my face	"		282	Or toads infect fair founts	"	850
Faced—like a bold-faced suitor	V A		6	to all fair eyes	"	1085
like a pale-faced coward	"		569	my life's fair end shall free it	"	1208
by this black-faced night	"		773	Nor why her fair cheeks	"	1225
when a black-faced cloud	R L		547	Of those fair suns	"	1230
Charging the sour-faced groom	"		1334	bid fair Lucrece speak	"	1268
such black-faced storms	"		1518	So fair a form	"	1530
Fact—ay, if the fact be known	"		239	hath thy fair colour spent	"	1600
powers to whom I pray abhor this				ere I name him, you fair lords	"	1688
fact	"		349	'tis a meritorious, fair design	"	1692
Faculty—Have faculty by nature	Son	122	6	'He, he, fair lords	"	1721
Fade—eternal summer shall not fade	"	18	9	that fair, fresh mirror	"	1760
and unrespected fade	"	54	10	by whom thy fair wife bleeds	"	1824
Fadeth—sunset fadeth in the west	"	73	6	from forth her fair streets chased	"	1834
Fading—and all her fading sweets	"	19	7	By heaven's fair sun	"	1837
upon thy fading mansion	"	146	6	This fair child of mine	Son	2 10
Fain—now she fain would speak	V A		221	where is she so fair	"	3 5
Faint—Who is so faint	"		401	thou art much too fair	"	6 13
she faint with dearth	"		545	Who lets so fair a house	"	13 9
Hot, faint, and weary	"		559	Inward worth nor outward fair	"	16 11
Grew I not faint	"		645	every fair from fair sometime de-		
make my faint heart bleed	"		669	clines	"	18 7
agues pale and faint	"		739	of that fair thou owest	"	18 10
Faint—Affection faints not	"		569	my love's fair brow	"	19 9
Faint not, faint heart	R L		1299	every fair with his fair doth re-		
Here manly Hector faints	"		1486	hearse	"	21 4
O, how I faint	Son	80	1	my love is as fair	"	21 10
Fainted—with grief or travail he				their fair leaves spread	"	25 5
had fainted	R L		1543	with fair aspect	"	26 10
Faintly—faintly she up-heaveth	V A		482	thy fair imperfect shade	"	43 11
He faintly flies	R L		740	Of thy fair health	"	45 12
Fair—her fair immortal hand	V A		80	thy fair appearance lies	"	46 8
those fair lips of thine	"		115	The rose looks fair	"	54 3
mine be not so fair	"		116	of fair were born	"	68 3
Fair flowers that are not	"		131	To thy fair flower	"	69 12
o'erwhelming his fair sight	"		183	ever yet the fair	"	70 2
Speak, fair; but speak fair words	"		208	such fair assistance	"	78 2
Of the fair breeder	"		282	Of their fair subject	"	82 4
With one fair hand	"		351	Thou art as fair	"	82 5
his fair cheek feels	"		352	Thou truly fair	"	82 11
his youth's fair fee	"		393	to your fair no painting set	"	83 2
Fair fall the wit	"		472	one of your fair eyes	"	83 13
Like the fair sun	"		483	cause of this fair gift	"	87 7
'Fair queen,' quoth he	"		523	But what's so blessed fair	"	92 13
framing thee so fair	"		744	things turn to fair	"	95 12
so fair a hope is slain	"		762	To me, fair friend	"	104 1
Of those fair arms	"		812	'Fair, kind, and true	"	105 9
lost the fair discovery	"		828	'Fair, kind, and true	"	105 10

FAIR 92 FALSE

Fair—'Fair, kind, and true	Son 105	13
hallow'd thy fair name	" 108	8
black was not counted fair	" 127	1
At such who, not born fair	" 127	11
no fair acceptance shine	" 135	8
no fair beseechers kill	" 135	13
To put fair truth	" 137	12
Is a man right fair	" 144	3
have sworn thee fair	" 147	13
if that be fair	" 148	5
have sworn thee fair	" 152	13
when in his fair parts	L C	83
from many a several fair	"	206
annexions of fair gems	"	208
Showing fair nature	"	311
is a man right fair	P P	2 3
with her fair pride	"	2 8
Then, thou fair sun	"	3 10
she on her back, fair queen	"	4 13
Fair is my love, but not so fair as fickle	"	7 1
Fair was the morn when the fair queen of love	"	9 1
did I see a fair sweet youth	"	9 9
Sweet rose, fair flower	"	10 1
Fair creature, kill'd too soon	"	10 4
Spied a blossom passing fair	"	17 3
That are either true or fair	P T	66
Fairer—Thrice fairer than myself	V A	7
Shall hate be fairer lodged	Son 10	10
but fairer we it deem	" 54	3
Grows fairer than at first	" 119	12
made fairer by their place	L C	117
None fairer, nor none falser	P P 7	6
Fairest—O fairest mover on this mortal round	V A	368
From fairest creatures	Son 1	1
descriptions of the fairest wights	" 106	2
Thou art the fairest	" 131	4
Thy black is fairest	" 131	12
The fairest votary took up that fire	" 154	5
the fairest one of three	P P 16	1
the fair'st that eye could see	" 16	3
Fairing—Fairing the foul	Son 127	6
Fairly—which fairly doth excel	" 5	4
Fairy—Or, like a fairy, trip	V A	146
Faith—plight your honourable faiths to me	R L	1690
And purest faith unhappily foresworn	Son 66	4
Yet, in good faith	" 131	5
In faith, I do not love thee	" 141	1
and new faith torn	" 152	3
And all my honest faith	" 152	6
O never faith could hold	P P 5	2
Her faith, her oaths	" 7	12
Faith's defying	" 18	6
Where her faith was firmly fix'd	" 18	11
In faith, you had not had it	" 19	24
Faithful—Faithful friends are hard to find	" 21	34
Faithful friend from flattering foe	" 21	58
Fulchion—His falchion on a flint	R L	176
under his insulting falchion	"	509
by Tarquin's falchion	"	1046
With shining falchion	"	1626
Falcon—As falcons to the lure	V A	1027
Which like a falcon	R L	506
as fowl hear falcon's bells	"	511
Fall—Hindering their present fall	R L	551
with their fresh falls' haste	"	650
not in smiling pomp, nor falls	Son 124	6
And falls through wind before the fall should be	P P 10	6
By shallow rivers, by whose falls	" 20	7
Fall—Fair fall the wit	V A	472
mellow plum doth fall	"	527
fall to the earth	"	546
He on her belly falls	"	594
and going I shall fall	"	719
But if thou fall	"	721
you will fall again	"	769
falls an orient drop beside	"	981
rise up and fall	R L	466
falls into thy boundless flood	"	653
shall thereon fall and die	"	1139
why should so many fall	"	1483
For every tear he falls	"	1551
He falls, and bathes the pale fear	"	1775
so fair a house fall to decay	Son 13	9
fall by thy side	" 151	12
for whose dear love I rise and fall	" 151	14
that lets not bounty fall	L C	41
Fall'n—As apt as new-fall'n snow	V A	354
Falleth—she flatly falleth down	"	463
With this, she falleth in the place	"	1121
Falling—like a falling plume	"	314
False—Gives false alarum	"	651
sometime false doth bring	"	658
a false sound enter there	"	780
but thy false dart	"	941
with false bethinking grieves	"	1024
false and full of fraud	"	1141
trustless wings of false desire	R L	2
O rash-false heat	"	48
this false lord arrived	"	50
triumph in so false a foe	"	77
suspecteth the false worshippers	"	86
my false heart bleed	"	228
Unto a view so false	"	292
will prison false desire	"	642
thou traitor, thou false thief	"	888
false slave to false delight	"	927
of this false night's abuses	"	1075
serve thou false Tarquin so	"	1197
fear that false hearts have	"	1512
false Sinon's tears	"	1560
and that false Tarquin stain'd	"	1743
as is false women's fashion	Son 20	4
less false in rolling	" 20	5
being false to me	" 41	14
Why should false painting	" 67	5
To show false Art	" 68	14
true love may seem false in this	" 72	9
Thou mayst be false	" 92	14
the false heart's history	" 93	7
that I was false of heart	" 109	1
others' false adulterate eyes	" 121	5
with art's false borrow'd face	" 127	6
with a false esteem	" 127	12
belied with false compare	" 130	14
that is not false I swear	" 131	9
And to this false plague	" 137	14
in the world's false subtleties	" 138	4
And seal'd false bonds	" 142	7
whereon my false eyes dote	" 148	5
'O false blood, thou register of lies	L C	52
Of this false jewel	"	154

FALSE 93 FAULT

False—O, that false fire	L C	324
in the world's false forgeries	P P	1 4
to this false perjury	"	3 3
False-creeping—False-creeping craft	R L	1517
Falsehood—To unmask falsehood	"	910
From hands of falsehood	Son	48 4
Why of eye's falsehood	"	137 7
Falsely—That censures falsely	"	118 4
Falseness—Did livery falseness in a pride of youth	L C	105
Falser—nor none falser to deface her	P P	7 6
False-speaking—credit her false-speaking tongue	Son	138 7
credit her false-speaking tongue	P P	1 7
Faltering—the .... feeble souls	R L	1768
Fame—espoused to more fame	"	20
should underprop her fame	"	53
to her ears her husband's fame	"	106
a badge of fame	"	1054
shall my fame be bred	"	1188
that did my fame confound	"	1202
And all my fame	"	1203
with fame and not with fire	"	1491
My fame, and thy perpetual infamy	"	1638
speaking of your fame	Son	80 4
Give my love fame	"	100 13
her fame so to herself	L C	243
fear, law, kindred, fame	"	270
Fame—shall fame his wit	Son	84 11
Familiar—that affable, ... ghost	"	86 9
Famine—making a famine	"	1 7
Famish—But rather famish them	V A	20
Famish'd—mine eye is famish'd	Son	47 3
Famoused—warrior .... for fight	"	25 9
Fan—To fan and blow them dry	V A	52
Fancy—to be soft fancy's slave	R L	200
by dreadful fancy waking	"	450
Towards this afflicted fancy	L C	61
wounded fancies sent me	"	197
Her fancy fell a-turning	P P	16 4
As well as fancy	"	19 4
Fang—Under whose sharp fangs	V A	663
Fangled—garments, though new-fangled ill	Son	91 3
Fanning—Fanning the hairs	V A	306
Fantastic—humour of fantastic wits	"	850
Fantasy—'tis a causeless fantasy	"	897
Far—he scuds far off	"	301
far off upon a hill	"	697
By this, far off	"	973
Which far exceeds	R L	81
Far from the purpose	"	113
doth so far proceed	"	251
far poorer than before	"	693
I thus far can dispense	"	1279
Met far from home	"	1596
And far the weaker	"	1647
From far where I abide	Son	27 5
How far I toil	"	28 8
From limits far remote	"	44 4
Thus far the miles	"	50 4
So far from home	"	61 6
From me far off	"	61 14
So far from variation	"	76 2
inferior far to his	"	80 7
How far a modern quill	"	83 7
smell far worse than weeds	"	94 14
more strong, far greater	"	119 12
builded far from accident	"	124 5
Far—Coral is far more red	Son	130 2
a far more pleasing sound	"	130 10
Thus far for love	"	136 4
Thus far I count my gain	"	141 13
Fare—Tarquin fares this night	R L	698
So fares it with this faultful lord	"	715
To ask the spotted princess how she fares	"	721
to ask her how she fares	"	1594
Fare well I could not	P P	14 6
Farewell—Bids him farewell	V A	580
Farewell! thou art too dear	Son	87 1
'Farewell,' quoth she	P P	14 5
Farewell, sweet lass	"	18 49
Then farewell his great renown	"	21 48
Faring—her babe from faring ill	Son	22 12
Far-off—See those far-off eyes	R L	1386
Farther—still farther off from thee	Son	28 8
For thou not farther	"	47 11
seeing farther than the eye	"	69 8
flesh stays no farther reason	"	151 8
Farthest—Upon the farthest earth	"	44 6
transport me farthest	"	117 8
Fashion—tears may grace the	R L	1319
as is false women's fashion	Son	20 4
inviting time our fashion calls	"	124 8
Fast—the green sticks fast	V A	527
twenty locks kept fast	"	575
The dove sleeps fast	R L	360
While in his hold-fast foot	"	555
sour-faced groom to hie as fast	"	1334
that forced him on so fast	"	1670
As fast as thou shalt wane, so fast thou grow'st	Son	11 1
And die as fast	"	12 12
As fast as objects	"	114 8
that him as fast doth bind	"	134 8
Fast—eagle, sharp by fast	V A	55
feasting to a public fast	R L	891
Fasten—Nimbly she fastens	V A	38
Fasten'd—So fasten'd in her arms	"	68
Faster—and then it faster rock'd	R L	262
faster than Time wastes life	Son	100 13
Fastly—afflicted fancy fastly drew	L C	61
Fat—that breeds the fat earth's store	R L	1837
Fatal—Wreathed up in fatal folds	V A	879
And kiss'd the fatal knife	R L	1843
Fate—I am the mistress of my fate	"	1069
look upon myself, and curse my fate	Son	29 4
Father—this was thy father's guise	V A	1177
Here was thy father's bed	"	1183
I their father had not been	R L	210
Their father was too weak	"	863
doting father of his fruit	"	1064
Till Lucrece' father	"	1732
the father's image lies	"	1753
Thy father die, and not thy father thee	"	1771
Then son and father weep	"	1791
The father says 'She's mine	"	1795
You had a father	Son	13 11
decrepit father takes delight	"	37 1
'Father,' she says	L C	71
'O father, what a hell	"	288
Fault—And 'tis your fault	V A	381
the cold fault cleanly out	"	694
'Tis not my fault	"	1003
The shame and fault	R L	238

Fault—the fault is thine	R L	482	Fear—If but for fear of this	R L	614
The fault unknown	"	527	sweating with guilty fear	"	740
Are nature's faults	"	509	That dying fear	"	1246
When pattern'd by thy fault	"	629	a kind of heavy fear	"	1435
Men's faults do seldom	"	653	Nor ashy-pale the fear	"	1512
And by their mortal fault	"	724	weaker with so strong a fear	"	1647
That all the faults	"	804	the pale fear in his face	"	1775
Nor fold my fault	"	1073	Is it for fear to wet a widow's eye	Son	9	1
are their own faults' books	"	1253	Who with his fear is put	"	23	2
Poor women's faults	"	1258	So I, for fear of trust	"	23	5
Yet with the fault	"	1279	I was not sick of any fear	"	86	12
can give the fault amending	"	1614	For fear of which	"	104	13
All men make faults	Son	35	5	Not mine own fears	"	107	1
For to thy sensual fault	"	35	9	Applying fears to hopes, and hopes
Of faults conceal'd	"	88	7	to fears	"	119	3
forsake me for some fault	"	89	1	For fear of harms	L C	165
Some say, thy fault is youth	"	96	1	Of wealth, of filial fear	"	27
Both grace and faults	"	96	3	all forces, shocks, and fears	"	273
Thou makest faults graces	"	96	4	my sober guards and civil fears	"	298
grew to faults assured	"	118	10	All fears scorn I	P P	18	20
And in our faults	"	138	14	Fear—I thy death should fear	V A	660
thy foul faults should find	"	148	14	bids them fear no more	"	899
Lest guilty of my faults	"	151	4	you need not fear	"	1083
Outfacing faults in love	P T	1	8	he would not fear him	"	1094
our faults in love thus smother'd be	"	1	14	It shall not fear	"	1154
then it is no fault of mine	"	3	12	no secret bushes fear	R L	88
Faultful—this faultful lord of Rome	R L	715	Who fears a sentence	"	244
Favour—If thou wilt deign this	V A	15	Then who fears sinking	"	280
Some favour, some remorse	"	257	so heedful fear	"	281
Both favour, savour	"	747	The merchant fears, ere rich at
in favour with their stars	Son	25	1	home	"	336
The most sweet favour	"	113	10	now I need not fear to die	"	1032
dwellers on form and favour	"	125	5	thou wilt be stol'n, I fear	Son	48	13
A thousand favours	L C	36	that which it fears to lose	"	64	14
favours to allure his eye	P P	4	6	to fear the worst of wrongs	"	92	5
Favour'd—Were I hard-favour'd	V A	133	that fears no blot	"	92	13
Hard-favour'd tyrant	"	931	It fears not policy	"	124	9
"For some hard-favour'd groom	R L	1632	Yet fear her, O thou minion	"	126	9
Favourite—Great princes' favourites	Son	25	5	But, soft! enough,—too much, I
Fawn—Hasting to feed her fawn	V A	876	fear	P P	19	49
that I do fawn upon	Son	149	6	Fear'd—I fear'd thy fortune	V A	642
Fawn'd—They that fawn'd on him				nor fear'd no hooks	R L	103
before	P P	21	49	still are fear'd for love	"	611
Fawneth—lion .... o'er his prey	R L	421	I fear'd by Tarquin's falchion	"	1046
Fear—breeder full of fear	V A	320	But when I fear'd	"	1048
for fear of slips	"	515	Feareth—th' other feareth harm	"	172
signs of fear lurk	"	644	Fearful—As fearful of him, part	V A	630
fear doth teach it	"	670	Pursue these fearful creatures	"	677
wit waits on fear	"	690	Whereon with fearful eyes	"	927
The fear whereof doth make	"	880	in this fearful flood	R L	1741
doubt and bloodless fear	"	891	O fearful meditation	Son	65	9
A second fear through all	"	903	Fearfully—Where fearfully the dogs	V A	886
I felt a kind of fear	"	998	The roses fearfully on thorns	Son	99	8
thou art so full of fear	"	1021	Fearfully	P P	18	44
where is no cause of fear	"	1153	Fearing—fearing my love's decease	V A	1002
Put fear to valour	"	1158	fearing to creep forth	"	1036
mother of dread and fear	R L	117	Fearing some hard news	R L	235
But honest fear	"	173	fearing no such thing	"	363
Here pale with fear	"	183	fearing of Time's tyranny	Son	115	9
the fear doth still exceed	"	229	the loss thereof still fearing	P P	7	10
extreme fear can neither fight	"	230	Feast—the feast might ever last	V A	447
O, how her fear	"	257	disturb the feast	"	450
tremble with her loyal fear	"	261	then my eye doth feast	Son	47	5
Then, childish fear, avaunt	"	274	feasts so solemn and so rare	"	52	5
Yet still pursues his fear	"	308	To any sensual feast	"	141	8
fear's frost hath dissolution	"	355	For feasts of love	L C	181
confounded in a thousand fears	"	456	Feast-finding—Feast-finding min-
With trembling fear	"	511	strels	R L	817
will make thee only loved for fear	"	610	Feasting—Thy private feasting	"	891

FEASTING 95 FIELD

Feasting—Justice is feasting	R L	905
all full with feasting	Son 75	9
Feat—With sleided silk feat and affectedly	L C	48
Feather—on feathers, flesh, and bone V A		56
at stirring of a feather	"	302
with thought's feathers flies	R L	1216
Have added feathers	Son 78	7
Feather'd—wave like .... wings	V A	306
hollow-swelling feather'd breasts	R L	1122
One of her feather'd creatures	Son 143	2
Save the eagle, feather'd king	P T	11
Feature—it shapes them to your....	Son 113	12
Featured—Featured like him	" 29	6
Featureless—Harsh, ..., and rude	" 11	10
Fed—with thy increase be fed	V A	170
eye so full hath fed	"	399
simple semblance he hath fed	"	795
He fed them with his sight	"	1104
that those shrunk pipes had fed	R L	1455
Within be fed, without be rich	Son 146	12
Fee—his youth's fair fee	V A	393
The honey fee of parting	"	538
hath deserved a greater fee	"	609
but sin ne'er gives a fee	R L	913
now becomes a fee	Son 120	13
Feeble—Thy mark is feeble age	V A	941
Feeble Desire, all recreant	R L	710
faltering feeble souls alive	"	1768
Like feeble age, he reeleth	Son 7	10
Her feeble force	P P	21
Feed—why shouldst thou feed	V A	169
Feed where thou wilt	"	232
glutton-like she feeds	"	548
that did feed her sight	"	822
Hasting to feed her fawn	"	876
feeds his vulture folly	R L	556
while the oppressor feeds	"	905
To feed oblivion	"	947
mountain-spring that feeds a dale	"	1077
justice feeds iniquity	"	1687
Feeds on the rarities	Son 60	11
So shalt thou feed on Death, that feeds on men	"	146 13
My flocks feed not	P P	18 1
Shepherds feed their flocks	" 20	6
Feeder—Being nurse and feeder	V A	446
Feed'st—Feed'st thy light's flame	Son 1	6
Feedeth—She feedeth on the steam	V A	63
Feeling—by feeding is allay'd	Son 56	3
did I frame my feeding	" 118	6
Feeding on that which doth preserve	" 147	3
Feel—and canst not feel	V A	201
scorns the heat he feels	"	311
his fair cheek feels	"	352
'why dost thou feel it	"	373
May feel her heart, poor citizen	R L	465
what helpless shame I feel	"	756
though I feel thou art	Son 48	10
which I then did feel	" 120	2
Feel'st—when thou feel'st it cold	" 2	14
Feeling—that the sense of feeling	V A	439
numbs each feeling part	"	892
life and feeling of her passion	R L	1317
Being from the feeling	"	1578
Not by our feeling	Son 121	4
Nor tender feeling	" 141	6
some feeling pity	L C	178

Feeling—Feeling it break	L C	275
Feelingly—sorrow then is feelingly sufficed	R L	1112
Here feelingly she weeps	"	1492
Feeling-painful—More feeling-painful: let it then suffice	"	1679
Fee-simple—And was my own	L C	144
Feign—goal of both, as poets feign	P P	8 13
Feigned—your feigned tears	V A	425
Fell—in fell battle's rage	R L	145
fell exploits effecting	"	429
tragedies and murders fell	"	766
by Time's fell hand defaced	Son 64	1
when that fell arrest	" 74	1
but spite of heaven's fell rage	L C	13
Fell—fell I not downright	V A	643
When their dress fell	R L	1526
as she wrought thee, fell a-doting	Son 20	10
that so fell sick of you	" 118	14
laid by his brand and fell asleep	" 153	1
I fell, and yet do question make	L C	321
Then fell she on her back	P P	4 13
and yet she fell a-turning	" 7	16
And as he fell to her, so fell she to him	"	11 4
Her fancy fell a-turning	"	16 4
As it fell upon a day	"	21 1
Fellow—All thy .... birds do sing	"	21 23
Fellowship—And fellowship in woe	R L	790
Felt—were it with thy hand felt	V A	143
having felt the sweetness	"	553
I felt a kind of fear	"	998
When more is felt than one hath power to tell	R L	1288
What freezings have I felt	Son 97	3
Female—proud, as females are	V A	309
to hell, my female evil	Son 144	5
to hell, my female evil	P P	2 5
Fence—the red should .... the white	R L	64
Fester—Lilies that fester	Son 94	14
Fetched—And as she fetched breath	P P	11 11
Fetlock—fetlocks shag and long	V A	295
Fever—As burning fevers	"	739
of this madding fever	Son 119	8
My love is as a fever	" 147	1
Augur of the fever's end	P T	7
Few—enjoy'd but of a few	R L	22
'Few words,' quoth she	"	1613
nor none, or few, do hang	Son 73	2
Fickle—It shall be fickle	V A	1141
Dost hold Time's fickle glass	Son 126	2
a fickle maid full pale	L C	5
but not so fair as fickle	P P	7 1
Fortune, cursed fickle dame	"	18 15
Whilst as fickle fortune smiled	"	21 29
Fie—'Fie, no more of love	V A	185
'Fie, lifeless picture	"	211
'Fie, fie,' he says	"	611
'Fie, fie, fond love	"	1021
'Fie, fie, fie,' now would she cry	P P	21 13
Field—The field's chief flower	V A	8
Making my arms his field	"	108
tempest to the field	"	454
dare not stay the field	"	894
doth challenge that fair field	R L	58
in her fair face's field	"	72
the fields of fruitful Italy	"	107
bold Hector, march'd to field	"	1430
in thy beauty's field	Son 2	2

Entry	Ref	No.
Field—valleys, dales, and fields	P P	20 3
Fiend—with such foul fiends	V A	638
my angel be turn'd fiend	Son	144 9
night, who, like a fiend	"	145 11
The naked and concealed fiend	L C	317
my angel be turn'd fiend	P P	2 9
Foul precurrer of the fiend	P T	6
Fierce—from the fierce tiger's jaws	Son	19 3
Or some fierce thing	"	23 3
Fiery—Red cheeks and fiery eyes	V A	219
in his fiery race	Son	51 11
Fiery-pointed—the fair and .... sun	R L	372
Fight—foil'd the god of fight	V A	114
fight brings beauty under	"	746
to use it in the fight	R L	62
makes them still to fight	"	68
with life's strength doth fight	"	124
can neither fight nor fly	"	230
The coward fights	"	273
Desire doth fight with Grace	"	712
an eager combat fight	"	1298
encouraging the Greeks to fight	"	1402
warrior famoused for fight	Son	25 9
'gainst his glory fight	"	60 7
against myself I'll fight	"	88 3
that love with love did fight	P P	16 5
vanquish'd men in bloody fight	"	18 36
Fighting—note the fighting conflict	V A	345
slaves for pillage fighting	R L	428
but fighting outwardly	L C	203
Figure—but figures of delight	Son	98 11
Steal from his figure	"	104 10
Laundering the silken figures	L C	17
Figured— ... to thee my true spirit	Son	108 2
to take her figured proffer	P P	4 10
Figuring—Figuring that their passions	L C	199
Filching—Doubting the filching age	Son	75 6
Filed—by all the Muses filed	"	85 4
Smooth not thy tongue with filed talk	P P	19 8
Filial—Of wealth, of filial fear	L C	270
Fill—as minutes fill up hours	R L	297
To fill with worm-holes	"	946
although to-day thou fill	Son	56 5
doth the impression fill	"	112 1
Ay, fill it full with wills	"	136 6
Fill'd—'My daughter' and 'my wife' with clamours fill'd	R L	1804
If it were fill'd	Son	17 2
drain'd his blood and fill'd his brow	"	63 3
countenance fill'd up his line	"	86 13
Fillet—Some in her threaden fillet	L C	33
Filleth—she feeds, yet never filleth	V A	548
Filling—coral cisterns filling	R L	1234
Filth—fly with the filth away	"	1010
Find—she in him finds missing	V A	605
in a brake she finds a hound	"	913
Find sweet beginning	"	1138
shall he think to find a stranger just	R L	159
finds no excuse nor end	"	238
from thence, where it may find	"	760
To find some desperate instrument	"	1038
Will we find out	"	1146
To find a face	"	1414
And who she finds forlorn	"	1500
It cannot be, I find	"	1539
That he finds means	"	1561
Find—Who finds his Lucrece	R L	1585
this refuge let me find	"	1654
Find no determination	Son	13 6
that I in heaven find	"	14 8
To find where your true image	"	24 6
for myself no quiet find	"	27 14
Both find each other	"	42 11
Shall reasons find	"	49 8
will my poor beast then find	"	51 5
your praise shall still find room	"	55 10
To find out shames	"	61 7
and thou shalt find	"	77 10
Wherein it finds a joy	"	91 6
O, what a happy title do I find	"	92 11
thou in this shalt find thy monument	"	107 13
when it alteration finds	"	116 3
and find the lesson true	"	118 13
now I find true	"	119 9
And thou shalt find it	"	142 4
thy foul faults should find	"	148 14
find their sepulchres in mud	L C	46
to do will aptly find	"	88
which abroad they find	"	137
that so their shame did find	"	187
All unseen 'gan passage find	P P	17 6
A cripple soon can find a halt	"	19 10
Faithful friends are hard to find	"	21 34
Finding—Finding their enemy	V A	887
Feast-finding minstrels	R L	817
Finding thy worth	Son	82 6
Finding the first conceit	"	108 13
Finding myself in honour	L C	150
Fine—to fine the hate of foes	R L	936
belongs to love's fine wit	Son	23 14
the fine point of seldom pleasure	"	52 4
Finger—locks her lily fingers one in one	V A	228
He bends her fingers	"	476
the needle his finger pricks	R L	319
As on the finger of a throned queen	Son	96 5
With thy sweet fingers	"	128 3
O'er whom thy fingers walk	"	128 11
Give them thy fingers	"	128 14
Fire—coals of glowing fire	V A	35
yet her fire must burn	"	94
all compact of fire	"	149
darts forth the fire	"	196
scornfully glisters like fire	"	275
love's fire doth assuage	"	334
It flash'd forth fire	"	348
set the heart on fire	"	388
To touch the fire	"	402
or in the fire	"	494
do abate the fire	"	654
Mine eyes are turn'd to fire	"	1072
melt at mine eyes' red fire	"	1073
matter is to fire	"	1162
bears the lightless fire	R L	4
sparks of fire do fly	"	177
I enforced this fire	"	181
Against love's fire	"	355
huge fires abide	"	647
Thou blow'st the fire	"	884
That two red fires	"	1353
the fire that burneth here	"	1475
with fame and not with fire	"	1491
His eye drops fire	"	1552
balls of quenchless fire	"	1554

FIRE 97 FLIGHT

Fire—in his fire doth quake	R L	1556
hot-burning fire doth dwell	"	1557
she gives her sorrow fire	"	1604
slight air and purging fire	Son 45	1
nor war's quick fire shall burn	" 55	7
the glowing of such fire	" 73	9
And his love-kindling fire	" 153	3
from this holy fire of love	" 153	5
Where Cupid got new fire	" 153	11
votary took up that fire	" 154	5
Which from Love's fire	" 154	10
Love's fire heats water	" 154	11
Both fire from hence	L C	294
O, that false fire	"	324
is music and sweet fire	P P 5	12
as straw with fire flameth	" 7	13
Fire—wind that fires the torch	R L	315
fire my good one out	Son 144	14
fire my good one out	P P 2	14
Fired—Love's brand new-fired	Son 153	9
Firm—And the firm soil win	" 64	7
Firmly—on that he firmly doted	R L	116
faith was firmly fix'd in love	P P 18	11
First—Struck dead at first	V A	250
who shall cope him first	"	888
who first should dry his tears	"	1092
I should have kill'd him first	"	1118
First red as roses	R L	258
First, like a trumpet	"	470
First, hovering o'er the paper	"	1297
wert thou first created	Son 20	9
The first my thought	" 45	3
that made me first your slave	" 58	1
at first in character was done	" 59	8
At first the very worst	" 90	12
when first your eye I eyed	" 104	2
Since first I saw you fresh	" 104	8
when first I hallow'd	" 108	8
Finding the first conceit	" 108	13
O, 'tis the first	" 114	9
mine eye loves it and doth first begin	" 114	14
Grows fairer than at first	" 119	12
when first it 'gins to bud	P P 13	3
First-born—With April's first-born flowers	Son 21	7
Fish—The fishes spread on it	V A	1100
Fisher—No fisher but the ungrown fry forbears	"	526
Fit—season once more fits	"	327
gouts and painful fits	R L	856
shall fit the trespass best	"	1613
which wounded bosoms fits	Son 120	12
Fitted—out of their spheres been fitted	" 119	7
Five—five hundred courses	" 59	6
my five wits nor my five senses	" 141	9
Fix—Will fix a sharp knife	R L	1138
Fixed—Whose beams upon his hairless face are fix'd	V A	487
eyes are sadly fixed	R L	561
from their fixed places	"	1525
candles fix'd in heaven's air	Son 21	12
with his colour fix'd	" 101	6
it is an ever-fixed mark	" 116	5
and nowhere fix'd	L C	27
was firmly fix'd in love	P P 18	11
Flame—with embracing flames	R L	6
And to the flame	"	180
Flame—Feed'st thy light's flame	Son 1	6
seem'd my flame to qualify	" 109	2
My most full flame	" 115	4
Not one whose flame	L C	191
In a mutual flame	P T	24
Flame—That flame through water	L C	287
Flameth—as straw with fire	P P 7	113
Flaming—by his flaming torch	R L	418
with a flaming light	"	1627
Flaming in the phœnix' sight	P T	35
Flank—In his soft flank	V A	1053
nuzzling in his flank	"	1115
Flap-mouth'd—flap-mouth'd mourner, black and grim	"	920
Flash'd—It flash'd forth fire	"	318
Flatly—she flatly falleth down	"	463
Flatter—And flatters her	"	978
one doth flatter thee	"	989
Th' one sweetly flatters	R L	172
To flatter thee	"	1061
Only to flatter fools	"	1559
false Sinon's tears doth flatter	"	1560
So flatter I the swart-complexion'd night	Son 28	11
Flatter the mountain-tops	" 33	2
as a dream doth flatter	" 87	13
Every one that flatters thee	P P 21	31
Flatter'd—flatter'd by their leader's jocund show	R L	296
by lies we flatter'd be	Son 138	14
Flatterer—To critic and to flatterer	" 112	11
Flattering—His flattering 'Holla	V A	284
and flattering thoughts retire	R L	644
And with such-like flattering	P P 21	41
Faithful friend from flattering foe	" 21	58
Flattery—your feigned tears, your flattery	V A	425
Sweet flattery! then she loves	Son 42	14
the monarch's plague, this flattery	" 114	2
'tis flattery in my seeing	" 114	9
Flaw—gusts and foul flaws	V A	456
Fled—Love to heaven is fled	"	793
at him should have fled	"	947
her eyes are fled	"	1037
to the world that I am fled	Son 71	3
whore is my judgement fled	" 148	3
And blushing fled	P P 9	14
All our evening sport from us is fled	" 18	47
Phœnix and the turtle fled	P T	23
Fleece—Till with her own white	R L	678
Ere beauty's dead fleece	Son 68	8
Fleetest—sorry seasons as thou	" 19	5
Fleet-foot—Or as the fleet-foot roe	V A	561
Fleeting—a froth of fleeting joy	R L	212
the pleasure of the fleeting year	Son 97	2
Fleet-wing'd—For fleet-wing'd duty	R L	1216
Flesh—feathers, flesh, and bone	V A	56
My flesh is soft and plump	"	142
The flesh being proud	R L	712
with her nails her flesh doth tear	"	739
the dull substance of my flesh	Son 44	1
Shall neigh,—no dull flesh	" 51	11
flesh stays no farther reason	" 151	8
Flew—observed as they flew	L C	60
Flight—tender smell or speedy	R L	695
cross Tarquin in his flight	"	968
scars of battle 'scapeth by the flight	L C	244

7

Flint—Nay, more than flint	V A	200	Fly—the eyes fly from their lights	R L	461
His fulchion on a flint	R L	176	He faintly flies	"	740
As from this cold flint	"	181	fly with the filth away	"	1010
Flint-hearted—'O, pity,' 'gan she cry, 'flint-hearted boy	V A	95	wheresoe'er they fly determining which way to fly	" "	1014 1150
Flinty—flinty, hard as steel	"	199	with thought's feathers flies	"	1216
Flock—among a flock of sheep	"	685	and from his lips did fly	"	1406
My flocks feed not	P P 18	1	and through her wounds doth fly	"	1728
Flocks all sleeping	" 18	42	A crow that flies	Son 70	4
shepherds feed their flocks	" 20	6	Ignorance aloft to fly	" 78	6
Flood—jewel in the flood	V A	824	which flies before her face	" 143	7
drown'd him in the flood	R L	266	that which flies from thee	" 143	9
into thy boundless flood	"	653	the caged cloister fly	L C	249
forward like a gentle flood	"	1118	from his heart did fly	"	325
no flood by raining slaketh	"	1677	Fly—poor flies in his fume	V A	316
in this fearful flood	"	1741	Flying—The timorous flying hare	V A	674
and gave the flood	L C	44	Foam—They join and shoot their		
why was not I a flood	P P 6	14	foam	R L	1442
Flood-gates—But through the	V A	959	Foe—so white a foe	V A	364
Flourish—the flourish set on youth	Son 60	9	that ever threat his foes	"	620
Flow—And to his flow	R L	651	to amaze his foes	"	684
Thus ebbs and flows	"	1569	if his foes pursue him	"	699
an eye, unused to flow	Son 30	5	triumph in so false a foe	R L	77
Flow'd—downward flow'd apace	L C	284	a parley to his heartless foe	"	471
Flower—The field's chief flower	V A	8	to fine the hate of foes	"	936
gardens full of flowers	"	65	to see his friends his foes	"	988
Fair flowers that are not	"	131	to scratch her wicked foe	"	1035
These forceless flowers	"	152	will kill myself, thy foe	"	1196
fresh flowers being shed	"	665	to ban her cruel foes	"	1460
thou pluck'st a flower	"	946	ta'en prisoner by the foe	"	1609
No flower was nigh	"	1055	revenged on my foe	"	1683
The flowers are sweet	"	1079	the hateful foe bewray'd	"	1698
A purple flower sprung up	"	1168	that should have slain her foe	"	1827
the new-sprung flower	"	1171	Thyself thy foe	Son 1	8
'Poor flower,' quoth she	"	1177	yet we must not be foes	" 40	14
my sweet love's flower	"	1188	even so as foes commend	" 69	4
take root with precious flowers	R L	870	from my face she turns my foes	" 139	11
Each flower moisten'd	"	1227	Faithful friend from flattering		
against the wither'd flower	"	1254	foe	P P 21	58
that the flower hath kill'd	"	1255	Foggy—vaporous and foggy Night	R L	771
But flowers distill'd	Son 5	13	Foil—which remain'd the foil	L C	153
would bear your living flowers	" 16	7	Foil'd—foil'd the god of fight	V A	114
With April's first-born flowers	" 21	7	victories once foil'd	Son 25	10
is no stronger than a flower	" 65	4	she foil'd the framing	P P 7	15
and died as flowers do now	" 68	2	Foison—spring and .... of the year	Son 53	9
To thy fair flower	" 69	12	Foist—What thou dost foist upon us	" 123	6
The summer's flower	" 94	9	Fold—The sheep are gone to fold	V A	532
But if that flower	" 94	11	Wreathed up in fatal folds	"	879
Of different flowers	" 98	6	in her lips' sweet fold	R L	679
More flowers I noted	" 99	14	Fold—Fold in the object	V A	822
Of bird, of flower, of shape	" 113	6	Nor fold my fault	R L	1073
or flowers with flowers gather'd	" 124	4	Here folds she up	"	1310
have been a spreading flower	L C	75	Folded—Shame folded up	"	675
and gave him all my flower	"	147	Of folded schedules	L C	43
Sweet rose, fair flower	P P 10	1	Follow—What follows more	V A	54
A flower that dies	" 13	3	imagination she did follow	"	975
a gloss, a glass, a flower	" 13	5	shame that follows sweet delight	R L	357
As flowers dead lie wither'd	" 13	9	temptation follows where thou art	Son 41	4
shine, sun, to succour flowers	" 15	16	To follow that which flies	" 143	7
A cup of flowers	" 20	11	Doth follow night	" 143	11
Flown—to hell is flown away	Son 145	12	Follow'd—That .... it as gentle day	" 145	10
Fluxive—bathed she in her fluxive eyes	• L C	50	Following—What following sorrow following where he haunted	R L L C	186 130
Fly—fly they know not whither	V A	304	Folly—love is wise in folly	V A	838
strive to over-fly them	"	324	feeds his vulture folly	R L	556
They basely fly	"	894	folly lurk in gentle breasts	"	851
away she flies	"	1027	His time of folly	"	992
sparks of fire do fly	R L	177	wound his folly's show	"	1810
can neither fight nor fly	"	230	folly, age, and cold decay	Son 11	6

FOLLY   99   FOR

Folly—And folly, doctor-like, controlling skill	Son	66	10
Fond—' Fie, fie, fond love	V. A.	....	1021
are with gain so fond	R. L.	....	134
Or what fond beggar	"	....	216
and full of fond mistrust	"	....	284
which fond desire doth scorch	"	....	314
True grief is fond	"	....	1094
Thy heat of lust, fond Paris	"	....	1473
Or who is he so fond	Son	3	7
Being fond on praise	"	84	14
Fondling—' Fondling,' she saith	V. A.	....	229
Fondly—how fondly I did dote	R. L.	....	207
Food—that pines beholding food	"	....	1115
my thoughts as food to life	Son	75	1
Fool—The poor fool prays her	V. A.	....	578
how much a fool was I	"	....	1015
and teach the fool	"	....	1146
merry fools to mock him	R. L.	....	989
servants to shallow fools	"	....	1016
Only to flatter fools	"	....	1559
' Fool, fool!' quoth she	"	....	1568
my unsounded self, supposed a fool	"	....	1819
So true a fool is love	Son	57	13
Love's not Time's fool	"	116	9
I witness call the fools of time	"	124	13
Thou blind fool, Love	"	137	1
fools that in the imagination set	L. C.	....	136
what fool is not so wise	P. P.	3	13
ah, fool too froward	"	4	14
Foolish—and uttering .... things	R. L.	....	1813
Dissuade one foolish heart	Son	141	10
Foolish-witty—love is wise in folly, foolish-witty	V. A.	....	838
Foot—or as the fleet-foot roe	"	....	561
when thou hast on foot	"	....	679
While in his hold-fast foot	R. L.	....	555
to the base shrub's foot	"	....	664
he sets his foot upon the light	"	....	673
A hand, a foot, a face	"	....	1427
under Pyrrhus' proud foot lies	"	....	1448
although my foot did stand	Son	44	5
can hold his swift foot back	"	63	11
Of hand, of foot, of lip	"	106	6
Footed—whate'er thou wilt, swift-footed Time	"	19	6
Footing—and yet no footing seen	V. A.	....	148
The earth, in love with thee, thy footing trips	"	....	722
For—this favour for thy meed	"	....	15
He, red for shame	"	....	36
For to a pretty ear	"	....	74
ready for his pay	"	....	89
More thirst for drink than she for this good turn	"	....	92
And begg'd for that	"	....	102
for my sake hath learn'd	"	....	105
For mastering her	"	....	114
for then I were not for thee	"	....	137
beauty for the use	"	....	164
Herbs for their smell	"	....	165
For, where they lay	"	....	176
make a shadow for thee	"	....	191
for stone at rain relenteth	"	....	200
for one poor kiss	"	....	207
And one for interest	"	....	210
For men will kiss	"	....	216
how doth she now for wits	"	....	249
What cares he now for curb	"	....	285

For—For rich caparisons	V. A.	....	286
For nothing else	"	....	288
For through his mane	"	....	305
For lovers say, the heart	"	....	329
For all askance	"	....	342
For one sweet look	"	....	371
' For shame,' he cries	"	....	379
For all my mind	"	....	383
For I have heard	"	....	413
For where a heart	"	....	426
For from the stillitory	"	....	443
For looks kill love	"	....	464
For sharply he did think	"	....	470
For on the grass	"	....	473
But for thy piteous lips	"	....	504
kiss each other, for this cure	"	....	505
for fear of slips	"	....	515
Say, for non-payment	"	....	521
For pity now she can	"	....	577
For my sick heart	"	....	584
mounted for the hot encounter	"	....	596
For where Love reigns	"	....	649
For there his smell	"	....	691
For misery is trodden on	"	....	707
for thou shalt not rise	"	....	710
For love can comment	"	....	714
Cynthia for shame	"	....	728
For stealing moulds	"	....	730
for framing thee so fair	"	....	744
For, by this black-faced night	"	....	773
For know, my heart	"	....	779
You do it for increase	"	....	791
for Love to heaven is fled	"	....	793
for having so offended	"	....	810
For lovers' hours are long	"	....	842
For who hath she	"	....	847
She hearkens for his hounds and for his horn	"	....	868
For now she knows	"	....	883
rate the boar for murther	"	....	906
asks the weary caitiff for his master	"	....	914
curse thee for this stroke	"	....	945
for thy mortal vigour	"	....	953
consulting for foul weather	"	....	972
For now reviving joy	"	....	977
and grave for kings	"	....	995
For he being dead	"	....	1019
Struggling for passage	"	....	1047
For oft the eye mistakes	"	....	1058
my grief for one	"	....	1069
still looketh for a grave	"	....	1106
For every little grief	"	....	1179
For he the night before	R. L.	....	15
For by our ears our hearts oft tainted be	"	....	38
beauty would blush for shame	"	....	54
For unstain'd thoughts do seldom dream	"	....	87
For that he colour'd with his high estate	"	....	92
he pineth still for more	"	....	98
so greets heaven for his success	"	....	112
He makes excuses for his being there	"	....	114
For then is Tarquin brought	"	....	120
For after supper long he questioned	"	....	122
Despair to gain doth traffic oft for gaining	"	....	131

For—That one for all, or all for one	R L 144	For—For me, I am the mistress	R L 1069
As life for honour	" 145	For day hath nought to do	" 1092
Honour for wealth	" 146	drowns for want of skill	" 1009
for that which we expect	" 149	For mirth doth search	" 1109
all for want of wit	" 153	For burden-wise I'll hum	" 1133
And for himself himself he must forsake	" 157	'And for, poor bird both were kept for heaven	" ..... 1142 " 1146
hold it for no sin	" 209	shall for him be spent	" 1182
For one sweet grape	" 215	For in my death	" 1189
Urging the worser sense for vantage still	" 249	And, for my sake For fleet-wing'd duty	" ..... 1197 " 1216
And gazed for tidings	" 254	For why her face wore sorrow's livery	" 1222
Why hunt I then for colour or excuses	" 267	For men have marble	" 1240
He takes for accidental things of trial	" 326	dost weep for grief For more it is	" ..... 1272 " 1286
That for his prey	" 342	for I have them here	" 1290
for standing by her side	" 425	For then the eye interprets	" 1325
slaves for pillage fighting	" 428	For Lucrece thought	" 1344
That even for anger	" 478	For now 'tis stale to sigh	" 1362
Shall plead for me	" 480	Pausing for means	" 1365
For those thine eyes betray thee	" 483	made for Priam's Troy	" 1367
marks thee for my earth's delight	" 487	For Helen's rape	" 1369
For in thy bed	" 514	Shed for the slaughter'd husband	" 1376
For lawful policy remains enacted	" 529	As, but for loss	" 1420
'Then, for thy husband	" 533	For much imaginary work was there	" 1422
For marks descried	" 538		
for his sake spare me	" 582	That for Achilles' image	" 1424
for thine own sake leave me	" 583	Stood for the whole	" 1428
For stones dissolved to water do convert	" 592	for trespass of thine eye For one's offence	" ..... 1476 " 1483
For kings, like gods, should govern	" 602	For sorrow, like a heavy-hanging bell	" 1493
only loved for fear	" 610		
are fear'd for love	" 611	For perjured Sinon	" 1521
If but for fear of this	" 614	for his wondrous skill	" 1528
For princes are the glass	" 615	'For even as subtle Sinon	" 1541
Authority for sin, warrant for blame	" 620	For every tear he falls For Sinon in his fire	" ..... 1551 " 1556
For it was lent thee	" 627	She looks for night, and then she longs for morrow	" 1571
I sue for exiled majesty's repeal	" 640		
For light and lust are deadly	" 674	'For in the dreadful dead of dark	" 1625
For with the nightly linen	" 680	'For some hard-favour'd groom plead for justice there	" ..... 1632 " 1649
Unapt for tender smell	" 695		
For there it revels	" 713	'And for my sake	" 1681
The guilty rebel for remission prays	" 714	For she that was thy Lucrece	" 1682
For now against himself	" 717	For sparing justice	" 1687
hates himself for his offence	" 738	For 'tis a meritorious fair design	" 1692
looks for the morning light	" 745	for daughter or for wife	" 1792
'For day,' quoth she	" 747	He weeps for her, for she was only mine	" 1798
For they their guilt	" 754		
Black stage for tragedies	" 766	For sportive words	" 1813
dark harbour for defame	" 768	is woe the cure for woe	" 1821
For Collatine's dear love	" 821	For his foul act	" 1824
a theme for disputation	" 822	For where is she so fair	Son 3 5
Yet for thy honour	" 842	For having traffic with thyself alone	" 4 9
For it had been dishonour	" 844	For never-resting time leads summer on	" 5 5
O unlook'd-for evil	" 846		
The sweets we wish for	" 867	That's for thyself	" 6 7
such numbers seek for thee	" 896	be it ten for one	" 6 8
cry out for thee	" 902	for thou art much too fair	" 6 13
no time for charitable deeds	" 908	Is it for fear to wet a widow's eye	" 9 1
For who so base	" 1000	for still the world enjoys it	" 9 10
For greatest scandal	" 1006	For shame! deny that	" 10 1
For me, I force not	" 1021	Who for thyself art so unprovident	" 10 2
For if I die	" 1032	For thou art so possessed	" 10 5
for yielding so	" 1036	for love of me	" 10 13
more vent for passage of her breath	" 1040	whom Nature hath not made for store	" 11 9
Yet for the self-same purpose	" 1047		
that is gone for which I sought	" 1051	she carved thee for her seal	" 11 13

Phrase		Son	
For—for love of you	Son	13	13
For beauty's pattern	"	19	12
And for a woman wert thou	"	20	9
she prick'd thee out for women's pleasure	"	20	13
heaven itself for ornament	"	21	3
For all that beauty	"	22	5
As I, not for myself, but for thee will	"	22	10
So I, for fear of trust	"	23	5
Who plead for love and look for recompense	"	23	11
For through the painter must you see	"	24	5
good turns eyes for eyes have done	"	24	9
and thine for me	"	24	10
Unlook'd for joy in that I honour most	"	25	4
For at a frown	"	25	8
famoused for fight	"	25	9
all the rest forgot for which he toil'd	"	25	12
repose for limbs	"	27	2
For then my thoughts	"	27	5
For thee and for myself	"	27	14
For thy sweet love remember'd	"	29	13
For precious friends hid	"	30	6
Reserve them for my love, not for their rhyme	"	32	7
Theirs for their style I'll read, his for his love	"	32	14
him for this my love	"	33	13
For no man well of such a salve can speak	"	34	7
For to thy sensual fault	"	35	9
For whether beauty	"	37	5
For every vulgar paper	"	38	4
For who's so dumb	"	38	7
Even for this	"	39	5
if for my love	"	40	5
I cannot blame thee for my love thou usest	"	40	6
For still temptation follows	"	41	4
And for my sake	"	42	7
my friend for my sake	"	42	8
both for my sake	"	42	12
For all the day	"	43	2
For then, despite of space	"	44	3
For nimble thought can jump	"	44	7
For when these quicker elements is famish'd for a look	"	45	5
	"	47	3
For thou not farther than my thoughts	"	47	11
For truth proves thievish for a prize so dear	"	48	14
For that same groan	"	50	13
But love, for love	"	51	12
For blunting the fine point	"	52	4
But you like none, none you for constant heart	"	53	14
For that sweet odour	"	54	4
But, for their virtue	"	54	9
watch the clock for you	"	57	6
labouring for invention	"	59	3
but for his scythe to mow	"	60	12
ever for thy sake	"	61	2
For thee watch I	"	61	13
And for this sin	"	62	3
And for myself	"	62	7

Phrase		Son	
For—that for myself I praise	Son	62	13
For such a time	"	63	9
for restful death I cry	"	66	1
For she hath no exchequer	"	67	11
him as for a map	"	68	13
For slander's mark	"	70	2
For canker vice	"	70	7
No longer mourn for me	"	71	1
for I love you so	"	71	6
For you in me	"	72	4
do more for me	"	72	6
That you for love speak well	"	72	10
For I am shamed	"	72	13
Which for memorial	"	74	4
And for the peace	"	75	3
starved for a look	"	75	10
For as the sun	"	76	13
invoke thee for my Muse	"	78	1
thank him not for that	"	79	13
This silence for my sin	"	83	9
For I impair not beauty	"	83	11
others for the breath of words respect	"	85	13
Me for my dumb thoughts	"	85	14
Bound for the prize	"	86	2
too dear for my possessing	"	87	1
For how do I hold thee	"	87	5
And for that riches where is my deserving	"	87	6
For bending all my loving thoughts	"	88	10
That for thy right	"	88	14
forsake me for some fault	"	89	1
For thee, against myself	"	89	13
For I must ne'er love him	"	89	14
do not drop in for an after-loss	"	90	4
For term of life	"	92	2
For it depends	"	92	4
For there can live no hatred	"	93	5
For sweetest things turn sourest	"	94	13
for their habitation	"	95	10
and for true things deem'd	"	96	8
For summer and his pleasures	"	97	11
for complexion dwells	"	99	4
condemned for thy hand	"	99	6
But, for his theft	"	99	12
For thy neglect of truth	"	101	2
Excuse not silence so, for 't lies in thee	"	101	10
For to no other pass	"	103	11
For as you were	"	104	2
For fear of which	"	104	13
And, for they look'd	"	106	11
For we, which now behold antiquity for aye his page	"	106	13
	"	108	12
bring water for my stain	"	109	8
leave for nothing all thy sum	"	109	12
For nothing this wide universe I call	"	109	13
O, for my sake	"	111	1
for my life provide	"	111	3
For what care I	"	112	3
For it no form delivers	"	113	5
For if it see	"	113	9
And for that sorrow	"	120	2
For if you were	"	120	5
For why should others' false adulterate eyes	"	121	5
For thy records and what we see doth lie	"	123	11

For—It might for Fortune's bastard	*Son* 124	2
Which die for goodness, who have lived for crime	" 124	14
great bases for eternity	" 125	3
For compound sweet	" 125	7
only me for thee	" 125	12
For since each hand	" 127	5
For well thou know'st	" 131	3
To mourn for me	" 132	11
For that deep wound	" 133	2
for I, being pent in thee	" 133	13
For thou art covetous	" 134	6
to write for me	" 134	7
came debtor for my sake	" 134	11
Thus far for love	" 136	4
For nothing hold me	" 136	11
for my name is 'Will'	" 136	14
For, if I should despair	" 140	9
For they in thee	" 141	2
languish'd for her sake	" 145	3
For that which longer	" 147	2
For I have sworn thee fair	" 147	13
for thy sake	" 149	4
for now I know thy mind	" 149	13
For, thou betraying me	" 151	5
for whose dear love	" 151	14
For all my vows are oaths	" 152	7
For I have sworn deep oaths	" 152	9
For I have sworn thee fair	" 152	13
The boy for trial	" 153	10
the bath for my help lies	" 153	13
For men diseased	" 154	12
Came there for cure	" 154	13
For some, untuck'd, descended	*L C*	31
For on his visage was in little drawn	"	90
For maiden-tongued he was	"	100
Came for additions	"	118
For his advantage still	"	123
And dialogued for him	"	132
Experience for me many bulwarks builded	"	152
For when we rage	"	160
For fear of harms	"	165
For further I could say	"	169
For feasts of love	"	181
For these, of force, must	"	223
What me your minister, for you obeys	"	229
For she was sought by spirits	"	236
Must for your victory	"	258
For thou art all	"	266
For, lo, his passion	"	295
What I should do again for such a sake	"	322
For being both to me	*P P* 2	11
Vows for thee broke	" 3	4
gone to the hedge for shade	" 6	2
tarriance for Adonis made	" 6	4
For his approach	" 6	8
Paler for sorrow	" 9	3
For Adon's sake	" 9	4
I weep for thee	" 10	7
For why thou left'st me nothing	" 10	8
For why I craved nothing	" 10	10
For methinks thou stay'st too long	" 12	12
beauty blemish'd once 's for ever lost	" 13	11
for I supp'd with sorrow	" 14	6
For—a word for shadows like myself	*P P* 14	11
For she doth welcome daylight	" 15	7
For why, she sigh'd	" 15	12
Yet not for me, shine sun	" 15	16
For of the two the trusty knight	" 16	11
For now my song is ended	" 16	16
Vow, alack! for youth unmeet	" 17	13
Thou for whom Jove would swear	" 17	15
And deny himself for Jove	" 17	17
Turning mortal for thy love	" 17	18
For now I see	" 18	16
All our love is lost, for Love is dead	" 18	48
For a sweet content	" 18	51
Other help for him	" 18	54
doth stand for nought	" 19	42
To sin and never for to saint	" 19	44
For her griefs so lively shown	" 21	17
For these dead birds sigh a prayer	*P T*	67
Forage—she begins to forage	*V A*	554
Forbade—... my tongue to speak	*R L*	1648
Forbade the boy	*P P* 9	8
Forbear—the ungrown fry forbears	*V A*	526
thou might'st my seat forbear	*Son* 41	9
forbear to glance thine eye	" 139	6
Forbid—But I forbid thee	" 19	8
That god forbid that made me	" 58	1
spoil of beauty can forbid	" 65	12
in honour so forbid	*L C*	150
Forbidden—That use is not forbidden usury	*Son* 6	5
Forbidding—all these poor forbiddings	*R L*	323
Forbod—To be forbod the sweets	*L C*	164
Force—desire doth lend her force	*V A*	29
then force must work my way	*R L*	513
by force, by fraud, or skill	"	1243
Sweet love, renew thy force	*Son* 56	1
some in their body's force	" 91	2
For these, of force	*L C*	223
did her force subdue	"	248
The aloes of all forces	"	273
Her feeble force will yield	*P P* 19	21
Force—Perforce will force it	*V A*	72
Lucrece must I force to my desire	*R L*	182
doth force a further strife	"	689
I force not argument a straw	"	1021
Forced—Forced to content	*V A*	61
Forced it to tremble	*R L*	261
This forced league	"	689
acquit my forced offence	"	1071
That was not forced	"	1657
forced him on so fast	"	1670
How may this forced stain	"	1701
Where thou art forced	*Son* 41	12
Or forced examples	*L C*	157
O, that forced thunder	"	326
Forceless—These forceless flowers	*V A*	152
Ford—Deep sounds make lesser noise than shallow fords	*R L*	1329
'Fore—The eyes 'fore duteous	*Son* 7	11
Fore-bemoaned—of .... moan	" 30	11
Fore-betray'd—betray the	*L C*	328
Forego—Mine eyes .... their light	*R L*	228
Foregoing—foregoing simple savour	*Son* 125	7
Foregone—grieve at grievances	" 30	9
Forehead—Brand not my forehead	*R L*	1091
Foreknowing—Foreknowing well	*V A*	245
Foresight—But her foresight	*R L*	728
Forest—Have from the forests shook	*Son* 104	4

Forestall—Thus I forestall thee	R L	484		**Forswore**—I forswore not thee	P P	3	6
could not forestall thy will	"	728		**Forsworn**—steal a kiss and die	V A		726
Foretell—Foretell new storms	"	1589		faith unhappily forsworn	Son	66	4
Forfeit—Supposed as forfeit	Son	107	4	though thou art forsworn	"	88	4
Myself I'll forfeit	"	134	3	thou know'st I am forsworn	"	152	1
Forged—Last full of forged lies	V A		804	But thou art twice forsworn	"	152	2
hast thou forged hooks	Son	137	7	If love make me forsworn	P P	5	1
Forgery—the weak brain's forgeries	R L		460	Though to myself forsworn	"	5	3
treason, forgery, and shift	"		920	**Fort**—Thy never-conquer'd fort	R L		482
in the world's false forgeries	P P	1	4	If in this blemish'd fort	"		1175
Forget—her joints forget to bow	V A		1061	**Forth**—Thine eye darts forth	V A		196
for fear of trust forget to say	Son	23	5	brought forth thee	"		201
dear love, forget me quite	"	72	3	blaze forth her wrong	"		219
Forget'st—that thou .... so long	"	100	1	But, lo, from forth	"		259
Forgetful—return, forgetful Muse	"	100	5	And forth she rushes	"		262
Forgetfulness—Were to import	"	122	14	drink the air, and forth again	"		273
Forgetting— .... shame's pure blush	V A		558	It flash'd forth fire	"		348
Forging—Till forging Nature	"		729	before one leaf put forth	"		416
Forgive—I do forgive thy robbery	Son	40	9	to creep forth again	"		1036
Forgot—that will never be forgot	R L		536	To set forth that	R L		32
And never be forgot	"		1644	Puffs forth another wind	"		315
And all the rest forgot	Son	25	12	Rushing from forth a cloud	"		373
in your sweet thoughts would be forgot	"	71	7	peeping forth this tumult to behold	"		447
Forgot upon your dearest love	"	117	3	From forth dull sleep	"		450
think on thee, when I forgot	"	149	3	breathes she forth her spite	"		762
All my merry jigs are quite forgot	P P	18	9	Is to let forth	"		1029
Forgotten—each part will be	Son	81	4	stol'n from forth thy gate	"		1068
Forlorn—in thine own law forlorn	V A		251	forth with bashful innocence	"		1341
Dian cloudy and forlorn	"		725	gleam'd forth their ashy light	"		1378
that was but late forlorn	"		1026	She throws forth Tarquin's name	"		1717
And who she finds forlorn	R L		1500	from forth her fair streets	"		1834
And from the forlorn world	Son	33	7	And make me travel forth	Son	34	2
Cytherea, all in love forlorn	P P	6	3	let him bring forth	"	38	11
She, poor bird, as all forlorn	"	21	9	Shall you pace forth	"	55	10
Forlorn—Love hath forlorn me	"	18	21	by that which I bring forth	"	72	13
Form—such saintlike forms	R L		1519	my Muse brings forth	"	103	1
So fair a form	"		1530	that put'st forth all to use	"	134	10
no form of thee hast left	Son	9	6	Breathed forth the sound	"	145	2
your sweet form should bear	"	13	8	those impediments stand forth	L C		269
Thy beauty's form	"	24	2	Forth their dye	P P	18	40
form of well-refined pen	"	85	8	And set thy person forth to sell	"	19	12
To set a form	"	89	6	**Forthwith**—forthwith he lighteth	R L		178
time and outward form	"	108	11	**Fortified**—Which .... her visage	L C		9
it no form delivers	"	113	5	**Fortify**—And fortify yourself	Son	16	3
dwellers on form and favour	"	125	5	do I now fortify	"	63	9
were beauteous as his form	L C		99	**Fortress'd**—Are weakly fortress'd	R L		28
which did no form receive	"		241	**Fortune**—I fear'd thy fortune	V A		642
all strange forms receives	"		303	Reckoning his fortune	R L		19
Form—that face should form another	Son	3	2	Love and Fortune be my gods	"		351
thy shadow's form form happy show	"	43	6	their cursed-blessed fortune	"		866
Formal—nor tied in formal plat	L C		29	Cancell'd my fortunes	"		934
Form'd—And therefore are they form'd	R L		1241	the giddy round of Fortune's wheel	"		952
Is form'd in them by force	"		1243	Nor can I fortune to brief minutes tell	Son	14	5
Former—sharpen'd in his .... might	Son	56	4	Whilst I, whom fortune	"	25	8
burthen of a former child	"	59	4	with fortune and men's eyes	"	29	1
the wits of former days	"	59	13	And shalt by fortune	"	32	3
dressings of a former sight	"	123	4	by fortune's dearest spite	"	37	3
Forsake—swiftly doth forsake him	V A		321	Join with the spite of fortune	"	90	3
himself he must forsake	R L		157	the very worst of fortune's might	"	90	12
beauties do themselves forsake	Son	12	11	do you with Fortune chide	"	111	1
thou didst forsake me	"	89	1	It might for Fortune's bastard	"	124	2
Forsaken—I am forsaken	"	133	7	O frowning Fortune, cursed fickle	P P	18	15
Forsook—himself himself forsook	V A		161	Whilst as fickle Fortune smiled	"	21	29
the shadow had forsook them	"		176	But if Fortune once do frown	"	21	47
she in that sense forsook	R L		1538	**Forty**—When forty winters	Son	2	1
Forswore—A woman I forswore	P P	3	5	**Forward**—Deep woes roll forward	R L		1118
				all forwards do contend	Son	60	4
				The forward violet	"	99	1

FOUGHT 104 FRESH

Fought—the strand of Dardan, where they fought	R L	1436
Foul—foul, or wrinkled-old	V A	133
Gusts and foul flaws	"	456
with such foul fiends	"	638
desire's foul nurse	"	773
consulting for foul weather	"	972
To wash the foul face	"	983
'Tis he, foul creature	"	1005
The foul boar's conquest	"	1030
But this foul, grim ambitious, foul infirmity	R L	1105 150
with lust's foul charm	"	173
O foul dishonour	"	198
including all foul harms	"	199
Full of foul hope	"	284
Who, like a foul usurper	"	412
his foul thoughts might compass	"	346
but his foul appetite	"	546
Yet, foul night-waking cat	"	554
not to foul desire	"	574
With foul offenders	"	612
foul sin may say	"	629
lived by foul devouring	"	700
with foul insurrection	"	722
Thou foul abettor	"	886
My life's foul deed	"	1208
By foul enforcement	"	1623
with the foul act dispense	"	1704
For his foul act	"	1824
Tarquin's foul offence	"	1852
limbecks foul as hell within	Son 119	2
Fairing the foul	" 127	6
And all they foul that thy	" 132	14
upon so foul a face	" 137	12
with her foul pride	" 144	8
thy foul faults should find	" 148	14
against the truth so foul a lie	" 152	14
the patterns of his foul beguiling	L C	170
of his foul adulterate heart	"	175
Foul precurrer of the fiend	P T	6
Foul-cankering— .... rust	V A	767
Foul-defiled—my foul-defiled blood	R L	1029
Fouler—and they thy fouler grave	"	661
Foul-reeking—furnace of .... smoke	"	799
Found—And swear I found you	"	1635
my friend hath found that loss	Son 42	10
'twixt a miser and his wealth is found	"	75 4
To new-found methods	"	76 4
And found such fair assistance	"	78 2
And found it in thy cheek	"	79 11
I found, or thought I found	"	83 3
found a kind of meetness	"	118 7
this advantage found	"	133 2
But found no cure	"	153 13
Found yet moe letters	L C	47
are seld or never found	P P 13	7
Foundation—earth's .... shakes	V A	1047
Fount—toads infect fair founts	R L	850
a river running from a fount	L C	283
Fountain—where the pleasant fountains lie	V A	234
Mud not the fountain	R L	577
The poison'd fountain	"	1707
And from the purple fountain	"	1734
and silver fountains mud	Son 35	2
In a cold valley-fountain	" 153	4
all their fountains in my well	L C	255

Four—feeder of the other four	V A	446
never four such lamps	"	489
My life, being made of four	Son 45	7
Fowl—Coucheth the fowl below	R L	507
as fowl hear falcon's bells	"	511
As lagging fowls	"	1335
Every fowl of tyrant wing	P T	10
Fox—Or at the fox	V A	675
Fragrant—a canker in the .... rose	Son 95	2
With a thousand fragrant posies	P P 20	10
Frail—my frail joints shake	R L	247
Frailer—why are frailer spies	Son 121	7
Frailty—All frailties that besiege	" 109	11
Or ou my frailties	" 121	7
Frame—with gentle work did frame	" 5	1
My body is the frame	" 24	3
wonder of your frame	" 59	10
did I frame my feeding	" 118	6
frame all thy ways	P P 19	25
Framed—Wherein she framed thee	V A	731
She framed the love	P P 7	15
Framing—For framing thee so fair	V A	744
yet she foll'd the framing	P P 7	15
Frank—And being frank	Son 4	4
Frantic—Frantic with grief	R L	762
Franticly—franticly she doteth	V A	1059
Frantic-mad — frantic-mad with evermore unrest	Son 147	10
Fraud—false and full of fraud	V A	1141
by force, by fraud or skill	R L	1243
Fraughted—Fraughted with gall	P P 18	26
Free—Free vent of words	V A	334
thy Lucrece is not free	R L	1624
she lends to those are free	Son 4	4
my oblation, poor but free	" 125	10
nor he will not be free	" 134	5
and yet am I not free	" 134	14
he was, and thereof free	L C	100
but mine own was free	"	195
Free—Or free that soul	R L	911
my life's fair end shall free it	"	1208
Freed—be freed from guilty woe	"	1482
Freedom—Steal thine own freedom	V A	163
the freedom of that right	Son 46	4
that did in freedom stand	L C	143
Freezing—parching heat nor freezing cold	R L	1145
What freezings have I felt	Son 97	3
Frenzy — pestilence and frenzies wood	V A	740
And his untimely frenzy	R L	1675
Frequent—That I have .... been	Son 117	5
Fresh—pale with fresh variety	V A	21
fresh beauty for the use	"	164
when in his fresh array	"	483
upon the fresh flowers	"	665
Upon fresh beauty	"	796
doth always fresh remain	"	801
colours fresh and trim	"	1079
with their fresh falls' haste	R L	650
But now that fair fresh mirror	"	1760
the world's fresh ornament	Son 1	9
Whose fresh repair	" 3	3
And that fresh blood	" 11	3
And in fresh numbers	" 17	6
Since first I saw you fresh	" 104	8
My love looks fresh	" 107	10
love in love's fresh case	" 108	9
Fresh to myself	L C	76

Fresh—in whose fresh regard	L C	213	Fright—And fright her with confusion	R L	443
lovely, fresh, and green	P P 4	2	fright her crying babe	"	814
Fresher—Some fresher stamps	Son 82	8	Frighted—As the poor frighted deer	"	1149
Fret—resistance made him fret	V A	69	From—pluck him from his horse	V A	30
still he lours and frets	"	75	From his soft bosom	"	81
when he doth fret	"	621	From morn till night	"	154
the hidden treasure frets	"	767	Seeds spring from seeds	"	167
the wind in greater fury fret	R L	648	shines from heaven	"	193
Fret—as frets upon an instrument	"	1140	The heat I have from thence	"	195
Friend—So white a friend	V A	364	And when from thence	"	227
with certain of his friends	"	588	from tempest and from rain	"	238
counsel of their friends	"	640	And from her twining arms	"	256
expected of my friends	"	718	from forth a copse	"	259
a late-embarked friend	"	818	As from a furnace	"	274
his affairs, his friends, his state	R L	45	lightning from the sky	"	348
were he not my dear friend	"	234	my palfrey from the mare	"	384
my kinsman, my dear friend	"	237	from his bending crest	"	395
and hears no heedful friends	"	495	from my unyielding heart	"	423
I rest thy secret friend	"	526	For from the stillitory	"	443
My husband is thy friend	"	582	As if from thence	"	488
the humble suppliant's friend	"	897	from the dangerous year	"	508
a thousand thousand friends	"	963	buys my heart from me	"	517
to see his friends his foes	"	988	nectar from his lips	"	572
Myself, thy friend, will kill myself, thy foe	"	1196	stealing moulds from heaven	"	730
Here friend by friend in bloody channel lies	"	1487	Yet from mine ear	"	778
			from the sweet embrace	"	811
And friend to friend gives unadvised wounds	"	1488	shooteth from the sky	"	815
			from Venus' eye	"	816
like him with friends possess'd	Son 29	6	From his moist cabinet mounts up	"	854
For precious friends hid in death's dateless night	" 30	6	from whose silver breast	"	855
			From whom each lamp	"	861
I think on thee, dear friend	" 30	13	from their strict embrace	"	874
And all those friends which I thought buried	" 31	4	from her two cheeks fair	"	957
			from their dark beds	"	1050
Had my friend's Muse grown	" 32	10	like a vapour from her sight	"	1166
Suffering my friend for my sake to approve her	" 42	8	reft from her by death	"	1174
			From the besieged Ardea	R L	1
my friend hath found that loss	" 42	10	fortress'd from a world of harms	"	28
my friend and I are one	" 42	13	From thievish ears	"	35
the miles are measured from thy friend	" 50	4	From Venus' doves doth challenge virtue claims from beauty beauty's red	"	58
by thy true-telling friend	" 82	12		"	59
To me, fair friend	" 104	1	Proving from world's minority their right	"	67
to try an older friend	" 110	11			
Pity me then, dear friend	" 111	13	pick no meaning from their parling looks	"	100
that deep wound it gives my friend and me	" 133	2	Far from the purpose of his coming	"	113
my sweet'st friend must be	" 133	4			
But then my friend's heart	" 133	10	unloose it from their bond	"	136
And sue a friend came debtor for my sake	" 134	11	leap'd from his bed	"	169
			That from the cold stone sparks of fire do fly	"	177
both to each friend	" 144	11			
that I do call my friend	" 149	5	'As from this cold flint I enforced	"	181
both to each friend	P P 2	11	hard news from the warlike band	"	255
O yes, dear friend	" 10	11	beats these from the stage	"	278
All thy friends are lapp'd in lead	" 21	24	He takes it from the rushes	"	318
Is no friend in misery	" 21	32	That shuts him from the heaven	"	338
Faithful friends are hard to find	" 21	34	Hath barr'd him from the blessed thing	"	340
Every man will be thy friend	" 21	35			
He that is thy friend indeed	" 21	51	So from himself impiety hath wrought	"	341
Faithful friend from flattering foe	" 21	58			
Friendly—Sorrow that friendly sighs sought still to dry	V A	964	Rushing from forth a cloud	"	373
			From this fair throne to heave	"	413
Friendship—and sweet friendship's oath	R L	569	From forth dull sleep	"	450
			From sleep disturbed	"	454
In scorn or friendship	P P 14	8	the eyes fly from their lights	"	461
Fright—fright the silly lamb	V A	1098	shame that from them no device can take	"	535
They fright him	R L	308			

From—From earth's dark womb some gentle gust doth get	R L	549
blows these pitchy vapours from their hiding	"	550
She puts the period often from his place	"	565
From vassal actors can be wiped away	"	608
From a pure heart command	"	625
That from their own misdeeds askance	"	637
wipe the dim mists from thy doting eyne	"	643
bids it leap from thence	"	760
as clear from this attaint	"	825
From me by strong assault it is bereft	"	835
Coming from thee	"	843
keep them from thy aid	"	912
From the creation to the general doom	"	924
To pluck the quills from ancient ravens' wings	"	949
coming from a king	"	1002
from her be-tumbled couch she started	"	1037
As smoke from Ætna that in air consumes	"	1042
which from discharged cannon fumes	"	1043
stol'n from forth thy gate	"	1068
As from a mountain-spring that feeds	"	1077
desert, seated from the way	"	1144
bark peel'd from the lofty pine	"	1167
wiped the brinish pearl from her bright eyes	"	1213
Those tears from thee	"	1271
'Tarquin from hence	"	1276
I commend me from our house in grief	"	1308
From that suspicion	"	1321
And from the towers of Troy	"	1382
and from his lips did fly	"	1406
And from the walls of strong-besieged Troy	"	1429
And from the strand of Dardan be freed from guilty woe	"	1436
	"	1482
stars shot from their fixed places	"	1525
from her tongue 'can lurk' from 'cannot' took	"	1537
steal effects from lightless hell	"	1555
beaten from her breast	"	1563
Being from the feeling of her own grief brought	"	1578
Met far from home	"	1596
From that, alas, thy Lucrece is not free	"	1624
From lips new-waxen pale begins to blow	"	1663
From what is past	"	1685
stain be wiped from me	"	1701
acquit me from this chance	"	1706
I from this compelled stain	"	1708
did vail it from the deep unrest	"	1725
date from cancell'd destiny	"	1729
And from the purple fountain Brutus drew	"	1734
And bubbling from her breast	"	1737
From—to this end from me derived	R L	1755
O, from thy cheeks my image thou hast torn	"	1762
starts Collatine as from a dream	"	1772
keep him from heart-easing words	"	1782
pluck'd the knife from Lucrece' side	"	1807
childish humour from weak minds proceeds	"	1825
from forth her fair streets chased	"	1834
From fairest creatures we desire increase	Son	1	1
when from highmost pitch	"	7	9
he reeleth from the day	"	7	10
From his low tract and look	"	7	12
from that which thou departest	"	11	2
when thou from youth convertest	"	11	4
Which erst from heat did canopy	"	12	6
Not from the stars do I my judgement pluck	"	14	1
But from thine eyes my knowledge I derive	"	14	9
If from thyself to store thou wouldst convert	"	14	12
As he takes from you	"	15	14
fair from fair sometime declines	"	18	7
Pluck the keen teeth from the fierce tiger's jaws	"	19	3
her babe from faring ill	"	22	12
Is from the book of honour razed	"	25	11
my thoughts, from far where I abide	"	27	5
I toil, still farther off from thee	"	28	8
From sullen earth, sings hymns	"	29	12
heavily from woe to woe	"	30	10
stol'n from mine eye	"	31	6
And from the forlorn world his visage hide	"	33	7
hath mask'd him from me now	"	33	12
which sourly robs from me	"	35	14
steal sweet hours from love's delight	"	36	8
take that honour from thy name	"	36	12
absent from thy heart	"	41	2
From limits far remote	"	44	4
removed from thee	"	44	6
return'd from thee	"	45	10
From bands of falsehood	"	48	4
From whence at pleasure thou mayst come	"	48	12
converted from the thing it was	"	49	7
measured from thy friend	"	50	4
being made from thee	"	50	8
when from thee I speed	"	51	2
From where thou art	"	51	3
Since from thee going	"	51	13
send'st from thee	"	61	5
So far from home into my deeds to pry	"	61	6
From me far off with others	"	61	14
never cut from memory	"	63	11
jewel from Time's chest lie hid	"	65	10
from these would I be gone	"	66	13
From this vile world	"	71	4
must from you be took	"	75	12
So far from variation or quick change	"	76	2
deliver'd from thy brain	"	77	11
From thy behaviour; beauty	"	79	10
From hence your memory death cannot take	"	81	3

From—Your name from hence immortal	*Son* 81	5
any fear from thence	" 86	12
Be absent from thy walks	" 89	9
husband nature's riches from expense	" 94	6
From thee, the pleasure	" 97	2
From you have I been absent	" 98	1
Or from their proud lap pluck them	" 98	8
If not from my love's breath	" 99	3
had stol'n from thee	" 99	15
Have from the forests shook	" 101	4
Steal from his figure	" 104	10
I from myself depart	" 109	3
As from my soul, which	" 109	4
praises from your tongue	" 112	6
farthest from your sight	" 117	8
Distill'd from limbecks foul	" 119	2
give them from me	" 122	11
builded far from accident	" 124	5
breath that from my mistress reeks	" 130	8
Me from myself thy cruel eye hath taken	" 133	5
therefore from my face she turns my foes	" 139	11
health from their physicians know	" 140	8
Dissuade one foolish heart from serving thee	" 141	10
not from those lips of thine	" 142	5
that which flies from thee	" 143	9
Tempteth my better angel from my side	" 144	6
being both from me	" 144	11
From heaven to hell is flown	" 145	12
'I hate' from hate away she threw	" 145	13
random from the truth	" 147	12
O, from what power hast thou this powerful might	" 150	1
borrow'd from this holy fire of Love	" 153	5
Which from Love's fire took heat perpetual	" 154	10
From off a hill	*L C*	1
from a sistering vale	"	2
fortified her visage from the sun	"	9
would not break from thence	"	34
from a maund she drew	"	36
If that from him there may be	"	68
his mettle from his rider takes	"	107
from judgement stand aloof	"	166
from many a several fair	"	206
was sent me from a nun	"	232
a river running from a fount	"	283
Both fire from hence	"	294
thunder from his heart	"	325
Tempteth my better angel from my side	*P T*	2 6
each moving sense from idle rest	" 15	3
Ne'er to pluck thee from thy thorn	" 17	12
All our evening sport from us is fled	" 18	47
Scarce I could from tears refrain	" 21	16
Faithful friend from flattering foe	" 21	58
From this session interdict	*P T*	9
In a mutual flame from hence	"	24
Front—in summer's front doth sing	*Son* 102	7
Frost—Sap check'd with frost	"	3 7
Like little frosts	*R L*	331
fear's frost hath dissolution	"	355
Frosty—but frosty in desire	*V A*	36
Froth—a froth of fleeting joy	*R L*	212
Frothy—Whose frothy mouth	*V A*	901
Froward—the froward infant still'd	"	562
when most his choice is froward	"	570
ah, fool too froward	*P P*	1 14
Frown—wounding of a frown	*V A*	463
Foul words and frowns	"	573
For at a frown they in their glory die	*Son* 25	8
frowns and wrinkles strange	" 93	8
within the level of your frown	" 117	11
Frown—now doth he frown	*V A*	45
When he did frown	"	571
see thee frown on my defects	*Son* 49	2
But if Fortune once do frown	*P P* 21	47
Frown'st—On whom frown'st thou	*Son* 149	6
Frowning—O frowning Fortune	*P P* 18	15
her frowning brows be bent	" 19	13
Frozen—What wax so frozen	*V A*	565
'Tween frozen conscience	*R L*	247
Fruit—doting father of his fruit	"	1064
and unfather'd fruit	*Son* 97	10
Fruitful—Won in the fields of fruitful Italy	*R L*	107
Fruitless—despite of .... chastity	*V A*	751
Fry—the ungrown fry, forbears	"	526
Fuel—with self-substantial fuel	*Son* 1	6
Fulfil—how canst thou fulfil	*R L*	628
where you did fulfil	"	1635
My love-suit, sweet, fulfil	*Son* 136	4
'Will' will fulfil the treasure	" 136	5
Fulfilled—that they are so fulfilled	*R L*	1258
Full—gardens full of flowers	*V A*	65
Broad breast, full eye	"	296
breeder, full of fear	"	320
Full gently now she takes him	"	361
eye so full hath fed	"	399
Whose full perfection	"	634
Lust full of forged lies	"	804
My face is full of shame	"	808
Full of respects	"	911
as one full of despair	"	935
thou art so full of fear	"	1021
false and full of fraud	"	1141
and too full of riot	"	1147
Full of foul hope and full of fond mistrust	*R L*	284
gives the watch-word to his hand full soon	"	370
His face, though full of cares	"	1503
Full many a glorious morning	*Son* 33	1
thy years full well befits	" 41	3
have full as deep a dye	" 54	5
winter, which being full of care	" 56	13
Sometime all full with feasting	" 75	9
Was it the proud full sail	" 86	1
My most full flame	" 115	4
To give full growth	" 115	14
Even so, being full	" 118	5
Full character'd with lasting memory	"	122 2
murderous, bloody, full of blame	"	129 3
Nor that full star	"	132 7
Ay, fill it full with wills	"	136 6
espied a fickle maid full pale	*L C*	5
Youth is full of pleasance, age is full of care	*P P*	12 2
Youth is full of sport	"	12 5
heard it said full oft	"	19 41
Full-fed—Look, as the .... hound	*R L*	694

Fullness—even till they wink with fullness	Son	56	6		
Fume—bites the poor flies in his	V A		316		
which from discharged cannon fumes	R L		1043		
Function—Doth part his function	Son	113	3		
Furnace—As from a furnace	V A		274		
thou furnace of foul-reeking smoke	R L		799		
Furrow—time's furrows I behold	Son	22	3		
Further—now she will no further	V A		905		
doth force a further strife	R L		689		
For further I could say	L C		169		
Fury—his fury was assuaged	V A		318		
With blindfold fury	"		554		
the headlong fury of his speed	R L		501		
with the wind in greater fury fret	"		648		
Spend'st thou thy fury	Son	100	3		
Gage—or all for one we gage	R L		144		
but laid no words to gage	"		1351		
Gain—Despair to gain doth traffic	"		131		
are with gain so foud	"		134		
bankrupt in this poor-rich gain	"		140		
A captive victor that hath lost in gain	"		730		
Having no other pleasure of his gain	"		860		
my loss is my love's gain	Son	42	9		
lives upon his gains	"	67	12		
thus far I count my gain	"	141	13		
to turn them both to gain	P P	16	10		
Gain—if I gain the thing I seek	R L		211		
I have seen the hungry ocean gain	Son	64	5		
And gain by ill thrice more	"	119	14		
it was to gain my grace	L C		79		
Gain'd—Thy grace being gain'd	"	3	8		
Gainer—I by this will be a gainer too	Son	88	9		
Gaining—doth traffic oft for gaining	R L		131		
Or, gaining more	"		138		
'Gainst—'Gainst venom'd sores	V A		916		
dotes on what he looks 'gainst law or duty	R L		497		
That 'gainst thyself	Son	10	6		
nothing 'gainst Time's scythe	"	12	13		
And 'gainst myself	"	35	11		
'Gainst death and all oblivious enmity	"	55	9		
Crooked eclipses 'gainst his glory	"	60	7		
'gainst my strong infection	"	111	10		
'gainst her own content	L C		157		
'gainst rule, 'gainst sense, 'gainst shame	"		271		
the battery that you make 'gainst mine	"		277		
'Gainst whom the world	P P	3	2		
Gait—comforter, with weary gait	V A		529		
with slow-sad gait descended	R L		1081		
An humble gait, calm looks	"		1508		
fingers walk with gentle gait	Son	128	11		
Gall—Thy honey turns to gall	R L		889		
water-galls in her dim element	"		1588		
Fraughted with gall	P P	18	26		
Gallant—or kill the gallant knight	"	16	6		
Galled—To break upon the galled shore	R L		1440		
'Gan—'O, pity,' 'gan she cry	V A		95		
with swelling drops 'gan wet	R L		1228		
and often 'gan to tear	L C		51		
'Gan—Till thus he 'gan besiege me	L C		177		
All unseen 'gan passage find	P P	17	6		
Gaol—in a gaol of snow	V A		362		
use rigour in my gaol	Son	133	12		
Gaping—a press of gaping faces	R L		1408		
Garden—gardens full of flowers	V A		65		
And many maiden gardens	Son	16	6		
Garment—Who wears a garment	V A		415		
Some in their garments	Son	91	3		
prouder than garments cost	"	91	10		
with the garment of a grace	L C		316		
Gash—That makes more gashes	V A		1066		
Gate—it will not ope the gate	"		424		
But through the flood-gates	"		959		
Soft pity enters at an iron gate	R L		595		
but stol'n from forth thy gate	"		1068		
Sings hymns at heaven's gate	Son	29	12		
Nor gates of steel so strong	"	65	8		
Who glazed with crystal gate	L C		286		
Gather'd—flowers that are not	V A		131		
Or flowers with flowers gather'd	Son	124	4		
Gaudy—The gaudy sun would peep	V A		1088		
his gaudy banner is display'd	R L		272		
herald to the gaudy spring	Son	1	10		
Gave—crystal tears gave light	V A		491		
O, had she then gave over	"		571		
The kiss I gave you	"		771		
entertainment that he gave	"		1108		
virtue gave the golden age	R L		60		
fountain that gave drink	"		577		
by him that gave it thee	"		624		
art gave lifeless life	"		1374		
no guilty instance gave	"		1511		
whom the best endow'd she gave the more	Son	11	11		
thy sour leisure gave sweet leave	"	39	10		
And Time that gave doth now	"	60	8		
gave my heart another youth	"	110	7		
gave eyes to blindness	"	152	11		
sigh'd, tore, and gave the flood	L C		44		
habitude gave life and grace	"		114		
and gave him all my flower	"		147		
to the stream gave grace	"		285		
gave the tempter place	"		318		
Gavest—the hours thou gavest me to repose	R L		933		
Thou gavest me thine	Son	22	14		
Thyself thou gavest	"	87	9		
me, to whom thou gavest it	"	87	11		
Gay—caparisons or trapping gay	V A		286		
dead fleece made another gay	Son	68	8		
thy outward walls so costly gay	"	146	4		
the learned man hath got the lady gay	P P	16	15		
Gaze—eyes pay tributary gazes	V A		632		
an eye to gaze on beauty	R L		496		
deer, that stands at gaze	"		1149		
The lovely gaze where every eye	Son	5	2		
to gaze therein on thee	"	24	12		
anon their gazes lend	L C		26		
mine eyes throw gazes to the east	P P	15	1		
Gazed—they long have gazed	V A		927		
gazed for tidings in my eager eyes	R L		254		
gazed upon with every eye	"		1015		
wistly on him gazed	"		1355		
on him she gazed, and gazing still	"		1531		
livery so gazed on now	Son	2	3		
Gazer—That the star-gazers	V A		509		
gazer late did wonder	"		748		

Gazer—How many gazers mightst thou lead	Son	96 11
Gazeth—Now gazeth she on him	V A	224
gazeth on her yet unstained bed	R L	366
object whereupon it gazeth	Son 20	6
Gazing—. . . . upon a late-embarked	V A	818
wonder of still-gazing eyes	R L	84
rage of lust by gazing qualified	"	424
Gazing upon the Greeks	"	1384
on him she gazed, and gazing still	"	1531
in their gazing spent	Son 125	8
Gem—with earth and sea's rich gems	"	21 6
With annexions of rich gems	L C	208
Gender—That thy sable . . . . makest	P T	18
General—to the general doom	R L	924
a private sin in general	"	1484
I better in one general best	Son 91	8
this general evil they maintain	"	121 13
the general of hot desire	"	154 7
did in the general bosom reign	L C	127
Gentle—whose gentle wind	V A	189
With gentle majesty	"	278
thy courser, gentle boy	"	403
Distempering gentle Love	"	653
Love's gentle spring	"	801
Lo, here the gentle lark	"	853
it is no gentle chase	"	883
Then, gentle shadow	"	1001
beast that knows no gentle right	R L	545
some gentle gust doth get	"	549
folly lurk in gentle breasts	"	851
roll forward like a gentle flood	"	1118
let beasts bear gentle minds	"	1148
Their gentle sex to weep	"	1237
Know, gentle wench	"	1273
with gentle work did frame	Son 5	1
fairer lodged than gentle love	"	10 10
A woman's gentle heart	"	20 3
thy robbery, gentle thief	"	40 9
Gentle thou art, and therefore	"	41 5
Within the gentle closure	"	48 11
had all thy gentle grace	"	79 2
shall be my gentle verse	"	81 9
youth and gentle sport	"	96 2
In gentle numbers	"	100 6
fingers walk with gentle gait	"	128 11
used in giving gentle doom	"	145 7
that follow'd it as gentle day	"	145 10
Then, gentle cheater	"	151 3
he 'gan besiege me: "Gentle maid	L C	177
jest at every gentle offer	P P	4 12
Gentlest—the rudest or . . . . sight	Son 113	9
Gently—Full gently now	V A	361
and gently bear him	"	1096
when thou gently sway'st	Son 128	3
Gentry—By knighthood, gentry	R L	569
Get—help she cannot get	V A	93
to get it is thy duty	"	168
how to get my palfrey	"	384
Or sells eternity to get a toy	R L	214
some gentle gust doth get	"	549
where he the lamb may get	"	878
Go, get me hither paper	"	1289
unless thou get a son	Son 7	11
that did his picture get	L C	134
Ghastly—beheld some . . . . sprite	R L	451
Let ghastly shadows	"	971
a jewel hung in ghastly night	Son 27	11
Ghost—Grim-grinning ghost	V A	933
Ghost—that affable familiar ghost	Son 86	9
Giddy—and turn the giddy round	R L	952
Gift—Which bounteous gift	Son 11	12
doth now his gift confound	"	60 8
The cause of this fair gift	"	87 7
So thy great gift	"	87 11
and your gifts to tell	"	103 12
Thy gift, thy tables	"	122 1
Which by a gift of learning	P P	16 11
Gild—the golden age to gild	R L	60
Gilded—nor the gilded monuments	Son 55	1
And gilded honour shamefully	"	66 5
much outlive a gilded tomb	"	101 11
were gilded in his smiling	L C	172
Gild'st—thou gild'st the even	Son 28	12
Gilding—Gilding the object	"	20 6
Gilding pale streams	"	33 4
Gills—their golden gills	V A	1100
'Gin—suitor 'gins to woo him	"	6
And 'gins to chide	"	45
when first it 'gins to bud	P P	13 3
Girded—all girded up in sheaves	Son 12	7
Girdle—. . . . with embracing flames	R L	6
Girl—'My girl,' quoth she	"	1270
But tell me, girl, when went	"	1275
Girth—now his woven girths	V A	266
Give—So offers he to give	"	88
Give me one kiss, I'll give	"	209
'Give me my hand,' saith he	"	373
'Give me my heart,' saith she	"	374
O, give it me	"	375
Gives false alarms	"	651
gives a deadly groan	"	1044
she securely gives good cheer	R L	89
And give the sneaped birds	"	333
Which gives the watch-word	"	370
Gives the hot charge	"	434
but he that gives them knows	"	833
Give physic to the sick	"	901
but sin ne'er gives a fee	"	913
disdained scraps to give	"	987
at least I give	"	1053
she doth give demure good-morrow	"	1219
To give her so much grief	"	1463
And friend to friend gives	"	1488
and give the harmless show	"	1507
smilingly with this gives o'er	"	1567
that we may give redress	"	1603
she gives her sorrow fire	"	1604
can give the fault amending	"	1614
to give this wound to me	"	1722
give his sorrow place	"	1773
and busy winds give o'er	"	1790
I did give that life	"	1800
to give thyself a blow	"	1823
plausibly did give consent	"	1854
Nature's bequest gives nothing	Son 4	3
largess given thee to give	"	4 6
your sweet semblance to some other give	"	13 4
To give away yourself	"	16 13
this gives life to thee	"	18 14
not to give back again	"	22 14
of me to thee did give	"	31 11
give physic to my grief	"	34 9
the shadow doth such substance give	"	37 10
O, give thyself the thanks	"	38 5
dost give invention	"	38 8

Give—by this separation I may give	Son	39	7
and give him leave	"	51	14
worthiness gives scope	"	52	13
which truth doth give	"	54	2
give thee that due	"	69	3
give thee so thine own	"	69	6
give warning to the world	"	71	3
will give thee memory	"	77	6
doth give another place	"	79	4
beauty doth he give	"	79	10
others would give life	"	83	12
charter of thy worth gives thee releasing	"	87	3
Give not a windy night	"	90	7
which gives thee all	"	100	2
And gives thy pen	."	100	8
Give my love fame	"	100	13
Nor gives to necessary wrinkles	"	108	11
Then give me welcome	"	110	13
To give full growth	"	115	14
Give salutation to my sportive blood	"	121	6
Therefore to give them	"	122	11
Give them thy fingers	"	128	14
It gives my friend and me	"	133	2
give the lie to my true sight	"	150	3
Nor gives it satisfaction	L C		162
Given—largess given thee to give	Son	4	6
have given admiring praise	"	59	14
And given grace a double majesty	"	78	8
And given to time	"	117	6
Givest—With the breath thou givest and takest	P T		19
Giving—shall claim excuse's giving	R L		1715
Giving him aid, my verse	Son	86	8
in giving gentle doom	"	145	7
consecrations giving place	L C		263
Glad—Make glad and sorry seasons	Son	19	5
but then no longer glad	"	45	13
Gladly—which thou receivest not gladly	"	8	3
Glance—But the mild glance	R L		1399
do I not glance aside	Son	76	3
forbear to glance thine eye aside	"	139	6
Glass—like pearls in glass	V A		980
Two glasses, where herself	"		1129
For princes are the glass	R L		615
Wilt thou be glass	"		619
When their glass fell	"		1526
Poor broken glass	"		1758
all the beauty of my glass	"		1763
Look in thy glass	Son	3	1
Thou art thy mother's glass	"	3	9
pent in walls of glass	"	5	10
My glass shall not persuade me	"	22	1
my glass shows me myself	"	62	9
Thy glass will show thee	"	77	1
which thy glass will truly show	"	77	5
Look in your glass	"	103	6
Your own glass shows you	"	103	14
Dost hold Time's fickle glass	"	126	2
Brighter than glass, and yet, as glass is, brittle	P P	7	3
A brittle glass	"	13	4
a gloss, a glass, a flower	"	13	5
As broken glass	"	13	10
Glassy—Writ in the glassy margents of such books	R L		102
Glazed—glazed with thine eyes	Son	24	8
Who glazed with crystal gate	L C		286
Gleam'd—gleam'd forth their ashy lights	R L		1378
Glide—So glides he in the night	V A		816
Glister—scornfully glisters like fire	"		275
Glittering—their.... golden towers	R L		945
Globe—ivory globes circled with blue	"		407
Gloomy—possession of thy .... place	"		803
Glorify—bright sun glorifies the sky	V A		485
Glorious—glorious by his manly chivalry	R L		109
kings glorious day	"		1013
Full many a glorious morning	Son	33	1
look'd on the world with glorious eye	P P	6	11
Gloriously—so gloriously behold	V A		857
his triumph and his glories	"		1014
Glory—Time's glory is to calm	R L		939
burnt the shining glory	"		1523
they in their glory die	Son	25	8
a part of all thy glory live	"	37	12
'gainst his glory fight	"	60	7
shall be most my glory	"	83	10
lends not some small glory	"	84	6
losing me shalt win much glory	"	88	8
Doth half that glory	"	132	8
Glory—Some glory in their birth	"	91	1
Gloss—Gloss on the rose	V A		936
A shining gloss that radeth	P P	13	2
a gloss, a glass, a flower	"	13	5
As vaded gloss no rubbing	"	13	8
Glove—Lucretia's glove, wherein	R L		317
This glove to wanton tricks	"		320
The doors, the wind, the glove	"		325
Glow—and begins to glow	V A		337
which in his liver glows	R L		47
Glow'd—which in his cheek so	L C		324
Glowing—coals of glowing fire	V A		35
see'st the glowing of such fire	Son	73	9
with crystal gate the glowing roses	L C		286
Glow-worm—His eyes, like glow-worms	V A		621
Glued—Their lips together glued	"		546
Glutton—With his glutton eye	"		399
Lust like a glutton dies	"		805
or else this glutton be	Son	1	13
Gluttoning—Or gluttoning on all	"	75	14
Glutton-like—And .... she feeds	V A		548
Gnat—Gnats are unnoted	R L		1014
Go—to her straight goes he	V A		264
His testy master goeth about	"		319
let go, and let me go	"		379
you crush me; let me go	"		611
where'er he goes	"		622
through the which he goes	"		683
bleeding as they go	"		924
with swift intent he goes	R L		46
that would let him go	"		76
yet ere he go to bed	"		776
to mark how slow time goes	"		990
Go, get me hither paper	"		1289
which shall go before	"		1302
with his own weight goes	"		1494
with the blunt swains he goes	"		1504
a watery rigol goes	"		1745
among the wastes of time must go	Son	12	10
if it shall go well	"	14	7
I'll run and give him leave to go	"	51	14
with that which goes before	"	60	3
over-goes my blunt invention	"	103	7

Go—which governs me to go about	Son	113	2	Gone—was Tarquin gone away	R L	1281
I never saw a goddess go	"	130	11	Her maid is gone	"	1296
thy proud heart go wide	"	140	14	the duteous vassal scarce is gone	"	1360
and had let go by	L C		59	nature calls thee to be gone	Son 4	11
'Mongst our mourners shalt thou				and lusty leaves quite gone	" 5	7
go	P T		20	trophies of my lovers gone	" 31	10
God—direful god of war	V A		98	miles when thou art gone	" 44	10
foil'd the god of fight	"		114	these quicker elements are gone	" 45	5
O thou clear god	"		860	from these would I be gone	" 66	13
be my gods, my guide	R L		351	after I am gone	" 71	14
thou art a god, a king	"		601	Though I, once gone	" 81	6
For kings, like gods	"		602	I have gone here and there	" 110	1
God wot, it was defect	"		1315	gone to the hedge for shade	P P 6	2
The painter was no god	"		1461	Good—to do a goddess good	V A	28
To rouse our Roman gods	"		1831	she for this good turn	"	92
That god forbid that made me first				by her good will	"	479
your slave	Son	58	1	and use good dealing	"	514
A god in love	"	110	12	good queen, it will not be	"	607
The little Love-god lying	"	154	1	but know, it is as good	"	1181
One god is god of both	P P	8	13	she securely gives good cheer	R L	89
how god Mars did try her	"	11	3	And with good thoughts	"	218
the warlike god embraced me	"	11	5	done to a great good end	"	528
the warlike god unlaced me	"	11	7	petty ills shall change thy good	"	656
All my lady's love is lost, God wot	"	18	10	Let my good name	"	820
Goddess—to do a goddess good	V A		28	We have no good that we can say		
The guilty goddess of my harmful	Son	111	2	is ours	"	873
I never saw a goddess go	"	130	11	both to good and bad	"	993
Thou being a goddess	P P	3	6	indeed to do me good	"	1028
Goest—As thou goest onwards	Son	126	6	that would do it good	"	1117
Goeth—goeth about to take him	V A		319	mine own would do me good	"	1274
Going—going I shall fall	"		719	This is too curious-good	"	1390
thyself, out-going in thy noon	Son	7	13	of good or evil luck	Son 14	3
Since from thee going	"	51	13	Now see what good turns	" 24	9
Gold—gold that's put to use more				some good conceit of thine	" 26	7
gold begets	V A		768	mine is thy good report	" 36	14
hills seem burnish'd gold	"		858	And each doth good turns	" 47	2
that colliers up his gold	R L		855	captive good attending captain ill	" 66	12
Basely with gold	"		1068	So thou be good	" 70	5
is his gold complexion dimm'd	Son	18	6	I think good thoughts, whilst		
As those gold candles	"	21	12	other write good words	" 85	5
of posied gold and bone	L C		45	mine is thy good report	" 96	14
Golden—sighs and golden hairs	V A		51	all thy sum of good	" 109	12
Love's golden arrow	"		947	o'er-green my bad, my good allow	" 112	4
their golden gills	"		1100	count bad what I think good	" 121	8
Against the golden splendour	R L		25	Yet, in good faith	" 131	5
That golden hap	"		42	fire my good one out	" 144	14
the golden age to gild	"		66	the sweets that seem so good	L C	164
an eye-sore in my golden coat	"		205	fire my good one out	P P 2	14
Her hair, like golden threads	"		400	with more than love's good will	" 9	7
clouds about his golden head	"		777	a vain and doubtful good	" 13	1
their glittering golden towers	"		945	a doubtful good, a gloss	" 13	5
of Nestor's golden words	"		1420	And as goods lost	" 13	7
this thy golden time	Son	3	12	Good night, good rest	" 14	1
on his golden pilgrimage	"	7	8	She bade good night	" 14	2
kissing with golden face	"	33	3	good-day, or night now borrow	" 15	17
the golden tresses of the dead	"	68	5	Goodly—like a goodly champaign	R L	1247
with golden quill	"	85	3	and of goodly pride	Son 80	12
The golden bullet beats it down	P P	19	30	The goodly objects	L C	137
Gone—or prey be gone	V A		58	Good-morrow - with this fair	V A	859
makest thou to be gone	"		188	give demure good-morrow	R L	1219
he struggles to be gone	"		227	Goodness—Which, rank of goodness	Son 118	12
my horse is gone	"		380	Which die for goodness	" 124	11
though thy horse be gone	"		390	Good-night—and bid good-night	V A	534
told and quickly gone	"		520	Now let me say 'Good-night	"	555
The sheep are gone to fold	"		532	'Good-night,' quoth she	"	537
Thou hadst been gone	"		613	Gore—a churlish swine to gore	"	616
my salt tears gone	"		1071	all stain'd with gore	"	664
blow it off, and being gone	"		1089	Gored—Gored mine own thoughts	Son 110	3
O, that is gone for which	R L		1051	Gorge—Till either gorge be stuff'd	V A	58

Gorged—full-fed hound or....hawk	R L	694	Granting—hold thee but by thy....	Son	87	5
Got—every alien pen hath got my use	Son	78	3	Grape—deceived with painted....	V A	601
a mansion have those vices got	"	95	9	For one sweet grape	R L	215
Where Cupid got new fire	"	153	14	Grass—Sweet bottom-grass	V A	236
the learned man hath got the lady gay	P P	16	15	For on the grass	"	473
Gout—cramps and gouts and painful fits	R L	856	The grass stoops not	"	1028
			no grass, herb, leaf or weed	"	1053
Gouty—Than the true....landlord	L C	140	an April daisy on the grass	"	395
Govern—should govern every thing	R L	602	Grate—The threshold grates the door	"	306
governs me to go about	Son	113	2	Gratis—He gratis comes	"	914
Govern'd—govern'd him in strength	V A	42	Grave—but a swallowing grave	V A	757
Governess—Where their dear....	R L	443	king of graves, and grave for kings	"	995
Government—regard and smiling government	"	1400	still looketh for a grave	"	1106
			to my household's grave	R L	198
Grace—heavenly moisture, air of grace	V A	64	and they thy fouler grave	"	661
			by the grave and thee	Son	1	14
to her oratory adds more grace	R L	564	Thou art the grave	"	31	9
Desire doth fight with grace	"	712	Of mouthed graves	"	77	6
In great commanders grace and majesty	"	1387	can yield me but a common grave	"	81	7
			Grace—can never grave it	V A	376
but with several graces	"	1410	And grave, like water, that doth eat in steel	R L	755
number all your graces	Son	17	6	you see grave Nestor stand	"	1401
And dost him grace	"	28	10	Graven—If Time have any wrinkle graven there	Son	100	10
Lascivious grace, in whom	"	40	13	Gravity—reasons find of settled..	"	49	8
In all external grace	"	53	13	Graze—Graze on my lips	V A	233
given grace a double majesty	"	78	8	Grazed—that grazed his cattle nigh	L C	57
with thy sweet graces graced be	"	78	12	Great—Or what great danger	V A	206
had all thy gentle grace	"	79	4	either being so great	R L	69
do inherit heaven's graces	"	94	5	And when great treasure	"	132
thy grace is youth	"	96	2	The guilt being great	"	229
Doth grace and faults	"	96	3	to a great good end	"	528
Thou makest faults graces	"	96	4	thy guilt is great	"	876
Than of your graces and your gifts	"	103	12	great strifes to end	"	899
it was to gain my grace	L C	79	Great grief grieves most	"	1117
gave life and grace	"	114	In great commanders	"	1387
Pieced not his grace	"	119	so great a sum of sums	Son	4	8
disciplined, ay, dieted in grace	"	261	Great princes' favourites	"	25	5
to the stream gave grace	"	285	Duty so great, which wit	"	26	5
with the garment of a Grace	"	316	though much is not so great	"	61	9
Thy grace being gain'd	P P	3	8	full sail of his great verse	"	86	1
Grace in all simplicity	P T	54	So thy great gift	"	87	11
Grace—and tears may grace the fashion	R L	1319	And my great mind	"	114	10
			your great deserts repay	"	117	2
eyes this cunning want to grace their art	Son	24	13	great bases for eternity	"	125	3
with his presence grace impiety	"	67	2	In things of great receipt	"	136	7
since mourning doth thee grace	"	132	11	Then must the love he great	P P	8	3
doth not grace the day	"	150	4	That to hear it was great pity	"	21	12
with damask dye to grace her	P P	7	5	Then farewell his great renown	"	21	48
Graced—with thy sweet graces....be	Son	78	12	Greater—deserved a greater fee	V A	699
but were all graced by him	L C	119	blinded with a greater light	R L	375
Graceless—Thus graceless holds he	R L	246	Unto a greater uproar	"	427
Gracious—With the gracious light	Son	7	1	In greater fury fret	"	476
gracious and kind	"	10	11	should not the greater hide	"	663
no face so gracious is as mine	"	62	5	perplex'd in greater pain	"	733
my gracious numbers are decay'd	"	79	3	with greater patience bear it	"	1158
in others seem right gracious	"	135	7	till meeting greater ranks	"	1441
Graciously—Points on me graciously	"	26	10	it is a greater grief	Son	40	11
Graff—This bastard graff	R L	1062	Thy worth the greater	"	70	6
Grained—upon his grained bat	L C	64	more strong, far greater	"	119	12
Grant—As well to hear as grant	R L	915	Greatest—For greatest scandal waits on greatest state	R L	1006
Grant, if thou wilt	Son	16	3				
I grant, sweet love	"	79	5	now my greatest grief	Son	48	6
I grant thou wert not married	"	82	1	Grecian—And you in....tires are	"	53	8
I grant I never saw	"	130	11	Greece—is drawn the power of....	R L	1368
Granted—ere he desire, have....	L C	131	Greedy—Rolling his greedy eyeballs	"	368
Grant'st—Thou grant'st no time	R L	908	Greeing—what with his gust is....	Son	114	11
Granteth—but his heart granteth	"	558	Greek—Gazing upon the Greeks	R L	1384

Greek—encouraging the Greeks to fight	R L	1102
Of all the Greeks	"	1470
Green—trip upon the green	V A	146
the green sticks fast	"	527
the orator too green	"	806
On the green coverlet	R L	394
And summer's green all girded	Son	12 7
with golden face the meadows green	"	33 3
and he in them still green	"	63 14
summer of another's green	"	68 11
which yet are green	"	104 8
The deep-green emerald	L C	213
lovely, fresh, and green	P P	4 2
on the brook's green brim	"	6 10
Like a green plum	"	10 5
Green plants bring not	"	18 39
Green-dropping—Green-dropping sap, which she compares to tears	V A	1176
Greet—wordless, so greets heaven	R L	112
And scarcely greet me	Son	49 6
to greet it with my lays	"	102 6
thus anew to greet	"	145 8
Greeteth—wife that greeteth thee	R L	1303
Grew—Grew kinder, and his fury	V A	318
Grew I not faint	"	645
where your equal grew	Son	84 4
the womb wherein they grew	"	86 4
pluck them where they grew	"	98 8
grew to faults assured	"	118 10
And grew a seething bath	"	153 7
In others' orchards grew	L C	171
Grey—Mine eyes are grey, and bright	V A	140
the grey cheeks of the east	Son	132 6
Grief—make them droop with grief	V A	666
And now his grief	"	701
grief and damn'd despair	"	743
best become her grief	"	968
Grief hath two tongues	"	1007
express my grief	"	1069
For every little grief	"	1179
and such griefs sustain	R L	139
Frantic with grief	"	762
my grief with groans	"	797
turns to gall, thy joy to grief	"	889
True grief is fond	"	1094
Sometime her grief is dumb	"	1105
Grief best is pleased with grief's society	"	1111
Great grief grieves most	"	1117
Grief dallied with, nor law nor limit knows	"	1120
for grief of my sustaining	"	1272
Conceit and grief	"	1298
from our house in grief	"	1308
Her grief, but not her grief's true quality	"	1313
much grief and not a tongue	"	1463
As if with grief or travail he had fainted	"	1543
feeling of her own grief	"	1578
And tell thy grief	"	1603
The grief away that stops his answer	"	1661
To push grief on, and back the same grief draw	"	1673
or grief help grievous deeds	"	1822
night doth nightly make grief's strength seem stronger	Son	28 11
Grief—give physic to my grief	Son	34 9
it is a greater grief	"	40 11
It is not all my grief	"	42 1
now my greatest grief	"	48 6
My grief lies onward	"	50 14
When other petty griefs	"	90 10
Of grief and blushes	L C	200
For her griefs so lively shown	P P	21 17
Thus of every grief in heart	"	21 55
Grievance—grieve at grievances forgone	Son	30 9
Her grievance with his hearing	L C	67
Grieve—Thy coward heart with false bethinking grieves	V A	1024
Great grief grieves most at that would do it good	R L	1117
grieve at grievances forgone	Son	30 9
Grieved—No more be grieved at	"	35 1
Grieving—Grieving themselves to guess at others' smarts	R L	1238
Grievous—or grief help .... deeds	"	1822
Grim—mourner, black and grim	V A	920
grim and urchin-snouted boar	"	1105
As the grim lion fawneth	R L	421
Whose grim aspect	"	451
Grim cave of death	"	769
and grim care's reign	"	1451
Grim-grinning—.... ghost	V A	933
Grin—Or as the wolf doth grin	"	459
Grind—I never more will grind	Son	110 10
Grinning—grim-grinning ghost	V A	933
Gripe—hind under the gripe's sharp claws	R L	543
Griped—Griped in an armed hand	"	1425
Griping—and griping it, the needle	"	319
Grisly—carrier of grisly care	"	926
Groan—Then love's deep groans	V A	377
heavy groan advantage thee	"	950
gives a deadly groan	"	1014
nor mother's groans respecting	R L	431
my tears, my sighs, my groans	"	584
my grief with groans	"	797
in his bed with horrid groans	"	975
And with deep groans	"	1432
Till after a deep groan	"	1276
When sighs and groans	"	1319
he answers with a groan	Son	50 11
For that same groan	"	50 13
A thousand groans	"	131 10
with bleeding groans they pine	L C	275
Groan—my heart longs not to groan	V A	785
her heart, whereat it groans	"	829
to sigh, to weep, and groan	R L	1362
power to make love groan	Son	131 6
that makes my heart to groan	"	133 1
Groin—the tusk in his soft groin	V A	1116
Groom—bed of some rascal groom	R L	671
Poor grooms are sightless night	"	1013
charging the sour-faced groom	"	1334
When, silly groom! God wot	"	1345
For some hard-favour'd groom	"	1632
death of Lucrece and her groom	"	1645
Gross—Not gross to sink	V A	150
hold it her own gross abuse	R L	1345
Though my gross blood	"	1655
And their gross painting	Son	82 13
to my gross body's treason	"	151 6
Grossly—Grossly engirt with daring infamy	R L	1173

8

Grossly—thou hast too grossly dyed	Son	99	5
Ground—What see'st thou in the ground	V A		118
now on the ground	"		224
to the ground below	"		923
of the sluttish ground	"		983
imprison'd in the ground	"		1046
on the ground lay spill'd	"		1167
My sable ground of sin	R L		1074
to the skies and ground	"		1199
Then jointly to the ground	"		1846
showers are to the ground	Son	75	2
treads on the ground	"	130	12
valley-fountain of that ground	"	153	4
In brief the grounds and motives	L C		63
he should not pass those grounds	P P	9	8
lie wither'd on the ground	"	13	9
Through heartless ground	"	18	35
Grounded—.... on sinful loving	Son	142	2
It is so grounded inward	"	62	4
Grove—hasteth to a myrtle grove	V A		865
Make thy sad grove	R L		1129
in men, as in a rough-grown grove	"		1249
Which a grove of myrtles made	P P	21	4
Grow—spring doth yearly grow	V A		141
face grows to face	"		540
To grow unto himself	"		1180
still blasts, and ne'er grows old	R L		49
so their pride doth grow	"		298
as they see others grow	Son	12	12
consider every thing that grows	"	15	1
and straight grow sad	"	45	14
that thou dost common grow	"	69	14
what worth in you doth grow	"	83	8
doth thy beauty grow	"	93	13
to that which still doth grow	"	115	14
Grows fairer than at first	"	119	12
That it nor grows with heat	"	124	12
black wires grow on her head	"	130	4
I should grow mad	"	140	9
that, when it grows	"	142	11
Trees did grow and plants	P P	21	6
Saw division grow together	P T		42
Grow'st—so fast thou grow'st	Son	11	1
to time thou grow'st	"	18	12
as thy sweet self grow'st	"	126	4
Growing—Things.... to themselves	V A		166
the growing rose defends	R L		492
grown with this growing age	Son	32	10
upon misprision growing	"	87	11
Growing a bath and healthful	"	154	11
an osier growing by a brook	P P	6	5
Grown—as in a rough-grown grove	R L		1249
grown with this growing age	Son	32	10
And sweets grown common	"	102	12
Who hast by waning grown	"	126	3
world is grown so bad	"	140	11
Growth—are growth's abuse	V A		166
shall never come to growth	R L		1062
in pride of all his growth	Son	99	12
In growth of riper days	"	102	8
To give full growth to that	"	115	14
Guard—thy sword to.... iniquity	R L		626
To guard the lawful reasons	Son	49	12
let my heart be his guard	"	133	11
Shook off my sober guards	L C		298
Guarded—the honey guarded with a sting	R L		493
Guess—to guess at others' smart	"		1238
Guess—And that, in guess, thy measure	Son	69	10
I guess one angel	"	144	12
I guess one angel	P P	2	12
Guest—that sour, unwelcome guest	V A		449
welcome to her princely guest	R L		90
brooks not merry guests	"		1125
to that unhappy guest	"		1565
mine eye is my heart's guest	Son	47	7
a sad distemper'd guest	"	153	12
Guide—had his team to guide	V A		179
Fortune be my gods, my guide	R L		351
That guides this hand	"		1722
star that guides my moving	Son	26	9
Guile—that so much guile	R L		1534
The wiles and guiles that women work	P P	19	37
Guilt—The guilt being great	R L		229
This guilt would seem	"		635
For they their guilt with weeping	"		754
O Opportunity, thy guilt is great	"		876
But they whose guilt	"		1342
Lest my bewailed guilt	Son	36	10
Guiltless—So.... she securely gives	R L		89
To burn the guiltless casket	"		1057
Let guiltless souls be freed	"		1482
Guilty—his guilty hand pluck'd up the latch	"		358
The guilty rebel for remission	"		714
the burthen of a guilty mind	"		735
sweating with guilty fear	"		740
Since thou art guilty	"		772
guilty of thy honour's wrack	"		841
Guilty thou art of murder	"		918
Guilty of perjury and subornation	"		919
Guilty of treason	"		920
Guilty of incest	"		921
Be guilty of my death	"		931
Let guiltless souls be freed from guilty woes	"		1482
no guilty instance gave	"		1511
The guilty goddess of my harmful	Son	111	2
Lest guilty of my faults	"	151	4
Guise—this was thy father's guise	V A		1177
Gulf—A swallowing gulf	R L		557
Gull—Which nightly gulls him	Son	86	10
Gun—deadly bullet of a gun	V A		461
Gush—Shall gush pure streams	R L		1078
Gust—Gusts and foul flaws	V A		456
some gentle gust doth get	R L		549
Against the stormy gusts	Son	13	11
what with his gust is 'greeing	"	114	11
Gyves—sports in unconstrained	L C		242
Habit—throws that shallow ... by	R L		1814
O love's best habit	Son	138	11
O love's best habit	P P	1	11
Habitation—Which for their....	Son	95	10
Habitude—.... gave life and grace	L C		114
Had—Had ta'en his last leave	V A		2
the shadow had forsook	"		176
Adonis had his team to guide	"		179
O, had thy mother borne	"		203
She had not brought	"		204
they had not seen	"		357
had his nets made plain	"		359
or I had no hearing	"		428
I had my load before	"		430
Had I no eyes	"		433

HAD				115		HAND		

Had—Had not his clouded with his brow's	*V A*	499		**Hair**—sighs and golden hairs	*V A*		51
no more had seen	"	504		with long dishevell'd hair	"		147
O, had she then gave over	"	571		for thee of my hairs	"		191
she had not suck'd	"	572		Fanning the hairs	"		306
then he had spoke	"	913		Her hair like golden threads	*R L*		400
had lost his power	"	914		time to tear his curled hair	"		981
that the boar had trench'd	"	1052		in my dishevell'd hair	"		1129
If he had spoke	"	1097		had stol'n thy hair	*Son*	99	7
Had I been tooth'd	"	1117		If hairs be wires	"	130	4
the heavens had him lent	*R L*	17		Her hair, nor loose, nor tied	*L C*		29
sleep had closed up mortal eyes	"	163		behold these talents of their hair	"		204
their father had not bin	"	210		**Hairless**—upon his hairless face	*V A*		487
Had Collatinus kill'd	"	232		**Hairy**—with hairy bristles armed	"		625
nad Narcissus seen her	"	265		**Half**—ere summer half be done	"		802
Self-love had never drown'd him	"	266		They that lose half	*R L*		1158
had they in that darksome prison died	"	379		and shows not half your parts	*Son*	17	4
Then had they seen	"	380		disgrace me half so ill	"	89	5
had sheathed their light	"	397		Doth half that glory	"	132	8
For it had been dishonour	"	844		**Hallow'd**—I hallow'd thy fair name	"	108	8
Philomel had ended	"	1079		Hallow'd with sighs	*L C*		228
when sadly she had laid	"	1212		**Halt**—The poor, lame, blind, halt	*R L*		902
had stain'd her stain'd excuse	"	1316		and I straight will halt	*Son*	89	3
observance in this work was had	"	1385		A cripple soon can find a halt	*P P*	19	10
the painter had anatomized	"	1450		**Hammer'd**—antiquities of .... steel	*R L*		951
those shrunk pipes had fed	"	1455		brass or hammer'd steel	*Son*	120	4
Had doting Priam check'd	"	1490		**Hand**—her fair immortal hand	*V A*		80
Troy had been bright	"	1491		My smooth moist hand, were it with thy hand felt	"		143
with grief or travail he had fainted	"	1543		Can thy right hand	"		158
beauty had purloin'd his eyes	"	1654		and then his hand	"		223
When they had sworn	"	1849		With one fair hand	"		351
You had a father	*Son*	13	14	Her other tender hand	"		352
Had my friend's Muse grown	"	32	10	her soft hand's print	"		353
than this his love had brought	"	32	11	takes him by the hand	"		361
Being had, to triumph	"	52	14	'Give me my hand	"		373
to show what wealth she had	"	67	13	You hurt my hand	"		421
Save what is had	"	75	12	Not thy soft hands	"		633
had all thy gentle grace	"	79	2	whose desperate hands	"		765
Thus have I had thee	"	87	13	In hand with all things	"		912
marjoram had stol'n thy hair	"	99	7	She takes him by the hand	"		1124
nor white, had stol'n of both	"	99	10	Her joy with heaved-up hand	*R L*		111
robbery had annex'd thy breath	"	99	11	she took me kindly by the hand	"		253
colour it had stol'n from thee	"	99	15	And how her hand, in my hand being lock'd	"		260
They had not skill enough	"	106	12	his guilty hand pluck'd up the latch	"		358
and no sooner had	"	129	6	give the watchword to his hand full soon	"		370
Had, having, and in quest to have	"	129	10	Her lily hand her rosy cheek lies under	"		386
legions of true hearts had warm'd	"	154	6	Without the bed her other fair hand was	"		393
Time had not scythed	*L C*		12	His eye commends the leading to his hand	"		436
on it had conceited characters	"		16	His hand, as proud of such a dignity	"		437
woe had pelleted in tears	"		18	as his hand did scale	"		440
schedules had she many a one	"		43	His hand, that yet remains	"		463
and had let go by	"		59	that his hand shakes withal	"		467
if I had self-applied	"		76	my heaved-up hands appeal	"		638
He had the dialect	"		125	Such wretched hands such wretched blood should spill	"		999
My parts had power	"		260	Poor hand, why quiver'st thou	"		1030
Scarce had the sun dried up	*P P*	6	1	Yield to my hand; my hand shall conquer thee	"		1210
that often there had been	"	6	8	the other takes in hand	"		1235
Ah, that I had my lady	"	11	13	such sober action with his hand	"		1403
Had women been so strong as men	"	19	23	Here one man's hand lean'd	"		1415
you had not had it then	"	19	24	Griped in an armed hand	"		1425
Had the essence but in one	*P T*		26	A hand, a foot, a face	"		1427
Hadst—O, would thou hadst not, or I had	*V A*		428				
'Thou hadst been gone	"		613				
Hadst thou but bid beware	"		943				
more than thou hadst before	*Son*	40	2				
before thou hadst this more	"	40	4				
Hail—Could 'scape the hail	*L C*		310				

Hand—he takes her by the blood-		
less hand	R L	1597
That guides this hand	"	1722
This said, he struck his hand	"	1842
winter's ragged hand deface	Son 6	1
with Nature's own hand painted	" 20	1
shake hands to torture me	" 28	6
from hands of falsehood	" 48	4
my hand against myself uprear	" 49	11
Or at your hand the account of		
hours to crave	" 58	3
despite his cruel hand	" 60	14
With Time's injurious hand crush'd	" 63	2
by Time's fell hand defaced	" 64	1
Or what strong hand can hold	" 65	11
The hand that writ it	" 71	6
The lily I condemned for thy hand	" 99	6
beauty, like a dial-hand	" 104	9
Of hand, of foot, of lip	" 106	6
like the dyer's hand	" 111	7
For since each hand hath put on	" 127	5
tender inward of thy hand	" 128	6
Love's own hand did make	" 145	1
but in her maiden hand	" 154	4
by a virgin hand disarm'd	" 154	8
a careless hand of pride	L C	30
Or monarch's hands that lets not		
bounty fall	"	41
that never touch'd his hand	"	141
advance of yours that phraseless		
hand	"	225
But alas, my hand hath sworn	P P 17	11
Handled—idle, over-handled theme	V A	770
Handling—with too much handling	"	560
Handmaid—Her twinkling hand-		
maids too	R L	787
Hang—droop with grief and hang the		
head	V A	666
doth she hang her head	"	1058
Thy kinsmen hang their heads	R L	521
and hang their heads with mine	"	793
calls to mind where hangs a piece	"	1366
Hang on such thorns	Son 54	7
And hang more praise	" 72	7
or none, or few, do hang	" 73	2
did hang in crooked curls	L C	85
plum that hangs upon a tree	P P 10	5
Hang'd—to a cabin hang'd with care	" 14	3
Hanging—his braided hanging mane	V A	271
still hanging by his neck	"	593
like a heavy-hanging bell	R L	1493
in my bosom's shop is hanging	Son 24	7
Hanging her pale and pined cheek	L C	32
Hap—That golden hap which their		
superiors want	R L	42
issueless shalt hap to die	Son 9	3
Hapless—to end a hapless life	R L	1045
Haply—Haply that name of 'chaste'	"	8
Haply I think on thee	Son 29	10
And haply of our old acquaintance	" 89	12
wilt thou not haply say	" 101	5
Happier—Or ten times happier	" 6	8
were happier than thou art	" 6	9
the height of happier men	" 32	8
Happiness—O happiness enjoy'd but		
of a few	R L	22
Happy—And now the happy season	V A	327
treasure of his happy state	R L	16
But happy monarchs still are fear'd	"	611
Happy—some happy mean to end	R L	1045
sire, and child, and happy mother	Son 8	11
on the top of happy hours	" 16	5
Then happy I, that love	" 25	13
return in happy plight	" 28	1
then ten times happy me	" 37	14
shadow's form form happy show	" 43	6
how happy you make those	" 57	12
O, what a happy title	" 92	11
Happy to have thy love, happy to		
die	" 92	12
saucy jacks so happy are in this	" 128	13
Happy—which happies those that pay	" 6	6
Harbinger—But thou shrieking		
harbinger	P T	5
Harbour—dark harbour for defame	R L	768
Hard—flinty, hard as steel	V A	199
borne so hard a mind	"	203
with his hard hoof he wounds	"	267
best thy hard heart	"	375
hath made mine hard	"	378
where a heart is hard	"	426
holds her pulses hard	"	476
That hard heart of thine	"	500
with her hard embracing	"	559
Fearing some hard news	R L	255
Of hard misfortune	"	1713
how hard true sorrow hits	Son 120	10
why 'twas beautiful and hard	L C	211
Faithful friends are hard to find	P P 21	34
Hard-believing—O hard-believing		
love, how strange	V A	985
Harden—Tears harden lust	R L	560
Harden'd—Stone him with harden'd		
hearts	"	978
Harder—O, if no harder than a stone	"	593
hearts, harder than stones	"	978
thou harder hast engrossed	Son 133	6
Hardest—The hardest knife ill used	" 95	14
Hard-favour'd—Were I hard-fa-		
vour'd, foul	V A	133
Hard-favour'd tyrant	"	931
some hard-favour'd groom	R L	1632
Hare—at the timorous flying hare	V A	674
on foot the purblind hare	"	679
Harm—thence doth little harm	"	195
fortress'd from a world of harms	R L	28
no outward harm express'd	"	91
th' other feareth harm	"	172
including all foul harms	"	199
A little harm done	"	528
should right poor ladies' harms	"	1694
For fear of harms	L C	165
Harm have I done to them	"	194
Harmed—cannot be easily harmed	V A	627
but ne'er was harmed	L C	194
Harmful—A harmful knife	R L	1724
of my harmful deeds	Son 111	2
Harmless — Harmless Lucretia,		
marking what he tells	R L	510
Such harmless creatures	"	1347
and give the harmless show	"	1507
sheathed in her harmless breast	"	1723
Harmony—Lost the deceiving har-		
mony should run	V A	781
Harsh—churlish, harsh in voice	"	134
Harsh, featureless, and rude	Son 11	10
Harsh-sounding — heavenly tune		
harsh-sounding	V A	431

Harvest—the harvest of his wits	R L	859	Hate—and see just cause of hate	Son 150	10
should that harvest reap	Son 128	7	In vowing new hate	" 152	4
Hast—hast thou a tongue	V A	427	Hate—I hate not love, but your	V A	789
when thou hast on foot the pur-			hates himself for his offence	R L	738
blind hare	"	679	him whom thou dost hate	" 89	14
thou hast no eyes to see	"	939	Then hate me when thou wilt	Son 90	1
Why hast thou cast	"	951	the sound that said 'I hate	" 145	2
what treasure hast thou lost	"	1075	'I hate' she alter'd with an end	" 145	9
as thou hast pretended	R L	576	'I hate' from hate	" 145	13
Hast thou put on his shape	"	597	But, love, hate on	" 149	13
Hast thou command	"	624	Hated - Past reason hated	" 129	7
which thou hast here deprived	"	1752	Hateful—Hateful divorce of love	V A	932
my image thou hast torn	"	1762	to his hateful name	"	994
no form of thee hast left behind	Son 9	6	and wretched hateful days	R L	161
Hast thou, the master-mistress of			Hateful it is ; there is no hate	"	240
my passion	" 20	2	'O hateful, vaporous, and foggy Night'	"	771
hast all the all of me	" 31	14	hateful cuckoos hatch in sparrows'		
at that which thou hast done	" 35	1	nests	"	849
What hast thou then	" 40	2	the hateful foe bewray'd	"	1698
That thou hast her	" 42	1	Hatefully—But hatefully at random	V A	949
thou hast the strength of laws	" 49	13	Hateth—Who hateth thee that I do		
thou hast pass'd by the ambush	" 70	9	call my friend	Son 119	5
thou hast but lost the dregs of life	" 74	9	Hath—the world hath ending	V A	12
thou hast too grossly dyed	" 99	5	yet hath he been my captive	"	101
Who hast by waning grown	" 126	3	hath he hung his lance	"	103
thou harder hast engrossed	" 133	6	for my sake hath learn'd	"	105
thou hast both him and me	" 134	13	the heart hath treble wrong	"	329
thou hast thy 'Will	" 135	1	hath made mine hard	"	378
hast thou forged hooks	" 137	7	The sea hath bounds, but deep de-		
hast thou this powerful might	" 150	1	sire hath none	"	389
Whence hast thou this becoming	" 150	5	eye so full hath fed	"	399
Whilst thou hast wherewith to			hath done me double wrong	"	429
spend	P P 21	36	Hath taught them	"	501
Haste—devouring all in haste	V A	57	hath ended in the west	"	530
And all in haste	"	870	hath caught the yielding prey	"	547
Her more than haste	"	909	She hath assay'd as much	"	608
And in her haste	"	1029	hath deserved a greater fee	"	609
return again in haste	R L	321	he hath a battle set	"	619
So his unhallow'd haste	"	552	Beauty hath nought to do	"	618
with their fresh falls' haste	"	650	hath she bribed the Destinies	"	733
The cause craves haste	"	1295	semblance he hath fed	"	795
to my lord with more than haste	"	1332	Hath dropp'd a precious jewel	"	823
that doth behold his haste	"	1608	For who hath she to spend	"	847
by thy continual haste	Son 123	11	When he hath ceased	"	919
Haste—I haste me to my bed	" 27	1	web that she hath wrought	"	991
why should I haste me thence	" 51	3	that hath done thee wrong	"	1005
Hasten—minutes hasten to their end	" 60	2	Grief hath two tongues	"	1007
Hasteth—and hasteth to his horse	V A	258	when he hath sung	"	1095
hasteth to a myrtle grove	"	865	and hath kill'd him so	"	1110
Hasting—Hasting to feed her fawn	"	876	hath done her beauty wrong	R L	80
Hasty—Thy hasty spring still blasts	R L	49	that hath engirt	"	221
Hat—she heaveth up his hat	V A	351	Hath barr'd him	"	340
some, untuck'd, descended her			impiety hath wrought	"	341
sheaved hat	L C	31	fear's frost hath dissolution	"	355
Hatch—cuckoos hatch in sparrows'			That thinks she hath beheld	"	451
nests	R L	849	Thy beauty hath ensnared thee	"	485
Hate—To make thee hate	V A	731	Only he hath an eye to gaze	"	496
there is no hate in loving	R L	240	The wolf hath seized	"	677
if not, enforced hate	"	668	But she hath lost	"	687
to fine the hate of foes	"	936	And he hath won	"	688
or begets him hate	"	1005	that hath lost in gain	"	730
possess'd with murderous hate	Son 10	5	a wandering wasp hath crept	"	839
Shall hate be fairer lodged	" 10	10	And scarce hath eyes	"	857
is in my love and hate	" 35	12	'So then he hath it	"	862
than hate's known injury	" 40	12	which wretchedness hath chained	"	990
In your waken'd hate	" 117	12	what he hath said	"	915
Time's love or to Time's hate	" 124	3	'Why hath thy servant oppor-		
and thy dear virtue hate	" 142	1	tunities	"	932
Hate of my sin	" 142	2	hath Tarquin rifled me	"	1050

Hath—			Hath—In thee hath neither sting	L C	265
For day hath nought	R L	1092	and chill extincture hath	"	294
grief is dumb and hath no words	"	1103	how often hath she joined	P P	7 7
winter that the flower hath kill'd	"	1235	to please me hath she coined	"	7 9
one hath power to tell	"	1258	Heart hath his hope	"	15 10
So woe hath wearied woe	"	1363	learned man hath got the lady	"	16 15
that hath done him wrong	"	1467	my hand hath sworn	"	17 11
that hath transgressed so	"	1481	Love hath forlorn me	"	18 21
Whose deed hath made herself	"	1566	thine eye hath chose the dame	"	19 1
hath overslipp'd her thought	"	1576	hath taught her thus to say	"	19 22
with painted images hath spent	"	1577	Love hath reason, reason none	P T	47
He hath no power	"	1594	Hatred—no hatred in thine eye	Son	93 5
Hath thee betall'n	"	1599	Haunted—following where he….	L C	130
what spite hath thy fair colour spent	"	1600	Have—Which long have rain'd	V A	83
It hath to say	"	1618	I have been woo'd	"	97
sad task hath not said	"	1699	thou unask'd shalt have	"	102
Hath served a dumb arrest	"	1780	The heat I have from thence	"	195
and too late hath spill'd	"	1801	if thou wilt have twain	"	210
that she hath kill'd	"	1803	since I have hemm'd thee here	"	229
hath in the world an end	Son	9 11	what a horse should have	"	299
Nature hath not made	"	11 9	and thou shalt have it	"	374
hath all too short a date	"	18 4	For I have heard	"	413
that more hath more express'd	"	23 12	That they have murder'd	"	502
what silent love hath writ	"	23 13	you shall have a kiss	"	536
Mine eye hath play'd the painter and hath stell'd	"	24 1	though the rose have prickles	"	574
That hath his windows glazed	"	24 8	You have no reason	"	612
Thy merit hath my duty strongly knit	"	26 2	till they have singled	"	693
Hath dear religious love	"	31 6	time thou needs must have	"	739
region cloud hath mask'd him	"	33 12	If love have lent you	"	775
That she hath thee	"	42 3	what have you urged	"	787
my friend hath found	"	42 10	have seen him no more	"	819
thy love hath cast	"	49 3	they long have gazed	"	927
Since every one hath, every one, one shade	"	53 3	at him should have fled	"	947
Hath been before	"	59 2	they have wept till now	"	1062
Hath travell'd on to age's steepy night	"	63 5	That what they have not	R L	135
Ruin hath taught	"	64 11	by hoping more, they have but less	"	137
For she hath no exchequer	"	67 11	Of that we have	"	152
the eye hath shown	"	69 8	The thing we have	"	153
hath in this line some interest	"	74 3	true respect should have	"	201
every alien pen hath got my use	"	78 3	Might have excuse	"	235
such virtue hath my pen	"	81 13	Poor wretches have remorse	"	269
my heart hath 'scaped	"	90 5	to have him heard	"	306
humour hath its adjunct	"	91 5	might have reposed still	"	382
my life hath end	"	92 6	'I have debated	"	498
a winter hath my absence been	"	97 1	Shall have thy trespass	"	524
Hath put a spirit of youth	"	98 3	'Have done,' quoth he	"	645
It hath my added praise	"	103 4	Have batter'd down her consecrated wall	"	723
Hath motion, and mine eye may be deceived	"	104 12	true eyes have never practised	"	748
moon hath her eclipse	"	107 5	To have their unseen sin remain	"	753
Which hath not figured	"	108 2	So should I have	"	789
hath the mind no part	"	113 7	I have no one to blush	"	792
errors hath my heart committed	"	119 5	Have no perfection of my summer left	"	837
Whilst it hath thought	"	119 6	We have no good that we can say	"	873
hand hath put on nature's power	"	127 5	Truth and Virtue have to do with thee	"	911
beauty hath no name	"	127 7	would else have come	"	916
music hath a far more pleasing sound	"	130 10	'Let him have time	"	981
Thy face hath not the power	"	131 6	Let him have time	"	982
cruel eye hath taken	"	133 5	Let him have time	"	983
Whoever hath her wish	"	135 1	Let him have time	"	984
Hath left me, and I desperate	"	147 7	'Let him have time	"	985
what eyes hath Love	"	148 1	Let him have time	"	988
over me hath power	L C	74	Have time to wail	"	990
The one a palate hath	"	167	such an office have	"	994
Nature hath charged me	"	220	Have heard the cause	"	1000
			that dear jewel I have lost	"	1178
					1191

Have—For men have marble, women waxen minds	R L	1240	Have—and in quest to have	Son	129	10
			I have seen roses	"	130	5
for I have them here	"	1290	Have put on black	"	132	3
creatures have a true respect	"	1317	now I have confess'd	"	134	1
where cares have carved some	"	1445	Him have I lost	"	134	13
the fear that false hearts have	"	1542	heart and eyes have erred	"	137	13
She would have said	"	1535	to have years told	"	138	12
dolour others have endured	"	1582	looks have been mine enemies	"	139	10
should have slain her foe	"	1827	That have profaned	"	142	6
I have astronomy	Son	14	2	If thou dost seek to have	"	142	13
eyes for eyes have done	"	24	9	the thing she would have stay	"	143	4
eyes have drawn	"	24	10	mayst have thy 'Will	"	143	13
have supposed dead	"	31	2	Two loves I have of comfort	"	144	1
morning have I seen	"	33	1	For I have sworn thee fair	"	147	13
yet I have still the loss	"	34	10	Which have no correspondence	"	148	2
Roses have thorns	"	35	2	Or, if they have	"	148	3
This wish I have	"	37	11	For I have sworn deep oaths	"	152	9
till she have prevailed	"	41	8	I have sworn thee fair	"	152	13
Thee have I not	"	48	9	Ink would have seem'd	L C		51
you have some part	"	53	13	have been a spreading flower	"		75
canker-blooms have full as deep	"	54	5	ere he desire have granted	"		131
I have no precious time	"	57	3	'So many have, that never	"		141
When you have bid	"	57	8	Have of my suffering youth	"		178
subjects worse have given	"	59	11	I have been call'd unto	"		181
hours have drained	"	63	3	that mine eyes have seen	"		190
When I have seen	"	64	1	Harm have I done to them	"		191
When I have seen	"	64	5	I have received from many	"		206
have seen such interchange	"	64	9	The thing we have not	"		240
But weep to have that	"	64	14	Have emptied all their fountains	"		253
unless this miracle have might	"	65	13	loves not to have years told	P P	1	12
earth can have but earth	"	74	7	Two loves I have of comfort	"	2	1
So oft have I invoked thee	"	78	1	and yet no cause I have	"	10	7
Have added feathers	"	78	7	that wont to have play'd	"	18	29
Your name from hence immortal life shall have	"	81	5	Have you not heard it said	"	19	41
				They have at commandment	"	21	46
yet when they have devised	"	82	9	Having—But having no defects	V A		138
therefore have I slept	"	83	5	having writ on death	"		509
Thus have I had thee	"	87	13	And having felt the sweetness	"		553
griefs have done their spite	"	90	10	But having thee at vantage	"		685
Happy to have thy love	"	92	12	for having so offended	"		810
They that have power	"	94	1	Having lost the fair discovery	"		828
what a mansion have those vices got	"	95	9	Having no fair to lose	"		1083
what freezings have I felt	"	97	3	Which having all	R L		96
From you have I been absent	"	98	1	In having much, torments us	"		131
If Time have any wrinkle	"	100	10	Having solicited the eternal power	"		344
Have from the forests shook	"	104	4	Having no other pleasure	"		860
seasons have I seen	"	104	6	Who, having two sweet babes	"		1161
have often lived alone	"	105	13	For having traffic with thyself	Son	4	9
pen would have express'd	"	106	7	And having climb'd	"	7	5
Have eyes to wonder	"	106	14	And having thee	"	91	12
If I have ranged	"	109	5	That having such a scope	"	103	2
'tis true I have gone here and there	"	110	1	Had, having, and in quest to have	"	129	10
that I have look'd on truth	"	110	5	having so short a lease	"	146	5
done, have what shall have no end	"	110	9	Havings—Whose rarest havings	L C		235
lines that I before have writ	"	115	1	Hawk—full-fed hound or gorged	R L		694
that I have scanted all	"	117	1	Some in their hawks	Son	91	4
That I have frequent been	"	117	5	Of more delight than hawks	"	91	11
That I have hoisted sail	"	117	7	Hazard—Such hazard now must doting Tarquin make	R L		155
potions have I drunk	"	119	1				
How have mine eyes out of their spheres been fitted	"	119	7	He—Hunting he loved, but love he laugh'd to scorn	V A		4
thrice more than I have spent	"	119	14	He red for shame	"		36
You've pass'd a hell of time	"	120	6	as he was down	"		43
have no leisure taken	"	120	7	now doth he frown	"		45
might have remember'd	"	120	9	He burns with bashful	"		49
Have faculty by nature to subsist	"	122	6	He saith she is immodest	"		53
before have heard	"	123	8	Panting he lies and breatheth	"		62
who have lived for crime	"	124	14	still is he sullen, still he lours and frets	"		75
Have I not seen	"	125	5				

Entry	Ref	Page
He—Look how he can	V A	79
he take truce with her	"	82
did he raise his chin	"	85
so offers he to give	"	88
He winks and turns	"	90
conquers where he comes	"	100
yet hath he been	"	101
Hath he hung his lance	"	103
he that overruled	"	109
Yet was he servile	"	112
So he were like him	"	180
he will not in her arms	"	226
he struggles to be gone	"	227
He might be buried	"	244
there he came to lie	"	245
he could not die	"	246
away he springs	"	258
to her straight goes he	"	264
he leaps, he neighs, he bounds	"	265
he breaks asunder	"	266
his hard hoof he wounds	"	267
The iron bit he crusheth	"	269
what he was controlled with	"	270
vapours doth he send	"	274
he trots, as if he told the steps	"	277
Anon he rears upright	"	279
What recketh he	"	283
What cares he now	"	285
He sees his love, and nothing else he sees	"	287
he did not lack	"	299
he sends far off, and there he stares	"	301
Anon he starts	"	302
he now prepares	"	303
And whether he run or fly	"	304
He looks upon his love	"	307
Scorns the heat he feels	"	311
He vails his tail	"	314
he stamps and bites	"	316
how he is enraged	"	317
He sees her coming	"	337
He holds her in his eye	"	342
just before him as he sat	"	349
my hand,' saith he	"	373
' For shame,' he cries	"	379
Thy palfrey as he should	"	385
like a jade he stood	"	391
But when he saw	"	393
He held such petty bondage	"	394
' I know not love,' quoth he	"	409
before he barketh	"	459
For sharply he did think	"	470
He wrings her nose, he strikes her on	"	475
He bends her fingers	"	476
He chafes her lips; a thousand ways he seeks	"	477
He kisses her; and she	"	479
so he will kiss her	"	480
He cheers the morn	"	484
' Fair queen,' quoth he	"	523
and ere he says 'Adieu	"	537
Till breathless he	"	541
He with her plenty	"	545
He now obeys	"	563
When he did frown	"	571
prays her that he may	"	578
He carries thence	"	582
He tells her, no; to-morrow he intends	"	587
He—He on her belly falls	V A	594
He will not manage her, although he mount her	"	598
Fie, fie, he says	"	611
he whetteth still	"	617
he hath a battle set	"	619
when he doth fret	"	621
where'er he goes	"	622
Being moved, he strikes	"	623
on the lion he will venture	"	628
through whom he rushes	"	630
Alas, he nought esteems	"	631
as he roots the mead	"	636
How he outruns the wind	"	681
He cranks and crosses	"	682
through the which he goes	"	683
Sometime he runs	"	685
alarums he doth hear	"	700
' No matter where,' quoth he	"	715
' I am,' quoth he	"	718
He hath fed	"	795
With this, he breaketh	"	811
So glides he in the night	"	816
He replies with howling	"	918
When he hath ceased	"	919
when he lived	"	935
if he be dead	"	937
Then he had spoke	"	943
'Tis he, foul creature	"	1005
he's author of thy slander	"	1006
For he being dead	"	1010
He could not die, he is not dead	"	1060
he put his bonnet on	"	1087
he would not fear him	"	1094
when he hath sung	"	1095
If he had spoke	"	1097
When he beheld his shadow	"	1099
when he was by	"	1101
He fed them with	"	1104
livery that he wore	"	1107
entertainment that he gave	"	1108
If he did see his face	"	1109
He thought to kiss him	"	1110
He ran upon the boar	"	1112
But he is dead, and never did he bless	"	1119
he himself is reft	"	1174
for the night before	R L	15
he should keep unknown	"	34
with swift intent he goes	"	46
Well was he welcomed	"	51
Now thinks he that her husband's shallow tongue	"	78
For that he colour'd	"	92
he pineth still for more	"	98
He stories to her ears	"	106
He makes excuses	"	114
long he questioned	"	122
himself he must forsake	"	157
When shall he think	"	159
When he himself himself confounds	"	160
on a flint he softly smiteth	"	176
forthwith he lighteth	"	178
he doth premeditate	"	183
he doth debate	"	185
he doth despise	"	187
Will he not wake	"	219
Or were he not	"	234
But as he is my kinsman	"	237

	R L			R L	
He—holds he disputation		246	He—he that gives them		833
Quoth he, 'She took me	"	253	he did complain him	"	845
my captain, and he leadeth	"	271	like still-pining Tantalus he sits	"	858
Away he steals	"	283	'So then he hath it when he cannot use it	"	862
That now he vows	"	287			
he still pursues his fear	"	308	where he the lamb may get	"	878
by the light he spies	"	316	He gratis comes	"	911
He takes it from the rushes	"	318	what he hath said	"	915
He in the worst sense construes	"	324	but he was stay'd	"	917
He takes for accidental things	"	326	till he render right	"	943
'So, so,' quoth he	"	330	'The baser is he	"	1002
ere rich at home he lands	"	336	He shall not boast	"	1063
Now is he come	"	337	'Nor shall he smile	"	1065
the blessed thing he sought	"	340	He ten times pines	"	1115
to pray he doth begin	"	342	That he may vow	"	1179
Even there he starts: quoth he, 'I must deflower	"	348	Lest he should hold it when he is by	"	1315
					1318
the door he opens wide	"	359	though he blush'd	"	1344
wickedly he stalks	"	365	She thought he blush'd	"	1351
about he walks	"	367	she thought he spied	"	1358
What could he see but mightily he noted	"	414	till he return again	"	1359
			he saw them quake	"	1393
What did he note but strongly he desired	"	413	swears he did her wrong	"	1462
			with the blunt swains he goes	"	1504
What he beheld, on that he firmly doted	"	416	He entertain'd a show	"	1514
			he had fainted	"	1543
his wilful eye he tired	"	417	For every tear he falls	"	1551
admiration he admired	"	418	That he finds means	"	1561
Which he by dumb demeanour seeks	"	474	in her sad face he stares	"	1591
			He hath no power	"	1594
he commits this ill	"	476	At last he takes her	"	1597
Thus he replies	"	477	groom of thine,' quoth he	"	1632
Only he hath an eye	"	496	he set his sword	"	1640
dotes on what he looks	"	497	But wretched as he is, he strives in vain	"	1663
he shakes aloft	"	505			
if he mount he dies	"	508	What he breathes out	"	1666
marking what he tells	"	510	'He, he,' she says	"	1717
'Lucrece,' quoth he	"	512	But more than he	"	1718
He rouseth up himself	"	541	'He, he, fair lords, 'tis he	"	1721
he doth but dally	"	554	He falls, and bathes	"	1775
to his borrow'd bed he make retire	"	573	what he said	"	1785
He is no woodman	"	580	as if the name he tore	"	1787
Must he in thee	"	618	He weeps for her	"	1798
He learn'd to sin	"	630	He with the Romans	"	1811
'Have done,' quoth he	"	645	But now he throws	"	1814
'No more,' quoth he	"	667	quoth he, 'arise	"	1818
he sets his foot upon the light	"	673	This said, he struck his hand	"	1842
He pens her piteous clamours	"	681	He doth again repeat	"	1848
And he hath won what he would lose again	"	688	Or who is he so fond	Son 3	7
			he reeleth from the day	" 7	10
Ere he can see	"	704	when he takes thee hence	" 12	14
he sounds this doom	"	717	As he takes from you	" 15	14
he stands disgraced	"	718	forgot for which he toil'd	" 25	12
through the dark night he stealeth	"	729	But since he died	" 32	13
he left behind	"	734	he was but one hour mine	" 33	11
And he the burthen of a guilty mind	"	735	And he that calls on thee	" 38	11
			where he would be	" 41	8
He like a thievish dog creeps	"	736	he answers with a groan	" 50	11
He scowls, and hates himself	"	738	he went wilful-slow	" 51	13
He faintly flies	"	740	he will not every hour survey	" 52	3
He runs, and chides	"	742	he thinks no ill	" 57	14
He thence departs	"	743	whereof now he's king	" 61	6
He in his speed looks for the morning light	"	745	That he shall never cut	" 63	11
			and he in them still green	" 63	11
ere he go to bed	"	776	with infection should he live	" 67	1
Ere he arrive	"	781	Why should he live	" 67	9
as he is but Night's child	"	785	He robs thee of, and pays	" 79	8
he would distain	"	786	He lends thee virtue, and he stole that word	" 79	9
How he in peace is wounded	"	831			

HE 122 HEAR

He—beauty doth he give	Son	79	10
he can afford	"	79	11
that which he doth say	"	79	13
Since what he owes	"	79	14
he upon your soundless deep doth ride	"	80	10
He of tall building and of goodly pride	"	80	12
Then if he thrive	"	80	13
But he that writes of you, if he can tell	"	84	7
No, neither he, nor his compeers	"	86	7
He, nor that affable familiar ghost	"	86	9
he could his looks translate	"	96	10
Because he needs no praise	"	101	9
hence as he shows now	"	101	14
While he insults o'er dull and speechless tribes	"	107	12
confess'd that he is thine	"	134	1
nor he will not be free	"	134	5
and he is kind	"	134	6
He learn'd but surety-like to write	"	134	7
He pays the whole	"	134	14
tell my body that he may	"	151	7
He is contented	"	151	11
So slides he down upon his grained bat	L C	....	64
sits he by her side	"	....	65
When he again desires her	"	....	66
For maiden-tongued he was	"	....	100
was he such a storm	"	....	101
'Well could he ride	"	....	106
what stop he makes	"	....	109
Or he his manage	"	....	112
He had the dialect	"	....	125
'That he did in the general	"	....	127
following where he haunted	"	....	130
bewitch'd, ere he desire	"	....	131
for him what he would say	"	....	132
Till thus he 'gan besiege me	"	....	177
eyes he did dismount	"	....	281
as he to me appears	"	....	299
and he takes and leaves	"	....	305
whom he would maim	"	....	312
Against the thing he sought he would exclaim	"	....	313
When he most burn'd	"	....	314
He preach'd pure maid	"	....	315
concealed fiend he cover'd	"	....	317
Or he refused to take	P P	4	10
He rose and ran away	"	4	14
Anon he comes	"	6	9
He, spying her, bounced in, whereas he stood	"	6	13
to singing he betakes	"	8	12
the boy he should not pass	"	9	8
he saw more wounds than one	"	9	13
And as he fell to her	"	11	4
'he seized on my lips	"	11	9
fetched breath, away he skips	"	11	11
'Air,' quoth he	"	17	9
King Pandion he is dead	"	21	23
'Pity but he were a king	"	21	42
If he be addict to vice	"	21	43
If to women he be bent	"	21	45
He that is thy friend indeed	"	21	51
He will help thee in thy need	"	21	52
If thou sorrow, he will weep	"	21	53
If thou wake, he cannot sleep	"	21	54

He—He with thee doth bear a part	P P	21	56
Head—And rein his proud head	V A	....	14
hold up thy head	"	....	118
she shakes her head	"	....	223
small head and nostril wide	"	....	296
and hang the head	"	....	666
cabins of her head	"	....	1038
doth she hang her head	"	....	1058
She bows her head	"	....	1171
greedy eyeballs in his head	R L	....	368
her head entombed is	"	....	390
Thy kinsmen hang their heads	"	....	521
clamours in her head	"	....	681
about his golden head	"	....	777
and hang their heads with mine	"	....	793
lean'd on another's head	"	....	1415
a face, a leg, a head	"	....	1427
Upon his head that hath	"	....	1481
to rest thy weary head	"	....	1621
With head declined	"	....	1661
Lifts up his burning head	Son	7	2
Till then not show my head	"	26	14
begins a journey in my head	"	27	3
second life on second head	"	68	7
black wires grow on her head	"	130	4
hath Love put in my head	"	148	1
Upon her head a platted hive	L C	....	8
Take counsel of some wiser head	P P	19	5
Headlong—.... fury of his speed	R L	....	501
Heal—That heals the wounds	Son	34	8
Healeth—the wound that nothing healeth	R L	....	731
Health—Health to thy person	"	....	1305
Of thy fair health	Son	45	12
No news but health	"	140	8
Healthful—to medicine a .... state	"	118	11
a bath and healthful remedy	"	154	11
Hear—nor ears to hear nor see	V A	....	437
not see, nor hear, nor touch	"	....	446
alarums he doth bear	"	....	700
hears the passing-bell	"	....	702
and hear a little more	"	....	709
she hears no tidings	"	....	867
she hears them chant it	"	....	869
By this she hears	"	....	877
hears some huntsman holloa	"	....	973
she hears a merry horn	"	....	1025
and gently hear him	"	....	1096
husband's welfare did she hear	R L	....	263
and hears no heedful friends	"	....	495
as fowl hear falcon's bells	"	....	511
by heaven, I will not hear thee	"	....	667
As well to hear as grant	"	....	915
O, hear me then	"	....	930
when he is by to hear her	"	....	1318
more than hear them told	"	....	1324
of sorrow that we hear	"	....	1328
long to hear her words	"	....	1610
to hear the hateful foe	"	....	1698
Music to hear, why hear'st thou	Son	8	1
To hear with eyes	"	23	14
Than you shall hear the surly	"	71	2
hear this, thou age unbred	"	104	13
I love to hear her speak	"	130	9
The more I hear and see	"	150	10
O, hear me tell	L C	....	253
Thou lovest to hear	P P	8	9
Lest that my mistress hear my song	"	19	50
To hear her secrets	"	19	54

Hear—That to hear it was great pity	P P	21	12
That to hear her	"	21	15
they cannot hear thee	"	21	21
Heard—For I have heard	V A	....	413
As if they heard	"	....	1126
The threshold grates the door to have him heard	R L	....	306
Have heard the cause	"	....	1178
that we before have heard them told	Son	123	8
Heard where his plants	L C	....	171
Have you not heard it	P P	19	41
Hear'st—thou hear'st me moralize	V A	....	712
why hear'st thou music sadly	Son	8	1
Hearer—Will tie the hearers	R L	....	818
Hearing—or I had no hearing	V A	....	428
And hearing him	"	....	944
And in my hearing	R L	....	1123
Hearing you praised	Son	85	9
with his hearing to divide	"	....	67
Hearken—To hearken if his foes	V A	....	699
She hearkens for his hounds	"	....	868
Hearsay—Let them say more that like of hearsay well	Son	21	13
Hearsed—within a puddle's womb is hearsed	R L	....	637
Heart—Is thine own heart	V A	....	157
the heart hath treble wrong	"	....	329
the heart's attorney	"	....	335
heart all whole as thine, thy heart	"	....	370
'Give me my heart	"	....	374
thy hard heart do steel it	"	....	375
Because Adonis' heart	"	....	378
set the heart on fire	"	....	388
from my unyielding heart	"	....	423
where a heart is hard	"	....	426
heart's deep-sore wounding	"	....	432
that hard heart of thine	"	....	500
this poor heart of mine	"	....	502
buys my heart from me	"	....	517
look well to her heart	"	....	580
For my sick heart	"	....	584
My boding heart pants	"	....	647
Knocks at my heart	"	....	659
make my faint heart bleed	"	....	669
my heart stands armed	"	....	779
And then my little heart	"	....	783
my heart longs not	"	....	785
my heart of teen	"	....	808
now she beats her heart	"	....	829
enters to surprise her heart	"	....	890
cleaves an infant's heart	"	....	942
Thy coward heart	"	....	1024
never wound the heart	"	....	1042
my heart to lead	"	....	1072
Heavy hearts lead	"	....	1073
My throbbing heart	"	....	1186
our hearts oft tainted be	R L	....	38
my false heart bleed	"	....	228
the heart that shadows dreadeth	"	....	270
My heart shall never countermand	"	....	276
But with a pure appeal seeks to the heart	"	....	293
But his hot heart, which fond desire	"	....	314
is his heart misled	"	....	369
Anon his beating heart, alarums striking	"	....	433
His drumming heart cheers up	"	....	435
Heart—the heart of all her land	R L	....	439
May feel her heart, poor citizen	"	....	465
but his heart granteth	"	....	558
and wreck-threatening heart	"	....	590
From a pure heart	"	....	625
She wakes her heart	"	....	759
Stone him with harden'd hearts	"	....	978
against my heart	"	....	1137
Faint not, faint heart	"	....	1209
drown their eyes or break their hearts	"	....	1239
either cipher'd either's heart	"	....	1396
the fear that false hearts have	"	....	1512
And then against my heart	"	....	1640
as if her heart would break	"	....	1716
so thick come in his poor heart's aid	"	....	1784
do not steep thy heart	"	....	1828
A woman's gentle heart	Son	20	3
raiment of my heart	"	22	6
Bearing thy heart	"	22	11
Presume not on thy heart	"	22	13
weakens his own heart	"	23	4
table of my heart	"	24	2
know not the heart	"	24	14
endeared with all hearts	"	31	1
absent from thy heart	"	41	2
Mine eye and heart are at a mortal war	"	46	1
Mine eye my heart thy picture's sight	"	46	3
My heart mine eye the freedom of	"	46	4
My heart doth plead	"	46	5
tenants to the heart	"	46	10
dear heart's part	"	46	12
And my heart's right thine inward love of heart	"	46	14
Betwixt mine eye and heart	"	47	1
Or heart in love	"	47	4
bids my heart	"	47	6
mine eye is my heart's guest	"	47	7
Awakes my heart to heart's and eye's delight	"	47	14
But you like none, none you, for constant heart	"	53	14
It is so grounded inward in my heart	"	62	4
the thought of hearts can mend	"	69	2
kingdom of hearts shouldst owe	"	70	14
when my heart hath 'scaped	"	90	5
Thy looks with me, thy heart in other place	"	93	4
false heart's history	"	93	7
Whate'er thy thoughts or thy heart's workings be	"	93	11
Take heed, dear heart	"	95	13
never say that I was false of heart	"	109	1
gave my heart another youth	"	110	7
it no form delivers to the heart	"	113	5
What wretched errors hath my heart committed	"	119	5
so long as brain and heart	"	122	5
let me be obsequious in thy heart	"	125	9
my dear doting heart	"	131	3
thy heart torments me with disdain	"	132	2
let it then as well beseem thy heart	"	132	10
Beshrew that heart that makes my heart to groan	"	133	1
Prison my heart	"	133	9

Heart—But then my friend's heart let my poor heart bail	Son	133	10
let my heart be his guard	"	133	11
the judgement of my heart is tied	"	137	8
Why should my heart think	"	137	9
Which my heart knows	"	137	10
my heart and eyes have erred	"	137	13
That thy unkindness lays upon my heart	"	139	2
Dear heart, forbear	"	139	6
Though thy proud heart go wide	"	140	14
'tis my heart that loves	"	141	3
Dissuade one foolish heart	"	141	10
thy proud heart's slave	"	141	12
Root pity in thy heart	"	142	11
Straight in her heart did mercy come	"	145	5
With insufficiency my heart to sway	"	150	2
true hearts had warm'd	"	154	6
supposed them mistress of his heart	L C	.....	142
of his foul adulterate heart	"	.....	175
my heart so much as warmed	"	.....	191
Kept hearts in liveries	"	.....	195
Encamp'd in hearts	"	.....	203
Now all these hearts that do on mine depend	"	.....	274
What rocky heart to water will not wear	"	.....	291
That not a heart which in his level came	"	.....	309
that forced thunder from his heart did fly	"	.....	325
Persuade my heart	P P	3	3
To win his heart she touch'd him	"	4	7
My heart doth charge the watch	"	15	2
Heart hath his hope	"	15	10
Heart's renying	"	18	7
Heart is bleeding	"	18	23
Thus of every grief in heart	"	21	53
Hearts remote, yet not asunder	P T	.....	29
Heart-easing—keep him from heart-easing words	R L	.....	1782
Hearted—'gan she cry, 'flint-hearted boy	V A	.....	95
at least kind-hearted prove	Son	10	12
Hearten—And therein heartens up his servile powers	R L	.....	295
Heartily—I heartily beseech thee	V A	.....	404
Heart-inflaming—his .... brand	Son	154	2
Heartless—To sound a parley to his heartless foe	R L	.....	471
Which heartless peasants did so well resemble	"	.....	1392
Through heartless ground	P P	18	35
Heart-strings—Shall tune our	R L	.....	1141
Heart-wish'd—burn'd in .... luxury	L C	.....	314
Heat—passenger in summer's heat	V A	.....	91
tired in the mid-day heat	"	.....	177
Shall cool the heat	"	.....	190
The heat I have from thence	"	.....	193
scorns the heat he feels	"	.....	311
O rash-false heat	R L	.....	48
Can curb his heat	"	.....	706
knows not parching heat	"	.....	1145
Thy heat of lust	"	.....	1473
Which erst from heat did canopy	Son	12	6
That it nor grows with heat	"	124	12
A dateless, lively heat	"	153	6
Heat—from Love's fire took heat	Son	154	10
Love's fire heats water	"	154	14
Heating—by heating of the blood	V A	.....	742
Heave—to heave the owner out	R L	.....	413
labour hence to heave thee	"	.....	586
Oft did she heave her napkin	L C	.....	15
Heaved-up—Her joy with .... hand	R L	.....	111
my heaved-up hands appeal	"	.....	638
Heaven—that shines from heaven	V A	.....	193
resounds like heaven's thunder	"	.....	268
in earth or heaven	"	.....	493
that shadow heaven's light	"	.....	533
stealing moulds from heaven	"	.....	730
in high heaven's despite	"	.....	731
Love to heaven is fled	"	.....	793
as bright as heaven's beauties	R L	.....	13
the heavens had him lent	"	.....	17
greets heaven for his success	"	.....	112
from the heaven of his thought	"	.....	338
As if the heavens should countenance his sin	"	.....	343
The eye of heaven is out	"	.....	356
By heaven and earth	"	.....	572
To all the host of heaven	"	.....	598
by heaven, I will not hear thee	"	.....	667
for heaven and Collatine	"	.....	1106
As heaven, it seem'd	"	.....	1372
By heaven's fair sun	"	.....	1837
that I in heaven find	Son	14	8
Though yet, heaven knows, it is but as	"	17	3
the eye of heaven shines	"	18	5
Who heaven itself for ornament doth use	"	21	3
That heaven's air in this huge rondure hems	"	21	8
fix'd in heaven's air	"	21	12
when clouds do blot the heaven	"	28	10
And trouble deaf heaven	"	29	3
sings hymns at heaven's gate	"	29	12
when heaven's sun staineth	"	33	14
in heaven's sweetest air	"	70	4
But heaven in thy creation did decree	"	93	9
do inherit heaven's graces	"	94	5
welcome, next my heaven the best	"	110	13
To shun the heaven that leads men	"	129	14
And yet, by heaven, I think	"	130	13
not the morning sun of heaven	"	132	5
From heaven to hell	"	145	12
sees not till heaven clears	"	148	12
spite of heaven's fell rage	L C	.....	13
To sing heaven's praise	P P	5	14
Wish'd himself the heaven's breath	"	17	8
There is no heaven, by holy then	"	19	45
Heaven-hued—The .... sapphire	L C	.....	215
Heavenly—calls it .... moisture	V A	.....	64
this heavenly and earthly sun	"	.....	198
heavenly tune harsh-sounding	"	.....	431
The heavenly moisture	"	.....	542
her heavenly image sits	R L	.....	288
the steep-up heavenly hill	Son	7	5
Such heavenly touches ne'er touch'd	"	17	8
with heavenly alchemy	"	33	4
the heavenly rhetoric of thine eye	P P	3	1
thou a heavenly love	"	3	7
whose heavenly touch	"	8	5

Heaveth—she heaveth up his hat	V A	 351	Hell—the heaven that leads men to this hell	Son	129	14
faintly she up-heaveth	"	 482	To win me soon to hell	"	141	5
Heavily—And .... from woe to woe	Son	30 '10	one angel in another's hell	"	144	12
Which heavily he answers	"	50 11	From heaven to hell	"	145	12
Heaviness—request to know your heaviness	R L	 1283	Who art as black as hell	"	147	11
this moody heaviness	"	 1602	what a hell of witchcraft lies	L C	....	288
Heavy—think it heavy unto thee	V A	 156	To win me soon to hell	P P	2	5
heavy, dark, disliking eye	"	 182	one angel in another's hell	"	2	12
Her heavy anthem	"	 839	Hell-born—Or blot with .... sin	R L	....	1519
What may a heavy groan	"	 950	Help—Her help she sees, but help she cannot get	V A	....	93
Heavy hearts lead	"	 1073	thy help I would assure thee	"	....	371
in his ears a heavy tale	"	 1125	They buy thy help	R L	....	913
weariness with heavy spright	R L	 121	of time's help to despair	"	....	983
When heavy sleep had closed up	"	 163	my case is past the help of law	"	....	1022
With heavy eye, knit brow	"	 709	Poor helpless help	"	....	1036
departs a heavy convertite	"	 743	the help that thou shalt lend me	"	....	1685
The heavy motion that it doth	"	 1326	Without thy help	Son	36	4
a kind of heavy fear	"	 1435	Your shallowest help will hold me up	"	80	9
Though woe be heavy	"	 1574	the help of bath desired	"	153	11
Though heavy sleep on sightless eyes	Son	43 12	the bath for my help lies	"	153	13
But heavy tears, badges of either's woe	"	44 14	All help needing	P P	18	24
How heavy do I journey	"	50 1	Other help for him	"	18	54
My heavy eyelids to the weary night	"	61 2	Help—If tears could help	R L	....	1274
And heavy ignorance aloft to fly	"	78 6	Do wounds help wounds, or grief help grievous words	"	....	1822
That heavy Saturn laugh'd	"	98 4	and help to bear thy part	"	....	1830
Heavy-hanging—like a .... bell	R L	 1493	Alas, she could not help it	P P	16	12
Hector—bold ...., march'd to field	"	 1430	He will help thee	"	21	52
Here manly Hector faints	"	 1488	Helpless—that helpless berries saw	V A	....	604
Hecuba—despairing Hecuba beheld	"	 1447	what helpless shame I feel	R L	....	756
Lo, here weeps Hecuba	"	 1485	This helpless smoke of words	"	....	1027
Hedge—Behind some hedge	V A	 1094	Poor helpless help	"	....	1036
gone to the hedge for shade	P P	6 2	Hem—in this huge rondure hems	Son	21	8
Heed—Take heed, dear heart	Son	95 13	Hemm'd—Since I have hemm'd thee here	V A	....	229
Heedful—corn o'ergrown by weeds, so heedful fear	R L	 281	hemm'd with thieves	"	....	1022
hears no heedful friends	"	 495	Hence—I pray you hence	"	....	382
Heedfully—heedifully doth view	"	 454	labour hence to heave thee	R L	....	586
Heel—Beating his kind embracements with her heels	V A	 312	Tarquin from hence	"	....	1276
Height—His wonted height	R L	 776	when he takes thee hence	Son	12	14
at height decrease	Son	15 7	who doth hence remain	"	39	14
by the height of happier men	"	32 8	From hence your memory	"	81	3
although his height be taken	"	116 8	Your name from hence	"	81	5
Heinous—Thy heinous hours wait on them	R L	 910	To make him seem long hence as he shows now	"	101	14
one most heinous crime	Son	19 8	Hence, thou suborn'd informer	"	125	13
Heir—His tender heir might bear	"	1 4	hence a question takes	L C	....	110
and make worms thine heir	"	6 14	Both fire from hence	"	....	294
beauty's successive heir	"	127 3	In a mutual flame from hence	P T	....	24
Held—He held such petty bondage	V A	 394	Heaverbirth—.... no creature wear	V A	....	1081
Her blood, in poor revenge, held it in chase	R L	 1736	Her—trembling in her passion	"	....	27
Held back his sorrow's tide	"	 1789	doth lend her force	"	....	29
of small worth held	Son	2 4	Under her other was the tender boy	"	....	32
the frame wherein 'tis held	"	21 3	she with her tears	"	....	49
upon these terms I held my city	L C	 176	with her windy sighs	"	....	51
Helen—For Helen's rape	R L	 1369	blames her miss	"	....	53
On Helen's cheek all art of beauty set	Son	53 7	tires with her beak	"	....	56
Hell—Night, image of hell	R L	 764	shaking her wings	"	....	57
To ugly hell; when, lo	"	 1082	breatheth in her face	"	....	62
torture may be call'd a hell	"	 1287	wishing her cheeks were gardens	"	....	65
effects from lightless hell	"	 1555	fasten'd in her arms	"	....	68
though waiting so be hell	Son	58 13	she tunes her tale	"	....	74
limbecks foul as hell	"	119 2	Her best is better'd	"	....	78
you've pass'd a hell of time	"	120 6	by her fair immortal	"	....	80
			he take truce with her	"	....	82
			making her cheeks all wet	"	....	83

Entry	Ref	Line	Entry	Ref	Line
Her—But when her lips	V A	89	Her—obscures her silver shine	V A	728
Her help she sees	"	93	the sun by day and her by night	"	732
yet her fire must burn	"	94	bound him to her breast	"	812
mastering her that foil'd the god	"	114	Love upon her back	"	814
her pleading tongue	"	217	did feed her sight	"	822
blaze forth her wrong	"	219	discovery of her way	"	828
cannot right her cause	"	220	She beats her heart	"	829
her sobs do her intendments break	"	222	repetition of her moans	"	831
she shakes her head	"	223	Her heavy anthem	"	839
Sometimes her arms infold him	"	225	Her song was tedious	"	841
he will not in her arms	"	226	would say after her	"	852
She locks her lily fingers	"	228	no tidings of her love	"	867
Her words are done, her woes the more	"	254	catch her by the neck, some kiss her face	"	872
her object will away	"	255	twine about her thigh to make her stay	"	873
from her twining arms	"	256	Hasting to feed her fawn	"	876
to her straight goes he	"	264	Appals her senses and her spirit confounds	"	882
and neighs unto her	"	307	Sadly in her ear	"	889
to see him woo her	"	309	to surprise her heart	"	890
embracements with her heels	"	312	cheering up her senses	"	896
With her the horse	"	322	through all her sinews	"	903
He sees her coming	"	337	which madly hurries her	"	904
he holds her in his eye	"	342	bear her a thousand ways	"	907
conflict of her hue	"	345	Her more than haste	"	909
now her cheek was pale	"	347	draws up her breath	"	929
Her other tender hand	"	352	Since her best work	"	934
her soft hand's print	"	353	She vail'd her eyelids	"	956
Her eyes petitioners to his eyes	"	356	her two cheeks fair	"	957
His eyes saw her eyes	"	357	of her bosom dropp'd	"	958
Her eyes woo'd still	"	358	O, how her eyes	"	961
her eyes did rain	"	360	Her eyes seen in the tears, tears in her eye	"	962
engine of her thoughts	"	367	Sighs dry her cheeks	"	966
in her naked bed	"	397	throng her constant woe	"	967
His meaning struck her	"	462	best become her grief	"	968
Claps her pale cheeks	"	468	pleased her babe	"	974
think to reprehend her	"	470	bids her rejoice	"	977
that can so well defend her	"	472	flatters her it is	"	978
breatheth life in her	"	474	Whereat her tears began	"	979
He wrings her nose, he strikes her on the cheeks	"	475	prison'd in her eye	"	980
He bends her fingers, holds her pulses hard	"	476	which her cheek melts	"	982
He chafes her lips	"	477	Her rash suspect	"	1010
He kisses her; and she, by her good will	"	479	and in her haste	"	1029
so he will kiss her	"	480	on her fair delight	"	1030
Her two blue windows	"	482	her eyes as murder'd	"	1031
her face illumined with her eye	"	486	her eyes are fled	"	1037
Her arms do lend	"	539	cabins of her head	"	1038
her thirsty lips	"	543	her troubled brain	"	1040
He with her plenty	"	545	once more leap her eyes	"	1050
Her lips are conquerors	"	549	doth she hang her head	"	1058
Her face doth reek and smoke, her blood doth boil	"	555	Her voice is stopp'd, her joints forget	"	1061
her hard embracing	"	559	Her eyes are mad	"	1062
prays her that he may	"	573	her sight dazzling	"	1064
look well to her heart	"	580	her mangling eye	"	1065
He tells her, no	"	587	her face with his	"	1122
Usurps her cheek	"	591	by her side lay kill'd	"	1165
her yoking arms	"	592	like a vapour from her sight	"	1166
He on her belly falls, she on her back	"	594	She bows her head	"	1171
Her champion mounted	"	596	to her Adonis' breath	"	1172
He will not manage her, although he mount her	"	598	within her bosom	"	1173
worse than Tantalus' is her annoy	"	599	reft from her by death	"	1174
and to lack her joy	"	600	yokes her silver doves	"	1190
languisheth in her mishaps	"	603	in her light chariot	"	1192
Her pleading hath	"	609	should underprop her fame	R L	53
			in her fair face's field	"	72
			Now thinks he that her husband's	"	78

Entry	Ref	Line
Her—prodigal that praised her so	R L	79
hath done her beauty wrong	"	80
welcome to her princely guest	"	90
He stories to her ears her husband's fame	"	106
Her joy with heaved-up hand	"	111
And in her vaulty prison	"	119
To darken her whose light	"	191
I'll beg her love; but she is not her own	"	241
Where her beloved Collatinus lies	"	256
O, how her fear did make her colour rise	"	257
'And how her hand	"	260
with her loyal fear	"	261
Which struck her sad, and then	"	262
Until her husband's welfare	"	263
had Narcissus seen her as she stood	"	265
her heavenly image sits	"	288
That eye which looks on her	"	290
The locks between her chamber wherein her needle sticks	"	302
	"	317
gazeth on her yet unstained bed	"	366
Must sell her joy, her life, her world's delight	"	385
Her lily hand her rosy cheek lies under	"	386
her head entombed is	"	390
her other fair hand was	"	393
Her eyes, like marigolds	"	397
Her hair, like golden threads, play'd with her breath	"	400
Each in her sleep	"	404
Her breasts, like ivory globes	"	407
Her azure veins, her alabaster skin	"	419
Her coral lips, her snow-white dimpled chin	"	420
for standing by her side	"	425
On her bare breast, the heart of all her land	"	439
Do tell her she is dreadfully beset	"	444
And fright her with confusion	"	445
breaks ope her lock'd-up eyes	"	446
Imagine her as one in dead of night	"	449
ugly in her eyes	"	459
remains upon her breast	"	463
May feel her heart	"	465
Beating her bulk	"	467
o'er the white sheet peers her whiter chin	"	472
at her own disgrace	"	479
his unhallow'd haste her words delays	"	552
Her sad behaviour	"	556
His ear her prayers admits	"	558
entrance to her plaining	"	559
Her pity-pleading eyes	"	561
Her modest eloquence	"	563
Which to her oratory adds	"	564
so her accent breaks	"	566
By her untimely tears, her husband's love	"	570
Till with her own white fleece her voice controll'd	"	678
Entombs her outcry in her lips' sweet fold	"	679
He pens her piteous clamours in her head	"	681
Her tears should drop	"	686
Her—rifled of her store	R L	692
She says, her subjects	"	722
her consecrated wall	"	723
Her immortality, and made her thrall	"	725
Which in her prescience	"	727
But her foresight	"	728
with her nails her flesh doth tear	"	739
And bids her eyes hereafter still be blind	"	758
She wakes her heart by beating on her breast	"	759
breathes she forth her spite	"	762
Her twinkling handmaids	"	787
to still her child	"	813
And fright her crying babe	"	814
vestal violate her oath	"	883
daughters of her daughter	"	953
scratch her wicked foe	"	1035
Kill both thyself and her	"	1036
from her be-tumbled couch	"	1037
passage of her breath	"	1040
thronging through her lips	"	1041
her nightly sorrow	"	1080
seems to point her out	"	1087
but her passion's strength	"	1103
Sometime her grief is dumb	"	1105
Make her moans mad with their sweet melody	"	1108
her bark being peel'd	"	1169
Her house is sack'd, her quiet interrupted	"	1170
Her mansion batter'd	"	1171
Her sacred temple spotted	"	1172
from her bright eyes	"	1213
calls her maid	"	1214
to her mistress lies	"	1215
unto her maid seem so	"	1217
Her mistress she doth give	"	1219
to her lady's sorrow	"	1221
For why her face	"	1222
ask of her audaciously	"	1223
Why her two suns	"	1224
Nor why her fair cheeks	"	1225
Her circled eyne	"	1229
in her mistress' sky	"	1230
of her drops spilling	"	1236
By that her death, to do her husband wrong	"	1264
through all her body spread	"	1266
of her complaining	"	1269
Her maid is gone	"	1296
with her quill	"	1297
Throng her inventions	"	1302
the tenour of her woe	"	1310
Her certain sorrow	"	1311
Her grief, but not her grief's	"	1313
her own gross abuse	"	1315
her stain'd excuse	"	1316
feeling of her passion	"	1317
when he is by to hear her	"	1318
Of her disgrace, the better so to clear her	"	1320
the world might bear her	"	1321
Her letter now is seal'd	"	1331
villain court'sies to her low	"	1338
And blushing on her	"	1339
he blush'd to see her shame	"	1344
kindled her mistrust	"	1352

Her—Her earnest eye	R L	1356
in her some blemish	"	1358
That she her plaints	"	1364
With her old eyes	"	1448
In her the painter had anatomized	"	1450
Her cheeks with chaps	"	1452
Her blue blood changed	"	1454
Lucrece spends her eyes	"	1457
And shapes her sorrow	"	1458
answer her but cries	"	1459
to ban her cruel foes	"	1460
to lend her those	"	1461
swears he did her wrong	"	1462
To give her so much	"	1463
her beauty I may tear	"	1472
She throws her eyes	"	1499
came in her mind	"	1536
And from her tongue	"	1537
such passion her assails	"	1562
beaten from her breast	"	1563
with her nails	"	1564
the current of her sorrow	"	1569
with her complaining	"	1570
too long with her remaining	"	1572
hath overslipp'd her thought	"	1576
of her own grief brought	"	1578
Losing her woes	"	1580
her tear-distained eye	"	1586
in her dim clement	"	1588
her sad-beholding husband	"	1590
In her sad face	"	1591
Her eyes, though sod in tears	"	1592
Her lively colour kill'd	"	1593
to ask her how she fares	"	1594
At last he takes her	"	1597
she gives her sorrow fire	"	1604
Her honour is ta'en prisoner	"	1608
long to hear her words	"	1610
in her watery nest	"	1611
of her certain ending	"	1612
Lucrece and her groom	"	1645
Doth in her poison'd closet yet endure	"	1659
to her imposition	"	1697
that yet her sad task	"	1699
Her body's stain her mind untainted clears	"	1710
as if her heart would break	"	1716
her poor tongue could not speak	"	1718
in her harmless breast	"	1723
that thence her soul unsheathed	"	1724
Her contrite sighs	"	1727
Her winged spright, and through her wounds	"	1728
father, that beholds her bleed	"	1732
on her self-slaughter'd body	"	1733
Her blood, in poor revenge	"	1736
And bubbling from her breast	"	1737
Circles her body in	"	1739
Some of her blood	"	1742
to die with her	"	1776
revenged on her death	"	1778
The one doth call her his	"	1793
Replies her husband	"	1796
He weeps for her	"	1798
I owed her, and 'tis mine	"	1803
that should have slain her foe	"	1827
forth her fair streets chased	"	1834
Her wrongs to us	"	1840
Her—To show her bleeding body	R L	1851
April of her prime	Son	3 10
her husband's shape	"	9 8
carved thee for her seal	"	11 13
devour her own sweet brood	"	19 2
phœnix in her blood	"	19 4
and all her fading sweets	"	19 7
her babe from faring ill	"	22 12
and her old face new	"	27 12
Will sourly leave her	"	41 8
Hers, by thy beauty tempting her to thee	"	41 13
That thou hast her	"	42 1
I loved her dearly	"	42 2
Thou dost love her, because thou know'st I love her	"	42 6
for my sake to approve her	"	42 8
And losing her, my friend	"	42 10
in manners holds her still	"	83 1
And stops her pipe	"	102 8
Than when her mournful hymns	"	102 10
Therefore, like her I sometime	"	102 13
a scope to show her pride	"	103 2
moon hath her eclipse endured	"	107 5
this purpose, that her skill	"	126 7
Yet fear her, O thou minion of her pleasure	"	126 9
still keep, her treasure	"	126 10
Her audit, though delay'd	"	126 11
her quietus is to render thee	"	126 12
Her eyes so suited	"	127 10
more red than her lips' red	"	130 2
her breasts are dun	"	130 3
black wires grow on her head	"	130 4
see I in her cheeks	"	130 6
I love to hear her speak	"	130 9
Whoever hath her wish	"	135 1
I do believe her	"	138 2
her false-speaking tongue	"	138 7
Therefore I lie with her	"	138 13
Her pretty looks	"	139 10
One of her feather'd creatures	"	143 2
Sets down her babe	"	143 3
her neglected child holds her in chase	"	143 5
Cries to catch her	"	143 6
flies before her face	"	143 7
her poor infant's discontent	"	143 8
with her foul pride	"	144
languish'd for her sake	"	145 3
Straight in her heart	"	145 5
Her 'love' for whose dear love	"	151 14
but in her maiden hand	"	154 4
Storming her world	L C	7
Upon her head		8
Which fortified her visage		9
did she heave her napkin to her eyne	"	15
Sometimes her level'd eyes	"	22
Her hair, nor loose nor tied	"	29
Proclaim'd in her	"	30
descended her sheaved hat	"	31
Hanging her pale and pined cheek	"	32
Some in her threaden fillet	"	33
bathed she in her fluxive eyes	"	50
and motives of her woe	"	63
sits he by her side	"	65
When he again desires her	"	66
Her grievance with his hearing	"	67
Which may her suffering	"	69

HER 129 HID

Phrase	Work	Col1	Col2
Her—and made him her place	L C		82
'gainst her own content	"		157
by-past perils in her way	"		158
Which late her noble suit	"		234
To spend her living	"		238
She that her fame	"		243
And makes her absence valiant, not her might	"		245
brought me to her eye	"		247
did her force subdue	"		248
Believed her eyes	"		262
I do believe her	P P	1	2
her false-speaking tongue	"	1	7
with her fair pride	"	2	8
take her figured proffer	"	4	10
Then fell she on her back	"	4	13
He, spying her	"	6	13
damask dye to grace her	"	7	5
falser to deface her	"	7	6
Her lips to mine	"	7	7
Between each kiss her oaths	"	7	8
all her pure protestings	"	7	11
Her faith, her oaths, her tears	"	7	12
than her milk-white dove	"	9	3
Her stand she takes	"	9	5
and left her all alone	"	9	14
Adonis sitting by her	"	11	1
god Mars did try her	"	11	3
And as he fell to her	"	11	4
clipp'd Adonis in her arms	"	11	6
And with her lips on his	"	11	10
her meaning nor her pleasure	"	11	12
And wish her lays	"	15	6
daylight with her ditty	"	15	7
Were I with her	"	15	13
That liked of her master	"	16	2
Her fancy fell a-turning	"	16	4
Where her faith was firmly fix'd	"	18	11
thou lovest her well	"	19	11
though her frowning brows	"	19	13
Her cloudy looks will calm	"	19	14
dissembled her delight	"	19	16
strive to try her strength	"	19	19
Her feeble force	"	19	21
When craft hath taught her thus	"	19	22
And to her will frame all thy ways	"	19	25
To hear her secrets	"	19	54
Lean'd her breast up-till a thorn	"	21	10
to hear her so complain	"	21	15
her griefs so lively shown	"	21	17
Herald—The owl, night's herald	V A		531
the herald will contrive	R L		206
herald to the gaudy spring	Son	1	10
Herald sad and trumpet be	P T		3
Heraldry—.... in Lucrece' face	R L		64
Herb—Herbs for their smell	V A		165
herb, leaf, or weed	"		1055
Herd—to herdmen and to herds	"		456
with a herd of deer	"		689
from heat did canopy the herd	Son	12	6
And scarce the herd	P P	6	2
Herds stand weeping	"	18	41
Herdmen—to herdmen and to herds	V A		456
Here—Here come and sit	"		17
since I have hemm'd thee here	"		229
and leave me here alone	"		382
here the gentle lark	"		853
Here kennell'd in a brake	"		913
here she meets another	"		917
Here—Here overcome, as one here I prophesy	V A		935
	"		1135
Here was thy father's bed, here	"		1183
Here pale with fear	R L		183
Here with a cockatrice' dead-killing eye	"		540
Here she exclaims against	"		757
for I have them here	"		1290
Here folds she up	"		1310
And here and there the painter interlaces	"		1390
Here one man's hand lean'd	"		1415
Here one being throng'd	"		1417
the fire that burneth here	"		1475
And here in Troy	"		1476
here weeps Hecuba, here Priam	"		1485
Here manly Hector faints, here Troilus	"		1486
Here friend by friend	"		1487
Here feelingly she weeps	"		1492
Sinon here is painted	"		1541
Here all enraged, such passion	"		1562
here the hopeless merchant	"		1660
Here with a sigh	"		1716
Even here she sheathed	"		1723
which thou hast here deprived	"		1752
than you yourself here live	Son	13	2
By praising him here	"	39	11
But here's the joy	"	42	13
do I ensconce me here	"	49	9
I have gone here and there	"	110	1
more black and damned here	L C		54
Look here, what tributes	"		197
that is not warmed here	"		292
she touch'd him here and there	P P	4	7
Here in these brakes	"	9	10
here was the sore	"	9	12
here be it said	"	19	53
Here the anthem doth commence	P T		21
Here enclosed in cinders lie	"		55
Hereafter—hereafter shall attend	V A		1136
hereafter still be blind	R L		758
no dame hereafter living	"		1714
Herein—Herein lives wisdom, beauty	Son	11	5
Heretic—It fears not policy, that heretic	"	124	9
Hers—But hers, which through the crystal tears gave light	V A		491
Hers, by thy beauty tempting her to thee	Son	41	13
She showed hers; he saw	P P	9	13
Herself—with herself at strife	V A		11
where herself herself beheld	"		1129
Means to immure herself	"		1194
Lucrece shames herself to see	R L		1084
And to herself all sorrow	"		1102
So with herself is she	"		1153
made herself herself detest	"		1566
slay herself, that should have slain	"		1827
Since Rome herself in them	"		1833
beauty herself is black	Son	132	13
The destined ill she must herself assay	L C		156
so to herself contrives	"		243
Hid—hid in some brake	V A		876
Which in pale embers hid	R L		5
cannot be hid in clay	"		609
of many, almost hid behind	"		1413
and arm'd his long-hid wits	"		1816

HID 130 HIM

Hid—hid in death's dateless night	Son	30	6
from Time's chest lie hid	"	65	10
Hidden—rust the .... treasure frets	V A		767
that hidden in thee lie	Son	31	8
Hide—broad buttock, tender hide	V A		298
thrusts into his hide	Sm	50	10
Hide—hides his angry brow	V A		349
that hides the silver moon	R L		371
should not the greater hide	"		663
and hide their infamy	"		794
may hide them when they list	"		1008
To hide the truth	"		1075
To hide deceit and give the harmless show	"		1507
Which hides your life	Son	17	4
his visage hide	"	33	7
which the robe doth hide	"	52	10
to hide my will in thine	"	135	6
to have what thou dost hide	"	142	13
Hideous—a hideous shapeless devil	R L		973
To hideous winter	Son	5	6
Sunk in hideous night	"	12	2
Hiding—hiding base sin in plaits	R L		93
the aspiring mountains hiding	"		548
thy black all-hiding cloak	"		801
Hiding thy bravery in their rotten smoke	Son	34	4
Hie—unto the wood they hie them	V A		323
away she hies	"		1188
to her mistress hies	R L		1215
sour-faced groom to hie as fast	"		1334
with bashful innocence doth hie	"		1341
O, sweet shepherd, hie thee	P P	12	11
Hied—hied him to the chase	V A		3
And thither hied	Son	153	12
High—high delightful plain	V A		236
and his high desire	"		276
High crest, short ears	"		297
the high wind sings	"		305
pitch the price so high	"		551
in high heaven's despite	"		731
mounts up on high	"		854
but high or low	"		1139
In that high task	R L		80
colour'd with his high estate	"		92
Collatine's high name	"		108
Huge rocks, high winds	"		335
By their high treason	"		369
by high almighty Jove	"		568
Some high, some low	"		1412
with your most high deserts	Son	17	2
the dumb on high to sing	"	78	5
As high as learning	"	78	14
better than high birth to me	"	91	9
of all size, both high and low	L C		21
Higher—the higher by this let	R L		646
To jump up higher seem'd	"		1414
Highmost—But when from highmost pitch	Son	7	9
High-pitch'd—His .... thoughts	R L		41
High-proud—at such .... rate	"		19
Hild—O, let it not be hild			1257
Hill—if those hills be dry •	V A		233
far off upon a hill	"		697
hills seem burnish'd gold	"		858
Between whose hills	R L		390
the steep-up heavenly hill	Son	7	5
From off a hill	L C		1
upon a steep-up hill	P P	9	5

Hill—That hills and valleys	P P	20	3
Hillock—Round rising hillocks	V A		237
Him—hied him to the chase	"		3
makes amain unto him	"		5
'gins to woo him	"		6
pluck him from his horse	"		30
backward she push'd him	"		41
govern'd him in strength	"		42
resistance made him fret	"		69
Being red, she loves him	"		77
Leading him prisoner	"		110
So he were like him	"		160
gazeth she on him	"		224
infold him like a band	"		225
She answers him	"		308
to see him woo her	"		309
about to take him	"		319
swiftly doth forsake him	"		321
just before him as he sat	"		349
takes him by the hand	"		361
I am bereft him so	"		381
And learn of him	"		404
can no more detain him	"		577
no longer to restrain him	"		579
Bids him farewell	"		580
in him finds missing	"		605
As fearful of him	"		630
let him keep his loathsome cabin	"		637
his foes pursue him still	"		699
makes him stop	"		706
bound him to her breast	"		812
after him she darts	"		817
have him seen no more	"		819
Venus salutes him	"		859
that makes him bright	"		862
doth make him shake	"		880
who shall cope him	"		888
another answer him	"		922
And, hearing him	"		944
at him should have fled	"		947
to strike him dead	"		948
call'd him all to nought	"		993
clepes him king of graves	"		995
he wreak'd on him	"		1004
Tells him of trophies	"		1013
with him is beauty	"		1019
seem'd with him to bleed	"		1056
to rob him of his fair	"		1086
would not fear him	"		1094
and gently hear him	"		1096
bring him mulberries	"		1103
they him with berries	"		1104
He thought to kiss him, and hath killed him	"		1110
whet his teeth at him	"		1113
to persuade him there	"		1114
been tooth'd like him	"		1117
With kissing him I should have killed him	"		1118
takes him by the hand	"		1124
did him peculiar duties	R L		14
the heavens had him lent	"		17
that would let him go	"		76
that nothing in him seem'd	"		94
persuade him to abstaining	"		130
betake him to retire	"		174
drown'd him in the flood	"		266
So cross him with their opposite persuasions	"		286

Him—				Him—			
That eye which him beholds	R L		291	confounds him there	Son	5	6
Each one by him enforced	"		303	to brave him	"	12	14
to have him heard	"		306	Him in thy course untainted do			
to see him there	"		307	allow	"	19	11
They fright him	"		308	to please him thou art bright	"	28	9
portal yields him way	"		309	And dost him grace	"	28	10
to make him stay	"		311	Featured like him, like him with			
could not stay him	"		323	friends possess'd	"	29	6
that did delay him	"		325	hath mask'd him from me now	"	33	12
shuts him from the heaven	"		338	Yet him for this my love	"	33	13
Hath barr'd him	"		340	To him that bears	"	34	12
And him by oath	"		410	let him bring forth	"	38	11
This moves in him	"		468	By praising him here	"	39	14
I mean to place him	"		517	in him dost lie	"	46	5
Swearing I slew him, seeing thee				And says in him	"	46	8
embrace him	"		518	spur cannot provoke him on	"	50	9
She conjures him	"		568	and give him leave to go	"	51	14
to do him shame	"		597	Can bring him to his sweet up-			
by him that gave it thee	"		624	locked treasure	"	52	2
Let him return	"		641	That sin by him	"	67	3
by him defiled	"		787	O, him she stores	"	67	13
reproach to him allotted	"		824	In him those holy antique hours			
did I entertain him	"		842	are seen	"	68	9
could not put him back	"		843	And him as for a map doth Nature			
to disdain him	"		844	store	"	68	13
he did complain him	"		845	Then thank him not	"	79	13
where none may spy him	"		881	Let him but copy	"	84	9
wander by him	"		882	Giving him aid	"	86	8
And bring him where his suit	"		898	nightly gulls him	"	86	10
Lending him wit	"		904	must ne'er love him	"	89	14
To make him curse	"		970	and leap'd with him	"	98	4
Afflict him in his bed	"		975	eat him up to death	"	99	13
Let there bechance him	"		976	To make him much outlive	"	101	11
To make him moan	"		977	To make him seem	"	101	14
Stone him with harden'd hearts	"		978	spite of him	"	107	11
mild women to him lose	"		979	Like him that travels	"	109	6
Wilder to him	"		980	Drugs poison him	"	118	14
'Let him have time	"		981	Of him, myself, and thee, I am for-			
Let him have time	"		982	saken	"	133	7
Let him have time	"		983	bond that him as fast doth bind	"	134	8
Let him have time	"		984	So him I lose	"	134	12
Let him have time	"		985	Him have I lost; thou hast both			
Disdain to him	"		987	him and me	"	134	13
'Let him have time	"		988	If that from him there may be			
to mock at him	"		989	aught applied	L C		68
Let him have time	"		990	and made him her place	"		82
Teach me to curse him	"		996	Each eye that saw him	"		89
That makes him honour'd, or be-				Yet, if men moved him	"		101
gets him hate	"		1005	by him became his deed	"		111
Revenge on him	"		1180	but were all graced by him	"		119
Which by him tainted shall for				To dwell with him in thoughts	"		129
him be spent	"		1182	And dialogued for him	"		132
Bid him with speed	"		1204	and gave him all my flower	"		147
And blushing with him, wistly on				Demand of him	"		149
him gazed	"		1353	Appear to him	"		299
did make him more amazed	"		1356	and mine did him restore	"		301
About him were a press of gaping				In him a plenitude	"		302
faces	"		1408	She told him stories	P P	4	5
that hath done him wrong	"		1467	She show'd him favours	"	4	6
In him the painter	"		1501	she touch'd him here and there	"	4	7
still on him she gazed	"		1531	Yet not so wistly as this queen on			
as Priam him did cherish	"		1546	him	"	6	12
Comparing him to that	"		1565	began to woo him	"	11	2
forced him on so fast	"		1676	so fell she to him	"	11	4
But ere I name him	"		1688	Other help for him	"	18	54
bids him possess his breath	"		1777	Bountiful they will him call	"	21	40
keep him from heart-easing words	"		1782	Quickly him they will entice	"	21	44
policy did him disguise	"		1815	They that fawn'd on him before	"	21	49
Who, wondering at him	"		1845	Himself—so .... himself forsook	V A		161

Himself—if himself were slain	V A	.....	243
himself Affection's sentinel	"	.....	650
To recreate himself	"	.....	1095
Since he himself is reft	"	.....	1174
To grow unto himself	"	.....	1180
And for himself himself he must forsake	R L	.....	157
When he himself himself confounds	"	.....	160
from himself impiety hath wrought	"	.....	341
He rouseth up himself	"	.....	541
Self-will himself doth tire	"	.....	707
For now against himself	"	.....	717
hates himself for his offence	"	.....	738
against himself to rave	"	.....	982
Himself himself seek every hour to kill	"	.....	998
in an armed hand; himself behind	"	.....	1425
Himself on her self-slaughtered body	"	.....	1733
That in himself such murderous	Son	9	14
with sighs himself doth smother	"	47	4
Accomplish'd in himself	L C	.....	116
When as himself to singing he betakes	P P	8	12
Wish'd himself the heaven's breath	"	17	8
And deny himself for Jove	"	17	17
Hind—Like a white hind under the gripe's sharp claws	R L	.....	543
Hinder—Stands on his hinder legs	V A	.....	698
Hindering—Hindering their present fall	R L	.....	551
Hindmost—Though words come	Son	85	12
Hips—their elbows and their hips	V A	.....	44
His—Had ta'en his last leave	"	.....	2
And rein his proud head	"	.....	14
on his sweating palm	"	.....	25
him from his horse	"	.....	30
doth she stroke his cheek	"	.....	45
she stops his lips	"	.....	46
burning of his cheeks	"	.....	50
she kiss'd his brow, his cheek, his chin	"	.....	59
In his angry eyes	"	.....	70
From his soft bosom	"	.....	81
did he raise his chin	"	.....	85
ready for his pay	"	.....	89
turns his lips another way	"	.....	90
hath he hung his lance	"	.....	103
His batter'd shield, his uncontrolled crest	"	.....	104
Scorning his churlish drum	"	.....	107
Making my arms his field, his tent my bed	"	.....	108
his stronger strength	"	.....	111
Love keeps his revels	"	.....	123
to kiss his shadow	"	.....	162
Adonis had his team	"	.....	179
His lowering brows, o'erwhelming his fair sight	"	.....	183
Souring his cheek	"	.....	185
and then his hand	"	.....	223
hasteth to his horse	"	.....	258
Breaketh his rein	"	.....	264
And now his woven girths	"	.....	266
with his hard hoof	"	.....	267
crusheth 'tween his teeth	"	.....	269
His ears up-prick'd; his braided hanging mane	"	.....	271
His—Upon his compass'd crest	V A	.....	272
His nostrils drink the air	"	.....	273
His eye, which scornfully	"	.....	275
Shows his hot courage and his high desire	"	.....	276
what recketh he his rider's	"	.....	283
His flattering 'Holla' or his 'Stand, I say	"	.....	284
He sees his love	"	.....	287
with his proud sight	"	.....	288
His art with nature's	"	.....	291
For through his mane	"	.....	305
He looks upon his love	"	.....	307
as if she knew his mind	"	.....	308
Spurns at his love	"	.....	311
Beating his kind embracements	"	.....	312
He vails his tail	"	.....	314
to his melting buttock	"	.....	315
the poor flies in his fume	"	.....	316
His love, perceiving	"	.....	317
his fury was assuaged	"	.....	318
His testy master goeth	"	.....	319
his bolsterous and unruly	"	.....	326
desperate in his suit	"	.....	336
with his bonnet hides his angry brow	"	.....	339
he holds her in his eye	"	.....	342
heaveth up his hat	"	.....	351
his fair cheek feels	"	.....	352
His tenderer cheek	"	.....	353
to his eyes suing	"	.....	356
His eyes saw her eyes	"	.....	357
his eyes disdain'd	"	.....	358
had his acts made plain	"	.....	359
he saw his love, his youth's fair foe	"	.....	393
from his bending crest	"	.....	395
his mouth, his back, his breast	"	.....	396
Who sees his true love	"	.....	397
his glutton eye	"	.....	399
His other agents	"	.....	400
his proceedings teach thee	"	.....	406
Loseth his pride	"	.....	420
by his stealing in	"	.....	450
which to his speech	"	.....	452
His meaning struck her ere his words begun	"	.....	462
And at his look	"	.....	463
brake off his late intent	"	.....	469
his breath breatheth	"	.....	474
that his unkindness	"	.....	478
when in his fresh array	"	.....	483
upon his hairless face	"	.....	487
Had not his clouded with his brow's repine	"	.....	490
His day's hot task	"	.....	530
lend his neck a sweet embrace	"	.....	539
his lips obey	"	.....	549
his lips' rich treasure	"	.....	552
his choice is froward	"	.....	570
nectar from his lips	"	.....	572
in his breast	"	.....	582
certain of his friends	*	.....	588
she trembles at his tale	"	.....	591
and on his neck	"	.....	592
still hanging by his neck	"	.....	593
On his bow-back	"	.....	619
ever threat his foes	"	.....	620
His eyes like glow-worms	"	.....	621
His snout digs sepulchres	"	.....	622

His—whate'er is in his way	V.A	623
his crooked tushes slay	"	624
His brawny sides	"	625
His short thick neck	"	627
keep his loathsome cabin	"	637
not within his danger	"	639
gentle Love in his desire	"	653
on his back doth lie	"	663
to overshoot his trouble	"	680
to amaze his foes	"	684
For there his smell	"	691
Stands on his hinder legs	"	698
To hearken if his foes	"	699
And now his grief	"	701
his weary legs doth scratch	"	705
his oil to lend the world his light	"	756
reaves his son of life	"	766
In his bed-chamber	"	784
usurp'd his name	"	794
From his moist cabinet	"	854
ariseth in his majesty	"	856
hearkens for his hounds and for his horn	"	868
just in his way	"	879
for his master	"	914
licking of his wound	"	915
his ill-resounding noise	"	919
volleys out his voice	"	921
to steal his breath	"	934
his breath and beauty	"	935
Seeing his beauty	"	938
with his strong course	"	960
honours to his hateful name	"	994
that his beauty may	"	1011
His victories, his triumphs, and his glories	"	1014
To wail his death	"	1017
in his shelly cave	"	1034
at his bloody view	"	1037
perplexed in his throne	"	1043
that his wound wept	"	1053
In his soft flank	"	1054
But stole his blood	"	1056
upon his hurt she looks	"	1063
His face seems twain	"	1067
to rob him of his fair	"	1086
he put his bonnet on	"	1087
Play with his locks	"	1090
of his tender years	"	1091
first should dry his tears	"	1092
To see his face	"	1093
wolf would leave his prey	"	1097
When he beheld his shadow	"	1099
them with his sight	"	1104
if he did see his face	"	1109
with his sharp spear	"	1112
whet his teeth at him	"	1113
nuzzling in his flank	"	1115
in his soft groin	"	1116
My youth with his	"	1120
her face with his	"	1122
looks upon his lips	"	1123
whispers in his ears	"	1125
that close his eyes	"	1127
robbed of his effect	"	1132
not match his woe	"	1140
Sith in his prime	"	1163
And in his blood	"	1167
resembling well his pale	"	1169
His—to wet his eyes	V.A	1179
was his desire	"	1180
breast as in his blood	"	1182
on his keen appetite	R L	9
in that sky of his delight	"	12
treasure of his happy state	"	16
his beauteous mate	"	18
Reckoning his fortune	"	19
because it is his own	"	35
Perchance his boast	"	36
His high-pitch'd thoughts	"	41
His all-too timeless speed	"	44
His honour, his affairs, his friends, his state	"	45
which in his liver glows	"	47
his traitor eye encloses	"	73
his barren skill to show	"	81
with his high estate	"	92
wonder of his eye	"	93
so wanteth in his store	"	97
moralize his wanton sight	"	104
More than his eyes were open	"	105
by his manly chivalry	"	109
for his success	"	112
the purpose of his coming hither	"	113
for his being there	"	114
in his fair welkin once appear	"	116
brought unto his bed	"	120
of his will's obtaining	"	128
to obtain his will resolving	"	129
Pawning his honour to obtain his lust	"	156
No comfortable star did lend his light	"	164
leap'd from his bed	"	169
Throwing his mantle rudely o'er his arm	"	170
His falchion on a flint	"	176
to his lustful eye	"	179
of his loathsome enterprise	"	184
And in his inward mind	"	185
His naked armour	"	188
his thoughts unjust	"	189
that hath engirt his marriage	"	221
to work upon his wife	"	235
And when his gaudy banner	"	272
Within his thought her heavenly image sets	"	288
confounds his wits	"	290
heartens up his servile powers	"	295
Stuff up his lust	"	297
between her chamber and his will	"	302
Each one by him enforced, retires his ward	"	303
they all rate his ill	"	304
he still pursues his fear	"	308
The wind wars with his torch	"	311
smoke of it into his face	"	312
Extinguishing his conduct	"	313
But his hot heart	"	314
the needle his finger pricks	"	319
his course doth let	"	328
pays the hour his debt	"	329
from the heaven of his thought	"	338
That for his prey	"	342
countenance his sin	"	343
of his unfruitful prayer	"	344
That his foul thoughts might compass his fair fair	"	346

	R L	
His—his guilty hand		358
and with his knee	"	379
at the mercy of his mortal sting	"	364
Rolling his greedy eyeballs in his head	"	368
is his heart misled	"	369
to his hand full soon	"	370
the curtain drawn, his eyes begun	"	374
In his clear bed	"	382
to want his bliss	"	389
And in his will his wilful eye he tired	"	417
the grim lion fawneth o'er his prey	"	421
His rage of lust	"	424
His eye, which late	"	426
tempts his veins	"	427
Anon his beating heart	"	433
His drumming heart cheers up his burning eye	"	435
His eye commends the leading to his hand	"	436
His hand, as proud	"	437
smoking with pride, march'd on to make his stand	"	438
as his hand did scale	"	440
Are by his flaming torch	"	448
His hand, that yet remains	"	463
his hand shakes withal	"	467
doth his tongue begin	"	470
to his heartless foe	"	471
stop the headlong fury of his speed	"	501
shakes aloft his Roman blade	"	505
coucheth the fowl below with his wings' shade	"	507
So under his insulting falchion lies	"	509
His venom in effect	"	532
his foul appetite	"	546
In his dim mist	"	548
So his unhallow'd haste	"	552
While in his hold-fast foot	"	555
feeds his vulture folly	"	556
His ear her prayers admits, but his heart granteth	"	558
wrinkles of his face	"	562
She puts the period from his place	"	565
That to his borrow'd bed	"	573
He is no woodman that doth bend his bow	"	580
for his sake spare me	"	582
Hast thou put on his shape	"	597
Thou wrong'st his honour, wound'st his princely name	"	599
His true respect	"	642
Add to his flow, but alter not his taste	"	651
he sets his foot	"	673
The wolf hath seized his prey	"	677
Cooling his hot face	"	682
His taste delicious	"	699
Devours his will	"	700
must vomit his receipt	"	703
see his own abomination	"	704
While Lust is in his pride	"	705
Can curb his heat or rein his rash desire	"	706
bankrupt beggar wails his case	"	711
his soul's fair temple	"	719
Leaving his spoil	"	733
hates himself for his offence	"	738
His—chides his vanish'd loathed delight	R L	742
He in his speed	"	745
His wonted height	"	776
about his golden head	"	777
his weary noon-tide prick	"	781
his smother'd light	"	783
to deck his oratory	"	815
coffers up his gold	"	855
his treasure to behold	"	857
the harvest of his wits	"	859
pleasure of his gain	"	860
cannot cure his pain	"	861
master'd by his young	"	863
Or kills his life or else his quality	"	875
where his suit may be obtained	"	898
Tarquin in his flight	"	968
his lewd eyes affright	"	971
of his committed evil	"	972
'Disturb his hours of rest	"	974
Afflict him in his bed	"	975
but pity not his moans	"	977
to tear his curled hair	"	981
see his friends his foes	"	988
His time of folly and his time of sport	"	992
let his unrecalling crime	"	993
the abusing of his time	"	994
At his own shadow	"	997
To shame his hope	"	1003
bathe his coal-black wings	"	1009
the stain upon his silver down	"	1012
father of his fruit	"	1064
laugh with his companions	"	1066
his mood with nought agrees	"	1095
His leaves will wither and his sap decay	"	1168
and as his due writ in my testament	"	1183
My shame be his	"	1202
His kindled duty	"	1352
the blood his cheeks replenish	"	1357
such sober action with his hand	"	1403
his beard all silver white	"	1405
from his lips did fly	"	1406
his sound advice	"	1409
His nose being shadow'd by his neighbour's ear	"	1416
That for Achilles' image stood his spear	"	1424
Upon his head	"	1481
Priam check'd his son's desire	"	1490
Once set on ringing, with his own weight goes	"	1494
His face, though full of cares	"	1503
to scorn his woes	"	1505
the painter labour'd with his skill	"	1506
ensconced his secret evil	"	1515
for his wondrous skill	"	1523
in his plain face	"	1532
Priam wets his eyes	"	1548
His eye drops fire	"	1552
clear pearls of his that move thy pity	"	1553
For Sinon in his fire	"	1556
to burn his Troy	"	1561
'his wounds will not be sore	"	1568
Brings home his lord	"	1584
Who finds his Lucrece	"	1585
to answer his desire	"	1606

His—his consorted lords	R L	....	1009
against my heart he set his sword	"	....	1040
His scarlet lust	"	....	1650
had purloin'd his eyes	"	....	1651
stops his answer so	"	....	1664
his breath drinks up again	"	....	1666
that doth behold his haste	"	....	1668
Yet in the eddy boundeth in his pride	"	....	1669
his sighs, his sorrows	"	....	1672
Which speechless woe of his poor she attended	"	....	1674
And his untimely frenzy	"	....	1675
Thine, mine, his own	"	....	1684
all his lordly crew	"	....	1731
give his sorrow place	"	....	1773
pale fear in his face	"	....	1775
possess his breath	"	....	1777
of his inward soul	"	....	1779
arrest upon his tongue	"	....	1780
sorrow should his use control	"	....	1781
through his lips do throng	"	....	1783
In his poor heart's aid	"	....	1784
But through his teeth	"	....	1787
Held back his sorrow's tide	"	....	1789
The one doth call her his, the other his	"	....	1793
to clothe his wit	"	....	1809
his folly's show	"	....	1810
his long-hid wits	"	....	1816
For his foul act	"	....	1824
he struck his hand upon his breast	"	....	1842
to end his vow	"	....	1843
And to his protestation	"	....	1844
did his words allow	"	....	1845
His tender heir might bear his memory	Son	1	4
Proving his beauty	"	2	12
Of his self-love	"	3	8
Lifts up his burning head	"	7	2
to his new-appearing sight	"	7	3
his sacred majesty	"	7	4
in his middle age	"	7	6
adore his beauty still	"	7	7
on his golden pilgrimage	"	7	8
From his low tract	"	7	12
Shifts but his place	"	9	10
to each his thunder	"	14	6
is his gold complexion dimm'd	"	18	6
wander'st in his shade	"	18	11
A man in hue, all 'hues' in his controlling	"	20	7
Stirr'd by a painted beauty to his verse	"	21	2
every fair with his fair	"	21	4
Who with his fear is put besides his part	"	23	2
weakens his own heart	"	23	4
you see his skill	"	24	5
That has his windows	"	24	8
than this his love had brought	"	32	11
his for his love	"	32	14
on his celestial face	"	33	6
his visage hide	"	33	7
To see his active child	"	37	2
And in his thoughts	"	47	8
cast his utmost sum	"	49	3
His rider loved not speed	"	50	8
thrusts into his hide	"	50	10
His—spurring to his side	Son	50	12
in his fiery race	"	51	11
to his sweet up-locked treasure	"	52	2
unfolding his imprison'd pride	"	52	12
Nor Mars his sword	"	55	7
in his former might	"	56	4
'gainst his glory fight	"	60	7
now his gift confound	"	60	8
for his scythe to mow	"	60	12
despite his cruel hand	"	60	14
have drain'd his blood	"	63	3
when his youthful morn	"	63	4
treasure of his spring	"	63	8
His beauty shall	"	63	13
hold his swift foot back	"	65	11
Or who his spoil of beauty	"	65	12
with his presence grace	"	67	2
with his society	"	67	4
imitate his cheek	"	67	5
of his living hue	"	67	6
since his rose is true	"	67	8
no exchequer now but his	"	67	11
lives upon his gains	"	67	12
Thus is his cheek	"	68	1
to dress his beauty	"	68	12
ashes of his youth	"	73	10
which is his due	"	74	7
a miser and his wealth	"	75	4
will steal his treasure	"	75	6
spends all his might	"	80	3
inferior far to his	"	80	7
that to his subjects	"	84	6
dignifies his story	"	81	8
shall fame his wit	"	84	11
Making his style admired	"	84	12
holds his rank before	"	85	12
of his great verse	"	86	1
Was it his spirit	"	86	5
nor his compeers	"	86	7
fill'd up his line	"	86	13
hath his adjunct pleasure	"	91	5
outbraves his dignity	"	91	12
knife ill used doth lose his edge	"	95	14
his looks translate	"	96	10
For summer and his pleasures wait on thee	"	97	11
April dress'd in all his trim	"	98	2
And to his robbery	"	99	11
But, for his theft, in pride of all his growth	"	99	12
So thou prevent'st his scythe	"	100	14
with his colour fix'd	"	101	6
Steal from his figure	"	104	10
for nye his page	"	108	12
Doth part his function	"	113	3
Of his quick objects	"	113	7
Nor his own vision	"	113	8
objects to his beams assemble	"	114	8
what with his gust is 'greeing	"	114	11
And to his palate	"	114	12
although his height be taken	"	116	8
Within his bending sickle's compass	"	116	10
with his brief hours	"	116	11
Till each to razed oblivion yield his part	"	122	7
Time's fickle glass, his sickle, hour	"	126	2
let my heart be his guard	"	133	11
addeth to his store	"	135	10
Wooing his purity	"	144	8

His—Angry that his prescriptions	Son	147	6
As his triumphant prize	"	151	10
laid by his brand	"	153	1
And his love-kindling fire	"	153	3
Laid by his side his heart-inflaming brand	"	154	2
man that grazed his cattle	L C		57
upon his grained bat	"		64
with his hearing to divide	"		67
eyes stuck over all his face	"		81
And when in his fair parts	"		83
His browny locks did hang	"		85
Upon his lips their silken parcels	"		87
For on his visage	"		90
'Small show of man was yet upon his chin	"		92
His phœnix down began	"		93
Yet show'd his visage	"		96
His qualities were beauteous as his form	"		99
His rudeness so with his authorized youth	"		104
"That horse his mettle from his rider takes	"		107
by him became his deed	"		111
Or he his manage	"		112
His real habitude gave life	"		114
in himself, not in his case	"		116
Pieced not his grace	"		119
of his subduing tongue	"		120
For his advantage still	"		123
in his craft of will	"		126
that did his picture get	"		134
that never touch'd his hand	"		141
mistress of his heart	"		142
with his art in youth	"		145
in his charmed power	"		146
and his amorous spoil	"		154
of his foul beguiling	"		170
Heard where his plants	"		171
gilded in his smiling	"		172
Of his foul adulterate heart	"		175
commanding in his monarchy	"		196
his invised properties	"		212
'This said, his watery eyes	"		281
'For, lo, his passion	"		295
His poison'd me, and mine did him restore	"		301
which in his level came	"		309
of his all-hurting aim	"		310
moisture of his eye	"		323
in his cheek so glow'd	"		324
from his heart did fly	"		325
his spongy lungs bestow'd	"		326
Wooing his purity	P P	2	8
stories to delight his ear	"	4	5
favours to allure his eye	"	4	6
To win his heart	"	4	7
Study his bias leaves, and makes his book thine eyes	"	5	5
thy voice his dreadful thunder	"	5	11
used to cool his spleen	"	6	6
For his approach	"	6	8
and throws his mantle by	"	6	9
And with her lips on his	"	11	10
Heart hath his hope	"	15	10
farewell his great renown	"	21	48
Use his company no more	"	21	50
Lest the requiem lack his right	P T		16
His—'Twixt the turtle and his queen	P T		31
That the turtle saw his right	"		34
Hiss—where never serpent hisses	V A		17
and the wind doth hiss you	"		1084
The adder hisses	R L		871
History—the false heart's history	Son	93	7
Hit—at random dost thou hit	V A		940
tender horns being hit	"		1033
how hard true sorrow hits	Son	120	10
Hither—the purpose of his coming hither	R L		113
Post hither, this vile purpose	"		220
Go, get me hither paper	"		1289
Hive—In thy weak hive the young possess their hive	"		1769
a platted hive of straw	L C		8
Hoard—She hoards, to spend	R L		1318
that I hoard them not	L C		220
Hoarsely—she.... calls her maid	R L		1214
Hoisted—That I have hoisted sail	Son	117	7
Hold—hold up thy head	V A		118
he holds her in his eye	"		342
holds her pulses hard	"		476
will hold thee in disdain	"		761
and hold it for no sin	R L		209
holds he disputation	"		246
To hold their cursed-blessed fortune	"		866
Holds disputation with each thing	"		1101
Lest he should hold it	"		1315
These contraries such unity do hold	"		1558
which you hold in lease	Son	13	5
Holds in perfection	"	15	2
shall beauty hold a plea	"	65	3
honey breath hold out	"	65	5
can hold his swift foot back	"	65	11
I hold such strife	"	75	3
will hold me up afloat	"	80	9
in manners holds her still	"	85	1
holds his rank before	"	85	12
For how do I hold thee	"	87	5
I sometime hold my tongue	"	102	13
holds what it doth catch	"	113	8
could not so much hold	"	122	9
Dost hold Time's fickle glass	"	126	2
For nothing hold me, so it please thee hold	"	136	11
child holds her in chase	"	143	5
No want of conscience holds it	"	151	13
could not hold argument	P P	3	2
O never faith could hold	"	5	2
Hold-fast—While in his hold-fast foot	R L		555
Holding—Holding their course to Paphos	V A		1193
who, holding Lucrece' life	R L		1805
Hole—To fill with worm-holes	"		946
I make some hole	"		1175
through loop-holes thrust	"		1383
Hollest—sanctified of holiest note	L C		233
Holla—His fluttering 'Holla	V A		284
Halloo—hears some huntsman halloa	"		973
Hollow—Love made these hollows	"		243
Whose hollow womb	"		268
Lo, in this hollow cradle	"		1185
Hollow-swelling — hollow-swelling feather'd breasts	R L		1122
Holy—By holy human law	"		571
breach of holy wedlock vow	"		809

Holy—a holy and obsequious tear	Son	31	5
those holy antique hours	"	68	9
no name, no holy bower	"	127	7
this holy fire of Love	"	153	5
of my holy vows afraid	L C	....	179
There is no heaven, by holy then	P P	19	45
Holy-thoughted—And .... Lucrece	R L	....	384
Homage—homage to his new-appearing sight	Son	7	3
Home—ere rich at home he lands	R L	....	336
Brings home his lord	"	....	1584
Met far from home	"	....	1596
So far from home	Son	61	6
Comes home again	"	87	12
That is my home of love	"	109	5
Home-bred—than civil .... strife	V A	....	764
Homely—The .... villain court'sies	R L	....	1338
Homeward—Homeward through the dark lawnd	V A	....	813
Honest—But honest fear, bewitch'd	R L	....	173
Pawn'd honest looks	"	....	1351
And all my honest faith	Son	152	8
Honesty—Thou smother'st honesty	R L	....	885
With outward honesty	"	....	1545
Honey—A thousand honey secrets	V A	....	16
did honey passage yield	"	....	452
The honey fee of parting	"	....	538
I think the honey guarded	R L	....	493
My honey lost, and I	"	....	836
And suck'd the honey	"	....	840
Thy honey turns to gall	"	....	889
summer's honey breath	Son	65	5
Honour—pure blush and honour's wrack	V A	....	558
Now she adds honours	"	....	994
Honour and beauty	R L	....	27
His honour, his affairs	"	....	45
With honour, wealth, and ease	"	....	142
As life for honour	"	....	145
Honour for wealth	"	....	146
Pawning his honour	"	....	156
To kill thine honour	"	....	516
And stoop to honour	"	....	574
Thou wrong'st his honour	"	....	599
thine honour lay in me	"	....	834
of thy honour's wrack	"	....	841
Yet for thy honour	"	....	842
Honour thyself to rid me	"	....	1031
my honour lives in thee	"	....	1032
My honour I'll bequeath	"	....	1184
'Tis honour to deprive	"	....	1186
mine honour is new-born	"	....	1190
Mine honour be the knife's	"	....	1201
Her honour is ta'en prisoner	"	....	1608
My low-declined honour	"	....	1705
in honour might uphold	Son	13	10
Of public honour and proud titles	"	25	2
in that I honour most	"	25	4
Is from the book of honour	"	25	11
with public kindness honour me	"	36	11
that honour from thy name	"	36	12
gilded honour shamefully misplaced	"	66	5
Finding myself in honour so forbid	L C	....	150
I mine honour shielded	"	....	151
Honourable—plight your honourable faiths	R L	....	1690
Honoured—by oath they truly	"	....	410
that makes him honour'd	"	....	1005
Honouring—the outward honouring	Son	125	2
Hoof—with his hard hoof	V A	....	267
Hoof'd—Round-hoof'd, short-jointed	"	....	295
Hook—nor fear'd no hooks	R L	....	103
hast thou forged hooks	Son	137	7
Hope—Things out of hope	V A	....	567
so fair a hope is slain	"	....	762
This sound of hope	"	....	976
Despair, and hope	"	....	988
weak-built hopes persuade him	R L	....	130
Full of foul hope	"	....	284
If in thy hope thou darest	"	....	605
To shame his hope	"	....	1003
When their brave hope	"	....	1430
And to their hope	"	....	1433
one more rich in hope	Son	29	5
in hope my verse shall stand	"	60	13
But hope of orphans	"	97	10
fears to hopes and hopes to fears	"	119	3
But if thou catch thy hope	"	143	11
Heart hath his hope	P P	15	10
Hope—But that I hope	Son	26	7
being lack'd, to hope	"	52	14
Hopeless—a hopeless castaway	R L	....	744
hopeless merchant of this loss	"	....	1660
Hoping—Thus hoping that Adonis	V A	....	1009
And so by hoping more	R L	....	137
Horn—for his hounds and for his	V A	....	868
she hears a merry horn	"	....	1025
whose tender horns being hit	"	....	1053
comes with horn and hounds	P P	9	6
Horse—to pluck him from his horse	V A	....	30
and hasteth to his horse	"	....	258
So did this horse excel	"	....	293
Look, what a horse should have	"	....	299
With her the horse	"	....	322
my horse is gone	"	....	380
though thy horse be gone	"	....	390
on thy well-breath'd horse	"	....	678
Sin's pack-horse, virtue's snare	R L	....	928
Then can no horse	Son	51	9
Some in their horse	"	91	4
than hawks or horses be	"	91	11
"That horse his mettle from his rider takes	L C	....	107
Whether the horse by him	"	....	111
Hospitality—Reward not	R L	....	575
Host—leaves the Roman host	"	....	3
To all the host of heaven	"	....	598
Hostess—A woeful hostess brooks not merry guests	"	....	1125
Hot—hot as coals of glowing fire	V A	....	35
Shows his hot courage	"	....	276
His day's hot task	"	....	530
Hot, faint and weary	"	....	559
for the hot encounter	"	....	596
The hot scent-snuffing hounds	"	....	692
Which the hot tyrant stains	"	....	797
drops of hot desire	"	....	1074
But his hot heart	R L	....	314
Gives the hot charge	"	....	434
Cooling his hot face	"	....	682
This hot desire converts to cold disdain	"	....	691
Sometime too hot	Son	18	5
in three hot Junes burn'd	"	104	7
the general of hot desire	"	154	7
these trophies of affections hot	L C	....	218
cold modesty, hot wrath	"	....	293

Entry	Ref	Page	Line
Hot—Hot was the day	P P	6	7
Youth is hot and bold	"	12	7
Hot-burning—conscience and hot-burning will	R L	247	
hot-burning fire doth dwell	"	1557	
Hotly—did hotly overlook	V A	178	
Burneth more hotly	"	332	
accomplishment so hotly chased	R L	716	
Hotter—she hotter that did look	P P	6	7
Hound—keep with thy hounds	V A	678	
To make the cunning hounds	"	686	
hot scent-snuffing hounds	"	692	
She hearkens for his hounds	"	868	
the hounds are at a bay	"	877	
yelping of the hounds	"	881	
in a brake she finds a hound	"	913	
full-fed hound or gorged hawk	R L	694	
Some in their hawks and hounds	Son	91	4
comes with horn and hounds	P P	9	6
Hour—an hour but short	V A	23	
What hour is this	"	495	
And in a peaceful hour	"	652	
For lovers' hours are long	"	842	
one minute in an hour	"	1187	
as minutes fill up hours	R L	297	
pays the hour his debt	"	329	
stand auspicious to the hour	"	347	
slavish wipe or birth-hour's blot	"	537	
an hour great strifes to end	"	899	
Thy heinous hours wait	"	910	
the hours thou gavest me	"	933	
proud buildings with thy hours	"	944	
wouldst thou one hour come back	"	963	
Disturb his hours of rest	"	974	
seek every hour to kill	"	998	
in that sad hour of mine	"	1179	
Those hours that with gentle work	Son	5	1
on the top of happy hours	"	16	5
O, carve not with thy hours	"	19	9
he was but one hour mine	"	33	11
sweet hours from love's delight	"	36	8
he will not every hour survey	"	52	3
Upon the hours and times	"	57	2
the world-without-end hour	"	57	5
the account of hours to crave	"	58	3
shames and idle hours in me	"	61	7
When hours have drain'd his blood	"	63	3
those holy antique hours	"	68	9
with his brief hours and weeks	"	116	11
on leases of short-number'd hours	"	124	10
Time's fickle glass, his sickle, hour	"	126	2
in selling hours of dross	"	146	11
The swiftest hours	L C	60	
of many a blasting hour	"	72	
dead within an hour	P P	13	6
minutes added to the hours	"	15	14
Hourly—which stop the hourly dial	R L	327	
House—Her house is sack'd	"	1170	
from our house in grief	"	1308	
so fair a house	Son	13	9
Household—to my household's grave	R L	198	
Housewife—Lo, as a careful	Son	143	1
Hover'd—cherubin above them	L C	319	
Hovering—First ....o'er the paper	R L	1297	
How—O, how quick is love	V A	38	
Look, how a bird lies	"	67	
Look how he can	"	79	
how want of love tormenteth	"	202	
how doth she now for wits	"	249	
How—how he is enraged	V A	317	
How she came stealing	"	344	
How white and red	"	346	
how to get my palfrey	"	384	
How like a jade he stood	"	391	
How he outruns the wind	"	681	
Look, how a bright star	"	815	
How love makes young men	"	837	
How love is wise in folly	"	838	
how the world's poor people	"	925	
O, how her eyes and tears	"	961	
how strange it seems	"	985	
how much a fool was I	"	1015	
how fondly I did dote	R L	207	
O, how her fear did make	"	257	
And how her hand	"	266	
How can they then assist	"	350	
'How will thy shame	"	603	
how canst thou fulfil	"	628	
how vile a spectacle	"	631	
how are they wrapp'd in	"	636	
princess how she fares	"	721	
eyes have never practised how	"	748	
that knew not how	"	810	
How Tarquin wronged me	"	819	
How he in peace is wounded	"	831	
Alas, how many bear	"	832	
How comes it then	"	895	
mark how slow time goes	"	990	
and how swift and short	"	991	
How Tarquin must be used	"	1193	
How was I overseen	"	1206	
how listening Priam	"	1548	
time how slow it creeps	"	1575	
ask her how she fares	"	1594	
O, teach me how to make	"	1653	
How may this forced stain	"	1701	
How much more praise	Son	2	9
Then how, when nature calls me	"	4	11
Mark how one string	"	8	9
How can I then	"	22	8
boast how I do love	"	26	13
How can I then return	"	28	1
How far I toll	"	28	8
How many a holy	"	31	5
How can my Muse	"	38	1
O, how thy worth	"	39	1
teachest how to make	"	39	13
How would thy shadow's form	"	43	6
How would, I say	"	43	9
How to divide the conquest	"	46	2
How careful was I	"	48	1
How heavy do I journey	"	50	1
O, how much more doth beauty	"	54	1
how happy you make those	"	57	12
how are our brains beguiled	"	59	2
How with this rage	"	65	3
O, how shall summer's honey breath	"	65	5
how thy beauties wear	"	71	1
how thy precious minutes	"	77	2
O, how I faint	"	80	1
How far a modern quill	"	83	7
For how do I hold thee	"	87	5
How like Eve's apple	"	93	13
How sweet and lovely	"	95	1
How many lambs might	"	96	9
How many gazers might'st thou	"	96	11
How like a winter has my absence been	"	97	1

How—I teach thee how	Son	101	13	Hunting—Hunting he loved	V A 4
Mark how with my neglect	"	112	12	the hunting of the boar	" 715
How have mine eyes	"	119	7	Huntsman—she bears some	" 973
To weigh how once I suffer'd	"	120	8	Hurl—their silken parcels hurls	L C 87
how hard true sorrow hits	"	120	10	Hurry—Which madly hurries her	V A 904
How oft, when thou	"	128	1	Hurt—You hurt my hand	" 421
How can it? O, how can Love's eye	"	148	9	To mend the hurt	" 478
				Upon his hurt she looks	" 1063
taught thee how to make	"	150	9	They that have power to hurt	Son 91 1
Saw how deceits were gilded	L C		172	Hurting—his all-hurting aim	L C 310
By how much of me	"	.....	189	Husband—her husband's shallow tongue	R L 78
How mighty then you are	"	.....	253		
How coldly those impediments	"	.....	269	to her ears her husband's fame	" 106
O, how the channel	"	.....	285	Until her husband's welfare	" 263
how shall I swear to love	P P	5	1	So thy surviving husband	" 519
how often hath she joined	"	7	7	Then, for thy husband	" 533
How many tales to please me	"	7	9	her husband's love	" 570
how god Mars did try her	"	11	3	'My husband is thy friend	" 582
Lord, how I ine eyes	"	15	1	husband, do thou take	" 1200
How sighs resound	"	18	34	to do her husband wrong	" 1264
How true a twain	P T		45	One of my husband's men	" 1291
Howling—and he replies with	V A		918	Shed for the slaughter'd husband	" 1376
In howling wise, to see my doleful plight	P P	18	33	her sad-beholding husband	" 1590
				Dear husband, in the interest	" 1619
Hue—conflict of her hue	V A		345	Replies her husband	" 1796
a whiter hue than white	"	.....	398	sweet husband to another	Son 8 9
savour, hue and qualities	"	.....	747	her husband's shape in mind	" 9 8
A man in hue, all 'hues	Son	20	7	Like a deceived husband	" 93 2
fair in knowledge as in hue	"	82	5	Husband—And .... nature's riches	" 94 6
flowers in odour and in hue	"	98	6	Husbandry—the tillage of thy	" 3 6
seeing of his living hue	"	67	6	Which husbandry in honour	" 13 10
So your sweet hue	"	104	11	Hush—mournful hymns did hush	" 102 10
which their hue encloses	L C		287	Hush'd—Even as the wind is hush'd	V A 458
Hued—The heaven-hued sapphire	"	.....	215	Hymns—sings .... at heaven's gate	Son 29 12
Huge—Huge rocks, high winds	R L		553	To every hymn	" 85 7
huge fires abide	"	.....	647	her mournful hymns did hush	" 102 10
And waste huge stones	"	.....	959		
That this huge stage presenteth	Son	15	3	I—but a kiss I beg	V A 96
in this huge rondure hems	"	21	8	I have been woo'd, as I entreat	" 97
Hugely—alone stands hugely politic	"	124	11	overruled I oversway'd	" 109
Hunt—For burden-wise I'll hum	R L		1133	And I will wink	" 122
Human—By holy human law	"	.....	571	were I hard-favour'd	" 133
doth ravish human sense	P P	8	6	then I were not for thee	" 137
Humanity—Let fair .... abhor	R L		195	I will enchant thine ear	" 145
Humble—the .... suppliant's friend	"	.....	897	whereon I lie	" 151
An humble gait, calm looks	"	.....	1508	even where I list to sport me	" 154
The humble as the proudest	Son	80	6	I must remove	" 186
The humble salve	"	120	12	And, lo, I lie	" 194
And in thy suit be humble true	P P	19	32	The heat I have	" 195
Humbly—she .... doth insinuate	V A		1012	And were I not immortal	" 197
Humour—Soothing the humour	"	.....	850	What am I, that thou	" 205
Such childish humour	R L		1825	I have hemm'd thee here	" 229
And every humour hath	Son	91	5	I am such a park	" 239
on thy humour doth depend	"	92	8	And this I do	" 281
Hundred—What is ten .... touches	V A		519	'Stand, I say	" 284
twenty hundred kisses	"	.....	522	thou wert as I am, and I a man	" 369
five hundred courses of the sun	Son	59	6	I would assure thee	" 371
Hung—hath he hung his lance	V A		103	I never shall regard	" 377
a jewel hung in ghastly night	Son	27	11	I am bereft him so	" 381
Hung with the trophies	"	31	10	I pray you hence	" 382
Hunger—Sharp .... by the conquest	R L		422	I heartily beseech thee	" 404
Hungry—I have seen the .... ocean	Son	64	5	Though I were dumb	" 406
Thy hungry eyes even till	",	56	6	'I know not love	" 409
Hunt—To hunt the boar	V A		588	and then I chase it	" 410
thou wouldst hunt the boar	"	.....	614	and I will not owe it	" 411
if thou needs wilt hunt	"	.....	673	For I have heard it is	" 413
Why hunt I then for colour	R L		267	or I had no hearing	" 428
Hunted—Spied the hunted boar	V A		900	I had my load before	" 430
Past reason hunted	Son	129	6	Had I no eyes	" 433

I—Or were I deaf	*V A* 435	I—I will not hear thee	*R L* 667
should I be in love	" 438	I mean to bear thee	" 670
And that I could not see	" 440	shame I feel	" 756
'O, where am I?' quoth she	" 493	So should I have	" 789
Do I delight to die	" 496	'Where now I have no one	" 792
But now I lived	" 497	But I alone alone must sit	" 795
But now I died	" 498	Tarquin wronged me, I Collatine	" 819
bargains may I make	" 512	As I, ere this, was pure	" 826
I can be well contented	" 513	and I, a drone-like bee	" 836
Before I know myself	" 525	'Yet am I guilty	" 841
I fear'd thy fortune	" 642	did I entertain him	" 842
Grew I not faint? and fell I not downright	" 645	I could not put him back	" 843
		I could prevent this storm	" 966
if I thee, I thy death should fear	" 660	I force not argument	" 1021
What should I do	" 667	In vain I rail	" 1023
I prophesy thy death	" 671	In vain I cavil	" 1025
'Where did I leave	" 715	In vain I spurn	" 1026
'I am,' quoth he	" 718	For if I die	" 1032
going I shall fall	" 719	But if I live	" 1033
I perceive the reason	" 727	I live and seek in vain	" 1044
The kiss I gave you	" 771	I fear'd by Tarquin's falchion	" 1046
that I cannot reprove	" 787	But when I fear'd I was a loyal wife	" 1048
I hate not love	" 789	So am I now	" 1049
More I could tell, but more I dare not	" 805	for which I sought to live	" 1051
		I need not fear to die	" 1052
now I will away	" 807	at least I give	" 1053
Death, I did but jest	" 997	I will not wrong thy true affection so	" 1060
I felt a kind of fear	" 998	I am the mistress	" 1069
as I met the boar	" 999	'I will not poison thee	" 1072
truth I must confess	" 1001	I will not paint	" 1074
I rail'd on thee	" 1002	I at each sad strain will strain a tear	" 1131
I did but act	" 1006		
how much a fool was I	" 1015	woes waking, wretched I	" 1136
So shall I die	" 1074	I make some hole	" 1175
why then I know	" 1109	Through which I may convey	" 1176
Had I been tooth'd like him, I must confess	" 1117	'Yet die I will not	" 1177
		I murder shameful scorn	" 1189
more am I accurst	" 1120	dear jewel I have lost	" 1191
here I prophesy	" 1135	shall I bequeath to thee	" 1192
Wherein I will not kiss	" 1188	abridgement of my will I make	" 1198
I enforced this fire	*R L* 181	How was I overseen	" 1206
So Lucrece must I force	" 182	'Madam, ere I was up	" 1277
'Yea, though I die	" 204	I thus far can dispense	" 1279
how fondly I did dote	" 207	And ere I rose	" 1281
that I their father had not been	" 210	than I can well express	" 1286
'What win I, if I gain the thing I seek	" 211	for I have them here	" 1290
		What should I say	" 1291
Why hunt I then	" 267	So, I commend me	" 1308
quoth he, 'I must deflower	" 348	her beauty I may tear	" 1472
to whom I pray	" 349	'It cannot be, I find	" 1539
am I come to scale	" 481	So did I Tarquin	" 1547
'Thus I forestall thee	" 484	I will indict	" 1630
Which I to conquer sought	" 488	And swear I found you	" 1635
'I see what crosses	" 491	I did begin to start	" 1639
I know what thorns	" 492	I took all patiently	" 1641
I think the honey guarded	" 493	I should not live	" 1642
I have debated	" 498	when I might charm	" 1681
what sorrow I shall breed	" 499	'But ere I name him	" 1688
I know repentant tears	" 502	And why not I	" 1708
yet strive I to embrace	" 504	Where shall I live	" 1754
I must enjoy thee	" 512	I often did behold	" 1758
I purpose to destroy thee	" 514	That I no more can see what once I was	" 1764
I mean to place him	" 517		
Swearing I slew him	" 518	'I did give that life	" 1800
I rest thy secret friend	" 526	I owed her	" 1803
I did entertain thee	" 596	that I may change my mind	*Son* 10 9
I complain me	" 598	When I do count the clock	" 12 1
I sue for exiled majesty's repeal	" 640	When I behold the violet	" 12 3

Phrase	Ref	No.	Line
I—lofty trees I see barren of leaves	Son	12	5
do I question make	"	12	9
do I my judgement pluck	"	14	1
I have astronomy	"	14	2
Nor can I fortune to brief minutes tell	"	14	5
that I in heaven find	"	14	8
my knowledge I derive	"	14	9
in them I read such art	"	14	10
I prognosticate	"	14	13
When I consider every thing	"	15	1
When I perceive that men	"	15	5
I engraft you new	"	15	14
If I could write	"	17	5
Shall I compare thee	"	18	1
But I forbid thee one	"	19	8
I will not praise	"	21	14
persuade me I am old	"	22	1
time's furrows I behold	"	22	3
Then look I death	"	22	4
How can I then be elder	"	22	8
As I, not for myself, but for thee will	"	22	10
which I will keep so chary	"	22	11
So I, for fear of trust, forget to say	"	23	5
Whilst I, whom fortune	"	25	3
in that I honour most	"	25	4
Then happy I that love	"	25	13
Where I may not remove	"	25	14
To thee I send this	"	26	3
But that I hope some good	"	26	7
Then may I dare to boast how I do love thee	"	26	13
I haste me to my bed	"	27	1
from far where I abide	"	27	5
How can I then return	"	28	1
How far I toil	"	28	8
I tell the day	"	28	9
flatter I the swart-complexion'd night	"	28	11
I all alone beweep	"	29	2
With what I most enjoy	"	29	8
Haply I think on thee	"	29	10
then I scorn to change	"	29	14
I summon up remembrance	"	30	2
I sigh the lack of many a thing I sought	"	30	3
Then can I drown an eye	"	30	5
Then can I grieve	"	30	9
Which I new pay	"	30	12
the while I think on thee	"	30	13
Which I by lacking have supposed dead	"	31	2
which I thought buried	"	31	4
images I loved I view in thee	"	31	13
a glorious morning have I seen	"	33	1
I have still the loss	"	34	10
and even I in this	"	35	5
fault I bring in sense	"	35	9
That I an accessary needs must be	"	35	13
I may not evermore acknowledge	"	36	9
I love thee in such sort	"	36	13
So I, made lame by fortune	"	37	3
I make my love engrafted	"	37	8
So then I am not lame	"	37	9
That I in thy abundance am sufficed	"	37	11
that best I wish in thee	"	37	13
This wish I have	"	37	14
manners may I sing	"	39	1
I—when I praise thee	Son	39	4
by this separation I may give	"	39	7
I cannot blame thee	"	40	6
I do forgive thy robbery	"	40	9
When I am sometime absent	"	41	2
thus I will excuse ye	"	42	5
thou know'st I love her	"	42	6
If I lose thee	"	42	9
and I lose both twain	"	42	11
my friend and I are one	"	42	13
When most I wink	"	43	1
But when I sleep	"	43	3
How would, I say, my eyes	"	43	9
to see till I see thee	"	43	13
I would be brought	"	44	3
that I am not thought	"	44	9
I must attend time's leisure	"	44	12
wherever I abide	"	45	2
This told, I joy	"	45	13
I send them back again	"	45	14
And I am still with them	"	47	12
How careful was I, when I took my way	"	48	1
Thee have I not lock'd up	"	48	9
though I feel thou art	"	48	10
thou wilt be stol'n, I fear	"	48	13
When I shall see thee frown	"	49	2
do I ensconce me here	"	49	9
I can allege no cause	"	49	14
How heavy do I journey	"	50	1
When what I seek	"	50	2
from thee I speed	"	51	2
should I haste me thence	"	51	3
Till I return	"	51	4
Then should I spur	"	51	7
motion shall I know	"	51	8
So am I as the rich	"	52	1
what should I do but tend	"	57	1
I have no precious time	"	57	3
Nor dare I question	"	57	5
Whilst I, my sovereign, watch the clock	"	57	6
Nor dare I question	"	57	9
I should in thought control	"	58	2
I am to wait	"	58	13
That I might see	"	59	9
O, sure I am	"	59	13
For thee watch I	"	61	13
As I all other	"	62	8
quite contrary I read	"	62	11
that for myself I praise	"	62	13
shall be, as I am now	"	63	1
do I now fortify	"	63	9
When I have seen by Time's	"	64	1
towers I see down-razed	"	64	3
When I have seen the hungry	"	64	5
When I have seen such	"	64	9
for restful death I cry	"	66	1
from these would I be gone	"	66	13
I leave my love alone	"	66	14
for me when I am dead	"	71	1
world that I am fled	"	71	3
for I love you so	"	71	6
That I in your sweet thoughts	"	71	7
O, if, I say, you look	"	71	9
When I perhaps compounded am with clay	"	71	10
with me after I am gone	"	71	14
praise upon deceased I	"	72	7

Phrase		Son	Line
I—For I am shamed by that which I bring forth		Son 72	13
I hold such strife		" 75	3
Thus do I pine		" 75	13
do I not glance aside		" 76	3
Why write I still all one		" 76	5
I always write of you		" 76	9
'So oft have I invoked thee		" 78	1
of that which I compile		" 78	9
Whilst I alone did call		" 79	1
I grant, sweet love		" 79	5
O, how I faint when I of you do write		" 80	1
I am a worthless boat		" 80	11
and I be cast away		" 80	13
Or I shall live your epitaph to make		" 81	1
when I in earth am rotten		" 81	2
Though I, once gone, to all the world must die		" 81	6
I grant thou wert		" 82	1
I never saw that you		" 83	1
I found or thought I found		" 83	3
have I slept in your report		" 83	5
For I impair not beauty		" 83	11
I think good thoughts		" 85	5
I say "'Tis so, 'tis true		" 85	9
I was not sick		" 86	12
Then lack'd I matter		" 86	14
For how do I hold thee		" 87	5
Thus have I had thee		" 87	13
I can set down a story		" 88	6
wherein I am attainted		" 88	7
And I by this will be		" 88	9
that to myself I do		" 88	11
to thee I so belong		" 88	13
And I will comment		" 89	2
and I straight will halt		" 89	3
I will acquaintance strangle		" 89	8
Lest I, too much profane, should do it wrong		" 89	11
For I must ne'er love him		" 89	14
so shall I taste		" 90	11
I better in one general best		" 91	8
of all men's pride I boast		" 91	12
need I not to fear		" 92	5
I see a better state		" 92	7
happy title do I find		" 92	11
and yet I know it not		" 92	14
So shall I live		" 93	1
I cannot know thy change		" 93	6
I love thee in such sort		" 96	13
What freezings have I felt		" 97	3
have I been absent		" 98	1
Nor did I wonder		" 98	9
I with these did play		" 98	14
violet thus did I chide		" 99	1
The lily I condemned		" 99	6
More flowers I noted, yet I none could see		" 99	14
I teach thee how		" 101	13
I love not less		" 102	2
When I was wont to greet it		" 102	6
I sometime hold my tongue		" 102	13
Because I would not dull you		" 102	14
if I no more can write		" 103	5
first your eye I eyed		" 104	2
of the seasons have I seen		" 104	6
Since first I saw you fresh		" 104	8
I—I see descriptions		Son 106	2
I see their antique pen		" 106	7
I'll live in this poor rhyme		" 107	11
I must each day say o'er		" 108	6
thou mine, I thine		" 108	7
I hallow'd thy fair name		" 108	8
that I was false of heart		" 109	1
might I from myself depart		" 109	3
if I have ranged		" 109	5
I return again		" 109	6
wide universe I call		" 109	13
I have gone here and there		" 110	1
that I have look'd on truth		" 110	5
I never more will grind		" 110	10
to whom I am confined		" 110	12
and wish I were renew'd		" 111	8
like a willing patient, I will drink		" 111	9
that I will bitter think		" 111	11
and I assure ye		" 111	13
For what care I who calls		" 112	3
and I must strive		" 112	5
nor I to none alive		" 112	7
In so profound abysm I throw all care		" 112	9
my neglect I do dispense		" 112	12
Since I left you		" 113	1
Or whether shall I say		" 114	3
Those lines that I before have writ		" 115	1
I could not love you dearer		" 115	2
Might I not then say, 'Now I love you best		" 115	10
When I was certain		" 115	11
then might I not say so		" 115	13
I never writ		" 116	14
that I have scanted all		" 117	1
I should your great deserts repay		" 117	2
That I have frequent been		" 117	5
That I have hoisted sail		" 117	7
says I did strive to prove		" 117	13
did I frame my feeding		" 118	6
But thence I learn		" 118	13
What potions have I drunk		" 119	1
when I saw myself to win		" 119	4
now I find true		" 119	9
So I return rebuked		" 119	13
more than I have spent		" 119	14
which I then did feel		" 120	2
I under my transgression bow		" 120	3
As I by yours, you've pass'd		" 120	6
And I, a tyrant, have no leisure taken		" 120	7
once I suffer'd in your crime		" 120	8
count bad what I think good		" 121	8
No, I am that I am		" 121	9
I may be straight		" 121	11
Nor need I tallies		" 122	10
to give them from me was I bold		" 122	11
boast that I do change		" 123	1
and thee I both defy		" 123	9
This I do vow		" 123	13
I will be true		" 123	14
To this I witness call		" 124	13
I bore the canopy		" 125	1
Have I not seen dwellers		" 125	5
Do I envy those jacks		" 128	5
I have seen roses		" 130	5
roses see I in her cheeks		" 130	6
I love to hear her speak, yet well I know		" 130	9

IDIOT

Entry	Ref	#
I—I grant I never saw	Son 130	11
I think my love as rare	" 130	13
I dare not be so bold	" 131	7
Although I swear it to myself	" 131	8
that is not false I swear	" 131	9
as I think, proceeds	" 131	14
Thine eyes I love	" 132	1
Then will I swear beauty	" 132	13
and thee, I am forsaken	" 133	7
for I, being pent in thee	" 133	13
So, now I have confess'd	" 134	1
And I myself am mortgaged	" 134	2
So him I lose	" 134	12
Him have I lost	" 134	13
and yet am I not free	" 134	14
am I that vex thee still	" 135	3
that I was thy 'Will	" 136	2
account I one must be	" 136	10
I do believe her, though I know she lies	" 138	2
Simply I credit her false-speaking tongue	" 138	7
say not I that I am old	" 138	10
Therefore I lie with her	" 138	13
since I am near slain	" 139	13
If I might teach thee wit	" 140	5
if I should despair, I should grow mad	" 140	9
That I may not be so	" 140	13
I do not love thee	" 141	1
thus far I count my gain	" 141	13
Be it lawful I love thee	" 142	9
Whilst I thy babe chase thee	" 143	10
So will I pray	" 143	13
Two loves I have of comfort	" 144	1
Suspect I may	" 144	10
I guess one angel	" 144	12
Yet this shall I ne'er know	" 144	13
the sound that said 'I hate	" 145	2
'I hate' she alter'd	" 145	9
'I hate' from hate away	" 145	13
And I desperate now approve	" 147	7
Past cure I am	" 147	9
For I have sworn thee fair	" 147	13
Say I love thee not	" 149	1
When I against myself	" 149	2
Do I not think on thee when I forgot	" 149	3
that I do call my friend	" 149	5
that I do fawn upon	" 149	6
do I not spend	" 149	7
do I in myself respect	" 149	9
now I know thy mind and I am blind	" 149	13
The more I hear	" 149	14
O, though I love	" 150	10
worthy I to be beloved	" 150	11
betraying me, I do betray	" 150	14
hold it what I call	" 151	5
for whose dear love I rise and fall	" 151	13
know'st I am forsworn	" 151	14
do I accuse thee	" 152	1
When I break twenty? I am perjured most	" 152	5
For I have sworn	" 152	6
For I have sworn thee fair; more perjured I	" 152	9
I, sick withal, the help of bath desired	" 152	13
	" 153	11
I—but I, my mistress' thrall	Son 154	12
and this by that I prove	" 154	13
And down I laid	L C	4
tell your judgement I am old	"	73
I might as yet have been	"	75
if I had self-applied	"	76
too early I attended	"	78
'Yet did I not	"	148
I mine honour shielded	"	151
'For further I could say	"	169
upon these terms I held my city	"	176
I have been call'd unto	"	181
Harm have I done to them	"	194
I have received from many	"	206
that I hoard them not	"	220
I myself must render	"	221
Since I their altar	"	224
And mine I pour	"	256
I strong o'er them, and you o'er me	"	257
white stole of chastity I daff'd	"	297
Ay me! I fell	"	321
What I should do again	"	322
I do believe her, though I know she lies	P P	1 2
Although I know my years	"	1 6
I smiling credit her false-speaking tongue	"	1 7
wherefore say not I that I am old	"	1 10
Two loves I have	"	2 1
Suspect I may	"	2 10
I guess one angel	"	2 12
truth I shall not know	"	2 13
A woman I forswore; but I will prove	"	3 5
I forswore not thee	"	3 6
how shall I swear to love	"	5 1
that I thy parts admire	"	5 10
why was not I a flood	"	6 14
the one and I the other	"	8 4
And I in deep delight am chiefly drown'd	"	8 11
did I see a fair sweet youth	"	9 9
I weep for thee, and yet no cause I have	"	10 7
more than I did crave	"	10 9
For why I craved nothing	"	10 10
I pardon crave of thee	"	10 11
Ah, that I had my lady	"	11 13
clip me till I run away	"	11 14
Age, I do abhor thee; youth, I do adore thee	"	12 9
Age, I do defy thee	"	12 11
Fare well I could not, for I supp'd with sorrow	"	14 6
nill I construe whether	"	14 8
I sit and mark	"	15 5
I post unto my pretty	"	15 9
were I with her	"	15 13
Air, would I might triumph so	"	17 10
For now I see	"	18 16
In black mourn I	"	18 19
All fears scorn I	"	18 20
I see that there is none	"	18 54
too much I fear	"	19 49
There will I make	"	20 9
Scarce I could from tears refrain	"	21 16
Ah, thought I	"	21 19
Thou and I were both beguiled	"	21 30
Idiot—As silly-jeering idiots	R L	1812

Idle—leave this idle theme	V A	.....	422
idle over-handled theme	"	.....	770
But idle sounds	"	.....	848
Out, idle words, servants	R L	.....	1016
shames and idle hours in me	Son	61	7
above that idle rank remain	"	122	3
each moving sense from idle rest	P P	15	3
Idly—thue so idly spent	Son	100	6
Idol—Well-painted idol, image dull and dead	V A	.....	212
my beloved as an idol show	Son	105	2
Idolatry—my love be call'd idolatry	"	105	1
If—If thou wilt deign	V A	.....	15
If thou wilt chide	"	.....	48
If they burn too	"	.....	192
if thou wilt have twain	"	.....	210
and if those hills be dry	"	.....	233
if himself were slain	"	.....	243
if there he came to lie	"	.....	245
as if he told the steps	"	.....	277
As if the dead the living should exceed	"	.....	292
as if she knew his mind	"	.....	308
If springing things be	"	.....	417
As if from thence they borrow'd	"	.....	488
purchase if thou make	"	.....	515
if any love you owe me	"	.....	523
If you will say so	"	.....	536
If thou encounter	"	.....	672
if thou needs wilt hunt	"	.....	673
As if another chase were	"	.....	696
To hearken if his foes pursue	"	.....	699
But if thou fall	"	.....	721
If thou destroy them not	"	.....	760
If so, the world	"	.....	761
If love have lent you	"	.....	775
If pleased themselves	"	.....	843
if she said 'No	"	.....	852
If he be dead	"	.....	937
If he had spoke	"	.....	1097
If he did see his face	"	.....	1109
As if they heard	"	.....	1126
And, if possess'd	R L	.....	23
if none of those	"	.....	41
if there he self-trust	"	.....	158
if I gain the thing I seek	"	.....	211
'If Collatinus dream	"	.....	218
ay, if the fact be known	"	.....	239
As if the heavens should countenance	"	.....	343
As if between them twain there were no strife	"	.....	405
if thou mean to chide	"	.....	484
if he mount he dies	"	.....	508
If thou deny	"	.....	513
'But if thou yield	"	.....	526
If ever man were moved	"	.....	587
O, if no harder than a stone thou art	"	.....	593
and if the same	"	.....	600
If in thy hope thou darest do	"	.....	605
If but for fear of this, thy will remove	"	.....	614
If all these petty ills shall change	"	.....	656
if not, enforced hate	"	.....	668
Or if thou wilt permit	"	.....	775
If that be made a theme	"	.....	822
If, Collatine, thine honour lay in me	"	.....	834
But if the like the snow-white swan desire	"	.....	1011
If—For if I die	R L	.....	1032
But if I live	"	.....	1033
Who, If it wink	"	.....	1139
If in this blemish'd fort I make	"	.....	1175
If thou dost weep	"	.....	1272
If tears could help	"	.....	1278
But, lady, if your maid may be	"	.....	1282
'If it should be told	"	.....	1284
If ever, love, thy Lucrece	"	.....	1306
As if some mermaid did their ears entice	"	.....	1411
As if with grief or travail he had fainted	"	.....	1543
If thou my love's desire do contradict	"	.....	1631
as if her heart would break	"	.....	1716
If in the child the father's image lies	"	.....	1753
If children pre-decease progenitors	"	.....	1756
If they surcease to be	"	.....	1766
as if the name he tore	"	.....	1787
If thou couldst answer	Son	2	10
if now thou not renewest	"	3	3
But if thou live	"	3	13
If ten of thine ten times refigured thee	"	6	10
if thou shouldst depart	"	6	11
If the true concord of well tuned sounds	"	8	5
if thou issueless shalt hap to die	"	9	3
Grant, if thou wilt	"	10	3
If all were minded so	"	11	7
if it shall go well	"	14	7
If from thyself to store thou wouldst convert	"	14	12
If it were fill'd	"	17	2
If I could write	"	17	5
as if not paid before	"	30	12
But if the while I think on thee	"	30	13
If thou survive	"	32	1
if aught in me	"	38	5
If my slight Muse do please	"	38	13
If for my love thou my love receivest	"	40	5
if thou thyself deceivest	"	40	7
If I lose thee	"	42	9
If the dull substance of my flesh were thought	"	44	1
Or, if they sleep	"	47	13
if ever that time come	"	49	1
As if by some instinct the wretch did know	"	50	7
If there be nothing new	"	59	1
If some suspect of ill mask'd not thy show	"	70	13
Nay, if you read this line	"	71	5
If thinking on me then	"	71	8
O, if, I say, you look upon	"	71	9
Then if he thrive	"	80	13
of you, if he can tell	"	84	7
thou wilt; if ever now	"	90	1
If thou wilt leave me	"	90	9
If thy sweet virtue answer not	"	93	14
But if that flower with base infection meet	"	94	11
If like a lamb he could his looks translate	"	96	10
If thou wouldst use	"	96	12
Or, if they sing	"	97	13
If not from my love's breath	"	99	3

If—If Time have any wrinkle graven	Son	100	10	Ill—this blunt and ill	R L	....	1300
If any, be a satire to decay	"	100	11	lodged not a mind so ill	"	....	1530
if never intermix'd	"	101	8	'What uncouth ill event	"	....	1594
if I no more can write	"	103	5	her babe from faring ill	Son	22	12
if I have ranged	"	109	5	and ransom all ill deeds	"	34	11
For if it see the rudest	"	113	9	in whom all ill well shows	"	40	13
If it be poison'd	"	114	13	any thing, he thinks no ill	"	57	14
If this be error	"	116	13	be it ill or well	"	58	14
For if you were	"	120	5	captive good attending captain ill	"	66	12
If my dear love were but the child	"	124	1	If some suspect of ill	"	70	13
If Nature, sovereign mistress	"	126	5	disgrace me half so ill	"	89	5
Or if it were	"	127	2	though new-fangled ill	"	91	3
But is profaned, if not lives in disgrace	"	127	8	blesses an ill report	"	95	8
				The hardest knife ill used	"	95	14
If snow be white	"	130	3	who calls me well or ill	"	112	3
If hairs be wires	"	130	4	The ills that were not	"	118	10
If thy soul check thee	"	136	1	would by ill be cured	"	118	12
If eyes, corrupt by over-partial looks	"	137	5	O benefit of ill	"	119	9
				gain by ill thrice more	"	119	14
If I might teach thee	"	140	5	might speak ill of thee	"	140	10
For if I should despair	"	140	9	a woman colour'd ill	"	144	4
Or, if it do, not from those lips	"	142	5	which doth preserve the ill	"	147	3
If thou dost seek	"	142	13	this becoming of things ill	"	150	5
But if thou catch	"	143	11	The destined ill she must	L C	....	156
If thou turn back	"	143	14	faults in love with love's ill rest	P P	1	8
Or, if they have	"	148	3	a woman colour'd ill	"	2	4
If that be fair whereon	"	148	5	I'll—I'll smother thee with kisses	V A	....	18
If it be not, then love	"	148	7	I'll sigh celestial breath	"	....	188
if thou lour'st on me	"	149	7	I'll make a shadow	"	....	191
If thy unworthiness raised love in me	"	150	13	I'll quench them	"	....	192
				I'll give it thee again	"	....	209
If that from him there may be	L C	....	68	I'll be a park	"	....	231
if I had self-applied	"	....	76	this night I'll waste	"	....	583
If best were as it was	"	....	98	I'll beg her love	R L	....	241
Yet, if men moved him	"	....	101	worthless slave of thine I'll slay	"	....	515
If broken then it is no fault	P P	3	12	I'll hum on Tarquin still	"	....	1133
If by me broke	"	3	13	to Tarquin I'll bequeath	"	....	1181
If love make me forsworn	"	5	1	I'll bequeath unto the knife	"	....	1184
if not to beauty vowed	"	5	2	I'll tune thy woes	"	....	1465
If knowledge be the mark	"	5	7	I'll murder straight, and then I'll slaughter thee	"	....	1634
If music and sweet poetry agree	"	8	1				
As if the boy should use	"	11	8	for their style I'll read	Son	32	14
And if these pleasures may thee move	"	20	15	Towards thee I'll run	"	51	14
				against myself I'll fight	"	88	3
If that the world and love were young	"	20	17	As I'll myself disgrace	"	89	7
				against myself I'll vow debate	"	89	13
But if store of crowns be scant	"	21	37	Myself I'll forfeit	"	134	3
If that one be prodigal	"	21	39	Therefore I'll lie with love	P P	1	13
If he be addict to vice	"	21	43	to thee I'll constant prove	"	5	3
If to women he be bent	"	21	45	Ill-annexed—But .... Opportunity	R L	....	874
But if Fortune once do frown	"	21	47	Ilion—cloud-kissing Ilion with annoy	"	....	1370
If thou sorrow, he will weep	"	21	53	Of rich-built Ilion	"	....	1524
If thou wake, he cannot sleep	"	21	54	Illiterate—Yea, the illiterate that know not how	"	....	810
If what parts can so remain	P T	....	48				
Ignorance—ignorance aloft to fly	Son	78	6	Ill-nurtured—Ill-nurtured, crooked	V A	....	134
my rude ignorance	"	78	14	Ill-resounding—his .... noise	"	....	919
Ignorant—All ignorant that soul	P P	5	9	Illumined—illumined with her eye	"	....	486
Ill—This ill presage	V A	....	457	Ill-wresting—Now this .... world	Son	140	11
Whose inward ill no outward harm express'd	R L	....	91	Image—image dull and dead	V A	....	212
				An image like thyself	"	....	664
So that in venturing ill	"	....	148	her heavenly image sits	R L	....	288
they all rate his ill	"	....	304	image of hell	"	....	764
had they seen the period of their ill	"	....	380	That for Achilles' image	"	....	1424
he commits this ill	"	....	476	a wretched image bound	"	....	1501
End thy ill aim	"	....	579	this mild image drew	"	....	1520
If all these petty ills	"	....	656	That she with painted images	"	....	1577
that thou taught'st this ill	"	....	996	the father's image lies	"	....	1753
the slander of mine ill	"	....	1207	my image thou hast torn	"	....	1762
not the authors of their ill	"	....	1244	thine image dies with thee	Son	3	11

Image—your true image pictured lies	Son	24	6
Their images I loved	"	31	13
Show me your image	"	59	7
thy image should keep open	"	61	1
Imaginary—All is imaginary	V A		597
For much imaginary work	R L		1422
my soul's imaginary sight	Son	27	9
Imagination—tremble at the....	V A		668
The dire imagination	"		975
in still imagination	R L		702
that in the imagination set	L C		136
Imagine—O, then imagine this	V A		721
Imagine her as one	R L		449
imagine every eye	"		1343
Imagined—for the whole to be....	"		1428
else may be imagined	"		1622
Imitate—To imitate thee well	"		1137
to imitate the battle	"		1438
painting imitate his cheek	Son	67	5
Imitated—Is poorly.... after you	"	53	6
Immaculate—.... and spotless	R L		1636
Immodest—saith she is immodest	V A		53
Immodestly—.... lies martyr'd	R L		802
Immortal—by her fair.... hand	V A		80
And were I not immortal	"		197
immortal life shall have	Son	81	5
Immortality—Her immortality, and made her thrall	R L		725
Immure—Means to immure herself	V A		1194
Immured—immured is the store	Son	84	3
would she be immured	L C		251
Impair—For I impair not beauty	Son	83	11
Impannelled—To 'cide this title is...."		46	9
Impart—truth would willingly....	"	72	8
Imparteth—no tool imparteth	R L		1039
Impartial—Whereat the.... gazer	V A		748
Impatience—This said,.... chokes	"		217
Impeach'd—When most impeach'd	Son	125	14
Impediment—Admit impediments	"	116	2
those impediments stand forth	L C		260
Imperfect—thy fair imperfect shade	Son	43	11
Imperious—Imperious supreme of all	V A		996
Imperiously—Imperiously he leaps	"		265
Impiety—impiety hath wrought	R L		341
not be call'd impiety	"		1174
with his presence grace impiety	Son	67	2
Impious—O impious act	R L		199
The impious breach	"		809
Impleach'd—metal amorously....	L C		205
Import—Were to.... forgetfulness	Son	122	14
Importune—Whom thine eyes woo as mine importune thee	"	142	10
Imposition—in knighthood to her imposition	R L		1697
Imposthumes—Surfeits,...., grief	V A		743
Impregnable—When rocks....	Son	65	7
Impressest—When thou impressest	L C		267
Impression—to every light....	V A		566
the impression of strange kinds	R L		1242
which deep impression bears	"		1712
doth the impression fill	Son	112	1
Imprint—thy mind's.... will bear	"	77	3
Imprinted—my soft lips imprinted	V A		511
Imprison'd—.... in the ground	"		1046
imprison'd in a body dead	R L		1456
unfolding his imprison'd pride	Son	52	12
The imprison'd absence	"	58	6

Impure—with impure defeature	V A		736
to purge my impure tale	R L		1078
Impurity—That some impurity	"		854
Impute—for my sin you did impute	Son	83	9
In—In such time-beguiling	V A		24
trembling in her passion	"		27
in a dull disdain	"		33
but frosty in desire	"		36
govern'd him in strength, though not in lust	"		42
devouring all in haste	"		57
breatheth in her face	"		62
tangled in a net	"		67
fasten'd in her arms	"		68
in his angry eyes	"		70
ducks as quickly in	"		87
in summer's heat	"		91
She bathes in water	"		94
in battle ne'er did bow	"		99
in every jar	"		100
in a red-rose chain	"		110
see'st thou in the ground	"		118
Look in mine eyeballs	"		119
Since eyes in eyes	"		120
sport is not in sight	"		124
in their prime	"		131
in little time	"		132
churlish, harsh in voice	"		134
one wrinkle in my brow	"		139
quick in turning	"		140
Would in thy palm	"		144
his shadow in the brook	"		162
And so, in spite of death	"		173
In that thy likeness	"		174
tired in the mid-day heat	"		177
Being judge in love	"		220
in her arms he bound	"		226
fingers one in one	"		228
mountain or in dale	"		232
smiles as in disdain	"		241
That in each cheek	"		242
In a tomb so simple	"		244
in thine own law	"		251
smiles at thee in scorn	"		252
In limning out	"		290
In shape, in courage	"		294
poor flies in his fume	"		316
as desperate in his suit	"		336
holds her in his eye	"		342
in a gaol of snow	"		362
ivory in an alabaster band	"		363
bondage in disdain	"		394
in her naked bed	"		397
it is a life in death	"		413
wither in their prime	"		418
Each part in me	"		436
should I be in love	"		438
stealing in disturb the feast	"		450
breatheth life in her	"		474
When in his fresh array	"		483
In water seen by night	"		492
in earth or heaven	"		493
Or in the ocean drench'd, or in the fire	"		494
In my soft lips	"		511
hath ended in the west	"		530
Chiefly in love	"		568
incaged in his breast	"		582
I'll waste in sorrow	"		583

In—is she in the very lists	V A	595	In—here in my breast	V A	1183
in her mishaps	"	603	Lo, in this hollow cradle	"	1185
in him finds missing	"	605	one minute in an hour	"	1187
but all in vain	"	607	In her light chariot	"	1192
whate'er is in his way	"	623	all in post	R L	1
lurk in mine eye	"	644	in pale embers hid	"	5
in a peaceful hour	"	652	Which triumph'd in that sky	"	12
gentle Love in his desire	"	653	in Tarquin's tent	"	15
whispers in mine ear	"	679	In the possession	"	18
pursuers in their yell	"	688	in the owner's arms	"	27
were in the skies	"	696	which in his liver glows	"	47
'In night,' quoth she	"	720	wrapp'd in repentant cold	"	48
The earth in love	"	722	boasted blushes, in despite	"	55
in high heaven's despite	"	731	in that white intituled	"	57
But in one minute's fight	"	746	use it in the fight	"	62
in dark obscurity	"	760	in Lucrece' face was seen	"	64
will hold thee in disdain	"	761	in her fair face's field	"	72
Sith in thy pride	"	762	In their pure ranks	"	73
So in thyself	"	763	triumph in so false a foe	"	77
is bestow'd in vain	"	771	In that high task	"	80
all in vain you strive	"	772	In silent wonder	"	84
armed in mine ear	"	779	in plaits of majesty	"	93
In his bedchamber	"	784	That nothing in him seem'd	"	94
your device in love	"	789	so wanteth in his store	"	97
Therefore in sadness	"	807	Writ in the glassy margents	"	102
glides he in the night	"	816	Won in the fields	"	107
Fold in the object	"	822	Doth yet in his fair welkin once		
jewel in the flood	"	824	appear	"	116
in some mistrustful	"	826	And in her vaulty prison stows	"	119
in the dark she lay	"	827	In this poor-rich gain	"	140
wise in folly, foolish-witty	"	838	in waning age	"	142
Still concludes in woe	"	839	And in this aim there is	"	143
In such-like circumstance	"	844	in fell battle's rage	"	145
ariseth in his majesty	"	856	So that in venturing	"	148
And all in haste	"	870	In having much	"	151
The bushes in the way	"	871	And in his inward mind	"	185
hid in some brake	"	876	engraven in my face	"	203
up in fatal folds just in his way	"	879	in my golden coat	"	205
remaineth in one place	"	885	and in a desperate rage	"	219
rings sadly in her ear	"	889	Or lain in ambush	"	235
in a trembling ecstasy	"	895	As in revenge	"	236
In hand with all	"	912	there is no hate in loving	"	240
kennell'd in a brake	"	913	be kept in awe	"	243
In the sweet channel	"	958	Which in a moment	"	250
seen in the tears, tears in her eye	"	962	in my eager eyes	"	254
prison'd in her eye like pearls in			In my hand being lock'd	"	260
glass	"	980	him in the flood	"	266
In thoughts unlikely	"	989	remorse in poor abuses	"	269
In likely thoughts	"	990	Love thrives not in the heart	"	270
And in her haste	"	1029	And in the self-same seat	"	289
in his shelly cave	"	1034	extinguishing his conduct in this		
up in shade doth sit	"	1035	case	"	313
perplexed in his throne	"	1046	return again in haste	"	321
In his soft flank	"	1053	He in the worst sense	"	324
And straight, in pity	"	1091	But in the midst	"	344
his shadow in the brook	"	1099	assist me in the act	"	350
some other in their bills	"	1102	Rolling his greedy eyeballs in his		
And nuzzling in his flank	"	1115	head	"	368
in his soft groin	"	1116	in that darksome prison	"	379
in the place she stood	"	1121	In his clear bed	"	382
she whispers in his ear	"	1123	seems to part in sunder	"	388
in darkness lies	"	1128	And canopied in darkness	"	398
in a breathing while	"	1142	in the map of death	"	402
Sith in his prime	"	1163	in life's mortality	"	403
And in his blood	"	1167	Each in her sleep	"	404
Which in round drops	"	1170	life lived in death and death in life	"	406
and in the breach appears	"	1175	These worlds in Tarquin new am-		
To wither in my breast as in his			bition bred	"	411
blood	"	1182	And in his will	"	417

Entry	Ref	No.
In—In bloody death	R L	430
Swell in their pride	"	432
one in dead of night	"	449
but she in worser taking	"	453
in a thousand fears	"	456
ugly in her eyes	"	459
In darkness daunts them	"	462
This moves in him more rage	"	468
'The colour in thy face	"	477
even in my soul	"	498
towering in the skies	"	506
For in thy bed	"	514
And in thy dead arms	"	517
cited up in rhymes	"	524
in succeeding times	"	525
In a pure compound	"	531
His venom in effect	"	532
in men's nativity	"	538
Plead, in a wilderness	"	544
In his dim mist	"	548
While in his hold-fast foot	"	555
even in plenty wanteth	"	557
In the remorseless wrinkles	"	562
'In Tarquin's likeness	"	596
be seeded in thine age	"	603
If in thy hope	"	605
cannot be hid in clay	"	609
When they in thee the like offences prove	"	613
Must be in thee read	"	618
dishonour in thy name	"	621
trespass in another	"	632
death-worthy in thy brother	"	635
wrapp'd in with infamies	"	636
in greater fury fret	"	648
in thy sea dispersed	"	658
Thou loathed in their shame, they in thy pride	"	662
in this shameful doom	"	672
in blind concealing night	"	675
in her lips' sweet fold	"	679
He pens her piteous clamours in her head	"	681
Cooling his hot face in the chastest tears	"	682
in digestion souring	"	699
comprehend in still imagination	"	702
Lust is in his pride	"	705
brought in subjection	"	724
Which in her prescience she controlleth	"	727
Even in this thought	"	729
hath lost in gain	"	730
perplex'd in greater pain	"	733
He in his speed	"	745
still in darkness be	"	752
that doth eat in steel	"	755
That in their smoky ranks	"	783
co-partners in my pain	"	789
And fellowship in woe	"	790
which in thy reign are made	"	804
sepulchred in thy shade	"	805
character'd in my brow	"	807
writ in learned books	"	811
in my looks	"	812
stamp'd in Collatinus' face	"	829
How he in peace is wounded, not in war	"	831
honour lay in me	"	834
In—In thy weak hive a wandering wasp had crept	R L	839
profaned in such a devil	"	847
hatch in sparrows' nests	"	849
lurk in gentle breasts	"	851
Who in their pride	"	864
Even in the moment	"	868
And in thy shady cell	"	881
To stamp the seal of time in aged things	"	941
in themselves beguiled	"	957
in thy pilgrimage	"	960
minute in an age	"	962
Tarquin in his flight	"	968
Afflict him in his bed	"	975
tigers in their wildness	"	980
In time of sorrow	"	991
bathe his coal-black wings in mire	"	1009
in skill-contending schools	"	1018
'In vain I rail	"	1023
In vain I cavil	"	1025
In vain I spurn	"	1026
my honour lives in thee	"	1032
thou livest in my defame	"	1033
that in air consumes	"	1042
'In vain,' quoth she, 'I live, and seek in vain	"	1044
in secret thought	"	1065
in cleanly-coin'd excuses	"	1073
Still in night	"	1085
in a sea of care	"	1100
in merry company	"	1110
And in my hearing be you dumb	"	1123
drown in ken of shore	"	1114
In my dishevell'd hair	"	1129
sing'st not in the day	"	1142
Is she in mutiny	"	1153
swallow'd in confusion	"	1159
If in this blemish'd fort	"	1175
In that sad hour	"	1179
writ in my testament	"	1183
For in my death	"	1189
read it in me	"	1195
set in her mistress' sky	"	1230
Who in a salt-waved ocean	"	1231
the other takes in hand	"	1235
Is form'd in them	"	1243
In men, as in a rough-grown grove	"	1249
The precedent whereof in Lucrece view	"	1261
from our house in grief	"	1308
To talk in deeds	"	1348
in both their faces	"	1353
spied in her some blemish	"	1358
In scorn of nature	"	1374
burnt out in tedious nights	"	1379
observance in this work was had	"	1385
In great commanders	"	1387
triumphing in their faces	"	1388
In youth, quick bearing	"	1389
In Ajax and Ulysses	"	1394
In Ajax' eyes blunt rage and rigour roll'd	"	1398
In speech, it seem'd	"	1405
And in their rage	"	1419
Griped in an armed hand	"	1425
In her the painter had anatomized	"	1450
changed to black in every vein	"	1454
imprison'd in a body dead	"	1456

In—in Priam's painted wound	R L	....	1466
And here in Troy	"	....	1476
a private sin in general	"	....	1484
in bloody channel lies	"	....	1487
In him the painter	"	....	1506
some shape in Sinon's was abused	"	....	1529
in his plain face	"	....	1532
can lurk in such a look	"	....	1535
came in her mind	"	....	1536
she in that sense forsook	"	....	1538
For Sinon in his fire doth quake	"	....	1556
And in that cold, hot-burning fire doth dwell	"	....	1557
In sorrow's sharp sustaining	"	....	1573
in shows of discontent	"	....	1580
clad in mourning black	"	....	1585
like rainbows in the sky	"	....	1587
water-galls in her dim element	"	....	1588
Amazedly in her sad face	"	....	1591
though sod in tears	"	....	1592
in a trance	"	....	1595
attired in discontent	"	....	1601
swan in her watery nest	"	....	1611
In me moe woes	"	....	1615
in the interest of thy bed	"	....	1619
' For in the dreadful dead of dark midnight	"	....	1625
in my chamber came	"	....	1626
The lechers in their deed	"	....	1637
be forgot in mighty Rome	"	....	1644
Doth in her poison'd closet	"	....	1659
he strives in vain	"	....	1665
Yet in the eddy, boundeth in his pride	"	....	1669
In rage sent out, recall'd in rage	"	....	1671
As bound in knighthood	"	....	1697
carved in it with tears	"	....	1713
in her harmless breast	"	....	1723
Her blood, in poor revenge, held it in chase	"	....	1736
In two slow rivers	"	....	1738
Circles her body in	"	....	1739
in this fearful flood	"	....	1741
If in the child	"	....	1753
In thy sweet semblance	"	....	1759
And then in key-cold Lucrece' bleeding stream	"	....	1774
pale fear in his face	"	....	1775
come in his poor heart's aid	"	....	1784
emulation in their woe	"	....	1808
his wit in state	"	....	1809
Burying in Lucrece' wound	"	....	1810
in Collatinus' eyes	"	....	1817
In such relenting dew	"	....	1829
in them doth stand	"	....	1833
country rights in Rome maintained	"	....	1838
makes waste in niggarding	Son	1	12
in thy beauty's field	"	2	2
Look in thy glass	"	3	1
and she in thee	"	3	9
pent in walls of glass	"	5	10
In thee thy summer	"	6	2
Leaving thee living in posterity	"	6	12
Lo, in the orient	"	7	1
youth in his middle age	"	7	6
out-going in thy noon	"	7	13
joy delights in joy	"	8	2
In singleness the parts	"	8	8
Strikes each in each	"	8	10

In—Who all in one	Son	8	12
consumest thyself in single life	"	9	2
husband's shape in mind	"	9	8
in the world doth spend	"	9	9
hath in the world an end	"	9	11
in that bosom sits	"	9	13
live in thine or thee	"	10	14
In one of thine	"	11	2
shouldst in bounty cherish	"	11	12
sunk in hideous night	"	12	2
girded up in sheaves	"	12	7
which you hold in lease	"	13	5
in honour might uphold	"	13	10
that I in heaven find	"	14	8
in them I read such art	"	14	10
Holds in perfection	"	15	2
Vaunt in their youthful sap	"	15	7
in youth before my sight	"	15	10
And all in war with Time	"	15	13
fortify yourself in your decay	"	16	3
neither in inward worth	"	16	11
live yourself in eyes of men	"	16	12
In time to come	"	17	1
And in fresh numbers	"	17	6
live twice, in it and in my rhyme	"	17	14
wander'st in his shade	"	18	11
When in eternal lines	"	18	12
phœnix in her blood	"	19	4
Him in thy course	"	19	11
love shall in my verse	"	19	14
less false in rolling	"	20	5
A man in hue, all 'hues' in his controlling	"	20	7
In this huge rondure hems	"	21	8
O, let me, true in love	"	21	9
fix'd in heaven's air	"	21	12
in thee time's furrows I behold	"	22	3
Which in thy breast doth live, as thine in me	"	22	7
And in mine own love's strength	"	23	7
in table of my heart	"	24	2
Which in thy bosom's shop	"	24	7
who are in favour	"	25	1
joy in that I honour	"	25	4
And in themselves their pride lies buried	"	25	7
they in their glory die	"	25	8
to whom in vassalage	"	26	1
in wanting words to show it	"	26	6
In thy soul's thought	"	26	8
a journey in my head	"	27	3
hung in ghastly night	"	27	11
return in happy plight	"	28	1
in consent shake hands	"	28	6
When, in disgrace	"	29	1
more rich in hope	"	29	5
Yet in these thoughts	"	29	9
hid in death's dateless night	"	30	6
hidden in thee lie	"	31	8
I view in thee	"	31	13
To march in ranks	"	32	12
o'ertake me in my way	"	34	3
Hiding thy bravery in their rotten smoke	"	34	4
lives in sweetest bud	"	35	4
and even I in this	"	35	5
I bring in sense	"	35	9
war is in my love	"	35	12
In our two loves there is	"	36	5

In—Though in our lives	Son	36	6
I love thee in such sort	"	36	13
Entitled in thy parts	"	37	7
That I in thy abundance am sufficed	"	37	11
that best I wish in thee	"	37	13
if aught in me	"	38	5
ten times more in worth	"	38	9
in whom all ill	"	40	13
lead thee in their riot	"	41	11
A loss in love	"	42	4
In dreams they look	"	43	3
are bright in dark directed	"	43	4
in the living day	"	43	10
When in dead night	"	43	11
In tender embassy of love	"	45	6
thou in him dost lie	"	46	5
And says in him	"	46	8
Or heart in love	"	47	4
And in his thoughts	"	47	8
thy picture in my sight	"	47	13
In sure wards of trust	"	48	4
lock'd up in any chest	"	48	9
that weight in me	"	50	6
put this in my mind	"	50	13
In winged speed	"	51	8
in his fiery race	"	51	11
in the long year set	"	52	6
jewels in the carcanet	"	52	8
you in Grecian tires	"	53	8
in every blessed shape	"	53	12
in all external grace	"	53	13
which doth in it live	"	54	4
bright in these contents	"	55	3
Even in the eyes	"	55	11
You live in this, and dwell in lovers' eyes	"	55	14
In his former might	"	56	4
that in your will	"	57	13
should in thought control	"	58	2
in some antique book	"	59	7
in character was done	"	59	8
in sequent toil	"	60	4
in the main of light	"	60	5
in beauty's brow	"	60	10
in hope my verse shall stand	"	60	13
and idle hours in me	"	61	7
inward in my heart	"	62	4
in all worth surmounts	"	62	8
shall in these black lines be seen	"	63	13
he in them still green	"	63	14
That in black ink	"	65	14
trimm'd in jollity	"	66	3
in days long since	"	67	14
in him those holy antique hours are seen	"	68	9
In other accents	"	69	7
And that, in guess	"	69	10
that flies in heaven's sweetest air	"	70	4
in your sweet thoughts	"	71	7
merit lived in me	"	72	2
For you in me	"	72	4
seem false in this	"	72	9
mayst in me behold	"	73	1
In me thou see'st	"	73	5
fadeth in the west	"	73	6
seals up all in rest	"	73	8
In me thou see'st	"	73	9
Hath in this line some interest	"	74	3
in a noted weed	"	76	6
In—assistance in my verse	Son	78	2
In others' works thou dost but mend	"	78	11
found it in thy cheek	"	79	11
what in thee doth live	"	79	12
And in the praise thereof spends	"	80	3
when I in earth am rotten	"	81	2
in me each part will be forgotten	"	81	4
entombed in men's eyes	"	81	8
in the mouths of men	"	81	14
Thou art as fair in knowledge as in hue	"	82	5
In true plain words	"	82	12
in thee it is abused	"	82	14
slept in your report	"	83	5
what worth in you doth grow	"	83	8
in one of your fair eyes	"	83	13
poets can in praise devise	"	83	14
In whose confine immured	"	84	3
what in you is writ	"	84	9
Muse in manners holds her still	"	85	1
In polish'd form	"	85	8
that is in my thought	"	85	11
speaking in effect	"	85	14
thoughts in my brain	"	86	3
My bonds in thee	"	87	4
gift in me is wanting	"	87	7
In sleep a king	"	87	14
in the eye of scorn	"	88	2
thou in losing me	"	88	8
and in my tongue	"	89	9
do not drop in for an after-loss	"	90	4
Come in the rearward	"	90	6
But in the onset come	"	90	11
Some glory in their birth, some in their skill	"	91	1
Some in their wealth, some in their body's force	"	91	2
Some in their garments	"	91	3
Some in their hawks and hounds, some in their horse	"	91	4
I better In one general best	"	91	8
Wretched in this alone	"	91	13
When in the least	"	92	6
heart in other place	"	93	4
no hatred in thine eye	"	93	5
In that I cannot know	"	93	6
In many's looks	"	93	7
Is writ in moods	"	93	8
heaven in thy creation did decree	"	93	9
That in thy face	"	93	10
canker in the fragrant rose	"	95	2
O, in what sweets dost thou thy sins inclose	"	95	4
but in a kind of praise	"	95	7
that in thee are seen	"	96	7
I love thee in such sort	"	96	13
been absent in the spring	"	98	1
dress'd in all his trim	"	98	2
youth in every thing	"	98	3
flowers in colour and in hue	"	98	6
vermillion in the rose	"	98	10
In my love's veins	"	99	5
in pride of all his growth	"	99	12
In gentle numbers	"	100	6
truth in beauty dyed	"	101	2
for't lies in thee	"	101	10
more weak in seeming	"	102	1
but in the spring	"	102	5
in summer's front doth sing	"	102	7

IN 151 IN

Entry	Ref	Son	No
In—stops her pipe in growth of riper days	Son	102	8
Look in your glass	"	103	6
in my verse can sit	"	103	13
when you look in it	"	103	14
In process of the seasons have I seen	"	104	1
in three hot Junes burn'd	"	104	7
in a wondrous excellence	"	105	6
And in this change	"	105	11
Three themes in one	"	105	12
never kept seat in one	"	105	14
When in the chronicle	"	106	1
In praise of ladies dead	"	106	4
Then, in the blazon	"	106	5
I'll live in this poor rhyme	"	107	11
In this shalt find thy monument	"	107	13
What's in the brain	"	108	1
in love's fresh cause	"	108	9
in thy breast doth lie	"	109	4
in my nature reign'd	"	109	9
in it thou art my all	"	109	11
A god in love	"	110	12
To what it works in	"	111	7
In so profound abysm I throw	"	112	9
in my purpose bred	"	112	13
mine eye is in my mind	"	113	1
'tis flattery in my seeing	"	114	9
Creep in 'twixt vows	"	115	6
in your waken'd hate	"	117	12
Thus policy in love	"	118	9
In the distraction of this madding fever	"	119	8
I suffer'd in your crime	"	120	8
Which in their wills	"	121	8
in their badness reign	"	121	11
forgetfulness in me	"	122	14
It suffers not in smiling pomp	"	124	6
in their gazing spent	"	125	8
obsequious in thy heart	"	125	9
stands least in thy control	"	125	14
who in thy power	"	126	1
In the old age	"	127	1
If not lives in disgrace	"	127	8
so happy are in this	"	128	13
in a waste of shame	"	129	1
Is lust in action	"	129	2
Mad in pursuit, and in possession so	"	129	9
and in quest to have	"	129	10
A bliss in proof	"	129	11
see I in her cheeks	"	130	6
And in some perfumes	"	130	7
Than in the breath	"	130	8
Yet, in good faith	"	131	5
in my judgement's place	"	131	12
In nothing art thou black save in thy deeds	"	131	13
that ushers in the even	"	132	7
like in every part	"	132	12
in thy steel bosom's ward	"	133	9
use rigour in my gaol	"	133	12
for I, being pent in thee	"	133	13
and all that is in me	"	133	11
and 'Will,' in overplus	"	135	2
hide my will in thine	"	135	6
Shall will in others seem	"	135	7
And in my will	"	135	8
And in abundance	"	135	10
So thou, being rich in 'Will	"	135	11
In—and me in that one 'Will	Son	135	14
in things of great receipt	"	136	7
Then in the number	"	136	9
Though in thy store's account	"	136	10
Be anchor'd in the bay	"	137	6
In things right true	"	137	13
in the world's false subtleties	"	138	1
is in seeming trust	"	138	11
And age in love	"	138	12
And in our faults	"	138	14
but in my sight	"	139	5
And in my madness	"	140	10
In faith, I do not love thee	"	141	1
they in thee a thousand errors note	"	141	2
in despite of view	"	141	4
Root pity in thy heart	"	142	11
In pursuit of the thing	"	143	1
child holds her in chase	"	143	5
one angel in another's hell	"	144	12
but live in doubt	"	144	13
Straight in her heart	"	145	5
in giving gentle doom	"	145	7
in selling hours of dross	"	146	11
Love put in my head	"	148	1
do I in myself respect	"	149	9
That in the very refuse	"	150	6
That, in my mind, thy worst	"	150	8
raised love in me	"	150	13
Triumph in love	"	151	8
To stand in thy affairs	"	151	12
In loving thee	"	152	1
In act thy bed-vow broke	"	152	3
In vowing new hate	"	152	4
faith in thee is lost	"	152	8
In a cold valley-fountain	"	153	4
but in her maiden hand	"	154	4
in a cool well by	"	154	9
silken figures in the brine	L. C.		17
had pelleted in tears	"		18
In clamours of all size	"		21
nor tied in formal plat	"		29
in her a careless hand of pride	"		30
Some in her threaden fillet	"		33
braided in loose negligence	"		35
she in a river threw	"		38
find their sepulchres in mud	"		46
sadly penn'd in blood	"		47
she in her fluxive eyes	"		50
This said, in top of rage	"		55
In brief the grounds and motives	"		63
in the charity of age	"		70
though in me you behold	"		71
And when in his fair parts	"		83
did hang in crooked curls	"		85
was in little drawn	"		90
thinks in Paradise was sawn	"		91
wavering stood in doubt	"		97
falseness in a pride of truth	"		105
in himself, not in his case	"		116
catching all passions in his craft of will	"		126
in the general bosom reign	"		127
dwell with him in thoughts	"		129
In personal duty, following	"		130
and in it put their mind	"		135
that in the imagination set	"		136
theirs in thought assign'd	"		138
And labouring in moe pleasures	"		139
That did in freedom stand	"		143

In—fee-simple, not in part	L C	....	144
art in youth and youth in art	"	....	145
in his charmed power	"	....	146
myself in honour so forbid	"	....	150
To put the by-past perils in her way	"	....	158
that preach in our behoof	"	....	165
in others' orchards grew	"	....	171
were gilded in his smiling	"	....	172
of shame in me remains	"	....	188
Kept hearts in liveries	"	....	195
commanding in his monarchy	"	....	196
In bloodless white	"	....	201
Encamp'd in hearts	"	....	203
in whose fresh regard	"	....	213
parcels in combined sums	"	....	231
noble suit in court did shun	"	....	234
her living in eternal love	"	....	238
sports in unconstrained gyves	"	....	242
in that my boast is true	"	....	246
their fountains in my well	"	....	255
ay, dieted in grace	"	....	261
In thee hath neither sting	"	....	265
in the suffering pangs it bears	"	....	272
In the small orb of one	"	....	289
In him a plenitude of subtile matter	"	....	302
In either's aptness	"	....	306
which in his level came	"	....	309
And, veil'd in them, did win	"	....	312
burn'd in heart-wish'd luxury	"	....	314
which in his cheek so glow'd	"	....	324
in the world's false forgeries	P P	1	4
in love with love's ill rest	"	1	8
And age, in love	"	1	12
In love thus smother'd be	"	1	14
one angel in another's hell	"	2	12
but live in doubt	"	2	13
cures all disgrace in me	"	3	8
vow; in thee it is	"	3	11
all in love forlorn	"	6	3
bounced in, whereas he stood	"	6	13
Yet in the midst of all	"	7	11
Bad in the best, though excellent in neither	"	7	18
And I in deep delight	"	8	11
and both in thee remain	"	8	11
Here in these brakes	"	9	10
Deep in the thigh	"	9	11
See, in my thigh	"	9	12
Pluck'd in the bud and vaded in the spring	"	10	2
thou left'st me nothing in thy will	"	10	8
clipp'd Adonis in her arms	"	11	6
In spite of physic	"	13	12
In scorn of friendship	"	14	8
To put in practice either	"	16	7
Playing in the wanton air	"	17	1
firmly fix'd in love	"	18	11
More in women than in men remain	"	18	18
In black mourn I	"	18	19
Living in thrall	"	18	22
In howling wise, to see	"	18	33
men in bloody fight	"	18	36
In faith, you had not	"	19	24
ringing in thy lady's ear	"	19	28
And in thy suit be humble	"	19	32
toys that in them lurk	"	19	39
kisses all the joys in bed	"	19	47
in every shepherd's tongue	"	20	18
In the merry month	"	21	2
In—Sitting in a pleasant shade	P P	21	3
thou mourn'st in vain	"	21	19
All thy friends are lapp'd in lead	"	21	24
Is no friend in misery	"	21	32
help thee in thy need	"	21	52
Tins of every grief in heart	"	21	55
priest in surplice white	P T	....	13
In a mutual flame	"	....	24
loved, as love in twain	"	....	25
essence but in one	"	....	26
there in love was slain	"	....	28
But in them it were a wonder	"	....	32
Flaming in the phœnix' sight	"	....	37
Reason, in itself confounded	"	....	41
Grace in all simplicity	"	....	51
enclosed in cinders lie	"	....	55
Incaged—incaged in his breast	V A	....	782
Incapable—Incapable of more	Son	113	13
Incense—Offer pure incense	R L	....	194
Uncertainty — Uncertainties now crown themselves	Son	107	7
certain o'er uncertainty	"	115	11
Incest—Guilty of incest	R L	....	921
Inclination—An accessary by thine inclination	"	....	922
Incline—so false will not incline	"	....	202
Inclined—that never was inclined	"	....	1657
Inclose—dost thou thy sins inclose	Son	95	4
Including—.... all foul harms	R L	....	190
Income—the income of each precious thing	"	....	334
Inconstancy—Inconstancy	P P	18	17
Inconstant—of this inconstant stay	Son	15	9
vex me with inconstant mind	"	92	9
Incorporate—Incorporate then they seem	V A	....	540
Increase—Upon the earth's increase	"	....	169
with thy increase be fed	"	....	170
You do it for increase	"	....	791
we desire increase	Son	1	1
wisdom, beauty, and increase	"	11	5
big with rich increase	"	97	6
Increase—that men as plants increase	"	15	5
Increaseful — ploughman with increaseful crops	R L	....	958
Increasing—her woes the more	V A	....	254
Increasing store with loss	Son	64	8
Incur—fond Paris, did incur	R L	....	1473
Indeed—seeing thee so indeed	V A	....	667
indeed to do me good	R L	....	1028
shows me myself indeed	Son	62	9
He that is thy friend indeed	P P	21	51
Indenting—indenting with the way	V A	....	704
Indigest—monsters and things	Son	114	5
Indirectly—poor beauty .... seek	"	67	7
Infamy—To embrace mine infamy	R L	....	504
not their own infamy	"	....	539
wrapp'd in with infamies	"	....	636
and hide their infamy	"	....	791
I cavil with mine infamy	"	....	1025
A dying life to living infamy	"	....	1055
engirt with daring infamy	"	....	1173
and thy perpetual infamy	"	....	1638
Infant—Or like the froward infant	V A	....	562
cleaves an infant's heart	"	....	942
Old woes, not infant sorrows	R L	....	1096
her poor infant's discontent	Son	143	8
Infect—Or toads infect fair founts	R L	....	850
Infected—O, that infected moisture	L C	....	323

Infection—To drive infection	V A	508
while Infection breeds	R L	907
with infection should he live	Son 67	1
with base infection meet	" 94	11
'gainst my strong infection	" 111	10
Inferior—inferior far to his	" 80	7
Infirmity—beauty with infirmities	V A	735
ambitious foul infirmity	R L	150
'Twas not their infirmity	P T	60
Inflame—when thou wilt inflame	L C	268
Inflaming—by his side his heart-inflaming brand	Son 154	2
Inflict—this night I will inflict	R L	1636
Influence—The beauteous influence	V A	862
in secret influence comment	Son 15	4
Whose influence is thine	" 78	10
Infold—infold him like a band	V A	225
Informer—This sour informer	"	655
Hence, thou suborn'd informer	Son 125	13
Infringed—with an infringed oath	R L	1061
Infusing—Infusing them with dreadful prophecies	V A	928
Inhabit—inhabit on a living brow	Son 68	4
Inhearse—thoughts in my brain	" 86	3
Inherit—do inherit heaven's graces	" 94	5
Inheritor—inheritors of this excess	" 146	7
Iniquity—thy sword to guard	R L	626
What virtue breeds iniquity devours	"	872
justice feeds iniquity	"	1687
self-living were iniquity	Son 62	12
Injurious—ransack'd by .... theft	R L	838
injurious, shifting Time	"	930
Injurious distance should not	Son 44	2
With Time's injurious hand	" 63	2
Injury—than hate's known injury	" 40	12
Without accusing you of injury	" 58	8
The injuries that to myself I do	" 88	11
dust and injury of age	" 108	10
That they elsewhere might dart their injuries	" 139	12
The injury of many	L C	72
Injustice—To chase injustice with revengeful arms	R L	1693
Ink—paper, ink, and pen	"	1289
That in black ink	Son 65	14
that ink may character	" 108	1
Ink would have seem'd more black	L C	54
Innocence—And forth with bashful innocence doth hie	R L	1341
Inordinate—in him seem'd	"	94
Insinuate—she humbly doth	V A	1012
Instance—no guilty instance gave	R L	1511
Instant—some special instant special blest	Son 52	11
Instead—Instead of love's coy touch	R L	669
Instigate—untimely thought did instigate	"	43
Instinct—As if by some instinct	Son 50	7
Instrument—some desperate	R L	1038
as frets upon an instrument	"	1140
'Poor instrument,' quoth she	"	1464
Insufficiency—With insufficiency my heart to sway	Son 150	2
Insult—While he insults o'er dull and speechless tribes	" 107	12
Insulter—what ransom the insulter willeth	V A	550
Insulting—under his .... falchion	R L	509
Insurrection—her subjects with foul insurrection	R L	722
Intelligence—gulls him with	Son 86	10
Intend—to-morrow he intends	V A	587
Intend a zealous pilgrimage	Son 27	6
battery to the spheres intend	L C	23
Intending—Intending weariness with heavy sprite	R L	121
Intendment—do her intendments break	V A	222
Intent—brake off his late intent	"	469
with swift intent he goes	R L	46
Collatinus dream of my intent	"	218
blunt the sharp'st intents	Son 115	7
Interchange—.... each other's seat	R L	70
such interchange of state	Son 64	9
Interdict—From this session	P T	9
Interest—And one for interest	V A	210
thy interest was not bought	R L	1067
in the interest of thy bed	"	1619
My sorrow's interest	"	1797
As interest of the dead	Son 31	7
hath in this line some interest	" 74	3
Interim—Let this sad interim	" 56	9
Interlace—and there the painter interlaces	R L	1390
Intermix'd—best, if never	Son 101	8
Interpret—the eye interprets to the ear	R L	1325
Interrupted—her quiet interrupted	"	1170
Intituled—in that white intituled	P T	57
Into—Into your idle over-handled theme	V A	770
Into the quiet closure	"	782
cast into eternal sleeping	"	951
Into the deep dark	"	1038
the smoke of it into his face	R L	312
Into the chamber wickedly he stalks	"	365
there falls into thy boundless flood	"	653
Into so bright a day	"	1518
that pour'st into my verse	Son 38	2
thrusts into his hide	" 50	10
into my deeds to pry	" 61	6
into the beauty of thy mind	" 69	9
should look into your moan	" 71	13
resolved my reason into tears	L C	296
Intrude—worm .... the maiden bud	R L	848
Inundation—the .... of the eyes	L C	290
Inured—Is not ....; return again	R L	321
Invasion—vows a league, and now invasion	"	287
Inveigh—No man inveigh against	"	1254
Invent—want subject to invent	Son 38	1
thy poet doth invent	" 79	7
Invention—can my invention make	R L	225
Throng her inventions	"	1302
dust give invention light	Son 38	8
Which, labouring for invention	" 59	3
And keep invention	" 76	6
over-goes my blunt invention	" 103	7
is my invention spent	" 105	11
Invised—Whereto his invised properties	L C	212
Invisible—That inward beauty and invisible	V A	434
on him, invisible commander	"	1004
O unseen shame, invisible disgrace	R L	827

Entry	Ref	No.
Invite—Till now did ne'er invite	L C	182
Invited—desire to be invited	Son 141	7
Inviting—Where to the .... time	" 124	8
Invocate—which rhymers invocate	" 38	10
Invocation—Roman gods with invocations	R L	1831
Invoked—So oft have I invoked thee	Son 78	1
Inward—That inward beauty and invisible	V A	434
Whose inward ill	R L	91
And in his inward mind	"	183
With inward vice	"	1546
vexation of his inward soul	"	1779
Neither in inward worth	Son 16	11
thine inward love of heart	" 46	14
grounded inward in my heart	" 62	4
To kiss the tender inward	" 128	6
Ireful—Being ireful, on the lion	V A	628
Iron—the iron bit he crusheth	"	269
enters at an iron gate	R L	593
and yet as iron rusty	P P 7	4
Is—O, how quick is love	V A	38
The steed is stalled up	"	39
saith she is immodest	"	53
river that is rank	"	71
Still is he sullen	"	75
Her best is better'd	"	78
'Tis but a kiss I beg	"	96
sport is not in sight	"	124
My flesh is soft	"	142
Love is a spirit all compact	"	149
Is love so light, sweet boy	"	155
Is thine own heart	"	157
to get it is thy duty	"	168
Still is left alive	"	174
what 'tis to love	"	202
Within this limit is relief	"	235
The time is spent	"	253
thus my strength is tried	"	280
breeder that is standing by	"	282
how he is enraged	"	317
When it is barr'd	"	330
An oven that is stopp'd	"	331
attorney once is mute	"	335
that she is so nigh	"	341
My day's delight is past, my horse is gone	"	380
And 'tis your fault	"	381
Is how to get my palfrey	"	384
Affection is a coal	"	387
Who is so faint	"	401
lesson is but plain	"	407
'Tis much to borrow	"	411
is love but to disgrace it	"	412
For I have heard it is	"	413
The colt that's back'd	"	419
where a heart is hard	"	426
is hush'd before it raineth	"	458
believing she is dead	"	467
now is turn'd to day	"	481
So is her face illumined	"	486
What hour is this	"	493
the plague is banish'd	"	510
What is ten hundred	"	519
Is twenty hundred	"	522
is sour to taste	"	528
shrieks,—'tis very late	"	531
fee of parting tender'd is	"	538
roe that's tired with chasing	"	561
Is—his choice is froward	V A	570
yet 'tis pluck'd	"	574
She is resolved	"	579
is she in the very lists	"	595
All is imaginary	"	597
is her annoy	"	599
She's Love, she loves, and yet she is not loved	"	610
know'st not what it is	"	615
whate'er is in his way	"	623
is trodden on by many	"	707
The night is spent	"	717
and now 'tis dark	"	719
all is but to rob thee	"	723
What is thy body	"	737
so fair a hope is slain	"	762
Gold that's put to use	"	768
The kiss I gave you is bestow'd	"	771
tempting tune is blown	"	778
The path is smooth	"	788
When reason is the bawd	"	792
Love to heaven is fled	"	793
is tempest after sun	"	800
Love is all truth	"	804
The text is old	"	806
My face is full of shame	"	808
deeply is redoubled	"	832
How love is wise	"	838
"'Tis so?' they answer all, 'Tis so"	"	851
morning is so much o'erworn	"	866
it is no gentle chase	"	883
'tis a causeless fantasy	"	897
is mated with delays	"	909
Thy mark is feeble ago	"	941
her best work is ruin'd	"	954
But none is best	"	971
it is Adonis' voice	"	978
Who is but drunken	"	984
Death is not to blame	"	992
but is still severe	"	1060
'Tis not my fault	"	1063
'Tis he, foul creature	"	1065
that Adonis is alive	"	1009
with him is beauty slain	"	1019
he is not dead	"	1060
Her voice is stopp'd	"	1061
several limb is doubled	"	1067
Whose tongue is music now	"	1077
What face remains alive that's worth	"	1076
'Tis true, 'tis true	"	1111
But he is dead	"	1119
and that is cold	"	1124
this is my spite	"	1133
where is no cause	"	1153
matter is to tire	"	1162
is reft from her by death	"	1174
And so 'tis thine; but know, it is as good	"	1181
And 'tis thy right	"	1184
quickly is convey'd	"	1192
As is the morning's silver-melting dew	R L	24
that which is so singular	"	32
Or why is Collatine	"	33
because it is his own	"	35
For then is Tarquin brought	"	120
treasure is the meed proposed	"	132
there's no death supposed	"	133

Is—Is but to surfeit	R L	....	139
Is but to nurse the life	"	....	141
there is such thwarting strife	"	....	143
Then where is truth	"	....	158
Is madly toss'd	"	....	171
that which is divine	"	....	193
my digression is so vile	"	....	202
as he is my kinsman	"	....	237
'Shameful it is	"	....	239
Hateful it is; there is no hate in loving	"	....	240
but she is not her own	"	....	241
The worst is but denial	"	....	242
My will is strong	"	....	243
That what is vile shows like	"	....	252
Affection is my captain	"	....	271
when his gaudy banner is display'd	"	....	272
My part is youth	"	....	278
Desire my pilot is	"	....	279
Is almost choked	"	....	282
Is not inured	"	....	321
Now is he come	"	....	337
My will is back'd	"	....	352
sin is clear'd	"	....	354
The eye of heaven is out	"	....	356
By their high treason is his heart misled	"	....	369
Whether it is that she reflects	"	....	376
her head entombed is	"	....	390
she is dreadfully beset	"	....	444
What terror 'tis, but she	"	....	453
the fault is thine	"	....	482
But will is deaf	"	....	495
The fault unknown is as a thought unacted	"	....	527
The poisonous simple sometime is compacted	"	....	530
His venom in effect is purified	"	....	532
eloquence with sighs is mixed	"	....	563
He is no woodman	"	....	580
My husband is thy friend	"	....	582
Thy sea within a puddle's womb is hearsed	"	....	657
Pure Chastity is rifled	"	....	692
While Lust is in his pride	"	....	705
his soul's fair temple is defaced	"	....	719
he is but Night's child	"	....	785
To cipher what is writ	"	....	811
That is as clear	"	....	825
Reproach is stamp'd	"	....	829
he in peace is wounded	"	....	831
by strong assault it is bereft	"	....	835
When virtue is profaned	"	....	847
perfection is so absolute	"	....	853
Is plagued with cramps	"	....	856
we can say is ours	"	....	873
thy guilt is great	"	....	876
'Tis thou that executest	"	....	877
'Tis thou that spurn'st	"	....	880
when temperance is thaw'd	"	....	884
Justice is feasting	"	....	906
Advice is sporting	"	....	907
Time's office is to fine	"	....	936
'Time's glory is to calm	"	....	939
'The baser is he	"	....	1002
The mightier is the thing	"	....	1004
The moon being clouded presently is miss'd	"	....	1007
Since that my case is past the help	"	....	1022
Is—Is to let forth my foul defiled blood	R L	....	1029
'O, that is gone	"	....	1051
For day hath nought to do what's done by night	"	....	1092
True grief is fond	"	....	1094
her grief is dumb	"	....	1105
Sometime 'tis mad	"	....	1106
Grief best is pleased	"	....	1111
then is feelingly sufficed	"	....	1112
it is sympathized	"	....	1113
'Tis double death to drown	"	....	1114
time is kept	"	....	1127
is she in mutiny	"	....	1153
When life is shamed	"	....	1155
whose whole is swallow'd in confusion	"	....	1159
Her house is sack'd	"	....	1170
'Tis honour to deprive	"	....	1186
mine honour is new-born	"	....	1190
Is form'd in them	"	....	1243
Wherein is stamp'd the semblance	"	....	1246
Is worthy blame	"	....	1257
For more it is than I can well express	"	....	1286
When more is felt	"	....	1288
Her maid is gone	"	....	1296
What wit sets down is blotted straight	"	....	1299
This is too curious-good	"	....	1300
when he is by	"	....	1318
'Tis but a part of sorrow	"	....	1328
Her letter now is seal'd	"	....	1331
vassal scarce is gone	"	....	1360
For now 'tis stale to sigh	"	....	1362
Before the which is drawn the power of Greece	"	....	1368
is Lucrece come	"	....	1443
where all distress is stell'd	"	....	1444
subtle Sinon here is painted	"	....	1541
patience is quite beaten	"	....	1563
Her honour is ta'en prisoner	"	....	1608
thy Lucrece is not free	"	....	1624
when the judge is robb'd	"	....	1652
and spotless is my mind	"	....	1656
But wretched as he is	"	....	1665
From what is past	"	....	1685
For 'tis a meritorious fair design	"	....	1692
What is the quality	"	....	1702
'He, he, fair lords, 'tis he	"	....	1721
at that which is so putrified	"	....	1750
now Lucrece is unlived	"	....	1754
'She's mine.' 'O, mine she is	"	....	1795
'tis mine that she hath kill'd	"	....	1803
is woe the cure for woe	"	....	1821
Is it revenge to give thyself a blow	"	....	1823
Now is the time	Son	3	2
For where is she so fair	"	3	5
Or who is he so fond	"	3	7
That use is not forbidden	"	6	5
Is it for fear to wet a widow's eye	"	9	1
But that thou none lovest is most evident	"	10	4
He, as thy presence is, gracious and kind	"	10	11
Thy end is truth's	"	14	14
it is but as a tomb	"	17	3
And often is his gold	"	18	6
as is false women's fashion	"	20	4

Is—So is it not with me	Son	21	1
my love is as fair	"	21	10
Is but the seemly raiment	"	22	6
when mine is slain	"	22	13
Who with his fear is put besides his part	"	23	2
My body is the frame wherein 'tis held	"	24	3
It is best painter's art	"	24	4
Which in my bosom's shop is hanging still	"	24	7
Is from the book of honour razed quite	"	25	11
day's oppression is not eased by night	"	28	3
Thy bosom is endeared	"	31	1
That due of many now is thine alone	"	31	12
'Tis not enough that through	"	34	5
Thy adverse party is thy advocate	"	35	10
civil war is in my love	"	35	12
there is but one respect	"	36	5
mine is thy good report	"	36	14
Look, what is best	"	37	12
For who's so dumb	"	38	7
And what is't but my own	"	39	4
it is a greater grief	"	40	11
it is not all my grief	"	42	1
That she hath thee, is of my wailing chief	"	42	3
my loss is my love's gain	"	42	9
But here's the joy	"	42	13
this title is impanneled	"	46	9
verdict is determined	"	46	11
mine eye's due is thine outward part	"	46	13
Betwixt mine eye and heart a league is took	"	47	1
mine eye is famish'd for a look	"	47	3
mine eye is my heart's guest	"	47	7
of posting is no need	"	51	4
So is the time	"	52	9
What is your substance	"	53	1
Is poorly imitated	"	53	6
virtue only is their show	"	54	9
by feeding is allay'd	"	56	3
So true a fool is love	"	57	13
your charter is so strong	"	58	9
but that which is	"	59	1
Is it thy will	"	61	1
Is it thy spirit	"	61	5
thy love, though much, is not so great	"	61	9
It is my love	"	61	10
there is no remedy	"	62	3
It is so grounded	"	62	4
no face so gracious is as mine	"	62	5
'Tis thee, myself, that	"	62	13
This thought is as a death	"	64	13
Whose action is no stronger	"	65	4
since his rose is true	"	67	8
now Nature bankrupt is	"	67	9
Thus is his cheek the map	"	68	1
with outward praise is crown'd	"	69	5
The soil is this	"	69	14
The ornament of beauty is suspect	"	70	3
where my body is	"	72	11
which is his due	"	74	7
My spirit is thine	"	74	8
Is—is that which it contains	Son	74	13
And that is this	"	74	14
and his wealth is found	"	75	4
Save what is had	"	75	12
Why is my verse so barren	"	76	1
all my best is dressing old words new	"	76	11
what is already spent	"	76	12
the sun is daily new	"	76	13
So is my love still telling what is told	"	76	14
whose influence is thine	"	78	10
wide as the ocean is	"	80	5
in thee it is abused	"	82	14
Who is it that says most	"	84	1
immured is the store	"	84	3
what in you is writ	"	84	9
I say, 'tis so, 'tis true	"	85	9
But that is in my thought	"	85	11
where is my deserving	"	87	6
The cause of this fair gift in me is wanting	"	87	7
my patent back again is swerving	"	87	8
Such is my love	"	88	13
while the world is bent	"	90	2
Thy love is better	"	91	9
Is writ in moods	"	93	8
flower is to the summer sweet	"	94	9
thy fault is youth	"	96	1
thy grace is youth	"	96	2
mine is thy good report	"	96	14
'tis with so dull a cheer	"	97	13
But best is best	"	101	8
My love is strengthen'd	"	102	1
That love is merchandized	"	102	3
the summer is less pleasant now	"	102	9
argument, all bare, is of more worth	"	103	3
Kind is my love to-day	"	105	5
'Fair, kind, and true' is all my argument	"	105	9
in this change is my invention spent	"	105	11
What's in the brain	"	108	1
What's new to speak	"	108	3
That is my home of love	"	109	5
Alas, 'tis true	"	110	1
sold cheap what is most dear	"	110	3
true it is that I have look'd	"	110	5
Now all is done	"	110	9
my nature is subdued	"	111	6
your pity is enough to cure	"	111	14
mine eye is in my mind	"	113	1
and is partly blind	"	113	3
but effectually is out	"	113	4
O, 'tis the first; 'tis flattery	"	114	9
what with his gust is 'greeing	"	114	11
'tis the lesser sin	"	114	13
Love is a babe	"	115	13
Love is not love	"	116	2
it is an ever-fixed mark	"	116	5
and is never shaken	"	116	6
It is the star	"	116	7
Whose worth's unknown	"	116	8
Love's not Time's fool	"	116	9
That better is by evil	"	119	10
when it is built anew	"	119	11
'Tis better to be vile	"	121	1
which is so deemed	"	121	3

Is—foist upon us that is old	Son	123	6	Is—What breast so cold that is not warmed, here	L C		292
Which is not mix'd	"	125	11	nature is both kind and tame	"		311
her quietus is to render thee	"	126	12	that she is made of truth	P P	1	1
But now is black beauty's successive heir	"	127	3	my love that she is young	"	1	9
But is profaned	"	127	8	love's best habit is a soothing tongue	"	1	11
Is lust in action	"	129	2	My better angel is a man right fair	"	2	3
Is perjured, murderous	"	129	3	breath a vapour is	"	3	9
Coral is far more red	"	130	2	in thee it is	"	3	11
is there more delight	"	130	7	it is no fault of mine	"	3	12
that is not false I swear	"	131	9	what fool is not so wise	"	3	13
Thy black is fairest	"	131	12	Well learned is that tongue	"	5	8
beauty herself is black	"	132	13	Which is to me some praise	"	5	10
Is't not enough	"	133	3	Which, not to anger bent, is music and sweet fire	"	5	12
and all that is in me	"	133	14	Fair is my love	"	7	1
confess'd that he is thine	"	134	1	and yet, as glass is, brittle	"	7	3
art covetous and he is kind	"	134	6	Dowland to thee is dear	"	8	5
whose will is large and spacious	"	135	5	whose deep conceit is such	"	8	7
And will, thy soul knows, is admitted there	"	136	3	One god is god of both	"	8	13
Among a number one is reckon'd none	"	136	8	Youth is full of pleasance, age is full of care	"	12	2
for my name is 'Will	"	136	14	Youth is full of sport, age's breath is short	"	12	5
They know what beauty is	"	137	3	Youth is nimble, age is lame	"	12	6
what the best is take the worst to be	"	137	4	Youth is hot and bold, age is weak and cold	"	12	7
Whereto the judgement of my heart is tied	"	137	8	Youth is wild, and age is tame	"	12	8
say this is not	"	137	11	my love is young	"	12	10
that she is made of truth	"	138	1	Beauty is but a vain and doubtful good	"	13	1
thus is simple truth suppress	"	138	8	A brittle glass that's broken presently	"	13	4
But wherefore says she not she is unjust	"	138	9	beauty blemish'd once's for ever lost	"	13	11
love's best habit is in seeming trust	"	138	11	now my song is ended	"	16	16
Is more than my o'er-press'd	"	139	8	All is amiss	"	18	4
world is grown so bad	"	140	11	All my lady's love is lost	"	18	10
But 'tis my heart that loves	"	141	3	There a nay is placed without remove	"	18	12
Who, in despite of view, is pleased to dote	"	141	4	Heart is bleeding	"	18	23
Love is my sin	"	142	1	sport from us is fled	"	18	47
whose busy care is spent	"	143	6	our love is lost, for Love is dead	"	18	48
The better angel is a man right fair	"	144	3	I see that there is none	"	18	54
From heaven to hell is flown away	"	145	12	There is no heaven	"	19	45
is this thy body's end	"	146	8	King Pandion he is dead	"	21	23
My love is as a fever	"	147	1	Is no friend in misery	"	21	32
Desire is death	"	147	8	He that is thy friend	"	21	51
now reason is past care	"	147	9	constancy is dead	P T		22
where is my judgement fled	"	148	3	Death is now the phœnix' nest	"		56
to say it is not so	"	148	6	Beauty brag, but 'tis not she	"		63
Love's eye is not so true	"	148	8	Island—Who, like a late-sack'd	R L		1740
That is so vex'd	"	148	10	Issue—Sweet issue of a more sweet-smelling sire	V A		1178
That is so proud	"	149	10	this proud issue of a king	R L		37
There is such strength	"	150	7	Thy issue blurr'd	"		522
Love is too young to know what conscience is	"	151	1	When your sweet issue	Son	13	8
conscience is born of love	"	151	2	Yet this abundant issue	"	97	9
He is contented	"	151	11	Issueless—Ah! if thou issueless	"	9	3
faith in thee is lost	"	152	8	It—in her passion, calls it balm	V A		27
'Tis promised in the charity	L C		70	And calls it heavenly	"		64
But, woe is me	"		78	Perforce will force it	"		72
What's sweet to do	"		88	'Tis but a kiss I beg	"		96
'twixt May and April is to see	"		102	were it with thy hand felt	"		143
advice is often seen	"		160	sweet boy, and may it be	"		155
'It is thy last	"		168	thou shouldst think it	"		156
This man's untrue	"		169	to get it is thy duty	"		168
That's to ye sworn	"		180	What 'tis to love	"		202
neither party is nor true nor kind	"		186	I'll give it thee again	"		209
That is, to you my origin and ender	"		222	When it is barr'd	"		330
what labour is't to leave	"		239				
in that my boast is true	"		246				

Phrase	Work	Line
It—O, what a sight it was	V A	343
It flash'd forth fire	"	348
dost thou feel it	"	373
thou shalt have it	"	374
O, give it me, lest thy hard heart do steel it	"	375
can never grave it	"	376
And 'tis your fault	"	381
it will set the heart	"	388
nor will not know it	"	409
Unless it be a boar, and then I chase it	"	410
'Tis much to borrow, and I will not owe it	"	411
Is love but to disgrace it	"	412
for I have heard it is	"	413
It will not ope the gate	"	424
hush'd before it raineth	"	458
before it staineth	"	460
clapping makes it red	"	468
shrieks, 'tis very late	"	531
yet 'tis pluck'd	"	574
it will not be	"	607
Know'st not what it is	"	615
was it not white	"	643
The thought of it	"	669
teach it divination	"	670
and now 'tis dark	"	719
Making it subject	"	737
you do it for increase	"	791
Call it not love	"	793
blotting it with blame	"	796
whereat it groans	"	829
"'Tis so!' they answer all, ''Tis so	"	851
hears them chant it	"	869
it is no gentle chase	"	883
Through which it enters	"	890
'tis a causeless fantasy	"	897
And, sighing it again	"	930
O no, it cannot be	"	937
shouldst strike at it	"	938
O yes, it may; thou hast	"	939
it is Adonis' voice	"	978
scorning it should pass	"	982
how strange it seems	"	983
It was not she	"	993
'Tis not my fault	"	1003
'Tis he, foul creature	"	1005
she treads on it so light	"	1028
wind would blow it off	"	1089
on it their golden gills	"	1100
'Tis true, 'tis true	"	1111
It shall be waited on	"	1137
it shall be fickle	"	1141
shall it make most weak	"	1145
It shall be sparing	"	1147
shall it keep in quiet	"	1149
It shall be raging-mad	"	1151
It shall suspect	"	1153
It shall not fear where it should most mistrust	"	1154
It shall be merciful	"	1155
when it seems most just	"	1156
it shall be where it shows	"	1157
It shall be cause	"	1159
Comparing it to her Adonis'	"	1172
bosom it shall dwell	"	1173
And so 'tis thine; but know it is as good	"	1181
It—And 'tis thy right	V A	1184
because it is his own	R L	35
call'd it then their shield	"	61
thus to use it	"	62
it should be kill'd	"	74
unloose it from their bond	"	136
by augmenting it	"	154
and lend it not	"	190
That it will live	"	203
hold it for no sin	"	209
'Shameful it is	"	239
Hateful it is	"	240
Forced it to tremble	"	261
then it faster rock'd	"	262
blows the smoke of it	"	312
He takes it from the rushes where it lies	"	318
And griping it	"	319
Whether it is that she reflects	"	376
What terror 'tis	"	453
beat it dead	"	489
was it newly bred	"	490
To soften it	"	591
wherein it shall discern	"	619
him that gave it thee	"	624
For it was lent thee	"	627
how vile a spectacle it were	"	631
For there it revels	"	713
So fares it	"	715
And bids it leap from thence, where it may find	"	760
it is bereft	"	835
For it had been dishonour	"	844
that it cannot cure	"	861
'So then he hath it when he cannot use it	"	862
And leaves it to be master'd	"	863
presently abuse it	"	864
'Tis thou that executest	"	877
'Tis thou that spurn'st	"	880
How comes it then	"	895
where it lay	"	1057
Sometime 'tis mad	"	1106
with like semblance it is sympathized	"	1113
'Tis double death to drown	"	1114
would do it good	"	1117
Who, if it wink	"	1139
alack, what were it	"	1156
with greater patience bear it	"	1158
Then let it not be call'd	"	1174
'Tis honour to deprive	"	1186
read it in me	"	1195
thou shalt see it	"	1206
life's fair end shall free it	"	1208
'So be it	"	1209
O, let it not be hild	"	1257
It small avails my mood	"	1273
'if it should be told cannot make it less	"	1284
	"	1285
For more it is	"	1286
prepare to carry it	"	1294
It will soon be writ	"	1295
Lest he should hold it	"	1315
that it doth behold	"	1326
'Tis but a part of sorrow	"	1328
and on it writ	"	1331
and she delivers it	"	1333
God wot, it was defect	"	1345

Phrase	Work	Ref	Line
It—but do it leisurely	R L	1349	
For now 'tis stale to sigh	"	1362	
As heaven it seem'd	"	1372	
That it beguiled attention	"	1404	
In speech, it seem'd	"	1405	
It seem'd they would debate	"	1421	
'It cannot be,' quoth she	"	1534	
'It cannot be' she in that sense	"	1538	
And turn'd it thus, 'It cannot be, I find	"	1539	
yet it seldom sleeps	"	1574	
how slow it creeps	"	1575	
It easeth some, though none it ever cured	"	1581	
all the task it hath to say	"	1618	
let it then suffice	"	1679	
For 'tis a meritorious fair design	"	1692	
carved in it with tears	"	1713	
'He, he, fair lords, 'tis he	"	1721	
That blow did bail it	"	1725	
prison where it breathed	"	1726	
and, as it left the place	"	1735	
revenge, held it in chase	"	1736	
from her breast, it doth divide	"	1737	
till it blow up rain	"	1788	
to make it more	"	1789	
At last it rains	"	1790	
'tis mine that she hath kill'd	"	1803	
Is it revenge to give thyself a blow	"	1823	
thou feel'st it cold	Son	2	14
Nor it, nor no remembrance what it was	"	5	12
ere it be self-kill'd	"	6	4
be it ten for one	"	6	8
is it for fear	"	9	1
the world enjoys it	"	9	10
user so destroys it	"	9	12
if it shall go well	"	14	7
If it were fill'd	"	17	2
it is but as a tomb	"	17	3
In it and in my rhyme	"	17	14
whereupon it gazeth	"	20	6
So is it not with me	"	21	1
the frame wherein 'tis held	"	24	3
it is best painter's art	"	24	4
words to show it	"	26	6
all naked, will bestow it	"	26	8
'tis not enough that through	"	34	5
though it alter not	"	36	7
doth it steal sweet hours	"	36	8
And what is't but mine own	"	39	4
Were it not thy sour leisure	"	39	10
It is a greater grief	"	40	11
it is not all my grief	"	42	1
yet it may be said	"	42	2
recounting it to me	"	45	12
It might unceased stay	"	48	3
from the thing it was	"	49	7
but fairer we it deem	"	54	3
which doth in it live	"	54	4
be it not said	"	56	1
Or call it winter	"	56	13
to you It doth belong	"	58	11
be it ill or well	"	58	14
Is it thy will	"	61	1
Is it thy spirit	"	61	5
It is my love	"	61	10
It is so grounded	"	62	4
'Tis thee, myself, that	"	62	13
It—which it fears to lose	Son	64	14
The hand that writ it	"	71	6
whereon it must expire	"	73	11
which it was nourish'd by	"	73	12
that which it contains	"	74	13
and pays it thee again	"	79	8
And found it in thy cheek	"	79	11
in thee it is abused	"	82	14
Who is it that says most	"	84	1
I say "Tis so, 'tis true	"	85	9
Was it the proud full sail	"	86	1
Was it his spirit	"	86	5
gavest it, else mistaking	"	87	10
should do it wrong	"	89	11
Wherein it finds a joy	"	91	6
For it depends upon	"	92	4
and yet I know it not	"	92	14
Though to itself it only live	"	94	10
'tis with so dull a cheer	"	97	13
Yet seem'd it winter still	"	98	13
or colour it had stol'n	"	99	15
Excuse not silence so, for't lies in thee	"	101	10
great it with my lays	"	102	6
when it hath my added praise	"	103	4
Were it not sinful then	"	103	9
when you look in it	"	103	14
would show it dead	"	108	14
it could so preposterously be stain'd	"	109	11
In it thou art my all	"	109	14
Alas, 'tis true	"	110	1
Most true it is	"	110	5
Thence comes it that	"	111	5
To what it works in	"	111	7
For it no form delivers	"	113	5
which it doth latch	"	113	6
holds what it doth catch	"	113	8
For if it see the rudest	"	113	9
it shapes them to your feature	"	113	12
taught it this alchemy	"	114	4
O, 'tis the first, 'tis flattery	"	114	9
most kingly drinks it up	"	114	10
If it be poison'd, 'tis the lesser sin	"	114	13
That mine eye loves it	"	114	14
when it alteration finds	"	116	3
It is an ever-fixed mark	"	116	5
It is the star	"	116	7
But bears it out even	"	116	12
Whilst it hath thought	"	119	6
when it is built anew	"	119	11
'Tis better to be vile	"	121	1
It might for Fortune's bastard	"	124	2
No, it was builded	"	124	5
It suffers not in smiling	"	124	6
It fears not policy	"	124	9
That it nor grows	"	124	12
Were 't ought to me I bore	"	125	1
Or if it were, it bore not beauty's name	"	127	2
I swear it to myself alone	"	131	8
O, let it then as well	"	132	10
deep wound it gives	"	133	2
Is't not to torture me	"	133	3
fill it full with wills	"	136	6
so it please thee hold	"	136	11
see where it lies	"	137	3
If I might teach thee wit, better it were	"	140	5
But 'tis my heart that loves	"	141	3

It—it merits not reproving	Son	142	4
Or, if it do, not from those lips	"	142	5
Be it lawful I love thee	"	142	9
that, when it grows	"	142	11
taught it thus anew	"	145	8
follow'd it as gentle day	"	145	10
to say it is not so	"	148	6
If it be not, then love	"	148	7
How can it? O, how can	"	148	9
hold it that I call	"	151	13
think sometime it saw	L C		10
Which on it had	"		16
what contents it bears	"		19
'Tis promised in the charity	"		70
Let it not tell your judgement	"		73
it was to gain my grace	"		79
the web it seem'd to wear	"		95
If best were as it was	"		98
in it put their mind	"		135
'Nor gives it satisfaction	"		162
That we must curb it	"		163
and cry "It is thy last	"		168
why, 'twas beautiful and hard	"		211
what labour is 't to leave	"		239
the suffering pangs it bears	"		272
Feeling it break	"		275
as it best deceives	"		306
vapour vow; in thee it is	P P	3	11
then it is no fault of mine	"	3	12
when first it 'gins to bud	"	13	3
'T may be, she joy'd	"	14	9
'T may be, again to make me	"	14	10
It was a lording's daughter	"	16	1
alas, it was a spite	"	16	7
she could not help it	"	16	12
ere it be day	"	19	17
had not had it then	"	19	24
bullet beats it down	"	19	30
heard it said full oft	"	19	41
here be it said	"	19	53
it fell upon a day	"	21	1
to hear it was great pity	"	21	12
in them it were a wonder	P T		32
That it cried, How true	"		45
Whereupon it made	"		49
'Twas not their infirmity	"		60
It was married chastity	"		61
Beauty brag, but 'tis not she	"		63
Italy—in the fields of fruitful Italy	R L		107
Itself—Beauty within itself	V A		130
Beauty itself doth of itself	R L		29
Wounding itself to death	"		466
That jealousy itself	"		1516
fountain clears itself again	"		1707
Who heaven itself for ornament doth use	Son	21	3
Or state itself confounded	"	64	10
lace itself with his society	"	67	4
Without all ornament, itself and true	"	68	10
to itself it only live and die	"	94	10
thought itself so blessed never	"	119	6
The sun itself sees not	"	148	12
Reason in itself confounded	P T		41
Ivory—Of this ivory pale	V A		230
Ivory in an alabaster band	"		363
Her breasts, like ivory globes	R L		407
to batter such an ivory wall	"		464
Like ivory conduits	"		1234
Ivy—A belt of straw and ivy buds	P P	20	13
Jack—Do I envy those jacks	Son	128	5
Since saucy jacks so happy are	"	128	13
Jade—How like a jade he stood	V A		391
Till, like a jade	R L		707
thus shall excuse my jade	Son	51	12
Jar—he comes in every jar	V A		100
Javelin—With javelin's point	"		616
Jaw—from the fierce tiger's jaws	Son	19	3
Jealous—Jealous of catching	V A		321
Let not the jealous day	R L		800
question with my jealous thought	Son	57	9
Jealousy—Jealousy, that sour unwelcome guest	V A		449
Love reigns, disturbing Jealousy	"		649
dissentious Jealousy	"		657
waited on with jealousy	"		1137
That jealousy itself	R L		1516
tenour of thy jealousy	Son	61	8
Jeering—As silly-jeering idiots are with kings	R L		1812
Jennet—A breeding jennet	V A		260
Jest—daily, smile, and jest	R L		106
Death, I did but jest	"		997
But smile and jest	P P	4	12
she joy'd to jest	"	14	9
Jesting—and all were jestings	"	7	12
Jet—and of beaded jet	L C		37
Jewel—Torches are made to light, jewels to wear	V A		163
jewel in the flood	"		824
Of that rich jewel	R L		34
of that dear jewel I have lost	"		1191
a jewel hung in ghastly night	Son	27	11
to whom my jewels trifles are	"	48	5
Or captain jewels in the carcanet	"	52	8
Shall Time's best jewel	"	65	10
The basest jewel	"	96	6
fairest and most precious jewel	"	131	4
Of this false jewel	L C		154
Jig—All my merry jigs	P P	18	9
Jocund—their leader's jocund show	R L		296
Join—join they all together	V A		971
They join and shoot their foam	R L		1442
Join with the spite of fortune	Son	90	3
Joined—how often hath she joined	P P	7	7
Joint—my joints did tremble	V A		642
her joints forgot to bow	"		1061
my frail joints shake	R L		227
sets every joint a-shaking	"		452
Jointed—Round-hoof'd, short-jointed, fetlocks shag	V A		295
Jointly—All jointly listening	R L		1410
Then jointly to the ground	"		1846
Jollity—needy nothing trimm'd in jollity	Son	66	3
Jot—be any jot diminish'd	V A		417
Journey—a journey in my head	Son	27	3
How heavy do I journey	"	50	1
Jove—'O Jove,' quoth she	V A		1015
by high almighty Jove	R L		568
Thine eye Jove's lightning seems	P P	5	11
'O Jove,' quoth she	"	6	14
Thou for whom Jove would swear	"	17	15
And deny himself for Jove	"	17	17
Joy—oh presented joy	V A		405
and death was lively joy	"		498
and to lack her joy	"		600

Joy—joy bids her rejoice	V. A	977
Her joy with heaved-up hand	R L	111
a froth of fleeting joy	"	212
Must sell her joy	"	383
joy breeds months of pain	"	690
thy joy to grief	"	889
that tune their memory's joy	"	1107
Trojan mothers sharing joy	"	1431
their light joy seemed to appear	"	1434
joy delights in joy	Son 8	2
But here's the joy	" 42	13
and my joy behind	" 50	14
a joy above the rest	" 91	6
Before, a joy proposed	" 129	12
Were kisses all the joys in bed	P P 19	47
Joy—U'ylook'd-for joy in that I honour most	Son 25	4
This told I joy; but then no longer glad	" 45	13
Joy'd—she joy'd to jest	P P 14	9
Joyless—While with a joyless smile	R L	1711
Judge—Being judge in love	V. A	220
My bloody judge forbade	R L	1648
And when the judge is robb'd	"	1652
Judgement—do I my .... pluck	Son 14	1
So, till the judgement	" 55	13
on better judgement making	" 87	12
Yet then my judgement	" 115	3
in my judgement's place	" 131	12
the judgement of my heart	" 137	8
where is my judgement fled	" 148	3
Let it not tell your judgement	L C	73
from judgement stand aloof	"	166
Juice—lean and lacking juice	V. A	136
Jump—To jump up higher seem'd	R L	1414
can jump both sea and land	Son 44	7
June—in three hot Junes burn'd	" 104	7
Juno—Juno but an Ethlope were	P P 17	16
Just—Now was she just before him	V. A	349
fatal folds just in his way	"	879
when it seems most just	"	1156
to find a stranger just	R L	159
a show so seeming just	"	1514
Just to the time	Son 109	7
And on just proof	" 117	10
And the just pleasure lost	" 121	3
and see just cause of hate	" 150	10
Justice—Justice is feasting	R L	906
might plead for justice there	"	1649
For sparing justice feeds iniquity	"	1687
Justify—O call me not to justify the wrong	Son 139	1
Justly—And justly thus controls	R L	189
One justly weeps	"	1235
Keen—edge on his keen appetite	R L	9
Pluck the keen teeth	Son 19	3
to make our appetites more keen	" 118	1
to make our wits more keen	L C	161
Keep—Love keeps his revels	V. A	123
keep his loathsome cabin	"	637
keep with thy hounds	"	678
earth-delving conies keep	"	687
shall it keep in quiet	"	1149
he should keep unknown	R L	34
and keep themselves enclosed	"	678
Keep still possession	"	803
keep them from thy aid	"	912
To keep thy sharp woes waking	"	1136
Keep—keep him from heart-easing words	R L	1782
private widow well may keep yourself keeps yourself still	Son 9	7
	" 16	13
which I will keep so chary	" 22	11
keep my drooping eyelids	" 27	7
with my desire keep pace	" 51	9
that keeps you as my chest	" 52	9
thy image should keep open	" 61	1
that keeps mine eye awake	" 61	10
And keep invention	" 76	6
To keep an adjunct	" 122	13
She keeps thee to this purpose	" 126	7
but not still keep, her treasure	" 126	10
Whoe'er keeps me	" 133	11
that vow'd chaste life to keep	" 154	3
Keep the obsequy so strict	P T	12
Keep'st—with tears thou keep'st me blind	Son 148	13
Keeping—Cave-keeping evils that obscurely sleep	R L	1250
Ken—to drown in ken of shore	"	1114
Kennell'd—kennell'd in a brake	V. A	913
Kept—twenty locks kept fast	"	575
by a painted cloth be kept in awe	R L	245
dear love be kept unspotted	"	821
which thy chaste bee kept	"	840
when time is kept with tears	"	1127
both were kept for heaven	"	1166
And kept unused	Son 9	12
till now never kept seat in one	" 105	14
his prescriptions are not kept	" 147	6
Kept hearts in liveries	L C	195
But kept cold distance	"	237
that kept my rest away	P P 14	2
Key—as the rich, whose blessed key	Son 52	1
Key-cold—in key-cold Lucrece' bleeding stream	R L	1774
Kill—For looks kill love	V. A	464
thou didst kill me; kill me once again	"	499
butcher, bent to kill	"	618
doth cry 'Kill, kill!'	"	652
the other kills thee quickly	"	990
murder wakes to stain and kill	R L	168
doth confound and kill	"	230
this blessed league to kill	"	383
To kill thine honour	"	516
all that brood to kill	"	627
Or kills his life	"	875
seek every hour to kill	"	908
Kill both thyself and her	"	1036
'To kill myself,' quoth she	"	1136
will kill myself, thy foe	"	1196
act of lust, and so did kill	"	1636
Kill me with spites	Son 40	14
But, ah, thought kills me	" 44	9
To-morrow see again and do not kill	" 56	7
and wretched minutes kill	" 126	8
no fair beseechers kill	" 135	13
Kill me outright with looks	" 139	11
or kills the gallant knight	P P 16	6
Kill'd—and hath kill'd him so	V. A	1110
I should have kill'd him	"	1118
by her side lay kill'd	"	1165
between them both it should be kill'd	R L	71
kill'd my son or sire	"	232

Kill'd—Like to a new-kill'd bird	R L 457
that the flower hath kill'd	" 1253
kill'd with deadly cares	" 1593
'tis mine that she hath kill'd	" 1803
ere it be self-kill'd	Son 6 4
kill'd too soon by death's sharp sting	P P 10 4
Killing—a cockatrice' dead-killing eye	R L 540
O comfort-killing Night	" 764
Kind—I felt a kind of fear	V A 998
overthrow of mortal kind	" 1018
stern sad tunes, to change their kinds	R L 1147
the impression of strange kinds	" 1242
a kind of heavy fear	" 1433
but in a kind of praise	Son 95 7
besiege all kinds of blood	" 109 10
found a kind of meetness	" 118 7
All kind of arguments	L C 121
Kind—Beating his kind embracements	V A 312
deceitful, so compact, so kind	R L 1423
presence is, gracious and kind	Son 10 11
although their eyes were kind	" 69 11
Kind is my love to-day, to-morrow kind	" 105 5
Fair, kind, and true	" 105 9
Fair, kind, and true	" 105 13
Fair, kind, and true	" 105 13
covetous and he is kind	" 134 6
kiss me, be kind	" 143 12
is nor true nor kind	L C 186
Their kind acceptance	" 207
fair nature is both kind and tame	" 311
Kinder—Grew kinder, and his fury	V A 318
Kind-hearted—at least .... prove	Son 10 12
Kindle—She seeks to kindle	V A 606
Kindled—His kindled duty kindled her mistrust	R L 1352
Thy eye kindled the fire	" 1475
Kindling—his love-kindling fire did quickly steep	Son 153 3
Kindly—She took me kindly by the hand	R L 253
Kindness—with public kindness honour me	Son 36 11
deep oaths of thy deep kindness	" 152 9
Kindred—filial fear, law, ..., fame	L C 270
King—King of graves and grave for kings	V A 995
Who like a king	" 1043
That kings might be espoused	R L 20
But king nor peer	" 21
this proud issue of a king	" 37
what thou art, a god, a king	" 601
For kings, like gods	" 602
when once thou art a king	" 606
Then kings' misdeeds	" 609
'a sea, a sovereign king	" 652
So shall these slaves be king	" 659
Or kings be breakers	" 852
to calm contending kings	" 939
coming from a king	" 1002
grooms are sightless night, kings glorious day	" 1013
As silly-jeering idiots are with kings	" 1812
to change my state with kings	Son 29 14
beauties whereof now he is king	" 63 6
King—In sleep a king, but waking no such matter	Son 87 14
and change decrees of kings	" 115 6
King Pandion he is dead	P P 21 23
Pity but he were a king	" 21 42
Save the eagle, feather'd king	P T 11
Kingdom—on the .... of the shore	Son 64 6
kingdoms of hearts shouldst owe	" 70 14
Kingly—most kingly drinks it up	" 114 10
Kinsman—But as he is my kinsman	R L 237
Thy kinsmen hang their heads	" 521
Kirtle—A cap of flowers and a	P P 20 11
Kiss—I'll smother thee with kisses	V A 18
Ten kisses short as one	" 22
she murders with a kiss	" 54
And one sweet kiss	" 84
'Tis but a kiss I beg	" 96
The kiss shall be thine own	" 117
for one poor kiss	" 207
Give me one kiss	" 209
A thousand kisses	" 517
twenty hundred kisses	" 522
you shall have a kiss	" 536
to rob thee of a kiss	" 723
Lest she should steal a kiss	" 726
The kiss I gave you	" 771
by a kiss thought to persuade	" 1114
the pillow of a lawful kiss	R L 387
Between each kiss	P P 7 8
Were kisses all the joys	" 19 47
Kiss—Art thou ashamed to kiss	V A 121
to kiss his shadow	" 162
For men will kiss	" 216
He kisses her	" 479
he will kiss her still	" 480
they kiss each other	" 505
some kiss her face	" 872
ever strive to kiss you	" 1082
He thought to kiss him	" 1110
Wherein I will not kiss	" 1188
to kiss the turrets bowed	R L 1372
To kiss the tender inward	Son 128 6
me thy lips to kiss	" 128 14
kiss me, be kind	" 143 12
To kiss and clip me	P P 11 14
Kiss'd—Even so she kiss'd	V A 59
And kiss'd the fatal knife	R L 1843
And often kiss'd	L C 51
Kissing—And kissing speaks	V A 47
with continual kissing	" 606
With kissing him	" 1118
Threatening cloud-kissing Ilion	R L 1370
Kissing with golden face	Son 33 3
Knee—And with his knee	R L 359
their knees they bow	" 1846
Kneel—whom she kneels	V A 350
But kneel with me	R L 1830
Knell—rings out the doleful knell	" 1495
bell rings doleful knell	P P 18 28
Knew—as if she knew his mind	V A 308
her thirsty lips well knew	" 543
no bearing yoke they knew	R L 409
my judgement knew no reason	Son 115 3
that the ruffle knew	L C 58
And knew the patterns	" 170
Knew vows were ever brokers	" 173
Knife—for the self-same purpose seek a knife	R L 1047
Will fix a sharp knife	" 1138

Knife—I'll bequeath unto the knife	R L		1184
Mine honour be the knife's	"		1201
And with my knife scratch out	"		1469
A harmful knife	"		1724
The murderous knife	"		1735
Brutus, who pluck'd the knife	"		1807
and by this bloody knife	"		1840
And kiss'd the fatal knife	"		1843
confounding age's cruel knife	Son	63	10
conquest of a wretch's knife	"	74	11
The hardest knife ill used	"	95	14
his scythe and crooked knife	"	100	14
Knight—Knights by their oaths	R L		1694
ladies dead, and lovely knights	Son	106	4
One knight loves both	P P	8	14
or kill the gallant knight	"	16	6
the trusty knight was wounded	"	16	11
Knighthood—O shame to	R L		197
By knighthood, gentry	"		569
As bound in knighthood	"		1697
Knit—With heavy eye, knit brow	"		799
Knit poisonous clouds	"		777
my duty strongly knit	Son	26	2
Knock—Knocks at my heart	V A		659
Knot—neither sting, knot, nor confine	L C		265
Know—secrets shalt thou know	V A		16
nor know not what we mean	"		126
they know not whether	"		304
'I know not love,' quoth he, 'nor will not know it	"		409
know myself, seek not to know	"		325
For know, my heart	"		779
For now she knows	"		883
she knows not whither	"		904
Which knows no pity	"		1000
why then I know	"		1109
but know, it is as good	"		1181
of this rash alarm to know	R L		473
I know what thorns	"		492
I know repentant tears	"		502
that knows no gentle right	"		545
that know not how	"		810
but he that gives them knows	"		853
thou shalt not know	"		1058
But thou shalt know	"		1067
nor law, nor limit knows	"		1120
That knows not parching heat	"		1145
Know, gentle wench	"		1273
to know your heaviness	"		1283
Collatine may know	"		1312
prepares to let them know	"		1607
dear my love, you know	Son	13	13
Though yet, heaven knows	"	17	3
They draw but what they see, know not the heart	"	24	14
And yet, love knows	"	40	11
the wretch did know	"	50	7
no motion shall I know	"	51	8
every blessed shape we know	"	53	12
O, know, sweet love	"	76	9
Thou by thy dial's shady stealth mayst know	"	77	7
and yet I know it not	"	92	11
I cannot know thy change	"	93	6
To know my shames	"	112	6
mine eye well knows	"	114	11
Which is not mix'd with seconds, knows no art	"	125	11
Know—All this the world well knows, yet none knows well	Son	129	13
yet well I know	"	130	9
And will, thy soul knows	"	136	3
They know what beauty is	"	137	3
Which my heart knows	"	137	10
though I know she lies	"	138	2
Although she knows	"	138	6
ah, my love well knows	"	139	9
from their physicians know	"	140	8
this shall I ne'er know	"	144	13
now I know thy mind	"	149	13
Love is too young to know	"	151	1
Yet who knows not	"	151	2
by age, desires to know	L C		62
though I know she lies	P P	1	2
Although I know my years	"	1	6
The truth I shall not know	"	2	13
The cock that treads them shall not know	"	19	40
These are certain signs to know	"	21	57
Knowing—As.... Tarquin's lust	R L		1354
Knowing a better spirit	Son	80	2
thy own worth then not knowing	"	87	9
knowing thy will	"	89	7
Knowing thy heart torments me	"	132	2
Knowledge—my knowledge I derive	"	14	9
Within the knowledge of mine own desert	"	49	10
Thou art as fair in knowledge	"	82	5
If knowledge be the mark	P P	5	7
Known—if the fact be known	R L		239
than hate's known injury	Son	40	12
known to us poor swains	P P	18	45
Know'st—thou .... not what it is	V A		613
because thou know'st I love her	Son	42	6
thou know'st thy estimate	"	87	2
For well thou know'st to my dear doting heart	"	131	3
thou know'st I am forsworn	"	152	1
Labour—each passion labours so	V A		969
doth labour to expel	"		976
labour hence to heave thee	R L		586
With too much labour	"		1099
Yet save that labour	"		1290
what labour is 't to leave	L C		239
Labour'd—the painter labour'd with his skill	R L		1506
Labouring—you see the .... pioner	"		1380
Which, labouring for invention	Son	59	3
And labouring in moe pleasures	L C		139
Labyrinth—Are like a labyrinth	V A		684
Lace—And lace itself with his society	Son	67	4
Lack—he did not lack	V A		299
and to lack her joy	"		600
but lack tongues to praise	Son	106	14
not born fair, no beauty lack	"	127	11
they foul that thy complexion lack	"	132	14
Lest the requiem lack his right	P T		16
Lack—I sigh the lack of many a thing	Son	30	3
Lack'd—being lack'd, to hope	"	52	14
Then lack'd I matter	"	86	14
Love lack'd a dwelling	L C		82
Lackey—Thou ceaseless lackey to eternity	R L		97
Lacking—lean, and lacking juice	V A		136
Love-lacking vestals	"		752

Lacking—Which I by lacking	Son	31	2
Lad—Did court the lad	P P	4	3
Laden—one with treasure laden	V A	....	1022
Lady—No, lady, no; my heart	"	....	785
their dear governess and lady lies	R L	....	443
a sad look to her lady's sorrow	"	....	1221
But, lady, if your maid may be	"	....	1282
should right poor ladies' harms	"	....	1694
In praise of ladies dead	Son	106	4
Ah, that I had my lady	P P	11	13
learned man hath got the lady gay	"	16	15
All my lady's love is lost	"	18	10
By ringing in thy lady's ear	"	19	28
Unless thy lady prove unjust	"	19	33
Laid—when sadly she had laid	R L	....	1212
but laid no words to gage	"	....	1351
laid great bases for eternity	Son	125	3
On purpose laid to make the taker mad	"	129	8
Cupid laid by his brand	"	151	1
Laid by his side	"	154	2
And down I laid	L C	....	4
Lain—Or lain in ambush	R L	....	233
Lagging—As lagging fowls before the northern blast	V A	....	1335
Lamb—never fright the silly lamb	V A	....	1098
The silly lambs: pure thoughts	R L	....	167
the poor lamb cries	"	....	677
She like a wearied lamb	"	....	737
where he the lamb may get	"	....	878
How many lambs might the stern wolf betray	Son	96	9
If like a lamb he could his looks translate	"	96	10
Lame—The poor, lame, blind, halt, creep, cry out for thee	R L	....	902
So I, made lame by fortune's dearest spite	Son	37	3
So then I am not lame	"	37	9
Youth is nimble, age is lame	P P	12	6
Lameness—Speak of my lameness	Son	89	3
Lament—she finds forlorn, she doth lament	R L	....	1500
And my laments would be	"	....	1616
Lamentable—A thousand lamentable objects	"	....	1373
Lamentation—relenting dew of lamentations	"	....	1829
Lamenting—lamenting Philomel had ended	"	....	1079
with my lamenting tongue	"	....	1465
Lamp—Were never four such lamps	V A	....	489
the lamp that burns	"	....	755
each lamp and shining star	"	....	861
Where, lo, two lamps, burnt out, in darkness lies	"	....	1128
Lance—hath he hung his lance	"	....	103
Land—ere rich at home he lands	R L	....	336
the heart of all her land	"	....	439
can jump both sea and land	Son	44	7
Of lands and mansions	L C	....	138
Landlord—Than the true gouty landlord	"	....	140
Language—with lustful language	V A	....	47
Languish'd—To me that languish'd for her sake	Son	145	3
Languisheth—Even so she	V A	....	663
Languishment—weeps at thy	R L	....	1130
heartstrings to true languishment	"	....	1141
Lank—lank and lean discolour'd cheek	R L	....	708
Lap—Or from their proud lap	Son	98	8
Lapp'd—All thy friends are lapp'd in lead	P P	21	24
Large—To leap large lengths of land	Son	44	10
of this large privilege	"	95	13
whose will is large and spacious	"	135	5
to make thy large ' Will ' more	"	135	12
Why so large cost, having so short	"	146	5
Largeness—What largeness thinks in Paradise was sawn	L C	....	91
Largess—The bounteous largess given thee to give	Son	4	6
Lark—Lo, here the gentle lark	V A	....	853
Like to the lark at break of day	Son	29	11
were tuned like the lark	P P	15	6
Lascivious—.... grace, in whom	Son	40	13
Making lascivious comments	"	95	6
Lass—Farewell, sweet lass	P P	18	49
Last—had ta'en his last leave	V A	....	2
And yields at last	"	....	566
picks them all at last	"	....	576
At last she thus begins	R L	....	1303
At last she calls to mind	"	....	1366
At last she sees	"	....	1501
At last she smilingly	"	....	1567
At last he takes her	"	....	1597
At last it rains	"	....	1790
before these last so bad	Son	67	14
do not leave me last	"	90	9
and cry, ' It is thy last	L C	....	168
Last—wish the feast might ever last	V A	....	447
And us they last	"	....	507
Thy violent vanities can never last	R L	....	894
cease thou thy course and last no longer	"	....	1765
She bade love last	P P	7	16
Lasting—monuments of .... moans	R L	....	798
else lasting shame	"	....	1620
Life's lasting date	"	....	1729
character'd with lasting memory	Son	122	2
Latch—Which with a yielding	R L	....	339
pluck'd up the latch	"	....	358
or shape, which it doth latch	Son	113	6
Late—brake off his late intent	V A	....	469
shrieks,—'tis very late	"	....	531
gazer late did wonder	"	....	748
that was but late forlorn	"	....	1026
wherein they late excell'd	"	....	1131
which late this mutiny restrains	R L	....	426
Comes all too late	"	....	1686
and too late hath spill'd	"	....	1801
Lucrece' soul that late complained	"	....	1839
where late the sweet birds sang	Son	73	4
Which late her noble suit	L C	....	234
too late she will repent	P P	19	15
Late-embarked—a .... friend	V A	....	818
Late-sack'd—Who, like a late-sack'd island	R L	....	1740
Lattice—through .... of sear'd age	L C	....	14
Laud—against long-living laud	R L	....	622
plantest scandal and displacest laud	"	....	887
Laugh—That laughs and weeps	V A	....	414
Nor laugh with his companions	R L	....	1066
To make the weeper laugh, the laugher weep	L C	....	124
Laugh'd—love he laugh'd to scorn	V A	....	4

Laugh'd—Saturn laugh'd and leap'd *Son* 98	4	
Laugher — To make the weeper laugh, the laugher weep *L C*	124	
Laund—through the dark laund runs apace *V A*	813	
Laundering—Laundering the silken figures *L C*	17	
Law—By law of nature *V A*	171	
in thine own law forlorn "	251	
on what he looks, 'gainst law or duty *R L*	497	
where are no laws "	544	
By holy human law "	571	
at right, at law, at reason "	880	
is past the help of law "	1022	
nor law nor limit knows "	1120	
thou hast the strength of law *Son* 49	13	
filial fear, law, kindred fame *L C*	270	
Lawful—Cozening the pillow of a lawful kiss *R L*	387	
lawful policy remains enacted "	529	
the dowry of a lawful bed "	938	
a lawful plea commence *Son* 35	11	
lawful reasons on thy part " 49	12	
Be it lawful I love thee " 142	9	
Lawn—Like lawn being spread *V A*	590	
that on lawn we lay *R L*	258	
Then white as lawn "	259	
Lay—For, where they lay *V A*	176	
in the dark she lay "	827	
by her side lay kill'd "	1165	
that on the ground lay spill'd "	1167	
roses that on lawn we lay *R L*	258	
in darkness sweetly lay "	398	
night's 'scapes doth open lay "	747	
thine honour lay in me "	834	
the guiltless casket where it lay "	1057	
Lays open all the little worms "	1248	
and on that pillow lay "	1620	
possess the claim they lay "	1794	
lay on me this cross *Son* 42	12	
beauty's truth to lay " 101	7	
That thy unkindness lays upon my heart " 139	2	
Lay—Yet nor the lays of birds " 98	5	
that doth thy lays esteem " 100	7	
to greet it with my lays " 102	6	
And wish her lays *P P* 13	6	
Let the bird of loudest lay *P T*	1	
Lazy—with a lazy spright *V A*	181	
Lead—time leads summer on *Son* 5	5	
Who lead thee in their riot " 41	11	
many gazers mightst thou lead away " 96	11	
that leads men to this hell " 129	14	
Lead—turn'd to fire, my heart to lead *V A*	1072	
Heavy heart's lead, melt "	1073	
All thy friends are lapp'd in lead *P P*	24	
Leaden—With leaden appetite *V A*	34	
Now leaden slumber *R L*	124	
Leader—true leaders to their queen *V A*	503	
by their leader's jocund show *R L*	296	
Leadeth—leadeth on to danger *V A*	788	
my captain, and he leadeth *R L*	271	
Leading—Leading him prisoner *V A*	110	
the leading to his hand *R L*	436	
Leaf—before one leaf put forth *V A*	416	
do the tender leaves "	798	
herb, leaf, or weed "	1057	
Leaf—His leaves will wither *R L*	1168	
and lusty leaves quite gone *Son* 5	7	
trees I see barren of leaves " 12	5	
their fair leaves spread " 25	5	
When yellow leaves, or none " 73	2	
The vacant leaves " 77	3	
That leaves look pale " 97	14	
Study his bias leaves *P P* 5	5	
Through the velvet leaves " 17	5	
all with leaves of myrtle " 20	12	
League—That now he vows a *R L*	287	
this blessed league to kill "	383	
This forced league doth force "	689	
a league is took *Son* 47	1	
Lean—whereon we lean *V A*	125	
lean, and lacking juice "	136	
ugly, meagre, lean "	931	
and lean discolour'd cheek *R L*	708	
Lean penury within that pen *Son* 84	5	
Lean'd—lean'd on another's head *R L*	1415	
Lean'd her breast up-till a thorn *P P* 21	10	
Leaning—leaning on their elbows *V A*	44	
Leap—Imperiously he leaps "	265	
curvets and leaps "	279	
Whereat she leaps "	1026	
once more leap her eyes "	1050	
And bids it leap from thence *R L*	760	
To leap large lengths *Son* 44	10	
those jacks that nimble leap " 128	5	
Beasts did leap and birds did sing *P P* 21	5	
Leap'd—lustful lord leap'd from his bed *R L*	169	
Saturn laugh'd and leap'd with him *Son* 98	4	
Learn—And learn of him *V A*	404	
O, learn to love "	407	
Where subjects' eyes do learn *R L*	616	
the school where Lust shall learn "	617	
O, learn to read what silent love *Son* 23	13	
But thence I learn " 118	13	
Learned—learn'd to sport and dance *V A*	105	
He learn'd to sin *R L*	630	
what is writ in learned books "	811	
feathers to the learned's wings *Son* 78	7	
He learn'd but surety-like " 134	7	
Well learned is that tongue *P P* 5	8	
the learned man hath got the lady gay " 16	15	
Learning—this....mayst thou taste *Son* 77	4	
As high as learning " 78	14	
Which by a gift of learning *P P* 16	14	
Lease—which you hold in lease *Son* 13	5	
summer's lease hath all too short a date " 18	4	
Can yet the lease of my true love control " 107	3	
leases of short-number'd hours " 124	10	
having so short a lease " 146	5	
Least—And not the least *V A*	745	
by death, at least, I give *R L*	1053	
Or, at the least, this refuge "	1654	
at least kind-hearted prove *Son* 10	12	
With what I most enjoy contented least " 29	8	
When in the least of them my life hath end " 92	6	
Or, at the least " 122	5	
stands least in thy control " 125	11	
Leathern—with a leathern rein *V A*	392	
Leave—Had ta'en his last leave "	2	

LEAVE 166 LEST

Leave—leave exceeds commission	V A	....	568
thy sour leisure gave sweet leave	Son	39	10
and give him leave to go	"	51	14
Leave—leave me here alone	V A	....	382
And leave this idle theme	"	....	422
'Where did I leave	"	....	715
Leave me, and then the story	"	....	716
Leaves Love upon her back	"	....	814
Bid them leave quaking	"	....	809
wolf would leave his prey	"	....	1097
Tarquin leaves the Roman host	R L	....	3
in venturing ill we leave to be	"	....	148
for thine own sake leave me	"	....	583
And leaves it to be master'd	"	....	863
leave thy peeping	"	....	1089
And leave the faltering	"	....	1768
audit canst thou leave	Son	4	12
Will sourly leave her	"	41	8
To leave poor me	"	49	13
I leave my love alone	"	66	14
which thou must leave ere long	"	73	14
If thou wilt leave me	"	90	9
leaves out difference	"	105	8
To leave for nothing	"	109	12
Who leaves unsway'd	"	141	11
what labour is't to leave	L C	....	239
To leave the battery	"	....	277
and he takes and leaves	"	....	305
To leave the master loveless	P P	16	6
Leaving—Leaving his spoil perplex'd	R L	....	733
Leaving thee living in posterity	Son	6	12
Leaving no posterity	P T	....	59
Lecher—The lechers in their deed	R L	....	1637
a lover, or a lecher whether?	P P	7	17
Lecture — read lectures of such shame	R L	....	618
Led—desire thus madly led	"	....	300
Leese—Leese but their show	Son	5	14
Left—still is left alive	V A	....	174
and left Adonis there	"	....	322
the very smell were left me	"	....	441
Left their round turrets	R L	....	441
the load of lust he left behind	"	....	734
no perfection of my summer left	"	....	837
Was left unseen, save to the eye of mind	"	....	1426
and, as it left the place	"	....	1735
summer's distillation left	Son	5	9
no form of thee hast left behind	"	9	6
Art left the prey of every vulgar thief	"	48	8
Since I left you mine eye is in my mind	"	113	1
Hath left me, and I desperate	"	147	7
and left her all alone	P P	9	14
Left—seize love upon thy left	V A	....	158
Left'st—For why thou left'st me nothing	P P	10	2
And yet thou left'st me more	"	10	9
Leg—straight legs and passing strong	V A	....	297
Stands on his hinder legs	"	....	698
his weary legs doth scratch	"	....	705
a foot, a face, a leg, a head	R L	....	1427
Legacy—What legacy shall I bequeath	"	....	1192
thy beauty's legacy	Son	4	2
Legion—Which many legions of true hearts	"	....	154	6
Leisure—pay them at thy leisure	V A	....	518
Debate where leisur' serves	R L	....	1019
Leisure—thy sour leisure gave sweet leave	Son	39	10
I must attend time's leisure	"	44	12
bound to stay your leisure	"	58	4
have no leisure taken	"	120	7
Or any of my leisures	L C	....	193
Leisurely—but do it leisurely	R L	....	1349
Lend—desire doth lend her force	V A	....	29
Her arms do lend his neck	"	....	539
to lend the world his light	"	....	756
That lends embracements	"	....	790
May lend thee light, as thou dost lend	"	....	864
tears did lend and borrow	"	....	951
star did lend his light	R L	....	164
burn out thy light, and lend it not	"	....	190
that to bad debtors lends	"	....	964
Lends light to all fair eyes	"	....	1083
no god to lend her those	"	....	1461
She lends them words	"	....	1498
that thou shalt lend me	"	....	1685
gives nothing, but doth lend	Son	4	3
she lends to those are free	"	4	4
lends but weak relief	"	34	11
can every shadow lend	"	53	4
He lends thee virtue	"	79	9
What strained touches rhetoric can lend	"	82	10
lends not some small glory	"	84	6
to lend base subjects light	"	100	4
Lest sorrow lend me words	"	140	3
anon their gazes lend	L C	....	26
Lendeth—sorrow to my sorrow	R L	....	1676
Lending—Lending him wit	"	....	964
Lending soft audience to my sweet design	L C	....	278
Length—through the .... of times	R L	....	718
At length address'd	"	....	1606
To leap large lengths	Son	44	10
and length thyself to-morrow	P P	15	18
Her feeble force will yield at length	"	19	21
Lent—to his melting buttock lent	V A	....	313
If love have lent you	"	....	775
wealth the heavens had him lent	R L	....	17
For it was lent thee	"	....	626
glance that sly Ulysses lent	"	....	1399
to Phrygian shepherds lent	"	....	1502
their passions likewise lent me	L C	....	199
Less—they have but less	R L	....	137
cannot make it less	"	....	1283
men of less truth than tongue	Son	17	10
less false in rolling	"	20	1
are loved of more and less	"	96	3
I love not less, though less the show appear	"	102	2
summer is less pleasant	"	102	9
Made more or less	"	123	12
And so much less of shame	L C	....	188
Lesser—more rage and lesser pity	R L	....	468
The lesser thing should not the greater hide	"	....	663
lesser noise than shallow fords	"	....	1329
'tis the lesser sin	Son	114	13
Lesson—the lesson is but plain	V A	....	407
and find the lesson true	Son	113	13
Lest—lest thy hard heart	V A	....	375
Lest Jealousy, that sour	"	....	449
Lest she should steal a kiss	"	....	726
Lest the deceiving harmony	"	....	781

Lest—Where, lest between them both	R L		74
lest he should hold it	"		1345
Lest my bewailed guilt should do thee shame	Son	36	10
Lest the wise world should look	"	71	13
O, lest the world should task you	"	72	1
O, lest your true love may seem	"	72	9
Lest I, too much profane, should do it wrong	"	89	11
Lest sorrow lend me words	"	140	3
Lest eyes well seeing thy foul fault should find	"	148	14
Lest guilty of my faults thy sweet self prove	"	151	4
Lest she some subtle practice smell	P P	19	9
Lest that my mistress hear	"	19	56
Lest the requiem lack his right	P T		16
Let—let not advantage slip	V A		129
'let go, and let me go	"		379
Let me excuse thy courser	"		403
with wringing; let us part	"		421
let their crimson liveries	"		506
Now let me say	"		535
you crush me; let me go	"		611
O, let him keep	"		637
will not let a false sound	"		780
that would let him go	R L		76
Let fair humanity abhor	"		195
Let him return	"		641
So let thy thoughts	"		666
Let their exhaled unwholesome breaths make sick	"		779
And let thy misty vapours march	"		782
Let not the jealous Day behold	"		800
'Let my good name, that senseless reputation	"		820
Let ghastly shadows his lewd eyes affright	"		971
Let there bechance him	"		976
And let mild women to him lose	"		979
'Let him have time	"		981
Let him have time	"		982
Let him have time	"		983
Let him have time	"		984
Let him have time	"		985
'Let him have time	"		988
Let him have time	"		990
And ever let his unrecalling crime	"		993
let the thief run mad	"		997
Is to let forth my foul-defiled blood	"		1029
let beasts bear gentle minds	"		1148
Then let it not be called impiety	"		1174
O, let it not be hid	"		1257
Let sin, alone committed, light alone	"		1480
Let guiltless souls be free	"		1482
to let them know	"		1607
this refuge let me find	"		1654
let it then suffice	"		1679
yet let the traitor die	"		1686
let no mourner say	"		1797
Let my unsounded self, supposed a fool	"		1819
let not winter's ragged hand deface	Son	6	1
Let those whom Nature hath not	"	11	9
not let that copy die	"	11	14
Who lets so fair a house fall to decay	"	13	9

Let let your son say so	Son	13	14
O, let me, true in love, but truly write	"	21	9
Let them say more	"	21	13
O, let my books be then the eloquence	"	23	9
Let those who are in favour with their stars	"	25	1
To let base clouds o'ertake me	"	34	3
Let me confess	"	36	1
Let him bring forth	"	38	11
let us divided live	"	39	5
Let this sad interim like the ocean be	"	56	9
O, let me suffer	"	58	5
But let your love even with my life decay	"	71	12
Let him but copy	"	84	9
Let not my love be call'd idolatry	"	105	1
Let me not to the marriage	"	116	1
let me be obsequious	"	125	9
let it then as well beseem	"	132	10
let my poor heart hail	"	133	10
let my heart be his guard	"	133	11
Let no unkind, no fair beseechers kill	"	135	13
let me pass untold	"	136	9
Let me excuse thee	"	139	9
let that pine to aggravate thy store	"	146	10
that lets not bounty fall	L C		41
and had let go by	"		59
Let it not tell your judgement	"		73
Let reason rule things	P P	19	3
Let the bird of loudest lay	P T		1
Let the priest in surplice white	"		13
To this urn let those repair	"		65
Let—When Collatine unwisely did not let	R L		10
With a lingering stay his course doth let	"		328
Those lets attend the time	"		330
swells the higher by this let	"		646
Letter—A letter to my lord	"		1293
she would not blot the letter	"		1322
Her letter now is seal'd	"		1331
Found yet moe letters	L C		47
Level—within the level of your frown	Son	117	11
and they that level	"	121	9
which in his level came	L C		309
Levell'd—Sometimes her levell'd eyes	"		22
were levell'd on my face	"		282
Lewd—of lewd unhallow'd eyes	R L		392
shadows his lewd eyes affright	"		971
Liberty—wrongs that .... commits	Son	41	1
absence of your liberty	"	58	6
to tempt all, liberty procured	L C		252
Licking—licking of his wound	V A		915
Lid—She lifts the coffer-lids	"		1127
Lie—Panting he lies	"		62
Look, how a bird lies	"		57
in her arms Adonis lies	"		68
there thy beauty lies	"		119
bank whereon I lie	"		151
And, lo, I lie between	"		194
pleasant fountains lie	"		234
there he came to lie	"		245
on the grass she lies	"		473
whereon thou dost lie	"		646

Lie—on his back doth lie	*V A*	663
Lie quietly, and hear	"	709
lamps, burnt out, in darkness lies	"	1128
doth Tarquin lie revolving	*R L*	127
her beloved Collatinus lies	"	256
where such treasure lies	"	280
from the rushes where it lies	"	318
Lies at the mercy	"	364
her rosy cheek lies under	"	386
like a virtuous monument, she lies	"	391
their dear governess and lady lies	"	443
she trembling lies	"	457
under his insulting falchion lies	"	509
lamb lies panting there	"	737
Immodestly lies martyr'd	"	802
whose guilt within their bosoms lie	"	1342
under Pyrrhus' proud foot lies	"	1448
in bloody channel lies	"	1487
the father's image lies	"	1753
where abundance lies	*Son* 1	7
where all thy beauty lies	" 2	5
your true image pictured lies	" 24	6
their pride lies buried	" 25	7
that hidden in thee lie	" 31	8
that thou in him dost lie	" 46	5
thy fair appearance lies	" 46	8
My grief lies onward	" 50	14
from Time's chest lie hid	" 65	10
on the ashes of his youth doth lie	" 73	10
When you entombed in men's eyes shall lie	" 81	8
my life on thy revolt doth lie	" 92	10
for't lies in thee	" 101	10
which in thy breast doth lie	" 109	4
see where it lies	" 137	3
Therefore I lie with her	" 138	13
the bath for my help lies	" 153	13
what a hell of witchcraft lies	*L C*	288
Therefore I'll lie with love	*P P* 1	13
lie wither'd on the ground	" 13	9
Here enclosed in cinders lie	*P T*	55
Lie, n.—Lust full of forged lies	*V A*	804
devise some virtuous lie	*Son* 72	5
by lies we flatter'd be	" 138	14
give the lie to my true sight	" 150	3
against the truth so foul a lie	" 152	14
thou register of lies	*L C*	52
Lie, v.—would say this poet lies	*Son* 17	7
Those lines that I before have writ do lie	" 115	1
For thy records and what we see doth lie	" 123	11
though I know she lies	" 138	2
though I know she lies	*P P* 1	2
Life—ending with thy life	*V A*	12
life were done	"	197
would surpass the life	"	289
it is a life in death	"	413
breatheth life in her	"	474
or life desire	"	496
and life was death's annoy	"	497
reaves his son of life	"	766
with life's strength doth fight	*R L*	124
is but to nurse the life	"	141
As life for honour	"	145
to betray my life	"	233
Must sell her joy, her life	"	385
Showing life's triumph	"	402
death's dim look in life's mortality	"	403
Life—But that life lived in death and death in life	*R L*	406
with thy life's decay	"	516
Thou their fair life	"	661
lost a dearer thing than life	"	687
The life of purity	"	780
Or kills his life	"	875
to end a hapless life	"	1045
A dying life to living infamy	"	1055
Till life to death acquit	"	1071
When life is shamed	"	1155
to deprive dishonour'd life	"	1186
My life's foul deed, my life's fair end shall free it	"	1207
Besides, the life and feeling	"	1317
Of spirit, life, and bold audacity	"	1346
art gave lifeless life	"	1374
Show'd life imprison'd	"	1456
one man's lust these many lives confounds	"	1489
Life's lasting date	"	1729
That life was mine	"	1752
I did give that life	"	1800
who holding Lucrece' life	"	1805
consumest thyself in single life	*Son* 9	2
the lines of life that life repair	" 16	9
Which hides your life	" 17	4
this gives life to thee	" 18	14
Though in our lives	" 36	6
My life, being made of four, with two alone	" 45	7
Until life's composition	" 45	9
though my lover's life	" 63	12
To live a second life	" 68	7
Even with my life decay	" 71	12
My life hath in this line	" 74	3
lost the dregs of life	" 74	9
you are to my thoughts as food to life	" 75	1
immortal life shall have	" 81	5
others would give life	" 83	12
lives more life in one	" 83	13
For term of life	" 92	2
And life no longer	" 92	3
my life hath end	" 92	6
my life on thy revolt doth lie	" 92	10
than Time wastes life	" 100	13
better for my life provide	" 111	3
And saved my life	" 145	14
vow'd chaste life to keep	" 154	3
gave life and grace	*L C*	114
Lifeless—Fie, lifeless picture	*V A*	211
art gave lifeless life	*R L*	1374
Life-poisoning—Life-poisoning pestilence	*V A*	740
Lifts—She lifts the coffer-lids	"	1127
Lifts up his burning head	*Son* 7	2
Light, n.—the crystal tears gave	*V A*	491
that shadow heaven's light	"	533
lend the world his light	"	756
their light blown out	"	826
patron of all light	"	860
May lend thee light	"	864
office and their light	"	1039
threw unwilling light	"	1051
were open'd to the light	*R L*	105
No comfortable star did lend his light	"	164
Fair torch, burn out thy light	"	190

LIGHT 169 LIKE

Light, n.—To darken her whose light	R L	191
Mine eyes forego their light	"	228
by the light he spies	"	316
blinded with a greater light	"	375
had sheathed their light	"	397
eyes fly from their lights	"	461
Small lights are soon blown out	"	647
sets his foot upon the light	"	673
For light and lust	"	674
looks for the morning light	"	745
to meet the eastern light	"	773
in their smoky ranks his smother'd light	"	783
The light will show	"	807
and bring truth to light	"	940
Lends light to all fair eyes that light will borrow	"	1083
with thy piercing light	"	1091
ocean quench their light	"	1231
gleam'd forth their ashy lights.	"	1378
creature, with a flaming light	"	1627
Feed'st thy light's flame	Son 1	6
when the gracious light	" 7	1
dost give invention light	" 38	8
with thy much clearer light	" 43	7
once in the main of light	" 60	5
to lend base subjects light	" 100	4
Light, v.—Torches are made to light	V A	163
Let sin, alone committed, light alone	R L	1480
Light, adj.—but light and will aspire	V A	150
Is love so light, sweet boy	"	155
to every light impression	"	566
treads on it so light	"	1028
should yet be light	"	1134
in her light chariot	"	1192
That through their light joy seemed to appear	R L	1434
And every light occasion	L C	86
Light, adv.—When thou shalt be disposed to set me light	Son 88	1
Lighted—And being lighted	R L	316
Lighteth—torch forthwith he	"	178
Lightless—bears the lightless fire	"	4
steal effects from lightless hell	"	1555
Lightning—as .... from the sky	V A	348
Thine eye Jove's lightning seems	P P 5	11
Like—like a bold-faced suitor	V A	6
Like a dive-dapper	"	86
Or, like a fairy, trip	"	146
Or, like a nymph	"	147
flowers like sturdy trees	"	152
So he were like him	"	180
Like misty vapours	"	184
Thing like a man	"	214
like a band	"	225
like heaven's thunder	"	268
glisters like fire	"	275
wave like feather'd wings	"	306
Then, like a melancholy	"	313
that, like a falling plume	"	314
like a lowly lover	"	370
Show'd like two silver doves	"	366
How like a jade he stood	"	391
aim at like delight	"	400
Like a red morn	"	453
Like the deadly bullet	"	461
Like the fair sun	"	483
Like—Shone like the moon	V A	492
Like a wild bird	"	560
like the froward infant	"	562
like a pale-faced coward	"	569
Like lawn being spread	"	590
Like to a mortal butcher	"	618
eyes, like glow-worms	"	621
But, like an earthquake	"	648
An image like thyself	"	664
like a labyrinth	"	684
like the wanton mermaid's	"	777
Love comforteth like sunshine	"	799
Lust like a glutton dies	"	803
In such-like circumstance, with such-like sport	"	844
Like shrill-tongued tapsters	"	849
Like a milch doe	"	875
like one that spies	"	878
Like soldiers, when their captain	"	893
Like milk and blood	"	902
Like the proceedings	"	910
like sluices, stopp'd	"	956
But like a stormy day	"	963
Like many clouds	"	972
like pearls in glass	"	980
Like stars ashamed	"	1032
Who, like a king	"	1043
lurk'd like two thieves	"	1086
been tooth'd like him	"	1117
melted like a vapour	"	1166
shows like a virtuous deed	R L	252
Like little frosts	"	331
Where, like a virtuous monument	"	391
Show'd like an April daisy	"	395
Her eyes, like marigolds	"	397
Her hair, like golden threads	"	400
Her breasts, like ivory globes	"	407
Who, like a foul usurper	"	412
like straggling slaves	"	428
Like to a new-kill'd bird	"	457
First, like a trumpet	"	470
Which, like a falcon	"	506
Like a white hind	"	543
look'st not like deceit	"	585
My sighs, like whirlwinds	"	586
like a troubled ocean	"	589
For kings, like gods	"	602
the like offences prove	"	613
Till, like a jade	"	707
Like to a bankrupt	"	711
He like a thievish dog	"	736
She like a wearied lamb	"	737
like water that doth eat	"	755
But like still pining Tantalus	"	858
But if the like the snow-white swan desire		1011
mine eyes, like sluices	"	1076
Like an unpractised swimmer	"	1098
When with like semblance	"	1113
like a gentle flood	"	1118
moisten'd like a melting eye	"	1227
weep like the dewy night	"	1232
Like ivory conduits	"	1234
like a goodly champaign plain	"	1247
Much like a press of people	"	1301
Like dying coals burnt out	"	1379
Like bright things stain'd	"	1435
like a heavy-hanging bell	"	1493
like a constant and confirmed devil	"	1513

LIKE 170 LIP

Entry	Work	Act/Scene	Line
Like—Whose words, like wildfire	R L	....	1523
like rainbows in the sky	"	....	1587
stood, like old acquaintance	"	....	1595
Who, like a late-sack'd city	"	....	1740
Like feeble age	Son	7	10
like a makeless wife	"	9	4
Be scorn'd like old men	"	17	10
Which, like a jewel	"	27	11
Wishing me like to one	"	29	5
Featured like him, like him with friends possess'd	"	29	6
Like to the lark	"	29	11
Like stones of worth	"	52	7
interim like the ocean be	"	56	9
But like a sad slave	"	57	11
Like as the waves make towards shadows like to thee	"	60	1
	"	61	4
And, like unletter'd clerk	"	85	6
like enough thou know'st	"	87	2
Like a deceived husband	"	93	2
How like Eve's apple	"	93	13
Which, like a canker	"	95	2
If like a lamb	"	96	10
How like a winter	"	97	1
Like widow'd wombs	"	97	8
Therefore, like her, I sometime	"	102	13
like a dial-hand	"	104	9
but yet, like prayers divine	"	108	5
Like him that travels	"	109	6
like the dyer's hand	"	111	7
Whilst, like a willing patient	"	111	9
Like as to make our appetites	"	118	1
are nothing like the sun	"	130	1
And suit thy pity like in every part	"	132	12
He learn'd but surety-like to write	"	134	7
Which like two spirits	"	144	2
who, like a fiend	"	145	11
Like usury, applying wet to wet	L C	....	40
Like unshorn velvet	"	....	94
Like fools that in the imagination set	"	....	136
Which, like a cherubin	"	....	319
That like two spirits	P P	2	2
to me like oaks, to thee like osiers	"	5	4
Like a green plum	"	10	5
should use like loving charms	"	11	8
Youth like summer morn, age like winter weather	"	12	3
Youth like summer brave, age like winter bare	"	12	4
for shadows like myself	"	14	11
were tuned like the lark	"	15	6
Like a thousand vanquish'd men	"	18	36
Thy like ne'er was	"	18	50
Even so, poor bird, like thee	"	21	27
Words are easy, like the wind	"	21	33
Like—like you worse and worse	V A	....	774
Distress likes dumps	R L	....	1127
Let them say more that like of hearsay well	Son	21	13
But you like none, none you, for constant heart	"	53	14
Liked—That liked of her master	P P	16	2
Likely—In likely thoughts	V A	....	990
Likeness—In that thy likeness	"	....	174
In Tarquin's likeness	R L	....	596
the likeness of a man	Son	141	11
Liker—Much liker than your painted counterfeit	"	16	8
Likewise—May .... be sepulchred	R L	....	805
their passions likewise lent me	L C	....	199
Liking—to swallow Venus' liking	V A	....	248
bids them do their liking	R L	....	434
yoke thy liking to my will	"	....	1633
Lily—locks her lily fingers	V A	....	228
A lily prison'd	"	....	362
whose wonted lily white	"	....	1053
of lilies and of roses	R L	....	71
Her lily hand her rosy cheek lies under	"	....	386
anger makes the lily pale	"	....	478
Lilies that fester, smell far worse	Son	94	14
wonder at the lily's white	"	98	9
The lily I condemned	"	99	6
A lily pale, with damask dye	P P	7	5
Limb—each several limb is doubled	V A	....	1067
limbs with travel tired	Son	27	2
Lo, thus by day, my limbs	"	27	13
Limbeck—Distill'd from limbecks	"	119	2
Limed—Birds never limed no secret bushes fear	R L	....	88
Limit—Within this limit	V A	....	235
nor law, nor limit knows	R L	....	1120
From limits far remote	Son	44	4
a limit past my praise	"	82	6
Limning—In limning out	V A	....	290
Limping—by limping sway disabled	Son	66	8
Line—to attend each line	R L	....	813
So should the lines of life	Son	16	9
When in eternal lines to time thou grow'st	"	18	12
Nor draw no lines there	"	19	10
These poor rude lines	"	32	4
With lines and wrinkles	"	63	4
in these black lines be seen	"	63	13
Nay, if you read this line	"	71	5
My life hath in this line	"	74	3
your countenance fill'd up his line	"	86	13
Dulling my lines	"	103	8
Those lines that I before have writ	"	115	1
in top of rage the lines she rents	L C	....	55
Linen—the nightly linen that she wears	R L	....	680
Linger—To linger out a purposed overthrow	Son	90	8
Lingering—Who, with a .... stay	R L	....	328
Lion—on the lion he will venture	V A	....	628
rough bear, or lion proud	"	....	884
the lion walk'd along	"	....	1093
As the grim lion fawneth	R L	....	421
the unicorn and lion wild	"	....	956
Time, blunt thou the lion's paws	Son	19	1
Lip—lips with loathed satiety	V A	....	19
but soon she stops his lips	"	....	46
thy lips shall never open	"	....	48
her lips were ready	"	....	89
turns his lips another way	"	....	90
Touch but my lips with those fair lips of thine	"	....	115
why not lips on lips	"	....	120
upon thy tempting lip	"	....	127
thy lips the worse for one poor kiss	"	....	207
Graze on my lips	"	....	233
He chafes her lips	"	....	477
for thy piteous lips	"	....	504
Pure lips, sweet seals in my soft lips imprinted	"	....	511
on my wax-red lips	"	....	516

Lip—thirsty lips well knew	V A	....	543
their lips together glued	"	....	546
Her lips are conquerors, his lips obey	"	....	549
his lips' rich treasure	"	....	552
nectar from his lips	"	....	572
sweet lips and crystal eyne	"	....	633
so do thy lips	"	....	724
looks upon his lips	"	....	1123
Her coral lips	R L	....	420
In her lips' sweet fold	"	....	679
through her lips, so vanisheth	"	....	1041
and from his lips did fly	"	....	1406
From lips new-waxen pale	"	....	1663
through his lips do throng	"	....	1783
Of hand, of foot, of lip	Son	106	6
though rosy lips and cheeks	"	116	9
Whilst my poor lips	"	128	7
more blest than living lips	"	128	12
me thy lips to kiss	"	128	14
more red than her lips' red•	"	130	2
not from those lips of thine	"	142	5
Those lips that love's own hand did make	"	145	1
Upon his lips their silken parcels hurls	L C	....	87
Her lips to mine	P P	7	7
he seized on my lips	"	11	9
And with her lips on his	"	11	10
Liquid—A liquid prisoner pent in walls of glass	Son	5	10
List—where I list to sport me	V A	....	154
in the very lists of love	"	....	595
hide them when they list	R L	....	1008
lie where you list	Son	58	9
to list the sad-tuned tale	L C	....	4
Listening—with listening ear	V A	....	698
with open listening ear	R L	....	283
All jointly listening	"	....	1410
listening Priam wets his eyes	"	....	1548
Listeth—not all she listeth	V A	....	561
Little—themselves in little time	"	....	132
thence doth little harm	"	....	195
hear a little more	"	....	709
And then my little heart	"	....	783
For every little grief	"	....	1179
Little suspecteth the false worshipper	R L	....	86
through little vents and crannies	"	....	310
Like little frosts	"	....	331
A little harm done	"	....	528
huge stones with little water-drops	"	....	959
But little stars may hide	"	....	1004
The little birds that tune	"	....	1107
the little worms that creep	"	....	1248
each little mote will peep	"	....	1251
a little while doth stay	"	....	1364
the Greeks with little lust	"	....	1384
Then little strength rings out	"	....	1495
And little stars shot	"	....	1525
but a little moment	Son	15	2
The little Love-god	"	154	1
on his visage was in little drawn	L C	....	90
Live—That thine may live	V A	....	172
which lives by subtlety	"	....	675
There lives a son	"	....	863
Adonis lives, and Death	"	....	992
lives and must not die	"	....	1017
That it will live engraven	R L	....	203

Live—that doth live by slaughter	R L	....	955
Let him have time to live	"	....	984
one that by alms doth live	"	....	986
my honour lives in thee	"	....	1052
But if I live thou livest in my defame	"	....	1033
I live, and seek in vain	"	....	1044
for which I sought to live	"	....	1051
To live or die, which of the twain	"	....	1154
The one will live	"	....	1187
fame that lives disbursed be	"	....	1203
To those that live	"	....	1204
I should not live to speak	"	....	1612
Where shall I live	"	....	1754
live, sweet Lucrece, live again	"	....	1770
And live to be revenged	"	....	1778
But if thou live	Son	3	13
yet canst not live	"	4	8
lives th' executor to be	"	4	14
their substance still lives sweet	"	5	11
may live in thine or thee	"	10	14
Herein lives wisdom	"	11	5
you yourself here live	"	13	2
Can make you live	"	16	12
And you must live	"	16	14
You should live twice	"	17	14
So long lives this	"	18	14
My love shall in my verse ever live young	"	19	14
in thy breast doth live	"	22	7
where buried love doth live	"	31	9
canker lives in sweetest bud	"	35	4
of all thy glory live	"	37	12
let us divided live	"	39	6
which doth in it live	"	54	4
They live unwoo'd	"	54	10
You live in this	"	55	14
And they shall live	"	63	14
with infection should he live	"	67	1
Why should he live	"	67	9
lives upon his gains	"	67	12
To live a second life	"	68	7
And live no more	"	72	12
what in thee doth live	"	79	12
Or I shall live	"	81	1
You still shall live	"	81	13
There lives more life	"	83	13
So shall I live	"	93	1
For there can live	"	93	5
it only live and die	"	94	10
I'll live in this poor rhyme	"	107	11
if not lives in disgrace	"	127	8
but live in doubt	"	144	13
live thou upon thy servant's loss	"	146	9
I shall not know, but live in doubt	P P	2	13
Where all those pleasures live	"	5	6
age and youth cannot live together	"	12	1
Must live alone	"	18	53
Live with me and be my love	"	20	1
Then live with me and be my love	"	20	16
To live with thee and be thy love	"	20	20
Lived—there Love lived	V A	....	246
But now I lived	"	....	497
Who when he lived	"	....	935
lived and died with him	"	....	1080
But when Adonis lived	"	....	1083
life lived in death	R L	....	406
that lived by foul devouring	"	....	700
burn the long-lived phœnix	Son	19	4

Lived—When beauty lived and died	Son	68	2
What merit lived in me	"	72	2
have often lived alone	"	105	13
who have lived for crime	"	124	14
Livelihood—The precedent of pith and livelihood	V A		26
Lively—death was lively joy	"		498
Her lively colour kill'd	R L		1393
to blush through lively veins	Son	67	10
A dateless lively heat	"	153	6
For her griefs so lively shone	P P	21	17
Liver—which in his liver glows	R L		47
Livery—never let their crimson liveries wear	V A		506
livery that he wore	"		1107
A badge of fame to slander's livery	R L		1054
her face wore sorrow's livery	"		1222
Thy youth's proud livery	Son	2	3
Kept hearts in liveries	L C		195
Livery—Did livery falseness	"		105
Livest—thou livest in my defame	R L		1033
Living—As if the dead the living should exceed	V A		292
thy death my living sorrow	"		671
against long-living laud	R L		622
living death and pain perpetual	"		726
A dying life to living infamy	"		1055
no dame hereafter living	"		1714
Leaving thee living	Son	6	12
would bear your living flowers	"	16	7
looking on thee in the living day	"	43	10
The living record of your memory	"	55	8
steal dead seeing of his living hue	"	67	6
inhabit on a living brow	"	68	4
more blest than living lips	"	128	12
To spend her living	L C		238
Living in thrall	P P	18	22
Lo—And, lo, I lie between	V A		194
But, lo, from forth a copse	"		259
Lo, thus my strength is tried	"		280
When, lo, the unback'd	"		320
Lo, here the gentle lark	"		853
Where, lo, two lamps	"		1128
lo, here I prophesy	"		1135
Lo, in this hollow cradle	"		1185
lo, there falls into thy boundless flood	R L		653
when, lo, the blushing morrow	"		1082
Lo, here weeps Hecuba	"		1485
Lo, here the hopeless merchant	"		1660
Lo, in the orient	Son	7	1
Lo, thus by day my limbs	"	27	13
Lo, as a careful housewife	"	143	1
And, lo, behold these talents	L C		204
Lo, all these trophies	"		218
Lo, this device was sent me	"		232
For, lo, his passion	"		295
Load—I had my load before	V A		430
She bears the load of lust	R L		734
This load of wrath	"		1474
Loan—those that pay the willing loan	Son	6	6
Loathed—with loathed satiety	V A		19
Thou loathed in their shame	R L		662
his vanish'd loathed delight	"		742
turn to loathed sours	"		867
to live a loathed slave	"		984
Loathsome—keep his .... cabin still	V A		637
of his loathsome enterprise	R L		184
Loathsome—Some loathsome oath the herald will contrive	R L		206
write my loathsome trespass	"		812
The loathsome act of lust	"		1636
And loathsome canker lives	Son	35	4
Lock—under twenty locks	V A		575
Play with his locks	"		1090
The locks between her chamber	R L		302
His browny locks did hang	L C		85
Lock—locks her lily fingers	V A		228
bid Suspicion double-lock the door	"		448
Locked—in my hand being lock'd	R L		260
breaks ope her lock'd-up eyes	"		446
lock'd up in any chest	Son	48	9
his sweet up-locked treasure	"	52	2
Lode-star—.... to his lustful eye	R L		179
Lodged—lodged not a mind so ill	"		1530
be fairer lodged than gentle love	Son	10	10
She was new lodged	L C		84
Lofty—hark peel'd from the lofty pine	R L		1167
When lofty trees I see	Son	12	5
sometime lofty towers I see	"	64	3
Long—one long as twenty	V A		22
Which long have rain'd	"		83
with long dishevell'd hair	"		147
fetlocks shag and long	"		295
Long may they kiss	"		505
lovers' hours are long	"		842
they long have gazed	"		927
Long after fearing to creep forth	"		1036
Of things long since, or	"		1078
after supper long he questioned	R L		122
To hold their cursed-blessed fortune long	"		866
But long she thinks	"		1359
quench Troy that burns so long	"		1468
too long with her remaining	"		1572
Short time seems long	"		1573
would be drawn out too long	"		1616
from heart-easing words so long	"		1782
So long as men can breathe	Son	18	13
So long lives this	"	18	14
So long as youth and thou	"	22	2
weep afresh love's long-since-cancell'd woe	"	30	7
to outlive long date	"	38	12
In the long year set	"	52	6
In days long since	"	67	14
thou must leave ere long	"	73	14
that thou forget'st so long	"	100	1
make him seem long hence	"	101	14
so long as brain and heart	"	122	5
Ere long espied a fickle maid	L C		5
And long upon these terms	"		176
methinks thou stay'st too long	P P	12	12
Long was the combat doubtful	"	16	5
my tongue to be so long	"	19	52
Long—my heart longs much to groan	V A		785
and then she longs for morrow	R L		1571
long to hear her words	"		1610
Longer—no longer to restrain him	V A		579
cease then thy course and last no longer	R L		1765
No longer yours than you yourself live here	Son	13	2
draw my sorrows longer	"	28	13
but then no longer glad	"	45	13
No longer mourn for me	"	71	1

LONGER 173 LOSE

Longer—And life no longer than thy love	Son	92	3
longer nurseth the disease	"	147	2
Long-experienced — set thy long-experienced wit to school	R L	....	1820
Long-hid—his .... wits advisedly	"	....	1816
Longing—Longing to hear the hateful foe	"	....	1698
as a fever longing still	Son	147	1
A longing tarriance for Adonis	P P	6	4
Long-lived—burn the .... phœnix	Son	19	4
Long-living—reproach against long-living land	R L	....	622
Look—Look, how a bird lies	V A	....	67
Look how he can, she cannot choose	"	....	79
Look in mine eyeballs	"	....	119
Look, when a painter	"	....	289
Look, what a horse should have	"	....	299
He looks upon his love	"	....	307
Looks on the dull earth	"	....	340
Look, the world's comforter	"	....	529
and look well to her heart	"	....	580
Look, how a bright star	"	....	815
Look, how the world's poor people	"	....	925
looks so steadfastly	"	....	1063
looks upon his lips	"	....	1123
That eye which looks on her	R L	....	290
Look, as the fair and fiery-pointed sun	"	....	372
She dares not look	"	....	458
And dotes on what he looks	"	....	497
eyes do learn, do read, do look	"	....	616
Look, as the full-fed hound	"	....	694
looks for the morning light	"	....	745
look to her lady's sorrow	"	....	1221
those far-off eyes look sad	"	....	1386
Look, look, how listening Priam	"	....	1548
She looks for night	"	....	1571
Look in thy glass	Son	3	1
and look another way	"	7	12
Look, what an unthrift	"	9	9
Look, whom she best endow'd	"	11	11
Then look I death	"	22	4
and look for recompense	"	23	11
And look upon myself	"	29	4
Look, what is best	"	37	13
in dreams they look on thee	"	43	3
The rose looks fair	"	54	3
They look into the beauty	"	69	9
you look upon this verse	"	71	9
should look into your moan	"	71	13
Look, what thy memory	"	77	9
so oft as thou wilt look	"	77	13
strangle and look strange	"	89	8
That leaves look pale	"	97	14
Look in your glass	"	103	6
Your own glass shows you when you look in it	"	103	14
My love looks fresh	"	107	10
That looks on tempests	"	116	6
says beauty should look so	"	127	14
Look here, what tributes	L C	....	197
she hotter that did look	P P	6	7
Look—O, what a war of looks	V A	....	355
For one sweet look	"	....	371
And at his look	"	....	463
looks kill love, and love by looks reviveth	"	....	464
with looks again	"	....	1042

Look—no meaning from their parting looks	R L	....	106
And death's dim look	"	....	403
my loathsome trespass in my looks	"	....	812
with bold stern looks	"	....	1252
Pawn'd honest looks	"	....	1351
and she their looks doth borrow	"	....	1498
piteous looks to Phrygian shepherds lent	"	....	1502
calm looks, eyes wailing still	"	....	1508
can lurk in such a look	"	....	1535
Serving with looks	Son	7	4
Yet mortal looks	"	7	7
is famish'd for a look	"	47	3
with a backward look	"	59	5
clean starved for a look	"	75	10
Thy looks with me	"	93	4
In many's looks the false heart's history	"	93	7
Thy looks should nothing	"	93	12
could his looks translate	"	96	10
by over-partial looks	"	137	5
pretty looks have been mine enemies	"	139	10
Kill me outright with looks	"	139	14
with many a lovely look	P P	4	3
Such looks as none could look	"	4	4
Her cloudy looks will calm	"	19	14
Look'd—who, being look'd on	V A	....	87
look'd red and raw	R L	....	1592
And some look'd black	"	....	1743
look'd but with divining eyes	Son	106	11
that I have look'd on truth	"	110	5
The sun look'd on the world	P P	6	11
Look'st—Thou ... not like deceit	R L	....	585
Looketh—still looketh for a grave	V A	....	1106
Looking—Then looking scornfully	R L	....	187
Looking on darkness	Son	27	8
By looking on thee	"	43	10
Looking with pretty ruth	"	132	4
Till looking on an Englishman	P P	16	3
Loop-hole—through .... thrust	R L	....	1383
Loose—nor loose nor tied in formal plat	L C	....	29
braided in loose negligence	"	....	35
Lord—this false lord arrived	R L	....	50
And now this lustful lord	"	....	169
The Roman lord marcheth	"	....	301
Save of their lord	"	....	409
this faultful lord of Rome	"	....	715
Dear lord of that dear jewel	"	....	1191
those proud lords to blame	"	....	1259
A letter to my lord	"	....	1293
she thus begins: 'Thou worthy lord	"	....	1303
At Ardea to my lord	"	....	1332
Brings home his lord	"	....	1584
Collatine and his consorted lords	"	....	1609
Dear lord, thy sorrow	"	....	1676
ere I name him, you fair lords	"	....	1688
Each present lord began	"	....	1696
He, he, fair lords, 'tis he	"	....	1721
Thou wronged lord of Rome	"	....	1818
Lord of my love	Son	26	1
They are the lords	"	94	7
after their lord's decease	"	97	8
Lord, how mine eyes	P P	15	1
Lording—It was a lording's daughter	"	16	1
Lordly—and all his lordly crew	R L	....	1731
Lose—Having no fair to lose	V A	....	1083

Lose—what he would lose again	R L	688	Love—Why, there Love lived	V A	246
to him lose their mildness	"	979	Poor queen of love	"	251
They that lose half	"	1158	He sees his love	"	287
Nor lose possession of that fair	Son	18 10	He looks upon his love	"	307
lose name of single one	"	39 6	Spurns at his love	"	311
If I lose thee	"	42 9	His love, perceiving	"	317
and I lose both twain	"	42 11	Love-sick Love by pleading	"	328
which it fears to lose	"	64 14	love's fire doth assuage	"	334
knife ill used doth lose his edge	"	97 14	love's deep groans	"	377
lose their dear delight	"	102 12	But when he saw his love	"	393
Lose all and more	"	125 6	Who sees his true-love	"	397
So him I lose	"	134 12	'I know not love	"	409
Loseth—Loseth his pride	V A	420	My love to love is love but to disgrace it	"	412
Losing—Losing her woes in shows	R L	1580			
And losing her, my friend	Son	42 10	To love's alarms	"	424
That thou in losing me	"	88 8	should I be in love	"	438
Still losing when I saw myself	"	119 4	Yet would my love	"	442
Loss—for loss of Nestor's golden words	R L	1420	that breedeth love	"	444
			For looks kill love, and love by looks reviveth	"	464
the hopeless merchant of this loss	"	1660			
All losses are restored	Son	30 14	that by love so thriveth	"	466
yet I have still the loss	"	34 10	love did wittily prevent	"	471
A loss in love	"	42 4	If any love you owe me	"	523
my loss is my love's gain	"	42 9	Chiefly in love	"	568
my friend hath found that loss	"	42 10	Yet love breaks through	"	576
store with loss, loss with store	"	64 8	Tell me, love's master	"	585
drop in for an after-loss	"	90 4	the very lists of love	"	595
Compared with loss of thee	"	90 14	She's Love, she loves	"	610
live thou upon thy servant's loss	"	146 9	To which Love's eyes	"	632
the loss thereof still fearing	P P	7 10	For where Love reigns	"	649
Wrought all my loss	"	18 14	Distempering gentle Love	"	653
Lost—perfect, never lost again	V A	408	eats up Love's tender spring	"	656
lost the fair discovery	"	828	For love can comment	"	714
had lost his power	"	944	in love with thee	"	722
what treasure hast thou lost	"	1075	If love have lent you	"	775
Their virtue lost	"	1131	I hate not love, but your device in love	"	789
and all together lost	R L	147			
lost a dearer thing than life	"	687	Call it not love, for Love	"	793
captive victor that hath lost in gain	"	730	Love comforteth like sunshine	"	799
My honey lost, and I	"	836	Love's gentle spring	"	801
that dear jewel I have lost	"	1191	Love surfeits not	"	803
but lost the dregs of life	Son	74 9	Love is all truth	"	804
And the just pleasure lost	"	121 3	Leaves Love upon her back	"	814
Him have I lost	"	134 13	How love makes young	"	837
my honest faith in thee is lost	"	152 8	How love is wise	"	838
Lost, vaded, broken, dead	P P	13 6	tidings of her love	"	867
And as goods lost	"	13 7	Hateful divorce of love	"	932
once 's for ever lost	"	13 11	Love's golden arrow	"	947
All my lady's love is lost	"	18 10	love, how strange it seems	"	985
All our love is lost	"	18 48	fearing my love's decease	"	1002
Lot—bequeath not to their lot	R L	534	Fie, fie, fond love	"	1021
Loud—To stop the loud pursuers	V A	688	Sorrow on love	"	1136
Anon their loud alarums	"	700	all love's pleasure	"	1140
and my loud crying still	Son	143 14	doth my love destroy	"	1163
Loudest—Let the bird of loudest lay	P T	1	They that love best their loves shall not	"	1164
Lour—still he lours and frets	V A	75			
Lour'st—Nay, if thou lour'st on me	Son	149 7	kiss my sweet love's flower	"	1188
Louring—His louring brows	V A	183	Of Collatine's fair love	R L	7
Love—but love he laugh'd to scorn	"	4	love's modest snow-white weed	"	196
O, how quick is love	"	38	I'll beg her love; but she	"	241
Love keeps his revels	"	123	Self-love had never drown'd him	"	266
Love is a spirit	"	149	Love thrives not in the heart	"	270
Is love so light, sweet boy	"	155	Then Love and Fortune	"	351
seize love upon thy left	"	158	Against love's fire fear's frost	"	355
cries 'Fie, no more of love	"	185	untimely tears, her husband's love	"	570
What 'tis to love? how want of love tormenteth	"	202	still are fear'd for love	"	611
			Yield to my love	"	668
Being judge in love	"	220	Instead of love's coy touch	"	669
Love made those hollows	"	243	For Collatine's dear love	"	821

Love—Whose love of either	R L	.....	1165
My resolution, love, shall be thy boast	"	.....	1193
my lord, my love, my dear	"	.....	1293
If ever, love, thy Lucrece	"	.....	1366
Sweet love, what spite	"	.....	1690
And entertain my love	"	.....	1629
If thou my love's desire do contradict	"	.....	1631
Of his self-love, to stop posterity	Son	3	8
No love toward others	"	9	13
thou bear'st love to any	"	10	1
fairer lodged than gentle love	"	10	10
for love of me	"	10	13
but, love, you are	"	13	1
dear my love, you know	"	13	13
Time for love of thus	"	15	13
carve not with thy hours my love's fair brow	"	19	9
My love shall in my verse ever live young	"	19	14
Mine be thy love and thy love's use	"	20	14
O, let me, true in love	"	21	9
my love is as fair	"	21	10
O, therefore, love, be of thyself	"	22	9
ceremony of love's rite	"	23	6
mine own love's strength	"	23	7
of mine own love's might	"	23	8
Who plead for love	"	23	11
what silent love hath writ	"	23	13
belongs to love's fine wit	"	23	14
Lord of my love	"	26	1
For thy sweet love remember'd	"	29	13
love's long-since-cancell'd woe	"	30	7
And there reigns love and all love's loving parts	"	31	3
Hath dear religious love stol'n	"	31	6
buried love doth live	"	31	9
Reserve them for my love	"	32	7
this his love had brought	"	32	11
I'll read, his for his love	"	32	14
my love no whit disdaineth	"	33	13
which thy love sheds	"	34	13
Is in my love and hate	"	35	12
undivided loves are one	"	36	2
In our two loves	"	36	5
alter not love's sole effect	"	36	7
hours from love's delight	"	36	8
my love engrafted to this store	"	37	8
And our dear love	"	39	6
with thoughts of love	"	39	11
Take all my loves, my love, yea, take them all	"	40	1
No love, my love, that thou mayst true love call	"	40	3
If for my love thou my love receivest	"	40	5
my love thou usest	"	40	6
And yet, love knows	"	40	11
To bear love's wrong	"	40	12
A loss in love	"	42	4
my loss is my love's gain	"	42	9
embassy of love to thee	"	45	6
thine inward love of heart	"	46	14
Or heart in love	"	47	4
With my love's picture	"	47	5
thoughts of love doth share	"	47	8
thy picture or my love	"	47	9
When as thy love hath cast	"	49	3
Love—When love, converted	Son	49	7
Thus can my love	"	51	1
of perfect'st love being made	"	51	10
But love, for love, thus shall excuse	"	51	12
Sweet love, renew thy force	"	56	1
So, love, be thou	"	56	5
The spirit of love	"	56	8
Return of love	"	56	12
So true a fool is love	"	57	13
O, no! thy love	"	61	9
It is my love	"	61	10
sin of self-love possesseth all	"	62	1
Mine own self-love quite contrary	"	62	11
Against my love shall be	"	63	1
My sweet love's beauty	"	63	12
and take my love away	"	64	12
my love may still shine bright	"	65	14
I leave my love alone	"	66	14
But let your love	"	71	12
After my death, dear love	"	72	3
O, lest your true love	"	72	9
That you for love	"	72	10
makes thy love more strong	"	73	13
O, know, sweet love	"	76	9
and you and love	"	76	10
So is my love still telling	"	76	14
I grant, sweet love	"	79	5
my love was my decay	"	80	14
And do so, love; yet	"	82	9
whose love to you	"	85	11
Such is my love	"	88	13
Thou canst not, love, disgrace me	"	89	5
Thy love is better	"	91	9
than thy love will stay	"	92	3
upon that love of thine	"	92	4
Happy to have thy love	"	92	12
so love's face	"	93	2
May still seem love to me	"	93	3
in thy face sweet love should ever	"	93	10
If not from my love's breath	"	99	3
In my love's veins	"	99	5
my love's sweet face survey	"	100	9
Give my love fame faster	"	100	13
on my love depends	"	101	3
My love is strengthen'd	"	102	1
That love is merchandized	"	102	3
Our love was new	"	102	5
Let not my love	"	105	1
kind is my love to-day	"	105	5
of my true love control	"	107	3
My love looks fresh	"	107	10
That may express my love	"	108	4
So that eternal love in love's fresh case	"	108	9
conceit of love there bred	"	108	13
That is my home of love	"	109	5
proved thee my best of love	"	110	8
A god in love	"	110	12
Your love and pity	"	112	1
And that your love	"	114	4
Love is a babe	"	115	13
Love is not love	"	116	2
Love's not Time's fool	"	116	9
Love alters not with his brief hours	"	116	11
upon your dearest love	"	117	3
and virtue of your love	"	117	14
Thus policy in love	"	118	9
And ruin'd love when it is built anew	"	119	11

LOVE

Entry	Source	#	#
Love—thy dear love to score	Son	122	10
If my dear love	"	124	1
As subject to Time's love	"	124	3
I think my love as rare	"	130	13
to make love groan	"	131	6
Thus far for love	"	136	4
fulfil the treasure of thy love	"	136	5
Make but my name thy love, and love that still	"	136	13
Thou blind fool, Love	"	137	1
When my love swears	"	138	1
O, love's best habit	"	138	11
And age in love loves not to have years told	"	138	12
ah, my love well knows	"	139	9
Love is my sin	"	142	1
And seal'd false bonds of love	"	142	7
Two loves I have	"	144	1
that Love's own hand	"	145	1
My love is as a fever	"	147	1
the physician to my love	"	147	5
what eyes hath Love	"	148	1
then love doth well denote	"	148	7
Love's eye is not so true	"	148	8
O, how can Love's eye be true	"	148	9
O, cunning Love	"	148	13
But, love, hate on	"	149	13
raised love in me	"	150	13
Love is too young	"	151	1
conscience is born of love	"	151	2
Triumph in love	"	151	8
Her love for whose dear love	"	151	14
to me love swearing	"	152	2
after new love bearing	"	152	4
Oaths of thy love	"	152	10
this holy fire of love	"	153	5
Love's brand new-fired	"	153	9
Which from Love's fire	"	154	10
Love's fire heats water, water cools not	"	154	14
Love to myself and to no love beside	L C		77
Love lack'd a dwelling	"		82
For feasts of love	"		181
Love made them not	"		185
living in eternal love	"		238
Religious love put out Religion's eye	"		250
As compound love to physic	"		259
O most potential love	"		264
Love's arms are peace	"		271
When my love swears	P P	1	1
Out facing faults in love with love's ill rest	"	1	8
But wherefore says my love	"	1	9
O, love's best habit	"	1	11
And age in love loves not to have years told	"	1	12
Therefore I'll lie with love and love with me	"	1	13
in love thus smother'd be	"	1	14
Two loves I have	"	2	1
thou a heavenly love	"	3	7
If love make me forsworn, how shall I swear to love	"	5	1
all in love forlorn	"	6	3
Fair is my love	"	7	1
her oaths of true love swearing	"	7	8
Dreading my love	"	7	10
She burn'd with love	"	7	13
Love—She burn'd out love	P P	7	14
She framed the love	"	7	15
She bade love last	"	7	16
Then must the love be great	"	8	3
when the fair queen of love	"	9	1
with more than love's good will	"	9	7
O, my love, my love is young	"	12	10
that love with love did fight	"	16	5
Love, whose month was ever May	"	17	2
Turning mortal for thy love	"	17	18
Love's denying	"	18	5
All my lady's love is lost	"	18	10
was firmly fix'd in love	"	18	11
Love hath forlorn me	"	18	21
love is lost, for Love is dead	"	18	48
Live with me and be my love	"	20	1
Live with me and be my love	"	20	16
If that the world and love were young	"	20	17
To live with thee and be thy love	"	20	20
Love and constancy is dead	P T		22
Number there in love was slain	"		28
So between them love did shine	"		33
Love hath reason, reason none	"		47
Co-supremes and stars of love	"		51
Love—She loves him best	V A		77
she cannot choose but love	"		79
What 'tis to love? how want of love tormenteth	"		202
To love a cheek that smiles	"		252
O, learn to love	"		407
my ears would love	"		433
She's Love, she loves	"		610
That if I love thee	"		660
They that love best their loves shall not	"		1164
loves no stops nor rests	R L		1124
that love and am beloved	Son	25	13
how I do love thee	"	26	13
I love thee in such sort	"	36	13
Thou dost love her, because thou know'st I love her	"	42	6
then she loves but me alone	"	42	14
Since why to love I can allege	"	49	14
For canker vice the sweetest buds doth love	"	70	7
for I love you so	"	71	6
that you should love	"	72	2
to love things nothing worth	"	72	14
To love that well	"	73	14
For I must ne'er love him	"	89	14
I love thee in such sort	"	96	13
I love not less, though less the show appear	"	102	2
That mine eye loves it	"	114	14
I could not love you dearer	"	115	2
Now I love you best	"	115	10
I love to hear her speak	"	130	9
Thine eyes I love	"	132	1
Make but my name thy love, and love that still	"	136	13
And age in love loves not to have years told	"	138	12
not to love, yet, love, to tell	"	140	6
I do not love thee	"	141	1
my heart that loves what they despise	"	141	3
Be it lawful I love thee	"	142	9
say I love thee not	"	149	1

Love—				Loving—Loving offenders, thus I		
make me love thee more	Son	150	9	will	Son 42	5
I love what others do abhor	"	150	11	Self so self-loving were iniquity	" 62	12
And age in love loves not to have years told	P P	1	12	all my loving thoughts on me and most most loving breast	" 88 " 110	10 11
If love make me forsworn, how shall I swear to love	"	5	1	and loving mourners be grounded on sinful loving	" 132 " 142	3 2
O do not love that wrong	"	5	13	In loving thee thou know'st	" 152	1
One knight loves both	"	8	14	should use like loving charms	P P 11	8
So they lov'd, as love in twain	P T		25	Low—And being low never relieved		
Loved—Hunting he loved	V A		4	by any	V A	708
yet she is not loved	"	.....	610	Ne'er settled equally, but high or		
make thee only loved for fear	R L		610	low	"	1139
Their images I loved	Son	31	13	But low shrubs wither	R L	665
I loved her dearly	"	42	2	low vassals to thy state	"	666
His rider loved not speed	"	50	8	villain court'sies to her low	"	1338
are loved of more and less	"	96	3	Some high, some low	"	1412
nor no man ever loved	"	116	14	From his low tract	Son 7	12
So they loved, as love in twain	P T		25	both high and low	L C	21
Love-god—The little Love-god	Son	154	1	Low-declined—My .... honour	R L	1705
Love-kindling—his love-kindling fire	"	153	3	Lower—Stray lower, where the		
Love-lacking—Love-lacking vestals	V A	.....	752	pleasant fountains lie	V A	234
Loveless—To leave the master....	P P	16	6	Lowly—And like a lowly lover	"	350
Loveliness—Unthrifty loveliness, why dost thou spend	Son	4	1	Loyal—tremble with her loyal fear Since thou couldst not defend thy	R L	261
Lovely—more lovely than a man	V A	.....	9	loyal dame	"	1034
These lovely caves	"	.....	247	when I fear'd I was a loyal wife	"	1048
Calls back the lovely April	Son	3	10	And the turtle's loyal breast	P T	57
The lovely gaze where every eye	"	5	2	Luck—of good or evil luck	Son 14	3
Thou art more lovely	"	18	2	Lucrece—Lucrece the chaste	R L	7
beauteous and lovely youth	"	54	13	his boast of Lucrece' sovereignty	"	36
thy lovely argument	"	79	5	in Lucrece' face was seen	"	64
How sweet and lovely	"	95	1	with modest Lucrece	"	123
ladies dead and lovely knights	"	106	4	So Lucrece must I force	"	182
O thou, my lovely boy	"	126	1	marcheth to Lucrece' bed	"	301
lovely, fresh, and green	P P	4	2	by Lucrece' side	"	381
With many a lovely look	"	4	3	And holy-thoughted Lucrece	"	384
Lover—For lovers say, the heart	V A	.....	329	'Lucrece,' quoth he	"	512
And like a lowly lover	"	.....	350	But cloudy Lucrece	"	1084
must not repel a lover	"	.....	573	Poor Lucrece' cheeks	"	1217
For lovers' hours are long	"	.....	842	whereof in Lucrece view	"	1261
trophies of my lovers gone	Son	31	10	bid fair Lucrece speak	"	1268
rude lines of thy deceased lover	"	32	4	'O, peace!' quoth Lucrece	"	1284
and dwell in lovers' eyes	"	55	14	If ever, love, thy Lucrece	"	1306
though my lover's life	"	63	12	For Lucrece thought	"	1344
Thy lovers withering as thy sweet self grow'st	"	126	4	is Lucrece come Lucrece spends her eyes	" ..... "	1443 1457
Was this a lover	P P	7	17	And therefore Lucrece swears	"	1462
That the lover, sick to death	"	17	7	So Lucrece, set a-work	"	1496
Lover'd—would not be so lover'd	L C	.....	320	Who finds his Lucrece	"	1585
Love-sick—By this, the .... queen	V A	.....	175	thy Lucrece is not free	"	1621
That love-sick Love	"	.....	328	The adulterate death of Lucrece	"	1645
Lovest—Why lovest thou that	Son	8	3	For she that was thy Lucrece	"	1682
that thou none lovest	"	10	4	Till Lucrece' father	"	1732
And then thou lovest me	"	136	14	as pitying Lucrece' woes	"	1747
Tell me thou lovest elsewhere	"	139	5	now Lucrece is unlived	"	1754
as thou lovest those	"	142	9	Then live, sweet Lucrece	"	1770
Those that can see thou lovest	"	149	14	Lucrece' bleeding stream	"	1774
Because thou lovest the one	P P	8	4	holding Lucrece' life	"	1805
Thou lovest to hear	"	8	9	the knife from Lucrece' side	"	1807
plainly say thou lovest her well	"	19	11	Burying in Lucrece' wound	"	1810
Love-suit—my love-suit, sweet, fulfil	Son	136	4	And by chaste Lucrece' soul	"	1839
Loving—vestals and self-loving nuns	V A	.....	752	to bear dead Lucrece thence	"	1850
the loving swine	"	.....	1115	Lucretia—Lucretia's glove, wherein		
there is no hate in loving	R L	.....	240	her needle sticks	"	317
and tell my loving tale	"	.....	480	Lucretia, marking what he tells	"	510
apparel on my tatter'd loving	Son	26	11	Lucretius—dear daughter,' old Lu-		
and all love's loving parts	"	31	3	cretius cries	"	1751
vouchsafe me but this loving thought	"	32	9	bids Lucretius give his sorrow	"	1773

12

Lucretius—'O,' quoth Lucretius, 'I did give	R L	1800
Lullaby—Then, lullaby, the learned man	P P 16	15
Lung—that burning lungs did raise	L C	228
his spongy lungs bestow'd	"	326
Lure—As falcons to the lure	V A	1027
Lurk—lurk in mine eye	"	644
embers hid, lurks to aspire	R L	5
folly lurk in gentle breasts	"	851
can lurk in such a look	"	1535
'can lurk' from 'cannot' took	"	1537
tricks and toys that in them lurk	P P 19	39
Lark'd—lurk'd like two thieves	V A	1086
Lurking—Who sees the .... serpent	R L	362
Lust—though not in lust	V A	42
Careless lust stirs up	"	556
sweating Lust on earth	"	794
Lust's effect is tempest	"	800
Lust's winter comes ere summer	"	802
Lust like a glutton dies	"	803
Lust full of forged lies	"	804
to obtain his lust	R L	156
While lust and murder wakes	"	168
with lust's foul charm	"	173
armour of still-slaughter'd lust	"	188
choked by unresisted lust	"	282
Stuff up his lust	"	297
His rage of lust	"	424
Tears harden lust	"	560
school where Lust shall learn	"	617
Not to seducing lust	"	639
Black lust, dishonour, shame	"	654
light and lust are deadly enemies	"	674
O, that prone lust should stain	"	684
And Lust, the thief	"	693
While Lust is in his pride	"	705
She bears the load of lust	"	734
as knowing Tarquin's lust	"	1354
the Greeks with little lust	"	1384
Thy heat of lust, fond Paris	"	1473
And one man's lust	"	1489
The loathsome act of lust	"	1636
lust came evidence to swear	"	1650
Is lust in action; and till action lust	Son 129	2
Lust-breathed—Lust-breathed Tarquin leaves	R L	3
Lustful—with .... language broken	V A	47
And now this lustful lord	R L	169
lode-star to his lustful eye	"	179
Lustily—chant it lustily	V A	869
Lusty—lusty courser's rein	"	31
lusty, young, and proud	"	260
treasure of thy lusty days	Son 2	6
and lusty leaves quite gone	" 5	7
Lute—Upon the lute doth ravish	P P 8	6
Phœbus' lute, the queen of music	" 8	10
Luxury—in heart-wish'd luxury	L C	314
Lying—Love-god lying once asleep	Son 154	1
Mad—being mad before	V A	249
As they were mad	"	323
Of mad mischances	"	738
Her eyes are mad	"	1062
It shall be raging-mad	"	1151
let the thief run mad	R L	997
Sometime 'tis mad	"	1106
mad with their sweet melody	"	1108
Mad—Who, mad that sorrow should his use control	R L	1781
to make the taker mad	Son 129	8
Mad in pursuit, and in possession so	"	129 9
I should grow mad	"	140 9
Mad slanderers by mad ears believed he	"	140 12
frantic-mad with evermore unrest	"	147 10
Madam—'Madam, ere I was up	R L	1277
Madding—of this madding fever	Son	119 8
Made—Nature that made thee	V A	11
resistance made him fret	"	69
Torches are made to light	"	163
Love made those hollows	"	243
his acts made plain	"	359
made mine hard	"	378
And once made perfect	"	408
thyself art made away	"	763
then apologies be made	R L	31
Made glorious by his manly chivalry	"	109
and made her thrall	"	725
which in thy reign are made	"	804
If that be made a theme	"	822
the other made divine	"	1164
made me stop my breath	"	1180
Make weak-made women tenants	"	1260
made for Priam's Troy	"	1367
made herself herself detest	"	1566
vow, which Brutus made before	"	1847
This were to be new made	Son 2	13
hath not made for store	" 11	9
So I, made lame	" 37	3
mine eyes be blessed made	" 43	9
My life, being made of four	" 45	7
being made from thee	" 50	8
of perfect'st love being made	" 51	10
whereof are ye made	" 53	1
are sweetest odours made	" 54	12
that made me first your slave	" 58	1
And art made tongue-tied	" 66	9
dead fleece made another gay	" 68	8
what nature made so clear	" 84	10
made myself a motley	" 110	2
Made old offences	" 110	4
by evil still made better	" 119	10
Made more or less	" 123	12
that she is made of truth	" 138	1
made them swear against the thing they see	"	152 12
and made him her place	L C	82
made fairer by their place	"	117
and made their wills obey	"	133
Love made them not	"	185
smiled or made some moan	"	217
made the blossoms dote	"	235
that she is made of truth	P P 1	1
tarriance for Adonis made	" 6	4
which a grove of myrtles made	" 21	4
Made me think upon mine own	" 21	18
Whereupon it made this threne	P T	49
Madly—Which madly hurries her	V A	904
Is madly toss'd	R L	171
desire thus madly led	"	300
Madmen—My thoughts and my discourse as madmen's are	Son 147	11
Madness—And in my madness	"	140 10
Madrigal—Melodious birds sing madrigals	P P 20	8

Maid—she hoarsely calls her maid	R L	....	1214
cheeks unto her maid seem so	"	....	1217
Even so the maid	"	....	1228
Which makes the maid weep	"	....	1232
ere I was up,' replied the maid	"	....	1277
If your maid may be so bold	"	....	1282
Her maid is gone	"	....	1296
A maid of Dian's	Son	153	2
a fickle maid full pale	L C	....	5
he 'gan besiege me: 'Gentle maid	"	....	177
He preach'd pure maid	"	....	315
pervert a reconciled maid	"	....	329
did bear the maid away	P P	16	14
Maiden—quench the .... burning	V A	....	50
A pair of maiden worlds	R L	....	408
the worm intrude the maiden bud	"	....	848
And many maiden gardens	Son	16	6
maiden virtue rudely strumpeted	"	66	6
but in her maiden hand	"	154	4
maidens' eyes stuck over all his face	L C	....	81
Maiden-tongued—For .... he was	"	....	100
Main—did win whom he would	"	....	312
Main—once in the main of light	Son	60	5
win of the watery main	"	64	7
On your broad main	"	80	8
Maintain—this general evil they maintain	"	121	3
Maintained—rights in Rome	R L	....	1838
Majesty—With gentle majesty	V A	....	278
ariseth in his majesty	"	....	856
in plaits of majesty	R L	....	93
for exiled majesty's repeal	"	....	640
In great commanders grace and majesty	"	....	1387
his sacred majesty	Son	7	4
given grace a double majesty	"	78	8
Make—makes amain unto him	V A	....	5
Make use of time	"	....	129
I'll make a shadow	"	....	191
they make no battery	"	....	426
clapping makes it red	"	....	468
bargains may I make	"	....	512
purchase if thou make	"	....	515
wilt thou make the match	"	....	586
make them droop with grief	"	....	666
make my faint heart	"	....	669
To make the cunning hounds	"	....	686
shadow makes him stop	"	....	706
To make thee hate	"	....	711
make true men thieves	"	....	724
Make modest Dian	"	....	725
makes me like you	"	....	774
Make verbal repetition	"	....	831
makes young men thrall	"	....	837
that makes him bright	"	....	862
to make her stay	"	....	873
fear whereof doth make him shake	"	....	880
make them wet again	"	....	906
makes thee ridiculous	"	....	988
makes the wound seem three	"	....	1064
That makes more gashes	"	....	1066
shall it make most weak	"	....	1145
Make the young old	"	....	1152
Yet their ambition makes	R L	....	68
He makes excuses	"	....	114
Make something nothing	"	....	134
must doting Tarquin make	"	....	155
can my invention make	"	....	225

Make—And with good thoughts makes dispensation	R L	....	248
did make her colour rise	"	....	257
The wind wars with his torch to make him stay	"	....	311
march'd on to make his stand	"	....	438
The sight which makes	"	....	455
To make the breach	"	....	469
makes the lily pale	"	....	478
and makes a pause	"	....	541
That to his borrow'd bed he make retire	"	....	573
'This deed will make thee	"	....	610
Make slow pursuit	"	....	696
Make war against	"	....	774
Let their exhaled unwholesome breaths make sick	"	....	779
and make perpetual night	"	....	784
As palmers' chat makes short	"	....	791
'Make me not object	"	....	806
To make the child	"	....	954
to make amends	"	....	961
To make him curse	"	....	970
To make him moan	"	....	977
That makes him honour'd	"	....	1005
To make more vent	"	....	1040
Make her moans mad	"	....	1108
doth make the wound	"	....	1116
Make thy sad grove	"	....	1129
I make some hole	"	....	1175
abridgement of my will I make	"	....	1193
the knife that makes my wound	"	....	1201
Which makes the maid weep	"	....	1232
Make weak-made women	"	....	1260
cannot make it less	"	....	1285
dares not thereof make discovery	"	....	1314
Deep sounds make lesser noise	"	....	1329
did make him more amazed	"	....	1356
and make them bold	"	....	1559
to make mine own excuse	"	....	1653
his sorrows, make a saw	"	....	1672
make conquest of the stronger	"	....	1767
sorrow's tide, to make it more	"	....	1789
and make my old excuse	Son	2	11
Make sweet some vial	"	6	3
make worms thine heir	"	6	14
Make thee another self	"	10	13
would make the world away	"	11	8
do I question make	"	12	9
Time's scythe can make defence	"	12	13
Make war upon this bloody tyrant	"	16	2
Can make you live	"	16	12
And make the earth devour	"	19	2
Make glad and sorry seasons	"	19	5
May make seem bare	"	26	6
Makes black night beauteous	"	27	12
doth nightly make grief's strength	"	28	14
make me travel forth	"	34	2
All men make faults	"	35	5
I make my love engrafted	"	37	8
how to make one twain	"	39	13
shadow shadows doth make bright	"	43	5
make some special instant	"	52	11
Makes summer's welcome	"	56	14
how happy you make those	"	57	12
make towards the pebbled shore	"	60	1
should make you woe	"	71	8
makes thy love more strong	"	73	13
To make me tongue-tied	"	80	4

MAKE 180 MAN

Make—			
your epitaph to make	Son	81	1
makes your praises worse	"	84	14
the spite of fortune, make me bow	"	90	3
and me most wretched make	"	91	14
dost thou make the shame	"	95	1
make me any summer's story	"	98	7
And make Time's spoils	"	100	12
Make answer, Muse	"	101	5
To make him much outlive	"	101	11
To make him seem long hence	"	101	14
But makes antiquity	"	108	12
To make of monsters	"	114	5
to make our appetites	"	118	1
rather make them born	"	124	7
to make the taker mad	"	129	8
proudly make them cruel	"	131	2
the power to make love groan	"	131	6
makes my heart to groan	"	133	1
to make thy large 'Will' more	"	135	12
Make but my name	"	136	13
she that makes me sin	"	141	14
makes all swift dispatch	"	143	3
Love's own hand did make	"	145	1
To make me give the lie	"	150	3
to make me love thee more	"	150	9
what stop he makes	L C		109
To make the weeper laugh	"		124
to make our wits more keen	"		161
makes her absence valiant	"		245
that you make 'gainst mine	"		277
and yet do question make	"		321
If love make me forsworn	P P	5	1
and makes his book thine eyes	"	5	5
lute, the queen of music, makes	"	8	10
to make me wander thither	"	14	10
make thee a bed of roses	"	20	9
Makest —makest thou to be gone	V A		188
And makest fair reputation	R L		623
Thou makest the vestal	"		883
makest waste in niggarding	Son	1	12
Thou makest faults graces	"	96	4
That thy sable gender makest	P T		18
Maketh—too sensible thy passion maketh	R L		1678
thus maketh mine untrue	Son	113	14
Making—Making them red and pale	V A		21
making her cheeks all wet	"		83
Making my arms his field	"		108
Making it subject	"		737
Making such sober action	R L		1403
Making a famine	Son	1	7
Making a complement	"	21	5
Making no summer	"	68	11
Not making worse what nature	"	84	10
Making his style admired	"	84	12
Making their tomb	"	86	4
on better judgement making	"	87	12
making no defence	"	89	4
Making lascivious comments	"	95	6
making beautiful old rhyme	"	106	3
Making dead wood	"	128	12
making addition thus	"	135	4
Makeless —like a makeless wife	"	9	4
Malady—not the least of all these maladies	V A		745
our maladies unseen	Son	118	3
Against strange maladies	"	153	8
Malcontent—like a melancholy	V A		313
Man—more lovely than a man	"		9

Man—			
Thing like a man	V A		214
Thou art no man, though of a man's complexion	"		215
For men will kiss	"		216
and I a man	"		369
make true men thieves	"		724
young men thrall and old men dote	"		837
men's minds confound	"		1048
The eyes of men without an orator	R L		30
that meaner men should vaunt	"		41
A martial man to be	"		200
or an old man's saw	"		244
descried in men's nativity	"		538
If ever men were moved	"		587
Men's faults do seldom	"		633
man, that coffers up his gold	"		855
the child a man, the man a child	"		954
The mightier man	"		1004
Since men prove beasts	"		1148
For men have marble	"		1240
In men, as in a rough-grown grove	"		1249
Though men can cover crimes	"		1252
No man inveigh against	"		1254
With men's abuses	"		1259
One of my husband's men	"		1291
The very eyes of men	"		1383
Here one man's hand	"		1415
And one man's lust	"		1489
That no man could distinguish	"		1785
men as plants increase	Son	15	5
yourself in eyes of men	"	16	12
like old men of less truth	"	17	10
So long as men can breathe	"	18	13
pattern to succeeding men	"	19	12
A man in hue	"	20	7
Which steals men's eyes	"	20	8
with fortune and men's eyes	"	29	1
this man's art and that man's scope	"	29	7
by the height of happier men	"	32	8
For no man well of such a salve can speak	"	34	7
All men make faults	"	35	5
in men's eyes shall lie	"	81	8
even in the mouths of men	"	81	14
of all men's pride I boast	"	91	12
nor no man ever loved	"	116	14
All men are bad	"	121	14
that leads men to this hell	"	129	14
in the bay where all men ride	"	137	6
As testy sick men	"	140	7
the likeness of a man	"	141	11
is a man right fair	"	144	3
Death that feeds on men	"	146	13
true as all men's	"	148	8
which yet men prove	"	153	7
For men diseased	"	154	12
A reverend man	L C		57
Small show of man	"		92
Yet, if men moved him	"		101
and often men would say	"		106
This man's untrue	"		169
is a man right fair	P P	2	3
the learned man hath got the lady gay	"	16	15
More in women than in men	"	18	18
Like a thousand vanquish'd men	"	18	36
'Had women been so strong as men'	"	19	23
women still to strive with men	"	19	43
Every man will be thy friend	"	21	35

Man—No man will supply thy want	P P	21	38	Map—the map of days outworn	Son 68 1
Manage—He will not manage her	V A	....	598	And him as for a map	" 68 13
manage by the well-doing steed	L C	....	112	Mar—Mar not the thing	R L 578
Mane—his braided hanging mane	V A	....	271	To mar the subject	Son 103 10
Thin mane, thick tail	"	....	298	Marble—though marble wear with	
through his mane and tail	"	....	305	raining	R L 560
Mangling—reprehends her .... eye	V A	....	1065	For men have marble	" 1240
Manifold—With objects manifold	L C	....	216	are they form'd as marble will	" 1241
Manly—Made glorious by his manly				Not marble, nor the gilded	Son 55 1
chivalry	R L	....	109	March—thy misty vapours march	R L 782
Here manly Hector faints	"	....	1486	To march in ranks	Son 32 12
Till manly shame	"	....	1777	March'd—march'd on to make	R L 438
Manner—their manners most expressly told	"	....	1397	bold Hector march'd to field	" 1430
				Marcheth—marcheth to Lucrece' bed	" 361
with manners may I sing	Son	39	1	Marching—marching on with trembling paces	" 1391
in manners holds her still	"	85	1		
which public manners breeds	"	111	4	Mare—my palfrey from the mare	V A 384
manner of my pity-wanting pain	"	140	4	Margent—Writ in the glassy margents of such books	R L 102
Mansion—Her mansion batter'd	R L	....	1171		
what a mansion have those vices got	Son	95	9	upon whose weeping margent	L C 39
				Marigold—Her eyes like marigolds	R L 397
upon thy fading mansion spend	"	146	6	But as the marigold	Son 25 6
Of lands and mansions	L C	....	138	Marjoram—And buds of marjoram	" 99 7
Mantle—his .... rudely o'er his arm	R L	....	170	Mark—Didst thou not mark my face	V A 643
and throws his mantle by	P P	6	9	Mark the poor wretch	" 680
Manual—Set thy seal-manual	V A	....	516	My will that marks thee	R L 487
Many—The many musits	"	....	683	to mark how slow time goes	" 990
trodden on by many	"	....	707	Mark how one string	Son 8 9
Like many clouds	"	....	972	Mark how with my neglect	" 112 12
Alas, how many bear such shameful blows	R L	....	832	I sit and mark	P P 15 5
				Mark—Thy mark is feeble age	V A 941
Many a dry drop seem'd	"	....	1375	mark of every open eye	R L 520
The scalps of many, almost hid	"	....	1413	For marks descried in men's nativity	" 538
Stood many Trojan mothers	"	....	1431		
Many she sees where cares have	"	....	1445	true mark of modesty	" 1220
the public plague of many moe	"	....	1479	slander's mark was ever yet the fair	Son 70 2
why should so many fall	"	....	1483		
these many lives confounds	"	....	1489	it is an ever-fixed mark	" 116 5
Till after many accents	"	....	1719	If knowledge be the mark	P P 5 7
being many seeming one	Son	8	13	Marketh—advisedly she marketh	V A 457
thou art beloved of many	"	10	3	Marking—She, marking them, begins	" 835
And many maiden gardens	"	16	6	marking what he tells	R L 570
the lack of many a thing	"	30	3	Marr'd—To mend the hurt that his unkindness marr'd	V A 478
of many a vanish'd sight	"	30	8		
many a holy and obsequious tear	"	31	5	Marriage—that hath engirt his	R L 221
That due of many now is thine	"	31	12	to the marriage of true minds	Son 116 1
Full many a glorious morning	"	33	1	Married—By unions married	" 8 6
And, proud of many	"	67	12	wert not married to my muse	" 82 1
In many's looks the false heart's history	"	93	7	It was married chastity	P T 61
				Marrow—my marrow burning	V A 142
How many lambs might the stern wolf betray	"	96	9	Marrow-eating The .... sickness	" 741
				Mars—Nor Mars his sword	Son 55 7
How many gazers might'st thou lead	"	96	11	how god Mars did try her	P P 11 3
				Martial—A martial man to be	R L 200
many nymphs that vow'd	"	154	3	Martyr'd—lies martyr'd with disgrace	" 802
many legions of true hearts	"	154	6	Marvel—Therefore no marvel	V A 390
had she many a one	L C	....	43	No marvel then, though I	Son 148 11
Crack'd many a ring	"	....	45	Mask—To mask their brows	R L 794
many a blasting hour	"	....	72	Masked — The region cloud hath mask'd him from me	Son 33 12
Many there were that did	"	....	134		
many have, that never touch'd	"	....	141	their masked buds discloses	" 54 8
many bulwarks builded	"	....	152	mask'd not thy show	" 70 13
Among the many that mine eyes	"	....	190	Masonry—root out the work of	" 55 6
from many a several fair	"	....	206	Master—His testy master	V A 319
with many a lovely look	P P	4	3	Tell me, love's master, shall we meet	" 585
How many tales to please me	"	....	7		
Map—triumph in the map of death	R L	....	402	asks the weary caitiff for his master	" 914
The face, that map which deep impression bears	"	....	1712	That liked of her master	P P 16 2
				To leave the master loveless	" 16 6

Master—beauty as you master now	*Son*	106	8	May—that I may change	*Son*	10 9
Master'd—.... with a leathern rein	*V A*		392	beauty still may live	"	10 14
to be master'd by his young	*R L*		863	Where I may not remove	"	25 14
Mastering—For mastering her	*V A*		114	May make seem bare	"	26 6
mastering what not strives	*L C*		240	may I dare to boast	"	26 13
Master-mistress—the master-mistress of my passion	*Son*	20	2	Suns of the world may stain	"	33 14
Match—wilt thou make the match	*V A*		586	I may not evermore acknowledge thee	"	36 9
shall not match his woe	"		1140	with manners may I sing	"	39 1
Matcheth—thy odour matcheth not thy show	*Son*	69	13	separation I may give	"	39 7
				yet it may be said	"	42 2
Mate—In the possession of his beauteous mate	*R L*		18	more blest may be the view	"	56 12
				Where you may be	"	57 10
Mated—is mated with delays	*V A*		909	You yourself may privilege your time	"	58 10
Matter—'No matter where,' quoth he	"		715			
As dry combustious matter	"		1162	my love may still shine bright	"	65 14
mistook the matter so	*R L*		1826	your true love may seem	"	72 9
No matter then although	*Son*	44	5	the world may see my pleasure	"	75 8
Then lack'd I matter	"	86	14	May still seem love to me	"	93 3
but waking no such matter	"	87	14	mine eye may be deceived	"	104 12
a plenitude of subtle matter	*L C*		302	that ink may character	"	•108 1
Maturity—Crawls to maturity	*Son*	60	6	That may express my love	"	108 4
Maund—favours from a maund she drew	*L C*		36	I may be straight	"	121 11
				May time disgrace and wretched minutes kill	"	126 8
Maw—and pine the maw	*V A*		602			
May—sweet boy, and may it be	"		155	She may detain, but not still keep	"	126 10
That thine may live	"		172	That I may not be so	"	140 13
by pleading may be blest	"		328	Thy pity may deserve	"	142 12
sorrow may be said	"		333	Suspect I may	"	144 10
Long may they kiss	"		505	My soul doth tell my body that he may	"	151 7
May say, the plague is banish'd	"		510			
bargains may I make	"		512	there may be aught applied	*L C*	68
that he may depart	"		578	may her suffering ecstasy assuage	"	60
much as may be proved	"		608	counsel may stop awhile	"	159
may be compared well	"		701	with acture they may be	"	185
May lend thee light	"		864	Suspect I may, yet not	*P P*	2 10
O yes, it may; thou hast	"		939	'T may be she joy'd to jest	"	14 9
What may a heavy groan advantage	"		950	'T may be again	"	14 10
may the better thrive	"		1011	thy cheeks may blow	"	17 9
that they may surprise	*R L*		166	Where thy desert may merit praise	"	19 27
sorrow may on this arise	"		186	pleasures may thee move	"	20 15
May feel her heart	"		465	Truth may seem, but cannot be	*P T*	62
foul sin may say	"		629	*May*—the darling buds of May	*Son*	18 3
never may behold	"		746	oft 'twixt May and April	*L C*	102
where it may find	"		760	Love whose month was ever May	*P P*	17 2
May set at noon	"		784	In the merry month of May	"	21 2
May likewise be	"		805	**Mayst**—mayst thou well be tasted	*V A*	128
Tarquin's eye may read the mot	"		810	thou revenged mayst be	*R L*	1194
where he the lamb may get	"		878	Thou mayst call thine	*Son*	11 4
where none may spy him	"		881	where thou mayst prove	"	26 14
his suit may be obtained	"		898	that thou mayst true love call	"	40 3
stars may hide them	"		1008	thou mayst come and part	"	48 12
The crow may bathe	"		1009	thou mayst in me behold	"	73 1
I may convey this troubled soul	"		1176	this learning mayst thou taste	"	77 4
That he may vow	"		1179	by the dial's shady stealth mayst know	"	77 7
may be so bold	"		1282			
may be call'd a hell	"		1287	mayst without attaint o'erlook	"	82 2
Collatine may know	"		1312	that thou mayst take	"	91 13
may grace the fashion	"		1319	Thou mayst be false	"	92 14
her beauty I may tear	"		1472	mayst thou be denied	"	142 14
that we may give redress	"		1603	thou mayst have thy 'Will	"	143 13
may be imagined	"		1622	**Maze**—with a winding maze	*R L*	1151
'How may this forced stain be wiped	"		1701	**Me**—why dost abhor me	*V A*	138
				Bid me discourse	"	145
May thy pure mind with the foul act dispense	"		1704	trees support me	"	152
				draw me through the sky	"	153
May any terms acquit me	"		1706	I list to sport me	"	154
Yet neither may possess	"		1794	'Ay me,' quoth Venus	"	187
widow well may keep	*Son*	9	7	fire that burneth me	"	196

Me—shouldst contemn me this	*L A*	205
Give me one kiss	"	209
'Give me my hand	"	373
'Give me my heart	"	374
O give it me	"	375
and let me go	"	379
leave me here alone	"	382
Let me excuse thy courser	"	403
done me double wrong	"	429
Each part in me	"	436
feeling were bereft me	"	439
very smell were left me	"	441
O thou didst kill me, kill me once again	"	499
buys my heart from me	"	517
if any love you owe me	"	523
seek not to know me	"	525
Now let me say	"	535
Tell me, love's master	"	585
you crush me: let me go	"	611
to withhold me so	"	612
But that thou told'st me	"	614
be ruled by me	"	673
thou hear'st me moralize	"	712
Leave me, and then	"	716
makes me like you	"	774
'Ay me!' she cries	"	833
Yet pardon me, I felt	"	998
To cipher me	*R L*	207
thou shalt charge me	"	226
'She took me kindly	"	233
assist me in the act	"	350
Shall plead for me	"	480
for his sake spare me	"	582
for thine own sake leave me	"	583
do not then ensnare me	"	584
do not deceive me	"	585
I complain me	"	598
to blush with me	"	792
Make me not object to the tell-tale Day	"	806
Tarquin wronged me	"	819
thine honour lay in me	"	834
From me by strong assault	"	845
have come to me	"	916
O, hear me then	"	930
thou gavest me to repose	"	933
and enchained me	"	934
Teach me to curse him	"	996
For me, I force not	"	1021
doth me no right	"	1027
to do me good	"	1028
to rid me of this shame	"	1051
hath Tarquin rifled me	"	1050
For me, I am the mistress of my fate	"	1069
Ay me! the bark peel'd	"	1167
made me stop my breath	"	1180
read it to me	"	1195
think no shame of me	"	1204
mine own would do me good	"	1274
But tell me, girl, when went	"	1275
Go, get me hither paper	"	1289
speed to come and visit me	"	1307
So, I commend me	"	1308
Show me the strumpet	"	1471
To me came Tarquin armed	"	1544
In me moe woes	"	1615
might be done to me	"	1623
O, teach me how to make	"	1653

Me—this refuge let me find	*R L*	.....	1654
Lucrece, now attend me	"	.....	1682
suppose thou dost defend me	"	.....	1684
the help that thou shalt lend me	"	.....	1685
your honourable faiths to me	"	.....	1690
stain be wiped from me	"	.....	1701
acquit me from this chance	"	.....	1706
to give this wound to me	"	.....	1722
this end from me derived	"	.....	1755
Shows me a bare-boned death	"	.....	1761
But kneel with me	"	.....	1830
for love of me	*Son*	10	13
by addition me of thee defeated	"	20	11
So is it not with me	"	21	1
O, let me, true in love	"	21	9
And then believe me	"	21	10
persuade me I am old	"	22	1
as thine in me	"	22	7
Thou gavest me thine	"	22	14
Mine eyes have drawn thy shape, and thine for me	"	24	10
Points on me graciously	"	26	10
To show me worthy	"	26	12
where thou mayst prove me	"	26	14
I haste me to my bed	"	27	1
shake hands to torture me	"	28	6
Wishing me like to one	"	29	5
parts of me to thee did give	"	31	11
hast all the all of me	"	31	14
O, then vouchsafe me	"	32	9
mask'd him from me now	"	33	12
make me travel forth	"	34	2
o'ertake me in my way	"	34	3
sourly robs from me	"	35	14
Let me confess	"	36	1
that do with me remain	"	36	3
by me he borne alone	"	36	4
public kindness honour me	"	36	11
then ten times happy me	"	37	14
if aught in me	"	38	5
all the better part of me	"	39	2
Kill me with spites	"	40	14
Ay me! but yet thou	"	41	9
beauty being false to me	"	41	14
touches me more nearly	"	42	4
doth she abuse me	"	42	7
lay on me this cross	"	42	12
she loves but me alone	"	42	14
dreams do show thee me	"	43	14
thought kills me	"	44	9
recounting it to me	"	45	12
art present still with me	"	47	10
And scarcely greet me	"	49	6
do I ensconce me here	"	49	9
To leave poor me	"	49	13
The beast that bears me	"	50	5
to bear that weight in me	"	50	6
More sharp to me	"	50	12
should I haste me thence	"	51	3
made me first your slave	"	58	1
O, let me suffer	"	58	5
Show me your image	"	59	7
and idle hours in me	"	61	7
From me far off	"	61	14
shows me myself indeed	"	62	9
Ruin hath taught me	"	64	11
No longer mourn for me	"	71	1
If thinking on me	"	71	8
And mock you with me	"	71	14

Phrase	Ref	#	#
Me—What merit lived in me	Son	72	2
forget me quite	"	72	3
For you in me can nothing worthy prove	"	72	4
more for me than mine	"	72	6
speak well of me untrue	"	72	10
to shame nor me nor you	"	72	12
thou mayst in me behold	"	73	1
In me thou see'st	"	73	5
In me thou see'st	"	73	9
shall carry me away	"	74	2
the better part of me	"	74	8
To make me tongue-tied	"	80	4
will hold me up afloat	"	80	9
in me each part	"	81	4
yield me but a common grave	"	81	7
Me for my dumb thoughts	"	85	14
that struck me dead	"	86	6
gift in me is wanting	"	87	7
Or me, to whom thou gavest it	"	87	10
disposed to set me light	"	88	1
thou in losing me	"	88	8
Doing thee vantage, double-vantage me	"	88	12
forsake me for some fault	"	89	1
disgrace me half so ill	"	89	5
hate me when thou wilt	"	90	1
make me bow	"	90	3
If thou wilt leave me, do not leave me last	"	90	9
than high birth to me	"	91	9
and me most wretched make	"	91	14
state to me belongs	"	92	7
canst not vex me	"	92	9
still seem love to me	"	93	3
thy looks with me	"	93	4
issue seem'd to me	"	97	9
make me any summer's story tell	"	98	7
O, blame me not	"	103	5
and doing me disgrace	"	103	8
To me, fair friend, you never can be old	"	104	1
and Death to me subscribes	"	107	10
Then give me welcome	"	110	13
Pity me then	"	111	8
Pity me then, dear friend	"	111	13
is enough to cure me	"	111	14
who calls me well or ill	"	112	3
None else to me	"	112	7
governs me to go about	"	113	2
Let me not to the marriage	"	116	1
and upon me proved	"	116	13
Accuse me thus	"	117	1
do tie me day by day	"	117	4
transport me farthest from your sight	"	117	8
Bring me within the level	"	117	11
But shoot not at me	"	117	12
you were once unkind befriends me now	"	120	1
soon to you, as you to me	"	120	11
and yours must ransom me	"	120	14
to give them from me was I bold	"	122	11
forgetfulness in me	"	122	14
To me are nothing novel	"	123	3
Were't aught to me	"	125	1
let me be obsequious	"	125	9
render, only me for thee	"	125	12
me thy lips to kiss	"	128	14
Me—and they, as pitying me	Son	132	1
torments me with disdain	"	132	2
To mourn for me	"	132	11
it gives my friend and me	"	133	2
to torture me alone	"	133	3
Me from myself	"	133	5
Whoe'er keeps me	"	133	11
and all that is in me	"	133	14
surety-like to write for me	"	134	7
hast both him and me	"	134	13
and me in that one 'Will	"	135	14
let me pass untold	"	136	9
For nothing hold me	"	136	11
That nothing me, a something	"	136	12
And then thou lovest me	"	136	14
think me some untutor'd youth	"	138	3
she thinks me young	"	138	5
with her and she with me	"	138	13
O, call not me to justify	"	139	1
Wound me not	"	139	3
and slay me not by art	"	139	4
tell me thou lovest elsewhere	"	139	5
Let me excuse thee	"	139	9
Kill me outright with looks	"	139	14
sorrow lend me words	"	140	3
yet, love, to tell me so	"	140	6
she that makes me sin	"	141	14
turn back to me	"	143	11
kiss me, be kind	"	143	12
two spirits do suggest me still	"	144	2
To win me soon to hell	"	144	5
But being both from me	"	144	11
To me that languish'd	"	145	3
Hath left me	"	147	7
O me, what eyes hath love	"	148	1
thou keep'st me blind	"	148	13
Nay, if thou lour'st on me	"	149	7
make me give the lie	"	150	3
how to make me love thee	"	150	9
raised love in me	"	150	13
For, thou betraying me	"	151	5
to me love swearing	"	152	2
though in me you behold	L C		71
over me hath power	"	....	74
But woe is me	"	....	78
for me many bulwarks builded	"	....	132
Till thus he 'gan besiege me	"	....	177
less of shame in me remains	"	....	188
By how much of me	"	....	189
what tributes wounded fancies sent me	"	....	197
their passions likewise lent me	"	....	199
Nature hath charged me	"	....	220
Since I their altar, you empatron me	"	....	224
What me your minister	"	....	229
was sent me from a nun	"	....	232
O, pardon me, in that my boast	"	....	246
which brought me to her eye	"	....	247
O, hear me tell	"	....	253
that to me belong	"	....	254
and you o'er me being strong	"	....	257
as he to me appears	"	....	290
His poison'd me, and mine did him restore	"	....	301
Ay me! I felt	"	....	321
think me some untutor'd youth	P P	1	3
thinking that she thinks me young	"	1	5
and love with me	"	1	13
two spirits do suggest me still	"	2	2

Me—To win me soon to hell	P P	2 5
For being both to me	"	2 11
cures all disgrace in me	"	3 8
If by me broke	"	3 13
If love make me forsworn	"	5 1
These thoughts, to me like oaks	"	5 4
Which is to me some praise	"	5 10
many tales to please me	"	7 9
'twixt thee and me	"	8 3
Spenser to me, whose deep conceit	"	8 7
thou left'st me nothing	"	10 8
yet thou left'st me more	"	10 9
thou didst bequeath to me	"	10 12
the warlike god embraced me	"	11 5
the warlike god unlaced me	"	11 7
To kiss and clip me	"	11 14
And daff'd me to a cabin	"	14 3
to make me wander thither	"	14 10
and bade me come to-morrow	"	15 12
To spite me now	"	15 15
Yet not for me	"	15 16
Love hath forlorn me	"	18 21
to round me on th' ear	"	19 51
Live with me and be my love	"	20 1
Then live with me	"	20 16
pleasures might me move	"	20 19
Made me think upon	"	21 18
None alive will pity me	"	21 28
Mead—As he roots the mead	V A	636
As winter meads when sun	R L	1218
Meadow—the meadows green	Son 33	3
Meagre—ugly, meagre, lean	V A	931
Mean—know not what we mean	"	126
what dost thou mean	"	933
means to immure herself	"	1194
if thou mean to chide	R L	484
do I mean to place him	"	517
I mean to bear thee	"	670
What means the world	Son 148	6
Meaner—that .... men should vaunt	"	41
Meaning—His meaning struck her	V A	462
Could pick no meaning	R L	100
would not take her meaning	P P 11	12
Means—Some happy mean to end a hapless life	R L	1045
These means, as frets	"	1140
Pausing for means	"	1365
That he finds means	"	1561
With means more blessed	Son 16	4
Than public means	" 111	4
Meant—and meant thereby	" 11	13
Measure—Measure my strangeness with my unripe years	V A	524
to tread the measures	"	1148
they measure by thy deeds	Son 69	10
are not my measure	" 91	7
Measured—Thus far the miles are....	" 50	4
Mediator—be you mediators	R L	1020
Medicine—And brought to medicine	Son 118	11
Meditation—O, fearful meditation	" 65	9
Meed—this favour, for thy meed	V A	15
is the meed proposed	R L	132
Meek—all recreant, poor, and meek	"	710
Meet—shall we meet to-morrow	V A	585
here she meets another	"	917
to meet the eastern light	R L	773
ne'er meet with Opportunity	"	903
they with winter meet	Son 5	13
with base infection meet	" 94	11
Meeting—the .... clouds contend	V A	820
till meeting greater ranks	R L	1441
All our merry meetings	P P 18	46
Meetness—found a kind of meetness	Son 118	7
Melancholy—like a .... malcontent	V A	313
oppress'd with melancholy	Son 45	8
Mellow—The mellow plum doth fall	V A	527
Melodious—Melodious discord, heavenly tune	"	431
the sweet melodious sounds	P P 8	9
Melodious birds sing madrigals	" 20	8
Melody—with their sweet melody	R L	1108
Melt—or seem to melt	V A	144
melt with the midday sun	"	750
Which her cheek melts	"	982
melt at mine eyes' red fire	"	1073
Melt at my tears	R L	594
when sun doth melt	"	1218
Melted—Was melted like a vapour	V A	1166
Melting—to his melting buttock lent	"	315
morning's silver-melting dew	R L	24
moistened like a melting eye	"	1227
All melting; though our drops	L C	300
Memorial—Which for memorial still	Son 74	4
Memory—might bear his memory	" 1	4
their brave state out of memory	" 15	8
living record of your memory	" 55	8
shall never cut from memory	" 63	11
will give thee memory	" 77	6
what thy memory cannot contain	" 77	9
From hence your memory	" 81	3
with lasting memory	" 122	2
Mend—To mend the hurt	V A	478
the thought of hearts can mend	Son 69	2
thou dost but mend the style	" 78	11
sinful then, striving to mend	" 103	9
Mended—Whether we are mended	" 59	11
Merchandized—That love is merchandized whose rich esteeming	" 102	3
Merchant—The merchant fears	R L	336
merchant of this loss	"	1660
Merciful—It shall be merciful	V A	1155
Merciless—the .... and pitchy night	"	821
tries a merciless conclusion	R L	1160
Mercy—Lies at the mercy	"	364
in her heart did mercy come	Son 145	5
Merely—characters and words merely but art	L C	174
merely with the garment	"	316
Merit—Thy merit hath my duty	Son 26	2
What merit lived in me	" 72	2
And place my merit	" 88	2
or thy dear merit	" 108	4
it merits not reproving	" 142	4
What merit do I in myself respect	" 149	9
Where thy desert may merit	P P 19	27
Meritorious—a .... fair design	R L	1692
Mermaid—Thy mermaid's voice	V A	429
like the wanton mermaid's songs	"	777
As if some mermaid	R L	1411
Merry—she hears a merry horn	V A	1025
And merry fools	R L	989
slain in merry company	"	1110
brooks not merry guests	"	1125
All my merry jigs	P P 18	9
All our merry meetings	" 18	46
In the merry month of May	" 21	2
Messenger—the mindful messenger come back	R L	1583

Messenger—By those swift....	Son	45	10	Might—worst of fortune's might	Son	90	12
Met—When as I met the boar	V A		999	gives thee all thy might	"	100	2
Met far from home	R L		1596	built up with newer might	"	123	2
Metal—With twisted metal	L C		203	with cunning, when thy might	"	139	7
Methinks—And yet methinks	Son	14	2	hast thou this powerful might	"	150	1
Methinks no face so gracious	"	62	5	her absence valiant, not her might	L C		245
which methinks still doth stand	"	104	11	Mightier—The mightier man, the			
That all the world besides methinks are dead	"	112	14	mightier is the thing	R L		1004
methinks thou stay'st too long	P P	12	12	do not you a mightier way	Son	16	1
Method—To new-found methods	Son	76	4	Mightily—but mightily he noted	R L		414
Metre—And stretched metre	"	17	12	Mightst—Then mightst thou pause	V A		137
Mettle—That horse his mettle	L C		107	thou mightst my seat forbear	Son	41	9
Mickle—more mickle was the pain	P P	16	9	mightst thou lead away	"	96	11
Mid-day—tired in the mid-day heat	V A		177	Mighty—Thyself art mighty	R L		583
melts with the mid-day sun	"		750	forgot in mighty Rome	"		1644
Middle—strong youth in his middle age	Son	7	6	How mighty then you are	L C		253
Midnight—dead of dark midnight	R L		1625	Milch—Like a milch doe	V A		875
Midst—But in the midst	"		344	Mild—raging-mad and silly-mild	"		1151
And midst the sentence	"		566	And let mild women	R L		979
Yet in the midst of all	P P	7	11	not infant sorrows, bear them mild	"		1096
Might—He might be buried	V A		244	By this, mild patience	"		1268
the feast might ever last	"		447	But the mild glance	"		1399
kings might be espoused	R L		20	So mild that Patience	"		1505
Might have excuse to work	"		235	this mild image drew	"		1520
might compass his fair fair	"		346	so weary and so mild	"		1542
might have reposed still	"		382	Mild as a dove	P P	7	2
Till they might open	"		399	Mildness—to him lose their....	R L		979
and shame that might ensue	"		1263	Mile—To leap large lengths of miles	Son	44	10
which the world might bear her	"		1321	Thus far the miles are measured	"	50	4
might become them better	"		1323	Milk—Like milk and blood	V A		902
There might you see	"		1380	Milk-white—than her.... dove	P P	9	3
That one might see	"		1386	Million—That millions of strange shadows on you tend	Son	53	2
You might behold	"		1388	Million'd—Time, whose million'd accidents	"	115	5
might one behold	"		1395	Mind—so hard a mind	V A		203
Their pleading might you see	"		1401	if she knew his mind	"		308
might be done to me	"		1623	with disturbed mind	"		340
might plead for justice there	"		1649	For all my mind	"		383
when I might charm thee so	"		1681	weak and silly mind	"		1016
beauty's rose might never die	Son	1	2	doth men's minds confound	"		1048
might bear his memory	"	1	4	troubled minds that wake	R L		126
in honour might uphold	"	13	10	And in his inward mind	"		185
it might unused stay	"	48	3	burthen of a guilty mind	"		735
That I might see	"	59	9	to close so pure a mind	"		761
might be better used	"	82	13	let beasts bear gentle minds	"		1148
being extant, well might show	"	83	6	For men have marble, women waxen, minds	"		1240
might the stern wolf betray	"	96	9	At last she calls to mind	"		1366
might I from myself depart	"	109	3	to mock the mind	"		1414
Might I not then say	"	115	10	save to the eye of mind	"		1426
Then might I not say so	"	115	13	not a mind so ill	"		1530
might have remember'd	"	120	9	came in her mind the while	"		1536
It might for Fortune's bastard	"	124	2	should bear a wicked mind	"		1540
That she might think me	"	138	3	and spotless is my mind	"		1656
might dart their injuries	"	139	12	May my pure mind	"		1704
If I might teach thee	"	140	5	her mind untainted clears	"		1710
might speak ill of thee	"	140	10	from weak minds proceeds	"		1825
might think sometime it saw	L C		10	her husband's shape in mind	Son	9	8
I might as yet have been	"		75	that I may change my mind	"	10	9
That she might think me	P P	1	3	To work my mind	"	27	4
as well as well might be	"	16	2	by night my mind	"	27	13
Air, would I might triumph so	"	17	10	doth put this in my mind	"	50	13
pleasures might me move	"	20	19	Since mind at first	"	59	8
Might—nor brag not of thy might	V A		113	the beauty of thy mind	"	69	9
sought with all my might	R L		488	thy mind's imprint will bear	"	77	3
of mine own love's might	Son	23	8	new acquaintance of thy mind	"	77	12
sharpen'd in his former might	"	56	4	vex me with inconstant mind	"	92	9
unless this miracle have might	"	65	13	mine eye is in my mind	"	113	1
Spends all his might	"	80	3				

MIND 187 MINISTER

Mind—hath the mind no part	Son	113	7
My most true mind	"	113	14
Or whether doth my mind	"	114	1
And my great mind	"	114	10
Divert strong minds	"	115	8
the marriage of true minds	"	116	1
been with unknown minds	"	117	5
for now I know thy mind	"	149	13
That in my mind	"	150	8
The mind and sight	L C		28
did enchant the mind	"		89
and in it put their mind	"		135
none of the mind	"		184
Minded—If all were minded so	Son	11	7
Mindful—But now the mindful messenger come back	R L		1583
Mine—Though mine be not so fair	V A		116
The kiss shall be thine own as well as mine	"		117
Look in mine eyeballs	"		119
Mine eyes are grey	"		140
Adonis' heart hath made mine hard	"		378
this poor heart of mine	"		502
And these mine eyes	"		503
mine eyes to watch	"		584
lurk in mine eye	"		644
whispers in mine ear	"		659
presenteth to mine eye	"		661
Mine eyes forego their light	R L		228
never countermand mine eye	"		276
thine eyes betray thee unto mine	"		483
to embrace mine infamy	"		504
see thy state and pity mine	"		644
hang their heads with mine	"		793
from this attaint of mine	"		825
cavil with mine infamy	"		1025
mine eyes, like sluices	"		1076
to affright mine eye	"		1138
mine honour is new-born	"		1190
mine honour be the knife's	"		1201
the slander of mine ill	"		1207
mine own would do me good	"		1274
Mine enemy was strong	"		1646
to make mine own excuse	"		1653
Thine, mine, his own	"		1684
to 'venge this wrong of mine	"		1691
That life was mine	"		1752
'She's mine.' 'O, mine she is	"		1795
for she was only mine	"		1798
'tis mine that she hath kill'd	"		1803
'This fair child of mine	Son	2	10
Mine be thy love	"	20	14
thy heart when mine is slain	"	22	13
in mine own love's strength	"	23	7
of mine own love's might	"	23	8
Mine eye hath play'd	"	24	1
Mine eyes have drawn	"	24	10
which wit so poor as mine	"	26	5
love stol'n from mine eye	"	31	6
he was but one hour mine	"	33	11
As thou being mine, mine is the good report	"	36	14
The pain be mine	"	38	14
What can mine own praise to mine own self bring	"	39	3
what is't but mine own	"	39	4
All mine was thine	"	40	4
then do mine eyes best see	"	43	1
mine eyes be blessed made	"	43	9
Mine—Mine eye and heart are at a mortal war	Son	46	1
Mine eye my heart thy picture's sight	"	46	3
My heart mine eye the freedom	"	46	4
mine eye's due is thine	"	46	13
Betwixt mine eye and heart	"	47	1
When that mine eye	"	47	3
mine eye is my heart's guest	"	47	7
dearest and mine only care	"	48	7
knowledge of mine own desert	"	49	10
that keeps mine eye awake	"	61	10
Mine own true love	"	61	11
possesseth all mine eye	"	62	1
so gracious is as mine	"	62	5
mine own worth do define	"	62	7
Mine own self-love	"	62	11
than mine own desert	"	72	6
matter; that enfeebled mine	"	86	14
With mine own weakness	"	88	5
thou art assured mine	"	92	2
As thou being mine, mine is thy good report	"	96	14
and mine eye may be deceived	"	104	12
Not mine own fears	"	107	1
thou mine, I thine	"	108	7
Gored mine own thoughts	"	110	3
Mine appetite I never more	"	110	10
mine eye is in my mind	"	113	1
thus maketh mine untrue	"	113	14
mine eye saith true	"	114	3
Mine eye well knows	"	114	11
That mine eye loves it	"	114	14
How have mine eyes	"	119	7
Mine ransoms yours, and yours	"	120	14
that mine ear confounds	"	128	4
Myself I'll forfeit, so that other mine	"	134	3
One will of mine	"	135	12
dost thou to mine eyes	"	137	1
Or mine eyes seeing this	"	137	11
have been mine enemies	"	139	10
love thee with mine eyes	"	141	1
Nor are mine ears	"	141	5
O, but with mine compare	"	142	3
of love as oft as mine	"	142	7
thine eyes woo as mine importune thee	"	142	10
I mine honour shielded	L C		151
that mine eyes have seen	"		190
but mine own was free	"		195
And mine I pour	"		236
hearts that do on mine depend	"		274
that you make 'gainst mine	"		277
and mine did him restore	"		301
then it is no fault of mine	P P	3	12
Her lips to mine	"	7	7
Lord, how mine eyes	"	15	1
the office of mine eyes	"	15	4
think upon mine own	"	21	18
Either was the other's mine	P T		36
Mingle—To mingle beauty	V A		735
Mingled—with others being	"		691
being mingled both together	"		902
red nor pale, but mingled so	R L		1510
Mingling—Mingling my talk with tears	"		797
Minion—O thou....of her pleasure	Son	126	9
Minister—What me your minister	L C		229

Entry	Ref	No.
Minority—Proving from world's minority their right	R L	67
Minstrel—Feast-finding minstrels	"	817
Minute—But in one minute's fight	V A	746
one minute in an hour	"	1187
Who buys a minute's mirth	R L	213
as minutes fill up hours	"	297
Till every minute pays	"	329
One poor retiring minute	"	962
to brief minutes tell	Son 14	5
So do our minutes	" 60	2
thy precious minutes waste	" 77	2
and wretched minutes kill	" 126	8
But now are minutes added	P P 15	14
each minute seems a moon	" 15	15
Miracle—unless this .... have might	Son 65	13
Mire—his coal-black wings in mire	R L	1009
Mirror—now that fair fresh mirror	"	1760
Mirth—Who buys a minute's mirth	"	213
For mirth doth search	"	1109
Miscall'd—truth .... simplicity	Son 66	1
Mischance—Of mad mischances	V A	738
With some mischance	R L	968
bechance him pitiful mischances	"	976
Mischief—A mischief worse	V A	764
Why work'st thou mischief	R L	960
Misdeed—Then kings' misdeeds	"	609
That from their own misdeeds	"	637
Miser—As 'twixt a miser and his wealth	Son 75	4
Misery—For misery is trodden on	V A	707
and much misery	"	738
Is no friend in misery	P P 21	32
Misfortune—Of hard misfortune	R L	1713
Misgoverning—dishonour, shame, misgoverning	"	654
Mishap—languisheth in her mishaps	V A	603
Misplaced—honour shamefully	Son 66	5
Misprision—upon .... growing	" 87	11
Misled—is his heart misled	R L	369
Miss—blames her miss	V A	53
Miss'd—being clouded presently is miss'd	R L	1007
thy record never can be miss'd	Son 122	8
Mis-shapen—Mis-shapen Time, copesmate of ugly Night	R L	925
Missing—she in him finds missing	V A	605
Mistake—hounds .... their smell	"	686
Mistakes that aim, and cleaves	"	942
oft the eye mistakes	"	1068
though I mistake my view	Son 148	11
Mistaking—Or me, to whom thou gavest it, else mistaking	" 87	10
Mistook—mistook the matter so	R L	1826
Mist—In his dim mist	"	548
And wipe the dim mist	"	643
Muster thy mists to meet	"	773
Mistress—Their mistress, mounted, through the empty skies	V A	1191
our mistress' ornaments	R L	322
I am the mistress of my fate	"	1069
to her mistress hies	"	1215
Her mistress she doth give	"	1219
set in her mistress' sky	"	1230
the master-mistress of my passion	Son 20	2
sovereign mistress over wrack	" 126	5
Therefore my mistress' eyes	" 127	9
My mistress' eyes	" 130	1
that from my mistress reeks	" 130	8
Mistress—My mistress, when she walks	Son 130	12
But at my mistress' eye	" 153	9
got new fire, my mistress' eyes	" 153	14
but I, my mistress' thrall	" 154	12
Sweetly supposed them mistress of his heart	L C	142
Lest that my mistress hear	P P 19	50
Mistrust—where it should most	V A	1154
and full of fond mistrust	R L	284
duty kindled her mistrust	"	1392
itself could not mistrust	"	1516
Mistrustful—in some .... wood	V A	826
Misty—like misty vapours	"	184
eye of heaven is out, and misty night	R L	356
And let thy misty vapours	"	782
Misuse—are oaths but to misuse thee	Son 152	7
Mixed—such lamps together mix'd	V A	489
eloquence with sighs is mixed	R L	563
Which is not mix'd	Son 125	11
and solace mix'd with sorrow	P P 15	11
Moan—repetition of her moans	V A	831
moved with woman's moans	R L	587
monuments of lasting moans	"	798
To make him moan; but pity not his moans	"	977
Make her moans mad	"	1108
moan tired moan	"	1363
of fore-bemoaned moan	Son 30	11
time's leisure with my moan	" 44	12
should look into your moan	" 71	13
upon myself with present moan	" 149	8
smiled or made some moan	L C	217
the cause of all my moan	P P 18	51
Every thing did banish moan	" 21	7
Moan—To make him moan	R L	977
And moan the expense	Son 30	8
Mock—To mock the subtle in themselves beguiled	R L	957
fools to mock at him resort	"	989
Mock with thy tickling beams	"	1090
higher seem'd, to mock	"	1414
shadows like to thee do mock my sight	Son 61	4
And mock you with me	" 71	14
mock their own presage	" 107	6
Mocking—You mocking birds	R L	1121
Modern—How far a modern quill	Son 83	7
Modest—and modest pride	V A	278
Make modest Dian	"	725
With modest Lucrece	R L	123
love's modest snow-white weed	"	196
O modest wantons	"	401
Her modest eloquence with sighs is mixed	"	563
That ever modest eyes	"	683
Modestly—She modestly prepares	"	1607
Modesty—wanton modesty	"	401
true mark of modesty	"	1220
terror and dear modesty	L C	202
cold modesty, hot wrath	"	293
Moe—public plague of many moe	R L	1479
In me moe woes	"	1615
Found yet moe letters	L C	47
And labouring in moe pleasures	"	139
Moiety—The clear eye's moiety	Son 46	12
Moist—My smooth moist hand	V A	143
From his moist cabinet	"	854

Entry	Ref	No.
Moisten'd—.... like a melting eye	R L	1227
Moisture—calls it heavenly....	V A	64
The heavenly moisture	"	542
O, that infected moisture of his eye	L C	323
Moment—Which in a moment	R L	250
Even in the moment	"	868
but a little moment	Son 15	2
Upon the moment	L C	248
Momentary—This momentary joy	R L	690
Monarch—But happy monarchs	"	611
Drink up the monarch's plague	Son 114	2
Or monarch's hand	L C	41
Monarchy—commanding in his monarchy	"	196
'Mongst—'Mongst our mourners	P T	20
Monster—To make of monsters	Son 114	5
Month—joy breeds months of pain	R L	690
whose month was ever May	P P 17	2
In the merry month of May	" 21	2
Monument—Where, like a virtuous monument, she lies	R L	391
Poor wasting monuments	"	798
To fill with worm-holes stately monuments	"	946
nor the gilded monuments	Son 55	1
Your monument shall be	" 81	9
shalt find thy monument	" 107	13
Mood—his.... with nought agrees	R L	1095
it small avails my mood	"	1273
Is writ in moods	Son 93	8
and the encrimson'd mood	L C	201
Moody—And moody Pluto winks	R L	553
this moody heaviness	"	1002
Moon—Shone like the moon	V A	492
that hides the silver moon	R L	371
The moon being clouded	"	1007
With sun and moon	Son 21	6
stain both moon and sun	" 35	3
The mortal moon hath her eclipse endured	" 107	5
each minute seems a moon	P P 15	15
Moralize—thou hear'st me moralize	V A	712
Nor could she moralize	R L	104
More—more lovely than a man	V A	9
More white and red	"	10
What follows more she murders with a kiss	"	54
Which bred more beauty	"	70
with a more delight	"	78
More thirst for drink	"	92
Fie, no more of love	"	185
Nay, more than flint	"	200
her woes the more increasing	"	254
the happy season once more fits	"	327
Burneth more hotly, swelleth with more rage	"	332
Once more the engine	"	367
Once more the ruby-colour'd	"	451
no more had seen	"	504
now no more resisteth	"	563
no more detain him	"	577
And more than so	"	661
hear a little more	"	709
more gold begets	"	768
more moving than your own	"	776
More I could tell, but more I dare not say	"	865
him seen no more	"	819
bids them fear no more	"	899
More—Her more than haste	V A	909
once more leap her eyes	"	1050
That makes more gushes	"	1056
more am I accurst	"	1120
now no more reflect	"	1130
more sweet-smelling sire	"	1178
espoused to more fame	R L	20
he pineth still for more	"	94
More than his eyes	"	105
And so, by hoping more	"	137
Or gaining more	"	154
beholds as more divine	"	291
Paying more slavish tribute	"	299
To add a more rejoicing	"	332
birds more cause to sing	"	333
latch, and with no more	"	359
With more than admiration	"	418
with more dreadful sights	"	462
more rage and lesser pity	"	468
her oratory adds more grace	"	564
'No more,' quoth he	"	667
To make more vent	"	1040
doth make the wound ache more	"	1116
No more than wax	"	1245
The more to blame	"	1278
For more it is	"	1286
When more is felt	"	1283
moves more than hear them told	"	1324
with more than haste	"	1332
Speed more than speed	"	1336
Promise more speed	"	1349
make him more amazed	"	1356
The more she saw the blood	"	1357
The more she thought	"	1358
More feeling-painful	"	1679
But more than he	"	1718
That I no more can see	"	1764
to make it more	"	1789
How much more praise	Son 2	9
she gave thee more	" 11	11
Thou shouldst print more	" 11	14
With means more blessed	" 16	4
more lovely and more temperate	" 18	2
An eye more bright	" 20	5
Let them say more	" 21	13
More than that tongue that more hath more express'd	" 23	12
more rich in hope	" 29	5
once more re-survey	" 32	3
No more be grieved	" 35	1
more than thy sins are	" 35	8
or all, or more	" 37	6
ten times more in worth	" 38	9
What hast thou then more than thou hadst before	" 40	2
thou hadst this more	" 40	4
touches me more nearly	" 42	4
More sharp to me	" 50	12
O, how much more	" 54	1
shall shine more bright	" 55	3
more blest may be	" 56	12
thrice more wish'd, more rare	" 56	11
To do more for me	" 72	6
And hang more praise	" 72	7
live no more to shame	" 72	12
makes thy love more strong	" 73	13
There lives more life	" 83	13
Which can say more	" 84	1
of praise add something more	" 85	10

More—no more shall dwell	*Son*	89	10
Of more delight than hawks	"	91	11
loved of more and less	"	96	3
More flowers I noted	"	99	14
more weak in seeming	"	102	1
is of more worth	"	103	3
If I no more can write	"	103	5
And more, much more	"	103	13
I never more will grind	"	110	10
Incapable of more	"	113	13
our appetites more keen	"	118	1
more strong, far greater	"	119	12
more than I have spent	"	119	14
that receive thee more	"	122	12
Made more or less	"	123	12
Which prove more short	"	125	4
Lose all, and more	"	125	6
more blest than living lips	"	128	12
Coral is far more red	"	130	2
is there more delight	"	130	7
a far more pleasing sound	"	130	10
More than enough	"	135	3
make thy large 'Will' more	"	135	12
Is more than my o'er-press'd defence can bide	"	139	8
without be rich no more	"	146	12
there's no more dying then	"	146	14
make me love thee more	"	150	9
The more I hear and see	"	150	10
More worthy I to be	"	150	14
more perjured I	"	152	13
more black and damned here	*L C*		54
by that cost more dear	"	....	95
to make our wits more keen	"	....	161
with more than love's good will	*P P*	9	7
he saw more wounds than one	"	9	13
And yet thou left'st me more	"	10	9
more mickle was the pain	"	16	9
More in women than in men	"	18	18
Use his company no more	"	21	50
Morn—of the weeping morn	*V A*	....	2
From morn till night	"	....	154
Like a red morn	"	....	453
He cheers the morn	"	....	484
or morn or weary even	"	....	495
To wake the morn	*R L*	....	942
one early morn did shine	*Son*	33	9
when his youthful morn	"	63	4
dried up the dewy morn	*P P*	6	1
Fair was the morn	"	9	1
Youth like summer morn	"	12	3
Morning—And wakes the morning	*V A*	....	853
Musing the morning	"	....	866
morning's silver-melting dew	*R L*	....	24
looks for the morning light	"	....	745
ravish the morning air	"	....	778
that tune their morning's joy	"	....	1107
Full many a glorious morning	*Son*	33	1
the morning sun of heaven	"	132	5
watch; the morning rise	*P P*	15	2
Mortal—on this mortal round	*V A*	....	368
Like a mortal butcher	"	....	618
for thy mortal vigour	"	....	953
of all mortal things	"	....	996
overthrow of mortal kind	"	....	1018
Where mortal stars, as bright	*R L*	....	13
had closed up mortal eyes	"	....	163
at the mercy of his mortal sting	"	....	364
And by their mortal fault	"	....	724
Mortal—Yet mortal looks adore	*Son*	7	7
are at a mortal war	"	46	1
eternal slave to mortal rage	"	64	4
Above a mortal pitch	"	86	6
The mortal moon	"	107	5
Turning mortal for thy love	*P P*	17	16
Mortality—death's dim look in life's mortality	*R L*	....	403
sad mortality o'er-sways their power	*Son*	65	2
Mortgage—am mortgaged to thy will	"	134	2
Morrow—Venus salutes him with this fair good-morrow	*V A*	....	859
when lo, the blushing morrow	*R L*	....	1082
give demure good-morrow	"	....	1219
and then she longs for morrow	"	....	1571
a windy night, a rainy morrow	*Son*	90	7
Most—when most his choice	*V A*	....	570
shall it make most weak	"	....	1145
it should most mistrust	"	....	1154
And most deceiving when it seems most just	"	....	1156
it shows most toward	"	....	1157
When most unseen, then most doth tyrannize	*R L*	....	676
Great grief grieves most	"	....	1117
manners most expressly told	"	....	1397
Who should weep most	"	....	1792
thou none lovest is most evident	*Son*	10	4
Sets you most rich	"	15	10
with your most high deserts	"	17	2
one most heinous crime	"	19	8
in that I honour most	"	25	4
With what I most enjoy	"	29	8
When most I wink	"	43	1
Most worthy comfort, now my greatest grief	"	48	6
Yet be most proud	"	78	9
Where breath most breathes	"	81	14
shall be most my glory	"	83	10
Who is it that says most	"	84	1
And to the most of praise	"	85	10
and me most wretched make	"	91	14
they most do show	"	94	2
of this most balmy time	"	107	9
sold cheap what is most dear	"	110	3
Most true it is	"	110	5
and most most loving breast	"	110	14
The most sweet favour	"	113	10
My most true mind	"	113	14
most kingly drinks it up	"	114	10
My most full flame	"	115	4
When most impeach'd	"	125	14
and most precious jewel	"	131	4
I am perjured most	"	152	6
O most potential love	*L C*	....	264
When he most burn'd	"	....	314
Mot—may read the mot afar	*R L*	....	830
Mote—each little mote will peep	"	....	1251
Mother—O, had thy mother	*V A*	....	203
that suck'd an earthly mother	"	....	863
mother of dread and fear	*R L*	....	117
nor mothers' groans respecting	"	....	431
That mother tries a merciless conclusion	"	....	1160
many Trojan mothers sharing joy	"	....	1431
unbless some mother	*Son*	3	4
Thou art thy mother's glass	"	3	9
sire and child and happy mother	"	8	11

Mother—As any mother's child	Son	21	11
And play the mother's part	"	143	12
Motion—with their continual	R L		591
The heavy motion	"		1326
with swift motion slide	Son	45	4
no motion shall I know	"	51	8
Hath motion, and mine eye	"	104	12
woad whose motion sounds	"	128	2
the motion of thine eyes	"	149	12
all that borrow'd motion	L C		327
Motive—the grounds and motives of her woe	"		63
Motley—a motley to the view	Son	110	2
Mould—stealing moulds from heaven	V A		730
Mount—although he mount her	"		598
mounts up on high	"		854
if he mount he dies	R L		508
Mountain—on mountain or in dale	V A		232
As mountain snow melts	"		750
the aspiring mountains	R L		548
The mountain or the sea	Son	113	11
And all the craggy mountains yields	P P	20	4
Mountain-spring—As from a	R L		1077
Mountain-top—Flatter the mountain-tops	Son	33	2
Mounted—Her champion mounted	V A		396
mounted, through the empty skies	"		1191
though mounted on the wind	Son	51	7
Mourn—to mourn some newer way	R L		1365
No longer mourn for me	Son	71	1
Yet so they mourn	"	127	13
To mourn for me	"	132	11
In black mourn I	P P	18	19
Mourner—mourner, black and grim	V A		920
let no mourner say	R L		1797
and they mourners seem	Son	127	10
and loving mourners be	"	132	3
'Mongst our mourners	P T		26
Mourn'st—thou mourn'st in vain	P P	21	19
Mournful—her . . . . hymns did hush	Son	102	10
Mourning—clad in mourning black	R L		1585
the mourning and congealed face	"		1734
As those two mourning eyes	Son	132	9
mourning doth thee grace	"	132	11
Mouse—the weak mouse panteth	R L		535
Mouth—Open'd their mouths	V A		248
Enfranchising his mouth	"		396
that sweet coral mouth	"		542
they spend their mouths	"		695
Whose frothy mouth	"		901
even in the mouths of men	Son	81	14
Mouthed—Another flap-mouth'd mourner	V A		920
Of mouthed graves	Son	77	6
Move—thy outward parts would	V A		435
This moves in him more rage	R L		468
moves more than hear them told	"		1324
that move thy pity	"		1533
my thoughts canst move	Son	47	11
these pleasures may thee move	P P	20	15
pleasures might me move	"	20	19
Moved—Being moved, he strikes	V A		623
moved with woman's moans	R L		587
Be moved with my tears	"		588
Yet if men moved him	L C		101
Mover—O fairest mover	V A		368
Moving—more moving than your own	"		776
star that guides my moving	Son	26	9
Moving—Who, moving others	Son	91	3
Doth cite each moving sense	P P	15	3
Mow—but for his scythe to mow	Son	60	12
Much—'Tis much to borrow	V A		411
be still as much	"		412
with too much handling	"		560
as much as may be	"		608
With much ado	"		694
mischances and much misery	"		738
is so much o'erworn	"		865
how much a fool was I	"		1015
too much wonder of his eye	R L		95
That, cloy'd with much, he	"		98
Those that much covet	"		131
In having much	"		151
She, much amazed	"		416
With too much labour drowns	"		1099
and too much talk affords	"		1105
Much like a press of people	"		1301
much imaginary work was there	"		1422
To give her so much grief	"		1463
that so much guile	"		1534
How much more praise	Son	2	9
for thou art much too fair	"	6	13
Much liker than your painted counterfeit	"	16	8
replete with too much rage	"	23	3
with thy much clearer light	"	43	7
so much of earth and water	"	44	11
O, how much more	"	54	1
though much, is not so great	"	61	9
so much as my poor name	"	71	11
and much enrich thy book	"	77	14
shalt win much glory	"	88	8
Lest I too much profane	"	89	11
To make him much outlive	"	101	11
And more, much more, than in my verse	"	103	13
could not so much hold	"	122	9
by paying too much rent	"	125	6
with too much disdain	"	140	2
And so much less	L C		188
By how much of me	"		189
my heart so much as warmed	"		191
enough,—too much, I fear	P P	19	49
Mud—Mud not the fountain that gave drink to thee	R L		577
Infect fair founts with venom mud	"		850
and silver fountains mud	Son	35	2
find their sepulchres in mud	L C		46
Muffled—Blind muffled bawd	R L		768
Mulberry—Would bring him mulberries	V A		1103
Murder—To rate the boar for murther	"		906
While lust and murder wakes	R L		168
tragedies and murders fell	"		766
rape and murder's rages	"		909
of murder and of theft	"		918
Murder—she murders with a kiss	V A		54
I murder shameful scorn	R L		1189
I'll murder straight	"		1634
Murder'd—murder'd this poor heart	V A		502
murder'd with the view	"		1031
Murder'st—Thou murder'st troth	R L		885
and murder'st all that are	"		929
Murderous—The murderous knife	"		1735
such murderous shame commits	Son	9	11
possess'd with murderous hate	"	10	5
is perjur'd, murderous	"	129	3

Murmur—each murmur stay	V A	.....	706
Muse—with me as with that Muse	Son	21	1
Had my friend's Muse	"	32	10
How can my Muse	"	38	1
Be thou the tenth Muse	"	38	9
If my slight Muse do please	"	38	13
Invoked thee for my Muse	"	78	1
my sick Muse doth give	"	79	4
married to my Muse	"	82	1
My tongue-tied Muse	"	85	1
by all the Muses filed	"	85	4
Where art thou, Muse	"	100	1
Return, forgetful Muse	"	100	5
Rise, resty Muse	"	100	9
O truant Muse	"	101	1
Make answer, Muse	"	101	5
Then do thy office, Muse	"	101	13
my Muse brings forth	"	103	1
Music—Ear's deep-sweet music	V A	.....	432
Whose tongue is music now		.....	1077
Music to hear, why hear'st thou music sadly	Son	8	1
But that wild music	"	102	11
thou my music, music play'st	"	128	1
music hath a far more pleasing sound	"	130	10
is music and sweet fire	P P	5	12
If music and sweet poetry agree	"	8	1
lute, the queen of music, makes	"	8	10
That defunctive music can	P T	.....	14
Musing—Musing the morning	V A	.....	866
Musit—The many musits through the which he goes	"	.....	683
Must—yet her fire must burn	"	.....	94
I must remove	"	.....	186
that must be cool'd	"	.....	387
must not repel a lover	"	.....	573
thou needs must have	"	.....	739
truth I must confess	"	.....	1001
lives and must not die	"	.....	1017
like him, I must confess	"	.....	1117
must doting Tarquin make	R L	.....	155
himself he must forsake	"	.....	157
Which must be lode-star	"	.....	179
must I force to my desire	"	.....	182
quoth he, 'I must deflower	"	.....	348
But they must ope	"	.....	383
Must sell her joy, her life	"	.....	385
must my will abide	"	.....	486
this night I must enjoy thee	"	.....	512
force must work my way	"	.....	513
thou perforce must bear	"	.....	612
Must be in thee read lectures	"	.....	618
must vomit his receipt	"	.....	703
alone must sit and pine	"	.....	795
So must my soul	"	.....	1169
How Tarquin must be used	"	.....	1195
And only must be wail'd	"	.....	1799
must be tomb'd with thee	Son	4	13
among the wastes of time must go	"	12	10
And you must live	"	16	14
must you see his skill	"	24	5
an necessary needs must be	"	35	13
we two must be twain	"	36	1
yet we must not be foes	"	40	14
I must attend time's leisure	"	44	12
whereon it must expire	"	73	11
which thou must leave ere long	"	73	14
or must from you be took	"	75	12
Must—to all the world must die	Son	81	6
I must ne'er love him	"	89	14
I must each day say o'er	"	108	6
and I must strive	"	112	5
Needs must I under my transgression bow	"	120	3
and yours must ransom me	"	120	14
my deeds must not be shown	"	121	12
though delay'd, answer'd must be	"	126	11
my sweet'st friend must be	"	133	4
in thy stores' account I one must be	"	136	10
she must herself assay	L C	.....	156
That we must curb it	"	.....	163
where I myself must render	"	.....	221
must your oblations be	"	.....	223
Must for your victory	"	.....	258
As they must needs	P P	8	2
Then must the love be great	"	8	3
one must be refused	"	16	9
Must live alone	"	18	53
Muster—muster troops of cares	R L	.....	720
Muster thy mists	"	.....	773
Mustering—.... to the quiet cabinet	"	.....	442
Mute—or else be mute	"	.....	208
attorney once is mute	"	.....	335
Will not my tongue be mute	"	.....	227
be you mute and dumb	"	.....	1123
beauty being mute	Son	83	11
the very birds are mute	"	97	12
Mutiny—Gives false alarms, suggesteth mutiny	V A	.....	651
This mutiny each part	"	.....	1049
this mutiny restrains	R L	.....	426
with herself is she in mutiny	"	.....	1153
Mutual—Till mutual overthrow	V A	.....	1018
in each by mutual ordering	Son	8	10
But mutual render	"	125	12
In a mutual flame	P T	.....	24
My—my captive and my slave	V A	.....	101
Over my altars	"	.....	103
And for my sake	"	.....	105
Making my arms his field, his tent my bed	"	.....	108
to my coy disdain	"	.....	112
Touch but my lips	"	.....	115
one wrinkle in my brow	"	.....	139
My beauty as the spring	"	.....	141
My flesh is soft and plump, my marrow burning	"	.....	142
My smooth moist hand	"	.....	143
sun doth burn my face	"	.....	186
for thee of my hairs	"	.....	191
quench them with my tears	"	.....	192
dwells upon my suit	"	.....	206
thou shalt be my deer	"	.....	231
Graze on my lips	"	.....	233
Then be my deer	"	.....	239
thus my strength is tried	"	.....	280
My heart all whole as thine, thy heart my wound	"	.....	370
my body's bane would cure	"	.....	372
'Give me my hand	"	.....	373
'Give me my heart	"	.....	374
My day's delight is past, my horse is gone	"	.....	380
all my mind, my thought, my busy care	"	.....	383
my palfrey from the mare	"	.....	384
My love to love	"	.....	412

My—'You hurt my hand	V. A	421
my unyielding heart	"	423
I had my load	"	430
my ears would love	"	433
my love to thee	"	442
In my soft lips	"	511
on my wax-red lips	"	516
buys my heart from me	"	517
Measure my strangeness with my unripe years	"	524
my sick heart commands	"	584
my joints did tremble	"	642
not mark my face	"	643
Within my bosom	"	646
My boding heart pants	"	647
shakes thee on my breast	"	648
Knocks at my heart	"	659
my faint heart bleed	"	669
thy death, my living sorrow	"	671
expected of my friends	"	718
my heart stands armed	"	779
closure of my breast	"	782
then my little heart	"	783
my heart longs not	"	785
My face is full of shame, my heart of teen	"	808
fearing my love's decease	"	1002
my fault; the boar provoked my tongue	"	1003
'My tongue cannot express my grief for one	"	1069
My sighs are blown away, my salt tears gone	"	1071
my heart to lead	"	1072
My youth with his; the more am I accurst	"	1120
this is my spite	"	1133
doth my love destroy	"	1163
wither in my breast	"	1182
here in my breast	"	1183
My throbbing heart shall rock thee	"	1186
my sweet love's flower	"	1188
to my desire	R L	182
to my household's grave	"	198
Then my digression is so vile	"	202
engraven in my face	"	203
in my golden coat	"	205
That my posterity	"	208
Shall curse my bones	"	209
dream of my intent	"	218
can my invention make	"	225
Will not my tongue be mute, my frail joints shake	"	227
my false heart bleed	"	228
kill'd my son or sire	"	232
to betray my life	"	233
my dear friend	"	234
he is my kinsman, my dear friend	"	237
My will is strong	"	243
in my eager eyes	"	254
in my hand being lock'd	"	260
Affection is my captain	"	271
My heart shall never countermand	"	276
My part is youth	"	278
Desire my pilot is, beauty my prize	"	279
be my gods, my guide	"	351
My will is back'd	"	352
tell my loving tale	"	480
must my will abide	"	486
My—My will that marks thee for my earth's delight	R L	487
with all my might	"	488
my attempt will bring	"	491
even in my soul	"	498
force must work my way	"	513
Tender my suit	"	534
'My husband is thy friend	"	582
My sighs, like whirlwinds	"	586
with my tears, my sighs, my groans	"	588
Melt at my tears	"	591
my heaved-up hands	"	638
'my uncontrolled tide	"	645
Yield to my love	"	668
And my true eyes	"	748
Upon my cheeks	"	756
of my cureless crime	"	772
co-partners in my pain	"	789
Mingling my talk with tears, my grief with groans	"	797
character'd in my brow	"	807
my loathsome trespass in my looks	"	812
will tell my story	"	813
Will couple my reproach	"	816
tuning my defame	"	817
'Let my good name	"	820
My honey lost	"	836
no perfection of my summer left	"	837
My Collatine would else Be guilty of my death, since of my crime	"	916
	"	931
Cancell'd my fortunes	"	934
Since that my case	"	1022
my confirm'd despite	"	1026
let forth my foul-defiled blood	"	1029
my honour lives in me	"	1032
thou livest in my defame	"	1033
mistress of my fate	"	1069
with my trespass	"	1070
acquit my forced offence	"	1071
with my attaint	"	1072
Nor fold my fault	"	1073
My sable ground	"	1074
My tongue shall utter all	"	1076
purge my impure tale	"	1078
through my window	"	1089
Brand not my forehead	"	1091
And in my hearing	"	1123
My restless discord	"	1124
my dishevell'd hair	"	1129
against my heart	"	1137
But with my body my poor soul's pollution	"	1157
My body or my soul	"	1163
So must my soul	"	1160
till my Collatine	"	1177
of my untimely death	"	1178
stop my breath	"	1180
My stained blood	"	1181
in my testament	"	1183
'My honour I'll bequeath	"	1184
my body so dishonoured	"	1185
shall my fame be bred	"	1188
For in my death	"	1189
My shame so dead	"	1190
My resolution, love	"	1193
And, for my sake	"	1197
abridgement of my will	"	1198
My soul and body	"	1199

My—My resolution, husband	R L	1200	My—master-mistress of my passion	Son	20	2
that makes my wound	"	1201	to my purpose	"	20	12
My shame be his that did my fame			my love is as fair	"	21	10
confound	"	1202	My glass shall not	"	22	1
And all my fame	"	1205	my days should expiate	"	22	4
My blood shall wash	"	1207	raiment of my heart	"	22	6
My life's foul deed, my life's fair end	"	1208	O, let my books	"	23	9
Yield to my hand; my hand shall			of my speaking breast	"	23	10
conquer thee	"	1210	in table of my heart	"	24	2
'My girl,' quoth she	"	1270	My body is the frame	"	24	3
grief of my sustaining	"	1272	Which in my bosom's shop	"	24	7
it small avails my mood	"	1273	Are windows to my breast	"	24	11
my sluggard negligence	"	1278	Lord of my love	"	26	1
One of my husband's men	"	1291	my duty strongly knit	"	26	2
A letter to my lord, my love, my			not to show my wit	"	26	4
dear	"	1295	that guides my moving	"	26	9
My woes are tedious, though my			on my tatter'd loving	"	26	11
words are brief	"	1309	then not show my head	"	26	14
At Ardea to my lord	"	1332	haste me to my bed	"	27	1
with my lamenting tongue	"	1465	a journey in my head	"	27	3
And with my tears	"	1468	To work my mind	"	27	4
And with my knife	"	1469	For then my thoughts	"	27	5
That with my nails	"	1472	keep my drooping eyelids	"	27	7
so my Troy did perish	"	1547	my soul's imaginary sight	"	27	9
And my laments	"	1616	to my sightless view	"	27	10
in my chamber came	"	1626	by day my limbs, by night my mind	"	27	13
And entertain my love	"	1629	draw my sorrows longer	"	28	13
If thou my love's desire	"	1631	beweep my outcast state	"	29	2
yoke thy liking to my will	"	1633	with my bootless cries	"	29	3
My fame, and thy	"	1638	and curse my fate	"	29	4
And then against my heart	"	1640	and then my state	"	29	10
So should my shame	"	1643	my state with kings	"	29	14
my poor self weak	"	1646	my dear time's waste	"	30	4
My bloody judge forbade my			of my lovers gone	"	31	10
tongue to speak	"	1648	my well-contented day	"	32	1
That my poor beauty	"	1651	my bones with dust	"	32	2
Though my gross blood	"	1655	Reserve them for my love	"	32	7
spotless is my mind	"	1656	Had my friend's Muse	"	32	10
to my sorrow lendeth	"	1676	Even so my sun	"	33	9
My woe too sensible	"	1678	splendour on my brow	"	33	10
And for my sake	"	1681	for this my love	"	33	13
revenged on my foe	"	1683	travel forth without my cloak	"	34	2
the quality of my offence	"	1702	o'ertake me in my way	"	34	3
May my pure mind	"	1704	on my storm-beaten face	"	34	6
My low-declined honour	"	1705	physic to my grief	"	34	9
By my excuse	"	1715	war is in my love	"	35	12
my old age new born	"	1759	Lest my bewailed guilt	"	36	10
my image thou hast torn	"	1762	Take all my comfort	"	37	4
beauty of my glass	"	1763	I make my love	"	37	8
My sorrow's interest	"	1797	How can my Muse	"	38	1
'she was my wife	"	1802	pour'st into my verse	"	38	2
'My daughter' and 'my wife	"	1804	If my slight Muse	"	38	13
'my daughter' and 'my wife	"	1806	all my loves, my love	"	40	1
Let my unsounded self	"	1819	No love, my love, that thou	"	40	3
Shall sum my count and make my			if for my love thou my love re-			
old excuse	Son	2 11	ceivest	"	40	5
I may change my mind	"	10 9	for my love thou usest	"	40	6
my love, you know	"	13 13	thee all my poverty	"	40	10
do I my judgement pluck	"	14 1	mightst my seat forbear	"	41	9
my knowledge I derive	"	14 9	it is not all my grief	"	42	1
before my sight	"	15 10	is of my wailing chief	"	42	3
than my barren rhyme	"	16 4	And for my sake	"	42	7
or my pupil pen	"	16 10	Suffering my friend for my sake	"	42	8
believe my verse	"	17 1	my loss is my love's gain	"	42	9
So should my papers	"	17 9	my friend hath found	"	42	10
and in my rhyme	"	17 14	And both for my sake	"	42	12
my love's fair brow	"	19 9	my friend and I are one	"	42	13
My love shall in my verse ever			my flesh were thought	"	44	1
live young	"	19 14	not stop my way	"	44	2

	Son				Son		
My—my foot did stand	Son	44	5	My—So is my love	Son	76	14
leisure with my moan	"	44	12	invoked thee for my Muse	"	78	1
The first my thought, the other				assistance in my verse	"	78	2
my desire	"	45	3	pen hath got my use	"	78	3
My life, being made of four	"	45	7	thou art all my art	"	78	13
my heart thy picture's sight	"	46	3	my rude ignorance	"	78	14
My heart mine eye the freedom	"	46	4	My verse alone	"	79	2
My heart doth plead	"	46	5	But now my gracious numbers	"	79	3
And my heart's right	"	46	11	And my sick Muse	"	79	4
With my love's picture then my				My saucy bark	"	80	7
eye doth feast	"	47	5	my love was my decay	"	80	11
to the painted banquet bids my				be my gentle verse	"	81	9
heart	"	47	6	such virtue hath my pen	"	81	13
mine eye is my heart's guest	"	47	7	married to my Muse	"	82	1
thy picture or my love	"	47	9	a limit past my praise	"	82	6
my thoughts canst move	"	47	11	silence for my sin	"	83	9
thy picture in my sight	"	47	13	shall be most my glory	"	83	10
Awakes my heart	"	47	14	My tongue-tied Muse	"	85	1
when I took my way	"	48	1	that is in my thought	"	85	11
That to my use	"	48	3	for my dumb thoughts	"	85	14
my jewels trifles are	"	48	5	my ripe thoughts in my brain in-			
now my greatest grief	"	48	6	hearse	"	86	3
closure of my breast	"	48	11	my verse astonished	"	86	8
frown on my defects	"	49	2	of my silence cannot boast	"	86	11
And this my hand	"	49	11	too dear for my possessing	"	87	1
my weary travel's end	"	50	2	My bonds in thee	"	87	4
tired with my woe	"	50	5	where is my deserving	"	87	6
put this in my mind	"	50	13	so my patent back	"	87	8
My grief lies onward and my joy				And place my merit	"	88	2
behind	"	50	14	bending all my loving thoughts	"	88	10
Thus can my love	"	51	1	Such is my love	"	88	13
Of my dull bearer	"	51	2	Speak of my lameness	"	89	3
my poor beast then find	"	51	5	and in my tongue	"	89	9
with my desire keep pace	"	51	9	my deeds to cross	"	90	2
shall excuse my jade	"	51	12	my heart hath 'scaped	"	90	5
keeps you as my chest	"	52	9	are not my measure	"	91	7
Whilst I, my sovereign	"	57	6	my life hath end	"	92	6
with my jealous thought	"	57	9	Since that my life	"	92	10
my verse shall stand	"	60	13	hath my absence been	"	97	1
My heavy eyelids	"	61	2	from my love's breath	"	99	3
desire my slumbers	"	61	3	In my love's veins	"	99	5
do mock my sight	"	61	4	my love's sweet face	"	100	9
into my deeds to pry	"	61	6	Give my love fame	"	100	13
It is my love	"	61	10	on my love depends	"	101	3
doth my rest defeat	"	61	11	My love is strengthen'd	"	102	1
all my soul and all my every part	"	62	2	greet it with my lays	"	102	6
inward in my heart	"	62	4	sometime hold my tongue	"	102	13
But when my glass	"	62	9	dull you with my song	"	102	14
Painting my age	"	62	14	my Muse brings forth	"	103	1
Against my love	"	63	1	my added praise beside	"	103	4
My sweet love's beauty, though my				my blunt invention	"	103	7
lover's life	"	63	12	Dulling my lines	"	103	8
and take my love	"	64	12	to no other pass my verses tend	"	103	11
my love may still shine	"	65	14	in my verse can sit	"	103	13
I leave my love alone	"	66	14	Let not my love	"	105	1
my poor name rehearse	"	71	11	Nor my beloved	"	105	2
with my life decay	"	71	12	all alike my songs	"	105	3
After my death	"	72	3	Kind is my love to-day	"	105	5
My name be buried where my				Therefore my verse	"	105	7
body is	"	72	11	is all my argument	"	105	9
My life hath in this	"	71	3	is my invention spent	"	105	11
My spirit is thine	"	74	8	the lease of my true love	"	107	3
my body being dead	"	74	10	My love looks fresh	"	107	13
you to my thoughts as food	"	75	1	to thee my true spirit	"	108	2
may see my pleasure	"	75	8	That may express my love	"	108	4
Why is my verse so barren	"	76	1	seem'd my flame to qualify	"	109	2
almost tell my name	"	76	7	As from my soul	"	109	4
are still my argument	"	76	10	That is my home	"	109	5
So all my best is	"	76	11	bring water for my stain	"	109	8

My—in my nature reign'd	Son	109	9	My—my love-suit, sweet, fulfil	Son	136	4
Save thou, my rose; in it thou art my all	"	109	14	and my will one	"	136	6
my heart another youth	"	110	7	Make but my name	"	136	13
thee my best of love	"	110	8	for my name is 'Will	"	136	14
next my heaven the best	"	110	13	of my heart is tied	"	137	8
O, for my sake	"	111	1	Why should my heart	"	137	9
of my harmful deeds	"	111	2	Which my heart knows	"	137	10
for my life provide	"	111	3	things right true my heart	"	137	13
my name receives a brand	"	111	5	When my love swears	"	138	1
my nature is subdued	"	111	6	she knows my days are past	"	138	6
'gainst my strong infection	"	111	10	lays upon my heart	"	139	2
stamp'd upon my brow	"	112	2	but in my sight	"	139	5
O'er-green my bad, my good allow	"	112	4	more than my o'er-press'd defence	"	139	8
You are my all	"	112	5	my love well knows	"	139	9
To know my shames	"	112	6	from my face she turns my foes	"	139	11
That my steel'd sense	"	112	8	And rid my pain	"	139	14
that my adder's sense	"	112	10	My tongue-tied patience	"	140	2
how with my neglect	"	112	12	of my pity-wanting pain	"	140	4
in my purpose bred	"	112	13	And in my madness	"	140	10
mine eye is in my mind	"	113	1	But my five wits nor my five senses can	"	141	9
My most true mind	"	113	14	But 'tis my heart	"	141	3
Or whether doth my mind	"	114	1	Only my plague thus far I count my gain	"	141	13
'tis flattery in my seeing	"	114	9	Love is my sin	"	142	1
And my great mind	"	114	10	Hate of my sin	"	142	2
Yet then my judgement	"	115	3	and my loud crying	"	143	14
My most full flame	"	115	4	my female evil	"	144	5
Rook both my wilfulness	"	117	9	Tempteth my better angel from my side	"	144	6
Since my appeal says	"	117	13	would corrupt my saint	"	144	7
did I frame my feeding	"	118	6	my angel be turn'd fiend	"	144	9
hath my heart committed	"	119	5	Till my bad angel fire my good one out	"	144	14
rebuked to my content	"	119	13	saw my woeful state	"	145	4
under my transgression bow	"	120	3	And saved my life	"	145	14
Unless my nerves were brass	"	120	4	centre of my sinful earth	"	146	1
by my unkindness shaken	"	120	5	My love is as a fever	"	147	1
My deepest sense	"	120	10	My reason, the physician to my love	"	147	5
to my sportive blood	"	121	6	My thoughts and my discourse	"	147	11
Or on my frailties	"	121	7	Love put in my head	"	148	1
At my abuses reckon	"	121	10	is my judgement fled	"	148	3
my deeds must not be shown	"	121	12	my false eyes dote	"	148	5
are within my brain	"	122	1	I mistake my view	"	148	11
If my dear love	"	124	1	I do call my friend	"	149	5
With my extern	"	125	2	all my best doth worship	"	149	11
take thou my oblation	"	125	10	my heart to sway	"	150	2
O thou, my lovely boy	"	126	1	the lie to my true sight	"	150	3
Therefore my mistress' eyes	"	127	9	That, in my mind	"	150	8
my music, music play'st	"	128	1	not abhor my state	"	150	12
Whilst my poor lips	"	128	7	urge not my amiss	"	151	3
My mistress' eyes	"	130	1	guilty of my faults	"	151	4
from my mistress reeks	"	130	8	My nobler part to my gross body's treason	"	151	5
My mistress, when she walks	"	130	12	My soul doth tell my body	"	151	7
I think my love as rare	"	130	13	For all my vows	"	152	7
to my dear doting heart	"	131	3	And all my honest faith	"	152	8
In my judgement's place	"	131	12	But at my mistress' eye	"	153	9
ruth upon my pain	"	132	4	would touch my breast	"	153	10
makes my heart to groan	"	133	1	the balm for my help lies	"	153	13
gives my friend and me	"	133	2	my mistress' eyes	"	153	14
my sweet'st friend	"	133	4	but I, my mistress' thrall	"	154	12
And my next self	"	133	6	My spirits to attend	L C	....	3
Prison my heart	"	133	9	it was to gain my grace	"	....	79
my friend's heart let my poor heart bail	"	133	10	My woeful self	"	....	143
my heart be his guard	"	133	11	and was my own fee-simple	"	....	144
use rigour in my gaol	"	133	12	Threw my affections	"	....	146
to be my comfort still	"	134	4	gave him all my flower	"	....	147
debtor for my sake	"	134	11	as some my equals did	"	....	148
my unkind abuse	"	134	12				
hide my will in thine	"	135	6				
And in my will	"	135	8				

My—upon these terms I held my city	L C	...	176	Myself—Before I know myself	V A	...	525
of my suffering youth	"	...	178	Unlike myself thou hear'st	"	...	712
of my holy vows afraid	"	...	179	Myself a weakling	R L	...	584
All thy offences	"	...	183	'To kill myself,' quoth she	"	...	1156
my heart so much as warned	"	...	191	either to myself was nearer	"	...	1165
Or my affection put	"	...	192	Myself, thy friend, will kill myself,			
Or any of my leisures	"	...	193	thy foe	"	...	1196
my origin and ender	"	...	222	Myself was stirring	"	...	1280
But, O my sweet	"	...	239	As I, not for myself	Son	22	10
in that my boast is true	"	...	246	For thee and for myself	"	27	14
their fountains in my well	"	...	255	And look upon myself	"	29	4
My parts had power	"	...	260	myself almost despising	"	29	9
to my sweet design	"	...	278	Myself corrupting	"	35	7
and undertake my troth	"	...	280	And 'gainst myself	"	35	11
were levell'd on my face	"	...	282	against myself uprear	"	49	11
resolved my reason into tears	"	...	296	And for myself	"	62	7
my white stole of chastity I dafl'd	"	...	297	shows me myself indeed	"	62	9
Shook off my sober guards	"	...	298	'Tis thee, myself, that for myself	"	62	13
When my love swears	P P	1	1	against myself I'll fight	"	88	3
my years be past the best	"	1	6	that to myself I do	"	88	11
But wherefore says my love	"	1	9	myself will bear all wrong	"	88	14
My better angel is a man	"	2	3	As I'll myself disgrace	"	89	7
My worser spirit a woman	"	2	4	For thee against myself	"	89	13
soon to hell, my female evil	"	2	5	might I from myself depart	"	109	3
my better angel from my side	"	2	6	So that myself bring water	"	109	8
my saint to be a devil	"	2	7	And made myself a motley	"	110	2
my angel be turn'd fiend	"	2	9	when I saw myself to win	"	119	4
my bad angel fire my good one out	"	2	14	I swear it to myself alone	"	131	8
Persuade my heart	"	3	3	Me from myself	"	133	5
My vow was earthly	"	3	7	Of him, myself, and thee	"	133	7
My vow was breath	"	3	9	I myself am mortgaged	"	134	2
Fair is my love	"	7	1	Myself I'll forfeit	"	134	3
Dreading my love	"	7	10	I against myself	"	149	2
See, in my thigh,' quoth she	"	9	12	Am of myself, all tyrant	"	149	4
he seized on my lips	"	11	9	Revenge upon myself	"	149	8
my lady at this bay	"	11	13	do I in myself respect	"	149	9
O, my love, my love is young	"	12	10	Fresh to myself	L C	...	76
Ah, neither be my share	"	14	1	Love to myself	"	...	77
that kept my rest away	"	14	2	Finding myself in honour	"	...	150
on the doubts of my decay	"	14	4	where I myself must render	"	...	221
Yet at my parting	"	14	7	Though to myself forsworn	P P	5	3
to jest at my exile	"	14	9	a word for shadows like myself	"	14	11
My heart doth charge	"	15	2				
I post unto my pretty	"	15	9	Nail—with her nails her flesh doth			
For now my song is ended	"	16	16	tear	R L	...	739
my hand hath sworn	"	17	11	That with my nails	"	...	1472
My flocks feed not	"	18	1	senseless Sinon with her nails	"	...	1564
My ewes breed not	"	18	2	Naked—in her naked bed	V A	...	397
My rams speed not	"	18	3	His naked armour	R L	...	188
All my merry jigs	"	18	9	all naked, will bestow it	Son	26	8
All my lady's love	"	18	10	naked and concealed fiend	L C	...	317
Wrought all my loss	"	18	14	And stood stark naked	P P	6	10
My shepherd's pipe can sound	"	18	27	Name—usurp'd his name	V A	...	794
My wether's bell rings	"	18	28	to his hateful name	"	...	994
My curtal dog, that wont	"	18	29	Haply that name of chaste	R L	...	8
My sighs so deep	"	18	31	Collatine's high name	"	...	108
to see my doleful plight	"	18	33	wound'st his princely name	"	...	599
the cause of all my moan	"	18	51	dishonour in thy name	"	...	621
Lest that my mistress hear my song	"	19	50	her crying babe with Tarquin's			
To teach my tongue	"	19	52	name	"	...	814
Live with me and be my love	"	20	1	Let my good name	"	...	820
live with me and be my love	"	20	16	titles to a ragged name	"	...	892
Myrtle—hasteth to a myrtle grove	V A	...	865	throws forth Tarquin's name	"	...	1717
Under a myrtle shade	P P	11	2	as if the name he tore	"	...	1787
Embroider'd all with leaves of				that honour from thy name	Son	36	12
myrtle	"	20	12	lose name of single one	"	39	6
Which a grove of myrtles made	"	21	4	as my poor name rehearse	"	71	11
Myself—'Thrice fairer than myself	V A	...	7	My name be buried	"	72	11
To sell myself I can	"	...	513	doth almost tell my name	"	76	7

Entry	Ref	№	Line
Name—spirit doth use your name	Son	80	2
Your name from hence	"	81	5
Thy sweet beloved name	"	89	10
of thy budding name	"	95	3
Naming thy name	"	95	8
I hallow'd thy fair name	"	108	8
my name receives a brand	"	111	5
it bore not beauty's name	"	127	2
Sweet beauty hath no name	"	127	7
Make but my name thy love	"	136	13
for my name is 'Will	"	136	14
But rising at thy name	"	151	9
Single nature's double name	P T	....	39
Name—thou didst name the boar	V A	....	641
But ere I name him	R L	....	1688
Nameless—blurr'd with nameless bastardy	"	....	522
Naming—Naming thy name	Son	95	8
Napkin—her napkin to her eyne	L C	....	15
Narcissus—Narcissus so himself	V A	....	161
had Narcissus seen her	R L	....	265
Nativity—descried in men's nativity	"	....	538
Nativity, once in the main	Son	60	5
Nature—Nature that made thee	V A	....	11
By law of nature	"	....	171
with nature's workmanship	"	....	291
Till forging Nature	"	....	729
workmanship of nature	"	....	731
Swear Nature's death	"	....	744
Now Nature cares not	"	....	933
Are nature's faults	R L	....	529
by nature they delight	"	....	697
In scorn of nature	"	....	1374
Nature's bequest gives nothing	Son	4	3
nature calls thee to be gone	"	4	11
Nature hath not made	"	11	9
nature's changing course	"	18	8
with Nature's own hand	"	20	1
Nature as she wrought thee	"	20	10
rarities of nature's truth	"	60	11
now Nature bankrupt is	"	67	9
for a map doth Nature store	"	68	13
what nature made so clear	"	84	10
husband nature's riches	"	94	6
though in my nature reign'd	"	109	9
my nature is subdued	"	111	6
by nature to subsist	"	122	6
Nature, sovereign mistress	"	126	5
hath put on nature's power	"	127	5
of one by nature's outwards	L C	....	80
Each stone's dear nature	"	....	210
Nature hath charged me	"	....	226
Showing fair nature	"	....	311
Single nature's double name	P T	....	39
Nay—Nay, more than flint	V A	....	200
Nay, do not struggle	"	....	710
'Nay, then,' quoth Adon	"	....	769
Nay, if you read this line	Son	71	5
Nay, if thou lour'st on me	"	149	7
There a nay is placed	P P	18	12
and say thee nay	"	19	20
A woman's nay doth stand	"	19	42
Near—with others all too near	Son	61	14
dreading the winter's near	"	97	14
that I come so near	"	136	1
since I am near slain	"	139	13
when their deaths be near	"	140	7
come thou not near	P T	....	8
Nearer—to myself was nearer	R L	....	1165
Nearly—touches me more nearly	Son	42	4
Necessary—gives to .... wrinkles	"	108	11
Neck—Whose sinewy neck	V A	....	99
his neck a sweet embrace	"	....	539
And on his neck	"	....	592
still hanging by his neck	"	....	593
His short thick neck	"	....	627
some catch her by the neck	"	....	872
One on another's neck	Son	131	11
Neck'd—The strong-neck'd steed	V A	....	263
Nectar—Such nectar from his lips	"	....	572
Need—what needs a second striking	"	....	250
if thou needs wilt hunt	"	....	673
thou needs must have	"	....	739
you need not fear	"	....	1083
I need not fear to die	R L	....	1052
an accessary needs must be	Son	35	13
of posting is no need	"	51	4
Where checks need blood	"	82	14
that you did painting need	"	83	1
Then need I not to fear	"	92	5
Truth needs no colour	"	101	6
Because he needs no praise	"	101	9
Needs must I under my transgression how	"	120	3
Nor need I tallies	"	122	10
needs would touch my breast	"	133	10
that needs will taste	L C	....	167
As they must needs	P P	8	2
conceit needs no defence	"	8	8
He will help thee in thy need	"	21	52
Need'st—What need'st thou wound	Son	139	7
Needeth—needeth then apologies	R L	....	31
Needing—ere that there was true needing	Son	118	8
All help needing	P P	18	24
Needle—wherein her needle sticks	R L	....	317
the needle his finger pricks	"	....	319
Needy—And needy nothing	Son	66	3
Ne'er—in battle ne'er did bow	V A	....	99
ne'er pleased her babe	"	....	974
Ne'er saw the beauteous livery	"	....	1107
Ne'er settled equally	"	....	1139
still blasts and ne'er grows old	R L	....	49
But they ne'er meet	"	....	903
sin ne'er gives a fee	"	....	913
ne'er touch'd earthly faces	Son	17	8
I must ne'er love him	"	89	14
this shall I ne'er know	"	144	13
Till now did ne'er invite	L C	....	182
but ne'er was harmed	"	....	194
Ne'er to pluck thee	P P	17	12
Thy like ne'er was	"	18	50
Ne'er-cloying—your .... sweetness	Son	118	5
Neglect—so then we do neglect	R L	....	132
For thy neglect of truth	Son	101	2
Mark how with my neglect	"	112	12
Neglected—Neglected all, with swift intent	R L	....	46
Whilst her neglected child	Son	143	5
Negligence—blame my sluggard	R L	....	1278
braided in loose negligence	L C	....	35
Neigh—snorts and neighs aloud	V A	....	292
he neighs, he bounds	"	....	265
and neighs unto her	"	....	307
Shall neigh,—no dull flesh	Son	51	11
Neighbour—from forth a copse that neighbours by	V A	....	259
all the neighbour caves	"	....	830

NEIGHBOUR 199 NEWS

Neighbour—shadow'd by his neighbour's ear	R L	1416	Never—I never saw that you	Son	83	1
Neither—neither eyes nor ears	V A	437	I must ne'er love him	"	89	14
can neither fight nor fly	R L	230	if never intermix'd	"	101	8
Cheeks neither red nor pale	"	1510	you never can be old	"	101	1
Yet neither may possess	"	1791	never kept seat in one	"	105	14
Neither in inward worth	Son 16	11	O, never say that I was false	"	109	1
neither he nor his compeers	" 86	7	Never believe, though	"	109	9
neither party is nor true	L C	186	I never more will grind	"	110	10
neither sting, knot, nor confine	"	265	and is never shaken	"	116	6
but neither true nor trusty	P P 7	2	I never writ, nor no man	"	116	11
though excellent in neither	" 7	18	full of your ne'er-cloying sweetness	"	118	5
Ah, neither be my share	" 14	1	itself so blessed never	"	119	6
Neither too young	" 19	6	never can be miss'd	"	122	8
Neither two nor one	P T	40	I never saw a goddess go	"	130	11
To themselves yet either neither	"	43	this shall I ne'er know	"	144	13
Nerve—Unless my nerves were brass	Son 120	4	that never touch'd his hand	L C		141
Nest—birds to their nest	V A	532	ne'er invite, nor never woo	"		182
hatch in sparrows' nests	R L	849	but ne'er was harmed	"		191
swan in her watery nest	"	1611	O never faith could hold	P P	5	2
Death is now the phoenix' nest	P T	56	are seld or never found	"	13	7
Nestor—you see grave Nestor stand	R L	1401	Ne'er to pluck thee	"	17	12
loss of Nestor's golden words	"	1420	Thy like ne'er was	"	18	50
Net—lies tangled in a net	V A	67	Press never thou to choose anew	"	19	34
Never—where never serpent hisses	"	17	and never for to saint	"	19	41
thy lips shall never open	"	48	Never-conquer'd—Thy .... fort	R L		482
but never to obey	"	61	Never-ending—date of ... woes	"		935
never to remove	"	81	Never-resting—For .... time	Son	5	5
Never did passenger	"	91	New—in Tarquin new ambition bred	R L		411
in battle ne'er did bow	"	99	Foretell new storms	"		1589
Never can blab	"	126	my old age new born	"		1759
can never grave it	"	376	This were to be new made	Son	2	13
I never shall regard	"	377	I engraft you new	"	15	14
never lost again	"	408	and her old face new	"	27	12
never waxeth strong	"	420	new wail my dear time's waste	"	30	4
Will never rise	"	480	Which I new pay	"	30	12
never four such lamps	"	489	By new unfolding	"	52	12
O, never let their crimson liveries	"	506	in Grecian tires are painted new	"	53	8
feeds, yet never filleth	"	548	where two contracted new	"	56	10
tushes never sheathed	"	617	If there be nothing new	"	59	1
never relieved by any	"	708	to dress his beauty new	"	68	12
and are never done	"	846	so barren of new pride	"	76	1
ne'er pleased her babe	"	974	dressing old words new	"	76	11
and never woman yet	"	1067	sun is daily new and old	"	76	13
never wound the heart	"	1042	To take a new acquaintance	"	77	12
And never fright	"	1098	though alter'd new	"	93	3
Ne'er saw the beauteous livery	"	1107	Our love was new	"	102	5
never did he bless	"	1119	What's new to speak, what new to register	"	108	3
Ne'er settled equally	"	1139	offences of affections new	"	110	4
Still blasts and ne'er grows old	R L	49	and new faith torn	"	152	3
Birds never limed	"	88	In vowing new hate after new love bearing	"	152	4
But she, that never coped	"	99	Cupid got new fire	"	153	14
Self-love had never drown'd him	"	265	new lodged and newly deified	L C		84
shall never countermand mine eye	"	276	And new pervert a reconciled maid	"		329
that will never be forgot	"	556	New-appearing—to his .... sight	Son	7	3
she never may behold the day	"	746	New-bleeding—Of proofs	L C		153
have never practised how	"	748	New-born—mine honour is	R L		1190
vanities can never last	"	894	Newer—to mourn some newer way	"		1365
But they ne'er meet	"	963	On newer proof to try	Son	110	11
sin ne'er gives a fee	"	913	built up with newer might	"	123	2
shall never come to growths	"	1052	New-fall'n—As apt as .... snow	V A		354
trespass never will dispense	"	1070	New-fangled—though ill	Son	91	3
And never be forgot	"	1644	New-fired—Love's brand new-fired	"	153	9
that never was inclined	"	1657	New-found—To new-found methods	"	76	4
rose might never die	Son 1	2	New-kill'd—Like to a .... bird	R L		457
heavenly touches ne'er touch'd earthly faces	" 17	8	Newly—was it newly bred	"		490
A closet never pierced	" 46	6	new lodged and newly-deified	L C		84
shall never cut from memory	" 63	11	News—That sometime true news	V A		658

Entry	Ref	No.
News—news from the warlike band	R L	255
No news but health	Son 140	8
New-sprung—the new-sprung flower	V A	1171
New-waxen—From lips .... pale	R L	1663
Next—Thou art the next of blood	V A	1184
next vouchsafe t' afford	R L	1305
next my heaven the best	Son 110	13
And my next self	" 133	6
Nibbler—the tender nibbler	P P 4	11
Nice—the painter was so nice	R L	1412
And nice affections wavering	L C	97
Niggard—The niggard prodigal	R L	79
Then, beauteous niggard	Son 4	5
Than niggard truth	" 72	8
Niggarding—makest waste in	" 1	12
Nigh—that she is so nigh	V A	341
No flower was nigh	"	1055
that grazed his cattle nigh	L C	57
Night—so shall the day seem night	V A	122
From morn till night	"	154
The night of sorrow	"	481
in water seen by night	"	492
The owl, night's herald	"	531
and bid good-night	"	534
let me say "Good-night	"	535
'Good-night,' quoth she	"	537
this night I'll waste in sorrow	"	583
The night is spent	"	717
'In night,' quoth she	"	720
'Now of this dark night	"	727
and her by night	"	732
that burns by night	"	755
by this black-faced night	"	773
merciless and pitchy night	"	821
and outwore the night	"	841
to spend the night withal	"	847
consort with ugly night	"	1041
rock thee day and night	"	1186
For he the night before	R L	15
Till sable Night	"	117
and wore out the night	"	123
the dead of night	"	162
and misty night	"	356
resembling dew of night	"	396
one in dead of night	"	449
to this night	"	485
'this night I must	"	512
in blind concealing night	"	675
Tarquin fares this night	"	698
through the dark night	"	729
on the direful night	"	741
'night's 'scapes doth open lay	"	747
unseen secrecy of night	"	763
'O comfort-killing Night	"	764
vaporous and foggy Night	"	771
make perpetual night	"	784
Were Tarquin Night, as he is but Night's child	"	785
Through Night's black bosom	"	788
'O Night, thou furnace	"	799
copesmate of ugly Night	"	925
sentinel the night	"	942
O, this dread night	"	965
this cursed crimeful night	"	970
Poor grooms are sightless night	"	1013
and uncheerful Night	"	1024
this false night's abuses	"	1075
And solemn night	"	1081
And therefore still in night	"	1085
Night—what's done by night	R L	1092
weep like the dewy night	"	1232
Assail'd by night	"	1262
burnt out in tedious nights	"	1379
She looks for night	"	1571
this night I will inflict	"	1630
in hideous night	Son 12	2
change your day of youth to sullied night	" 15	12
hung in ghastly night	" 27	11
Makes black night beauteous	" 27	12
by night my mind	" 27	13
is not eased by night	" 28	3
But day by day by night, and night by day	" 28	4
the swart-complexion'd night	" 28	11
And night doth nightly	" 28	14
hid in death's dateless night	" 30	6
When in dead night	" 43	11
All days are nights	" 43	13
And nights bright days	" 43	14
to the weary night	" 61	2
to age's steepy night	" 63	5
by and by black night	" 73	7
his compeers by night	" 86	7
Give not a windy night	" 90	7
did hush the night	" 102	10
the day or night	" 113	11
that our night of woe	" 120	9
Doth follow night	" 145	11
as dark as night	" 147	14
Good night, good rest	P P 14	1
She bade good-night	" 14	2
dark dreaming night	" 15	8
The night so pack'd, I post	" 15	9
the night would post too soon	" 15	13
Pack night, peep day; good day, of night now borrow	" 15	17
Short, night, to-night, and length thyself	" 15	18
will calm ere night	" 19	14
Nightingale—Save the .... alone	P P 21	8
Nightly—For with the .... linen	R L	680
warble of her nightly sorrow	"	1080
doth nightly make grief's strength	Son 28	14
Which nightly gulls him	" 86	10
Night-owl—that this .... will catch	R L	360
Night-waking—foul .... cat	"	554
Night-wanderers—.... often are	V A	825
Night-wandering—.... weasels	R L	307
Nill—nill I construe whether	P P 14	8
Nimble—Relish your nimble notes	R L	1126
For nimble thought can jump	Son 44	7
those jacks that nimble leap	" 128	5
Youth is nimble	P P 12	6
Nimbly—Nimbly she fastens	V A	38
Nine—Than those old nine	Son 38	10
No—But having no defects	V A	138
and yet no footing seen	"	148
'Fie, no more of love	"	185
but of no woman bred	"	214
Thou art no man	"	215
No dog shall rouse thee	"	240
Taking no notice	"	341
Therefore no marvel	"	390
they make no battery	"	426
or I had no hearing	"	428
Had I no eyes	"	433
no more had seen	"	504
No fisher but the ungrown	"	526

Entry	Source	Line
No—now no more resisteth	V. 1	563
she can no more detain him	"	577
no longer to restrain him	"	579
He tells her, no; to-morrow	"	587
You have no reason	"	612
and takes no rest	"	647
which no encounter dare	"	676
No matter where	"	715
No, lady, no; my heart	"	785
have him seen no more	"	819
if she said 'No	"	852
no tidings of her love	"	867
it is no gentle chase	"	883
bids them fear no more	"	889
she will no further	"	905
O no, it cannot be	"	937
thou hast no eyes	"	939
'No, no,' quoth she	"	997
Which knows no pity	"	1000
No flower was nigh, no grass	"	1055
where no breach should be	"	1066
henceforth no creature wear	"	1081
Having no fair to lose	"	1083
now no more reflect	"	1130
is no cause of fear	"	1153
no secret bushes fear	R L	88
inward ill no outward harm	"	91
Could pick no meaning	"	100
She touch'd no unknown baits, nor fear'd no hooks	"	103
No cloudy show	"	115
there's no death supposed	"	133
if there be no self-trust	"	158
no comfortable star did lend	"	164
no noise but owls' and wolves'	"	165
hold it for no sin	"	209
finds no excuse nor end	"	238
no hate in loving	"	240
with no more	"	339
fearing no such thing	"	363
there were no strife	"	405
their lord no bearing yoke	"	409
and hears no heedful friends	"	495
no device can take	"	535
wilderness where are no laws	"	544
that knows no gentle right	"	545
No penetrable entrance	"	559
He is no woodman	"	580
O, if no harder	"	593
no outrageous thing	"	607
'No more,' quoth he	"	667
While Lust is in his pride, no exclamation	"	705
I have no one to blush	"	792
Have no perfection	"	837
But no perfection is so absolute	"	853
Having no other pleasure	"	860
We have no good	"	873
Thou grant'st no time	"	908
doth me no right	"	1027
But this no slaughterhouse	"	1039
O no, that cannot be	"	1049
No object but her passion's strength	"	1103
and hath no words	"	1105
loves no stops	"	1124
think no shame of me	"	1204
No cause, but company	"	1236
No more than wax	"	1245
No man inveigh	"	1254
No—without or yea or no	R L	1340
but laid no words	"	1351
no semblance did remain	"	1453
The painter was no god	"	1461
no guilty instance gave	"	1511
no water thence proceeds	"	1552
He hath no power	"	1594
Where no excuse can give	"	1614
No rightful plea	"	1649
no flood by raining slaketh	"	1677
'No, no,' quoth she, 'no dame hereafter living	"	1714
That I no more can see	"	1764
and last no longer	"	1765
That no man could distinguish	"	1785
let no mourner say	"	1797
nor no remembrance	Son	5 12
That thou no form	"	9 6
No love toward others	"	9 13
No longer yours	"	13 2
Find no determination	"	13 6
Nor draw no lines	"	19 10
for myself no quiet find	"	27 14
no whit disdaineth	"	33 13
For no man	"	34 7
No more be grieved	"	35 1
No love, my love	"	40 3
No matter then although	"	44 5
but then no longer glad	"	45 13
I can allege no cause	"	49 14
of posting is no need	"	51 4
no motion shall I know	"	51 8
Then can no horse	"	51 9
no dull flesh	"	51 11
I have no precious time	"	57 3
he thinks no ill	"	57 14
O, no! thy love	"	61 9
there is no remedy	"	62 3
no face so gracious	"	62 5
No shape so true, no truth of such account	"	62 6
is no stronger than a flower	"	65 4
no exchequer now but his	"	67 11
Making no summer	"	68 11
Robbing no old to dress	"	68 12
No longer mourn for me	"	71 1
And live no more to shame	"	72 12
pursuing no delight	"	75 11
no praise to thee	"	79 12
your fair no painting set	"	83 2
No, neither he	"	86 7
but waking no such matter	"	87 14
making no defence	"	89 4
no more shall dwell	"	89 10
And life no longer	"	92 3
that fears no blot	"	92 13
no hatred in thine eye	"	93 6
'Truth needs no colour	"	101 6
Beauty no pencil	"	101 7
because he needs no praise	"	101 9
if I no more can write	"	103 5
For to no other pass	"	103 11
and no pace perceived	"	104 10
Counting no old thing old	"	108 7
what shall have no end	"	110 9
No bitterness that I will bitter think	"	111 11
For it no form delivers	"	113 5
hath the mind no part	"	113 7
knew no reason why	"	115 3

No—O, no! it is an ever-fixed mark	Son	116	5
nor no man ever loved	"	116	14
have no leisure taken	"	120	7
No, I am that I am	"	121	9
No, Time, thou shalt not	"	123	1
No, it was builded far	"	124	5
No, let me be obsequious	"	125	9
knows no art	"	125	11
beauty hath no name, no holy bower	"	127	7
no beauty lack	"	127	11
Enjoy'd no sooner	"	129	5
and no sooner had	"	129	6
But no roses	"	130	6
no fair acceptance shine	"	135	8
Let no unkind, no fair beseechers kill	"	135	13
No news but health	"	140	8
be rich no more	"	146	12
no more dying then	"	146	14
Which have no correspondence	"	148	2
as all men's: no	"	148	8
No marvel then	"	148	11
stays no farther reason	"	151	8
No want of conscience	"	151	13
But found no cure	"	153	13
and to no love beside	L C		77
which did no form receive	"		241
it is no fault of mine	P P	3	12
conceit needs no defence	"	8	8
and yet no cause I have	"	10	7
no rubbing will refresh	"	13	8
no cement can redress	"	13	10
pipe can sound no deal	"	18	27
There is no heaven	"	19	45
Is no friend in misery	"	21	19
No man will supply thy want	"	21	38
Use his company no more	"	21	50
and no space was seen	P T		30
Leaving no posterity	"		59
Noble—with noble disposition	R L		1695
noble by the sway	L C		108
Which late her noble suit	"		234
Nobler—My nobler part	Son	151	6
Nobly—Thou nobly base	R L		660
Noise—his ill-resounding noise	V A		919
No noise but owls' and wolves' lesser noise than shallow fords	R L		165
	"		1329
None—deep desire hath none	V A		389
But none is best	"		971
if none of those	R L		44
when none may spy him	"		881
and be nurse to none	"		1162
But none where all distress	"		1446
though none it ever cured	"		1581
and thy none of ours	"		1757
Thou single wilt prove none	Son	8	14
that thou none lovest	"	10	4
O, none but unthrifts	"	13	13
But you like none, none you	"	53	14
O, none, unless this miracle	"	65	13
When yellow leaves, or none	"	73	2
power to hurt and will do none	"	94	1
yet I none could see	"	99	14
None else to me, nor I to none	"	112	7
yet none knows well	"	129	13
Among a number one is reckon'd none	"	136	8
to none was ever said	L C		180

None—none of the mind	L C		181
Such looks as none could look	P P	4	4
None fairer, nor none falser	"	7	6
I see that there is none	"	18	54
None takes pity on thy pain	"	21	20
None alive will pity me	"	21	28
Two distincts, division none	P T		27
Love hath reason, reason none	"		47
Non-payment—Say, for	V A		521
Noon—May set at noon	R L		784
out-going in thy noon	Son	7	13
Noon-tide—his weary .... prick	R L		781
Nor—nor brag not of thy might	V A		113
nor know not what we mean	"		126
nor will not know it	"		409
neither eyes nor ears, to hear nor see	"		437
nor hear, nor touch	"		440
Bonnet nor veil henceforth	"		1081
Nor sun nor wind	"		1082
But king nor peer to such	R L		21
Nor read the subtle-shining secrecies	"		101
nor fear'd no hooks	"		103
Nor could she moralize	"		104
can neither fight nor fly	"		230
finds no excuse nor end	"		238
Nor children's tears nor mothers' groans respecting	"		431
Nor aught obeys	"		546
Nor shall he smile at thee	"		1065
Nor laugh with his companions	"		1066
Nor fold my fault	"		1073
nor law nor limit knows	"		1120
loves no stops nor rests	"		1124
heat nor freezing cold	"		1145
Nor why her fair cheeks	"		1225
Checks neither red nor pale	"		1510
Nor ashy pale the fear that	"		1512
Nor it, nor no remembrance	Son	5	12
Nor can I fortune to brief minutes tell	"	14	5
nor outward fair	"	16	11
Nor lose possession	"	18	10
Nor shall Death brag	"	18	11
Nor draw no lines	"	19	10
remove nor be removed	"	25	14
Nor can thy shame	"	34	9
Nor thou with public kindness	"	36	11
poor, nor despised	"	37	9
nor the gilded monuments	"	55	1
Nor Mars his sword nor war's quick fire	"	55	7
Nor services to do	"	57	4
Nor dare I chide	"	57	5
Nor think the bitterness	"	57	7
Nor dare I question	"	57	9
nor stone, nor earth, nor boundless sea	"	65	1
Nor gates of steel	"	65	8
nor me nor you	"	72	12
neither he, nor his compeers	"	86	7
nor that affable familiar ghost	"	86	9
Yet nor the lays of birds, nor the sweet smell	"	98	5
Nor did I wonder	"	98	9
Nor praise the deep vermillion	"	98	10
nor red nor white	"	99	10
Nor my beloved	"	105	2

Nor—nor the prophetic soul	Son	107	1	Not—not all she listeth	V A 564
Nor gives to necessary wrinkles	"	108	11	not like a pale-faced coward	" 569
Nor double penance	"	111	12	she had not suck'd	" 572
nor I to none alive	"	112	7	must not repel a lover	" 573
Nor his own vision	"	113	8	He will not manage her	" 598
nor no man ever loved	"	116	14	good queen, it will not be	" 607
Nor need I tallies	"	122	10	yet she is not loved	" 610
at the present nor the past	"	123	10	know'st not what it is	" 615
not in smiling pomp, nor falls	"	124	6	Not thy soft hands	" 633
it nor grows with heat nor drowns				Come not within	" 639
with showers	"	124	12	not to dissemble	" 641
Nor that full star	"	132	7	Didst thou not mark my face? was		
nor he will not be free	"	134	5	it not white	" 643
nor thou belied	"	140	13	Saw'st thou not signs	" 644
Nor are mine ears	"	141	5	Grew I not faint, and fell I not		
Nor tender feeling	"	141	6	downright	" 645
Nor taste, nor smell	"	141	7	do not struggle, for thou shalt not		
nor my five senses can	"	141	9	rise	" 710
Nor youth all quit	L C	.....	13	And not the least	" 745
nor loose nor tied in formal plat	"	.....	29	not in dark obscurity	" 760
nor being desired yielded	"	.....	149	And will not let	" 780
Nor gives it satisfaction	"	.....	162	longs not to groan	" 785
ne'er invite, nor never woo	"	.....	182	I hate not love	" 789
is nor true nor kind	"	.....	186	Call it not love	" 793
vow, bond, nor space	"	.....	264	Love surfeits not	" 803
neither sting, knot, nor confine	"	.....	265	more I dare not say	" 805
neither true nor trusty	P P	7	2	dare not stay the field	" 894
None fairer nor none falser	"	7	6	she knows not whither	" 904
her meaning nor her pleasure	"	11	12	And not death's ebon dart	" 948
young nor yet unwed	"	19	6	Now Nature cares not	" 953
Neither two nor one	P T	.....	40	Not to believe	" 986
Northern—As lagging fowls before				Death is not to blame	" 992
the northern blast	R L	.....	1335	It was not she	" 993
Nose—He wrings her nose	V A	.....	475	'Tis not my fault	" 1003
His nose being shadow'd	R L	.....	1416	lives and must not die	" 1017
Nostril—His nostrils drink the air	V A	.....	273	The grass stoops not	" 1028
small head and nostril wide	"	.....	296	he could not die, he is not dead	" 1060
Not—And yet not cloy	"	.....	19	you need not fear	" 1083
though not in lust	"	.....	42	he would not fear him	" 1094
be not proud nor brag not	"	.....	113	Who did not wink	" 1113
mine be not so fair	"	.....	116	shall not match his woe	" 1140
why not lips on lips	"	.....	120	It shall not fear	" 1154
our sport is not in sight	"	.....	124	their loves shall not enjoy	" 1164
know not what we mean	"	.....	126	shall not be one minute	" 1187
let not advantage slip	"	.....	129	Wherein I will not kiss	" 1188
should not be wasted	"	.....	130	and not be seen	" 1194
not gather'd in their prime	"	.....	131	Collatine unwisely did not let	R L 10
I were not for thee	"	.....	137	all could not satisfy	" 96
Thou canst not see	"	.....	139	That what they have not	" 135
Not gross to sink	"	.....	150	and lend it not	" 193
And were I not immortal	"	.....	197	I their father had not bin	" 210
and canst not feel	"	.....	201	Will he not wake	" 219
had not brought forth thee	"	.....	204	Will not my tongue	" 227
he will not in her arms	"	.....	226	Or were he not	" 231
there he could not die	"	.....	246	is not her own	" 241
he did not lack	"	.....	299	Love thrives not	" 270
they know not whether	"	.....	304	will not be dismay'd	" 273
they had not seen them	"	.....	357	will not incline	" 292
dares not be so bold	"	.....	401	Is not inured	" 321
'I know not love,' quoth he, ' nor				could not stay him	" 328
will not know it	"	.....	409	Slack'd, not suppress'd	" 425
and I will not owe it	"	.....	411	she dares not look	" 458
it will not ope the gate	"	.....	424	bequeath not to their lot	" 504
O, would thou hadst not	"	.....	428	not their own infamy	" 539
Add that I could not see	"	.....	440	not to foul desire	" 574
Would they not wish	"	.....	447	'Reward not hospitality	" 575
Had not his clouded with	"	.....	490	Mud not the fountain	" 577
Are they not quickly told	"	.....	520	Mar not the thing	" 578
seek not to know me	"	.....	525	do not then ensnare me	" 584

Not—Thou look'st not like deceit;			
do not deceive me	R L	....	585
Thou art not what thou seem'st	"	....	600
Thou seem'st not what thou art	"	....	601
What darest thou not when once	"	....	606
Draw not thy sword	"	....	626
Not to seducing lust	"	....	639
Turns not, but swells	"	....	646
alter not his taste	"	....	651
And not the puddle	"	....	658
should not the greater hide	"	....	663
The cedar stoops not	"	....	664
I will not hear thee	"	....	667
If not, enforced hate	"	....	668
could not forestall their will	"	....	728
'They think not	"	....	750
should not peep again	"	....	788
Let not the jealous Day	"	....	800
'Make me not object	"	....	806
that know not how	"	....	810
in peace is wounded, not in war	"	....	831
Which not themselves	"	....	833
could not put him back	"	....	843
doth not pollute	"	....	854
Not spend the dowry	"	....	938
pity not his moans	"	....	977
I force not argument	"	....	1021
Since thou could'st not defend	"	....	1034
I need not fear to die	"	....	1052
thou shalt not know	"	....	1058
I will not wrong	"	....	1060
He shall not boast	"	....	1063
thy interest was not bought	"	....	1067
I will not poison	"	....	1072
I will not paint	"	....	1074
Brand not my forehead	"	....	1091
not infant sorrows	"	....	1096
A woeful hostess brooks not	"	....	1125
thou sing'st not	"	....	1142
That knows not parching heat	"	....	1145
Then let It not	"	....	1174
Yet die I will not	"	....	1177
Faint not, faint heart	"	....	1209
But durst not ask	"	....	1223
Thou call them not	"	....	1244
Not that devour'd	"	....	1256
O, let it not be hild	"	....	1257
but not her grief's	"	....	1313
She dares not thereof make	"	....	1314
She would not blot	"	....	1322
and not a tongue	"	....	1463
and not with fire	"	....	1491
could not mistrust	"	....	1516
lodged not a mind	"	....	1530
and yet not wise	"	....	1550
'his wounds will not be sore	"	....	1568
Lucrece is not free	"	....	1624
I should not live	"	....	1642
That was not forced	"	....	1657
hath not said	"	....	1699
And why not I	"	....	1708
could not speak	"	....	1718
Thou wast not to this end	"	....	1755
and not thy father thee	"	....	1771
'do not take away	"	....	1796
do not steep thy heart	"	....	1828
If now thou not renewest	Son	3	3
remember'd not to be	"	3	13
yet canst not live	"	4	8
Not—were not summer's distillation			
left	Son	5	9
Then let not winter's rugged hand			
deface	"	6	1
is not forbidden usury	"	6	5
Be not self-will'd	"	6	13
Sweets with sweets war not	"	8	2
thou receivest not gladly	"	8	3
stick'st not to conspire	"	10	6
hath not made for store	"	11	9
not let that copy die	"	11	14
Not from the stars	"	14	1
But not to tell	"	14	3
do not you a mightier way	"	16	1
shows not half your parts	"	17	4
summer shall not fade	"	18	9
O, carve not with thy hours	"	19	9
but not acquainted	"	20	3
So is it not with me	"	21	1
though not so bright	"	21	11
I will not praise that purpose not			
to sell	"	21	14
shall not persuade me	"	22	1
As I, not for myself	"	22	10
Presume not on thy heart	"	22	13
not to give back again	"	22	14
know not the heart	"	24	14
I may not remove	"	25	14
not to show my wit	"	26	4
then not show my head	"	26	14
Is not eased by night	"	28	3
When sparkling stars twire not	"	28	12
as if not paid before	"	30	12
not for their rhyme	"	32	7
'Tis not enough	"	34	5
cures not the disgrace	"	34	8
not love's sole effect	"	36	7
I may not evermore	"	36	9
But do not so	"	36	13
So then I am not lame	"	37	9
Were it not thy sour leisure	"	39	10
we must not be foes	"	40	14
It is not all my grief	"	42	1
should not stop my way	"	44	2
that I am not thought	"	44	9
For thou not farther	"	47	11
have I not lock'd up	"	48	9
where thou art not	"	48	10
rider loved not speed	"	50	8
will not every hour survey	"	52	3
Sweet roses do not so	"	54	11
Not marble, nor the gilded	"	55	1
be it not said	"	56	1
and do not kill	"	56	7
Not blame your pleasure	"	58	14
is not so great	"	61	9
rocks impregnable are not so stout	"	65	7
matcheth not thy show	"	69	13
shall not be thy defect	"	70	1
Either not assail'd	"	70	10
mask'd not thy show	"	70	13
this line, remember not	"	71	5
Do not so much	"	71	*1
do I not glance aside	"	76	3
Then thank him not	"	79	13
eyes not yet created	"	81	10
thou wert not married	"	82	1
For I impair not beauty	"	83	11
lends not some small glory	"	84	6

NOT

Phrase	Ref	Page	Line
Not—Not making worse	Son	84	10
I was not sick	"	86	12
worth then not knowing	"	87	9
Thou canst not, love	"	89	5
And do not drop	"	90	4
Ah, do not, when my heart	"	90	5
Give not a windy night	"	90	7
do not leave me last	"	90	9
will not seem so	"	90	14
are not my measure	"	91	7
need I not to fear	"	92	5
Thou canst not vex me	"	92	9
yet I know it not	"	92	11
answer not thy show	"	93	14
That do not do the thing	"	94	2
But do not so	"	96	13
If not from my love's	"	99	3
wilt thou not haply say	"	101	5
Excuse not silence	"	101	10
I love not less	"	102	2
Not that the summer	"	102	9
Because I would not	"	102	11
O, blame me not	"	103	5
Were it not sinful	"	103	9
Let not my love	"	105	1
They had not skill	"	106	12
Not mine own fears	"	107	1
Which hath not figured	"	108	2
Weighs not the dust	"	108	10
not with time	"	109	7
That did not better	"	111	3
I could not love you dearer	"	115	2
might I not then say	"	115	10
might I not say so	"	115	13
Let me not to the marriage	"	116	1
Love is not love	"	116	2
Love's not Time's fool	"	116	9
Love alters not	"	116	11
But shoot not at me	"	117	12
The ills that were not, grew	"	118	10
When not to be receives	"	121	2
Not by our feeling	"	121	4
must not be shown	"	121	12
could not so much hold	"	122	9
No, Time, thou shalt not boast	"	123	1
Not woundering at	"	123	10
It suffers not in smiling	"	124	6
It fears not policy	"	124	9
Have I not seen dwellers	"	125	5
which is not mix'd	"	125	11
but not still keep	"	126	10
black was not counted fair	"	127	1
bore not beauty's name	"	127	2
If not lives in disgrace	"	127	8
who, not born fair, no beauty lack	"	127	11
cruel, not to trust	"	129	4
face hath not the power	"	131	6
I dare not be so bold	"	131	7
is not false I swear	"	131	9
truly not the morning	"	132	5
Is't not enough	"	133	3
Thou canst not then	"	133	12
But thou wilt not, nor he will not be free	"	134	5
yet am I not free	"	134	11
Not once vouchsafe	"	135	6
see not what they see	"	137	2
say this is not	"	137	11
says she not she is unjust	"	138	9
Not—And wherefore say not	Son	138	10
not to have years told	"	138	12
O, call not me	"	139	1
Wound me not	"	139	3
slay me not by art	"	139	4
Yet do not so	"	139	13
do not press	"	140	1
Though not to love	"	140	6
I may not be so	"	140	13
I do not love thee	"	141	1
it merits not reproving	"	142	4
not from those lips	"	142	5
Not prizing her poor infant's	"	143	8
yet not directly tell	"	144	10
saying 'not you	"	145	14
prescriptions are not kept	"	147	6
to say it is not so	"	148	6
If it be not	"	148	7
Love's eye is not so true	"	148	8
sees not till heaven	"	148	12
say I love thee not	"	149	1
Do I not think on thee	"	149	3
do I not spend	"	149	7
doth not grace the day	"	150	4
not abhor my state	"	150	12
Yet who knows not	"	151	2
urge not my amiss	"	151	3
water cools not love	"	154	14
Time had not scythed	L C	.....	12
would not break from thence	"	.....	34
that lets not bounty fall	"	.....	41
Let it not tell your judgement	"	.....	73
Not age, but sorrow	"	.....	74
not in his case	"	.....	116
Pieced not his grace	"	.....	119
my own fee-simple not in part	"	.....	144
Yet did I not	"	.....	148
what will not stay	"	.....	159
And be not of my holy vows	"	.....	179
Love made them not	"	.....	185
Not one whose flame	"	.....	191
that I hoard them not	"	.....	220
The thing we have not, mastering what not strives	"	.....	240
her absence valiant, not her might	"	.....	243
Not to be tempted	"	.....	251
to water will not wear	"	.....	291
that is not warmed here	"	.....	292
That not a heart	"	.....	309
would not be so lover'd	"	.....	320
say not I that I am old	P P	1	10
loves not to have years told	"	1	12
yet not directly tell	"	2	10
I shall not know	"	2	13
Did not the heavenly rhetoric	"	3	1
could not hold argument	"	3	2
deserves not punishment	"	3	4
I forswore not thee	"	3	6
what fool is not so wise	"	3	13
would not touch the bait	"	4	11
if not to beauty vowed	"	5	2
Which, not to anger bent	"	5	12
O do not love that wrong	"	5	13
Yet not so wistly	"	6	12
why was not I a flood	"	6	11
but not so fair as fickle	"	7	1
he should not pass those grounds	"	9	8
And would not take	"	11	12
Fare well I could not	"	14	6

Not—Not daring trust	P P	15	4	Notice—Taking no notice	V A	....	341
Yet not for me	"	15	16	Notorious—thou notorious bawd	R L	....	586
Alas, she could not help it	"	16	12	Nought—Alas, he nought esteems	V A	....	631
My flocks feed not	"	18	1	Beauty hath nought	"	....	638
My ewes breed not	"	18	2	nought at all respecting	"	....	911
My rams speed not	"	18	3	nought at all effecting	"	....	912
Plays not at all	"	18	30	call'd him all to nought	"	....	993
Clear wells spring not	"	18	37	For day hath nought to do	R L	....	1092
Sweet birds sing not	"	18	38	his mood with nought agrees	"	....	1095
Green plants bring not	"	18	39	presenteth nought but show	Son	15	3
Smooth not thy tongue	"	19	8	Receiving nought by elements	"	44	13
you had not had it then	"	19	24	stay and think of nought	"	57	11
Spare not to spend	"	19	26	doth stand for nought	P P	19	42
be thou not slack	"	19	35	Nourish'd—that which it was.... by	Son	73	12
shall not know	"	19	40	Novel—To me are nothing novel	"	123	3
Have you not heard it said	"	19	41	Now—stalled up, and even now	V A	....	39
She will not stick to round me	"	19	51	Now doth she stroke his cheek,			
they will not cheer thee	"	21	22	now doth he frown	"	....	45
come thou not near	P T	....	8	as I entreat thee now	"	....	97
Hearts, remote, yet not asunder	"	....	29	And now Adonis	"	....	181
the self was not the same	"	....	38	now she weeps, and now she fain	"	....	221
'Twas not their infirmity	"	....	60	And now her sobs	"	....	222
Beauty brag, but 'tis not she	"	....	63	Now gazeth she on him, now on			
Notary—and notary of shame	R L	....	765	the ground	"	....	224
Note—To note the fighting conflict	V A	....	345	how doth she now for wits	"	....	249
begins a wailing note	"	....	835	Now which way	"	....	253
shamed with the note	R L	....	208	now his woven girths	"	....	266
What did he note	"	....	413	now stand on end	"	....	272
Relish your nimble notes	"	....	1126	What cares he now	"	....	285
one pleasing note do sing	Son	8	12	he now prepares	"	....	303
In thee a thousand errors note	"	141	2	now the happy season	"	....	327
sanctified, of holiest note	L C	....	231	now her cheek was pale	"	....	347
Noted—but mightily he noted	R L	....	414	Now was she just before him	"	....	349
Invention in a noted weed	Son	76	6	gently now she takes him	"	....	361
More flowers I noted	"	99	14	now press'd with bearing	"	....	430
Noteth—poor Venus noteth	V A	....	1057	now is turn'd to day	"	....	481
Nothing—nothing else he sees	"	....	287	But now I lived	"	....	497
For nothing else	"	....	288	But now I died	"	....	498
nothing but my body's bane	"	....	372	Now let me say	"	....	535
prove nothing worth	"	....	418	Now quick desire	"	....	547
nothing but the very smell	"	....	441	He now obeys, and now no more			
nothing in him seem'd	R L	....	94	resisteth	"	....	563
nothing by augmenting it	"	....	154	now she can no more	"	....	577
nothing can affection's course control	"	....	500	Now is she in the very lists	"	....	595
				And now his grief	"	....	701
the wound that nothing healeth	"	....	731	And now 'tis dark	"	....	719
Who nothing wants	"	....	1459	Now of this dark night	"	....	727
Nature's bequest gives nothing	Son	4	3	now it sleeps alone	"	....	786
And nothing 'gainst Time's scythe	"	12	13	now I will away	"	....	807
one thing to my purpose nothing	"	20	12	now she beats her heart	"	....	829
If there be nothing new	"	59	1	For now she knows	"	....	883
And nothing stands	"	60	3	now she will no further	"	....	905
And needy nothing	"	66	3	Now Nature cares not	"	....	933
Want nothing that the thoughts	"	69	2	now wind, now rain	"	....	965
can nothing worthy prove	"	72	4	For now reviving joy	"	....	977
to love things nothing worth	"	72	14	Now she unweaves	"	....	991
nothing thence but sweetness	"	93	12	Now she adds honours	"	....	994
Nothing, sweet boy	"	108	5	they have wept till now	"	....	1062
To leave for nothing	"	109	12	Whose tongue is music now	"	....	1077
For nothing this wide universe	"	109	13	now no more reflect	"	....	1130
To me are nothing novel, nothing strange	"	123	3	now thinks he	R L	....	78
				Now leaden slumber	"	....	124
are nothing like the sun	"	130	1	Such hazard now must	"	....	135
In nothing art thou black	"	131	13	now stole upon the time	"	....	162
For nothing hold me	"	136	11	Now serves the season	"	....	166
That nothing me, a something left'st me nothing	P P	136	12	And now this lustful lord	"	....	169
		10	8	That now he vows a league, and now invasion	"	....	287
nothing of thee still	,	19	10				
That nothing could be used	,	16	10	Now is he come	"	....	337

NOW 207 O

Now—For now against himself	R L	717	Now—For now I see	P P	18	16
Where now I have no one	"	792	'Fie, fie, fie,' now would she cry	"	21	13
So am I now	"	1049	Death is now the phœnix' nest	P T		56
And therefore now I need not	"	1052	Nowhere—and nowhere fix'd	L C		27
Her letter now is seal'd	"	1331	Numb—numbs each feeling part	V A		892
For now 'tis stale to sigh	"	1362	Number—numbers seek for thee	R L		896
But now the mindful messenger	"	1583	in fresh numbers number all	Son	17	6
And now this pale swan	"	1611	numbers to outlive long date	"	38	12
are now depending	"	1615	But now my gracious numbers	"	79	3
now attend me	"	1682	In gentle numbers	"	100	6
now Lucrece is unlived	"	1754	Among a number one is	"	136	8
But now that fair fresh mirror	"	1760	Then in the number	"	136	9
But now he throws	"	1814	Number there in love was slain	P T		28
now set thy long-experienced wit	"	1820	Number'd—leases of short-number'd			
now, by the Capitol	"	1835	hours	Son	124	10
that art now the world's	Son	1	9	Nun—and self-loving nuns	V A		752
livery, so gazed on now	"	2	3	was sent me from a nun	L C		232
Now is the time	"	3	2	to charm a sacred nun	"		260
if now thou not renewest	"	3	3	Nurse—Being nurse and feeder	V A		446
now converted are	"	7	11	desire's foul nurse	"		773
Now stand you on the top	"	16	5	A nurse's song ne'er pleased	"		974
Now see what good turns	"	24	9	nurse of blame	R L		767
which now appear	"	31	7	The nurse, to still her child	"		813
now is thine alone	"	31	12	and be nurse to none	"		1162
mask'd him from me now	"	33	12	As tender nurse	Son	22	12
but now come back again	"	45	11	Nurse—but to nurse the life	R L		141
turns now unto the other	"	47	2	Nursed—Those children nursed	Son	77	11
now my greatest grief	"	48	6	Nursest—Thou nursest all	R L		929
doth now his gift confound	"	60	8	Nurseth—longer nurseth the disease	Son	147	2
as I am now	"	63	1	Nurtured—Ill-nurtured, crooked	V A		134
whereof now he's king	"	63	6	Nuzzling—And nuzzling in his flank	"		1115
do I now fortify	"	63	9	Nymph—Stain to all nymphs			9
now Nature bankrupt is	"	67	9	Or, like a nymph	"		147
no exchequer now but his	"	67	11	Whilst many nymphs	Son	154	3
died as flowers do now	"	68	2	Nymphs back peeping	P P	18	43
Now proud as an enjoyer	"	75	5				
Now counting best	"	75	7	O—O, how quick is love	V A		38
But now my gracious numbers	"	79	3	'O, pity,' 'gan she cry	"		95
if ever, now	"	90	1	O, be not proud	"		113
Now, while the world	"	90	2	O, had thy mother borne	"		203
which now seem woe	"	90	13	O, what a sight it was	"		343
hence as he shows now	"	101	14	O, what a war of looks	"		355
is less pleasant now	"	102	9	O fairest mover	"		368
till now never kept seat	"	105	14	O, give it me	"		375
as you master now	"	106	8	O, learn to love	"		407
now behold these present days	"	106	13	O, would thou hadst not	"		428
Incertainties now crown themselves	"	107	7	But, O, what banquet	"		445
Now with the drops	"	107	9	'O, where am I	"		493
Now all is done	"	110	9	O, thou didst kill me	"		499
Now I love you best	"	115	10	O, never let their	"		506
now I find true	"	119	9	O, had she then	"		571
unkind befriends me now	"	120	1	O, be advised	"		615
now becomes a fee	"	120	13	O, let him keep	"		637
But now is black, beauty's successive heir	"	127	3	O, then imagine this	"		721
				O strange excuse	"		791
now I have confess'd	"	134	1	O thou clear god	"		860
are they now transferred	"	137	14	O no, it cannot be	"		937
Now this ill-wresting world	"	140	11	O yes, it may	"		939
I desperate now approve	"	147	7	O, how her eyes	"		961
now reason is past care	"	147	9	O hard-believing love	"		985
for now I know thy mind	"	149	13	'O Jove,' quoth she	'		1015
Till now did ne'er invite	L C	182		O happiness enjoy'd	R L		22
And now she would	"	249		O rash-false heat	"		48
And now, to tempt all	"	252		'O shame to knighthood	"		197
Now all these hearts	"	274		O foul dishonour	"		198
But now are minutes added	P P	15	14	O impious act	"		199
To spite me now	"	15	15	'O what excuse	"		225
good day, of night now borrow	"	15	17	O, how her fear	"		257
For now my song is ended	"	16	16	O, had they	"		379

O—O modest wanton	R L	401	O—O, love's best habit	Son	138	11
O, if no harder	"	593	O, call not me	"	139	1
O, be remember'd	"	607	O, but with mine compare	"	142	3
O, how are they wrapp'd	"	636	O me, what eyes	"	148	1
O, that prone lust	"	684	O, how can love's eye	"	148	9
O, deeper sin	"	701	O cunning Love	"	148	13
'O comfort-killing Night	"	764	Canst thou, O cruel	"	149	1
'O hateful, vaporous, and foggy	"	771	O, from what power	"	150	1
'O Night, thou furnace	"	790	O, though I love	"	150	11
'O unseen shame	"	827	Cried, 'O false blood	L C		52
O, unfelt sore	"	828	O appetite, from judgement	"		166
O unlook'd-for evil	"	846	O, then, advance	"		225
O Opportunity, thy guilt	"	876	But, O my sweet	"		239
O, hear me then	"	930	O, pardon me	"		246
O, this dread night	"	965	O, hear me tell	"		253
'O Time, thou tutor	"	995	O most potential love	"		264
O no, that cannot be	"	1049	O, how the channel	"		285
'O, that is gone	"	1051	O father, what a hell	"		288
she sobbing speaks: 'O eye of eyes	"	1088	O cleft effect	"		293
O, let it not be hild	"	1257	O, that infected moisture	"		323
'O, peace!' quoth Lucrece	"	1284	O, that false fire	"		324
Ulysses, O, what art	"	1394	O, that forced thunder	"		325
'O, teach me how to make	"	1653	O, that sad breath	"		326
'O, speak,' quoth she	"	1700	O, all that borrow'd motion	"		327
O, from thy cheeks	"	1762	O, love's best habit	P P	1	11
O Time, cease thou thy course	"	1765	O never faith could hold	"	5	2
'She's mine.' 'O, mine she is	"	1795	O do not love that wrong	"	5	13
'O,' quoth Lucretius, 'I did give	"	1800	'O Jove,' quoth she	"	6	14
O, change thy thought	Son	10	9	O yes, dear friend	"	10	11
O, that you were	"	13	1	O, my love, my love	"	12	10
O, none but unthrifts	"	13	13	O, sweet shepherd, hie thee	"	12	11
O, carve not with thy hours	"	19	9	O frowning Fortune	"	18	15
O, let me, true in love	"	21	9	O cruel speeding	"	18	23
O, therefore, love	"	22	9	Oak—To dry the old oak's sap	R L		950
O, let my books	"	23	9	those thoughts to me like oaks	P P	5	4
O, learn to read	"	23	13	Oath—And him by oath	R L		410
O, then vouchsafe	"	32	9	and sweet friendship's oath	"		569
O, give thyself	"	38	5	the vestal violate her oath	"		883
O, how thy worth	"	39	1	with an infringed oath	"		1061
O absence, what a torment	"	39	9	Knights, by their oaths	"		1694
O, what excuse	"	51	5	why of two oaths' breach	Son	152	5
O, how much more	"	54	1	For all my vows are oaths	"	152	7
O, let me suffer	"	58	5	For I have sworn deep oaths	"	152	9
O, that record	"	59	5	Oaths of thy love	"	152	10
O, sure I am	"	59	13	to that strong-bonded oath	L C		279
O, no! thy love	"	61	9	To break an oath	P P	3	14
O, how shall summer's	"	65	5	her oaths of true love	"	7	8
O fearful meditation	"	65	9	Her faith, her oaths, her tears	"	7	12
O, none, unless this	"	65	13	Obdurate—Art thou obdurate	V A		199
O, him she stores	"	67	13	Obdurate vassals fell exploits	R L		429
O, if, I sung	"	71	9	Obedience—Whose swift obedience	"		1215
O, lest the world	"	72	1	Obey—but never to obey	V A		61
O, lest your true love	"	72	9	conquerors, his lips obey	"		549
O, know, sweet love	"	76	9	He now obeys	"		563
O, how I faint	"	80	1	Nor aught obeys	R L		546
O, what a happy title	"	92	11	and made their wills obey	L C		133
O, in what sweets	"	95	4	your minister, for you obey	"		229
O, what a mansion	"	95	9	To whose sound chaste wings obey	P T		4
O truant Muse	"	101	1	Obeyed—his stronger strength	V A		111
O, blame me not	"	103	5	Object—her object will away	"		255
O, never say that I	"	109	1	Fold in the object	"		822
O, for my sake	"	111	1	Make me not object to the tell-tale			
O, 'tis the first	"	114	9	day	R L		806
O, no! it is an ever-fixed	"	116	5	No object but her passion's strength	"		1103
O benefit of Ill	"	119	9	thousand lamentable objects	"		1373
O, that our night	"	120	9	Gilding the object	Son	20	6
O thou, my lovely boy	"	126	1	Of his quick objects	"	113	7
O thou minion of her pleasure	"	126	9	As fast as objects	"	114	8
O, let it then as well	"	132	10	The goodly objects	L C		137

Object—With objects manifold	L C		216
Oblation—And take thou my must your oblations be	Son L C	125	10 223
Oblivion—Planting oblivion, beating reason back	V A		557
To feed oblivion	R L		947
Till each to razed oblivion	Son	122	7
Oblivious—'Gainst death and all-oblivious enmity	"	55	9
Obloquy—the author of their	R L		523
Obscure—brakes obscure and rough	V A		237
obscures her silver shine	"		728
Obscurely—evils that .... sleep	R L		1250
Obscurity—not in dark obscurity	V A		760
Obsequious—a holy and .... tear	Son	31	5
obsequious in thy heart	"	125	9
Obsequy—Keep the .... so strict	P T		12
Observance—Such sweet observance	R L		1385
Observed—observed as they flew	L C		60
Obtain—Yet ever to obtain	R L		129
to obtain his lust	"		156
Obtained—his suit may be obtained	"		898
Obtaining—dangers of his will's	"		128
Occasion—on what occasion	"		1270
And every light occasion	L C		86
Ocean—Or in the ocean drench'd	V A		494
like a troubled ocean	R L		589
to stain the ocean of thy blood	"		655
Who in a salt-waved ocean	"		1231
Let this sad interim like the ocean be	Son	56	9
I have seen the hungry ocean	"	64	5
wide as the ocean is	"	80	5
I pour your ocean	L C		256
Odd—they such odd action yield	R L		1433
Odour—For that sweet odour	Son	54	4
Of their sweet deaths are sweetest odours made	"	54	12
But why thy odour matcheth not	"	69	13
In odour and in hue	"	98	6
O'er—o'er the downs	V A		677
stain that o'er with silver white	R L		56
rudely o'er his arm	"		170
lion fawneth o'er his prey	"		421
So o'er this sleeping soul	"		423
Who o'er the white sheet	"		472
First hovering o'er the paper	"		1297
with this gives o'er	"		1567
and busy winds give o'er	"		1790
all silver'd o'er with white	Son	12	4
from woe to woe tell o'er	"	30	10
o'er dull and speechless tribes	"	107	12
say o'er the very same	"	108	6
I was certain o'er incertainty	"	115	11
O'er whom thy fingers walk	"	128	11
I strong o'er them, and you o'er me being strong	L C		257
O'ercharged—.... with burthen	Son	23	8
O'erflow—the bounding bank o'erflows	R L		1119
O'ergreen—So you .... my bad	Son	112	4
O'ergrown—As corn .... by weeds	R L		281
O'erlook—mayst without attaint o'erlook	Son	82	2
O'er-press'd—my .... defence	"	139	8
O'er-read—Which eyes not yet created shall o'er-read	"	81	10
O'ersnow'd—Beauty o'ersnow'd and bareness	"	5	8
O'erstraw'd—and the top	V A		1143
O'ersway—But sad mortality o'ersways their power	Son	65	2
O'ertake—o'ertake me in my way	"	34	3
O'erwhelming—.... his fair sight	V A		183
O'erworn—...., despised, rheumatic	"		135
is so much o'erworn	"		866
crush'd and o'erworn	Son	63	2
Of—leave of the weeping morn	V A		2
of pith and livelihood	"		26
coals of glowing fire	"		35
burning of his cheeks	"		50
moisture, air of grace	"		64
gardens full of flowers	"		65
direful god of war	"		98
brag not of thy might	"		113
the god of fight	"		114
those fair lips of thine	"		115
Make use of time	"		129
all compact of fire	"		149
be of thyself rejected	"		159
By law of nature	"		171
so in spite of death	"		173
'Fie, no more of love	"		185
heat of this descending	"		190
a shadow for thee of my hairs	"		191
how want of love	"		202
but of no woman bred	"		211
of a man's complexion	"		215
circuit of this ivory pale	"		230
Poor queen of love	"		251
Of the fair breeder	"		282
stirring of a feather	"		302
breeder, full of fear	"		320
Jealous of catching	"		321
aidance of the tongue	"		330
So of concealed sorrow	"		333
conflict of her hue	"		345
what a war of looks	"		355
prison'd in a gaol of snow	"		362
the engine of her thoughts	"		367
approach of sweet desire	"		386
And learn of him	"		404
Say, that the sense of feeling	"		439
the stillitory of thy face	"		443
feeder of the other four	"		446
deadly bullet of a gun	"		461
wounding of a frown	"		465
The night of sorrow	"		481
that hard heart of thine	"		500
this poor heart of mine	"		502
for fear of slips	"		515
The honey fee of parting	"		538
the sweetness of the spoil	"		553
Things out of hope	"		567
with certain of his friends	"		588
the very lists of love	"		595
Of bristly pikes	"		620
As fearful of him, part	"		630
that face of thine	"		631
counsel of their friends	"		640
signs of fear lurk	"		644
of an angry-chafing boar	"		662
The thought of it	"		669
among a flock of sheep	"		685
with a herd of deer	"		689
the hunting of the boar	"		711
'Why, what of that	"		717
expected of my friends	"		718

14

Of—desire sees best of all	*V A* 720	**Of**—Of that rich jewel	*R L* 34
rob thee of a kiss	" 723	boast of Lucrece' sovereignty	" 36
Now of this dark night	" 727	issue of a king	" 37
condemn'd of treason	" 729	envy of so rich a thing	" 39
workmanship of nature	" 734	if none of those	" 44
Of mad mischances	" 738	Which of them both	" 53
heating of the blood	" 742	Of either's colour	" 66
not the least of all	" 745	The sovereignty of either	" 69
despite of fruitless chastity	" 751	war of lilies and of roses	" 71
of daughters and of sons	" 754	wonder of still-gazing eyes	" 84
by the rights of time	" 759	in plaits of majesty	" 93
reaves his son of life	" 766	wonder of his eye	" 95
closure of my breast	" 782	margents of such looks	" 102
to be barr'd of rest	" 784	fields of fruitful Italy	" 107
Lust full of forged lies	" 804	wreaths of victory	" 110
full of shame, my heart of teen	" 808	purpose of his coming hither	" 113
Of those fair arms	" 812	show of stormy, blustering weather	" 115
discovery of her way	" 828	mother of dread and fear	" 117
repetition of her moans	" 831	As one of which	" 127
the choir of echoes	" 840	dangers of his will's obtaining	" 128
humor of fantastic wits	" 850	the profit of excess	" 138
lark, weary of rest	" 853	The aim of all	" 141
patron of all light	" 860	The death of all	" 147
no tidings of her love	" 867	Of that we have	" 152
yelping of the hounds	" 881	want of wit	" 153
proceedings of a drunken brain	" 910	the dead of night	" 162
Full of respects	" 911	sparks of fire do fly	" 177
licking of his wound	" 915	dangers of his loathsome enterprise	" 184
Hateful divorce of love	" 932	armour of still-slaughter'd lust	" 188
as one full of despair	" 955	a froth of fleeting joy	" 212
channel of her bosom dropp'd	" 958	dream of my intent	" 218
This sound of hope	" 976	quittal of such strife	" 236
face of the sluttish ground	" 983	Full of foul hope and full of fond	
both of them extremes	" 987	mistrust	" 284
clepes him king of graves	" 995	crannies of the place	" 310
of all mortal things	" 996	smoke of it into his face	" 312
I felt a kind of fear	" 998	things of trial	" 326
author of thy slander	" 1006	income of each precious thing	" 334
Tells him of trophies	" 1013	heaven of his thought	" 338
To be of such a weak	" 1016	in the midst of his unfruitful prayer	" 344
overthrow of mortal kind	" 1018	The eye of heaven	" 356
thou art so full of fear	" 1021	mercy of his mortal sting	" 364
stars ashamed of day	" 1032	period of their ill	" 380
cabins of her head	" 1038	cozening the pillow of a lawful kiss	" 387
disposing of her troubled brain	" 1040	admired of lewd, unhallow'd eyes	" 392
drops of hot desire	" 1074	dew of night	" 396
Of things long since	" 1078	in the map of death	" 402
to rob him of his fair	" 1086	A pair of maiden worlds	" 407
pity of his tender years	" 1091	Save of their lord	" 409
robb'd of his effect	" 1132	His rage of lust	" 424
'Wonder of time	" 1133	proud of such a dignity	" 437
false and full of fraud	" 1141	heart of all her land	" 439
and too full of riot	" 1147	Whose ranks of blue veins	" 440
is no cause of fear	" 1153	confusion of their cries	" 445
It shall be cause of war	" 1159	dead of night	" 449
of a more sweet-smelling sire	" 1178	reason of this rash alarm	" 473
art the next of blood	" 1184	fury of his speed	" 501
Thus weary of the world	" 1189	worthless slave of thine	" 515
wings of false desire	*R L* 2	mark of every open eye	" 520
Of Collatine's fair love	" 7	author of their obloquy	" 523
that name of 'chaste	" 8	picture of true piety	" 542
sky of his delight	" 12	wrinkles of his face	" 562
treasure of his happy state	" 16	all the form of both	" 572
possession of his beauteous mate	" 18	for fear of this	" 614
but of a few	" 22	lectures of such shame	" 618
splendour of the sun	" 23	the ocean of thy blood	" 655
from a world of harm	" 28	Instead of love's coy touch	" 668
doth of itself persuade	" 29	bed of some rascal groom	" 671
The eyes of men	" 30	breeds months of pain	" 690

OF 211 OF

	R L	
Of—rifled of her store	"	692
lord of Rome	"	713
the length of times	"	718
muster troops of cares	"	720
despite of cure	"	732
the load of lust	"	734
burthen of a guilty mind	"	735
secrecy of night	"	763
image of hell	"	764
notary of shame	"	765
nurse of blame	"	767
Grim cave of death	"	769
guilty of my cureless crime	"	772
course of time	"	774
The life of purity	"	780
showers of silver brine	"	796
monuments of lasting moans	"	798
furnace of foul-reeking smoke	"	799
possession of thy gloomy place	"	803
The story of sweet chastity's decay	"	808
breach of holy wedlock	"	809
The branches of another root	"	823
this attaint of mine	"	825
perfection of my summer	"	837
guilty of thy honour's wrack	"	841
Besides, of weariness he did complain	"	845
And talk'd of virtue	"	846
breakers of their own behests	"	852
the harvest of his wits	"	859
pleasure of his gain	"	860
Guilty thou art of murder and of theft	"	918
Guilty of perjury	"	919
Guilty of treason	"	920
Guilty of incest	"	921
copesmate of ugly Night	"	925
carrier of grisly care	"	926
Eater of youth	"	927
Base watch of woes	"	928
Be guilty of my death, since of my crime	"	931
date of never-ending woes	"	935
the hate of foes	"	936
dowry of a lawful bed	"	938
the seal of time	"	941
with decay of things	"	947
antiquities of hammer'd steel	"	951
round of Fortune's wheel	"	952
daughters of her daughter	"	953
thought of his committed evil	"	972
his hours of rest	"	974
have time of time's help to despair	"	983
In time of sorrow	"	991
His time of folly and his time of sport	"	992
the abusing of his time	"	994
the help of law	"	1022
smoke of words	"	1027
rid me of this shame	"	1031
instrument of death	"	1038
passage of her breath	"	1040
Of that true type	"	1050
A badge of fame	"	1054
The stained taste of violated troth	"	1059
father of his fruit	"	1064
mistress of my fate	"	1069
ground of sin	"	1074
truth of this false night's	"	1075

	R L	
Of—well-tuned warble of her nightly sorrow	"	1080
'O eye of eyes	"	1088
for want of skill	"	1099
In a sea of care	"	1100
the bottom of annoy	"	1109
in ken of shore	"	1114
that sing'st of ravishment	"	1128
which of the twain	"	1154
Whose love of either	"	1165
cause of my untimely death	"	1178
sad hour of mine	"	1179
So of shame's ashes shall my fame be bred	"	1188
lord of that dear jewel	"	1191
abridgement of my will	"	1198
no shame of me	"	1204
the slander of mine ill	"	1207
This plot of death	"	1212
true mark of modesty	"	1220
durst not ask of her	"	1223
Of those fair suns	"	1230
No cause, but company, of her drops spilling	"	1236
impression of strange kinds	"	1242
authors of their ill	"	1244
semblance of a devil	"	1246
Of present death	"	1263
counterfeit of her complaining	"	1269
grief of my sustaining	"	1272
the break of day	"	1280
One of my husband's men	"	1291
press of people at a door	"	1301
Of that unworthy wife	"	1304
the tenour of her woe	"	1310
feeling of her passion	"	1317
Of her disgrace	"	1320
a part of woe	"	1327
'Tis but a part of sorrow	"	1328
with wind of words	"	1330
Of spirit, life	"	1346
pattern of the worn-out age	"	1350
Of skilful painting	"	1367
the power of Greece	"	1368
In scorn of nature	"	1374
And from the towers of Troy	"	1382
The very eyes of men	"	1383
Of physiognomy might one behold	"	1395
The face of either	"	1396
a press of gaping faces	"	1408
The scalps of many	"	1413
such signs of rage	"	1419
loss of Nestor's	"	1420
the eye of mind	"	1426
walls of strong-besieged Troy	"	1429
a kind of heavy fear	"	1435
the strand of Dardan	"	1436
Of what she was no semblance	"	1453
Of all the Greeks	"	1470
Thy heat of lust	"	1473
This load of wrath	"	1474
trespass of thine eye	"	1476
pleasure of some one	"	1478
plague of many moe	"	1479
though full of cares	"	1503
Of rich-built Ilion	"	1524
signs of truth	"	1532
clear pearls of his	"	1553
balls of quenchless fire	"	1554

Of—			
the current of her sorrow	R L	.....	1569
feeling of her own grief	"	.....	1578
surmise of others' detriment	"	.....	1579
shows of discontent	"	.....	1580
one word of woe	"	.....	1605
dirge of her certain ending	"	.....	1612
the interest of thy bed	"	.....	1619
dead of dark midnight	"	.....	1625
groom of thine	"	.....	1632
act of lust	"	.....	1636
death of Lucrece	"	.....	1645
hopeless merchant of this loss	"	.....	1660
woe of his, poor she attendeth	"	.....	1674
one pair of weeping eyes	"	.....	1680
this wrong of mine	"	.....	1691
quality of my offence	"	.....	1702
Of hard misfortune	"	.....	1713
Of that polluted prison	"	.....	1726
Some of her blood	"	.....	1742
Of that black blood	"	.....	1745
they none of ours	"	.....	1757
the beauty of my glass	"	.....	1763
conquest of the stronger	"	.....	1767
vexation of his inward soul	"	.....	1779
lord of Rome	"	.....	1818
dew of lamentations	"	.....	1829
death of this true wife	"	.....	1841
of small worth held	Son	2	4
treasure of thy lusty days	"	2	6
'This fair child of mine	"	2	10
tillage of thy husbandry	"	3	6
Of his self-love	"	3	8
April of her prime	"	3	10
windows of thine age shalt see	"	3	11
Despite of wrinkles	"	3	12
So great a sum of sums	"	4	8
Thou of thyself thy sweet self dost deceive	"	4	10
pent in walls of glass	"	5	10
If ten of thine ten times	"	6	10
concord of well-tuned sounds	"	8	5
form of thee hast left behind	"	9	6
thou art beloved of many	"	10	3
for love of me	"	10	13
In one of thine	"	11	2
I see barren of leaves	"	12	5
Then of thy beauty do I question make	"	12	9
among the wastes of time must go	"	12	10
gusts of winter's day	"	13	11
rage of death's eternal cold	"	13	12
to tell of good or evil luck	"	14	3
Of plagues, of dearths	"	14	4
Or else of thee this I prognosticate	"	14	13
wear their brave state out of memory	"	15	8
conceit of this inconstant stay	"	15	9
day of youth to sullied night	"	15	12
Time for love of you	"	15	13
the top of happy hours	"	16	5
So should the lines of life	"	16	9
yourself in eyes of men	"	16	12
the beauty of your eyes	"	17	5
old men of less truth	"	17	10
metre of an antique song	"	17	12
some child of yours alive	"	17	13
the darling buds of May	"	18	3
the eye of heaven shines	"	18	5
possession of that fair	"	18	10
Of—master-mistress of my passion	Son	20	2
me of thee defeated	"	20	11
couplement of proud compare	"	21	5
that like of hearsay well	"	21	13
youth and thou are of one date	"	22	2
raiment of my heart	"	22	6
be of thyself so wary	"	22	9
So I, for fear of trust	"	23	5
ceremony of love's rite	"	23	6
burthen of mine own love's might	"	23	8
presagers of my speaking breast	"	23	10
in table of my heart	"	24	2
Of public honour	"	25	2
fortune of such triumphs bars	"	25	3
book of honour razed quite	"	25	11
Lord of my love	"	26	1
good conceit of thine	"	26	7
worthy of thy sweet respect	"	26	12
the benefit of rest	"	28	2
at break of day arising	"	29	11
sessions of sweet silent thought	"	30	1
remembrance of things past	"	30	2
the lack of many a thing	"	30	3
expense of many a vanish'd sight	"	30	8
account of fore-bemoaned moan	"	30	11
As interest of the dead	"	31	7
trophies of my lovers gone	"	31	10
parts of me to thee did give	"	31	11
That due of many	"	31	12
hast all the all of me	"	31	14
lines of thy deceased lover	"	32	4
bettering of the time	"	32	5
height of happier men	"	32	8
ranks of better equipage	"	32	12
Suns of the world may stain	"	33	14
of such a salve can speak	"	34	7
do deeds of youth	"	37	2
comfort of thy worth and truth	"	37	4
Or any of these all	"	37	6
by a part of all thy glory live	"	37	12
the better part of me	"	39	2
lose name of single one	"	39	6
with thoughts of love	"	39	11
taste of what thyself refusest	"	40	8
is of my wailing chief	"	42	3
substance of my flesh were thought	"	44	1
despite of space	"	44	3
large lengths of miles	"	44	10
so much of earth	"	44	11
badges of either's woe	"	44	14
embassy of love to thee	"	45	6
being made of four	"	45	7
Of thy fair health	"	45	12
conquest of thy sight	"	46	2
freedom of that right	"	46	4
A quest of thoughts	"	46	10
inward love of heart	"	46	14
thoughts of love doth share a part	"	47	8
From hands of falsehood, in sure wards of trust	"	48	4
Thou, best of dearest	"	48	7
prey of every vulgar thief	"	48	8
closure of my breast	"	48	11
reasons find of settled gravity	"	49	8
knowledge of mine own desert	"	49	10
the strength of laws	"	49	13
Of my dull bearer	"	51	2
of posting is no need	"	51	4
desire, of perfect'st love being made	"	51	10

Of—point of seldom pleasure	Son	52	4	Of—ashes of his youth doth lie	Son	73	10
Like stones of worth	"	52	7	the better part of me	"	74	8
millions of strange shadows	"	53	2	lost the dregs of life	"	74	9
all art of beauty set	"	53	7	The prey of worms	"	74	10
Speak of the spring and foison of the year	"	53	9	conquest of a wretch's knife	"	74	11
				Too base of thee	"	74	12
shadow of your beauty show	"	53	10	The worth of that is that	"	74	13
tincture of the roses	"	54	6	for the peace of you	"	75	3
Of their sweet deaths	"	54	12	so barren of new pride	"	76	1
And so of you	"	54	13	I always write of you	"	76	9
Of princes, shall outlive	"	55	2	And of this book this learning	"	77	4
the work of masonry	"	55	6	Of mouthed graves will give	"	77	6
record of your memory	"	55	8	acquaintance of thy mind	"	77	12
the eyes of all posterity	"	55	11	proud of that which I compile	"	78	9
The spirit of love	"	56	8	and born of thee	"	78	10
Return of love	"	56	12	travail of a worthier pen	"	79	6
being full of care	"	56	13	Yet what of thee	"	79	7
and times of your desire	"	57	2	He robs thee of, and pays it	"	79	8
bitterness of absence sour	"	57	7	when I of you do write	"	80	1
stay and think of nought	"	57	11	speaking of your fame	"	80	4
control your times of pleasure	"	58	2	He of tall building and of goodly pride	"	80	12
account of hours to crave	"	58	3				
absence of your liberty	"	58	6	breathers of this world are dead	"	81	12
accusing you of injury	"	58	8	even in the mouths of men	"	81	14
pardon of self-doing crime	"	58	12	Of their fair subject	"	82	4
burthen of a former child	"	59	4	stamp of the time-bettering days	"	82	8
Even of five hundred courses of the sun	"	59	6	tender of a poet's debt	"	83	4
				Speaking of worth	"	83	8
wonder of your frame	"	59	10	In one of your fair eyes	"	83	13
the wits of former days	"	59	13	But he that writes of you	"	84	7
once in the main of light	"	60	5	While comments of your praise	"	85	2
rarities of nature's truth	"	60	11	of well-refined pen	"	85	8
tenour of thy jealousy	"	61	8	And to the most of praise	"	85	10
Sin of self-love	"	62	1	breath of words respect	"	85	13
no truth of such account	"	62	6	sail of his great verse	"	86	1
with beauty of thy days	"	62	14	prize of all too precious you	"	86	2
or vanish'd out of sight	"	63	7	of my silence cannot boast	"	86	11
treasure of his spring	"	63	8	I was not sick of any fear	"	86	12
cost of outworn buried age	"	64	2	The charter of thy worth	"	87	3
kingdom of the shore	"	64	6	cause of this fair gift	"	87	7
win of the watery main	"	64	7	in the eye of scorn	"	88	2
interchange of state	"	64	9	Of faults conceal'd	"	88	7
siege of battering days	"	65	6	Speak of my lameness	"	89	1
Nor gates of steel	"	65	8	haply of our old acquaintance	"	89	12
his spoil of beauty	"	65	12	the spite of fortune	"	90	3
seeing of his living hue	"	67	6	rearward of a conquer'd woe	"	90	6
Roses of shadow	"	67	8	worst of fortune's might	"	90	12
Beggar'd of blood to blush	"	67	10	And other strains of woe	"	90	13
And, proud of many	"	67	12	with loss of thee	"	90	14
map of days outworn	"	68	1	Of more delight	"	91	11
signs of fair were born	"	68	3	of all men's pride I boast	"	91	12
tresses of the dead	"	68	5	For term of life	"	92	2
The right of sepulchres	"	68	6	that love of thine	"	92	4
summer of another's green	"	68	11	the worst of wrongs	"	92	5
what beauty was of yore	"	68	14	in the least of them	"	92	6
Those parts of thee	"	69	1	owners of their faces	"	94	7
thought of hearts can mend	"	69	2	stewards of their excellence	"	94	8
the voice of souls	"	69	3	beauty of thy budding name	"	95	3
the beauty of thy mind	"	69	9	the story of thy days	"	95	5
the rank smell of weeds	"	69	12	but in a kind of praise	"	95	7
The ornament of beauty	"	70	3	Take heed, dear heart, of this large privilege	"	95	13
being woo'd of time	"	70	6				
ambush of young days	"	70	9	loved of more and less	"	96	3
some suspect of ill	"	70	13	finger of a throned queen	"	96	5
kingdoms of hearts shouldst owe	"	70	14	strength of all thy state	"	96	12
speak well of me untrue	"	72	10	pleasure of the fleeting year	"	97	2
That time of year	"	73	1	burthen of the prime	"	97	7
twilight of such day	"	73	5	But hope of orphans	"	97	10
the glowing of such fire	"	73	9	spirit of youth in every thing	"	98	3

Of—Yet nor the lays of birds	Son	98	5
Of different flowers	"	98	6
but figures of delight	"	98	11
pattern of all those	"	98	12
And buds of marjoram	"	99	7
had stol'n of both	"	99	10
pride of all his growth	"	99	12
speak of that which gives	"	100	2
thy neglect of truth in beauty	"	101	2
praised of ages yet to be	"	101	12
in growth of riper days	"	102	8
is of more worth	"	103	3
Than of your graces	"	103	12
In process of the seasons	"	104	6
For fear of which	"	104	13
To one of one still such	"	105	4
chronicle of wasted time	"	106	1
descriptions of the fairest wights	"	106	2
In praise of ladies dead	"	106	4
in the blazon of sweet beauty's best	"	106	5
Of hand, of foot, of lip, of eye, of brow	"	106	6
Of this our time	"	106	10
Of the wide world's dreaming	"	107	2
lease of my true love control	"	107	3
olives of endless age	"	107	8
drops of this most balmy time	"	107	9
Since, spite of him	"	107	11
tombs of brass are spent	"	107	14
and injury of age	"	108	10
conceit of love there bred	"	108	13
I was false of heart	"	109	1
That is my home of love	"	109	5
besiege all kinds of blood	"	109	10
all thy sum of good	"	109	12
Made old offences of affections new	"	110	4
thee my best of love	"	110	8
guilty goddess of my harmful deeds	"	111	2
Potions of eisel	"	111	10
Of others' voices	"	112	10
Of bird, of flower	"	113	6
Of his quick objects	"	113	7
Incapable of more	"	113	13
To make of monsters	"	114	5
change decrees of kings	"	115	6
course of altering things	"	115	8
fearing of Time's tyranny	"	115	9
doubting of the rest	"	115	12
marriage of true minds	"	116	1
to the edge of doom	"	116	12
the level of your frown	"	117	11
virtue of your love	"	117	14
full of your ne'er-cloying sweetness	"	118	5
And sick of welfare found a kind of meetness	"	118	7
Which rank of goodness	"	118	12
so fell sick of you	"	118	14
drunk of Siren tears	"	119	1
out of their spheres	"	119	7
distraction of this maddling fever	"	119	8
O benefit of ill	"	119	9
pass'd a hell of time	"	120	6
our night of woe	"	120	9
reproach of being	"	121	2
Of thee, thy record	"	122	8
dressings of a former sight	"	123	4
but the child of state	"	124	1
blow of thralled discontent	"	124	7
of short-number'd hours	"	124	10
Of—call the fools of time	Son	124	13
minion of her pleasure	"	126	9
becoming of their woe	"	127	13
inward of thy hand	"	128	6
The expense of spirit in a waste of shame	"	129	1
bloody, full of blame	"	129	3
morning sun of heaven	"	132	5
grey cheeks of the east	"	132	6
Of him, myself, and thee	"	133	7
The statute of thy beauty	"	134	9
One will of mine	"	135	12
the treasure of thy love	"	136	5
In things of great receipt	"	136	7
Why of eyes' falsehood hast thou	"	137	7
judgement of my heart is tied	"	137	8
that she is made of truth	"	138	1
The manner of my pity-wanting pain	"	140	4
might speak ill of thee	"	140	10
Who, in despite of view	"	141	4
the likeness of a man	"	141	11
Hate of my sin	"	142	2
from those lips of thine	"	142	5
bonds of love as oft as mine	"	142	7
revenues of their rents	"	142	8
One of her feather'd creatures	"	143	2
In pursuit of the thing	"	143	4
Two loves I have of comfort	"	144	1
the centre of my sinful earth	"	146	1
inheritors of this excess	"	146	7
selling hours of dross	"	146	11
Am of myself, all tyrant	"	149	4
the motion of thine eyes	"	149	12
becoming of things ill	"	150	5
very refuse of thy deeds	"	150	6
and warrantise of skill	"	150	7
see just cause of hate	"	150	10
to be beloved of thee	"	150	14
conscience is born of love	"	151	2
Lest guilty of my faults	"	151	4
Proud of this pride	"	151	10
No want of conscience	"	151	13
why of two oaths' breach	"	152	5
oaths of thy deep kindness	"	152	9
Oaths of thy love	"	152	10
A maid of Dian's	"	153	2
valley-fountain of that ground	"	153	4
holy fire of love	"	153	5
help of bath desired	"	153	11
many legions of true hearts	"	154	6
the general of hot desire	"	154	7
Tearing of papers	L C		6
a platted hive of straw	"		8
The carcass of a beauty	"		11
spite of heaven's fell rage	"		13
through lattice of sear'd age	"		14
In clamours of all size	"		21
a careless hand of pride	"		30
Of amber, crystal, and of beaded jet	"		37
Of folded schedules	"		43
ring of posied gold	"		45
thou register of lies	"		52
This said, in top of rage	"		55
Of court, of city	"		59
and motives of her woe	"		63
in the charity of age	"		70
injury of many a blasting hour	"		72

Of—Of one by nature's outwards	L C	...	80
occasion of the wind	"		86
'Small show of man	"		92
in a pride of truth	"	...	105
Proud of subjection	"	.....	108
tip of his subduing tongue	"	.....	120
All kind of arguments	"	.....	121
in his craft of will	"	.....	126
Of young, of old, and sexes both enchanted	"	.....	128
Of lands and mansions	"	.....	138
mistress of his heart	"	.....	142
Demand of him	"	.....	149
Of proofs new-bleeding	"	.....	153
Of this false jewel	"	.....	154
For fear of harms	"	.....	165
patterns of his foul beguiling	"	.....	170
bastards of his foul adulterate heart	"	.....	175
Have of my suffering	"	.....	178
of my holy vows afraid	"	.....	179
For feasts of love	"	.....	181
Are errors of the blood, none of the mind	"	.....	184
less of shame in me	"	.....	188
By how much of me	"	.....	189
Or any of my leisures	"	.....	193
Of paled pearls	"	.....	198
Of grief and blushes	"	.....	200
Effects of terror	"	.....	202
these talents of their hair	"	.....	204
With the annexions of fair gems enrich'd	"	.....	208
trophies of affections hot	"	.....	218
Of pensived and subdued desires	"	.....	219
For these, of force must your oblations be	"	.....	223
'"O, then, advance of yours that phraseless hand	"	.....	225
the airy scale of praise	"	.....	226
sister sanctified, of holiest note	"	.....	233
spirits of richest coat	"	.....	236
The scars of battle	"	.....	244
Of stale example	"	.....	268
Of wealth, of filial fear	"	.....	270
The aloes of all forces	"	.....	273
a hell of witchcraft lies	"	.....	288
orb of one particular tear	"	.....	289
inundation of the eyes	"	.....	290
but an art of craft	"	.....	295
stole of chastity I daff'd	"	.....	297
a plenitude of subtle matter	"	.....	302
Of burning blushes, or of weeping water	"	.....	304
the hail of his all hurting aim	"	.....	310
the garment of a Grace	"	.....	316
moisture of his eye	"	.....	323
she is made of truth	P P	1	1
Two loves I have, of comfort and despair	"	2	1
rhetoric of thine eye	"	3	1
it is no fault of mine	"	3	12
oaths of true love swearing	"	7	8
of all her pure protestings	"	7	11
the queen of music, makes	"	8	10
One god is god of both	"	8	13
when the fair queen of love	"	9	1
a spectacle of ruth	"	9	11
nothing of thee still	"	10	10
I pardon crave of thee	"	10	11

Of—Youth is full of pleasance, age is full of care	P P	12	2
Youth is full of sport	"	12	5
In spite of physic	"	13	12
the doubts of my decay	"	14	4
the office of mine eyes	"	15	4
good day, of night now borrow	"	15	17
the fairest one of three	"	16	1
That liked of her master	"	16	2
For of the two the trusty knight	"	16	11
was victor of the day	"	16	13
a gift of learning	"	16	14
Causer of this	"	18	8
The cause of all my moan	"	18	51
counsel of some wiser head	"	19	5
make thee a bed of roses	"	20	9
A cap of flowers	"	20	11
with leaves of myrtle	"	20	12
A belt of straw	"	20	13
merry month of May	"	21	2
grove of myrtles made	"	21	4
careless of thy sorrowing	"	21	26
store of crowns be scant	"	21	37
Thus of every grief in heart	"	21	55
bird of loudest lay	P T	.....	1
precurrer of the fiend	"	.....	6
Augur of the fever's end	"	.....	7
fowl of tyrant wing	"	.....	10
and stars of love	"	.....	51
Off—Sometime he scuds far off	V A	.....	301
And all amazed brake off	"	.....	469
far off upon a hill	"	.....	697
By this, far off she hears	"	.....	973
wind would blow it off	"	.....	1099
those far-off eyes look sad	R L	.....	1386
still farther off from thee	Son	28	8
From me far off	"	61	14
From off a hill	L C	.....	1
Shook off my sober guards	"	.....	298
Offence—the like offences prove	R L	.....	613
hates himself for his offence	"	.....	734
To cloak offences	"	.....	749
acquit my forced offence	"	.....	1071
For one's offence	"	.....	1483
the quality of my offence	"	.....	1702
publish Tarquin's foul offence	"	.....	1852
bears the strong offences cross	Son	34	12
excuse the slow offence	"	51	1
comment upon that offence	"	89	2
Made old offences of affections new	"	110	4
All my offences	L C	.....	183
Offend—to offend thine ear	Son	8	6
Offended—for having so offended	V A	.....	810
Offender—With foul offenders	R L	.....	612
The offender's sorrow	Son	34	11
offenders, thus I will excuse ye	"	42	5
Offer—So offers he to give	V A	.....	88
Offer pure incense	R L	.....	194
jest at every gentle offer	P P	4	12
Office—their office and their light	V A	.....	1039
Thy princely office	R L	.....	628
Time's office is to fine the hate	"	.....	936
would such an office have	"	.....	1000
These offices, so oft	Son	77	13
Then do thy office, Muse	"	101	13
the office of mine eyes	P P	15	4
Offspring—We are their offspring	R L	.....	1757
Oft—compass'd oft with venturing	V A	.....	567
oft the eye mistakes	"	.....	1038

Oft—our hearts oft tainted be	R L	.....	38
That oft they interchanged	"	.....	70
doth traffic oft for gaining	"	.....	131
and oft that wealth doth cost	"	.....	146
oft betake him to retire	"	.....	174
By oft predict that I in heaven find	Son	14	8
so oft as thou wilt look	"	77	13
So oft have I invoked thee	"	78	1
How oft, when thou	"	128	1
of love as oft as mine	"	142	7
Oft did she heave	L C	.....	15
As oft 'twixt May and April	"	.....	102
Have you not heard it said full oft	P P	19	41
Often—as night-wanderers.... are	V A	.....	825
often from his place	R L	.....	565
to weep are often willing	"	.....	1237
I often did behold	"	.....	1758
often is his gold complexion dimm'd	Son	18	6
have often lived alone	"	105	13
And often reading	L C	.....	19
As often shrieking	"	.....	20
These often bathed she	"	.....	50
And often kiss'd and often 'gan to tear	"	.....	51
and often men would say	"	.....	106
advice is often seen	"	.....	160
that often there had been	P P	6	8
how often hath she joined	"	7	7
Oftentimes—stories .... begun	V A	.....	845
Oil—Dries up his oil	"	.....	756
Old—foul or wrinkled-old	"	.....	133
The text is old	"	.....	806
and old men dote	"	.....	837
Make the young old, the old become a child	"	.....	1152
blasts and ne'er grows old	R L	.....	49
or an old man's saw	"	.....	244
To blot old books	"	.....	948
To dry the old oak's sap	"	.....	950
Old woes, not infant sorrows	"	.....	1096
with her old eyes	"	.....	1448
The credulous old Priam	"	.....	1522
Priam, why art thou old	"	.....	1550
like old acquaintance in a trance	"	.....	1595
dear daughter,' old Lucretius cries	"	.....	1751
my old age new born	"	.....	1759
fresh mirror dim and old	"	.....	1760
The old bees die	"	.....	1769
and make my old excuse	Son	2	11
when thou art old	"	2	13
Be scorn'd like old men	"	17	10
do thy worst, old Time	"	19	13
persuade me I am old	"	22	1
and her old face new	"	27	12
And with old woes new wail	"	30	4
Than those old nine	"	38	10
what the old world could say	"	59	9
Robbing no old to dress his beauty new	"	68	12
dressing old words new	"	76	11
sun is daily new and old	"	76	13
of our old acquaintance tell	"	89	12
What old December's bareness	"	97	4
you never can be old	"	104	1
making beautiful old rhyme	"	106	3
Counting no old thing old	"	108	7
Old—Made old offences of affections new	Son	110	4
foist upon us that is old	"	123	6
In the old age	"	127	1
say not I that I am old	"	138	10
tell your judgement I am old	L C	.....	73
Of young, of old	"	.....	128
say not I that I am old	P P	1	10
Older—on newer proof to try an older friend	Son	110	11
Olive—olives of endless age	"	107	8
On—on his sweating palm	V A	.....	25
on a ragged bough	"	.....	37
leaning on their elbows	"	.....	44
Tires with her beak on feathers, flesh, and bone	"	.....	56
feedeth on the steam as on a prey	"	.....	63
Who, being look'd on	"	.....	87
Why not lips on lips	"	.....	120
Dance on the sands	"	.....	148
and complain on theft	"	.....	160
Now gazeth she on him, now on the ground	"	.....	224
on mountain or in dale	"	.....	232
Graze on my lips	"	.....	233
now stand on end	"	.....	272
on so proud a back	"	.....	300
puts on outward strangeness	"	.....	310
Looks on the dull earth	"	.....	340
mover on this mortal round	"	.....	368
it will set the heart on fire	"	.....	388
take advantage on presented joy	"	.....	403
For on the grass she lies	"	.....	473
strikes her on the cheeks	"	.....	475
having writ on death	"	.....	509
Set thy seal-manual on my waxred lips	"	.....	516
yet complain on drouth	"	.....	544
And on his neck	"	.....	592
He on her belly falls, she on her back	"	.....	594
On his bow-back	"	.....	619
on the lion he will venture	"	.....	628
shakes thee on my breast	"	.....	648
on his back doth lie	"	.....	663
And on thy well-breath'd	"	.....	678
And when thou hast on foot	"	.....	679
wit waits on fear	"	.....	690
Stands on his hinder legs	"	.....	698
trodden on by many	"	.....	707
Are on the sudden wasted	"	.....	749
That on the earth	"	.....	753
leadeth on to danger	"	.....	788
on earth usurp'd his name	"	.....	794
as one on shore	"	.....	817
Passion on passion	"	.....	832
mounts up on high	"	.....	854
exclaims on Death	"	.....	930
Gloss on the rose	"	.....	936
I rail'd on thee	"	.....	1002
Be wreak'd on him	"	.....	1004
she treads on it so light	"	.....	1028
conquest on her fair delight	"	.....	1030
would he put his bonnet on	"	.....	1087
The fishes spread on it	"	.....	1100
Sorrow on love hereafter	"	.....	1136
waited on with jealousy	"	.....	1137
on the ground lay spill'd	"	.....	1167
baseless edge on his keen appetite	R L	.....	9

On—seldom dream on evil	R L	....	87	On—he that calls on thee	Son	38	11
His falchion on a flint he softly				lay on me this cross	"	42	12
smiteth	"	....	176	dreams they look on thee	"	43	3
sorrow may on this arise	"	....	186	By looking on thee	"	43	10
roses that on lawn we lay	"	....	258	sleep on sightless eyes doth stay	"	43	12
reason wait on wrinkled age	"	....	275	frown on my defects	"	49	2
which looks on her	"	....	290	reasons on thy part	"	49	12
gazeth on her yet unstained bed	"	....	366	I journey on the way	"	50	1
Swelling on either side	"	....	389	Plods dully on	"	50	6
On the green coverlet	"	....	394	cannot provoke him on	"	50	9
an April daisy on the grass	"	....	395	mounted on the wind	"	51	7
on that he firmly doted	"	....	416	shadows on you tend	"	53	2
march'd on to make	"	....	438	On Helen's cheek all art of beauty set	"	53	7
On her bare breast	"	....	439	Hang on such thorns	"	54	7
to gaze on beauty	"	....	496	the flourish set on youth	"	60	9
And dotes on what he looks	"	....	497	Feeds on the rarities	"	60	11
put on his shape	"	....	597	travell'd on to age's steepy night	"	63	5
should drop on them	"	....	686	Advantage on the kingdom of the			
exclaiming on the direful night	"	....	741	shore	"	64	6
beating on her breast	"	....	759	inhabit on a living brow	"	68	4
blasts wait on the tender spring	"	....	869	live a second life on second head	"	68	7
wait on them	"	....	910	If thinking on me	"	71	8
waits on greatest state	"	....	1006	That on the ashes of his youth			
I'll hum on Tarquin still	"	....	1133	doth lie	"	73	10
While thou on Tereus	"	....	1134	feasting on your sight	"	75	9
Revenge on him that made me	"	....	1180	Or gluttoning on all	"	75	14
on what occasion break	"	....	1270	the dumb on high to sing	"	78	5
and on it writ	"	....	1331	On your broad main	"	80	8
And blushing on her	"	....	1339	Being fond on praise, which makes	"	84	14
wistly on him gazed	"	....	1355	Comes home again on better judge-			
Pale cowards, marching on	"	....	1391	ment making	"	87	12
lean'd on another's head	"	....	1415	bending all my loving thoughts			
Staring on Priam's wounds	"	....	1448	on thee	"	88	10
On this sad shadow Lucrece spends				that which on thy humour doth			
her eyes	"	....	1457	depend	"	92	8
And rail on Pyrrhus	"	....	1467	my life on thy revolt doth lie	"	92	10
Once set on ringing, with his	"	....	1494	comments on his sport	"	95	6
And still on him she gazed	"	....	1531	As on the finger of a throned queen	"	96	5
and on that pillow lay	"	....	1620	pleasures wait on thee	"	97	11
On thee and thine this night I will				Which on thy soft cheek for com-			
inflict	"	....	1630	plexion dwells	"	99	4
forced him on so fast	"	....	1670	on thorns did stand	"	99	8
To push grief on and back	"	....	1673	Spend'st thou thy fury on some			
revenged on my foe	"	....	1683	worthless song	"	100	3
Himself on her self-slaughter'd				beauty on my love depends	"	101	3
body threw	"	....	1733	dreaming on things to come	"	107	2
in on every side	"	....	1739	I have look'd on truth	"	110	5
to be revenged on her death	"	....	1778	On newer proof, to try	"	110	11
so gazed on now	Son	2	3	That looks on tempests	"	116	6
leads summer on	"	5	5	And on just proof surmise accu-			
on his golden pilgrimage	"	7	8	mulate	"	117	10
Unlook'd on diest	"	7	14	Or on my frailties why are frailer			
That on himself such murderous				spies	"	121	7
shame commits	"	9	14	Which works on leases	"	124	10
Borne on the bier	"	12	8	dwellers on form and favour	"	125	5
Now stand you on the top of				put on nature's power	"	127	5
happy hours	"	16	5	On purpose laid	"	129	8
Presume not on thy heart	"	22	13	wires grow on her head	"	130	4
actor on the stage	"	23	1	treads on the ground	"	130	12
gaze therein on thee	"	24	12	but thinking on thy face	"	131	10
Points on me graciously	"	26	10	One on another's neck	"	131	11
puts apparel on my tatter'd loving	"	26	11	Have put on black	"	132	3
Looking on darkness	"	27	8	On both sides thus	"	138	8
Haply I think on thee	"	29	10	grounded on sinful loving	"	142	2
I think on thee	"	30	13	shalt thou feed on Death, that			
rack on his celestial face	"	33	6	feeds on men	"	146	13
splendour on my brow	"	33	10	Feeding on that which doth pre-			
dry the rain on my storm-beaten				serve the ill	"	147	3
face	"	34	6	I not think on thee	"	149	3

On—On whom frown'st thou	Son	149	6	One—With one fair hand	V A	 351
if thou lour'st on me	"	149	7	For one sweet look	"	 371
But, love, hate on	"	149	13	before one leaf put forth	"	 416
Which on it had	L C	....	16	at thy leisure, one by one	"	 518
Their view right on	"	....	26	To one sore sick	"	 702
For on his visage	"	....	90	But in one minute's fight	"	 746
velvet, on that termless skin	"	....	94	As one on shore	"	 817
on this side the verdict went	"	....	113	as one that unaware	"	 823
So on the tip	"	....	120	like one that spies an adder	"	 878
that do on mine depend	"	....	274	remaineth in one place	"	 885
were levell'd on my face	"	....	282	as one full of despair	"	 955
that on this earth doth shine	P P	3	10	The one doth flatter thee	"	 989
Then fell she on her back	"	4	13	As one with treasure laden	"	 1022
on the brook's green brim	"	6	10	Over one shoulder doth she	"	 1058
The sun look'd on the world	"	6	11	express my grief for one	"	 1069
as this queen on him	"	6	12	shall not be one minute	"	 1187
he seized on my lips	"	11	9	And every one	R L	 125
And with her lips on his	"	11	10	As one of which	"	 127
lie wither'd on the ground	"	13	9	That one for all or all for one	"	 144
descant on the doubts of my decay	"	14	4	Th' one sweetly flatters	"	 172
Till looking on an Englishman	"	16	3	For one sweet grape	"	 215
On a day, aluck the day	"	17	1	Each one by him enforced	"	 303
meetings on the plains	"	18	46	Imagine her as one in dead of night	"	 449
to round me on th' ear	"	19	51	I have no one	"	 792
None takes pity on thy pain	"	21	20	One poor retiring minute	"	 962
They that fawned on him	"	21	49	wouldst thou one hour come back	"	 965
On the sole Arabian tree	P T	....	2	to see one that by alms doth live	"	 986
Once—season once more fits	V A	....	327	continuance tames the one	"	 1097
attorney once is mute	"	....	345	And as one shifts, another straight		
Once more the engine	"	....	367	ensues	"	 1104
And once made perfect	"	....	408	Or one encompass'd with a winding maze	"	 1151
Once more the ruby-colour'd	"	....	451			
kill me once again	"	....	499	two sweet babes, when death takes one	"	 1161
captain once doth yield	"	....	893			
once more leap her eyes	"	....	1050	When the one pure, the other	"	 1164
in his fair welkin once appear	R L	....	116	The one will live, the other	"	 1187
Which once corrupted	"	....	294	one justly weeps, the other	"	 1235
ere once she speaks	"	....	567	than one hath power to tell	"	 1288
when once thou art a king	"	....	606	One of my husband's men	"	 1291
Who wayward once	"	....	1095	That one might see	"	 1386
Once set on ringing	"	....	1494	That one would swear	"	 1393
Ere once she can discharge	"	....	1603	might one behold	"	 1395
all at once began to say	"	....	1709	Here one man's hand	"	 1415
can see what once I was	"	....	1764	Here one being throng'd	"	 1417
a thousand victories once foil'd	Son	25	10	'Why should the private pleasure of some one	"	 1478
by fortune once more re-survey	"	32	3			
bid your servant once adieu	"	57	8	For one's offence why should so many fall	"	 1483
once in the main of light	"	60	5			
Though I, once gone	"	81	6	And one man's lust	"	 1489
That you were once unkind	"	120	1	discharge one word of woe	"	 1605
how once I suffer'd	"	120	8	with one poor tired tongue	"	 1617
Not once vouchsafe	"	135	6	To drown one woe, one pair of weeping eyes	"	 1680
And Death once dead	"	146	14			
Love-god lying once asleep	"	154	1	The one doth call her his	"	 1793
To every place at once	L C	....	27	be it ten for one	Son	6 8
'Once,' quoth she	P P	9	9	Mark how one string	"	8 9
So beauty blemish'd once	"	13	11	Who, all in one, one pleasing note do sing	"	8 12
But if fortune once do frown	"	21	47			
One—Ten kisses short as one, one long as twenty	V A	....	22	being many, seeming one	"	8 13
				In one of thine	"	11 2
Over one arm the lusty courser's rein	"	....	31	one most heinous crime	"	19 8
				adding one thing to my purpose	"	20 12
And one sweet kiss	"	....	84	youth and thou are of one date	"	22 2
not see one wrinkle	"	....	139	The one by toil, the other	"	28 7
for one poor kiss	"	....	207	like to one more rich	"	29 5
Give me one kiss	"	....	209	my sun one early morn	"	33 9
And one for interest	"	....	210	was but one hour mine	"	33 11
lily fingers one in one	"	....	228	undivided loves are one	"	36 2
excel a common one	"	....	293	there is but one respect	"	36 5

One—lose name of single one	Son	39	6	Ope—it will not ope the gate	V A	......	424
how to make one twain	"	39	13	But they must ope	R L	......	383
my friend and I are one	"	42	13	breaks ope her lock'd-up eyes	"	......	416
Since every one hath, every one,				Open—thy lips shall never open	V A	......	48
one shade	"	53	3	course opens them again	"	......	960
And you, but one, can every	"	53	4	But as they open	R L	......	304
The one doth shadow	'	53	10	the door he opens wide	"	......	359
Why write I still all one	"	76	5	Till they might open	"	......	399
in one of your fair eyes	"	83	13	Open—with open listening ear	"	......	283
I better in one general best	"	91	8	mark of every open eye	"	......	520
One blushing shame	"	99	9	night's 'scapes doth open lay	"	......	747
To one, of one, still such, and				turns to open shame	"	......	890
ever so	"	105	4	Lays open all the little worms	"	......	1218
One thing expressing	"	105	8	keep my drooping eyelids open			
Three themes in one	"	105	12	wide	Son	27	7
never kept seat in one	"	105	14	thy image should keep open	"	61	1
One on another's neck	"	131	10	Open'd—Open'd their mouths	V A	......	248
One will of mine	"	135	12	ruby-colour'd portal open'd	"	......	451
Think all but one, and me in that				And being open'd	"	......	1051
one ' Will	"	135	14	were open'd to the light	R L	......	105
full with wills, and my will one	"	136	6	Opinion—errors by opinion bred	"	......	937
Among a number one is reckon'd				Opportunity—But ill-annex'd....	"	......	874
none	"	136	8	O Opportunity, thy guilt is great	"	......	876
in thy stores' account I one must be	"	136	10	How comes it then, vile Opportunity	"	......	895
Dissuade one foolish heart	"	141	10	ne'er meet with Opportunity	"	......	903
One of her feather'd creatures	"	143	2	thy servant Opportunity	"	......	932
I guess one angel	"	144	12	In vain I rail at Opportunity	"	......	1023
fire my good one out	"	144	14	Opposite—with their .... persuasion	"	......	286
Which one by one	L C	......	38	Oppress'd—The weak oppress'd, the			
schedules had she many a one	"	......	43	impression of strange kinds	"	......	1242
Of one by nature's outwards so				and night by day oppress'd	Son	28	4
commended	"	......	80	oppress'd with melancholy	"	45	8
The one a palate hath	"	......	167	Oppression—When day's oppression			
Not one whose flame	"	......	191	is not eased	"	28	3
orb of one particular tear	"	......	289	Oppressor—while the .... feeds	R L	......	905
I guess one angel	P P	2	12	Or—than doves or roses are	V A	......	10
fire my good one out	"	2	14	or prey be gone	"	......	58
Because thou lovest the one	"	8	4	foul, or wrinkled-old	"	......	133
One god is god of both	"	8	13	dissolve, or seem to melt	"	......	144
One knight loves both	"	8	14	Or, like a fairy, trip	"	......	146
he saw more wounds than one	"	9	13	Or, like a nymph	"	......	147
the fairest one of three	"	16	1	Or what great danger	"	......	206
But one must be refused	"	16	9	fair words, or else be mute	"	......	208
One silly cross	"	18	13	mountain or in dale	"	......	232
One woman would another wed	"	19	48	for curb or pricking spur	"	......	285
Every one that flatters thee	"	21	31	caparisons or trapping gay	"	......	286
If that one be prodigal	"	21	39	whether he ran or fly	"	......	304
Had the essence but in one	P T	......	26	stopp'd, or river stay'd	"	......	331
Neither two nor one	"	......	40	or ivory in an alabaster	"	......	363
Seemeth this concordant one	"	......	46	or I had no hearing	"	......	428
Only—the only sovereign plaster	V A	......	916	Or were I deaf	"	......	435
Only he hath an eye	R L	......	497	Or as the wolf doth grin	"	......	459
will make thee only loved for fear	"	......	610	Or as the berry breaks	"	......	460
Only to flatter fools	"	......	1559	Or like the deadly bullet	"	......	461
for she was only mine	"	......	1798	in earth or heaven	"	......	493
And only must be wail'd	"	......	1799	or in the ocean drench'd, or in the			
And only herald to the gaudy				fire	"	......	494
spring	Son	1	10	or morn or weary even	"	......	495
dearest and mine only care	"	48	7	delight to die, or life desire	"	......	496
their virtue only is their show	"	54	9	Or being early pluck'd	"	......	528
Though to itself it only live and die	"	94	10	Or as the fleet-foot roe	"	......	561
render, only me for thee	"	125	12	Or like the froward infant	"	......	562
Only my plague thus far	"	141	13	Or at the fox	"	......	675
Onset—the onset still expecting	R L	......	432	Or at the roe	"	......	676
But in the onset come	Son	90	11	Or theirs whose desperate hands	"	......	765
Onward—Onward to Troy	R L	......	1504	Or butcher-sire that reaves	"	......	766
My grief lies onward	Son	50	14	Or 'stonish'd as night-wanderers	"	......	825
As thou goest onwards	"	126	6	rough bear or lion proud	"	......	884
Opal—sapphire and the opal blend	L C	......	215	unwitnessed with eye or ear	"	......	1023

Or—Or, as the snail	V A 1033	Or—thy picture or my love	Son 47 9
grass, herb, leaf, or weed	" 1055	Or, if they sleep	" 47 13
or any thing ensuing	" 1078	Or captain jewels in the carcanet	" 52 8
but high or low	" 1139	Or as the wardrobe	" 52 10
Or why is Collatine	R L 33	Or call it winter	" 56 13
Or, gaining more	" 138	Where you may be, or your affairs	
one for all or all for one	" 144	suppose	" 57 10
Or sells eternity	" 214	Or at your hand	" 58 3
Or what fond beggar	" 216	be it well or ill	" 58 14
my son or sire	" 232	we are mended, or whether better	
Or lain in ambush	" 233	they	" 59 11
Or were he not	" 234	Or whether revolution	" 59 12
revenge or quittal of such strife	" 236	Are vanishing or vanish'd out of	
a sentence or an old man's saw	" 244	sight	" 63 7
for colour or excuses	" 267	Or state itself confounded	" 64 10
Or as those bars	" 327	Or what strong hand	" 65 11
dazzleth them, or else some shame		Or who his spoil	" 65 12
supposed	" 377	Or durst inhabit on a living brow	" 68 4
'gainst law or duty	" 497	Either not assail'd or victor being	
Or stop the headlong fury	" 501	charged	" 70 10
slavish wipe or birth-hour's blot	" 537	yellow leaves, or none, or few	" 73 2
full-fed hound or gorged hawk	" 694	Or as sweet-season'd showers	" 75 2
tender smell or speedy flight	" 695	Possessing or pursuing	" 75 11
slow pursuit, or altogether balk	" 696	what is had or must from you be	
curb his heat, or rein his rash de-		took	" 75 12
sire	" 706	Or gluttoning on all, or all away	" 75 14
Or if thou wilt permit	" 775	variation or quick change	" 76 2
Or hateful cuckoos	" 849	Or, being wreck'd	" 80 11
Or toads infect fair founts	" 850	Or I shall live	" 81 1
Or tyrant fully lurk	" 851	Or you survive	" 81 2
Or kings be breakers	" 852	I found, or thought I found	" 83 3
Or kills his life or else his quality	" 875	Or me, to whom thou gavest it	" 87 10
Or free that soul	" 900	hawks or horses be	" 91 11
makes him honour'd or begets		thy thoughts or thy heart's work-	
him hate	" 1005	ings be	" 93 11
Or that which from discharged		Or, if they sing	" 97 13
cannon fumes	" 1043	Or from their proud lap	" 98 8
Or one encompass'd	" 1151	But sweet or colour	" 99 15
To live or die	" 1154	my love, or thy dear merit	" 108 4
'My body or my soul	" 1163	calls me well or ill	" 112 3
drown their eyes or break their		my steel'd sense or changes right	
hearts	" 1239	or wrong	" 112 8
by force, by fraud, or skill	" 1243	Of bird, of flower, or shape	" 113 6
without or yea or no	" 1340	rudest or gentlest sight	" 113 9
Or blot with hell-born sin	" 1519	favour or deformd'st creature	" 113 10
As if with grief or travail	" 1543	The mountain or the sea, the day	
Or, at the least, this refuge	" 1654	or night	" 113 11
Or keep him from heart-easing	" 1782	The crow or dove	" 113 12
for daughter or for wife	" 1792	Or whether doth my mind	" 114 1
help wounds, or grief help griev-		Or whether shall I say	" 114 3
ous deeds	" 1822	Or bends with the remover	" 116 4
Pity the world, or else this glut-		brass or hammer'd steel	" 120 4
ton be	Son 1 13	Or on my frailties	" 121 7
Or who is he so fond	" 3 7	Or, at the least	" 122 5
Or ten times happier	" 6 8	Made more or less	" 123 12
Or else receivest with pleasure	" 8 4	Time's love or to Time's hate	" 124 3
Or to thyself at least	" 10 12	weeds, or flowers with flowers	" 124 4
live in thine or thee	" 10 14	Or laid great bases	" 125 3
of good or evil luck	" 14 3	than waste or ruining	" 125 4
of dearths, or seasons' quality	" 14 4	Or if it were	" 127 2
Or say with princes	" 14 7	Or mine eyes seeing	" 137 11
Or else of thee	" 14 13	Or, if it do	" 142 5
Time's pencil, or my pupil pen	" 16 10	Or, if they have	" 148 3
chance or nature's changing course	" 18 8	Or made them swear	" 152 12
men can breathe, or eyes can see	" 18 13	Or monarch's hands	L C 41
Or some fierce thing	" 23 3	as it was, or best without	" 98
birth, or wealth, or wit	" 37 5	Or be his manage	" 112
Or any of these all, or all, or more	" 37 6	in thoughts, or to remain	" 129
Or heart in love	" 47 4	Or forced examples	" 157

Or—Or my affection put	L C		192
Or any of my leisures	"		193
smiled or made some moan	"		217
Or sister sanctified	"		233
blushes, or of weeping water	"		304
Or swounding paleness	"		305
Or to turn white	"		308
Or he refused to take	P P	4	10
a lover, or a lecher whether	"	7	17
are seld or never found	"	13	7
In scorn or friendship	"	14	8
or kill the gallant knight	"	16	6
That are either true or fair	P T		66
Orator—the orator too green	V A		806
of men without an orator	R L		30
All orators are dumb	"		268
The orator, to deck his oratory	"		815
Oratory—to her .... adds more grace	"		564
The orator, to deck his oratory	"		815
Orb—In the small orb	L C		289
Orbed—To the orbed earth	"		25
Orchard—in others' orchards grew	"		171
Ordering—in each by mutual	Son	8	10
Orient—an orient drop beside	V A		981
in the orient when the gracious light	Son	7	1
Bright orient pearl	P P	10	3
Origin—my origin and ender	L C		222
Ornament—our mistress' ornaments are chaste	R L		322
the world's fresh ornament	Son	1	9
for ornament doth use	"	21	3
By that sweet ornament	"	54	2
Without all ornament	"	68	10
The ornament of beauty	"	70	3
profaned their scarlet ornaments	"	142	6
appertainings or to ornaments	L C		115
Orphan—The orphan pines while the oppressor feeds	R L		905
But hope of orphans	Son	97	10
Orpheus—Pluto winks while Orpheus plays	R L		553
Orts—a beggar's orts to crave	"		985
Osier—to thee like osiers bowed	P P	5	4
Under an osier growing by a brook	"	6	5
Other—Under her other was	V A		32
each other did destroy	"		346
Her other tender hand	"		352
His other agents aim	"		400
feeder of the other four	"		446
may they kiss each other	"		505
with others being mingled	"		691
others, they think	"		843
as thou dost lend to other	"		864
all other eyes to see	"		952
view'd each other's sorrow	"		963
The other kills thee quickly	"		990
some other in their bills	"		1102
was the other queen	R L		66
Interchange each other's seat	"		70
th' other feareth harm	"		172
her other fair hand was	"		393
no other pleasure of his gain	"		860
tames the one; the other wild	"		1007
Will slay the other	"		1162
the other made divine	"		1164
the other being dead	"		1187
the other takes in hand	"		1235
to guess at others' smart	"		1258
Other—while others sanctify	R L		1348
surmise of others' detriment	"		1579
their dolour others have endured	"		1582
his lord and other company	"		1594
wondering each other's chance	"		1596
call her his, the other his	"		1793
love toward others	Son	9	13
they see others grow	"	12	12
to some other give	"	13	4
the other to complain	"	28	7
Both find each other	"	42	11
The other two	"	45	1
the other my desire	"	45	3
doth good turns now unto the other	"	47	2
The other as your bounty	"	53	11
with others all too near	"	61	14
As I all other	"	62	8
In other accents	"	69	7
In others' works	"	78	11
When others would give	"	83	12
whilst other write good words	"	85	5
Then others for the breath	"	85	13
When other petty griefs	"	90	10
And other strains of woe	"	90	13
thy heart in other place	"	93	4
Who, moving others	"	94	3
Others but stewards	"	94	8
For to no other pass	"	103	11
varying to other words	"	105	10
Of others' voices	"	112	10
but by others' seeing	"	121	4
should others' false adulterate eye	"	121	5
forfeit, so that other mine	"	134	3
Shall will in others	"	135	7
Robb'd others' beds' revenues	"	142	8
what others do abhor	"	150	11
With others thou shouldst	"	150	12
must curb it upon others' proof	L C		163
in others' orchards grew	"		171
thou lovest the one and I the other	P P	8	4
other help for him	"	18	54
Either was the other's mine	P T		36
Our—our sport is not in sight	V A		124
by our ears our hearts oft tainted be	R L		38
our mistress' ornaments are chaste	"		322
from forth a cloud, bereaves our sight	"		373
that we call them ours	"		868
that we can say is ours	"		873
Shall tune our heart-strings	"		1141
from our house in grief	"		1598
and they are none of ours	"		1757
To rouse our Roman gods	"		1831
By our strong arms	"		1834
By all our country rights	"		1838
Our undivided loves are one	Son	36	2
In our two loves	"	36	5
Though in our lives	"	36	6
And our dear love	"	39	6
how are our brains beguiled	"	59	2
So do our minutes hasten	"	60	2
of our old acquaintance tell	"	89	12
Our love was new	"	102	5
Of this our time	"	106	10
to make our appetites more keen	"	118	1
we our palate urge	"	118	2
to prevent our maladies	"	118	3

Our—O, that our night of woe	Son 120	9
Not by our feeling	" 121	4
Our dates are brief	" 123	5
make them born to our desire	" 123	7
inviting time our fashion calls	" 124	8
And in our faults	" 138	14
to make our wits more keen	L C	161
satisfaction to our blood	"	162
that preach in our behoof	"	165
our drops this difference bore	"	300
Since that our faults	P P 1	14
All our pleasure known	" 18	45
All our merry meetings	" 18	46
All our evening sport	" 18	47
All our love is lost	" 18	48
'Mongst our mourners	P T	20
Out—In liming out	V A	299
Things out of hope	"	567
the cold fault cleanly out	"	694
Their light blown out	"	826
volleys out his voice	"	921
lo, two lamps burn out	"	1128
and wore out the night	R L	123
'Fair torch, burn out thy light	"	190
The eye of heaven is out	"	356
to heave the owner out	"	413
Small lights are soon blown out	"	647
halt, creep, cry out for thee	"	902
'Out, idle words, servants to shallow fools	"	1016
And seems to point her out	"	1087
Will we find out	"	1146
tread the way out readily	"	1152
pattern of the worn-out age	"	1350
burnt out in tedious nights	"	1379
scratch out the angry eyes	"	1469
rings out the doleful knell	"	1495
would be drawn out too long	"	1616
What he breathes out	"	1666
In rage sent out	"	1671
wear their brave state out	Son 15	8
prick'd thee out for women's pleasure	" 20	13
But, out, alack! he was but one hour mine	" 33	11
root out the work of masonry	" 55	6
wear this world out	" 55	12
To find out shames	" 61	7
or vanish'd out of sight	" 63	7
summer's honey breath hold out	" 65	5
To linger out a purposed overthrow	" 90	8
habitation choose out thee	" 93	10
leaves out difference	" 105	8
but effectually is out	" 113	4
But bears it out even to the edge	" 116	12
out of their spheres been fitted	" 119	7
fire my good one out	" 144	14
doth point out thee	" 151	9
love put out Religion's eye	L C	250
fire my good one out	P P 2	14
She burned out love	" 7	14
Out-brage'd—Whose bare .... the web it seem'd to wear	L C	95
Out-brave—out-braves his dignity	Son 94	12
Out-burneth—as soon as straw	P P 7	14
Outcast—beweep my outcast state	Son 29	2
Outcry—Entombs her outcry	R L	679
Outfacing—Outfacing faults in love	P P 1	8
Out-going—out-going in thy noon	Son 7	13

Outlive—to outlive long date	Son 38	12
outlive this powerful rhyme	" 55	2
much outlive a gilded tomb	" 101	11
Outrage—darest do such outrage	R L	605
Outrageous—no outrageous thing	"	607
Outright—Kill me .... with looks	Son 139	14
Outrun—How he outruns the wind	V A	681
'Outruns the eye	R L	1667
Out-stripp'd—they be out-stripp'd by every pen	Son 32	6
Out-stripping—Out-stripping crows	V A	324
Outward—puts on .... strangeness	"	310
thy outward parts would move	"	435
no outward harm express'd	R L	91
With outward honesty	"	1345
inward worth nor outward fair	Son 16	11
nine eye's due is thine outward part	" 46	13
outward thus with outward praise	" 69	5
Where time and outward form	" 108	14
the outward honouring	" 125	2
Painting thy outward walls	" 146	4
outwards so commended	L C	80
with an outward show	P P 19	38
Outwardly—but fighting outwardly	L C	203
Outwore—and outwore the night	V A	841
Outworn—death by time outworn	R L	1761
of outworn buried age	Son 64	2
the map of days outworn	" 68	1
Oven—An oven that is stopp'd	V A	331
Over—one arm the lusty	"	31
Over my altars hath he	"	103
O, had she then gave over	"	571
Over one shoulder doth she	"	1058
sovereign mistress over wrack	Son 126	5
sorrow over me hath power	L C	74
eyes stuck over all his face	"	81
Overcome—Who, ... by doubt	V A	891
Overcome, as one	"	955
Overflow—will force it overflow	"	72
Over-fly—strive to over-fly them	"	324
Over-go—That over-goes my blunt invention	Son 103	7
Over-handled—your idle over-handled theme	V A	770
Overlook—did hotly overlook them	"	178
Over-partial—corrupt by .... looks	Son 137	5
Overplus—and 'Will' in overplus	" 135	2
Overruled—Thus he that	V A	109
Oversee—shalt oversee this will	R L	1205
Overseen—How was I overseen	"	1206
Over-shoot—to .... his troubles	V A	680
Over-slipp'd—hath over-slipp'd her thought	R L	1576
Oversway'd—overruled I	V A	109
Overthrow—Till mutual overthrow	"	1018
a purposed overthrow	Son 90	8
Overturn—war shall statues overturn	" 55	5
Over-wash'd—cheeks .... with woe	R L	1225
Owe—and I will not owe it	V A	411
if any love you owe me	"	523
which Collatine doth owe	R L	82
more slavish tribute than they owe	"	299
kingdoms of hearts shouldst owe	Son 70	14
Since what he owes thee	" 79	14
landlord which doth owe them	L C	140
Owed—I owed her, and 'tis mine	R L	1803
borrow'd motion seeming owed	L C	327
Owest—of that fair thou owest	Son 18	10

Entry	Ref	No.
Owl—The owl, night's herald	V A	531
No noise but owls' and wolves'	R L	165
that this night-owl will catch	"	360
Own—The kiss shall be thine own	V A	117
Is thine own heart to thine own face	"	157
Steal thine own freedom	"	160
by their own direction	"	216
in thine own law forlorn	"	251
more moving than your own	"	776
because it is his own	R L	35
but she is not her own	"	241
blush at her own disgrace	"	479
not their own infamy	"	539
for thine own sake leave me	"	583
Their own transgressions	"	634
That from their own misdeeds	"	637
Till with her own white fleece	"	678
can see his own abomination	"	704
breakers of their own behests	"	852
At his own shadow	"	997
are their own faults' books	"	1253
mine own would do me good	"	1274
her own gross abuse	"	1315
with his own weight goes	"	1494
the feeling of her own grief	"	1578
to make mine own excuse	"	1653
Thine, mine, his own	"	1684
thine own bright eyes	Son 1	5
Within thine own bud	" 1	11
thine own deep-sunken eyes	" 2	7
by your own sweet skill	" 16	14
her own sweet brood	" 19	2
Nature's own hand	" 20	1
weakens his own heart	" 23	4
mine own love's strength	" 23	7
mine own love's might	" 23	8
Thine own sweet argument	" 38	3
mine own praise to mine own self bring	" 39	3
mine own when I praise	" 39	4
of mine own desert	" 49	10
Mine own true love	" 61	11
mine own worth do define	" 62	7
Mine own self-love	" 62	11
give thee so thine own	" 69	6
than mine own desert	" 72	6
thy own worth then not knowing	" 87	9
With mine own weakness	" 88	5
Your own glass shows	" 103	14
Not mine own fears	" 107	1
Mock their own presage	" 107	6
Gored mine own thoughts	" 110	3
his own vision holds	" 113	8
your own dear-purchased right	" 117	6
reckon up their own	" 121	10
thou thine own state	" 142	3
Love's own hand did make	" 145	1
Ask'd their own wills	L C	133
was my own fee-simple	"	144
'gainst her own content	"	157
but mine own was free	"	193
to your own command	"	227
Made me think upon mine own	P P 21	18
Owner—beauty, in the owners' arms	R L	27
From this fair throne to heave the owner out	"	413
and owners of their faces	Son	94 7
The owner's tongue doth publish	"	102 4
Pace—colour, pace, and bone	V A	294
knit brow and strengthless pace	R L	709
marching on with trembling paces	"	1391
with my desire keep pace	Son 51	9
and no pace perceived	" 104	10
Pace—Shall you pace forth	"	55 10
Pack—Pack night, peep day	P P 13	17
Pack'd—The night so pack'd, I post	" 15	8
Pack-horse—sin's pack-horse, virtue's snare	R L	928
Page—wait on them as their pages	"	919
antiquity for aye his page	Son 108	12
Paid—as if not paid before	" 30	12
Pain—In his shelly cave with pain	V A	1034
Pain pays the income	R L	334
joy breeds months of pain	"	690
living death and pain perpetual	"	726
perplex'd in greater pain	"	743
have co-partners in my pain	"	789
it cannot cure his pain	"	861
The pain be mine	Son 38	14
with pretty ruth upon my pain	" 132	4
and rid my pain	" 139	14
The manner of my pity-wanting pain	" 140	4
she that makes me sin awards me pain	" 141	14
painting pain and cost	P P 13	12
As take the pain	" 14	12
more mickle was the pain	" 16	9
None takes pity on thy pain	" 21	20
Pained—ease to the pained	R L	901
Painful—gouts and painful fits	"	856
More feeling-painful	"	1679
The painful warrior famoused	Son 25	9
Paint—ground of sin I will not	R L	1074
Painted—Well-painted idol	V A	212
deceived with painted grapes	"	601
Shall by a painted cloth	R L	245
To this well-painted piece	"	1443
in Priam's painted wound	"	1466
she weeps Troy's painted woes	"	1492
Sinon here is painted	"	1541
That she with painted images	"	1577
than your painted counterfeit	Son 16	8
with Nature's own hand painted	" 20	1
Stirr'd by a painted beauty	" 21	2
And to the painted banquet	" 47	6
in Grecian tires are painted new	" 53	8
Painter—Look, when a painter	V A	289
Which the conceited painter drew so proud	R L	1371
to show the painter's strife	"	1377
and there the painter interlaces	"	1390
the painter was so nice	"	1412
In her the painter had anatomized	"	1450
The painter was no god	"	1461
In him the painter labour'd	"	1506
And chid the painter	"	1528
Mine eye hath play'd the painter	Son 24	1
it is best painter's art	" 24	4
For through the painter	" 24	5
Painting—Of skilful painting	R L	1367
about the painting round	"	1499
Painting my age with beauty	Son 62	14
Why should false painting imitate	" 67	5
And their gross painting	" 82	13
that you did painting need	" 83	1
to your fair no painting set	" 83	2

Painting—Painting thy outward walls	Son	146	4
painting pain and cost	P P	13	12
Pair—A pair of maiden worlds	R L		408
one pair of weeping eyes	"		1680
Palate—And to his palate doth prepare	Son	114	12
we our palate urge	"	118	2
The one a palate hath	L C		167
Pale—Making them red and pale	V A		21
shame and anger ashy-pale	"		76
But now her cheek was pale	"		347
Claps her pale cheek	"		468
whereat a sudden pale	"		589
agues pale and faint	"		739
With cold-pale weakness numbs	"		892
and they are pale	"		1123
Resembling well his pale cheeks	"		1169
Which in pale embers hid	R L		5
Here pale with fear	"		183
round turrets destitute and pale	"		441
anger pale as the lily pale	"		478
Pale cowards marching on	"		1391
Cheeks neither red nor pale	"		1510
Nor ashy-pale the fear	"		1512
And now this pale swan	"		1611
From lips new-waxen pale	"		1663
the pale fear in his face	"		1775
Gilding pale streams	Son	33	4
That leaves look pale	"	97	14
a fickle maid full pale	L C		5
her pale and pined cheek	"		32
A lily pale with damask dye	P P	7	5
Pale—Within the circuit of this ivory pale	V A		230
Paled—Of paled pearls and rubies	L C		198
Pale-faced—like a .... coward	V A		569
Paleness—Or swounding paleness	"		303
Paler—Paler for sorrow	P P	9	3
Palfrey—how to get my palfrey	"		384
Thy palfrey, as he should	"		385
Palm—on his sweating palm	"		25
Would in thy palm dissolve	"		144
Palmer—As palmers' chat makes short their pilgrimage	R L		791
Pandion—King Pandion he is dead	P P	21	23
Pang—In the suffering pangs it bears	L C		272
Pant—My boding heart pants	V A		647
Panteth—the weak mouse panteth	R L		555
Panting—Panting he lies	V A		62
wearied lamb lies panting there	R L		737
Paper—paper, ink, and pen	"		1289
o'er the paper with her quill	"		1297
So should my papers	Son	17	9
For every vulgar paper	"	38	4
Tearing of papers, breaking	L C		6
Paphos—Holding their course to...	V A		1193
Paradise—thinks in .... was sown	L C		91
to win a Paradise	P P	3	14
Parallel—And delves the parallels	Son	60	10
Parasite—sounds resembling parasites	V A		848
Parcel—their silken parcels hurls	L C		87
Their distract parcels in combined sums	"		231
Parching—not parching heat nor freezing cold	R L		1145
Pardon—Yet pardon me	V A		998
Pardon—Yourself to pardon	Son	58	12
"O, pardon me, in that my boast	L C		246
I pardon crave of thee	P P	10	11
Paris—Thy heat of lust, fond Paris	R L		1473
Park—I'll be a park	V A		231
I am such a park	"		239
Parley—parley to his heartless foe	R L		471
Parling—from their parling looks	"		100
Part—thy outward parts would move	V A		433
Each part in me	"		436
numbs each feeling part	"		892
This mutiny each part doth surprise	"		1049
My part is youth	R L		298
corrupted takes the worser part	"		294
against a thorn thou bear'st thy part	"		1135
every part a part of woe	"		1327
'Tis but a part of sorrow	"		1328
help to bear thy part	"		1830
In singleness the parts that thou shows not half your parts	Son	8	8
	"	17	4
put besides his part	"	23	2
all love's loving parts	"	31	3
all their parts of me	"	31	11
in thy parts do crowned sit	"	37	7
by a part of all thy glory live	"	37	12
the better part of me	"	39	2
eye's moiety and the dear heart's part	"	46	12
mine eye's due is thine outward part	"	46	13
love doth share a part	"	47	8
To guard the lawful reasons on thy part	"	49	12
you have some part	"	53	13
and all my every part	"	62	2
Those parts of thee	"	69	1
The very part was consecrate	"	74	6
the better part of me	"	74	8
each part will be forgotten	"	81	4
Upon thy part	"	88	6
hath the mind no part	"	113	7
oblivion yield his part	"	122	7
like in every part	"	132	12
And play the mother's part	"	143	12
My nobler part to my gross body's treason	"	151	6
And when in his fair parts	L C		85
my own fee-simple not in part	"		144
My parts had power to charm	"		260
that I thy parts admire	P P	5	10
He with thee doth bear a part	"	21	56
Part—with wringing; let us part	V A		421
Do summon us to part	"		534
As fearful of him, part; through	"		630
seems to part in sunder	R L		388
thou mayst come and part	Son	48	12
Which parts the shore	"	56	10
Doth part his function	"	113	3
If what parts can so remain	P T		48
Partake—against myself with thee partake	Son	149	2
Partial—corrupt by over-partial looks	"	137	5
As well as fancy, partial wight	P P	19	4
Partially—partially they smother	R L		631
Particular—But these particulars	Son	91	7
of one particular tear	L C		289
Parting—The honey fee of parting	V A		538

Parting—Yet at my parting		P P	14	7		
Partly—and is partly blind		Son	113	3		
Partner—To be thy partner		R L		672		
Party—Thy adverse party		Son	35	10		
Where neither party		L C		186		
Pass—as scorning it should pass		V A		982		
when thou shalt strangely pass		Son	49	5		
For to no other pass		"	103	11		
let me pass untold		"	136	9		
he should not pass these grounds		P P	9	8		
Passage—did honey passage yield		V A		452		
Struggling for passage		"		1047		
for passage of her breath		R L		1040		
All unseen 'gan passage find		P P	17	6		
Pass'd—Thou hast pass'd by		Son	70	9		
you've pass'd a hell of time		"	120	6		
Passenger—.... in summer's heat		V A		91		
Passing—straight legs and ....strong		"		297		
As passing all conceit		P P	8	8		
Spied a blossom passing fair		"	17	3		
Passing-bell—that bears the		V A		702		
Passion—trembling in her passion		"		27		
swelling passion doth provoke		"		218		
Passion on passion deeply is re-doubled		"		832		
Variable passions throng		"		967		
each passion labours so		"		969		
her passion's strength renews		R L		1103		
life and feeling of her passion		"		1317		
such passion her assails		"		1562		
too sensible thy passion maketh		"		1678		
the master-mistress of my passion		Son	20	2		
Catching all passions		L C		126		
their passions likewise lent me		"		199		
For, lo, his passion, but an art		"		295		
Passion—Dumbly she passions		V A		1059		
Past—My day's delight is past		"		380		
past reason's weak removing		R L		243		
To all sins past		"		923		
is past the help of law		"		1022		
recall'd in rage being past		"		1671		
From what is past		"		1685		
the violet past prime		Son	12	3		
remembrance of things past		"	30	2		
a limit past my praise		"	82	6		
at the present nor the past		"	123	10		
Past reason hunted		"	129	6		
Past reason hated		"	129	7		
my days are past the best		"	138	6		
Past cure I am, now reason is past care		"	147	9		
To put the by-past perils		L C		158		
my years be past the best		P P	1	6		
Patent—so my patent back again is swerving		Son	87	8		
Path—The path is smooth		V A		788		
She treads the path		"		908		
Patience—Where thou with		R L		486		
with greater patience bear it		"		1158		
By this, mild patience		"		1268		
Patience seem'd to scorn		"		1305		
That patience is quite beaten		"		1563		
And patience, tame to sufferance		Son	58	7		
My tongue-tied patience		"	140	2		
Patient—The patient dies while the physician sleeps		R L		904		
Whilst, like a willing patient		Son	111	9		
Playing patient sports		L C		242		
Patiently—unless I took all		R L		1641		
Patron—god and patron of all light		V A		860		
Pattern—Even so this pattern		R L		1350		
beauty's pattern to succeeding men		Son	19	12		
you pattern of all those		"	98	12		
patterns of this foul beguiling		L C		170		
Pattern'd—When .... by thy fault		R L		629		
Pause—Then mightst thou pause		V A		137		
doth provoke a pause		"		218		
Sad pause and deep regard		R L		277		
and makes a pause		"		541		
Pausing — Pausing for means to mourn		"		1365		
Paw—blunt thou the lion's paws		Son	19	1		
Pawn'd—Pawn'd honest looks		R L		1351		
Pawning—Pawning his honour		"		156		
Pay—one sweet kiss shall pay		V A		84		
So thou wilt buy, and pay		"		514		
pay them at thy leisure		"		518		
Love's eyes pay tributary gazes		"		632		
every minute pays the hour		R L		329		
Pain pays the income		"		334		
streams that pay a daily debt		"		649		
those that pay the willing loan		Son	6	6		
Which I new pay as if not paid		"	30	12		
and pays it thee again		"	79	8		
thou thyself dost pay		"	79	14		
He pays the whole		"	134	14		
Pay—her lips were ready for his pay		V A		89		
Paying—Paying what ransom		"		550		
by paying too much rent		Son	125	6		
Paying more slavish tribute		R L		229		
Payment—Say, for non-payment		V A		521		
With such black payment		R L		576		
Peace—How he in peace is wounded		"		831		
"O peace!" quoth Lucrece		"		1284		
And for the peace of you		Son	75	3		
And peace proclaims		"	107	8		
Love's arms are peace		L C		271		
Peaceful—And in a peaceful hour		V A		652		
Pearl—like pearls in glass		"		980		
And wiped the brinish pearl		R L		1213		
Those round clear pearls		"		1553		
Ah, but those tears are pearl		Son	34	13		
Of paled pearls and rubies		L C		198		
Bright orient pearl		P P	10	3		
Pearly—With pearly sweat		R L		396		
Peasant—Which heartless peasants		"		1392		
Pebbled—waves make towards the pebbled shore		Son	60	1		
Peculiar—did him peculiar duties		R L		14		
Peel'd—the bark peel'd from the lofty pine		"		1167		
her bark being peel'd away		"		1169		
Peep—the gaudy sun would peep		V A		1088		
should not peep again		R L		788		
each little mote will peep		"		1251		
Delights to peep		Son	24	12		
Pack night, peep day		P P	15	17		
Peep'd—Some beauty peep'd		L C		14		
Peeping—leave thy peeping		R L		1089		
Nymphs back peeping		P P	18	43		
peeping forth this tumult		R L		447		
Peer—peer to such a peerless dame		"		21		
o'er the white sheet peers her whiter chin		"		472		
Peering—peering through a wave		V A		86		
Peerless—peer to such a ....dame		R L		21		
Pelf—but cannot pluck the pelf		P P	11	12		
Pelleted—woe had pelleted in tears		L C		18		

15

Pelt—seems to pelt and swear	R L	.....	1418
Pen—paper, ink, and pen	"	.....	1289
Time's pencil, or my pupil pen	Son	16	10
with thine antique pen	"	19	10
they be outstripp'd by every pen	"	32	6
as every alien pen	"	78	3
travail of a worthier pen	"	79	6
such virtue hath my pen	"	81	13
within that pen doth dwell	"	84	5
of well refined pen	"	85	8
And gives thy pen	"	100	8
I see their antique pen	"	106	7
Pen—He pens her piteous clamours	R L	.....	681
Penance—Nor double penance, to correct correction	Son	111	12
Pencil—Time's...., or my pupil pen	"	16	10
Beauty no pencil, beauty's truth	"	101	7
Pencill'd—To pencill'd pensiveness	R L	.....	1497
Penetrable—No penetrable entrance	"	.....	559
Penn'd—sadly penn'd in blood	L C	.....	47
Pensived—Of pensived and subdued desires	"	.....	219
Pensiveness—To pencill'd....	R L	.....	1497
Pent—pent in walls of glass	Son	5	10
for 1, being pent in thee	"	133	13
Penury—Lean.... within that pen	"	84	5
People—poor people are amazed	V A	.....	925
a press of people at a door	R L	.....	1301
Perceive—I perceive the reason	V A	.....	727
When I perceive that men	Son	15	5
Perceived—and no pace perceived	"	104	10
Perceivest—This thou perceivest	Son	73	13
Perceiving—perceiving how he is enraged	V A	.....	317
Perchance—Perchance his boast	R L	.....	36
Perchance that envy	"	.....	39
Perfect—And once made perfect	V A	.....	408
The perfect ceremony	Son	23	6
every bad a perfect best	"	114	7
whose perfect white	R L	.....	394
Perfect'st—of .... love being made	Son	51	10
Perfection—Whose full perfection	V A	.....	634
And pure perfection	"	.....	736
Have no perfection	R L	.....	837
But no perfection is so absolute	"	.....	853
Holds in perfection	Son	15	2
And right perfection wrongfully disgraced	"	66	7
Perforce—Perforce will force it	V A	.....	72
thou perforce must bear	R L	.....	612
Perforce am thine	Son	133	14
Perfume—Three April perfumes	"	104	7
And in some perfumes	"	130	7
Perfumed—Comes breath perfumed	V A	.....	444
As the perfumed tincture	Son	54	6
Perhaps—When I perhaps compounded am with clay	"	71	10
Peril—To put the by-past perils	L C	.....	158
Period—had they seen the period of their ill	R L	.....	380
She puts the period	"	.....	565
Perish—so my Troy did perish	"	.....	1547
rude, barrenly perish	Son	11	10
Perjured—For perjured Sinon	R L	.....	1521
Is perjured, murderous	Son	129	3
I am perjured most	"	152	6
sworn thee fair; more perjured I	"	152	13
Perjury—Guilty of perjury	R L	.....	919
craft and perjury should thrust	"	.....	1517
Perjury—to this false perjury	P P	3	8
Permit—permit the sun to climb	R L	.....	775
permit the basest clouds	Son	33	5
Perpetual—death and pain....	R L	.....	726
and make perpetual night	"	.....	784
and thy perpetual infamy	"	.....	1638
with a perpetual dullness	Son	56	8
took heat perpetual	"	154	10
Perpetually—drop on them	R L	.....	686
Perplexed—..... in his throne	V A	.....	1043
perplex'd in greater pain	R L	.....	733
Person—Health to thy person	"	.....	1305
And set thy person forth	P P	19	12
Personal—In personal duty	L C	.....	130
Perspective—perspective it is best painter's art	Son	24	4
Persuade—to persuade him there	V A	.....	1114
doth of itself persuade	R L	.....	29
persuade him to abstaining	"	.....	130
My glass shall not persuade me	Son	22	1
Persuade my heart	P P	3	3
Persuasion—with their opposite persuasion	R L	.....	286
Perusal—Worthy perusal stand	Son	38	6
Perused—she advisedly perused	R L	.....	1527
Which she perused	L C	.....	44
Perverse—Perverse it shall be	V A	.....	1157
Pervert—And new pervert	L C	.....	329
Pestilence—Life-poisoning....	V A	.....	740
Petitioners—petitioners to his eyes	"	.....	356
Petty—such petty bondage	"	.....	394
the petty streams that pay	R L	.....	649
If all these petty ills	"	.....	656
When other petty griefs	Son	90	10
Philomel—lamenting Philomel had ended	R L	.....	1079
Come, Philomel, that sing'st	"	.....	1128
Philomel on summer's front	Son	102	7
Philomela—While Philomela sits and sings	P P	15	5
Phoebus—That Phoebus' lute	"	8	10
Phoenix—turn the long-lived	Son	19	4
His phoenix down began	L C	.....	93
Phoenix and the turtle fled	P T	.....	23
Flaming in the phoenix' sight	"	.....	35
To the phoenix and the dove	"	.....	50
Death is now the phoenix' nest	"	.....	56
Phrase—And precious phrase	Son	85	4
Phraseless—that phraseless hand	L C	.....	225
Phrygian—to .... shepherds lent	R L	.....	1502
Physic—Give physic to the sick	"	.....	901
give physic to my grief	Son	34	9
which physic did except	"	147	8
to physic your cold breast	L C	.....	259
In spite of physic	P P	13	12
Physician—while the .... sleeps	R L	.....	904
from their physicians know	Son	140	8
the physician to my love	"	147	5
Physiognomy—Of .... might one	R L	.....	1395
Pick—picks them all at last	V A	.....	576
Could pick no meaning	R L	.....	100
Picture—Fie, lifeless picture	V A	.....	211
picture of an angry-chafing boar	"	.....	662
the picture of true piety	R L	.....	542
This picture she advisedly perused	"	.....	1527
the picture was belied	"	.....	1533
thy picture's sight would bar	Son	46	3
With my love's picture	"	47	5
by thy picture or my love	"	47	9

Picture—thy picture in my sight	Son 47	13
that did his picture get	L C	134
Pictured—your true image.... lies	Son 21	6
Piece—where hangs a piece	R L	1366
To this well-painted piece	"	1413
Pieced—Pieced not his grace	L C	119
Pied—When proud-pied April	Son 98	2
Pierced—A closet never pierced	" 46	6
Piercing—with thy piercing light	R L	1091
Piety—the picture of true piety	"	542
Pike—Of bristly pikes	V A	620
Pilgrimage—makes short their,...	R L	791
mischief in thy pilgrimage	"	960
Attending on his golden pilgrimage	Son 7	8
a zealous pilgrimage to thee	" 27	6
Pillage—slaves for pillage fighting	R L	428
Pillow—Cozening the pillow	"	387
and on that pillow lay	"	1620
Pilot—Desire my pilot is	"	279
Pine—surfeit by the eye and pine the maw	V A	602
alone must sit and pine	R L	795
The orphan pines while the oppressor feeds	"	905
He ten times pines, that pines beholding	"	1115
Thus do I pine and surfeit	Son 75	13
Why dost thou pine	" 146	3
And let that pine to aggravate	" 146	10
with bleeding groans they pine	L C	275
Pine—peel'd from the lofty pine	R L	1167
Pined—pale and pined cheek beside	L C	32
Pineth—he pineth still for more	R L	98
Pining—like still-pining Tantalus	"	858
Pioner—you see the labouring pioner	"	1380
Pipe—those shrunk pipes had fed	"	1455
And stops her pipe in growth of	Son 102	8
My shepherd's pipe can sound	P P 18	27
Pirate—strong pirates, shelves, and sands	R L	335
Pit—these round enchanting pits	V A	247
Pitch—doth pitch the price	"	551
when from highmost pitch	Son 7	9
Above a mortal pitch	" 86	6
Pitch'd—His high-pitch'd thoughts	R L	41
Pitchy—merciless and pitchy night	V A	821
pitchy vapours from their biding	R L	550
Piteous—But for thy piteous lips	V A	504
pens her piteous clamours	R L	681
piteous looks to Phrygian shepherds lent	"	1502
Pith—The precedent of pith	V A	26
Pitied—may deserve to pitied be	Son 142	12
Pitiful—bechance him pitiful mischances	R L	976
Pitiful thrivers, in their gazing	Son 125	8
Pity—'O, pity,' 'gan she cry	V A	95
'Pity,' she cries, 'some favour	"	257
For pity now she can no more detain him	"	577
Which knows no pity	"	1000
in pity of his tender years	"	1091
more rage and lesser pity	R L	468
Soft pity enters at an iron gate	"	595
pearls of his that move thy pity	"	1553
your pity is enough to cure me	Son 111	14
Your love and pity	" 112	1
And suit thy pity	" 132	12

Pity—Root pity in thy heart	Son 142	11
Thy pity may deserve	" 142	12
Have of my suffering youth some feeling pity	L C	178
That to hear it was great pity	P P 21	12
None takes pity on thy pain	" 21	24
Pity but he were a king	" 21	42
Pity—see thy state and pity mine	R L	644
but pity not his moans	"	977
Pity the world, or else	Son 1	13
Pity me then and wish	" 111	8
Pity me then, dear friend	" 111	13
None alive will pity me	P P 21	28
Pitying—as pitying Lucrece' woes	R L	1747
and they, as pitying me	Son 132	1
Pity-pleading—Her .... eyes	R L	561
Pity-wanting—of my .... pain	Son 140	1
Place—remaineth in one place	V A	883
she falleth in the place	"	1121
vents and crannies of the place	R L	310
the period often from his place	"	565
possession of thy gloomy place	"	803
shot from their fixed places	"	1325
and, as it left the place	"	1745
to weep upon the tainted place	"	1746
give his sorrow place	"	1773
treasure thou some place	Son 6	3
Shifts but his place	" 9	10
the place where he would be	" 44	8
Each changing place	" 60	3
doth give another place	" 79	4
thy heart in other place	" 93	4
Nor gives to necessary wrinkles place	" 108	11
in my judgement's place	" 131	12
the wide world's common place	" 137	10
To every place at once	L C	27
and made him her place	"	82
made fairer by their place	"	117
Playing the place	"	241
and conseerations giving place	"	263
gave the tempter place	"	318
Place—do I mean to place him	R L	517
And place my merit	Son 84	2
Placed—they thinly placed are	" 52	7
a nay is placed without remove	P P 18	42
Plague—the plague is banish'd	V A	510
Become the public plague	R L	1479
of plagues, of dearths, or seasons	Son 14	4
Drink up the monarch's plague	" 114	2
And to this false plague	" 137	14
Only my plague thus far	" 141	13
Plague—To plague a private sin	R L	1484
Plagued—Is plagued with cramps	"	856
Plain—high delightful plain	V A	236
like a goodly champaign plain	R L	1247
All our merry meetings on the plains	P P 18	46
Plain—had his acts made plain	V A	379
the lesson is but plain	"	407
in his plain face she spied	R L	1552
'Tarquin' was pronounced plain	"	1786
In true plain words	Son 82	12
Plaining—entrance to her plaining	R L	559
Plainly—But plainly say thou lov'st her	P P 19	11
Plaint—That she her plaints	R L	1364
Plaintful—A plaintful story	L C	2
Plait—in plaits of majesty	R L	93

Plant—sappy plants to bear	V A		165
that men as plants increase	Son	15	5
He tr'd where his plants	L C		171
Green plants bring not	P P	18	39
Trees did grow and plants did spring	"	21	6
Plantest—Thou plantest scandal	R L		887
Planting—Planting oblivion, beating reason back	V A		557
Plaster—the only sovereign plaster	"		916
Plat—nor tied in formal plat	L C		29
Platted—a platted hive of straw	"		8
Plausibly—....did give consent	R L		1854
Play—all this dumb play	V A		359
Play—Be bold to play	"		124
Play with his locks	"		1090
Pluto winks while Orpheus plays	R L		553
Will play the tyrants	Son	5	3
and play as wantonly	"	54	7
To play the watchman	"	61	12
I with these did play	"	98	14
And play the mother's part	"	143	12
Plays not at all, but seems afraid	P P	18	30
Play'd—play'd with her breath	R L		400
Mine eye hath play'd	Son	24	1
that wont to have play'd	P P	18	29
Play'st—thou, my music, music	Son	128	1
Playing—Playing the place	L C		241
Playing patient sports	"		242
Playing in the wanton air	P P	17	4
Plea—No rightful plea might plead	R L		1649
a lawful plea commence	Son	35	11
doth that plea deny	"	46	7
shall beauty hold a plea	"	65	3
Plead—Shall plead for me	R L		480
Pleads in a wilderness	"		544
No rightful plea might plead	"		1649
Who plead for love	Son	23	11
My heart doth plead	"	46	5
Pleadeth—are dumb when beauty pleadeth	R L		268
Pleading—her pleading tongue	V A		217
by pleading may be blest	"		328
pleading hath deserved	"		609
Her pity-pleading eyes	R L		561
There pleading might you see	"		1401
Pleasance—Youth is full of....	P P	12	2
Pleasant—pleasant fountains lie	V A		234
summer is less pleasant now	Son	102	9
Sitting in a pleasant shade	P P	21	3
Please—to please him thou art bright	Son	28	9
do please these curious days	"	38	13
so it please thee hold	"	136	11
sickly appetite to please	"	147	4
How many tales to please me	P P	7	9
Pleased—If....themselves, others	V A		843
ne'er pleased her babe	"		974
pleased with grief's society	R L		1111
is pleased to dote	Son	141	4
Pleasing—nimble notes to....ears	R L		1126
one pleasing note do sing	Son	8	12
hath a far more pleasing sound	"	130	10
Pleasure—birds such pleasure took	V A		1101
That all love's pleasure	"		1140
Having no other pleasure	R L		860
Thy secret pleasure turns	"		890
the private pleasure of some one	"		1478
Or else receivest with pleasure	Son	8	4
prick'd thee out for women's pleasure	"	20	13
Pleasure—From whence at pleasure	Son	48	12
the fine point of seldom pleasure	"	52	4
control your times of pleasure	"	58	2
Not blame your pleasure	"	58	14
the world may see my pleasure	"	75	8
hath his adjunct pleasure	"	91	5
the pleasure of the fleeting year	"	97	2
his pleasures wait on thee	"	97	11
And the just pleasure lost	"	121	3
O thou minion of her pleasure	"	126	9
in moe pleasures to bestow	L C		139
Where all those pleasures live	P P	5	6
take her meaning nor her pleasure	"	11	12
All our pleasure known	"	18	45
we will all the pleasures prove	"	20	2
And if these pleasures may thee move	"	20	15
These pretty pleasures might me move	"	20	19
Plenitude—In him a plenitude of subtle matter	L C		302
Plenty—amid their plenty with her plenty press'd	V A		20
"		545
that even in plenty wanteth	R L		557
Plight—Shall plight your honourable faiths	"		1690
return in happy plight	Son	28	1
to see my doleful plight	P P	18	33
Plod—Plods dully on	Son	50	6
Plot—Whoever plots the sin	R L		879
This plot of death	"		1212
heart think that a several plot	Son	137	9
Ploughman—To cheer the....	R L		958
Pluck—pluck him from his horse	V A		30
Who plucks the bud	"		416
Pluck down the rich	"		1130
To pluck the quills	R L		949
do I my judgement pluck	Son	14	1
Pluck the keen teeth	"	19	3
pluck them where they grew	"	98	8
still will pluck thee back	"	126	6
but cannot pluck the pelf	P P	14	12
Ne'er to pluck thee	"	17	12
Youth so apt to pluck a sweet	"	17	14
Pluck'd—being early pluck'd	V A		528
guilty hand pluck'd up the latch	R L		358
Brutus, who pluck'd the knife	"		1807
untimely pluck'd, soon vaded	P P	10	1
Pluck'd in the bud	"	10	2
Pluck'st—thou pluck'st a flower	V A		946
Plum—The mellow plum doth fall	"		527
Like a green plum	P P	10	5
Plume—like a falling plume	V A		314
Plump—flesh is soft and plump	"		142
Plunging—unpractised swimmer plunging	R L		1098
Pluto—Pluto winks while Orpheus plays	"		553
Poesy—under thee their poesy disperse	Son	78	4
Poet—would say, 'This poet lies	"	17	7
be term'd a poet's rage	"	17	11
and poets better prove	"	32	13
thy poet doth invent	"	79	7
The barren tender of a poet's debt	"	83	4
Than both your poets	"	83	14
god of both, as poets feign	P P	8	13
Poetry—If music and sweet poetry agree	"	8	1

Point—With javelin's point a churlish swine to gore	*V A*		616
thy spear's point can enter	"		626
the fine point of seldom pleasure	*Son* 52		4
Point—And seems to point her out	*R L*		1087
Points on me graciously	*Son* 26		10
doth point out thee	"	151	9
Pointed—the fair and fiery-pointed sun	*R L*		372
Point'st—thou point'st the season	"		879
Pointing—Pointing to each his thunder	*Son* 14		6
Poison—The bottom poison, and the top o'erstraw'd	*V A*		1143
I will not poison thee	*R L*		1072
Drugs poison him	*Son* 118		14
Poison'd—Doth in her poison'd closet yet endure	*R L*		1659
The poison'd fountain clears	"		1707
If it be poison'd	*Son* 114		13
His poison'd me	*L C*		301
Poisoning—Life-poisoning pestilence	*V A*		740
Poisonous—The poisonous simple	*R L*		530
Knit poisonous clouds	"		777
Policy—For lawful policy remains	"		529
policy did him disguise	"		1815
Thus policy in love	*Son* 118		9
It fears not policy, that heretic	" 124		9
Polish'd—In polish'd form	"	85	8
Politic—alone stands hugely politic	" 124		11
Pollute—impurity doth not pollute	*R L*		854
who did thy stock pollute	"		1063
Polluted—Of that polluted prison	"		1726
Pollution—my poor soul's pollution	"		1157
Pomp—suffers not in smiling pomp	*Son* 124		6
Poor—the worse for one poor kiss	*V A*		207
Poor queen of love	"		251
bites the poor flies	"		316
this poor heart of mine	"		502
the poor fool prays	"		578
Even as poor birds	"		601
As those poor birds	"		604
Mark the poor wretch	"		680
By this, poor Wat	"		697
how the world's poor people	"		925
poor Venus noteth	"		1057
Alas, poor world	"		1075
enrich the poor with treasures	"		1150
'Poor flower,' quoth she	"		1177
Poor wretches have remorse in poor abuses	*R L*		269
But all these poor forbiddings	"		323
May feel her heart, poor citizen	"		465
a poor unseasonable doe	"		581
the poor lamb cries	"		677
all recreant, poor and meek	"		710
Poor wasting monuments	"		798
The poor, lame, blind	"		902
One poor retiring minute	"		962
Poor grooms are sightless night	"		1013
'Poor hand, why quiver'st thou	"		1030
Poor helpless help, the treasure	"		1056
And for, poor bird	"		1142
As the poor frighted deer	"		1149
my poor soul's pollution	"		1157
Poor Lucrece' cheeks	"		1217
Poor women's faces	"		1253
Poor women's faults	"		1258
To the poor counterfeit	"		1269
Poor—'Poor instrument,' quoth she	*R L*		1464
with one poor tired tongue	"		1617
was strong, my poor self weak	"		1646
That my poor beauty	"		1651
Which speechless woe of his poor she attendeth	"		1674
should right poor ladies' harms	"		1694
her poor tongue could not speak	"		1718
Her blood in poor revenge	"		1736
Poor broken glass	"		1758
come in his poor heart's aid	"		1784
which wit so poor as mine	*Son* 26		5
These poor rude lines	"	32	4
lame, poor, nor despised	"	37	9
To leave poor me	"	49	13
will my poor beast then find	"	51	5
Why should poor beauty	"	67	7
as my poor name rehearse	"	71	11
I'll live in this poor rhyme	"	107	11
That poor retention	"	122	9
my oblation poor but free	"	125	10
Whilst my poor lips	"	128	7
my friend's heart let my poor heart bail	"	133	10
her poor infant's discontents	"	143	8
Poor soul, the centre of my sinful	"	146	1
thy poor drudge to be	"	151	11
their poor balls are tied	*L C*		24
known to us poor swains	*P P*	18	45
Poor Corydon	"	18	52
She, poor bird, as all forlorn	"	21	9
Even so, poor bird, like thee	"	21	27
Poorer—far poorer than before	*R L*		693
Poorly—But, poorly rich, so wanteth	"		97
Is poorly imitated after you	*Son* 53		6
Poor-rich—they prove bankrupt in this poor-rich gain	*R L*		140
Portal—Once more the ruby-colour'd portal open'd	*V A*		451
As each unwilling portal	*R L*		309
Posied—ring of .... gold and bone	*L C*		45
Possess—that which they possess	*R L*		135
the young possess their hive	"		1769
bids him possess his breath	"		1777
may possess the claim they lay	"		1794
Possess'd—And, if possess'd, as soon	"		23
For thou art so possess'd	*Son* 10		5
like him with friends possess'd	"	29	6
Possesseth—possesseth all mine eye	"	62	1
Possessing—Possessing or pursuing	"	75	11
too dear by my possessing	"	87	1
Possession—In the possession of his beauteous mate	*R L*		18
Keep still possession	"		803
Nor lose possession	*Son* 18		10
and in possession so	"	129	9
Post—besieged Arden all in post	*R L*		1
swift subtle post	"		926
The post attends	"		1333
Post—Post hither, this vile purpose	"		220
I post unto my pretty	*P P*	15	9
the night would post too soon	"	15	13
Posterity—to bury that posterity	*V A*		758
That my posterity	*R L*		208
to stop posterity	*Son* 3		8
Leaving thee living in posterity	"	6	12
in the eyes of all posterity	"	55	11
Leaving no posterity	*P T*		59
Posting—of posting is no need	*Son* 51		4

Entry	Ref	Line	No.
Posy—a thousand fragrant posies	P P	20	10
Potential—O most potential love	L C		264
Potion—Potions of eisel 'gainst	Son	111	10
What potions have I drunk	"	119	1
Pour—And mine I pour your ocean all among	L C		256
Pour'st—that pour'st into my verse	Son	38	2
Pouted—Who blush'd and pouted	V A		33
Poverty—Although thou steal thee all my poverty	Son	40	10
what poverty my Muse brings forth	"	103	1
Power—thy .... had lost his	V A		944
heartens up his servile powers	R L		295
solicited the eternal power	"		345
The powers to whom I pray	"		349
and all the power of both	"		572
than one hath power to tell	"		1288
is drawn the power of Greece	"		1368
He hath no power to ask	"		1594
Another power; no flood o'ersways their power	Son	65	2
They that have power	"	94	1
Darkening thy power	"	100	4
my lovely boy, who in my power	"	126	1
hath put on nature's power	"	127	5
Thy face hath not the power	"	131	6
Use power with power	"	139	4
these rebel powers that thee array	"	146	2
O, from what power	"	150	1
over me hath power	L C		74
affections in his charmed power	"		146
'"My parts had power to charm	"		260
Powerful—shall outlive this powerful rhyme	Son	55	2
hast thou this powerful might	"	150	1
Practice—To put in practice either	P P	16	7
Lest she some subtle practice smell	"	19	9
Practised—eyes have never practised how	R L		748
Praise—Therefore that praise which Collatine	"		82
And decks with praises	"		108
shame and thriftless praise	Son	2	8
How much more praise	"	2	9
thine shall be the praise	"	38	14
What can mine own praise	"	39	3
your praise shall still find room	"	55	10
have given admiring praise	"	59	14
with outward praise is crown'd	"	69	5
accents do this praise confound	"	69	7
Yet this thy praise cannot be so thy praise	"	70	11
hang more praise upon deceased I	"	72	7
No praise to thee	"	79	12
And in the praise thereof	"	80	3
a limit past my praise	"	82	6
can in praise devise	"	83	11
Than this rich praise	"	84	2
Being fond on praise, which makes your praises worse	"	84	14
While comments of your praise	"	85	2
But to the most of praise	"	85	10
but in a kind of praise	"	95	7
Because he needs no praise	"	101	9
hath my added praise beside	"	103	4
alike my songs and praises be	"	105	3
In praise of ladies dead	"	106	4
So all their praises	"	106	9
To know my shames and praises	"	112	6

Entry	Ref	Line	No.
Praise—weighs down the airy scale of praise	L C		226
Which is to me some praise	P P	5	10
To sing heaven's praise	"	5	14
When thy desert may merit praise	"	19	27
Praise—To praise the clear unmatched red	R L		11
I will not praise that purpose not to sell	Son	21	14
mine own when I praise thee	"	39	4
that for myself I praise	"	62	13
Nor praise the deep vermillion	"	98	10
but lack tongues to praise	"	106	14
Praised—prodigal that .... her so	R L		79
Hearing you praised, I say	Son	85	9
And to be praised of ages yet to be	"	101	12
and praised cold chastity	L C		313
Praising—By praising him here	Son	39	14
Praising thy worth	"	60	14
Pray—I pray you hence	V A		382
The poor fool prays her	"		578
to pray he doth begin	R L		342
The powers to whom I pray	"		349
rebel for remission prays	"		714
She prays she never may behold	"		746
So will I pray that thou	Son	143	13
Prayer—in the midst of his unfruitful prayer	R L		344
she with vehement prayer	"		475
His ear her prayers admits	"		558
but yet, like prayers divine	Son	108	5
For these dead birds sigh a prayer	P T		67
Preach—that preach in our behoof	L C		165
Preach'd—He preach'd pure maid	"		315
Precedent—The precedent of pith	V A		26
The precedent whereof	R L		1261
ever shunn'd by precedent	L C		155
Precept—what are precepts worth	"		267
Precious—Whose precious taste dropp'd a precious jewel	V A		543
Income of each precious thing	R L		334
take root with precious flowers	"		870
For precious friends hid	Son	30	6
I have no precious time	"	57	3
thy precious minutes waste	"	77	2
And precious phrase	"	85	4
of all too precious you	"	86	2
fairest and most precious jewel	"	131	4
Precurrer—Foul .... of the fiend	P T		6
Pre-decease—If children pre-decease progenitors	R L		1756
Predict—By oft predict that I in heaven find	Son	14	8
Prefer—That shall prefer and undertake	L C		280
Prefiguring—all you prefiguring	Son	106	10
Premeditate—he doth premeditate	R L		183
Prepare—bid the wind a base he now prepares	V A		303
prepare to carry it	R L		1294
and she prepares to write	"		1295
prepares to let them know	"		1607
you should prepare	Son	13	3
doth prepare the cup	"	114	12
Preposterously—could so preposterously be stain'd	"	109	11
Presage—This ill presage	V A		457
augurs mock their own presage	Son	107	6
Presager—And dumb presagers	"	23	10

Prescience—Which in her	R L	727
Prescription—his prescriptions are not kept	Son 117	6
Presence—Be as thy presence is	" 10	11
And with his presence	" 67	2
Present—That every present sorrow	V A	970
Hindering their present fall	R L	551
To view thy present trespass	"	632
Of present death, and shame	"	1263
Some present speed to come	"	1307
Each present lord began	"	1696
Presents thy shadow	Son 27	10
Thyself away art present	" 47	10
behold these present days	" 105	13
Crowning the present	" 115	12
at the present nor the past	" 123	10
upon myself with present moan	" 119	8
Present-absent—These present-absent with swift motion slide	" 45	4
Presented—advantage on .... joy	V A	105
Present'st—And thou present'st	Son 70	8
Presenteth—presenteth to mine eye	V A	661
this huge stage presenteth	Son 15	3
Presently—do presently abuse it	R L	861
being clouded presently is missed	"	1007
that's broken presently	P P 13	1
Preserve—which doth .... the ill	Son 147	3
Press—Much like a press of people	R L	1301
a press of gaping faces	"	1408
as thou art cruel; do not press	Son 140	1
Press never thou to choose	P P 19	31
Press'd—now press'd with bearing	V A	430
with her plenty press'd	"	545
my o'er-press'd defence can bide	Son 139	8
Presume—Presume not on thy heart	" 22	13
Pretended—as thou hast pretended	R L	576
Prettily—entreats, and .... entreats	V A	73
Pretty—For to a pretty ear	"	71
appears a pretty dimple	"	242
A pretty while these pretty creatures stand	R L	1233
Those pretty wrongs	Son 41	1
Looking with pretty ruth	" 132	4
Her pretty looks have been	" 139	10
I post unto my pretty	P P 15	9
These pretty pleasures	" 20	19
Prevailed—till she have prevailed	Son 41	8
Prevent—did wittily prevent	V A	471
this vile purpose to prevent	R L	220
I could prevent this storm	"	966
to prevent our maladies	Son 118	3
Prevent'st—thou .... his scythe	" 100	14
Prey—or prey be gone	V A	58
on the steam as on a prey	"	63
caught the yielding prey	"	547
Rich preys make true men	"	724
the wolf would leave his prey	"	1097
That for his prey	R L	542
lion fawneth o'er his prey	"	421
The wolf hath seized his prey	"	677
The prey wherein by nature they delight	"	—
Art left the prey	Son 48	8
The prey of worms	" 74	10
Priam—painting, made for Priam's Troy	R L	1367
Staring on Priam's wounds	"	1448
in Priam's painted wound	"	1466
weeps Hecuba, here Priam dies	"	1485

Priam—Had doting Priam check'd	R L	1490
The credulous old Priam	"	1522
as Priam him did cherish	"	1546
listening Priam wets his eyes	"	1548
Priam, why art thou old	"	1550
To Priam's trust false Sinon's tears	"	1560
Price—pitch the price so high	V A	551
Priceless—What priceless wealth	R L	17
Prick—the needle his finger pricks	"	319
his weary noon-tide prick	"	781
Prick'd—His ears up-prick'd	V A	271
but since she prick'd thee out	Son 20	13
Pricking—curb of pricking spur	V A	285
Prickles—What though the rose have prickles	"	574
Pride—and modest pride	"	278
Loseth his pride	"	429
Sith in thy pride	"	762
so their pride doth grow	R L	298
Swell in their pride	"	432
Smoking with pride	"	438
they in thy pride	"	662
While Lust is in his pride	"	705
Who in their pride	"	861
boundeth in his pride	"	1669
his wit in state and pride	"	1809
their pride lies buried	Son 25	7
his imprison'd pride	"	52 12
so barren of new pride	"	76 1
and of goodly pride	"	80 12
of all men's pride I boast	"	91 12
my love's breath? The purple pride	"	99 3
in pride of all his growth	"	99 12
such a scope to show her pride	"	103 2
shook three summers' pride	"	104 4
with her foul pride	"	144 8
Proud of this pride	"	151 10
a careless hand of pride	L C	30
falseness in a pride of truth	"	105
with her fair pride	P P 2	8
Priest—Let the priest in surplice white	P T	13
Prime—gather'd in their prime	V A	131
wither in their prime	"	418
Sith in his prime	"	1163
rejoicing to the prime	R L	332
the lovely April of her prime	Son 3	10
behold the violet past prime	" 12	3
a pure unstained prime	" 70	8
wanton burthen of the prime	" 97	7
Primrose—this primrose bank	V A	151
Prince—For princes are the glass	R L	615
Or say with princes	Son 14	7
Great princes' favorites	" 25	5
Of princes, shall outlive	" 55	2
Princely—welcome to her princely guest	R L	90
wound'st his princely name	"	599
Thy princely office	"	628
Princess—To ask the spotted	"	721
Print—her soft hand's print	V A	353
Thou shouldst print more	Son 11	14
Prison—And in her vaulty prison	R L	119
in that darksome prison died	"	379
will prison false desire	"	642
Of that polluted prison	"	1726
Prison my heart	Son 133	9
Prison'd—A lily prison'd	V A	362
prison'd in her eye	"	980

Prisoner—Leading him prisoner	V A	110	Proof—Of proofs new-bleeding		
ta'en prisoner by the foe	R L	1608	which remain	L C	153
judge is robb'd, the prisoner dies	"	1632	curb it upon other's proof	"	163
A liquid prisoner pent in walls	Son 5	10	Property—his invised properties did		
Private—crest-wounding, ... scar	R L	828	tend	"	212
Thy private feasting	"	891	Property was thus appalled	P T	37
Why should the private pleasure	"	1478	Prophecy—with dreadful prophecies	V A	928
To plague a private sin	"	1484	praises are but prophecies	Son 106	9
When every private widow	Son 9	7	Prophesy—I prophesy thy death	V A	671
Privilege—To privilege dishonour	R L	621	lo, here I prophesy	"	1133
may privilege your time	Son 58	10	Prophetic—nor the prophetic soul	Son 107	1
of this large privilege	" 95	13	Proportion'd—a well-proportion'd		
Privileged—And, privileged by age	L C	62	steed	V A	290
Prize—Desire my pilot is, beauty			Make war against proportion'd		
my prize	R L	270	course of time	R L	774
thievish for a prize so dear	Son 48	14	Proposed—great treasure is the		
bound for the prize	" 86	2	mead proposed	"	132
As his triumphant prize	" 151	10	Before, a joy proposed	Son 129	12
Prizing—Not .... her poor infant	" 143	8	Protest—she doth protest	V A	581
Proceed—and doth so far proceed	R L	251	Protestation—The .... stops	R L	1790
no water thence proceeds	"	1352	to his protestation urged	"	1844
from weak minds proceeds	"	1825	Protesting—of all her pure protest-		
and where they did proceed	Son 76	8	ings	P P 7	11
the slander, as I think, proceeds	" 131	14	Proud—And rein his proud head	V A	14
Proceeding—yet his proceedings			O, be not proud	"	113
teach thee	V A	406	lusty, young, and proud	"	260
Like the proceedings	"	910	with his proud sight	"	288
Process—In process of the season	Son 104	6	proud rider on so proud a back	"	300
Proclaim—And peace proclaims			Being proud, as females are	"	309
olives of endless age	" 107	8	rough bear, or lion proud	"	884
Proclaim'd—.... in her a careless	L C	30	Clapping their proud tails	"	923
Procure—Procure to weep	P P 18	32	at such high-proud rate	R L	19
Procured—to tempt all, liberty pro-			this proud issue of a king	"	37
cured	L C	252	proud of such a dignity	"	437
Prodigal—Be prodigal: the lamp	V A	755	The flesh being proud	"	712
The niggard prodigal	R L	79	To ruinate proud buildings	"	944
If that one be prodigal	P P 21	39	those proud lords to blame	"	1239
Prodigies—apparitions, signs, and			painter drew so proud	"	1371
prodigies	V A	926	under Pyrrhus' proud foot	"	1448
Profane—Lest I, too much profane	Son 89	11	Thy youth's proud livery	Son 2	3
Profaned—profaned in such a devil	R L	847	couplement of proud compare	" 21	5
But is profaned, if not	Son 127	8	and proud titles boast	" 25	2
profaned their scarlet ornaments	" 142	6	The rich-proud cost	" 64	2
Proffer—to take her figured proffer	P P 4	10	And, proud of many, lives	" 67	12
To proffer, though she put thee			Now proud as an enjoyer	" 75	5
back	" 10	36	Yet be most proud	" 78	9
Profit—the profit of excess	R L	138	Was it the proud full sail	" 86	1
Shall profit thee	Son 77	14	Or from their proud lap	" 98	8
Profitless—Profitless usurer, why			though thy proud heart go wide	" 140	14
dost thou use	" 4	7	Thy proud heart's slave	" 141	12
Profound—In so profound abysm	" 112	9	That is so proud	" 149	10
Progenitor—children pre-decease			Proud of this pride	" 151	10
progenitors	R L	1756	Proud of subjection	L C	108
Prognosticate—this I prognosticate	Son 14	13	a youngster proud and wild	P P 9	4
Progress—progress to eternity	" 77	8	Prouder—.... than garments' cost	Son 91	10
Promise—Upon this promise	V A	85	Proudest—as the .... sail doth bear	" 80	6
Promise more speed	R L	1349	Proudly—proudly make them cruel	" 131	2
lord began to promise aid	"	1696	Proud-pied—When proud-pied April	" 98	2
Why didst thou promise	Son 34	1	Prove—she begins to prove	V A	40
Promised—'Tis .... in the charity	L C	70	prove nothing worth	"	418
Prompt—All replication prompt	"	122	she doth prove	"	597
Prone—O, that .... lust should stain	R L	684	That they prove bankrupt	R L	140
to base touches prone	Son 141	6	the like offences prove	"	613
Pronounced—'Tarquin' was pro-			Since men prove beasts	"	1148
nounced plain	R L	1786	Thou single wilt prove none	Son 8	14
Proof—Are better proof	V A	626	at least kind-hearted prove	" 10	12
On newer proof, to try	Son 110	11	where thou mayst prove me	" 26	14
And on just proof	" 117	10	and poets better prove	" 32	13
A bliss in proof, and proved	" 129	11	what a torment wouldst thou prove	" 39	9

Prove—For truth proves thievish	Son	48	14
can nothing worthy prove	"	72	4
And prove thee virtuous	"	88	4
says I did strive to prove	"	117	13
Which prove more short	"	125	4
things of great receipt with ease we prove	"	136	7
thy sweet self prove	"	151	4
which yet men prove	"	153	7
and this by that I prove	"	154	13
but I will prove	P P	3	5
to thee I'll constant prove	"	5	3
Unless thy lady prove unjust	"	19	33
will all the pleasures prove	"	20	2
Proved—as may be proved	V A	....	608
proved thee my best of love	Son	110	6
error and upon me proved	"	116	13
and proved a very woe	"	129	11
Provide—better for my life provide	"	111	3
Proving—Proving from world's minority	R L	....	67
Proving his beauty by succession	Son	2	12
Provoke—doth provoke a pause	V A	....	218
cannot provoke him on	Son	50	9
Provoked—provoked my tongue	V A	....	1003
Provokest—provokest such weeping	"	....	949
Pry—into my deeds to pry	Son	61	6
Pry'st—Why pry'st thou through	R L	....	1089
Public—to a public fast	"	....	891
Become the public plague	"	....	1479
Of public honour and proud titles	Son	25	2
Nor thou with public kindness	"	36	11
public means which public manners	"	111	4
Publish—And so to publish	R L	....	1852
doth publish everywhere	Son	102	4
Publisher—why is Collatine the publisher	R L	....	33
Puddle—The sea within a puddle's womb	"	....	657
And not the puddle	"	....	658
Puff—Puffs forth another wind	"	....	315
Pulse—holds her pulses hard	V A	....	476
Punishment—deserve not	P P	3	4
Pupil—Time's pencil or my .... pen	Son	16	10
Purblind—the purblind hare	V A	....	679
Purchase—Which .... if thou make	"	....	515
Would purchase thee a thousand	R L	....	963
Purchased—Your own dear-purchased right	Son	117	6
Pure—Pure shame and awed resistance	V A	....	69
Pure lips, sweet seals	"	....	511
Forgetting shame's pure blush	"	....	558
And pure perfection	"	....	736
In their pure ranks	R L	....	73
Pure thoughts are dead	"	....	167
Offer pure incense to so pure	"	....	194
All pure effects, and doth	"	....	251
But with a pure appeal	"	....	283
In a pure compound	"	....	531
From a pure heart command	"	....	625
should stain so pure a bed	"	....	684
Pure chastity is rifled	"	....	692
to close so pure a mind	"	....	761
was pure to Collatine	"	....	826
Shall gush pure streams	"	....	1078
When the one pure yieldings, but still pure	"	....	1164
	"	....	1658
May my pure mind	"	....	1701
Pure—still pure and red remain'd	R L	....	1742
a pure unstained prince	Son	70	8
pure and most most loving	"	110	14
He preach'd pure maid	L C	....	315
all her pure protestings	P P	7	11
Purer—Some purer chest to close	R L	....	761
Purest—And purest faith unhappily forsworn	Son	66	4
Purge—to purge my impure tale	R L	....	1078
shun sickness when we purge	Son	118	4
Purging—slight air and purging fire	"	45	1
Purified—in effect is purified	R L	....	532
Purify—could weeping purify	"	....	685
Purity—The life of purity	"	....	780
Wooing his purity	Son	144	8
Wooing his purity	P P	2	8
Purl'd—which purl'd up to the sky	R L	....	1407
Purloin'd—had purloin'd his eyes	"	....	1651
Purple—With purple tears	V A	....	1054
a purple flower sprung up	"	....	1168
And from the purple fountain	R L	....	1734
The purple pride	Son	99	3
Purple-colour'd—with .... face	V A	....	1
Purpose—the purpose of his coming hither	R L	....	113
This vile purpose to prevent	"	....	220
Yet for the self-same purpose	"	....	1047
one thing to my purpose	Son	20	12
strongly in my purpose bred	"	112	13
She keeps thee to this purpose	"	126	7
On purpose laid to make the taker mad	"	129	8
Purpose—I purpose to destroy thee	R L	....	514
that purpose not to sell	Son	21	14
Purposed—linger out a purposed overthrow	"	90	8
Yet their purposed trim	L C	....	118
Pursue—.... these fearful creatures	V A	....	677
his foes pursue him still	"	....	699
yet he still pursues his fear	R L	....	308
Pursuers—stop the loud pursuers	V A	....	688
Pursuing—or pursuing no delight	Son	75	11
Pursuit—Make slow pursuit	R L	....	696
With swift pursuit to venge	"	....	1691
Mad in pursuit	Son	129	9
In pursuit of the thing	"	143	4
Push—To push grief on	R L	....	1673
Push'd—Backward she push'd him	V A	....	41
Put—puts on outward strangeness	"	....	310
before one leaf put forth	"	....	416
gold that's put to use	"	....	768
put his bonnet on	"	....	1087
put fear to valour	"	....	1158
I could not put him back	R L	....	843
She puts the period	"	....	565
Hast thou put on his shape	"	....	597
is put besides his part	Son	23	2
And puts apparel on	"	26	11
doth put this in my mind	"	50	13
Hath put a spirit	"	98	3
hath put on nature's power	"	127	5
Have put on black	"	132	3
To put fair truth	"	137	12
hath Love put in my head	"	148	1
and in it put their mind	L C	....	135
put the by-past perils in her way	"	....	158
put to the smallest teen	"	....	192
love put out Religion's eye	"	....	250
To put in practice either	P P	16	7

Put—with scorn she put away	P P	19	18
though she put thee back	"	19	36
Put'st—that put'st forth all to use	Son	134	10
Putrified—that which is so putrified	R L		1750
Pyramid—Thy pyramids built up	Son	123	2
Pyrrhus—under Pyrrhus' proud foot lies	R L		1448
And rail on Pyrrhus	"		1467
Quake—tributary subject quakes	V A		1045
saw them quake and tremble	R L		1393
In his fire doth quake with cold	"		1536
Quaking—bids them leave quaking	V A		899
Qualified—lust by gazing qualified	R L		424
Qualify—seem'd my flame to qualify	Son	109	2
Quality—savour, hue, and qualities	V A		747
his life or else his quality	R L		875
her grief's true quality	"		1313
What is the quality	"		1702
of dearths or season's quality	Son	14	4
His qualities were beauteous	L C		99
nature, worth, and quality	"		210
Queen—the love-sick queen began	V A		175
Poor queen of love	"		251
leaders to their queen	"		503
'Fair queen,' quoth he	"		523
All in vain; good queen	"		607
where their queen	"		1193
was the other queen	R L		66
The silver-shining queen	"		786
on the finger of a throned queen	Son	96	5
could look but beauty's queen	P P	4	4
on her back, fair queen, and toward	"	4	13
as this queen on him	"	6	12
the queen of music, makes	"	8	10
when the fair queen of love	"	9	1
She, silly queen	"	9	7
'Twixt the turtle and his queen	P T		31
Quench—.... the maiden burning	V A		50
I'll quench them with my tears	"		192
To quench the coal	R L		47
ocean quench their light	"		1231
with my tears quench Troy	"		1468
Quenched—This brand she	Son	154	9
Quenchless—are balls of .... fire	R L		1554
Quest—A quest of thoughts	Son	46	9
and in quest to have	"	129	10
Question—do I question make	"	12	9
Nor dare I question	"	57	9
hence a question takes	L C		110
arguments and question deep	"		121
and yet do question make	"		321
Questioned—after supper long he questioned	R L		122
Quick—O, how quick is love	V A		38
bright, and quick in turning	"		140
Now quick desire	"		547
In youth, quick bearing	R L		1387
nor war's quick fire shall burn	Son	55	7
variation or quick change	"	76	2
Of his quick objects	"	113	7
Quicker—these quicker elements are gone	"	45	5
Quickly—ducks as quickly in	V A		87
quickly told and quickly gone	"		520
other kills thee quickly	"		990
quickly is convey'd	"		1192
fire did quickly steep	Son	153	3
But quickly on this side	L C		113

Quickly—Quickly him they will entice	P P	21	44
Quick-shifting—Quick-shifting auties	R L		459
Quiet—Into the quiet closure	V A		782
shall it keep in quiet	"		1149
mustering to the quiet cabinet	R L		442
her quiet interrupted	"		1170
for myself no quiet find	Son	27	14
Quietly—Lie quietly, and hear	V A		709
Quietus—her .... is to render thee	Son	126	12
Quill—To pluck the quills	R L		949
o'er the paper with her quill	"		1297
How far a modern quill	Son	83	7
their character with golden quill	"	85	3
Quit—Nor youth all quit	L C		13
Quite—heart were quite undone	V A		783
quite beaten from her breast	R L		1363
and lusty leaves quite gone	Son	5	7
book of honour rased quite	"	25	11
quite contrary I read	"	62	11
dear love, forget me quite	"	72	3
over-goes my blunt invention quite	"	103	7
All my merry jigs are quite forgot	P P	18	9
Quittal—a quittal of such strife	R L		236
Quiver'st—why quiver'st thou at this decree	"		1030
Quote—.... my loathsome trespass	"		812
Quoth—' Ay me,' quoth Venus	V A		187
' I know not love,' quoth he	"		409
canst thou talk?' quoth she	"		427
where am I?' quoth she	"		493
' Fair queen,' quoth he	"		523
' Good-night,' quoth she	"		537
' The boar,' quoth she	"		589
' Thou hadst been gone,' quoth she	"		613
' No matter where,' quoth he	"		715
what of that?' quoth she	"		717
' I am,' quoth he	"		718
' In night,' quoth she	"		720
' Nay, then,' quoth Adon	"		769
' No, no,' quoth she	"		997
' O Jove,' quoth she	"		1015
' And yet,' quoth she	"		1070
' Wonder of time,' quoth she	"		1133
' Poor flower,' quoth she	"		1177
Quoth he, ' She took me kindly	R L		253
' So, so,' quoth he, ' these lets	"		330
quoth he, ' I must deflower	"		348
' Lucrece,' quoth he, ' this night	"		512
Quoth she, ' Reward not	"		575
' Have done,' quoth he	"		645
' Thou art,' quoth she, ' a sea	"		652
' No more,' quoth he; ' by heaven	"		667
' For day,' quoth she	"		747
' In vain,' quoth she, ' I live	"		1044
' You mocking birds,' quoth she	"		1121
' To kill myself,' quoth she	"		1156
' My girl,' quoth she	"		1270
' O, peace !' quoth Lucrece	"		1284
' Poor instrument,' quoth she	"		1464
' It cannot be,' quoth she	"		1534
' Fool, fool !' quoth she	"		1568
' Few words,' quoth she	"		1613
groom of thine,' quoth he	"		1632
you fair lords,' quoth she	"		1688
' O, speak,' quoth she	"		1700
' No, no,' quoth she	"		1714
' O,' quoth Lucretius, ' I did give	"		1800

Quoth—' Woe, woe,' quoth Collatine	R L	....	1802
quoth he, ' arise	"	....	1818
'O Jove,' quoth she	P P	6	14
' Once,' quoth she, 'did I see	"	9	9
See, in my thigh,' quoth she	"	9	12
' Even thus,' quoth she	"	11	5
' Even thus,' quoth she	"	11	7
' Even thus,' quoth she	"	11	9
' Farewell,' quoth she	"	14	5
' Air,' quoth he	"	17	9
Race—no dull flesh in his fiery race	Son	51	11
Rack—With ugly rack on his celestial face	"	33	6
Radiance—their sickly radiance do amend	L C	....	214
Rage—swelleth with more rage	V A	....	332
In fell battle's rage	R L	....	145
and in a desperate rage	"	....	219
His rage of lust by gazing	"	....	424
more rage and lesser pity	"	....	468
treason, rape, and murder's rages	"	....	909
blunt rage and rigour roll'd	"	....	1398
such signs of rage they bear	"	....	1419
In rage sent out, recall'd in rage, being past	"	....	1671
rage of death's eternal cold	Son	13	12
be term'd a poet's rage	"	17	11
replete with too much rage	"	23	3
eternal slave to mortal rage	"	64	4
How with this rage shall beauty	"	65	3
but spite of heaven's fell rage	L C	....	13
This said, in top of rage	"	....	55
For when we rage, advice is often seen	"	....	160
Ragged—on a ragged bough	V A	....	37
titles to a ragged name	R L	....	892
winter's ragged hand deface	Son	6	1
Raging-mad—It shall be	V A	....	1151
Rail—In vain I rail at Opportunity	R L	....	1023
And rail on Pyrrhus	"	....	1467
Rail'd—I rail'd on thee	V A	....	1002
Raiment—the seemly raiment of my heart	Son	22	6
Rain—Rain added to a river	V A	....	71
stone at rain relenteth	"	....	200
from tempest and from rain	"	....	238
like sunshine after rain	"	....	799
breaks the silver rain	"	....	959
now wind, now rain	"	....	965
This windy tempest till it blow up rain	R L	....	1788
to each his thunder, rain, and wind	Son	14	6
To dry the rain on my storm-beaten face	"	34	6
yet receives rain still	"	153	9
with sorrow's wind and rain	L C	....	7
Rain—chorus-like her eyes did rain	V A	....	360
At last it rains, and busy winds	R L	....	1790
Rainbow—like rainbows in the sky	"	....	1587
Rain'd—Which long have rain'd	V A	....	83
Raineth—hush'd before it raineth	"	....	458
Raining—though marble wear with raining	R L	....	560
that down thy cheeks are raining	"	....	1271
no flood by raining slacketh	"	....	1677
Rainy—a windy night, a rainy morrow	Son	90	7

Raise—did he raise his chin	V A	....	85
that burning lungs did raise	L C	....	228
Raised—thy unworthiness raised love in me	Son	150	13
Ram—Rude ram, to batter such an ivory wall	R L	....	464
My rams speed not	P P	18	3
Ran—He ran upon the boar	V A	....	1112
To Simois' reedy banks the red blood ran	R L	....	1437
He rose and ran away	P P	4	14
Random—hatefully at random	V A	....	940
At random from the truth	Son	147	12
Ranged—love; if I have ranged	"	109	5
Rank—a river that is rank	V A	....	71
add the rank smell of weeds	Son	69	12
By their rank thoughts	"	121	12
To blush at speeches rank	L C	....	307
Rank—In their pure ranks	R L	....	73
Whose ranks of blue veins	"	....	440
that in their smoky ranks	"	....	783
ridges; and their ranks began till meeting greater ranks	"	....	1439
	"	....	1441
To march in ranks	Son	32	12
holds his rank before	"	85	12
Which rank of goodness	"	118	12
above that idle rank remain	"	122	3
Ransack'd—But robb'd and	R L	....	838
Ransom—Paying what ransom	V A	....	530
are rich and ransom all	Son	34	14
Mine ransom yours, and yours must ransom me	"	120	14
Rape—treason, rape, and murder's rages	R L	....	909
For Helen's rape the city	"	....	1369
Rare—first-born flowers and all things rare	Son	21	7
feasts so solemn and so rare	"	52	5
thrice more wish'd, more rare	"	56	14
by heaven, I think my love as rare	"	130	13
Rarest—Whose rarest havings made the blossoms dote	L C	....	235
Rarity—the rarities of nature's truth	Son	60	11
Beauty, truth, and rarity	P T	....	53
Rascal—base bed of some .... groom	R L	....	671
Rash—Her rash suspect she doth	V A	....	1010
The reason of this rash alarm	R L	....	473
seducing lust, thy rash relief	"	....	639
or rein his rash desire	"	....	706
Rash-false—O rash-false heat	"	....	48
Rate—to rate the boar	V A	....	906
at such high-proud rate	R L	....	19
they all rate his ill	"	....	304
Rather—but rather famish them	V A	....	20
Rather than triumph	R L	....	77
And rather make them born	Son	123	7
Rave—time against himself to rave	R L	....	982
Raven—quills from ancient raven's wings	"	....	949
my mistress' eyes are raven black	Son	127	9
Ravish—ravish the morning air	R L	....	778
doth ravish human sense	P P	8	6
Ravisher—treason and the ravisher	R L	....	770
Thou ravisher, thou traitor	"	....	888
Ravishment—death and ravishment	"	....	430
that sing'st of ravishment	"	....	1128
Raw—though sod in tears, look'd red and raw	"	....	1592

Razed—Is from the book of honour			
razed quite	Son	25	11
towers I see down-razed	"	64	3
Till each to razed oblivion	"	122	7
Read—Nor read the subtle-shining			
secrecies	R L		101
eyes do learn, do read, do look	"		616
read lectures of such shame	"		618
may read the mot afar	"		830
must be used, read it in me	"		1195
In them I read such art	Son	14	10
O, learn to read	"	23	13
Theirs for their style I'll read	"	32	14
quite contrary I read	"	62	11
Nay, if you read this line	"	71	5
eyes not yet created shall o'er-read	"	81	10
Readily—tread the way out readily	R L		1152
Reading—reading what contents it			
bears	L C		19
Ready—were ready for his pay	V A		89
Bid thou be ready by and by	R L		1292
Real—His real habitude gave life	L C		114
Reap—should that harvest reap	Son	128	7
Rear—Anon, he rears upright	V A		279
Rearward—Come in the rearward	Son	90	6
Reason—beating reason back	V A		557
You have no reason	"		612
I perceive the reason	"		727
When reason is the bawd	"		792
past reason's weak removing	R L		243
Respect and reason wait	"		277
The reason of this rash alarm	"		473
reproof and reason beat it dead	"		489
spurn'st at right, at law, at reason	"		880
reasons find of settled gravity	Son	49	8
To guard the lawful reasons	"	49	12
Against thy reasons making	"	89	4
my judgement knew no reason	"	113	3
Past reason hunted	"	129	6
Past reason hated	"	129	7
My reason, the physician	"	147	5
now reason is past care	"	147	9
flesh stays no farther reason	"	151	8
prompt and reason strong	L C		122
Though Reason weep and cry	"		168
resolved my reason into tears	"		296
Let reason rule things	P P	19	3
Reason in itself confounded	P T		41
Love hath reason, reason none	"		47
Reave—reaves his son of life	V A		766
Rebel—command thy rebel will	R L		625
The guilty rebel for remission	"		714
these rebel powers that thee array	Son	146	2
Rebuked—So I return rebuked	"	119	13
Recall'd—In rage sent out, recall'd			
in rage	R L		1671
Receipt—Desire must vomit his re-			
ceipt	"		703
In things of great receipt	Son	136	7
Receive—receives her soft hand's			
print	V A		353
Receives the scroll	R L		1340
my name receives a brand	Son	111	5
receives reproach of being	"	121	2
tables that receive thee more	"	122	12
yet receives rain still	"	135	9
which did no form receive	L C		241
all strange forms receives	"		303
Received—I have .... from many	"		206
Receivest—that which thou .... not	Son	8	3
Or else receivest with pleasure	"	8	4
thou my love receivest	"	40	5
Receiving—Receiving nought by			
elements	"	44	13
Recite—world should task you to....	"	72	1
Recketh—What recketh he his			
rider's angry stir	V A		283
Reckon—At my abuses reckon up			
their own	Son	121	10
Reckon'd—one is reckon'd none	"	136	8
Reckoning—Reckoning his fortune	R L		19
But reckoning Time	Son	115	5
Recompense—and look for	"	23	11
Reconciled—pervert a .... maid	L C		329
Record—So should my shame still			
rest upon record	R L		1643
The living record of your memory	Son	55	8
record could with a backward look	"	59	5
thy record never can be miss'd	"	122	8
thy records and what we see doth			
lie	"	123	11
Recounting—recounting it to me	"	45	12
Recreant—all ...., poor, and meek	R L		710
Recreate—To recreate himself	V A		1095
Recure—A smile .... the wounding	"		465
Recured—life's composition be	Son	45	9
Red—white and red than doves	V A		10
Making them red and pale	"		21
She red and hot as coals	"		35
He red for shame	"		36
Being red, she loves him	"		77
drum and ensign red	"		107
not as fair, yet are they red	"		116
Red cheeks and fiery eyes	"		219
How white and red	"		346
Like a red morn	"		453
till clapping makes it red	"		468
on my wax-red lips	"		516
bepainted all with red	"		901
mine eyes' red fire	"		1073
mulberries and ripe-red cherries	"		1103
clear unmatched red and white	R L		11
claims from beauty beauty's red	"		59
the red should fence the white	"		63
Argued by beauty's red	"		65
First red as roses	"		258
And the red rose blush	"		479
two red fires in both their faces	"		1353
The red blood reek'd	"		1377
bears back all boll'n and red	"		1417
reedy banks the red blood ran	"		1437
Cheeks neither red nor pale	"		1510
blushing red no guilty instance	"		1511
sod in tears, look'd red and raw	"		1592
still pure and red remain'd	"		1742
untainted still doth red abide	"		1749
A third, nor red nor white	Son	99	10
more red than her lips' red	"	130	2
roses damask'd, red and white	"	130	5
paled pearls and rubies red as blood	L C		198
Redeem—Return, forgetful Muse,			
and straight redeem	Son	100	5
Redress—that we may give redress	R L		1603
broken glass nocement can redress	P P	13	10
Redoubled—Passion on passion deep-			
ly is redoubled	V A		832
Red-rose—in a red-rose chain	"		110
Reedy—To Simois' reedy banks	R L		1437

Reek—Her face doth reek	V A	.....	555
that from my mistress reeks	Son	130	8
Reek'd—The red blood reek'd	R L	.....	1377
Reeking—furnace of foul-reeking smoke	"	.....	790
Reeleth—he reeleth from the day	Son	7	10
Refigured—ten times refigured thee	"	6	10
Refined—form of well refined-pen	"	85	8
Reflect—and now no more reflect	V A	.....	1130
that she reflects so bright	R L	.....	376
Refrain—I could from tears refrain	P P	21	16
Refresh—no rubbing will refresh	"	13	8
Reft—reft from her by death	V A	.....	1174
Refuge—this refuge let me find	R L	.....	1654
Refuse—the very refuse of thy deeds	Son	150	6
Refused—Or he refused to take her figured	P P	4	10
But one must be refused	"	16	9
Refusest—of what thyself refusest	Son	40	8
Regard—I never shall regard	V A	.....	377
deep regard beseems the sage	R L	.....	277
creeping thief to some regard	"	.....	305
Show'd deep regard	"	.....	1400
emerald, in whose fresh regard	L C	.....	213
Region—The region cloud hath mask'd him	Son	33	12
Register—Dim register and notary	R L	.....	765
what new to register	Son	108	3
Thy registers and thee	"	123	9
O false blood, thou register of lies	L C	.....	52
Rehearse—with his fair doth	Son	21	4
every vulgar paper to rehearse	"	38	4
as my poor name rehearse	"	71	11
your being shall rehearse	"	81	11
Reign—For when love reigns	V A	.....	649
And there reigns love	Son	31	3
and in their badness reign	"	121	11
in the general bosom reign	L C	.....	127
Reign—which in thy reign are made	R L	.....	804
beauty's wreck and grim care's reign	"	.....	1451
enemies to either's reign	Son	28	5
Reign'd—though in my nature	"	109	9
And reign'd commanding	L C	.....	196
Rein—And rein his proud head	V A	.....	14
the lusty courser's rein	"	.....	31
Breaketh his rein	"	.....	264
master'd with a leathern rein	"	.....	392
or rein his rash desire	R L	.....	706
Rejected—be of thyself rejected	V A	.....	159
Rejoice—joy bids her rejoice	"	.....	977
Rejoicing—more rejoicing to the prime	R L	.....	332
Releasing—doth urge releasing	V A	.....	256
thy worth gives thee releasing	Son	87	3
Relenteth—at rain relenteth	V A	.....	200
Relenting—In such relenting dew	R L	.....	1829
Relief—Within this limit is relief enough	V A	.....	235
sorrow lends but weak relief	Son	34	11
Relier—seducing lust, thy rash	R L	.....	639
Relieved—never relieved by any	V A	.....	708
Relieveth—all the earth relieveth	"	.....	484
Religion—put out Religion's eye	L C	.....	250
Religious—Hath dear religious love	Son	31	6
Religious love put out Religion's	L C	.....	250
Relish—Relish your nimble notes	R L	.....	1126
Remain—doth always fresh remain	V A	.....	801
What face remains alive	"	.....	1076
Remain—that yet remains upon her breast	R L	.....	463
surviving husband shall remain	"	.....	519
lawful policy remains	"	.....	529
despite of cure, remain	"	.....	732
remains a hopeless castaway	"	.....	744
their unseen sin remain untold	"	.....	753
in a rough-grown grove, remain	"	.....	1249
no semblance did remain	"	.....	1453
blots that do with me remain	Son	36	3
him here who doth hence remain	"	39	14
This with thee remains	"	74	14
above that idle rank remain	"	122	8
with him in thoughts, or to remain	L C	.....	129
much less of shame in me remain	"	.....	184
and both in thee remain	P P	8	14
More in women than in men remain	"	18	18
If what parts can so remain	P T	.....	48
Remain'd—still pure and red	R L	.....	1742
which remain'd the foil	L C	.....	153
Remaineth—.... in one place	V A	.....	885
Remaining—too long with her	R L	.....	1572
Remedy—The remedy indeed to do me good	"	.....	1028
for this sin there is no remedy	Son	62	3
a bath and healthful remedy	"	154	11
Remember—read this line, ... not	"	71	5
an adjunct to remember thee	"	122	13
Remember'd—O, be remember'd, no outrageous	R L	.....	607
remember'd not to be	Son	3	13
For thy sweet love remember'd	"	29	13
of thee to be remember'd	"	74	12
night of woe might have remember'd	"	120	9
Remembrance—no .... what it was	"	5	13
I summon up remembrance	"	30	2
Remission—rebel for .... prays	R L	.....	714
Remorse—'some favour, some	V A	.....	257
have remorse in poor abuses	R L	.....	269
Remorseless—In the .... wrinkles	"	.....	563
Remote—From limits far remote	Son	44	4
Hearts remote, yet not asunder	P T	.....	29
Remove—never to remove	V A	.....	81
I must remove	"	.....	186
Remove your siege	"	.....	423
fear of this thy will remove	R L	.....	611
may not remove nor be removed	Son	25	11
with the remover to remove	"	116	4
and did thence remove	L C	.....	237
a way is placed without remove	P P	18	12
Removed—not remove nor be	Son	25	14
But things removed that hidden	"	31	8
earth removed from thee	"	44	6
And yet this time removed	"	97	5
Remover—with the .... to remove	"	116	4
Removing—past reason's weak	R L	.....	243
Render—the wronger till he render right	"	.....	943
But mutual render only me for thee	Son	125	12
her quietus is to render thee	"	126	12
when I myself must render	L C	.....	221
Renew—but her passion's strength renews	R L	.....	1103
Sweet love, renew thy force	Son	56	1
Renew'd—and wish I were renew'd	"	111	8

Renewest—if now thou not....	Son	3	3
Renown—farewell his great....	P P	21	48
Rent—by paying too much rent	Son	126	6
beds' revenues of their rents	"	142	8
In top of rage the lines she rents	L C		55
Renying—Heart's renying	P P	18	7
Repair—Whose fresh repair if now	Son	3	3
Which to repair should be	"	10	8
lines of life that life repair	"	16	9
To this urn let those repair	P T		65
Repay—your great deserts repay	Son	117	2
Repeal—for exiled majesty's repeal	R L		640
Repeat—He doth again repeat	"		1848
Repel—must not repel a lover	V A		573
Repent—Though thou repent, yet I have	Son	34	10
too late, she will repent	P P	19	15
Repentant—wrapp'd in .... cold	R L		48
repentant tears ensue the deed	"		502
Repetition—repetition of her moans	V A		831
repetition cannot make it less	R L		1285
Repine—with his brows repine	V A		490
Replenish—the blood his cheeks....	R L		1357
Replete—replete with too much rage	Son	23	3
Incapable of more, replete with you	"	113	13
Replication—All replication prompt	L C		122
Replied—ere I was up,' replied the maid	R L		1277
Reply—Thus she replies	V A		385
spend their mouths; Echo replies	"		695
and he replies with howling	"		918
Thus he replies: 'The colour	R L		477
Replies her husband, 'do not take	"		1796
Report—mine is thy good report	Son	36	14
have I slept in your report	"	83	5
thy name blesses an ill report	"	95	8
mine is thy good report	"	96	14
Repose—against repose and rest	R L		757
thou gavest me to repose	"		933
The dear repose for limbs	Son	27	2
and that repose to say	"	50	3
Reposed—might have reposed still	R L		382
Reprehend—think to reprehend her	V A		470
reprehends her mangling eye	"		1065
Reproach—Reproach, disdain and deadly enmity	R L		503
Thou back'st reproach against	"		622
reproach to Tarquin's shame	"		816
And undeserved reproach	"		824
Reproach is stamp'd	"		829
and death reproach's debtor	"		1135
receives reproach of being	Son	121	2
By how much of me their reproach contains	L C		189
Reprobate—By reprobate desire	R L		300
Reproof—But as reproof and reason	"		489
Reprove—that I cannot reprove	V A		787
Reproving—but denial and	R L		242
it merits not reproving	Son	142	4
Reputation—fair .... but a bawd	R L		623
that senseless reputation	"		820
Request—request to know your heaviness	"		1283
At this request, with noble	"		1695
Requiem—the .... lack his right	P T		16
Require—services to do till you....	Son	57	4
Resemble—peasants did so well	R L		1392
as your sweet self resemble	Son	114	6
Resembling—idle sounds resembling parasites	V A		848
resembling well his pale cheeks	"		1169
resembling dew of night	R L		396
Resembling strong youth	Son	7	6
Resembling sire and child	"	8	11
Reserve—Reserve them for my love	"	32	7
Reserve their character	"	85	3
Reserved—Reserved the stalk and gave him all my flower	L C		147
Resign—Where they resign	"		1039
Resistance—.... made him fret	"		69
to resistance did belong	R L		1265
Resisteth—now no more resisteth	V A		563
Resolution—will is back'd with....	R L		352
My resolution, love, shall be thy boast	"		1193
My resolution, husband, do thou take	"		1200
Resolved—She is resolved no longer	V A		579
resolved my reason into tears	L C		296
Resolving—to obtain his will	R L		129
Resound—resounds like heaven's thunder	V A		268
How sighs resound	P P	18	34
Resounding—ill-resounding noise	V A		919
Resort—fools to mock at him resort	R L		989
graces that to thee resort	Son	96	4
Respect—Full of respects	V A		911
a true respect should have	R L		201
Respect and reason wait	"		275
true respect will prison false desire	"		642
creatures have a true respect	"		1347
worthy of thy sweet respect	Son	26	12
there is but one respect	"	36	5
Call'd to that audit by advised respects	"	49	4
Respect—others for the breath of words respect	"	85	13
What merit do I in myself respect	"	149	9
Respecting—nought at all	V A		911
nor mothers' groans respecting	R L		431
Rest—beats, and takes no rest	V A		647
to be barr'd of rest	"		784
the gentle lark, weary of rest	"		853
in this hollow cradle take thy rest	"		1185
to rest themselves betake	R L		125
exclaims against repose and rest	"		757
Disturb his hours of rest	"		974
loves no stops nor rests	"		1114
debarr'd the benefit of rest	Son	28	2
that doth my rest defeat	"	61	11
that seals up all in rest	"	73	8
in love with love's ill rest	P P	1	8
Good night, good rest	"	14	1
that kept my rest away	"	14	2
each moving sense from idle rest	"	15	3
Rest—protestation urged the rest	R L		1844
And all the rest forgot	Son	25	12
a joy above the rest	"	91	6
doubting of the rest	"	115	12
Rest—I rest thy secret friend	R L		526
want to rest thy weary head	"		1621
So should my shame still rest upon record	"		1643
To eternity doth rest	P T		58
Restful—for restful death I cry	Son	66	1
Restless—with restless trances	R L		974
My restless discord loves	"		1124

Resting—For never-resting time leads summer on		Son	5	5	Rhyme—for my love, not for their rhyme	Son 32	7
Restore—Thou wilt restore, to be my comfort		"	134	4	shall outlive this powerful rhyme	" 55	2
nine did him restore		L C		301	making beautiful old rhyme	" 106	3
Restored—All losses are restored		Son	30	14	I'll live in this poor rhyme	" 107	11
Restrain—no longer to .... him		V A		579	Rhymer—those old nine which rhymers invocate	" 38	10
which late this mutiny restrains		R L		426	Rich—For rich caparisons	V A	286
Resty—Rise, resty Muse, my love's sweet face		Son	100	9	draw his lips' rich treasure	"	552
Re-survey—And shalt by fortune once more re-survey		"	32	3	Rich preys make true men	"	724
Retention—That poor .... could		"	122	9	Pluck down the rich	"	1150
Retire—But back retires to rate the boar		V A		906	Of that rich jewel he should keep	R L	34
oft betake him to retire		R L		174	envy of so rich a thing	"	39
by him enforced, retires his ward		"		303	But, poorly rich, so wanteth	"	97
That to his borrow'd bed he make retire		"		573	bankrupt in this poor-rich gain	"	140
and flattering thoughts retire		"		641	ere rich at home be lands	"	336
Retire again, till meeting		"		1441	Sets you most rich in youth	Son 15	10
Retiring—One poor retiring minute		"		962	with earth and sea's rich gems	" 21	6
Return—Turn, and return		V A		704	to one more rich in hope	" 29	5
return again in haste		R L		321	And they are rich	" 34	14
Let him return, and flattering		"		641	So am I as the rich	" 52	1
return to make amends		"		961	Than this rich praise	" 84	2
till he return again		"		1359	big with rich increase	" 97	6
How can I then return		Son	28	1	merchandized whose rich esteeming	" 102	8
Till I return, of posting		"	51	4	So thou, being rich in 'Will	" 135	1.
Return of love, more blest		"	56	12	without be rich no more	" 146	12
Return, forgetful Muse		"	100	5	Rich-built—Of rich-built Ilion	R L	1524
Like him that travels, I return again		"	109	6	Richer—Richer than wealth, prouder than garments' cost	Son 91	10
So I return rebuked		"	119	13	Riches—And for that riches	" 87	6
Return'd—messengers .... from thee		"	45	10	And husband nature's riches	" 94	6
Revealing—Revealing day through every cranny		R L		1086	Richest—by spirits of richest coat	L C	236
Revels—Love keeps his revels		V A		123	Richly—of your praise, richly compiled	Son 85	2
For there it revels		R L		713	Rich-proud—The rich-proud cost	" 64	2
Revenge—As in revenge or quittal		"		236	Rid—to rid me of this shame	R L	1031
Revenge on him that made me		"		1180	outright with looks, and rid my pains	Son 139	14
Her blood, in poor revenge		"		1736	Ride—permit the basest clouds to ride	" 33	5
Is it revenge to give thyself		"		1823	upon your soundless deep doth ride	" 80	10
We will revenge the death		"		1841	in the bay where all men ride	" 137	6
Revenge upon myself		Son	149	8	her levell'd eyes their carriage ride	L C	22
Revenged—thou revenged mayst be		R L		1194	Well could he ride, and often	"	106
Be suddenly revenged on my foe		"		1683	Rider—To tie the rider	V A	40
And live to be revenged		"		1778	his rider's angry stir	"	283
Revengeful—injustice with .... arms		"		1693	Save a proud rider	"	300
Revenue—beds' .... of their rents		Son	142	8	His rider loved not speed	Son 50	8
Reverend—And reverend welcome		R L		90	his mettle from his rider takes	L C	107
A reverend man that grazed		L C		57	Ridge—Whose ridges with the meeting clouds	V A	820
Reviewest—When thou reviewedst this, thou dost review		Son	74	5	With swelling ridges; and their ranks	R L	1439
Revive—coal revives with wind		V A		338	Ridiculous—makes thee ridiculous	V A	988
Reviveth—love by looks reviveth		"		464	Rifled—Chastity is .... of her store	R L	692
Reviving—For now reviving joy		"		977	hath Tarquin rifled me	"	1050
Revolt—on thy revolt doth lie		Son	92	10	Right—by the rights of time	V A	759
Revolution—revolution be the same		"	59	12	and 'tis thy right	"	1184
Revolving—doth Tarquin lie		R L		127	from world's minority their right	R L	67
Reward—Reward not hospitality		"		575	beast that knows no gentle right	"	543
Rewarded—whose concave womb rewarded		L C		1	at right, at law, at reason	"	880
Rhetoric—touches rhetoric can lend		Son	82	10	the wronger till be render right	"	943
heavenly rhetoric of thine eye		P P	3	1	doth me no right	"	1027
Rheumatic—despised, ..., and cold		V A		135	By all our country rights	"	1838
Rhyme—trespass cited up in rhymes		R L		524	your true rights be term'd	Son 17	11
more blessed than my barren rhyme		Son	16	4	the freedom of that right	" 46	4
In it and in my rhyme		"	17	14	And my heart's right	" 46	14
					The right of sepulchres	" 68	6

Right—That for thy right	Son	88	14	Rock—rock thee day and night	V A	 1186
your own dear-purchased right	"	117	6	Huge rocks, high winds	R L	 343
Lest the requiem lack his right	P T	....	16	When rocks impregnable	Son	65 7
That the turtle saw his right	"	....	34	There will we sit upon the rocks	P P	20 5
Right—Can thy right hand	V A	....	158	Rock'd—and then it faster rock'd	R L	 262
And right perfection wrongfully disgraced	Son	66	7	Rocky—rocky and wreck-threatening heart	"	 590
or changes right or wrong	"	112	8	What rocky heart to water will not wear	L C	 291
in others seem right gracious	"	135	7			
In things right true	"	137	13	Roe—Or as the fleet-foot roe	V A	 561
The better angel is a man right fair	"	144	3	Or at the roe	"	 676
Their view right on	L C	....	26	Roll—Deep woes roll forward	R L	 1118
My better angel is a man right fair	P P	2	3	Roll'd—blunt rage and rigour roll'd	"	 1398
Right—cannot right her cause	V A	....	220	Rolling—Rolling his greedy eyeballs	"	 368
should right poor ladies' harms	"	....	1694	less false in rolling	Son	20 5
Rightful—No rightful plea might plead	R L	....	1649	Roman—leaves the Roman host	R L	 3
				welcomed by the Roman dame	"	 51
Rightly—They rightly do inherit	Son	94	5	The Roman lord marcheth	"	 301
Rigol—a watery rigol goes	R L	....	1745	shakes aloft his Roman blade	"	 505
Rigour—ruin'd with thy rigour	V A	....	954	Awake, thou Roman dame	"	 1628
blunt rage and rigour roll'd	R L	....	1398	He with the Romans	"	 1811
then use rigour in my gaol	Son	133	12	Courageous Roman, do not stoop	"	 1828
Ring—rings sadly in her ear	V A	....	889	To rouse our Roman gods	"	 1831
rings out the doleful knell	R L	....	1495	The Romans plausibly did give	"	 1854
breaking rings a-twain	L C	....	6	Rome—this faultful lord of Rome	"	 715
a ring of posied gold and bone	"	....	45	never be forgot in mighty Rome	"	 1644
My wether's bell rings doleful knell	P P	13	28	thou wronged lord of Rome	"	 1818
				Since Rome herself on them	"	 1833
Ringing—Once set on ringing	R L	....	1494	country rights in Rome maintained	"	 1838
By ringing in thy lady's ear	P P	19	28	her bleeding body thorough Rome	"	 1851
Riot—and too full of riot	V A	....	1347	Rondure—In this huge .... hems	Son	21 8
in their riot even there	Son	41	11	Roof—that beauteous roof to ruinate	"	10 7
Ripe—That did my ripe thoughts	"	86	3	Room—your praise shall still find room	"	55 10
Riper—But as the riper should	"	1	3			
in growth of riper days	"	102	8	Root—Would root these beauties as he roots the mead	V A	 636
Ripe-red—and ripe-red cherries	V A	....	1103			
Rise—Will never rise so he will kiss her	"	....	480	root out the work of masonry	Son	55 6
				Root pity in thy heart	"	142 11
for thou shalt not rise	"	....	710	Root—wither at the cedar's root	R L	 603
fear did make her colour rise	R L	....	257	of another root are rotted	"	 823
itself to death, rise up and fall	"	....	466	take root with precious flowers	"	 870
Rise, resty Muse, my love's sweet face survey	Son	100	9	Rose—than doves or roses are	V A	 10
				prisoner in a red-rose chain	"	 110
dear love I rise and fall	"	151	14	What though the rose	"	 574
Rise—My heart doth charge the watch; the morning rise	P P	15	2	upon the blushing rose	"	 590
				Gloss on the rose	"	 936
Rising—Round rising hillocks	V A	....	237	war of lilies and of roses	R L	 71
But rising at thy name	Son	151	9	First red as roses	"	 258
Rite—ceremony of love's rite	"	23	6	white as lawn the roses took away	"	 259
River—Rain added to a river	V A	....	71	And the red rose blush	"	 479
is stopp'd, or river stay'd	"	....	331	thorns the growing rose defends	"	 492
In two slow rivers	R L	....	1738	beauty's rose might never die	Son	1 2
a river running from a fount	L C	....	283	Roses have thorns and silver fountains mud	"	35 2
By shallow rivers by whose falls	P P	20	7			
one by one she in a river threw	L C	....	38	The rose looks fair	"	54 3
Roaring—the violent roaring tide	R L	....	1667	perfumed tincture of the roses	"	54 6
Rob—To rob thee of a kiss	V A	....	723	Sweet roses do not so	"	54 11
to rob him of his fair	"	....	1085	Roses of shadow, since his rose	"	67 8
which sourly robs from m-	Son	35	14	a canker in the fragrant rose	"	95 2
He robs thee of, and pays it thee	"	79	8	the deep vermillion in the rose	"	98 10
Robb'd—robb'd of his effect	V A	....	1132	The roses fearfully on thorns	"	99 8
But robb'd and ransack'd	R L	....	838	Save thou, my rose	"	109 14
And when the judge is robb'd	"	....	1652	I have seen roses damask'd	"	130 5
Robb'd others' beds' revenues	Son	142	8	But no such roses see I	"	130 6
Robbery—I do forgive thy robbery	"	40	9	with crystal gate the glowing roses	L C	 286
And to his robbery had annex'd	"	99	11	Sweet rose, fair flower	P P	10 1
Robbing—Robbing no old to dress	"	68	12	make thee a bed of roses	"	20 9
Robe—wardrobe which the robe doth hide	"	52	10	Rose—And ere I rose was Tarquin	R L	 1281
				He rose and ran away	P P	4 14

Rose-cheek'd—Rose-cheek'd Adonis bied him	V A	3	Ruminate—taught me thus to....	Son 64	11
Rosy—her rosy cheek lies under	R L	386	Run—Whether he run or fly	V A	304
though rosy lips and cheeks	Son 116	9	Sometime he runs	"	685
Rot—Rot and consume themselves	V A	132	harmony should run	"	781
Rotted—of another root are rotted	R L	823	through the dark lawnd runs	"	813
Rotten—With rotten damps ravish	"	778	And as she runs	"	871
Shall rotten death make conquest	"	1767	This way she runs	"	905
in their rotten smoke	Son 34	4	He runs and chides	R L	742
when I in earth am rotten	" 81	2	let the thief run mad	"	997
Rough brakes obscure and rough	V A	237	Towards thee I'll run	Son 51	14
Rough bear or lion proud	"	884	careful housewife runs to catch	" 143	1
To the rough beast	R L	545	kiss and clip me till I run away	P P 11	14
But chide rough winter	"	1255	Runn'st—So runn'st thou after that	Son 143	9
Rough winds do shake	Son 18	3	Running—a river.... from a fount	L C	283
Rough-grown—In men, as in a rough-grown grove	R L	1249	Rush—And forth she rushes through whom he rushes	V A "	262 630
Round—Round rising hillocks	V A	237	from the rushes where it lies	R L	318
round enchanting pits	"	247	Rushing—Rushing from forth a cloud	"	373
Which in round drops	"	1170	Rust—Foul-cankering rust	V A	767
Left their round turrets destitute	R L	441	Rusty—and yet as iron rusty	P P 7	4
And turn the giddy round	"	952	Ruth—Looking with pretty ruth	Son 132	4
her eyes about the painting round	"	1499	a spectacle of ruth	P P 9	11
Those round clear pearls of his	"	1553	Ruthless—Ruthless beasts they will not cheer thee	" 21	22
And round about her tear-distained to round me on th' ear	" P P 19	1586 51			
Round—on this mortal round	R L	368	Sable—sable Night, mother of dread	R L	117
What rounds, what bounds	L C	109	My sable ground of sin	"	1074
Round-hoof'd—Round-hoof'd, short-jointed	V A	295	sable curls all silver'd o'er That thy sable gender makest	Son 12 P T	4 18
Rouse—No dog shall rouse thee	"	240	Sack'd—Her house is sack'd	R L	1170
To rouse our Roman gods	R L	1831	Who, like a late-sack'd island	"	1740
Rouseth—He rouseth up himself	"	541	Sacred—Her sacred temple spotted	"	1172
Rubbing—As vaded gloss no rubbing will refresh	P P 13	8	Serving with looks his sacred majesty	Son 7	4
Ruby—and rubies red as blood	L C	198	Tan sacred beauty	" 115	7
Ruby-colour'd—the.... portal	V A	451	power to charm a sacred nun	L C	260
Rude—by brain-sick rude desire	R L	175	Sad—at these sad signs	V A	929
Rude ram, to batter	"	464	Which struck her sad	R L	262
Harsh, featureless, and rude	Son 11	10	Sad pause and deep regard	"	277
These poor rude lines	" 32	4	Her sad behaviour feeds	"	556
learning my rude ignorance	" 78	14	with slow-sad gait descended	"	1081
Savage, extreme, rude, cruel	" 129	4	Sad souls are slain in merry company	"	1110
Rudeness—His rudeness so with his authorized youth	L C	104	Make thy sad grove	"	1129
Rudely—his mantle rudely o'er his arm	R L	170	So I at each sad strain stern, sad tunes to change their	"	1131
shall rudely tear thee	"	669	kinds	"	1147
maiden virtue rudely strumpeted	Son 66	6	in that sad hour of mine	"	1179
Rudest—the rudest or gentlest sight	" 113	9	And sorts a sad look	"	1221
Ruffian—The staring ruffian	V A	1149	To see sad sights moves more	"	1324
Ruffle—blusterer that the ruffle knew	L C	58	see those far-off eyes look sad On this sad shadow	" "	1386 1457
Ruin—To whose weak ruins muster	R L	720	set a-work, sad tales doth tell	"	1496
Time's ruin, beauty's wreck	"	1451	So sober-sad, so weary	"	1542
Ruin has taught me thus	Son 64	11	in her sad face he stares	"	1591
Ruinate—To.... proud buildings	R L	944	With sad attention long	"	1610
that beauteous roof to ruinate	Son 10	7	Begins the sad dirge	"	1612
Ruin'd—ruin'd with thy rigour	V A	954	her sad task hath not said	"	1699
Bare ruin'd choirs, where late	Son 73	4	sad account of fore-bemoaned		
And ruin'd love when it is built	" 119	11	moan	Son 30	11
Ruining—more short than waste or ruining	" 123	4	and straight grow sad Let this sad interim	" 45 " 56	14 9
Rule—Could rule them both	V A	1008	like a sad slave, stay and think	" 57	11
'gainst rule, 'gainst sense	L C	271	sad mortality o'er-sway	" 65	2
Let reason rule things worthy	P P 19	3	And the sad augurs mock	" 107	6
Ruled—Thus he that overruled I			a sad distemper'd guest	" 153	12
oversway'd	V A	109	O, that sad breath	L C	326
be ruled by me	"	673	Herald sad and trumpet be	P T	5

16

Sad-beholding—her sad-beholding			Sake—all tyrant, for thy sake	Son 149	4
husband saw	R L	1590	should do again for such a sake	L C	322
Saddle-bow—to the saddle-bow	V A	14	For Adon's sake	P P 9	4
Sadly—rings sadly in her ear	"	889	Salt—my salt tears gone	V A	1071
another sadly scowling	"	917	To their salt sovereign	R L	650
pity-pleading eyes are sadly fixed	R L	561	Salt-waved—Who in a .... ocean	"	1231
thievish dog creeps sadly thence	"	736	Salutation—Give salutation to my		
when sadly she had laid	"	1212	sportive blood	Son 21	6
why hear'st thou music sadly	Son 8	1	Salute—Venus salutes him	V A	859
letters sadly penn'd in blood	L C	47	Salve—Earth's sovereign salve	"	28
Sadness—Therefore, in sadness, now			To see the salve doth make	R L	1116
I will away	V A	807	well of such a salve can speak	Son 34	7
Sad-set—sad-set eyes and wretched			salve which wounded bosoms fits	" 120	12
arms	R L	1662	Salving—salving thy amiss	" 35	7
Sad-tuned—to list the .... tale	L C	4	Same—in the self-same seat sits Col-		
Safest—With safest distance	"	151	latine	R L	289
Sage—this sorrow to the sage	R L	222	and if the same	"	600
deep regard beseems the sage	"	277	The same disgrace which they	"	751
Said—This said, impatience chokes	V A	217	for the self-same purpose seek	"	1047
sorrow may be said	"	333	and back the same grief draw	"	1673
if she said 'No	"	852	tyrants to the very same	Son 5	3
This said, she hasteth	"	865	even by the self-same sky	" 15	6
This said, his guilty hand	R L	358	For that same groan	" 50	13
This said, he shakes aloft	"	505	whether revolution be the same	" 59	12
This said, he sets his foot	"	673	But those same tongues	" 69	6
as grant what he hath said	"	915	still all one, e'er the same	" 76	5
This said, from her be-tumbled			each day say o'er the very same	" 108	6
couch	"	1037	That thy wife was not the same	P T	38
She would have said	"	1533	Sanctified—Or sister sanctified	L C	233
her sad task hath not said	"	1699	Sand—Dance on the sands	V A	148
could distinguish what he said	"	1785	strong pirates, shelves, and sands	R L	335
This said, he struck his hand	"	1842	Sang—where late the sweet birds		
And yet it may be said	Son 42	2	sang	Son 73	4
renew thy force; be it not said	" 56	1	Sap—Green-dropping sap, which she		
those that said I could not love	" 115	2	compares	V A	1176
the sound that said 'I hate	" 145	2	To dry the old oak's sap	R L	950
This said, in top of rage	L C	55	leaves will wither and his sap decay	"	1168
to none was ever said	"	180	Sap check'd with frost	Son 5	7
This said, his watery eyes	"	281	Vaunt in their youthful sap	" 15	7
Have you not heard it said	P P	41	Sapphire—The heaven-hued	L C	213
Yet will she blush, here be it said	"	53	Sappy—Sappy plants to bear	V A	165
Sail—as the proudest sail doth bear	Son 80	6	Sat—before him as he sat	"	349
Was it the proud full sail	" 86	1	again desires her, being sat	L C	66
That I have hoisted sail	" 117	7	Satiety—And yet not cloy thy lips		
Saint—This earthly saint, adored	R L	85	with loathed satiety	V A	19
corrupt my saint to be a devil	Son 144	7	Satire—If any, be a satire to decay	Son 100	11
corrupt my saint to be a devil	P P 2	7	Satisfaction—Nor gives it	L C	162
To sin and never for to saint	" 19	44	Satisfied—by the conquest satisfied	R L	422
Saint-like—Or blot with hell-born			Satisfy—all could not satisfy	"	96
sin such saint-like forms	R L	1519	Saturn—That heavy Saturn laugh'd	Son 98	4
Saith—Saith thou the world	V A	12	Sauce—To bitter sauces did I frame	" 118	6
He saith she is immodest	"	53	Saucily—while others saucily	R L	1348
'Fondling,' she saith	"	229	Saucy—My saucy bark inferior far	Son 80	7
'Give me my hand,' saith he	"	373	Since saucy jacks so happy are	" 128	13
'Give me my heart,' saith she	"	374	Savage—Savage, extreme, rude, cruel	" 129	4
shall I say mine eye saith truth	Son 114	3	Save—Save a proud rider	V A	300
Sake—And for my sake	V A	105	Save sometime too much wonder	R L	95
and thy children's sake	R L	533	Save thieves and cares	"	126
for his sake spare me	"	582	Save of their lord	"	409
for thine own sake leave me	"	583	Yet save that labour	"	1290
And for my sake	"	1197	save to the eye of mind	"	1426
And for my sake	"	1681	Save breed, to brave him	Son 12	14
And for my sake	Son 42	7	Save that my soul's imaginary sight	" 27	9
for my sake to approve her	" 42	8	Save where thou art not	" 48	10
And both for my sake	" 42	12	Save, where you are	" 57	12
watchman ever for thy sake	" 61	12	Save that to die I leave my love	" 66	14
O, for my sake do you	" 111	1	Save what is had	" 75	12
a friend came debtor for my sake	" 134	11	Save thou, my rose	" 109	14
that languish'd for her sake	" 143	3	save in thy deeds	" 131	13

Save—Save the nightingale alone	P P	21	8	Say—the old world could say	Son	59	9
Save the eagle, feather'd king	P T	....	11	O, if, I say, you look	"	71	9
Saved—And saved my life	Son	145	14	which he doth say	"	79	13
Savour—savour, hue, and qualities	V A	....	747	Who is it that says most? which			
foregoing simple savour	Son	125	7	can say more	"	84	1
Saw—His eyes saw her eyes	V A	....	337	you praised, I say 'Tis so	"	85	9
But when he saw his love	"	....	393	Say that thou didst forsake	"	89	1
that helpless berries saw	"	....	604	Some say, thy fault is youth	"	96	1
Ne'er saw the beauteous livery	"	....	1107	Some say, thy grace is youth	"	96	2
The more she saw the blood	R L	....	1357	say o'er the very same	"	108	6
he saw them quake and tremble	"	....	1393	O, never say that I	"	109	1
her sad-beholding husband saw	"	....	1590	Or whether shall I say	"	114	3
I never saw that you	Son	83	1	Might I not then say	"	115	10
Since first I saw you fresh	"	104	8	then might I not say so	"	115	13
when I saw myself to win	"	119	4	Since my appeal says I did strive	"	117	13
I never saw a goddess go	"	130	11	every tongue says beauty	"	127	14
when she saw my woeful state	"	145	4	some say that thee behold	"	131	5
might think sometime it saw	L C	....	10	To say they err	"	131	7
Each eye that saw him	"	....	89	say this is not	"	137	11
Saw how deceits were gilded	"	....	172	But wherefore says she	"	138	9
he saw more wounds than one	P P	9	13	And wherefore say not	"	138	10
the turtle saw his right	P T	....	34	to say it is not so	"	148	6
Saw division grow together	"	....	42	say I love thee not	"	149	1
Saw—a sentence or an old man's saw	R L	....	244	'Father,' she says, 'though in me	L C	....	71
his sighs, his sorrows make a saw	"	....	1672	often men would say	"	....	106
Saw'st—.... thou not signs of fear	V A	....	644	what he would say	"	....	152
Sawn—What largeness thinks in				For further I could say	"	....	169
Paradise was sawn	L C	....	91	But wherefore says my love	P P	1	9
Say—what shall she say	V A	....	253	And wherefore say not I	"	1	10
As who should say	"	....	280	say thou lovest her well	"	19	11
or his 'Stand, I say	"	....	284	ban and brawl, and say thee nay	"	19	20
For lovers say the heart	"	....	329	taught her thus to say	"	19	22
Say, that the sense	"	....	439	Saying—Saying, some shape in			
May say, the plague	"	....	510	Sinon's was abused	R L	....	1529
Say, for non-payment	"	....	521	saved my life, saying 'not you	Son	145	14
'Now let me say, "Good-night,"				Scale—as his hand did scale	R L	....	440
and so say you	"	....	535	am I come to scale	"	....	481
if you will say so	"	....	536	weighs down the airy scale of			
and ere he says 'Adieu	"	....	537	praise	L C	....	226
'Sweet boy,' she says	"	....	583	Scalp—The scalps of many	R L	....	1413
Say, shall we? shall we? wilt thou	"	....	586	Scandal—the scandal will survive	"	....	204
'Fie, fie,' he says	"	....	611	Thou plantest scandal	"	....	887
more I dare not say	"	....	805	For greatest scandal waits	"	....	1006
She says 'Tis so	"	....	851	Which vulgar scandal stamp'd	Son	112	2
And would say after her	"	....	852	Scant—if store of crowns be scant	P P	21	37
And says, within her bosom	"	....	1173	Scanted—that I have scanted all	Son	117	1
As who should say	R L	....	320	'Scape—night's 'scapes doth open lay	R L	....	747
foul sin may say	"	....	629	Could 'scape the hail	L C	....	310
She says her subjects	"	....	722	'Scaped—my heart hath 'scaped	Son	90	5
that we can say is ours	"	....	873	'Scapeth—battle ....by the flight	L C	....	244
but stontly say 'So be it	"	....	1209	Scar—The scar that will, despite	R L	....	732
What should I say	"	....	1291	crest-wounding private scar	"	....	828
all the task it hath to say	"	....	1618	The scars of battle 'scapeth	L C	....	244
at once began to say	"	....	1709	Scarce—And scarce hath eyes	R L	....	857
'He, be,' she says	"	....	1717	duteous vassal scarce is gone	"	....	1360
The father says 'She's mine	"	....	1795	Scarce had the sun dried up	P P	6	1
let no mourner say	"	....	1797	And scarce the herd gone	"	6	2
To say, within thine own	Son	2	7	Scarce I could from tears refrain	"	21	16
let your son say so	"	13	14	Scarcely—And scarcely greet me	Son	49	6
Or say with princes if it shall go				Scarcity—would breed a scarcity	V A	....	753
well	"	14	7	Scarlet—His scarlet lust came	R L	....	1650
age to come would say	"	17	7	profaned their scarlet ornaments	Son	142	6
wilt thou not haply say	"	21	5	Scatter—They scatter and unloose it	R L	....	136
Let them say more that like	"	21	13	Scene—As chorus to their tragic	P T	....	52
forget to say	"	23	5	Scent-snuffing—hot .... hounds	V A	....	692
How would, I say, mine eyes	"	43	9	Sceptre—with the sceptre straight			
And says in him thy fair appearance lies	"	46	6	be strucken down	R L	....	217
and that repose to say	"	50	3	Schedule—By this short schedule	"	....	1312
				Of folded schedules had she many	L C	....	43

School—the glass, the ..., the book	R L	....	615
And wilt thou be the school	"	....	617
In skill-contending schools	"	....	1018
thy long-experienced wit to school	"	....	1820
Scope—Desiring this man's art and that man's scope	Son	29	7
whose worthiness gives scope	"	52	13
The scope and tenour	"	61	8
That having such a scope	"	103	2
which wondrous scope affords	"	105	12
Scorch—which fond desire doth	R L	....	314
Score—thy dear love to score	Son	122	10
Scorn—love he laugh'd to scorn	V A	....	4
smiles at thee in scorn	"	....	252
I murder shameful scorn	R L	....	1189
In scorn of nature	"	....	1374
my merit in the eye of scorn	Son	88	2
In scorn or friendship	P P	14	8
That which with scorn she put away	"	19	18
Scorns—scorns the heat he feels	V A	....	311
The sun doth scorn you	"	....	1084
Patience seem'd to scorn his woes	R L	....	1505
That then I scorn to change	Son	29	14
All fears scorn I	P P	18	20
Scorn'd—Be scorn'd like old men	Son	17	10
Scornful—taught them ... tricks	V A	....	501
The scornful mark of every open eye	R L	....	520
Scornfully—.... glisters like fire	V A	....	275
Then looking scornfully	R L	....	187
Scorning—Scorning his churlish drum	V A	....	107
scorning it should pass	"	....	982
Scowl—He scowls and hates himself	R L	....	738
Scowling—another sadly scowling	V A	....	917
Scrap—disdained scraps to give	R L	....	987
Scratch—briar his weary legs doth scratch	V A	....	705
to scratch her wicked foe	R L	....	1035
scratch out the angry eyes	"	....	1469
Scratch'd—Shaking their .... ears	V A	....	924
Scroll—Receives the scroll	R L	....	1340
Scud—he scuds far off	"	....	301
Scythe—'gainst Time's .... can make	Son	12	13
but for his scythe to mow	"	60	12
his scythe and crooked knife	"	100	14
despite thy scythe and thee	"	123	14
Scythed—Time had not scythed	L C	....	12
Sea—The sea hath bounds	V A	....	389
a sea, a sovereign king	R L	....	652
Thy sea within a puddle's womb	"	....	657
the paddle in thy sea dispersed	"	....	658
deep-drenched in a sea of care	"	....	1100
with earth and sea's rich gems	Son	21	6
can jump both sea and land	"	44	7
nor earth, nor boundless sea	"	65	1
The mountain or the sea	"	113	11
The sea, all water	"	135	9
Seal—Pure lips, sweet seals	V A	....	511
To stamp the seal of Time	R L	....	941
She carved thee for her seal	Son	11	13
that seals up all in rest	"	73	8
Seal'd—Her letter now is seal'd	R L	....	1331
And seal'd false bonds	Son	142	7
and seal'd to curious secrecy	L C	....	49
Sealing—still to be sealing	V A	....	512
Seal-manual—Set thy seal-manual	"	....	516
Seaman—Wreck to the seaman	"	....	454
Search—search the bottom of annoy	R L	....	1109
Sear'd—through lattice of sear'd age	L C	....	14
Season—now the happy season	V A	....	327
Now serves the season	R L	....	166
thou point'st the season	"	....	879
of dearths, or seasons' quality	Son	14	4
Make glad and sorry seasons	"	19	5
In process of the seasons	"	104	6
Seasoned—Or as sweet-season'd showers are to the ground	"	75	2
season'd woe had pelleted with tears	L C	....	18
Seasoning—Seasoning the earth with showers	R L	....	796
Seat—Interchange each other's seat	"	....	70
And in the self-same seat	"	....	289
thou mightst my seat forbear	Son	41	9
till now never kept seat in one	"	105	14
Seated—deep desert, seated from the way	R L	....	1144
Second—What needs a .... striking	V A	....	250
A second fear through all	"	....	903
To live a second life on second head	Son	68	7
Death's second self	"	73	8
The second burthen of a former child	"	59	4
Second—Which is not mix'd with seconds	"	125	11
Secrecy—the subtle-shining secrecies	R L	....	101
the unseen secrecy of night	"	....	763
seal'd to curious secrecy	L C	....	49
Secret—no secret bushes fear	R L	....	88
I rest thy secret friend	"	....	526
Thy secret pleasure turns	"	....	890
smile at thee in secret thought	"	....	1065
so ensconced his secret evil	"	....	1515
in secret influence comment	Son	13	4
Secret—A thousand honey secrets	V A	....	16
To hear her secrets	P P	19	54
Securely—she .... gives good cheer	R L	....	89
Seducing—Not to seducing lust	"	....	639
See—Her help she sees	V A	....	93
Thou canst not see	"	....	139
He sees his love, and nothing else he sees	"	....	287
to see him woo her	"	....	309
He sees her coming	"	....	337
Who sees his true love	"	....	397
to hear nor see	"	....	437
I could not see	"	....	440
Then shalt thou see	"	....	703
desire sees best of all	"	....	720
thou hast no eyes to see	"	....	939
taught all other eyes to see	"	....	952
To see his face, the lion	"	....	1093
If he did see his face	"	....	1109
weasels shriek to see him there	R L	....	307
Who sees the lurking serpent	"	....	362
What could he see	"	....	414
I see what crosses my attempt	"	....	491
That thou shalt see thy state	"	....	644
Ere he can see his own abomination	"	....	704
but that every eye can see	"	....	750
And time to see one	"	....	986
to see his friends his foes	"	....	988
Lucrece shames herself to see	"	....	1084
with every thing she sees	"	....	1093
To see the salve doth make	"	....	1116
overseen that thou shalt see it	"	....	1206

Entry	Ref	Line
See—thy Lucrece thou wilt see	R L	1305
To see sad sights moves more	"	1324
be blush'd to see her shame	"	1344
might you see the labouring pioner	"	1380
see those far-off eyes look sad	"	1386
might you see grave Nestor	"	1401
To see their youthful sons	"	1432
Many she sees where cares	"	1445
she sees a wretched image	"	1501
To see those borrow'd tears	"	1549
see time how slow it creeps	"	1575
can see what once I was	"	1764
sweet Lucrece, live again, and see	"	1770
And see thy blood	Son 2	14
through windows of thine age shalt see	" 3	11
And see the brave day sunk	" 12	2
trees I see barren of leaves	" 12	5
as they see others grow	" 12	12
men can breathe, or eyes can see	" 18	13
you see his skill	" 24	5
Now see what good turns	" 24	9
but what they see	" 24	14
which the blind do see	" 27	8
To see his active child	" 37	2
do mine eyes best see	" 43	1
to see till I see thee	" 43	13
When I shall see thee	" 49	2
To-morrow see again	" 56	7
to the banks, that, when they see	" 56	11
That I might see	" 59	9
towers I see down-razed	" 64	3
may see my pleasure	" 75	8
I see a better state	" 92	7
things turn to fair that eyes can see	" 95	12
yet I none could see	" 99	14
I see descriptions	" 106	2
I see their antique pen	" 106	7
if it see the rudest or gentlest sight	" 113	9
what we see doth lie	" 123	11
roses see I in her cheeks	" 130	6
and see not what they see	" 137	2
see where it lies	" 137	3
what they see aright	" 148	4
sees not till heaven	" 148	12
that can see thou lovest	" 149	11
see just cause to hate	" 150	10
the thing they see	" 152	12
'twixt May and April is to see	L C	102
offences that abroad you see	"	183
that soul that sees this	P P	5 9
did I see a fair sweet youth	"	9 9
See, in my thigh,' quoth she	"	9 12
the fair'st that eye could see	"	16 3
For now I see	"	18 16
to see my doleful plight	"	18 33
I see that there is none	"	18 54
And see the shepherds feed	"	20 6
Seed—Seeds spring from seeds	V A	167
Seeded—shame be … in t'ine age	R L	603
Seeing—seeing thee so indeed	V A	667
Seeing his beauty	"	938
seeing thee embrace him	R L	518
Seeing such emulation	"	1808
seeing of his living hue	Son 67	6
seeing farther than the eye	" 69	8
Seems seeing, but effectually	" 113	1
'tis flattery in my seeing	" 114	9
but by others' seeing	" 121	4
Seeing—Or mine eyes seeing this	Son 137	11
Lest eyes well-seeing thy foul faults	" 148	14
Seek—try again she seeks	V A	52
a thousand ways he seeks	"	477
seek not to know me	"	525
She seeks to kindle	"	606
a pure appeal seeks to the heart	R L	293
by dumb demeanour seeks to show	"	474
Who seek to stain the ocean	"	655
such numbers seek for thee	"	896
seek every hour to kill	"	998
I live, and seek in vain	"	1044
for the self-same purpose seek a knife	"	1047
Then what I seek	Son 50	2
poor beauty indirectly seek	" 67	7
art enforced to seek anew	" 82	7
If thou dost seek to have	" 142	13
Seeking—…. that beauteous roof	" 10	7
Seem—seem an hour but short	V A	23
so shall the day seem night	"	122
dissolve or seem to melt	"	144
strangeness, seems unkind	"	310
Incorporate then they seem	"	540
hills seem burnish'd gold	"	858
how strange it seems	"	985
makes the wound seem three	"	1064
His face seems twain	"	1067
when it most seems just	"	1156
seems to part in sunder	R L	388
This guilt would seem death-worthy	"	635
And seems to point her out	"	1087
unto her maid seem so	"	1217
seems to pelt and swear	"	1418
Short time seems long	"	1573
Which seems to weep	"	1746
love's strength seem to decay	Son 23	7
May make seem bare	" 26	6
make grief's strength seem stronger	" 28	14
extremity can seem but slow	" 51	6
doth beauty beauteous seem	" 54	1
true love may seem false in this	" 72	9
strains of woe which now seem woe	" 90	13
with loss of thee will not seem so	" 90	11
May still seem love to me	" 93	3
To make him seem long hence	" 101	14
Such seems your beauty still	" 104	3
Seems seeing, but effectually	" 113	4
and they mourners seem	" 127	10
in others seem right gracious	" 135	7
the sweets that seem so good	L C	164
Thine eye Jove's lightning seems	P P	5 11
each minute seems a morn	"	15 15
Plays not at all, but seems afraid	"	18 30
Truth may seem, but cannot be	P T	62
Seem'd—seem'd with him to bleed	V A	1056
nothing in him seem'd inordinate	R L	94
As heaven, it seem'd, to kiss	"	1372
Many a dry drop seem'd	"	1375
In speech, it seem'd	"	1405
Which seem'd to swallow up	"	1409
To jump up higher seem'd	"	1414
It seem'd they would debate	"	1421
their light joy seem'd to appear	"	1431
Patience seem'd to scorn his woes	"	1505
that seem'd to welcome woe	"	1500
this abundant issue seem'd to me	Son 97	9
Yet seem'd it winter still	" 98	13
absence seem'd my claim to qualify	" 109	2

Seem'd—Ink would have seem'd more black	L C	54	**Self**—thy sweet self dost deceive	Son	4	10
the web it seem'd to wear	"	95	Make thee another self	"	10	13
Seem'st—Thou art not what thou seem'st	R L	600	to mine own self bring	"	39	3
			Self so self-loving were iniquity	"	62	12
Thou seem'st not what thou art	"	601	Death's second self	"	73	8
Seemeth—sorrow seemeth chief	V A	970	as your sweet self resemble	"	114	6
when she seemeth drown'd	"	984	as thy sweet self grow'st	"	126	4
Seemeth this concordant one	P T	46	And my next self	"	133	6
Seeming—Seeming to bury	V A	738	thy sweet self prove	"	151	4
as seeming troubled	"	830	My woeful self	L C		143
though seeming short	"	842	That the self was not the same	P T		38
a show so seeming just	R L	1314	**Self-applied**—if I had self-applied	L C		76
being many, seeming one	Son	8	13	**Self-doing**—Yourself to pardon of self-doing crime	Son	58	12
though more weak in seeming	"	102	1	**Self-example**—By .... mayst thou	"	142	14
best habit is in seeming trust	"	138	11	**Self-kill'd**—ere it be self-kill'd	"	6	4
borrow'd motion seeming owed	L C		327	**Self-love**— .... had never drown'd him	R L		266
Seemly—Is but the seemly raiment	Son	22	6	Of his self-love, to stop	Son	3	8
Seen—and yet no footing seen	V A	148	Sin of self-love possesseth all	"	62	1
as they had not seen them	"	357	self-love quite contrary I read	"	62	11
in water seen by night	"	492	**Self-loving**—and self-loving nuns	V A		752
lips no more had seen	"	504	Self so self-loving were iniquity	Son	62	12
have him seen no more	"	819	**Self-same**—And in the .... seat	R L		289
Her eyes seen in the tears	"	962	Yet for the self-same purpose	"		1047
Which seen, her eyes	"	1031	even by the self-same sky	Son	15	6
immure herself and not be seen	"	1194	**Self-slaughter'd**—on her .... body	R L		1733
in Lucrece' face was seen	R L	64	**Self-substantial**—with .... fuel	Son	1	6
had Narcissus seen her	"	265	**Self-trust**—if there be no self-trust	R L		158
Then had they seen	"	380	**Self-will**— .... himself doth tire	"		707
glorious morning have I seen	Son	33	1	**Self-will'd**—Be not self-will'd	Son	6	13
in these black lines be seen	"	63	13	**Sell**—To sell myself	V A		513
seen by Time's fell hand	"	64	1	Or sells eternity to get a toy	R L		214
I have seen the hungry ocean	"	64	5	Must sell her joy, her life	"		385
seen such interchange	"	64	9	that purpose not to sell	Son	21	14
holy antique hours are seen	"	68	9	set thy person forth to sell	P P	19	12
errors that in thee are seen	"	96	7	**Selling**—in selling hours of dross	Son	146	11
what dark days seen	"	97	3	**Semblance**—whose simple	V A		795
In process of the seasons have I seen	"	104	6	When with like semblance	R L		1113
Have I not seen dwellers	"	125	5	the semblance of a devil	"		1246
I have seen roses damask'd	"	130	5	no semblance did remain	"		1453
advice is often seen	L C		160	In thy sweet semblance	"		1759
many that mine eyes have seen	"		190	And your sweet semblance	Son	13	4
Distance and no space was seen	P T		30	**Send**—vapours doth he send	V A		274
See'st—What see'st thou in the ground	V A		118	I send this written ambassage	Son	26	3
			I send them back again	"	45	14
Thou see'st our mistress' ornaments	R L		322	**Send'st**—that thou send'st from thee	"	61	5
			Sense—that the sense of feeling	V A		439
Thou see'st the twilight	Son	73	5	appals her senses	"		882
thou see'st the glowing	"	73	9	her senses all dismay'd	"		896
Seething—And grew a seething bath	"	153	7	Urging the worser sense	R L		249
Seize—Seize love upon thy left	V A		158	He in the worst sense	"		324
Sits Sin, to seize the souls	R L		882	she in that sense forsook	"		1538
Seized—wolf hath .... his prey	"		677	I bring in sense	Son	35	9
he seized on my lips	P P	11	9	That my steel'd sense	"	112	8
Seizeth—With this she seizeth	V A		25	that my adder's sense	"	112	10
Seizure—on his did act the seizure	P P	11	10	My deepest sense, how hard	"	120	10
Seld—goods lost are seld or never found	"	13	7	nor my five senses can	"	141	9
			'gainst rule, 'gainst sense	L C		271
Seldom—do seldom dream on evil	R L		87	doth ravish human sense	P P	8	6
seldom to themselves appear	"		633	Doth cite each moving sense	"	15	3
yet it seldom sleeps	"		1574	**Senseless**—cold and senseless stone	V A		211
the fine point of seldom pleasure	Son	52	4	that senseless reputation	R L		820
Since, seldom coming, in the long year set	"	52	6	She tears the senseless Sinon	"		1564
			Senseless trees they cannot bear	P P	21	21
Self—Mine enemy was strong, my poor self weak	R L		1646	**Sensible**—that were but sensible	V A		436
			My woe too sensible thy passion maketh	R L		1678
Let my unsounded self	"		1819				
to thy sweet self too cruel	Son	1	8	**Sensual**—For to thy sensual fault	Son	35	9

Sensual—To any sensual feast	Son	141	8	Set—To set a form	Son	89	6
Sent—In rage sent out	R L	....	1671	Sets down her babe	"	143	3
what tributes wounded fancies sent	L C	....	197	Upon whose weeping margent she			
was sent me from a nun	"	....	232	was set	L C	....	39
Sentence—Who fears a sentence	R L	....	244	in the imagination set	"	....	136
And midst the sentence	"	....	566	And set thy person forth	P P	19	12
Sentinel—himself affection's	V A	....	650	Set'st—Thou set'st the wolf	R L	....	878
and sentinel the night	R L	....	942	Settled—Ne'er settled equally	V A	....	1139
Separable—in our lives a .... spite	Son	36	6	reasons find of settled gravity	Son	49	8
Separation—That by this separation	"	39	7	Several—each several limb	V A	....	1067
Sepulchre—His snout digs sepulchres	V A	....	622	but with several graces	R L	....	1410
				think that a several plot	Son	137	9
The right of sepulchres	Son	68	6	from many a several fair	L C	....	206
find their sepulchres in mud	L C	....	46	each several stone	"	....	216
Sepulchred—be .... in thy shade	R L	....	805	Severe—but is still severe	V A	....	1000
Sequent—In .... toil all forwards	Son	60	4	merciful and too severe	"	....	1155
Serpent—where never serpent hisses	V A	....	17	Sex—Their gentle sex to weep	R L	....	1237
Who sees the lurking serpent	R L	....	362	and sexes both enchanted	L C	....	128
Servant—Why hath thy servant Opportunity	"	....	932	Shade—smother'd up in shade	V A	....	1035
				below with his wings' shade	R L	....	507
servants to shallow fools	"	....	1016	be sepulchred in thy shade	"	....	805
bid your servant once adieu	Son	57	8	thou wander'st in his shade	Son	18	11
live thou upon thy servant's loss	"	146	9	thy shade shines so	"	43	8
Serve—Now serves the season	R L	....	166	thy fair imperfect shade	"	43	11
leisure serve with dull debaters	"	....	1019	every one, one shade	"	53	3
serve thou false Tarquin so	"	....	1197	Under a myrtle shade	P P	6	2
To serve their eyes	L C	....	135	gone to the hedge for shade	"	11	2
Serve always with assured trust	P P	19	51	Sitting in a pleasant shade	"	21	3
When time shall serve	"	19	35	Shaded—alack, too timely shaded	"	10	3
Served—Hath served a dumb arrest	R L	....	1780	Shadow—died to kiss his shadow	V A	....	162
Service—Nor services to do	Son	57	4	the shadow had forsook	"	....	176
thy service to despise	"	149	10	I'll make a shadow	"	....	191
Servile—Yet was he servile	V A	....	112	shadow to his melting buttock lent	"	....	315
Subject and servile	"	....	1161	Each shadow makes him stop	"	....	706
heartens up his servile powers	R L	....	295	Then, gentle shadow	"	....	1001
Servilely—Servilely master'd with	V A	....	392	When he beheld his shadow	"	....	1099
Serving—Serving with looks	Son	7	4	in the heart that shadows dreadeth	R L	....	270
one foolish heart from serving	"	141	10				
Servitor—as servitors to the unjust	R L	....	285	Such shadows are the weak	"	....	460
Session—When to the sessions	Son	30	1	shadows his lewd eyes affright	"	....	971
From this session interdict	P T	....	9	At his own shadow	"	....	997
Set—And being set, I'll smother	V A	....	18	On this sad shadow	"	....	1457
it will set the heart on fire	"	....	388	Presents thy shadow	Son	27	10
Set thy seal-manual	"	....	516	Whilst that this shadow	"	37	10
he hath a battle set	"	....	619	whose shadow shadows doth make	"	43	5
his breath and beauty set	"	....	935	How would thy shadow's form	"	43	6
set dissension 'twixt the son	"	....	1160	strange shadows on you tend	"	53	2
name of 'chaste' unhappily set	R L	....	8	can every shadow lend	"	53	4
To set forth that which	"	....	32	shadow of your beauty show	"	53	10
sets every joint a-shaking	"	....	452	While shadows like to thee	"	61	4
sets his foot upon the light	"	....	673	Roses of shadow	"	67	8
May set at noon	"	....	784	As with your shadow	"	98	14
the sun being set	"	....	1226	'Wander,' a word for shadows	P P	14	11
set in her mistress' sky	"	....	1230	Shadow—clouds that shadow heaven's light	V A	....	533
What wit sets down	"	....	1299				
Once set on ringing	"	....	1494	Shadow'd—His nose being	R L	....	1416
So Lucrece, set a-work	"	....	1496	Shady—And in thy shady cell	"	....	881
against my heart he set his sword	"	....	1640	dial's shady stealth mayst know	Son	77	7
With sad-set eyes and wretched arms	"	....	1662	Shag—fetlocks shag and long	V A	....	295
				Shake—Sometimes she shakes her head	"	....	223
set thy long-experienced wit	"	....	1820				
Sets you most rich in youth	Son	15	10	Shakes thee on my breast	"	....	648
in the long year set	"	52	6	make him shake and shudder	"	....	880
On Helen's cheek all art of beauty set	"	53	7	earth's foundation shakes	"	....	1047
				my frail joints shake	R L	....	227
the flourish set on youth	"	60	9	that his hand shakes withal	"	....	467
to your fair no painting set	"	83	2	shakes aloft his Roman blade	"	....	505
disposed to set me light	"	88	1	Rough winds do shake	Son	18	3
I can set down a story	"	88	6	shake hands to torture me	"	28	6

Shake—which shake against the cold	Son	73	3	Shall—' shall fit the trespass best	R L	 1613
Shaken—and is never shaken	"	116	6	Shall plight your honorable faiths	"	 1696
by my unkindness shaken	"	120	5	By my excuse shall claim	"	 1715
Shaking—Shaking her wings	V A	....	57	Where shall I live	"	 1754
Shaking their scratch'd ears	"	....	924	Shall rotten death make conquest	"	 1767
sets every joint a-shaking	R L	....	452	winters shall besiege	Son	2 1
Shall—thy lips shall never open	V A	....	48	Shall sum my count	"	2 11
one sweet kiss shall pay	"	....	84	Shall hate be fairer lodged	"	10 10
The kiss shall be thine	"	....	117	if it shall go well	"	14 7
Shall the day seem night	"	....	122	shall together thrive	"	14 11
Shall cool the heat	"	....	190	Shall I compare thee	"	18 1
No dog shall rouse thee	"	....	240	summer shall not fade	"	18 9
which way shall she turn, what				Nor shall Death brag	"	18 11
shall she say	"	....	253	love shall in my verse ever live	"	19 14
I never shall regard	"	....	377	my glass shall not persuade me	"	22 1
you shall have a kiss	"	....	536	Death my bones with dust shall		
shall we meet to-morrow	"	....	585	cover	"	32 2
Say, shall we? shall we? wilt	"	....	586	So shall those blots	"	36 3
and going I shall fall	"	....	719	thine shall be the praise	"	38 14
who shall cope him first	"	....	888	When shall I see	"	49 2
So shall I die	"	....	1074	Shall reasons find	"	49 8
hereafter shall attend	"	....	1136	no motion shall I know	"	51 8
It shall be waited on	"	....	1137	Shall neigh,—no dull flesh	"	51 11
Shall not match his woe	"	....	1140	shall excuse my jade	"	51 12
It shall be fickle	"	....	1141	When that shall vade	"	54 14
shall the truest sight beguile	"	....	1144	shall outlive this powerful rhyme	"	55 2
shall make it most weak	"	....	1145	But you shall shine	"	55 5
It shall be sparing	"	....	1147	war's quick fire shall burn	"	55 7
shall it keep in quiet	"	....	1149	Shall you pace forth; your praise		
It shall be raging-mad	"	....	1151	shall still find room	"	55 10
It shall suspect	"	....	1153	in hope my verse shall stand	"	60 13
It shall not fear	"	....	1154	Against my love shall be	"	63 1
It shall be merciful	"	....	1155	he shall never cut	"	63 11
Perverse it shall be	"	....	1157	shall in these black lines be seen	"	63 13
It shall be cause of war	"	....	1159	And they shall live	"	63 14
their loves shall not enjoy	"	....	1164	shall beauty hold a plea	"	65 3
within her bosom it shall dwell	"	....	1173	O, how shall summer's honey		
My throbbing heart shall rock thee	"	....	1186	breath hold out	"	65 5
There shall not be one minute	"	....	1187	Shall Time's best jewel from Time's		
When shall he think	R L	....	159	chest lie hid	"	65 10
Shall curse my bones	"	....	209	shall not be thy defect	"	70 1
Shall by a painted cloth be kept	"	....	245	Than you shall hear	"	71 2
My heart shall never countermand	"	....	276	Shall carry me away	"	74 2
Shall plead for me	"	....	480	with thee shall stay	"	74 4
what sorrow I shall breed	"	....	499	Shall profit thee	"	77 14
husband shall remain	"	....	519	Or I shall live	"	81 1
where Lust shall learn	"	....	617	immortal life shall have	"	81 5
wherein it shall discern	"	....	619	In men's eyes shall lie	"	81 8
shall change thy good	"	....	656	shall be my gentle verse	"	81 9
'So shall these slaves be king	"	....	659	created shall o'er-read	"	81 10
shall rudely tear thee	"	....	669	your being shall rehearse	"	81 11
shall never come	"	....	1062	You still shall live	"	81 13
He shall not boast	"	....	1063	Which shall be most my glory	"	83 10
'Nor shall he smile	"	....	1065	such a counterpart shall fame his		
My tongue shall utter all	"	....	1076	wit	"	84 11
Shall gush pure streams	"	....	1078	no more shall dwell	"	89 10
shall thereon fall and die	"	....	1139	so shall I taste	"	90 11
Shall tune our heart-strings	"	....	1141	So shall I live	"	93 1
shall for him be spent	"	....	1182	what shall be thy amends	"	101 1
shall my fame be bred	"	....	1188	what shall have no end	"	110 9
What legacy shall I bequeath	"	....	1192	Or whether shall I say	"	114 3
shall be thy boast	"	....	1193	Which shall above that idle rank		
My blood shall wash	"	....	1207	remain	"	122 3
life's fair end shall free it	"	....	1208	this shall ever be	"	123 13
my hand shall conquer thee	"	....	1210	Shall will in others seem	"	135 7
both shall victors be	"	....	1211	this shall I ne'er know	"	144 13
shall be accounted evil	"	....	1245	Shall worms, inheritors of this suc-		
which shall go before	"	....	1302	cess	"	146 7

Shall—That shall prefer	L C	280		**Shame**—what helpless shame I feel	R L		756
The truth I shall not know	P P	2	13	Dim register and notary of shame	"		765
how shall I swear to love	"	5	1	reproach to Tarquin's shame	"		816
to know thee shall suffice	"	5	7	'O unseen shame! invisible	"		827
When time shall serve	"	19	35	pleasure turns to open shame	"		890
the cock that treads them shall not know	"	19	40	to rid me of this shame	"		1031
with age shall them attain	"	19	46	So of shame's ashes	"		1188
Shallow—her husband's.... tongue	R L		78	My shame so dead	"		1190
servants to shallow fools	"		1016	My shame be his	"		1202
make lesser noise than shallow fords	"		1329	live and think no shame of me	"		1204
throws that shallow habit by	"		1814	women tenants to their shame	"		1260
By shallow rivers by whose falls	P P	20	7	and shame that might ensue	"		1263
Shallowest—Your shallowest help will hold me	Son	80	9	he blush'd to see her shame	"		1344
				else lasting shame	"		1629
Shalt—secrets shalt thou know	V A		16	my shame still rest upon record	"		1643
thou unask'd shalt have	"		102	Till manly shame bids him	"		1777
thou shalt be my deer	"		231	Were an all-eating shame	Son	2	8
and thou shalt have it	"		374	such murderous shame commits	"	9	14
Then shalt thou see	"		703	For shame! deny that thou	"	10	1
for thou shalt not rise	"		710	Nor can thy shame give physic	"	34	9
When thou shalt charge me	R L		226	guilt should do thee shame	"	36	10
Shalt have thy trespass cited up	"		524	To find out shame	"	61	7
That thou shalt see thy state	"		644	dost thou make the shame	"	95	1
Collatine, thou shalt not know	"		1058	One blushing shame	"	99	9
But thou shalt know thy interest	"		1067	To know my shames	"	112	6
Shalt oversee this will	"		1205	slander'd with a bastard shame	"	127	4
that thou shalt see it	"		1206	expense of spirit in a waste of shame	"	129	1
that thou shalt lend me	"		1685	They sought their shame and so their shame did find	L C		187
windows of thine age shalt see	Son	3	11	And so much less of shame	"		188
issueless shalt hap to die	"	9	3	'gainst rule, 'gainst sense, 'gainst shame	"		271
As fast as thou shalt wane	"	11	6				
And shalt by fortune once more re-survey	"	32	3	**Shame**—To shame the sun by day and her	V A		732
when thou shalt strangely pass	"	49	5	To shame his hope	R L		1003
and thou shalt find	"	77	10	Lucrece shames herself to see	"		1084
When thou shalt be disposed	"	88	1	live no more to shame nor me nor you	Son	72	12
shalt win much glory	"	88	8	**Shamed**—shamed with the note	R L		208
in this shalt find thy monument	"	107	13	When life is shamed	"		1155
thou shalt not boast	"	123	1	For I am shamed by that	Son	72	13
thou shalt find it merits not reproving	"	142	4	**Shameful**—Shameful it is	R L		239
So shalt thou feed on Death	"	146	13	partner in this shameful doom	"		672
'Mongst our mourners shalt thou go	P T		20	bear such shameful blows	"		832
				I murder shameful scorn	"		1189
Shame—He red for shame	V A		36	**Shamefully**—honour.... misplaced	Son	66	5
He burns with bashful shame	"		49	**Shaming**—As shaming any eye	R L		1143
Pure shame and awed resistance	"		69	**Shape**—In shape, in courage	V A		294
'Twixt crimson shame	"		76	Hast thou put on his shape	R L		597
'For shame,' he cries	"		379	Shape every bush	"		973
Forgetting shame's pure blush	"		558	And shapes her sorrow	"		1458
Cynthia for shame obscures	"		728	some shape in Sinon's was abused	"		1529
My face is full of shame	"		808	Tarquin's shape came in her mind	"		1536
beauty would blush for shame	R L		54	her husband's shape in mind	Son	9	8
When shame assail'd	"		63	Mine eyes have drawn thy shape	"	24	10
O, shame to knighthood	"		197	in every blessed shape we know	"	53	12
this surviving shame	"		223	No shape so true	"	62	6
The shame and fault finds no excuse	"		238	Of bird, of flower, or shape	"	113	6
				it shapes them to your feature	"	113	12
Covers the shame that follows	"		357	**Shapeless**—shapeless and unfinish'd	V A		415
or else some shame supposed	"		377	a hideous, shapeless devil	R L		973
What wrong, what shame	"		499	**Share**—doth share a part	Son	47	8
The shame that from them	"		535	Ah, neither be my share	P P	14	1
put on his shape to do him shame	"		597	**Sharing**—Trojan mothers.... joy	R L		1431
shame be seeded in thine age	"		603	**Sharp**—empty eagle, sharp by fast	V A		55
read lectures of such shame	"		618	Under whose sharp fangs	"		663
dishonour, shame, misgoverning	"		651	sun and sharp air	"		1085
Thou loathed in their shame	"		602	with his sharp spear	"		1112
Shame folded up	"		675	Sharp hunger by the conquest	R L		422

Sharp—under the gripe's....claws	R L	543
To keep thy sharp woes waking	"	1136
Will fix a sharp knife	"	1138
in sorrow's sharp sustaining	"	1573
More sharp to me	Son 30	12
by death's sharp sting	P P 10	4
Sharpen'd—To-morrow sharpen'd in his former might	Son 56	4
Sharp'st—blunt the sharp'st intents	" 115	7
Sharply—sharply he did think	V A	470
She—thus she began	"	7
With this she seizeth	"	25
She red and hot	"	35
Nimbly she fastens	"	38
she begins to prove	"	40
Backward she push'd him, as she would be thrust	"	41
So soon was she along	"	43
Now doth she stroke	"	45
soon she stops his lips	"	46
she with her tears	"	49
blow them dry again she seeks	"	52
He saith she is immodest	"	53
she murders with a kiss	"	54
Even so she kiss'd his brow	"	59
And where she ends she doth anew begin	"	60
She feedeth on the steam	"	63
Still she entreats	"	73
she tunes her tale	"	74
she loves him best	"	77
she cannot chuse but love	"	79
immortal hand she swears	"	80
what she did crave	"	88
she for this good turn	"	92
Her help she sees, but help she cannot get	"	93
She bathes in water	"	94
'O, pity,' 'gan she cry	"	95
She had not brought forth	"	204
she cannot right her cause	"	220
And now she weeps, and now she fain would speak	"	221
she shakes her head	"	223
Now gazeth she on him	"	224
She would, he will not	"	226
She locks her lily fingers	"	228
'Foudling,' she saith	"	229
how doth she now	"	240
shall she turn? what shall she say	"	253
'Pity,' she cries, 'some favour	"	257
And forth she rushes	"	262
She answers him, as if she knew his mind	"	308
She puts on outward strangeness	"	310
that she is so nigh	"	341
How she came stealing	"	344
Now was she just before him	"	349
down she kneels	"	350
she heaveth up his hat	"	351
she takes him by the hand	"	361
'Give me my heart,' saith she	"	374
Thus she replies	"	385
quoth she, 'hast thou a tongue	"	427
advisedly she marketh	"	457
she flatly falleth down	"	463
believing she is dead	"	467
on the grass she lies as she were slain	"	473
She—and she by her good will	V A	479
faintly she upheaveth	"	482
'O, where am I?' quoth she	"	493
'Good-night,' quoth she	"	537
she faint with dearth	"	545
glutton-like she feeds	"	548
she will draw his lips	"	552
she begins to forage	"	554
she takes all she can, not all she listeth	"	564
O, had she then gave over	"	571
she had not suck'd	"	572
she can no more detain him	"	577
She is resolved no longer	"	579
by Cupid's bow she doth protest	"	581
'Sweet boy,' she says	"	583
'The boar!' quoth she	"	589
she trembles at his tale	"	591
yoking arms she throws	"	592
She sinketh down	"	593
she on her back	"	594
Now is she in the very lists	"	595
imaginary she doth prove	"	597
so she languisheth	"	603
which she in him finds missing	"	605
She seeks to kindle	"	606
She hath assay'd	"	608
She's Love, she loves, and yet she is not loved	"	610
hadst been gone,' quoth she	"	613
what of that?' quoth she	"	717
'In night,' quoth she	"	720
Lest she should steal	"	726
Wherein she framed thee	"	731
hath she bribed the Destinies	"	733
after him she darts	"	817
In the dark she lay	"	827
now she beats her heart	"	829
'Ay me!' she cries	"	833
She, marking them, begins	"	835
who hath she to spend	"	847
She says '"Tis so;' they answer if she said 'No	"	851
	"	852
This said, she hasteth	"	863
yet she hears no tidings	"	867
She hearkens for his hounds	"	868
Anon she hears them	"	869
she coasteth to the cry	"	870
And as she runs	"	871
She wildly breaketh	"	874
she hears the hounds	"	877
Whereat she starts	"	878
For now she knows	"	883
Thus stands she	"	895
She tells them 'tis	"	897
with that word she spied	"	900
she knows not whither	"	904
This way she runs, and now she will no further	"	905
She treads the path that she untreads	"	908
She finds a hound	"	913
here she meets another	"	917
To whom she speaks	"	918
she at these sad signs draws up	"	929
thus chides she Death	"	932
She vail'd her eyelids	"	956
far off she hears	"	973
Imagination she did follow	"	975

She—when she seemeth drown'd	V A	984	She—She stays, exclaiming	R L	741
she unweaves the web that she hath wrought	"	991	She there remains	"	744
It was not she that call'd	"	993	She prays she never may behold	"	746
Now she adds honours	"	994	'For day,' quoth she	"	747
She clepes him king	"	995	Here she exclaims	"	757
'No, no,' quoth she	"	997	She wakes her heart	"	759
she doth extenuate	"	1010	thus breathes she forth	"	762
she humbly doth insinuate	"	1012	from her be-tumbled couch she starteth	"	1037
'O Jove,' quoth she	"	1015	'In vain,' quoth she	"	1044
she hears a merry horn	"	1025	where she sits weeping	"	1087
Whereat she leaps	"	1026	To whom she sobbing speaks	"	1088
to the lure, away she flies	"	1027	Thus cavils she with every thing she sees	"	1093
she treads on it so light	"	1028	So she, deep-drenched	"	1100
doth she hang her head	"	1058	each thing she views	"	1101
Dumbly she passions, franticly she doteth	"	1059	'You mocking birds,' quoth she	"	1121
She thinks he could not	"	1060	is she in mutiny	"	1153
she looks so steadfastly	"	1063	'To kill myself,' quoth she	"	1156
And then she reprehends	"	1065	when sadly she had laid	"	1212
'And yet,' quoth she	"	1070	she hoarsely calls her maid	"	1214
With this, she falleth in the place she stood	"	1121	Her mistress she doth give	"	1219
She looks upon his lips	"	1123	'My girl,' quoth she	"	1270
She takes him by the hand	"	1124	and there she stay'd	"	1275
She whispers in his ears	"	1125	She would request	"	1283
woeful words she told	"	1126	she prepares to write	"	1296
She lifts the coffer-lids	"	1127	At last she thus begins	"	1303
'Wonder of time,' quoth she	"	1133	Here folds she up	"	1310
She bows her head	"	1171	She dares not thereof make discovery	"	1314
She crops the stalk	"	1175	Ere she with blood had stain'd	"	1316
which she compares to tears	"	1176	She hoards, to spend	"	1318
'Poor flower,' quoth she	"	1177	she would not blot the letter	"	1322
weary of the world, away she hies	"	1189	she delivers it	"	1333
she securely gives	R L	89	dull and slow she deems	"	1335
But she that never coped	"	99	She thought he blush'd	"	1354
She touch'd no unknown baits	"	103	The more she saw	"	1357
Nor could she moralize	"	104	The more she thought	"	1358
she doth express	"	111	But long she thinks	"	1359
but she is not her own	"	241	she cannot entertain	"	1361
She took me kindly	"	253	That she her plaints a little while	"	1364
her husband's welfare she did hear	"	263	she calls to mind	"	1366
Whereat she smiled	"	264	Many she sees	"	1445
seen her as she stood	"	265	Till she despairing Hecuba beheld	"	1447
But she, sound sleeping	"	363	Of what she was	"	1453
that she reflects so bright	"	376	'Poor instrument,' quoth she	"	1464
a virtuous monument, she lies	"	391	Here feelingly she weeps	"	1492
she is dreadfully beset	"	444	She lends them words, and she their looks doth borrow	"	1498
She, much amazed, breaks ope	"	446			
That thinks she hath beheld	"	451	She throws her eyes about	"	1499
but she, in worser taking	"	453	And who she finds forlorn she doth lament	"	1500
she trembling lies	"	457			
She dares not look	"	458	At last she sees	"	1501
But she with vehement prayers	"	475	she advisedly perused	"	1527
While she, the picture	"	542	on him she gazed	"	1531
She puts the period	"	565	in his plain face she spied	"	1532
That thrice she doth begin ere once she speaks	"	567	That she concludes	"	1533
			'It cannot be,' quoth she	"	1534
She conjures him	"	568	She would have said	"	1535
Quoth she, 'Reward not hospitality	"	575	she in that sense forsook	"	1558
'Thou art,' quoth she	"	632	She tears the senseless Sinon	"	1564
linen that she wears	"	680	At last she smilingly	"	1567
But she hath lost	"	687	'Fool, fool!' quoth she	"	1568
how she fares	"	721	She looks for night, and then she longs for morrow	"	1571
She says, her subjects	"	722			
she controlled still	"	727	And both she thinks too long	"	1572
She bears the load	"	734	That she with painted images	"	1577
She like a wearied lamb	"	737	how she fares	"	1594
she, desperate, with her nails	"	739	she gives her sorrow fire	"	1604

Phrase	Ref	Col1	Col2
She—she can discharge	R L	.....	1605
She modestly prepares	"	.....	1607
'Few words,' quoth she	"	.....	1613
Which speechless woe of his poor she attendeth	"	.....	1674
For she that was	"	.....	1682
you fair lords,' quoth she	"	.....	1688
But she that yet	"	.....	1699
'O, speak,' quoth she	"	.....	1700
with a joyless smile she turns away	"	.....	1711
'No, no,' quoth she	"	.....	1714
She throws forth Tarquin's name; 'He, he,' she says	"	.....	1717
She utters this	"	.....	1721
Even here she sheathed	"	.....	1723
The father says 'She's mine.' 'O, mine is she	"	.....	1795
for she was only mine	"	.....	1798
Which she too early	"	.....	1801
'she was my wife	"	.....	1802
that she hath kill'd	"	.....	1803
where is she so fair	Son	3	5
and she in thee	"	3	9
she lends to those	"	4	4
whom she best endow'd she gave the more	"	11	11
She carved thee for her seal	"	11	13
as she wrought thee	"	20	10
But since she prick'd thee out	"	20	13
till she have prevailed	"	41	8
That she hath thee	"	42	3
so doth she abuse me	"	42	7
she loves but me alone	"	42	14
she hath no exchequer	"	67	11
O, him she stores, to show what wealth she had	"	67	13
She keeps thee	"	126	7
She may detain	"	126	10
when she walks	"	130	12
As any she belied with false	"	130	14
she is made of truth	"	138	1
though I know she lies	"	138	2
That she might think	"	138	3
she thinks me young	"	138	5
Although she knows	"	138	6
wherefore says she not she is unjust	"	138	9
and she with me	"	138	13
she turns my foes	"	139	11
That she that makes me sin	"	141	14
the thing she would have stay	"	143	4
she saw my woeful state	"	145	4
'I hate' she alter'd	"	145	9
hate away she threw	"	145	13
brand she quenched	"	154	9
Oft did she heave her napkin	L C	.....	15
from a maund she drew	"	.....	26
one by one she in a river threw	"	.....	38
Upon whose weeping margent she was set	"	.....	39
schedules had she many a one	"	.....	43
Which she perused, sigh'd	"	.....	44
bathed she in her fluxive eye	"	.....	50
In top of rage the lines she rents	"	.....	55
'Father,' she says, 'though in me	"	.....	71
in his fair parts she did abide	"	.....	83
She was new lodged	"	.....	84
she must herself away	"	.....	156
For she was sought	"	.....	236
She that her fame	"	.....	243
She—she would the caged cloister fly	L C	.....	249
would she be immured	"	.....	251
swears that she is made of truth	P P	1	1
though I know she lies	"	1	2
That she might think me	"	1	3
that she thinks me young	"	1	5
says my love that she is young	"	1	9
She told him stories	"	4	5
She show'd him favour	"	4	6
she touch'd him here and there	"	4	7
Then fell she on her back	"	4	13
she hotter that did look	"	6	7
'O Jove,' quoth she	"	6	14
how often hath she joined	"	7	7
to please me hath she coined	"	7	9
She burn'd with love	"	7	13
She burn'd out love	"	7	14
She framed the love, and yet she foil'd the framing	"	7	15
She bade love last, and yet she fell a-turning	"	7	16
Her stand she takes	"	9	5
She, silly queen	"	9	7
'Once,' quoth she, 'did I see	"	9	9
'See, in my thigh,' quoth she	"	9	12
She showed hers	"	9	13
She told the youngling	"	11	3
so fell she to him	"	11	4
'Even thus,' quoth she	"	11	5
And then she clipp'd Adonis	"	11	6
'Even thus,' quoth she	"	11	7
'Even thus,' quoth she	"	11	9
And as she fetched breath	"	11	11
She bade good-night	"	14	2
'Farewell,' quoth she	"	14	5
sweetly did she smile	"	14	7
she joy'd to jest at my exile	"	14	9
For she doth welcome	"	15	7
For why, she sigh'd	"	15	12
Alas, she could not help it	"	16	12
Lest she some subtle practice smell	"	19	9
too late she will repent	"	19	15
with scorn she put away	"	19	18
though she strive to try her strength	"	19	19
though she put thee back	"	19	36
She will not stick to round me	"	19	51
Yet will she blush	"	19	53
She, poor bird, as all forlorn	"	21	9
now would she cry	"	21	13
Beauty brag, but 'tis not she	P T	.....	63
Sheathed—tushes never sheathed	V A	.....	617
Sheathed unaware the tusk	"	.....	1116
had sheathed their light	R L	.....	397
she sheathed in her harmless breast	"	.....	1723
Sheave—all girded up in sheaves	Son	12	7
Sheaved—descended her .... hat	L C	.....	31
Shed—fresh flowers being shed			
ever modest eyes with sorrow shed	R L	.....	683
Shed for the slaughter'd husband	"	.....	1376
borrow'd tears that Sinon sheds	V A	.....	1549
which thy love sheds	Son	34	13
Sheep—sheep are gone to fold	V A	.....	532
among a flock of sheep	"	.....	685
Sheet—Teaching the sheets	"	.....	398
Who o'er the white sheet peers	R L	.....	472
Shelly—backward in his shelly cave	V A	.....	1034
Shelter—To .... thee from tempest	"	.....	235
Shelve—strong pirates, shelves, and sands	R L	.....	335

Shepherd—Sorrow to shepherds	V. A.	455
to Phrygian shepherds lent	R L	1592
O sweet shepherd, hie thee	P P	12 11
My shepherd's pipe can sound	"	18 27
see the shepherds feed their flocks	"	20 6
truth in every shepherd's tongue	"	20 18
Shield—His batter'd shield	V. A.	104
and call'd it then their shield	R L	61
Shielded—I mine honour shielded	L C	151
Shift—Danger deviseth shifts	V. A.	690
And as one shifts	R L	1104
treason, forgery, and shift	"	920
Shifts but his place	Son	9 10
Shifting—With shifting change	"	20 4
Quick-shifting antics, ugly	R L	459
injurious, shifting Time	"	930
Shine—The sun that shines from heaven shines but warm	V. A.	193
shine when he doth fret	"	621
too hot the eye of heaven shines	Son	18 5
one early morn did shine	"	33 9
thy shade shines so	"	43 8
But you shall shine	"	55 3
my love may still shine bright	"	65 14
no fair acceptance shine	"	135 8
that on this earth doth shine	P P	3 10
shine, sun, to succour flowers	"	15 16
So between them love did shine	P T	33
Shine—borrow'd all their shine	V. A.	488
obscures her silver shine	"	728
Shining—shining star doth borrow	"	861
read the subtle-shining secrecies	R L	101
and to shining arms	"	197
The silver-shining queen	"	786
burnt the shining glory	"	1523
With shining falchion	"	1626
A shining gloss that vadeth	P P	13 2
Shiver'd—And .... all the beauty	R L	1763
Shock—forces, shocks, and fears	L C	273
Shone—Shone like the moon	V. A.	492
Shook—shook three summers' pride	Son	104 4
Shook off my sober guards	L C	298
Shoot—to over-shoot his troubles	V. A.	680
before thy shoot be ended	R L	579
join and shoot their foam	"	1442
But shoot not at me	Son	117 12
Shooteth—Shooteth from the sky	V. A.	815
Shop—Which in my bosom's shop	Son	24 7
Shore—as one on shore	V. A.	817
to drown in ken of shore	R L	1114
To break upon the galled shore	"	1440
Which parts the shore	Son	56 10
make towards the pebbled shore	"	60 1
on the kingdom of the shore	"	64 6
Shorn—right of sepulchres were shorn away	"	68 6
Short—Ten kisses short as one	V. A.	22
an hour but short	"	53
High crest, short ears	"	297
His short thick neck	"	627
though seeming short	"	842
makes short their pilgrimage	R L	791
and how swift and short	"	991
By this short schedule	"	1312
Short time seems long	"	1573
sick and short assays	"	1720
hath all too short a date	Son	18 4
quilt doth come too short	"	83 7
more short than waste or ruining	"	125 4
Short—having so short a lease	Son	146 5
age's breath is short	P P	12 5
Short—Short, night, to-night, and length thyself to-morrow	"	15 18
Short-jointed—Round-hoof'd, ...	V. A.	295
Short-number'd—leases of short-number'd hours	Son	124 10
Shot—And little stars shot	R L	1525
Should—should not be wasted	V. A.	139
As who should say	"	280
the living should exceed	"	292
what a horse should have	"	299
Thy palfrey, as he should	"	385
Yet should I be in love	"	438
Should by his stealing in disturb	"	450
that the debt should double	"	521
I thy death should fear	"	660
What should I do	"	667
Lest she should steal	"	726
harmony should run	"	781
at him should have fled	"	947
who should best become	"	968
as scorning it should pass	"	982
where no breach should be	"	1066
should dry his tears	"	1092
the day should yet be light	"	1134
should most mistrust	"	1151
he should keep unknown	R L	34
meaner men should vaunt	"	41
should underprop her fame	"	53
the reed should fence the white	"	63
it should be kill'd	"	74
respect should have	"	201
As who should say	"	320
should countenance his sin	"	343
should govern every thing	"	602
The lesser thing should not	"	663
should stain so pure a bed	"	684
Her tears should drop	"	683
should not peep again	"	788
So should I have	"	789
'Why should the worm intrude	"	848
wretched blood should spill	"	999
should thee behold	"	1143
'if it should be told	"	1284
What should I say	"	1291
Lest he should hold	"	1315
'Why should the private pleasure	"	1478
why should so many fall	"	1483
perjury should thrust	"	1517
should bear a wicked mind	"	1540
I should not live	"	1612
So should my shame	"	1643
should right poor ladies' harms	"	1694
that should survive	"	1764
should his use control	"	1784
Who should weep most	"	1792
that should have slain her foe	"	1827
should by time decease	Son	1 3
that face should form another	"	3 2
to repair should be thy chief desire	"	10 8
the times should cease	"	11 7
you should prepare	"	13 3
So should that beauty	"	13 5
your sweet form should bear	"	13 8
So should the lines of life	"	16 9
So should my papers	"	17 9
You should live twice	"	17 11
death my days should expiate	"	22 4

Should—guilt should do thee shame	Son	36	10
distance should not stop my way	"	44	2
why should I haste me	"	51	3
Then should I spur	"	51	7
Thy edge should blunter be	"	56	2
what should I do but tend	"	57	1
I should in thought control	"	58	2
image should keep open	"	61	1
slumbers should be broken	"	61	3
with infection should he live	"	67	1
advantage should achieve	"	67	3
Why should false painting	"	67	5
Why should poor beauty	"	67	7
Why should he live	"	67	9
then should make you woe	"	71	8
world should look into your moan	"	71	13
the world should task you	"	72	1
that you should love	"	72	2
And so should you	"	72	14
Which should example	"	84	4
should do it wrong	"	89	11
love should ever dwell	"	93	10
Thy looks should nothing	"	93	12
should afterwards burn clear	"	115	4
I should your great deserts repay	"	117	2
Which should transport	"	117	8
For why should others' false	"	121	5
beauty should look so	"	127	14
should that harvest reap	"	128	7
Why should my heart	"	137	9
For, if I should despair, I should grow mad	"	140	9
foul faults should find	"	148	14
What I should do again	L C		322
he should not pass those grounds	P P	9	8
before the fall should be	"	10	6
should use like loving charms	"	11	8
Shoulder—Over one shoulder	V A		1058
Shouldst—thou shouldst think it	"		156
why shouldst thou feed	"		169
shouldst contemn me	"		205
thou shouldst strike at it	"		938
If thou shouldst depart	Son	6	11
the parts that thou shouldst bear	"	8	8
thou shouldst in bounty cherish	"	11	12
Thou shouldst print more	"	11	14
kingdoms of hearts shouldst owe	"	70	14
shouldst not abhor my state	"	150	12
the deer that thou shouldst strike	P P	19	2
Show—Shows thee unripe	V A		128
Shows his hot courage	"		276
it shows most toward	"		1157
his barren skill to show	R L		81
shows like a virtuous deed	"		252
demeanour seeks to show	"		474
The light will show	"		807
To show the beldam daughters	"		933
to show the painter's strife	"		1377
Show me the strumpet	"		1471
some watery token shows	"		1748
Shows me a bare-boned death	"		1761
To show her bleeding body	"		1851
shows not half your parts	Son	17	4
not to show my wit	"	26	4
in wanting words to show it	"	26	6
To show me worthy	"	26	12
Till then not show my head	"	26	14
In whom all ill well shows	"	40	13
when dreams do show thee me	"	43	14

Show—shadow of your beauty show	Son	53	10
Show me your image	"	59	7
shows me myself indeed	"	62	9
to show what wealth she had	"	67	13
To show false Art	"	68	14
Thy glass will show thee	"	77	1
thy glass will truly show	"	77	5
being extant well might show	"	83	6
the thing they most do show	"	94	2
long hence as he shows now	"	101	14
such a scope to show her pride	"	103	2
Your own glass shows you	"	103	14
Nor my beloved as an idol show	"	105	2
outward form would show it dead	"	108	14
Show—No cloudy show	R L		115
their leader's jocund show	"		296
and give the harmless show	"		1307
He entertain'd a show	"		1514
in shows of discontent	"		1580
wound his folly's show	"		1810
Leese but their show	Son	5	14
presenteth nought but shows	"	15	3
shadow's form form happy show	"	43	6
their virtue only is their show	"	54	9
thy odour matcheth not thy show	"	69	13
suspect of ill mask'd not thy show	"	70	13
virtue answer not thy show	"	93	14
less the show appear	"	102	2
Small show of man	L C		92
swound at tragic shows	"		308
Dissembled with an outward show	P P	19	38
Showed—Show'd like two silver doves	V A		366
Show'd like an April daisy	R L		395
Show'd deep regard	"		1400
Show'd life imprison'd	"		1456
full of cares, yet show'd content	"		1503
Yet show'd his visage	L C		96
She show'd him favours	P P	4	6
She showed hers	"	9	13
Shower—With such distilling showers	V A		66
with showers of silver brine	R L		796
Or as sweet-season'd showers	Son	75	2
nor drowns with showers	"	124	12
Show'st—grown, and therein show'st	"	126	3
Showing—Showing their birth	"	76	8
Showing life's triumph	R L		402
Showing fair nature	L C		311
Shown—farther than the eye hath shown	Son	69	8
my deeds must not be shown	"	121	12
For her griefs so lively shown	P P	21	17
Shrewd—Thy eyes' shrewd tutor	V A		500
Shriek—night's herald, shrieks	"		531
shriek to see him there	R L		307
Shrieking—As often shrieking	L C		20
But thou shrieking harbinger	P T		5
Shrill-tongued—Like .... tapsters	V A		849
Shrine—incense to so pure a shrine	R L		194
Shrink—Shrinks backward in his shelly cave	V A		1034
Shrub—stoops not to the base shrub's foot	R L		664
But low shrubs wither	"		665
Shrunk—those shrunk pipes had fed	"		1455
Shudder—make him shake and	V A		880
Shun—prevent this storm and shun thy wrack	R L		966

| SHUN | 255 | SIGN |

Shun—To shun this blot	*R L* 1322	
We sicken to shun sickness	*Son* 118 4	
To shun the heaven	" 129 14	
her noble suit in court did shun	*L C* 234	
Shunn'd—who ever shunn'd by precedent	" 155	
Shut—That shuts him from the heaven	*R L* 338	
Sick—By this, the love-sick queen began	*V A* 175	
That love-sick Love by pleading	" 328	
For my sick heart	" 584	
by brain-sick rude desire	*R L* 175	
To one sore sick	" 762	
unwholesome breaths make sick	" 779	
Give physic to the sick	" 901	
sick and short assays	" 1720	
And my sick Muse	*Son* 79 4	
I was not sick of any fear	" 86 12	
And sick of welfare	" 118 7	
him that so fell sick of you	" 118 14	
As testy sick men	" 140 7	
I, sick withal, the help of bath desired	" 153 11	
That the lover, sick to death	*P P* 17 7	
Sicken—We sicken to shun sickness	*Son* 118 4	
Sickle—Within his bending sickle's compass come	" 116 10	
Time's fickle glass, his sickle, hour	" 126 2	
Sickly—The uncertain sickly appetite	" 147 4	
their sickly radiance do amend	*L C* 214	
Sickness—marrow-eating sickness	*V A* 741	
We sicken to shun sickness	*Son* 118 4	
Sick-thoughted—.... Venus	*V A* 5	
Side—and by Venus' side	" 180	
His brawny sides	" 625	
by her side lay kill'd	" 1165	
Collatine again by Lucrece' side	*R L* 381	
Swelling on either side	" 389	
for standing by her side	" 425	
her body in on every side	" 1739	
pluck'd the knife from Lucrece' side	" 1807	
than spurring to his side	*Son* 50 12	
Upon thy side against myself	" 88 3	
On both sides thus	" 138 8	
my better angel from my side	" 144 6	
fall by thy side	" 151 12	
Laid by his side	" 154 2	
sits he by her side	*L C* 65	
on this side the verdict went	" 113	
my better angel from my side	*P P* 2 6	
Siege—Remove your siege	*V A* 423	
This siege that hath engirt	*R L* 221	
Against the wreckful siege	*Son* 65 6	
Sigh—Then with her windy sighs	*V A* 51	
sighs can never grave it	" 376	
Sorrow that friendly sighs sought	" 964	
Sighs dry her cheeks	" 966	
My sighs are blown away	" 1071	
eloquence with sighs is mixed	*R L* 563	
My sighs, like whirlwinds	" 586	
my tears, my sighs, my groans	" 588	
When sighs and groans and tears	" 1319	
Three times with sighs	" 1604	
Even so his sighs	" 1672	
Here with a sigh	" 1716	
Her contrite sighs	" 1727	
Sigh—with sighs himself doth smother	*Son* 47 4	
Hallow'd with sighs	*L C* 228	
their sighs to you extend	" 276	
My sighs so deep	*P P* 18 31	
How sighs resound	" 18 34	
Sigh—I'll sigh celestial breath	*V A* 189	
For now 'tis stale to sigh	*R L* 1362	
I sigh the lack of many a thing	*Son* 30 3	
For these dead birds sigh a prayer	*P T* 67	
Sigh'd—sigh'd, tore, and gave the flood	*L C* 44	
For why she sigh'd	*P P* 15 12	
Sighing—And sighing it again	*V A* 930	
Sight—our sport is not in sight	" 124	
o'erwhelming his fair sight	" 183	
with his proud sight agrees	" 288	
O, what a sight it was	" 343	
that did feed her sight	" 822	
That her sight dazzling	" 1064	
He fed them with his sight	" 1104	
the truest sight beguile	" 1144	
like a vapour from her sight	" 1166	
moralize his wanton sight	*R L* 104	
a cloud, bereaves our sight	" 373	
Lucrece to their sight	" 384	
The sight which makes supposed terror	" 455	
daunts them with more dreadful sights	" 462	
To see sad sights moves more	" 1324	
beguiled attention, charm'd the sight	" 1404	
to his new-appearing sight	*Son* 7 3	
rich in youth before my sight	" 15 10	
my soul's imaginary sight	" 27 9	
expense of many a vanish'd sight	" 30 8	
stand against thy sight	" 38 6	
the conquest of thy sight	" 46 2	
thy picture's sight would bar	" 46 3	
thy picture in my sight	" 47 13	
like to thee do mock my sight	" 61 4	
or vanish'd out of sight	" 63 7	
all full with feasting on your sight	" 75 9	
the rudest or gentlest sight	" 113 9	
transport me farthest from your sight	" 117 8	
dressings of a former sight	" 123 4	
but in my sight	" 139 5	
no correspondence with true sight	" 148 2	
give the lie to my true sight	" 150 3	
The mind and sight distractedly	*L C* 28	
Weak sights their sickly radiance	" 214	
Whose sights till then	" 282	
eyes their wished sight	*P P* 15 10	
Flaming in the phoenix' sight	*P T* 35	
Sighted—Thick-sighted, barren, lean	*V A* 136	
Sightless—Poor grooms are sightless night	*R L* 1013	
thy shadow to my sightless view	*Son* 27 10	
on sightless eyes doth stay	" 43 12	
Sign—Saw'st thou not signs	*V A* 644	
signs and prodigies	" 926	
at these sad signs	" 929	
such signs of rage they bear	*R L* 1419	
Such signs of truth	" 1532	
Before these bastard signs	*Son* 68 3	
These are certain signs to know	*P P* 21 57	

SILENCE 256 SING

Silence—This silence for my sin *Son* 83 9
  of my silence cannot boast " 86 11
  Excuse not silence so " 101 10
Silent—This silent war of lilies *R L* 71
  In silent wonder " 84
  what silent love hath writ *Son* 23 13
  the sessions of sweet silent thought " 30 1
Silk—With sleided silk *L C* 48
Silken—Laundering the .... figures " 17
  their silken parcels burls " ..... '87
Silly—The silly boy, believing *V A* 467
  a weak and silly mind " 1016
  fright the silly lamb " 1098
  The silly lambs *R L* 167
  When, silly groom! God wot " 1345
  She, silly queen, with more *P P* 9 7
  Unto the silly damsel " 16 8
  One silly cross " 18 13
Silly-jeering—As .... idiots *R L* 1812
Silly-mild—raging-mad and .... *V A* 1151
Silver—like two silver doves " 366
  obscure her silver shine " 728
  from whose silver breast " 855
  breaks the silver rain " 950
  yokes the silver doves " 1190
  Their silver cheeks *R L* 61
  that hides the silver moon " 371
  with showers of silver brine " 796
  The stain upon his silver down " 1012
  his beard all silver-white " 1405
  and silver fountains mud *Son* 35 2
Silver'd—all silver'd o'er with white " 12 4
Silver-melting—morning's....dew *R L* 24
Silver-shining—The .... queen " 786
Silver-white—stain that o'er with
  silver-white " 56
Simile—Take all these similes *L C* 227
Simois—To Simois' reedy banks *R L* 1437
  shoot their foam at Simois' banks " 1442
Simple—in a tomb so simple *V A* 244
  Under whose simple semblance " 795
  simple truth miscall'd simplicity *Son* 66 11
  foregoing simple savour " 125 7
  thus is simple truth supprest " 138 8
  Who, young and simple *L C* 320
  And was my own fee-simple " 144
  Simple were so well compounded *P T* 44
Simple—The poisonous simple some-
  time is compacted *R L* 530
Simplicity—simple truth miscall'd
  simplicity *Son* 66 11
  Grace in all simplicity *P T* 54
Simply—Simply I credit *Son* 138 7
Sin—Hiding base sin *R L* 93
  and hold it for no sin " 209
  should countenance his sin " 343
  The blackest sin is clear'd " 354
  Authority for sin " 620
  by thy fault foul sin may say " 629
  deeper sin than bottomless conceit " 701
  To have their unseen sin " 753
  Whoever plots the sin " 879
  Sits Sin to seize the souls " 882
  but Sin ne'er gives a fee " 913
  To all sins past " 923
  sin's pack-horse, virtue's snare " 928
  My sable ground of sin " 1074
  Let sin, alone committed " 1480
  To plague a private sin " 1481

Sin—Or blot with hell-born sin *R L* 1519
  Excusing thy sins more than thy
  sins are *Son* 35 8
  Sin of self-love possesseth all mine
  eye " 62 1
  for this sin there is no remedy " 62 3
  That sin by him advantage should " 67 3
  This silence for my sin " 83 9
  dost thou thy sins inclose " 95 4
  'tis the lesser sin " 114 13
  Love is my sin " 142 1
  Hate of my sin " 142 2
Sin—He learn'd to sin *R L* 630
  she that makes me sin *Son* 141 14
  To sin and never for to saint *P P* 19 44
Since—since eyes in eyes *V A* 120
  since I have homm'd thee here " 229
  since I am such a park " 239
  Since sweating Lust on earth
  usurp'd " 794
  Since her best work is ruin'd " 954
  Since thou art dead " 1135
  Since he himself is reft " 1174
  Since thou art guilty *R L* 772
  guilty of my death since of my
  crime " 931
  Since that my case is past " 1022
  Since thou couldst not defend " 1034
  Since men prove beasts " 1148
  And ever since, as pitying " 1747
  Since Rome herself in them " 1833
  Since sweets and beauties do them-
  selves forsake *Son* 12 11
  But since she prick'd thee out " 20 13
  But since he died " 32 13
  Since why to love I can allege " 49 14
  Since from thee going " 51 13
  Since, seldom coming " 52 6
  Since every one hath " 53 3
  Since mind at first " 59 8
  Since brass, nor stone, nor earth " 65 1
  since his rose is true " 67 8
  Since what he owes thee " 79 14
  But since your worth " 80 5
  Since that my life " 92 10
  Since first I saw you fresh " 104 8
  Since all alike my songs " 105 3
  Since, spite of him, I'll live " 107 11
  Since I left you " 113 1
  Since my appeal says " 117 13
  For since each hand " 127 5
  Since saucy jacks so happy are " 128 13
  since mourning doth thee grace " 132 11
  but since I am near slain " 139 13
  Since I their altar *L C* 224
  Since that our faults in love *P P* 1 14
Since—Of things long since, or *V A* 1078
  love's long-since-cancell'd woe *Son* 30 7
  In days long since " 67 14
Sinew—all her sinews spread *V A* 767
Sinewy—Whose sinewy neck " 903
  .... " 99
Sinful—Were it not sinful then *Son* 103 9
  grounded on sinful loving " 142 2
  the centre of my sinful earth " 146 1
Sing—the high wind sings *V A* 305
  and sings extemporally " 836
  That some would sing " 1102
  birds more cause to sing *R L* 333

Sing—where the sweet birds sing	*R L*	871
one pleasing note do sing	*Son* 8	12
Sings this to thee	" 8	14
sings hymns at heaven's gate	" 29	12
with manners may I sing	" 39	1
taught the dumb on high to sing	" 78	5
Or, if they sing	" 97	13
Sing to the ear	" 100	7
in summer's front doth sing	" 102	7
skill enough your worth to sing	" 106	12
To sing heaven's praise	*P P* 5	14
While Philomela sits and sings	" 15	5
Sweet birds sing not	" 18	38
Melodious birds sing madrigals	" 20	8
Beasts did leap and birds did sing	" 21	5
All thy fellow birds do sing	" 21	25
Sing'st—Philomel that sing'st of ravishment	*R L*	1128
thou sing'st not in the night	"	1142
Singing—to singing he betakes	*P P* 8	12
Single—Die single, and thine image dies with thee	*Son* 3	14
'Thou single wilt prove none	" 8	14
consumest thyself in single life	" 9	2
lose name of single one	" 39	6
Single nature's double name	*P T*	39
Singled—till they have singled	*V A*	693
Singleness—In singleness the parts	*Son* 8	8
Singular—that which is so singular	*R L*	32
Sink—Not gross to sink	*V A*	150
Sinks down to death	*Son* 45	8
Sinketh—She sinketh down	*V A*	593
Sinking—Then who fears sinking where such treasure lies	*R L*	280
Sinon—perjured Sinon, whose enchanting story	"	1521
some shape in Sinon's was abused	"	1529
subtle Sinon here is painted	"	1541
borrow'd tears that Sinon sheds	"	1549
For Sinon in his fire	"	1556
false Sinon's tears doth flatter	"	1560
She tears the senseless Sinon	"	1564
Sire—Or butcher-sire that reaves	*V A*	766
dissension 'twixt the son and sire	"	1160
a more sweet-smelling sire	"	1178
kill'd my son or sire	*R L*	232
The sire, the son, the dame	"	1477
Resembling sire and child	*Son* 8	11
Siren—have I drunk of Siren tears	" 119	1
Sister—Or sister sanctified	*L C*	233
the sister and the brother	*P P* 8	2
Sistering—from a sistering vale	*L C*	2
Sit—Here come and sit	*V A*	17
chafing, down Adonis sits	"	325
doves that sit a-billing	"	366
up in shade doth sit	"	1035
her heavenly image sits	*R L*	288
In the self-same seat sits Collatine	"	289
alone must sit and pine	"	795
like still-pining Tantalus he sits	"	858
Sits Sin to seize the souls	"	882
where she sits weeping	".	1087
in that bosom sits	*Son* 9	13
in thy parts do crowned sit	" 37	7
than in my verse can sit	" 103	13
sits he by her side	*L C*	65
Philomela sits and sings, I sit and mark	*P P* 15	5
There will we sit	" 20	5

Sith—Sith in thy pride so fair a hope	*V A*	762
Sith in his prime death doth	"	1163
Sitting—Sweet Cytherea, sitting by a brook	*P P* 4	1
with young Adonis sitting by her	" 11	1
Sitting in a pleasant shade	" 21	9
Situation—And situation with those dancing chips	*Son* 128	10
Size—In clamours of all size	*L C*	21
Skilful—Of skilful painting	*R L*	1367
Skill—far exceeds his barren skill	"	81
drowns for want of skill	"	1099
on Tereus descant'st better skill	"	1134
by force, by fraud, or skill	"	1243
labour'd with his skill	"	1506
for his wondrous skill	"	1528
drawn by your own sweet skill	*Son* 16	14
must you see his skill	" 24	5
folly doctor-like controlling skill	" 66	10
some in their skill	" 91	1
both skill and argument	" 100	8
They had not skill enough	" 106	12
to this purpose, that her skill	" 126	7
strength and warrantise of skill	" 150	7
the dialect and different skill	*L C*	125
Skill-contending—in .... schools	*R L*	1018
Skill'd—well-skill'd workman	"	1520
Skin—her alabaster skin	"	419
on that termless skin	*L C*	94
Skip—away he skips	*P P* 11	11
Sky—draw me through the sky	*V A*	153
when they blot the sky	"	184
as lightning from the sky	"	348
sun glorifies the sky	"	485
chase were in the skies	"	696
shooteth from the sky	"	815
through the empty skies	"	1191
in that sky of his delight	*R L*	11
a falcon towering in the skies	"	506
to the skies and ground	"	1199
suns set in her mistress' sky	"	1230
which purl'd up to the sky	"	1407
that the skies were sorry	"	1524
like rainbows in the sky	"	1587
even by the self-same sky	*Son* 15	6
Slack—be thou not slack	*P P* 19	35
Slack'd—Slack'd, not suppress'd	*R L*	425
Slackly—Though slackly braided	*L C*	35
Slain—if himself were slain	*V A*	243
she lies as she were slain	"	473
so fair a hope is slain	"	762
with him is beauty slain	"	1019
thus was Adonis slain	"	1111
by Tarquin's falchion to be slain	*R L*	1046
slain in merry company	"	1110
that should have slain her foe	"	1827
when mine is slain	*Son* 22	13
but since I am near slain	" 139	13
Number there in love was slain	*P T*	28
Slaketh—no flood by raining	*R L*	1677
Slander—author of thy slander	*V A*	1006
a badge of fame to slander's livery	*R L*	1054
wash the slander of mine ill	"	1207
For slander's mark was ever yet	*Son* 70	2
slander doth but approve	" 70	5
And thence this slander	" 131	14
Slander'd—And beauty slander'd	" 127	4
Slanderer—Mad slanderers by mad ears believed be	" 140	12

17

Slandering — Slandering creation with a false esteem		*Son*	127	12		
Slanderous—To slanderous tongues	*R L*			161		
As slanderous deathsman	"			1001		
Slaughter—that doth live by....	"			955		
and then I'll slaughter thee	"			1634		
Slaughter'd—armour of still-slaughter'd lust	"			188		
shed for the slaughter'd husband	"			1376		
on her self-slaughter'd body threw	"			1733		
Slaughterhouse—But this no....	"			1039		
Slave—my captive and my slave	*V A*			101		
to be soft fancy's slave	*R L*			200		
And they, like straggling slaves	"			428		
some worthless slave of thine	"			515		
these slaves be king and thou their slave	"			659		
false slave to false delight	"			927		
to live a loathed slave	"			984		
deathsman to so base a slave	"			1001		
Being your slave, what should I do	*Son*	57	1			
But, like a sad slave, stay	"	57	11			
that made me first your slave	"	58	1			
slave to mortal rage	"	64	4			
But slave to slavery	"	133	4			
Thy proud heart slave	"	141	12			
Slavery—But slave to slavery	"	133	4			
Slavish—Paying more.... tribute	*R L*			299		
Worse than a slavish wipe	"			537		
Slay—his crooked tushes slay	*V A*			624		
themselves do slay	"			765		
worthless slave of thine I'll slay	*R L*			515		
To slay the tiger	"			955		
Will slay the other	"			1162		
To slay herself	"			1827		
and slay me not by art	*Son*	139	4			
Sleep—sleeps, while now it sleeps	*V A*			786		
When heavy sleep had closed	*R L*			163		
The dove sleeps fast.	"			360		
Each in her sleep	"			404		
From forth dull sleep	"			450		
From sleep disturbed	"			454		
while the physician sleeps	"			904		
evils that obscurely sleep	"			1250		
yet it seldom sleeps	"			1574		
But when I sleep	*Son*	43	3			
Through heavy sleep	"	43	12			
Or, if they sleep	"	47	13			
In sleep a king	"	87	14			
still did wake and sleep	*L C*			123		
If thou wake he cannot sleep	*P P*	21	54			
Sleeping—into eternal sleeping	*V A*			951		
But she, sound sleeping, fearing	*R L*			363		
So o'er this sleeping soul	"			423		
eyes that are sleeping	"			1090		
Was sleeping by a virgin hand disarm'd	*Son*	154	8			
Flocks all sleeping	*P P*	18	42			
Sleided—With sleided silk	*L C*			48		
Slept—have I slept in your report	*Son*	83	5			
Slew—Swearing I slew him	*R L*			518		
old Priam after slew	"			1522		
Slide—with swift motion slide	*Son*	45	4			
So slides he down	*L C*			64		
Slight—If my slight Muse do please	*Son*	38	13			
slight air and purging fire	"	45	1			
Slip—let not advantage slip	*V A*			129		
for fear of slips	"			515		
Slipp'd—time hath over-slipp'd her thought	*R L*			1576		
Slow—Make slow pursuit	"			696		
to mark how slow time goes	"			900		
With soft-slow tongue	"			1220		
but dull and slow she deems	"			1336		
see time how slow it creeps	"			1575		
In two slow rivers	"			1738		
by elements so slow	*Son*	44	13			
excuse the slow offence	"	51	1			
extremity can seem but slow	"	51	6			
going he went wilful-slow	"	51	13			
cold and to temptation slow	"	94	4			
Slow-sad—with.... gait descended	*R L*			1081		
Sluggard—blame my.... negligence	"			1278		
Sluice—who like sluices stopp'd	*V A*			956		
mine eyes like sluices	*R L*			1076		
Slumber—Now leaden slumber	"			124		
my slumbers should be broken	*Son*	61	3			
Sluttish—of the sluttish ground	*V A*			983		
besmear'd with sluttish time	*Son*	55	4			
Sly—that sly Ulysses lent	"			1399		
Small—small head and nostril wide	*V A*			296		
Small lights are soon blown out	*R L*			647		
of small worth held	*Son*	2	4			
lends not some small glory	"	84	6			
Small show of man	*L C*			92		
In the small orb	"			289		
Small—it small avails my mood	*R L*			1273		
Smallest—put to the smallest teen	*L C*			192		
Smart—to guess at others' smarts	*R L*			1238		
Smear—And smear with dust	"			945		
Smeared—smeared all with dust	"			1381		
Smell—Herbs for their smell	*V A*			165		
the very smell were left me	"			441		
hounds mistake their smell	"			686		
his smell with others	"			691		
smell to the violet	"			936		
Unapt for tender smell	*R L*			695		
add the rank smell of weeds	*Son*	69	12			
nor the sweet smell	"	98	5			
Nor taste nor smell	"	141	7			
Smell—the new-sprung flower to smell	*V A*			1171		
smell far worse than weeds	*Son*	94	14			
steal thy sweet that smells	"	99	2			
some subtle practice smell	*P P*	19	9			
Smelling—breedeth love by....	*V A*			444		
a more sweet-smelling sire	"			1178		
Smile—A smile recures the wounding	"			465		
While with a joyless smile	*R L*			1711		
Smile—dally, smile, and jest	*V A*			106		
smiles as in disdain	"			241		
smiles at thee in scorn	"			252		
Nor shall he smile at thee	*R L*			1065		
But smile and jest	*P P*	4	12			
sweetly did she smile	"	14	7			
Smiled—Whereat she smiled	*R L*			264		
smiled or made some moan	*L C*			217		
Whilst as fickle Fortune smiled	*P P*	21	29			
Smiling—regard and smiling government	*R L*			1400		
It suffers not in smiling pomp	*Son*	124	6			
were gilded in his smiling	*L C*			172		
I smiling credit her false-speaking	*P P*	1	7			
Smilingly—.... with this gives o'er	*R L*			1367		
Smiteth—on a flint he softly smiteth	"			176		
Smoke—And blows the smoke of it	"			312		
furnace of foul-reeking smoke	"			799		

SMOKE 259 SO

Smoke—This helpless .... of words	R L	....	1027
As smoke from .Etna	"	....	1012
in their rotten smoke	Son	34	4
Smoke—Her face doth reek and	V A	....	555
Smoking—Smoking with pride	R L	....	428
Smoky—That in their smoky ranks	"	....	783
Smooth—My smooth moist hand	V A	....	143
the path is smooth	"	....	788
Smooth not thy tongue	P P	19	8
Smoothing—Thy smoothing titles	R L	....	892
Smoothness — smoothness, like a goodly champaign plain	"	....	1247
Smother—I'll smother thee	V A	....	18
partially they smother	R L	....	634
with sighs himself doth smother	Son	47	4
Smother'd—smother'd up in shade	V A	....	1035
his smother'd light	R L	....	783
Another smother'd seems to pelt	"	....	1418
in love thus smother'd be	P P	1	14
Smother'st—Thou .... honesty	R L	....	885
Snail—Or, as the snail	V A	....	1033
Snare—sin's pack-horse, virtue's snare	R L	....	928
Sneaped—And give the sneaped birds	"	....	333
Snort—snorts and neighs aloud	V A	....	262
Snout—His snout digs sepulchres	"	....	622
Snouted—grim, and urchin-snouted boar	"	....	1105
Snow—apt as new-fall'n snow	"	....	354
in a gaol of snow	"	....	362
As mountain snow melts	"	....	750
when sun doth melt their snow	R L	....	1218
If snow be white	Son	130	3
Snow-white—love's modest snow-white weed	R L	....	196
her snow-white dimpled chin	"	....	420
like the snow-white swan	"	....	1011
Snuffing—the hot scent-snuffing hounds	V A	....	692
So—Being so enraged	"	....	29
So soon was she along	"	....	43
Even so she kiss'd his brow	"	....	59
So they were dew'd	"	....	66
So fasten'd in her arms	"	....	68
So offers he to give	"	....	88
mine be not so fair	"	....	116
so shall the day seem night	"	....	122
Is love so light	"	....	155
Narcissus so himself	"	....	161
And so, in spite of death	"	....	173
So he were like him	"	....	180
'young' and so unkind	"	....	187
borne so hard a mind	"	....	203
in a tomb so simple	"	....	244
So did this horse excel	"	....	293
on so proud a back	"	....	300
So of concealed sorrow	"	....	333
that she is so nigh	"	....	341
So white a friend engirts so white a foe	"	....	364
I am bereft him so	"	....	381
so full hath fed	"	....	399
Who is so faint, that dares not be so bold	"	....	401
by love so thriveth	"	....	466
can so well defend her	"	....	472
so he will kiss her still	"	....	480
So is her face illumined	"	....	486
So thou wilt buy	"	....	514
So—and so say you	V A	....	535
If you will say so	"	....	536
pitch the price so high	"	....	551
What wax so frozen	"	....	565
so she languisheth	"	....	611
to withhold me so	"	....	612
And more than so, presenteth	"	....	651
seeing thee so indeed	"	....	667
this to that, and so to so	"	....	713
so do thy lips	"	....	724
framing thee so fair	"	....	744
If so, the world	"	....	761
so fair a hope is slain	"	....	762
So in thyself thyself art	"	....	763
for having so offended	"	....	810
So glides he in the night	"	....	816
So did the merciless	"	....	821
Even so confounded	"	....	827
twenty times cry so	"	....	834
of echoes answer so	"	....	840
She says "Tis so:" they answer all "Tis so	"	....	851
so gloriously behold	"	....	857
is so much o'erworn	"	....	866
Even so the timorous	"	....	881
enemy to be so curst	"	....	887
So she at these sad signs	"	....	929
each passion labours so	"	....	969
pleased her babe so well	"	....	974
thou art so full of fear	"	....	1021
treads on it so light	"	....	1028
So, at his bloody view	"	....	1037
each part doth so surprise	"	....	1049
she looks so steadfastly	"	....	1063
So shall I die by drops	"	....	1074
and hath kill'd him so	"	....	1110
And so 'tis thine	"	....	1181
which is so singular	R L	....	32
envy of so rich a thing	"	....	39
being so great	"	....	69
in so false a foe	"	....	77
that praised her so	"	....	79
So guiltless she	"	....	89
so wanteth in his store	"	....	97
so greets heaven	"	....	112
are with gain so fond	"	....	134
And so, by hoping more	"	....	137
So that in venturing	"	....	148
So then we do neglect	"	....	152
So Lucrece must I force	"	....	182
to so pure a shrine	"	....	194
is so vile, so base	"	....	202
with so black a deed	"	....	226
doth so far proceed	"	....	251
with so sweet a cheer	"	....	264
so heedful fear	"	....	281
So cross him	"	....	286
a view so false	"	....	292
so their pride doth grow	"	....	298
'So, so,' quoth he	"	....	330
So from himself	"	....	341
Even so, the curtain drawn	"	....	374
she reflects so bright	"	....	376
themselves so beautify	"	....	404
So o'er this sleeping soul	"	....	423
So under his insulting falchion	"	....	509
'So thy surviving husband	"	....	519
being so applied	"	....	531
So his unhallow'd haste	"	....	552

So—so her accent breaks	R L	566	So—He with the Romans was esteemed so	R L	1811
So shall these slaves	"	659	wife mistook the matter so	"	1826
'So let thy thoughts	"	666	blood so unjustly stained	"	1836
stain so pure a bed	"	684	And so to publish	"	1832
So surfeit-taking Tarquin	"	698	so gazed on now	Son	2 3
So fares it	"	715	where is she so fair	"	3 5
so hotly chased	"	716	who is he so fond	"	3 7
to close so pure a mind	"	761	So thou through windows	"	3 11
vapours march so thick	"	782	So great a sum	"	4 8
So should I have	"	789	So thou, thyself	"	7 13
is so absolute	"	833	user so destroys it	"	9 12
'So then he hath it	"	862	art so unprovident	"	10 2
Being so bad	"	896	thou art so possess'd	"	10 5
For who so base	"	1000	so fast thou grow'st	"	11 1
to so base a slave	"	1001	If all were minded so	"	11 7
for yielding so	"	1036	So shall that beauty	"	13 5
through her lips, so vanisheth	"	1041	Who lets so fair a house	"	13 9
So am I now	"	1049	let your son say so	"	13 14
thy true affection so	"	1060	So shall the lines	"	16 9
So she, deep-drenched	"	1100	So should my papers	"	17 9
So I at each sad strain	"	1131	So long as men	"	18 13
So with himself	"	1153	So long lives this	"	18 14
So must my soul	"	1169	So is it not with me	"	21 1
my body so dishonoured	"	1185	though not so bright	"	21 11
So of shame's ashes	"	1188	So long as youth	"	22 2
My shame so dead	"	1190	be of thyself so wary	"	22 9
serve thou false Tarquin so	"	1197	I will keep so chary	"	22 11
"So be it	"	1209	So I, for fear	"	23 5
unto her maid seem so	"	1217	Duty so great, which wit so poor		
her two suns were cloud-eclipsed so	"	1224	as mine	"	26 5
Even so the maid	"	1228	So flatter I	"	28 11
that they are so fulfill'd	"	1258	Even so my sun	"	33 9
may be so bold	"	1282	So shall those blots	"	36 3
So, I commend me	"	1308	But do not so	"	36 13
better so to clear her	"	1320	So I, made lame	"	37 3
Even so this pattern	"	1350	So then I am not lame	"	37 9
So woe hath wearied woe	"	1363	For who's so dumb	"	38 7
painter drew so proud	"	1371	so sweetly doth deceive	"	39 12
did so well resemble	"	1392	even so doth she abuse	"	42 7
the painter was so nice	"	1412	thy shade shines so	"	43 8
so compact, so kind	"	1423	so much of earth	"	44 11
give her so much grief	"	1463	by elements so slow	"	44 13
that burns so long	"	1468	So, either by thy picture	"	47 9
that hath transgressed so	"	1481	for a prize so dear	"	48 14
why should so many fall	"	1483	So am I as the rich	"	52 1
So Lucrece, set a-work	"	1496	so solemn and so rare	"	52 5
So mild that Patience	"	1505	So is the time	"	52 9
but mingled so	"	1510	Sweet roses do not so	"	54 11
a show so seeming just	"	1514	And so of you	"	54 13
And therein so ensconced	"	1515	So, till the judgement	"	55 13
Into so bright a day	"	1518	So, love, be thou	"	56 5
So fair a form lodged not a mind so ill	"	1530	So true a fool is love	"	57 13
that so much guile	"	1534	your charter is so strong	"	58 9
So sober-sad, so weary, and so mild	"	1542	waiting so be hell	"	58 13
Tarquin armed; so beguiled	"	1544	So do our minutes	"	60 2
So did I Tarquin; so my Troy did perish	"	1547	So far from home	"	61 6
So Priam's trust	"	1550	is not so great	"	61 9
act of lust, and so did kill	"	1636	It is so grounded	"	62 4
So should my shame	"	1643	so gracious is as mine	"	62 5
with so strong a fear	"	1647	No shape so true	"	62 6
that stops his answer so	"	1664	Self so self-loving	"	62 12
forced him on so fast	"	1670	are not so stout	"	63 7
Even so his sighs	"	1672	gates of steel so strong	"	65 8
when I might charm thee so	"	1681	before these last so bad	"	67 14
that which is so putrified	"	1750	so as foes commend	"	69 4
from heart-easing words so long	"	1782	that give thee so thine own	"	69 6
Weak words, so thick come	"	1784	So thou be good	"	70 5
			cannot be so thy praise	"	70 11

Phrase	Source	Line/Page	No.
So—for I love you so	Son	71	6
Do not so much	"	71	11
And so should you	"	72	14
So then thou hast	"	74	9
So are you to my thoughts as	"	75	1
so barren of new pride	"	76	1
So far from variation	"	76	2
So all my best is	"	76	11
So is my love still	"	76	14
so oft as thou wilt look	"	77	13
So oft have I	"	78	1
And do so, love	"	82	9
so dignifies his story	"	84	8
nature made so clear	"	84	10
"Tis so, 'tis true	"	85	9
And so my patent back	"	87	8
So thy great gift	"	87	11
to thee I so belong	"	88	13
disgrace me half so ill	"	89	5
so shall I taste	"	90	11
will not seem so	"	90	14
But what's so blessed-fair	"	92	13
So shall I live	"	93	1
so love's face	"	93	2
So are those errors	"	96	7
But do not so	"	96	13
'tis with so dull a cheer	"	97	13
thou forget'st so long	"	100	1
time so idly spent	"	100	6
So thou prevent'st	"	100	14
So dost thou too	"	101	4
Excuse not silence so	"	101	10
So your sweet hue	"	104	11
still such, and ever so	"	105	4
So all their praises	"	106	9
So that eternal love	"	108	9
So that myself	"	109	8
could so preposterously	"	109	11
So you o'er-green	"	112	4
In so profound abysm	"	112	9
You are so strongly	"	112	13
might I not say so	"	115	13
Even so, being full	"	118	5
that so fell sick	"	118	14
itself so blessed never	"	119	6
So I return rebuked	"	119	13
which is so deemed	"	121	3
so long as brain and heart	"	122	5
could not so much behold	"	122	9
Her eyes so suited	"	127	10
Yet so they mourn	"	127	13
beauty should look so	"	127	14
To be so tickled	"	128	9
so happy are in this	"	128	13
and in possession so	"	129	9
so as thou art	"	131	1
I dare not be so bold	"	131	1
So, now I have confess'd	"	134	1
so that other mine	"	134	3
So him I lose	"	134	12
So thou, being rich in ' Will	"	135	11
that I come so near	"	136	1
so it please thee hold	"	136	11
upon so foul a face	"	137	12
Yet do not so	"	139	13
yet, love, to tell me so	"	140	6
world is grown so bad	"	140	11
That I may not be so	"	140	13
So runn'st thou	"	143	9
So—So will I pray	Son	143	13
walls so costly gay	"	146	4
Why so large cost, having so short a lease	"	146	5
So shalt thou feed	"	146	13
to say it is not so	"	148	6
eye is not so true	"	148	8
That is so vex'd	"	148	10
That is so proud	"	149	10
swear against the truth so foul a lie	"	152	14
And so the general of hot desire	"	154	7
so breaking their contents	L C		56
So slides he down	"		61
by nature's outwards so commended	"		80
so with his authorized youth	"		104
So on the tip of his subduing tongue	"		120
So many have, that never touch'd	"		141
in honour so forbid	"		150
the sweets that seem so good	"		164
that so their shame did find	"		187
And so much less of shame	"		188
my heart so much as warmed	"		191
so to herself contrives	"		243
What breast so cold	"		292
would not be so lover'd	"		320
which in his cheek so glow'd	"		324
what fool is not so wise	P P	3	13
Touches so soft still conquer	"	4	8
Yet not so wistly	"	6	12
but not so fair as fickle	"	7	1
so fell she to him	"	11	4
So beauty blemish'd once	"	13	11
The night so pack'd	"	15	9
Air, would I might triumph so	"	17	10
Youth, so apt to pluck a sweet	"	17	14
My sighs so deep	"	18	31
Had women been so strong	"	19	23
teach my tongue to be so long	"	19	52
hear her secrets so bewray'd	"	19	54
to hear her so complain	"	21	15
her griefs so lively shown	"	21	17
Even so, poor bird, like thee	"	21	27
Keep the obsequy so strict	P T		12
So they loved as love in twain	"		26
So between them love did shine	"		33
Simple were so well compounded	"		44
If what parts can so remain	"		48
Sob—And now her sobs	V A		222
Sobbing—To whom she .... speaks	R L		1088
Sober—Making such sober action	"		1403
glory to the sober west	Son	132	8
Shook off my sober guards	L C		298
Sober-sad—So sober-sad, so weary	R L		1542
Society—pleased with grief's society	"		1111
lace itself with his society	Son	67	4
Sod—Her eyes, though sod in tears	R L		1592
Soft—From his soft bosom	V A		81
my flesh is soft	"		142
her soft hand's print	"		353
soft sighs can never grave it	"		376
in my soft lips imprinted	"		511
Not thy soft hands	"		633
In his soft flank	"		1053
tusk in his soft groin	"		1116
to be soft fancy's slave	R L		200
Soft pity enters at an iron gate	"		595
Which on thy soft cheek	Son	99	4
Lending soft audience	L C		278

Soft—Touches so soft still conquer	P P	4	8	Some—some special instant	Son	52	11
But soft! enough	"	19	49	you have some part	"	53	13
Soften—soften it with their continual motion	R L		591	in some antique book	"	59	7
				If some suspect	"	70	13
Softer—Softer than wax	P P	7	4	devise some virtuous lie	"	72	5
Softly—on a flint he softly smiteth	R L		176	'life hath in this line some interest	"	74	3
And softly cried "Awake	"		1628	Some fresher stamp	"	82	8
Soft-slow—With soft-slow tongue	"		1220	not some small glory	"	84	6
Soil—And the firm soil win	Son	64	7	forsake me for some fault	"	89	1
The soil is this, that thou dost	"	69	14	Some glory in their birth, some in their skill	"	91	1
Solace—Sorrow changed to solace, and solace mix'd with sorrow	P P	15	11	Some in their wealth, some in their body's force	"	91	2
Sold—sold cheap what is most dear	Son	110	3	Some in their garments	"	91	3
Soldier—Like soldiers, when their captain	V A		893	Some in their hawks and hounds, some in their horse	"	91	4
Sole—alter not love's sole effect	Son	36	7	Some say thy fault is youth, some wantonness	"	96	1
On the sole Arabian tree	P T		2				
Solemn—This solemn sympathy	V A		1057	Some say thy grace is youth	"	96	2
And solemn night with slow-sad gait	R L		1081	some worthless song	"	100	3
				And in some perfumes	"	130	7
feasts so solemn and so rare	Son	52	5	some say that thee behold	"	131	5
Solicited—.... the eternal power	R L		345	think me some untutor'd youth	"	138	3
Some—'some favour, some remorse	V A		257	Some beauty peep'd through	L C		14
in some mistrustful wood	"		826	For some, untuck'd, descended	"		31
Some catch her by the neck, some kiss her face	"		872	Some in her threaden fillet	"		33
Some twine about her thigh	"		873	Where want cries some, but	"		42
fawn hid in some brake	"		876	as some my equals did	"		148
some huntsman holloa	"		973	some feeling pity	"		178
Behind some hedge	"		1094	smiled or made some moan	"		217
That some would slug, some other in their bills	"		1102	think me some untutor'd youth	P P	1	3
				Which is to me some praise	"	5	10
But some untimely thought	R L		43	Take counsel of some wiser head	"	19	5
Some loathsome dash	"		206	some subtle practice smell	"	19	9
Fearing some hard news	"		255	Something—Make .... nothing	R L		154
to some regard	"		305	add something more	Son	85	10
or else some shame supposed	"		377	a something sweet to thee	"	136	12
beheld some ghastly sprite	"		451	Sometime—Sometime he trots	V A		277
some worthless slave	"		513	Sometime he sends	"		301
some gentle gust	"		549	That sometime true news, sometime false doth bring	"		658
some rascal groom	"		671				
Some purer chest	"		761	Sometime he runs among	"		685
That some impurity	"		854	And sometime where	"		687
With some mischance cross Tarquin	"		938	And sometime sorteth	"		689
some desperate instrument	"		1038	Save sometime too much wonder	R L		95
Some happy mean	"		1045	that sometime threat the spring	"		331
Some dark deep desert	"		1144	sometime is compacted	"		530
I make some hole	"		1175	Sometime her grief is dumb	"		1105
Some present speed	"		1307	Sometime 'tis mad	"		1106
in her some blemish	"		1358	Yet sometime Tarquin	"		1786
to mourn some newer way	"		1365	Sometime too hot	Son	18	5
As if some mermaid	"		1411	from fair sometime declines	"	18	7
Some high, some low	"		1412	When I am sometime absent	"	41	2
where cares have carved some	"		1445	When sometime lofty towers	"	64	3
pleasure of some one	"		1478	Sometime all full with feasting	"	75	9
Saying, some shape	"		1529	I sometime hold my tongue	"	102	13
It caseth some	"		1581	might think sometime	L C		10
'? For some hard-favour'd groom	"		1632	Sometime diverted their poor balls	"		24
Some of her blood	"		1742	Sometime a blusterer	"		58
And some look'd black	"		1743	Sometimes—Sometimes she shakes	V A		223
some watery token shows	"		1748	Sometimes her arms	"		225
unbless some mother	Son	3	4	Yet sometimes falls	"		981
Make sweet some vial, treasure thou some place	"	6	3	That sometimes anger thrusts	Son	50	10
				Sometimes her levell'd eyes	L C		22
to some other give	"	13	4	sometimes they do extend	"		25
But were some child	"	17	13	Son—Art thou a woman's son	V A		201
Or some fierce thing	"	23	3	dearth of daughters and of sons	"		754
I hope some good conceit	"	26	7	reaves his son of life	"		766
As if by some instinct	"	50	7	There lives a son	"		863

Son—'twixt the son and sire	V.A	1160
kill'd my son or sire	R L	232
To see their youthful sons	"	1432
The sire, the son, the dame	"	1477
check'd his son's desire	"	1490
Then son and father weep	"	1791
unless thou get a son	Son 7	14
let your son say so	" 13	14
when a woman woos, what woman's son	" 41	7
Song—wanton mermaid's songs	V.A	777
Her song was tedious	"	841
A nurse's song	"	974
Whose speechless song	Son 8	13
metre of an antique song	" 17	12
on some worthless song	" 100	3
not dull you with my song	" 102	14
my songs and praises be	" 105	3
For now my song is ended	P P 16	16
Lest that my mistress hear my song	" 19	50
Sonnet—And deep-brain'd sonnets	L C	209
Soon—So soon was she along	V.A	45
soon she stops his lips	"	46
stains and soon bereaves	"	797
as soon decay'd and done	R L	24
to his hand full soon	"	570
Small lights are soon blown out	"	647
and it will soon be writ	"	1295
As soon as think the place	Son 44	8
And soon to you	" 120	11
To win me soon to hell	" 144	5
To win me soon to hell	P P 2	5
as soon as straw out-burneth	" 7	11
untimely pluck'd, soon vaded	" 10	1
kill'd too soon by death's sharp sting	" 10	4
the night would post too soon	" 15	13
A cripple soon can find a halt	" 19	10
Sooner—Enjoy'd no sooner	Son 129	5
and no sooner had	" 129	6
Soothing—Soothing the humour	V.A	850
best habit is a soothing tongue	P P 1	11
Sore—heart's deep-sore wounding	V.A	452
To one sore sick	"	702
'Gainst venom'd sores	"	916
an eye-sore in my golden coat	R L	205
O unfelt sore	"	828
'his wounds will not be sore	"	1568
'here was the sore	P P 9	12
Sorrow—So of concealed sorrow	V.A	333
Sorrow to shepherds	"	455
The night of sorrow	"	481
this night I'll waste in sorrow	"	583
thy death, my living sorrow	"	671
view'd each other's sorrow	"	963
Sorrow that friendly sighs	"	964
sorrow seemeth chief	"	970
Sorrow on love hereafter	"	1136
What following sorrow	R L	186
this sorrow to the sage	"	222
what sorrow I shall breed	"	499
modest eyes with sorrow shed	"	683
In time of sorrow	"	991
true sorrow then is feelingly suffic'd	"	1012
warble of her nightly sorrow	"	1080
Old woes, not infant sorrows	"	1096
to herself all sorrow doth compare	"	1102
sad look to her lady's sorrow	"	1221
her face wore sorrow's livery	"	1222

Sorrow—Her certain sorrow writ uncertainly	R L	1411
'Tis but a part of sorrow	"	1328
And sorrow ebbs, being blown	"	1330
And shapes her sorrow	"	1458
sorrow, like a heavy-hanging bell	"	1493
pensiveness and colour'd sorrow	"	1497
the current of her sorrow	"	1569
in sorrow's sharp sustaining	"	1573
she gives her sorrow fire	"	1604
his sorrows, make a saw	"	1672
thy sorrow to my sorrow lendeth	"	1676
give his sorrow place	"	1773
Who, mad that sorrow	"	1781
Held back his sorrow's tide	"	1789
My sorrow's interest; let	"	1797
draw my sorrows longer	Son 28	13
losses are restored and sorrows end	" 30	14
The offender's sorrow lends	" 34	11
my heart hath 'scaped this sorrow	" 90	5
And for that sorrow	" 120	2
how hard true sorrow hits	" 120	10
Lest sorrow lend me words	" 140	3
with sorrow's wind and rain	L C	7
Not age, but sorrow	"	74
Paler for sorrow	P P 9	3
for I supp'd with sorrow	" 11	6
Sorrow changed to solace and solace mix'd with sorrow	" 15	11
Sorrow—If thou sorrow, he will weep	" 21	53
Sorrowing—Careless of thy....	" 21	26
Sorry—that the skies were sorry	R L	1524
Make glad and sorry seasons	Son 19	5
Sort—When wilt thou sort an hour	R L	899
And sorts a sad look	"	1221
I love thee in such sort	Son 36	13
I love thee in such sort	" 96	13
Sorteth—sorteth with a herd of deer	V.A	689
Sought—sought still to dry	"	964
from the blessed thing he sought	R L	340
sought with all my might	"	488
for which I sought to live	"	1051
to imitate the battle sought	"	1458
many a thing I sought	Son 30	3
They sought their shame	L C	187
For she was sought by spirits	"	236
Against the thing he sought	"	313
Soul—So o'er this sleeping soul	R L	423
debated even in my soul	"	498
his soul's fair temple is defaced	"	719
to seize the souls that wander	"	882
Or free that soul	"	911
Sad souls are slain	"	1110
my poor soul's pollution	"	1157
My body or my soul	"	1163
So must my soul	"	1169
I may convey this troubled soul	"	1175
My soul and body to the skies	"	1109
Let guiltless souls be freed	"	1482
thence her soul unsheathed	"	1724
the faltering feeble souls	"	1766
vexation of his inward soul	"	1779
And by chaste Lucrece' soul	"	1839
and women's souls amazeth	Son 20	8
In thy soul's thought	" 26	8
my soul's imaginary sight	" 27	9
And all my soul	" 62	2
All tongues the voice of souls	" 69	3

Soul—nor the prophetic soul	Son	107	1	Spare—Spare not to spend	P P	19 26
As from my soul	"	109	4	Sparing—It shall be sparing	V A	 1147
suborn'd informer! a true soul	"	125	13	sparing justice feeds iniquity	R L	 1687
If thy soul check thee	"	136	1	Spark—sparks of fire do fly	"	 177
Swear to thy blind soul	"	136	2	Sparkling—When sparkling stars		
And will, thy soul knows, is admitted	"	136	3	twire not	Son	28 12
				Sparrow—hatch in sparrows' nests	R L	 849
Poor soul, the centre of my sinful earth	"	146	1	Speak—And kissing speaks	V A	 47
				Speak, fair; but speak fair words	"	 208
Then, soul, live thou	"	146	9	now she fain would speak	"	 221
My soul doth tell my body	"	151	7	To whom she speaks	"	 918
And credent soul to that strong-bonded oath	L C	....	279	teach the fool to speak	"	 1146
				thus speaks advisedly	E L	 180
All ignorant that soul that sees thee	P P	5	9	begin ere once she speaks	"	 567
				To whom she sobbing speaks	"	 1088
Sound—false sound enter there	V A	....	780	patience bid fair Lucrece speak	"	 1268
But idle sounds	"	....	848	I should not live to speak	"	 1642
This sound of hope	"	....	976	forbade my tongue to speak	"	 1648
Unprofitable sounds, weak	R L	....	1017	'O, speak,' quoth she	"	 1700
Deep sounds make lesser noise	"	....	1329	her poor tongue could not speak	"	 1718
quoth she, 'without a sound	"	....	1464	of such a salve can speak	Son	34 7
concord of well tuned sounds	Son	8	5	Speak of the spring and foison	"	53 9
a far more pleasing sound	"	130	10	you for love speak well of me	"	72 10
Breathed forth the sound	"	145	2	Speak of my lameness	"	89 3
the sweet melodious sound	P P	8	9	To speak of that	"	100 2
To whose sound chaste wings obey	P T		4	What's new to speak	"	108 3
Sound—But she, sound sleeping	R L	....	363	I love to hear her speak	"	130 9
swallow up his sound advice	"	....	1409	might speak ill of thee	"	140 10
Sound—To sound a parley	"	....	471	Speaking—.... to those that came	R L	 1689
against himself he sounds this doom	"	....	717	presagers of my speaking breast	Son	23 10
				speaking of your fame	"	80 4
wood whose motion sounds	Son	128	2	Speaking of worth	"	83 8
pipe can sound no deal	P P	18	27	dumb thoughts, speaking in effect	"	85 14
Sounding—heavenly tune harsh-sounding	V A	....	431	credit her false-speaking tongue	"	138 7
				credit her false-speaking tongue	P P	1 7
Soundless—upon your .... deep	Son	80	10	Spear—spear's point can enter	V A	... 626
Soundly—But soundly sleeps	V A	....	786	with his sharp spear	"	 1112
Sour—that sour unwelcome guest	"	....	449	for Achilles' image stood his spear	R L	 1424
is sour to taste	"	....	528	Special—special instant special blest	Son	52 11
'This sour informer	"	....	655	Spectacle—how vile a .... it were	R L	 631
turn to loathed sours	R L	....	867	a spectacle of ruth	P P	9 11
Were it not thy sour leisure	Son	39	10	Speech—Which to his speech	V A	 452
the bitterness of absence sour	"	57	7	In speech, it seem'd	R L	 1405
Sourest—turn sourest by their deeds	"	94	13	To blush at speeches rank	L C	 307
Sour-faced—charging the sour-faced groom	R L	....	1334	Speechless—Which .... woe of his	R L	 1674
				Whose speechless song	Son	8 13
Souring—Souring his cheeks, cries 'Fie	V A	....	185	o'er dull and speechless tribes	"	107 12
				Speed—His all-too-timeless speed	R L	 4
In digestion souring	R L	....	699	the headlong fury of his speed	"	 501
Sourly—which sourly robs from me	Son	35	14	He in his speed looks	"	 745
Will sourly leave her	"	41	8	Bid him with speed prepare	"	 1294
Sovereign—Earth's sovereign salve	V A	....	28	Some present speed to come	"	 1307
only sovereign plaster	"	....	919	Speed more than speed but dull and slow she deems	"	 1336
a sea, a sovereign king	R L	....	632			
Flatter the mountain-tops with sovereign eye	Son	33	2	Promise more speed	"	 1349
				His rider loved not speed	Son	50 8
sovereign mistress over wrack	"	126	5	In winged speed no motion	"	51 8
maladies a sovereign cure	"	153	8	Speed—when from thee I speed	Son	51 2
Sovereign—To their salt sovereign	R L	....	650	My rams speed not	P P	18 3
Whilst I, my sovereign, watch	Son	57	6	Speeding—O, cruel speeding	"	18 25
Sovereignty—his boast of Lucrece' sovereignty	R L	....	36	Speedy—tender smell or .... flight	R L	 695
				done with speedy diligence	"	 1853
The sovereignty of either	"	....	69	Spend—spend their mouths	V A	 695
Space—to die with her a space	"	....	1776	to spend the night	"	 847
For then, despite of space	Son	44	3	Not spend the dowry	R L	 948
vow, bond, nor space	L C	....	264	She hoards, to spend	"	 1318
Distance, and no space was seen	P T	....	30	Lucrece spends her eyes	"	 1457
Spacious—whose will is large and....	Son	135	5	why dost thou spend	Son	4 1
Spare—for his sake spare me	R L	....	582	in the world doth spend	"	9 9

Spend—no precious time at all to	Son	57	3	**Spleen**—A thousand spleens	V A 907
in the praise thereof spends all	"	80	3	Adon used to cool his spleen	P P 6 6
thy fading mansion spend	"	146	6	**Splendour**—Against the golden.... R L 25
lour'st on me, do I not spend	"	149	7	with all-triumphant splendour	Son 33 10
To spend her living in eternal love	L C	....	238	**Spoil**—sweetness of the spoil	V A 553
thou hast wherewith to spend	P P	21	36	Leaving his spoil perplex'd	R L 733
Spare not to spend	"	19	26	To spoil antiquities	" 951
Spend'st—spend'st thou thy fury	Son	100	3	his spoil of beauty	Son 65 12
Spending—Spending again what is	"	76	12	make Time's spoils despised	" 100 12
Spenser—Spenser to me, whose deep				and his amorous spoil	L C 154
conceit is such	P P	8	7	**Spoil'd**—spotted, spoil'd, corrupted	R L 1172
Spent—The time is spent	V A	....	255	**Spoke**—then he had spoke	V A 943
The night is spent	"	....	717	If he had spoke	" 1097
shall for him be spent	R L	....	1182	**Spongy**—his spongy lungs bestow'd	L C 326
with painted images hath spent	"	....	1577	**Sport**—such time-beguiling sport	V A 24
to those already spent	"	....	1589	our sport is not in sight	" 124
hath thy fair colour spent	"	....	1600	with such-like sport	" 844
what is already spent	Son	76	12	and his time of sport	R L 992
time so idly spent	"	100	6	comments on thy sport	Son 95 6
is my invention spent	"	105	11	thy grace is youth and gentle sport	" 96 2
and tombs of brass are spent	"	107	14	Playing patient sports	L C 242
more than I have spent	"	119	14	Youth is full of sport	P P 12 5
in their gazing spent	"	125	8	All our evening sport	" 18 47
a beauty spent and done	L C	....	11	**Sport**—learn'd to sport and dance	V A 105
Sphere—out of their spheres been				where I list to sport me	" 154
fitted	Son	119	7	**Sporting**—Advice is sporting	R L 907
battery to the spheres intend	L C	....	23	**Sportive**—For sportive words	" 1813
Spied—spied the hunted boar	V A	....	900	salutation to my sportive blood	Son 121 6
he spied in her some blemish	R L	....	1358	**Spot**—That spots and stains	R L 196
in his plain face she spied	"	....	1532	The spots whereof could weeping	
Spied a blossom passing fair	P P	17	3	purify	" 685
Spill—hands such wretched blood				To clear this spot by death	" 1053
should spill	R L	....	999	Doth spot the beauty	Son 95 3
Spill'd—on the ground lay spill'd	V A	....	1167	**Spotless**—Immaculate and spotless	R L 1656
and too late have spill'd	R L	....	1801	**Spotted**—To ask the spotted princess	" 721
Spilling—of her drops spilling	"	....	1236	spotted, spoil'd, corrupted	" 1172
Spirit—Love is a spirit	V A	....	149	**Spread**—.... upon the blushing rose	V A 590
and her spirit confounds	"	....	882	through all her sinews spread	" 903
spirit, life, and bold audacity	R L	....	1346	The fishes spread on it	" 1100
The spirit of love	Son	56	8	through all her body spread	R L 1236
Is it thy spirit	"	61	5	their fair leaves spread	Son 25 5
My spirit is thine	"	74	8	**Spreading**—have been a .... flower	L C 75
Knowing a better spirit	"	80	2	**Spright**—with a lazy spright	V A 181
that able spirit affords	"	85	7	weariness with heavy spright	R L 121
Was it his spirit, by spirits taught	"	86	5	Her winged spright	" 1728
Hath put a spirit of youth	"	98	3	**Spring**—The tender spring upon	V A 127
figured to thee my true spirit	"	108	2	Spring doth yearly grow	" 141
The expense of spirit in a waste	"	129	1	Love's tender spring	" 656
Which like two spirits	"	114	2	Love's gentle spring	" 801
The worser spirit a woman	"	144	4	Thy hasty spring still blasts	R L 49
My spirits to attend	L C	....	3	sometime threat the spring	" 331
spirits of richest coat	"	....	236	thy vices bud before thy spring	" 604
That like two spirits	P P	2	2	wait on the tender spring	" 869
My worser spirit a woman	"	2	4	and cherish springs	" 950
Spite—so in spite of death	V A	....	173	Wanting the spring	" 1455
this is my spite	"	....	1133	herald to the gaudy spring	Son 1 10
thus breathes she forth her spite	R L	....	762	Speak of the spring	" 53 9
what spite hath thy fair colour				the treasure of his spring	" 63 8
spent	"	....	1600	have I been absent in the spring	" 98 1
in our lives a separable spite	Son	36	6	and then but in the spring	" 102 5
by fortune's dearest spite	"	37	3	Three beauteous springs	" 104 5
Kill me with spites	"	40	14	and vaded in the spring	P P 10 2
Join with the spite of fortune	"	90	3	**Spring**—Seeds spring from seeds	V A 167
petty griefs have done their spite	"	90	10	Away he springs	" 258
Since, spite of him, I'll live	"	107	11	a mountain-spring that feeds a dale	R L 1077
but spite of heaven's fell rage	L C	....	44	Trees did grow and plants did	
In spite of physic	P P	13	12	spring	P P 21 6
alas, it was a spite	"	16	7	Clear wells spring not	" 18 37
Spite—To spite me now	"	15	15	**Springing**—If springing things	V A 417

Sprite—beheld some ghastly sprite	*R L*	....	451
Sprung—A purple flower sprung up	*V A*	....	1168
the new-sprung flower to smell	"	....	1171
Spur—curb or pricking spur	"	....	285
The bloody spur cannot provoke him	*Son*	50	9
Then should I spur	"	51	7
Spurn—Spurns at his love	*V A*	....	311
In vain I spurn at my confirm'd	*R L*	....	1026
Spurn'st—'Tis thou that spurn'st at right	"	....	880
Spurring—Spurring to his side	*Son*	50	12
Spy—one that spies an adder	*V A*	....	878
in her haste unfortunately spies	"	....	1029
by the light he spies	*R L*	....	316
where none may spy him	"	....	681
through every cranny spies	"	....	1086
Spy—this bate-breeding spy	*V A*	....	655
why are frailer spies	*Son*	121	7
Spying—He spying her, bounced in	*P P*	6	13
Stage—and beats these from the stage	*R L*	....	278
Black stage for tragedies	"	....	766
That this huge stage presenteth	*Son*	15	3
an unperfect actor on the stage	"	23	1
Stain—Stain to all nymphs	*V A*	....	9
The stain upon his silver down	*R L*	....	1012
How many this forced stain	"	....	1701
from this compelled stain	"	....	1708
Her body's stain	"	....	1710
bring water for my stain	*Son*	109	8
Stain—stains and soon bereaves	*V A*	....	797
And stains her face	"	....	1122
Virtue would stain that o'er with	*R L*	....	56
murder wakes to stain	"	....	168
stains love's modest snow-white weed	"	....	196
Who seeks to stain the ocean should stain so pure a bed	"	....	655
	"	....	684
Suns of the world may stain	*Son*	33	14
stain both moon and sun	"	35	3
Stained—all stain'd with gore	*V A*	....	664
stained taste of violated troth	*R L*	....	1059
My stained blood to Tarquin	"	....	1181
had stain'd her stain'd excuse	"	....	1316
Like bright things stain'd	"	....	1433
be stain'd with this abuse	"	....	1655
and that false Tarquin stain'd	"	....	1743
this chaste blood so unjustly stained	"	....	1836
so preposterously he stain'd	*Son*	109	11
Staineth—breaks before it staineth	*V A*	....	460
when heaven's sun staineth	*Son*	33	14
Stale—For now 'tis stale to sigh	*R L*	....	1362
Of stale example	*L C*	....	268
Stalk—She crops the stalk	*V A*	....	1175
wickedly he stalks	*R L*	....	365
Reserved the stalk	*L C*	....	147
Stalled—The steed is stalled up	*V A*	....	39
And stall'd the deer	*P P*	19	2
Stamp—He stamps and bites	*V A*	....	316
To stamp the seal of time	*R L*	....	941
Some fresher stamp	*Son*	82	8
Stamp'd—Reproach is stamp'd	*R L*	....	829
stamp'd the semblance	"	....	1246
stamp'd upon my brow	*Son*	112	2
Stand—now stand on end	*V A*	....	272
or his 'Stand, I say	"	....	284
Stands on his hinder legs	"	....	698

Stand—my heart stands armed	*V A*	....	779
Thus stands she	"	....	895
And they would stand auspicious	*R L*	....	347
he stands disgraced	"	....	718
deer that stands at gaze	"	....	1149
these pretty creatures stand	"	....	1233
you see grave Nestor stand	"	....	1401
that thou dost trembling stand	"	....	1599
in them doth stand disgraced	"	....	1833
Now stand you on the top	*Son*	16	5
stand against thy sight	"	38	6
although my foot did stand	"	44	5
And nothing stands	"	60	12
in hope my verse shall stand	"	60	13
fearfully on thorns did stand	"	99	8
which methinks still doth stand	"	104	11
all alone stands hugely politic	"	124	11
stands least in thy control	"	125	14
by thee blushing stand	"	128	8
To stand in thy affairs	"	151	12
that did in freedom stand	*L C*	....	143
from judgement stand aloof	"	....	166
these impediments stand forth	"	....	269
Herds stand weeping	*P P*	18	41
A woman's nay doth stand for nought	"	19	42
Stand—march'd on to make his stand	*R L*	....	438
Her stand she takes	*P P*	9	5
Standing—that is standing by	*V A*	....	282
for standing by her side	*R L*	....	423
Star—Look, how a bright star	*V A*	....	815
shining star doth borrow	"	....	861
stars ashamed of day	"	....	1032
Where mortal stars, as bright	*R L*	....	13
No comfortable star did lend	"	....	164
Which must be lode-star	"	....	179
But little stars may hide them	"	....	1008
And little stars shot	"	....	1325
Not from the stars	*Son*	14	1
And constant stars	"	14	10
the stars in secret influence	"	15	4
are in favour with their stars	"	25	1
Till whatsoever star	"	26	9
sparkling stars twire not	"	28	12
the star to every wandering bark	"	116	7
Nor that full star	"	132	7
Co-supremes and stars of love	*P T*	....	51
Stars—and there he stares	*V A*	....	301
in her sad face he stares	*R L*	....	1591
Star-gazers—That the star-gazers	*V A*	....	509
Staring—the staring ruffian	"	....	1149
Staring on Priam's wounds	*R L*	....	1448
Stark—And stood stark naked	*P P*	6	17
Start—Anon he starts	*V A*	....	302
Whereat she starts	"	....	878
Even there he starts	*R L*	....	348
I did begin to start and cry	"	....	1639
By this starts Collatine	"	....	1772
Starteth—from her be-tumbled couch she starteth	"	....	1037
Starved—clean starved for a look	*Son*	75	10
State—of his happy state	*R L*	....	16
his affairs, his friends, his state	"	....	45
That thou shalt see thy state	"	....	644
low vassals to thy state	"	....	666
scandal waits on greatest state	"	....	1006
companions at thy state	"	....	1006
clothes his wit in state and pride	"	....	1809
And wear their brave state	*Son*	15	8

State—beweep my outcast state	Son	29	2	Steam—feedeth on the steam	V. A	63
and then my state	"	29	10	Steed—to alight thy steed	"	13
change my state with kings	"	29	11	The steed is stalled up	"	39
such interchange of state	"	64	9	The strong-neck'd steed	"	263
Or state itself confounded	"	64	10	a well-proportion'd steed	"	290
I see a better state	"	92	7	by the well-doing steed	L C	112
the strength of all thy state	"	96	12	Steel—strong-temper'd steel	V. A	111
to medicine a healthful state	"	118	11	flinty, hard as steel	"	199
were but the child of state	"	124	1	water that doth eat in steel	R L	755
they would change their state	"	128	9	antiquities of hammer'd steel	"	951
compare thou thine own state	"	142	3	Nor gates of steel so strong	Son	65	8
she saw my woeful state	"	145	4	were brass or hammer'd steel	"	120	4
shouldst not abhor my state	"	150	12	in thy steel bosom's ward	"	133	9
Stately—fill with worm-holes stately monuments	R L	946	Steel—thy hard heart do steel it	V. A	375
Statue—Statue contenting but the eye	V. A	213	Steel'd—And being steel'd	"	376
statues, tombs, and stories	"	1013	That my steel'd sense	Son	112	8
war shall statues overturn	Son	55	5	Steep—do not steep thy heart	R L	1828
Statute—The statute of thy beauty	"	134	9	love-kindling fire did quickly steep	Son	153	3
Stay—each murmur stay	V. A	706	Steep-up—the steep-up heavenly hill	"	7	5
to make her stay	"	875	stand she takes upon a steep-up hill	P P	9	5
dare not stay the field	"	894	Steepy—travelled on to age's steepy night	Son	63	5
with his torch to make him stay	R L	311	Still'd—where all distress is....	R L	1144
could not stay him	"	323	hath play'd the painter and hath still'd	Son	24	1
doth Tarquin stay	"	423	Step—as if he told the steps	V. A	277
She stays, exclaiming	"	711	lurking serpent steps aside	R L	362
upon his silver down will stay	"	1012	Stern—by the stern and direful god	V. A	98
a little while doth stay	"	1364	To creatures stern sad tunes	R L	1147
on sightless eyes doth stay	Son	43	12	cover crimes with bold stern looks	"	1252
where thou dost stay	"	44	4	might the stern wolf betray	Son	96	9
it might unused stay	"	48	3	Steward—but stewards of their excellence	"	94	8
stay and think of nought	"	57	11	Stick—the green sticks fast	V. A	527
bound to stay your leisure	"	58	4	wherein her needle sticks	R L	317
still with thee shall stay	"	74	4	She will not stick to round me	P P	19	51
no longer than thy love will stay	"	92	3	Stick'st—thou stick'st not to conspire	Son	10	6
the thing she would have stay	"	143	4	Stifle—To stifle beauty	V. A	934
flesh stays no farther reason	"	151	8	Still—Still she entreats	"	73
what will not stay	L C	159	Still is he sullen, still he lours and frets	"	75
Stay—Who with a lingering stay	R L	328	still is left alive	"	174
conceit of this inconstant stay	Son	15	9	Her eyes woo'd still	"	358
Stay'd—or river stay'd	V. A	331	he still as much	"	442
but he was stay'd by thee	R L	917	So he will kiss her still	"	480
and there she stay'd	"	1275	their verdure still endure	"	507
Stay'st—thou stay'st too long	P P	12	12	still to be sealing	"	512
Steadfast—with a steadfast eye	R L	1339	still hanging by his neck	"	593
Steadfastly—looks so steadfastly	V. A	1063	he whetteth still	"	617
Steal—Steal thine own freedom	"	160	let him keep his loathsome cabin still	"	637
Lest she should steal a kiss	"	726	foes pursue him still	"	699
and to steal his breath	"	934	still concludes in woe	"	839
Away he steals	R L	283	And still the choir of echoes answers	"	840
Such devils steal effects	"	1555	Sought still to dry	"	964
Which steals men's eyes	Son	20	8	but is still severe	"	1000
Yet doth it steal sweet hours	"	36	8	bids them still consort	"	1041
steal thee all my poverty	"	40	10	still looketh for a grave	"	1106
And steal dead seeing of his living hue	"	67	6	Thy hasty spring still blasts	R L	49
the filching age will steal	"	75	6	makes them still to fight	"	68
to steal thyself away	"	92	1	pineth still for more	"	98
whence didst thou steal thy sweet	"	99	2	True valour still, a true	"	201
Steal from his figure	"	104	10	the fear doth still exceed	"	229
Stealeth—through the dark night he stealeth	R L	729	for vantage still	"	249
Stealing—How she came stealing	V. A	344	yet he still pursues	"	308
by his stealing in	"	459	might have reposed still	"	382
stealing moulds from heaven	"	730	the onset still expecting	"	432
Stealing unseen to west	Son	33	8			
Stealing away the treasure	"	63	8			
Stealth—by thy dial's shady stealth	"	77	7			

Still—she with vehement prayers urgeth still	R L	....	475
monarchs still are fear'd for love	"	....	611
she controlled still	"	....	727
And therefore would they still	"	....	752
hereafter still be blind	"	....	758
Keep still possession	"	....	804
And therefore still in night	"	....	1085
unpractised swimmer plunging still	"	....	1098
I'll hum on Tarquin still	"	....	1133
Extremity still urgeth	"	....	1337
eyes wailing still	"	....	1508
And still on him she gazed, and gazing still	"	....	1531
should my shame still rest	"	....	1643
To accessary yieldings, but still pure	"	....	1658
of her blood still pure	"	....	1742
still doth red abide	"	....	1749
substance still lives	Son	5	14
adore his beauty still	"	7	7
and still weep	"	9	5
still the world enjoys it	"	9	10
beauty still may live	"	10	14
To give away yourself keeps yourself still	"	16	13
In my bosom's shop is hanging still	"	24	7
still farther off	"	28	8
yet I have still the loss	"	34	10
For still temptation follows	"	41	4
art present still with me	"	47	10
And I am still with them	"	47	12
praise shall still find room	"	55	10
and he in them still green	"	63	14
may still shine	"	65	14
still will thee shall stay	"	74	4
Why write I still all one	"	76	5
you and love are still my argument	"	76	10
So is my love still telling	"	76	14
You still shall live	"	81	13
Muse in manners holds her still	"	85	1
still cry 'Amen	"	85	6
May still seem love	"	93	3
Yet seem'd it winter still	"	98	13
Such seems your beauty still	"	104	3
still such, and ever so	"	105	4
Still constant in a wondrous excellence	"	105	6
that which still doth grow	"	115	14
Still losing when I saw myself	"	119	4
by evil still made better	"	119	10
still will pluck thee back	"	126	6
She may detain, but not still keep, her treasure	"	126	10
to be my comfort still	"	134	4
am I that vex thee still	"	135	3
yet receives rain still	"	135	9
and love that still	"	136	13
spirits do suggest me still	"	144	2
a fever, longing still	"	147	1
still to endure	"	153	6
In her threaden fillet still did bide	L C	....	33
still did wake and sleep	"	....	123
two spirits do suggest me still	P P	2	2
Touches so soft still conquer chastity	"	4	8
the loss thereof still fearing	"	7	10
I craved nothing of thee still	"	10	10

Still—still to strive with men	P P	19	43
Still—pure thoughts are dead and still	R L	....	167
in still imagination	"	....	702
The nurse, to still her child	"	....	813
Stone-still, astonish'd with	"	....	1730
which methinks still doth stand	Son	104	11
and my loud crying still	"	143	14
Still'd—still'd with dandling	V A	....	562
Still-gazing—wonder of .... eyes	R L	....	84
Stillitory—the stillitory of thy face	V A	....	443
Still-pining—But like still-pining Tantalus	R L	....	858
Still-slaughter'd—armour of still-slaughter'd lust	"	....	188
Sting—disdainfully did sting	"	....	40
at the mercy of his mortal sting	"	....	364
honey guarded with a sting	"	....	493
hath neither sting, knot, nor	L C	....	265
by death's sharp sting	P P	10	4
Stir—rider's angry stir	V A	....	283
careless lust stirs up	"	....	556
the strumpet that began this stir	R L	....	1471
Stirr'd—stirr'd by a painted beauty	Son	21	2
Stirring—at stirring of a feather	V A	....	302
Myself was stirring	R L	....	1063
Stock—who did thy stock pollute	"	....	1063
Stole—But stole his blood	V A	....	1056
Now stole upon the time	R L	....	162
and he stole that word	Son	79	9
my white stole of chastity	L C	....	297
Stol'n—the treasure stol'n away	R L	....	1056
but stol'n from forth thy gate	"	....	1068
religious love stol'n from mine eye	Son	31	6
thou wilt be stol'n, I fear	"	48	13
buds of marjoram had stol'n	"	99	7
nor red, nor white, had stol'n	"	99	10
it had stol'n from thee	"	99	15
Stone—stone at rain relenteth	V A	....	200
cold and senseless stone	"	....	211
That from the cold stone	R L	....	177
For stones dissolved to water	"	....	592
no harder than a stone	"	....	593
And waste huge stones	"	....	959
Stone him with hurden'd hearts, harder than stones	"	....	978
Like stones of worth	Son	52	7
than unswept stone	"	55	4
Since brass, nor stone	"	65	1
are themselves as stone	"	94	3
Each stone's dear nature	L C	....	210
each several stone	"	....	216
Stone-still—Stone-still, astonish'd	R L	....	1730
'Stonished—'stonish'd as night-wanderers	V A	....	825
Stood—How like a jade he stood	"	....	391
falleth in the place she stood	"	....	1121
upon their whiteness stood	"	....	1170
had Narcissus seen her as she stood	R L	....	265
for Achilles' image stood his spear	"	....	1424
Stood for the whole	"	....	1428
Stood many Trojan mothers	"	....	1431
both stood like old acquaintance	"	....	1595
Stood Collatine and all	"	....	1731
like a late-sack'd island vastly stood	"	....	1740
wavering stood in doubt	L C	....	97
And stood stark naked	P P	6	10
bounced in, whereas he stood	"	6	13

Stoop—The grass stoops not	V. A.	1628
And stoop to honour	R L	574
The cedar stoops not	"	664
Stop—soon she stops his lips	V. A.	46
stop the loud pursuers	"	688
Each shadow makes him stop	"	706
which stop the hourly dial	R L	327
Or stop the headlong fury	"	501
made me stop my breath	"	1180
that stops his answers so	"	1064
The protestation stops	"	1700
to stop posterity	Son 3	8
should not stop my way	" 41	2
And stops her pipe	" 102	8
Counsel may stop awhile	L C	159
Stop—loves no stops nor rests	R L	1124
what course, what stop he makes	L C	109
Stopped—An oven that is stopp'd	V. A.	331
who, like sluices, stopp'd	"	956
Her voice is stopp'd	"	1061
Who, being stopp'd, the bounding	R L	1119
and to flatterer stopped are	Son 112	11
Store—so wanteth in his store	R L	97
is rifled of her store	"	692
that breeds the fat earth's store	"	1837
Nature hath not made for store	Son 11	9
to store thou wouldst convert	" 14	12
engrafted to this store	" 37	8
Increasing store with loss and loss with store	" 64	8
Immured is the store	" 84	3
addeth to his store	" 135	10
Though in thy store's account	" 136	10
to aggravate thy store	" 146	10
But if store of crowns be scant	P P 21	37
Store—O, him she stores	Son 67	13
as for a map doth Nature store	" 68	13
Storm—I could prevent this storm	R L	966
such black-faced storms	"	1518
Foretell new storms	"	1589
was he such a storm	L C	101
Storm-beaten—on my .... face	Son 34	6
Storming—Storming her world	L C	7
Stormy—But like a stormy day	V. A.	965
of stormy blustering weather	R L	115
Against the stormy gusts of winter's day	Son 13	11
Story—the story aptly ends	V. A.	716
Their copious stories	"	845
statues, tombs, and stories	"	1013
The story of sweet chastity's decay	R L	808
to still her child will tell my story	"	813
Sinon whose enchanting story	"	1521
so dignifies his story	Son 84	8
I can set down a story	" 88	6
tells the story of thy days	" 93	5
any summer's story tell	" 98	7
A plaintful story	L C	2
She told him stories	P P 4	5
Story—He stories to her ears	R L	106
Stout—are not so stout	Son 65	7
Stoutly—but stoutly say "So be it	R L	1209
Stow—in her vaulty prison stows the day	"	119
Straggling—And they like straggling slaves	"	428
Straight—to her straight goes he	V. A.	261
And straight in pity	"	1091
straight he strucken down	R L	217
Straight—as one shifts, another straight ensues	R L	1104
Is blotted straight with will	"	1299
I'll murder straight	"	1634
and straight grow sad	Son 45	14
and I straight will halt	" 89	3
Return, forgetful Muse, and straight	" 100	5
but despised straight	" 129	5
Straight In her heart	" 145	5
Straight—straight legs and passing strong	V. A.	297
I may be straight	Son 121	11
Bear thine eyes straight	" 140	14
Strain - They all strain courtesy	V. A.	888
at each sad strain will strain	R L	1131
And other strains of woe	Son 90	13
Strained—What strained touches	" 82	10
Strait—back to the strait	R L	1670
Strand—And from the strand of Dardan	"	1436
Strange—O strange excuse	V. A.	791
how strange it seems	"	985
the Impression of strange kinds	R L	1242
millions of strange shadows	Son 53	2
and to compounds strange	" 76	4
strangle and look strange	" 89	8
frowns and wrinkles strange	" 93	8
nothing novel, nothing strange	" 123	3
Against strange maladies	" 153	8
all strange forms receives	L C	303
Strangely—when thou shalt strangely pass	Son 49	5
askance and strangely	" 110	6
Strangeness—puts on outward	V. A.	310
Measure my strangeness	"	524
Stranger—unto every stranger	"	790
never coped with stranger eyes	R L	99
to find a stranger just	"	159
A stranger came, and on that pillow	"	1620
Strangle—strangle and look strange	Son 89	8
Straw—I force not argument a	R L	1021
a platted hive of straw	L C	8
as straw with fire flameth	P P 7	13
as soon as straw out-burneth	" 7	14
A belt of straw and ivy buds	" 20	13
Stray—Stray lower, where the pleasant	V. A.	234
Straying—thy beauty and thy straying youth	Son 41	10
Stream—strive against the stream	V. A.	772
The petty streams that pay	R L	649
Shall gush pure streams	"	1078
Lucrece' bleeding stream	"	1774
Gilding pale streams	Son 33	4
to the stream gave grace	L C	285
Stream'd—Blue circles stream'd	R L	1587
Street—from forth her fair streets	"	1814
Strength—govern'd him in ...	V. A.	42
his stronger strength obeyed	"	111
thus my strength is tried	"	280
with life's strength doth fight	R L	124
her passion's strength renews	"	1103
Then little strength rings out	"	1495
Whose strength's abundance	Son 23	4
And in mine own love's strength	" 23	7
make grief's strength seem stronger	" 28	14
thou hast the strength of laws	" 49	13
strength by limping sway disabled	" 66	8
the strength of all thy state	" 96	12

Strength—There is such strength	Son	150	7
strive to try her strength	P P	19	19
Strengthen'd—My love is	Son	102	1
Strengthless—Two .... doves	V A	.....	153
knit brow, and strengthless pace	R L	.....	709
Stretched—And stretched metre	Son	17	12
Strict—From their strict embrace	V A	.....	874
Keep the obsequy so strict	P T	.....	12
Strife—with herself at strife	V A	.....	11
workmanship at strife	"	.....	291
civil home-bred strife	"	.....	764
revenge or quittal of such strife	R L	.....	236
there were no strife	"	.....	405
doth force a further strife	"	.....	689
sort an hour great strifes to end	"	.....	899
to show the painter's strife	"	.....	1377
weep with equal strife	"	.....	1791
I hold such strife	Son	75	3
Strike—strikes her on the cheeks	V A	.....	475
strikes whate'er is in his way	"	.....	623
And whom he strikes	"	.....	624
thou shouldst strike at it	"	.....	938
to strike him dead	"	.....	948
Strike the wise dumb	"	.....	1146
strike a poor unseasonable doe	R L	.....	581
Strikes each in each	Son	8	10
the deer that thou shouldst strike	P P	19	2
Striking—what needs a second	V A	.....	250
his beating heart, alarum striking	R L	.....	433
String—Shall tune our heart-strings	"	.....	1141
Mark how one string, sweet husband to another	Son	8	9
Stripp'd—they be out-stripp'd by every pen	"	32	6
Stripping—Out-stripping crows that strive	V A	.....	324
Strive—strive to overfly them	"	.....	324
all in vain you strive	"	.....	772
ever strive to kiss you	"	.....	1082
They both would strive	"	.....	1092
Yet strive I to embrace	R L	.....	504
as he is, he strives in vain	"	.....	1665
all the world, and I must strive	Son	112	5
I did strive to prove	"	117	13
mastering what not strives	L C	.....	240
she strive to try her strength	P P	19	19
still to strive with men	"	19	43
Strived—beauty and virtue strived	R L	.....	52
Striving—As striving who should then, striving to mend	V A	.....	968
	Son	103	9
Stroke—doth she stroke his cheek	V A	.....	45
curse thee for this stroke	"	.....	945
Strong—straight legs and passing	"	.....	297
never waxeth strong	"	.....	420
with his strong course	"	.....	960
My will is strong	R L	.....	243
strong pirates, shelves, and sands	"	.....	335
From me by strong assault	"	.....	835
and they too strong	"	.....	865
with circumstances strong	"	.....	1262
Mine enemy was strong	"	.....	1646
with so strong a fear	"	.....	1647
By our strong arms	"	.....	1831
Resembling strong youth	Son	7	6
the strong offence's cross	"	34	11
your charter is so strong	"	58	9
Nor gates of steel so strong	"	65	8
what strong hand can hold	"	65	11
which makes thy love more strong	"	73	13
Strong—'gainst my strong infection	Son	111	10
Divert strong minds	"	115	8
more strong, far greater	"	119	12
replication prompt and reason strong	L C	.....	122
I strong o'er them, and you o'er me being strong	"	.....	257
Had women been so strong	P P	19	23
Strong-besieged—the walls of strong-besieged Troy	R L	.....	1429
Strong-bonded—to that .... oath	L C	.....	279
Stronger—his .... strength obey'd	V A	.....	111
make conquest of the stronger	R L	.....	1767
make grief's strength seem stronger	Son	28	14
is no stronger than a flower	"	65	4
Strongest—The strongest body	V A	.....	1145
The strongest castle	P P	19	29
Strongly—but strongly he desired	R L	.....	415
my duty strongly knit	Son	26	2
You are so strongly in my purpose bred	"	112	13
Strong-neck'd—The .... steed	V A	.....	263
Strong-temper'd—.... steel	"	.....	111
Struck—Struck dead at first	"	.....	250
His meaning struck her	"	.....	462
Which struck her sad, and	R L	.....	262
he struck his hand upon his breast	"	.....	1842
that struck me dead	Son	86	6
Strucken—straight be .... down	R L	.....	217
Struggle—he struggles to be gone	V A	.....	227
Nay, do not struggle	"	.....	710
Struggling—Struggling for passage	"	.....	1047
Strumpet—Show me the strumpet	R L	.....	1471
Strumpeted—maiden virtue rudely strumpeted	Son	66	6
Stuck—stuck o'er all his face	L C	.....	81
Stud—coral clasps and amber studs	P P	20	14
Studded—The studded bridle	V A	.....	37
Study—Study his bias leaves	P P	5	5
Stuff—Stuff up his lust	R L	.....	297
Stuff'd—Till either gorge be stuff'd	V A	.....	58
Sturdy—like sturdy trees support me	"	.....	152
Style—Theirs for their style	Son	32	14
thou dost but mend the style	"	78	11
Making his style admired	"	84	12
Subdue—did her force subdue	L C	.....	248
Subdued—my nature is subdued	Son	111	6
pensive and subdued desires	L C	.....	219
Subduing—tip of his subduing tongue	"	.....	120
Subject—tributary subject quakes	V A	.....	1045
Where subjects' eyes do learn	R L	.....	616
her subjects with foul insurrection	"	.....	722
want subject to invent	Son	38	1
To subjects worse have given	"	59	14
Of their fair subject	"	82	4
That to his subject lends	"	84	6
to lend base subjects light	"	100	4
To mar the subject	"	103	10
Subject—Making it subject	V A	.....	737
Subject and servile	"	.....	1161
As subject to Time's love	Son	124	3
Subjection—by their mortal fault brought in subjection	R L	.....	724
Proud of subjection	L C	.....	108
Subornation—perjury and	R L	.....	919
Suborn'd—Hence, thou .... informer	Son	125	13
Subscribe—and Death to me subscribes	"	107	10

Subsist—by nature to subsist	Son	122	6		
Substance—their substance still lives	"	5	14		
doth such substance give	"	37	10		
If the dull substance	"	44	1		
What is your substance	"	53	1		
Substantial—Feed'st thy light's flame with self-substantial fuel	"	1	6		
Subtle—Swift subtle post, carrier	R L		926		
To mock the subtle	"		957		
even as subtle Sinon	"		1541		
a plenitude of subtle matter	L C		302		
some subtle practice smell	P P	19	9		
Subtle-shining—the .... secrecies	R L		101		
Subtlety—which lives by subtlety	V A		675		
in the world's false subtleties	Son	138	4		
Succour—shine sun to .... flowers	P P	15	16		
Succeeding—in succeeding times	R L		525		
pattern to succeeding men	Son	19	12		
Success—greets heaven for his	R L		112		
Succession—Proving his beauty by succession thine	Son	2	12		
Successive—beauty's successive heir	"	127	3		
Such—such time-beguiling sport	V A		24		
with such distilling showers	"		66		
I am such a park	"		239		
He held such petty bondage	"		394		
Were never four such lamps	"		489		
tricks, and such disdain	"		501		
kisses such a trouble	"		522		
Such nectar from his lips	"		572		
with such foul fiends	"		638		
thou provokest such weeping	"		949		
such a weak and silly mind	"		1016		
the birds such pleasure took	"		1101		
at such high-proud rate	R L		19		
to such a peerless dame	"		21		
margents of such books	"		102		
and such griefs sustain	"		139		
there is such thwarting strife	"		143		
Such hazard now	"		155		
quittal of such strife	"		236		
where such treasure lies	"		280		
fearing no such thing	"		363		
proud of such a dignity	"		437		
Such shadows are	"		460		
batter such an ivory wall	"		464		
With such black payment	"		576		
darest do such outrage	"		605		
of such shame	"		618		
bear such shameful blows	"		832		
in such a devil	"		847		
such numbers seek for thee	"		896		
Such wretched hands such wretched blood	"		999		
would such an office have	"		1000		
Such danger to resistance	"		1265		
still urgeth such extremes	"		1337		
Such harmless creatures	"		1347		
Such sweet observance	"		1385		
Making such sober action	"		1403		
such signs of rage	"		1419		
such old action yield	"		1433		
such black-faced storms	"		1518		
hell-born sin such saint-like forms	"		1519		
Such signs of truth	"		1532		
can lurk in such a look	"		1535		
But such a face	"		1540		
Such devils steal effects	"		1555		
such unity do hold	"		1558		
Such—such passion her assails	R L		1562		
Seeing such emulation	"		1808		
Such childish humour	"		1825		
In such relenting dew	"		1829		
such murderous shame	Son	9	14		
I read such art	"	11	10		
Such heavenly touches	"	17	8		
of such triumph bars	"	25	3		
such wealth brings	"	29	13		
such a beauteous day	"	34	1		
of such a salve can speak	"	34	7		
Such civil war	"	35	12		
I love thee in such sort	"	36	13		
doth such substance give	"	37	10		
Hang on such thorns	"	54	7		
truth of such account	"	62	6		
For such a time	"	63	9		
such interchange of state	"	64	9		
the twilight of such day	"	73	5		
the glowing of such fire	"	73	9		
I hold such strife	"	75	3		
found such fair assistance	"	78	2		
such virtue hath my pen	"	81	13		
And such a counterpart	"	84	11		
but waking no such matter	"	87	14		
Such is my love	"	88	13		
I love thee in such sort	"	96	13		
having such a scope	"	103	2		
Such seems your beauty	"	104	3		
still such, and ever so	"	105	4		
Even such a beauty	"	106	8		
Such cherubins as your sweet self resemble	"	114	6		
At such who, not born fair	"	127	11		
But no such roses	"	130	6		
There is such strength	"	150	7		
was he such a storm	L C		101		
do again for such a sake	"		322		
Such looks as none could look	P P	4	4		
with such an earthly tongue	"	5	14		
whose deep conceit is such	"	8	7		
Such-like—In such-like circumstance, with such-like sport	V A		844		
And with such-like flattering	P P	21	41		
Suck'd—she had not suck'd	V A		572		
suck'd an earthly mother	"		863		
And suck'd the honey	R L		840		
Sudden—whereat a suden pale	V A		589		
Are on a sudden wasted	"		749		
Suddenly—Be suddenly revenged	R L		1683		
that vadeth suddenly	P P	13	2		
Sue—sue for exiled majesty's repeal	R L		641		
And sue a friend	Son	134	11		
Suffer—suffer these abominations	R L		1632		
O, let me suffer	Son	58	5		
It suffers not in smiling pomp	"	124	6		
pine within and suffer dearth	"	146	3		
Sufferance—patience, tame to	"	58	7		
Suffer'd—....., it will set the heart	V A		388		
I suffer'd in your crime	Son	120	8		
Suffering—Suffering my friend	"	42	8		
her suffering ecstasy assuage	L C		69		
Have of my suffering youth	"		178		
In the suffering pangs it bears	"		272		
Suffice—let it then suffice	R L		1679		
to know thee shall suffice	P P	5	7		
Sufficed—then is feelingly sufficed	R L		1112		
in thy abundance am sufficed	Son	37	11		
Sugar'd—Thy sugar'd tongue	R L		893		

Suggest—two spirits do suggest me	*Son*	144	2
two spirits do suggest me still	*P P*	2	2
Suggested—.... this proud issue	*R L*		37
Suggesteth—alarms, ... mutiny	*V A*		651
Suggestion—By their suggestion	"		1044
Suing—to his eyes suing	"		356
Suit—dwells upon my suit	"		206
as desperate in his suit	"		316
Tender my suit	*R L*		534
where his suit may be obtained	"		898
my love-suit, sweet, fulfil	*Son*	136	4
A youthful suit,—it was	*L C*		79
Which late her noble suit	"		234
And in thy suit be humble	*P P*	19	32
Suit—And suit thy pity	*Son*	132	12
Suited—Her eyes so suited	"	127	10
Suitor—suitor 'gins to woo him	*V A*		6
Sullen—Still is he sullen	"		75
From sullen earth, sings	*Son*	29	12
the surly sullen bell	"	71	2
Sullied—your day of youth to sullied night	"	15	12
Sum—Shall sum my count	"	2	11
So great a sum of sums	"	4	8
hath cast his utmost sum	"	49	3
all thy sum of good	"	109	12
parcels in combined sums	*L C*		231
Summer—A summer's day will seem	*V A*		23
In summer's heat	"		91
ere summer half be done	"		802
perfection of my summer	*R L*		837
time leads summer on	*Son*	5	5
Summer's distillation left	"	5	9
In thee thy summer	"	6	2
And summer's green all girded	"	12	7
compare thee to a summer's day	"	18	1
And summer's lease	"	13	4
thy eternal summer	"	18	9
When summer's breath	"	54	8
Make summer's welcome	"	56	14
summer's honey breath	"	65	5
summer of another's green	"	68	11
The summer's flower is to the summer sweet	"	94	9
this time removed was summer's time	"	97	5
For summer and his pleasures	"	97	11
any summer's story tell	"	98	7
in summer's front doth sing	"	102	7
the summer is less pleasant	"	102	9
shook three summers' pride	"	104	4
was beauty's summer dead	"	104	14
Youth like summer morn	*P P*	12	3
Youth like summer brave	"	12	4
Summon—Do summon us to part	*V A*		531
I summon up remembrance	*Son*	30	2
Sun—Even as the sun	*V A*		1
The sun doth burn my face	"		186
of this descending sun	"		190
The sun that shines	"		193
between that sun and thee	"		194
heavenly and earthly sun	"		198
Like the fair sun	"		483
sun glorifies the sky	"		485
To shame the sun	"		732
melts with the mid-day sun	"		750
is tempest after sun	"		800
The sun ariseth	"		856
Nor sun nor wind	"		1082
Sun—The sun doth scorn you	*V A*		1084
sun and sharp air	"		1085
gaudy sun would peep	"		1088
golden splendour of the sun	*R L*		25
fair and fiery-pointed sun	"		372
permit the sun to climb	"		775
when sun doth melt their snow	"		1218
Why her two suns	"		1224
the sun being set	"		1226
Of those fair suns	"		1230
By heaven's fair sun	"		1837
With sun and moon	*Son*	21	6
where-through the sun	"	24	11
the marigold at the sun's eye	"	25	6
stain both moon and sun	"	35	3
Even so my sun one early morn	"	33	9
Suns of the world may stain when heaven's sun staineth	"	33	14
with that sun thine eye	"	49	6
five hundred courses of the sun	"	59	6
the sun is daily new and old	"	76	13
are nothing like the sun	"	130	1
not the morning sun of heaven	"	132	5
The sun itself sees not	"	148	12
fortified her visage from the sun	*L C*		9
Then, thou fair sun	*P P*	3	10
Scarce had the sun	"	6	1
The sun look'd on the world	"	6	11
shine sun to succour flowers	"	15	16
Sunder—seems to part in sunder	*R L*		388
Sundry—The sundry dangers	"		128
Sung—when he hath sung	*V A*		1095
And sung by children	*R L*		525
sung the dolefull'st ditty	*P P*	21	11
Sunk—brave day sunk in hideous night	*Son*	12	2
Sunken—thine own deep-sunken eyes	"	2	7
Sunset—sunset fadeth in the west	"	73	6
Sunshine—comforteth like	*V A*		799
Superior—which their superiors want	*R L*		42
Supp'd—for I supp'd with sorrow	*P P*	14	6
Supper—after supper long he questioned	*R L*		122
Suppliant—the humble suppliant's friend	"		897
Suppliant—And .... their sighs	*L C*		276
Supply—No man will .... thy want	*P P*	21	38
Support—sturdy trees support me	*V A*		152
Suppose—.... thou dost defend me	*R L*		1684
or your affairs suppose	*Son*	57	10
Supposed—there's no death	*R L*		133
or else some shame supposed	"		377
makes supposed terror true	"		455
my unsounded self, supposed a fool	"		1819
1 by lacking have supposed dead	*Son*	31	2
Supposed as forfeit	"	107	4
Sweetly supposed them	*L C*		142
Supposing—supposing thou art true	*Son*	93	1
Suppress'd—slack'd, not suppress'd	*R L*		425
thus is simple truth supprest	*Son*	138	8
Supreme—Imperious supreme of all	*V A*		996
the supreme fair	*R L*		780
Surcease—If they surcease to be	"		1766
Sure—in sure wards of trust	*Son*	48	4
O, sure I am, the wits	"	59	13
And to be sure	"	131	9
Surety-like—He learn'd but	"	134	7
Surfeit—Whereon they surfeit	*V A*		544

Surfeit—Do surfeit by the eye	V A	602
Surfeits, imposthumes, grief	"	743
Love surfeits not	"	803
Is but to surfeit	R L	139
pine and surfeit day by day	Son 75	13
Surfeit-taking—So.... Tarquin	R L	698
Surly—hear the surly sullen bell	Son 71	2
Surmise—Tarquin answers with surmise	R L	83
By deep surmise	"	1579
on just proof surmise accumulate	Son 117	10
Surmount—in all worths surmount	" 62	8
Surpass—would surpass the life	V A	289
Surplice—Let the priest in surplice white	P T	13
Surprise—to surprise her heart	V A	890
doth so surprise	"	1019
that they may surprise	R L	166
Survey—he will not every hour	Son 52	3
my love's sweet face survey	" 100	9
Survive—thou dost survive	V A	173
the scandal will survive	R L	204
surcease to be that should survive	"	1766
If thou survive my well-contented day	Son 32	1
Or you survive when I in earth	" 81	2
Surviving—this surviving shame	R L	223
So thy surviving husband	"	519
Suspect—It shall suspect where is	V A	1153
Suspect I may, yet not	Son 144	10
Suspect I may, yet not	P P 2	10
Suspect—Her rash suspect	V A	1010
The ornament of beauty is suspect	Son 70	3
If some suspect of ill	" 70	13
Suspecteth—Little suspecteth the false worshipper	R L	86
Suspicion—And bid suspicion	V A	448
From that suspicion	R L	1321
Sustain—and such griefs sustain	"	139
Sustaining—for grief of my....	"	1272
long in sorrow's sharp sustaining	"	1573
Swallow—to swallow Venus' liking	V A	248
swallow up his sound advice	R L	1409
Swallow'd—whole is,... in confusion	"	1159
as a swallow'd bait	Son 129	7
Swallowing—but a.... grave	V A	757
A swallowing gulf	R L	557
Swain—with the blunt swains he goes	"	1504
known to us poor swains	P P 18	45
Swan—the snow-white swan desire	R L	1011
And now this pale swan	"	1611
Be the death-divining swan	P T	15
Swart-complexion'd — the swart-complexion'd night	Son 28	11
Sway—by limping sway disabled	" 66	8
my heart to sway	" 150	2
noble by the sway	L C	108
Sway'd—'Thus he that overruled I oversway'd	V A	109
Sway'st—when thou gently sway'st	Son 128	3
Swear—immortal hand she swears	V A	80
Swear Nature's death	"	744
That one would swear	R L	1393
seems to pelt and swear	"	1418
swears he did her wrong	"	1462
And swear I found you	"	1635
came evidence to swear	"	1650
I swear it to myself alone	Son 131	8
that is not false I swear	" 131	9

Swear—Then will I swear	Son 132	13
Swear to thy blind soul	" 136	2
swears that she is made of truth	" 138	1
And swear that brightness	" 150	4
swear against the thing they see	" 152	12
To swear against the truth	" 152	14
When my love swears	P P 1	1
how shall I swear to love	" 5	1
Thou for whom Jove would swear	" 17	15
Swearing—Swearing I slew him	R L	518
Swearing unless I took all	"	1641
to me love swearing	Son 152	2
her oaths of true love swearing	P P 7	8
Sweat—queen began to sweat	V A	175
With pearly sweat	R L	396
Begrimed with sweat	"	1381
Sweating—on his sweating palm	V A	25
Since sweating Lust	"	794
sweating with guilty fear	R L	740
Sweet—sweet above compare	V A	8
And one sweet kiss	"	84
sweet boy, and may it be	"	155
Sweet bottom-grass	"	236
For one sweet look	"	371
approach of sweet desire	"	386
Ear's deep-sweet music	"	432
Pure lips, sweet seals	"	511
his neck a sweet embrace	"	539
that sweet coral mouth	"	542
'Sweet boy,' she says	"	583
'sweet boy, ere this	"	613
sweet lips and crystal eyne	"	633
from the sweet embrace	"	811
In the sweet channel	"	958
sweet Death, I did but jest	"	997
The flowers are sweet	"	1079
But true-sweet beauty lived	"	1080
Find sweet beginning	"	1138
Sweet issue of a more	"	1178
my sweet love's flower	"	1188
For one sweet grape	R L	215
with so sweet a cheer	"	264
that follows sweet delight	"	357
and enter this sweet city	"	469
and sweet friendship's oath	"	569
in her lips' sweet fold	"	679
of sweet chastity's decay	"	808
where the sweet birds sing	"	871
mad with their sweet melody	"	1108
Who, having two sweet babes	"	1161
Such sweet observance	"	1385
And drop sweet balm	"	1466
Sweet love, what spite	"	1600
In thy sweet semblance	"	1759
Then live, sweet Lucrece	"	1770
to thy sweet self too cruel	Son 1	8
thy sweet self dost deceive	" 4	10
substance still lives sweet	" 5	11
Make sweet some vial	" 6	3
sweet husband to another	" 8	9
And your sweet semblance	" 13	4
your sweet issue your sweet form should bear	" 13	8
drawn by your own sweet skill	" 16	11
her own sweet brood	" 19	2
worthy of thy sweet respect	" 26	12
For thy sweet love	" 29	13
of sweet silent thought	" 30	1
To that sweet thief	" 35	14

18

SWEET 274 TABLE

Entry	Ref	Page	Line
Sweet—Yet doth it steal sweet hours	Son	36	8
Thine own sweet argument	"	38	3
sour leisure gave sweet leave	"	39	10
Sweet flattery! then she loves	"	42	14
sweet up-locked treasure	"	52	2
By that sweet ornament	"	54	2
For that sweet odour	"	54	4
Sweet roses do not so	"	54	11
Of their sweet deaths	"	54	12
Sweet love, renew thy force	"	56	1
My sweet love's beauty	"	63	11
That I in your sweet thoughts	"	71	7
late the sweet birds sang	"	73	4
O, know, sweet love	"	76	9
with thy sweet graces graced be	"	78	12
I grant, sweet love	"	79	5
Thy sweet beloved name	"	89	10
in thy face, sweet love	"	93	10
If thy sweet virtue	"	93	14
is to the summer sweet	"	94	9
How sweet and lovely	"	95	1
nor the sweet smell	"	98	5
They were but sweet	"	98	11
my love's sweet face	"	100	9
So your sweet hue	"	104	11
blazon of sweet beauty's best	"	106	5
Nothing, sweet boy	"	108	5
The most sweet favour	"	113	10
your sweet self resemble	"	114	6
as thy sweet self grow'st	"	126	4
Sweet beauty hath no name	"	127	7
With thy sweet fingers	"	128	3
To thy sweet will making	"	135	4
my love-suit, sweet, fulfil	"	136	4
a something sweet to thee	"	136	12
that tongue that ever sweet	"	145	6
thy sweet self prove	"	151	4
What's sweet to do	L C		88
When winds breathe sweet	"		103
But, O my sweet	"		239
to my sweet design	"		278
Sweet Cytherea, sitting	P P	4	1
is music and sweet fire	"	5	12
If music and sweet poetry agree	"	8	1
the sweet melodious sound	"	8	9
did I see a fair sweet youth	"	9	9
Sweet rose, fair flower	"	10	1
O, sweet shepherd, hie thee	"	12	11
Sweet birds sing not	"	18	38
Farewell, sweet lass	"	18	49
For a sweet content	"	18	51
Sweet—With sweets that shall	V A		1144
The sweets we wish for	R L		867
Sweets with sweets war not	Son	8	2
Since sweets and beauties	"	12	11
all her fading sweets	"	19	7
O, in what sweets	"	95	4
Sweet thief, whence didst thou steal thy sweet	"	99	2
But sweet or colour	"	99	15
And sweets grown common	"	102	12
For compound sweet	"	125	7
To be forbod the sweets	L C		164
Youth, so apt to pluck a sweet	P P	17	14
Sweeten—sweetens in the suffering pangs	L C		272
Sweetest—canker lives in .... bud	Son	35	4
are sweetest odours made	"	54	12
in heaven's sweetest air	"	70	4
Sweetest—canker vice the sweetest buds doth love	Son	70	7
For sweetest things turn sourest	"	94	13
my sweet'st friend must be	"	133	4
Sweetly—in darkness sweetly lay	R L		398
They do but sweetly chide thee	Son	8	7
so sweetly doth deceive	"	39	12
Sweetly supposed them	L C		142
sweetly did she smile	P P	14	7
Th' one sweetly flatters	R L		172
Sweetness—sweetness of the spoil	V A		553
nothing thence but sweetness	Son	93	12
your ne'er-cloying sweetness	"	118	5
Sweet-season'd—Or as .... showers	"	75	2
Sweet-smelling—a more .... sire	V A		1178
Swell—Swell in their pride	R L		432
swells the higher by this let	"		646
Swelleth—swelleth with more rage	V A		332
Swelling—And swelling passion	"		218
swelling dugs do ache	"		875
Swelling on either side	R L		389
your hollow-swelling feather'd breasts	"		1122
with swelling drops 'gan wet	"		1228
With swelling ridges	"		1439
Swerving—my patent back again is swerving	Son	87	8
Swift—by whose swift aid	V A		1190
with swift intent he goes	R L		46
Swift subtle post, carrier	"		926
and how swift and short	"		991
Whose swift obedience	"		1215
With swift pursuit to venge	"		1691
with swift motion slide	Son	45	4
By those swift messengers	"	45	10
When swift extremity	"	51	6
can hold his swift foot back	"	65	11
and makes all swift despatch	"	143	3
Swiftest—The .... hours observed	L C		60
Swift-footed—whate'er thou wilt, swift-footed Time	Son	19	6
Swiftly—swiftly doth forsake him	V A		321
Swimmer—Like an unpractised	R L		1098
Swine—a churlish swine to gore	V A		616
the loving swine	"		1115
Swoln—All swoln with chafing	"		325
Swore—and that they swore	R L		1848
Sworn—When they had sworn	"		1849
For I have sworn thee fair	Son	147	13
For I have sworn deep oaths	"	152	9
For I have sworn thee fair	"	152	13
But, alas! my hand hath sworn	P P	17	11
That's to ye sworn	L C		180
Swound—Here Troilus swounds	R L		1486
and swound at tragic shows	L C		308
Swounding—Or swounding paleness	"		305
Sword—Draw not thy sword	R L		626
they would debate with angry swords	"		1421
against my heart he set his sword	"		1640
Nor Mars his sword	Son	55	7
Sympathized—with like semblance it is sympathized	R L		1113
Thou truly fair wert truly sympathized	Son	82	11
Sympathy—This solemn sympathy	V A		1057
enforced by sympathy	R L		1229
Table—In table of my heart	Son	24	2

Table—thy tables, are within my brain	*Son*	122	1	**Tale**—she trembles at his tale	*V.A* 591
To trust those tables	"	122	12	This curry-tale, dissentious Jealousy "	 657
Ta'en—Had ta'en his last leave	*V.A*	.....	2	in his ears a heavy tale	" 1125
is ta'en prisoner by the foe	*R L*	.....	1608	and tell my loving tale	*R L* 480
Tail—Thin mane, thick tail	*V A*	.....	298	object to the tell-tale Day	" 806
through his mane and tail	"	.....	395	to purge my impure tale	" 1078
He vails his tail	"	.....	314	sad tales doth tell	" 1496
Clapping their proud tails	"	.....	923	to list the sad-tuned tale	*L C* 4
Tainted—our hearts oft tainted be	*R L*	.....	38	How many tales to please me	*P P* 7 9
Which by him tainted	"	.....	1182	thou comest thy tale to tell	" 19 7
weep upon the tainted place	"	.....	1746	**Talent**—these talents of their hair	*L C* 204
Take—Till he take truce	*V A*	.....	82	**Talk** 'What! canst thou talk	*V.A* 427
goeth about to take him	"	.....	319	To talk in deeds	*R L* 1348
snow takes any dint	"	.....	354	Begins to talk; but through	" 1783
now she takes him	"	.....	361	*Talk*—to your wanton talk	*V.A* 809
To take advantage	"	.....	405	Mingling my talk with tears	*R L* 797
she takes all she can	"	.....	564	and too much talk affords	" 1106
take counsel of their friends	"	.....	640	thy tongue with filed talk	*P P* 19 8
and takes no rest	"	.....	647	**Talk'd**—And talk'd of virtue	*R L* 846
she takes him by the hand	"	.....	1124	**Tall**—He of tall building	*Son* 80 12
in this hollow cradle take thy rest	"	.....	1185	**Tally**—Nor need I tallies	" 122 10
takes the worser part	*R L*	.....	294	**Tame**—tame and gently hear him	*V.A* 1096
He takes it from the rushes	"	.....	318	And patience, tame to sufferance	*Son* 58 7
He takes for accidental things	"	.....	326	nature is both kind and tame	*L C* 311
no device can take	"	.....	535	Youth is wild and age is tame	*P P* 12 8
take root with precious flowers	"	.....	870	*Tame*—To tame the unicorn	*R L* 956
when death takes one	"	.....	1161	Continuance tames the one	" 1097
husband, do thou take	"	.....	1200	**Tamed**—tamed with too much	*V.A* 560
the other takes in hand	"	.....	1235	**Tan**—Tan sacred beauty	*Son* 115 7
At last he takes her	"	.....	1597	**Tangled**—tangled in a net	*V.A* 67
do not take away	"	.....	1796	**Tann'd**—chopp'd with tann'd antiquity	*Son* 62 10
when he takes thee hence	*Son*	12	14	**Tantalus**—worse than Tantalus'	*V.A* 599
As he takes from you	"	15	14	like still-pining Tantalus	*R L* 858
Unless thou take that honour	"	36	12	**Tapster**—Like shrill-tongued tapsters	*V.A* 849
decrepit father takes delight	"	37	1		
Take all my comfort	"	37	4	**Tarquin**—.... leaves the Roman	*R L* 3
Take all my loves, my love, yea, take them all	"	40	1	In Tarquin's tent	" 15
come and take my love	"	64	12	Which Tarquin view'd	" 72
black night doth take away	"	73	7	Enchanted Tarquin answers	" 83
To take a new acquaintance	"	77	12	For then is Tarquin	" 120
your memory death cannot take	"	81	3	doth Tarquin lie revolving	" 127
that thou mayst take	"	91	13	now must doting Tarquin make	" 183
Take heed, dear heart	"	95	13	These worlds in Tarquin	" 411
And take thou my oblation	"	125	10	doth Tarquin stay	" 423
thy beauty thou wilt take	"	134	9	'In Tarquin's likeness	" 596
take the worst to be	"	137	4	So surfeit-taking Tarquin	" 698
his metal from his rider takes	*L C*	.....	107	'Were Tarquin Night	" 785
hence a question takes	"	.....	110	with Tarquin's name	" 814
Take all these similes	"	.....	227	reproach to Tarquin's shame	" 816
and he takes and leaves	"	.....	305	How Tarquin wronged me	" 819
to take her figured proffer	*P P*	4	10	And Tarquin's eye	" 830
Her stand she takes	"	9	5	When Tarquin did, but he	" 917
And would not take her meaning	"	11	12	some mischance cross Tarquin	" 968
As take the pain	"	14	12	At Time, at Tarquin	" 1024
Take counsel of some wiser head	"	19	5	I fear'd by Tarquin's fulchion	" 1046
None takes pity on thy pain	"	21	20	hath Tarquin rifled me	" 1050
Taken—Had ta'en his last leave	*V A*	.....	2	I'll hum on Tarquin still	" 1133
is ta'en prisoner for the foe	*R L*	.....	1608	my stained blood to Tarquin	" 1181
although his height be taken	*Son*	116	8	How Tarquin must be used	" 1195
have no leisure taken	"	120	7	serve thou false Tarquin so	" 1197
thy cruel eye hath taken	"	133	5	'Tarquin from hence	" 1276
Taker—to make the taker mad	"	120	8	Tarquin gone away	" 1284
Takest—breath thou givest and....	*P T*	.....	19	as knowing Tarquin's lust	" 1354
Taking—Taking no notice	*V.A*	.....	341	But Tarquin's shape	" 1536
but she, in worser taking	*R L*	.....	453	To me came Tarquin armed	" 1544
So surfeit-taking Tarquin fares	"	.....	698	So did I Tarquin	" 1547
Tale—she tunes her tale	*V A*	.....	74	She throws forth Tarquin s name	" 1717
				and that false Tarquin stain'd	" 1743

Tarquin—sometime 'Tarquin' was pronounced plain	R L	1786	Tear—Tears harden lust	R L	560
to publish Tarquin's foul offence	"	1852	By her untimely tears	"	570
Tarquin's everlasting banishment	"	1855	Be moved with my tears	"	588
Tarriance—longing .... for Adonis	V A 6	4	Melt at my tears	"	594
Task—His day's hot task	V A	539	in the chastest tears	"	682
In that high task	R L	80	Her tears should drop	"	686
the task it hath to say	"	1618	Mingling my talk with tears	"	797
her sad task hath not said	"	1699	when time is kept with tears	"	1127
should task you to recite	Son 72	1	at each sad strain will strain a tear	"	1131
Taste—Dainties to taste	V A	164	Those tears from thee	"	1271
is sour to taste	"	528	If tears could help	"	1274
this learning mayst thou taste	Son 77	4	and tears may grace	"	1319
so shall I taste	" 90	11	seem'd a weeping tear	"	1375
that needs will taste	L C	167	And with my tears quench Troy	"	1468
Taste—wert thou to the taste	V A	445	To see those borrow'd tears	"	1549
Whose precious taste	"	543	For every tear he falls	"	1551
but alter not his taste	R L	651	false Sinon's tears doth flatter	"	1560
His taste delicious	"	699	Her eyes, though sod in tears	"	1592
to bitter wormwood taste	"	893	carved in it with tears	"	1713
The stained taste of violated troth	"	1059	To check the tears	"	1817
By wilful taste of what thyself	Son 40	8	a holy and obsequious tear	Son 31	5
Nor taste, nor smell	" 141	7	Ah! but those tears are pearl	" 34	13
Tasted—mayst thou well be tasted	V A	128	heavy tears, badges of either's woe	" 44	14
Tatter'd—Will be a tatter'd weed	Son 2	4	potions have I drunk of Siren tears	" 119	1
on my tatter'd loving	" 26	11	with watching and with tears	" 148	10
Taught—.... them scornful tricks	V A	501	with tears thou keep'st me blind	" 148	13
Those eyes that taught all other eyes	"	952	woe had pelleted in tears	L C	18
Ruin hath taught me	Son 64	11	orb of one particular tear	"	289
taught the dumb on high	" 78	5	resolved my reason into tears	"	296
by spirits taught to write	" 86	5	Her faith, her oaths, her tears	P P 7	12
love taught it this alchemy	" 114	4	Scarce I could from tears refrain	" 21	16
And taught it thus anew	" 145	1	Tear—shall rudely tear thee	R L	669
Who taught thee how	" 150	9	her nails her flesh doth tear	"	739
hath taught her thus to say	P P 19	22	to tear his curled hair	"	981
Taught'st—that thou .... this ill	R L	996	her beauty I may tear	"	1472
Teach—his proceedings teach thee	V A	406	She tears the senseless Sinon	"	1564
doth teach it divination	"	670	and often 'gan to tear	"	51
teach the fool to speak	"	1146	Tear-distained—about her .... eye	R L	1586
and thou didst teach the way	R L	630	Tearing—Tearing of papers, breaking rings	L C	6
Teach me to curse him	"	996	Tedious—Her song was tedious	V A	841
O, teach me how to make	"	1653	My woes are tedious	R L	1309
To teach my tongue	Son 19	52	burnt out in tedious nights	"	1379
Doth teach that ease	" 50	3	Teeming—The teeming autumn	Son 97	6
I teach thee how	" 101	13	Teen—my heart of teen	V A	808
If I might teach thee wit	" 140	5	put to the smallest teen	L C	192
Teachest—And that thou teachest	" 39	13	Teeth—'tween his teeth	V A	269
Teaching—Teaching the sheets	V A	398	whet his teeth at him	"	1113
Teaching decrepit age	"	1148	But through his teeth	R L	1787
Teaching them thus to use it	R L	62	Pluck the keen teeth	Son 19	3
Team—had his team to guide	V A	179	Tell—Tell me, love's master	V A	585
Tear—she with her tears	"	49	He tells her, no; to-morrow	"	587
with her contending tears	"	82	More I could tell	"	805
quench them with my tears	"	192	She tells them 'tis	"	897
With tears, which chorus-like	"	360	Tells him of trophies	"	1013
your feigned tears	"	425	Do tell her she is dreadfully beset	R L	444
the crystal tears gave light	"	491	and tell my loving tale	"	480
Dost thou drink tears	"	949	marking what he tells	"	510
O, how her eyes and tears	"	961	will tell my story	"	813
seen in the tears, tears in her eye	"	962	But tell me, girl, when went	"	1275
tears make them wet again	"	966	than one hath power to tell	"	1288
Whereat her tears began	"	979	sad tales doth tell	"	1495
With purple tears, that his wound wept	"	1054	And tell thy grief	"	1603
my salt tears gone	"	1071	To tell them all	"	1617
first should dry his tears	"	1092	and tell the face thou viewest	Son 3	1
which she compares to tears	"	1176	count the clock that tells the time	" 12	1
Nor children's tears	R L	431	But not to tell of good	" 14	3
tears ensue the deed	"	502	fortune to brief minutes tell	" 14	5
			I tell the day to please him	" 28	9

Tell—from woe to woe tell o'er	Son 30	10
doth almost tell my name	" 76	7
if he can tell	" 84	7
of our old acquaintance tell	" 89	12
nothing thence but sweetness tell	" 93	12
That tongue that tells	" 95	5
any summer's story tell	" 98	7
and your gifts to tell	" 103	12
Tell me thou lovest elsewhere	" 139	5
yet, love, to tell me so	" 140	6
yet not directly tell	" 144	10
My soul doth tell my body	" 151	7
Let it not tell your judgement	L C	73
you are, O, hear me tell	"	253
yet not directly tell	P P	2 10
thou comest thy tale to tell	"	19 7
Telling—still telling what is told	Son 76	14
by thy true-telling friend	" 82	12
Tell-tale—object to the tell-tale Day	R L	806
Temperance—when.... is thaw'd	"	884
Temperate—lovely and more....	Son 18	2
Temper'd—Strong-temper'd steel his stronger strength obey'd	V A	111
Tempering—dissolves with tempering	"	565
Tempest—from.... and from rain	"	238
tempest to the field	"	454
tempest after sun	"	800
This windy tempest	R L	1788
That looks on tempests	Son 116	6
Temple—his soul's fair temple	R L	719
Her sacred temple spotted	"	1172
Tempt—uproar tempts his veins	"	427
And now, to tempt all	L C	252
Temptation—For still.... follows	Son 41	4
and to temptation slow	" 94	4
Tempted—Not to be tempted	L C	251
Tempter—gave the tempter place	"	318
Tempteth—Tempteth my better angel	Son 144	6
Tempteth my better angel	P P	2 6
Tempting—Upon thy tempting lip	V A	127
the tempting tune is blown	"	778
tempting her to thee	Son 41	13
Ten—Ten kisses short as one	V A	22
What is ten hundred	"	519
without ten women's wit	"	1008
He ten times pines	R L	1115
Or ten times happier be it ten for one	Son 6	8
Ten times thyself	" 6	9
If ten of thine ten times	" 6	10
then ten times happy me	" 37	14
ten times more in worth	" 38	9
Tenant—tenants to their shame	R L	1260
all tenants to the heart	Son 46	10
Tend—strange shadows on you tend	" 53	2
What should I do but tend	" 57	1
to no other pass my verses tend	" 103	11
his lovised properties did tend	L C	212
Tender—was the tender boy	V A	32
The tender spring	"	127
broad buttock, tender hide	"	298
Her other tender hand	"	352
eats up Love's tender spring	"	656
do the tender leaves	"	798
whose tender horns being hit	"	1033
in pity of his tender years	"	1091
Unapt for tender smell	R L	695
wait on the tender spring	"	869

Tender—His tender heir might bear	Son 1	4
And, tender churl	" 1	12
As tender nurse	" 22	12
In tender embassy of love	" 45	6
To kiss the tender inward	" 128	6
Nor tender feeling	" 141	6
The tender nibbler	P P	4 11
Tender—Tender my suit	R L	534
The barren tender	Son 83	4
Of pensived and subdued desires the tender	L C	219
Tender'd—fee of parting.... is	V A	538
as you to me then tender'd	Son 120	11
Tenderer—His tenderer cheek	V A	353
Tenour—the tenour of her woe	R L	1310
The scope and tenour	Son 61	8
Tent—his tent my bed	V A	108
the night before in Tarquin's tent	R L	15
Tenth—Be thou the tenth Muse	Son 38	9
Tereu—' Tereu, Tereu !' by and by	P P	21 14
Tereus—While thou on Tereus	R L	1134
Term—May any terms acquit me	"	1706
For term of life	Son 92	2
Buy terms divine	" 146	11
And long upon these terms	L C	176
Term'd—be term'd a poet's rage	Son 17	11
Termless—on that termless skin	L C	94
Terror—Which with cold terror	V A	1048
with trembling terror die	R L	231
What terror 'tis	"	452
makes supposed terror true	"	455
Effects of terror	L C	202
Testament—writ in my testament	R L	1183
Testy—His testy master	V A	319
fond and testy as a child	R L	1094
As testy sick men	Son 140	7
Text—The text is old	V A	806
Than—' Thrice fairer than myself	"	7
more lovely than a man	"	9
than doves or roses are	"	10
than she for this good turn	"	92
Nay, more than flint	"	200
a whiter hue than white	"	398
That worse than Tantalus	"	599
than thy spear's point	"	626
And more than so	"	661
than civil home-bred strife	"	764
more moving than your own	"	776
Her more than haste	"	909
Rather than triumph	R L	77
More than his eyes	"	105
more slavish tribute than they owe	"	299
With more than admiration	"	418
Worse than a slavish wipe	"	537
no harder than a stone	"	593
a dearer thing than life	"	687
far poorer than before	"	693
deeper sin than bottomless conceit	"	701
hearts, harder than stones	"	978
Wilder to him than tigers	"	980
Than they whose whole	"	1159
No more than wax	"	1245
than I can well express	"	1286
than one hath power to tell	"	1288
more than hear them told	"	1324
lesser noise than shallow fords	"	1329
with more than haste	"	1352
Speed more than speed	"	1336
In me moe words than woes	"	1615

Than—But more than he happier than thou art	R L ...... Son	6	1718 9
fairer lodged than gentle love	"	10	10
than you yourself here live	"	13	2
more blessed than my barren rhyme	"	16	4
than your painted counterfeit	"	16	8
of less truth than tongue	"	17	10
eye more bright than theirs	"	20	5
be elder than thou art	"	22	8
More than that tongue	"	23	12
A dearer birth than this	"	32	11
more than thy sins are	"	35	8
Than those old nine	"	38	10
more than thou hadst before	"	40	2
than hate's known injury	"	40	12
not farther than my thoughts	"	47	11
than spurring to his side	"	50	12
Than unswept stone	"	55	4
should blunter be than appetite	"	56	2
is no stronger than a flower	"	65	4
than the eye hath shown	"	69	8
Than you shall hear	"	71	2
than mine own desert	"	72	6
than niggard truth	"	72	8
Than both your poets	"	83	14
Than this rich praise	"	84	2
than high birth to me	"	91	9
Richer than wealth, prouder than garments' cost	"	91	10
more delight than hawks or horses	"	91	11
than thy love will stay	"	92	3
Than that which on thy humour	"	92	8
smell far worse than weeds	"	94	14
faster than Time wastes life	"	100	13
Than when her mournful hymns	"	102	10
Than when it hath	"	103	4
Than of your graces	"	103	12
than in my verse can sit	"	103	13
Than public means	"	111	4
Grows fairer than at first	"	119	12
more than I have spent	"	119	14
to be vile than vile esteemed	"	121	1
Than think that we before have heard	"	123	8
more short than waste or ruining	"	124	4
more blest than living lips	"	128	12
more red than her lips' red	"	130	2
Than in the breath	"	130	8
more than enough am I	"	135	3
more than o'er-press'd defence	"	139	8
Than the true gouty landlord	L C		140
Brighter than glass	P P	7	3
Softer than wax	"	7	4
Paler for sorrow than her milk-white dove	"	9	3
with more than love's good will	"	9	7
he saw more wounds than one	"	9	13
more than I did crave	"	10	9
More in women than in men	"	18	18
Than—To break upon the galled shore and than	R L		1440
Thank—O, give thyself the thanks	Son	38	5
Then thank him not	"	79	13
That—Nature that made thee, with	V A		11
Saith that the world hath ending	"	......	12
a river that is rank	"	......	71
And begg'd for that which thou unmask'd shalt have	"	......	102
he that overruled I oversway'd	"	......	109

That—mastering her that foil'd the god of fight	V A		114
flowers that are not gather'd	"	......	131
That thou shouldst think it heavy	"	......	156
That thine may live when thou	"	......	172
In that thy likeness still is left	"	......	174
The sun that shines from heaven	"	......	193
I lie between that sun and thee	"	......	194
the fire that burneth me	"	......	196
'What am I, that thou shouldst contemn me this	"	......	203
That in each cheek appears a pretty dimple	"	......	242
To love a cheek that smiles at thee	"	......	252
a copse that neighbours by	"	......	259
Of the fair breeder that is standing by	"	......	282
his tail, that, like a falling plume	"	......	314
crows that strive to overfly them	"	......	324
That love-sick Love by pleading may be blest	"	......	328
An oven that is stopp'd	"	......	331
Taking no notice that she is so nigh	"	......	341
doves that sit a-billing	"	......	366
a coal that must be cool'd	"	......	387
Who is so faint, that dares not be so bold	"	......	401
That laughs and weeps, and all	"	......	414
The colt that's back'd	"	......	419
That inward beauty and invisible	"	......	434
Each part in me that were but sensible	"	......	436
That the sense of feeling were bereft me	"	......	439
And that I could not see, nor hear	"	......	440
breath perfumed that breedeth love by smelling	"	......	444
Jealousy, that sour unwelcome guest	"	......	449
a red morn that ever yet betoken'd	"	......	453
bankrupt that by love so thriveth	"	......	466
the wit that can so well defend her	"	......	472
the hurt that his unkindness marr'd	"	......	478
Thy eyes' shrewd tutor, that hard heart of thine	"	......	500
That they have murder'd this poor heart	"	......	502
That the star-gazers, having writ	"	......	509
Say, for non-payment that the debt should double	"	......	521
clouds that shadow heaven's light	"	......	533
The heavenly moisture, that sweet coral mouth	"	......	542
That she will draw his lips' rich treasure dry	"	......	552
roe that's tired with chasing	"	......	561
prays her that he may depart	"	......	578
That worse than Tantalus' is her annoy	"	......	599
birds that helpless berries saw	"	......	604
But that thou told'st me thou wouldst	"	......	614
pikes that ever threat his foes	"	......	620
esteems that face of thine	"	......	631
They that thrive well	"	......	640
This canker that eats up	"	......	656
That sometime true news, sometime false doth bring	"	......	658
That if I love thee, I thy death	"	......	660
That tremble at the imagination	"	......	668
To one sore-sick that hears the passing-bell	"	......	702

THAT 279 THAT

That—Applying this to that, and so to so	V.A	713
'Why, what of that?' quoth she	"	717
For stealing moulds from heaven that were divine	"	730
That on the earth would breed	"	753
lamp that burns by night	"	755
to bury that posterity	"	758
Or butcher-sire that reaves his son of life	"	766
gold that's put to use	"	768
'What have you urged that I cannot reprove	"	787
The path is smooth that leadeth on to danger	"	788
That lends embracements unto every stranger	"	790
Mine ears, that to your wanton talk	"	809
the object that did feed her sight	"	822
as one that unaware	"	823
That all the neighbour caves	"	830
That cedar-tops and hills seem	"	858
influence that makes him bright	"	862
a son that suck'd an earthly mother	"	863
like one that spies an adder	"	878
And childish error, that they are afraid	"	898
And with that word	"	900
the path that she untreads again	"	908
Mistakes that aim, and cleaves	"	912
'Dost thou drink tears, that thou provokest	"	949
Those eyes that taught	"	952
tide that from her two cheeks	"	957
Sorrow that friendly sighs sought	"	964
That every present sorrow seemeth	"	970
web that she hath wrought	"	991
It was not she that call'd	"	993
the boar, that bloody beast	"	999
creature, that hath done thee wrong	"	1005
hoping that Adonis is alive	"	1009
And that his beauty may the better thrive	"	1011
Whereat she leaps that was but late forlorn	"	1026
That from their dark beds once more leap	"	1030
wound that the boar had trench'd	"	1052
tears, that his wound wept	"	1054
Her eyes are mad that they have wept	"	1062
That her sight dazzling makes the wound	"	1064
That makes more gashes	"	1066
What face remains alive that's worth the viewing	"	1076
the silly lamb that day	"	1098
That some would sing	"	1102
livery that he wore	"	1107
entertainment that he gave	"	1108
She takes him by the hand, and that is cold	"	1124
coffer-lids that close	"	1127
That, thou being dead, the day should yet be light	"	1134
That all love's pleasure shall not match	"	1140
With sweets that shall the truest sight beguile	"	1144

That—they that love best	V.A	1164
the boy that by her side lay kill'd	"	1165
blood, that on the ground lay spill'd	"	1167
Haply that name of 'chaste'	R.L	8
Which triumph'd in that sky	"	12
That kings might be espoused	"	20
To set forth that which is so singular	"	32
Of that rich jewel	"	34
Perchance that envy	"	39
that meaner men should vaunt	"	41
That golden hap which	"	42
Virtue would stain that o'er beauty, in that white intituled	"	56
	"	57
challenge that fair field	"	58
That oft they interchange armies, that would let him go	"	70
	"	76
Now thinks he that her husband's	"	78
prodigal that praised her so	"	79
In that high task hath done	"	80
Therefore that praise which	"	82
For that he colour'd with his high estate	"	92
That nothing in him seem'd	"	94
That, cloy'd with much, he pineth	"	98
But she, that never coped	"	99
troubled minds that wake	"	126
Those that much covet	"	134
That what they have not, that which they possess	"	135
That they prove bankrupt	"	140
That one for all	"	144
oft that wealth doth cost	"	146
So that in venturing ill	"	148
The things we are for that which we expect	"	149
Of that we have	"	152
Now serves the season that they may surprise	"	166
That from the cold stone	"	177
that which is divine	"	193
That spots and stains	"	196
That it will live engraven	"	203
That my posterity	"	208
To wish that I their father	"	210
This siege that hath engirt	"	221
That which is vile	"	252
roses that on lawn we lay	"	258
That had Narcissus seen her	"	265
the heart that shadows dreadeth	"	270
That now he vows a league	"	287
That eye which looks	"	290
That eye which him beholds	"	291
wind that fires the torch	"	315
The doors, the wind, the glove that did delay him	"	325
Like little frosts that sometime	"	331
That shuts him from the heaven	"	338
That for his prey	"	342
That his foul thoughts	"	346
the shame that follows sweet delight	"	357
The dove sleeps fast that this night-owl will catch	"	360
draw the cloud that hides	"	371
Whether it is that she reflects so bright	"	376
That dazzleth them	"	377
in that darksome prison died	"	379

		R L	
That—But that life lived in death			406
What he beheld, on that he firmly doted		"	416
That thinks she hath beheld		"	451
Who, angry that the eyes		"	461
His hand, that yet remains		"	463
her bulk that his hand shakes withal		"	467
That even for anger makes		"	478
Under that colour		"	481
My will that marks thee		"	487
That done, some worthless slave		"	513
The shame that from them		"	535
The blemish that will never be forgot		"	536
beast that knows no gentle right		"	545
gulf that even in plenty		"	557
That twice she doth begin		"	567
That to his borrow'd bed		"	573
Mud not the fountain that gave drink		"	577
the thing that cannot be amended		"	578
woodman that doth bend his bow		"	580
by him that gave it thee		"	624
all that brood to kill		"	627
That from their own misdeeds		"	637
That thou shalt see thy state		"	644
streams that pay a daily debt		"	649
That done, despitefully I mean		"	670
linen that she wears		"	680
That ever modest eyes		"	683
O, that prone lust should stain		"	684
his will, that lived by foul devouring		"	700
and when that decays		"	713
That through the length		"	718
victor that hath lost in gain		"	730
the wound that nothing healeth		"	731
The scar that will, despite of cure, remain		"	732
but that every eye		"	750
like water that doth eat in steel		"	755
That in their smoky rauks		"	783
Day behold that face		"	800
That all the faults which		"	804
the illiterate, that know not how		"	810
good name, that senseless reputation		"	820
If that be made a theme		"	822
That is as clear		"	825
he that gives them		"	833
That some impurity doth		"	851
aged man that coffers up his gold		"	855
torment that it cannot cure		"	861
in the moment that		"	868
no good that we can say		"	873
thou that executest		"	877
'Tis thou that spurn'st		"	880
souls that wander		"	882
free that soul which		"	900
incest, that abomination		"	921
all that are to come		"	923
murder'st all that are		"	929
the tiger that doth live		"	955
Lending him wit that to bad debtors lends		"	964
see one that by alms doth live		"	986
curse him that thou taught'st this ill		"	996
That makes him honour'd		"	1005
That—Since that my case		R L	1022
smoke from Ætna that in air consumes		"	1042
Or that which from discharged cannon fumes		"	1043
that cannot be		"	1049
Of that true type		"	1050
O, that is gone		"	1051
That thou art doting father		"	1064
mountain-spring that feeds a dale		"	1077
eyes that light will borrow		"	1083
eyes that are sleeping		"	1090
little birds that tune		"	1107
He ten times pines that pines beholding food		"	1115
grief grieves most at that would		"	1117
Philomel, that sing'st of ravishment		"	1128
That knows not parching heat		"	1145
deer, that stands at gaze		"	1149
That cannot tread the way		"	1152
They that lose half		"	1158
That mother tries		"	1160
That he may vow, in that sad hour		"	1179
Revenge on him that made me		"	1180
That wounds my body		"	1185
'Dear lord of that dear jewel		"	1191
Mine honour be the knife's that makes my wound		"	1201
My shame be his that did my fame		"	1202
my fame that lives		"	1203
To those that live		"	1204
How was I overseen that thou shalt see it		"	1206
little worms that creep		"	1248
that obscurely sleep		"	1250
winter that the flower hath kill'd		"	1255
not that devour'd, but that which doth devour		"	1256
Poor women's faults, that they are so fulfill'd		"	1258
shame that might ensue		"	1263
By that her death		"	1264
That dying fear		"	1266
Those tears from thee, that down thy cheeks		"	1271
And that deep torture		"	1287
Yet save that labour		"	1290
Of that unworthy wife that greeteth thee		"	1304
From that suspicion which		"	1321
motion that it doth behold		"	1326
a part of sorrow that we hear		"	1328
That two red fires		"	1353
That she her plaints		"	1364
That one might see		"	1386
That one would swear		"	1393
glance that sly Ulysses lent		"	1399
That it beguiled attention		"	1401
That for Achilles' image		"	1424
That through their light joy		"	1434
the spring that those shrunk pipes		"	1455
Pyrrhus that hath done him wrong		"	1467
quench Troy that burns so long		"	1468
Greeks that are thine enemies		"	1470
strumpet that began this stir		"	1471
That with my nails		"	1472
load of wrath that burning Troy		"	1474
the fire that burneth here		"	1475

That—his head that hath transgressed so	R L 1481
That piteous looks to Phrygian shepherds lent	" 1502
So mild that Patience seem'd to scorn	" 1505
A brow unbent, that seem'd to welcome	" 1509
That blushing red no guilty instance gave	" 1511
the fear that false hearts have	" 1512
That jealousy itself could not	" 1516
Of rich-built Ilion, that the skies were	" 1524
That she concludes the picture was belied	" 1533
'It cannot be,' quoth she, 'that so much guile	" 1534
she in that sense forsook	" 1538
those borrow'd tears that Sinon sheds	" 1549
clear pearls of his that move thy pity	" 1553
And in that cold hot-burning fire doth dwell	" 1557
That he finds means to burn	" 1561
That patience is quite beaten	" 1563
Comparing him to that unhappy guest	" 1565
And they that watch see time	" 1575
That she with painted images	" 1577
Hath thee befall'n, that thou dost tell thy grief, that we may give redress	" 1599
A stranger came, and on that pillow lay	" 1603
From that, alas, thy Lucrece is not	" 1620
That my poor beauty had purloin'd	" 1624
That was not forced; that never was	" 1651
The grief away that stops his answer so	" 1657
the eye that doth behold his haste	" 1664
the strait that forced him on	" 1668
For she that was thy Lucrece	" 1670
the help that thou shalt lend me	" 1682
Speaking to those that came with	" 1685
But she, that yet her sad task	" 1689
The face, that map which deep	" 1699
That guides this hand to give	" 1712
knife, that thence her soul unsheathed	" 1722
That blow did bail it	" 1724
Of that polluted prison where Lucrece' father, that beholds her bleed	" 1725
rivers, that the crimson blood some look'd black, and that false Tarquin	" 1732
	" 1738
	" 1743
Of that black blood a watery rigol	" 1745
Blushing at that which is	" 1750
'That life was mine	" 1752
But now that fair fresh mirror	" 1760
That I no more can see what once	" 1764
If they surcease to be that should survive	" 1766
Who, mad that sorrow should his use	" 1781
That no man could distinguish	" 1785
'I did give that life	" 1800
That—'tis mine that she hath kill'd	R L 1803
he throws that shallow habit by	" 1814
To slay herself, that should have slain	" 1827
That they will suffer these	" 1832
by the Capitol that we adore	" 1835
By heaven's fair sun that breeds	" 1837
Lucrece' soul that late complained	" 1839
And that deep vow, which Brutus made	" 1847
again repeat, and that they swore	" 1848
That thereby beauty's rose	Son 1 2
Thou that art now	" 1 9
the time that face should form another	" 3 2
hours that with gentle work	" 5 1
And that unfair which	" 5 4
That use is not forbidden	" 6 5
Which happies those that pay the willing loan	" 6 6
That's for thyself	" 6 7
Why lovest thou that which	" 8 3
the parts that thou shouldst bear	" 8 8
That thou consumest thyself	" 9 2
That thou no form	" 9 6
in that bosom sits	" 9 13
That on himself such murderous shame	" 9 14
deny that thou bear'st love to any	" 10 1
But that thou none lovest	" 10 4
That 'gainst thyself thou stick'st not to conspire	" 10 6
Seeking that beauteous roof to ruinate	" 10 7
that I may change my mind	" 10 9
That beauty still may live	" 10 14
from that which thou departest	" 11 2
And that fresh blood which	" 11 3
not let that copy die	" 11 14
clock that tells the time	" 12 1
That thou among the wastes	" 12 10
that you were yourself	" 13 1
So should that beauty which	" 13 5
By oft predict that I in heaven find	" 14 8
every thing that grows	" 15 1
That this huge stage	" 15 3
perceive that men as plants increase	" 15 5
the lines of life that life repair	" 16 9
child of yours alive that time	" 17 13
possession of that fair thou owest	" 18 10
as with that Muse	" 21 1
That heaven's air	" 21 8
Let them say more that like of hearsay well	" 21 13
I will not praise that purpose not to sell	" 21 14
For all that beauty that doth cover thee	" 22 5
More than that tongue that more	" 23 12
That hath his windows	" 24 8
joy in that I honour most	" 25 4
I, that love and am beloved	" 25 13
But that I hope	" 26 7
star that guides my moving	" 26 9
Save that my soul's imaginary sight	" 27 9
That am debarr'd	" 28 2
and that man's scope	" 29 7
That then I scorn to change	" 29 14

That—things removed that hidden in thee lie	Son	31	8	That—Each changing place with that which goes before	Son	60	3
That due of many now is	"	31	12	And Time that gave	"	60	8
When that churl Death	"	32	2	thy spirit that thou send'st from thee	"	61	5
'Tis not enough that through the cloud	"	34	5	It is my love that keeps mine eye	"	61	10
That heals the wound	"	34	8	love that doth my rest	"	61	11
To him that bears grieved at that which thou hast done	"	34	12	'Tis thee, myself, that for myself I praise	"	62	13
	"	35	1	That he shall never cut	"	63	11
That I am accessary	"	35	13	That time will come	"	64	12
To that sweet thief confess that we two must be twain	"	35	14	weep to have that which it fears to lose	"	64	14
	"	36	1	That in black ink my love	"	65	14
blots that do with me remain	"	36	3	Save that, to die I leave	"	66	14
take that honour from thy name	"	36	12	That sin by him advantage	"	67	3
Whilst that this shadow	"	37	10	Those parts of thee that the world's eye doth view	"	69	1
That I in thy abundance am	"	37	11				
what is best that best I wish in thee	"	37	13	Want nothing that the thought of hearts	"	69	2
thou dost breathe, that pour'st into my verse	"	38	2	give thee that due	"	69	3
For who's so dumb that cannot write to thee	"	38	7	tongues, that give thee so thine own	"	69	6
And he that calls on thee	"	38	11	And that, in guess they measure by thy deeds	"	69	10
That by this separation I may	"	39	7	The soil is this, that thou dost common grow	"	69	14
That due to thee which	"	39	8				
And that thou teachest how	"	39	13	That thou art blamed shall not	"	70	1
No love, my love, that thou mayst true love call	"	40	3	A crow that flies	"	70	4
wrongs that liberty commits	"	41	1	Give warning to the world that I am fled	"	71	3
That thou hast her, it is	"	42	1				
That she hath thee, is	"	42	3	The hand that writ it	"	71	6
A loss in love that touches me more nearly	"	42	4	That I in your sweet thoughts	"	71	7
hath found that loss	"	42	10	What merit lived in me, that you should love	"	72	2
thought kills me, that I am not thought	"	44	9	That you for love speak well	"	72	10
But that, so much of earth	"	44	11	by that which I bring forth	"	72	13
the freedom of that right	"	46	4	That time of year thou mayst	"	73	1
plead that thou in him	"	46	5	Death's second self, that seals up all in rest	"	73	8
doth that plea deny	"	46	7	That on the ashes consumed with that which it was nourish'd by	"	73	10
When that mine eye is	"	47	3				
That to my use it might	"	48	3		"	73	12
Against that time, if ever that time come	"	49	1	To love that well which when that fell arrest	"	73	14
					"	74	1
Call'd to that audit	"	49	4	The worth of that is that which it	"	74	13
Against that time when	"	49	5	And that is this, and this	"	74	14
greet me with that sun	"	49	6	Then better'd that the world	"	75	8
Against that time do I	"	49	9	That every word doth	"	76	7
Doth teach that ease and that repose to say	"	50	3	Thine eyes that taught thee dumb	"	78	5
				proud of that which I compile	"	78	9
The beast that bears me	"	50	5	and he stole that word	"	79	9
bear that weight in me	"	50	6	thank him not for that which he doth say	"	79	13
That sometimes anger thrusts	"	50	10				
For that same groan doth	"	50	13	saw that you did painting need	"	83	1
is the time that keeps you	"	52	9	That you yourself, being extant	"	83	6
That millions of strange shadows	"	53	2	Who is it that says most	"	84	1
By that sweet ornament	"	54	2	Than this rich praise, that you alone are you	"	84	2
For that sweet colour	"	54	4				
When that shall vade	"	54	14	within that pen doth dwell	"	84	5
That wear this world out	"	55	12	That to his subject lends	"	84	6
the judgement that yourself arise	"	55	13	But he that writes of you	"	84	7
to the banks, that, when they see	"	56	11	That you are you	"	84	8
is love that in your will	"	57	13	To every hymn that able spirit affords	"	85	7
That god forbid that made me first your slave	"	58	1				
				But that is in my thought	"	85	11
That you yourself may privilege	"	58	10	That did my ripe thoughts	"	86	3
nothing new but that which is	"	59	1	mortal pitch, that struck me dead	"	86	6
O, that record could with	"	59	5	He, nor that affable familiar ghost	"	86	9
That I might see what	"	59	9	that enfeebled mine	"	86	14

That—And for that riches where is my deserving	Son	87	6
That thou in losing me	"	88	8
The injuries that to myself I do	"	88	11
That for thy right myself will bear	"	88	14
Say that thou didst forsake	"	89	1
comment upon that offence	"	89	2
Wretched in this alone, that thou mayst take	"	91	13
It depends upon that love of thine	"	92	4
Than that which on thy humour	"	92	8
Since that my life on thy revolt	"	92	10
what's so blessed fair that fears no blot	"	92	13
Therefore in that I cannot know	"	93	6
That in thy face sweet love should	"	93	10
They that have power	"	94	1
That do not do the thing	"	94	2
But if that flower	"	94	11
Lilies that fester smell far worse	"	94	14
That tongue that tells	"	95	5
all things turn to fair that eyes can see	"	95	12
graces that to thee resort	"	96	4
errors that in thee are seen	"	96	7
That leaves look pale	"	97	14
That heavy Saturn laugh'd	"	98	4
steal thy sweet that smells	"	99	2
Where art thou, Muse, that thou forget'st so long	"	100	1
To speak of that which gives	"	100	2
ear that doth thy lays esteem	"	100	7
That love is merchandized	"	102	3
Not that the summer is	"	102	9
But that wild music burthens	"	102	11
That having such a scope	"	103	2
That over-goes my blunt	"	103	7
To mar the subject that before was well	"	103	10
What's in the brain, that ink may character	"	108	1
That may express my love	"	108	4
So that eternal love	"	108	9
never say that I was false of heart	"	109	1
That is my home of love	"	109	5
Like him that travels	"	109	6
So that myself bring water	"	109	8
All frailties that besiege	"	109	10
That it could so preposterously	"	109	11
Most true it is that I have look'd	"	110	5
That did not better for my life	"	111	3
Thence comes it that my name receives a brand	"	111	5
bitterness that I will bitter think	"	111	11
Even that your pity is enough	"	111	14
That my steel'd sense	"	112	8
that my adder's sense	"	112	10
That all the world besides	"	112	14
And that which governs	"	113	2
And that your love taught it	"	114	4
That mine eye loves it	"	114	14
lines that I before have writ	"	115	1
Even those that said I could not love	"	115	2
To give full growth to that which still doth grow	"	115	11
That looks on tempests	"	116	6
Accuse me thus: that I have scanted all	"	117	1
That I have frequent been	"	117	5
That—That I have hoisted sail	Son	117	7
ere that there were true needing	"	118	8
The ills that were not, grew	"	118	10
Drugs poison him that so fell sick of you	"	118	14
That better is by evil still made	"	119	10
That you were once unkind	"	120	1
And for that sorrow which	"	120	2
O, that our night of woe	"	120	9
But that your trespass now becomes	"	120	13
No, I am that I am, and they that level	"	121	9
Which shall above that idle rank remain	"	122	3
That poor retention could not	"	122	9
those tables that receive thee more	"	122	12
Time, thou shalt not boast that I do change	"	123	1
What thou dost foist upon us that is old	"	123	6
Than think that we before	"	123	8
not policy, that heretic	"	124	9
That it nor grows with heat	"	124	12
to this purpose that her skill	"	126	7
That every tongue says beauty	"	127	14
Upon that blessed wood	"	128	2
concord that mine ear confounds	"	128	4
those jacks that nimble leap	"	128	5
which should that harvest reap	"	128	7
the heaven that leads men to this hell	"	129	14
the breath that from my mistress reeks	"	130	8
That music hath a far more	"	130	10
some say that thee behold	"	131	5
that is not false I swear	"	131	9
Nor that full star that ushers in the even	"	132	7
Doth half that glory to the sober west	"	132	8
all they foul that thy complexion lack	"	132	14
Beshrew that heart that makes my heart	"	133	1
For that deep wound it gives	"	133	2
and all that is in me	"	133	14
confess'd that he is thine	"	134	1
Myself I'll forfeit, so that other mine	"	134	3
Under that bond that him as fast doth bind	"	134	8
Thou usurer that put'st forth all to use	"	134	10
am I that vex thee still	"	135	3
and me in that one 'Will	"	135	14
If thy soul check thee that I come so near	"	136	1
Swear to thy blind soul that I was thy 'Will	"	136	2
That nothing me, a something	"	136	12
Make but my name thy love, and love that still	"	136	13
That they behold, and see not	"	137	2
Why should my heart think that a several plot	"	137	9
swears that she is made	"	138	1
That she might think me	"	138	3
thinking that she thinks me young	"	138	5
say not I that I am old	"	138	10

That—That thy unkindness lays upon my heart	Son	139	2	That—a palate hath that needs will taste	L C	167
That they elsewhere might dart	"	139	12	That's to ye sworn to none	"	180
That I may not be so	"	140	13	offences that abroad you see	"	188
'tis my heart that loves what they despise	"	141	3	They sought their shame that so their shame did find	"	187
That she that makes me sin	"	141	14	the many that mine eyes have seen	"	190
That have profaned	"	142	6	Figuring that they their passions	"	199
Root pity in thy heart, that, when it grows	"	142	11	sonnets that did amplify	"	209
To follow that which flies before her	"	143	7	charged me that I hoard them not	"	220
So runn'st thou after that which flies from thee	"	143	9	That is to you my origin	"	222
I pray that thou mayst have thy 'Will	"	143	13	yours that phraseless hand	"	225
And whether that my angel be	"	144	9	sighs that burning lungs did raise	"	228
lips that Love's own hand did make	"	145	1	She that her fame	"	243
the sound that said 'I hate	"	145	2	in that my boast is true	"	246
To me that languish'd for her sake	"	145	3	bosoms that to me belong	"	254
Chiding that tongue that ever sweet	"	145	6	hearts that do on mine depend	"	274
That follow'd it	"	145	10	battery that you make 'gainst mine	"	277
powers that thee array	"	146	2	credent soul to that strong-bonded oath	"	279
And let that pine	"	146	10	That shall prefer and undertake	"	280
Death, that feeds on men	"	146	13	That flame through water	"	287
For that which longer nurseth	"	147	2	What breast so cold that is not warmed	"	292
Feeding on that which doth	"	147	3	That not a heart which	"	309
Angry that his prescriptions	"	147	6	That the unexperient gave	"	318
That censures falsely what	"	148	4	O, that infected moisture	"	323
If that be fair whereon	"	148	5	O, that false fire	"	324
That is so vex'd with watching	"	148	10	O, that forced thunder	"	325
thee that I do call my friend	"	149	5	O, that sad breath	"	326
On whom frown'st thou that I do fawn upon	"	149	6	O, all that borrowed motion swears that she is made of truth	P P	1	1
That is so proud	"	149	10	that she might think me	"	1	3
Those that can see	"	149	14	thinking that she thinks me young	"	1	5
And swear that brightness	"	150	4	says my love that she is young	"	1	9
That in the very refuse	"	150	6	say not I that I am old	"	1	10
That, in my mind, thy worst all best exceeds	"	150	8	Since that our faults	"	1	14
tell my body that he may	"	151	7	That like two spirits do	"	2	2
hold it that I call	"	151	13	whether that my angel be	"	2	9
valley-fountain of that ground	"	153	4	Sun, that on this earth doth shine	"	3	10
nymphs that vow'd chaste life to keep	"	154	3	those pleasures live that art can comprehend	"	5	6
votary took up that fire	"	154	5	learned is that tongue that well	"	5	8
and this by that I prove	"	154	13	ignorant that soul that sees	"	5	8
scythed all that youth begun	L C		12	some praise, that I thy parts admire	"	5	10
That season'd woe had	"		18	O do not love that wrong	"	5	13
hands that lets not bounty fall	"		41	she hotter that did look	"	6	7
A reverend man that grazed his cattle	"		57	His approach that often there had been	"	6	8
a blusterer, that the ruffle knew	"		58	That Phœbus' lute, the queen of music, makes	"	8	10
If that from him there may	"		68	plum that hangs upon a tree	"	10	5
That maidens' eyes stuck over all	"		81	Ah, that I had my lady	"	11	13
Each eye that saw him	"		89	gloss that vadeth suddenly	"	13	2
velvet, on that termless skin	"		94	A flower that dies	"	13	3
his visage by that cost more dear	"		96	glass that's broken presently	"	13	4
That horse his mettle	"		107	that kept my rest away	"	14	2
'That he did in the general bosom reign	"		127	that liked of her master	"	16	2
'Many there were that did his picture get	"		134	an Englishman, the fair'st that eye could	"	16	3
fools that in the imagination set	"		136	the combat doubtful that love with love did fight	"	16	5
'So many have, that never touch'd his hand	"		141	That nothing could be used	"	16	10
self, that did in freedom stand	"		143	That the lover, sick to death	"	17	7
That we must curb it	"		163	My curtal dog, that went to have play'd	"	18	29
the sweets that seem so good	"		164	Other help for him I see that there is none	"	18	54
harms that preach in our behoof	"		165	the deer that thou shouldst strike	"	19	2

That—That thus dissembled her delight	L C	19	16
That which with scorn she put away	"	19	18
gulfs that women work	"	19	37
toys that in them lurk	"	19	39
The cock that treads them	"	19	40
Lest that my mistress hear	"	19	50
That hills and valleys	"	20	3
If that the world	"	20	17
That to hear it was great pity	"	21	12
That to hear her so complain	"	21	15
Every one that flatters thee	"	21	31
If that one be prodigal	"	21	39
they that fawn'd on him before	"	21	49
He that is thy friend	"	21	51
That defunctive music can	P T		14
That thy sable gender makest	"		18
That the turtle saw his right	"		34
That the self was not the same	"		38
That it cried, 'How true a twain	"		45
That are either true or fair	"		66
Thaw'd—wasted, thaw'd, and done	V A		749
when temperance is thaw'd	R L		884
The—Even as the sun	V A		1
of the weeping morn	"		2
hied him to the chase	"		3
The field's chief flower	"		8
Saith that the world	"		12
to the saddle-bow	"		14
The precedent of pith	"		26
the lusty courser's rein	"		31
was the tender boy	"		32
The studded bridle	"		37
The steed is stalled up	"		39
To tie the rider	"		40
quench the maiden burning	"		50
feedeth on the steam	"		63
overflow the bank	"		72
by the stern and direful	"		98
foil'd the god of fight	"		114
The kiss shall be thine own	"		117
What seest thou in the ground	"		118
the day seem night	"		122
The tender spring	"		127
The spring doth yearly grow	"		141
trip upon the green	"		146
Dance on the sands	"		148
draw me through the sky	"		153
shadow in the brook	"		162
fresh beauty for the use	"		164
Upon the earth's increase	"		169
Unless the earth	"		170
By this the love-sick queen	"		175
the shadow had forsook them	"		176
tired in the mid-day heat	"		177
when they blot the sky	"		184
The sun doth burn	"		186
Shall cool the heat	"		190
The sun that shines	"		193
The heat I have	"		195
darts forth the fire	"		196
the worse for one poor kiss	"		207
but the eye alone	"		213
now on the ground	"		224
Within the circuit	"		230
the pleasant fountains lie	"		234
her woes the more increasing	"		254
The time is spent	"		255
The strong-neck'd steed	"		263
The—The bearing earth	V A		267
The iron bit he eruseth	"		269
His nostrils drink the air	"		273
as if he told the steps	"		277
to captivate the eye	"		281
Of the fair breeder	"		282
would surpass the life	"		289
as if the dead the living	"		292
To bid the wind a base	"		303
the high wind sings	"		305
Fanning the hairs	"		306
scorns the heat he feels	"		311
and bites the poor flies	"		316
the unback'd breeder	"		320
With her the horse	"		322
unto the wood they hie	"		323
And now the happy season	"		327
the heart hath treble wrong	"		329
the aidance of the tongue	"		330
when the heart's attorney	"		335
The client breaks	"		336
Looks on the dull earth	"		340
to the wayward boy	"		344
note the fighting conflict	"		345
Lightning from the sky	"		348
disdain'd the wooing	"		358
takes him by the hand	"		361
once more the engine	"		367
palfrey from the mare	"		384
Welcomes the warm approach	"		386
set the heart on fire	"		388
The sea hath bounds	"		389
tied to the tree	"		391
Throwing the base thong	"		395
Teaching the sheets	"		398
To touch the fire, the weather being able	"		402
the lesson is but plain	"		407
Who plucks the bud	"		416
The colt that's back'd	"		419
it will not ope the gate	"		424
that the sense of feeling	"		439
but the very smell	"		441
from the stillitory	"		443
wert thou to the taste	"		445
of the other four	"		446
not wish the feast	"		447
double-lock the door	"		448
disturb the feast	"		450
Once more the ruby-colour'd	"		451
Wreck to the seaman, tempest to the field	"		454
woe unto the birds	"		455
Even as the wind is hush'd	"		458
Or as the wolf doth grin	"		459
Or as the berry breaks	"		460
like the deadly bullet	"		461
the wounding of a frown	"		465
The silly boy, believing	"		467
Fair fall the wit	"		472
on the grass she lies	"		473
strikes her on the cheeks	"		475
To mend the hurt	"		478
The night of sorrow	"		481
Like the fair sun	"		483
He cheers the morn, and all the earth relieveth	"		484
And as the bright sun glorifies the sky	"		485

The—the crystal tears gave light	V A	....	491	The—I perceive the reason	V A 727
Shone like the moon	"	....	492	To shame the sun	" 732
Or in the ocean drench'd, or in the fire	"	....	494	the curious workmanship	" 734
				subject to the tyranny	" 737
from the dangerous year	"	....	508	the marrow-eating sickness	" 741
That the star-gazers	"	....	509	heating of the blood	" 742
the plague is banish'd	"	....	510	And not the least	" 745
the debt should double	"	....	521	Whereat the impartial gazer	" 748
the ungrown fry forbears	"	....	526	on the sudden wasted	" 749
The mellow plum doth fall, the green sticks fast	"	....	527	with the mid-day sun	" 750
				That on the earth	" 753
'Look, the world's comforter ended in the west	"	....	529	the lamp that burns	" 755
	"	....	530	lend the world his light	" 756
The owl, night's herald	"	....	531	by the rights of time	" 759
The sheep are gone	"	....	532	the world will hold thee	" 761
The honey fee of parting	"	....	538	the hidden treasure frets	" 767
The heavenly moisture	"	....	542	The kiss I gave you	" 771
fall to the earth	"	....	546	strive against the stream	" 772
caught the yielding prey	"	....	547	the wanton mermaid's songs	" 777
the insulter willeth	"	....	550	the tempting tune is blown	" 778
pitch the price so high	"	....	551	the deceiving harmony	" 781
the sweetness of the spoil	"	....	553	Into the quiet closure	" 782
as the fleet-foot roe	"	....	561	The path is smooth	" 788
Or like the froward infant	"	....	562	is the bawd to lust's abuse	" 792
though the rose have prickles	"	....	574	the hot tyrant stains	" 797
The poor fool prays	"	....	578	do the tender leaves	" 798
The which, by Cupid's bow	"	....	581	The text is old, the orator too green	" 806
make the match	"	....	586	from the sweet embrace	" 811
To hunt the boar	"	....	588	through the dark lawnd	" 813
'The boar!' quoth she	"	....	589	Shooteth from the sky	" 815
upon the blushing rose	"	....	590	glides he in the night	" 816
the very lists of love	"	....	595	Till the wild waves	" 819
for the hot encounter	"	....	596	with the meeting clouds	" 820
by the eye and pine the maw	"	....	602	did the merciless and pitchy night	" 821
The warm effects	"	....	605	Fold in the object	" 822
thou wouldst hunt the boar	"	....	614	jewel in the flood	" 824
on the lion he will venture	"	....	628	in the dark she lay	" 827
the thorny brambles	"	....	629	the fair discovery	" 828
all the world amazes	"	....	634	all the neighbour caves	" 830
as he roots the mead	"	....	636	And still the choir	" 840
thou didst name the boar	"	....	641	and outwore the night	" 841
do abate the fire	"	....	654	to spend the night withal	" 847
The picture of an angry-chafing	"	....	662	Soothing the humour	" 850
upon the fresh flowers	"	....	665	Lo, here the gentle lark	" 853
and hang the head	"	....	666	And wakes the morning	" 855
tremble at the imagination	"	....	668	The sun ariseth	" 856
The thought of it	"	....	669	Who doth the world	" 857
with the boar to-morrow	"	....	672	The beauteous influence	" 862
the timorous flying hare	"	....	674	Musing the morning	" 866
Or at the fox	"	....	675	she coasteth to the cry	" 870
Or at the roe	"	....	676	the bushes in the way	" 871
creatures o'er the downs	"	....	677	catch her by the neck	" 872
on foot the purblind hare	"	....	679	she hears the hounds	" 877
Mark the poor wretch	"	....	680	The fear whereof	" 008
he outruns the wind	"	....	681	the timorous yelping of the hounds	" 881
The many musits, through the which he goes	"	....	683	But the blunt boar	" 884
				the cry remaineth	" 885
make the cunning hounds	"	....	686	the dogs exclaim aloud	" 886
stop the loud pursuers	"	....	688	dare not stay the field	" 894
The hot scent-snuffing	"	....	692	she spied the hunted boar	" 900
the cold fault cleanly out	"	....	694	to rate the boar	" 906
were in the skies	"	....	696	She treads the path	" 908
hears the passing-bell	"	....	702	Like the proceedings	" 910
the dew-bedabbled wretch	"	....	703	asks the weary caitiff	" 914
indenting with the way	"	....	704	The only sovereign plaster	" 916
the hunting of the boar	"	....	711	Against the welkin	" 921
the story aptly ends	"	....	716	to the ground below	" 923
The night is spent	"	....	717	how the world's poor people	" 925
The earth, in love	"	....	722	Gloss on the rose, smell to the violet	" 936

The—The Destinies will curse	V.A	 945
The crystal tide	"	 957
In the sweet channel	"	 958
through the flood-gates breaks the silver rain	"	 959
Her eyes seen in the tears	"	 962
The dire imagination	"	 975
To wash the foul face of the sluttish ground	"	 983
The one doth flatter	"	 989
the other kills thee	"	 990
she unweaves the web	"	 991
as I met the boar	"	 999
the boar provoked my tongue	"	 1003
may the better thrive	"	 1011
As falcons to the lure	"	 1027
The grass stoops not	"	 1028
The boar's foul conquest	"	 1030
murder'd with the view	"	 1031
Or, as the snail	"	 1033
Into the deep-dark cabins	"	 1038
To the disposing	"	 1040
And never wound the heart	"	 1042
As when the wind, imprison'd in the ground	"	 1046
Upon the wide wound that the boar had trench'd	"	 1052
makes the wound seem three	"	 1064
oft the eye mistakes, the brain being troubled	"	 1068
that's worth the viewing	"	 1076
The flowers are sweet	"	 1079
The sun doth scorn you, and the wind doth hiss you	"	 1084
the gaudy sun would peep	"	 1088
The wind would blow it	"	 1089
the lion walk'd along	"	 1093
The tiger would be tame	"	 1096
the wolf would leave	"	 1097
never fright the silly lamb	"	 1098
his shadow in the brook	"	 1099
The fishes spread on it	"	 1100
the birds such pleasure took	"	 1101
Ne'er saw the beauteous livery	"	 1107
Witness the entertainment	"	 1108
He ran upon the boar	"	 1112
the loving swine	"	 1115
the tusk in his soft groin	"	 1116
the more am I accurst	"	 1120
she falleth in the place	"	 1121
takes him by the hand	"	 1124
the woeful words she told	"	 1126
She lifts the coffer-lids	"	 1127
the day should yet be light	"	 1134
The bottom poison, and the top o'erstraw'd	"	 1143
the truest sight beguile	"	 1144
The strongest body	"	 1145
Strike the wise dumb, and teach the fool	"	 1146
to tread the measures	"	 1148
The staring ruffian	"	 1149
Pluck down the rich, enrich the poor	"	 1150
the young old, the old become	"	 1152
courage to the coward	"	 1158
'twixt the son and sire	"	 1160
By this the boy	"	 1165
on the ground lay spill'd	"	 1167
pale cheeks and the blood	"	 1169
The—the new-spring flower to smell	V.A	 1171
She crops the stalk, and in the breach appears	"	 1175
Thou art the next of blood	"	 1184
weary of the world	"	 1189
through the empty skies	"	 1191
From the besieged	R.L.	 1
Borne by the trustless wings	"	 2
leaves the Roman host	"	 3
bears the lightless fire	"	 4
with embracing flames the waist	"	 6
Lucrece the chaste	"	 7
To praise the clear	"	 11
For he the night before	"	 15
Unlock'd the treasure	"	 16
the heavens had him lent	"	 17
In the possession	"	 18
As is the morning's	"	 24
Against the golden splendour of the sun	"	 25
In the owner's arms	"	 27
The eyes of men	"	 30
Collatine the publisher	"	 33
to quench the coal	"	 47
by the Roman dame	"	 51
the golden age to gild	"	 60
use it in the fight	"	 62
the red should fence the white	"	 63
the other queen	"	 66
The sovereignty of either	"	 69
The coward captive	"	 75
The niggard prodigal	"	 79
the false worshipper	"	 86
the subtle-shining secrecies	"	 101
Writ in the glassy margents	"	 102
open'd to the light	"	 105
Won in the fields	"	 107
Far from the purpose	"	 113
Upon the world	"	 118
stows the day	"	 119
wore out the night	"	 123
The sundry dangers	"	 128
is the meed proposed	"	 132
the profit of excess	"	 138
The aim of all is but to nurse the life	"	 141
The death of all	"	 147
The things we are	"	 149
The thing we have	"	 153
Now stole upon the time the dead of night	"	 162
Now serves the season	"	 166
The silly lambs	"	 167
Th' one sweetly flatters, th' other feareth harm	"	 172
That from the cold stone	"	 177
And to the flame	"	 180
The dangers of his loathsome humanity abhor the deed	"	 184
	"	 195
the scandal will survive	"	 204
the herald will contrive	"	 206
shamed with the note	"	 208
if I gain the thing	"	 211
who will the vine destroy	"	 215
but to touch the crown	"	 216
Would with the sceptre	"	 217
sorrow to the sage	"	 222
The guilt being great, the fear doth still exceed	"	 229

The—	R L		The—As the grim lion	R L	
The shame and fault		238	by the conquest satisfied		421
ay, if the fact be known	"	239	the onset still expecting	"	422
The worst is but denial	"	242	Gives the hot charge	"	432
Urging the worser sense	"	249	commends the leading	"	434
kindly by the hand	"	253	the heart of all her land	"	436
from the warlike band	"	255	to the quiet cabinet	"	439
the roses took away	"	259	The sight which makes	"	442
In the flood	"	266	the weak brain's forgeries	"	453
Love thrives not in the heart	"	270	Who, angry that the eyes	"	460
The coward fights	"	273	To make the breach	"	461
beseems the sage	"	277	Who o'er the white sheet	"	469
from the stage	"	278	The reason of this rash alarm	"	472
to the unjust	"	285	The colour in thy face	"	473
And in the self-same seat	"	289	makes the lily pale	"	477
seeks to the heart	"	293	And the red rose	"	478
takes the worser part	"	294	the fault is thine	"	479
The Roman lord	"	301	the growing rose defends	"	482
The locks between	"	302	I think the honey	"	492
Which drives the creeping thief	"	305	Or stop the headlong fury	"	493
The threshold grates the door	"	306	tears ensue the deed	"	501
crannies of the place	"	310	towering in the skies	"	502
The wind wars	"	311	Coucheth the fowl below	"	506
And blows the smoke	"	312	The scornful mark	"	507
wind that fires the torch	"	315	And thou, the author	"	520
by the light he spies	"	316	The fault unknown	"	523
He takes it from the rushes	"	318	The poisonous simple	"	527
the needle his finger pricks	"	319	The shame that from them	"	530
He in the worst sense	"	324	The blemish that will never	"	535
The doors, the wind, the glove	"	325	the picture of true piety	"	536
stop the hourly dial	"	327	under the gripe's sharp claws	"	542
pays the hour his debt	"	329	To the rough beast	"	543
those lets attend the time	"	330	the world doth threat	"	545
sometime threat the spring	"	331	the aspiring mountains	"	547
rejoicing to the prime	"	332	the weak mouse panteth	"	548
And give the sneaped birds	"	333	In the remorseless wrinkles	"	555
Pain pays the income	"	334	She puts the period	"	562
The merchant fears	"	336	And midst the sentence	"	565
unto the chamber door	"	337	all the power of both	"	566
from the heaven	"	338	Mud not the fountain	"	572
from the blessed thing	"	340	Mar not the thing	"	577
As if the heavens	"	343	To all the host	"	578
But in the midst	"	344	and if the same	"	598
the eternal power	"	345	the like offences prove	"	600
auspicious to the hour	"	347	princes are the glass, the school, the book	"	613
The powers to whom	"	349	And wilt thou be the school	"	615
assist me in the act	"	350	thou didst teach the way	"	617
The blackest sin	"	354	And wipe the dim mist	"	630
The eye of heaven is out	"	356	swells the higher	"	643
Covers the shame	"	357	And with the wind	"	646
pluck'd up the latch	"	358	The petty streams	"	648
the door he opens wide	"	359	the ocean of thy blood	"	649
The dove sleeps fast	"	360	And not the puddle	"	655
Who sees the lurking serpent	"	362	The lesser thing should not the greater hide	"	658
Lies at the mercy	"	364	The cedar stoops not to the base shrub's foot	"	663
Into the chamber	"	365	at the cedar's root	"	664
The curtains being close	"	367	Unto the base bed	"	665
Which gives the watch-word	"	370	upon the light	"	671
To draw the cloud that hides the silver moon	"	371	The wolf hath seized his prey, the poor lamb cries	"	673
Look, as the fair	"	372	with the nightly linen	"	677
the curtain drawn	"	374	In the chastest tears	"	680
the period of their ill	"	380	The spots whereof	"	682
Cozening the pillow	"	387	And Lust, the thief	"	685
Without the bed	"	393	as the full-fed hound	"	693
On the green coverlet	"	394	The prey wherein	"	694
daisy on the grass	"	395			697
to adorn the day	"	399			
in the map of death	"	402			
to heave the owner out	"	413			

The—The flesh being proud	*R L*	712	**The**—To dry the old oak's sap	*R L*	950
The guilty rebel	"	714	the giddy round	"	952
through the length of times	"	718	the beldam daughters	"	953
To ask the spotted princess	"	721	make the child a man	"	954
through the dark night	"	729	slay the tiger	"	955
Bearing away the wound	"	731	tame the unicorn	"	956
The scar that will	"	732	To mock the subtle in themselves	"	957
She bears the load	"	734	cheer the ploughman	"	958
And he the burthen	"	735	And the dire thought	"	972
on the direful night	"	741	the abusing of his time	"	994
looks for the morning light	"	745	the thief run mad	"	997
behold the day	"	746	'The baser is he	"	1002
The same disgrace	"	751	The mightier man, the mightier		
Against the unseen	"	763	is the thing	"	1004
and the ravisher	"	770	The moon being clouded	"	1007
to meet the eastern light	"	773	'The crow may bathe	"	1009
permit the sun to climb	"	775	with the filth away	"	1010
ravish the morning air	"	778	But if the like the snow-white		
The life of purity, the supreme fair	"	780	swan desire	"	1011
The silver-shining queen	"	786	The stain upon his silver down	"	1012
Seasoning the earth	"	796	past the help of law	"	1022
Let not the jealous Day	"	800	The remedy indeed	"	1028
That all the faults	"	804	the self-same purpose	"	1047
to the tell-tale Day	"	806	the treasure stol'n away	"	1056
The light will show	"	807	the guiltless casket	"	1057
The story of sweet chastity	"	808	The stained taste	"	1059
The impious breach	"	809	I am the mistress	"	1069
Yea, tho illiterate	"	810	hide the truth	"	1075
The nurse, to still her child	"	813	The well tuned warble	"	1080
The orator, to deck	"	815	the blushing morrow	"	1082
Will tie the hearers	"	818	Continuance tames the one; the		
The branches of another root	"	823	other wild	"	1097
read the mot afar	"	830	The little birds	"	1107
And suck'd the honey	"	840	the bottom of annoy	"	1109
the worm intrude the maiden bud	"	848	To see the salve doth make the		
The aged man	"	855	wound ache more	"	1116
the harvest of his wits	"	859	the bounding banks o'erflows	"	1119
The sweets we wish for	"	867	As the dank earth	"	1130
Even in the moment	"	868	the diapason bear	"	1132
wait on the tender spring	"	869	sing'st not in the day	"	1142
The adder hisses where the sweet			seated from the way	"	1144
birds sing	"	871	As the poor frighted deer	"	1149
the traitor's treason	"	877	tread the way	"	1152
Thou set'st the wolf where he the			which of the twain	"	1154
lamb may get	"	878	Will slay the other	"	1162
Whoever plots the sin, thou point'st			which was the dearer	"	1163
the season	"	879	When the one pure, the other		
to seize the souls	"	882	made divine	"	1164
Thou makest the vestal	"	883	the bark peel'd from the lofty pine	"	1167
Thou blow'st the fire	"	884	batter'd by the enemy	"	1171
the humble suppliant's friend	"	897	Have heard the cause	"	1178
Give physic to the sick, ease to the			unto the knife	"	1181
pained	"	901	The one will live, the other being		
The poor, lame, blind	"	902	dead	"	1187
The patient dies while the physi-			to the skies	"	1199
cian sleeps	"	904	Mine honour be the knife's	"	1201
The orphan pines while the op-			wash the slander	"	1207
pressor feeds	"	905	And wiped the brinish pearl	"	1213
while the widow weeps	"	906	But as the earth doth weep, the		
From the creation to the general			sun being set	"	1226
doom	"	924	Even so the maid	"	1228
Betray'd the hours	"	933	Which makes the maid weep like		
fine the hate of foes	"	936	the dewy night	"	1232
Not spend the dowry	"	934	the other takes in hand	"	1235
To stamp the seal	"	941	The weak oppress'd, the impres-		
To wake the morn and sentinel			sion of strange kinds	"	1242
the night	"	942	the authors of their ill	"	1244
To wrong the wronger	"	943	the semblance of a devil	"	1246
To pluck the quills	"	949	all the little worms	"	1248

19

The—against the wither'd flower	R L	1254	The—the private pleasure	R L	1478
the flower hath kill'd	"	1255	Become the public plague	"	1479
The precedent whereof	"	1261	rings out the doleful knell	"	1495
To the poor counterfeit	"	1269	about the painting round	"	1499
replied the maid	"	1277	with the blunt swains	"	1504
'The more to blame	"	1278	In him the painter	"	1506
Yet with the fault	"	1279	give the harmless show	"	1507
ere the break of day	"	1280	the fear that false hearts	"	1512
The repetition cannot	"	1285	The well-skill'd workman	"	1520
The cause craves haste	"	1295	The credulous old Priam	"	1522
o'er the paper	"	1297	burnt the shining glory	"	1523
the tenour of her woe	"	1310	that the skies were sorry	"	1524
the life and feeling	"	1317	And chid the painter	"	1528
may grace the fashion	"	1319	the picture was belied	"	1533
the better so to clear her	"	1320	in her mind the while	"	1536
which the world	"	1321	She tears the senseless Sinon	"	1564
would not blot the letter	"	1322	the current of her sorrow	"	1569
For then the eye interprets to the ear	"	1325	Being from the feeling	"	1578
The heavy motion	"	1326	But now the mindful messenger come back	"	1583
The post attends	"	1333	rainbows in the sky	"	1587
Charging the sour-faced groom	"	1334	by the bloodless hand	"	1597
before the northern blast	"	1335	by the foe	"	1608
The homely villain	"	1338	Begins the sad dirge	"	1612
Receives the scroll	"	1340	shall fit the trespass best	"	1613
the worn-out age	"	1350	the fault amending	"	1614
The more she saw the blood	"	1357	Then be this all the task	"	1618
The more she thought	"	1358	in the interest	"	1619
And yet the duteous vassal	"	1360	'For in the dreadful dead	"	1625
The weary time	"	1361	The loathsome act	"	1636
Before the which is drawn the power of Greece	"	1368	The lechers in their deed	"	1637
			The adulterate death	"	1645
the city to destroy	"	1369	And far the weaker	"	1647
Which the conceited painter	"	1371	the judge is robb'd, the prisoner dies	"	1652
kiss the turrets bow'd	"	1372			
Shed for the slaughter'd husband by the wife	"	1376	Or, at the least	"	1654
			the hopeless merchant	"	1660
The red blood reek'd, to show the painter's strife	"	1377	The grief away	"	1664
			the violent roaring tide	"	1667
the labouring pioner	"	1380	Outruns the eye	"	1668
And from the towers	"	1382	Yet in the eddy	"	1669
The very eyes	"	1383	Back to the strait	"	1670
Gazing upon the Greeks	"	1384	back the same grief draw	"	1673
the painter interlaces	"	1390	the help that thou	"	1685
The face of either	"	1396	yet let the traitor die	"	1686
But the mild glance	"	1399	the hateful foe bewray'd	"	1698
encouraging the Greeks to fight	"	1402	The protestation stops	"	1700
charm'd the sight	"	1404	'What is the quality	"	1702
purl'd up to the sky	"	1407	with the foul act dispense	"	1704
the painter was so nice	"	1412	The poison'd fountain	"	1707
The scalps of many	"	1413	The face, that map	"	1712
to mock the mind	"	1414	from the deep unrest	"	1725
to the eye of mind	"	1426	unto the clouds bequeathed	"	1727
Stood for the whole	"	1428	And from the purple fountain	"	1734
And from the walls	"	1429	The murderous knife, and, as it left the place	"	1735
And from the strand	"	1436			
the red blood ran	"	1437	that the crimson blood	"	1738
the battle sought	"	1438	About the mourning	"	1744
upon the galled shore	"	1440	upon the tainted place	"	1746
In her the painter	"	1450	If in the child the father's image lies	"	1753
Wanting the spring	"	1455			
to the beldam's woes	"	1458	And shiver'd all the beauty	"	1763
The painter was no god	"	1461	conquest of the stronger	"	1767
scratch out the angry eyes	"	1469	the faltering feeble souls	"	1768
Of all the Greeks	"	1470	The old bees die, the young possess their hive	"	1769
Show me the strumpet	"	1471			
kindled the fire	"	1475	the pale fear	"	1775
The sire, the son, the dame, and daughter	"	1477	The deep vexation	"	1779
			as if the name he tore	"	1787

The—			
The one doth call her his, the other his	R L	....	1793
the claim they lay	"	....	1794
The father says 'She's mine	"	....	1795
The dispersed air, who, holding	"	....	1805
Brutus, who pluck'd the knife	"	....	1807
He with the Romans	"	....	1811
To check the tears	"	....	1817
is woe the cure for woe	"	....	1821
mistook the matter so	"	....	1826
Now by the Capitol	"	....	1835
breeds the fat earth's store	"	....	1837
the death of this true wife	"	....	1841
And kiss'd the fatal knife	"	....	1843
protestation urged the rest	"	....	1844
Then jointly to the ground	"	....	1846
The Romans plausibly did give	"	....	1854
But as the riper	Son	1	3
the world's fresh ornament	"	1	9
to the gaudy spring	"	1	10
Pity the world	"	1	13
To eat the world's due, by the grave and thee	"	1	14
Where all the treasure	"	2	6
tell the face thou viewest	"	3	1
Now is the time	"	3	2
dost beguile the world	"	3	4
Disdains the tillage	"	3	6
will be the tomb	"	3	7
Calls back the lovely April	"	3	10
The bounteous largess	"	4	6
lives th' executor to be	"	4	14
The lovely gaze	"	5	2
Will play the tyrants to the very same	"	5	3
pay the willing loan	"	6	6
Lo, in the orient when the gracious light	"	7	1
the steep-up heavenly hill	"	7	5
he reeleth from the day	"	7	10
The eyes, 'fore duteous	"	7	11
If the true concord	"	8	5
In singleness the parts	"	8	8
The world will wail thee	"	9	4
The world will be thy widow	"	9	5
In the world doth spend	"	9	9
still the world enjoys it	"	9	10
hath in the world an end	"	9	11
the user so destroys it	"	9	12
the times should cease	"	11	7
make the world away	"	11	8
she gave the more	"	11	11
When I do count the clock	"	12	1
And see the brave day	"	12	2
the violet past prime	"	12	3
did canopy the herd	"	12	6
Borne on the bier	"	12	8
among the wastes of time	"	12	10
Against the stormy gusts	"	13	11
Not from the stars	"	14	1
Whereon the stars	"	15	4
even by the self-same sky	"	15	6
Then the conceit of this	"	15	9
on the top of happy hours	"	16	5
So should the lines of life	"	16	9
I could write the beauty	"	17	5
The age to come would say	"	17	7
the darling buds	"	18	3
the eye of heaven shines	"	18	5
blunt thou the lion's paws	Son	19	1
make the earth devour	"	19	2
Pluck the keen teeth from the fierce tiger's jaws	"	19	3
And burn the long-lived	"	19	4
To the wide world	"	19	7
the master-mistress	"	20	2
Gilding the object	"	20	6
Is but the seemly raiment	"	22	6
actor on the stage	"	23	1
The perfect ceremony	"	23	6
be then the eloquence	"	23	9
eye hath play'd the painter	"	24	1
My body is the frame	"	24	3
For through the painter	"	24	5
where-through the sun	"	24	11
know not the heart	"	24	14
the marigold at the sun's eye	"	25	6
The painful warrior	"	25	9
Is from the book	"	25	11
And all the rest	"	25	12
The dear repose for limbs	"	27	2
which the blind do see	"	27	8
the benefit of rest	"	28	2
The one by toil, the other to complain	"	28	7
I tell the day	"	28	9
do blot the heaven	"	28	10
the swart-complexion'd night	"	28	11
thou gibi'st the even	"	28	12
Like to the lark	"	29	11
When to the sessions	"	30	1
I sigh the lack	"	30	3
And moan the expense	"	30	8
The sad account	"	30	11
But if the while I think	"	30	13
As interest of the dead	"	31	7
Thou art the grave	"	31	9
Hung with the trophies	"	31	10
hast all the all of me	"	31	14
the bettering of the time	"	32	5
the height of happier men	"	32	8
Flatter the mountain-tops	"	33	2
the meadows green	"	33	3
the basest clouds to ride	"	33	5
And from the forlorn world	"	33	7
The region cloud	"	33	12
Suns of the world may stain	"	33	14
that through the cloud thou break	"	34	5
To dry the rain	"	34	6
heals the wound and cures not the disgrace	"	34	8
yet I have still the loss	"	34	10
The offender's sorrow	"	34	11
bear the strong offence's cross	"	34	12
O, give thyself the thanks	"	38	5
Be thou the tenth Muse	"	38	9
The pain be mine, but thine shall be the praise	"	38	14
all the better part of me	"	39	2
To entertain the time	"	39	11
But here's the joy	"	42	13
For all the day	"	43	2
To the clear day	"	43	7
In the living day	"	43	10
If the dull substance	"	44	1
Upon the farthest earth	"	44	6
As soon as think the place	"	44	8
The other two	"	45	1

Entry		Son	
The—The first my thought, the other my desire	Son	45	3
the conquest of thy sight	"	46	2
the freedom of that right	"	46	4
But the defendant	"	46	7
all tenants to the heart	"	46	10
The clear eye's moiety and the dear heart's part	"	46	12
now unto the other	"	47	2
And to the painted banquet	"	47	6
Are left the prey	"	48	8
Within the gentle closure	"	48	11
from the thing it was	"	49	7
Within the knowledge of mine	"	49	10
To guard the lawful reasons	"	49	12
the strength of laws	"	49	13
I journey on the way	"	50	1
'Thus far the miles	"	50	4
The beast that bears me	"	50	5
the wretch did know	"	50	7
The bloody spur	"	50	9
excuse the slow offence	"	51	1
mounted on the wind	"	51	7
So am I as the rich	"	52	1
The which he will not	"	52	3
For blunting the fine point	"	52	4
In the long year set	"	52	6
jewels in the carcanet	"	52	8
So is the time	"	52	9
the wardrobe which the robe doth hide	"	52	10
and the counterfeit	"	53	5
Speak of the spring and foison of the year	"	53	9
The one doth shadow	"	53	10
The other as your bounty	"	53	11
The rose looks fair	"	54	3
The canker-blooms	"	54	5
As the perfumed tincture of the roses	"	54	6
nor the gilded monuments	"	55	1
root out the work of masonry	"	55	6
The living record	"	55	8
Even in the eyes	"	55	11
out to the ending doom	"	55	12
So, till the judgement	"	55	13
The spirit of love	"	56	8
like the ocean be	"	56	9
Which parts the shore	"	56	10
Come daily to the banks	"	56	11
may be the view	"	56	12
Upon the hours	"	57	2
chide the world-without-end hour	"	57	5
watch the clock for you	"	57	6
Nor think the bitterness	"	57	7
at your hand the account	"	58	3
The imprison'd absence	"	58	6
The second burthen	"	59	4
courses of the sun	"	59	6
what the old world could say	"	59	9
revolution be the same	"	59	12
the wits of former days	"	59	13
Like as the waves make towards the pebbled shore	"	60	1
once in the main of light	"	60	5
the flourish set on youth	"	60	9
delves the parallels	"	60	10
Feeds on the rarities	"	60	11
eyelids to the weary night	"	61	2
The—The scope and tenour	Son	61	8
To play the watchman	"	61	12
the treasure of his spring	"	63	8
The rich proud cost	"	64	2
the hungry ocean gain	"	64	5
the kingdom of the shore	"	64	6
And the firm soil win of the watery main	"	64	7
Against the wreckful siege	"	65	6
The map of days outworn	"	68	1
Before the golden tresses of the dead	"	68	5
The right of sepulchres	"	68	6
the world's eye doth view	"	69	1
the thought of hearts can mend	"	69	2
the voice of souls	"	69	3
the eye hath shown	"	69	8
the beauty of thy mind	"	69	9
the rank smell of weeds	"	69	12
The soil is this	"	69	14
was ever yet the fair	"	70	2
The ornament of beauty	"	70	3
Thy worth the greater	"	70	6
the sweetest buds doth love	"	70	7
the ambush of young days	"	70	9
the surly sullen bell	"	71	2
the world that I am fled	"	71	3
The hand that writ it	"	71	6
Lest the wise world	"	71	13
O, lest the world	"	72	1
shake against the cold	"	73	3
late the sweet birds sang	"	73	4
the twilight of such day	"	73	5
fadeth in the west	"	73	6
the glowing of such fire	"	73	9
That on the ashes	"	73	10
As the death-bed	"	73	11
The very part	"	74	6
The earth can have	"	74	7
the better part of me	"	74	8
lost the dregs of life	"	74	9
The prey of worms	"	74	10
The coward conquest	"	74	11
The worth of that	"	74	13
showers are to the ground	"	75	2
And for the peace of you	"	75	3
Doubting the filching age	"	75	6
the world may see my pleasure	"	75	8
Why with the time	"	76	3
ever the same	"	76	5
For as the sun	"	76	13
The vacant leaves	"	77	3
The wrinkles which thy glass	"	77	5
the dumb on high	"	78	5
to the learned's wing	"	78	7
but mend the style	"	78	11
Deserves the travail of a worthier pen	"	79	6
And in the praise thereof	"	80	3
wide as the ocean is	"	80	5
The humble as the proudest	"	80	6
The worst was this	"	80	14
to all the world must die	"	81	6
The earth can yield me	"	81	7
When all the breathers	"	81	12
even in the mouths of men	"	81	14
The dedicated words	"	82	3
the time-bettering days	"	82	8
The barren tender	"	83	4

	Son		
The—immured is the store	Son	84	3
by all the Muses filed	"	85	4
to the most of praise	"	85	10
for the breath of words	"	85	13
Was it the proud	"	86	1
Bound for the prize	"	86	2
the womb wherein they grew	"	86	4
The charter of thy worth	"	87	3
The cause of this fair gift	"	87	7
in the eye of scorn	"	88	2
The injuries that to myself	"	88	11
while the world is bent	"	90	2
with the spite of fortune	"	90	3
Come in the rearward	"	90	6
But in the onset come	"	90	11
At first the very worst	"	90	12
a joy above the rest	"	91	6
the worst of wrongs	"	92	5
When in the least of them	"	92	6
the false heart's history	"	93	7
do not do the thing	"	94	2
They are the lords and owners	"	94	7
The summer's flower is to the summer sweet	"	94	9
The basest weed	"	94	12
dost thou make the shame	"	95	1
a canker in the fragrant rose	"	95	2
Doth spot the beauty	"	95	3
the story of thy days	"	95	5
The hardest knife	"	95	14
As on the finger	"	96	5
The basest jewel	"	96	6
the stern wolf betray	"	96	9
the strength of all thy state	"	96	12
the pleasure of the fleeting year	"	97	2
The teeming autumn	"	97	6
the wanton burthen of the prime	"	97	7
the very birds are mute	"	97	12
dreading the winter's near	"	97	14
been absent in the spring	"	98	1
Yet nor the lays of birds, nor the sweet smell	"	98	5
at the lily's white	"	98	9
the deep vermillion in the rose	"	98	10
The forward violet	"	99	1
The purple pride	"	99	3
The lily I condemned	"	99	6
The roses fearfully	"	99	8
Sing to the ear	"	100	7
though less the show	"	102	2
The owner's tongue	"	102	4
and then but in the spring	"	102	5
Not that the summer	"	102	9
did hush the night	"	102	10
The argument, all bare	"	103	3
To mar the subject	"	103	10
Have from the forests	"	104	4
the seasons have I seen	"	104	6
When in the chronicle	"	106	1
of the fairest wights	"	106	2
Then, in the blazon	"	106	5
nor the prophetic soul	"	107	1
Of the wide world	"	107	2
Can yet the lease	"	107	3
The mortal moon	"	107	5
And the sad augurs mock	"	107	6
Now with the drops	"	107	9
What's in the brain	"	108	1
say o'er the very same	"	108	6
The—Weighs not the dust	Son	108	10
Finding the first conceit	"	108	13
Just to the time, not with the time exchanged	"	109	7
a motley to the view	"	110	2
next my heaven the best	"	110	13
The guilty goddess	"	111	2
like the dyer's hand	"	111	7
doth the impression fill	"	112	1
You are my all the world	"	112	5
That all the world besides	"	112	14
delivers to the heart	"	113	5
hath the mind no part	"	113	7
the rudest or gentlest sight	"	113	9
The most sweet favour	"	113	10
The mountain or the sea, the day or night	"	113	11
The crow or dove	"	113	12
the monarch's plague	"	114	2
O, 'tis the first	"	114	9
doth prepare the cup	"	114	12
'tis the lesser sin	"	114	13
blunt the sharp'st intents	"	115	7
to the course of altering	"	115	8
Crowning the present, doubting of the rest	"	115	12
Let me not to the marriage	"	116	1
the remover to remove	"	116	4
It is the star	"	116	7
even to the edge of doom	"	116	12
sail to all the winds	"	117	7
the level of your frown	"	117	11
The constancy and virtue	"	117	14
The ills that were not	"	118	10
and find the lesson true	"	118	13
In the distraction	"	119	8
The humble salve	"	120	12
And the just pleasure	"	121	3
Or, at the least	"	122	5
at the present nor the past	"	123	10
but the child of state	"	124	1
Under the blow	"	124	7
Whereto th' inviting time	"	124	8
call the fools of time	"	124	13
I bore the canopy	"	125	1
the outward honouring	"	125	2
In the old age	"	127	1
Fairing the foul	"	127	6
The wiry concord	"	128	4
To kiss the tender inward	"	128	6
At the wood's boldness	"	128	8
The expense of spirit	"	129	1
make the taker mad	"	129	8
this the world well knows	"	129	13
To shun the heaven	"	129	11
are nothing like the sun	"	130	1
Than in the breath	"	130	8
treads on the ground	"	130	12
Thou art the fairest	"	131	4
hath not the power	"	131	6
truly not the morning sun	"	132	5
the grey cheeks of the east	"	132	6
that ushers in the even	"	132	7
to the sober west	"	132	8
The statute of thy beauty	"	134	9
He pays the whole	"	134	14
The sea, all water	"	135	9
the treasure of thy love	"	136	5
Then in the number	"	136	9

The—Yet what the best is take the worst to be	*Son*	137	4	The—To be forbod the sweets *L C*	164
Be anchor'd in the bay	"	137	6	The one a palate hath "	167
Whereto the judgement	"	137	8	And knew the patterns "	170
the wide world's common place	"	137	10	Are errors of the blood, none of	
in the world's false subtleties	"	138	4	the mind "	184
are past the best	"	138	6	Among the many "	190
to justify the wrong	"	139	1	put to the smallest teen "	192
The manner of my pity-wanting	"	140	4	the encrimson'd mool "	201
the likeness of a man	"	141	11	With the annexions "	208
In pursuit of the thing	"	143	4	'" The diamond, why "	211
And play the mother's part	"	143	12	The deep-green emerald "	213
The better angel is	"	144	3	The heaven-hued sapphire and	
The worser spirit	"	144	4	the opal blend "	215
forth the sound that said	"	145	2	desires the tender "	219
the centre of my sinful earth	"	146	1	the airy scale of praise "	226
nurseth the disease	"	147	2	made the blossoms dote "	235
doth preserve the ill	"	147	3	The thing we have not "	240
The uncertain sickly	"	147	4	Playing the place "	241
the physician to my love	"	147	5	The scars of battle 'scapeth by the	
the truth vainly express'd	"	147	12	flight "	244
What means the world	"	148	6	The accident which brought "	247
The sun itself sees not	"	148	12	Upon the moment "	248
the motion of thine eyes	"	149	12	the caged cloister fly "	249
the lie to my true sight	"	150	3	The broken bosoms "	254
doth not grace the day	"	150	4	the suffering pangs it bears "	272
That in the very refuse	"	150	6	The aloes of all forces "	273
The more I hear	"	150	10	To leave the battery "	277
swear against the thing they see	"	152	12	the channel to the stream "	285
against the truth so foul a lie	"	152	14	the glowing roses "	286
The boy for trial needs	"	153	10	In the small orb "	289
the help of bath desired	"	153	11	the inundation of the eyes "	290
the bath for my help	"	153	13	could 'scape the hail "	310
The little Love-god	"	154	1	Against the thing "	313
The fairest votary	"	154	5	the garment of a Grace "	316
the general of hot desire	"	154	7	The naked and concealed "	317
list the sad-tuned tale	*L C*		4	That the unexperient gave the	
her visage from the sun	"		9	templer place "	318
Whereon the thought	"		10	betray the fore-betray'd "	328
The carcass of a beauty	"		11	Unskilful in the world's *P P*	1 4
the silken figures in the brine	"		17	my years be past the best "	1 6
to the spheres intend	"		23	The truth I shall not know "	2 13
To the orbed earth	"		25	Did not the heavenly rhetoric "	3 1
The mind and sight	"		28	'Gainst whom the world "	3 2
and gave the flood	"		44	Did court the lad "	4 3
the lines she rents	"		55	The tender nibbler would not	
that the ruffle knew	"		58	touch the bait "	4 11
The swiftest hours	"		60	If knowledge be the mark "	5 7
In brief the grounds	"		63	the sun dried up the dewy morn "	6 1
in the charity of age	"		70	the herd gone to the hedge "	6 2
The injury of many	"		72	Hot was the day "	6 7
occasion of the wind	"		86	on the brook's green brim "	6 10
did enchant the mind	"		89	sun look'd on the world "	6 11
the web it seem'd to wear	"		95	the loss thereof still fearing "	7 10
noble by the sway	"		108	Yet in the midst "	7 11
Whether the horse by him	"		111	She framed the love, and yet she	
by the well-doing steed	"		112	foil'd the framing "	7 15
the verdict went	"		113	Bad in the best "	7 18
'So on the tip of his	"		120	the sister and the brother- "	8 2
the weeper laugh, the laugher weep	"		124	must the love be great "	8 3
He had the dialect	"		125	Because thou lovest the one and I	
In the general bosom reign	"		127	the other "	8 4
In the imagination set	"		136	Upon the lute "	8 6
The goodly objects which abroad	"		137	the sweet melodious sound "	8 9
Than the true gouty	"		140	the queen of music, makes "	8 10
Reserved the stalk	"		147	Fair was the morn when the fair	
which remain'd the foil	"		153	queen of love "	9 1
The destined ill	"		156	Forbade the boy "	9 8
To put the by-past perils	"		158	Deep in the thigh "	9 11
				' here was the sore "	9 12

THE 295 THEE

Phrase	Ref	Col	Line
The—Pluck'd in the bud and vaded in the spring	P P	10	2
before the fall should be	"	10	6
She told the youngling	"	11	3
the warlike god embraced me	"	11	5
the warlike god unlaced me	"	11	7
As if the boy should use	"	11	8
did act the seizure	"	11	10
wither'd on the ground	"	13	9
on the doubts of my decay	"	14	4
As take the pain, but cannot pluck the pelf	"	14	12
throw gazes to the east	"	15	1
heart doth charge the watch; the morning rise	"	15	2
the office of mine eyes	"	15	4
were tuned like the lark	"	15	6
The night so pack'd	"	15	9
the night would post	"	15	13
added to the hours	"	15	11
the fairest one of three	"	16	1
the fair'st that eye could see	"	16	3
was the combat doubtful	"	16	5
leave the master loveless, or kill the gallant knight	"	16	6
Unto the silly damsel	"	16	8
more mickle was the pain	"	16	9
For of the two the trusty knight	"	16	11
was victor of the day	"	16	13
did bear the maid away	"	16	14
the learned man hath got the lady gay	"	16	15
alack the day	"	17	1
in the wanton air	"	17	4
Through the velvet leaves the wind	"	17	5
That the lover	"	17	7
the heaven's breath	"	17	8
meetings on the plains	"	18	46
the cause of all my mean	"	18	51
hath chose the dame	"	19	1
And stall'd the deer	"	19	2
The strongest castle	"	19	29
The golden bullet	"	19	30
The wiles and guiles	"	19	37
The tricks and toys	"	19	39
The cock that treads	"	19	40
all the joys in bed	"	19	47
to round me on th' ear	"	19	51
all the pleasures prove	"	20	2
the craggy mountains yields	"	20	4
we sit upon the rocks	"	20	5
see the shepherds feed	"	20	6
If that the world	"	20	17
In the merry month	"	21	2
Save the nightingale	"	21	8
the dolefull'st ditty	"	21	11
like the wind	"	21	33
Let the bird of loudest lay	P T		1
On the sole Arabian tree	"		2
precurrer of the fiend	"		6
of the fever's end	"		7
Save the eagle	"		11
Keep the obsequy	"		12
Let the priest in surplice	"		13
Be the death-divining	"		15
Lest the requiem	"		16
With the breath	"		19
Here the anthem	"		21
and the turtle died	"		23

Phrase	Ref	Line
The—Had the essence	P T	26
'Twixt the turtle	"	31
That the turtle saw	"	34
in the phœnix' sight	"	35
was the other's mine	"	36
the self was not the same	"	38
To the phœnix and the dove	"	50
the phœnix' nest	"	56
And the turtle's loyal	"	57
Thee—Nature that made thee	V A	11
I'll smother thee with kisses	"	18
as I entreat thee now	"	97
Shews thee unripe	"	128
then I were not for thee	"	137
think it heavy unto thee	"	156
a shadow for thee	"	191
that sun and thee	"	194
not brought forth thee	"	204
I'll give it thee again	"	209
I have hemm'd thee here	"	229
To shelter thee from tempest	"	238
No dog shall rouse thee	"	240
smiles at thee in scorn	"	252
I would assure thee	"	371
bane would cure thee	"	372
I heartily beseech thee	"	404
his proceedings teach thee	"	406
love by touching thee	"	438
to thee be still as much	"	442
hundred touches unto thee	"	519
But having thee at vantage	"	635
shakes thee on my breast	"	648
That if I love thee	"	660
seeing thee so indeed	"	667
To make thee hate	"	711
in love with thee	"	722
to rob thee of a kiss	"	723
Wherein she framed thee	"	731
framing thee so fair	"	714
will hold thee in disdain	"	761
May lend thee light	"	864
curse thee for this stroke	"	945
bid thee crop a weed	"	946
groan advantage thee	"	950
makes thee ridiculous	"	988
one doth flatter thee	"	989
the other kills thee quickly	"	990
I rail'd on thee	"	1002
that hath done thee wrong	"	1005
rock thee day and night	"	1186
thine eyes betray thee	R L	483
'Thus I forestall thee	"	484
hath ensnared thee	"	485
My will that marks thee	"	487
must enjoy thee	"	512
to destroy thee	"	514
seeing thee embrace him	"	518
gave drink to thee	"	577
labour hence to heave thee	"	586
I did entertain thee	"	595
will make thee only loved	"	610
When they in thee	"	613
Must he in thee	"	618
by him that gave it thee	"	624
'To thee, to thee, my heaved-up hands appeal	"	638
I will not hear thee	"	667
shall rudely tear thee	"	669
I mean to bear thee	"	670

Thee—				Thee—			
Coming from thee	P. L.		843	Although thou steal thee	Son	40	10
such numbers seek for thee	"		896	lead thee in their riot	"	41	11
cry out for thee	"		902	tempting her to thee	"	41	13
have to do with thee	"		911	That she hath thee	"	42	3
but he was stay'd by thee	"		917	If I lose thee	"	42	9
Would purchase thee	"		963	In dreams they look on thee	"	43	3
my honour lives in thee	"		1032	By looking on thee	"	43	10
To flatter thee	"		1061	to see till I see thee	"	43	13
smile at thee	"		1065	dreams do show thee me	"	43	14
I will not poison thee	"		1072	removed from thee	"	44	6
To imitate thee well	"		1137	Are both with thee	"	43	2
should thee behold	"		1143	embassy of love to thee	"	45	6
shall I bequeath to thee	"		1192	messengers return'd from thee	"	45	10
my hand shall conquer thee	"		1210	and they with thee	"	47	12
Those tears from thee	"		1271	Thee have I not	"	48	9
wife that greeteth thee	"		1304	When I shall see thee frown	"	49	2
Hath thee befall'n	"		1599	being made from thee	"	50	8
On thee and thine	"		1630	when from thee I speed	"	51	2
and then I'll slaughter thee	"		1634	Since from thee going	"	51	13
when I might charm thee so	"		1681	Towards thee I'll run	"	51	14
Thy father die, and not thy father thee	"		1771	shadows like to thee do mock	"	61	4
				that thou send'st from thee	"	61	5
by the grave and thee	Son	1	14	For thee watch I	"	61	13
and she in thee	"	3	9	'Tis thee, myself, that for myself I praise	"	62	13
thine image dies with thee	"	3	14	Those parts of thee	"	69	1
largess given thee to give	"	4	6	give thee that due	"	69	3
nature calls thee to begone	"	4	11	that give thee so thine own	"	69	6
must be tomb'd with thee	"	4	13	still with thee shall stay	"	74	4
In thee thy summer	"	6	2	was consecrate to thee	"	74	6
to breed another thee	"	6	7	Too base of thee	"	74	12
ten times refigured thee	"	6	10	and this with thee remains	"	74	14
Leaving thee living in posterity	"	6	12	Thy glass will show thee	"	77	1
do but sweetly chide thee	"	8	7	will give thee memory	"	77	6
Sings this to thee	"	8	14	Shall profit thee	"	77	14
The world will wail thee	"	9	4	invoked thee for my Muse	"	78	1
form of thee hast left behind	"	9	6	under thee their poesy	"	78	4
Make thee another self	"	10	13	is thine and born of thee	"	78	10
live in thine or thee	"	10	14	Yet what of thee thy poet	"	79	7
She carved thee for her seal	"	11	13	He robs thee of, and pays it thee again	"	79	8
when he takes thee hence	"	12	14	He lends thee virtue	"	79	9
of thee this I prognosticate	"	14	13	No praise to thee but what in thee doth live	"	79	12
compare thee to a summer's day	"	18	1	Since what he owes thee	"	79	14
and this gives life to thee	"	18	14	gives thee releasing	"	87	1
But I forbid thee	"	19	8	My bonds in thee	"	87	4
as she wrought thee	"	20	10	For how do I hold thee	"	87	5
me of thee defeated	"	20	11	Thus have I had thee	"	87	13
she prick'd thee out	"	20	13	And prove thee virtuous	"	88	4
when in thee time's furrows	"	22	3	my loving thoughts on thee	"	88	10
beauty that doth cover thee	"	22	6	Doing thee vantage	"	88	12
myself, but for thee will	"	22	10	to thee I so belong	"	88	13
to gaze therein on thee	"	24	12	For thee, against myself	"	89	13
To thee I send this	"	26	3	Compared with loss of thee	"	90	4
how I do love thee	"	26	13	And having thee	"	91	12
a zealous pilgrimage to thee	"	27	6	chose out thee	"	95	10
For thee and for myself	"	27	14	graces that to thee resort	"	96	4
still farther off from thee	"	28	8	that in thee are seen	"	96	7
Haply I think on thee	"	29	10	I love thee in such sort	"	96	13
the while I think on thee	"	30	13	From thee, the pleasure	"	97	2
that hidden in thee lie	"	31	8	his pleasures wait on thee	"	97	11
parts of me to thee did give	"	31	11	it had stol'n from thee	"	99	14
evermore acknowledge thee	"	36	9	gives thee all my might	"	100	2
should do thee shame	"	36	10	for't lies in thee	"	101	10
I love thee in such sort	"	36	13	I teach thee how	"	101	13
that best I wish in thee	"	37	13	to thee my true spirit	"	108	2
that cannot write to thee	"	38	7	proved thee my best of love	"	110	8
And he that calls on thee	"	38	11	of thee, thy record	"	122	8
when I praise thee	"	39	4				
That due to thee	"	39	8				
I cannot blame thee	"	40	6				

Thee—that receive thee more	*Son*	122	12	Thee—To live with thee	*P P*	20	20
to remember thee	"	122	13	they cannot hear thee	"	21	21
Thy registers and thee I both defy	"	123	9	they will not cheer thee	"	21	22
despite thy scythe and thee	"	123	14	Even so, poor bird, like thee	"	21	27
only me for thee	"	125	12	Every one that flatters thee	"	21	31
still will pluck thee back	"	126	6	He will help thee	"	21	52
keeps thee to this purpose	"	126	7	He with thee doth bear a part	"	21	56
quietus is to render thee	"	126	12	Theft—and complain on theft	*V A*	....	160
by thee blushing stand	"	128	8	ransack'd by injurious theft	*R L*	....	838
some say that thee behold	"	131	5	of murder and of theft	"	....	918
mourning doth thee grace	"	132	11	But for his theft	*Son*	99	12
Of him, myself, and thee	"	133	7	Their—amid their plenty	*V A*	....	20
for I, being pent in thee	"	133	13	their elbows and their hips	"	....	44
am I that vex thee still	"	135	3	gather'd in their prime	"	....	131
If thy soul check thee	"	136	1	Herbs for their smell	"	....	165
so it please thee hold	"	136	11	by their own direction	"	....	216
a something sweet to thee	"	136	12	Open'd their mouths	"	....	248
Let me excuse thee	"	139	9	wither in their prime	"	....	418
If I might teach thee wit	"	140	5	borrow'd all their shine	"	....	488
might speak ill of thee	"	140	10	true leaders to their queen	"	....	503
I do not love thee	"	141	1	let their crimson liveries	"	....	506
in thee a thousand errors note	"	141	2	their verdure still endure	"	....	507
feast with thee alone	"	141	8	birds to their nest	"	....	532
from serving thee	"	141	10	Their lips together	"	....	546
Be it lawful I love thee	"	142	1	take counsel of their friends	"	....	610
as mine importune thee	"	142	10	hounds mistake their smell	"	....	686
that which flies from thee	"	143	9	pursuers in their yell	"	....	688
chase thee afar behind	"	143	10	their clamorous cry	"	....	693
powers that thee array	"	146	2	do they spend their mouths	"	....	695
For I have sworn thee fair, and				their loud alarums	"	....	700
thought thee bright	"	147	13	Their light blown out	"	....	826
say I love thee not	"	149	1	Their copious stories	"	....	845
myself with thee partake	"	149	2	from their strict embrace	"	....	874
Do I not think on thee	"	149	3	Finding their enemy	"	....	887
Who hateth thee	"	149	5	their captain once doth yield	"	....	893
Who taught thee how to make me				clapping their proud tails	"	....	923
love thee more	"	150	9	Shaking their scratch'd ears	"	....	924
I to be beloved of thee	"	150	14	began to turn their tide	"	....	979
doth point out thee	"	151	9	their office and their light	"	....	1039
In loving thee	"	152	1	By their suggestion	"	....	1044
breach do I accuse thee	"	152	5	from their dark beds	"	....	1050
but to misuse thee	"	152	7	their colours fresh and trim	"	....	1079
faith in thee is lost	"	152	8	on it their golden gills	"	....	1100
And, to enlighten thee	"	152	11	some other in their bills	"	....	1102
For I have sworn thee fair	"	152	13	Their virtue lost	"	....	1131
In thee hath neither sting	*L C*	....	265	their lives shall not enjoy	"	....	1164
Vows for thee broke	*P P*	3	4	upon their whiteness stood	"	....	1170
I forswore not thee	"	3	6	Their mistress mounted	"	....	1191
in thee it is	"	3	11	Holding their course to Paphos,			
to thee I'll constant prove	"	5	3	where their queen	"	....	1193
to thee like osiers bowed	"	5	4	hap which their superiors want	*R L*	....	42
to know thee shall suffice	"	5	7	Their silver cheeks, and call'd it			
that well can thee commend	"	5	8	then their shield	"	....	61
that sees thee without wonder	"	5	9	from world's minority their right	"	....	67
be great 'twixt thee and me	"	8	3	Yet their ambition	"	....	68
Dowland to thee is dear	"	8	5	In their pure ranks	"	....	73
and both in thee remain	"	8	14	from their parling looks	"	....	100
I weep for thee	"	10	7	unloose it from their bond	"	....	136
I craved nothing of thee	"	10	10	that I their father had not been	"	....	210
I pardon crave of thee	"	10	11	Mine eyes forego their light	"	....	228
Age, I do abhor thee; youth, I do				with their opposite persuasion	"	....	286
adore thee	"	12	9	flatter'd by their leader's jocund			
Age, I do defy thee; O, sweet shep-				show	"	....	296
herd, hie thee	"	12	11	And as their captain, so their			
Ne'er to pluck thee	"	17	12	pride doth grow	"	....	298
and say thee nay	"	19	20	construes their denial	"	....	324
though she put thee back	"	19	36	till their effects be tried	"	....	353
make thee a bed of roses	"	20	9	By their high treason	"	....	369
these pleasures may thee move	"	20	15	the period of their ill	"	....	380

Their—Lucrece to their sight	R L	384
had sheathed their light	"	397
Save of their lord	"	409
Swell in their pride	"	432
bids them do their liking	"	434
Left their round turrets	"	441
Where their dear governess	"	443
confusion of their cries	"	445
fly from their lights	"	461
Thy kinsmen hang their heads	"	521
the author of their obloquy	"	523
bequeath not to their lot	"	534
not their own infamy	"	539
from their biding	"	550
Hindering their present fall	"	551
with their continual motion	"	591
Their own transgressions	"	634
That from their own misdeeds askance their eyes	"	637
To their salt sovereign, with their fresh falls' haste	"	650
and thou their slave	"	659
Thou their fair life	"	641
loathed in their shame	"	662
And by their mortal fault	"	724
forestall their will	"	728
To have their unseen sin	"	753
For they their guilt	"	754
Let their exhaled	"	779
That in their smoky ranks	"	783
makes short their pilgrimage	"	791
To cross their arms and hang their heads	"	793
To mask their brows and hide their infamy	"	794
of their own behests	"	852
Who in their pride	"	864
Their father was too weak	"	865
To hold their cursed-blessed as their pages	"	866
their glittering golden towers	"	910
alter their contents	"	945
lose their mildness	"	948
in their wildness	"	979
tune their morning's joy	"	980
their sweet melody	"	1107
to change their kinds	"	1108
doth melt their snow	"	1117
quench their light	"	1218
Their gentle sex	"	1231
they drown their eyes or break their hearts	"	1237
authors of their ill	"	1239
Their smoothness, like a goodly	"	1247
are their own faults' books	"	1253
tenants to their shame	"	1266
guilt within their bosoms lie	"	1342
beholds their blame	"	1343
both their faces blazed	"	1353
gleam'd forth their ashy lights	"	1378
in their faces	"	1388
Their face their manners most expressly told	"	1397
did their ears entice	"	1411
And in their rage	"	1419
When their brave hope	"	1430
To see their youthful sons	"	1432
And to their hope	"	1433
That through their light	"	1434
Their—and their ranks began	R L	1439
shoot their foam	"	1442
she their looks doth borrow	"	1498
shot from their fixed places	"	1523
When their glass fell wherein they view'd their faces	"	1526
To think their dolour	"	1582
The lechers in their deed	"	1637
Knights, by their oaths	"	1694
We are their offspring	"	1757
The young possess their hive	"	1769
Answer'd their cries	"	1806
such emulation in their woe	"	1808
to the ground their knees they bow	"	1846
Lease but their show; their substance still lives	Son	5	14
Vaunt in their youthful sap	"	15	7
And wear their brave state	"	15	8
yellow'd with their age	"	17	9
eye more bright than theirs	"	20	5
thy love's use their treasure	"	20	14
want to grace their art	"	24	13
favour with their stars	"	25	1
their fair leaves spread	"	25	5
their pride lies buried	"	25	7
they in their glory die	"	25	8
Who all their parts	"	31	11
Their images I loved	"	31	13
not for their rhyme	"	32	7
Theirs for their style	"	32	14
in their rotten smoke	"	34	4
Who lead thee in their riot	"	41	11
And by their verdict	"	46	11
their masked buds disclose	"	54	8
But, for their virtue only is their show	"	54	9
Of their sweet deaths	"	54	12
hasten to their end	"	60	2
o'ersways their power	"	65	2
Then, churls, their thoughts, although their eyes were kind	"	69	11
Showing their birth	"	76	8
their poesy disperse	"	78	4
Of their fair subject	"	82	4
And their gross painting	"	82	13
Reserve their character	"	85	3
Making their tomb	"	86	4
have done their spite	"	90	10
glory in their birth, some in their skill	"	91	1
In their wealth, some in their body's force	"	91	2
Some in their garments	"	91	3
Some in their hawks and hounds, some in their horse	"	91	4
owners of their faces	"	94	7
of their excellence	"	94	8
turn sourest by their deeds	"	94	13
Which for their habitation	"	95	10
after their lords' decease	"	97	8
Or from their proud lap	"	98	8
lose their dear delight	"	102	12
I see their antique pen	"	106	7
So all their praises	"	106	9
mock their own presage	"	107	6
their spheres been fitted	"	119	7
Which in their wills	"	121	8
reckon up their own	"	121	10
By their rank thoughts	"	121	12

Their—			
and in their badness reign	Son	121	14
in their gazing spent	"	125	8
becoming of their woe	"	127	13
would change their state	"	128	9
might dart their injuries	"	139	12
when their deaths be near	"	140	7
from their physicians know	"	140	8
their scarlet ornaments	"	142	6
revenues of their rents	"	142	8
levell'd eyes their carriage ride	L C		22
their poor balls are tied	"	.....	24
Their view right on; anon their gazes lend	"	.....	26
their sepulchres in mud	"	.....	46
so breaking their contents	"	.....	56
their silken parcels	"	.....	87
made fairer by their place	"	.....	117
yet their purposed trim	"	.....	118
Ask'd their own wills, and made their wills obey	"	.....	133
To serve their eyes, and in it put their mind	"	.....	135
They sought their shame that so their shame did find	"	.....	187
their reproach contains	"	.....	189
their passions likewise lent	"	.....	199
these talents of their hair	"	.....	204
Their kind acceptance	"	.....	207
their sickly radiance do	"	.....	214
Since I their altar	"	.....	224
Their distract parcels	"	.....	231
their fountains in my well	"	.....	255
suppliant their sighs	"	.....	276
which their hue encloses	"	.....	287
and eyes their wished sight	P P	13	10
Forth their dye	"	18	40
shepherds feed their flocks	"	20	6
to their tragic scene	P T	.....	52
not their infirmity	"	.....	60
Theirs— .... whose desperate hands	V A	.....	765
theirs in thought assign'd	L C	.....	158
Them— But rather famish them	V A	.....	20
Making them red and pale	"	.....	21
fan and blow them dry	"	.....	52
the shadow had forsook them	"	.....	176
hotly overlook them	"	.....	178
quench them with my tears	"	.....	192
unto the wood they hie them	"	.....	323
strive to overfly them	"	.....	324
was then between them	"	.....	353
as they had not seen them	"	.....	357
taught them scornful tricks	"	.....	501
pay them at thy leisure	"	.....	518
picks them all at last	"	.....	576
Doth make them droop	"	.....	666
If thou destroy them not	"	.....	760
She, marking them	"	.....	845
she hears them chant it	"	.....	869
She tells them	"	.....	897
Bids them leave quaking, bids them fear no more	"	.....	899
Infusing them with dreadful prophecies	"	.....	928
opens them again	"	.....	960
makes them wet again	"	.....	966
are both of them extremes	"	.....	987
Could rule them both	"	.....	1098
bids them still consort	"	.....	1041
He fed them with his sight	"	.....	1104

Them—			
Which of them both	R L	.....	53
Teaching them thus	"	.....	62
makes them still to fight	"	.....	68
lest between them both	"	.....	74
That dazzleth them	"	.....	377
As if between them twain	"	.....	405
bids them do their liking	"	.....	431
In darkness daunts them	"	.....	462
from them no device can take	"	.....	555
drop on them perpetually	"	.....	686
but he that gives them knows	"	.....	833
that we call them ours	"	.....	868
wait on them as their pages	"	.....	910
keep them from thy aid	"	.....	912
little stars may hide them	"	.....	1008
sorrows bear them mild	"	.....	1096
Is form'd in them by force	"	.....	1243
Then call them not the authors for I have them here	"	.....	1244
	"	.....	1290
might become them better	"	.....	1323
more than hear them told	"	.....	1324
he saw them quake and tremble	"	.....	1393
She lends them words	"	.....	1498
and make them bold	"	.....	1559
prepares to let them know	"	.....	1607
To tell them all	"	.....	1617
in them doth stand disgraced	"	.....	1833
in them I read such art	Son	14	10
Let them say more	"	21	13
Compare them with	"	32	5
Reserve them for my love	"	32	7
yea, take them all	"	40	1
I send them back again	"	45	14
And I am still with them	"	47	12
and he in them still green	"	63	14
When in the least of them	"	92	6
pluck them where they grew	"	98	8
it shapes them to your feature	"	113	12
Therefore to give them	"	122	11
rather make them born	"	123	7
before have heard them told	"	123	8
Give them thy fingers	"	128	14
proudly make them cruel	"	131	2
Or made them swear	"	152	12
Bidding them find	L C	.....	46
moe pleasures to bestow them	"	.....	139
which doth owe them	"	.....	140
supposed them mistress	"	.....	142
Love made them not	"	.....	185
Harm have I done to them	"	.....	194
that I hoard them not	"	.....	220
But yield them up	"	.....	221
I strong o'er them	"	.....	257
And, veil'd in them	"	.....	312
cherubin, above them hover'd	"	.....	319
to turn them both to gain	P P	16	10
toys that in them lurk	"	19	39
The cock that treads them	"	19	40
time with age shall them attaint	"	19	46
But in them it were a wonder	P T	.....	32
So between them love did shine	"	.....	33
Theme— leave this idle theme	V A	.....	422
your idle, overhandled theme	"	.....	770
If that he made a theme	R L	.....	822
Three themes in one	Son	105	12
Themselves— Rot and consume	V A	.....	132
Things growing to themselves	"	.....	166
hands themselves do slay	"	.....	765
Do burn themselves	"	.....	810

Themselves—If pleased themselves	V A	 843	Then—How comes it then	R L	....	895
of day, themselves withdrew	"	 1032	O, hear me then	"	.....	930
to rest themselves betake	R L	 125	True sorrow then	"	.....	1112
keep themselves enclosed	"	 378	Then let it not	"	.....	1174
themselves so beautify	"	 404	And then they drown their eyes	"	....	1259
do seldom to themselves appear	"	 633	Then call them not	"	.....	1244
which they themselves behold	"	 731	For then the eye	"	.....	1325
Which not themselves	"	 853	Then little strength rings out	"	.....	1495
in themselves beguiled	"	 957	and then she longs	"	.....	1571
Grieving themselves to guess	"	 1238	Then be this all the task	"	.....	1618
beauties do themselves forsake	Son	12 11	and then I'll slaughter thee	"	.....	1634
And in themselves their pride	"	25 7	And then against my heart	"	.....	1640
Die to themselves	"	54 11	let it then suffice	"	.....	1679
are themselves as stone	"	94 3	Then live, sweet Lucrece	"	.....	1770
now crown themselves assured	"	107 7	And then in key-cold	"	.....	1774
though they themselves be bevel	"	121 11	Then son and father weep	"	.....	1791
All aids, themselves made fairer	L C	 117	Then jointly to the ground	"	.....	1846
To themselves yet either	P T	 43	Then being ask'd	Son	2	5
Then—Then with her windy sighs	V A	 51	Then, beauteous niggard	"	4	5
Then why not lips on lips	"	 120	Then how, when nature calls	"	4	11
then wink again	"	 121	Then, were not summer's	"	5	9
Then mightst thou pause, for then			Then let not winter's	"	6	1
I were not for thee	"	 137	Then what could death do	"	6	11
Then woo thyself	"	 159	Then of thy beauty	"	12	9
and then his hand	"	 223	then you were	"	13	6
Then be my deer	"	 239	Then the conceit of this	"	15	9
Then, like a melancholy	"	 313	And then believe me	"	21	10
was then between them	"	 355	Then look I death	"	22	4
then love's deep groans	"	 377	How can I then be older	"	22	8
and then I chase it	"	 410	be then the eloquence	"	23	9
Incorporate then they seem	"	 540	Then happy I	"	25	13
But then woos best	"	 570	Then may I dare to boast	"	26	13
O, had she then gave over	"	 571	then not show my head	"	26	14
Then do they spend	"	 595	then begins a journey	"	27	3
Then shalt thou see	"	 703	For then my thoughts	"	27	5
then the story aptly ends	"	 716	How can I then return	"	28	1
O, then imagine this	"	 721	and then my state	"	29	10
'Nay, then,' quoth Adon	"	 769	That then I scorn	"	29	14
And then my little heart	"	 783	Then can I drown an eye	"	30	5
then he had spoke	"	 943	Then can I grieve	"	30	9
then join they all together	"	 971	O, then vouchsafe me	"	32	9
Then, gentle shadow	"	 1001	So then I am not lame	"	37	9
and then she reprehends	"	 1065	then ten times happy me	"	37	14
then would Adonis weep	"	 1090	hast thou then more	"	40	2
why then I know	"	 1109	Then, if for my love	"	40	5
What needeth then	R L	 31	then she loves but me alone	"	42	14
Then virtue claims	"	 59	then do mine eyes best see	"	43	1
call'd it then their shield	"	 61	Then thou, whose shadow	"	43	5
For then is Tarquin	"	 120	For then, despite of space	"	44	3
so then we do neglect	"	 152	No matter then although	"	44	5
Then where is truth	"	 158	then no longer glad	"	45	13
Then looking scornfully	"	 187	then my eye doth feast	"	47	9
Then my digression	"	 202	my poor beast then find	"	51	5
Then white as lawn	"	 259	Then should I spur	"	51	7
and then it faster rock'd	"	 262	Then can no horse	"	51	9
'Why hunt I then	"	 267	Then, churls, their thoughts	"	69	11
'Then, childish fear, avaunt	"	 274	Then thou alone kingdoms	"	70	1
Then who fears sinking	"	 280	then should make you woe	"	71	8
How can they then	"	 350	So then thou hast but lost	"	74	9
'Then Love and Fortune	"	 351	Then better'd that the world	"	75	8
Then had they seen	"	 380	Then thank him not	"	79	13
Then Collatine again	"	 381	Then if he thrive	"	80	13
then force must work	"	 513	Then others for the breath	"	83	13
'Then, for thy husband	"	 533	Then lack'd I matter	"	86	14
do not then ensnare me	"	 584	worth then not knowing	"	87	9
Then kings' misdeeds	"	 649	Then hate me	"	90	1
then most doth tyrannize	"	 676	Then need I not to fear	"	92	5
And then with lank	"	 708	Then do thy office, Muse	"	101	13
'So then he hath it	"	 862	and then but in the spring	"	102	5

Then—Were it not sinful then	Son	103	9	There—to persuade him there	V A	 1114
Then, in the blazon	"	106	5	There shall not be	"	 1187
Then give me welcome	"	110	13	for his being there	R L	 114
Pity me then and wish	"	111	8	there's no death supposed	"	 133
Pity me then, dear friend	"	111	13	there is such thwarting strife	"	 143
Yet then my judgement	"	115	3	if there be no self-trust	"	 158
Might I not then say	"	115	10	there is no hate	"	 240
Then might I not say so	"	115	13	shriek to see him there	"	 307
which I then did feel	"	120	2	Even there he starts	"	 348
you to me, then tender'd	"	120	11	there were no strife	"	 405
then her breasts are dun	"	130	3	yet, winking, there appears	"	 458
let it then as well beseem	"	132	10	And, lo, there falls	"	 653
Then will I swear	"	132	13	For there it revels	"	 713
But then my friend's heart	"	133	10	lies panting there	"	 737
Thou canst not then use rigour	"	133	12	She there remains	"	 744
Then in the number	"	136	9	Let there bechance him	"	 976
And then thou lovest me	"	136	14	and there we will unfold	"	 1146
Then, soul, live thou	"	146	9	and there she stay'd	"	 1275
there's no more dying then	"	146	14	lamentable objects there	"	 1373
then love doth well denote	"	148	7	There might you see	"	 1390
No marvel then	"	148	11	there would appear	"	 1382
Then, gentle cheater	"	151	3	And here and there	"	 1390
O, then, advance of yours	L C	....	225	There pleading might you see	"	 1401
'"How mighty then you are	"	....	253	imaginary work was there	"	 1422
Whose sights till then	"	....	282	plead for justice there	"	 1649
Then thou, fair sun	P P	3	10	and confounds him there	Son	5 6
then it is no fault of mine	"	3	12	Nor draw no lines there	"	19 10
Then fell she on her back	"	4	13	And there reigns love	"	31 3
Then must the love be great	"	8	3	there is but one respect	"	36 5
And then she clipp'd Adonis	"	11	6	in their riot even there	"	41 11
Then, lullaby, the learned man	"	16	15	If there be nothing new	"	59 1
And then too late	"	19	15	there is no remedy	"	62 3
you had not had it then	"	19	24	There lives more life	"	83 13
Then live with me	"	20	16	For there can live no hatred	"	93 5
Then farewell his great renown	"	21	48	have any wrinkle graven there	"	100 10
Then—There is no heaven by holy then	"	19	45	and there appears a face	"	103 6
				conceit of love there bred	"	108 13
Then—the galled shore, and than	R L	....	1440	I have gone here and there	"	110 1
Thence—thence doth little harm	V A	....	195	ere that there was true needing	"	118 8
And when from thence	"	....	227	is there more delight	"	130 7
As if from thence	"	....	488	And will, thy soul knows, is admitted there	"	136 3
He carries thence incaged	"	....	582			
creeps sadly thence	R L	....	736	there's no more dying then	"	146 14
He thence departs	"	....	743	There is such strength	"	150 7
And bids it leap from thence	"	....	760	Came there for cure	"	154 13
no water thence proceeds	"	....	1552	there may be aught applied	L C	 68
that thence her soul	"	....	1724	Many there were that did	"	 134
to bear dead Lucrece thence	"	....	1850	Even there resolved my reason	"	 296
thence thou wilt be stol'n	Son	48	13	There my white stole	"	 297
why should I haste me thence	"	51	3	she touch'd him here and there	P P	4 7
of any fear from thence	"	86	12	that often there had been	"	6 8
nothing thence but sweetness	"	93	12	There a nay is placed	"	18 12
Thence comes it that my name	"	111	5	I see that there is none	"	18 54
And almost thence my nature	"	111	6	and chiefly there	"	19 26
But thence I learn	"	118	13	There is no heaven	"	19 45
And thence this slander	"	131	14	There will we sit upon the rocks	"	20 5
would not break from thence	L C	....	34	There will I make thee	"	20 9
and did thence remove	"	....	237	And there sung the dolefull'st ditty	"	21 11
There—There thy beauty lies	V A	....	119	Number there in love was slain	P T	 28
where there are but twain	"	....	123	Thereby—That .... beauty's rose	Son	1 2
if there he came to lie	"	....	245	her seal, and meant thereby	"	11 13
There Love lived, and there he	"	....	246	Therefore—Therefore no marvel	V A	 390
and there he stares	"	....	301	And therefore hath she	"	 733
and left Adonis there	"	....	322	Therefore, despite of	"	 751
For there his smell	"	....	691	Therefore, in sadness	"	 807
false sound enter there	"	....	780	And therefore would he	"	 1087
There lives a son	"	....	863	Therefore that praise	R L	 82
And there another	"	....	915	Who, therefore angry	"	 388
And there all smother'd up in shade	"	....	1035	And therefore would they still	"	 752

Therefore—....now I need not fear	R L	....	1032	These—Tired with all these, from			
And therefore still in night	"	....	1085	these would I	Son	66	13
And therefore are they form'd	"	....	1241	before these last so bad	"	67	14
And therefore Lucrece swears	"	....	1452	Before these bastard signs	"	68	3
O therefore, love, be of thyself	Son	22	9	Commit to these waste blanks	"	77	10
and therefore to be won	"	41	5	These offices, so oft as thou wilt look	"	77	13
therefore to be assailed	"	41	6	But these particulars are not	"	91	7
Therefore desire, of perfect'st love	"	51	10	All these I better	"	91	8
Therefore are feasts	"	52	5	I with these did play	"	98	14
And therefore mayst without attain	"	82	2	behold these present days	"	106	13
And therefore art enforced	"	82	7	These blenches gave my heart	"	110	7
And therefore to your fair	"	83	2	these rebel powers that thee array	"	146	2
And therefore have I slept	"	83	5	These often bathed she	L C	....	50
Therefore in that I cannot	"	93	6	And long upon these terms	"	....	176
Therefore, like her, I sometime	"	102	13	these talents of their hair	"	....	204
Therefore my verse to constancy confined	"	105	7	Lo, all these trophies	"	....	218
Therefore to give them	"	122	11	For these, of force, must your	"	....	223
and therefore we admire	"	123	5	Take all these similes	"	....	227
Therefore my mistress' eyes	"	127	9	Now all these hearts	"	....	274
Therefore I lie with her	"	138	13	Here in these brakes	P P	9	10
therefore from my face	"	139	11	If these pleasures may thee move	"	20	15
Therefore I'll lie with love	P P	1	13	These pretty pleasures might me move	"	20	19
Therein—And therein heartens up	R L	....	295	These are certain signs	"	21	57
And therein so ensconced	"	....	1315	For these dead birds sigh	P T	....	67
to gaze therein on thee	Son	24	12	They—So they were dew'd	V A	....	66
and therein dignified	"	101	4	yet are they red	"	....	116
and therein show'st	"	126	3	For, where they lay	"	....	176
Thereof—not...., make discovery	R L	....	1314	when they blot the sky	"	....	184
And in the praise thereof	Son	80	3	If they burn too	"	....	192
the loss thereof still fearing	P P	7	10	fly they know not whether	"	....	304
and thereof free	L C	....	100	As they were mad, unto the wood they hie them	"	....	323
Thereon—shall thereon fall and die	R L	....	1139	as they had not seen them	"	....	357
These—These blue-vein'd violets	V A	....	125	They wither in their prime	"	....	413
These forceless flowers	"	....	152	they make no battery	"	....	426
These lovely caves, these round enchanting pits	"	....	247	Would they not wish	"	....	447
And these mine eyes	"	....	503	they borrow'd all their shine	"	....	488
Would root these beauties	"	....	636	That they have murder'd	"	....	502
Pursue these fearful creatures	"	....	677	Long may they kiss	"	....	505
of all these maladies	"	....	745	And as they last	"	....	507
she at these sad signs	"	....	929	Are they not quickly told	"	....	520
and bents these from the stage	R L	....	278	Incorporate then they seem	"	....	540
these poor forbiddings could not	"	....	323	Whereon they surfeit	"	....	544
these lets attend the time	"	....	330	They that thrive well	"	....	640
These worlds in Tarquin new ambition bred	"	....	411	till they have singled	"	....	693
blow these pitchy vapours	"	....	550	they spend their mouths	"	....	695
If all these petty ills shall change	"	....	656	others, they think, delight	"	....	843
So shall these slaves be king	"	....	659	they answer all "Tis so	"	....	851
These means, as frets upon an instrument	"	....	1140	They all strain courtesy	"	....	888
these pretty creatures stand	"	....	1233	They busely fly	"	....	894
These many lives confound	"	....	1489	that they are afraid	"	....	898
These contraries such unity do hold	"	....	1558	bleeding as they go	"	....	924
These water-galls in her dim element	"	....	1588	they long have gazed	"	....	927
will suffer these abominations	"	....	1832	They bid thee crop	"	....	946
Yet in these thoughts	Son	29	9	they view'd each other's sorrow	"	....	963
These poor rude lines	"	32	4	then join they all together	"	....	971
Or any of these all	"	37	6	Where they resign	"	....	1039
do please these curious days	"	38	13	they have wept till now	"	....	1062
These present-absent with swift motion glide	"	45	4	They both would strive	"	....	1092
when these quicker elements are gone	"	45	5	they him with berries	"	....	1104
more bright in these contents	"	55	3	and they are pale	"	....	1123
In these black lines be seen	"	63	13	As if they heard	"	....	1126
Tired with all these	"	66	1	wherein they late excell'd	"	....	1131
				They that love best	"	....	1164
				That oft they interchange	R L	....	70
				what they have not, that which they possess	"	....	135
				They scatter and unloose it	"	....	136

They—they have but less	R L	....	137
That they prove bankrupt	"	....	140
that they may surprise	"	....	166
tribute than they owe	"	....	299
But, as they open, they all rate his ill	"	....	364
They fright him	"	....	308
And they would stand	"	....	347
How can they then assist	"	....	350
But blind they are	"	....	378
O, had they in that darksome prison	"	....	379
Then had they seen	"	....	380
But they must ope	"	....	383
Till they might open	"	....	399
no bearing yoke they knew	"	....	409
by oath they truly honoured	"	....	410
And they, like straggling slaves	"	....	428
They, mustering to the quiet	"	....	442
When they in thee	"	....	613
partially they smother	"	....	634
how are they wrapp'd in	"	....	636
they basely dignified	"	....	660
they thy fouler grave	"	....	661
they in thy pride	"	....	662
by nature they delight	"	....	697
They think not	"	....	750
which they themselves behold	"	....	751
would they still in darkness be	"	....	752
For they their guilt	"	....	754
and they too strong	"	....	865
they ne'er meet with Opportunity	"	....	903
They buy thy help	"	....	913
hide them when they list	"	....	1068
wheresoe'er they fly	"	....	1014
They that lose half	"	....	1158
Than they whose whole	"	....	1159
And then they drown their eyes	"	....	1239
are they form'd as marble will	"	....	1241
that they are so fulfill'd	"	....	1258
But they whose guilt	"	....	1342
such signs of rage they bear	"	....	1419
It seem'd they would debate	"	....	1421
they such odd action yield	"	....	1433
the strand of Dardan where they fought	"	....	1436
They join and shoot their foam	"	....	1442
wherein they view'd their faces	"	....	1526
And they that watch see time	"	....	1575
they all at once began to say	"	....	1709
and they none of ours	"	....	1737
If they surcease to be	"	....	1766
possess the claim they lay	"	....	1794
That they will suffer	"	....	1832
their knees they bow	"	....	1846
and that they swore	"	....	1848
When they had sworn	"	....	1849
They did conclude to bear	"	....	1830
they with winter meet	Son	5	13
They do but sweetly	"	8	7
as they see others	"	12	12
They draw but what they see	"	24	14
they in their glory die	"	25	8
And thou, all they, hast all	"	31	14
And though they be	"	32	6
And they are rich	"	34	14
they view things unrespected	"	43	2
they look on thee	"	43	3
and they with thee	"	47	12
They—Or, if they sleep	Son	47	13
they thinly placed are	"	52	7
They live unwoo'd	"	54	10
they wink with fullness	"	56	6
that, when they see	"	56	11
mended, or whether better they	"	59	11
And they shall live	"	63	14
They look into the beauty	"	69	9
they measure by thy deeds	"	69	10
where they did proceed	"	76	8
when they have devised	"	82	9
wherein they grew	"	86	4
they most do show	"	94	2
They rightly do inherit	"	94	5
They are the lords	"	94	7
Or, if they sing	"	97	13
pluck them where they grew	"	98	8
They were but sweet	"	98	11
And, for they look'd	"	106	11
They had not skill	"	106	12
and they that level	"	121	9
they themselves be bevel	"	121	11
evil they maintain	"	121	13
They are but dressings	"	123	4
and they mourners seem	"	127	10
Yet so they mourn	"	127	13
they would change their state	"	128	9
To say they err	"	131	7
and they, as pitying me	"	132	1
And all they foul	"	132	14
That they behold, and see not what they see	"	137	2
They know what beauty is	"	137	3
are they now transferred	"	137	14
That they elsewhere	"	139	12
For they in thee	"	141	2
loves what they despise	"	141	3
Or, if they have	"	148	3
what they see aright	"	148	4
against the thing they see	"	152	12
As they did battery to the spheres	L C	....	23
sometimes they do extend	"	....	25
observed as they flew .	"	....	60
unruly though they be	"	....	103
which abroad they find	"	....	137
with acture they may be	"	....	185
They sought their shame	"	....	187
they their passions likewise lent	"	....	199
when they to assail begun	"	....	262
with bleeding groans they pine	"	....	275
As they must needs	P P	8	2
they cannot hear thee	"	21	21
they will not cheer thee	"	21	22
Bountiful him they will him call	"	21	40
Quickly him they will entice	"	21	44
They have at commandment	"	21	46
They that fawn'd on him	"	21	49
So they lived, as love in twain	P T	....	25
Thick—Thin mane, thick tail	V A	....	298
His short thick neck	"	....	627
misty vapours march so thick	R L	....	782
so thick come in his poor heart's aid	"	....	1784
Thick-sighted—Thick-sighted, barren	V A	....	136
Thief—hemm'd with thieves	"	....	1022
Lurk'd like two thieves	"	....	1086
drives the creeping thief	R L	....	305
And Lust, the thief, far poorer	"	....	693

THIEF				304	THING			
Thief—thou traitor, thou false	R L		888		Thine—give thee so thine own	Son	69	6
let the thief run mad	"		997		My spirit is thine	"	74	8
To that sweet thief	Son	35	14		Thine eyes, that taught	"	78	5
thy robbery, gentle thief	"	40	9		is thine and born of thee	"	78	10
the prey of every vulgar thief	"	48	8		upon that love of thine	"	92	4
Sweet thief, whence didst thou steal	"	99	2		no hatred in thine eye	"	93	5
Thievish—From thievish ears	R L		35		thou mine, I thine	"	108	7
He like a thievish dog	"		736		Thine eyes I love	"	132	1
For truth proves thievish	Son	48	14		Perforce am thine	"	133	14
Time's thievish progress	"	77	8		confess'd that he is thine	"	134	1
Thigh—twine about her thigh	V A		873		to hide my will in thine	"	135	6
Deep in the thigh	P P	9	11		Wound me not with thine eye	"	139	3
'See, in my thigh,' quoth she	"	9	12		to glance thine eye	"	139	6
Thin—Thin mane, thick tail	V A		298		Bear thine eyes straight	"	140	14
Thin winding breath	R L		1407		compare thou thine own state	"	142	3
Thine—those fair lips of thine	V A		115		from those lips of thine	"	142	5
The kiss shall be thine own	"		117		Whom thine eyes woo	"	142	10
I will enchant thine ear	"		145		the motion of thine eyes	"	149	12
thine own heart to thine own face	"		157		all things else are thine	L C		266
Steal thine own freedom	"		160		the heavenly rhetoric of thine eye	P P	3	1
That thine may live	"		172		makes his book thine eyes	"	5	5
Thine eye darts forth	"		196		Thine eye Jove's lightning seems	"	5	11
in thine own law forlorn	"		251		When as thine eye hath chose	"	19	1
all whole as thine	"		370		Thing—Things growing to themselves	V A		166
that hard heart of thine	"		500		Thing like a man	"		214
that face of thine	"		631		If springing things	"		417
And so 'tis thine	"		1181		Things out of hope	"		567
whose light excelleth thine	R L		191		in hand with all things	"		912
the fault is thine	"		482		of all mortal things	"		996
thine eyes betray thee	"		483		Of things long since, or any thing ensuing	"		1078
some worthless slave of thine	"		515		envy of so rich a thing	R L		39
To kill thine honour	"		516		The things we are	"		149
for thine own sake leave me	"		583		The thing we have	"		153
shame be seated in thine age	"		603		if I gain the thing I seek	"		211
thine honour lay in me	"		834		accidental things of trial	"		326
necessary by thine inclination	"		922		income of each precious thing	"		334
that are thine enemies	"		1470		the blessed thing he sought	"		340
for trespass of thine eye	"		1476		fearing no such thing	"		363
On thee and thine	"		1630		Mar not the thing	"		578
some hard-favour'd groom of thine	"		1632		should govern every thing	"		602
Thine, mine, his own	"		1684		no outrageous thing	"		607
thine own bright eyes	Son	1	5		The lesser thing should not	"		663
thine own bud	"	1	11		a dearer thing than life	"		687
thine own deep-sunken eyes	"	2	7		the seal of time in aged things	"		941
by succession thine	"	2	12		with decay of things	"		947
of thine age shalt see	"	3	11		the mightier is the thing	"		1004
thine image dies with thee	"	3	14		with every thing she sees	"		1093
If ten of thine ten times	"	6	10		with each thing she views	"		1101
make worms thine heir	"	6	14		Like bright things stain'd	"		1435
with pleasure thine annoy	"	8	4		and uttering foolish things	"		1813
do offend thine ear	"	8	6		every thing that grows	Son	15	1
live in thine or thee	"	10	14		By adding one thing	"	20	12
In one of thine	"	11	2		and all things rare	"	21	7
Thou mayst call thine	"	11	4		Or some fierce thing replete	"	23	3
But from thine eyes	"	14	9		remembrance of things past	"	30	2
with thine antique pen	"	19	10		many a thing I sought	"	30	3
doth live as thine in me	"	22	7		But things removed, that hidden	"	31	8
thou gavest me thine	"	22	14		they view things unrespected	"	43	2
glazed with thine eyes	"	24	8		converted from the thing	"	49	7
and thine for me	"	24	10		Though you do any thing	"	57	14
some good conceit of thine	"	26	7		to love things nothing worth	"	72	14
now is thine alone	"	31	12		That do not do the thing	"	94	2
Thine own sweet argument	"	38	3		sweetest things turn sourest	"	94	13
but thine shall be the praise	"	38	14		And all things turn to fair	"	95	12
All mine was thine	"	40	4		and for true things deem'd	"	96	8
Thine by thy beauty	"	41	14		a spirit of youth in every thing	"	98	3
is thine outward part	"	46	13		One thing expressing	"	105	8
thine inward love of heart	"	46	14					
with that sun thine eye	"	49	6					

Thing—dreaming on things to come	Son	107	2	This—shouldst contemn me this	V.A	205
Counting no old thing new	"	108	7	This said, impatience	"	217
monsters and things indigest	"	114	5	of this ivory pale	"	230
to the course of altering things	"	115	8	Within this limit	"	235
In things of great receipt	"	136	7	At this Adonis smiles	"	241
In things right true	"	137	13	And this I do	"	281
In pursuit of the thing	"	143	4	So did this horse excel	"	293
this becoming of things ill	"	150	5	And all this dumb play	"	359
against the thing they see	"	152	12	This beauteous combat	"	365
The thing we have not	L C		240	on this mortal round	"	368
and all things else are thine	"		266	this idle theme, this bootless chat	"	422
Against the thing he sought	"		313	This ill presage	"	457
rule things worthy blame	P P	19	3	What hour is this	"	495
Every thing did banish moan	"	21	7	this poor heart of mine	"	502
Think—think it heavy unto thee	V.A		156	kiss each other for this cure	"	505
did think to reprehend her	"		470	this night I'll waste	"	583
others, they think, delight	"		843	sweet boy, ere this	"	613
She thinks he could not	"		1060	This sour informer, this bate-		
Now thinks he that her husband	R L		78	breeding spy	"	655
When shall he think	"		159	This canker that eats	"	656
That thinks she hath beheld	"		451	This carry-tale, dissentious	"	657
I think the honey guarded	"		493	By this, poor Wat	"	697
Think but how vile a spectacle	"		631	Applying this to that	"	713
They think not but that every eye	"		750	O, then imagine this	"	721
and think no shame of me	"		1201	Now of this dark night	"	727
But long she thinks	"		1359	For, by this black-faced night	"	773
And both she thinks too long	"		1372	With this, he breaketh	"	811
To think their dolour	"		1582	with this fair good-morrow	"	859
Haply I think on thee	Son	29	10	This said, she hasteth	"	865
I think on thee, dear friend	"	30	13	By this she hears	"	877
As soon as think the place	"	44	8	This dismal cry rings	"	889
Nor think the bitterness	"	57	7	This way she runs	"	905
stay and think of nought	"	57	11	curse thee for this stroke	"	945
he thinks no ill	"	57	14	By this, far off	"	973
I think good thoughts	"	85	5	This sound of hope	"	976
that I will bitter think	"	111	11	Even at this word	"	1025
count bad what I think good	"	121	8	This mutiny each part	"	1049
Than think that we	"	123	8	This solemn sympathy	"	1057
I think my love as rare	"	130	13	this foul, grim, and urchin-snouted		
as I think, proceeds	"	131	14	boar	"	1105
Think all but one	"	135	14	With this, she falleth	"	1121
think that a several plot	"	137	9	this is my spite	"	1133
That she might think me	"	138	3	By this the boy	"	1165
that she thinks me young	"	138	5	this was thy father's guise	"	1177
Do I not think on thee	"	149	3	in this hollow cradle	"	1185
might think sometime it saw	L C		10	This bateless edge	R L	9
thinks in Paradise was sawn	"		91	Suggested this proud issue	"	37
That she might think me	P P	1	3	this false lord arrived	"	50
that she thinks me young	"	1	5	This heraldry in Lucrece' face	"	64
Think women still to strive	"	19	43	This silent war	"	71
Made me think upon mine own	"	21	18	This earthly saint, adored by this		
Thinking—If thinking on me then	Son	71	8	devil	"	85
but thinking on thy face	"	131	10	in this poor-rich gain	"	140
Thus vainly thinking	"	138	5	And in this aim	"	143
Thus vainly thinking	P P	1	5	And this ambitious	"	150
Thinly—they thinly placed are	Son	52	7	And now this lustful lord	"	169
Third—A third, nor red nor white	"	99	10	'As from this cold flint I enforced		
Thirst—More thirst for drink	V.A		92	this fire	"	181
Thirsty—her thirsty lips well knew	"		543	on this arise	"	186
This—wilt deign this favour	"		15	this vile purpose	"	220
With this she seizeth	"		25	This siege that hath	"	221
pay this countless debt	"		84	This blur to youth, this sorrow to		
Upon this promise	"		85	to the sage	"	222
for this good turn	"		92	This dying virtue, this surviving		
this primrose bank	"		151	shame	"	223
By this the love-sick queen	"		175	dear friend, this desire	"	234
of this descending sun	"		190	his conduct in this case	"	313
Between this heavenly and earthly				'This glove to wanton tricks	"	320
sun	"		198	abhor this fact	"	349

20

This—This said, his guilty hand	R L	358	This—this night I will inflict	R L	1630
this night-owl will catch	"	360	this act will be	"	1637
this blessed league to kill	"	383	'With this, I did begin	"	1639
From this fair throne	"	413	this refuge let me find	"	1654
So o'er this sleeping soul	"	423	stain'd with this abuse	"	1655
which late this mutiny	"	426	merchant of this loss	"	1660
this tumult to behold	"	447	this wrong of mine	"	1691
This moves in him	"	468	At this request	"	1695
enter this sweet city	"	469	'How may this forced stain	"	1701
this rash alarm to know	"	473	acquit me from this chance		1706
he commits this ill	"	476	from this compelled stain	"	1708
to this night	"	485	With this, they all	"	1709
All this beforehand	"	494	She utters this	"	1721
This said, he shakes aloft	"	505	That guides this hand to give this		
'this night I must enjoy	"	512	wound to me	"	1722
at this disdain	"	521	with this deadly deed	"	1730
by this dividing	"	551	in this fearful flood	"	1741
'This deed will make thee	"	610	wast not to this end	"	1755
If but for fear of this	"	614	By this starts Collatine	"	1772
This guilt would seem	"	635	This windy tempest	"	1788
the higher by this let	"	646	And by this chaste blood	"	1836
in this shameful doom	"	672	by this bloody knife	"	1840
This said, he sets	"	673	the death of this true wife	"	1841
This forced league	"	689	This said, he struck his hand	"	1842
This momentary joy	"	690	sworn to this advised doom	"	1849
This hot desire	"	691	or else this glutton be	Son	1 13
Tarquin fares this night	"	698	'This fair child of mine	"	2 10
with this faultful lord	"	715	This were to be new-made	"	2 13
Who this accomplishment	"	716	this thy golden time	"	3 12
he sounds this doom	"	717	Sings this to thee	"	8 14
Even in this thought	"	729	Without this, folly	"	11 6
from this attaint of mine	"	825	Against this coming end	"	13 3
As I, ere this	"	826	this I prognosticate	"	14 13
O, this dread night	"	965	That this huge stage	"	15 3
I could prevent this storm	"	966	of this inconstant stay	"	15 9
this cursed, crimeful night	"	970	war upon this bloody tyrant	"	16 2
thou taught'st this ill	"	996	Which this, Time's pencil	"	16 10
This helpless smoke of words	"	1027	'This poet lies	"	17 7
at this decree	"	1030	So long lives this, and this gives		
to rid me of this shame	"	1031	life to thee	"	18 14
This said, from her	"	1037	this huge rondure hems	"	21 8
But this no slaughterhouse	"	1039	Yet eyes this cunning	"	24 13
To clear this spot	"	1053	this written ambassage	"	26 3
This bastard graff	"	1062	Desiring this man's art	"	29 7
this false night's abuses	"	1075	but this loving thought	"	32 9
By this, lamenting Philomel	"	1079	with this growing age	"	32 10
If in this blemish'd fort	"	1175	A dearer birth than this	"	32 11
convey this troubled soul	"	1176	with this disgrace	"	33 8
'This brief abridgement	"	1198	Yet him for this my love	"	33 13
shalt oversee this will	"	1205	and even I in this	"	35 5
This plot of death	"	1212	engrafted to this store	"	37 8
By this, mild patience	"	1268	Whilst that this shadow	"	37 10
This is too curious-good, this			This wish I have	"	37 14
blunt and ill	"	1300	Even for this	"	39 5
By this short schedule	"	1312	That by this separation	"	39 7
To shun this blot	"	1322	thou hadst this more	"	40 4
Even so this pattern	"	1350	lay on me this cross	"	42 12
in this work was had	"	1385	This told, I joy	"	43 13
To this well-painted piece	"	1443	To 'cide this title	*	46 9
On this sad shadow	"	1457	And this my hand	"	49 11
that began this stir	"	1471	put this in my mind	"	50 13
This load of wrath	"	1474	this powerful rhyme	"	55 2
this mild image drew	"	1520	That wear this world out	"	55 12
This picture she advisedly perused	"	1527	You live in this	"	55 14
with this gives o'er	"	1567	Let this sad interim	"	56 9
Which all this time	"	1576	To this composed	"	59 10
this moody heaviness	"	1602	And for this sin	"	62 3
And now this pale swan	"	1611	This thought is as a death	"	64 13
Then be this all	"	1618	How with this rage	"	65 3

THIS				THOSE			
This—O, none, unless this miracle	Son	65	13	This—as this queen on him	P P	6	12
do this praise confound	"	69	7	Was this a lover	"	7	17
The soil is this	"	69	14	my lady at this bay	"	11	13
Yet this thy praise	"	70	11	Causer of this	"	18	8
From this vile world	"	71	4	To this troop come thou not near	P T	.....	8
Nay, if you read this line	"	71	5	From this session interdict	"	.....	9
you look upon this verse	"	71	9	Seemeth this concordant one	"	.....	46
may seem false in this	"	72	9	Whereupon it made this throne	"	.....	49
This thou perceivest	"	73	13	To this urn let those repair	"	.....	65
in this line some interest	"	74	3	Thither—And thither hied	Son	153	12
When thou reviewest this	"	74	5	to make me wander thither	P P	14	10
And that is this, and this with thee	"	74	14	Thong—Throwing the base thong	V.A	.....	395
And of this book this learning	"	77	4	Thorn—I know what thorns	R L	.....	492
The worst was this	"	80	14	against a thorn thou bear'st	"	.....	1135
breathers of this world	"	81	12	Roses have thorns	Son	35	2
This silence for my sin	"	83	9	Hang on such thorns	"	54	7
Than this rich praise	"	84	2	on thorns did stand	"	99	8
The cause of this fair gift	"	87	7	Ne'er to pluck thee from thy thorn	P P	17	12
And I by this will be	"	88	9	Lean'd her breast up-till a thorn	"	21	10
hath 'scaped this sorrow	"	90	5	Thorny—The thorny brambles	V.A	.....	629
Wretched in this alone	"	91	13	Thorough—her bleeding body thor-			
All this away	"	91	14	ough Rome	R L	.....	1851
of this large privilege	"	95	13	Those—those fair lips of thine	V.A	.....	115
And yet this time	"	97	5	if those hills be dry	"	.....	233
Yet this abundant issue	"	97	9	Love made those hollows	"	.....	243
For fear of which, hear this	"	104	13	As those poor birds	"	.....	604
And in this change	"	105	11	Of those fair arms	"	.....	812
Of this our time	"	106	10	Those eyes that taught	"	.....	952
of this most balmy time	"	107	9	if none of those	R L	.....	44
live in this poor rhyme	"	107	11	To those two armies	"	.....	76
And thou in this shalt find	"	107	13	Those that much covet	"	.....	134
this wide universe I call	"	109	13	Or as those bars	"	.....	327
monarch's plague, this flattery	"	114	2	For those thine eyes betray thee	"	.....	483
taught it this alchemy	"	114	4	To those that live	"	.....	1204
If this be error	"	116	13	Of those fair suns	"	.....	1280
of this madding fever	"	119	8	those proud lords to blame	"	.....	1259
Unless this general evil	"	121	13	Those tears from thee	"	.....	1271
This I do vow and this shall ever be	"	123	13	those far-off eyes look sad	"	.....	1386
To this I witness	"	124	13	that those shrunk pipes have fed	"	.....	1455
She keeps thee to this	"	126	7	no gol to lend her those	"	.....	1461
so happy are in this	"	128	13	To see those borrow'd tears	"	.....	1549
All this the world	"	129	13	Those round clear pearls	"	.....	1553
leads men to this hell	"	129	14	to those already spent	"	.....	1589
And thence this slander	"	131	14	Speaking to those that came	"	.....	1689
seeing this, say this is not	"	137	11	lends to those are free	Son	4	4
And to this false plague	"	137	14	Those hours that with gentle	"	5	1
Now this ill-wresting world	"	140	11	Which happies those that pay	"	6	6
Yet this shall I ne'er	"	144	13	Let those whom Nature	"	11	9
inheritors of this excess	"	146	7	As those gold candles	"	21	12
is this thy body's end	"	146	8	Let those who are	"	25	1
hast thou this powerful might	"	150	1	And all those friends	"	31	4
this becoming of things ill	"	150	5	Ah, but those tears	"	34	13
Proud of this pride	"	151	10	So shall those blots	"	36	3
this advantage found	"	153	2	Than those old nine	"	38	10
this holy fire of Love	"	153	5	Those pretty wrongs	"	41	1
This brand she quenched	"	154	9	By those swift messengers	"	45	10
and this by that I prove	"	154	13	how happy you make those	"	57	12
this double voice accorded	L C	.....	3	And all those beauties	"	63	6
This said, in top of rage	"	.....	55	In him those holy antique	"	68	9
Towards this afflicted fancy	"	.....	61	Those parts of thee	"	69	1
But quickly on this side	"	.....	113	But those same tongues	"	69	6
Of this false jewel	"	.....	154	Upon those boughs	"	73	3
"This man's untrue	"	.....	169	Those children nursed	"	77	11
Lo, this device was sent me	"	.....	232	have those vices got	"	95	9
This said, his watery eyes	"	.....	281	So are those errors	"	96	7
our drops this difference bore	"	.....	300	you pattern of all those	"	98	12
to this false perjury	P P	3	3	Those lines that I before	"	115	1
that on this earth doth shine	"	3	10	Even those that said	"	115	2
Exhale this vapour vow	"	3	11	To trust those tables	"	122	12

THOSE				THOU			
Those—Do I envy those jacks	Son	128	5	Thou—thou hast no eyes to see	V A	.....	939
with those dancing chips	"	128	10	at random dost thou hit	"	.....	940
As those whose beauties	"	131	2	Hadst thou but bid	"	.....	943
As those two mourning eyes	"	132	9	thou pluck'st a flower	"	.....	946
not from those lips of thine	"	142	5	'Dost thou drink tears, that thou			
as thou lovest those	"	142	9	provokest such weeping	"	.....	949
Those lips that Love's own hand	"	145	1	Why hast thou cast	"	.....	951
Those that can see	"	149	14	thou art so full of fear	"	.....	1021
those impediments stand forth	L C	.....	269	treasure hast thou lost	"	.....	1075
Those thoughts, to me like oaks	P P	5	4	what canst thou boast	"	.....	1077
Where all those pleasures live	"	5	6	That, thou being dead	"	.....	1134
he should not pass those grounds	"	9	8	'Since thou art dead	"	.....	1135
To this urn let those repair	P T	.....	65	Thou art the next	"	.....	1184
Thou—Vouchsafe, thou wonder	V A	.....	13	When thou shalt charge me	R L	.....	226
If thou wilt deign	"	.....	15	Thou see'st our mistress	"	.....	322
secrets shalt thou know	"	.....	16	if thou mean to chide	"	.....	484
If thou wilt chide	"	.....	48	Where thou with patience	"	.....	486
why art thou coy	"	.....	96	If thou deny	"	.....	513
thou unask'd shalt have	"	.....	102	And thou, the author	"	.....	523
What see'st thou in the ground	"	.....	118	'But if thou yield	"	.....	526
Art thou ashamed to kiss	"	.....	121	as thou hast pretended	"	.....	576
mayst thou well be tasted	"	.....	128	Thou look'st not like deceit	"	.....	585
Then mightst thou pause	"	.....	137	a stone thou art	"	.....	593
Thou canst not see	"	.....	139	Hast thou put on	"	.....	597
That thou shouldst think	"	.....	156	Thou wrong'st his honour	"	.....	599
Thou wast begot	"	.....	168	Thou art not what thou seem'st	"	.....	600
why shouldst thou feed	"	.....	169	Thou seem'st not what thou art	"	.....	601
thou art bound to breed	"	.....	171	thou darest do such outrage	"	.....	605
when thou thyself art dead	"	.....	172	What darest thou not when once			
thou dost survive	"	.....	173	thou art a king	"	.....	606
makest thou to be gone	"	.....	188	thou perforce must bear	"	.....	612
Art thou obdurate	"	.....	199	'And wilt thou be	"	.....	617
Art thou a woman's son	"	.....	201	Wilt thou be glass	"	.....	619
that thou shouldst contemn me	"	.....	205	Thou back'st reproach	"	.....	622
if thou wilt have twain	"	.....	210	'Hast thou command	"	.....	624
Thou art no man	"	.....	215	how canst thou fulfil	"	.....	628
thou shalt be my deer	"	.....	231	thou didst teach the way	"	.....	630
Feed where thou wilt	"	.....	232	That thou shalt see	"	.....	644
thou wert as I am	"	.....	369	'Thou art,' quoth she	"	.....	652
'why dost thou feel it	"	.....	373	and thou their slave	"	.....	659
'and thou shalt have it	"	.....	374	Thou nobly base	"	.....	660
What! canst thou talk?' quoth				Thou their fair life	"	.....	661
she, 'hast thou a tongue	"	.....	427	Thou loathed in their shame	"	.....	662
O, would thou hadst not	"	.....	428	Since thou art guilty	"	.....	772
wert thou to the taste	"	.....	445	Or if thou wilt	"	.....	773
O, thou didst kill me	"	.....	499	'O Night, thou furnace	"	.....	799
So thou wilt buy	"	.....	514	'Tis thou that executest	"	.....	877
Which purchase if thou make	"	.....	515	Thou set'st the wolf	"	.....	878
wilt thou make the match	"	.....	586	thou point'st the season	"	.....	879
Thou hadst been gone	"	.....	613	'Tis thou that spurn'st at right	"	.....	880
thou told'st me thou wouldst hunt	"	.....	614	Thou makest the vestal	"	.....	883
thou knowst not what it is	"	.....	615	Thou blow'st the fire	"	.....	884
When thou didst name the boar	"	.....	641	Thou smother'st honesty, thou			
'Didst thou not mark	"	.....	643	murder'st truth	"	.....	885
Saw'st thou not signs	"	.....	644	Thou foul abettor! thou notorious			
whereon thou dost lie	"	.....	646	bawd	"	.....	886
If thou encounter	"	.....	672	Thou plantest scandal	"	.....	887
But if thou needs wilt hunt	"	.....	673	Thou ravisher, thou traitor, thou			
And when thou hast on foot	"	.....	679	false thief	"	.....	888
Then shalt thou see	"	.....	703	'When wilt thou be	"	.....	897
for thou shalt not rise	"	.....	710	When wilt thou sort	"	.....	899
thou hear'st me moralize	"	.....	712	Thou grant'st no time	"	.....	908
But if thou fall	"	.....	721	thou art well appaid	"	.....	914
thou needs must have	"	.....	759	'Guilty thou art	"	.....	918
If thou destroy them not	"	.....	760	Thou nursest all	"	.....	929
O, thou clear god	"	.....	860	the hours thou gavest me	"	.....	933
as thou dost lend to other	"	.....	864	'Why work'st thou mischief	"	.....	960
what dost thou mean	"	.....	933	Unless thou couldst return	"	.....	961
thou shouldst strike at it	"	.....	938	wouldst thou one hour come back	"	.....	965

Phrase	Ref	Col	Line
Thou—'Thou ceaseless lackey	R L	...	967
'O Time, thou tutor	"	...	995
thou taught'st this ill	"	...	996
why quiver'st thou	"	...	1030
thou livest in my defame	"	...	1033
Since thou couldst not	"	...	1031
thou shalt not know	"	...	1058
That thou art	"	...	1064
But thou shalt know	"	...	1067
Why pry'st thou	"	...	1089
While thou on Tereus	"	...	1134
thou bear'st thy part	"	...	1135
thou sing'st not	"	...	1142
thou revenged mayst be	"	...	1194
serve thou false Tarquin so	"	...	1197
do thou take	"	...	1200
'Thou, Collatine, shalt oversee	"	...	1205
that thou shalt see it	"	...	1206
Thou dead, both die	"	...	1211
If thou dost weep	"	...	1272
Bid thou be ready	"	...	1292
'Thou worthy lord	"	...	1303
thy Lucrece thou wilt see	"	...	1306
Priam, why art thou old	"	...	1550
that thou dost trembling stand	"	...	1599
Why art thou thus attired	"	...	1601
where thou wast wont	"	...	1621
"Awake, thou Roman dame	"	...	1628
If thou my love's desire	"	...	1631
"Unless thou yoke	"	...	1633
suppose thou dost defend me	"	...	1684
that thou shalt lend me	"	...	1685
which thou hast here deprived	"	...	1752
Thou wast not	"	...	1755
my image thou hast torn	"	...	1762
cease thou thy course	"	...	1765
'Thou wronged lord of Rome	"	...	1818
But thou, contracted to thine own	Son	1	5
Thou that art now	"	1	9
If thou couldst answer	"	2	10
when thou art old	"	2	13
when thou feel'st it cold	"	2	14
tell the face thou viewest	"	3	1
if now thou not renewest	"	3	3
Thou dost beguile	"	3	4
Thou art thy mother's glass	"	3	9
So thou through windows	"	3	11
But if thou live	"	3	13
why dost thou spend	"	4	1
why dost thou abuse	"	4	5
why dost thou use	"	4	7
Thou of thyself	"	4	10
canst thou leave	"	4	12
ere thou be distill'd	"	6	2
treasure thou some place	"	6	3
happier than thou art	"	6	9
if thou shouldst depart	"	6	11
for thou art much too fair	"	6	13
So thou, thyself out-going	"	7	13
unless thou get a son	"	7	14
hear'st thou music sadly	"	8	1
Why lovest thou that which thou receivest not gladly	"	8	3
that thou shouldst bear	"	8	8
'Thou single wilt prove none	"	8	14
That thou consumest	"	9	2
Ah! if thou issueless	"	9	3
That thou no form of thee hast left	"	9	6
thou bear'st love to any	"	10	1
Thou—Grant, if thou wilt, thou art beloved of many	Son	10	3
thou none lovest	"	10	4
For thou art so possess'd	"	10	5
thou stick'st not to conspire	"	10	6
As fast as thou shalt wane, so fast thou grow'st	"	11	1
from that which thou departest	"	11	2
which youngly thou bestow'st	"	11	3
Thou mayst call thine when thou from youth convertest	"	11	4
thou shouldst in bounty	"	11	12
Thou shouldst print more	"	11	14
That thou among the wastes	"	12	10
thou wouldst convert	"	14	12
Thou art more lovely	"	18	2
of that fair thou owest	"	18	10
thou wander'st in his shade	"	18	11
to time thou grow'st	"	18	12
blunt thou the lion's paws	"	19	1
seasons as thou fleet'st	"	19	5
And do whate'er thou wilt	"	19	6
Hast thou, the master-mistress	"	20	2
wert thou first created	"	20	9
youth and thou are of one date	"	22	2
be elder than thou art	"	22	8
Thou gavest me thine	"	22	14
where thou mayst prove one	"	26	14
please him thou art bright	"	28	9
thou gild'st the even	"	28	12
Thou art the grave	"	31	9
And thou, all they, hast all	"	31	14
If thou survive	"	32	1
Why didst thou promise	"	34	1
that through the cloud thou break	"	34	5
Though thou repent	"	34	10
which thou hast done	"	35	1
Nor thou with public kindness honour me	"	36	11
Unless thou take that honour	"	36	12
As thou being mine	"	36	14
While thou dost breathe	"	38	2
When thou thyself dost give	"	38	8
Be thou the tenth Muse	"	38	9
When thou art all	"	39	2
which thou deservest	"	39	8
wouldst thou prove	"	39	9
And that thou teachest	"	39	13
What hast thou then more than thou hadst	"	40	2
thou mayst true love call	"	40	3
before thou hadst this more	"	40	4
thou my love receivest	"	40	5
for my love thou usest	"	40	6
if thou thyself deceivest	"	40	7
Although thou steal thee	"	40	10
follows where thou art	"	41	4
Gentle thou art	"	41	5
Beauteous thou art	"	41	6
thou mightst my seat forbear	"	41	9
Where thou art forced	"	41	12
That thou hast her	"	42	1
Thou dost love her, because thou know'st I love her	"	42	6
Then thou, whose shadow shadows doth	"	43	5
where thou dost stay	"	44	4
when thou art gone	"	44	10
that thou in him dost lie	"	46	5

Entry	Work	Line	No.
Thou—thou not farther than my thoughts canst move	Son	47	11
But thou, to whom	"	48	5
Thou, best of dearest	"	48	7
thou art not, though I feel thou art	"	48	10
thou mayst come and part	"	48	12
thence thou wilt be stol'n	"	48	13
thou shalt strangely pass	"	49	5
To leave poor me thou hast the strength	"	49	13
From where thou art	"	51	3
So, love, be thou; although to-day thou fill	"	56	5
Dost thou desire	"	61	3
thou send'st from thee	"	61	5
whilst thou dost wake	"	61	13
that thou dost common grow	"	69	14
That thou art blamed	"	70	1
So thou be good	"	70	5
And thou present'st	"	70	8
Thou hast pass'd	"	70	9
Then thou alone	"	70	14
thou mayst in me behold	"	73	1
In me thou see'st	"	73	5
In me thou see'st the glowing	"	73	9
This thou perceivest	"	73	13
thou must leave	"	73	14
When thou reviewest this, thou dost review	"	74	5
So then thou hast	"	74	9
learning mayst thou taste	"	77	4
Thou by thy dial's shady stealth	"	77	7
and thou shalt find	"	77	10
oft as thou wilt look	"	77	13
thou dost but mend	"	78	11
But thou art all my art	"	78	13
thou thyself dost pay	"	79	14
I grant thou wert not	"	82	1
Thou art as fair	"	82	5
Thou truly fair wert truly	"	82	11
Farewell! thou art too dear	"	87	1
thou know'st thy estimate	"	87	2
Thyself thou gavest	"	87	9
to whom thou gavest it	"	87	10
When thou shalt be	"	88	1
though thou art forsworn	"	88	4
That thou in losing me	"	88	8
Say that thou didst forsake	"	89	1
whom thou dost hate	"	89	14
hate me when thou wilt	"	90	1
If thou wilt leave me	"	90	9
that thou mayst take	"	91	13
thou art assured mine	"	92	2
Thou canst not vex me	"	92	9
Thou mayst be false	"	92	14
supposing thou art true	"	93	1
dost thou make the shame	"	95	1
thou thy sins inclose	"	95	4
Thou makest faults graces	"	96	4
mightst thou lead away	"	96	11
If thou wouldst use	"	96	12
As thou being mine	"	96	14
And, thou away, the very birds	"	97	12
whence didst thou steal	"	99	2
thou hast too grossly dyed	"	99	5
Where art thou, Muse, that thou forget'st	"	100	1
Spend'st thou thy fury	"	100	3
So thou prevent'st his scythe	"	100	14
Thou—So dost thou too	Son	101	4
wilt thou not haply say	"	101	5
wilt thou be dumb	"	101	9
thou age unbred	"	104	13
And thou in this shalt find	"	107	13
thou mine, I thine	"	108	7
Save thou, my rose; in it thou art my all	"	109	14
No, Time, thou shalt not	"	123	1
What thou dost foist	"	123	6
And take thou my oblation	"	125	10
thou suborn'd informer	"	125	13
O thou, my lovely boy	"	126	1
As thou goest onwards	"	126	6
Yet fear her, O thou minion	"	126	9
How oft, when thou, my music	"	128	1
when thou gently sway'st	"	128	3
Thou art as tyrannous, so as thou art	"	131	1
For well thou know'st	"	131	3
Thou art the fairest	"	131	4
In nothing art thou black	"	131	13
thou harder hast engrossed	"	133	6
Thou canst not then use	"	133	12
And yet thou wilt	"	133	13
Thou wilt restore	"	134	4
But thou wilt not	"	134	5
For thou art covetous	"	134	6
The statute of thy beauty thou wilt	"	134	9
Thou usurer, that put'st forth	"	134	10
thou hast both him and me	"	134	13
thou hast thy 'Will	"	135	1
Wilt thou, whose will is large	"	135	5
So thou, being rich	"	135	11
And then thou lovest me	"	136	14
Thou blind fool, Love, what dost thou	"	137	1
hast thou forged hooks	"	137	7
Tell me thou lovest elsewhere	"	139	5
What need'st thou wound	"	139	7
Be wise as thou art cruel	"	140	1
I may not be so, nor thou belied	"	140	13
compare thou thine own state	"	142	3
thou shalt find it merits not	"	142	4
as thou lovest those	"	142	9
If thou dost seek to have what thou dost hide	"	142	13
mayst thou be denied	"	142	14
So runn'st thou after that	"	143	9
But if thou catch	"	143	11
thou mayst have thy 'Will	"	143	13
If thou turn back	"	143	14
Why dost thou pine	"	146	3
Dost thou upon thy fading	"	146	6
Then, soul, live thou	"	146	9
So shalt thou feed on death	"	146	13
thou keep'st me blind	"	148	13
Canst thou, O cruel	"	149	1
On whom frown'st thou	"	149	6
Nay, if thou lour'st on me	"	149	7
Those that can see thou lovest	"	149	14
thou this powerful might	"	150	1
Whence hast thou this	"	150	5
thou shouldst not abhor	"	150	12
For, thou betraying me	"	151	5
In loving thee thou know'st	"	152	1
But thou art twice forsworn	"	152	2
thou register of lies	L C	....	52
witness dost thou bear	"	....	53
For thou art all	"	....	266

Thou—"When thou impressest	L C	....	267	Though—though more weak in seeming	Son 102	1
When thou wilt inflame	"	....	268	though less the show appear	" 102	2
Thou being a goddess	P P	3	6	Though absence seem'd	" 109	2
thou a heavenly love	"	3	7	though in my nature reign'd	" 109	9
Then, thou fair sun	"	3	10	though rosy lips and cheeks	" 116	9
Celestial as thou art	"	5	13	though they themselves be bevel	" 121	11
Because thou lovest the one	"	8	4	Her audit, though delay'd	" 126	11
Thou lovest to hear	"	8	9	Though in thy stores' account	" 136	10
For why thou left'st me nothing	"	10	8	though I know she lies	" 138	2
And yet thou left'st me more	"	10	9	Though not to love	" 140	6
thou didst bequeath to me	"	10	12	though thy proud heart	" 140	11
thou stay'st too long	"	12	12	though I mistake my view	" 148	11
Thou for whom Jove	"	17	15	O, though I love what others	" 7	18
that thou shouldst strike	"	19	2	Though slackly braided	L C	35
And when thou comest	"	19	7	though in me you behold	"	71
thou lovest her well	"	19	11	unruly though they be	"	103
thou to choose anew	"	19	34	Though Reason weep, and cry	"	168
be thou not slack	"	19	35	though our drops this difference bore	"	300
thou mourn'st in vain	"	21	19	though I know she lies	P P 1	2
Thou and I were both	"	21	30	Though to myself forsworn	" 5	3
Whilst thou hast	"	21	36	though excellent in neither	" 7	18
If thou sorrow	"	21	53	What though her frowning brows	" 19	13
If thou wake	"	21	54	What though she strive	" 19	19
But thou shrieking harbinger	P T		5	though she put thee back	" 19	36
come thou not near	"	....	8	Thought—of her thoughts began	V A	367
And thou treble-dated crow	"	....	17	my thought, my busy care	"	383
thou givest and takest	"	....	19	Whose vulture thought	"	551
shalt thou go	"	....	20	The thought of it	"	609
Though—though not in lust	V A		42	in thoughts unlikely	"	989
Though mine be not so fair	"	....	116	In likely thoughts	"	990
though of a man's complexion	"	....	215	His high-pitch'd thoughts	R L	41
though a thousand bark	"	....	240	But some untimely thought	"	43
Though nothing but	"	....	372	For unstain'd thoughts	"	87
though thy horse be gone	"	....	390	pure thoughts are dead and still	"	167
Though I were dumb	"	....	406	controls his thoughts unjust	"	189
Though neither eyes nor ears	"	....	437	And die, unhallow'd thoughts	"	192
though the rose have prickles	"	....	574	with good thoughts makes dispensation	"	248
though seeming short	"	....	842	Within his thought	"	288
Though weak-built hopes	R L		130	from the heaven of his thought	"	334
Though death be adjunct	"	....	133	That his foul thoughts	"	346
Yea, though I die	"	....	204	Thoughts are but dreams	"	353
though marble wear with raining	"	....	560	is as a thought unacted	"	527
Though men can cover crimes	"	....	1252	and flattering thoughts retire	"	641
though my words are brief	"	....	1309	So let thy thoughts	"	666
His face, though full of cares	"	....	1503	Even in this thought	"	729
Though woe be heavy	"	....	1574	And the dire thought	"	972
though none it ever cured	"	....	1581	smile at thee in secret thought	"	1065
Her eyes, though sod in tears	"	....	1392	duty with thought's feathers flies	"	1216
Though my gross blood he stain'd	"	....	1635	hath oversllpp'd her thought	"	1576
though they with winter	Son 5		13	O, change thy thought	Son 10	9
Though yet heaven knows	"	17	3	In the soul's thought	" 26	8
though not so bright	"	21	11	For then my thoughts	" 27	5
though enemies to either's reign	"	28	5	Yet in these thoughts	" 29	9
And though they be	"	32	6	of sweet silent thought	" 30	1
Though thou repent	"	34	10	but this loving thought	" 32	9
Though in our lives	"	34	6	with thoughts of love	" 39	11
Which though it alter not	"	36	7	Which time and thoughts	" 39	12
Though I feel thou art	"	48	10	If the dull substance of my flesh were thought	" 44	1
though mounted on the wind	"	51	7	For nimble thought	" 44	7
Though you do any thing	"	57	11	thought kills me, that I am not thought	" 44	9
though waiting so be hell	"	58	13	The first my thought	" 45	3
thy love, though much	"	61	9	A quest of thoughts	" 46	10
though my lover's life	"	63	12	And in his thoughts	" 47	8
Though I, once gone	"	81	6	than my thoughts canst move	" 47	11
Though words come hindmost	"	85	12			
though thou art forsworn	"	88	4			
Though new-fangled ill	"	91	3			
though alter'd new	"	93	3			
Though to itself	"	94	10			

Thought—with my jealous thought	*Son*	57	9
I should in thought	"	58	2
This thought is as a death	"	64	13
the thought of hearts can mend	"	69	2
Then, churls, their thoughts	"	69	11
In your sweet thoughts	"	71	7
So are you to my thoughts	"	75	1
I think good thoughts	"	85	5
But that is in my thought	"	85	11
Me for my dumb thoughts	"	85	14
That did my ripe thoughts	"	86	3
loving thoughts on thee	"	88	10
Whate'er thy thoughts	"	93	11
Gored mine own thoughts	"	110	3
their rank thoughts my deeds	"	121	12
My thoughts and my discourse	"	147	11
Whereon the thought	*L C*		10
To dwell with him in thoughts	"	....	129
theirs in thought assign'd	"	....	138
Those thoughts, to me like oaks	*P P*	5	4
Thought—He thought to kiss him	*V A*	....	1110
thought to persuade him	"	....	1114
Lucrece thought he blush'd	*R L*	....	1314
She thought he blush'd	"	....	1354
The more she thought	"	....	1358
which I thought buried	*Son*	31	4
I found, or thought I found	"	83	3
it hath thought itself so blessed	"	119	6
and thought thee bright	"	147	13
Thought characters and words merely but art	*L C*	....	174
Ah, thought I, thou mourn'st	*P P*	21	19
Thoughted—Sick-thoughted Venus makes amain	*V A*		5
And holy-thoughted Lucrece	*R L*	....	384
Thousand—A .... honey secrets	*V A*	....	16
though a thousand bark	"	....	240
a thousand ways he seeks	"	....	477
A thousand kisses	"	....	517
with a thousand doubles	"	....	682
twenty thousand tongues	"	....	775
A thousand spleens bear her a thousand ways	"	....	907
A thousand times	"	....	1130
confounded in a thousand fears	*R L*	....	456
A thousand crosses keep them	"	....	912
A thousand thousand friends	"	....	963
a thousand lamentable objects	"	....	1373
After a thousand victories	*Son*	25	10
A thousand groans	"	131	10
A thousand errors note	"	141	2
A thousand favours from a maund	*L C*	....	36
Like a thousand vanquish'd men	*P P*	18	36
With a thousand fragrant posies	"	20	10
Thrall—makes young men thrall	*V A*	....	837
and made her thrall	*R L*	....	725
but I my mistress' thrall	*Son*	154	12
Living in thrall	*P P*	18	22
Thralled—blow of .... discontent	*Son*	124	7
Threads—Her hair like golden	*R L*	....	400
Threaden—Some in her .... fillet	*L C*	....	33
Threat—ever threat his foes	*V A*	....	620
that sometime threat the spring	*R L*	....	331
threats if he mounts he dies	"	....	508
the world doth threat	"	....	547
Threatening- thy rocky and wreck-threatening heart	"	....	590
Threatening cloud-kissing Ilion	"	....	1370
Three—makes the wound seem	*V A*	....	1064
Three—Three times with sighs	*R L*	....	1604
Three winters cold	*Son*	104	3
shook three summers' pride	"	104	4
Three beauteous springs	"	104	5
Three April perfumes in three hot Junes burn'd	"	104	7
Three themes in one	"	105	12
Which three till now	"	105	14
the fairest one of three	*P P*	16	1
Threefold—A torment thrice	*Son*	133	8
Threescore—And threescore year would make	"	11	8
Threne—Whereupon it made this threne	*P T*	....	49
Threshold—The .... grates the door	*R L*	....	306
Threw—threw unwilling light	*V A*	....	1054
on her self-slaughter'd body threw	*R L*	....	1733
from hate away she threw	*Son*	145	13
she in a river threw	*L C*	....	38
Threw my affections	"	....	146
Thrice—' Thrice fairer than myself	*V A*	....	7
thrice more wish'd, more rare	*Son*	56	14
thrice more than I have spent	"	119	14
A torment thrice threefold	"	133	8
Thriftless—all-eating shame and thriftless praise	*Son*	2	8
Thrive—They that thrive well	*V A*	....	640
may the better thrive	"	....	1011
Love thrives not in the heart	*R L*	....	270
shall together thrive	*Son*	14	11
Then if he thrive	"	80	13
Thrivers—Pitiful thrivers, in their gazing	"	125	8
Thriveth—that by love so thriveth	*V A*	....	466
Throbbing—My throbbing heart	"	....	1186
Throne—perplexed in his throne	"	....	1043
From this fair throne	*R L*	....	413
Throned—finger of a throned queen	*Son*	96	5
Throng—throng her constant woe	*V A*	....	967
Throng her inventions	*R L*	....	1302
through his lips do throng	"	....	1783
Throng'd—Here one being throng'd	"	....	1417
Thronging— Which, thronging through her lips	"	....	1041
Through—peering through a wave	*V A*	....	86
draw me through the sky	"	....	153
through his mane and tail the high wind sings	"	....	395
through the crystal tears gave light	"	....	491
Yet love breaks through	"	....	576
through whom he rushes	"	....	630
through the which he goes	"	....	683
through the dark lawnd runs apace	"	....	813
Through which it enters	"	....	890
Through all her sinews spread	"	....	903
But through the flood-gates breaks	"	....	959
mounted, through the empty skies	"	....	1191
Through little vents and crannies	*R L*	....	310
That through the length of times	"	....	718
through the dark night he stealeth	"	....	729
Through Night's black bosom	"	....	788
Which thronging through her lips	"	....	1041
through every cranny spies	"	....	1086
Why pry'st thou through my window	"	....	1089
Through which I may convey	"	....	1176
Through crystal walls	"	....	1251
through all her body spread	"	....	1266
through loop-holes thrust	"	....	1383

Through—through their light joy	R L	1434
As through an arch	"	1667
through her wounds doth fly	"	1728
through his lips do throng	"	1783
But through his teeth	"	1787
through windows of thine age	Son 3	11
For through the painter	" 24	5
where-through the sun	" 24	11
that through the cloud thou break	" 34	5
Through heavy sleep	" 43	12
to blush through lively veins	" 67	10
through my unkind abuse	" 134	12
through lattice of seared age	L C	14
That flame through water	"	287
And falls through wind	P P 10	6
Through the velvet leaves	" 17	5
Through heartless ground	" 18	35
Throw—her yoking arms she throws	V A	592
She throws her eyes about	R L	1499
She throws forth Tarquin's name	"	1717
throws that shallow habit by	"	1814
I throw all care	Son 112	9
and throws his mantle by	P P 6	9
throw gazes to the east	" 15	1
Throwing — Throwing the base thong	V A	395
Throwing his mantle rudely	"	170
Thrust—she would be thrust	"	41
through loop-holes thrust	R L	1383
craft and perjury should thrust	"	1517
under truest bars to thrust	Son 48	2
anger thrusts into his hide	" 50	10
Thunder — resounds like heaven's thunder	V A	268
Pointing to each his thunder	Son 14	6
O that forced thunder	L C	325
thy voice his dreadful thunder	P P 5	11
Thus—thus she began	V A	7
Thus he that overruled	"	109
thus my strength is tried	"	280
Thus she replies	"	385
Thus stands she	"	895
thus chides she Death	"	932
Thus hoping that Adonis	"	1009
thus was Adonis slain	"	1111
Thus weary of the world	"	1189
Teaching them thus to use it	R L	62
thus speaks advisedly	"	180
And justly thus controls	"	189
Thus graceless holds he	"	246
desire thus madly led	"	300
Thus treason works	"	361
Thus he replies	"	477
'Thus I forestall thee	"	484
When thus thy vices bud	"	604
thus breathes she forth her spite	"	762
Thus cavils she with every thing	"	1093
I thus far can dispense	"	1279
At last she thus begins	"	1303
And turn'd it thus	"	1539
Thus ebbs and flows	"	1569
And thus begins	"	1598
thus attired in discontent	"	1601
frenzy thus awaketh	"	1675
Lo, thus by day my limbs	Son 27	13
thus I will excuse thee	" 42	5
As thus; mine eyes' due	" 46	13
Thus far the miles	" 50	4
Thus can my love excuse	" 51	1
Thus—thus shall excuse my jade	Son 51	12
taught me thus to ruminate	" 64	11
Thus is his cheek the map	" 68	1
Thy outward thus with outward	" 69	5
Thus do I pine	" 75	13
Thus have I had thee	" 87	13
violet thus did I chide	" 99	1
thus maketh mine untrue	" 113	14
Accuse me thus	" 117	1
Thus policy in love	" 118	9
threefold thus to be crossed	" 133	8
making addition thus	" 135	4
Thus far for love	" 136	4
Thus vainly thinking	" 138	5
thus is simple truth supprest	" 138	8
thus far I count my gain	" 141	13
taught it thus anew to greet	" 145	8
Till thus he 'gan besiege me	L C	177
Thus merely with the garment	"	316
Thus vainly thinking	P P 1	5
in love thus smother'd be	" 1	14
'Even thus,' quoth she	" 11	5
'Even thus,' quoth she	" 11	7
'Even thus,' quoth she	" 11	9
Thus art with arms contending	" 16	13
That thus dissembled	" 19	16
taught her thus to say	" 19	22
Thus of every grief in heart	" 21	55
Property was thus appalled	P T	37
Thwarting—there is such thwarting strife	R L	143
Thy—hath ending with thy life	V A	12
to alight thy steed	"	13
this favour, for thy meed	"	15
yet not cloy thy lips	"	19
thy lips shall never open	"	48
brag not of thy might	"	113
hold up thy head	"	118
there thy beauty lies	"	119
upon thy tempting lip	"	127
were it with thy hand felt	"	143
in thy palm dissolve	"	144
Can thy right hand seize love upon thy left	"	158
to get it is thy duty	"	168
with thy increase be fed	"	170
In that thy likeness	"	174
O, had thy mother	"	203
What were thy lips	"	207
thy heart my wound	"	370
thy help I would assure thee	"	371
lest thy hard heart	"	375
'Thy palfrey, as he should	"	385
though thy horse be gone	"	390
'Let me excuse thy courser	"	403
Thy mermaid's voice	"	429
thy outward parts would move	"	435
the stillitory of thy face	"	443
Thy eyes' shrewd tutor	"	500
But for thy piteous lips	"	504
banish'd by thy breath	"	510
Set thy seal-manual	"	516
pay them at thy leisure	"	518
thy spear's point can enter	"	626
not thy soft hands	"	633
danger by thy will	"	639
I fear'd thy fortune	"	642
I thy death should fear	"	660
I prophesy thy death	"	671

Thy—on thy well-breath'd horse keep with thy hounds	V A	.....	678
thy footing trips	"	.....	722
so do thy lips	"	.....	724
'What is thy body	"	.....	757
Sith in thy pride	"	.....	762
Thy mark is feeble age; but thy false dart	"	.....	941
hearing him, thy power	"	.....	944
for thy mortal vigour	"	.....	953
ruin'd with thy rigour	"	.....	954
Thy weal and woe	"	.....	987
author of thy slander	"	.....	1006
Thy coward heart	"	.....	1024
this was thy father's guise	"	.....	1177
'Here was thy father's bed	"	.....	1183
and 'tis thy right	"	.....	1184
in this hollow cradle take thy rest	"	.....	1185
Thy hasty spring still blasts	R L	.....	49
burn out thy light	"	.....	190
'The colour in thy face	"	.....	477
Thy never-conquer'd fort	"	.....	482
Thy beauty hath ensnared	"	.....	485
By thy bright beauty	"	.....	490
For in thy bed	"	.....	514
with thy life's decay	"	.....	516
And in thy dead arms	"	.....	517
So thy surviving husband	"	.....	519
Thy kinsmen hang their heads	"	.....	521
Thy issue blurr'd	"	.....	522
Shalt have thy trespass	"	.....	524
I rest thy secret friend	"	.....	526
'Then, for thy husband and thy children's sake	"	.....	533
End thy ill aim before thy shoot be ended	"	.....	579
'My husband is thy friend	"	.....	582
Beat at thy rocky and	"	.....	590
'How will thy shame	"	.....	603
thy vices bud before thy spring	"	.....	604
If in thy hope	"	.....	605
thy will remove	"	.....	614
in thy name	"	.....	621
command thy rebel will	"	.....	625
Draw not thy sword	"	.....	626
Thy princely office	"	.....	628
When pattern'd by thy fault	"	.....	629
To view thy present trespass	"	.....	632
death-worthy in thy brother	"	.....	635
thy rash relier	"	.....	639
from thy doting eyne	"	.....	643
That thou shalt see thy state	"	.....	644
into thy boundless flood	"	.....	653
the ocean of thy blood	"	.....	655
shall change thy good	"	.....	656
Thy sea within	"	.....	657
In thy sea dispersed	"	.....	658
and they thy fouler grave	"	.....	661
they in thy pride	"	.....	662
'So let thy thoughts, low vassals to thy state	"	.....	666
To be thy partner	"	.....	672
Muster thy mists	"	.....	773
And let thy misty vapours	"	.....	782
thy black all-hiding cloak	"	.....	801
of thy gloomy place	"	.....	808
which in thy reign are made	"	.....	804
sepulchred in thy shade	"	.....	805
In thy weak hive	"	.....	839

Thy—which thy chaste bee kept	R L	.....	840
of thy honour's wrack	"	.....	841
Yet for thy honour	"	.....	842
thy guilt is great	"	.....	876
And in thy shady cell	"	.....	881
Thy honey turns to gall, thy joy to grief	"	.....	889
Thy secret pleasure	"	.....	890
Thy private feasting	"	.....	891
Thy smoothing titles	"	.....	892
Thy sugar'd tongue	"	.....	893
Thy violent vanities	"	.....	894
Thy heinous hours	"	.....	910
keep them from thy aid	"	.....	912
They buy thy help	"	.....	913
'Why hath thy servant	"	.....	932
with thy hours	"	.....	944
in thy pilgrimage	"	.....	960
shun thy wrack	"	.....	966
defend thy loyal dame	"	.....	1034
wrong thy true affection	"	.....	1060
did thy stock pollute	"	.....	1063
at thy state	"	.....	1066
thy interest was not bought	"	.....	1067
from forth thy gate	"	.....	1068
leave thy peeping	"	.....	1089
Mock with thy tickling beams	"	.....	1090
with thy piercing light	"	.....	1091
Make thy sad grove	"	.....	1129
at thy languishment	"	.....	1130
thou bear'st thy part	"	.....	1135
To keep thy sharp woes	"	.....	1136
shall be thy boast	"	.....	1193
Myself, thy friend, will kill myself, thy foe	"	.....	1196
that down thy checks	"	.....	1271
Health to thy person	"	.....	1305
thy Lucrece thou wilt see	"	.....	1306
I'll tune thy woes	"	.....	1465
Thy heat of lust, fond Paris	"	.....	1473
Thy eye kindled the fire	"	.....	1475
pearls of his that move thy pity	"	.....	1553
fire to burn thy city	"	.....	1554
hath thy fair colour spent	"	.....	1600
And tell thy grief	"	.....	1603
in the interest of thy bed	"	.....	1619
to rest thy weary head	"	.....	1621
thy Lucrece is not free	"	.....	1624
yoke thy liking to my will	"	.....	1633
and thy perpetual infamy	"	.....	1638
Dear lord, thy sorrow	"	.....	1676
too sensible thy passion maketh	"	.....	1678
For she that was thy Lucrece	"	.....	1682
In thy sweet semblance	"	.....	1759
O, from thy cheeks	"	.....	1762
cease thou thy course	"	.....	1765
Thy father die, and not thy father thee	"	.....	1771
Now set thy long-experienced wit	"	.....	1820
by whom thy fair wife bleeds	"	.....	1824
Thy wretched wife mistook	"	.....	1826
do not steep thy heart	"	.....	1828
and help to bear thy part	"	.....	1830
Feed'st thy light's flame	Son	1	6
Thyself thy foe, to thy sweet self	"	1	8
buriest thy content	"	1	11
Shall besiege thy brow	"	2	1
In thy beauty's field	"	2	2
Thy youth's proud livery	"	2	3

Thy—where all thy beauty lies	Son	2	5
treasure of thy lusty days	"	2	6
deserved thy beauty's use	"	2	9
And see thy blood	"	2	11
Look in thy glass	"	3	1
tillage of thy husbandry	"	3	6
Thou art thy mother's glass	"	3	9
this thy golden time	"	3	12
thy beauty's legacy	"	4	2
thyself thy sweet self dost deceive	"	4	10
Thy unused beauty	"	4	13
In thee thy summer	"	6	2
thyself out-going in thy noon	"	7	13
The world will be thy widow	"	9	5
should be thy chief desire	"	10	8
O, change thy thought	"	10	9
Be, as thy presence is	"	10	11
Then of thy beauty	"	12	9
Thy end is truth's	"	14	14
But thy eternal summer	"	18	9
O, carve not with thy hours	"	19	9
in thy course untainted do allow	"	19	11
Yet do thy worst, old Time, despite thy wrong	"	19	13
thy love, and thy love's use	"	20	14
Which in thy breast doth live	"	22	7
Bearing thy heart	"	22	11
Presume not on thy heart	"	22	13
Thy beauty's form	"	24	2
have drawn thy shape	"	24	10
Thy merit hath my duty	"	26	2
In thy soul's thought	"	26	8
of thy sweet respect	"	26	12
Presents thy shadow	"	27	10
For thy sweet love	"	29	13
Thy bosom is endeared	"	31	1
of thy deceased lover	"	32	4
Hiding thy bravery	"	34	4
Nor can thy shame	"	34	9
which thy love sheds	"	34	13
thy trespass with compare	"	35	6
salving thy amiss	"	35	7
Excusing thy sins more than thy sins are	"	35	8
For to thy sensual fault	"	35	9
Thy adverse party is thy advocate	"	35	10
Without thy help	"	36	4
honour from thy name	"	36	12
mine is thy good report	"	36	14
of thy worth and truth	"	37	4
Entitled in thy parts	"	37	7
That I in thy abundance	"	37	11
of all thy glory live	"	37	12
stand against thy sight	"	38	6
O, how thy worth	"	39	1
Were it not thy sour leisure	"	39	10
I do forgive thy robbery	"	40	9
absent from thy heart	"	41	2
Thy beauty and thy years	"	41	3
And chide thy beauty and thy straying youth	"	41	10
Hers, by thy beauty	"	41	13
Thine, by thy beauty	"	41	14
would thy shadow's form	"	43	6
thy much clearer light	"	43	7
thy shade shines so	"	43	8
thy fair imperfect shade	"	43	11
Of thy fair health	"	45	12
the conquest of thy sight	"	46	2
Thy—thy picture's sight would bar	Son	46	3
thy fair appearance lies	"	46	8
So, either by thy picture	"	47	9
thy picture in my sight	"	47	13
When as thy love hath cast	"	49	3
reasons on thy part	"	49	12
measured from thy friend	"	50	4
renew thy force	"	56	1
Thy edge should blunter be	"	56	2
Thy hungry eyes	"	56	6
Praising thy worth	"	60	14
Is it thy will thy image should keep open	"	61	1
Is it thy spirit	"	61	5
tenour of thy jealousy	"	61	8
O, no! thy love	"	61	9
watchman ever for thy sake	"	61	12
with beauty of thy days	"	62	14
Thy outward thus with outward	"	69	5
the beauty of thy mind	"	69	9
measure by thy deeds	"	69	10
To thy fair flower	"	69	12
But why thy odour matcheth not thy show	"	69	13
shall not be thy defect	"	70	1
Thy worth the greater	"	70	6
this thy praise cannot be so thy praise	"	70	11
mask'd not thy show	"	70	13
makes thy love more strong	"	73	13
Thy glass will show thee how thy beauties wear	"	77	1
Thy dial how thy precious minutes	"	77	2
thy mind's imprint	"	77	3
thy glass will truly show	"	77	5
Thou by thy dial's	"	77	7
what thy memory cannot contain	"	77	9
deliver'd from thy brain	"	77	11
acquaintance of thy mind	"	77	12
and much enrich thy book	"	77	14
thy sweet graces graced be	"	78	12
did call upon thy aid	"	79	1
had all thy gentle grace	"	79	2
thy lovely argument	"	79	5
thy poet doth invent	"	79	7
From thy behaviour	"	79	10
And found it in thy cheek	"	79	11
Finding thy worth	"	82	6
by thy true-telling friend	"	82	12
know'st thy estimate	"	87	2
The charter of thy worth	"	87	3
but by thy granting	"	87	5
thy own worth then not knowing	"	87	9
So thy great gift	"	87	11
Upon thy side against myself	"	88	3
Upon thy part I can	"	88	6
That for thy right	"	88	14
Against thy reasons	"	89	4
knowing thy will	"	89	7
Be absent from thy walks	"	89	9
Thy sweet beloved name	"	89	10
Thy love is better	"	91	9
But do thy worst	"	92	1
than thy love will stay	"	92	3
on thy humour doth depend	"	92	8
on thy revolt doth lie	"	92	10
Happy to have thy love	"	92	12
Thy looks with me, thy heart in other place	"	93	4

Thy—I cannot know thy change	Son	93	6	Thy—To thy sweet will	Son	135	4
in thy creation did decree	"	93	9	'Will,' add to thy 'Will	"	135	11
That in thy face	"	93	10	make thy large 'Will' more	"	135	12
Whate'er thy thoughts or thy heart's workings be	"	93	11	If thy soul check thee	"	136	1
Thy looks should nothing	"	93	12	Swear to thy blind soul that I was thy 'Will	"	136	2
doth thy beauty grow	"	93	13	And will, thy soul knows	"	136	3
If thy sweet virtue answer not thy show	"	93	14	the treasure of thy love	"	136	5
of thy budding name	"	95	3	Though in thy stores	"	136	10
dost thou thy sins inclose	"	95	4	Make but my name thy love	"	136	13
the story of thy days	"	95	5	That thy unkindness	"	139	2
comments on thy sport	"	95	6	but with thy tongue	"	139	3
Naming thy name	"	95	8	when thy might	"	139	7
Some say, thy fault is youth	"	96	1	thy proud heart go wide	"	140	14
Some say, thy grace is youth	"	96	2	thy tongue's tune delighted	"	141	5
the strength of all thy state	"	96	12	Thy proud heart's slave	"	141	12
mine is thy good report	"	96	14	and thy dear virtue hate	"	142	1
whence didst thou steal thy sweet	"	99	2	Root pity in thy heart	"	142	11
Which on thy soft cheek	"	99	4	Thy pity may deserve	"	142	12
condemned for thy hand	"	99	6	Whilst I, thy babe, chase	"	143	10
had stol'n thy hair	"	99	7	But if thou catch thy hope	"	143	11
had annex'd thy breath	"	99	11	mayst have thy 'Will	"	143	13
gives thee all thy might	"	100	2	Painting thy outward walls	"	146	4
Spend'st thou thy fury	"	100	3	thy fading mansion spend	"	146	6
Darkening thy power	"	100	4	Eat up thy charge? is this thy body's end	"	146	8
that doth thy lays esteem	"	100	7	upon thy servant's loss	"	146	9
And gives thy pen	"	100	8	to aggravate thy store	"	146	10
what shall be thy amends	"	101	1	thy foul faults should find	"	148	14
For thy neglect	"	101	2	all tyrant for thy sake	"	149	4
Then do thy office	"	101	13	thy service to despise	"	149	10
shalt find thy monument	"	107	13	doth worship thy defect	"	149	11
or thy dear merit	"	108	4	now I know thy mind	"	149	13
I hallow'd thy fair name	"	108	8	refuse of thy deeds	"	150	6
In thy breast doth lie	"	109	4	thy worst all best exceeds	"	150	8
all thy sum of good	"	109	12	If thy unworthiness raised love	"	150	13
Even to thy pure	"	110	14	thy sweet self prove	"	151	4
Thy gift, thy tables	"	122	1	But rising at thy name	"	151	9
Of thee, thy record	"	122	8	thy poor drudge to be	"	151	11
thy dear love to score	"	122	10	To stand in thy affairs, fall by thy side	"	151	12
Thy pyramids built up	"	123	2	In act thy bed-vow broke	"	152	3
Thy registers and thee	"	123	9	of thy deep kindness	"	152	9
For thy records and what	"	123	11	Oaths of thy love, thy truth, thy constancy	"	152	10
by thy continual haste	"	123	12	It is thy last	L C	.....	168
despite thy scythe and thee	"	123	14	Thy grace being gain'd	P P	3	8
obsequious in thy heart	"	125	9	that I thy parts admire	"	5	10
stands least in thy control	"	125	14	thy voice his dreadful thunder	"	5	11
who in thy power	"	126	1	left'st me nothing in thy will	"	10	8
Thy lovers withering as thy sweet self grow'st	"	126	4	Thy discontent thou didst bequeath	"	10	12
With thy sweet fingers	"	128	3	thy cheeks may blow	"	17	9
tender inward of thy hand	"	128	6	pluck thee from thy thorn	"	17	12
O'er whom thy fingers walk	"	128	11	Turning mortal for thy love	"	17	18
Give them thy fingers, me thy lips to kiss	"	128	14	Thy like ne'er was	"	18	50
Thy face hath not the power	"	131	6	thou comest thy tale to tell	"	19	7
but thinking on thy face	"	131	10	Smooth not thy tongue	"	19	8
Thy black is fairest	"	131	12	And set thy person forth	"	19	12
black save in thy deeds	"	131	13	frame all thy ways	"	19	25
Knowing thy heart torments	"	132	2	Where thy desert may merit	"	19	27
eyes become thy face	"	132	9	By ringing in thy lady's ear	"	19	28
as well beseem thy heart	"	132	10	And in thy suit be humble true	"	19	32
And suit thy pity	"	132	12	Unless thy lady prove unjust	"	19	33
that thy complexion lack	"	132	14	To live with thee and be thy love	"	20	20
thy cruel eye	"	133	5	None takes pity on thy pain	"	21	20
thy steel bosom's ward	"	133	9	All thy friends are lapp'd in lead	"	21	24
am mortgaged to thy will	"	134	2	All thy fellow birds do sing	"	21	25
The statute of thy beauty	"	134	9	Careless of thy sorrowing	"	21	26
thou hast thy 'Will	"	135	1	Every man will be thy friend	"	21	35

Thy—No man will supply thy want	P P	21	38	Till—till they have singled	V A		693
He that is thy friend indeed	"	21	51	Till forging Nature	"		729
He will help thee in thy need	"	21	52	Till the wild waves	"		819
That thy sable gender makest	P T		18	Till, cheering up	"		896
Thyself—Then woo thyself, be of thyself rejected	V A		159	Till mutual overthrow	"		1018
				that they have wept till now	"		1062
when thou thyself art dead	"		172	Till sable Night, mother of dread	R L		117
An image like thyself	"		664	Till every minute pays	"		329
So in thyself, thyself art	"		763	till their effects be tried	"		353
Thyself art mighty	R L		583	Till they might open	"		399
Honour thyself to rid me	"		1031	Till with her own white fleece	"		678
Kill both thyself and her	"		1036	Till, like a jade	"		707
to give thyself a blow	"		1823	till he render right	"		943
Thyself thy foe	Son	1	8	Till life to death acquit	"		1071
thyself thy beauty's legacy	"	4	2	I will not till my Collatine	"		1177
with thyself alone	"	4	9	Till after a deep groan	"		1276
Thou of thyself thy sweet self	"	4	10	till action might become them	"		1323
That's for thyself to breed	"	6	7	till he return again	"		1359
Ten times thyself	"	6	9	till meeting greater ranks	"		1441
So thou, thyself out-going	"	7	13	Till she despairing Hecuba beheld	"		1447
consumest thyself in single life	"	9	2	Till after many accents	"		1719
thyself art so unprovident	"	10	2	Till Lucrece' father	"		1732
That 'gainst thyself	"	10	6	Till manly shame bids him	"		1777
Or to thyself at least	"	10	12	till it blow up rain	"		1788
If from thyself to store	"	14	12	Till Nature, as she wrought thee	Son	20	10
be of thyself so wary	"	22	9	Till whatsoever star	"	26	9
O, give thyself the thanks	"	38	5	Till then not show my head	"	26	14
When thou thyself	"	38	8	till she have prevailed	"	41	8
if thou thyself deceivest	"	40	7	to see till I see thee	"	43	13
of what thyself refusest	"	40	8	Till I return, of posting	"	51	4
Thyself away art present still	"	47	10	So, till the judgement	"	55	13
thou thyself dost pay	"	79	14	even till they wink with fullness	"	56	6
Thyself thou gavest	"	87	9	to do, till you require	"	57	4
to steal thyself away	"	92	1	till now never kept seat	"	105	14
and length thyself to-morrow	P P	15	18	Till each to razed oblivion	"	122	7
Tickled—To be so tickled	Son	128	9	and till action, lust	"	129	2
Tickling—Mock with thy tickling beams	R L		1090	Till my bad angel fire	"	144	14
				sees not till heaven clears	"	148	12
Tide—The crystal tide	V A		957	Till thus he 'gan besiege me	L C		177
began to turn their tide	"		979	Till now did ne'er invite	"		182
my uncontrolled tide	R L		645	till then were levell'd	"		282
his weary noon-tide prick	"		781	Till my bad angel fire	P P	2	14
the violent roaring tide	"		1667	Till looking on an Englishman	"	16	3
Held back his sorrow's tide	"		1789	Lean'd her breast up-till a thorn	"	21	10
Tidings—no tidings of her love	V A		847	Tillage—Disdains the tillage	Son	3	6
And gazed for tidings	R L		254	Time—Make use of time	V A		129
Tie—To tie the rider	V A		40	Themselves in little time	"		132
Will tie the hearers	R L		818	The time is spent	"		255
To tie up envy evermore	Son	70	12	by the rights of time	"		759
do tie me day by day	"	117	4	and twenty times, 'Woe, woe	"		833
Tied—being tied unto a tree	V A		263	twenty times cry so	"		834
tied to the tree	"		391	A thousand times	"		1130
made tongue-tied by authority	Son	66	9	Wonder of time	"		1133
To make me tongue-tied	"	80	4	Now stole upon the time	R L		162
My tongue-tied Muse	"	85	1	these lets attend the time	"		330
judgement of my heart is tied	"	137	8	by children in succeeding times	"		525
My tongue-tied patience	"	140	2	That through the length of times	"		718
their poor balls are tied	L C		24	proportion'd course of time	"		774
Her hair, nor loose nor tied	"		29	Thou grant'st no time	"		908
Tiger—The tiger would be tame	V A		1096	Mis-shapen Time, copesmate	"		925
To slay the tiger	R L		955	injurious, shifting Time	"		930
than tigers in their wildness	"		980	Time's office is to pine	"		936
from the fierce tiger's jaws	Son	19	3	Time's glory is to calm	"		939
Till—Till either gorge be stuff'd	V A		58	To stamp the seal of time	"		941
Till he take truce	"		82	time to tear his curled hair	"		981
From morn till night	"		154	time against himself to rave	"		982
Till clapping makes it red	"		468	time of time's help to despair	"		983
Till his breath breatheth	"		474	Let him have time to live	"		984
Till breathless he disjoin'd	"		541	time a beggar's orts to crave	"		985

Time—And time to see one	R L	....	986	Time—but Time decays	Son	65	8
Let him have time to see	"	....	988	Shall Time's best jewel from Time's chest lie hid	"	65	10
Let him have time to mark how slow time goes	"	....	990	being woo'd of time	"	70	6
In time of sorrow	"	....	991	That time of year	"	73	1
His time of folly and his time of sport	"	....	992	Why with the time	"	76	3
				Time's thievish progress	"	77	8
Have time to wail the abusing of his time	"	....	994	And yet this time removed was summer's time	"	97	5
'O Time, thou tutor	"	....	995	time so idly spent	"	100	6
At Time, at Tarquin	"	....	1024	If Time have any wrinkle	"	100	10
He ten times pines	"	....	1115	And make Time's spoils despised	"	100	12
when time is kept with tears	"	....	1127	faster than Time wastes life	"	100	13
The weary time she cannot	"	....	1361	chronicle of wasted time	"	106	1
Time's ruin, beauty's wreck	"	....	1451	Of this our time	"	106	10
time doth weary time	"	....	1570	of this most balmy time	"	107	9
Short time seems long	"	....	1573	Where time and outward form	"	108	14
see time how slow it creeps	"	....	1575	Just to the time, not with the time exchanged	"	109	7
Which all this time	"	....	1576				
Three times with sighs	"	....	1604	But reckoning Time	"	115	5
death by time outworn	"	....	1761	fearing of Time's tyranny	"	115	9
O Time, cease thou thy course	"	....	1765	Love's not Time's fool	"	116	9
should by time decease	Son	1	3	And given to time	"	117	6
Now is the time	"	3	2	you've pass'd a hell of time	"	120	6
this thy golden time	"	3	12	No, Time, thou shalt not boast	"	123	1
time leads summer on	"	5	5	As subject to Time's love or to Time's hate	"	124	3
Or ten times happier	"	6	8				
Ten times thyself	"	6	9	inviting time our fashion calls	"	124	8
ten times refigured thee	"	6	10	call the fools of time	"	124	13
the times should cease	"	11	7	hold Time's fickle glass	"	126	2
the clock that tells the time	"	12	1	May time disgrace	"	126	8
wastes of time must go	"	12	10	Time had not scythed all	L C	....	12
'gainst Time's scythe	"	12	13	When time shall serve	P P	19	35
Where wasteful Time	"	15	11	When time with age	"	19	46
Time for love of you	"	15	13	Time-beguiling—Such .... sport	V A	....	24
this bloody tyrant, Time	"	16	2	Time-bettering—of the .... days	Son	82	8
Which this, Time's pencil	"	16	10	Timeless—His all-too-timeless speed	R L	....	44
in time to come	"	17	1	Timely—alack, too timely shaded	P P	10	3
of yours alive that time	"	17	13	Timorous—the .... flying hare	V A	....	674
to time thou grow'st	"	18	12	so the timorous yelping	"	....	881
Devouring Time, blunt thou	"	19	1	Tincture—tincture of the roses	Son	54	6
swift-footed Time	"	19	6	Tip—So on the tip	L C	....	120
do thy worst, old Time	"	19	10	Tire—Tires with her beak	V A	....	56
time's furrows I behold	"	22	3	Self-will himself doth tire	R L	....	707
my dear time's waste	"	30	4	And you in Grecian tires	Son	53	8
the bettering of the time	"	32	5	Tired—tired in the mid-day heat	V A	....	177
ten times happy me	"	37	14	that's tired with chasing	"	....	561
ten times more in worth	"	38	9	his wilful eye be tired	R L	....	417
To entertain the time	"	39	11	moan tired moan	"	....	1363
Which time and thoughts	"	39	12	with one poor tired tongue	"	....	1617
I must attend time's leisure	"	44	12	for limbs with travel tired	Son	27	2
Another time mine eye	"	47	7	tired with my woe	"	50	5
Against that time, if ever that time come	"	49	1	Tired with all these	"	66	1
				Tired with all these	"	66	13
Against that time when thou	"	49	5	'Tis—'Tis but a kiss I beg	V A	....	96
Against that time do I	"	49	9	What 'tis to love	"	....	202
So is the time	"	52	9	And 'tis your fault	"	....	381
besmear'd with sluttish time	"	55	4	'Tis much to borrow	"	....	411
and times of your desire	"	57	2	shrieks,—'tis very late	"	....	531
I have no precious time	"	57	8	yet 'tis pluck'd	"	....	574
control your times of pleasure	"	58	2	and now 'tis dark	"	....	719
may privilege your time	"	58	10	'''Tis so:' they answer all ''Tis so	"	....	851
And Time that gave	"	60	8	'tis a causeless fantasy	"	....	897
Time doth transfix	"	60	9	'Tis not my fault	"	....	1003
And yet to times in hope	"	60	13	'Tis he, foul creature	"	....	1005
With Time's injurious	"	63	2	'Tis true, 'tis true	"	....	1111
For such a time	"	63	9	And so 'tis thine	"	....	1181
by Time's fell hand defaced	"	64	1	And 'tis thy right	"	....	1184
That Time will come	"	64	12	What terror 'tis	R L	....	453

'Tis—'Tis thou that executest	R L	877	To—To love a cheek	V A		252
'Tis thou that spurn'st	"	880	hasteth to his horse	"		258
Sometime 'tis mad	"	1106	to her straight goes he	"		264
'Tis double death to drown	"	1114	to captivate the eye	"		281
'Tis honour to deprive	"	1186	To bid the wind a base	"		303
'Tis but a part of sorrow	"	1328	to see him woo her	"		309
For now 'tis stale to sigh	"	1362	to his melting buttock lent	"		315
For 'tis a meritorious fair design	"	1692	about to take him	"		319
'He, he, fair lords, 'tis he	"	1721	strive to over-fly them	"		324
'tis mine that she hath kill'd	"	1803	and begins to glow	"		337
the frame wherein 'tis held	Son	24 5	wistly to view	"		343
'Tis not enough that through	"	34 5	to the wayward boy	"		344
'Tis thee, myself, that	"	62 13	To note the fighting conflict	"		345
I say "Tis so, 'tis true	"	83 9	to his eyes suing	"		356
'tis with so dull a cheer	"	97 13	to get my palfrey	"		384
Alas, 'tis true	"	110 1	tied to the tree	"		391
O, 'tis the first ; 'tis flattery	"	114 9	To touch the fire	"		402
'tis the lesser sin	"	114 13	To take advantage	"		405
'Tis better to be vile	"	121 1	O, learn to love	"		407
But 'tis my heart that loves	"	141 3	'Tis much to borrow	"		411
'Tis promised in the charity	L C	70	to love is love but to disgrace it	"		412
Beauty brag, but 'tis not she	P T	63	To love's alarms	"		424
Titan—And Titan, tired	V A	177	to hear nor see	"		437
Title—Thy smoothing titles	R L	892	to thee be still as much	"		442
and proud titles boast	Son	25 2	wert thou to the taste	"		445
To 'cide this title	"	46 9	Which to his speech	"		452
O what a happy title	"	92 11	Wreck to the seaman, tempest to the field	"		454
To—hied him to the chase	V A	3	sorrow to shepherds	"		455
love he laugh'd to scorn	"	4	to herdmen and to herds	"		456
'gins to woo him	"	6	to reprehend her	"		470
Stain to all nymphs	"	9	To mend the hurt	"		478
to alight thy steed	"	13	now is turn'd to day	"		481
to the saddle-bow	"	14	Do I delight to die	"		496
to do a goddess good	"	28	leaders to their queen	"		503
to pluck him from his horse	"	30	to drive infection	"		508
unapt to toy	"	34	still to be sealing	"		512
To tie the rider she begins to prove	"	40	To sell myself I can be	"		513
and 'gins to chide	"	46	seek not to know me	"		525
To fan and blow them	"	52	is sour to taste	"		528
Forced to content, but never to obey	"	61	gone to fold, birds to their nest	"		532
added to a river	"	71	Do summon us to part	"		534
to a pretty ear	"	74	face grows to face	"		540
never to remove	"	81	fall to the earth	"		546
So offers he to give	"	88	she begins to forage	"		554
to sport and dance	"	105	to every light impression	"		566
To toy, to wanton	"	106	longer to restrain him	"		579
to my coy disdain	"	112	look well to her heart	"		580
Art thou ashamed to kiss	"	121	mine eyes to watch	"		584
Be bold to play	"	124	To hunt the boar	"		588
or seem to melt	"	144	To clip Elysium, and to lack her joy	"		600
Not gross to sink	"	150	She seeks to kindle	"		606
where I list to sport me	"	154	to withhold me so	"		612
to thine own face affected	"	157	a churlish swine to gore	"		616
And died to kiss	"	162	Like to a mortal butcher, bent to kill	"		618
Torches are made to light, jewels to wear	"	163	To which Love's eyes	"		632
Dainties to taste	"	164	hath nought to do	"		638
sappy plants to bear	"	165	not to dissemble	"		641
growing to themselves	"	166	presenteth to mine eye	"		661
to get it is thy duty	"	168	to overshoot his troubles	"		680
thou art bound to breed	"	171	to amaze his foes	"		684
queen began to sweat	"	175	To make the cunning hounds	"		686
bad his team to guide	"	179	to stop the loud pursuers	"		688
makest thou to be gone	"	188	are driven to doubt	"		692
What 'tis to love	"	202	to hearken if his foes	"		699
struggles to be gone	"	227	To one sore sick	"		702
To shelter thee	"	238	To make thee hate	"		711
there he came to lie	"	245	this to that and so to so	"		713
to swallow Venus' liking	"	248				

To—to rob thee of a kiss	V A	.....	723
To shame the sun	"	.....	732
To cross the curious workmanship	"	.....	734
To mingle beauty	"	.....	735
subject to the tyranny	"	.....	737
to lend the world his light	"	.....	756
to bury that posterity	"	.....	758
gold that's put to use	"	.....	768
to be barr'd of rest	"	.....	784
longs not to groan	"	.....	785
that leadeth on to danger	"	.....	788
bawd to lust's abuse	"	.....	792
Love to heaven is fled	"	.....	793
to your wanton talk	"	.....	809
bound him to her breast	"	.....	812
to spend the night withal	"	.....	847
as thou dost lend to other	"	.....	864
hasteth to a myrtle grove	"	.....	865
she coasteth to the cry	"	.....	870
to make her stay	"	.....	873
Hasting to feed her fawn	"	.....	876
to be so curst	"	.....	887
to surprise her heart	"	.....	890
to rate the boar	"	.....	906
To whom she speaks	"	.....	918
to the ground below	"	.....	923
To stifle beauty and to steal his	"	.....	934
smell to the violet	"	.....	936
thou hast no eyes to see	"	.....	939
to strike him dead	"	.....	948
all other eyes to see	"	.....	952
sought still to dry	"	.....	964
doth labour to expel	"	.....	976
to turn their tide	"	.....	979
To wash the foul face	"	.....	983
Not to believe	"	.....	986
Death is not to blame	"	.....	992
call'd him all to nought	"	.....	993
to his hateful name	"	.....	994
To be of such a weak	"	.....	1016
To wail his death	"	.....	1017
As falcons to the lure	"	.....	1027
to creep forth again	"	.....	1036
To the disposing of her troubled	"	.....	1040
seem'd with him to bleed	"	.....	1056
her joints forgot to bow	"	.....	1061
eyes are turn'd to fire, my heart to lead	"	.....	1072
ever strive to kiss you	"	.....	1082
Having no fair to lose	"	.....	1083
to rob him of his fair	"	.....	1086
To see his face	"	.....	1093
To recreate himself	"	.....	1095
He thought to kiss him	"	.....	1110
to persuade him there	"	.....	1114
teach the fool to speak	"	.....	1146
to tread the measures	"	.....	1148
Put fear to valour, courage to the coward	"	.....	1158
servile to all discontents	"	.....	1161
matter is to fire	"	.....	1162
the new-sprung flower to smell	"	.....	1171
to her Adonis' breath	"	.....	1172
which she compares to tears	"	.....	1176
To wet his eyes	"	.....	1179
To grow unto himself	"	.....	1180
To wither in my breast	"	.....	1182
their course to Paphos	"	.....	1193
Means to immure herself	"	.....	1194
To—And to Collatium	R L	.....	4
lurks to aspire	"	.....	5
To praise the clear	"	.....	11
espoused to more fame	"	.....	20
to such a peerless dame	"	.....	21
To set forth	"	.....	32
To quench the coal	"	.....	47
the golden age to gild	"	.....	60
thus to use it	"	.....	62
makes them still to fight	"	.....	68
To those two armies	"	.....	76
his barren skill to show	"	.....	81
to her princely guest	"	.....	90
open'd to the light	"	.....	103
He stories to her ears	"	.....	106
And every one to rest	"	.....	125
yet ever to obtain	"	.....	129
persuade him to abstaining	"	.....	130
Despair to gain	"	.....	131
Is but to surfeit	"	.....	139
to nurse the life	"	.....	141
we leave to be	"	.....	148
to obtain his lust	"	.....	156
to find a stranger just	"	.....	159
To slanderous tongues	"	.....	161
wakes to stain and kill	"	.....	168
betake him to retire	"	.....	174
to his lustful eye	"	.....	179
And to the flame	"	.....	180
I force to my desire	"	.....	182
To darken her	"	.....	191
to so pure a shrine	"	.....	194
'O shame to knighthood, and to shining arms	"	.....	197
to my household's grave	"	.....	198
to be soft fancy's slave	"	.....	200
To cipher me	"	.....	207
To wish that I	"	.....	210
to wail a week	"	.....	213
to get a toy	"	.....	214
but to touch the crown	"	.....	216
this vile purpose to prevent	"	.....	220
This blur to youth, this sorrow to the sage	"	.....	222
to betray my life	"	.....	233
to work upon his wife	"	.....	235
Forced it to tremble	"	.....	261
to the unjust	"	.....	283
appeal seeks to the heart	"	.....	293
marcheth to Lucrece' bed	"	.....	301
to some regard	"	.....	305
to have him heard	"	.....	306
shriek to see him there	"	.....	307
to make him stay	"	.....	311
'This glove to wanton tricks	"	.....	320
To add a more rejoicing to the prime	"	.....	332
more cause to sing	"	.....	333
to pray he doth begin	"	.....	342
auspicious to the hour	"	.....	347
The powers to whom	"	.....	349
to his hand full soon	"	.....	370
To draw the cloud	"	.....	371
To wink, being blinded	"	.....	375
league to kill	"	.....	383
Lucrece to their sight	"	.....	384
seems to part in sunder	"	.....	388
to want his bliss	"	.....	389
To be admired	"	.....	392

To—to adorn the day	R L	399	To—To cipher what is writ	R L		811
to heave the owner out	"	413	to still her child	"		813
leading to his hand	"	436	to deck his oratory	"		815
to make his stand	"	438	to Tarquin's shame	"		816
to the quiet cabinet	"	442	to attend each line	"		818
this tumult to behold	"	447	to him allotted	"		824
Like to a new-kill'd bird	"	457	was pure to Collatine	"		826
to batter such an ivory wall	"	464	to disdain him	"		844
Wounding itself to death	"	466	his treasure to behold	"		857
To make the breach	"	469	to be master'd	"		863
To sound a parley to his heartless foe	"	471	To hold their cursed-blessed fortune	"		866
this rash alarm to know	"	473	turn to loathed sours	"		867
seeks to show	"	474	to seize the souls	"		882
I come to scale	"	481	Thy honey turns to gall, thy joy to grief	"		889
if thou mean to chide	"	484				
to this night	"	485	turns to open shame	"		890
Which I to conquer sought	"	488	to a public fast	"		891
to gaze on beauty	"	496	to a ragged name	"		892
to embrace mine infamy	"	504	to bitter wormwood taste	"		893
I purpose to destroy thee	"	514	great strifes to end	"		899
To kill thine honour	"	516	Give physic to the sick, ease to the pained	"		901
I mean to place him	"	517				
to a great good end	"	528	have to do with thee	"		911
bequeath not to their lot	"	534	As well to hear	"		915
To the rough beast	"	545	have come to me	"		916
to her plaining	"	559	To all sins past and all that are to come	"		923
Which to her oratory	"	564				
That to his borrow'd bed	"	573	to the general doom	"		924
And stoop to honour, not to foul desire	"	574	slave to false delight	"		927
			thou gavest me to repose	"		933
gave drink to thee	"	577	To endless date	"		935
To strike a poor unseasonable doe	"	581	Time's office is to fine	"		936
labour hence to heave thee	"	586	To eat up errors	"		937
To soften it	"	591	to calm contending kings	"		939
dissolved to water	"	592	To unmask falsehood and bring truth to light	"		940
to do him shame	"	597				
To all the host of heaven	"	598	To stamp the seal	"		941
To privilege dishonour	"	621	To wake the morn	"		942
to guard iniquity	"	626	To wrong the wronger	"		943
all that brood to kill	"	627	To ruinate proud buildings	"		944
He learn'd to sin	"	630	'To fill with worm-holes	"		946
To view thy present trespass	"	632	To feed oblivion	"		947
to themselves appear	"	633	To blot old books	"		948
'To thee, to thee	"	638	To pluck the quills	"		949
Not to seducing lust	"	639	To dry the old oak's sap	"		950
To their salt sovereign	"	650	To spoil antiquities	"		951
Add to his flow	"	651	'To show the bedlam daughters	"		953
Who seek to stain	"	653	To make the child a man	"		954
to the base shrub's foot	"	664	To slay the tiger	"		955
low vassals to thy state	"	666	To tame the unicorn	"		956
Yield to my love	"	668	To mock the subtle	"		957
I mean to bear thee	"	670	To cheer the ploughman	"		958
To be thy partner	"	672	return to make amends	"		961
converts to cold disdain	"	691	to bad debtors	"		964
Like to a bankrupt	"	711	lackey to eternity	"		967
To whose weak ruins	"	720	To make him curse	"		970
To ask the spotted princess	"	721	To make him moan	"		977
To living death	"	726	to him lose their mildness	"		979
To cloak offences	"	749	Wilder to him than tigers	"		980
To have their unseen sin	"	753	to tear his curled hair	"		981
to close so pure a mind	"	761	against himself to rave	"		982
to meet the eastern light	"	773	of time's help to despair	"		983
the sun to climb	"	775	to live a loathed slave	"		984
ere he go to bed	"	776	a beggar's orts to crave	"		985
to blush with me	"	792	And time to see	"		986
To cross their arms	"	793	Disdain to him disdained scraps to give	"		987
To mask their brows	"	794				
to the tell-tale Day	"	806	to see his friends	"		988

21

To—to mock at him	R L	989	To—A letter to my lord	R L	1293
to mark how slow	"	990	prepare to carry it	"	1294
Have time to wail	"	994	she prepares to write	"	1296
to good and bad	"	995	Health to thy person next vouch-		
Teach me to curse him	"	996	safe t' afford	"	1305
every hour to kill	"	998	Some present speed to come	"	1307
to so base a slave	"	1001	She hoards, to spend when he is		
To shame his hope	"	1003	by to bear her	"	1318
servants to shallow fools	"	1016	better so to clear her	"	1320
To trembling clients	"	1020	To shun this blot	"	1322
to do me good	"	1028	To see sad sights	"	1324
Is to let forth	"	1029	interprets to the ear	"	1325
to rid me of this shame	"	1031	'At Ardea to my lord	"	1332
to scratch her wicked foe	"	1035	to hie as fast	"	1334
To find some desperate instrument	"	1038	court'sies to her low	"	1338
To make more vent	"	1040	to see her shame	"	1344
to end a hapless life	"	1045	To talk in deeds	"	1348
by Tarquin's falchion to be slain	"	1046	no words to gage	"	1351
I sought to live	"	1051	'tis stale to sigh, to weep	"	1362
not fear to die	"	1052	to mourn some newer way	"	1365
To clear this spot	"	1053	she calls to mind	"	1366
to slander's livery	"	1054	the city to destroy	"	1369
to living infamy	"	1055	to kiss the turrets bow'd	"	1372
To burn the guiltless casket	"	1057	to show the painter's strife	"	1377
To flatter thee	"	1061	the Greeks to fight	"	1402
come to growth	"	1062	purl'd up to the sky	"	1407
Till life to death	"	1071	to swallow up	"	1409
To hide the truth	"	1075	To jump up higher seem'd to mock		
to purge my impure tale	"	1078	the mind	"	1414
To ugly hell	"	1082	seems to pelt and swear	"	1418
light to all fair eyes	"	1083	save to the eye	"	1426
shames herself to see	"	1084	to be imagined	"	1428
to point her out	"	1087	march'd to field	"	1430
To whom she sobbing speaks	"	1088	To see their youthful sons	"	1432
hath nought to do	"	1092	And to their hope	"	1433
And to herself all sorrow	"	1102	joy seemed to appear	"	1434
to drown in ken of shore	"	1114	To Simois' reedy banks	"	1437
To see the salve	"	1116	To imitate the battle	"	1438
to pleasing ears	"	1126	To break upon the galled shore	"	1440
To keep thy sharp woes	"	1136	To this well-painted piece	"	1443
To imitate thee well	"	1137	To find a face	"	1444
to affright mine eye	"	1138	changed to black	"	1454
to true languishment	"	1141	to the beldam's woes	"	1458
To creatures stern sad tunes, to			wants to answer	"	1459
change their kinds	"	1147	to ban her cruel foes	"	1460
which way to fly	"	1150	to lend her those	"	1461
To live or die	"	1154	To give her so much	"	1463
'To kill myself	"	1156	To plague a private sin	"	1484
be nurse to none	"	1162	And friend to friend	"	1488
to myself was nearer	"	1165	To pencill'd pensiveness	"	1497
to Tarquin I'll bequeath	"	1181	to Phrygian shepherds lent	"	1502
'Tis honour to deprive	"	1186	Onward to Troy	"	1504
bequeath to thee	"	1192	seem'd to scorn his woes	"	1505
to the skies and ground	"	1199	To hide deceit	"	1507
To those that live	"	1204	seem'd to welcome woe	"	1509
Yield to my hand	"	1210	To me came Tarquin armed	"	1544
to her mistress hies	"	1215	To see those borrow'd tears	"	1549
to her lady's sorrow	"	1221	to burn thy city	"	1554
Their gentle sex to weep	"	1237	Only to flatter fools	"	1559
Grieving themselves to guess	"	1238	to burn his Troy	"	1561
those proud lords to blame	"	1259	to that unhappy guest	"	1565
tenants to their shame	"	1260	To think their dolour	"	1582
to do her husband wrong	"	1264	to those already spent	"	1589
Such danger to resistance	"	1265	to ask her how	"	1594
To the poor counterfeit	"	1269	to answer his desire	"	1606
'The more to blame	"	1278	to let them know	"	1607
to know your heaviness	"	1283	to hear her words	"	1610
that one hath power to tell	"	1288	To tell them all	"	1617
by and by to bear	"	1292	It hath to say	"	1618

Phrase	Ref	Num	Phrase	Ref	Num	Num
To—might be done to me	R. L.	1623	To—to wet a widow's eye	Son	9	1
thy liking to my will	"	1633	shalt hap to die	"	9	3
to start and cry	"	1639	bear'st love to any	"	10	1
should not live to speak	"	1642	stick'st not to conspire	"	10	6
my tongue to speak	"	1648	roof to ruinate	"	10	7
came evidence to swear	"	1650	Which to repair	"	10	8
to make mine own excuse	"	1653	Or to thyself at least	"	10	12
To necessary yieldings	"	1658	Save breed, to brave him	"	12	14
begins to blow	"	1661	to some other give	"	13	4
Back to the strait	"	1670	a house fall to decay	"	13	9
To push grief on	"	1673	But not to tell	"	14	3
to my sorrow lendeth	"	1676	to brief minutes tell	"	14	5
To drown one woe	"	1680	Pointing to each his thunder	"	14	6
Speaking to those	"	1689	from thyself to store	"	14	12
honourable faiths to me	"	1690	To change your day of youth to			
to venge this wrong	"	1691	sullied night	"	15	12
To chase injustice	"	1693	To give away yourself	"	16	13
began to promise aid	"	1696	my verse in time to come	"	17	1
to her imposition	"	1697	The age to come	"	17	7
Longing to hear	"	1698	compare thee to a summer's day	"	18	1
honour to advance	"	1705	to time thou grow'st	"	18	12
at once began to say	"	1709	this gives life to thee	"	18	14
to give this wound to me	"	1722	To the wide world	"	19	7
Which seems to weep	"	1746	pattern to succeeding men	"	19	12
to this end	"	1755	to my purpose nothing	"	20	12
If they surcease to be	"	1766	beauty to his verse	"	21	2
And counterfeits to die	"	1776	that purpose not to sell	"	21	14
And live to be revenged	"	1778	not to give back again	"	22	14
Begins to talk	"	1783	forget to say	"	23	5
to make it more	"	1789	strength seem to decay	"	23	7
Began to clothe his wit	"	1809	O, learn to read	"	23	13
To check the tears	"	1817	To hear with eyes belongs to love's			
set thy long-experienced wit to			fine wit	"	23	14
school	"	1820	To find where your true image	"	24	6
to give thyself a blow	"	1823	Are windows to my breast	"	24	11
To slay herself	"	1827	Delights to peep, to gaze therein	"	24	12
to bear thy part	"	1830	want to grace their art	"	24	13
To rouse our Roman gods	"	1831	to whom in vassalage	"	26	1
Her wrongs to us	"	1840	To thee I send this	"	26	3
to end his vow	"	1843	To witness duty, not to show my wit	"	26	4
And to his protestation	"	1844	wanting words to show it	"	26	6
to the ground	"	1846	To show me worthy	"	26	12
to this advised doom	"	1849	may I dare to boast	"	26	13
to bear dead Lucrece thence	"	1850	I haste me to my bed	"	27	1
To show her bleeding body	"	1851	To work my mind	"	27	4
to publish Tarquin's foul offence	"	1852	pilgrimage to thee	"	27	6
To Tarquin's everlasting banishment	"	1855	to my sightless view	"	27	10
contracted to thine own bright			enemies to either's reign	"	28	5
eyes	Son	1	5	shake hands to torture me	"	28	6
to thy sweet self too cruel	"	1	8	the other to complain	"	28	7
herald to the gaudy spring	"	1	10	to please him	"	28	9
To eat the world's due	"	1	14	Wishing me like to one	"	29	5
To say, within thine own	"	2	7	Like to the lark	"	29	11
were to be new made	"	2	13	then I scorn to change	"	29	14
to stop posterity	"	3	8	When to the sessions	"	30	1
remember'd not to be	"	3	13	unused to flow	"	30	5
lends to those are free	"	4	4	woe to woe tell o'er	"	30	10
given thee to give	"	4	6	of me to thee did give	"	31	11
calls thee to be gone	"	4	11	To march in ranks	"	32	12
lives th' executor to be	"	4	14	basest clouds to ride	"	33	5
to the very same	"	5	3	Stealing unseen to west	"	33	8
To hideous winter	"	5	6	To let base clouds	"	34	3
to breed another thee	"	6	7	To dry the rain	"	34	6
To be death's conquest	"	6	14	give physic to my grief	"	34	9
to his new-appearing	"	7	3	To him that bears	"	34	12
Music to hear	"	8	1	For to thy sensual fault	"	35	9
sweet husband to another	"	8	9	To that sweet thief	"	35	14
Sings this to thee	"	8	14	To see his active child	"	37	2
				engrafted to this store	"	37	8

To—want subject to invent	Son	38	1	To—thus to ruminate	Son	64	11
paper to rehearse	"	38	4	But weep to have that which it			
cannot write to thee	"	38	7	fears to lose	"	64	14
to outlive long date	"	38	12	As, to behold desert	"	66	2
to mine own self bring	"	39	3	Save that, to die	"	66	14
That due to thee	"	39	8	Beggar'd of blood to blush	"	67	10
To entertain the time	"	39	11	to show what wealth	"	67	13
how to make one twain	"	39	13	To live a second life	"	68	7
To bear love's wrong	"	40	12	to dress his beauty new	"	68	12
and therefore to be won	"	41	5	To show false Art	"	68	14
therefore to be assailed	"	41	6	To thy fair flower	"	69	12
to break a twofold truth	"	41	12	To tie up envy	"	70	12
tempting her to thee	"	41	13	Give warning to the world	"	71	3
being false to me	"	41	14	with vilest worms to dwell	"	71	4
my sake to approve her	"	42	8	task you to recite	"	72	1
To the clear day	"	43	7	To do more for me	"	72	6
When to unseeing eyes	"	43	8	no more to shame	"	72	12
to see till I see thee	"	43	13	to love things nothing worth	"	72	14
To leap large lengths	"	44	10	To love that well	"	73	14
embassy of love to thee	"	45	6	was consecrate to thee	"	74	6
Sinks down to death	"	45	8	of thee to be remembered	"	74	12
recounting it to me	"	45	12	So are you to my thoughts as food			
How to divide	"	46	2	to life	"	75	1
To 'cide this title	"	46	9	showers are to the ground	"	75	2
tenants to the heart	"	46	10	to be with you alone	"	75	7
And to the painted banquet	"	47	6	To new-found methods and to com-			
to heart's and eye's delight	"	47	14	pounds strange	"	76	4
truest bars to thrust	"	48	2	progress to eternity	"	77	8
That to my use	"	48	3	Commit to these waste blanks	"	77	10
to whom my jewels trifles are	"	48	5	To take a new acquaintance	"	77	12
Call'd to that audit	"	49	4	on high to sing	"	78	5
To guard the lawful	"	49	12	ignorance aloft to fly	"	78	6
To leave poor me	"	49	13	to the learned's wing	"	78	7
Since why to love	"	49	14	No praise to thee	"	79	12
and that repose to say	"	50	3	To make me tongue-tied	"	80	4
to bear that weight	"	50	6	inferior far to his	"	80	7
More sharp to me than spurring				your epitaph to make	"	81	1
to his side	"	50	12	to all the world must die	"	81	6
give him leave to go	"	51	14	tongues to be your being	"	81	11
bring him to his sweet up-locked	"	52	2	married to my Muse	"	82	1
To make some special	"	52	11	enforced to seek anew	"	82	7
Being had, to triumph, being				And therefore to your fair	"	83	2
lack'd, to hope	"	52	14	That to his subject	"	84	6
Die to themselves	"	54	11	You to your beauteous	"	84	13
out to the ending doom	"	55	12	To every hymn	"	85	7
Come daily to the banks	"	56	11	And to the most of praise	"	85	10
time at all to spend	"	57	3	whose love to you	"	85	11
Nor services to do	"	57	4	by spirits taught to write	"	86	5
of hours to crave	"	58	3	to whom thou gavest	"	87	10
to stay your leisure	"	58	4	to set me light	"	88	1
tame to sufferance	"	58	7	that to myself I do	"	88	11
To what you will; to you it doth				to thee I so belong	"	88	13
belong	"	58	11	To set a form	"	89	6
Yourself to pardon	"	58	12	my deeds to cross	"	90	2
I am to wait	"	58	13	To linger out a purposed	"	90	8
To this composed wonder	"	59	10	than high birth to me	"	91	9
To subjects worse have given	"	59	14	to steal thyself away	"	92	1
hasten to their end	"	60	2	Then need I not to fear	"	92	5
crawls to maturity	"	60	6	state to me belongs	"	92	7
for his scythe to mow	"	60	12	Happy to have thy love, happy to			
And yet to times	"	60	13	die	"	92	12
to the weary night	"	61	2	still seem love to me	"	93	3
shadows like to thee do mock	"	61	4	have power to hurt	"	94	1
into my deeds to pry	"	61	6	to temptation slow	"	94	4
To find out shames	"	61	7	is to the summer sweet	"	94	9
To play the watchman	"	61	12	Though to itself	"	94	10
to age's steepy night	"	63	5	turn to fair that eyes can see	"	95	12
slave to mortal rage	"	64	4	graces that to thee resort	"	96	4
confounded to decay	"	64	10	To truths translated	"	96	8

To—issue seem'd to me	Son	97	9	To—grow to faults assured	Son	118	10
And to his robbery	"	99	11	And brought to medicine	"	118	11
eat him up to death	"	99	13	Applying fears to hopes and hopes			
To speak of that	"	100	2	to fears	"	119	3
power to lend base subjects	"	100	4	I saw myself to win	"	119	4
Sing to the ear	"	100	7	rebuked to my content	"	119	13
be a satire to decay	"	100	11	To weigh how once	"	120	8
beauty's truth to lay	"	101	7	And soon to you	"	120	11
To make him much	"	101	11	'Tis better to be vile	"	121	1
And to be praised of ages yet to be	"	101	12	When not to be receives	"	121	2
To make him seem long	"	101	14	to my sportive blood	"	121	6
I was wont to greet it	"	102	6	even to eternity	"	122	4
a scope to show her pride	"	103	2	by nature to subsist	"	122	6
striving to mend	"	103	9	Till each to razed oblivion	"	122	7
To mar the subject	"	103	10	thy dear love to score	"	122	10
For to no other pass	"	103	11	Therefore to give them	"	122	11
and your gifts to tell	"	103	12	To trust those tables	"	122	12
To me, fair friend, you never can	"	104	1	To keep an adjunct to remember			
to yellow autumn turn'd	"	104	5	thee	"	122	13
To one, of one, still such	"	105	4	Were to import forgetfulness	"	122	14
to constancy confined	"	105	7	To me are nothing novel	"	123	3
varying to other words	"	105	10	born to our desire	"	123	7
your worth to sing	"	106	12	to Time's love or to Time's hate	"	124	3
Have eyes to wonder, but lack				To this I witness call	"	124	13
tongues to praise	"	106	14	Were't aught to me	"	125	1
dreaming on things to come	"	107	2	keeps thee to this purpose	"	126	7
forfeit to a confined doom	"	107	4	is to render thee	"	126	12
and Death to me subscribes	"	107	10	To kiss the tender inward	"	128	6
to thee my true spirit	"	108	2	To be so tickled	"	128	9
What's new to speak, what new				me thy lips to kiss	"	128	14
to register	"	108	3	rude, cruel, not to trust	"	129	4
Nor gives to necessary wrinkles	"	108	11	to make the taker mad	"	129	8
seem'd my flame to quality	"	109	2	in quest to have, extreme	"	129	10
Just to the time	"	109	7	To shun the heaven that leads men			
To leave for nothing	"	109	12	to this hell	"	129	14
a motley to the view	"	110	2	I love to hear her speak	"	130	9
to try an older friend	"	110	11	to my dear doting heart	"	131	3
to whom I am confined	"	110	12	to make love groan	"	131	6
Even to thy pure and most	"	110	14	To say they err	"	131	7
To what it works in	"	111	7	swear it to myself alone	"	131	8
to correct correction	"	111	12	And to be sure	"	131	9
is enough to cure me	"	111	14	to the sober west	"	132	8
To know my shames	"	112	6	To mourn for me	"	132	11
None else to me, nor I to none alive	"	112	7	my heart to groan	"	133	1
To critic and to flatterer stopped				to torture me alone	"	133	3
are	"	112	11	But slave to slavery	"	133	4
which governs me to go about	"	113	2	thus to be crossed	"	133	8
delivers to the heart	"	113	5	mortgaged to thy will	"	134	2
it shapes them to your feature	"	113	12	to be my comfort still	"	134	4
To make of monsters	"	114	5	surety-like to write for me	"	134	7
to his beams assemble	"	114	8	that put'st forth all to use	"	134	10
And to his palate	"	114	12	And 'Will' to boot	"	135	2
Divert strong minds to the course	"	115	8	To thy sweet will	"	135	4
To give full growth to that which				to hide my will	"	135	6
still doth grow	"	115	14	addeth to his store	"	135	10
Let me not to the marriage	"	116	1	add to thy 'Will	"	135	11
the remover to remove	"	116	4	Swear to thy blind soul	"	136	2
to every wandering bark	"	116	7	something sweet to thee	"	136	12
even to the edge of doom	"	116	12	dost thou to mine eyes	"	137	1
dearest love to call	"	117	3	take the worst to be	"	137	4
And given to time	"	117	6	To put fair truth	"	137	12
to all the winds	"	117	7	And to this false plague	"	137	14
I did strive to prove	"	117	13	not to have years told	"	138	12
to make our appetites	"	118	1	call not me to justify	"	139	1
to prevent our maladies	"	118	3	forbear to glance thine eye	"	139	6
sicken to shun sickness	"	118	4	Though not to love, yet, love, to			
To bitter sauces did I frame	"	118	6	tell me so	"	140	6
To be diseased	"	118	8	is pleased to dote	"	141	4
in love, to anticipate	"	118	9	to base touches prone	"	141	6

Entry	Source	Page	Line
To—desire to be invited	Son	141	7
To any sensual feast	"	141	8
and vassal wretch to be	"	141	12
deserve to pitied be	"	142	12
thou dost seek to have	"	142	13
housewife runs to catch	"	143	1
Cries to catch her	"	143	6
To follow that which flies	"	143	7
turn back to me	"	143	11
To win me soon to hell	"	144	5
my saint to be a devil	"	144	7
both to each friend	"	144	11
To me that languish'd	"	145	3
taught it thus anew to greet	"	145	8
From heaven to hell	"	145	12
to aggravate thy store	"	146	10
appetite to please	"	147	4
the physician to my love	"	147	5
to say it is not so	"	148	6
thy service to despise	"	149	10
my heart to sway	"	150	2
To make me give the lie to my true sight	"	150	8
thee how to make me love	"	150	9
to be beloved of thee	"	150	14
to know what conscience is	"	151	1
to my gross body's treason	"	151	6
thy poor drudge to be	"	151	11
To stand in thy affairs	"	151	12
to me love swearing	"	152	2
but to misuse thee	"	152	7
And, to enlighten thee, gave eyes to blindness	"	152	11
To swear against the truth	"	152	14
still to endure	"	153	6
vow'd chaste life to keep	"	154	3
My spirits to attend	L C	.....	3
to list the sad-tuned tale	"	.....	4
her napkin to her eyne	"	.....	15
to the spheres intend	"	.....	23
To the orbed earth	"	.....	25
To every place at once	"	.....	27
And, true to bondage	"	.....	34
applying wet to wet	"	.....	40
seal'd to curious secrecy	"	.....	49
often 'gan to tear	"	.....	51
desires to know	"	.....	62
his hearing to divide	"	.....	67
Fresh to myself	"	.....	75
Love to myself, and to no love beside	"	.....	77
it was to gain my grace	"	.....	79
sweet to do, to do will aptly find	"	.....	88
began but to appear	"	.....	93
web it seem'd to wear	"	.....	95
May and April is to see	"	.....	102
To appertainings and to ornament	"	.....	115
To make the weeper laugh	"	.....	124
To dwell with him in thoughts, or to remain	"	.....	129
To serve their eyes	"	.....	135
pleasures to bestow them	"	.....	139
To put the by-past perils	"	.....	158
to make our wits more keen	"	.....	161
satisfaction to our blood	"	.....	162
To be forbod the sweets	"	.....	164
ever brokers to defiling	"	.....	173
That's to ye sworn to none was	"	.....	180
put to the smallest teen	"	.....	192
To—Harm have I done to them	L C	.....	194
That is, to you	"	.....	222
to your own command	"	.....	227
and to your audit comes	"	.....	230
To spend her living	"	.....	238
what labour is't to leave	"	.....	239
so to herself contrives	"	.....	243
brought 'me to her eye	"	.....	247
Not to be tempted	"	.....	251
And now, to tempt all	"	.....	252
that to me belong	"	.....	254
to physic your cold breast	"	.....	259
to charm a sacred nun	"	.....	260
when they to assail begun	"	.....	262
sighs to you extend	"	.....	270
To leave the battery	"	.....	277
to my sweet design	"	.....	278
to that strong bonded oath	"	.....	279
to the stream gave grace	"	.....	285
to water will not wear	"	.....	291
Appear to him, as he to me	"	.....	299
Applied to cautels	"	.....	303
To blush at speeches rank, to weep at woes	"	.....	307
Or to turn white	"	.....	308
love not to have years told	P P	1	12
To win me soon to hell	"	2	5
my saint to be a devil	"	2	7
both to me, both to each friend	"	2	11
to this false perjury	"	3	3
To break an oath, to win a paradise	"	3	14
stories to delight his ear	"	4	5
favours to allure	"	4	6
To win his heart	"	4	7
to take her figured proffer	"	4	10
how shall I swear to love	"	5	1
if not to beauty vowed	"	5	2
Though to myself forsworn, to thee I'll constant prove	"	5	3
to me like oaks, to thee like osiers bowed	"	5	4
to know thee shall suffice	"	5	7
Which is to me some praise	"	5	10
Which, not to anger bent	"	5	12
To sing heaven's praise	"	5	14
to the hedge for shade	"	6	2
used to cool his spleen	"	6	6
damask dye to grace her	"	7	5
none fairer to deface her	"	7	6
Her lips to mine	"	7	7
many tales to please	"	7	9
Dowland to thee is dear	"	8	5
Spenser to me	"	8	7
Thou lovest to hear	"	8	9
to singing he betakes	"	8	12
didst bequeath to me	"	10	12
began to woo him	"	11	2
And as he fell to her, so fell she to him	"	11	4
To kiss and clip me	"	11	14
when first it 'gins to bud	"	13	3
And daff'd me to a cabin	"	14	3
To descant on the doubts	"	14	4
she joy'd to jest	"	14	9
again to make me wander	"	14	10
throw gazes to the east	"	15	1
Sorrow changed to solace	"	15	11
added to the hours	"	15	14
To spite me now	"	15	15

Phrase	Work	Col1	Col2
To—To leave the master loveless	P P	16	6
To put in practice either	"	16	7
to turn them both to gain	"	16	10
sick to death	"	17	7
Ne'er to pluck thee	"	17	12
so apt to pluck a sweet	"	17	14
that wont to have play'd	"	18	29
Procure to weep	"	18	32
to see my doleful plight	"	18	33
known to us poor swains	"	18	45
thy tale to tell	"	19	7
thy person forth to sell	"	19	12
to try her strength	"	19	19
taught her thus to say	"	19	22
And to her will frame	"	19	25
Spare not to spend	"	19	26
thou to choose anew	"	19	34
To proffer though she put	"	19	36
still to strive with men	"	19	43
To sin and never for to saint	"	19	44
stick to round me on th' ear	"	19	51
To teach my tongue to be so long	"	19	52
To hear her secrets	"	19	54
To live with thee	"	20	20
That to hear it was great pity	"	21	12
That to hear her so	"	21	15
are hard to find	"	21	34
wherewith to spend	"	21	36
be addict to vice	"	21	43
to women he be bent	"	21	45
certain signs to know	"	21	57
To whose sound chaste wings obey	P T	....	4
To this troop come thou not near	"	....	8
To themselves yet either neither	"	....	43
To the phœnix and the dove	"	....	50
chorus to their tragic scene	"	....	52
To eternity doth rest	"	....	58
To this urn let those repair	"	....	65
Toad—Or toads infect fair founts	R L	....	856
To-day—Which but to-day	Son	56	3
although to-day thou fill	"	56	5
Kind is my love to-day	"	105	5
Together—such lamps .... mix'd	V A	....	489
Their lips together glued	"	....	546
mingled both together	"	....	902
join they all together	"	....	971
and all together lost	R L	....	147
All which together	"	....	589
shall together thrive	Son	14	11
age and youth cannot live together	P P	12	1
Saw division grow together	P T	....	42
Toil—Weary with toil, I haste me	Son	27	1
The one by toil, the other	"	28	7
How far I toil, still farther	"	28	8
In sequent toil all forward	"	60	4
Toil'd—forgot for which he toil'd	"	25	12
Token—some watery token shows	R L	....	1748
Told—as if he told the steps	V A	....	277
told and quickly gone	"	....	520
woeful words she told	"	....	1126
if it should be told	R L	....	1284
more than hear them told	"	....	1324
manners most expressly told	"	....	1397
This told, I joy	Son	45	13
still telling what is told	"	76	14
we before have heard them told	"	123	8
loves not to have years told	"	138	12
loves not to have years told	P P	1	12
Told—She told him stories	P P	4	5
She told the youngling	"	11	3
Told'st—that thou told'st me	V A	....	611
Tomb—in a tomb so simple	"	....	244
statues, tombs, and stories	"	....	1013
so fond will be the tomb	Son	3	7
it is but as a tomb	"	17	3
give life and bring a tomb	"	83	12
Making their tomb the womb	"	86	4
outlive a gilded tomb	"	101	11
and tombs of brass are spent	"	107	14
Tomb'd—must be tomb'd with thee	"	4	13
To-morrow—shall we meet	V A	....	585
to-morrow he intends	"	....	587
with the boar to-morrow	"	....	672
To-morrow sharpen'd in his former might	Son	56	4
To-morrow see again	"	56	7
to-day, to-morrow kind	"	105	5
and come again to-morrow	P P	14	5
and bade me come to-morrow	"	15	12
and length thyself to-morrow	"	15	18
Tongue—chokes her pleading	V A	....	217
aidance of the tongue	"	....	330
'hast thou a tongue	"	....	427
twenty thousand tongues	"	....	775
every tongue more moving	"	....	776
the boar provoked my tongue	"	....	1003
Grief hath two tongues	"	....	1007
my tongue cannot express	"	....	1069
Whose tongue is music now	"	....	1077
her husband's shallow tongue	R L	....	78
To slanderous tongues	"	....	161
Will not my tongue be mute	"	....	227
doth his tongue begin	"	....	470
Thy sugar'd tongue	"	....	893
My tongue shall utter all	"	....	1076
With untuned tongue	"	....	1214
With soft-slow tongue	"	....	1220
so much grief and not a tongue	"	....	1463
with my lamenting tongue	"	....	1465
And from her tongue 'can lurk	"	....	1537
with one poor tired tongue	"	....	1617
forbade my tongue to speak	"	....	1648
her poor tongue could not speak	"	....	1718
dumb arrest upon his tongue	"	....	1780
of less truth than tongue	Son	17	10
More than that tongue	"	23	12
All tongues, the voice of souls	"	69	3
But those same tongues	"	69	6
And tongues to be	"	81	11
and in my tongue	"	89	9
That tongue that tells the story	"	95	5
The owner's tongue doth publish	"	102	4
I sometime hold my tongue	"	102	13
but lack tongues to praise	"	106	14
and praises from your tongue	"	112	6
That every tongue says beauty	"	127	14
her false-speaking tongue	"	138	7
but with thy tongue	"	139	3
with thy tongue's tune	"	141	5
Chiding that tongue	"	145	6
tip of his subduing tongue	L C	....	120
credit her false-speaking tongue	P P	1	7
is a soothing tongue	"	1	11
Well learned is that tongue	"	5	8
with such an earthly tongue	"	5	14
Smooth not thy tongue	"	19	8
To teach my tongue	"	19	52

Tongue—in every shepherd's	P P	20	18	Tool—But this no slaughterhouse no tool imparteth	R L	1039
Tongued—Like shrill-tongued tapsters	V A		849	Tooth'd—Had I been tooth'd	V A	1117
With close-tongued treason	R L		770	Top—That cedar-tops and hills seem	"	858
For maiden-tongued he was	L C		100	and the top o'erstraw'd	"	1143
Tongue-tied—made tongue-tied by authority	Son	66	9	on the top of happy hours	Son	16	5
To make me tongue-tied	"	80	4	Flatter the mountain-tops	"	33	2
My tongue-tied Muse	"	85	1	This said, in top of rage	L C	55
My tongue-tied patience	"	140	2	Torch—Torches are made to light	V A	163
To-night—Short, night, to-night	P P	13	18	Whereat a waxen torch	R L	178
Too—If they burn too, I'll	V A		192	'Fair torch, burn out thy light	"	190
with too much handling	"		569	The wind wars with his torch	"	311
the orator too green	"		806	wind that fires the torch	"	315
and yet too credulous	"		986	Are by his flaming torch	"	448
and too full of riot	"		1147	Tore—as if the name he tore	"	1787
merciful and too severe	"		1155	sigh'd, tore, and gave the flood	L C	44
His all-too-timeless speed	R L		44	Torment—torments us with defect	R L	151
sometime too much wonder	"		95	But torment that it cannot	"	861
Both too too oft betake him	"		174	what a torment wouldst thou prove	Son	39	9
handmaids too, by him defiled	"		787	torments me with disdain	"	132	2
Their father was too weak, and they too strong	"		865	A torment thrice threefold	"	133	8
With too much labour	"		1099	Tormenteth—want of love	V A	202
and too much talk affords	"		1106	Torn—my image thou hast torn	R L	1702
This is too curious-good	"		1300	and new faith torn	Son	152	3
too long with her remaining	"		1572	Torture—And that deep torture	R L	1287
would be drawn out too long	"		1616	shake hands to torture me	Son	28	6
My woe too sensible	"		1678	to torture me alone	"	133	3
Comes all too late	"		1686	Toss'd—Is madly toss'd	R L	171
she too early and too late hath spill'd	"		1801	Touch—'Touch but my lips	V A	115
				To touch the fire	"	402
to thy sweet self too cruel	Son	1	8	not see, nor hear, nor touch	"	440
for thou art much too fair	"	6	13	but to touch the crown	R L	216
hath all too short a date	"	18	4	that touches me more nearly	Son	42	4
Sometime too hot	"	18	5	needs would touch my breast	"	153	10
replete with too much rage	"	23	3	would not touch the bait	P P	4	11
sweet argument too excellent	"	38	3	Touch—ten hundred touches	V A	519
with others all too near	"	61	14	Instead of love's coy touch	R L	669
Too base of thee	"	74	12	Such heavenly touches	Son	17	8
doth come too short	"	83	7	What strained touches	"	82	10
of all too precious you	"	86	2	to have touches prone	"	141	6
Farewell, thou art too dear	"	87	1	Touches so soft	P P	4	8
be a gainer too	"	88	9	whose heavenly touch	"	8	5
Lest I too much profane	"	89	11	Touch'd—touch'd no unknown bait	R L	103
thou hast too grossly dyed	"	90	5	ne'er touch'd earthly faces	Son	17	8
So dost thou too	"	101	4	that never touch'd his hand	L C	141
by paying too much rent	"	125	6	she touch'd him here and there	P P	4	7
with too much disdain	"	140	2	Touching—by touching thee	V A	438
Love is too young	"	151	1	Toward—where it shows most toward	"	1157
too early I attended	L C		78	No love toward others	Son	9	13
Ah, fool too froward	P P	4	14	Then fell she on her back, fair queen, and toward	P P	4	13
alack! too timely shaded	"	10	3	Towards—Towards thee I'll run	Son	51	14
Fair creature, kill'd too soon	"	10	4	make towards the pebbled shore	"	60	1
methinks thou stay'st too long	"	12	12	Towards this afflicted fancy	L C	61
the night would post too soon	"	13	13	Tower—glittering golden towers	R L	945
Neither too young	"	19	6	And from the towers of Troy	"	1382
And then too late	"	19	15	lofty towers I see down-razed	Son	64	3
But, soft! enough,—too much	"	19	49	The strongest castle, tower, and town	P P	19	29
Took—birds such pleasure took	V A		1101	Towering—towering in the skies	R L	506
She took me kindly by the hand	R L		253	Town—The strongest castle, tower, and town	P P	19	29
the roses took away	"		259	Toy—appetite, unapt to toy	V A	34
'can lurk' from 'cannot' took	"		1537	To toy, to wanton	"	106
I took all patiently	"		1611	Or sells eternity to get a toy	R L	214
and heart a league is took	Son	47	1	The tricks and toys	P P	19	39
when I took my way	"	48	1	Tract—From his low tract	Son	7	12
or must from you be took	"	75	12	Traffic—doth traffic oft for gaining	R L	131
votary took up that fire	"	154	5	For having traffic with thyself	Son	4	9
took heat perpetual	"	154	10			

Tragedy—Black stage for tragedies	*R L*	766	**Tree**—Trees did grow	*P P*	21	6
Tragic—and swound at tragic shows	*t. C*	308	Senseless trees they cannot hear thee	"	21	21
As chorus to their tragic scene	*P T*	52	On the sole Arabian tree	*P T*		2
Traitor—his traitor eye encloses	*R L*	73	**Tremble**—she trembles at his tale	*V A*		591
ere traitors be espied	"	361	my joints did tremble	"		642
executest the traitor's treason	"	877	tremble at the imagination	"		668
thou traitor, thou false thief	"	888	tremble with her loyal fear	*R L*		261
yet let the traitor die	"	1686	he saw them quake and tremble	"		1393
Trampling—Adonis'.... courser	*V A*	261	**Trembling**—trembling in her passion	*V A*		27
Trance—with restless trances	*R L*	974	In a trembling ecstasy	"		895
old acquaintance in a trance	"	1595	with trembling terror die	*R L*		231
Transferred—are they now....	*Son*	137	11	she trembling lies	"		457
Transfix—Time doth.... the flourish	"	60	9	With trembling fear	"		511
Transgressed—that hath.... so	*R L*	1481	To trembling clients	"		1020
Transgression—Their own transgressions	"	634	marching on with trembling paces	"		1391
under my transgression bow	*Son*	120	3	thou dost trembling stand	"		1599
Translate—he could his looks,...	"	96	10	**Trench**—And dig deep trenches	*Son*	2	2
Translated—To truths translated	"	96	8	**Trench'd**—that the boar had....	*V A*		1052
Transport—Which should.... me	"	117	8	**Trespass**—Shalt have thy trespass	*R L*		524
Trapping—or trapping gay	*V A*	286	To view thy present trespass	"		632
Travail—As if with grief or travail	*R L*	1543	Will quote my loathsome trespass	"		812
Deserves the travail	*Son*	79	6	And with my trespass	"		1070
Travel—for limbs with travel tired	"	27	2	for trespass of thine eye	"		1476
And make me travel forth	"	34	2	shall fit the trespass best	"		1613
my weary travel's end	"	50	2	Authorizing thy trespass	*Son*	35	6
Like him that travels	"	109	6	But that your trespass	"	120	13
Travell'd—Hath travell'd on	"	63	5	**Tress**—Before the golden tresses	"	68	5
Tread—She treads the path	*V A*	908	**Trial**—accidental things of trial	*R L*		326
she treads on it so light	"	1028	The boy for trial	*Son*	153	10
to tread the measures	"	1148	**Tribe**—insults o'er dull and speechless tribes	"	107	12
That cannot tread the way	*R L*	1152				
treads on the ground	*Son*	130	12	**Tributary**—pay tributary gazes	*V A*		632
The cock that treads them	*P P*	19	40	tributary subject quakes	"		1045
Treason—condemn'd of treason	*V A*	729	**Tribute**—Paying more slavish....	*R L*		299
Thus treason works	*R L*	361	Look here, what tributes	*L C*		197
By their high treason	"	369	**Trick**—taught them scornful tricks	*V A*		501
With close-tongued treason	"	770	'This glove to wanton tricks	*R L*		320
executest the traitor's treason	"	877	The tricks and toys	*P P*	19	39
Wrath, envy, treason, rape	"	909	**Tried**—Thus my strength is tried	*V A*		280
Guilty of treason	"	920	till their effects be tried	*R L*		353
to my gross body's treason	*Son*	151	6	**Trifle**—Trifles unwitnessed	*V A*		1023
Treasure—his lips' rich treasure	*V A*	552	Each trifle under truest bars	*Son*	48	2
the hidden treasure frets	"	767	to whom my jewels trifles are	"	48	5
As one with treasure laden	"	1022	**Trim**—colours fresh and trim	*V A*		1079
what treasure hast thou lost	"	1075	dress'd in all his trim	*Son*	98	2
enrich the poor with treasures	"	1150	yet their purposed trim	*L C*		118
Unlock'd the treasure	*R L*	16	**Trimm'd**—nothing.... in jollity	*Son*	66	3
And when great treasure	"	132	**Trip**—trip upon the green	*V A*		146
sinking where such treasure lies	"	280	thy footing trips	"		722
his treasure to behold	"	857	**Tripping**—Came tripping by	*Son*	154	4
the treasure stol'n away	"	1056	**Triumph**—his triumphs and his glories	*V A*		1014
Where all the treasure	*Son*	2	6				
With beauty's treasure	"	6	4	Showing life's triumph	*R L*		402
thy love's use Showing their treasure	"	20	14	fortune of such triumph	*Son*	25	3
to his sweet uplocked treasure	"	52	2	*Triumph*—Rather than triumph	*R L*		77
the treasure of his spring	"	63	8	Being had, to triumph	*Son*	52	14
will steal his treasure	"	75	6	Triumph in love	"	151	8
but not still keep her treasure	"	126	10	would I might triumph so	*P P*	17	10
fulfil the treasure of thy love	"	136	5	**Triumphant**—With all-triumphant splendour	*Son*	33	10
Treasure—treasure thou some place	"	6	3				
Treatise—Your treatise makes me	*V A*	774	As his triumphant prize	"	151	10
Treble—heart hath treble wrong	"	329	**Triumph'd**—Which triumph'd in that sky	*R L*		12
Treble-dated—And thou.... crow	*P T*	17				
Tree—like sturdy trees	*V A*	182	**Triumphing**—.... in their faces	"		1388
tied unto a tree	"	263	**Trodden**—trodden on by many	*V A*		707
tied to the tree	"	391	**Troilus**—here Troilus swounds	*R L*		1486
When lofty trees I see	*Son*	12	5	**Trojan**—Stood many Trojan mothers	"		1431
that hangs upon a tree	*P P*	10	5				

Trojan—be falls, a Trojan bleeds	R L	1551	True—of my true love control	Son	107	8
Troop—muster troops of cares	"	720	figured to thee my true spirit	"	108	2
To this troop come thou not near	P T	8	Alas, 'tis true	"	110	1
Trophy—Tells him of trophies	V A	1013	Most true it is that I	"	110	5
Hung with the trophies	Son	31 10	My most true mind	"	113	14
' " Lo, all these trophies of affec-			mine eye saith true	"	114	3
tions hot	L C	218	to the marriage of true minds	"	116	1
Trot—Sometime he trots	V A	277	ere that there was true needing	"	118	8
Troth—human law and common			and find the lesson true	"	118	13
troth	R L	571	now I find true	"	119	9
taste of violated troth	"	1059	how hard true sorrow hits	"	120	10
and undertake my troth	L C	280	I will be true	"	123	14
Trouble—such a trouble	V A	522	thou suborn'd informer! a true soul	"	125	13
to overshoot his troubles	"	680	In things right true	"	137	13
And trouble deaf heaven	Son	29 3	no correspondence with true sight	"	148	2
Troubled—as seeming troubled	V A	830	Love's eye is not so true	"	148	8
of her troubled brain	"	1040	O, how can Love's eye be true	"	148	9
the brain being troubled	"	1068	give the lie to my true sight	"	150	3
troubled minds that wake	R L	126	many legions of true hearts	"	154	6
like a troubled ocean	"	589	And, true to bondage	L C	34
I may convey this troubled soul	"	1176	Than the true gouty landlord	"	140
Troy—made for Priam's Troy	"	1367	party is nor true nor kind	"	186
And from the towers of Troy	"	1382	in that my boast is true	"	246
walls of strong-besieged Troy	"	1429	but neither true nor trusty	P P	7	2
quench Troy that burns so long	"	1468	her oaths of true love swearing	"	7	8
that burning Troy doth bear	"	1474	And in my suit be humble true	"	19	32
And here in Troy	"	1476	How true a twain	P T	45
Troy had been bright with fame	"	1491	That are either true or fair	"	66
weeps Troy's painted woes	"	1492	True-love—Who sees his true-love	V A	397
Onward to Troy	"	1504	Truest—the truest sight beguile	"	1144
so my Troy did perish	"	1547	under truest bars to thrust	Son	48	2
to burn his Troy with water	"	1561	True-sweet—But true-sweet beauty	V A	1080
Truant—O .... Muse, what shall be	Son	101 1	True-telling—by thy .... friend	Son	82	12
Truce—Till he take truce	V A	82	Truly—by oath they truly honoured	R L	410
True—true leaders to their queen	"	503	true in love, but truly right	Son	21	9
That sometime true news	"	658	thy glass will truly show	"	77	5
makes true men thieves	"	724	truly fair wert truly sympathized	"	82	11
True valour still a true respect	R L	201	And truly not the morning sun	"	132	5
makes supposed terror true	"	455	Trumpet—First like a trumpet	R L	470
the picture of true piety	"	542	Herald sad and trumpet be	P T	3
His true respect will prison	"	542	Trust—if there be no self-trust	R L	158
And my true eyes have never	"	748	So Priam's trust false Sinon's tears	"	1560
Of that true type	"	1050	So I, for fear of trust	Son	23	5
thy true affection so	"	1060	in sure wards of trust	"	48	4
True grief is fond and testy	"	1094	best habit is in seeming trust	"	138	11
True sorrow then is feelingly	"	1112	Serve always with assured trust	P P	19	31
heart-strings to true languishment	"	1141	Trust—To trust those tables	Son	122	12
true mark of modesty	"	1220	rude, cruel, not to trust	"	129	4
her grief's true quality	"	1313	Not daring trust the office	P P	15	4
creatures have a true respect	"	1347	Trustless—borne by the .... wings	R L	2
the death of this true wife	"	1841	Trusty—but neither true nor trusty	P P	7	2
If the true concord	Son	8 5	For of the two the trusty knight	"	16	11
And your true rights	"	17 11	Truth—Love is all truth	V A	804
O, let me, true in love	"	21 9	truth I must confess	"	1001
your true image pictured lies	"	24 6	Then where is truth	R L	158
that thou mayst true love call	"	40 3	When Truth and Virtue	"	911
So true a fool is love	"	57 13	and bring truth to light	"	940
Mine own true love	"	61 11	To hide the truth	"	1075
No shape so true	"	62 6	Such signs of truth	"	1532
since his truth is true	"	67 8	As truth and beauty	Son	14	11
itself and true	"	68 10	Thy end is truth's	"	14	14
O, lest your true love	"	72 9	of less truth than tongue	"	17	10
In true plain words	"	82 12	of thy worth and truth	"	37	4
"Tis so, 'tis true	"	85 9	to break a twofold truth	"	41	12
supposing thou art true	"	93 1	For truth proves thievish	"	48	14
and for true things deem'd	"	96 8	which truth doth give	"	54	2
Fair, kind, and true	"	105 9	by verse distills your truth	"	54	14
Fair, kind, and true	"	105 10	rarities of nature's truth	"	60	11
Fair, kind, and true	"	105 13	no truth of such account	"	62	6

Truth—simple truth miscall'd simplicity	Son	66	11	
Uttering bare truth	"	69	4	
Than niggard truth	"	72	8	
To truths translated	"	96	8	
For thy neglect of truth	"	101	2	
Both truth and beauty	"	101	3	
'Truth needs no colour	"	101	6	
beauty's truth to lay	"	101	7	
that I have look'd on truth	"	110	5	
To put fair truth	"	137	12	
that she is made of truth	"	138	1	
thus is simple truth supprest	"	138	8	
from the truth vainly express'd	"	147	12	
thy truth, thy constancy	"	152	10	
To swear against the truth	"	152	14	
in a pride of truth	L C	...	105	
that she is made of truth	P P	1	1	
The truth I shall not know	"	2	13	
truth in every shepherd's tongue	"	20	18	
Beauty, truth, and rarity	P T	...	53	
Truth may seem, but cannot be	"	...	62	
Truth and beauty buried be	"	...	64	
Try—tries a merciless conclusion	R L	...	1160	
to try an older friend	Son	110	11	
how god Mars did try her	P P	11	3	
though she strive to try her strength	"	19	19	
Tumbled — from her be-tumbled couch	R L	...	1037	
Tumult—this tumult to behold	"	...	447	
Tune—heavenly tune harsh-sounding	V A	...	431	
the tempting tune is blown	"	...	778	
quoth she, 'your tunes entomb	R L	...	1124	
To creatures stern sad tunes	"	...	1147	
with thy tongue's tune delighted	Son	141	5	
Tune—she tunes her tale	V A	...	74	
that tune their memory's joy	R L	...	1107	
Shall tune our heart-strings	"	...	1141	
I'll tune thy woes	"	...	1465	
Tuned—The well-tuned warble of well-tuned sounds	Son	8	5	
to list the sad-tuned tale	L C	...	1	
were tuned like the lark	P P	15	6	
Tuning—minstrels, ... my defame	R L	...	817	
Turn—than she for this good turn	V A	...	92	
Turn, and return	"	...	704	
Now see what good turns	Son	24	9	
doth good turns now unto the other	"	47	2	
Turn—He winks, and turns his lips	V A	...	90	
Now which way shall she turn	"	...	253	
began to turn their tide	"	...	979	
Turns not, but swells	R L	...	616	
turn to loathed sours	"	...	867	
Thy honey turns to gall	"	...	889	
pleasure turns to open shame	"	...	890	
And turn the giddy round	"	...	952	
with a joyless smile she turns away	"	...	1711	
turn sourest by their deeds	Son	94	13	
And all things turn to fair	"	95	12	
from my face she turns my foes	"	139	11	
turn back to me	"	143	11	
If thou turn back	"	143	14	
Or to turn white and swound	L C	...	308	
to turn them both to gain	P P	16	10	
Turn'd—now is Iurn'd to day	V A	...	481	
mine eyes are turn'd	"	...	1072	
And turn'd it thus	R L	...	1539	
to yellow autumn turn'd	Son	104	5	

Turn'd—my angel be turn'd fiend	Son	144	9	
my angel be turn'd fiend	P P	2	9	
Turning—and quick in turning	V A	...	140	
and yet she fell a-turning	P P	7	16	
Her fancy fell a-turning	"	16	4	
Turning mortal for thy love	"	17	18	
Turret—left their round turrets	R L	...	441	
to kiss the turrets bow'd	"	...	1372	
Turtle—Phoenix and the turtle fled	P T	...	23	
'Twixt the turtle and his queen	"	...	31	
That the turtle saw his right	"	...	34	
And the turtle's loyal breast	"	...	57	
Tushes—tushes never sheathed	V A	...	617	
his crooked tushes slay	"	...	624	
Tusk—the tusk in his soft groin	"	...	1116	
Tutor—Thy eyes' shrewd tutor	"	...	500	
O Time, thou tutor	R L	...	995	
Twain—there are but twain	V A	...	123	
if thou wilt have twain	"	...	210	
His face seems twain	"	...	1067	
As if between them twain	R L	...	405	
which of the twain were better	"	...	1154	
that we two must be twain	Son	36	1	
how to make one twain	"	39	13	
and I love both twain	"	42	11	
breaking rings a-twain	L C	...	6	
So they loved, as love in twain	P T	...	25	
How true a twain	"	...	45	
'Twas—why, 'twas beautiful and hard	L C	...	211	
'Twas not their infirmity	P T	...	60	
'Tween—crusheth 'tween his teeth	V A	...	269	
'Tween frozen conscience	R L	...	247	
Twenty—one long as twenty	V A	...	22	
Is twenty hundred kisses	"	...	522	
under twenty locks	"	...	575	
twenty thousand tongues	"	...	775	
and twenty times, 'Woe, woe	"	...	833	
twenty echoes twenty times	"	...	834	
when I break twenty	Son	152	6	
'Twere—As 'twere encouraging	R L	...	1402	
Twice—That twice she doth begin	"	...	567	
You should live twice	Son	17	14	
But thou art twice forsworn	"	152	2	
And twice desire	P P	19	17	
Twilight—the twilight of such day	Son	73	5	
Twine—twine about her thigh	V A	...	873	
Twining—from her twining arms	"	...	256	
Twinkling—Her....handmaids too	R L	...	787	
Twire—When sparkling stars twire not	Son	28	12	
Twisted—With twisted metal	L C	...	205	
'Twixt—'Twixt crimson shame	V A	...	76	
'twixt the son and sire	"	...	1160	
As 'twixt a miser	Son	75	4	
creep in 'twixt vows	"	115	6	
As oft 'twixt May and April	L C	...	102	
be great 'twixt thee and me	P P	8	3	
'Twixt the turtle and his queen	P T	...	31	
Two—Two strengthless doves	V A	...	153	
Show'd like two silver doves	"	...	366	
Her two blue windows	"	...	482	
from her two cheeks fair	"	...	957	
Grief hath two tongues	"	...	1007	
behold two Adons dead	"	...	1070	
Lurk'd like two thieves	"	...	1086	
Where, lo, two lamps	"	...	1128	
Two glasses, where herself	"	...	1129	
To those two armies	R L	...	76	

Two—Who, having two sweet babes	R L	1161	Under—Under whose sharp fangs	V A	663
Why her two suns	"	1224	fight brings beauty under	"	746
That two red fires	"	1353	Under whose simple semblance	"	793
In two slow rivers	"	1738	Under whose brim	"	1088
that we two must be twain	Son 36	1	her rosy cheek lies under	R L	386
In our two loves	" 36	5	Under what colour he commits	"	476
The other two, slight air	" 45	1	Under that colour I am come	"	481
made of four, with two alone	" 45	7	under his insulting falchion	"	509
where two contracted new	" 56	10	under the gripe's sharp claws	"	543
As those two mourning eyes	" 132	9	under Pyrrhus' proud foot lies	"	1449
Two loves I have	" 144	1	burning head, each under eye	Son 7	2
Which like two spirits	" 144	2	under truest bars to thrust	" 48	2
But why of two oaths' breach	" 152	5	under thee thy poesy disperse	" 78	4
Two loves I have	P P 2	1	under my transgression bow	" 120	3
That like two spirits	" 2	2	Under the blow of thralled	" 124	7
For of the two the trusty knight	" 16	11	Under that bond that him	" 134	8
Two distincts, division none	P T	27	Works under you	L C	230
Neither two nor one was called	"	40	Under an osier growing	P P 6	5
Twofold—to break a twofold truth	Son 41	12	Under a myrtle shade	" 11	2
Type—of that true type	R L	1050	Underneath—underneath thy black		
Tyrannize—then most doth tyrannize	"	676	all-hiding cloak	R L	801
Tyrannous—Thou art as tyrannous	Son 131	1	Underprop—should .... her fame	"	53
Tyranny—subject to the tyranny	V A	737	Understood—blushes, aptly	L C	200
fearing of Time's tyranny	Son 115	9	Undertake—prefer and .... my troth	"	280
Tyrant—the hot tyrant stains	V A	797	Undeserved—And .... reproach	R L	824
Hard-favour'd tyrant	"	931	Undistinguished—shrieking undis-		
Or tyrant fully lurk in gentle	R L	851	tinguished woe	L C	20
Will play the tyrants	Son 5	3	Undivided—our .... loves are one	Son 36	2
this bloody tyrant, Time	" 16	2	Undone—heart were quite undone	V A	783
When tyrants' crests	" 107	14	Unear'd—so fair whose .... womb	Son 3	5
And I, a tyrant	" 120	7	Unexperient—That the .... gave	L C	318
Am of myself all tyrant	" 149	4	Unfair—And that .... which fairly	Son 5	4
Every fowl of tyrant wing	P T	14	Unfather'd—Fortune's bastard be		
			unfather'd	" 124	2
Ugly—ugly, meagre, lean	V A	931	and unfather'd fruit	" 97	10
consort with ugly night	"	1041	Unfelt—O unfelt sore! crest-wound-		
ugly in her eyes	R L	459	ing	R L	827
copesmate of ugly Night	"	925	Unfinish'd—shapeless and	V A	415
To ugly hell; when, to	"	1082	Unfold—with weeping will unfold	R L	754
With ugly rack on his	Son 33	6	and there we will unfold	"	1146
Ulysses—In Ajax and Ulysses	R L	1394	Unfolding—By new unfolding	Son 52	12
glance that sly Ulysses lent	"	1399	Unfortunately—in her haste unfor-		
Unacted—is as a thought unacted	"	527	tunately spies	V A	1029
Unadvised—gives .... wounds	"	1488	Unfruitful—midst of his unfruit-		
Unapproved—What .... witness	L C	53	ful prayer	R L	344
Unapt—unapt to toy	V A	34	Ungrown—the .... fry forbears	V A	526
Unapt for tender smell	R L	695	Unhallow'd—die, ... thoughts	R L	192
Unask'd—thou unask'd shalt have	V A	102	of lewd unhallow'd eyes	"	392
Unaware—as one that unaware	"	823	So his unhallow'd haste	"	552
Sheathed unaware the tusk	"	1116	Unhappily—name of 'chaste' un-		
Unback'd—lo, the unback'd breeder	"	320	happily set	"	8
Unbent—A brow .... that seem'd	R L	1509	faith unhappily forsworn	Son 66	4
Unbless—unbless some mother	Son 3	4	Unhappy—to that unhappy guest	R L	1565
Unbred—hear this, thou age unbred	" 104	13	Unicorn—To tame the unicorn	"	956
Uncertain—The .... sickly appetite	" 117	4	Union—By unions married	Son 8	6
Uncertainly—sorrow writ	R L	1311	Unity—such unity do hold	R L	1558
Uncheerful—at Tarquin and un-			Universe—this wide universe I call	Son 109	13
cheerful Night	"	1024	Unjust—controls his thoughts	R L	189
Uncleanness—With your	"	193	as servitors to the unjust	"	285
Unconquered—maiden worlds	"	408	says she not she is unjust	Son 138	9
Unconstrained—sports in uncon-			Unless thy lady prove unjust	P P 19	33
strained gyves	L C	242	Unjustly—blood so unjustly stained	R L	1836
Uncontrolled—his .... crest	V A	104	Unkind—' young, and so unkind	V A	187
quoth he; 'my uncontrolled tide	R L	645	but died unkind	"	204
Uncouple—Uncouple at the timor-			strangeness, seems unkind	"	310
ous flying hare	V A	674	That you were once unkind	Son 120	1
Uncouth—What uncouth ill event	R L	1598	through my unkind abuse	" 134	12
Under—Under her other was	V A	32	Let no unkind	" 135	13
Under twenty locks	"	575	Unkindness—his .... marr'd	V A	478

Unkindness—by my .... shaken	Son	120	5	Unseen—Stealing unseen to west	Son 33 4
That thy unkindness lays	"	139	2	prevent our maladies unseen	" 118 3
Unknown—he should keep	R L		34	All unseen 'gan passage find	P P 17 6
She touch'd no unknown baits	"		103	Unset—maiden gardens, yet unset	Son 16 6
The fault unknown	"		527	Unsheathed—thence her soul	R L 1724
Whose worth's unknown	Son	116	8	Unshorn—Like unshorn velvet	L C 94
frequent been with unknown minds	"	117	5	Unskillful — Unskillful in the world's false forgeries	P P 1 4
Unlaced—the warlike god .... me	P P	11	7	Unsounded—Let my .... self	R L 1819
Unlearned—Unlearned in the world's false subtleties	Son	138	4	Unspotted—dear love be kept	" 821
Unless—Unless the earth with thy increase be fed	V A		170	Unstained—For unstain'd thoughts on her yet unstained bed	" .... 87 " 366
Unless it be a bear	"		410	a pure unstained prime	Son 70 8
Unless thou couldst return	R L		961	Unsway'd—Who leaves unsway'd	" 141 11
Unless thou yoke thy liking	"		1633	Unswept—Than unswept stone	" 55 4
unless I took all patiently	"		1641	Untainted—her mind .... clears	R L 1710
unless thou get a son	Son	7	14	And blood untainted	" 1749
Unless thou take that honour	"	36	12	untainted do allow	Son 19 11
unless this miracle have might	"	65	13	Unthrift—Look, what an unthrift	" 9 9
Unless you would devise	"	72	5	O, none but unthrifts	" 13 13
Unless my nerves were brass	"	120	4	Unthrifty — Unthrifty loveliness, why dost thou spend	" 4 1
Unless this general evil they maintain	"	121	13	Until—Until her husband's welfare	R L 263
Unless thy lady prove unjust	P P	19	33	Until life's composition	Son 45 9
Unletter'd—And, like .... clerk	Son	85	6	Untimely—But some .... thought	R L 43
Unlike—Unlike myself thou hear'st	V A		712	By her untimely tears	" 570
Unlikely—in thoughts unlikely	"		989	the cause of my untimely death	" 1178
Unlived—now Lucrece is unlived	R L		1754	And his untimely frenzy	" 1675
Unlock'd—Unlock'd the treasure	"		16	Untimely breathings, sick	" 1720
Unlook'd—Unlook'd on diest	Son	7	14	untimely pluck'd, soon vaded	P P 10 1
Unlook'd for joy	"	25	4	Unto—makes unain unto him	V A 5
Unlook'd-for—O unlook'd-for evil	R L		846	think it heavy unto thee	" 156
Unloose—.... it from their bond	"		136	being tied unto a tree	" 263
Unmask—To unmask falsehood	"		940	and neighs unto her	" 307
Unmask, dear dear, this	"		1602	unto the wood they hie	" 323
Unmatched—the clear unmatched red and white	"		11	woe unto the birds	" 455
				hundred touches unto thee	" 519
Unmeet—Vow, alack! for youth unmeet	P P	17	13	unto every stranger	" 790
				To grow unto himself	" 1180
Unmoved—Unmoved, cold, and to temptation slow	Son	94	4	brought unto his bed	R L 120
				Unto a view so false	" 292
Unnoted—Gnats are unnoted	R L		1014	unto the chamber door	" 337
Unpeopled—Bare and unpeopled	"		1741	Unto a greater uproar	" 427
Unperceived—And unperceived fly	"		1010	betray thee unto mine	" 483
Unperfect—As an unperfect actor	Son	23	1	Unto the base bed	" 671
Unpractised—Like an unpractised swimmer	R L		1098	I'll bequeath unto the knife	" 1184
				cheeks unto her maid seem so	" 1217
Unprofitable—.... sounds, weak	"		1017	unto the clouds bequeathed	" 1727
Unprovident—art so unprovident	Son	10	2	turns now unto the other	Son 47 2
Unrecalling—let his .... crime	R L		993	I have been call'd unto	L C 181
Unrest—hail it from the deep unrest	"		1725	I post unto my pretty	P P 15 9
with evermore unrest	Son	147	16	Unto the silly damsel	" 16 8
Unresisted—choked by .... lust	R L		282	Untold—To have their unseen sin remain untold	R L 753
Unrespected—they view things	Son	43	2	let me pass untold	Son 136 9
unwoo'd and unrespected fade	"	54	10	Untread—that she untreads again	V A 908
Unripe—Shews thee unripe	V A		128	Untrimm'd—changing course	Son 18 8
with my unripe years	"		524	Untrue—speak well of me untrue	" 72 10
But whether unripe years	P P	4	9	thus maketh mine untrue	" 113 14
Unruly—boisterous and .... beast	V A		326	"This man's untrue	L C 169
Unruly blasts wait	R L		869	Untuck'd—For some, ..., descended	" 31
unruly though they be	L C		103	Untuned—With untuned tongue	R L 1214
Unsavoury—but unsavoury end	V A		1138	Untutor'd—think me some untutor'd youth	Son 138 3
Unseasonable—a poor .... doe	R L		581	think me some untutor'd youth	P P 1 3
Unseeing—When to unseeing eyes	Son	43	8	Unused—Thy unused beauty	Son 4 13
Unseen—When most unseen	R L		676	And kept unused	" 9 12
To have their unseen sin	"		753	an eye unused to flow	" 30 5
Against the unseen secrecy	"		763	it might unused stay	" 48 3
O unseen shame	"		827		
Was left unseen	"		1426		

Unweave—Now she unweaves the web	V A	.....	991
Unwed—Neither too young nor yet unwed	P P	19	6
Unwelcome—that sour .... guest	V A	.....	449
Unwholesome—unwholesome truths make sick	R L	.....	779
Unwholesome weeds take root	"	.....	870
Unwilling—wilful and unwilling	V A	.....	365
threw unwilling light	"	.....	1051
As each unwilling portal	R L	.....	309
Unwisely—unwisely did not let	"	.....	10
Unwitnessed—.... with eye or ear	V A	.....	1023
Unwoo'd—They live unwoo'd and unrespected	Son	54	10
Unworthiness—If thy unworthiness	"	150	13
Unworthy—Of that unworthy wife	R L	.....	1304
Unyielding—from my .... heart	V A	.....	423
Up—The steed is stalled up	"	.....	39
hold up thy head	"	.....	118
She heaveth up his hat	"	.....	351
stirs up a desperate courage	"	.....	556
eats up Love's tender spring	"	.....	656
dries up his oil	"	.....	756
From his moist cabinet mounts up on high	"	.....	854
Wreathed up in fatal folds	"	.....	879
cheering up her senses	"	.....	896
draws up her breath	"	.....	929
smother'd up in shade	"	.....	1035
A purple flower sprung up	"	.....	1168
Her joy with heaved-up hand	R L	.....	111
had closed up mortal eyes	"	.....	163
And therein heartens up his servile powers	"	.....	295
Stuff up his lust, as minutes fill up hours	"	.....	297
pluck'd up the latch	"	.....	358
cheers up his burning eye	"	.....	435
breaks ope her lock'd-up eyes	"	.....	446
to death, rise up and fall	"	.....	466
cited up in rhymes	"	.....	524
He rouseth up himself	"	.....	541
my heaved-up hands appeal	"	.....	638
Shame folded up in blind concealing night	"	.....	675
that coffers up his gold	"	.....	855
To eat up errors	"	.....	937
'Madam, ere I was up	"	.....	1277
Here folds she up the tenour of her woe	"	.....	1310
Wagg'd up and down	"	.....	1406
which purl'd up to the sky	"	.....	1407
Which seem'd to swallow up his sound advice	"	.....	1409
To jump up higher seem'd	"	.....	1414
voice damm'd up with woe	"	.....	1661
his breath drinks up again	"	.....	1666
till it blow up rain	"	.....	1788
Lifts up his burning head	Son	7	2
the steep-up heavenly hill	"	7	5
all girded up in sheaves	"	12	7
I summon up remembrance	"	30	2
lock'd up in any chest	"	48	9
To tie up envy evermore	"	70	12
that seals up all in rest	"	73	8
will hold me up afloat	"	80	9
countenance fill'd up his line	"	86	13
eat him up to death	"	99	13
Up—Drink up the monarch's plague	Son	114	2
most kingly drinks it up	"	114	10
reckon up their own	"	121	10
built up with newer might	"	123	2
Eat up thy charge	"	146	8
votary took up that fire	"	154	5
But yield them up	L C	.....	221
dried up the dewy morn	P P	6	1
Up-heaveth—faintly she	V A	.....	482
Uphold—in honour might uphold	Son	13	10
Up-locked—to his sweet up-locked treasure	"	52	2
Upon—Upon this promise	V A	.....	85
'The tender spring upon thy tempting lip	"	.....	127
trip upon the green	"	.....	146
seize love upon thy left	"	.....	158
'Upon the earth's increase why shouldst thou feed	"	.....	169
dwells upon my suit	"	.....	206
Upon his compass'd crest now stand on end	"	.....	272
He looks upon his love	"	.....	307
beams upon his hairless face are fix'd	"	.....	487
spread upon the blushing rose	"	.....	590
blood upon the fresh flowers being shed	"	.....	665
far off upon a hill	"	.....	697
comment upon every woe	"	.....	714
Upon fresh beauty, blotting	"	.....	796
Leaves Love upon her back	"	.....	814
Gazing upon a late-embarked friend	"	.....	818
Upon the wide wound	"	.....	1052
Upon his hurt she looks	"	.....	1063
He ran upon the boar	"	.....	1112
She looks upon his lips	"	.....	1123
upon their whiteness stood	"	.....	1170
Upon the world dim darkness doth display	R L	.....	118
Now stole upon the time	"	.....	162
to work upon his wife	"	.....	235
yet remains upon her breast	"	.....	463
sets his foot upon the light	"	.....	673
Upon my checks what helpless shame I feel	"	.....	756
upon his silver down will stay	"	.....	1012
gazed upon with every eye	"	.....	1015
as frets upon an instrument	"	.....	1140
Gazing upon the Greeks	"	.....	1384
break upon the galled shore	"	.....	1440
Upon his head that hath	"	.....	1481
still rest upon record	"	.....	1643
weep upon the tainted place	"	.....	1746
served a dumb arrest upon his tongue	"	.....	1780
struck his hand upon his breast	"	.....	1842
Upon thyself thy beauty's legacy	Son	4	2
war upon this bloody tyrant	"	16	2
And look upon myself	"	29	4
Upon the farthest earth	"	44	6
Upon the hours	"	57	2
lives upon his gains	"	67	12
you look upon this verse	"	71	9
hang more praise upon deceased I	"	72	7
Upon those bows which shake	"	73	3
did call upon thy aid	"	79	1
upon your soundless deep doth ride	"	80	10
upon misprision growing	"	87	11

UPON — VALLEY-FOUNTAIN

Upon—Upon thy side against myself
I'll fight .... Son 88 3
Upon thy part I can set down a
story .... " 88 6
comment upon that offence .... " 89 2
set a form upon desired change .... " 89 6
For it depends upon that love .... " 92 4
stamp'd upon my brow .... " 112 2
and upon me proved .... " 116 13
upon your dearest love to call .... " 117 3
thou dost foist upon us .... " 123 6
Upon that blessed wood .... " 128 2
Looking with pretty ruth upon
my pain .... " 132 4
put fair truth upon so foul a face .... " 137 12
lays upon my heart .... " 139 2
upon thy fading mansion spend .... " 146 6
live thou upon thy servant's loss .... " 146 9
that I do fawn upon .... " 149 6
Revenge upon myself .... " 149 8
Upon her head a platted hive .... L C 8
Upon whose weeping margent .... " 39
slides he down upon his grained bat .. " 64
Upon his lips their silken parcels
hurls .... " 87
was yet upon his chin .... " 92
curb it upon other's proof .... " 163
And long upon these terms I held ...... " 176
Upon the moment .... " 248
Upon the lute doth ravish .... P P 8 6
upon a steep-up hill .... " 9 5
that hangs upon a tree .... " 10 5
There will we sit upon the rocks .... " 20 5
As it fell upon a day .... " 21 1
Made me think upon my own .... " 21 18
Up-prick'd—His ears up-prick'd .... V A 271
Uprear—against myself uprear .... Son 49 11
Upright—Anon he rears upright .... V A 279
Uproar—Unto a greater uproar .... R L 427
Up-till—Lean'd her breast up-till a
thorn .... P P 21 10
Urchin-snouted—and .... boar .... V A 1105
Urge—arms doth urge releasing .... " 256
we our palate urge .... Son 118 2
urge not my amiss .... " 151 3
Urged—'What have you urged .... V A 787
protestation urged the rest .... R L 1844
Urgeth—she with vehement prayers
urgeth still .... " 475
still urgeth such extremes .... " 1337
Urging—Urging the worser sense ...... " 249
Urn—To this urn let those repair .... P T 65
Us—let us part .... V A 421
Do summon us to part .... " 534
torments us with defect .... R L 131
Her wrongs to us .... " 1840
let us divided live .... Son 39 5
What thou dost foist upon us .... " 123 6
By blunting us to make our wits .... L C 161
your victory us all congest .... " 258
known to us poor swains .... P P 18 45
sport from us is fled .... " 18 47
Use—Make use of time .... V A 129
fresh beauty for the use .... " 164
gold that's put to use .... " 768
sorrow should his use control .... R L 1781
deserved thy beauty's use .... Son 2 9
That use is not forbidden .... " 6 5
thy love's use their treasure .... " 20 14

Use—That to my use it might .... Son 48 3
every alien pen hath got my use .... " 78 3
that put'st forth all to use .... " 134 10
Use—and use good dealing .... V A 514
thus to use it in the fight .... R L 62
when he cannot use it .... " 862
why dost thou use .... Son 4 7
for ornament doth use .... " 21 3
spirit doth use your name .... " 80 2
words which writers use .... " 82 3
If thou wouldst use the strength .... " 96 12
use rigour in my gaol .... " 133 12
Use power with power .... " 139 4
should use like loving charms .... P P 11 8
Use his company no more .... " 21 50
Used—How Tarquin must be used ..... R L 1195
Was used in giving gentle doom .... Son 145 7
Which, used, lives .... " 4 14
might be better used .... " 82 13
The hardest knife, ill used .... " 95 14
Adon used to cool his spleen .... P P 6 6
That nothing could be used .... " 16 10
Useless—And .... barns the harvest .. R L 859
User—the user so destroys it .... Son 9 12
Usest—for my love thou usest .... " 40 6
Usher—that ushers in the even .... " 132 7
Usurer—Profitless usurer, why dost
thou use .... " 4 7
Thou usurer, that put'st forth all
to use .... " 134 10
Usurp—Usurps her cheek .... V A 591
Usurp'd—on earth usurp'd his name . " 794
Usurper—Who, like a foul usurper ... R L 412
Usury—use is not forbidden usury .... Son 6 5
Like usury, applying wet to wet .... L C 40
Utmost—hath cast his utmost sum .... Son 49 3
Utter—My tongue shall utter all .... R L 1076
She utters this: 'He, he, fair lords ..... " 1721
Uttering—and uttering foolish things " 1813
Uttering bare truth .... Son 69 4

Vacant—The vacant leaves .... Son 77 3
Vade—When that shall vade .... " 54 14
Vaded—untimely pluck'd, soon .... P P 10 1
and vaded in the spring .... " 10 2
Lest, vaded, broken .... " 13 6
vaded gloss no rubbing will refresh .. " 13 8
Vadeth—gloss that vadeth suddenly . " 13 2
Vail—He vails his tail .... V A 314
Vail'd—She vail'd her eyelids .... " 956
Vain—But all in vain .... " 607
is bestow'd in vain .... " 771
And all in vain you strive .... " 772
'In vain I rail at Opportunity .... R L 1023
In vain I cavil .... " 1025
In vain I spurn .... " 1026
'In vain,' quoth she, 'I live, and
seek in vain .... " 1044
he strives in vain .... " 1665
a vain and doubtful good .... P P 13 1
thou mourn'st in vain .... " 21 19
Vainly—Thus vainly thinking .... Son 138 5
from the truth vainly express'd .... " 147 12
Thus vainly thinking .... P P 1 5
Vale—from a sistering vale .... L C 2
Valiant—makes her absence valiant . " 245
Valley—hills and valleys, dales and
fields .... P P 20 3
Valley-fountain—In a cold .... Son 153 4

Valour—Put fear to valour	V A	....	1158
True valour still a true respect	"	.....	201
Vanish'd—his .... loathed delight	R L	.....	742
of many a vanish'd sight	Son	30	8
or vanish'd out of sight	"	63	7
Vanisheth—through her lips, so	R L	.....	1041
Vanishing—Are .... or vanish'd	Son	63	7
Vanity—Thy violent vanities	R L	.....	894
Vanquish'd—captive .... doth yield	"	.....	75
Like a thousand vanquish'd men	P P	18	36
Vantage—having thee at vantage	V A	.....	635
sense for vantage still	R L	.....	249
Doing thee vantage, double-vantage me	Son	88	12
Vapour—Like misty vapours	V A	.....	184
vapours doth he send	"	.....	274
melted like a vapour	"	.....	1166
Which blows these pitchy vapours	R L	.....	550
misty vapours march so thick	"	.....	782
and breath a vapour is	P P	3	9
Exhale this vapour vow	"	3	11
Vaporous—.... and foggy Night	R L	.....	771
Variable—variable passions throng	V A	.....	967
Variation—So far from variation	Son	76	2
Variety—pale with fresh variety	V A	.....	21
Varying—varying to other words	Son	105	10
Vassal—Obdurate vassals, full exploits	R L	.....	429
From vassal actors	"	.....	608
low vassals to thy state	"	.....	666
the duteous vassal scarce is gone	"	.....	1360
Being your vassal	Son	58	9
and vassal wretch to be	"	141	12
Vassalage—to whom in vassalage	"	26	1
Vast—Vast sin-concealing chaos	R L	.....	767
Vastly—like a late-sack'd island, vastly stood	"	.....	1740
Vaulty—And in her vaulty prison	"	.....	119
Vaunt—Vaunt in their youthful sap	Son	15	7
Vehement—But she with vehement prayers	R L	.....	473
Veil—'Bonnet nor veil	V A	.....	1081
beauty's veil doth cover	Son	95	11
Veil'd—And, veil'd in them	L C	.....	312
Vein—Her azure veins	R L	.....	419
uproar tempts his veins	"	.....	427
Whose ranks of blue veins	"	.....	440
changed to black in every vein	"	.....	1454
to blush through lively veins	Son	67	10
In my love's veins	"	99	5
Vein'd—These blue-vein'd violets	V A	.....	125
Velvet—Like unshorn velvet	L C	.....	94
Through the velvet leaves	P P	17	5
Venge—to venge this wrong of mine	V A	.....	1691
Vengeful—A .... canker eat him up	Son	99	13
Venom—His venom in effect	R L	.....	532
fair founts with venom mud	"	.....	850
Venom'd—'Gainst venom'd sores	V A	.....	916
Vent—Free vent of words	"	.....	334
Through little vents and crannies	R L	.....	310
To make more vent for passage	"	.....	1040
Venture—on the lion he will	V A	.....	628
Venturing—compass'd oft with	"	.....	567
So that in venturing ill	R L	.....	148
Venus—Sick-thoughted Venus	V A	.....	5
and by Venus' side	"	.....	180
'Ay me,' quoth Venus	"	.....	187
to swallow Venus' liking	"	.....	248
in the night from Venus' eye	"	.....	316

Venus—Venus salutes him	V A	.....	859
poor Venus noteth	"	.....	1037
From Venus' doves doth challenge	R L	.....	58
Venus with young Adonis	P P	11	1
Verbal—Make verbal repetition	V A	.....	831
Verdict—And by their verdict is determined	Son	46	11
On this side the verdict went	L C	.....	113
Verdure—their verdure still endure	V A	.....	507
Vermillion—Nor praise the deep	Son	98	10
Verse—Who will believe my verse	"	17	1
My love shall in my verse	"	19	14
beauty to his verse	"	21	2
that pour'st into my verse	"	38	2
by verse distills your truth	"	54	14
in hope my verse shall stand	"	60	13
you look upon this verse	"	71	9
Why is my verse so barren	"	76	1
such fair assistance in my verse	"	78	2
My verse alone had all	"	79	2
shall be my gentle verse	"	81	9
full sail of his great verse	"	86	1
my verse astonished	"	86	8
to no other pass my verses tend	"	103	11
than in my verse can sit	"	103	13
my verse to constancy confined	"	105	7
Very—nothing but the very smell	V A	.....	441
shrieks,—'tis very late	"	.....	531
in the very lists of love	"	.....	595
The very eyes of men	R L	.....	1383
tyrants to the very same	Son	5	3
The very part was consecrate	"	74	6
At first the very worst	"	90	12
the very birds are mute	"	97	12
say o'er the very same	"	108	6
and proved, a very woe	"	129	11
the very refuse of thy deeds	"	150	6
Vestal—Love-lacking vestals	V A	.....	752
makest the vestal violate her oath	R L	.....	883
Vex—Thou canst not vex me	Son	92	9
am I that vex thee still	"	133	3
Vexation—The deep vexation	R L	.....	1779
Vex'd—That is so .... with watching	Son	148	10
Vial—Make sweet some vial	"	6	3
Vice—When thus thy vices bud	R L	.....	604
With inward vice	"	.....	1546
For canker vice	Son	70	7
have those vices got	"	95	9
If he be addict to vice	P P	21	43
Victor—A captive victor that hath	R L	.....	730
and both shall victors be	"	.....	1211
or victor being charged	Son	70	10
As victors, of my silence	"	86	11
was victor of the day	P P	16	13
Victory—His victories, his triumphs	V A	.....	1014
arms and wreaths of victory	R L	.....	110
After a thousand victories	Son	25	10
Must for your victory	L C	.....	258
View—wistly to view	V A	.....	343
as murder'd with the view	"	.....	1031
So, at his bloody view	"	.....	1037
Their view right on	R L	.....	26
Unto a view so false	"	.....	292
to my sightless view	Son	27	10
more blest may be the view	"	56	12
a motley to the view	"	110	2
Who, in despite of view	"	141	4
though I mistake my view	"	148	11

View—disturbed, heedfully doth view	*R L*	454	
To view thy present trespass	"	632	
with each thing she views	"	1101	
The precedent whereof in Lucrece view	"	1261	
I loved, I view in thee	*Son*	31	13
they view things unrespected	"	43	2
that the world's eye doth view	"	69	1
View'd—view'd each other's sorrow	*V A*	963	
Which Tarquin view'd	*R L*	72	
wherein they view'd their faces	"	1526	
Viewest—and tell the face thou	*Son*	3	1
Viewing—that's worth the viewing	*V A*	1076	
Vigour—for thy mortal vigour	"	953	
Vile—digression is so vile, so base	*R L*	202	
this vile purpose to prevent	"	220	
That what is vile	"	252	
how vile a spectacle it were	"	631	
How comes it then, vile Opportunity	"	895	
From this vile world	*Son*	71	4
to be vile than vile esteemed	"	121	1
Vilest—with vilest worms to dwell	"	71	4
Villain—The homely .... court'sies	*R L*	1338	
Vine—who will the vine destroy	"	215	
Violate—the vestal violate her oath	"	883	
Violated—taste of violated troth	"	1059	
Violent—Thy .... vanities can never	"	894	
the violent roaring tide	"	1667	
Violet—These blue-vein'd violets	*V A*	125	
smell to the violet	"	936	
the violet past prime	*Son*	12	3
The forward violet	"	99	1
Virgin—by a virgin hand disarm'd	"	154	8
Virtue—Their virtue lost	*V A*	1131	
beauty and virtue strived	*R L*	52	
When virtue bragg'd, beauty would	"	54	
Virtue would stain o'er	"	56	
Then virtue claims from beauty	"	59	
which virtue gave the golden age	"	60	
beauty's red and virtue's white	"	65	
Thus dying virtue	"	223	
And talk'd of virtue	"	846	
When virtue is profaned	"	847	
What virtue breeds	"	872	
When Truth and Virtue	"	911	
sin's pack-horse, virtue's snare	"	928	
But, for their virtue	*Son*	54	9
virtue rudely strumpeted	"	66	6
He lends thee virtue	"	79	9
such virtue hath my pen	"	81	13
If thy sweet virtue	"	93	14
virtue of your love	"	117	14
and thy dear virtue hate	"	142	1
Virtuous—shows like a .... deed	*R L*	252	
Where like a virtuous monument	"	391	
With virtuous wish	*Son*	16	7
devise some virtuous lie	"	72	5
And prove thee virtuous	"	88	4
Visage—his visage hide	"	33	7
Which fortified her visage	*L C*		9
For on his visage	"		90
Yet show'd his visage	"		96
Vision—Nor his own vision holds	*Son*	113	8
Visit—to come and visit me	*R L*	1307	
Voice—churlish, harsh in voice	*V A*	134	
Thy mermaid's voice	"	429	

Voice—volleys out his voice	*V A*	921	
It is Adonis' voice	"	974	
Her voice is stopp'd	"	1061	
her voice controll'd	*R L*	678	
and voice damn'd up with woe	"	1661	
All tongues the voice of souls	*Son*	69	3
Of others' voices	"	112	10
this double voice accorded	*L C*		3
thy voice his dreadful thunder	*P P*	5	11
Volley—volleys out his voice	*V A*	921	
Vomit—must vomit his receipt	*R L*	703	
Votary—The fairest votary took up	*Son*	154	5
Vouchsafe—Vouchsafe, thou wonder	*V A*		13
next vouchsafe t' afford	*R L*	1305	
O then vouchsafe me	*Son*	32	9
Not once vouchsafe to hide	"	135	6
Vow—Dismiss your vows	*V A*	425	
breach of holy wedlock vow	*R L*	809	
the fatal knife to end his vow	"	1813	
And that deep vow	"	1847	
Creep in 'twixt vows	*Son*	115	6
In act thy bed-vow broke	"	152	3
For all my vows are oaths	"	152	7
Knew vows were ever brokers	*L C*		173
of my holy vows afraid	"		179
All vows and consecrations	"		263
vow, bond, nor space	"		264
Vows for thee broke	*P P*	3	4
My vow was earthly	"	3	7
My vow was breath	"	3	9
Exhale this vapour vow	"	3	11
Vow, alack! for youth unmeet	"	17	13
Vow—That now he vows a league	*R L*	287	
That he may vow	"	1179	
against myself I'll vow	*Son*	89	13
This I do vow	"	123	13
Vowed—that vow'd chaste life to keep	"	154	3
if not to beauty vowed	*P P*	5	2
Vowing—In vowing new hate	*Son*	152	4
Vulgar—For every vulgar paper	"	38	4
prey of every vulgar thief	"	48	8
Which vulgar scandal	"	112	2
Vulture—Whose vulture thought	*V A*	551	
feeds his vulture folly	*R L*	556	
Wagg'd—Wagg'd up and down	*R L*	1406	
Wail—To wail his death	*V A*	1017	
to wail a week	*R L*	213	
beggar wails his case	"	711	
wail the abusing of his time	"	994	
The world will wail thee	*Son*	9	4
new wail my dear time's waste	"	30	9
Wail'd—must be wail'd by Collatine	*R L*	1799	
Wailing—begins a wailing note	*V A*	835	
calm look, eyes wailing still	*R L*	1508	
is of my wailing chief	*Son*	42	3
Waist—girdle with embracing flames the waist	*R L*		6
Wait—wit waits on fear	*V A*	690	
wait on wrinkled age	*R L*	275	
wait on the tender spring	"	869	
wait on them as their pages	"	910	
scandal waits on greatest state	"	1006	
I am to wait	*Son*	58	13
his pleasures wait on thee	"	57	11
Waited—It shall be waited on	*V A*	1137	
Waiting—though waiting so be hell	*Son*	58	13
Wake—And wakes the morning	*V A*	855	
and troubled minds that wake	*R L*	126	

22

Wake—wakes to stain and kill	R L	....	168
Will he not wake	"	....	219
She wakes her heart	"	....	759
To wake the morn	"	....	942
thou dost wake elsewhere	Son	61	13
still did wake and sleep	L C	....	123
If thou wake, he cannot sleep	P P	21	54
Waken'd—in your waken'd hate	Son	117	12
Waking—by dreadful fancy....	R L	....	450
Yet, foul night-waking cat	"	....	554
To keep thy sharp woes waking	"	....	1136
but waking no such matter	Son	87	14
Walk—curtains being close, about			
he walks	R L	....	367
Be absent from thy walks	Son	89	9
thy fingers walk with gentle gait	"	128	11
My mistress, when she walks	"	130	12
Walk'd—the lion walk'd along	V A	....	1093
Wall—to batter such an ivory wall	R L	....	464
batter'd down her consecrated wall	"	....	723
Through crystal walls	"	....	1231
the walls of strong-besieged Troy	"	....	1429
pent in walls of glass	Son	5	10
Painting thy outward walls	"	146	4
Wander—the souls that...., by him	R L	....	882
to make me wander thither	P P	14	10
Wander, a word for shadows	"	14	11
Wanderer—as night-wanderers often are	V A	....	825
Wander'st—thou .... in his shade	Son	18	11
Wandering—Night-wandering weasels shriek	R L	....	307
a wandering wasp hath crept	"	....	839
to every wandering bark	Son	116	7
Wane—As fast as thou shalt wane	"	11	1
Waning—wealth and ease in waning age	R L	....	142
Who hast by waning grown	Son	126	3
Want—how .... of love tormenteth	V A	....	202
which their superiors want	R L	....	42
and all, for want of wit	"	....	153
to want his bliss	"	....	389
drowns for want of skill	"	....	1099
nothing wants to answer	"	....	1459
cunning want to grace their art	Son	24	13
want subject to invent	"	38	1
Want nothing that the thought	"	69	2
No want of conscience	"	151	13
Where want cries some, but	L C	....	42
unripe years did want conceit	P P	4	9
No man will supply thy want	"	21	38
Wanteth—so wanteth in his store	R L	....	97
that even in plenty wanteth	"	....	557
Wanting—Wanting the spring	"	....	1455
in wanting words to show it	Son	26	6
this fair gift in me is wanting	"	87	7
manner of my pity-wanting pain	"	140	4
Wanton—to toy, to wanton	V A	....	106
the wanton mermaid's songs	"	....	777
to your wanton talk	"	....	809
moralize his wanton sight	R L	....	104
'This glove to wanton tricks	"	....	320
O modest wantons! wanton modesty	"	....	401
Bearing the wanton burthen	Son	97	7
Playing in the wanton air	P P	17	4
Wantonly—and play as wantonly	Son	54	7
Wantonness—Some say, thy fault is youth, some wantonness	"	96	1
War—direful god of war	V A	....	98
War—what a war of looks	V A	....	355
It shall be cause of war	"	....	1159
This silent war of lilies	R L	....	71
Make war against proportion'd course of time	"	....	774
in peace is wounded, not in war	"	....	831
And all in war with Time	Son	15	13
Make war upon this bloody tyrant	"	16	2
Such civil war is in my love and hate	"	35	12
are at a mortal war	"	46	1
When wasteful war shall statues	"	55	5
nor war's quick fire shall burn	"	55	7
War—The wind wars with his torch	R L	....	311
Sweets with sweets war not	Son	8	2
Warble—The well-tuned warble	R L	....	1080
Ward—by him enforced, retires his ward	"	....	303
in sure wards of trust	Son	48	4
in thy steel bosom's ward	"	133	9
Wardrobe—Or as the wardrobe	"	52	10
Warlike—hard news from the warlike band	R L	....	255
'the warlike god embraced me	P P	11	5
'the warlike god unlaced me	"	11	7
Warm—'The sun that shines from heaven shines but warm	V A	....	193
Welcomes the warm approach	"	....	386
The warm effects	"	....	605
And see thy blood warm	Son	2	14
Warm'd—legions of true hearts had warm'd	"	154	6
my heart so much as warm'd	L C	....	191
that is not warmed here	"	....	292
Warning—Give .... to the world	Son	71	3
Warrant—warrant for blame	R L	....	620
Warrantise—strength and warrantise of skill	Son	150	7
Warrior—The painful .... famoused	"	25	9
Wary—be of thyself so wary	"	22	9
Was—Under her other was the tender boy	V A	....	32
So soon was she along as he was down	"	....	43
Yet was he servile	"	....	112
what he was controlled with	"	....	270
his fury was assuaged	"	....	318
O, what a sight it was	"	....	343
now her cheek was pale	"	....	347
Now was she just before him	"	....	349
a war of looks was then between them	"	....	355
life was death's annoy	"	....	497
death was lively joy	"	....	498
was it not white	"	....	643
Her song was tedious	"	....	841
It was not that she call'd him	"	....	993
how much a fool was I	"	....	1015
was but late forlorn	"	....	1026
that his wound wept, was drench'd	"	....	1054
No flower was nigh	"	....	1055
When he was by	"	....	1101
thus was Adonis slain	"	....	1111
Was melted like a vapour	"	....	1166
this was thy father's guise	"	....	1177
unto himself was his desire	"	....	1180
Here was thy father's bed	"	....	1183
Well was he welcomed	R L	....	31
in Lucrece' face was seen	"	....	64

Was—was the other queen	R L	66
Without the bed her other fair hand was	"	393
was it newly bred	"	490
For it was lent thee	"	627
was pure to Collatine	"	826
was too weak	"	845
he was stay'd by thee	"	917
I was a loyal wife	"	1048
thy interest was not bought	"	1067
which was the dearer	"	1163
to myself was nearer	"	1165
How was I overseen	"	1206
'Madam, ere I was up	"	1277
Myself was stirring	"	1280
was Tarquin gone away	"	1284
God wot, it was defect	"	1345
in this work was had	"	1385
the painter was so nice	"	1412
imaginary work was there	"	1422
Was left unseen, save	"	1426
Of what she was	"	1453
The painter was no god	"	1461
in Sinon's was abused	"	1529
the picture was belied	"	1533
Mine enemy was strong	"	1646
That was not forced; that never was inclined	"	1657
For she that was thy Lucrece	"	1682
'That life was mine	"	1752
what once I was	"	1764
'Tarquin' was pronounced	"	1786
for she was only mine	"	1798
'She was my wife	"	1802
with the Romans was esteemed so	"	1811
nor no remembrance what it was	Son	5 12
he was but one hour mine	"	33 11
All mine was thine	"	40 4
How careful was I	"	48 1
from the thing it was	"	49 7
in character was done	"	59 8
what beauty was of yore	"	68 14
slander's mark was ever yet the fair	"	70 2
which it was nourish'd by	"	73 12
part was consecrate to thee	"	74 6
The worst was this; my love was my decay	"	80 14
Was it the proud full sail	"	86 1
Was it his spirit	"	86 5
I was not sick	"	86 12
time removed was summer's time	"	97 5
Our love was new	"	102 5
When I was wont to greet	"	102 6
that before was well	"	103 10
was beauty's summer dead	"	104 14
that I was false of heart	"	109 1
When I was certain	"	115 11
that there was true needing	"	118 8
from me was I hold	"	122 11
No, it was builded	"	124 5
black was not counted	"	127 1
that I was thy 'Will	"	136 2
Was used in giving gentle doom	"	145 7
Was sleeping by a virgin hand	"	154 8
weeping margent she was set	L C	39
it was to gain my grace	"	79
She was new lodged	"	84
on his visage was in little drawn	"	90
thinks in Paradise was sawn	"	91
Was—was yet upon his chin	L C	92
If best were as it was	"	98
For maiden-tongued he was	"	100
was he such a storm	"	101
And was my own fee-simple	"	144
to none was ever said	"	180
but ne'er was harmed	"	194
but mine own was free	"	195
why, 'twas beautiful and hard	"	211
was sent me from a nun	"	232
For she was sought	"	236
My vow was earthly	P P	3 7
My vow was breath	"	3 9
Hot was the day	"	6 7
'why was not I a flood	"	6 14
Was this a lover	"	7 17
Fair was the morn	"	9 1
'here was the sore	"	9 12
It was a lording's daughter	"	16 1
Long was the combat doubtful	"	16 5
alas, it was a spite	"	16 7
more mickle was the pain	"	16 9
was wounded with disdain	"	16 11
was victor of the day	"	16 13
Love, whose month was ever May	"	17 2
faith was firmly fix'd in love	"	18 11
Thy like ne'er was	"	18 50
That to hear it was great pity	"	21 12
Number there in love was slain	P T	28
Distance and no space was seen	"	30
Either was the other's mine	"	36
Property was thus appalled	"	37
That the self was not the same	"	38
Neither two nor one was called	"	40
It was married chastity	"	61
Wash—To wash the foul face	V A	983
wash the slander of my ill	R L	1207
Wash'd—cheeks over-wash'd with woe	"	1225
Wasp—a wandering .... hath crept	"	839
Wast—Thou wast begot	V A	168
And wast afeard to scratch	R L	1035
Where thou wast wont	"	1621
Thou wast not to this end	"	1755
Waste—I'll waste in sorrow	V A	583
And waste huge stones	R L	959
how thy precious minutes waste	Son	77 2
faster than Time wastes life	"	100 13
Waste—makest waste in niggarding	"	1 12
But beauty's waste	"	9 11
among the wastes of time	"	12 10
my dear time's waste	"	30 4
more short than waste or ruining	"	125 4
in a waste of shame	"	129 1
Waste—to these waste blanks	"	77 10
Wasted—wasted in such time-beguiling	V A	24
should not be wasted	"	130
wasted, thaw'd, and done	"	749
the chronicle of wasted time	Son	106 1
Wasteful—wasteful Time debateth	"	15 11
When wasteful war	"	55 5
Wasting—Poor .... monuments	R L	798
Wat—'By this, poor Wat	V A	697
Watch—mine eyes to watch	"	581
And they that watch	R L	1575
watch the clock for you	Son	57 6
For thee watch I	"	61 13
Watch—Base watch of woes	R L	928

Watch—My heart doth charge the watch	P P	15	2	Wayward—to the wayward boy	V A 344
Watching—That is so vex'd with	Son	148	9	Who wayward once	R L 1095
Watchman—To play the watchman	"	61	12	We—whereon we lean	V A 125
Watchword—Which gives the	R L	.....	370	know not what we mean	" 126
Water—She bathes in water	V A	.....	94	shall we meet to-morrow	" 585
in water seen by night	"	.....	492	Say, shall we? shall we	" 586
As air and water	"	.....	654	all for one we gage	R L 144
stones dissolved to water	R L	.....	592	venturing ill we leave to be	" 148
And grave like water	"	.....	755	The things we are for that which we expect	" 149
no water thence proceeds	"	.....	1552	we have; so then we do	" 152
to burn his Troy with water	"	.....	1561	The thing we have	" 153
of earth and water wrought	Son	44	11	that on lawn we lay	" 238
bring water for my stain	"	109	8	The sweets we wish for	" 867
The sea, all water	"	135	9	that we call them ours	" 868
Love's fire heats water, water cools	"	154	14	We have no good that we can say is ours	" 873
That flame through water	L C	.....	287	Will we find out; and there we will unfold	" 1146
to water will not wear	"	.....	291	of sorrow that we hear	" 1328
or of weeping water	"	.....	304	that we may give redress	" 1603
Water-drops — huge stones with little water-drops	R L	.....	959	We are their offspring	" 1757
Water-gall — These water-galls in her dim element	"	.....	1588	the Capitol that we adore	" 1835
Watery—swan in her watery nest	"	.....	1611	We will revenge the death	" 1841
a watery rigol goes	"	.....	1745	creatures we desire increase	Son 1 1
some watery token shows	"	.....	1748	that we two must be twain	" 36 1
win of the watery main	Son	64	7	yet we must not be foes	" 40 14
his watery eyes he did dismount	L C	.....	281	in every blessed shape we know	" 53 12
Wave—peering through a wave	V A	.....	86	but fairer we it deem	" 54 3
wave like feather'd wings	"	.....	306	Whether we are mended	" 59 11
Till the wild waves	"	.....	819	For we, which now behold	" 106 13
Whose waves to imitate	R L	.....	1438	with eager compounds we our palate urge	" 118 2
Like as the waves make	Son	60	1	We sicken to shun sickness when we purge	" 118 4
Waved—Who in a salt-waved ocean	R L	.....	1231	and therefore we admire	" 123 5
Wavering—wavering stood in doubt	L C	.....	97	we before have heard them	" 123 8
Wax—What wax so frozen	V A	.....	565	and what we see doth lie	" 123 11
No more than wax	R L	.....	1245	with ease we prove	" 136 7
Softer than wax	P P	7	4	by lies we flatter'd be	" 138 14
Waxen—Whereat a waxen torch	R L	.....	178	For when we rage	L C 160
men have marble, women waxen, minds	"	.....	1240	That we must curb it	" 162
From lips new-waxen pale	"	.....	1663	The thing we have not	" 240
Waxeth—never waxeth strong	V A	.....	420	we will all the pleasures prove	P P 20 2
Wax-red—on my wax-red lips	"	.....	516	There will we sit upon the rocks	" 20 5
Way—his lips another way	"	.....	90	Weak—weak and silly mind	V A 1016
which way shall she turn	"	.....	253	shall it make most weak	" 1145
a thousand ways he seeks	"	.....	477	past reason's weak removing	R L 243
whate'er is in his way	"	.....	623	are the weak brain's forgeries	" 460
indenting with the way	"	.....	704	the weak mouse panteth	" 555
discovery of her way	"	.....	828	To whose weak ruins muster	" 720
the bushes in the way	"	.....	871	In thy weak hive	" 839
just in his way	"	.....	879	Their father was too weak	" 865
This way she runs	"	.....	905	Unprofitable sounds, weak arbitrators	" 1017
bear her a thousand ways	"	.....	907	The weak oppress'd	" 1242
unwilling portal yields him way	R L	.....	309	my poor self weak	" 1646
force must work my way	"	.....	513	Weak words, so thick come	" 1784
thou didst teach the way	"	.....	630	from weak minds proceeds	" 1825
seated from the way	"	.....	1144	lends but weak relief	Son 34 11
determining which way to fly	"	.....	1150	though more weak in seeming	" 102 1
tread the way out readily	"	.....	1152	Weak sights their sickly radiance	L C 214
to mourn some newer way	"	.....	1365	age is weak and old	P P 12 7
and look another way	Son	7	12	Weak-built—Though .... hopes	R L 130
do not you a mightier way	"	16	1	Weaken—Whose strength's abundance weakens his own heart	Son 23 4
o'ertake me in my way	"	34	3		
should not stop my way	"	44	2		
when I took my way	"	48	1	Weaker—And far the weaker	R L 1647
do I journey on the way	"	50	1	Weakling—Myself a weakling	" 584
by-past perils in her way	L C	.....	158	Weakly—Are weakly fortress'd	" 28
And to her will frame all thy ways	P P	19	25		

Weak-made—Make .... women	R L	1260	Weed—The basest weed out-braves	Son	91 12
Weakness—with cold-pale	V A	892	smell far worse than weeds	"	91 11
With mine own weakness	Son	88 5	weeds among weeds	"	121 4
Weal—Thy weal and woe	V A	987	Week—a minute's mirth to wail a		
Wealth—What priceless wealth	R L	17	week	R L	213
honour, wealth, and ease in waning			with his brief hours and weeks	Son	116 11
age	"	142	Weep—that laughs and weeps	V A	414
Honour for wealth; and oft that			then would Adonis weep	"	1090
wealth doth cost	"	146	while the widow weeps	R L	906
thy sweet love remember'd such			weeps at thy languishment	"	1130
wealth brings	Son	29 13	But as the earth doth weep	"	1226
birth, or wealth, or wit	"	37 5	Which makes the maid weep	"	1232
to show what wealth she had	"	67 13	One justly weeps	"	1235
'twixt a miser and his wealth	"	75 4	to weep are often willing	"	1237
Some in their wealth	"	91 2	If thou dost weep for grief	"	1272
Richer than wealth	"	91 10	to sigh, to weep, and groan	"	1362
Of wealth, of filial fear	L C	270	Lo, here weeps Hecuba	"	1485
Weapon—bright weapons wield	R L	1432	she weeps Troy's painted woes	"	1492
Wear—jewels to wear	V A	163	to weep upon the tainted place	"	1746
Who wears a garment	"	415	Who should weep most	"	1791
their crimson liveries wear	"	506	weep with equal strife	"	1792
henceforth no creature wear	"	1084	He weeps for her	"	1798
And wear their brave state	Son	13 8	be thy widow, and still weep	Son	9 5
That wear this world out	"	55 12	And weep afresh	"	30 7
how thy beauties wear	"	77 1	But weep to have that	"	64 14
though marble wear with raining	R L	560	the laugher weep	L C	121
the nightly linen that she wears	"	680	Though Reason weep, and cry	"	168
the web it seem'd to wear	L C	95	to weep at woes	"	307
to water will not wear	"	291	I weep for thee and yet	P P	10 7
Wearied—She like a wearied lamb	R L	737	Procure to weep	"	18 32
So woe hath wearied woe	"	1363	If thou sorrow, he will weep	"	21 53
Weariness— .... with heavy spright	"	121	Weeper—To make the weeper laugh	L C	121
of weariness he did complain him	"	845	Weeping—of the weeping morn	V A	2
Weary—or morn or weary even	V A	495	thou provokest such weeping	"	919
comforter, with weary gait	"	529	could weeping purify	R L	685
Hot, faint, and weary	"	539	with weeping will unfold	"	754
brier his weary legs doth scratch	"	705	where she sits weeping	"	1087
lark, weary of rest	"	853	seem'd a weeping tear	"	1375
asks the weary caitiff	"	914	one pair of weeping eyes	"	1680
Thus weary of the world	"	1189	Upon whose weeping margent	L C	39
his weary noon-tide prick	R L	781	or of weeping water	"	301
The weary time she cannot			Herds stand weeping	P P	18 41
so weary, and so mild	"	1361	Weepingly—acceptance weepingly		
to rest thy weary head	"	1542	beseech'd	L C	207
from highmost pitch, with weary	"	1621	Weigh—Weighs not the dust	Son	108 10
car	Son	7 9	To weigh how once I suffer'd	"	120 8
Weary with toil I haste me	"	27 1	Whose white weighs down	L C	226
my weary travel's end	"	50 2	Weight—with his own weight goes	R L	1494
to the weary night	"	61 2	to bear that weight in me	Son	50 6
Weary—And time doth weary time	R L	1570	Welcome—Welcomes the warm approach	V A	386
Weasel—Night-wandering weasels			welcome to her princely guest	R L	90
shriek to see him	"	307	that seem'd to welcome woe	"	1309
Weather—the weather being cold	V A	402	Makes summer's welcome	Son	56 11
consulting for foul weather	"	972	Then give me welcome	"	110 13
of stormy blustering weather	R L	115	For she doth welcome daylight	P P	15 7
age like winter weather	P P	12 3	Welcomed—Well was he welcomed	R L	51
Web—She unweaves the web	V A	991	Welfare—Until her husband's	"	263
the web it seem'd to wear	L C	95	And sick of welfare	Son	118 7
Wed—One woman would another			Welkin—Against the welkin	V A	921
wed	P P	19 48	in his fair welkin once appear	R L	116
Wedlock—breach of holy .... vow	R L	809	Well—As well as mine	V A	117
Weed—bid thee crop a weed	V A	946	mayst thou well be tasted	"	128
herb, leaf, or weed	"	1053	Well-painted idol	"	212
love's modest snow-white weed	R L	196	For knowing well, if there	"	245
As corn o'ergrown by weeds	"	281	a well-proportion'd steed	"	290
Unwholesome weeds take root	"	870	can so well defend her	"	472
Will be a tatter'd weed	Son	2 4	I can be well contented	"	513
add the rank smell of weeds	"	69 12	her thirsty lips well knew	"	543
Invention in a noted weed	"	76 6			

Well—and look well to her heart	V A	580	Were—then I were not for thee	V A		137
They that thrive well	"	640	were it with thy band felt	"		143
on thy well-breath'd horse	"	678	So he were like him	"		180
grief may be compared well	"	701	And were I not immortal, life			
pleased her babe so well	"	974	were done	"		197
resembling well his pale cheeks	"	1169	What were thy lips the worse	"		207
cancell'd ere well begun	R L	26	if himself were slain	"		243
Well was he welcomed	"	51	As they were mad	"		323
and thou art well appaid	"	914	Though I were dumb	"		406
As well to hear as grant	"	915	Or were I deaf	"		435
' Well, well, dear Collatine	"	1058	that were but sensible	"		436
To imitate thee well	"	1137	feeling were bereft me	"		439
than I can well express	"	1286	but the very smell were left me	"		441
peasants did so well resemble	"	1392	she lies as she were slain	"		473
private widow well may keep	Son	9 7	Were never four such lamps	"		489
if it shall go well	"	14 7	Were beauty under twenty locks	"		575
that like of hearsay well	"	21 13	As if another chase were in the			
my well-contented day	"	32 1	skies	"		696
well of such a salve can speak	"	34 7	moulds from heaven that were			
in whom all ill well shows	"	40 13	divine	"		730
thy years full well befits	"	41 3	heart were quite undone	"		783
be it ill or well	"	58 14	were open'd to the light	R L		105
you for love speak well of me untrue	"	72 10	Or were he not my dear friend	"		234
To love that well	"	73 14	between them twain there were			
being extant, well might show	"	83 6	no strife	"		405
will be well esteem'd	"	96 6	If ever man were moved	"		587
subject that before was well	"	103 10	a spectacle it were	"		631
who calls me well or ill	"	112 3	Were Tarquin Night, as he is	"		785
Mine eye well knows	"	114 11	which of the twain were better	"		1154
All this the world well knows; yet			alack, what were it	"		1156
none knows well	"	129 13	When both were kept for heaven	"		1166
yet well I know	"	130 9	were cloud-eclipsed so	"		1224
For well thou know'st	"	131 3	As 'twere encouraging the Greeks	"		1402
as well beseem thy heart	"	132 10	About him were a press	"		1408
ah, my love well knows	"	139 9	with chaps and wrinkles were dis-			
then love doth well denote	"	148 7	guised	"		1452
Well could he ride	L C	106	that the skies were sorry	"		1524
With wit well blazon'd	"	217	Were an all-eating shame	Son	2	8
Well learned is that tongue that			This were to be new made	"	2	13
well can thee commend	P P	5 8	Then, were not summer's distilla-			
Fare well I could not	"	14 6	tion left	"	5	9
as well as well might be	"	16 2	Beauty's effect with beauty were			
As well as fancy	"	19 4	bereft	"	5	11
say thou lovest her well	"	19 11	Ten times thyself were happier	"	6	9
Simple were so well compounded	P T	44	If all were minded so	"	11	7
Well—quenched in a cool well by	Son	154 9	O, that you were yourself	"	13	1
all their fountains in my well	L C	255	determination; then you were	"	13	6
Clear wells spring not	P P	18 37	If it were fill'd with your	"	17	2
Well-contented—my .... day	Son	32 1	But were some child of yours alive	"	17	13
Well-doing—by the well-doing steed	L C	112	Were it not thy sour leisure	"	39	10
Well-painted—Well-painted idol	V A	212	substance of my flesh were thought	"	44	1
To this well-painted piece	R L	1443	self-loving were iniquity	"	62	12
Well-proportion'd—.... steed	V A	290	signs of fair were born	"	68	3
Well-refined—form of .... pen	Son	85 8	sepulchres, were shorn away	"	68	6
Well-seeing—Lost eyes well-seeing	"	148 14	although their eyes were kind	"	69	11
Well-skill'd—The .... workman	R L	1520	They were but sweet	"	98	11
Well-tuned—the well-tuned warble	"	1080	Were it not sinful then	"	103	9
concord of well-tuned sounds	Son	8 5	For as you were when first	"	104	2
Wench—Know, gentle wench, it	"	127 3	Ere you were born	"	104	14
Went—like a foul usurper .... about	R L	412	and wish I were renew'd	"	111	8
' But tell me, girl, when went	"	1275	The ills that were not	"	118	10
going he went wilful-slow	Son	51 13	That you were once unkind	"	120	1
on this side the verdict went	L C	113	Unless my nerves were brass	"	120	4
Wept—that his wound wept	V A	1054	If you were by my unkindness			
they have wept till now	"	1062	shaken	"	120	5
Were—her cheeks were gardens	"	65	Were to import forgetfulness	"	122	14
So they were dew'd	"	66	were but the child of state	"	124	1
when her lips were ready	"	89	Were 't aught to me	"	125	1
Were I hard-favour'd	"	133	Or if it were, it bore	"	127	2

Were—			
teach thee wit, better it were	Son	140	5
If best were as it was	L C		98
His qualities were beauteous	"		99
but were all graced by him	"		119
'Many there were	"		134
were gilded in his smiling	"		172
vows were ever brokers	"		173
till then were levell'd on my face	"		282
her tears, and all were jestings	P P	7	12
were tuned like the lark	"	15	6
Were I with her	"	15	13
Juno but an Ethiop were	"	17	16
Were kisses all the joys	"	19	47
the world and love were young	"	20	17
Thou and I were both beguiled	"	21	30
'Pity but he were a king	"	21	42
But in them it were a wonder	P T		32
Simple were so well compounded	"		44
Wert—			
Would thou wert as I am	V A		369
O, what banquet wert thou	"		445
for a woman wert thou first created	Son	20	9
I grant thou wert not married	"	82	1
Thou truly fair wert truly	"	82	11
West—			
hath ended in the west	V A		530
Stealing unseen to west	Son	33	8
sunset fadeth in the west	"	73	6
glory to the sober west	"	132	8
Wet—			
making her cheeks all wet	V A		83
make them wet again	"		966
To wet his eyes	"		1179
with swelling drops 'gan wet	R L		1228
how listening Priam wets his eyes	"		1548
to wet a widow's eye	Son	9	1
applying wet to wet	L C		40
Wether—			
My wether's bell rings	P P	18	28
What—			
What follows more	V A		54
what she did crave	"		88
What see'st thou	"		118
know not what we mean	"		126
What bare excuses	"		188
What 'tis to love	"		202
'What am I	"		205
Or what great danger	"		206
What were thy lips	"		207
what needs a second striking	"		250
what shall she say	"		253
what he was controlled with	"		270
What recketh he	"		283
What cares he now	"		285
what a horse should have	"		299
O, what a sight it was	"		343
O, what a war of looks	"		355
'What! canst thou talk	"		427
what banquet wert thou	"		445
What hour is this	"		495
What bargains may I make	"		512
What is ten hundred	"		519
Paying what ransom	"		550
What wax so frozen	"		565
What though the rose	"		574
thou know'st not what	"		615
'What should I do	"		667
and with what care	"		681
'Why, what of that	"		717
'What is thy body	"		757
'What have you urged	"		787
what dost thou mean	"		953
What may a heavy groan	"		950
what treasure hast thou lost	"		1075

What—			
What face remains	V A		1076
what canst thou boast	"		1077
What priceless wealth	R L		17
What needeth then apologies	"		31
That what they have not	"		135
What following sorrow	"		186
'What win I	"		211
Or what fond beggar	"		216
'O what excuse	"		225
That what is vile	"		252
What could he see	"		414
What did he note	"		415
What he beheld	"		416
What terror 'tis	"		453
Under what colour	"		476
'I see what crosses	"		491
I know what thorns	"		492
on what he looks	"		497
What wrong, what shame, what sorrow I shall breed	"		499
marking what he tells	"		510
what thou seem'st	"		600
what thou art	"		601
What darest thou not	"		606
what he would lose again	"		688
what helpless shame	"		756
To cipher what is writ	"		811
What virtue breeds	"		872
what he hath said	"		915
what's done by night	"		1092
'alack, what were it	"		1156
What legacy shall I bequeath	"		1192
'on what occasion break	"		1270
What should I say	"		1291
What wit sets down	"		1299
Ulysses, O, what art	"		1394
Of what she was	"		1453
What uncouth ill event	"		1598
Sweet love, what spite	"		1600
And what wrong else	"		1622
What he breathes out	"		1666
From what is past	"		1683
What is the quality	"		1702
can see what once I was	"		1764
distinguish what he said	"		1785
What acceptable audit	Son	4	12
remembrance what it was	"	5	12
Then what could death do	"	6	11
Look, what an unthrift	"	9	9
what silent love	"	23	13
Now see what good turns	"	24	9
They draw but what they see	"	24	14
With what I most enjoy	"	29	8
Look, what is best	"	37	13
What can mine own praise	"	39	3
And what is't but mine	"	39	4
O absence, what a torment	"	39	9
What hast thou then	"	40	2
taste of what thyself refusest	"	40	8
what woman's son	"	41	7
When what I seek	"	50	2
O, what excuse will my poor beast	"	51	5
What is your substance	"	53	1
what should I do	"	57	1
To what you will	"	58	11
what the old world could say	"	59	9
Or what strong hand	"	65	11
to show what wealth	"	67	13
what beauty was of yore	"	68	14

What—What merit lived in me	Son	72	2	What—What though she strive	PP	19	19
Save what is had	"	75	12	what parts can so remain	PT	.....	48
what is already spent	"	76	12	Whate'er—whate'er is in his way	VA	.....	623
still telling what is told	"	76	14	And do whate'er thou wilt	Son	19	6
Look, what thy memory	"	77	9	Whate'er thy thoughts	"	93	11
Yet what of thee	"	79	7	Whatsoever—Till whatsoever star	"	26	9
what in thee doth live	"	79	12	Wheel—giddy round of Fortune's			
Since what he owes	"	79	14	wheel	RL	.....	952
What strained touches	"	82	10	When—But when her lips	VA	.....	89
what worth in you doth grow	"	83	8	when thou thyself art dead	"	.....	172
what in you is writ	"	84	9	when they blot the sky	"	.....	184
what nature made	"	84	10	And when from thence	"	.....	227
O, what a happy title	"	92	11	Look, when a painter	"	.....	289
But what's so blessed-fair	"	92	13	When, lo, the unback'd breeder	"	.....	320
O, in what sweets	"	95	4	When it is barr'd	"	.....	330
O, what a mansion	"	95	9	When the heart's attorney	"	.....	335
What freezings have I felt, what				when he saw his love	"	.....	393
dark days seen	"	97	3	But, when his glutton eye	"	.....	399
What old December's bareness	"	97	4	when in his fresh array	"	.....	483
what shall be thy amends	"	101	1	when most his choice	"	.....	570
Alack, what poverty	"	103	1	When he did frown	"	.....	571
What's in the brain	"	108	1	shine when he doth fret	"	.....	621
What's new to speak, what new				When thou didst name	"	.....	641
to register	"	108	3	And when thou hast on foot	"	.....	679
sold cheap what is most dear	"	110	3	When reason is the bawd	"	.....	792
have what shall have no end	"	110	9	when their captain once	"	.....	893
To what it works in	"	111	7	When he hath ceased	"	.....	919
For what care I	"	112	3	Who when he lived	"	.....	953
what it doth catch	"	113	8	when she seemeth drown'd	"	.....	984
what with his gust is 'greeing	"	114	11	When as I met the boar	"	.....	999
What potions have I drunk	"	119	1	As when the wind	"	.....	1046
What wretched errors	"	119	5	But when Adonis lived	"	.....	1083
what I think good	"	121	8	When he hath sung	"	.....	1095
What thou dost foist	"	123	6	When he beheld his shadow	"	.....	1099
what we see doth lie	"	123	11	When he was by	"	.....	1101
what dost thou	"	137	1	when it seems most just	"	.....	1136
see not what they see	"	137	2	When Collatine unwisely	RL	.....	10
They know what beauty is	"	137	3	When at Collatium	"	.....	50
Yet what the best is	"	137	4	When virtue bragg'd	"	.....	54
What need'st thou wound	"	139	7	When beauty boasted blushes	"	.....	55
that loves what they despise	"	141	3	When shame assail'd	"	.....	63
what thou dost hide	"	142	13	And when great treasure	"	.....	132
what eyes hath Love	"	148	1	When shall he think	"	.....	159
what they see aright	"	148	4	When he himself	"	.....	160
What means the world	"	148	6	When heavy sleep	"	.....	163
What merit do I	"	149	9	When thou shalt charge me	"	.....	226
O, from what power	"	150	1	when beauty pleadeth	"	.....	268
what others do abhor	"	150	11	And when his gaudy banner	"	.....	272
to know what conscience is	"	151	1	But when a black-faced cloud	"	.....	547
what contents it bears	LC	.....	19	When thus thy vices	"	.....	604
What unapproved witness	"	.....	53	when once thou art	"	.....	606
What's sweet to do	"	.....	88	When they in thee	"	.....	613
What largeness thinks in Paradise	"	.....	91	When, pattern'd by thy fault	"	.....	629
What rounds, what bounds, what				When must unseen	"	.....	676
course, what stop he makes	"	.....	109	and when that decays	"	.....	713
for him what he would say	"	.....	132	When virtue is profaned	"	.....	847
What with his art in youth	"	.....	145	when he cannot use it	"	.....	862
what will not stay	"	.....	159	when temperance is thaw'd	"	.....	884
what tributes wounded fancies	"	.....	197	'When wilt thou be	"	.....	897
What me your minister	"	.....	229	When wilt thou sort an hour	"	.....	899
what labour is't to leave	"	.....	239	'When Truth and Virtue	"	.....	911
mastering what not strives	"	.....	240	When Tarquin did	"	.....	917
what are precepts worth	"	.....	267	when they list	"	.....	1008
what a hell of witchcraft lies	"	.....	288	But when I fear'd	"	.....	1048
What rocky heart	"	.....	291	when lo, the blushing morrow	"	.....	1082
What breast so cold	"	.....	292	When with like semblance	"	.....	1113
What I should do again	"	.....	322	when time is kept with tears	"	.....	1127
what fool is not so wise	PP	3	13	When life is shamed	"	.....	1153
What though her frowning brows	"	19	13	when death takes one	"	.....	1191

When—When the one pure, the other	R L	....	1164	When—But when my glass	Son	62	9
When both were kept for heaven	"	....	1166	When hours have drain'd	"	63	3
when sadly she had laid	"	....	1212	when his youthful morn	"	63	4
when sun doth melt their snow	"	....	1218	When I have seen	"	64	1
But tell me, girl, when went	"	....	1275	When sometime lofty towers	"	64	3
When more is felt	"	....	1288	When I have seen the hungry	"	64	5
when he is by to hear her	"	....	1318	When I have seen such interchange	"	64	9
When sighs and groans	"	....	1319	When rocks impregnable	"	65	7
When every part a part of woe	"	....	1327	When beauty lived	"	68	2
When, silly groom! Got wot	"	....	1343	for me when I am dead	"	71	1
When their brave hope	"	....	1430	When I perhaps compounded am	"	71	10
When their glass fell	"	....	1526	When yellow leaves	"	73	2
Which when her sad-beholding	"	....	1590	when that fell arrest	"	74	1
And when the judge is robb'd	"	....	1652	When thou reviewest	"	74	5
when I might charm thee so	"	....	1684	when I of you do write	"	80	1
When they had sworn	"	....	1849	when I in earth am rotten	"	81	2
When forty winters	Son	2	1	When you entombed in men's eyes	"	81	8
when thou art old	"	2	13	When all the breathers	"	81	12
when thou feel'st it cold	"	2	14	when they have devised	"	82	9
when nature calls thee	"	4	11	When others would give life	"	83	12
when the gracious light	"	7	1	But when your countenance	"	86	13
But when from highmost pitch	"	7	9	When thou shalt be disposed	"	88	1
When every private widow	"	9	7	hate me when thou wilt	"	90	1
when thou from youth	"	11	4	when my heart hath 'scaped	"	90	5
When I do count the clock	"	12	1	When other petty griefs	"	90	10
When I behold the violet	"	12	3	When in the least	"	92	6
When lofty trees I see	"	12	5	When proud-pied April	"	98	2
when he takes thee hence	"	12	14	When I was wont to greet	"	102	6
When your sweet issue	"	13	8	when her mournful hymns	"	102	10
When I consider every thing	"	15	1	when it hath my added praise	"	103	4
When I perceive that men	"	15	5	when you look in it	"	103	14
When in eternal lines	"	18	12	when first your eye	"	104	2
But when in thee	"	22	3	When in the chronicle	"	106	1
when mine is slain	"	22	13	When tyrants' crests	"	107	14
when body's work's expired	"	27	4	when first I hallow'd	"	108	8
When day's oppression	"	28	3	When I was certain	"	115	11
when clouds do blot	"	28	10	when it alteration finds	"	116	3
When sparkling stars	"	28	12	sickness when we purge	"	118	4
When, in disgrace	"	29	1	when I saw myself to win	"	119	4
When to the sessions	"	30	1	when it is built	"	119	11
When that churl Death	"	32	2	When not to be receives	"	121	2
when heaven's sun staineth	"	33	14	When most impeach'd stands least	"	125	14
When thou thyself	"	38	6	when thou, my music	"	128	1
When thou art all	"	39	2	when thou gently sway'st	"	128	3
when I praise thee	"	39	4	My mistress, when she walks	"	130	12
When I am sometime absent	"	41	1	When my love swears	"	138	1
And when a woman woos	"	41	7	when thy might	"	139	7
When most I wink	"	43	1	when their deaths be near	"	140	7
But when I sleep	"	43	3	that, when it grows	"	142	11
When to unseeing eyes	"	43	8	But when she saw	"	145	4
When in dead night	"	43	11	When I against myself	"	149	2
when dreams do show	"	43	14	think on thee, when I forgot	"	149	3
when thou art gone	"	44	10	When all my best	"	149	11
For when these quicker	"	45	5	When I break twenty	"	152	6
When that mine eye	"	47	3	When he again desires her	L C	....	66
when I took my way	"	48	1	And when in his fair parts	"	....	83
When I shall see	"	49	2	When winds breathe sweet	"	....	103
When as thy love hath cast	"	49	3	For when we rage	"	....	160
when thou shalt strangely pass	"	49	5	when they to assail begun	"	....	262
When love, converted	"	49	7	When thou impressest	"	....	267
When what I seek	"	50	2	When thou wilt inflame	"	....	268
when from thee I speed	"	51	2	When he most burn'd	"	....	314
When swift extremity	"	51	6	When my love swears	P P	1	1
When summer's breath	"	54	8	When Cytherea, all in love	"	6	3
When that shall vade	"	54	14	When as himself to singing he betakes	"	8	12
When wasteful war shall statues	"	55	5	when the fair queen of love	"	9	1
that, when they see	"	56	11	When first it 'gins to bud	"	13	3
When you have bid	"	57	8	When as thine eye hath chose	"	19	1

WHEN 346 WHEREIN

Entry	Work	Page	Line
When—And when thou comest	P P	19	7
When craft hath taught her	"	19	22
When time shall serve	"	19	35
When time with age	"	19	46
Whence—From whence at pleasure	Son	48	12
whence didst thou steal	"	99	2
Whence hast thou this	"	150	5
Where—where never serpent hisses	V A	.....	17
And where she ends she doth	"	.....	60
conquers where he comes	"	.....	100
where there are but twain	"	.....	123
where I list to sport me	"	.....	154
For, where they lay	"	.....	176
Feed where thou wilt	"	.....	232
where the pleasant fountains lie	"	.....	234
For where a heart is hard	"	.....	426
'O, where am I	"	.....	493
For where Love reigns	"	.....	649
where earth-delving conies keep	"	.....	687
'Where did I leave?' 'No matter where	"	.....	715
Where fearfully the dogs	"	.....	886
where they view'd each other's	"	.....	963
Where they resign their office	"	.....	1039
where no breach should be	"	.....	1066
Where, lo, two lamps	"	.....	1128
where herself herself beheld	"	.....	1129
where is no cause of fear	"	.....	1153
where it should most mistrust	"	.....	1154
where it shows most toward	"	.....	1157
to Paphos, where their queen	"	.....	1193
Where mortal stars, as bright	R L	.....	13
Where, lest between them both	"	.....	74
Then where is truth	"	.....	158
Where her beloved Collatinus lies	"	.....	256
where such treasure lies	"	.....	280
from the rushes where it lies	"	.....	318
Where, like a virtuous monument	"	.....	391
Where their dear governess	"	.....	443
Where thou with patience	"	.....	486
In a wilderness where are no laws	"	.....	544
Where subjects' eyes do learn	"	.....	616
school where Lust shall learn	"	.....	617
where it may find	"	.....	760
'Where now I have	"	.....	792
where the sweet birds sing	"	.....	871
where he the lamb may get	"	.....	878
where none may spy him	"	.....	881
where his suit may be obtained	"	.....	898
Debate where leisure serves	"	.....	1019
where it lay	"	.....	1057
where she sits weeping	"	.....	1087
where hangs a piece	"	.....	1366
of Dardan, where they fought	"	.....	1436
a face where all distress is still'd	"	.....	1441
where cares have carved some	"	.....	1445
But none where all distress	"	.....	1446
Where no excuse can give	"	.....	1611
Where thou wast wont	"	.....	1621
where you did fulfil	"	.....	1635
prison where it breathed	"	.....	1726
Where shall I live	"	.....	1754
where abundance lies	Son	1	7
where all thy beauty lies	"	2	5
Where all the treasure	"	2	6
For where is she	"	3	5
where every eye doth dwell	"	5	2
bareness every where	"	5	8
where wasteful Time	"	15	11
Where—where your true image	Son	24	6
Where I may not remove	"	25	14
where thou mayst prove me	"	26	14
from far where I abide	"	27	5
where buried love doth live	"	31	9
follows where thou art	"	41	4
Where thou art forced	"	41	12
where thou dost stay	"	44	4
where he would be	"	44	8
Save where thou art not	"	48	10
From where thou art	"	51	3
where two contracted new	"	56	10
Where you may be	"	57	10
Save, where you are	"	57	12
Be where you list	"	58	9
meditation! where, alack	"	65	9
buried where my body is	"	72	11
where late the sweet birds sang	"	73	4
and where they did proceed	"	76	8
Where breath most breathes	"	81	14
Where cheeks need blood	"	82	14
where your equal grew	"	84	4
admired every where	"	84	12
where is my deserving	"	87	6
Where beauty's veil	"	95	11
December's bareness every where	"	97	4
where they grew	"	98	8
Where art thou, Muse	"	100	1
Time's spoils despised every where	"	100	12
tongue doth publish every where	"	102	4
Where time and outward form	"	108	14
see where it lies	"	137	3
where all men ride	"	137	6
where is my judgement	"	148	3
Where Cupid got new fire	"	153	14
Where want cries some, but where excess begs all	L C	.....	42
following where he haunted	"	.....	130
Heard where his plants	"	.....	171
Where neither party is	"	.....	186
where I myself must render	"	.....	221
Where all those pleasures live	P P	5	6
A brook where Adon used	"	6	6
Where her faith was firmly fix'd	"	18	11
Where thy desert may merit	"	19	27
Whereas—bounced in, ... he stood	"	6	13
Whereat—whereat a sudden pale	V A	.....	589
Whereat the impartial gazer	"	.....	748
Whereat amazed, as one	"	.....	823
whereat it groans	"	.....	829
Whereat she starts	"	.....	878
Whereat her tears began	"	.....	979
Whereat she leaps	"	.....	1026
Whereat each tributary	"	.....	1045
Whereat a waxen torch	R L	.....	178
Whereat she smiled	"	.....	264
Wherefore—But .... do not you	Son	16	1
Ah, wherefore with infection	"	67	1
But wherefore says she not	"	138	9
And wherefore say not I	"	138	10
But wherefore says my love	P P	1	9
And wherefore say not I	"	1	10
Wherein—Wherein she framed thee	V A	.....	734
wherein they late excell'd	"	.....	1134
Wherein I will not kiss	"	.....	1188
wherein her needle sticks	R L	.....	317
wherein it shall discern	"	.....	619
wherein by nature they delight	"	.....	697
Wherein is stamp'd	"	.....	1246

Wherein—wherein they view'd their faces	R L	1526
Wherein deep policy	"	1815
the frame wherein 'tis held	Son 24	3
the womb wherein they grew	" 86	4
wherein I am attainted	" 88	7
Wherein it finds a joy	" 91	6
Wherein I should	" 117	2
Whereof—The fear whereof	V A	880
The spots whereof could weeping purify	R L	685
whereof in Lucrece' view	"	1261
whereof are you made	Son 53	1
whereof now he's king	" 63	6
Whereon—violets whereon we lean	V A	125
primrose bank whereon I lie	"	151
Whereon they surfeit	"	544
whereon thou dost lie	"	646
Whereon with fearful eyes	"	927
Whereon the stars	Son 15	4
whereon it must expire	" 73	11
whereon my false eyes dote	" 148	5
Whereon the thought	L C	10
Wheresoe'er—wheresoe'er they fly	R L	1014
Where-through—.... the sun	Son 24	11
Whereto—Whereto all bonds do tie me	" 117	4
Whereto the inviting time	" 124	8
Whereto the judgement	" 137	8
Whereto his invised properties	L C	212
Whereupon—whereupon it gazeth	Son 20	6
Whereupon it made this threne	P T	49
Wherever—where'er he goes	V A	622
wherever I abide	Son 45	2
Wherewith—.... being crown'd	" 60	6
hast wherewith to spend	P P 21	36
Whet—did not whet his teeth	V A	1113
Whether—And whe'r he run or fly they know not whether	"	304
Whether it is that she	R L	376
For whether beauty, birth	Son 37	5
Whether we are mended, or whether better they	" 39	11
Or whether revolution be	" 59	12
Or whether doth my mind	" 114	1
Or whether shall I say	" 114	3
And whether that my angel	" 144	9
Whether the horse by him	L C	111
And whether that my angel	P P 2	9
But whether unripe years	" 4	9
or a lecher whether	" 7	17
nill I construe whether	" 14	8
Whetteth—he whetteth still	V A	617
Which—Which bred more beauty	"	70
Which long have rain'd	"	83
that which thou unask'd shalt have	"	102
which way shall she turn	"	253
His eye, which scornfully glisters	"	275
tears, which chorus-like her eyes	"	360
Which to his speech	"	452
Which cunning love	"	471
hers, which through the crystal tears	"	491
Which purchase if thou make	"	515
The which, by Cupid's bow	"	581
effects which she in him finds missing	"	605
To which Love's eyes	"	632
fox which lives by subtlety	"	675
roe which no encounter dare	"	676
Which—through the which he goes	V A	683
Which by the rights of time	"	759
Which the hot tyrant	"	797
arms which bound him to her breast	"	812
Which after him she darts	"	817
Through which it enters	"	890
Which madly hurries her	"	904
Which her cheek melts	"	982
Which knows no pity	"	1000
Which seen, her eyes	"	1031
Which with cold terror	"	1048
Which in round drops	"	1170
sap, which she compares	"	1176
Which in pale embers hid	R L	5
Which triumph'd in that sky	"	12
that which is so singular	"	32
hap which their superiors want	"	42
coal which in his liver glows	"	47
Which of them both	"	53
Which virtue gave	"	60
Which Tarquin view'd	"	72
Which far exceeds	"	81
praise which Collatine doth owe	"	82
Which, having all	"	96
As one of which	"	127
that which they possess	"	135
for that which we expect	"	149
Which must be lode-star	"	179
that which is divine	"	193
Which in a moment	"	250
Which struck her sad, and then	"	262
Both which, as servitors	"	285
That eye which looks	"	290
That eye which him beholds	"	291
Which once corrupted	"	294
Which drives the creeping thief heart, which fond desire	"	305
	"	314
bars which stop the hourly dial	"	327
Which with a yielding latch	"	339
Which gives the watch-word	"	370
His eye, which late this mutiny restrains	"	426
The sight which makes	"	453
Which he by dumb demeanour	"	474
Which I to conquer sought	"	488
Which like a falcon	"	506
Which blows these pitchy vapours	"	550
Which to her oratory	"	564
'All which together, like a	"	589
Which in her prescience	"	727
disgrace which they themselves behold	"	751
Which underneath thy black faults which in thy reign	"	801
	"	804
Which not themselves	"	833
honey which thy chaste bee kept	"	840
that soul which wretchedness hath chained	"	909
Which thronging through her lips	"	1041
Or that which from discharged cannon fumes	"	1043
that is gone for which I sought	"	1051
determining which way to fly	"	1150
which of the twain	"	1154
'My body or my soul, which was the dearer	"	1163
Through which I may convey	"	1176
Which by him tainted	"	1182
Which makes the maid weep	"	1232

Which—but that which doth devour	*R L*		1256
Throng her inventions, which shall go before	"		1302
suspicion which the world might bear	"		1321
Before the which is drawn	"		1368
Which the conceited painter	"		1371
Which heartless peasants	"		1392
breath, which purl'd up	"		1407
Which seem'd to swallow up	"		1409
Which bleeding under Pyrrhus'	"		1449
Which all this time	"		1576
Which when her sad-beholding husband saw	"		1590
Which speechless woe of his	"		1674
map which deep impression bears	"		1712
Which seems to weep	"		1746
that which is so putrified	"		1750
That life was mine which thou hast here deprived	"		1752
Which she too early	"		1801
vow, which Brutus made before	"		1847
Which being done with speedy	"		1853
Which, used, lives	*Son*	4	14
And that unfair which fairly doth excel	"	5	4
Which happies those	"	6	6
that which thou receivest	"	8	3
Which to repair should be thy	"	10	8
from that which thou departest	"	11	2
blood which youngly thou bestow'st	"	11	3
Which bounteous gift	"	11	12
Which erst from heat	"	12	6
beauty which you hold in lease	"	13	5
Which husbandry in honour	"	13	10
Which this Time's pencil	"	16	10
Which hides your life	"	17	4
Which steals men's eyes	"	20	8
Which in thy breast	"	22	7
thy heart, which I will keep	"	22	11
Which in my bosom's shop	"	24	7
forgot for which he toil'd	"	25	12
Duty so great which wit so poor	"	26	5
darkness which the blind do see	"	27	8
Which, like a jewel hung in	"	27	11
Which I new-pay	"	30	12
Which I by lacking	"	31	2
friends which I thought buried	"	31	4
As interest of the dead, which now appear	"	31	7
those tears are pearl which thy love sheds	"	34	13
at that which thou hast done	"	35	1
thief which sourly robs from me	"	35	14
Which though it alter not	"	36	7
those old nine which rhymers invocate	"	38	10
That due to thee which thou deservest	"	39	8
Which time and thoughts	"	39	12
Which heavily he answers	"	50	11
The which he will not	"	52	3
wardrobe which the robe doth hide	"	52	10
ornament which truth doth give	"	54	2
odour which doth in it live	"	54	4
Which but to-day	"	56	3
Which parts the shore	"	56	10
winter, which, being full of care	"	56	13
new, but that which is	"	59	1
Which—Which, labouring for invention	*Son*	59	3
that which goes before	"	60	3
death, which cannot choose	"	64	13
that which it fears to lose	"	64	14
that which I bring forth	"	72	13
those boughs which shake	"	73	3
Which by and by black night	"	73	7
that which it was nourish'd by	"	73	12
This thou perceivest which makes thy love	"	73	13
To love that well which thou must leave	"	73	14
Which for memorial	"	74	4
earth, which is his due	"	74	7
is that which it contains	"	74	13
The wrinkles which thy glass	"	77	5
of that which I compile	"	78	9
for that which he doth say	"	79	13
Which eyes not yet created	"	81	10
words which writers use	"	82	3
Which shall be most my glory	"	83	10
most? which can say more	"	84	1
Which should example where your praise, which makes your praises worse	"	84	4
	"	84	14
Which nightly gulls him	"	86	10
strains of woe, which now seem woe	"	90	13
that which on thy humour	"	92	8
Which, like a cauker	"	95	2
Which for their habitation	"	95	10
Which on thy soft cheek	"	99	4
that which gives thee all thy might	"	100	2
Since first I saw you fresh, which yet are green	"	104	8
hue, which methinks still doth stand	"	104	11
For fear of which	"	104	13
Three themes in one, which wondrous scope affords	"	105	12
Which three till now	"	105	14
For we, which now behold	"	106	13
Which hath not figured	"	108	2
soul, which in thy breast doth lie	"	109	4
means which public manners breeds	"	111	4
Which vulgar scandal	"	112	2
And that which governs me	"	113	2
or shape, which it doth latch	"	113	6
to that which still doth grow	"	115	14
Which alters when it alteration	"	116	3
Which should transport me	"	117	8
Which, rank of goodness	"	118	12
that sorrow which I then did feel	"	120	2
salve which wounded bosoms fits	"	120	12
pleasure lost, wĺıch is so deem'd	"	121	3
Which in their wills	"	121	8
Which shall above that	"	122	3
Which works on leases	"	124	10
Which die for goodness	"	124	14
Which prove more short	"	125	4
Which is not mix'd	"	125	11
lips, which should that harvest	"	128	7
Which my heart knows	"	137	10
that which flies before	"	143	7
that which flies from thee	"	143	9
Which like two spirits	"	144	2
For that which longer nurseth	"	147	2
that which doth preserve	"	147	3
Desire is death, which physic did except	"	147	8

WHICH 349 WHO

Which—Which have no correspondence	Son	148 2
Which borrow'd from this holy fire	"	153 5
a seething bath which yet men prove	"	153 7
Which many legions	"	154 6
Which from Love's fire	"	154 10
Which fortified her visage	L C	9
Which on it had	"	16
Which one by one	"	38
Which she perused	"	44
Which may her suffering objects which abroad they find	"	69
	"	137
landlord which doth owe them	"	140
proofs new-bleeding, which remain'd the foil	"	153
Which late her noble suit	"	234
the place which did no form receive	"	241
accident which brought me to her eye	"	247
water which their hue encloses	"	287
heart which in his level came	"	309
Which, like a cherubin	"	319
fire which in his cheek so glow'd	"	324
Which is to me some praise	P P	5 10
Which, not to anger bent	"	5 12
Which by a gift of learning	"	16 14
That which with scorn	"	19 18
Which a grove of myrtles made	"	21 4
While—While she takes all	V A	564
while now it sleeps alone	"	786
While lust and murder wakes	R L	168
winks while Orpheus plays	"	553
While in his hold-fast foot	"	555
While Lust is in his pride	"	703
dies while the physician sleeps	"	904
pines while the oppressor feeds	"	905
feasting while the widow weeps	"	906
sporting while infection breeds	"	907
While thou on Tereus descant'st	"	1134
while others saucily	"	1348
While Collatine and his consorted lords	"	1609
While with a joyless smile	"	1711
While thou dost breathe	Son	38 2
While shadows like to thee	"	61 4
While comments of your praise	"	85 2
Now, while the world is bent	"	90 2
While he insults	"	107 12
While Philomela sits and sings	P P	15 5
While—in a breathing-while	V A	1142
A pretty while these pretty creatures stand	R L	1233
a little while doth stay	"	1364
came in her mind the while	"	1536
But if the while I think	Son	30 13
Whiles—And whiles against a thorn	R L	1135
Whilst—Whilst I, whom fortune	Son	25 3
Whilst that this shadow	"	37 10
Whilst I, my sovereign, watch	"	57 6
whilst thou dost wake elsewhere	"	61 13
Whilst I alone did call	"	79 1
Whilst he upon your	"	80 10
whilst other write good words	"	85 5
Whilst, like a willing patient	"	111 9
Whilst it hath thought	"	119 6
Whilst my poor lips	"	128 7
Whilst her neglected child	"	143 5
Whilst I thy babe	"	143 10
Whilst—Whilst many nymphs	Son	154 3
Whilst as fickle Fortune	P P	21 29
Whilst thou hast wherewith	"	21 36
Whirlwind—My sighs, like whirlwinds	R L	586
Whisper—whispers in mine ear	V A	659
She whispers in his ear	"	1125
Whispering—.... conspirator	R L	769
Whit—my love no whit disdaineth	Son	33 13
White—More white and red	V A	10
best; and being white	"	77
How white and red	"	316
So white a friend engirts so white a foe	"	364
a whiter hue than white	"	398
was it not white	"	643
whose wonted lily white	"	1053
chequer'd with white	"	1168
clear unmatched red and white	R L	11
stain that o'er with silver-white	"	56
in that white intituled	"	57
the red should fence the white	"	63
beauty's red and virtue's white	"	65
love's modest snow-white weed	"	196
Then white as lawn	"	259
coverlet; whose perfect white	"	394
her snow-white dimpled chin	"	420
Who o'er the white sheet	"	472
Like a white hind	"	542
Till with her own white fleece	"	678
like the snow-white swan	"	1011
his beard all silver-white	"	1405
all silver'd o'er with white	Son	12 4
with white and bristly beard	"	12 8
wonder at the lily's white	"	98 9
shame, another white despair	"	99 9
A third, nor red, nor white	"	99 10
If snow be white	"	130 3
roses damask'd red and white	"	130 5
In bloodless white	L C	201
Whose white weighs down	"	226
There my white stole of chastity	"	297
Or to turn white and swound	"	308
than her milk-white dove	P P	9 3
Let the priest in surplice white	P T	13
Whiteness—upon their .... stood	V A	1170
Whiter—a whiter hue than white	"	398
peers her whiter chin	R L	472
Whither—she knows not whither	V A	904
Who—Who blush'd and pouted	"	33
Who, being looked on	"	87
Who conquers where he comes	"	100
As who should say	"	280
hairs, who wave like feather'd wings	"	306
Who sees his true-love	"	397
Who is so faint	"	401
Who wears a garment	"	415
Who plucks the bud	"	416
For who hath she	"	817
Who doth the world	"	857
Who shall cope him first	"	888
Who, overcome by doubt	"	891
Who when he lived	"	935
eyelids, who, like sluices, stopp'd	"	956
As striving who should best become	"	968
Who is but drunken	"	984
To wail his death who lives and	"	1017
Who bids them still	"	1041

Who—Who, like a king	V A	1043
They both would strive who first should dry his tears	"	1092
Who did not whet his teeth	"	1113
Who buys a minute's mirth	R L	213
who will the vine destroy	"	215
Who fears a sentence	"	244
Then who fears sinking	"	280
Who, flatter'd by their leader's	"	296
As who should say	"	320
Who with a lingering stay	"	328
Who sees the lurking serpent	"	362
Who, therefore angry	"	388
Who, like a foul usurper	"	412
Who, peeping forth	"	447
Who, angry that the eyes	"	461
Who o'er the white sheet	"	472
Who seek to stain	"	655
Who this accomplishment	"	716
Who in their pride	"	864
For who so base	"	1000
He shall not boast who did thy stock pollute	"	1063
Who wayward once, his mood	"	1095
Who, being stopp'd	"	1119
Who, if it wink	"	1139
Who, having two sweet babes	"	1161
Who in a salt-waved ocean	"	1231
And who cannot abuse	"	1267
Who nothing wants	"	1459
And who she finds forlorn	"	1500
Who finds his Lucrece	"	1585
Who, like a late-sack'd island	"	1740
Who, mad that sorrow	"	1781
Who should weep most	"	1792
air, who, holding Lucrece' life	"	1805
Brutus, who pluck'd the knife	"	1807
Who, wondering at him	"	1845
Or who is he so fond	Son	3 7
chide thee, who confounds	"	8 7
Who, all in one	"	8 12
Who for thyself	"	10 2
Who lets so fair a house	"	13 9
Who will believe my verse	"	17 1
Who heaven itself	"	21 3
Who with his fear is put besides	"	23 2
Who plead for love	"	23 11
Let those who are in favour	"	25 1
Who all their parts of me	"	31 11
For who's so dumb	"	38 7
him here who doth hence remain	"	39 14
Who lead thee in their riot	"	41 11
Who even but now come back	"	45 11
Or who his spoil of beauty	"	65 12
Who is it that says most	"	84 1
Who, moving others, are	"	94 3
what care I who calls me	"	112 3
who have lived for crime	"	124 14
lovely boy, who in thy power	"	126 1
Who hast thy waning grown	"	126 3
At such who, not born fair	"	127 11
Who, in despite of view	"	141 4
Who leaves unsway'd	"	141 11
night, who like a fiend	"	145 11
Who art as black as hell	"	147 14
Who hateth thee	"	149 5
Who taught thee how to make	"	150 9
Yet who knows not conscience	"	151 2
who ever shunn'd by precedent	L C	155
Who—Who disciplined, ay, dieted	L C	261
Who glazed with crystal gate	"	286
Who, young and simple	"	630
Whoever—Whoever plots the sin	R L	879
Whoe'er keeps me, let my heart	Son 133	11
Whoever hath her wish	" 135	1
Whole—My heart all whole as thine	V A	370
whose whole is swallow'd	R L	1139
Stood for the whole	"	1428
He pays the whole, and yet am I	Son 134	14
Whom—And whom he strikes	V A	624
part; through whom he rushes	"	630
From whom each lamp	"	861
To whom she speaks	"	918
The powers to whom I pray	R L	349
To whom she sobbing speaks	"	1086
by whom thy fair wife bleeds	"	1824
Let those whom Nature	Son 11	9
Look, whom she best endow'd	" 11	11
Whilst I, whom fortune	" 25	3
my love, to whom in vassalage	" 26	1
in whom all ill well shows	" 40	13
to whom my jewels trifles are	" 48	5
Or me, to whom thou gavest it	" 87	10
him whom thou dost hate	" 89	14
to whom I am confined	" 110	12
O'er whom thy fingers walk	" 128	10
Whom thine eyes woo	" 142	10
On whom frown'st thou	" 149	6
did win whom he would maim	L C	312
'Gainst whom the world	P P 3	2
Thou for whom Jove would swear	" 17	15
Whose—Whose sinewy neck	V A	99
breath, whose gentle wind	"	189
Whose hollow womb resounds	"	268
Whose beams upon his hairless	"	487
Whose precious taste	"	543
Whose vulture thought	"	551
love, whose leave exceeds	"	568
Whose tushes never sheathed	"	617
Whose full perfection	"	634
Under whose sharp fangs	"	663
Whose blood upon the fresh sickness, whose attaint	"	665 741
theirs whose desperate hands	"	765
Under whose simple semblance	"	795
Whose ridges with the meeting	"	820
from whose silver breast	"	855
whose swelling dugs do ache	"	875
Whose frothy mouth	"	901
whose tender horns being hit	"	1033
flank; whose wonted lily white	"	1053
Whose tongue is music now	"	1077
Under whose brim	"	1088
Whose downward eye	"	1106
doves, by whose swift aid	"	1190
Within whose face	R L	52
Whose inward ill	"	91
her whose light excelleth thine	"	191
Whose crime will bear	"	224
Between whose hills	"	390
coverlet; whose perfect white	"	394
Whose ranks of blue veins	"	440
Whose grim aspect sets every	"	452
Whose crooked beak threats	"	508
To whose weak ruins muster troops	"	720
Then they whose whole is	" "	1159
Whose love of either	"	1165
By whose example	"	1194

WHOSE					WILD		
Whose—Whose swift obedience to her mistress hies		R L	1215	Why—why hear'st thou music sadly	Son	8	1
But they whose guilt		"	1342	Why lovest thou that which	"	8	3
Whose waves to imitate		"	1438	Why didst thou promise	"	34	1
Sinon, whose enchanting story		"	1521	Since why to love	"	49	14
Whose words, like wildfire		"	1523	why should I haste me thence	"	51	3
Whose deed hath made herself		"	1566	Why should false painting	"	67	5
Whose fresh repair	Son	3	3	Why should poor beauty	"	67	7
she so fair whose uncar'd womb	"	3	5	Why should he live	"	67	9
Whose speechless song	"	8	13	But why thy colour matcheth not	"	69	13
Whose strength's abundance	"	23	4	Why is my verse so barren	"	76	1
Then thou, whose shadow	"	43	5	Why with the time do I not	"	76	3
the rich, whose blessed key	"	52	1	Why write I still all one	"	76	5
you, whose worthiness gives scope	"	52	13	my judgement knew no reason why	"	115	3
Whose action is no stronger	"	65	4	why, fearing of Time's tyranny	"	115	9
Whose influence is thine	"	78	10	For why should others' false adulterate eyes	"	121	5
In whose confine immured	"	84	3	why are frailer spies	"	121	7
my thought, whose love to you	"	85	11	why then her breasts are dun	"	130	3
That love is merchandized whose rich esteeming	"	102	3	Why of eyes' falsehood	"	137	7
Time, whose million'd accidents	"	115	5	Why should my heart think	"	137	9
Whose worth's unknown	"	116	8	Why dost thou pine within	"	146	3
wood whose motion sounds	"	128	2	Why so large cost	"	146	5
As those whose beauties	"	131	2	why of two oaths' breach	"	152	5
Wilt thou, whose will	"	135	5	why 'twas beautiful and hard	L C		211
her whose busy care is bent	"	143	6	' why was not I a flood	P P	6	14
for whose dear love I rise	"	151	14	For why thou left'st me	"	10	8
a hill whose concave womb	L C		1	For why I craved nothing	"	10	10
Upon whose weeping margent	"		39	For why she sigh'd	"	15	12
Whose bare out-bragg'd the web	"		95	Wicked—to scratch her wicked foe	R L		1035
Not one whose flame	"		191	should bear a wicked mind	"		1540
emerald, in whose fresh regard	"		213	Wickedly—wickedly he stalks	"		365
Whose white weighs down	"		226	Wide—small head and nostril wide	V A		296
Whose rarest havings	"		235	Upon the wide wound	"		1052
Whose sights till then were	"		282	the door he opens wide	R L		359
to thee is dear, whose heavenly touch	P P	8	5	To the wide world	Son	19	7
whose deep conceit is such	"	8	7	my drooping eyelids open wide	"	27	7
Love, whose month was ever May	"	17	2	wide as the ocean is	"	80	5
By shallow rivers by whose falls	"	20	7	Of the wide world	"	107	2
To whose sound chaste wings	P T		4	this wide universe I call	"	109	13
Why—why art thou coy	V A		96	the wide world's common place	"	137	10
why not lips on lips	"		120	though thy proud heart go wide	"	140	14
why dost abhor me	"		138	Widow—while the widow weeps	R L		906
why shouldst thou feed	"		169	to wet a widow's eye	Son	9	1
Why, there Love lived	"		246	The world will be thy widow	"	9	5
' why dost thou feel it	"		373	When every private widow	"	9	7
'Why, what of that	"		717	Widow'd—Like widow'd wombs	"	97	8
Why hast thou cast	"		951	Wield—youthful sons bright weapons wield	R L		1432
why then I know	"		1109	Wife—to work upon his wife	"		235
Or why is Collatine	R L		33	I was a loyal wife	"		1048
'Why hunt I then for colour	"		267	Of that unworthy wife	"		1304
'Why should the worm intrude	"		848	slaughter'd husband by the wife	"		1376
'Why hath thy servant	"		932	for daughter or for wife	"		1792
'Why work'st thou mischief	"		960	quoth Collatine, 'she was my wife	"		1802
why quiver'st thou at this	"		1030	'My daughter' and 'my wife	"		1804
Why pry'st thou through	"		1089	'my daughter' and 'my wife	"		1806
For why her face	"		1222	by whom thy fair wife bleeds	"		1824
Why her two suns	"		1224	Thy wretched wife mistook	"		1826
Nor why her fair cheeks	"		1225	the death of this true wife	"		1841
Why should the private pleasure	"		1478	like a makeless wife	Son	9	4
why should so many fall	"		1483	Wight—descriptions of the fairest wights	"	106	2
Priam, why art thou old	"		1550	As well as fancy, partial wight	P P	19	4
Why art thou thus attired	"		1601	Wild—Like a wild bird	V A		560
And why not I from this	"		1708	Till the wild waves	"		819
'Why, Collatine, is woe the cure	"		1821	the unicorn and lion wild	R L		956
why dost thou spend	Son	4	1	tames the one; the other wild	"		1097
niggard, why dost thou abuse	"	4	5	But that wild music	Son	102	11
usurer, why dost thou use	"	4	7	a youngster proud and wild	P P	9	4

Wild—Youth is wild, and age is tame	*P P*	12	8
Wilder—Wilder to him than tigers	*R L*	....	980
Wilderness—Pleads, in a wilderness	"	....	544
Wildfire—Whose words like wildfire	"	....	1523
Wildly—She wildly breaketh	*V A*	....	874
Wildly determining which way	*R L*	....	1150
Wildness—than tigers in their....	"	....	980
Wile—The wiles and gulles	*P P*	19	37
Wilful—wilful and unwilling	*V A*	....	365
his wilful eye he tired	*R L*	....	417
By wilful taste of what	*Son*	40	8
Wilfully—doth wilfully appear	"	80	8
Wilfulness—Book hath my wilfulness	"	117	9
Wilful-slow—going he went....	"	51	13
Will—I'll smother thee with kisses	*V A*	....	18
A summer's day will seem	"	....	23
Perforce will force it	"	....	72
And I will wink	"	....	122
I will enchant thine ear	"	....	145
light, and will aspire	"	....	150
will draw me through the sky	"	....	153
I'll sigh celestial breath	"	....	189
I'll make a shadow	"	....	191
I'll quench them with my tears	"	....	192
I'll give it thee again	"	....	209
For men will kiss	"	....	216
he will not in her arms be bound	"	....	226
I'll be a park	"	....	231
her object will away	"	....	255
will set the heart on fire	"	....	388
'nor will not know it	"	....	409
and I will not owe it	"	....	411
it will not ope the gate	"	....	424
Will never rise, so he will kiss her still	"	....	480
If you will say so	"	....	536
That she will draw	"	....	552
'this night I'll waste	"	....	583
He will not manage her	"	....	598
good queen, it will not be	"	....	607
on the lion he will venture	"	....	628
world will hold thee	"	....	761
you will fall again	"	....	769
will not let a false sound enter	"	....	780
now I will away	"	....	807
will have him seen no more	"	....	819
now she will no further	"	....	905
The Destinies will curse thee	"	....	945
will ever strive to kiss you	"	....	1082
Wherein I will not kiss	"	....	1188
That it will live	*R L*	....	203
the scandal will survive	"	....	204
the herald will contrive	"	....	206
who will the vine destroy	"	....	215
Will he not wake	"	....	219
Whose crime will bear	"	....	224
Will not my tongue be mute	"	....	227
I'll beg her love	"	....	241
will not be dismay'd	"	....	273
will not incline	"	....	292
this night-owl will catch	"	....	360
my attempt will bring	"	....	491
some worthless slave of thine I'll slay	"	....	515
that will never be forgot	"	....	536
'How will thy shame be seeded	"	....	603
'This deed will make thee	"	....	610
will prison false desire	"	....	642
I will not hear thee	"	....	667

Will—The scar that will, despite of cure, remain	*R L*	....	732
with weeping will unfold	"	....	754
The light will show	"	....	807
Will quote my loathsome trespass	"	....	812
will tell my story	"	....	813
Will couple my reproach	"	....	816
Will tie the hearers	"	....	818
upon his silver down will stay	"	....	1012
I will not wrong	"	....	1060
never will dispense	"	....	1070
'I will not poison thee	"	....	1072
I will not paint	"	....	1074
that light will borrow	"	....	1083
will strain a tear	"	....	1131
I'll hum on Tarquin still	"	....	1133
Will fix a sharp knife	"	....	1138
Will we find out; and there we will unfold	"	....	1146
Will slay the other	"	....	1162
His leaves will wither	"	....	1168
'Yet die I will not	"	....	1177
to Tarquin I'll bequeath	"	....	1181
I'll bequeath unto the knife	"	....	1184
The one will live	"	....	1187
will kill myself	"	....	1196
are they form'd as marble will	"	....	1241
each little mote will peep	"	....	1251
it will soon be writ	"	....	1295
I'll tune thy woes	"	....	1465
wounds will not be sore	"	....	1568
this night I will inflict	"	....	1630
I'll murder straight, and then I'll slaughter thee	"	....	1634
this act will be	"	....	1637
That they will suffer	"	....	1672
We will revenge the death	"	....	1841
Will be a tatter'd weed	*Son*	2	4
will be the tomb	"	3	7
Will play the tyrants	"	5	3
The world will wail thee	"	9	4
world will be thy widow	"	9	5
Who will believe	"	17	1
I will not praise	"	21	14
I, not for myself, but for thee will	"	22	10
I will keep so chary	"	22	11
all naked, will bestow	"	26	8
for their style I'll read	"	32	14
Will sourly leave her	"	41	8
thus I will excuse ye	"	42	5
what excuse will my poor beast	"	51	5
Towards thee I'll run	"	51	14
he will not every hour survey	"	52	3
To what you will	"	58	11
That Time will come	"	64	12
will steal his treasure	"	75	6
Thy glass will show	"	77	1
thy mind's imprint will bear	"	77	3
thy glass will truly show	"	77	5
will give thee memory	"	77	6
will hold me up afloat	"	80	9
each part will be forgotten	"	81	4
against myself I'll fight	"	88	3
will be a gainer too	"	88	9
will bear all wrong	"	88	14
And I will comment	"	89	2
and I straight will halt	"	89	3
As I'll myself disgrace	"	89	7
I will acquaintance strangle	"	89	8

WILL			
Will—against myself I'll vow debate	Son	89	13
will not seem so	"	90	14
thy love will stay	"	92	3
and will do none	"	94	1
will be well esteem'd	"	96	6
I'll live in this poor rhyme	"	107	11
I never more will grind	"	110	10
willing patient, I will drink	"	111	9
that I will bitter think	"	111	11
I will be true	"	123	14
still will pluck thee back	"	126	6
Then will I swear	"	132	13
Myself I'll forfeit	"	134	3
he will not be free	"	134	5
to do will aptly find	L C	....	88
may stop awhile what will not	"	....	159
that needs will taste	"	....	167
to water will not wear	"	....	291
Therefore I'll lie with love	P P	1	13
but I will prove	"	3	5
to thee I'll constant prove	"	5	3
no rubbing will refresh	"	13	8
looks will calm ere night	"	19	14
too late she will repent	"	19	15
force will yield at length	"	19	21
She will not stick to round	"	19	51
Yet will she blush	"	19	53
we will all the pleasures prove	"	20	2
There will we sit	"	20	5
There will I make thee	"	20	9
they will not cheer thee	"	21	12
None alive will pity me	"	21	28
Every man will be thy friend	"	21	35
No man will supply thy want	"	21	38
Bountiful they will him call	"	21	40
Quickly him they will entice	"	21	44
He will help thee in thy need	"	21	52
If thou sorrow, he will weep	"	21	53
Will—and she, by her good will	V A	....	479
Come not within his danger by thy will	"	....	639
of his will's obtaining	R L	....	128
his will resolving	"	....	129
My will is strong	"	....	243
frozen conscience and hot-burning will	"	....	247
between her chamber and his will	"	....	302
My will is back'd	"	....	352
And in his will his wilful eye	"	....	417
must my will abide	"	....	486
My will that marks thee	"	....	487
But will is deaf	"	....	495
thy will remove	"	....	614
command thy rebel will	"	....	625
Devours his will	"	....	706
Self-will himself doth tire	"	....	707
could not forestall their will	"	....	728
abridgement of my will I make	"	....	1198
shalt oversee this will	"	....	1205
blotted straight with will	"	....	1299
thy liking to my will	"	....	1633
that in your will	Son	57	13
Is it thy will	"	61	1
knowing thy will	"	89	7
Which in their wills	"	121	8
am mortgaged to thy will	"	134	2
thou hast thy 'Will'	"	135	1
And 'Will' to boot, and 'Will' in overplus	"	135	2
Will—To thy sweet will	Son	135	4
whose will is large	"	135	5
to hide my will in thine	"	135	6
Shall will in others	"	135	7
And in my will	"	135	8
rich in 'Will,' add to thy 'Will'	"	135	11
One will of mine, to make thy large 'Will' more	"	135	12
me in that one 'Will'	"	135	14
that I was thy 'Will'	"	136	2
And will, thy soul knows	"	136	3
'Will' will fulfil the treasure	"	136	5
full with wills, and my will one	"	136	6
for my name is 'Will'	"	136	14
So will I pray that thou mayst have thy 'Will'	"	143	13
in his craft of will	L C	....	126
Ask'd their own wills, and made their wills obey	"	....	133
with more than love's good will	P P	9	7
left'st me nothing in thy will	"	10	8
And to her will frame all thy ways	"	19	23
Will'd—Be not self-will'd	Son	6	13
Willeth—the insulter willeth	V A	....	550
Willing—to weep are often willing	R L	....	1237
that pay the willing loan	Son	6	6
Whilst like a willing patient	"	111	9
Willingly—would willingly impart	"	72	8
Wilt—wilt thou make the match	V A	....	586
But if thou needs wilt hunt	"	....	673
And wilt thou be the school	R L	....	617
Wilt thou be glass wherein	"	....	619
Or if thou wilt permit	"	....	773
When wilt thou be humble	"	....	897
When wilt thou sort an hour	"	....	899
thy Lucrece thou wilt see	"	....	1306
Thou single wilt prove none	Son	8	14
Grant, if thou wilt	"	10	3
And do whate'er thou wilt	"	19	6
thou wilt be stol'n, I fear	"	48	13
so oft as thou wilt look	"	77	13
Then hate me when thou wilt	"	90	1
If thou wilt leave me	"	90	9
wilt thou not haply say	"	101	5
wilt thou be dumb	"	101	9
And yet thou wilt	"	133	13
Thou wilt restore	"	134	4
But thou wilt not	"	134	5
of thy beauty thou wilt take	"	134	9
Wilt thou, whose will	"	135	5
When thou wilt inflame	L C	....	268
Win—'What win I' if I gain	R L	....	211
win of the watery main	Son	64	7
shalt win much glory	"	83	8
when I saw myself to win	"	119	4
To win me soon to hell	"	144	5
did win whom he would maim	L C	....	312
To win me soon to hell	P P	2	5
to win a paradise	"	3	14
To win his heart	"	4	7
Wind—breath, whose gentle wind	V A	....	189
To bid the wind a base	"	....	303
the high wind sings	"	....	305
coal revives with wind	"	....	338
Even as the wind is hush'd	"	....	458
How he outruns the wind	"	....	681
now wind, now rain	"	....	965
As when the wind	"	....	1046
Nor sun nor wind	"	....	1082

WIND 354 WITH

Entry	Ref	Page	Line
Wind—the wind doth hiss you	V A	1084	
The wind would blow it off	"	1089	
The wind wars with his torch	R L	311	
Puffs forth another wind	"	315	
The doors, the wind, the glove	"	325	
Huge rocks, high winds	"	335	
And with the wind	"	648	
blown with wind of words	"	1390	
and busy winds give o'er	"	1790	
his thunder, rain, and wind	Son	14	6
Rough winds do shake	"	18	3
though mounted on the wind	"	51	7
hoisted sail to all the winds	"	117	7
with sorrow's wind and rain	L C		7
light occasion of the wind	"		86
When winds breathe sweet	"		103
and falls through wind	P P	10	6
Through the velvet leaves the wind	"	17	5
Words are easy, like the wind	"	21	33
Winding—with a winding maze	R L		1151
Thin winding breath	"		1407
Window—Her two blue windows	V A		482
pry'st thou through my window	R L		1089
So then through windows	Son	3	11
That hath his windows glazed	"	24	8
Are windows to my breast	"	24	11
Windy—Then with her .... sighs	V A		51
This windy tempest	R L		1788
Give not a windy night	Son	90	7
Wing—Shaking her wings	V A		57
wave like feather'd wings	"		306
Borne by the trustless wings	R L		2
with his wings' shade	"		507
from ancient ravens' wings	"		949
his coal-black wings in mire	"		1009
feathers to the learned's wing	Son	78	7
To whose sound chaste wings obey	P T		4
Every fowl of tyrant wing	"		10
Winged—For fleet-wing'd duty	R L		1216
Her winged spright	"		1728
In winged speed no motion	Son	51	8
Wink—He winks and turns his lips	V A		90
then wink again	"		121
And I will wink	"		122
To wink, being blinded	R L		375
And moody Pluto winks	"		553
Who if it wink	"		1139
When most I wink	Son	43	1
till they wink with fullness	"	56	6
Winking—yet .... there appears	R L		458
Winter—Lust's winter comes	V A		802
As winter meads	R L		1218
But chide rough winter	"		1255
Why forty winters shall besiege thy brow	Son	2	1
To hideous winter	"	5	6
though they with winter meet	"	5	13
let not winter's ragged hand	"	6	1
gusts of winter's day	"	13	11
Or call it winter	"	56	13
How like a winter hath my absence	"	97	1
dreading the winter's near	"	97	14
Yet seem'd it winter still	"	98	13
Three winters cold	"	104	3
age like winter weather	P P	12	9
age like winter bare	"	12	4
Wipe—Worse than a slavish wipe	R L		537
And wipe the dim mist	"		643
Wiped—can be wiped away	"		606
Wiped—wiped the brinish pearl	R L		1213
forced stain be wiped from me	"		1701
Wire—If hairs be wires, black wires grow on her head	Son	130	4
Wiry—The wiry concord, that mine ear	"	128	4
Wisdom—Herein lives wisdom	"	11	5
Wise—love is wise in folly	V A		838
Strike the wise dumb	"		1146
old and yet not wise	R L		1550
List the wise world	Son	71	13
Be wise as thou art cruel	"	140	1
what fool is not so wise	P P	3	13
Wise—In howling wise, to see	"	18	33
Wiser—Take counsel of some wiser head	"	19	5
Wish—Would they not wish	V A		447
To wish that I their father	R L		210
The sweets we wish for	"		867
that best I wish in thee	Son	37	13
and wish I were renew'd	"	111	8
And wish her lays	P P	15	6
Wish—With virtuous wish would	Son	16	7
This wish I have	"	37	14
Whoever hath her wish	"	135	1
Wish'd—thrice more...., more rare	"	56	14
eyes their wished sight	P P	15	10
Wish'd himself the heaven's breath	"	17	8
buru'd in heart-wish'd luxury	L C		314
Wishing—Wishing her checks	V A		65
Wishing Adonis had his team	"		179
Wishing me like to one	Son	29	5
Wistly—wistly to view	V A		343
wistly on him gazed	R L		1355
Yet not so wistly	P P	6	12
Wit—how doth she now for wits	V A		249
Fair fall the wit	"		472
wit waits on fear	"		690
humour of fantastic wits	"		850
without ten women's wit	"		1008
and, all for want of wit	R L		153
confounds his wits	"		290
the harvest of his wits	"		859
Lending him wit	"		964
What wit sets down	"		1299
Began to clothe his wit	"		1809
And arm'd his long-hid wits	"		1816
long-experienced wit to school	"		1820
belongs to love's fine wit	Son	23	14
not to show my wit	"	26	4
which wit so poor as mine	"	26	5
birth, or wealth, or wit	"	37	5
the wits of former days	"	59	13
shall fame his wit	"	84	11
If I might teach thee wit	"	140	5
But my five wits nor my five senses	"	141	9
to make our wits more keen	L C		161
With wit well blazon'd	"		217
Witchcraft—what a hell of	"		288
With—the sun with purple-colour'd face	V A		1
with herself at strife	"		11
hath ending with thy life	"		12
smother thee with kisses	"		18
cloy thy lips with loathed satiety	"		19
pale with fresh variety	"		21
With this she seizeth	"		25
With leaden appetite, unapt	"		34
with lustful language broken	"		47

Phrase	Ref	Line
With—He burns with bashful shame; she with her tears	V. A	49
Then with her windy sighs	"	51
she murders with a kiss	"	54
Tires with her beak	"	56
dew'd with such distilling showers	"	66
better'd with a more delight	"	78
take truce with her contending tears	"	82
'Touch but my lips with those fair lips	"	115
with thy hand felt	"	143
a nymph, with long dishevell'd hair	"	147
with thy increase be fed	"	170
With burning eye did hotly overlook	"	178
Adonis, with a lazy spright	"	181
with a heavy, dark, disliking eye	"	182
quench them with my tears	"	192
with his hard hoof he wounds	"	267
what he was controlled with	"	270
With gentle majesty	"	278
with his proud sight agrees	"	288
His art with nature's workmanship at strife	"	291
Beating his kind embracements with her heels	"	312
With her the horse, and	"	322
All swoln with chafing	"	325
swelleth with more rage	"	332
coal revives with wind	"	338
And with his bonnet hides	"	339
Looks on the dull earth with disturbed mind	"	340
With one fair hand she heaveth	"	351
With tears, which chorus-like master'd with a leathern rein	"	360
	"	392
and all but with a breath	"	414
hurt my hand with wringing	"	421
now press'd with bearing	"	430
illumined with her eye	"	486
clouded with his brow's repine	"	490
Measure my strangeness with my unripe years	"	524
comforter, with weary gait	"	529
with her plenty press'd, she faint with dearth	"	545
With blindfold fury she begins	"	554
weary, with her hard embracing	"	559
tamed with too much handling	"	560
that's tired with chasing	"	561
still'd with dandling	"	562
but dissolves with tempering	"	565
compass'd oft with venturing	"	567
with certain of his friends	"	588
deceived with painted grapes	"	601
kindle with continual kissing	"	606
With javelin's point	"	616
with hairy bristles arm'd	"	625
to do with such foul fiends	"	638
all stain'd with gore	"	664
make them droop with grief	"	666
encounter with the boar	"	672
keep with thy hounds	"	678
and with what care	"	681
crosses with a thousand doubles	"	682
sorteth with a herd of deer	"	689
with others being mingled	"	691
With much ado	"	694
With—with listening ear	V. A	698
indenting with the way	"	704
in love with thee	"	722
mingle beauty with infirmities	"	735
with impure defeature	"	736
melts with the mid-day sun	"	750
blotting it with blame	"	796
With this, he breaketh	"	811
with the melting clouds contend	"	820
with such-like sport	"	844
salutes him with this fair good-morrow	"	859
With cold-pale weakness numbs	"	892
And with that word she spied	"	900
bepainted all with red	"	901
is mated with delays	"	909
In hand with all things	"	912
he replies with howling	"	918
Whereon with fearful eyes they long have gazed	"	927
Infusing them with dreadful prophecies	"	928
ruin'd with thy rigour	"	954
And with his strong course opens	"	960
With Death she humbly doth insinuate	"	1012
with him is beauty slain	"	1019
As one with treasure laden, hemm'd with thieves	"	1022
unwitnessed with eye or ear	"	1023
with false bethinking grieves	"	1024
as murder'd with the view	"	1031
in his shelly cave with pain	"	1034
consort with ugly night	"	1041
wound the heart with looks again	"	1042
Which with cold terror doth	"	1048
With purple tears, that his wound wept, was drench'd	"	1054
seem'd with him to bleed	"	1056
lived and died with him	"	1080
Play with his locks	"	1090
fed them with his sight, they him with berries	"	1104
ran upon the boar with his sharp spear	"	1112
With kissing him I should have kill'd him	"	1118
My youth with his; the more	"	1120
With this she falleth	"	1121
stains her face with his congealed blood	"	1122
waited on with jealousy	"	1137
With sweets that shall	"	1144
enrich the poor with treasures	"	1150
chequer'd with white	"	1168
girdle with embracing flames	R. L	6
With pure aspects did him	"	14
with swift intent he goes	"	46
stain that o'er with silver white	"	56
answers with surmise	"	83
colour'd with his high estate	"	92
cloy'd with much	"	98
coped with stranger eyes	"	99
And decks with praises	"	108
With bruised arms	"	110
Her joy with heaved-up hand she doth express	"	111
with heavy spright	"	121
With modest Lucrece	"	123

Entry		
With—with life's strength doth fight	R L	124
are with gain so fond	"	134
With honour, wealth, and ease	"	142
torments us with defect	"	*151
bewitch'd with lust's foul charm	"	173
Here pale with fear	"	183
With your uncleanness	"	193
shamed with the note	"	208
Would with the sceptre straight be strucken down	"	217
charge me with so black a deed	"	226
with trembling terror die	"	231
And with good thoughts makes dispensation	"	248
tremble with her loyal fear	"	261
smiled with so sweet a cheer	"	264
steals with open listening ear	"	283
cross him with their opposite persuasion	"	286
But with a pure appeal seeks	"	293
wars with his torch	"	311
Who with a lingering stay his course doth let	"	328
Which with a yielding latch, and with no more	"	339
will is back'd with resolution	"	352
sin is clear'd with absolution	"	354
And with his knee the door he opens	"	359
blinded with a greater light	"	375
With pearly sweat	"	396
play'd with her breath	"	400
circled with blue	"	407
With more than admiration he admired	"	418
Smoking with pride	"	438
And fright her with confusion	"	445
daunts them with more dreadful sights	"	462
with vehement prayers urgeth	"	475
Where thou with patience must	"	486
sought with all my might	"	488
guarded with a sting	"	493
Coucheth the fowl below with his wings' shade	"	507
With trembling fear	"	511
kill thine honour with thy life's decay	"	516
blurr'd with nameless bastardy	"	522
Here with a cockatrice' dead-killing eye	"	540
though marble wear with raining	"	560
eloquence with sighs is mixed	"	563
With such black payment	"	576
moved with woman's moans	"	587
Be moved with my tears	"	588
wounded with their continual motion	"	591
With foul offenders thou perforce must bear	"	612
wrapp'd in with infamies	"	636
with the wind in greater fury fret	"	648
with their fresh falls' haste	"	650
Till with her own white fleece	"	678
For with the nightly linen	"	680
eyes with sorrow shed	"	683
with lank and lean discolour'd cheek	"	708
With heavy eye	"	709
doth fight with Grace	"	712
So fares it with this faultful lord	"	715

Entry		
With—with foul insurrection	R L	722
with her nails her flesh doth tear	"	739
sweating with guilty fear	"	740
cloak offences with a cunning brow	"	749
with weeping will unfold	"	754
Frantic with grief	"	762
With close-tongued treason	"	770
'With rotten damps ravish	"	778
I have no one to blush with me	"	792
hang their heads with mine	"	793
Seasoning the earth with showers	"	796
Mingling my talk with tears, my grief with groans	"	797
lies martyr'd with disgrace	"	802
fright her crying babe with Tarquin's name	"	814
infect fair founts with venom mud	"	850
Is plagued with cramps	"	856
take root with precious flowers	"	870
meet with Opportunity	"	903
have to do with thee	"	911
ruinate proud buildings with thy hours	"	944
smear with dust	"	945
fill with worm-holes	"	946
To feed oblivion with decay of things	"	947
cheer the ploughman with increaseful crops	"	958
waste huge stones with little water drops	"	959
With some mischance cross	"	963
Disturb his hours of rest with restless trances	"	974
Afflict him in his bed with bedrid groans	"	975
Stone him with harden'd hearts	"	978
shame his hope with deeds degenerate	"	1003
fly with the filth	"	1010
gazed upon with every eye	"	1015
serves with dull debaters	"	1019
cavil with mine infamy	"	1025
flatter thee with an infringed oath	"	1061
laugh with his companions	"	1066
Basely with gold	"	1068
And with my trespass never will dispense	"	1070
poison thee with my attaint	"	1072
night with slow-sad gait descended	"	1081
Mock with thy tickling beams	"	1090
Brand not my forehead with thy piercing light	"	1091
cavils she with every thing	"	1093
his mood with nought agrees	"	1095
With too much labour drowns	"	1099
Holds disputation with each thing	"	1101
Make her moans mad with their sweet melody	"	1108
pleased with grief's society	"	1111
When with like semblance	"	1113
Grief dallied with nor law nor limit knows	"	1120
kept with tears	"	1127
And with deep groans	"	1132
encompass'd with a winding maze	"	1151
So with herself is she in mutiny	"	1153
But with my body	"	1157
with greater patience bear it	"	1158

With—engirt with daring infamy	R L	1173
With untuned tongue she hoarsely calls	"	1214
duty with thought's feathers flies	"	1216
With soft-slow tongue	"	1220
over-wash'd with woe	"	1225
with swelling drops 'gan wet	"	1228
cover crimes with bold stern looks	"	1252
With men's abuses	"	1259
Assail'd by night with circumstances strong	"	1262
Yet with the fault I thus far can dispense	"	1279
Bid him with speed prepare	"	1294
hovering o'er the paper with her quill	"	1297
blotted straight with will	"	1299
Ere she with blood had stain'd	"	1316
With words, till action	"	1323
blown with wind of words	"	1330
with more than haste	"	1352
blushing on her with a steadfast eye	"	1359
with bashful innocence doth hie	"	1341
And blushing with him	"	1355
Threatening cloud-kissing Ilion with annoy	"	1370
Begrimed with sweat, and smeared all with dust	"	1381
Gazing upon the Greeks with little lust	"	1384
marching on with trembling paces	"	1391
Making such sober action with his hand	"	1403
listening, but with several graces	"	1410
debate with angry swords	"	1421
With swelling ridges; and	"	1439
Staring on Priam's wounds with her old eyes	"	1448
Her cheeks with chaps and wrinkles were disguised	"	1452
tune thy woes with my lamenting tongue	"	1465
with my tears quench Troy	"	1468
with my knife scratch out	"	1469
with my nails her beauty I may tear	"	1472
bright with fame and not with fire	"	1491
with his own weight goes	"	1494
with the blunt swains he goes	"	1504
labour'd with his skill	"	1506
blot with hell-born sin	"	1519
with grief or travail he had fainted	"	1543
With outward honesty	"	1545
With inward vice	"	1546
doth quake with cold	"	1556
burn his Troy with water	"	1561
tears the senseless Sinon with her nails	"	1564
with this gives o'er	"	1567
weary time with her complaining	"	1570
too long with her remaining	"	1572
she with painted images hath spent	"	1577
kill'd with deadly cares	"	1593
Three times with sighs she gives	"	1604
With sad attention long to hear	"	1610
tell them all with one poor tired tongue	"	1617
With shining falchion in my chamber came	"	1626
With—with a flaming light	R L	1627
'With this, I did begin	"	1639
with so strong a fear	"	1647
stain'd with this abuse	"	1655
With head declined, and voice damm'd up with woe	"	1661
With sad-set eyes	"	1662
that came with Collatine	"	1689
With swift pursuit to venge	"	1691
chase injustice with revengeful arms	"	1693
with noble disposition	"	1695
constrain'd with dreadful circumstance	"	1703
with the foul act dispense	"	1704
With this, they all	"	1709
While with a joyless smile	"	1711
carved in it with tears	"	1713
Here with a sigh	"	1716
astonish'd with this deadly deed	"	1730
to die with her	"	1776
weep with equal strife	"	1791
with clamours fill'd	"	1804
He with the Romans was esteem'd	"	1811
idiots are with kings	"	1812
But kneel with me	"	1830
rouse our Roman gods with invocations	"	1831
done with speedy diligence	"	1853
Feed'st thy light's flame with self-substantial fuel	Son	1 6
thine image dies with thee	"	3 14
having traffic with thyself alone	"	4 9
must be tomb'd with thee	"	4 13
that with gentle work did frame	"	5 1
Sap check'd with frost	"	5 7
Beauty's effect with beauty were bereft	"	5 11
they with winter meet	"	5 13
With beauty's treasure	"	6 4
Serving with looks	"	7 4
with weary car	"	7 9
Sweets with sweets war not	"	8 2
receivest with pleasure thine annoy	"	8 4
possess'd with murderous hate	"	10 5
silver'd o'er with white	"	12 4
Borne on the bier with white and bristly beard	"	12 8
Or say with princes	"	14 7
Time debateth with Decay	"	15 11
all in war with Time	"	15 13
With means more blessed	"	16 4
With virtuous wish would bear	"	16 7
fill'd with your most high deserts	"	17 2
yellow'd with their age	"	17 9
O, carve not with thy hours	"	19 9
draw no lines there with thine antique pen	"	19 10
with nature's own hand painted	"	20 1
With shifting change	"	20 4
So is it not with me as with that Muse	"	21 1
every fair with his fair doth rehearse	"	21 4
With sun and moon, with earth and sea's rich gems	"	21 6
With April's first-born	"	21 7
Who with his fear is put besides	"	23 2
replete with too much rage	"	23 3

With—O'ercharged with burthen	Son	23	8	With—lace itself with his society	Son	67	4
To hear with eyes	"	23	14	with outward praise is crown'd	"	69	5
glazed with thine eyes	"	24	8	with vilest worms to dwell	"	71	4
in favour with their stars	"	25	1	compounded am with clay	"	71	10
graciously with fair aspect	"	26	10	even with my life decay	"	71	12
Weary with toil	"	27	1	mock you with me	"	71	14
with travel tired	"	27	2	Consumed with that	"	73	12
in disgrace with fortune	"	29	1	still with thee shall stay	"	74	4
with my bootless cries	"	29	3	this with thee remains	"	74	14
like him with friends possess'd	"	29	6	to be with you alone	"	75	7
With what I most enjoy contented	"	29	8	all full with feasting	"	75	9
change my state with kings	"	29	14	with the time do I not glance aside	"	76	3
And with old woes new wail	"	30	4	And arts with thy sweet graces			
bosom is endeared with all hearts	"	31	1	graced be	"	78	12
Hung with the trophies	"	31	10	Reserve their character with gold-			
my bones with dust shall cover	"	32	3	en quill	"	85	3
Compare them with the bettering				gulls him with intelligence	"	86	10
of the time	"	32	5	With mine own weakness being			
grown with this growing age	"	32	10	best acquainted	"	88	5
with sovereign eye	"	33	2	Join with the spite of fortune	"	90	3
Kissing with golden face	"	33	3	Compared with loss of thee	"	90	14
Gilding pale streams with heav-				vex me with inconstant mind	"	92	9
enly alchemy	"	33	4	thy looks with me	"	93	4
With ugly rack	"	33	6	with base infection meet	"	94	11
with this disgrace	"	33	8	big with rich increase	"	97	6
With all triumphant splendour	"	33	10	'tis with so dull a cheer	"	97	13
Authorizing thy trespass with				laugh'd and leap'd with him	"	98	4
compare	"	35	6	As with your shadow I with these			
that do with me remain	"	36	3	did play	"	98	14
with public kindness honour me	"	36	11	with his colour fix'd	"	101	6
with manners may I sing	"	39	1	greet it with my lays	"	102	6
entertain the time with thoughts				dull you with my song	"	102	14
of love	"	39	11	look'd but with divining eyes	"	106	11
Kill me with spites	"	40	14	Now with the drops	"	107	9
with thy much clearer light	"	43	7	not with the time exchanged	"	109	7
attend time's leisure with my moan	"	44	12	do you with Fortune chide	"	111	1
Are both with thee	"	45	2	with my neglect I do dispense	"	112	12
with swift motion slide	"	45	4	replete with you	"	113	13
with two alone	"	45	7	being crown'd with you	"	114	1
oppress'd with melancholy	"	45	8	with his gust is 'greeing	"	114	11
pierced with crystal eyes	"	46	6	bends with the remover to remove	"	116	4
heart in love with sighs	"	47	4	alters not with his brief hours	"	116	11
With my love's picture then my				been with unknown minds	"	117	5
eye doth feast	"	47	5	With eager compounds we our pal-			
art present still with me	"	47	10	ate urge	"	118	2
And I am still with them and they				character'd with lasting memory	"	122	2
with me	"	47	12	built up with newer might	"	123	2
greet me with that sun	"	49	6	flowers with flowers gather'd	"	124	4
tired with my woe	"	50	5	nor grows with heat nor drowns			
he answers with a groan	"	50	11	with showers	"	124	12
with my desire keep pace	"	51	9	With my extern the outward hon-			
besmear'd with sluttish time	"	55	2	ouring	"	125	2
they wink with fullness	"	56	6	not mix'd with seconds	"	125	11
with a perpetual dullness	"	56	8	slander'd with a bastard shame	"	127	4
question with my jealous thought	"	57	9	Fairing the foul with art's false			
could with a backward look	"	59	5	borrow'd face	"	127	6
changing place with that which	"	60	3	Slandering creation with a false			
with others all too near	"	61	14	esteem	"	127	12
chopp'd with tann'd antiquity	"	62	10	With thy sweet fingers	"	128	3
Painting my age with beauty	"	62	14	with those dancing chips	"	128	10
With Time's injurious hand crush'd	"	63	2	fingers walk with gentle gait	"	128	11
With lines and wrinkles	"	63	4	boiled with false compare	"	130	14
Increasing store with loss and loss				torments me with disdain	"	132	2
with store	"	64	8	Looking with pretty ruth	"	132	4
How with this rage shall beauty	"	65	3	fill it full with wills	"	136	6
Tired with all these	"	66	1	with ease we prove	"	136	7
Tired with all these	"	66	13	I lie with her and she with me	"	138	13
with infection should he live	"	67	1	Wound me not with thine eye, but			
And with his presence grace	"	67	2	with thy tongue	"	139	3

WITH   359   WITHOUT

With—			
Use power with power	Son	139	4
wound with cunning	"	139	7
Kill me outright with looks	"	139	14
with too much disdain	"	140	2
love thee with mine eyes	"	141	1
with thy tongue's tune delighted	"	141	5
To any sensual feast with thee alone	"	141	8
but with mine compare	"	142	3
Wooing his purity with her foul pride	"	144	8
she alter'd with an end	"	145	9
frantic-mad with evermore unrest	"	147	10
correspondence with true sight	"	148	2
vex'd with watching and with tears	"	148	10
with tears thou keep'st me	"	148	13
myself with thee partake	"	149	2
Revenge upon myself with present moan	"	149	8
With insufficiency my heart to sway	"	150	2
With others thou shouldst not abhor	"	150	12
Storming her world with sorrow's wind	L C		7
With sickled silk feat	"	.....	48
with his hearing to divide	"	.....	67
with his authorized youth	"	.....	104
To dwell with him	"	.....	129
What with his art in youth	"	.....	145
With safest distance I mine honour shielded	"	.....	151
with acture they may be	"	.....	185
With twisted metal amorously impleach'd	"	.....	205
With the annexions of fair gems enrich'd	"	.....	208
With objects manifold	"	.....	216
With wit well blazon'd	"	.....	217
Hallow'd with sighs	"	.....	228
with bleeding groans they pine	"	.....	275
With brinish current downward flow'd	"	.....	284
glazed with crystal gate	"	.....	286
But with the inundation	"	.....	290
with the garment of a Grace	"	.....	316
Outfacing faults in love with love's ill rest	P P	1	8
He with love, and love with me	"	1	13
Wooing his purity with her fair pride	"	2	8
With young Adonis	"	4	2
with many a lovely look	"	4	3
with such an earthly tongue	"	5	14
look'd on the world with glorious eye	"	6	11
with damask dye to grace	"	7	5
as straw with fire flameth	"	7	13
Adonis comes with horn	"	9	6
with more than love's good will	"	9	7
deep-wounded with a boar	"	9	10
with young Adonis sitting	"	11	1
And with her lips on him	"	11	10
cabin hang'd with care	"	14	3
for I supp'd with sorrow	"	14	6
welcome daylight with her ditty	"	15	7
solace mix'd with sorrow	"	15	11
Were I with her	"	15	13
love with love did fight	"	16	5
was wounded with disdain	"	16	11
Thus art with arms contending	"	16	13
Fraughted with gall	"	18	26

With—			
Smooth not thy tongue with filed talk	P P	19	8
with scorn she put away	"	19	18
Serve always with assured trust	"	19	31
Dissembled with an outward show	"	19	38
still to strive with men	"	19	43
When time with age shall them attaint	"	19	46
Live with me	"	20	1
With a thousand fragrant posies	"	20	10
with leaves of myrtle	"	20	12
With coral clasps	"	20	14
Then live with me	"	20	16
To live with thee	"	20	20
And with such-like	"	21	41
He with thee doth bear a part	"	21	56
With the breath thou givest	P T	.....	19
Withal—spend the night withal	V A	.....	847
that his hand shakes withal	R L	.....	467
I, sick withal, the help	Son	153	11
Withdrew—themselves withdrew	V A	.....	1032
Wither—they wither in their prime	"	.....	418
To wither in my breast	"	.....	1182
wither at the cedar's root	R L	.....	663
His leaves will wither	"	.....	1168
Wither'd—against the .... flower	"	.....	1254
As flowers dead lie wither'd	P P	13	9
Withering—Thy lovers withering	Son	126	4
Withhold—to withhold me so	V A	.....	612
Within—Beauty within itself	"	.....	130
Within the circuit	"	.....	230
Within this limit	"	.....	235
Come not within his danger	"	.....	639
Within my bosom	"	.....	646
within her bosom it shall dwell	"	.....	1173
Within whose face	R L	.....	52
Within his thought	"	.....	288
Thy sea within a puddle's womb is hearsed	"	.....	657
Within your hollow-swelling	"	.....	1122
within their bosoms lie	"	.....	1342
Within thine own bud	Son	1	11
within thine own deep-sunken eyes	"	2	7
Within the gentle closure	"	48	11
Within the knowledge	"	49	10
within that pen doth dwell	"	84	5
Within his bending sickle's compass	"	116	10
within the level of your frown	"	117	11
foul as hell within	"	119	2
are within my brain	"	122	1
pine within and suffer dearth	"	146	3
Within be fed, without	"	146	12
dead within an hour	P P	13	6
Without—End without audience	V A	.....	846
without ten women's wit	"	.....	1008
eyes of men without an orator	R L	.....	30
Without the bed her other	"	.....	393
without or yea or no	"	.....	1340
quoth she, 'without a sound	"	.....	1464
Without this, folly	Son	11	6
travel forth without my cloak	"	34	2
Without thy help	"	36	4
the world-without-end hour	"	57	5
Without accusing you	"	58	8
Without all ornament	"	68	10
Without all hail	"	74	2
mayst without attaint o'erlook	"	82	2
fed, without be rich no more	"	146	12
As it was, or best without	L C	.....	98

Without—sees thee without wonder	P P	5	9
a nay is placed without remove	"	18	12
Witness—'Witness this primrose bank	V A		151
Witness the entertainment	"		1103
To witness duty, not to show	Son	26	4
To this I witness call	"	124	13
on another's neck do witness bear	"	131	11
What unapproved witness	L C		53
Wittily—love did wittily prevent	V A		471
Witty—wise in folly, foolish-witty	"		838
Woe—her woes the more increasing	"		254
woe unto the birds	"		455
comment upon every woe	"		714
and twenty times, 'Woe, woe	"		833
still concludes in woe	"		839
throng her constant woe	"		967
Thy weal and woe	"		987
shall not match his woe	"		1140
fellowship in woe doth woe assuage	R L		790
Base watch of woes	"		928
date of never-ending woes	"		935
old woes, not infant sorrows	"		1096
Deep woes roll forward	"		1118
To keep thy sharp woes waking	"		1136
fair cheeks over-washed with woe	"		1225
My woes are tedious	"		1309
the tenour of her woe	"		1310
a part of woe doth bear	"		1327
So woe hath wearied woe	"		1363
her sorrow to the beldam's woes	"		1458
I'll tune thy woes	"		1465
be freed from guilty woe	"		1482
she weeps Troy's painted woes	"		1492
Patience seem'd to scorn his woes	"		1505
that seem'd to welcome woe	"		1509
Though woe be heavy	"		1574
Losing her woes in shows	"		1580
discharge one word of woe	"		1605
In me moe woes than words	"		1615
voice damm'd up with woe	"		1661
Which speechless woe of his	"		1674
My woe too sensible	"		1678
To drown one woe	"		1680
as pitying Lucrece' woes	"		1747
'Woe, woe,' quoth Collatine	"		1802
such emulation in their woe	"		1808
is woe the cure for woe	"		1821
And with old woes new wail	Son	30	4
love's long-since-cancell'd woe	"	30	7
from woe to woe tell o'er	"	30	10
badges of either's woe	"	44	14
tired with my woe	"	50	5
then should make you woe	"	71	8
in the rearward of a conquered woe	"	90	6
strains of woe which now seem woe	"	90	13
O, that our night of woe	"	120	9
becoming of their woe	"	127	13
and proved, a very woe	"	129	11
That season'd woe had pelleted	L C		18
shrieking undistinguish'd woe	"		20
grounds and motives of her woe	"		63
'But, woe is me	"		78
Woeful—a woeful ditty	V A		836
the woeful words she told	"		1126
A woeful hostess brooks not	R L		1125
she saw my woeful state	Son	145	4
Woeful—My woeful self	L C		143
Wolf—Or as the wolf doth grin	V A		459
the wolf would leave his prey	"		1097
No noise but owls' and wolves'	R L		165
The wolf hath seized his prey	"		677
Thou set'st the wolf	"		878
might the stern wolf betray	Son	96	9
Woman—Art thou a woman's son	V A		201
but of no woman bred	"		214
and never woman yet	"		1007
without ten women's wit	"		1008
moved with woman's moans	R L		587
And let mild women	"		979
men have marble, women waxen, minds	"		1240
Poor women's faces	"		1253
Poor women's faults	"		1258
Make weak-made women	"		1260
A woman's face	Son	20	1
A woman's gentle heart	"	20	3
as is false women's fashion	"	20	4
and women's souls amazeth	"	20	8
And for a woman wert thou pricked thee out for women's pleasure	"	20	9
	"	20	13
when a woman woos, what woman's son	"	41	7
a woman colour'd ill	"	144	4
a woman colour'd ill	P P	2	4
A woman I forswore	"	3	5
More in women than in men	"	18	18
Had women been so strong	"	19	23
gulfs that women work	"	19	37
A woman's nay doth stand	"	19	42
Think women still to strive	"	19	43
One woman would another wed	"	19	48
If to women he be bent	"	21	45
Womb—Whose hollow.... resounds	V A		268
From earth's dark womb	R L		549
Thy sea within a puddle's womb	"		657
so fair whose unear'd womb	Son	3	5
the womb wherein they grew	"	86	4
Like widow'd wombs	"	97	8
whose concave womb reworded	L C		1
Won—Won in the fields	R L		107
And he hath won	"		688
and therefore to be won	Son	41	5
Wonder—Vouchsafe, thou wonder	V A		13
gazer late did wonder	"		748
'Wonder of time	"		1133
In silent wonder	R L		84
too much wonder of his eye	"		95
wonder of your frame	Son	59	10
Nor did I wonder	"	98	9
Have eyes to wonder	"	106	14
that sees thee without wonder	P P	5	9
But in them it were a wonder	P T		32
Wondering—wondering each other's chance	R L		1596
Who wondering at him	"		1845
Not wondering at the present	Son	123	10
Wondrous—at vantage,—....dread	V A		635
the painter for his wondrous skill	R L		1528
in a wondrous excellence	Son	105	6
which wondrous scope affords	"	105	12
Wont—Where thou wast wont to rest	R L		1621
When I was wont to greet it	Son	102	6
that wont to have play'd	P P	18	29

Wonted—whose wonted lily white	V A	.....	1053
His wonted height	R L	.....	776
Woo—'gins to woo him	V A	.....	6
Then woo thyself	"	.....	159
to see him woo her	"	.....	309
But then woos best	"	.....	570
And when a woman woos	Son	41	7
Whom thine eyes woo	"	142	10
did ne'er invite, nor never woo	L C	.....	182
began to woo him	P P	11	2
Wood—unto the wood they hie	V A	.....	323
in some mistrustful wood	"	.....	826
Upon that blessed wood	Son	128	2
At the wood's boldness	"	128	8
Making dead wood more blest	"	128	12
Wood—pestilence and frenzies wood	V A	.....	740
Woodman—He is no woodman	R L	.....	580
Woo'd—I have been woo'd	V A	.....	97
Her eyes woo'd still	"	.....	358
being woo'd of time	Son	70	6
Wooing—eyes disdain'd the	V A	.....	358
wooing his purity	Son	144	8
Wooing his purity	P P	2	8
Word—but speak fair words	V A	.....	208
Her words are done	"	.....	254
Free vent of words	"	.....	334
ere his words began	"	.....	462
Foul words and frowns	"	.....	573
And with that word	"	.....	900
Even at this word	"	.....	1025
the woeful words she told	"	.....	1126
haste her words delays	R L	.....	552
Out, idle words, servants	"	.....	1016
This helpless smoke of words	"	.....	1027
Sometime her grief is dumb and hath no words	"	.....	1105
though my words are brief	"	.....	1309
With words, till action might become them	"	.....	1323
being blown with wind of words	"	.....	1330
but laid no words to gage	"	.....	1351
loss of Nestor's golden words	"	.....	1420
And bitter words to ban	"	.....	1460
She lends them words	"	.....	1498
Whose words, like wildfire discharge one word of woe	"	.....	1605
long to hear her words	"	.....	1610
'Few words,' quoth she	"	.....	1613
In me moe woes than words	"	.....	1615
live to speak another word	"	.....	1642
heart-easing words so long	"	.....	1782
Weak words, so thick come	"	.....	1784
For sportive words	"	.....	1813
did his words allow	"	.....	1845
wanting words to show it	Son	26	6
That every word doth almost tell	"	76	7
dressing old words new	"	76	11
and he stole that word	"	79	9
The dedicated words	"	82	3
In true plain words	"	82	12
whilst other write good words	"	85	5
Though words come hindmost	"	85	12
the breath of words respect	"	85	13
varying to other words	"	105	10
Lest sorrow lend me words, and words express	"	140	3
and words merely but art	L C	.....	174
a word for shadows like myself	P P	14	11
Words are easy like the wind	"	21	33
Wordless—.... so greets heaven	R L	.....	112
Wore—livery that he wore	V A	.....	1107
and wore out the night	R L	.....	123
her face wore sorrow's livery	"	.....	1222
Work—her best work is ruin'd	V A	.....	954
to work upon his wife	R L	.....	235
Thus treason works	"	.....	361
force must work my way	"	.....	513
In this work was had	"	.....	1385
imaginary work was there	"	.....	1422
So Lucrece set a-work	"	.....	1496
with gentle work did frame	Son	5	1
To work my mind, when body's work's expired	"	27	4
the work of masonry	"	55	6
In others' works	"	78	11
To what it works in	"	111	7
Which works on leases	"	124	10
Works under you	L C	.....	230
gulles that women work	P P	19	37
Work'st—Why .... thou mischief	R L	.....	960
Working—thy heart's workings be	Son	93	11
Workman—The well-skill'd	R L	.....	1320
Workmanship—.... at strife	V A	.....	291
workmanship of nature	"	.....	734
World—the world hath ending	"	.....	12
Look, the world's comforter	"	.....	529
all the world amazes	"	.....	634
lend the world his light	"	.....	756
the world will hold thee	"	.....	761
Who doth the world	"	.....	857
Look, how the world's poor people	"	.....	925
Alas, poor world, what treasure	"	.....	1075
Thus weary of the world	"	.....	1189
fortress'd from a world of harms	R L	.....	28
Proving from world's minority	"	.....	67
Upon the world dim darkness	"	.....	118
her life, her world's delight	"	.....	385
A pair of maiden worlds	"	.....	408
These worlds in Tarquin	"	.....	411
the world doth threat	"	.....	547
which the world might bear	"	.....	1321
the world's fresh ornament	Son	1	9
Pity the world	"	1	13
To eat the world's due	"	1	14
Thou dost beguile the world	"	3	4
The world will wail thee	"	9	4
The world will be thy widow	"	9	5
in the world doth spend	"	9	9
for still the world enjoys it	"	9	10
hath in the world an end	"	9	11
make the world away	"	11	8
To the wide world	"	19	7
from the forlorn world his visage hide	"	33	7
Suns of the world may stain	"	33	14
That wear this world out	"	55	12
the old world could say	"	59	9
world's eye doth view	"	69	1
Give warning to the world	"	71	3
From this vile world	"	71	4
Lest the wise world	"	71	13
O, lest the world should task you	"	72	1
the world may see	"	75	8
to all the world must die	"	81	6
breathers of this world are dead	"	81	12
Now while the world is bent	"	90	2
Of the wide world dreaming	"	107	2
You are my all-the-world	"	112	5

World—That all the world	Son	112	14	Worth—The charter of thy worth Son 87	3
All this the world well knows	"	129	13	thy own worth then not knowing " 87	9
wide world's common place	"	137	10	all bare, is of more worth " 103	3
in the world's false subtleties	"	138	4	skill enough your worth to sing " 106	12
world is grown so bad	"	140	11	Whose worth's unknown " 116	8
What means the world to say	"	148	6	dear nature, worth, and quality L C	210
Storming her world	L C	....	7	what are precepts worth "	267
in the world's false forgeries	P P	1	4	Worthier—the travail of a .... pen Son 79	6
'Gainst whom the world	"	3	2	Worthiness—whose .... gives scope " 52	13
The sun look'd on the world	"	6	11	Worthless—some .... slave of thine R L	513
If that the world and love	"	20	17	I am a worthless boat Son 80	11
World-without-end—the .... hour	Son	57	5	on some worthless song " 100	3
Worm—eyes, like glow-worms	V A	.....	621	Worthy—seem death-worthy in thy	
earth's worm, what dost thou	"	.....	933	brother R L	635
Why should the worm intrude	R L	.....	848	Is worthy blame "	1237
the little worms that creep	"	.....	1248	thus begins: 'Thou worthy lord "	1303
and make worms thine heir	Son	6	14	To show me worthy Son 26	12
with vilest worms to dwell	"	71	4	Worthy perusal stand " 38	6
The prey of worms	"	74	10	Most worthy comfort " 48	6
Shall worms, inheritors of this	"	146	7	can nothing worthy prove " 72	4
Worm-hole—To fill with worm-holes	R L	.....	946	More worthy I to be " 150	14
Wormwood—to bitter .... taste	"	.....	893	rule things worthy blame P P 19	3
Worn-out—pattern of the .... age	"	.....	1350	Wot—God wot, it was defect R L	1345
Worse—were thy lips the worse	V A	.....	207	Would—as she would be thrust V A	41
worse than Tantalus' is her annoy	"	.....	599	Would in thy palm dissolve "	144
mischief worse than civil home-				and now she fain would speak "	221
bred strife	"	.....	764	She would, he will not "	226
like you worse and worse	"	.....	774	would surpass the life "	289
Worse than a slavish wipe	R L	.....	537	Would thou wert as I am "	369
To subjects worse have given	Son	59	14	I would assure thee "	371
Not making worse what nature	"	84	10	bane would cure thee "	372
which makes your praises worse	"	84	14	O, would thou hadst not "	428
smell far worse than weeds	"	94	14	my ears would love "	433
And worse essays prove thee	"	110	8	thy outward parts would move "	435
Worser—Urging the worser sense	R L	.....	249	Yet would my love to thee be "	442
takes the worser part	"	.....	294	Would they not wish "	447
but she, in worser taking	"	.....	453	Would root these beauties "	636
The worser spirit a woman	Son	144	4	would breed a scarcity "	753
My worser spirit a woman	P P	2	4	And would say after her "	832
Worship—doth worship thy defect	Son	149	11	would he put his bonnet on "	1087
Worshipper—suspecteth the false				the gaudy sun would peep "	1088
worshipper	R L	.....	86	The wind would blow it off "	1089
Worst—The worst is but denial	"	.....	242	then would Adonis weep "	1090
He in the worst sense construes	"	.....	324	They both would strive "	1092
Yet do thy worst, old Time	Son	19	13	he would not fear him "	1094
The worst was this	"	80	14	tiger would be tame "	1096
At first the very worst	"	90	12	wolf would leave his prey "	1097
But do thy worst	"	92	1	That some would sing "	1102
fear the worst of wrongs	"	92	5	Would bring him mulberries "	1103
take the worst to be	"	137	4	beauty would blush for shame R L	54
thy worst all best exceeds	"	150	8	Virtue would stain that o'er "	56
Worth—prove nothing worth	V A	.....	418	that would let him go "	76
that's worth the viewing	"	.....	1076	Would with the sceptre straight	
of small worth held	Son	2	4	be strucken "	217
Neither in inward worth	"	16	11	And they would stand "	347
of thy worth and truth	"	37	4	This guilt would seem "	635
ten times more in worth	"	38	9	what he would lose again "	688
O, how thy worth with manners	"	39	1	And therefore would they still in	
Like stones of worth	"	52	7	darkness be "	752
Praising thy worth	"	60	14	queen he would distain "	786
mine own worth do define	"	62	7	Collatine would else have come to	
in all worths surmount	"	62	8	me "	916
Thy worth the greater	"	70	6	Would purchase thee a thousand "	963
to love things nothing worth	"	72	14	who so base would such an office	
The worth of that	"	74	13	have "	1000
But since your worth	"	80	5	in night would cloister'd be "	1085
Finding thy worth a limit	"	82	6	at that would do it good "	1117
Speaking of worth, what worth in				mine own would do me good "	1274
you doth grow	"	83	8	She would request to know "	1283

Entry	Source	Line	No.
Would—she .... not blot the letter	R L		1322
of Troy there would appear	"		1382
That one would swear	"		1393
It seem'd they would debate	"		1421
She would have said	"		1535
would be drawn out too long	"		1616
as if her heart would break	"		1716
would make the world away	Son	11	8
would bear your living flowers	"	16	7
The age to come would say	"	17	7
How would thy shadow's form happy show	"	43	6
How would, I say, mine eyes be blessed made	"	43	9
despite of space, I would be brought	"	44	3
the place where he would be	"	44	5
thy picture's sight would bar	"	46	3
from these would I be gone	"	66	13
I in your sweet thoughts would be forgot	"	71	7
Unless you would devise	"	72	5
truth would willingly impart	"	72	8
others would give life	"	83	12
Because I would not dull you	"	102	14
antique pen would have express'd	"	106	7
outward form would show it	"	108	14
would by ill be cured	"	118	12
they would change their state	"	128	9
the thing she would have stay	"	143	4
And would corrupt my saint	"	144	7
needs would touch my breast	"	153	10
would not break from thence	L C		34
Ink would have seem'd	"		54
and often men would say	"		106
for him what he would say	"		132
she would the caged cloister fly	"		249
would she be immured	"		251
did win whom he would maim	"		312
he would exclaim	"		313
would not be so lover'd	"		320
Would yet again betray	"		328
And would corrupt my saint	P P	2	7
would not touch the bait	"	4	11
And would not take	"	11	12
the night would post too soon	"	15	13
Air, would I might triumph	"	17	10
Thou for whom Jove would swear	"	17	15
One woman would another wed	"	19	48
Fie, fie, fie, now would she cry	"	21	13
Wouldst—wouldst hunt the boar	V A		614
wouldst thou one hour come back	R L		965
to store thou wouldst convert	Son	14	12
what a torment wouldst thou prove	"	39	9
If thou wouldst use	"	96	12
Wound—thy heart my wound	V A		370
licking of his wound	"		915
Upon the wide wound	"		1052
that his wound wept	"		1054
makes the wound seem three	"		1064
Bearing away the wound	R L		731
make the wound ache more	"		1116
that makes my wound	"		1201
Staring on Priam's wounds	"		1448
in Priam's painted wound	"		1466
gives unadvised wounds	"		1488
his wounds will not be sore	"		1568
to give this wound to me	"		1722
and through her wounds doth fly	"		1728
Do wounds help wounds	"		1822
Wound—That heals the wound	Son	34	8
For that deep wound	"	133	2
he saw more wounds than one	P P	9	13
Wound—with his hard hoof he wounds	V A		267
And never wound the heart	"		1042
That wounds my body	R L		1185
Wound his folly's show	"		1810
Wound me not with thine eye	Son	139	3
What needst thou wound	"	139	7
Wounded—How he in peace is....	R L		831
salve which wounded bosoms fits	Son	120	12
wounded fancies sent me	L C		197
deep-wounded with a boar	P P	9	10
was wounded with disdain	"	16	11
Wound'st—.... his princely name	R L		599
Wounding—heart's deep-sore	V A		432
the wounding of a frown	"		465
Wounding itself to death	R L		466
crest-wounding private scar	"		828
Woven—And now his woven girths	V A		266
Wrack—pure blush and honour's wrack	"		558
guilty of thy honour's wrack	R L		841
and shun thy wrack	"		966
sovereign mistress over wrack	Son	126	5
Wrapp'd—.... In repentant cold	R L		48
Wrapp'd and confounded	"		456
wrapp'd in with infamies	"		636
Wrath—Wrath, envy, treason, rape	"		909
This load of wrath	"		1474
cold modesty, hot wrath	L C		293
Wreak'd—Be wreak'd on him	V A		1004
Wreath—and wreaths of victory	R L		110
Wreathed—Wreathed up in fatal folds	V A		879
Wreck—Wreck to the seaman	"		454
Time's ruin, beauty's wreck	R L		1451
Wreck'd—Or being wreck'd	Son	80	11
Wreckful—Against the .... siege	"	65	6
Wreck-threatening—.... heart	R L		590
Wresting—Now this ill-wresting world	Son	140	11
Wretch—Mark the poor wretch	V A		680
the dew-bedabbled wretch	"		703
Poor wretches have remorse	R L		269
the wretch did know	Son	50	7
conquest of a wretch's knife	"	74	11
and vassal wretch to be	"	141	12
Wretched—and .... hateful days	R L		161
Such wretched hands such wretched blood should spill	"		999
woes making, wretched I	"		1136
a wretched image bound	"		1501
and wretched arms across	"		1652
But wretched as he is	"		1665
Thy wretched wife mistook	"		1826
Wretched in this alone	Son	91	13
and me most wretched make	"	91	14
What wretched errors	"	119	5
and wretched minutes kill	"	126	8
Wretchedness—free that soul which wretchedness hath chained	R L		900
Wring—He wrings her nose	V A		475
Wringing—hurt my hand with	"		421
Wrinkle—one wrinkle in my brow	"		139
In the remorseless wrinkles	R L		562
chaps and wrinkles were disguised	"		1452
Despite of wrinkles	Son	3	12

Wrinkle—With lines and wrinkles	Son	63	4	Ye—thus I will excuse ye	Son	42	5
The wrinkles which thy glass	"	77	5	dear friend, and I assure ye	"	111	13
and frowns and wrinkles strange	"	93	8	That's to ye sworn	L C	....	180
any wrinkle graven there	"	100	10	Yea—Yea, though I die	R L	....	204
Nor give to necessary wrinkles	"	108	11	Yea, the illiterate, that know not	"	....	810
Wrinkled—wait on wrinkled age	R L	....	275	without or yea or no	"	....	1340
Wrinkled-old—foul or wrinkled-old	V A	....	133	my love, yea, take them all	Son	40	1
Writ—having writ on death	"	....	509	Year—from the dangerous year	V A	....	508
Writ in the glassy margents	R L	....	162	with my unripe years	"	....	524
what is writ in learned books	"	....	811	of his tender years	"	....	1091
writ in my testament	"	....	1183	And threescore year would make	Son	11	8
and it will soon be writ	"	....	1295	Thy beauty and thy years	"	41	3
sorrow writ uncertainly	"	....	1311	In the long year set	"	52	6
now is seal'd and on it writ	"	....	1331	spring and foison of the year	"	53	9
what silent love hath writ	Son	23	13	That time of year	"	73	1
The hand that writ it	"	71	6	the pleasure of the fleeting year	"	97	2
what in you is writ	"	84	9	loves not to have years told	"	138	12
Is writ in moods	"	93	8	my years be past the best	P P	1	6
that I before have writ	"	115	1	loves not to have years told	"	1	12
I never writ, nor no man	"	116	14	unripe years did want	"	4	9
Write—and she prepares to write	R L	....	1296	Yearly—spring doth yearly grow	V A	....	141
If I could write the beauty	Son	17	5	Yell—loud pursuers in their yell	"	....	688
let me, true in love, but truly write	"	21	9	Yellow—When .... leaves or none	Son	73	2
that cannot write to thee	"	38	7	to yellow autumn turn'd	"	104	5
Why write I still	"	76	5	Yellowed—yellow'd with their age	"	17	9
I always write of you	"	76	9	Yelping—the timorous yelping of			
when I of you do write	"	80	1	the hounds	V A	....	881
But he that writes of you	"	84	7	Yes—O, yes it may	"	....	939
whilst other write good words	"	85	5	O, yes, dear friend	P P	10	11
by spirits taught to write	"	86	5	Yet—And yet not cloy	V A	....	19
If I no more can write	"	103	5	yet her fire must burn	"	....	94
but surety-like to write for me	"	134	7	Yet hath he been	"	....	101
Writer—words which writers use	"	82	3	Yet was he servile	"	....	112
Written—this written ambassage	"	26	3	yet are they red	"	....	116
Wrong—blaze forth her wrong	V A	....	210	yet mayst thou well	"	....	128
the heart hath treble wrong	"	....	329	and yet no footing seen	"	....	148
hath done me double wrong	"	....	429	yet his proceedings teach thee	"	....	406
hath done thee wrong	"	....	1005	Yet should I be	"	....	438
hath done her beauty wrong	R L	....	80	Yet would my love	"	....	442
What wrong, what shame	"	....	499	that ever yet betoken'd	"	....	453
to do her husband wrong	"	....	1264	yet complain on drouth	"	....	544
swears he did her wrong	"	....	1462	she feeds, yet never filleth	"	....	548
that hath done him wrong	"	....	1467	yet 'tis pluck'd	"	....	574
And what wrong else	"	....	1622	Yet love breaks through	"	....	576
to venge this wrong of mine	"	....	1691	yet she is not loved	"	....	610
Her wrongs to us	"	....	1840	Yet from mine ear	"	....	778
despite thy wrong	Son	19	13	And yet she hears	"	....	867
to bear love's wrong	"	40	12	yet nought at all	"	....	911
Those petty wrongs	"	41	1	Yet sometimes falls	"	....	981
myself will bear all wrong	"	88	14	and yet too credulous	"	....	986
should do it wrong	"	89	11	Yet pardon me, I felt	"	....	998
to fear the worst of wrongs	"	92	5	and never woman yet	"	....	1007
or changes right or wrong	"	112	8	'And yet,' quoth she	"	....	1070
to justify the wrong	"	139	1	day should yet be light	"	....	1134
O do not love that wrong	P P	5	13	Yet their ambition makes	R L	....	68
Wrong—To wrong the wronger	R L	....	943	Doth yet in his fair welkin	"	....	116
I will not wrong thy true affection so	"	....	1060	Yet ever to obtain	"	....	129
				yet he still pursues	"	....	308
Wronged—How Tarquin .... me	"	....	819	on her yet unstained bed	"	....	366
'Thou wronged lord of Rome	"	....	1818	yet, winking, there appears	"	....	458
Wronger—To wrong the wronger	"	....	943	that yet remains	"	....	463
Wrong'st—Thou .... his honour	"	....	599	Yet strive I	"	....	504
Wrongfully—perfection wrongfully disgraced	Son	66	7	Yet, foul night-waking cat	"	....	554
				yet ere he go to bed	"	....	776
Wrought—that she hath wrought	V A	....	991	'Yet am I guilty	"	....	841
Impiety hath wrought	R L	....	341	Yet for thy honour	"	....	842
Till Nature as she wrought	Son	20	10	Yet for the self-same purpose	"	....	1047
of earth and water wrought	"	44	11	'Yet die I will not	"	....	1177
Wrought all my loss	P P	18	14	Yet with the fault	"	....	1279

Yet—Yet save that labour	R L	1290	Yet—yet their purposed trim	L C		118
And yet the duteous vassal	"	1360	'Yet did I not	"		148
yet show'd content	"	1503	and yet do question make	"		321
but yet defiled	"	1545	Would yet again betray	"		328
and yet not wise	"	1550	yet not directly tell	P P	2	10
yet it seldom sleeps	"	1574	Yet not so wistly	"	6	12
in her poison'd closet yet endure	"	1659	and yet, as glass is, brittle	"	7	3
Yet in the eddy	"	1669	and yet as iron rusty	"	7	4
yet let the traitor die	"	1686	Yet in the midst of all	"	7	11
that yet her sad task	"	1699	yet she foil'd the framing	"	7	15
Yet sometime ' Tarquin	"	1786	and yet she fell a-turning	"	7	16
Yet neither may possess	"	1794	and yet no cause I have	"	10	7
yet canst not live	Son	4	8	And yet thou left'st me more	"	10	9
Yet mortal looks adore	"	7	7	Yet at my parting sweetly	"	14	7
And yet methinks I have	"	14	2	Yet not for me	"	15	16
maiden gardens, yet unset	"	16	6	too young, nor yet unwed	"	19	6
Though yet, heaven knows	"	17	3	Yet will she blush	"	19	53
Yet do thy worst	"	19	13	Hearts remote, yet not asunder	P T		29
Yet eyes this cunning want	"	24	13	To themselves yet either neither	"		43
Yet in these thoughts	"	29	9	Yield—did honey passage yield	V A		452
Yet him for this my love	"	33	13	And yields at last	"		566
yet I have still the loss	"	34	10	captain once doth yield	"		803
Yet doth it steal	"	36	8	captive vanquished doth yield	R L		75
But yet be blamed	"	40	7	portal yields him way	"		309
And yet, love knows	"	40	11	But if thou yield	"		526
yet we must not be foes	"	40	14	Yield to my love	"		668
but yet thou mightst	"	41	9	Yield to my hand	"		1210
And yet it may be said	"	42	2	they such old action yield	"		1433
And yet to times in hope	"	60	13	The earth can yield me	Son	81	7
was ever yet the fair	"	70	2	to razed oblivion yield	"	122	7
Yet this thy praise	"	70	11	But yield them up	L C		221
Yet be most proud	"	78	9	will yield at length	P P	19	21
Yet what of thee	"	79	7	the craggy mountains yields	"	20	4
eyes yet not created	"	81	10	Yielded—nor being desired yielded	L C		149
yet when they have devised	"	82	9	Yielding—caught the yielding prey	V A		547
for my sin you did impute	"	83	9	Which with a yielding latch	R L		339
and yet I know it not	"	92	14	and her for yielding so	"		1036
And yet this time	"	97	5	To accessary yieldings	"		1658
Yet this abundant issue	"	97	9	Yoke—yokes her silver doves	V A		1190
Yet nor the lays of birds	"	98	5	no bearing yoke they knew	R L		409
Yet seem'd it winter still	"	98	13	Unless thou yoke thy liking	"		1633
yet I none could see	"	99	14	Yoking—her .... arms she throws	V A		592
of ages yet to be	"	101	12	Yore—what beauty was of yore	Son	68	14
which yet are green	"	104	8	You—I pray you hence	V A		382
Ah, yet doth beauty	"	104	9	'You hurt my hand	"		421
Can yet the lease	"	107	3	'if any love you owe me	"		523
but yet, like prayers	"	108	5	"Good night," and so say you	"		535
Yet then my judgement	"	115	3	If you will say so, you shall have			
Yet fear her, O thou minion	"	126	9	a kiss	"		536
Yet so they mourn	"	127	13	' you crush me; let me go	"		611
yet none knows well	"	129	13	You have no reason	"		612
yet well I know	"	130	9	' you will fall again	"		769
And yet, by heaven	"	130	13	The kiss I gave you	"		771
Yet, in good faith	"	131	5	all in vain you strive	"		772
And yet thou wilt	"	133	13	like you worse and worse	"		774
and yet am I not free	"	134	14	'If love have lent you	"		775
yet receives rain still	"	135	9	'What have you urg'd	"		787
Yet what the best is	"	137	4	You do it for increase	"		791
Yet do not so	"	139	13	ever strive to kiss you	"		1082
yet, love, to tell me so	"	140	6	you need not fear	"		1083
yet not directly tell	"	144	10	The sun doth scorn you, and the			
Yet this shall I ne'er know	"	144	13	wind doth hiss you	"		1084
Yet who knows not	"	151	2	thoughts, before you blot	R L		192
which yet men prove	"	153	7	be you mediators	"		1020
Found yet moe letters	L C		47	' You mocking birds,' quoth she	"		1121
I might as yet have been	"		75	be you mute and dumb	"		1123
was yet upon his chin	"		92	There might you see	"		1380
Yet show'd his visage	"		96	You might behold	"		1388
Yet, if men moved him	"		101	you see grave Nestor stand	"		1401

You—And swear I found you where you did		R L	1635	You—You still shall live		Son	81	13
ere I name him, you fair lords		"	1688	that you did painting need		"	83	1
that you were yourself! but, love, you are		Son	13	1	you did exceed		"	83	3
					That you yourself, being extant		"	83	6
you yourself here live	"	13	2	worth in you doth grow	"	83	8
you should prepare	"	13	3	my sin you did impute	"	83	9
which you hold in lease	"	13	5	that you alone are you	"	84	2
then you were	"	13	6	But he that writes of you	"	84	7
dear my love, you know	"	13	13	That you are you	"	84	8
You had a father	"	13	14	what in you is writ	"	84	9
Sets you most rich	"	15	10	You to your beauteous blessings	"	84	13
Time for love of you	"	15	13	Hearing you praised	"	85	9
As he takes from you, I engraft you new	"	15	14	whose love to you	"	85	11
				of all too precious you	"	86	2
do not you a mightier way	"	16	1	From you have I been absent	"	98	1
Now stand you on the top	"	16	5	Drawn after you, you pattern	"	98	12
Can make you live	"	16	12	and, you away	"	98	13
And you must live	"	16	14	dull you with my song	"	102	14
You should live twice	"	17	14	your own glass shows you when you look in it	"	103	14
must you see his skill	"	24	5	you never can be old	"	104	1
keeps you as my chest	"	52	9	For as you were	"	104	2
Blessed are you	"	52	13	Since first I saw you fresh	"	104	8
whereof are you made	"	53	1	Ere you were born	"	104	14
shadows on you tend	"	53	2	as you master now	"	106	8
And you, but one imitated after you	"	53	4	all you prefiguring	"	106	10
					do you with Fortune chide	"	111	1
And you in Grecian tires	"	53	6	So, you o'er-green my bad	"	112	4
you in every blessed shape	"	53	12	You are my all-the-world	"	112	5
grace you have some part	"	53	13	You are so strongly	"	112	13
you like none, none you	"	53	14	Since I left you	"	113	1
And so of you	"	54	13	replete with you	"	113	13
But you shall shine	"	55	3	being crown'd with you	"	114	1
Shall you pace forth	"	55	10	I could not love you	"	115	2
You live in this	"	55	14	'Now I love you best	"	115	10
till you require	"	57	4	that so fell sick of you	"	118	14
watch the clock for you	"	57	6	That you were once unkind	"	120	1
When you have bid	"	57	8	For if you were	"	120	5
Where you may be	"	57	10	you've pass'd a hell of time	"	120	6
Save, where you are how happy you make those	"	57	12	soon to you, as you to me	"	120	11
				saying 'not you	"	145	14
Though you do any thing	"	57	14	though in me you behold	L C		71
accusing you of injury	"	58	8	offences that abroad you see	"		183
Be where you list	"	58	9	That is to you, my origin	"		222
That you yourself	"	58	10	I their altar, you enpatron me	"		224
To what you will; to you it doth belong	"	58	11	What me your minister, for you obeys	"		229
Than you shall hear	"	71	2	Works under you	"		230
if you read this line	"	71	5	How mighty then you are	"		253
for I love you so	"	71	6	and you o'er me being strong	"		257
should make you woe	"	71	8	their sighs to you extend	"		276
you look upon this verse	"	71	9	that you make 'gainst mine	"		277
And mock you with me	"	71	14	you had not had it then	P P	19	24
task you to recite	"	72	1	Have you not heard it said	"	19	41
that you should love	"	72	2	Young—young, and so unkind	V A		187
For you in me	"	72	4	lusty, young, and proud	"		260
Unless you would devise	"	72	5	and burdened being young	"		419
That you for love	"	72	10	love makes young men thrall	"		837
nor me nor you	"	72	12	Make the young old	"		1152
And so should you	"	72	14	to be master'd by his young	R L		803
So are you to my thoughts	"	75	1	the young possess their hive	"		1769
And for the peace of you	"	75	3	in my verse ever live young	Son	19	14
to be with you alone	"	75	7	the ambush of young days	"	70	9
must from you be took	"	75	12	thinking that she thinks me young	"	138	5
I always write of you	"	76	9	Love is too young to know	"	151	1
And you and love are still my	"	76	10	Of young, of old	L C		128
when I of you do write	"	80	1	Who, young and simple	"		320
Or you survive	"	81	2	that she thinks me young	P P	1	5
When you entombed	"	81	8	says my love that she is young	"	1	9

Young—With young Adonis	P P	4	2
Venus, with young Adonis	"	11	1
O, my love, my love is young	"	12	10
Neither too young nor yet	"	19	6
the world and love were young	"	20	17
Youngling—She told the youngling	"	11	3
Youngly—blood which youngly thou bestow'st	Son	11	3
Youngster—a.... proud and wild	"	9	4
Your—And 'tis your fault	V A	.....	381
Remove your siege	"	.....	423
your vows, your feigned tears, your flattery	"	.....	425
your idle over-handled theme	"	.....	770
Your treatise makes me	"	.....	774
more moving than your own	"	.....	776
but your device in love	"	.....	789
to your wanton talk	"	.....	809
With your uncleanness	R L	.....	193
your tunes entomb	"	.....	1121
Within your hollow-swelling feather'd breasts	"	.....	1122
Relish your nimble notes	"	.....	1126
if your maid may be so bold	"	.....	1282
to know your heaviness	"	.....	1283
plight your honourable faiths	"	.....	1690
And your sweet semblance	Son	13	4
When your sweet issue your sweet form should bear	"	13	8
let your son say so	"	13	14
change your day of youth	"	15	12
fortify yourself in your decay	"	16	3
bear your living flowers	"	16	7
your painted counterfeit	"	16	8
by your own sweet skill	"	16	14
your most high deserts	"	17	2
Which hides your life and shows not half your parts	"	17	4
the beauty of your eyes	"	17	5
number all your graces	"	17	6
And your true rights	"	17	11
To find where your true image	"	24	6
What is your substance	"	53	1
shadow of your beauty show	"	53	10
us your bounty doth appear	"	53	11
by verse distills your truth	"	54	14
record of your memory	"	55	8
your praise shall still find room	"	55	10
Being your slave	"	57	1
and times of your desire	"	57	2
bid your servant once adieu	"	57	8
or your affairs suppose	"	57	10
love that in your will	"	57	13
made me first your slave	"	58	1
your times of pleasure	"	58	2
Or at your hand	"	58	3
Being your vassal, bound to stay your leisure	"	58	4
being at your beck	"	58	5
absence of your liberty	"	58	6
your charter is so strong	"	58	9
may privilege your time	"	58	10
Not blame your pleasure	"	58	14
Show me your image	"	59	7
wonder of your frame	"	59	10
That I in your sweet thought	"	71	7
But let your love	"	71	12
look into your moan	"	71	13
O, lest your true love	"	72	9
Your—feasting on your sight	Son	75	9
doth use your name	"	80	2
speaking of your fame	"	80	4
But since your worth	"	80	5
On your broad main	"	80	8
Your shallowest help	"	80	9
upon your soundless deep	"	80	10
your epitaph to make	"	81	1
From hence your memory	"	81	3
Your name from hence	"	81	5
Your monument shall be	"	81	9
tongues to be your being shall rehearse	"	81	11
therefore to your fair no painting set	"	83	2
I slept in your report	"	83	5
in one of your fair eyes	"	83	13
Then both your poets	"	83	14
where your equal grew	"	84	4
you to your beauteous blessings	"	84	13
makes your praises worse	"	84	14
While comments of your praise	"	85	2
But when your countenance	"	86	13
As with your shadow	"	98	14
Look in your glass	"	103	6
Than of your graces and your gifts	"	103	12
Your own glass shows you	"	103	14
when first your eye I eyed	"	104	2
Such seems your beauty	"	104	3
So your sweet hue	"	104	11
your worth to sing	"	106	12
Even that your pity	"	111	14
Your love and pity	"	112	1
and praises from your tongue	"	112	6
shapes them to your feature	"	113	12
And that your love	"	114	4
as your sweet self resemble	"	114	6
your great deserts repay	"	117	2
your dearest love to call	"	117	3
your own dear-purchased right	"	117	6
farthest from your sight	"	117	8
level of your frown	"	117	11
in your waken'd hate	"	117	12
and virtue of your love	"	117	14
bring full your ne'er-cloying sweetness	"	118	5
I suffer'd in your crime	"	120	8
that your trespass	"	120	13
Let it not tell your judgement	L C	.....	73
must your oblations be	"	.....	223
to your own command	"	.....	227
What me your minister	"	.....	229
and to your audit comes	"	.....	230
I pour your ocean all among	"	.....	256
Must for your victory	"	.....	258
to physic your cold breast	"	.....	259
Yours—No longer yours than you yourself	Son	13	2
were some child of yours alive	"	17	13
As I by yours	"	120	6
Mine ransoms yours, and yours must ransom me	"	120	14
'O, then, advance of yours that phraseless hand	L C	.....	225
Yourself—Busy yourselves in skill-contending schools	R L	.....	1018
O, that you were yourself	Son	13	1
No longer yours than you yourself here live	"	13	2

Yourself—Yourself again, after yourself's decease	*Son*	13	7	**Youth**—These blenches gave my heart another youth	*Son*	110	7
And fortify yourself	"	16	3	scythed all that youth begun	*L C*	.....	12
Can make you live yourself	"	16	12	Nor youth all quit	"	.....	13
To give away yourself keeps yourself still	"	16	13	with his authorized youth	"	.....	104
				art in youth and youth in art	"	.....	145
judgement that yourself arise	"	55	13	of my suffering youth	"	.....	178
That you yourself may privilege	"	58	10	did I see a fair sweet youth	*P P*	9	9
Yourself to pardon	"	58	12	Crabbed age and youth	"	12	1
That you yourself, being extant	"	83	6	Youth is full of pleasance	"	12	2
Youth—his youth's fair fee	*V A*	.....	393	Youth like summer morn	"	12	3
My youth with his	"	.....	1120	Youth like summer brave	"	12	4
This blur to youth	*R L*	.....	222	Youth is full of sport	"	12	5
My part is youth	"	.....	278	Youth is nimble	"	12	6
Eater of youth, false slave	"	.....	927	Youth is hot and bold	"	12	7
In youth, quick bearing	"	.....	1389	Youth is wild	"	12	8
Thy youth's proud livery	*Son*	2	3	youth, I do adore thee	"	12	9
Resembling strong youth	"	7	6	Vow, alack! for youth unmeet	"	17	13
when thou from youth convertest	"	11	4	Youth so apt to pluck a sweet	"	17	14
Sets you most rich in youth	"	15	10	*Youth*—beauteous and lovely youth	*Son*.	54	13
change your day of youth	"	18	12	she might think me some untutor'd youth	"	138	3
So long as youth and thou	"	22	2				
To see his active child do deeds of youth	"	37	2	she might think me some untutor'd youth	*P P*	1	3
and thy straying youth	"	41	10	**Youthful**—To see their .... sons	*R L*	.....	1432
the flourish set on youth	"	60	9	Vaunt in their youthful sap	*Son*	15	7
on the ashes of his youth	"	73	10	when his youthful morn	"	63	4
Some say, thy fault is youth	"	96	1	A youthful suit,—it was	*L C*	.....	79
thy grace is youth and gentle sport	"	96	2				
a spirit of youth in every thing	"	98	3	**Zealous**—Intend a .... pilgrimage	*Son*	27	6

VENUS AND ADONIS

EVEN as the sun with purple-colour'd face
Had ta'en his last leave of the weeping morn,
Rose-cheek'd Adonis hied him to the chase;
Hunting he loved, but love he laugh'd to scorn;
Sick-thoughted Venus makes amain unto him, 5
And like a bold-faced suitor 'gins to woo him.

'Thrice fairer than myself,' thus she began,
'The field's chief flower, sweet above compare,
Stain to all nymphs, more lovely than a man,
More white and red than doves or roses are; 10
Nature that made thee, with herself at strife,
Saith that the world hath ending with thy life.

'Vouchsafe, thou wonder, to alight thy steed,
And rein his proud head to the saddle-bow;
If thou wilt deign this favour, for thy meed 15
A thousand honey secrets shalt thou know;
Here come and sit, where never serpent hisses,
And, being set, I'll smother thee with kisses;

'And yet not cloy thy lips with loathed satiety,
But rather famish them amid their plenty, 20
Making them red and pale with fresh variety;
Ten kisses short as one, one long as twenty;
A summer's day will seem an hour but short,
Being wasted in such time-beguiling sport.'

With this she seizeth on his sweating palm, 25
The precedent of pith and livelihood,
And, trembling in her passion, calls it balm,
Earth's sovereign salve to do a goddess good;
Being so enraged, desire doth lend her force
Courageously to pluck him from his horse. 30

Over one arm the lusty courser's rein,
Under her other was the tender boy,
Who blush'd and pouted in a dull disdain,
With leaden appetite, unapt to toy;
She red and hot as coals of glowing fire, 35
He red for shame, but frosty in desire.

The studded bridle on a ragged bough
Nimbly she fastens,—O, how quick is love!—
The steed is stalled up, and even now
To tie the rider she begins to prove; 40
Backward she push'd him, as she would be
thrust,
And govern'd him in strength, though not in lust.

So soon was she along as he was down,
Each leaning on their elbows and their hips:
Now doth she stroke his cheek, now doth he
frown, 45
And 'gins to chide, but soon she stops his lips,

And kissing speaks, with lustful language
broken,
'If thou wilt chide, thy lips shall never open.'

He burns with bashful shame; she with her tears
Doth quench the maiden burning of his cheeks; 50
Then with her windy sighs and golden hairs
To fan and blow them dry again she seeks;
He saith she is immodest, blames her miss;
What follows more she murders with a kiss.

Even as an empty eagle, sharp by fast, 55
Tires with her beak on feathers, flesh, and bone,
Shaking her wings, devouring all in haste,
Till either gorge be stuff'd or prey be gone;
Even so she kiss'd his brow, his cheek, his chin,
And where she ends she doth anew begin. 60

Forced to content, but never to obey,
Panting he lies and breatheth in her face;
She feedeth on the steam as on a prey,
And calls it heavenly moisture, air of grace; 64
Wishing her cheeks were gardens full of flowers,
So they were dew'd with such distilling showers.

Look, how a bird lies tangled in a net,
So fasten'd in her arms Adonis lies;
Pure shame and awed resistance made him fret,
Which bred more beauty in his angry eyes; 70
Rain added to a river that is rank
Perforce will force it overflow the bank.

Still she entreats, and prettily entreats,
For to a pretty ear she tunes her tale;
Still is he sullen, still he lours and frets, 75
'Twixt crimson shame and anger ashy-pale;
Being red, she loves him best; and being white,
Her best is better'd with a more delight.

Look how he can, she cannot choose but love;
And by her fair immortal hand she swears 80
From his soft bosom never to remove,
Till he take truce with her contending tears,
Which long have rain'd, making her cheeks all
wet;
And one sweet kiss shall pay this countless debt.

Upon this promise did he raise his chin, 85
Like a dive-dapper peering through a wave,
Who, being look'd on, ducks as quickly in;
So offers he to give what she did crave;
But when her lips were ready for his pay,
He winks, and turns his lips another way. 90

Never did passenger in summer's heat
More thirst for drink than she for this good turn.

Her help she sees, but help she cannot get;
She bathes in water, yet her fire must burn;
'O, pity,' 'gan she cry, 'flint-hearted boy! 95
'Tis but a kiss I beg; why art thou coy?

'I have been woo'd, as I entreat thee now,
Even by the stern and direful god of war,
Whose sinewy neck in battle ne'er did bow,
Who conquers where he comes in every jar; 100
  Yet hath he been my captive and my slave,
  And begg'd for that which thou unask'd shalt
    have.

'Over my altars hath he hung his lance,
His batter'd shield, his uncontrolled crest,
And for my sake hath learn'd to sport and dance,
To toy, to wanton, dally, smile and jest; 106
  Scorning his churlish drum and ensign red,
  Making my arms his field, his tent my bed.

'Thus he that overruled I overway'd,
Leading him prisoner in a red-rose chain; 110
Strong-tempered steel his stronger strength
  obey'd,
Yet was he servile to my coy disdain.
  O, be not proud, nor brag not of thy might,
  For mastering her that foil'd the god of fight!

'Touch but my lips with those fair lips of thine,—
Though mine be not so fair, yet are they red,— 116
The kiss shall be thine own as well as mine;
What see'st thou in the ground? hold up thy head;
  Look in mine eyeballs, there thy beauty lies;
  Then why not lips on lips, since eyes in eyes? 120

'Art thou ashamed to kiss? then wink again,
And I will wink; so shall the day seem night;
Love keeps his revels where there are but twain;
Be bold to play, our sport is not in sight;
  These blue-vein'd violets whereon we lean 125
  Never can blab, nor know not what we mean.

'The tender spring upon thy tempting lip
Shews thee unripe; yet mayst thou well be tasted;
Make use of time, let not advantage slip;
Beauty within itself should not be wasted; 130
  Fair flowers that are not gather'd in their prime
  Rot and consume themselves in little time.

'Were I hard-favour'd, foul, or wrinkled-old,
Ill-nurtured, crooked, churlish, harsh in voice,
O'erworn, despised, rheumatic and cold, 135
Thick-sighted, barren, lean, and lacking juice,
  Then mightst thou pause, for then I were not
    for thee;
  But having no defects, why dost abhor me?

'Thou canst not see one wrinkle in my brow;
Mine eyes are grey, and bright, and quick in
  turning; 140
My beauty as the spring doth yearly grow,
My flesh is soft and plump, my marrow burning;
  My smooth, moist hand, were it with thy hand
    felt,
  Would in thy palm dissolve, or seem to melt.

'Bid me discourse, I will enchant thine ear, 145
Or, like a fairy, trip upon the green,
Or, like a nymph with long dishevell'd hair,
Dance on the sands, and yet no footing seen;

Love is a spirit all compact of fire,
Not gross to sink, but light, and will aspire. 150

'Witness this primrose bank whereon I lie;
These forceless flowers like sturdy trees support
  me;
Two strengthless doves will draw me through the
  sky,
From morn till night, even where I list to sport me;
  Is love so light, sweet boy, and may it be 155
  That thou shouldst think it heavy unto thee?

'Is thine own heart to thine own face affected?
Can thy right hand seize love upon thy left?
Then woo thyself, be of thyself rejected,
Steal thine own freedom, and complain on theft.
  Narcissus so himself himself forsook, 161
  And died to kiss his shadow in the brook.

'Torches are made to light, jewels to wear,
Dainties to taste, fresh beauty for the use, 164
Herbs for their smell, and sappy plants to bear;
Things growing to themselves are growth's abuse;
  Seeds spring from seeds and beauty breedeth
    beauty;
  Thou wast begot; to get it is thy duty.

'Upon the earth's increase why shouldst thou feed,
Unless the earth with thy increase be fed? 170
By law of nature thou art bound to breed,
That thine may live when thou thyself art dead;
  And so, in spite of death, thou dost survive,
  In that thy likeness still is left alive.'

By this, the love-sick queen began to sweat, 175
For, where they lay, the shadow had forsook them,
And Titan, tired in the mid-day heat,
With burning eye did hotly overlook them,
  Wishing Adonis had his team to guide,
  So he were like him and by Venus' side. 180

And now Adonis, with a lazy spright,
And with a heavy, dark, disliking eye,
His louring brows o'erwhelming his fair sight,
Like misty vapours when they blot the sky, 184
  Souring his cheeks, cries 'Fie, no more of love!
  The sun doth burn my face; I must remove.'

'Ay me,' quoth Venus, 'young, and so unkind!
What bare excuses makest thou to be gone!
I'll sigh celestial breath, whose gentle wind
Shall cool the heat of this descending sun; 190
  I'll make a shadow for thee of my hairs;
  If they burn too, I'll quench them with my tears.

'The sun that shines from heaven shines but warm,
And, lo, I lie between that sun and thee;
The heat I have from thence doth little harm, 195
Thine eye darts forth the fire that burneth me;
  And were I not immortal, life were done
  Between this heavenly and earthly sun.

'Art thou obdurate, flinty, hard as steel?
Nay, more than flint, for stone at rain relenteth;
Art thou a woman's son, and canst not feel 201
What 'tis to love? how want of love tormenteth?
  O, had thy mother borne so hard a mind,
  She had not brought forth thee, but died unkind.

'What am I, that thou shouldst contemn me this?
Or what great danger dwells upon my suit? 206
What were thy lips the worse for one poor kiss?
Speak, fair; but speak fair words, or else be mute;
  Give me one kiss, I'll give it thee again,
  And one for interest, if thou wilt have twain. 210

'Fie, lifeless picture, cold and senseless stone,
Well-painted idol, image dull and dead,
Statue contenting but the eye alone,
Thing like a man, but of no woman bred!
  Thou art no man, though of a man's complexion, 215
  For men will kiss even by their own direction.'

This said, impatience chokes her pleading tongue,
And swelling passion doth provoke a pause;
Red cheeks and fiery eyes blaze forth her wrong;
Being judge in love, she cannot right her cause;
  And now she weeps, and now she fain would speak, 221
  And now her sobs do her intendments break.

Sometimes she shakes her head, and then his hand,
Now gazeth she on him, now on the ground;
Sometimes her arms infold him like a band; 225
She would, he will not in her arms be bound;
  And when from thence he struggles to be gone,
  She locks her lily fingers one in one.

'Fondling,' she saith, 'since I have hemm'd thee here
Within the circuit of this ivory pale, 230
I'll be a park, and thou shalt be my deer;
Feed where thou wilt, on mountain or in dale;
  Graze on my lips, and if those hills be dry,
  Stray lower, where the pleasant fountains lie.

'Within this limit is relief enough, 235
Sweet bottom-grass and high delightful plain,
Round rising hillocks, brakes obscure and rough,
To shelter thee from tempest and from rain;
  Then be my deer, since I am such a park;
  No dog shall rouse thee, though a thousand bark.' 240

At this Adonis smiles as in disdain,
That in each cheek appears a pretty dimple;
Love made those hollows, if himself were slain,
He might be buried in a tomb so simple;
  Foreknowing well, if there he came to lie, 245
  Why, there Love lived, and there he could not die.

These lovely caves, these round enchanting pits,
Open'd their mouths to swallow Venus' liking.
Being mad before, how doth she now for wits? 249
Struck dead at first, what needs a second striking?
  Poor queen of love, in thine own law forlorn,
  To love a cheek that smiles at thee in scorn!

Now which way shall she turn? what shall she say?
Her words are done, her woes the more increasing;
The time is spent, her object will away, 255
And from her twining arms doth urge releasing.
  'Pity,' she cries, 'some favour, some remorse!'
  Away he springs, and hasteth to his horse.

But, lo, from forth a copse that neighbours by,
A breeding jennet, lusty, young, and proud, 260
Adonis' trampling courser doth espy,
And forth she rushes, snorts and neighs aloud;

The strong-neck'd steed, being tied unto a tree,
Breaketh his rein and to her straight goes he.
  Imperiously he leaps, he neighs, he bounds, 265
  And now his woven girths he breaks asunder;
The bearing earth with his hard hoof he wounds,
Whose hollow womb resounds like heaven's thunder;
  The iron bit he crusheth 'tween his teeth,
  Controlling what he was controlled with. 270

His ears up-prick'd; his braided hanging mane
Upon his compass'd crest now stand on end;
His nostrils drink the air, and forth again,
As from a furnace, vapours doth he send;
  His eye, which scornfully glisters like fire, 275
  Shows his hot courage and his high desire.

Sometime he trots, as if he told the steps,
With gentle majesty and modest pride;
Anon he rears upright, curvets and leaps,
As who should say 'Lo, thus my strength is tried';
  And this I do to captivate the eye 281
  Of the fair breeder that is standing by.'

What recketh he his rider's angry stir,
His flattering 'Holla' or his 'Stand, I say'?
What cares he now for curb or pricking spur? 285
For rich caparisons or trapping gay?
  He sees his love, and nothing else he sees,
  For nothing else with his proud sight agrees.

Look, when a painter would surpass the life,
In limning out a well-proportion'd steed, 290
His art with nature's workmanship at strife,
As if the dead the living should exceed;
  So did this horse excel a common one
  In shape, in courage, colour, pace, and bone.

Round-hoof'd, short-jointed, fetlocks shag and long, 295
Broad breast, full eye, small head and nostril wide,
High crest, short ears, straight legs and passing strong,
Thin mane, thick tail, broad buttock, tender hide;
  Look, what a horse should have he did not lack,
  Save a proud rider on so proud a back. 300

Sometime he scuds far off, and there he stares;
Anon he starts at stirring of a feather;
To bid the wind a base he now prepares,
And whe'r he run or fly they know not whether;
  For through his mane and tail the high wind sings, 305
  Fanning the hairs, who wave like feather'd wings.

He looks upon his love and neighs unto her;
She answers him, as if she knew his mind; 308
Being proud, as females are, to see him woo her,
She puts on outward strangeness, seems unkind,
  Spurns at his love and scorns the heat he feels,
  Beating his kind embracements with her heels.

Then, like a melancholy malcontent,
He vails his tail, that, like a falling plume,
Cool shadow to his melting buttock lent; 315
He stamps, and bites the poor flies in his fume.
  His love, perceiving how he is enraged,
  Grew kinder, and his fury was assuaged.

His testy master goeth about to take him;
When, lo, the unback'd breeder, full of fear, 320
Jealous of catching, swiftly doth forsake him,
  With her the horse, and left Adonis there;
As they were mad, unto the wood they hie them,
Out-stripping crows that strive to over-fly them.

All swoln with chafing, down Adonis sits, 325
Banning his boisterous and unruly beast;
And now the happy season once more fits,
  That love-sick Love by pleading may be blest;
For lovers say the heart hath treble wrong
When it is barr'd the aidance of the tongue. 330

An oven that is stopp'd, or river stay'd,
Burneth more hotly, swelleth with more rage;
So of concealed sorrow may be said:
  Free vent of words love's fire doth assuage;
But when the heart's attorney once is mute, 335
The client breaks, as desperate in his suit.

He sees her coming, and begins to glow,
Even as a dying coal revives with wind,
And with his bonnet hides his angry brow,
  Looks on the dull earth with disturbed mind; 340
Taking no notice that she is so nigh,
For all askance he holds her in his eye.

O, what a sight it was, wistly to view
How she came stealing to the wayward boy!
To note the fighting conflict of her hue, 345
  How white and red each other did destroy!
But now her cheek was pale, and by and by
It flash'd forth fire, as lightning from the sky.

Now was she just before him as he sat,
And like a lowly lover down she kneels; 350
With one fair hand she heaveth up his hat,
  Her other tender hand his fair cheek feels;
His tenderer cheek receives her soft hand's print,
As apt as new-fall'n snow takes any dint.

O, what a war of looks was then between them! 355
Her eyes petitioners to his eyes suing;
His eyes saw her eyes as they had not seen them;
  Her eyes woo'd still, his eyes disdain'd the wooing;
And all this dumb play had his acts made plain
With tears, which chorus-like her eyes did rain. 360

Full gently now she takes him by the hand,
A lily prison'd in a gaol of snow,
Or ivory in an alabaster band;
  This beauteous combat, wilful and unwilling, 365
Show'd like two silver doves that sit a-billing.

Once more the engine of her thoughts began:
'O fairest mover on this mortal round,
Would thou wert as I am, and I a man, 369
  My heart all whole as thine, thy heart my wound;
For one sweet look thy help I would assure thee,
Though nothing but my body's bane would cure thee.'

'Give me my hand,' saith he; 'why dost thou feel it?'
'Give me my heart,' saith she, 'and thou shalt have it;

'O, give it me, lest thy hard heart do steel it, 375
And being steel'd, soft sighs can never grave it;
  Then love's deep groans I never shall regard,
Because Adonis' heart hath made mine hard.'

'For shame,' he cries, 'let go, and let me go;
My day's delight is past, my horse is gone, 380
And 'tis your fault I am bereft him so;
  I pray you hence, and leave me here alone;
For all my mind, my thought, my busy care,
Is how to get my palfrey from the mare.'

Thus she replies: 'Thy palfrey, as he should, 385
Welcomes the warm approach of sweet desire;
Affection is a coal that must be cool'd;
  Else, suffered, it will set the heart on fire; 388
The sea hath bounds, but deep desire hath none;
Therefore no marvel though thy horse be gone.

'How like a jade he stood, tied to the tree,
Servilely master'd with a leathern rein!
But when he saw his love, his youth's fair fee,
  He held such petty bondage in disdain; 394
Throwing the base thong from his bending crest,
Enfranchising his mouth, his back, his breast.

'Who sees his true-love in her naked bed,
Teaching the sheets a whiter hue than white,
But, when his glutton eye so full hath fed,
  His other agents aim at like delight? 400
Who is so faint, that dares not be so bold
To touch the fire, the weather being cold?

'Let me excuse thy courser, gentle boy;
And learn of him, I heartily beseech thee,
To take advantage on presented joy; 405
  Though I were dumb, yet his proceedings teach thee;
O, learn to love; the lesson is but plain,
And once made perfect, never lost again.'

'I know not love,' quoth he, 'nor will not know it,
Unless it be a boar, and then I chase it; 410
'Tis much to borrow, and I will not owe it;
  My love to love is love but to disgrace it;
For I have heard it is a life in death,
That laughs, and weeps, and all but with a breath.

'Who wears a garment shapeless and unfinish'd?
Who plucks the bud before one leaf put forth? 416
If springing things be any jot diminish'd,
  They wither in their prime, prove nothing worth;
The colt that's back'd and burden'd being young
Loseth his pride, and never waxeth strong. 420

'You hurt my hand with wringing; let us part,
And leave this idle theme, this bootless chat;
Remove your siege from my unyielding heart;
  To love's alarms it will not ope the gate;
Dismiss your vows, your feigned tears, your flattery; 425
For where a heart is hard they make no battery.'

'What! canst thou talk?' quoth she, 'hast thou a tongue?
O, would thou hadst not, or I had no hearing!
  Thy mermaid's voice hath done me double wrong;
I had my load before, now press'd with bearing; 430

Melodious discord, heavenly tune harsh-sound-
  ing,
Ear's deep-sweet music, and heart's deep-sore
  wounding.

'Had I no eyes but ears, my ears would love
That inward beauty and invisible;
Or were I deaf, thy outward parts would move 435
Each part in me that were but sensible;
  Though neither eyes nor ears, to hear nor see,
  Yet should I be in love by touching thee.

'Say, that the sense of feeling were bereft me,
And that I could not see, nor hear, nor touch, 440
And nothing but the very smell were left me,
Yet would my love to thee be still as much;
  For from the stillitory of thy face excelling
  Comes breath perfumed, that breedeth love by
    smelling.

'But, O, what banquet wert thou to the taste, 445
Being nurse and feeder of the other four!
Would they not wish the feast might ever last,
And bid Suspicion double-lock the door,
  Lest Jealousy, that sour unwelcome guest,
  Should by his stealing in disturb the feast?' 450

Once more the ruby-colour'd portal open'd,
Which to his speech did honey passage yield;
Like a red morn that ever yet betoken'd
Wreck to the seaman, tempest to the field,
  Sorrow to shepherds, woe unto the birds, 455
  Gusts and foul flaws to herdmen and to herds.

This ill presage advisedly she marketh;
Even as the wind is hush'd before it raineth,
Or as the wolf doth grin before he barketh,
Or as the berry breaks before it staineth, 460
  Or like the deadly bullet of a gun,
  His meaning struck her ere his words begun.

And at his look she flatly falleth down,
For looks kill love, and love by looks reviveth;
A smile recures the wounding of a frown; 465
But blessed bankrupt, that by love so thriveth!
  The silly boy, believing she is dead,
  Claps her pale cheek, till clapping makes it red;

And all amazed brake off his late intent,
For sharply he did think to reprehend her, 470
Which cunning love did wittily prevent;
Fair fall the wit that can so well defend her!
  For on the grass she lies as she were slain,
  Till his breath breatheth life in her again.

He wrings her nose, he strikes her on the cheeks,
He bends her fingers, holds her pulses hard, 476
He chafes her lips; a thousand ways he seeks
To mend the hurt that his unkindness marr'd;
  He kisses her; and she, by her good will,
  Will never rise, so he will kiss her still. 480

The night of sorrow now is turn'd to day;
Her two blue windows faintly she up-heaveth,
Like the fair sun, when in his fresh array
He cheers the morn, and all the earth relieveth;
  And as the bright sun glorifies the sky, 485
  So is her face illumined with her eye;

Whose beams upon his hairless face are fix'd,
As if from thence they borrow'd all their shine.
Were never four such lamps together mix'd,
Had not his clouded with his brow's repine;
  But hers, which through the crystal tears gave
    light, 491
  Shone like the moon in water seen by night.

'O, where am I?' quoth she; 'in earth or heaven,
Or in the ocean drench'd, or in the fire?
What hour is this? or morn or weary even? 495
Do I delight to die, or life desire?
  But now I lived, and life was death's annoy;
  But now I died, and death was lively joy.

'O, thou didst kill me; kill me once again; 499
Thy eyes' shrewd tutor, that hard heart of thine,
Hath taught them scornful tricks, and such dis-
    dain,
That they have murder'd this poor heart of mine;
  And these mine eyes, true leaders to their queen,
  But for thy piteous lips no more had seen.

'Long may they kiss each other, for this cure! 505
O, never let their crimson liveries wear!
And as they last, their verdure still endure,
To drive infection from the dangerous year!
  That the star-gazers, having writ on death, 509
  May say, the plague is banish'd by thy breath.

'Pure lips, sweet seals in my soft lips imprinted,
What bargains may I make, still to be sealing?
To sell myself I can be well contented,
So thou wilt buy, and pay, and use good dealing;
  Which purchase if thou make, for fear of slips
  Set thy seal-manual on my wax-red lips. 516

'A thousand kisses buys my heart from me;
And pay them at thy leisure, one by one.
What is ten hundred touches unto thee?
Are they not quickly told and quickly gone? 520
  Say, for non-payment that the debt should
    double,
  Is twenty hundred kisses such a trouble?'

'Fair queen,' quoth he, 'if any love you owe me,
Measure my strangeness with my unripe years;
Before I know myself, seek not to know me; 525
No fisher but the ungrown fry forbears;
  The mellow plum doth fall, the green sticks fast,
  Or being early pluck'd is sour to taste.

'Look, the world's comforter, with weary gait,
His day's hot task hath ended in the west; 530
The owl, night's herald, shrieks,—'tis very late;
The sheep are gone to fold, birds to their nest;
  And coal-black clouds that shadow heaven's
    light
  Do summon us to part, and bid good-night.

'Now let me say "Good-night," and so say you;
If you will say so, you shall have a kiss.' 536
'Good-night,' quoth she; and, ere he says 'Adieu,'
The honey fee of parting tender'd is;
  Her arms do lend his neck a sweet embrace; 539
  Incorporate then they seem; face grows to face.

Till breathless he disjoin'd, and backward drew
The heavenly moisture, that sweet coral mouth,
Whose precious taste her thirsty lips well knew,
Whereon they surfeit, yet complain on drouth;

He with her plenty pressed, she faint with
    dearth, 545
Their lips together glued, fall to the earth.

Now quick desire hath caught the yielding prey,
And glutton-like she feeds, yet never filleth;
Her lips are conquerors, his lips obey,
Paying what ransom the insulter willeth; 550
  Whose vulture-thought doth pitch the price so
    high,
  That she will draw his lips' rich treasure dry.

And having felt the sweetness of the spoil,
With blindfold fury she begins to forage; 554
Her face doth reek and smoke, her blood doth boil,
And careless lust stirs up a desperate courage,
  Planting oblivion, beating reason back,
  Forgetting shame's pure blush and honour's
    wrack.

Hot, faint, and weary, with her hard embracing,
Like a wild bird being tamed with too much hand-
    ling, 560
Or as the fleet-foot roe that's tired with chasing,
Or like the froward infant still'd with dandling,
  He now obeys, and now no more resisteth,
  While she takes all she can, not all she listeth.

What wax so frozen but dissolves with tempering,
And yields at last to every light impression? 566
Things out of hope are compass'd oft with ven-
    turing,
Chiefly in love, whose leave exceeds commission;
  Affection faints not like a pale-faced coward,
  But then woos best when most his choice is
    froward. 570

When he did frown, O, had she then gave over,
Such nectar from his lips she had not suck'd.
Foul words and frowns must not repel a lover;
What though the rose have prickles, yet 'tis
    pluck'd;
  Were beauty under twenty locks kept fast, 575
  Yet love breaks through, and picks them all at
    last.

For pity now she can no more detain him;
The poor fool prays her that he may depart;
She is resolved no longer to restrain him;
Bids him farewell, and look well to her heart, 580
  The which, by Cupid's bow she doth protest,
  He carries thence incaged in his breast.

'Sweet boy,' she says, 'this night I'll waste in
    sorrow,
For my sick heart commands mine eyes to watch.
Tell me, love's master, shall we meet to-mor-
    row? 585
Say, shall we? shall we? wilt thou make the
    match?'
  He tells her, no; to-morrow he intends
  To hunt the boar with certain of his friends.

'The boar!' quoth she; whereat a sudden pale,
Like lawn being spread upon the blushing rose, 590
Usurps her cheek; she trembles at his tale,
And on his neck her yoking arms she throws;
  She sinketh down, still hanging by his neck,
  He on her belly falls, she on her back.

Now is she in the very lists of love, 595
Her champion mounted for the hot encounter;
All is imaginary she doth prove,
He will not manage her, although he mount her;
  That worse than Tantalus' is her annoy,
  To clip Elysium, and to lack her joy. 600

Even as poor birds, deceived with painted grapes,
Do surfeit by the eye and pine the maw,
Even so she languisheth in her mishaps,
As those poor birds that helpless berries saw. 604
  The warm effects which she in him finds missing
  She seeks to kindle with continual kissing.

But all in vain; good queen, it will not be;
She hath assay'd as much as may be proved;
Her pleading hath deserved a greater fee;
She's Love, she loves, and yet she is not loved. 610
  'Fie, fie,' he says, 'you crush me; let me go;
  You have no reason to withhold me so.'

'Thou hadst been gone,' quoth she, 'sweet boy, ere
    this,
But that thou told'st me thou wouldst hunt the
    boar.
O, be advised; thou know'st not what it is 615
With javelin's point a churlish swine to gore,
  Whose tushes never sheathed he whetteth still,
  Like to a mortal butcher, bent to kill.

'On his bow-back he hath a battle set
Of bristly pikes, that ever threat his foes; 620
His eyes, like glow-worms, shine when he doth
    fret;
His snout digs sepulchres where'er he goes;
  Being moved, he strikes whate'er is in his way;
  And whom he strikes his crooked tushes slay.

'His brawny sides, with hairy bristles arm'd, 625
Are better proof than thy spear's point can enter;
His short thick neck cannot be easily harm'd;
Being ireful, on the lion he will venture:
  The thorny brambles and embracing bushes, 629
  As fearful of him, part; through whom he rushes.

'Alas, he nought esteems that face of thine,
To which Love's eyes pay tributary gazes;
Nor thy soft hands, sweet lips and crystal eyne,
Whose full perfection all the world amazes; 634
  But having thee at vantage,—wondrous dread!—
  Would root these beauties as he roots the mead.

'O, let him keep his loathsome cabin still;
Beauty hath nought to do with such foul fiends;
Come not within his danger by thy will; 639
They that thrive well take counsel of their friends.
  When thou didst name the boar, not to dissemble,
  I fear'd thy fortune, and my joints did tremble.

'Didst thou not mark my face? was it not white?
Saw'st thou not signs of fear lurk in mine eye?
Grew I not faint? and fell I not downright? 645
Within my bosom, whereon thou dost lie,
  My boding heart pants, beats, and takes no rest,
  But, like an earthquake, shakes thee on my
    breast.

'For where Love reigns, disturbing Jealousy
Doth call himself Affection's sentinel; 650
Gives false alarms, suggesteth mutiny,
And in a peaceful hour doth cry "Kill, kill!"

Distempering gentle Love in his desire,
As air and water do abate the fire.

'This sour informer, this bate-breeding spy, 655
This canker that eats up Love's tender spring,
This carry-tale, dissentious Jealousy,
That sometime true news, sometime false doth
 bring,
Knocks at my heart, and whispers in mine ear,
That if I love thee, I thy death should fear; 660

'And more than so, presenteth to mine eye
The picture of an angry-chafing boar,
Under whose sharp fangs on his back doth lie
An image like thyself, all stained with gore;
Whose blood upon the fresh flowers being shed
Doth make them droop with grief and hang the
 head. 666

'What should I do, seeing thee so indeed,
That tremble at the imagination?
The thought of it doth make my faint heart bleed,
And fear doth teach it divination; 670
 I prophesy thy death, my living sorrow,
 If thou encounter with the boar to-morrow.

'But if thou needs wilt hunt, be ruled by me;
Uncouple at the timorous flying hare,
Or at the fox which lives by subtlety, 675
Or at the roe which no encounter dare;
 Pursue these fearful creatures o'er the downs,
 And on thy well-breath'd horse keep with thy
  hounds.

'And when thou hast on foot the purblind hare,
Mark the poor wretch, to overshoot his troubles, 681
How he outruns the wind, and with what care
He cranks and crosses with a thousand doubles;
 The many musits through the which he goes
 Are like a labyrinth to amaze his foes.

'Sometime he runs among a flock of sheep, 685
To make the cunning hounds mistake their smell,
And sometime where earth-delving conies keep,
To stop the loud pursuers in their yell;
 And sometime sorteth with a herd of deer:
 Danger deviseth shifts; wit waits on fear; 690

'For there his smell with others being mingled,
The hot scent-snuffing hounds are driven to doubt,
Ceasing their clamorous cry till they have singled
With much ado the cold fault cleanly out;
 Then do they spend their mouths; Echo replies,
 As if another chase were in the skies. 696

'By this, poor Wat, far off upon a hill,
Stands on his hinder legs with listening ear,
To hearken if his foes pursue him still;
Anon their loud alarums he doth hear; 700
 And now his grief may be compared well
 To one sore sick that hears the passing-bell.

'Then shalt thou see the dew-bedabbled wretch
Turn, and return, indenting with the way;
Each envious brier his weary legs doth scratch, 705
Each shadow makes him stop, each murmur stay;
 For misery is trodden on by many,
 And being low never relieved by any.

'Lie quietly, and hear a little more;
Nay, do not struggle, for thou shalt not rise; 710
To make thee hate the hunting of the boar,
Unlike myself thou hear'st me moralize,
 Applying this to that, and so to so;
 For love can comment upon every woe.

'Where did I leave?' 'No matter where,' quoth he;
'Leave me, and then the story aptly ends; 716
The night is spent.' 'Why, what of that?' quoth
 she.
'I am,' quoth he, 'expected of my friends;
 And now 'tis dark, and going I shall fall.'
 'In night,' quoth she, 'desire sees best of all. 720

'But if thou fall, O, then imagine this,
The earth, in love with thee, thy footing trips,
And all is but to rob thee of a kiss.
Rich preys make true men thieves; so do thy lips
 Make modest Dian cloudy and forlorn, 725
 Lest she should steal a kiss, and die forsworn.

'Now of this dark night I perceive the reason:
Cynthia for shame obscures her silver shine,
Till forging Nature be condemn'd of treason, 729
For stealing moulds from heaven that were divine;
 Wherein she framed thee, in high heaven's
  despite,
 To shame the sun by day and her by night.

'And therefore hath she bribed the Destinies
To cross the curious workmanship of nature,
To mingle beauty with infirmities 735
And pure perfection with impure defeature;
 Making it subject to the tyranny
 Of mad mischances and much misery;

'As burning fevers, agues pale and faint,
Life-poisoning pestilence and frenzies wood, 740
The marrow-eating sickness, whose attaint
Disorder breeds by heating of the blood;
 Surfeits, imposthumes, grief and damn'd despair,
 Swear Nature's death for framing thee so fair.

'And not the least of all these maladies 745
But in one minute's fight brings beauty under;
Both favour, savour, hue and qualities,
Whereat the impartial gazer late did wonder,
 Are on the sudden wasted, thaw'd and done, 749
 As mountain snow melts with the mid-day sun.

'Therefore, despite of fruitless chastity,
Love-lacking vestals and self-loving nuns,
That on the earth would breed a scarcity
And barren dearth of daughters and of sons,
 Be prodigal; the lamp that burns by night 755
 Dries up his oil to lend the world his light.

'What is thy body but a swallowing grave,
Seeming to bury that posterity
Which by the rights of time thou needs must have,
If thou destroy them not in dark obscurity? 760
 If so, the world will hold thee in disdain,
 Sith in thy pride so fair a hope is slain.

'So in thyself thyself art made away;
A mischief worse than civil home-bred strife,
Or theirs whose desperate hands themselves do
 slay, 765
Or butcher-sire that reaves his son of life.

Foul-cankering rust the hidden treasure frets,
But gold that's put to use more gold begets.'

'Nay, then,' quoth Adon, 'you will fall again
Into your idle over-handled theme; 770
The kiss I gave you is bestow'd in vain,
And all in vain you strive against the stream;
For, by this black-faced night, desire's foul
 nurse,
Your treatise makes me like you worse and
 worse.

'If love have lent you twenty thousand tongues,
And every tongue more moving than your own, 776
Bewitching like the wanton mermaid's songs,
Yet from mine ear the tempting tune is blown;
For know, my heart stands armed in mine ear,
And will not let a false sound enter there; 780

'Lest the deceiving harmony should run
Into the quiet closure of my breast;
And then my little heart were quite undone,
In his bedchamber to be barr'd of rest.
No, lady, no; my heart longs not to groan, 785
But soundly sleeps, while now it sleeps alone.

'What have you urged that I cannot reprove?
The path is smooth that leadeth on to danger;
I hate not love, but your device in love
That lends embracements unto every stranger. 790
 You do it for increase: O strange excuse,
 When reason is the bawd to lust's abuse!

'Call it not love, for Love to heaven is fled
Since sweating Lust on earth usurp'd his name;
Under whose simple semblance he hath fed 795
Upon fresh beauty, blotting it with blame;
Which the hot tyrant stains and soon bereaves,
As caterpillars do the tender leaves.

'Love comforteth like sunshine after rain,
But Lust's effect is tempest after sun; 800
Love's gentle spring doth always fresh remain,
Lust's winter comes ere summer half be done;
 Love surfeits not, Lust like a glutton dies;
 Love is all truth, Lust full of forged lies.

'More I could tell, but more I dare not say; 805
The text is old, the orator too green.
Therefore, in sadness, now I will away;
My face is full of shame, my heart of teen;
 Mine ears, that to your wanton talk attended,
 Do burn themselves for having so offended.' 810

With this, he breaketh from the sweet embrace
Of those fair arms which bound him to her breast,
And homeward through the dark lawnd runs
 apace;
Leaves Love upon her back deeply distress'd.
 Look, how a bright star shooteth from the sky,
 So glides he in the night from Venus' eye; 816

Which after him she darts, as one on shore
Gazing upon a late-embarked friend,
Till the wild waves will have him seen no more,
Whose ridges with the meeting clouds contend; 820
 So did the merciless and pitchy night
 Fold in the object that did feed her sight.

Whereat amazed, as one that unaware
Hath dropp'd a precious jewel in the flood,
Or 'stonish'd as night-wanderers often are, 825
Their light blown out in some mistrustful wood;
 Even so confounded in the dark she lay,
 Having lost the fair discovery of her way.

And now she beats her heart, whereat it groans,
That all the neighbor caves, as seeming troubled,
Make verbal repetition of her moans; 831
Passion on passion deeply is redoubled;
 'Ay me!' she cries, and twenty times, 'Woe, woe!'
 And twenty echoes twenty times cry so.

She, marking them, begins a wailing note, 835
And sings extemporally a woeful ditty;
How love makes young men thrall, and old men
 dote;
How love is wise in folly, foolish-witty;
 Her heavy anthem still concludes in woe,
 And still the choir of echoes answer so. 840

Her song was tedious, and outwore the night,
For lovers' hours are long, though seeming short;
If pleased themselves, others, they think, delight
In such-like circumstance, with such-like sport;
 Their copious stories, oftentimes begun, 845
 End without audience, and are never done.

For who hath she to spend the night withal,
But idle sounds resembling parasites;
Like shrill-tongued tapsters answering every call,
Soothing the humour of fantastic wits? 850
 She says ''Tis so;' they answer all ''Tis so;'
 And would say after her, if she said 'No.'

Lo, here the gentle lark, weary of rest,
From his moist cabinet mounts up on high,
And wakes the morning, from whose silver breast
The sun ariseth in his majesty; 856
 Who doth the world so gloriously behold,
 That cedar-tops and hills seem burnish'd gold.

Venus salutes him with this fair good-morrow;
'O thou clear god, and patron of all light, 860
From whom each lamp and shining star doth bor-
 row
The beauteous influence that makes him bright,
 There lives a son, that suck'd an earthly mother,
 May lend thee light, as thou dost lend to other.'

This said, she hasteth to a myrtle grove, 865
Musing the morning is so much o'erworn,
And yet she hears no tidings of her love;
She hearkens for his hounds and for his horn;
 Anon she hears them chant it lustily,
 And all in haste she coasteth to the cry. 870

And as she runs, the bushes in the way
Some catch her by the neck, some kiss her face,
Some 'twine about her thigh to make her stay;
She wildly breaketh from their strict embrace, 874
 Like a milch doe, whose swelling dugs do ache,
 Hasting to feed her fawn hid in some brake.

By this she hears the hounds are at a bay;
Whereat she starts, like one that spies an adder
Wreathed up in fatal folds just in his way,
The fear whereof doth make him shake and shud-
 der; 880

Even so the timorous yelping of the hounds
Appals her senses and her spirit confounds.

For now she knows it is no gentle chase,
But the blunt boar, rough bear, or lion proud,
Because the cry remaineth in one place, 885
Where fearfully the dogs exclaim aloud;
Finding their enemy to be so curst,
They all strain courtesy who shall cope him first.

This dismal cry rings sadly in her ear,
Through which it enters to surprise her heart; 890
Who, overcome by doubt and bloodless fear,
With cold-pale weakness numbs each feeling part;
  Like soldiers, when their captain once doth
    yield,
  They basely fly, and dare not stay the field.

Thus stands she in a trembling ecstasy; 895
Till, cheering up her senses all dismay'd,
She tells them 'tis a causeless fantasy,
And childish error, that they are afraid;
  Bids them leave quaking, bids them fear no
    more; 899
  And with that word she spied the hunted boar;

Whose frothy mouth, bepainted all with red,
Like milk and blood being mingled both together,
A second fear through all her sinews spread,
Which madly hurries her she knows not whither;
  This way she runs, and now she will no further,
  But back retires to rate the boar for murther. 906

A thousand spleens bear her a thousand ways;
She treads the path that she untreads again;
Her more than haste is mated with delays,
Like the proceedings of a drunken brain, 910
  Full of respects, yet nought at all respecting;
  In hand with all things, nought at all effecting.

Here kennell'd in a brake she finds a hound,
And asks the weary caitiff for his master;
And their another licking of his wound, 915
'Gainst venom'd sores the only sovereign plaster;
  And here she meets another sadly scowling,
  To whom she speaks, and he replies with howl-
    ing.

When he hath ceased his ill-resounding noise,
Another flap-mouth'd mourner, black and grim,
Against the welkin volleys out his voice; 921
Another and another answer him,
  Clapping their proud tails to the ground below,
  Shaking their scratch'd ears, bleeding as they go.

Look, how the world's poor people are amazed
At apparitions, signs, and prodigies, 926
Whereon with fearful eyes they long have gazed,
Infusing them with dreadful prophecies;
  So she at these sad signs draws up her breath,
  And, sighing it again, exclaims on Death. 930

'Hard-favour'd tyrant, ugly, meagre, lean,
Hateful divorce of love,'—thus chides she Death,—
'Grim-grinning ghost, earth's worm, what dost
    thou mean
To stifle beauty and to steal his breath,
  Who when he lived, his breath and beauty set
  Gloss on the rose, smell to the violet? 936

'If he be dead,—O no, it cannot be,
Seeing his beauty, thou shouldst strike at it;—
O yes, it may; thou hast no eyes to see,
But hatefully at random dost thou hit. 940
  Thy mark is feeble age; but thy false dart
  Mistakes that aim, and cleaves an infant's heart.

'Hadst thou but bid beware, then he had spoke,
And, hearing him, thy power had lost his power.
The Destinies will curse thee for this stroke; 945
They bid thee crop a weed, thou pluck'st a flower;
  Love's golden arrow at him should have fled,
  And not Death's ebon dart, to strike him dead.

'Dost thou drink tears, that thou provokest such
    weeping?
What may a heavy groan advantage thee? 950
Why hast thou cast into eternal sleeping
Those eyes that taught all other eyes to see?
  Now Nature cares not for thy mortal vigour,
  Since her best work is ruin'd with thy rigour.'

Here overcome, as one full of despair, 955
She vail'd her eyelids, who, like sluices, stopp'd
The crystal tide that from her two cheeks fair
In the sweet channel of her bosom dropp'd;
  But through the flood-gates breaks the silver
    rain,
  And with his strong course opens them again. 960

O, how her eyes and tears did lend and borrow!
Her eyes seen in the tears, tears in her eye;
Both crystals, where they view'd each other's
    sorrow,
Sorrow that friendly sighs sought still to dry;
  But like a stormy day, now wind, now rain, 965
  Sighs dry her cheeks, tears make them wet again.

Variable passions throng her constant woe,
As striving who should best become her grief;
All entertain'd, each passion labours so
That every present sorrow seemeth chief, 970
  But none is best; then join they all together,
  Like many clouds consulting for foul weather.

By this, far off she hears some huntsman holloa;
A nurse's song ne'er pleased her babe so well;
The dire imagination she did follow 975
This sound of hope doth labour to expel;
  For now reviving joy bids her rejoice,
  And flatters her it is Adonis' voice.

Whereat her tears began to turn their tide,
Being prison'd in her eye like pearls in glass; 980
Yet sometimes falls an orient drop beside,
Which her cheek melts, as scorning it should pass
  To wash the foul face of the sluttish ground,
  Who is but drunken when she seemeth drown'd.

O hard-believing love, how strange it seems 985
Not to believe, and yet too credulous!
Thy weal and woe are both of them extremes;
Despair, and hope, makes thee ridiculous; 988
  The one doth flatter thee in thoughts unlikely,
  In likely thoughts the other kills thee quickly.

Now she unweaves the web that she hath wrought;
Adonis lives, and Death is not to blame;
It was not she that call'd him all to nought;
Now she adds honours to his hateful name;

She clepes him king of graves, and grave for
   kings, 995
Imperious supreme of all mortal things.

'No, no,' quoth she, 'sweet Death, I did but jest;
Yet pardon me, I felt a kind of fear
Whenas I met the boar, that bloody beast,
Which knows no pity, but is still severe; 1000
Then, gentle shadow,—truth I must confess,—
I rail'd on thee, fearing my love's decease.

"'Tis not my fault; the boar provoked my tongue;
Be wreak'd on him, invisible commander; 1004
'Tis he, foul creature, that hath done thee wrong;
I did but act, he's author of thy slander;
   Grief hath two tongues; and never woman yet
   Could rule them both without ten women's wit.'

Thus hoping that Adonis is alive,
Her rash suspect she doth extenuate; 1010
And that his beauty may the better thrive,
With Death she humbly doth insinuate;
   Tells him of trophies, statues, tombs, and stories
   His victories, his triumphs and his glories.

'O Jove,' quoth she, 'how much a fool was I
To be of such a weak and silly mind 1016
To wail his death who lives and must not die
Till mutual overthrow of mortal kind!
   For he being dead, with him is beauty slain,
   And, beauty dead, black chaos comes again. 1020

'Fie, fie, fond love, thou art so full of fear
As one with treasure laden, hemm'd with thieves;
Trifles unwitnessed with eye or ear
Thy coward heart with false bethinking grieves.'
   Even at this word she hears a merry horn, 1025
   Whereat she leaps that was but late forlorn.

As falcons to the lure, away she flies;
The grass stoops not, she treads on it so light;
And in her haste unfortunately spies
The foul boar's conquest on her fair delight; 1030
   Which seen, her eyes, as murder'd with the view,
   Like stars ashamed of day, themselves withdrew;

Or, as the snail, whose tender horns being hit,
Shrinks backward in his shelly cave with pain,
And there all smother'd up in shade doth sit, 1035
Long after fearing to creep forth again;
   So, at his bloody view, her eyes are fled
   Into the deep-dark cabins of her head;

Where they resign their office and their light
To the disposing of her troubled brain; 1040
Who bids them still consort with ugly night,
And never wound the heart with looks again;
   Who, like a king perplexed in his throne,
   By their suggestion gives a deadly groan,

Whereat each tributary subject quakes; 1045
As when the wind, imprison'd in the ground,
Struggling for passage, earth's foundation shakes,
Which with cold terror doth men's minds confound.
   This mutiny each part doth so surprise,
   That from their dark beds once more leap her
      eyes; 1050

And being open'd threw unwilling light
Upon the wide wound that the boar had trench'd
In his soft flank; whose wonted lily white
With purple tears, that his wound wept, was
   drench'd. 1054
   No flower was nigh, no grass, herb, leaf, or weed,
   But stole his blood and seem'd with him to bleed.

This solemn sympathy poor Venus noteth;
Over one shoulder doth she hang her head;
Dumbly she passions, franticly she doteth;
She thinks he could not die, he is not dead; 1060
   Her voice is stopp'd, her joints forget to bow;
   Her eyes are mad that they have wept till now.

Upon his hurt she looks so steadfastly
That her sight dazzling makes the wound seem
   three; 1064
And then she reprehends her mangling eye,
That makes more gashes where no breach should
   be;
   His face seems twain, each several limb is doubled;
   For oft the eye mistakes, the brain being troubled.

'My tongue cannot express my grief for one,
And yet,' quoth she, 'behold two Adons dead! 1070
My sighs are blown away, my salt tears gone,
Mine eyes are turn'd to fire, my heart to lead;
   Heavy heart's lead, melt at mine eyes' red fire!
   So shall I die by drops of hot desire.

'Alas, poor world, what treasure hast thou lost! 1075
What face remains alive that's worth the viewing?
Whose tongue is music now? what canst thou boast
Of things long since, or any thing ensuing?
   The flowers are sweet, their colours fresh and
      trim; 1079
   But true-sweet beauty lived and died with him.

'Bonnet nor veil henceforth no creature wear!
Nor sun nor wind will ever strive to kiss you;
Having no fair to lose, you need not fear;
The sun doth scorn you, and the wind doth hiss
   you; 1084
   But when Adonis lived, sun and sharp air
   Lurk'd like two thieves, to rob him of his fair.

'And therefore would he put his bonnet on,
Under whose brim the gaudy sun would peep;
The wind would blow it off, and, being gone,
Play with his locks; then would Adonis weep; 1090
   And straight, in pity of his tender years,
   They both would strive who first should dry his
      tears.

'To see his face the lion walk'd along
Behind some hedge, because he would not fear him;
To recreate himself when he hath sung, 1095
The tiger would be tame and gently hear him;
   If he had spoke, the wolf would leave his prey,
   And never fright the silly lamb that day.

'When he beheld his shadow in the brook,
The fishes spread on it their golden gills; 1100
When he was by, the birds such pleasure took,
That some would sing, some other in their bills

Would bring him mulberries and ripe-red cher-
  ries;
He fed them with his sight, they him with berries.

'But this foul, grim, and urchin-snouted boar, 1105
Whose downward eye still looketh for a grave,
Ne'er saw the beauteous livery that he wore;
Witness the entertainment that he gave;
If he did see his face, why then I know   1109
He thought to kiss him, and hath kill'd him so.

'Tis true, 'tis true; thus was Adonis slain;
He ran upon the boar with his sharp spear,
Who did not whet his teeth at him again,
But by a kiss thought to persuade him there;
  And muzzling in his flank, the loving swine 1115
  Sheathed unaware the tusk in his soft groin.

'Had I been tooth'd like him, I must confess,
With kissing him I should have kill'd him first;
But he is dead, and never did he bless
My youth with his; the more am I accurst.' 1120
  With this, she falleth in the place she stood,
  And stains her face with his congealed blood.

She looks upon his lips, and they are pale;
She takes him by the hand, and that is cold;
She whispers in his ears a heavy tale,   1125
As if they heard the woeful words she told;
  She lifts the coffer-lids that close his eyes,
  Where, lo, two lamps, burnt out, in darkness lies;

Two glasses, where herself herself beheld
A thousand times, and now no more reflect; 1130
Their virtue lost, wherein they late excell'd,
And every beauty robb'd of his effect;
  'Wonder of time,' quoth she, 'this is my spite,
  That, thou being dead, the day should yet be
    light.

'Since thou art dead, lo, here I prophesy,   1135
Sorrow on love hereafter shall attend;
It shall be waited on with jealousy,
Find sweet beginning but unsavoury end;
  Ne'er settled equally, but high or low,   1139
  That all love's pleasure shall not match his woe.

'It shall be fickle, false, and full of fraud;
Bud, and be blasted, in a breathing while;
The bottom poison, and the top o'erstraw'd
With sweets that shall the truest sight beguile;
  The strongest body shall it make most weak, 1145
  Strike the wise dumb, and teach the fool to speak.

'It shall be sparing and too full of riot,
Teaching decrepit age to tread the measures;
The staring ruffian shall it keep in quiet,
Pluck down the rich, enrich the poor with treas-
  ures;   1150

It shall be raging-mad, and silly-mild,
Make the young old, the old become a child.

'It shall suspect where is no cause of fear;
It shall not fear where it should most mistrust;
It shall be merciful and too severe,   1155
And most deceiving when it seems most just;
  Perverse it shall be where it shows most toward,
  Put fear to valour, courage to the coward.

'It shall be cause of war and dire events,
And set dissension 'twixt the son and sire; 1160
Subject and servile to all discontents,
As dry combustious matter is to fire;
  Sith in his prime death doth my love destroy,
  They that love best their loves shall not enjoy.'

By this the boy that by her side lay kill'd   1165
Was melted like a vapour from her sight,
And in his blood, that on the ground lay spill'd,
A purple flower sprung up, chequer'd with white,
  Resembling well his pale cheeks and the blood
  Which in round drops upon their whiteness
    stood.   1170

She bows her head, the new-sprung flower to smell,
Comparing it to her Adonis' breath;
And says, within her bosom it shall dwell,
Since he himself is reft from her by death;
  She crops the stalk, and in the breach appears
  Green-dropping sap, which she compares to
    tears.   1176

'Poor flower,' quoth she, 'this was thy father's
  guise,—
Sweet issue of a more sweet-smelling sire,—
For every little grief to wet his eyes;
To grow unto himself was his desire,   1180
And so 'tis thine; but know, it is as good
  To wither in my breast as in his blood.

'Here was thy father's bed, here in my breast;
Thou art the next of blood, and 'tis thy right;
Lo, in this hollow cradle take thy rest;   1185
My throbbing heart shall rock thee day and night;
  There shall not be one minute in an hour
  Wherein I will not kiss my sweet love's flower.'

Thus weary of the world, away she hies,   1189
And yokes her silver doves; by whose swift aid
Their mistress, mounted, through the empty skies
In her light chariot quickly is convey'd;
  Holding their course to Paphos, where their
    queen
  Means to immure herself and not be seen.

THE RAPE OF LUCRECE

From the besieged Ardea all in post,
Borne by the trustless wings of false desire,
Lust-breathed Tarquin leaves the Roman host,
And to Collatium bears the lightless fire
Which, in pale embers hid, lurks to aspire   5
   And girdle with embracing flames the waist
   Of Collatine's fair love, Lucrece the chaste.

Haply that name of 'chaste' unhappily set
This hateless edge on his keen appetite;
When Collatine unwisely did not let   10
To praise the clear unmatched red and white
Which triumph'd in that sky of his delight,
   Where mortal stars, as bright as heaven's beauties,
   With pure aspects did him peculiar duties.

For he the night before, in Tarquin's tent,   15
Unlock'd the treasure of his happy state;
What priceless wealth the heavens had him lent
In the possession of his beauteous mate;
Reckoning his fortune at such high-proud rate,
   That kings might be espoused to more fame,   20
   But king nor peer to such a peerless dame.

O happiness enjoy'd but of a few!
And, if possess'd, as soon decay'd and done
As is the morning's silver-melting dew
Against the golden splendour of the sun!   25
An expired date, cancell'd ere well begun:
   Honour and beauty, in the owner's arms,
   Are weakly fortress'd from a world of harms.

Beauty itself doth of itself persuade
The eyes of men without an orator;   30
What needeth then apologies be made,
To set forth that which is so singular?
Or why is Collatine the publisher
   Of that rich jewel he should keep unknown
   From thievish ears, because it is his own?   35

Perchance his boast of Lucrece' sovereignty
Suggested this proud issue of a king;
For by our ears our hearts oft tainted be;
Perchance that envy of so rich a thing,
Braving compare, disdainfully did sting   40
   His high-pitch'd thoughts, that meaner men should vaunt
   That golden hap which their superiors want.

But some untimely thought did instigate
His all-too-timeless speed, if none of those;
His honour, his affairs, his friends, his state, 45
Neglected all, with swift intent he goes
To quench the coal which in his liver glows.
   O rash-false heat, wrapp'd in repentant cold,
   Thy hasty spring still blasts, and ne'er grows old!

When at Collatium this false lord arrived,   50
Well was he welcomed by the Roman dame,
Within whose face beauty and virtue strived
Which of them both should underprop her fame;
When virtue bragg'd, beauty would blush for shame;
   When beauty boasted blushes, in despite   55
   Virtue would stain that o'er with silver white.

But beauty, in that white intituled,
From Venus' doves doth challenge that fair field;
Then virtue claims from beauty beauty's red,
Which virtue gave the golden age to gild   60
Their silver cheeks, and call'd it then their shield;
   Teaching them thus to use it in the fight,
   When shame assail'd, the red should fence the white.

This heraldry in Lucrece' face was seen,
Argued by beauty's red and virtue's white;   65
Of either's colour was the other queen,
Proving from world's minority their right;
Yet their ambition makes them still to fight;
   The sovereignty of either being so great,
   That oft they interchange each other's seat. 70

This silent war of lilies and of roses,
Which Tarquin view'd in her fair face's field,
In their pure ranks his traitor eye encloses;
Where, lest between them both it should be kill'd,
The coward captive vanquished doth yield   75
   To those two armies, that would let him go
   Rather than triumph in so false a foe.

Now thinks he that her husband's shallow tongue,
The niggard prodigal that praised her so,
In that high task hath done her beauty wrong,   80
Which far exceeds his barren skill to show;
Therefore that praise which Collatine doth owe
   Enchanted Tarquin answers with surmise,
   In silent wonder of still-gazing eyes.

This earthly saint, adored by this devil,   85
Little suspecteth the false worshipper;
For unstain'd thoughts do seldom dream on evil;
Birds never limed no secret bushes fear;
So guiltless she securely gives good cheer
   And reverend welcome to her princely guest,   90
   Whose inward ill no outward harm express'd;

For that he colour'd with his high estate,
Hiding base sin in plaits of majesty;
That nothing in him seem'd inordinate,
Save sometime too much wonder of his eye,   95
Which, having all, all could not satisfy;
   But, poorly rich, so wanteth in his store,
   That, cloy'd with much, he pineth still for more.

But she, that never coped with stranger eyes,
Could pick no meaning from their parling looks,
Nor read the subtle-shining secrecies   101
Writ in the glassy margents of such books;
She touch'd no unknown baits, nor fear'd no
    hooks;
Nor could she moralize his wanton sight,
More than his eyes were open'd to the light.   105

He stories to her ears her husband's fame,
Won in the fields of fruitful Italy;
And decks with praises Collatine's high name,
Made glorious by his manly chivalry
With bruised arms and wreaths of victory;   110
Her joy with heaved-up hand she doth express,
And wordless so greets heaven for his success.

Far from the purpose of his coming hither,
He makes excuses for his being there;
No cloudy show of stormy blustering weather
Doth yet in his fair welkin once appear;   116
Till sable Night, mother of dread and fear,
Upon the world dim darkness doth display,
And in her vaulty prison stows the day.

For then is Tarquin brought unto his bed,   120
Intending weariness with heavy spright;
For after supper long he questioned
With modest Lucrece, and wore out the night;
Now leaden slumber with life's strength doth
    fight;
And every one to rest themselves betake,   125
Save thieves and cares and troubled minds that
    wake.

As one of which doth Tarquin lie revolving
The sundry dangers of his will's obtaining;
Yet ever to obtain his will resolving,
Though weak-built hopes persuade him to ab-
    staining;   130
Despair to gain doth traffic oft for gaining,
And when great treasure is the meed proposed,
Though death be adjunct, there's no death sup-
    posed.

Those that much covet are with gain so fond
That what they have not, that which they possess,
They scatter and unloose it from their bond,   136
And so, by hoping more, they have but less;
Or, gaining more, the profit of excess
Is but to surfeit, and such griefs sustain,
That they prove bankrupt in this poor-rich gain.

The aim of all is but to nurse the life   141
With honour, wealth, and ease, in waning age;
And in this aim there is such thwarting strife
That one for all or all for one we gage;
As life for honour in fell battle's rage;   145
Honour for wealth; and oft that wealth doth cost
The death of all, and all together lost.

So that in venturing ill we leave to be
The things we are for that which we expect;
And this ambitious, foul infirmity,   150
In having much, torments us with defect
Of that we have; so then we do neglect
The thing we have, and, all for want of wit,
Make something nothing by augmenting it.

Such hazard now must doting Tarquin make,
Pawning his honor to obtain his lust;   156
And for himself himself he must forsake;
Then where is truth, if there be no self-trust?
When shall he think to find a stranger just,
When he himself himself confounds, betrays
To slanderous tongues and wretched hateful
    days?   161

Now stole upon the time the dead of night,
When heavy sleep had closed up mortal eyes;
No comfortable star did lend his light,   164
No noise but owls' and wolves' death-boding cries;
Now serves the season that they may surprise
The silly lambs: pure thoughts are dead and still,
While lust and murder wakes to stain and kill.

And now this lustful lord leap'd from his bed,
Throwing his mantle rudely o'er his arm;   170
Is madly toss'd between desire and dread;
Th' one sweetly flatters, th' other feareth harm;
But honest fear, bewitch'd with lust's foul charm,
Doth too too oft betake him to retire,
Beaten away by brain-sick rude desire.   175

His falchion on a flint he softly smiteth,
That from the cold stone sparks of fire do fly;
Whereat a waxen torch forthwith he lighteth,
Which must be lode-star to his lustful eye;
And to the flame thus speaks advisedly: 180
'As from this cold flint I enforced this fire,
So Lucrece must I force to my desire.'

Here pale with fear he doth premeditate
The dangers of his loathsome enterprise,
And in his inward mind he doth debate   185
What following sorrow may on this arise;
Then looking scornfully he doth despise
His naked armour of still-slaughter'd lust,
And justly thus controls his thoughts unjust:

'Fair torch, burn out thy light, and lend it not
To darken her whose light excelleth thine;   191
And die, unhallow'd thoughts, before you blot
With your uncleanness that which is divine;
Offer pure incense to so pure a shrine;
Let fair humanity abhor the deed   195
That spots and stains love's modest snow-white
    weed.

'O shame to knighthood and to shining arms!
O foul dishonour to my household's grave!
O impious act, including all foul harms!
A martial man to be soft fancy's slave!   200
True valour still a true respect should have;
Then my digression is so vile, so base,
That it will live engraven in my face.

'Yea, though I die, the scandal will survive,
And be an eye-sore in my golden coat;   205
Some loathsome dash the herald will contrive,
To cipher me how fondly I did dote;
That my posterity, shamed with the note,
Shall curse my bones, and hold it for no sin
To wish that I their father had not bin.   210

'What win I, if I gain the thing I seek?
A dream, a breath, a froth of fleeting joy.
Who buys a minute's mirth to wail a week?
Or sells eternity to get a toy?   214
For one sweet grape who will the vine destroy?

Or what fond beggar, but to touch the crown,
Would with the sceptre straight be strucken
    down?

'If Collatinus dream of my intent,
Will he not wake, and in a desperate rage
Post hither, this vile purpose to prevent? 220
This siege that hath engirt his marriage,
This blur to youth, this sorrow to the sage,
  This dying virtue, this surviving shame,
  Whose crime will bear an ever-during blame?

'O what excuse can my invention make, 225
When thou shalt charge me with so black a deed?
Will not my tongue be mute, my frail joints shake,
Mine eyes forego their light, my false heart bleed?
The guilt being great, the fear doth still exceed;
  And extreme fear can neither fight nor fly, 230
  But coward-like with trembling terror die.

'Had Collatinus kill'd my son or sire,
Or lain in ambush to betray my life,
Or were he not my dear friend, this desire
Might have excuse to work upon his wife, 235
As in revenge or quittal of such strife;
  But as he is my kinsman, my dear friend,
  The shame and fault finds no excuse nor end.

'Shameful it is; ay, if the fact be known;
Hateful it is; there is no hate in loving; 240
I'll beg her love; but she is not her own;
The worst is but denial and reproving;
My will is strong, past reason's weak removing.
  Who fears a sentence or an old man's saw
  Shall by a painted cloth be kept in awe.' 245

Thus graceless holds he disputation
'Tween frozen conscience and hot-burning will,
And with good thoughts makes dispensation,
Urging the worser sense for vantage still;
Which in a moment doth confound and kill 250
  All pure effects, and doth so far proceed
  That what is vile shows like a virtuous deed.

Quoth he, 'She took me kindly by the hand,
And gazed for tidings in my eager eyes,
Fearing some hard news from the warlike band,
Where her beloved Collatinus lives. 256
  O, how her fear did make her colour rise!
  First red as roses that on lawn we lay,
  Then white as lawn, the roses took away.

'And how her hand, in my hand being lock'd, 260
Forced it to tremble with her loyal fear!
Which struck her sad, and then it faster rock'd,
Until her husband's welfare she did hear;
Whereat she smiled with so sweet a cheer
  That had Narcissus seen her as she stood 265
  Self-love had never drown'd him in the flood.

'Why hunt I then for colour or excuses?
All orators are dumb when beauty pleadeth;
Poor wretches have remorse in poor abuses;
Love thrives not in the heart that shadows dreadeth; 270
  Affection is my captain, and he leadeth;
  And when his gaudy banner is display'd,
  The coward fights, and will not be dismay'd.

'Then, childish fear, avaunt! debating, die!
Respect and reason wait on wrinkled age! 275
My heart shall never countermand mine eye;
Sad pause and deep regard beseems the sage;
My part is youth, and beats these from the stage;
  Desire my pilot is, beauty my prize;
  Then who fears sinking where such treasure
    lies?' 280

As corn o'ergrown by weeds, so heedful fear
Is almost choked by unresisted lust.
Away he steals with open listening ear,
Full of foul hope and full of fond mistrust;
Both which, as servitors to the unjust, 285
  So cross him with their opposite persuasion,
  That now he vows a league, and now invasion.

Within his thought her heavenly image sits,
And in the self-same seat sits Collatine;
That eye which looks on her confounds his wits;
That eye which him beholds, as more divine, 291
Unto a view so false will not incline;
  But with a pure appeal seeks to the heart,
  Which once corrupted takes the worser part;

And therein heartens up his servile powers, 295
Who, flatter'd by their leader's jocund show,
Stuff up his lust, as minutes fill up hours;
And as their captain, so their pride doth grow,
Paying more slavish tribute than they owe.
  By reprobate desire thus madly led, 300
  The Roman lord marcheth to Lucrece' bed.

The locks between her chamber and his will,
Each one by him enforced, retires his ward;
But, as they open, they all rate his ill, 304
Which drives the creeping thief to some regard;
The threshold grates the door to have him heard;
  Night-wandering weasels shriek to see him
    there;
  They fright him, yet he still pursues his fear.

As each unwilling portal yields him way,
Through little vents and crannies of the place 310
The wind wars with his torch to make him stay,
And blows the smoke of it into his face,
Extinguishing his conduct in this case;
  But his hot heart, which fond desire doth scorch,
  Puffs forth another wind that fires the torch; 315

And being lighted, by the light he spies
Lucretia's glove, wherein her needle sticks;
He takes it from the rushes where it lies,
And griping it, the needle his finger pricks; 319
As who should say, 'This glove to wanton tricks
  Is not inured; return again in haste;
  Thou see'st our mistress' ornaments are chaste.'

But all these poor forbiddings could not stay him;
He in the worst sense construes their denial;
The doors, the wind, the glove, that did delay him,
He takes for accidental things of trial; 326
Or as those bars which stop the hourly dial,
  Who with a lingering stay his course doth let,
  Till every minute pays the hour his debt.

'So, so,' quoth he, 'these lets attend the time, 330
Like little frosts that sometime threat the spring,

To add a more rejoicing to the prime,
And give the sneaped birds more cause to sing,
Pain pays the income of each precious thing;
    Huge rocks, high winds, strong pirates, shelves,
        and sands,   335
    The merchant fears, ere rich at home he lands.'

Now is he come unto the chamber door,
That shuts him from the heaven of his thought,
Which with a yielding latch, and with no more,
Hath barr'd him from the blessed thing he sought.
So from himself impiety hath wrought,   341
    That for his prey to pray he doth begin,
    As if the heavens should countenance his sin.

But in the midst of his unfruitful prayer,
Having solicited the eternal power   345
That his foul thoughts might compass his fair fair,
And they would stand auspicious to the hour,
Even there he starts: quoth he 'I must deflower;
    The powers to whom I pray abhor this fact;
    How can they then assist me in the act?   350

'Then Love and Fortune be my gods, my guide!
My will is back'd with resolution;
Thoughts are but dreams till their effects be tried;
The blackest sin is clear'd with absolution;   354
Against love's fire fear's frost hath dissolution.
    The eye of heaven is out, and misty night
    Covers the shame that follows sweet delight.'

This said, his guilty hand pluck'd up the latch,
And with his knee the door he opens wide.
The dove sleeps fast that this night-owl will catch;
Thus treason works ere traitors be espied;   361
Who sees the lurking serpent steps aside;
    But she, sound sleeping, fearing no such thing,
    Lies at the mercy of his mortal sting.

Into the chamber wickedly he stalks,   365
And gazeth on her yet unstained bed.
The curtains being close, about he walks,
Rolling his greedy eyeballs in his head;
By their high treason is his heart misled;
    Which gives the watch-word to his hand full
        soon   370
    To draw the cloud that hides the silver moon.

Look, as the fair and fiery-pointed sun,
Rushing from forth a cloud, bereaves our sight;
Even so, the curtain drawn, his eyes begun
To wink, being blinded with a greater light;
Whether it is that she reflects so bright,   376
    That dazzleth them, or else some shame sup-
        posed;
    But blind they are, and keep themselves en-
        closed.

O, had they in that darksome prison died!
Then had they seen the period of their ill;   380
Then Collatine again, by Lucrece' side,
In his clear bed might have reposed still;
But they must ope, this blessed league to kill;
    And holy-thoughted Lucrece to their sight
    Must sell her joy, her life, her world's delight.

Her lily hand her rosy cheek lies under,   386
Cozening the pillow of a lawful kiss;
Who, therefore angry, seems to part in sunder,
Swelling on either side to want his bliss;
Between whose hills her head entombed is;   390

Where, like a virtuous monument, she lies,
To be admired of lewd unhallowed eyes.

Without the bed her other fair hand was,
On the green coverlet; whose perfect white
Show'd like an April daisy on the grass,   395
With pearly sweat, resembling dew of night.
Her eyes, like marigolds, had sheathed their light,
    And canopied in darkness sweetly lay,
    Till they might open to adorn the day.

Her hair, like golden threads, play'd with her
    breath;   400
O modest wantons! wanton modesty!
Showing life's triumph in the map of death,
And death's dim look in life's mortality;
Each in her sleep themselves so beautify   404
As if between them twain there were no strife,
    But that life lived in death and death in life.

Her breasts, like ivory globes circled with blue,
A pair of maiden worlds unconquered,
Save of their lord no bearing yoke they knew,
And him by oath they truly honoured.   410
These worlds in Tarquin new ambition bred;
    Who, like a foul usurper, went about
    From this fair throne to heave the owner out.

What could he see but mightily he noted?
What did he note but strongly he desired?   415
What he beheld, on that he firmly doted,
And in his will his wilful eye he tired.
With more than admiration he admired
    Her azure veins, her alabaster skin,   419
    Her coral lips, her snow-white dimpled chin.

As the grim lion fawneth o'er his prey,
Sharp hunger by the conquest satisfied,
So o'er this sleeping soul doth Tarquin stay,
His rage of lust by gazing qualified;   424
Slack'd, not suppress'd; for standing by her side,
    His eye, which late this mutiny restrains,
    Unto a greater uproar tempts his veins;

And they, like straggling slaves for pillage fight-
    ing,
Obdurate vassals fell exploits effecting,   429
In bloody death and ravishment delighting,
Nor children's tears nor mothers' groans respect-
    ing,
Swell in their pride, the onset still expecting;
    Anon his beating heart, alarum striking,
    Gives the hot charge, and bids them do their
        liking.

His drumming heart cheers up his burning eye,
His eye commends the leading to his hand;   436
His hand, as proud of such a dignity,
Smoking with pride, march'd on to make his stand
On her bare breast, the heart of all her land;
    Whose ranks of blue veins, as his hand did scale,
    Left their round turrets destitute and pale. 441

They, mustering to the quiet cabinet
Where their dear governess and lady lies,
Do tell her she is dreadfully beset,   444
And fright her with confusion of their cries;
    She, much amazed, breaks ope her lock'd-up eyes,

Who, peeping forth this tumult to behold,
Are by his flaming torch dimm'd and controll'd.

Imagine her as one in dead of night   449
From forth dull sleep by dreadful fancy waking,
That thinks she hath beheld some ghastly sprite,
Whose grim aspect sets every joint a-shaking;
What terror 'tis, but she, in worser taking,
  From sleep disturbed, heedfully doth view   454
  The sight which makes supposed terror true.

Wrapp'd and confounded in a thousand fears,
Like to a new-kill'd bird she trembling lies;
She dares not look; yet, winking, there appears
Quick-shifting antics, ugly in her eyes;   459
Such shadows are the weak brain's forgeries;
  Who, angry that the eyes fly from their lights,
  In darkness daunts them with more dreadful
    sights.

His hand, that yet remains upon her breast,—
Rude ram, to batter such an ivory wall!—
May feel her heart, poor citizen! distress'd,   465
Wounding itself to death, rise up and fall,
Beating her bulk, that his hand shakes withal.
  This moves in him more rage and lesser pity,
  To make the breach and enter this sweet city.

First, like a trumpet, doth his tongue begin   470
To sound a parley to his heartless foe;
Who o'er the white sheet peers her whiter chin,
The reason of this rash alarm to know,
Which he by dumb demeanour seeks to show;
  But she with vehement prayers urgeth still
  Under what colour he commits this ill.   476

Thus he replies: 'The colour in thy face,
That even for anger makes the lily pale
And the red rose blush at her own disgrace,
Shall plead for me and tell my loving tale;   480
Under that colour am I come to scale
  Thy never-conquer'd fort; the fault is thine,
  For those thine eyes betray thee unto mine.

'Thus I forestall thee, if thou mean to chide;
Thy beauty hath ensnared thee to this night,   485
Where thou with patience must my will abide;
My will that marks thee for my earth's delight,
Which I to conquer sought with all my might;
  But as reproof and reason beat it dead,
  By thy bright beauty was it newly bred.   490

'I see what crosses my attempt will bring;
I know what thorns the growing rose defends;
I think the honey guarded with a sting;
All this beforehand counsel comprehends;   494
But will is deaf and hears no heedful friends;
  Only he hath an eye to gaze on beauty,
  And dotes on what he looks, 'gainst law or duty.

'I have debated, even in my soul,
What wrong, what shame, what sorrow I shall
  breed;
But nothing can affection's course control,   500
Or stop the headlong fury of his speed.
I know repentant tears ensue the deed,
  Reproach, disdain, and deadly enmity;
  Yet strive I to embrace mine infamy.'

This said, he shakes aloft his Roman blade,   505
Which, like a falcon towering in the skies,
Coucheth the fowl below with his wings' shade,
Whose crooked beak threats if he mount he dies;
So under his insulting falchion lies   509
  Harmless Lucretia, marking what he tells
  With trembling fear, as fowl hear falcon's bells.

'Lucrece,' quoth he, 'this night I must enjoy thee;
If thou deny, then force must work my way,
For in thy bed I purpose to destroy thee;
That done, some worthless slave of thine I'll slay,
To kill thine honour with thy life's decay;   516
And in thy dead arms do I mean to place him,
  Swearing I slew him, seeing thee embrace him.

'So thy surviving husband shall remain
The scornful mark of every open eye;   520
Thy kinsmen hang their heads at this disdain,
Thy issue blurr'd with nameless bastardy;
And thou, the author of their obloquy,
  Shalt have thy trespass cited up in rhymes
  And sung by children in succeeding times.

'But if thou yield, I rest thy secret friend;   526
The fault unknown is as a thought unacted;
A little harm done to a great good end
For lawful policy remains enacted.
The poisonous simple sometime is compacted
  In a pure compound; being so applied,   531
  His venom in effect is purified.

'Then, for thy husband and thy children's sake,
Tender my suit; bequeath not to their lot
The shame that from them no device can take,
The blemish that will never be forgot;   536
Worse than a slavish wipe or birth-hour's blot;
  For marks descried in men's nativity
  Are nature's faults, not their own infamy.'

Here with a cockatrice' dead-killing eye   540
He rouseth up himself, and makes a pause;
While she, the picture of true piety,
Like a white hind under the gripe's sharp claws,
Pleads, in a wilderness where are no laws,
  To the rough beast that knows no gentle right,
  Nor aught obeys but his foul appetite.   546

But when a black-faced cloud the world doth
  threat,
In his dim mist the aspiring mountains hiding,
From earth's dark womb some gentle gust doth get,
Which blows these pitchy vapours from their bid-
  ing,   550
Hindering their present fall by this dividing;
  So his unhallow'd haste her words delays,
  And moody Pluto winks while Orpheus plays.

Yet, foul night-waking cat, he doth but dally,
While in his hold-fast foot the weak mouse pant-
  eth;   555
Her sad behaviour feeds his vulture folly,
A swallowing gulf that even in plenty wanteth;
His ear her prayers admits, but his heart granteth
  No penetrable entrance to her plaining;
  Tears harden lust, though marble wear with
    raining.   560

Her pity-pleading eyes are sadly fixed
In the remorseless wrinkles of his face;
Her modest eloquence with sighs is mixed,
Which to her oratory adds more grace.
She puts the period often from his place,   565
 And midst the sentence so her accent breaks
 That twice she doth begin ere once she speaks.

She conjures him by high almighty Jove,
By knighthood, gentry, and sweet friendship's
  oath,
By her untimely tears, her husband's love,   570
By holy human law and common troth,
By heaven and earth, and all the power of both,
 That to his borrow'd bed he make retire,
 And stoop to honour, not to foul desire.

Quoth she, 'Reward not hospitality   575
With such black payment as thou hast pretended;
Mud not the fountain that gave drink to thee;
Mar not the thing that cannot be amended;
End thy ill aim before thy shoot be ended;
 He is no woodman that doth bend his bow
  To strike a poor unseasonable doe.   581

'My husband is thy friend; for his sake spare me;
Thyself art mighty; for thine own sake leave me;
Myself a weakling; do not then ensnare me;
Thou look'st not like deceit; do not deceive me.
My sighs, like whirlwinds, labour hence to heave
  thee;   586
 If ever man were moved with woman's moans,
 Be moved with my tears, my sighs, my groans;

'All which together, like a troubled ocean,
Beat at thy rocky and wreck-threatening heart,
To soften it with their continual motion;   591
For stones dissolved to water do convert.
O, if no harder than a stone thou art,
 Melt at my tears, and be compassionate!
 Soft pity enters at an iron gate.   595

'In Tarquin's likeness I did entertain thee;
Hast thou put on his shape to do him shame?
To all the host of heaven I complain me,
Thou wrong'st his honour, wound'st his princely
  name.   599
Thou art not what thou seem'st; and if the same,
 Thou seem'st not what thou art, a god, a king;
 For kings, like gods, should govern every thing.

'How will thy shame be seeded in thine age,
When thus thy vices bud before thy spring!
If in thy hope thou darest do such outrage,   605
What darest thou not when once thou art a king?
O, be remember'd, no outrageous thing
 From vassal actors can be wiped away;
 Then kings' misdeeds cannot be hid in clay.

'This deed will make thee only loved for fear;
But happy monarchs still are fear'd for love;
With foul offenders thou perforce must bear,   612
When they in thee the like offences prove;
If but for fear of this, thy will remove;
 For princes are the glass, the school, the book,
 Where subjects' eyes do learn, do read, do look.

'And wilt thou be the school where Lust shall
  learn?   617
Must he in thee read lectures of such shame?
Wilt thou be glass wherein it shall discern

Authority for sin, warrant for blame,   620
To privilege dishonour in thy name?
 Thou back'st reproach against long-living laud,
 And makest fair reputation but a bawd.

'Hast thou command? by him that gave it thee,
From a pure heart command thy rebel will;   625
Draw not thy sword to guard iniquity,
For it was lent thee all that brood to kill.
Thy princely office how canst thou fulfil,
 When, pattern'd by thy fault, foul sin may say
 He learn'd to sin and thou didst teach the way?

'Think but how vile a spectacle it were,   631
To view thy present trespass in another.
Men's faults do seldom to themselves appear;
Their own transgressions partially they smother;
This guilt would seem death-worthy in thy bro-
  ther.
 O, how are they wrapp'd in with infamies
 That from their own misdeeds askance their
  eyes!   637

'To thee, to thee, my heaved-up hands appeal,
Not to seducing lust, thy rash relier;
I sue for exiled majesty's repeal;   640
Let him return, and flattering thoughts retire;
His true respect will prison false desire,
 And wipe the dim mist from thy doting eyne,
 That thou shalt see thy state and pity mine.'

'Have done,' quoth he; 'my uncontrolled tide
Turns not, but swells the higher by this let.   646
Small lights are soon blown out, huge fires abide,
And with the wind in greater fury fret;
The petty streams that pay a daily debt
 To their salt sovereign, with their fresh falls'
  haste   650
 Add to his flow, but alter not his taste.'

'Thou art,' quoth she, 'a sea, a sovereign king
And, lo, there falls into thy boundless flood
Black lust, dishonour, shame, misgoverning,
Who seek to stain the ocean of thy blood.   655
If all these petty ills shall change thy good,
 Thy sea within a puddle's womb is hearsed,
 And not the puddle in thy sea dispersed.

'So shall these slaves be king, and thou their slave;
Thou nobly base, they basely dignified;   660
Thou their fair life, and they thy fouler grave;
Thou loathed in their shame, they in thy pride;
The lesser thing should not the greater hide;
 The cedar stoops not to the base shrub's foot,
 But low shrubs wither at the cedar's root.   665

'So let thy thoughts, low vassals to thy state'—
'No more,' quoth he; 'by heaven, I will not hear
  thee;
Yield to my love; if not, enforced hate,
Instead of love's coy touch, shall rudely tear thee;
That done, despitefully I mean to bear thee   670
 Unto the base bed of some rascal groom,
 To be thy partner in this shameful doom.'

This said, he sets his foot upon the light,
For light and lust are deadly enemies;
Shame folded up in blind concealing night,   675
When most unseen, then most doth tyrannize.
The wolf hath seized his prey, the poor lamb cries;
 Till with her own white fleece her voice con-
  tr ll'd
 Entombs her outcry in her lips' sweet fold:

For with the nightly linen that she wears   680
He pens her piteous clamours in her head,
Cooling his hot face in the chastest tears
That ever modest eyes with sorrow shed.
O, that prone lust should stain so pure a bed!
  The spots whereof could weeping purify,   685
  Her tears should drop on them perpetually.

But she hath lost a dearer thing than life,
And he hath won what he would lose again;
This forced league doth force a further strife;
This momentary joy breeds months of pain;
This hot desire converts to cold disdain;   690
  Pure Chastity is rifled of her store,
  And Lust, the thief, far poorer than before.

Look, as the full-fed hound or gorged hawk,
Unapt for tender smell or speedy flight,   695
Make slow pursuit, or altogether balk
The prey wherein by nature they delight,
So surfeit-taking Tarquin fares this night:
  His taste delicious, in digestion souring,   699
  Devours his will, that lived by foul devouring.

O, deeper sin than bottomless conceit
Can comprehend in still imagination!
Drunken Desire must vomit his receipt,
Ere he can see his own abomination.
While Lust is in his pride, no exclamation   705
  Can curb his heat or rein his rash desire,
  Till, like a jade, Self-will himself doth tire.

And then with lank and lean discolour'd cheek,
With heavy eye, knit brow, and strengthless pace,
Feeble Desire, all recreant, poor, and meek,   710
Like to a bankrupt beggar wails his case:
The flesh being proud, Desire doth fight with
  Grace,
  For there it revels, and when that decays
  The guilty rebel for remission prays.

So fares it with this faultful lord of Rome,   715
Who this accomplishment so hotly chased;
For now against himself he sounds this doom,
That through the length of times he stands disgraced;
Besides, his soul's fair temple is defaced,   719
  To whose weak ruins muster troops of cares,
  To ask the spotted princess how she fares.

She says, her subjects with foul insurrection
Have batter'd down her consecrated wall,
And by their mortal fault brought in subjection
Her immortality, and made her thrall   725
To living death and pain perpetual;
  Which in her prescience she controlled still,
  But her foresight could not forestall their will.

Even in this thought through the dark night he
  stealeth,
A captive victor that hath lost in gain;   730
Bearing away the wound that nothing healeth,
The scar that will, despite of cure, remain;
Leaving his spoil perplex'd in greater pain.
  She bears the load of lust he left behind,
  And he the burthen of a guilty mind.   735

He like a thievish dog creeps sadly thence;
She like a wearied lamb flies panting there;
He scowls, and hates himself for his offence;
She, desperate, with her nails her flesh doth tear;
He faintly flies, sweating with guilty fear;   740

She stays, exclaiming on the direful night;
He runs, and chides his vanish'd, loathed delight.

He thence departs a heavy convertite;
She there remains a hopeless cast-away;
He in his speed looks for the morning light;   745
She prays she never may behold the day,
'For day,' quoth she, 'night's 'scapes doth open
  lay,
  And my true eyes have never practiced how
  To cloak offences with a cunning brow.

'They think not but that every eye can see   750
The same disgrace which they themselves behold;
And therefore would they still in darkness be,
To have their unseen sin remain untold;
For they their guilt with weeping will unfold,
  And grave, like water that doth eat in steel,
  Upon my cheeks what helpless shame I feel.'

Here she exclaims against repose and rest,   757
And bids her eyes hereafter still be blind.
She wakes her heart by beating on her breast,
And bids it leap from thence, where it may find
Some purer chest to close so pure a mind.   761
  Frantic with grief thus breathes she forth her
    spite
  Against the unseen secrecy of night:

'O comfort-killing Night, image of hell!
Dim register and notary of shame!   765
Black stage for tragedies and murders fell!
Vast sin-concealing chaos! nurse of blame!
Blind, muffled bawd! dark harbour for defame!
  Grim cave of death! whispering conspirator
  With close-tongued treason and the ravisher!

'O hateful, vaporous, and foggy Night!   771
Since thou art guilty of my cureless crime,
Muster thy mists to meet the eastern light,
Make war against proportion'd course of time;
Or if thou wilt permit the sun to climb   775
His wonted height, yet ere he go to bed,
Knit poisonous clouds about his golden head.

'With rotten damps ravish the morning air;
Let their exhaled unwholesome breaths make sick
The life of purity, the supreme fair,   780
Ere he arrive his weary noon-tide prick;
And let thy misty vapours march so thick
That in their smoky ranks his smother'd light
  May set at noon and make perpetual night!

'Were Tarquin Night, as he is but Night's child,
The silver-shining queen he would distain;   786
Her twinkling handmaids too, by him defiled,
Through Night's black bosom should not peep
  again;
So should I have co-partners in my pain;   789
  And fellowship in woe doth woe assuage,
  As palmers' chat makes short their pilgrimage.

'Where now I have no one to blush with me,
To cross their arms and hang their heads with
  mine,
To mask their brows and hide their infamy;
But I alone alone must sit and pine,   795
Seasoning the earth with showers of silver brine,
  Mingling my talk with tears, my grief with
    groans,
  Poor wasting monuments of lasting moans.

'O Night, thou furnace of foul-reeking smoke,
Let not the jealous Day behold that face   800
Which underneath thy black all-hiding cloak
Immodestly lies martyr'd with disgrace!
Keep still possession of thy gloomy place,
That all the faults which in thy reign are made
May likewise be sepulchred in thy shade!   805

'Make me not object to the tell-tale Day!
The light will show, character'd in my brow,
The story of sweet chastity's decay,
The impious breach of holy wedlock vow;
Yea, the illiterate, that know not how   810
To cipher what is writ in learned books,
Will quote my loathsome trespass in my looks.

'The nurse, to still her child, will tell my story,
And fright her crying babe with Tarquin's name;
The orator, to deck his oratory,   815
Will couple my reproach to Tarquin's shame;
Feast-finding minstrels, tuning my defame,
Will tie the hearers to attend each line,
How Tarquin wronged me, I Collatine.

'Let my good name, that senseless reputation,
For Collatine's dear love be kept unspotted;   821
If that be made a theme for disputation,
The branches of another root are rotted,
And undeserved reproach to him allotted
That is as clear from this attaint of mine
As I, ere this, was pure to Collatine.   826

'O unseen shame! invisible disgrace!
O unfelt sore! crest-wounding, private scar!
Reproach is stamp'd in Collatinus' face,
And Tarquin's eye may read the mot afar,   830
How he in peace is wounded, not in war.
Alas, how many bear such shameful blows,
Which not themselves, but he that gives them
   knows!

'If, Collatine, thine honour lay in me,
From me by strong assault it is bereft.   835
My honey lost, and I, a drone-like bee,
Have no perfection of my summer left,
But robb'd and ransack'd by injurious theft;
In thy weak hive a wandering wasp hath crept,
And suck'd the honey which thy chaste bee
   kept.   840

'Yet am I guilty of thy honour's wrack;
Yet for thy honour did I entertain him;
Coming from thee, I could not put him back,
For it had been dishonour to disdain him;
Besides, of weariness he did complain him,   845
And talk'd of virtue: O unlook'd-for evil,
When virtue is profaned in such a devil!

'Why should the worm intrude the maiden bud?
Or hateful cuckoos hatch in sparrows' nests?
Or toads infect fair founts with venom mud?
Or tyrant folly lurk in gentle breasts?   851
Or kings be breakers of their own behests?
But no perfection is so absolute
That some impurity doth not pollute.

'The aged man that coffers up his gold   855
Is plagued with cramps and gouts and painful fits,
And scarce hath eyes his treasure to behold,
But like still-pining Tantalus he sits
And useless barns the harvest of his wits,
Having no other pleasure of his gain   860
But torment that it cannot cure his pain.

'So then he hath it when he cannot use it,
And leaves it to be master'd by his young;
Who in their pride do presently abuse it;
Their father was too weak, and they too strong,
To hold their cursed-blessed fortune long.   866
The sweets we wish for turn to loathed sours
Even in the moment that we call them ours.

'Unruly blasts wait on the tender spring;
Unwholesome weeds take root with precious flow-
   ers;   870
The adder hisses where the sweet birds sing;
What virtue breeds iniquity devours;
We have no good that we can say is ours
But ill-annexed Opportunity
Or kills his life or else his quality.   875

'O Opportunity, thy guilt is great!
'Tis thou that executest the traitor's treason;
Thou set'st the wolf where he the lamb may get;
Whoever plots the sin, thou point'st the season;
'Tis thou that spurn'st at right, at law, at reason;
And in thy shady cell, where none may spy him,
Sits Sin, to seize the souls that wander by him.

'Thou makest the vestal violate her oath;   883
Thou blow'st the fire when temperance is thaw'd;
Thou smother'st honesty, thou murder'st troth;
Thou foul abettor! thou notorious bawd!   886
Thou plantest scandal and displacest laud;
Thou ravisher, thou traitor, thou false thief,
Thy honey turns to gall, thy joy to grief!

'Thy secret pleasure turns to open shame,   890
Thy private feasting to a public fast,
Thy smoothing titles to a ragged name,
Thy sugar'd tongue to bitter wormwood taste;
Thy violent vanities can never last.
How comes it then, vile Opportunity,   895
Being so bad, such numbers seek for thee?

'When wilt thou be the humble suppliant's friend,
And bring him where his suit may be obtained?
When wilt thou sort an hour great strifes to end?
Or free that soul which wretchedness hath
   chained?   900
Give physic to the sick, ease to the pained?
The poor, lame, blind, halt, creep, cry out for
   thee;
But they ne'er meet with Opportunity.

'The patient dies while the physician sleeps;
The orphan pines while the oppressor feeds;
Justice is feasting while the widow weeps;   906
Advice is sporting while infection breeds;
Thou grant'st no time for charitable deeds;
Wrath, envy, treason, rape, and murder's rages,
Thy heinous hours wait on them as their pages.

'When Truth and Virtue have to do with thee,
A thousand crosses keep them from thy aid;   912
They buy thy help, but Sin ne'er gives a fee;
He gratis comes, and thou art well appaid
As well to hear as grant what he hath said.

My Collatine would else have come to me 916
When Tarquin did, but he was stay'd by thee.

'Guilty thou art of murder and of theft,
Guilty of perjury and subornation,
Guilty of treason, forgery, and shift, 920
Guilty of incest, that abomination;
An accessory by thine inclination
To all sins past and all that are to come,
From the creation to the general doom.

'Mis-shapen Time, copesmate of ugly Night,
Swift subtle post, carrier of grisly care, 926
Eater of youth, false slave to false delight,
Base watch of woes, sin's pack-horse, virtue's snare;
Thou nursest all and murder'st all that are;
O, hear me then, injurious shifting time! 930
Be guilty of my death, since of my crime.

'Why hath thy servant Opportunity
Betray'd the hours thou gavest me to repose,
Cancell'd my fortunes, and enchained me
To endless date of never-ending woes? 935
Time's office is to fine the hate of foes,
To eat up errors by opinion bred,
Not spend the dowry of a lawful bed.

'Time's glory is to calm contending kings,
To unmask falsehood and bring truth to light,
To stamp the seal of time in aged things, 941
To wake the morn and sentinel the night,
To wrong the wronger till he render right,
To ruinate proud buildings with thy hours,
And smear with dust their glittering golden towers; 945

'To fill with worm-holes stately monuments,
To feed oblivion with decay of things,
To blot old books and alter their contents,
To pluck the quills from ancient ravens' wings,
To dry the old oak's sap and cherish springs,
To spoil antiquities of hammer'd steel, 951
And turn the giddy round of Fortune's wheel;

'To show the beldam daughters of her daughter,
To make the child a man, the man a child,
To slay the tiger that doth live by slaughter,
To tame the unicorn and lion wild, 956
To mock the subtle in themselves beguiled,
To cheer the ploughman with increaseful crops,
And waste huge stones with little water-drops.

'Why work'st thou mischief in thy pilgrimage,
Unless thou couldst return to make amends?
One poor retiring minute in an age 962
Would purchase thee a thousand thousand friends,
Lending him wit that to bad debtors lends;
O, this dread night, wouldst thou one hour come back, 965
I could prevent this storm and shun thy wrack!

'Thou ceaseless lackey to eternity,
With some mischance cross Tarquin in his flight;
Devise extremes beyond extremity, 969
To make him curse this cursed crimeful night;
Let ghastly shadows his lewd eyes affright,
And the dire thought of his committed evil
Shape every bush a hideous shapeless devil.

'Disturb his hours of rest with restless trances,
Afflict him in his bed with bedrid groans; 975
Let there bechance him pitiful mischances,
To make him moan; but pity not his moans;
Stone him with harden'd hearts, harder than stones;
And let mild women to him lose their mildness,
Wilder to him than tigers in their wildness.

'Let him have time to tear his curled hair, 981
Let him have time against himself to rave,
Let him have time of time's help to despair,
Let him have time to live a loathed slave,
Let him have time a beggar's orts to crave, 985
And time to see one that by alms doth live
Disdain to him disdained scraps to give.

'Let him have time to see his friends his foes,
And merry fools to mock at him resort; 989
Let him have time to mark how slow time goes
In time of sorrow, and how swift and short
His time of folly and his time of sport;
And ever let his unrecalling crime
Have time to wail the abusing of his time.

'O Time, thou tutor both to good and bad, 995
Teach me to curse him that thou taught'st this ill!
At his own shadow let the thief run mad,
Himself himself seek every hour to kill!
Such wretched hands such wretched blood should spill;
For who so base would such an office have 1000
As slanderous deathsman to so base a slave?

'The baser is he, coming from a king,
To shame his hope with deeds degenerate;
The mightier man, the mightier is the thing
That makes him honour'd or begets him hate;
For greatest scandal waits on greatest state. 1006
The moon being clouded presently is miss'd,
But little stars may hide them when they list.

'The crow may bathe his coal-black wings in mire,
And unperceived fly with the filth away; 1010
But if the like the snow-white swan desire,
The stain upon his silver down will stay.
Poor grooms are sightless night, kings glorious day;
Gnats are unnoted wheresoe'er they fly,
But eagles gazed upon with every eye. 1015

'Out, idle words, servants to shallow fools!
Unprofitable sounds, weak arbitrators!
Busy yourselves in skill-contending schools;
Debate where leisure serves with dull debaters;
To trembling clients be you mediators; 1020
For me, I force not argument a straw,
Since that my case is past the help of law.

'In vain I rail at Opportunity,
At Time, at Tarquin, and uncheerful Night;
In vain I cavil with mine infamy, 1025
In vain I spurn at my confirm'd despite;
This helpless smoke of words doth me no right.
The remedy indeed to do me good
Is to let forth my foul-defiled blood.

'Poor hand, why quiver'st thou at this decree?
Honour thyself to rid me of this shame;
For if I die, my honour lives in thee, 1032

But if I live, thou livest in my defame;
Since thou couldst not defend thy loyal dame,
And wast afeard to scratch her wicked foe,
Kill both thyself and her for yielding so.' 1036

This said, from her be-tumbled couch she starteth,
To find some desperate instrument of death;
But this no slaughterhouse no tool imparteth
To make more vent for passage of her breath; 1040
Which thronging through her lips, so vanisheth
As smoke from Ætna that in air consumes,
Or that which from discharged cannon fumes.

'In vain,' quoth she, 'I live, and seek in vain
Some happy mean to end a hapless life. 1045
I fear'd by Tarquin's falchion to be slain,
Yet for the self-same purpose seek a knife;
But when I fear'd I was a loyal wife;
So am I now; O no, that cannot be; 1049
Of that true type hath Tarquin rifled me.

'O, that is gone for which I sought to live,
And therefore now I need not fear to die.
To clear this spot by death, at least I give
A badge of fame to slander's livery,
A dying life to living infamy; 1055
Poor helpless help, the treasure stol'n away,
To burn the guiltless casket where it lay!

'Well, well, dear Collatine, thou shalt not know
The stained taste of violated troth;
I will not wrong thy true affection so, 1060
To flatter thee with an infringed oath;
This bastard graff shall never come to growth;
He shall not boast who did thy stock pollute
That thou art doting father of his fruit. 1064

'Nor shall he smile at thee in secret thought,
Nor laugh with his companions at thy state;
But thou shalt know thy interest was not bought
Basely with gold, but stol'n from forth thy gate.
For me, I am the mistress of my fate, 1069
And with my trespass never will dispense,
Till life to death acquit my forced offence.

'I will not poison thee with my attaint,
Nor fold my fault in cleanly-coin'd excuses;
My sable ground of sin I will not paint, 1074
To hide the truth of this false night's abuses;
My tongue shall utter all; mine eyes, like sluices,
As from a mountain-spring that feeds a dale,
Shall gush pure streams to purge my impure tale.'

By this, lamenting Philomel had ended 1079
The well tuned warble of her nightly sorrow,
And solemn night with slow-sad gait descended
To ugly hell; when, lo, the blushing morrow
Lends light to all fair eyes that light will borrow;
But cloudy Lucrece shames herself to see,
And therefore still in night would cloister'd be.

Revealing day through every cranny spies, 1086
And seems to point her out where she sits weeping;
To whom she sobbing speaks: 'O eye of eyes,
Why pry'st thou through my window? leave thy peeping;
Mock with thy tickling beams eyes that are sleeping; 1090

Brand not my forehead with thy piercing light,
For day hath nought to do what's done by night.'

Thus cavils she with every thing she sees;
True grief is fond and testy as a child, 1094
Who wayward once, his mood with nought agrees;
Old woes, not infant sorrows, bear them mild;
Continuance tames the one; the other wild,
Like an unpractised swimmer plunging still
With too much labour drowns for want of skill.

So she, deep-drenched in a sea of care, 1100
Holds disputation with each thing she views,
And to herself all sorrow doth compare;
No object but her passion's strength renews,
And as one shifts, another straight ensues; 1104
Sometime her grief is dumb and hath no words;
Sometime 'tis mad and too much talk affords.

The little birds that tune their morning's joy
Make her moans mad with their sweet melody;
For mirth doth search the bottom of annoy;
Sad souls are slain in merry company; 1110
Grief best is pleased with grief's society;
True sorrow then is feelingly sufficed
When with like semblance it is sympathized.

'Tis double death to drown in ken of shore; 1114
He ten times pines that pines beholding food;
To see the salve doth make the wound ache more;
Great grief grieves most at that would do it good;
Deep woes roll forward like a gentle flood,
Who, being stopp'd, the bounding banks o'erflows; 1119
Grief dallied with nor law nor limit knows.

'You mocking birds,' quoth she, 'your tunes entomb
Within your hollow-swelling feather'd breasts,
And in my hearing be you mute and dumb;
My restless discord loves no stops nor rests;
A woeful hostess brooks not merry guests; 1125
Relish your nimble notes to pleasing ears;
Distress likes dumps when time is kept with tears.

'Come, Philomel, that sing'st of ravishment,
Make thy sad grove in my dishevell'd hair;
As the dank earth weeps at thy languishment,
So I at each sad strain will strain a tear, 1131
And with deep groans the diapason bear;
For burden-wise I'll hum on Tarquin still,
While thou on Tereus descant'st better skill.

'And whiles against a thorn thou bear'st thy part,
To keep thy sharp woes waking, wretched I,
To imitate thee well, against my heart 1137
Will fix a sharp knife, to affright mine eye;
Who, if it wink, shall thereon fall and die.
These means, as frets upon an instrument,
Shall tune our heart-strings to true languishment. 1141

'And for, poor bird, thou sing'st not in the day,
As shaming any eye should thee behold,
Some dark deep desert, seated from the way,
That knows not parching heat nor freezing cold,
Will we find out; and there we will unfold

To creatures stern sad tunes, to change their
  kinds;   1147
Since men prove beasts, let beasts bear gentle
  minds.'

As the poor frighted deer, that stands at gaze,
Wildly determining which way to fly,   1150
Or one encompass'd with a winding maze,
That cannot tread the way out readily;
So with herself is she in mutiny,
To live or die, which of the twain were better,
When life is shamed and death reproach's
  debtor.   1155

'To kill myself,' quoth she, 'alack, what were it,
But with my body my poor soul's pollution?
They that lose half with greater patience bear it
Than they whose whole is swallow'd in confusion.
That mother tries a merciless conclusion   1160
Who, having two sweet babes, when death takes
  one,
Will slay the other and be nurse to none.

'My body or my soul, which was the dearer,
When the one pure, the other made divine?
Whose love of either to myself was nearer,   1165
When both were kept for heaven and Collatine?
Ay me! the bark peel'd from the lofty pine,
His leaves will wither and his sap decay;
So must my soul, her bark being peel'd away.

'Her house is sack'd, her quiet interrupted,
Her mansion batter'd by the enemy;   1171
Her sacred temple spotted, spoil'd, corrupted,
Grossly engirt with daring infamy;
Then let it not be call'd impiety,
If in this blemish'd fort I make some hole
Through which I may convey this troubled soul.

'Yet die I will not till my Collatine   1177
Have heard the cause of my untimely death;
That he may vow, in that sad hour of mine,
Revenge on him that made me stop my breath.
My stained blood to Tarquin I'll bequeath,   1181
Which by him tainted shall for him be spent,
And as his due writ in my testament.

'My honour I'll bequeath unto the knife
That wounds my body so dishonoured.   1185
'Tis honour to deprive dishonour'd life;
The one will live, the other being dead;
So of shame's ashes shall my fame be bred;
For in my death I murder shameful scorn;
My shame so dead, mine honour is new-born.

'Dear lord of that dear jewel I have lost,   1191
What legacy shall I bequeath to thee?
My resolution, love, shall be thy boast,
By whose example thou revenged mayst be.
How Tarquin must be used, read it in me;   1195
Myself, thy friend, will kill myself, thy foe,
And, for my sake, serve thou false Tarquin so.

'This brief abridgement of my will I make:
My soul and body to the skies and ground;
My resolution, husband, do thou take;   1200
Mine honour be the knife's that makes my wound;
My shame be his that did my fame confound;
And all my fame that lives disbursed be
To those that live and think no shame of me.

'Thou, Collatine, shalt oversee this will;   1205
How was I overseen that thou shalt see it!
My blood shall wash the slander of mine ill;
My life's foul deed, my life's fair end shall free it.
Faint not, faint heart, but stoutly say "So be it;"
Yield to my hand; my hand shall conquer thee;
Thou dead, both die and both shall victors be.'

This plot of death when sadly she had laid,   1212
And wiped the brinish pearl from her bright eyes,
With untuned tongue she hoarsely calls her maid,
Whose swift obedience to her mistress hies;
For fleet-wing'd duty with thought's feathers flies.
Poor Lucrece' cheeks unto her maid seem so
As winter meads when sun doth melt their snow.

Her mistress she doth give demure good-morrow,
With soft slow tongue, true mark of modesty,
And sorts a sad look to her lady's sorrow,   1221
For why her face wore sorrow's livery,
But durst not ask of her audaciously
Why her two suns were cloud-eclipsed so,   1224
Nor why her fair cheeks over-wash'd with woe.

But as the earth doth weep, the sun being set,
Each flower moisten'd like a melting eye,
Even so the maid with swelling drops 'gan wet
Her circled eyne, enforced by sympathy
Of those fair suns set in her mistress' sky,   1230
Who in a salt-waved ocean quench their light,
Which makes the maid weep like the dewy
  night.

A pretty while these pretty creatures stand,
Like ivory conduits coral cisterns filling;   1234
One justly weeps; the other takes in hand
No cause, but company, of her drops spilling;
Their gentle sex to weep are often willing,
Grieving themselves to guess at others' smarts,
And then they drown their eyes or break their
  hearts.   1239

For men have marble, women waxen, minds,
And therefore are they form'd as marble will;
The weak oppress'd, the impression of strange
  kinds
Is form'd in them by force, by fraud, or skill;
Then call them not the authors of their ill,   1244
No more than wax shall be accounted evil
Wherein is stamp'd the semblance of a devil.

Their smoothness, like a goodly champaign plain,
Lays open all the little worms that creep;
In men, as in a rough-grown grove, remain
Cave-keeping evils that obscurely sleep;   1250
Through crystal walls each little mote will peep;
Though men can cover crimes with bold stern
  looks,
Poor women's faces are their own faults' books.

No man inveigh against the wither'd flower,
But chide rough winter that the flower hath kill'd;
Not that devour'd, but that which doth devour,
Is worthy of blame. O, let it not be hild   1257
Poor women's faults, that they are so fulfill'd
With men's abuses; those proud lords to blame
Make weak-made women tenants to their shame.

The precedent whereof in Lucrece view,   1261
Assail'd by night with circumstances strong
Of present death, and shame that might ensue

By that her death, to do her husband wrong;
Such danger to resistance did belong,   1263
 That dying fear through all her body spread;
 And who cannot abuse a body dead?

By this, mild patience bid fair Lucrece speak
To the poor counterfeit of her complaining;
'My girl,' quoth she, 'on what occasion break
These tears from thee, that down thy cheeks are
 raining?   1271
If thou dost weep for grief of my sustaining,
 Know, gentle wench, it small avails my mood;
 If tears could help, mine own would do me good.

'But tell me, girl, when went'—and there she
 stay'd   1275
Till after a deep groan—'Tarquin from hence?'
'Madam, ere I was up,' replied the maid,
 'The more to blame my sluggard negligence;
Yet with the fault I thus far can dispense;
 Myself was stirring ere the break of day, 1280
 And ere I rose was Tarquin gone away.

'But, lady, if your maid may be so bold,
She would request to know your heaviness.'
'O, peace!' quoth Lucrece; 'if it should be told,
The repetition cannot make it less,   1285
 For more it is than I can well express;
 And that deep torture may be call'd a hell
 When more is felt than one hath power to tell.

Go, get me hither paper, ink, and pen;   1289
Yet save that labour, for I have them here.
What should I say? One of my husband's men
Bid thou be ready by and by to bear
A letter to my lord, my love, my dear;
 Bid him with speed prepare to carry it;   1294
 The cause craves haste and it will soon be writ.'

Her maid is gone, and she prepares to write,
First hovering o'er the paper with her quill;
Conceit and grief an eager combat fight;
What wit sets down is blotted straight with will;
This is too curious-good, this blunt and ill; 1300
 Much like a press of people at a door,
 Throng her inventions, which shall go before.

At last she thus begins: 'Thou worthy lord
Of that unworthy wife that greeteth thee,
Health to thy person! next vouchsafe t' afford,—
If ever, love, thy Lucrece thou wilt see,— 1306
Some present speed to come and visit me.
 So, I commend me from our house in grief;
 My woes are tedious, though my words are
 brief.'

Here folds she up the tenour of her woe,   1310
Her certain sorrow writ uncertainly.
By this short schedule Collatine may know
Her grief, but not her grief's true quality;
She dares not thereof make discovery,   1314
 Lest he should hold it her own gross abuse,
 Ere she with blood had stain'd her stain'd ex-
 cuse.

Besides, the life and feeling of her passion
She hoards, to spend when he is by to hear her,
When sighs and groans and tears may grace the
 fashion

Of her disgrace, the better so to clear her   1320
From that suspicion which the world might bear
 her.
 To shun this blot, she would not blot the letter
 With words, till action might become them
 better.

To see sad sights moves more than hear them told;
For then the eye interprets to the ear   1325
The heavy motion that it doth behold,
When every part a part of woe doth bear.
'Tis but a part of sorrow that we hear;
 Deep sounds make lesser noise than shallow
 fords,
 And sorrow ebbs, being blown with wind of
 words.   1330

Her letter now is seal'd and on it writ
'At Ardea to my lord with more than haste.'
The post attends, and she delivers it,
Charging the sour-faced groom to hie as fast
As lagging fowls before the northern blast;
 Speed more than speed but dull and slow she
 deems;   1336
 Extremity still urgeth such extremes.

The homely villain court'sies to her low,
And blushing on her, with a steadfast eye
Receives the scroll without or yea or no,   1340
And forth with bashful innocence doth hie.
But they whose guilt within their bosoms lie
 Imagine every eye beholds their blame;
 For Lucrece thought he blush'd to see her
 shame;

When, silly groom! God wot, it was defect
Of spirit, life and bold audacity,   1346
Such harmless creatures have a true respect
To talk in deeds, while others saucily
Promise more speed but do it leisurely;   1349
Even so this pattern of the worn-out age
 Pawn'd honest looks, but laid no words to gage.

His kindled duty kindled her mistrust,
That two red fires in both their faces blazed;
She thought he blush'd, as knowing Tarquin's lust,
And blushing with him, wistly on him gazed; 1355
Her earnest eye did make him more amazed:
 The more she saw the blood his cheeks replenish,
 The more she thought he spied in her some
 blemish.

But long she thinks till he return again,
And yet the duteous vassal scarce is gone.
The weary time she cannot entertain,   1361
For now 'tis stale to sigh, to weep and groan;
So woe hath wearied woe, moan tired moan,
 That she her plaints a little while doth stay,
 Pausing for means to mourn some newer way.

At last she calls to mind where hangs a piece
Of skilful painting, made for Priam's Troy;
Before the which is drawn the power of Greece,
For Helen's rape the city to destroy,   1369
Threatening cloud-kissing Ilion with annoy;
 Which the conceited painter drew so proud,
 As heaven, it seem'd, to kiss the turrets bow'd

A thousand lamentable objects there,
In scorn of nature, art gave lifeless life;
Many a dry drop seem'd a weeping tear, 1375
Shed for the slaughter'd husband by the wife;
The red blood reek'd, to show the painter's strife;
And dying eyes gleam'd forth their ashy lights,
Like dying coals burnt out in tedious nights.

There might you see the labouring pioner 1380
Begrimed with sweat and smeared all with dust;
And from the towers of Troy there would appear
The very eyes of men through loop-holes thrust,
Gazing upon the Greeks with little lust; 1384
Such sweet observance in this work was had
That one might see those far-off eyes look sad.

In great commanders grace and majesty
You might behold, triumphing in their faces;
In youth, quick bearing and dexterity;
And here and there the painter interlaces 1390
Pale cowards, marching on with trembling paces,
Which heartless peasants did so well resemble,
That one would swear he saw them quake and tremble.

In Ajax and Ulysses, O, what art
Of physiognomy might one behold! 1395
The face of either cipher'd either's heart;
Their face their manners most expressly told;
In Ajax' eyes blunt rage and rigour roll'd;
But the mild glance that sly Ulysses lent 1399
Show'd deep regard and smiling government.

There pleading might you see grave Nestor stand,
As 'twere encouraging the Greeks to fight,
Making such sober action with his hand 1403
That it beguiled attention, charm'd the sight;
In speech, it seem'd, his beard all silver white
Wagg'd up and down, and from his lips did fly
Thin winding breath which purl'd up to the sky.

About him were a press of gaping faces,
Which seem'd to swallow up his sound advice;
All jointly listening, but with several graces,
As if some mermaid did their ears entice, 1411
Some high, some low, the painter was so nice;
The scalps of many, almost hid behind,
To jump up higher seem'd, to mock the mind.

Here one man's hand lean'd on another's head,
His nose being shadow'd by his neighbour's ear;
Here one being throng'd bears back, all boll'n and red; 1417
Another smother'd seems to pelt and swear;
And in their rage such signs of rage they bear
As, but for loss of Nestor's golden words,
It seem'd they would debate with angry swords.

For much imaginary work was there; 1422
Conceit deceitful, so compact, so kind,
That for Achilles' image stood his spear
Griped in an armed hand; himself behind
Was left unseen, save to the eye of mind; 1426
A hand, a foot, a face, a leg, a head,
Stood for the whole to be imagined.

And from the walls of strong-besieged Troy
When their brave hope, bold Hector, march'd to field, 1430
Stood many Trojan mothers sharing joy
To see their youthful sons bright weapons wield;
And to their hope they such odd action yield

That through their light joy seemed to appear,
Like bright things stain'd, a kind of heavy fear.

And from the strand of Dardan, where they fought,
To Simois' reedy banks the red blood ran, 1437
Whose waves to imitate the battle sought
With swelling ridges; and their ranks began
To break upon the galled shore, and than 1440
Retire again, till meeting greater ranks
They join and shoot their foam at Simois' banks.

To this well-painted piece is Lucrece come,
To find a face where all distress is stell'd. 1444
Many she sees where cares have carved some,
But none where all distress and dolour dwell'd,
Till she despairing Hecuba beheld,
Staring on Priam's wounds with her old eyes,
Which bleeding under Pyrrhus' proud foot lies.

In her the painter had anatomized 1450
Time's ruin, beauty's wreck, and grim care's reign;
Her cheeks with chaps and wrinkles were disguised;
Of what she was no semblance did remain;
Her blue blood changed to black in every vein,
Wanting the spring that those shrunk pipes have fed, 1455
Show'd life imprison'd in a body dead.

On this sad shadow Lucrece spends her eyes,
And shapes her sorrow to the beldam's woes,
Who nothing wants to answer her but cries,
And bitter words to ban her cruel foes; 1460
The painter was no god to lend her those;
And therefore Lucrece swears he did her wrong,
To give her so much grief and not a tongue.

'Poor instrument,' quoth she, 'without a sound,
I'll tune thy woes with my lamenting tongue,
And drop sweet balm in Priam's painted wound,
And rail on Pyrrhus that hath done him wrong,
And with my tears quench Troy that burns so long,
And with my knife scratch out the angry eyes
Of all the Greeks that are thine enemies. 1470

'Show me the strumpet that began this stir,
That with my nails her beauty I may tear.
Thy heat of lust, fond Paris, did incur
This load of wrath that burning Troy doth bear;
Thy eye kindled the fire that burneth here; 1475
And here in Troy, for trespass of thine eye,
The sire, the son, the dame, and daughter die.

'Why should the private pleasure of some one
Become the public plague of many moe?
Let sin, alone committed, light alone 1480
Upon his head that hath transgressed so;
Let guiltless souls be freed from guilty woe;
For one's offence why should so many fall,
To plague a private sin in general?

'Lo, here weeps Hecuba, here Priam dies, 1485
Here manly Hector faints, here Troilus swounds,
Here friend by friend in bloody channel lies
And friend to friend gives unadvised wounds,
And one man's lust these many lives confounds;
Had doting Priam check'd his son's desire,
Troy had been bright with fame and not with fire.' 1491

Here feelingly she weeps Troy's painted woes;
For sorrow, like a heavy-hanging bell,
Once set on ringing, with his own weight goes;
Then little strength rings out the doleful knell;
So Lucrece, set a-work, sad tales doth tell   1496
    To pencill'd pensiveness and colour'd sorrow;
    She lends them words, and she their looks doth
        borrow.

She throws her eyes about the painting round,
And who she finds forlorn she doth lament.
At last she sees a wretched image bound,   1501
That piteous looks to Phrygian shepherds lent;
His face, though full of cares, yet show'd content;
    Onward to Troy with the blunt swains he goes,
    So mild that Patience seem'd to scorn his woes.

In him the painter labour'd with his skill   1506
To hide deceit and give the harmless show
An humble gait, calm looks, eyes wailing still,
A brow unbent, that seem'd to welcome woe;
Cheeks neither red nor pale, but mingled so   1510
    That blushing red no guilty instance gave,
    Nor ashy pale the fear that false hearts have.

But, like a constant and confirmed devil,
He entertain'd a show so seeming just,
And therein so ensconced his secret evil,   1515
That jealousy itself could not mistrust
False-creeping craft and perjury should thrust
    Into so bright a day such black-faced storms,
    Or blot with hell-born sin such saint-like forms.

The well-skill'd workman this mild image drew
For perjured Sinon, whose enchanting story
The credulous old Priam after slew;   1522
Whose words, like wildfire, burnt the shining
        glory
Of rich-built Ilion, that the skies were sorry,
    And little stars shot from their fixed places,
    When their glass fell wherein they view'd their
        faces.   1526

This picture she advisedly perused,
And chid the painter for his wondrous skill,
Saying, some shape in Sinon's was abused;
So fair a form lodged not a mind so ill;   1530
And still on him she gazed, and gazing still
Such signs of truth in his plain face she spied
    That she concludes the picture was belied.

'It cannot be,' quoth she, 'that so much guile'—
She would have said 'can lurk in such a look;'
But Tarquin's shape came in her mind the while,
And from her tongue 'can lurk' from 'cannot'
        took;   1537
'It cannot be' she in that sense forsook,
    And turn'd it thus, 'It cannot be, I find,
    But such a face should bear a wicked mind;

For even as subtle Sinon here is painted,   1541
So sober-sad, so weary, and so mild,
As if with grief or travail he had fainted,
To me came Tarquin armed; so beguiled
With outward honesty, but yet defiled   1545
    With inward vice; as Priam him did cherish,
    So did I Tarquin; so my Troy did perish.

Look, look, how listening Priam wets his eyes,
To see those borrow'd tears that Sinon sheds!
Priam, why art thou old and yet not wise?   1550

For every tear he falls a Trojan bleeds;
His eye drops fire, no water thence proceeds;
    Those round clear pearls of his that move thy
        pity
    Are balls of quenchless fire to burn thy city.

'Such devils steal effects from lightless hell;
For Sinon in his fire doth quake with cold,   1556
And in that cold hot-burning fire doth dwell;
These contraries such unity do hold,
Only to flatter fools and make them bold;
    So Priam's trust false Sinon's tears doth flatter,
    That he finds means to burn his Troy with
        water.'   1561

Here, all enraged, such passion her assails,
That patience is quite beaten from her breast.
She tears the senseless Sinon with her nails,
Comparing him to that unhappy guest   1565
Whose deed hath made herself herself detest;
    At last she smilingly with this gives o'er;
    'Fool, fool!' quoth she, 'his wounds will not be
        sore.'   1568

Thus ebbs and flows the current of her sorrow,
And time doth weary time with her complaining.
She looks for night, and then she longs for morrow,
And both she thinks too long with her remaining;
Short time seems long in sorrow's sharp sustain-
        ing;   1573
    Though woe be heavy, yet it seldom sleeps,
    And they that watch see time how slow it creeps.

Which all this time hath overslipp'd her thought,
That she with painted images hath spent;
Being from the feeling of her own grief brought
By deep surmise of others' detriment,
Losing her woes in shows of discontent.   1580
    It easeth some, though none it ever cured,
    To think their dolour others have endured.

But now the mindful messenger come back
Brings home his lord and other company;
Who finds his Lucrece clad in mourning black;
And round about her tear-distained eye   1586
Blue circles stream'd, like rainbows in the sky;
    These water-galls in her dim element
    Foretell new storms to those already spent.

Which when her sad-beholding husband saw,
Amazedly in her sad face he stares;   1591
Her eyes, though sod in tears, look'd red and raw,
Her lively colour kill'd with deadly cares.
He hath no power to ask her how she fares;
    Both stood, like old acquaintance in a trance,
    Met far from home, wondering each other's
        chance.   1596

At last he takes her by the bloodless hand,
And thus begins: 'What uncouth ill event
Hath thee befall'n, that thou dost trembling stand?
Sweet love, what spite hath thy fair colour spent?
Why art thou attired in discontent?   1601
    Unmask, dear dear, this moody heaviness,
    And tell thy grief, that we may give redress.'

Three times with sighs she gives her sorrow fire,
Ere once she can discharge one word of woe;
At length address'd to answer his desire,   1606

She modestly prepares to let them know
Her honour is ta'en prisoner by the foe;
While Collatine and his consorted lords 1609
With sad attention long to hear her words.

And now this pale swan in her watery nest
Begins the sad dirge of her certain ending;
'Few words,' quoth she, 'shall fit the trespass best,
Where no excuse can give the fault amending;
In me moe woes than words are now depending;
And my laments would be drawn out too long,
To tell them all with one poor tired tongue.

'Then be this all the task it hath to say: 1618
Dear husband, in the interest of thy bed
A stranger came, and on that pillow lay
Where thou wast wont to rest thy weary head;
And what wrong else may be imagined
By foul enforcement might be done to me,
From that, alas, thy Lucrece is not free. 1624

'For in the dreadful dead of dark midnight,
With shining falchion in my chamber came
A creeping creature, with a flaming light,
And softly cried "Awake, thou Roman dame,
And entertain my love; else lasting shame
On thee and thine this night I will inflict,
If thou my love's desire do contradict. 1631

'"For some hard-favour'd groom of thine," quoth he,
"Unless thou yoke thy liking to my will,
I'll murder straight, and then I'll slaughter thee,
And swear I found you where you did fulfil
The loathsome act of lust, and so did kill 1636
The lechers in their deed; this act will be
My fame, and thy perpetual infamy."

'With this, I did begin to start and cry;
And then against my heart he set his sword,
Swearing, unless I took all patiently, 1641
I should not live to speak another word;
So should my shame still rest upon record,
And never be forgot in mighty Rome
The adulterate death of Lucrece and her groom.

'Mine enemy was strong, my poor self weak, 1646
And far the weaker with so strong a fear;
My bloody judge forbade my tongue to speak;
No rightful plea might plead for justice there;
His scarlet lust came evidence to swear 1650
That my poor beauty had purloin'd his eyes;
And when the judge is robb'd, the prisoner dies.

'O teach me how to make mine own excuse!
Or, at the least, this refuge let me find; 1654
Though my gross blood be stain'd with this abuse,
Immaculate and spotless is my mind;
That was not forced; that never was inclined
To accessary yieldings, but still pure
Doth in her poison'd closet yet endure.'

Lo, here, the hopeless merchant of this loss,
With head declined, and voice damm'd up with woe, 1661
With sad-set eyes and wretched arms across,
From lips new-waxen pale begins to blow
The grief away that stops his answer so;
But, wretched as he is, he strives in vain;
What he breathes out his breath drinks up again. 1666

As through an arch the violent roaring tide
Outruns the eye that doth behold his haste,
Yet in the eddy boundeth in his pride 1669
Back to the strait that forced him on so fast,
In rage sent out, recall'd in rage, being past;
Even so his sighs, his sorrows, make a saw,
To push grief on and back the same grief draw

Which speechless woe of his poor she attendeth,
And his untimely frenzy thus awaketh: 1675
'Dear lord, thy sorrow to my sorrow lendeth
Another power; no flood by raining slaketh.
My woe too sensible thy passion maketh
More feeling-painful; let it then suffice 1679
To drown one woe, one pair of weeping eyes.

'And for my sake, when I might charm thee so,
For she that was thy Lucrece, now attend me;
Be suddenly revenged on my foe,
Thine, mine, his own; suppose thou dost defend me
From what is past; the help that thou shalt lend me 1685
Comes all too late, yet let the traitor die;
For sparing justice feeds iniquity.

'But ere I name him, you fair lords,' quoth she,
Speaking to those that came with Collatine,
'Shall plight your honourable faiths to me, 1690
With swift pursuit to venge this wrong of mine;
For 'tis a meritorious fair design
To chase injustice with revengeful arms;
Knights, by their oaths, should right poor ladies' harms.'

At this request, with noble disposition 1695
Each present lord began to promise aid,
As bound in knighthood to her imposition,
Longing to hear the hateful foe bewray'd. 1698
But she, that yet her sad task hath not said,
The protestation stops. 'O, speak,' quoth she,
'How may this forced stain be wiped from me?

'What is the quality of my offence,
Being constrain'd with dreadful circumstance?
May my pure mind with the foul act dispense,
My low-declined honour to advance? 1705
May any terms acquit me from this chance?
The poison'd fountain clears itself again;
And why not I from this compelled stain?'

With this, they all at once began to say, 1709
Her body's stain her mind untainted clears;
While with a joyless smile she turns away
The face, that map which deep impression bears
Of hard misfortune, carved in it with tears.
'No, no,' quoth she, 'no dame hereafter living
By my excuse shall claim excuse's giving.' 1715

Here with a sigh, as if her heart would break,
She throws forth Tarquin's name; 'He, he,' she says,
But more than 'he' her poor tongue could not speak;
Till after many accents and delays, 1719
Untimely breathings, sick and short assays,
She utters this: 'He, he, fair lords, 'tis he,
That guides this hand to give this wound to me.'

Even here she sheathed in her harmless breast
A harmful knife, that thence her soul unsheathed;
That blow did bail it from the deep unrest   1725
Of that polluted prison where it breathed;
Her contrite sighs unto the clouds bequeathed
  Her winged sprightly, and through her wounds
      doth fly
  Life's lasting date from cancell'd destiny.

Stone-still, astonish'd with this deadly deed,
Stood Collatine and all his lordly crew;   1731
Till Lucrece' father, that beholds her bleed,
Himself on her self-slaughter'd body threw;
And from the purple fountain Brutus drew
  The murderous knife, and, as it left the place,
  Her blood, in poor revenge, held it in chase;

And bubbling from her breast, it doth divide
In two slow rivers, that the crimson blood
Circles her body in on every side,
Who, like a late-sack'd island, vastly stood   1740
Bare and unpeopled in this fearful flood.
  Some of her blood still pure and red remain'd,
  And some look'd black, and that false Tarquin
      stain'd.

About the mourning and congealed face
Of that black blood a watery rigol goes,   1745
Which seems to weep upon the tainted place;
And ever since, as pitying Lucrece' woes,
Corrupted blood some watery token shows;
  And blood untainted still doth red abide,
  Blushing at that which is so putrified.   1750

'Daughter, dear daughter,' old Lucretius cries,
'That life was mine which thou hast here deprived.
If in the child the father's image lies,
Where shall I live now Lucrece is unlived?
Thou wast not to this end from me derived.
  If children pre-decease progenitors,   1756
  We are their offspring, and they none of ours.

Poor broken glass, I often did behold
In thy sweet semblance my old age new born;
But now that fair fresh mirror, dim and old,   1760
Shows me a bare-boned death by time outworn;
O, from thy cheeks my image thou hast torn,
  And shiver'd all the beauty of my glass,
  That I no more can see what once I was.

'O time, cease thou thy course and last no longer,
If they surcease to be that should survive.   1766
Shall rotten death make conquest of the stronger,
And leave the faltering, feeble souls alive?
The old bees die, the young possess their hive;
  Then live, sweet Lucrece, live again, and see
  Thy father die, and not thy father thee!'   1771

By this, starts Collatine as from a dream,
And bids Lucretius give his sorrow place;
And then in key-cold Lucrece' bleeding stream
He falls, and bathes the pale fear in his face,
And counterfeits to die with her a space;   1776
  Till manly shame bids him possess his breath,
  And live to be revenged on her death.

The deep vexation of his inward soul   1779
Hath served a dumb arrest upon his tongue;
Who, mad that sorrow should his use control

Or keep him from heart-easing words so long,
Begins to talk; but through his lips do throng
Weak words, so thick come in his poor heart's
    aid   1784
That no man could distinguish what he said.

Yet sometime 'Tarquin' was pronounced plain,
But through his teeth, as if the name he tore.
This windy tempest, till it blow up rain,
Held back his sorrow's tide, to make it more;
At last it rains, and busy winds give o'er;   1790
  Then son and father weep with equal strife
  Who should weep most, for daughter or for wife.

The one doth call her his, the other his,
Yet neither may possess the claim they lay.
The father says 'She's mine.' 'O, mine she is,'
Replies her husband; 'do not take away   1796
My sorrow's interest; let no mourner say
  He weeps for her, for she was only mine,
  And only must be wail'd by Collatine.'

'O,' quoth Lucretius, 'I did give that life   1800
Which she too early and too late hath spill'd.'
'Woe, woe,' quoth Collatine, 'she was my wife;
I owed her, and 'tis mine that she hath kill'd.'
'My daughter' and 'my wife' with clamours fill'd
  The dispersed air, who, holding Lucrece' life,
  Answer'd their cries, 'my daughter' and 'my
      wife.'   1806

Brutus, who pluck'd the knife from Lucrece' side,
Seeing such emulation in their woe,
Began to clothe his wit in state and pride,
Burying in Lucrece' wound his folly's show.
He with the Romans was esteemed so   1811
As silly-jeering idiots are with kings,
For sportive words and uttering foolish things;

But now he throws that shallow habit by
Wherein deep policy did him disguise,   1815
And arm'd his long-hid wits advisedly
To check the tears in Collatinus' eyes.
'Thou wronged lord of Rome,' quoth he, 'arise;
  Let my unsounded self, supposed a fool,
  Now set thy long-experienced wit to school.

'Why, Collatine, is woe the cure for woe?   1821
Do wounds help wounds, or grief help grievous
    deeds?
Is it revenge to give thyself a blow
For his foul act by whom thy fair wife bleeds?
Such childish humour from weak minds proceeds;
  Thy wretched wife mistook the matter so,
  To slay herself that should have slain her foe.

'Courageous Roman, do not steep thy heart
In such relenting dew of lamentations,   1829
But kneel with me and help to bear thy part
To rouse our Roman gods with invocations
That they will suffer these abominations,
  Since Rome herself in them doth stand disgraced,
  By our strong arms from forth her fair streets
      chased.

'Now, by the Capitol that we adore,   1835
And by this chaste blood so unjustly stained,
By heaven's fair sun that breeds the fat earth's
    store,

By all our country rights in Rome maintained,
And by chaste Lucrece' soul that late complained
Her wrongs to us, and by this bloody knife,
We will revenge the death of this true wife!'

This said, he struck his hand upon his breast,
And kiss'd the fatal knife, to end his vow,
And to his protestation urged the rest,   1844
Who, wondering at him, did his words allow;
Then jointly to the ground their knees they bow;

And that deep vow, which Brutus made before,
He doth again repeat, and that they swore.

When they had sworn to this advised doom,   1849
They did conclude to bear dead Lucrece thence,
To show her bleeding body thorough Rome,
And so to publish Tarquin's foul offence;
Which being done with speedy diligence,
The Romans plausibly did give consent
To Tarquin's everlasting banishment.   1855

SONNETS

1

From fairest creatures we desire increase,
That thereby beauty's rose might never die,
But as the riper should by time decease,
His tender heir might bear his memory;   4
But thou, contracted to thine own bright eyes,
Feed'st thy light's flame with self-substantial fuel,
Making a famine where abundance lies,
Thyself thy foe, to thy sweet self too cruel.
Thou that art now the world's fresh ornament
And only herald to the gaudy spring,   10
Within thine own bud buriest thy content
And, tender churl, makest waste in niggarding.
Pity the world, or else this glutton be,
To eat the world's due, by the grave and thee.

2

When forty winters shall besiege thy brow
And dig deep trenches in thy beauty's field,
Thy youth's proud livery, so gazed on now,
Will be a tatter'd weed, of small worth held;
Then being ask'd where all thy beauty lies,   5
Where all the treasure of thy lusty days,
To say, within thine own deep-sunken eyes,
Were an all-eating shame and thriftless praise.
How much more praise deserved thy beauty's use,
If thou couldst answer ' This fair child of mine
Shall sum my count and make my old excuse,'
Proving his beauty by succession thine!   12
This were to be new made when thou art old,
And see thy blood warm when thou feel'st it cold.

3

Look in thy glass, and tell the face thou viewest
Now is the time that face should form another;
Whose fresh repair if now thou not renewest,
Thou dost beguile the world, unbless some mother.
For where is she so fair whose unear'd womb
Disdains the tillage of thy husbandry?   6
Or who is he so fond will be the tomb
Of his self-love, to stop posterity?
Thou art thy mother's glass, and she in thee
Calls back the lovely April of her prime;   10
So thou through windows of thine age shalt see,
Despite of wrinkles, this thy golden time.

But if thou live, remember'd not to be,
Die single, and thine image dies with thee.

4

Unthrifty loveliness, why dost thou spend
Upon thyself thy beauty's legacy?
Nature's bequest gives nothing, but doth lend,
And being frank, she lends to those are free.
Then, beauteous niggard, why dost thou abuse   5
The bounteous largess given thee to give?
Profitless usurer, why dost thou use
So great a sum of sums, yet canst not live?
For having traffic with thyself alone,
Thou of thyself thy sweet self dost deceive.   10
Then how, when nature calls thee to be gone,
What acceptable audit canst thou leave?
Thy unused beauty must be tomb'd with thee,
Which, used, lives th' executor to be.

5

Those hours that with gentle work did frame
The lovely gaze where every eye doth dwell,
Will play the tyrants to the very same
And that unfair which fairly doth excel;
For never-resting time leads summer on   5
To hideous winter and confounds him there;
Sap cheek'd with frost and lusty leaves quite gone,
Beauty o'ersnow'd and bareness every where;
Then, were not summer's distillation left,
A liquid prisoner pent in walls of glass,   10
Beauty's effect with beauty were bereft,
Nor it, nor no remembrance what it was;
But flowers distill'd, though they with winter meet,
Leese but their show; their substance still lives sweet.

6

Then let not winter's ragged hand deface
In thee thy summer, ere thou be distill'd;
Make sweet some vial; treasure thou some place
With beauty's treasure, ere it be self-kill'd.
That use is not forbidden usury,   5
Which happies those that pay the willing loan;
That's for thyself to breed another thee,
Or ten times happier, be it ten for one;

6

Ten times thyself were happier than thou art,
If ten of thine ten times refigured thee;　　10
Then what could death do, if thou shouldst depart,
Leaving thee living in posterity?
　Be not self-will'd, for thou art much too fair
　To be death's conquest and make worms thine
　　heir.

7

Lo, in the orient when the gracious light
Lifts up his burning head, each under eye
Doth homage to his new-appearing sight,
Serving with looks his sacred majesty;
And having climb'd the steep-up heavenly hill, 5
Resembling strong youth in his middle age,
Yet mortal looks adore his beauty still,
Attending on his golden pilgrimage;
But when from highmost pitch, with weary car,
Like feeble age, he reeleth from the day,　　10
The eyes, 'fore duteous, now converted are
From his low tract, and look another way;
　So thou, thyself out-going in thy noon,
　Unlook'd on diest, unless thou get a son.

8

Music to hear, why hear'st thou music sadly?
Sweets with sweets war not, joy delights in joy.
Why lovest thou that which thou receivest not
　gladly,
Or else receivest with pleasure thine annoy?
If the true concord of well tuned sounds,　　5
By unions married, do offend thine ear,
They do but sweetly chide thee, who confounds
In singleness the parts that thou shouldst bear.
Mark how one string, sweet husband to another,
Strikes each in each by mutual ordering;　　10
Resembling sire and child and happy mother,
Who, all in one, one pleasing note do sing;
　Whose speechless song, being many, seeming
　　one,
　Sings this to thee: 'Thou single wilt prove
　　none.'

9

Is it for fear to wet a widow's eye
That thou consumest thyself in single life?
Ah! if thou issueless shalt hap to die,
The world will wail thee, like a makeless wife;
The world will be thy widow, and still weep　5
That thou no form of thee hast left behind,
When every private widow well may keep
By children's eyes her husband's shape in mind.
Look, what an unthrift in the world doth spend
Shifts but his place, for still the world enjoys it;
But beauty's waste hath in the world an end,　11
And kept unused, the user so destroys it.
　No love toward others in that bosom sits
　That on himself such murderous shame com-
　　mits.

10

For shame! deny that thou bear'st love to any,
Who for thyself art so unprovident.
Grant, if thou wilt, thou art beloved of many,
But that thou none lovest is most evident;
For thou art so possess'd with murderous hate 5
That 'gainst thyself thou stick'st not to conspire,
Seeking that beauteous roof to ruinate
Which to repair should be thy chief desire.

O, change thy thought, that I may change my
　mind!
Shall hate be fairer lodged than gentle love?　10
Be, as thy presence is, gracious and kind,
Or to thyself at least kind-hearted prove;
　Make thee another self, for love of me,
　That beauty still may live in thine or thee.

11

As fast as thou shalt wane, so fast thou growest
In one of thine, from that which thou departest;
And that fresh blood which youngly thou be-
　stowest
Thou mayst call thine when thou from youth
　convertest.
Herein lives wisdom, beauty, and increase;　5
Without this, folly, age, and cold decay;
If all were minded so, the times should cease
And threescore year would make the world away.
Let those whom Nature hath not made for store,
Harsh, featureless, and rude, barrenly perish;
Look, whom she best endow'd she gave the more;
Which bounteous gift thou shouldst in bounty
　cherish;　　12
　She carved thee for her seal, and meant thereby
　Thou shouldst print more, not let that copy die.

12

When I do count the clock that tells the time,
And see the brave day sunk in hideous night;
When I behold the violet past prime,
And sable curls all silver'd o'er with white;
When lofty trees I see barren of leaves,　5
Which erst from heat did canopy the herd,
And summer's green all girded up in sheaves,
Borne on the bier with white and bristly beard,
Then of thy beauty do I question make,
That thou among the wastes of time must go,
Since sweets and beauties do themselves forsake
And die as fast as they see others grow;　　12
　And nothing 'gainst Time's scythe can make
　　defence
　Save breed, to brave him when he takes thee
　　hence.

13

O, that you were yourself! but, love, you are
No longer yours than you yourself here live;
Against this coming end you should prepare,
And your sweet semblance to some other give.
So should that beauty which you hold in lease 5
Find no determination; then you were　6
Yourself again, after yourself's decease,
When your sweet issue your sweet form should
　bear.
Who lets so fair a house fall to decay,
Which husbandry in honour might uphold　10
Against the stormy gusts of winter's day
And barren rage of death's eternal cold?
　O, none but unthrifts; dear my love, you know
　You had a father; let your son say so.

14

Not from the stars do I my judgement pluck;
And yet methinks I have astronomy,
But not to tell of good or evil luck,
Of plagues, of dearths, or seasons' quality;
Nor can I fortune to brief minutes tell,　5
Pointing to each his thunder, rain, and wind,
Or say with princes if it shall go well,
By oft predict that I in heaven find;

But from thine eyes my knowledge I derive,
And, constant stars, in them I read such art,
As truth and beauty shall together thrive, 11
If from thyself to store thou wouldst convert;
 Or else of thee this I prognosticate:
 Thy end is truth's and beauty's doom and date.

15

When I consider every thing that grows
Holds in perfection but a little moment,
That this huge stage presenteth nought but shows
Whereon the stars in secret influence comment;
When I perceive that men as plants increase, 5
Cheered and check'd even by the self-same sky,
Vaunt in their youthful sap, at height decrease,
And wear their brave state out of memory;
Then the conceit of this inconstant stay
Sets you most rich in youth before my sight
Where wasteful Time debateth with Decay, 11
To change your day of youth to sullied night;
 And all in war with Time for love of you,
 As he takes from you, I engraft you new.

16

But wherefore do not you a mightier way
Make war upon this bloody tyrant, Time?
And fortify yourself in your decay
With means more blessed than my barren rhyme?
Now stand you on the top of happy hours, 5
And many maiden gardens, yet unset,
With virtuous wish would bear your living flowers
Much liker than your painted counterfeit;
So should the lines of life that life repair, 9
Which this, Time's pencil, or my pupil pen,
Neither in inward worth nor outward fair,
Can make you live yourself in eyes of men.
 To give away yourself keeps yourself still;
 And you must live, drawn by your own sweet skill.

17

Who will believe my verse in time to come,
If it were fill'd with your most high deserts?
Though yet, heaven knows, it is but as a tomb
Which hides your life and shows not half your parts.
If I could write the beauty of your eyes 5
And in fresh numbers number all your graces,
The age to come would say 'This poet lies;
Such heavenly touches ne'er touch'd earthly faces.'
So should my papers, yellow'd with their age,
Be scorn'd, like old men of less truth than tongue,
And your true rights be termed a poet's rage
And stretched metre of an antique song; 12
 But were some child of yours alive that time,
 You should live twice, in it and in my rhyme.

18

Shall I compare thee to a summer's day?
Thou art more lovely and more temperate;
Rough winds do shake the darling buds of May,
And summer's lease hath all too short a date;
Sometime too hot the eye of heaven shines, 5
And often is his gold complexion dimm'd;
And every fair from fair sometimes declines,
By chance or nature's changing course untrimm'd;
But thy eternal summer shall not fade,
Nor lose possession of that fair thou owest; 10
Nor shall Death brag thou wander'st in his shade,
When in eternal lines to time thou growest;

So long as men can breathe, or eyes can see,
So long lives this, and this gives life to thee.

19

Devouring Time, blunt thou the lion's paws,
And make the earth devour her own sweet brood;
Pluck the keen teeth from the fierce tiger's jaws,
And burn the long-lived phoenix in her blood;
Make glad and sorry seasons as thou fleet'st, 5
And do whate'er thou wilt, swift-footed Time,
To the wide world and all her fading sweets;
But I forbid thee one most heinous crime;
O, carve not with thy hours my love's fair brow,
Nor draw no lines there with thine antique pen;
Him in thy course untainted do allow 11
For beauty's pattern to succeeding men.
 Yet do thy worst, old Time; despite thy wrong,
 My love shall in my verse ever live young.

20

A woman's face with Nature's own hand painted
Hast thou, the master-mistress of my passion;
A woman's gentle heart, but not acquainted
With shifting change, as is false women's fashion;
An eye more bright than theirs, less false in rolling, 5
Gilding the object whereupon it gazeth;
A man in hue, all 'hues' in his controlling,
Which steals men's eyes and women's souls amazeth.
And for a woman wert thou first created;
Till Nature, as she wrought thee, fell a-doting,
And by addition me of thee defeated, 11
By adding one thing to my purpose nothing.
 But since she prick'd thee out for women's pleasure,
 Mine be thy love, and thy love's use their treasure.

21

So is it not with me as with that Muse
Stirr'd by a painted beauty to his verse,
Who heaven itself for ornament doth use
And every fair with his fair doth rehearse,
Making a couplement of proud compare, 5
With sun and moon, with earth and sea's rich gems,
With April's first-born flowers, and all things rare
That heaven's air in this huge rondure hems.
O, let me, true in love, but truly write,
And then believe me, my love is as fair 10
As any mother's child, though not so bright
As those gold candles fix'd in heaven's air;
 Let them say more that like of hearsay well;
 I will not praise that purpose not to sell.

22

My glass shall not persuade me I am old,
So long as youth and thou are of one date;
But when in thee time's furrows I behold,
Then look I death my days should expiate.
For all that beauty that doth cover thee 5
Is but the seemly raiment of my heart,
Which in thy breast doth live, as thine in me;
How can I then be elder than thou art?
O, therefore, love, be of thyself so wary
As I, not for myself, but for thee will; 10
Bearing thy heart, which I will keep so chary
As tender nurse her babe from faring ill.

Presume not on thy heart when mine is slain;
Thou gavest me thine, not to give back again.

23

As an unperfect actor on the stage,
Who with his fear is put besides his part,
Or some fierce thing replete with too much rage,
Whose strength's abundance weakens his own heart;
So I, for fear of trust, forget to say   5
The perfect ceremony of love's rite,
And in mine own love's strength seem to decay,
O'ercharged with burthen of mine own love's might.
O, let my books be then the eloquence
And dumb presagers of my speaking breast;   10
Who plead for love, and look for recompense,
More than that tongue that more hath more expressed.
O, learn to read what silent love hath writ;
To hear with eyes belongs to love's fine wit.

24

Mine eye hath play'd the painter and hath stell'd
Thy beauty's form in table of my heart;
My body is the frame wherein 'tis held,
And perspective it is best painter's art.
For through the painter must you see his skill,   5
To find where your true image pictured lies;
Which in my bosom's shop is hanging still,
That hath his windows glazed with thine eyes.
Now see what good turns eyes for eyes have done:
Mine eyes have drawn thy shape, and thine for me   10
Are windows to my breast, where-through the sun
Delights to peep, to gaze therein on thee;
Yet eyes this cunning want to grace their art,
They draw but what they see, know not the heart.

25

Let those who are in favour with their stars
Of public honour and proud titles boast,
Whilst I, whom fortune of such triumph bars,
Unlook'd for joy in that I honour most.
Great princes' favourites their fair leaves spread
But as the marigold at the sun's eye,   6
And in themselves their pride lies buried,
For at a frown they in their glory die.
The painful warrior famoused for fight,
After a thousand victories, once foil'd,   10
Is from the book of honour razed quite,
And all the rest forgot for which he toil'd;
Then happy I, that love and am beloved
Where I may not remove nor be removed.

26

Lord of my love, to whom in vassalage
Thy merit hath my duty strongly knit,
To thee I send this written ambassage,
To witness duty, not to show my wit;
Duty so great, which wit so poor as mine   5
May make seem bare, in wanting words to show it,
But that I hope some good conceit of thine
In thy soul's thought, all naked, will bestow it;
Till whatsoever star that guides my moving,
Points on me graciously with fair aspect,   10
And puts apparel on my tatter'd loving,
To show me worthy of thy sweet respect;
Then may I dare to boast how I do love thee;
Till then not show my head where thou mayst prove me.

27

Weary with toil, I haste me to my bed,
The dear repose for limbs with travel tired;
But then begins a journey in my head,
To work my mind, when body's work's expired;
For then my thoughts, from far where I abide,
Intend a zealous pilgrimage to thee,   6
And keep my drooping eyelids open wide,
Looking on darkness which the blind do see;
Save that my soul's imaginary sight
Presents thy shadow to my sightless view,   10
Which, like a jewel hung in ghastly night,
Makes black night beauteous and her old face new.
Lo, thus, by day my limbs, by night my mind,
For thee and for myself no quiet find.

28

How can I then return in happy plight,
That am debarr'd the benefit of rest?
When day's oppression is not eased by night,
But day by night, and night by day, oppress'd?
And each, though enemies to either's reign,   5
Do in consent shake hands to torture me;
The one by toil, the other to complain
How far I toil, still farther off from thee.
I tell the day, to please him thou art bright,
And dost him grace when clouds do blot the heaven;   10
So flatter I the swart-complexion'd night;
When sparkling stars twire not thou gild'st the even.
But day doth daily draw my sorrows longer,
And night doth nightly make grief's strength seem stronger.

29

When, in disgrace with fortune and men's eyes,
I all alone beweep my outcast state,
And trouble deaf heaven with my bootless cries,
And look upon myself, and curse my fate,
Wishing me like to one more rich in hope,   5
Featured like him, like him with friends possess'd,
Desiring this man's art, and that man's scope,
With what I most enjoy contented least;
Yet in these thoughts myself almost despising,
Haply I think on thee, and then my state,   10
Like to the lark at break of day arising
From sullen earth, sings hymns at heaven's gate;
For thy sweet love remember'd such wealth brings
That then I scorn to change my state with kings.

30

When to the sessions of sweet silent thought
I summon up remembrance of things past,
I sigh the lack of many a thing I sought,
And with old woes new wail my dear time's waste;
Then can I drown an eye, unused to flow,   5
For precious friends hid in death's dateless night,
And weep afresh love's long-since-cancell'd woe,
And moan the expense of many a vanish'd sight;
Then can I grieve at grievances foregone,
And heavily from woe to woe tell o'er   10
The sad account of fore-bemoaned moan,
Which I new pay as if not paid before.

But if the while I think on thee, dear friend,
All losses are restored and sorrows end.

31

Thy bosom is endeared with all hearts,
Which I by lacking have supposed dead;
And there reigns love, and all love's loving parts,
And all those friends which I thought buried.
How many a holy and obsequious tear   5
Hath dear religious love stol'n from mine eye,
As interest of the dead, which now appear
But things removed that hidden in thee lie!
Thou art the grave where buried love doth live,
Hung with the trophies of my lovers gone,   10
Who all their parts of me to thee did give;
That due of many now is thine alone;
  Their images I loved I view in thee,
  And thou, all they, hast all the all of me.

32

If thou survive my well-contented day,
When that churl Death my bones with dust shall cover,
And shalt by fortune once more re-survey
These poor rude lines of thy deceased lover,   4
Compare them with the bettering of the time,
And though they be outstripp'd by every pen,
Reserve them for my love, not for their rhyme,
Exceeded by the height of happier men.
O, then vouchsafe me but this loving thought:
'Had my friend's Muse grown with this growing age,   10
A dearer birth than this his love had brought,
To march in ranks of better equipage;
  But since he died, and poets better prove,
  Theirs for their style I'll read, his for his love.'

33

Full many a glorious morning have I seen
Flatter the mountain-tops with sovereign eye,
Kissing with golden face the meadows green,
Gilding pale streams with heavenly alchemy;
Anon permit the basest clouds to ride   5
With ugly rack on his celestial face,
And from the forlorn world his visage hide,
Stealing unseen to west with this disgrace;
Even so my sun one early morn did shine   9
With all-triumphant splendour on my brow;
But, out, alack! he was but one hour mine,
The region cloud hath mask'd him from me now.
  Yet him for this my love no whit disdaineth;
  Suns of the world may stain when heaven's sun staineth.

34

Why didst thou promise such a beauteous day,
And make me travel forth without my cloak,
To let base clouds o'ertake me in my way,
Hiding thy bravery in their rotten smoke?
'Tis not enough that through the cloud thou break,
To dry the rain on my storm-beaten face,   6
For no man well of such a salve can speak
That heals the wound and cures not the disgrace;
Nor can thy shame give physic to my grief;
Though thou repent, yet I have still the loss;
  The offender's sorrow lends but weak relief   11
  To him that bears the strong offence's cross.

Ah, but those tears are pearl which thy love sheds,
And they are rich and ransom all ill deeds.

35

No more be grieved at that which thou hast done;
Roses have thorns, and silver fountains mud;
Clouds and eclipses stain both moon and sun,
And loathsome canker lives in sweetest bud.
All men make faults, and even I in this,   5
Authorizing thy trespass with compare,
Myself corrupting, salving thy amiss,
Excusing thy sins more than thy sins are;
For to thy sensual fault I bring in sense,—
Thy adverse party is thy advocate,—   10
And 'gainst myself a lawful plea commence;
Such civil war is in my love and hate,
  That I an accessary needs must be
  To that sweet thief which sourly robs from me.

36

Let me confess that we two must be twain,
Although our undivided loves are one;
So shall those blots that do with me remain,
Without thy help, by me be borne alone.
In our two loves there is but one respect,   5
Though in our lives a separable spite,
Which though it alter not love's sole effect,
Yet doth it steal sweet hours from love's delight.
I may not evermore acknowledge thee,
Lest my bewailed guilt should do thee shame,   10
Nor thou with public kindness honour me,
Unless thou take that honour from thy name;
  But do not so; I love thee in such sort,
  As thou being mine, mine is thy good report.

37

As a decrepit father takes delight
To see his active child do deeds of youth,
So I, made lame by fortune's dearest spite,
Take all my comfort of thy worth and truth;
For whether beauty, birth, or wealth, or wit,   5
Or any of these all, or all, or more,
Entitled in thy parts do crowned sit,
I make my love engrafted to this store;
So then I am not lame, poor, nor despised,
Whilst that this shadow doth such substance give
That I in thy abundance am sufficed   11
And by a part of all thy glory live.
  Look, what is best, that best I wish in thee;
  This wish I have; then ten times happy me!

38

How can my Muse want subject to invent,
While thou dost breathe, that pour'st into my verse
Thine own sweet argument, too excellent
For every vulgar paper to rehearse?
O, give thyself the thanks, if aught in me   5
Worthy perusal stand against thy sight;
For who's so dumb that cannot write to thee,
When thou thyself dost give invention light?
Be thou the tenth Muse, ten times more in worth
Than those old nine which rhymers invocate;   10
And he that calls on thee, let him bring forth
Eternal numbers to outlive long date.
  If my slight Muse do please these curious days,
  The pain be mine, but thine shall be the praise

39

O, how thy worth with manners may I sing,
When thou art all the better part of me?
What can mine own praise to mine own self bring?
And what is't but mine own when I praise thee?
Even for this let us divided live, 5
And our dear love lose name of single one,
That by this separation I may give
That due to thee which thou deservest alone.
O absence, what a torment wouldst thou prove,
Were it not thy sour leisure gave sweet leave 10
To entertain the time with thoughts of love,
Which time and thoughts so sweetly doth deceive,
  And that thou teachest how to make one twain,
  By praising him here who doth hence remain!

40

Take all my loves, my love, yea, take them all;
What hast thou then more than thou hadst before?
No love, my love, that thou mayst true love call;
All mine was thine before thou hadst this more.
Then, if for my love thou my love receivest, 5
I cannot blame thee for my love thou usest;
But yet be blamed, if thou thyself deceivest
By wilful taste of what thyself refusest.
I do forgive thy robbery, gentle thief,
Although thou steal thee all my poverty; 10
And yet, love knows, it is a greater grief
To bear love's wrong than hate's known injury.
  Lascivious grace, in whom all ill well shows,
  Kill me with spites; yet we must not be foes.

41

Those pretty wrongs that liberty commits,
When I am sometime absent from thy heart,
Thy beauty and thy years full well befits,
For still temptation follows where thou art.
Gentle thou art, and therefore to be won, 5
Beauteous thou art, therefore to be assailed;
And when a woman woos, what woman's son
Will sourly leave her till she have prevailed?
Ay me! but yet thou mightst my seat forbear,
And chide thy beauty and thy straying youth,
Who lead thee in their riot even there 11
Where thou art forced to break a twofold truth,
  Hers, by thy beauty tempting her to thee,
  Thine, by thy beauty being false to me.

42

That thou hast her, it is not all my grief,
And yet it may be said I loved her dearly;
That she hath thee, is of my wailing chief,
A loss in love that touches me more nearly.
Loving offenders, thus I will excuse ye: 5
Thou dost love her, because thou know'st I love her;
And for my sake even so doth she abuse me,
Suffering my friend for my sake to approve her.
If I lose thee, my loss is my love's gain,
And losing her, my friend hath found that loss;
Both find each other, and I lose both twain. 11
And both for my sake lay on me this cross:
  But here's the joy; my friend and I are one;
  Sweet flattery! then she loves but me alone.

43

When most I wink, then do mine eyes best see,
For all the day they view things unrespected;
But when I sleep, in dreams they look on thee,
And, darkly bright, are bright in dark directed.
Then thou, whose shadow shadows doth make bright, 5
How would thy shadow's form form happy show
To the clear day with thy much clearer light,
When to unseeing eyes thy shade shines so!
How would, I say, mine eyes be blessed made
By looking on thee in the living day, 10
When in dead night thy fair imperfect shade
Through heavy sleep on sightless eyes doth stay!
  All days are nights to see till I see thee,
  And nights bright days when dreams do show thee me.

44

If the dull substance of my flesh were thought,
Injurious distance should not stop my way;
For then, despite of space, I would be brought,
From limits far remote, where thou dost stay.
No matter then although my foot did stand 5
Upon the farthest earth removed from thee;
For nimble thought can jump both sea and land,
As soon as think the place where he would be.
But, ah, thought kills me, that I am not thought,
To leap large lengths of miles when thou art gone,
But that, so much of earth and water wrought,
I must attend time's leisure with my moan;
  Receiving nought by elements so slow 13
  But heavy tears, badges of either's woe.

45

The other two, slight air and purging fire,
Are both with thee, wherever I abide;
The first my thought, the other my desire,
These present-absent with swift motion slide.
For when these quicker elements are gone 5
In tender embassy of love to thee,
My life, being made of four, with two alone
Sinks down to death, oppress'd with melancholy;
Until life's composition be recured 9
By those swift messengers return'd from thee,
Who even but now come back again assured
Of thy fair health, recounting it to me;
  This told, I joy; but then no longer glad,
  I send them back again, and straight grow sad.

46

Mine eye and heart are at a mortal war,
How to divide the conquest of thy sight;
Mine eye my heart thy picture's sight would bar,
My heart mine eye the freedom of that right.
My heart doth plead that thou in him dost lie,
A closet never pierced with crystal eyes, 6
But the defendant doth that plea deny,
And says in him thy fair appearance lies.
To 'cide this title is impannelled
A quest of thoughts, all tenants to the heart;
And by their verdict is determined 11
The clear eye's moiety and the dear heart's part:
  As thus: mine eye's due is thine outward part,
  And my heart's right thine inward love of heart.

47

Betwixt mine eye and heart a league is took,
And each doth good turns now unto the other;
When that mine eye is famish'd for a look,
Or heart in love with sighs himself doth smother,
With my love's picture then my eye doth feast,
And to the painted banquet bids my heart; 6
Another time mine eye is my heart's guest,
And in his thoughts of love doth share a part;

So, either by thy picture or my love,
Thyself away art present still with me;
For thou not farther than my thoughts canst move,
And I am still with them and they with thee;
  Or, if they sleep, thy picture in my sight
  Awakes my heart to heart's and eye's delight.

48

How careful was I, when I took my way,
Each trifle under truest bars to thrust,
That to my use it might unused stay
From hands of falsehood, in sure wards of trust!
But thou, to whom my jewels trifles are,
Most worthy comfort, now my greatest grief,
Thou, best of dearest and mine only care,
Art left the prey of every vulgar thief.
Thee have I not lock'd up in any chest,
Save where thou art not, though I feel thou art,
Within the gentle closure of my breast,
From whence at pleasure thou mayst come and part;
  And even thence thou wilt be stol'n, I fear,
  For truth proves thievish for a prize so dear.

49

Against that time, if ever that time come,
When I shall see thee frown on my defects,
When as thy love hath cast his utmost sum,
Call'd to that audit by advised respects;
Against that time when thou shalt strangely pass,
And scarcely greet me with that sun, thine eye,
When love, converted from the thing it was,
Shall reasons find of settled gravity;
Against that time do I ensconce me here
Within the knowledge of mine own desert,
And this my hand against myself uprear,
To guard the lawful reasons on thy part;
  To leave poor me thou hast the strength of laws,
  Since why to love I can allege no cause.

50

How heavy do I journey on the way,
When what I seek, my weary travel's end,
Doth teach that ease and that repose to say,
'Thus far the miles are measured from thy friend!'
The beast that bears me, tired with my woe,
Plods dully on, to bear that weight in me,
As if by some instinct the wretch did know
His rider loved not speed, being made from thee;
The bloody spur cannot provoke him on
That sometimes anger thrusts into his hide;
Which heavily he answers with a groan,
More sharp to me than spurring to his side;
  For that same groan doth put this in my mind
  My grief lies onward, and my joy behind.

51

Thus can my love excuse the slow offence
Of my dull bearer when from thee I speed;
From where thou art why should I haste me thence?
Till I return, of posting is no need.
O, what excuse will my poor beast then find,
When swift extremity can seem but slow?
Then should I spur, though mounted on the wind,
In winged speed no motion shall I know;

Then can no horse with my desire keep pace;
Therefore desire, of perfect'st love being made,
Shall neigh,—no dull flesh,—in his fiery race;
But love, for love, thus shall excuse my jade;
  Since from thee going he went wilful-slow,
  Towards thee I'll run and give him leave to go.

52

So am I as the rich, whose blessed key
Can bring him to his sweet up-locked treasure,
The which he will not every hour survey,
For blunting the fine point of seldom pleasure.
Therefore are feasts so solemn and so rare,
Since, seldom coming, in the long year set,
Like stones of worth they thinly placed are,
Or captain jewels in the carcanet.
So is the time that keeps you as my chest,
Or as the wardrobe which the robe doth hide,
To make some special instant special blest,
By new unfolding his imprison'd pride.
  Blessed are you, whose worthiness gives scope,
  Being had, to triumph, being lack'd, to hope.

53

What is your substance, whereof are you made,
That millions of strange shadows on you tend?
Since every one hath, every one, one shade,
And you, but one, can every shadow lend.
Describe Adonis, and the counterfeit
Is poorly imitated after you;
On Helen's cheek all art of beauty set,
And you in Grecian tires are painted new;
Speak of the spring and foison of the year,
The one doth shadow of your beauty show,
The other as your bounty doth appear;
And you in every blessed shape we know.
  In all external grace you have some part,
  But you like none, none you, for constant heart.

54

O, how much more doth beauty beauteous seem
By that sweet ornament which truth doth give!
The rose looks fair, but fairer we it deem
For that sweet odour which doth in it live.
The canker-blooms have full as deep a dye
As the perfumed tincture of the roses,
Hang on such thorns, and play as wantonly
When summer's breath their masked buds discloses;
But, for their virtue only is their show,
They live unwoo'd and unrespected fade;
Die to themselves. Sweet roses do not so;
Of their sweet deaths are sweetest odours made;
  And so of you, beauteous and lovely youth,
  When that shall vade, by verse distills your truth.

55

Not marble, nor the gilded monuments
Of princes, shall outlive this powerful rhyme;
But you shall shine more bright in these contents
Than unswept stone, besmear'd with sluttish time.
When wasteful war shall statues overturn,
And broils root out the work of masonry,
Nor Mars his sword nor war's quick fire shall burn
The living record of your memory.

'Gainst death and all-oblivious enmity
Shall you pace forth; your praise shall still find
   room   10
Even in the eyes of all posterity
That wear this world out to the ending doom.
  So, till the judgement that yourself arise,
  You live in this, and dwell in lovers' eyes.

56

Sweet love, renew thy force; be it not said
Thy edge should blunter be than appetite,
Which but to-day by feeding is allay'd,
To-morrow sharpen'd in his former might;
So, love, be thou; although to-day thou fill   5
Thy hungry eyes even till they wink with full-
   ness,
To-morrow see again, and do not kill
The spirit of love with a perpetual dullness.
Let this sad interim like the ocean be   9
Which parts the shore, where two contracted new
Come daily to the banks, that, when they see
Return of love, more blest may be the view;
  Or call it winter, which, being full of care,
  Makes summer's welcome thrice more wish'd,
    more rare.

57

Being your slave, what should I do but tend
Upon the hours and times of your desire?
I have no precious time at all to spend,
Nor services to do, till you require.   4
Nor dare I chide the world-without-end hour
Whilst I, my sovereign, watch the clock for you,
Nor think the bitterness of absence sour
When you have bid your servant once adieu;
Nor dare I question with my jealous thought
Where you may be, or your affairs suppose,   10
But, like a sad slave, stay and think of nought
Save, where you are how happy you make those.
  So true a fool is love that in your will,
  Though you do any thing, he thinks no ill.

58

That god forbid that made me first your slave,
I should in thought control your times of pleasure,
Or at your hand the account of hours to crave,
Being your vassal, bound to stay your leisure!
O, let me suffer, being at your beck,   5
The imprison'd absence of your liberty;
And patience, tame to sufferance, bide each check,
Without accusing you of injury.
Be where you list, your charter is so strong
That you yourself may privilege your time   10
To what you will; to you it doth belong
Yourself to pardon of self-doing crime.
  I am to wait, though waiting so be hell,
  Not blame your pleasure, be it ill or well.

59

If there be nothing new, but that which is
Hath been before, how are our brains beguil'd,
Which, labouring for invention, bear amiss
The second burthen of a former child!
O, that record could with a backward look,   5
Even of five hundred courses of the sun,
Show me your image in some antique book,
Since mind at first in character was done,

That I might see what the old world could say
To this composed wonder of your frame;   10
Whether we are mended, or whether better they,
Or whether revolution be the same.
  O, sure I am, the wits of former days
  To subjects worse have given admiring praise.

60

Like as the waves make towards the pebbled shore,
So do our minutes hasten to their end;
Each changing place with that which goes before,
In sequent toil all forwards do contend.
Nativity, once in the main of light,   5
Crawls to maturity, wherewith being crown'd,
Crooked eclipses 'gainst his glory fight,
And Time that gave doth now his gift confound.
Time doth transfix the flourish set on youth,
And delves the parallels in beauty's brow,   10
Feeds on the rarities of nature's truth,
And nothing stands but for his scythe to mow;
  And yet to times in hope my verse shall stand,
  Praising thy worth, despite his cruel hand.

61

Is it thy will thy image should keep open
My heavy eyelids to the weary night?
Dost thou desire my slumbers should be broken,
While shadows like to thee do mock my sight?
Is it thy spirit that thou send'st from thee   5
So far from home into my deeds to pry,
To find out shames and idle hours in me,
The scope and tenour of thy jealousy?
O, no! thy love, though much, is not so great;
It is my love that keeps mine eye awake;   10
Mine own true love that doth my rest defeat,
To play the watchman ever for thy sake;
  For thee watch I whilst thou dost wake else-
   where,
  From me far off, with others all too near.

62

Sin of self-love possesseth all mine eye
And all my soul and all my every part;
And for this sin there is no remedy,
It is so grounded inward in my heart.
Methinks no face so gracious is as mine,   5
No shape so true, no truth of such account;
And for myself mine own worth do define,
As I all other in all worths surmount.
But when my glass shows me myself indeed,
Beated and chopp'd with tann'd antiquity,   10
Mine own self-love quite contrary I read;
Self so self-loving were iniquity.
  'Tis thee, myself, that for myself I praise,
  Painting my age with beauty of thy days.

63

Against my love shall be, as I am now,
With Time's injurious hand crush'd and o'erworn;
When hours have drain'd his blood and fill'd his
   brow
With lines and wrinkles; when his youthful morn
Hath travell'd on to age's steepy night,   5
And all those beauties whereof now he's king
Are vanishing or vanish'd out of sight,
Stealing away the treasure of his spring;
For such a time do I now fortify
Against confounding age's cruel knife,   10
That he shall never cut from memory
My sweet love's beauty, though my lover's life;

His beauty shall in these black lines be seen,
And they shall live, and he in them still green.

64.

When I have seen by Time's fell hand defaced
The rich-proud cost of outworn buried age;
When sometime lofty towers I see down-razed,
And brass eternal slave to mortal rage;
When I have seen the hungry ocean gain 5
Advantage on the kingdom of the shore,
And the firm soil win of the watery main,
Increasing store with loss and loss with store;
When I have seen such interchange of state,
Or state itself confounded to decay; 10
Ruin hath taught me thus to ruminate,
That Time will come and take my love away.
  This thought is as a death, which cannot choose
  But weep to have that which it fears to lose.

65.

Since brass, nor stone, nor earth, nor boundless sea,
But sad mortality o'er-sways their power,
How with this rage shall beauty hold a plea,
Whose action is no stronger than a flower?
O, how shall summer's honey breath hold out 5
Against the wreckful siege of battering days,
When rocks impregnable are not so stout,
Nor gates of steel so strong, but Time decays?
O fearful meditation! where, alack, 9
Shall Time's best jewel from Time's chest lie hid?
Or what strong hand can hold his swift foot back?
Or who his spoil of beauty can forbid?
  O, none, unless this miracle have might,
  That in black ink my love may still shine bright.

66.

Tired with all these, for restful death I cry,
As, to behold desert a beggar born,
And needy nothing trimm'd in jollity,
And purest faith unhappily forsworn,
And gilded honour shamefully misplaced, 5
And maiden virtue rudely strumpeted,
And right perfection wrongfully disgraced,
And strength by limping sway disabled,
And art made tongue-tied by authority,
And folly, doctor-like, controlling skill, 10
And simple truth miscall'd simplicity,
And captive good attending captain ill;
  Tired with all these, from these would I be gone,
  Save that, to die, I leave my love alone.

67.

Ah, wherefore with infection should he live
And with his presence grace impiety,
That sin by him advantage should achieve
And lace itself with his society?
Why should false painting imitate his cheek, 5
And steal dead seeing of his living hue?
Why should poor beauty indirectly seek
Roses of shadow, since his rose is true?
Why should he live, now Nature bankrupt is,
Beggar'd of blood to blush through lively veins?
For she hath no exchequer now but his, 11
And, proud of many, lives upon his gains.
  O, him she stores, to show what wealth she had
  In days long since, before these last so bad.

68.

Thus is his cheek the map of days outworn,
When beauty lived and died as flowers do now,
Before these bastard signs of fair were born,
Or durst inhabit on a living brow;
Before the golden tresses of the dead, 5
The right of sepulchres, were shorn away,
To live a second life on second head;
Ere beauty's dead fleece made another gay;
In him those holy antique hours are seen,
Without all ornament, itself and true, 10
Making no summer of another's green,
Robbing no old to dress his beauty new;
  And him as for a map doth Nature store,
  To show false Art what beauty was of yore.

69.

Those parts of thee that the world's eye doth view
Want nothing that the thought of hearts can mend;
All tongues, the voice of souls, give thee that due,
Uttering bare truth, even so as foes commend.
Thy outward thus with outward praise is crown'd;
But those same tongues, that give thee so thine own, 6
In other accents do this praise confound
By seeing farther than the eye hath shown.
They look into the beauty of thy mind,
And that, in guess, they measure by thy deeds;
Then, churls, their thoughts, although their eyes were kind, 11
To thy fair flower add the rank smell of weeds;
  But why thy odour matcheth not thy show,
  The soil is this, that thou dost common grow.

70.

That thou art blamed shall not be thy defect,
For slander's mark was ever yet the fair;
The ornament of beauty is suspect,
A crow that flies in heaven's sweetest air.
So thou be good, slander doth but approve 5
Thy worth the greater, being woo'd of time;
For canker vice the sweetest buds doth love,
And thou present'st a pure unstained prime.
Thou hast pass'd by the ambush of young days,
Either not assail'd, or victor being charged; 10
Yet this thy praise cannot be so thy praise,
To tie up envy evermore enlarged;
  If some suspect of ill mask'd not thy show,
  Then thou alone kingdoms of hearts shouldst owe.

71.

No longer mourn for me when I am dead
Than you shall hear the surly sullen bell
Give warning to the world that I am fled
From this vile world, with vilest worms to dwell;
Nay, if you read this line, remember not 5
The hand that writ it; for I love you so,
That I in your sweet thoughts would be forgot,
If thinking on me then should make you woe.
O, if, I say, you look upon this verse 9
When I perhaps compounded am with clay,
Do not so much as my poor name rehearse,
But let your love even with my life decay;
  Lest the wise world should look into your moan,
  And mock you with me after I am gone.

72

O, lest the world should task you to recite
What merit lived in me, that you should love
After my death, dear love, forget me quite,
For you in me can nothing worthy prove;
Unless you would devise some virtuous lie, 5
To do more for me than mine own desert,
And hang more praise upon deceased I
Than niggard truth would willingly impart;
O, lest your true love may seem false in this,
That you for love speak well of me untrue, 10
My name be buried where my body is,
And live no more to shame nor me nor you.
  For I am shamed by that which I bring forth,
  And so should you, to love things nothing worth.

73

That time of year thou mayst in me behold
When yellow leaves, or none, or few, do hang
Upon those boughs which shake against the cold,
Bare ruin'd choirs, where late the sweet birds sang.
In me thou see'st the twilight of such day 5
As after sunset fadeth in the west;
Which by and by black night doth take away,
Death's second self, that seals up all in rest.
In me thou see'st the glowing of such fire,
That on the ashes of his youth doth lie, 10
As the death-bed whereon it must expire,
Consumed with that which it was nourish'd by.
  This thou perceivest, which makes thy love more strong,
  To love that well which thou must leave ere long.

74

But be contented; when that fell arrest
Without all bail shall carry me away,
My life hath in this line some interest,
Which for memorial still with thee shall stay.
When thou reviewest this, thou dost review 5
The very part was consecrate to thee;
The earth can have but earth, which is his due;
My spirit is thine, the better part of me;
So then thou hast but lost the dregs of life,
The prey of worms, my body being dead; 10
The coward conquest of a wretch's knife,
Too base of thee to be remembered.
  The worth of that is that which it contains,
  And that is this, and this with thee remains.

75

So are you to my thoughts as food to life,
Or as sweet-season'd showers are to the ground;
And for the peace of you I hold such strife
As 'twixt a miser and his wealth is found;
Now proud as an enjoyer, and anon 5
Doubting the filching age will steal his treasure;
Now counting best to be with you alone,
Then better'd that the world may see my pleasure;
Sometime all full with feasting on your sight,
And by and by clean starved for a look; 10
Possessing or pursuing no delight,
Save what is had or must from you be took.
  Thus do I pine and surfeit day by day,
  Or gluttoning on all, or all away.

76

Why is my verse so barren of new pride,
So far from variation or quick change?
Why with the time do I not glance aside
To new-found methods and to compounds strange?
Why write I still all one, ever the same, 5
And keep invention in a noted weed,
That every word doth almost tell my name,
Showing their birth and where they did proceed?
O, know, sweet love, I always write of you,
And you and love are still my argument; 10
So all my best is dressing old words new,
Spending again what is already spent;
  For as the sun is daily new and old,
  So is my love still telling what is told.

77

Thy glass will show thee how thy beauties wear,
Thy dial how thy precious minutes waste;
The vacant leaves thy mind's imprint will bear,
And of this book this learning mayst thou taste.
The wrinkles which thy glass will truly show 5
Of mouthed graves will give thee memory;
Thou by thy dial's shady stealth mayst know
Time's thievish progress to eternity.
Look, what thy memory cannot contain
Commit to these waste blanks, and thou shalt find
Those children nursed, deliver'd from thy brain,
To take a new acquaintance of thy mind. 12
  These offices, so oft as thou wilt look,
  Shall profit thee and much enrich thy book.

78

So oft have I invoked thee for my Muse
And found such fair assistance in my verse
As every alien pen hath got my use
And under thee their poesy disperse.
Thine eyes, that taught the dumb on high to sing
And heavy ignorance aloft to fly, 6
Have added feathers to the learned's wing
And given grace a double majesty.
Yet be most proud of that which I compile,
Whose influence is thine and born of thee; 10
In others' works thou dost but mend the style,
And arts with thy sweet graces graced be;
  But thou art all my art, and dost advance
  As high as learning my rude ignorance.

79

Whilst I alone did call upon thy aid,
My verse alone had all thy gentle grace;
But now my gracious numbers are decay'd,
And my sick Muse doth give another place.
I grant, sweet love, thy lovely argument 5
Deserves the travail of a worthier pen;
Yet what of thee thy poet doth invent
He robs thee of, and pays it thee again.
He lends thee virtue, and he stole that word
From thy behaviour; beauty doth he give, 10
And found it in thy cheek; he can afford
No praise to thee but what in thee doth live.
  Then thank him not for that which he doth say,
  Since what he owes thee thou thyself dost pay.

80

O, how I faint when I of you do write,
Knowing a better spirit doth use your name,
And in the praise thereof spends all his might,
To make me tongue-tied, speaking of your fame!
But since your worth, wide as the ocean is, 5
The humble as the proudest sail doth bear,
My saucy bark, inferior far to his,
On your broad main doth wilfully appear.

Your shallowest help will hold me up afloat,
Whilst he upon your soundless deep doth ride;
Or, being wreck'd, I am a worthless boat, 11
He of tall building and of goodly pride;
 Then if he thrive and I be cast away,
 The worst was this; my love was my decay.

81

Or I shall live your epitaph to make,
Or you survive when I in earth am rotten;
From hence your memory death cannot take,
Although in me each part will be forgotten. 4
Your name from hence immortal life shall have,
Though I, once gone, to all the world must die;
The earth can yield me but a common grave,
When you entombed in men's eyes shall lie.
Your monument shall be my gentle verse,
Which eyes not yet created shall o'er-read; 10
And tongues to be your being shall rehearse,
When all the breathers of this world are dead;
 You still shall live,—such virtue hath my pen,—
 Where breath most breathes, even in the mouths
  of men.

82

I grant thou wert not married to my Muse,
And therefore mayst without attaint o'erlook
The dedicated words which writers use
Of their fair subject, blessing every book.
Thou art as fair in knowledge as in hue, 5
Finding thy worth a limit past my praise;
And therefore art enforced to seek anew
Some fresher stamp of the time-bettering days.
And do so, love; yet when they have devised
What strained touches rhetoric can lend, 10
Thou truly fair wert truly sympathized
In true plain words by thy true-telling friend;
 And their gross painting might be better used
 Where cheeks need blood; in thee it is abused.

83

I never saw that you did painting need,
And therefore to your fair no painting set;
I found, or thought I found, you did exceed
The barren tender of a poet's debt;
And therefore have I slept in your report, 5
That you yourself, being extant, well might show
How far a modern quill doth come too short,
Speaking of worth, what worth in you doth grow.
This silence for my sin you did impute,
Which shall be most my glory, being dumb; 10
For I impair not beauty being mute,
When others would give life and bring a tomb.
 There lives more life in one of your fair eyes
 Than both your poets can in praise devise.

84

Who is it that says most? which can say more
Than this rich praise, that you alone are you?
In whose confine immured is the store
Which should example where your equal grew.
Lean penury within that pen doth dwell 5
That to his subject lends not some small glory;
But he that writes of you, if he can tell
That you are you, so dignifies his story,
Let him but copy what in you is writ,
Not making worse what nature made so clear, 10
And such a counterpart shall fame his wit, 11
Making his style admired every where.

You to your beauteous blessings add a curse,
Being fond on praise, which makes your praises
 worse.

85

My tongue-tied Muse in manners holds her still,
While comments of your praise, richly compiled,
Reserve their character with golden quill,
And precious phrase by all the Muses filed.
I think good thoughts, whilst other write good
 words, 5
And, like unletter'd clerk, still cry 'Amen'
To every hymn that able spirit affords,
In polish'd form of well refined pen.
Hearing you praised, I say "Tis so, 'tis true,'
And to the most of praise add something more; 10
But that is in my thought, whose love to you, 11
Though words come hindmost, holds his rank
 before.
 Then others for the breath of words respect,
 Me for my dumb thoughts, speaking in effect.

86

Was it the proud full sail of his great verse,
Bound for the prize of all too precious you,
That did my ripe thoughts in my brain inhearse,
Making their tomb the womb wherein they grew?
Was it his spirit, by spirits taught to write 5
Above a mortal pitch, that struck me dead?
No, neither he, nor his compeers by night
Giving him aid my verse astonished.
He, nor that affable familiar ghost
Which nightly gulls him with intelligence,
As victors, of my silence cannot boast; 11
I was not sick of any fear from thence;
 But when your countenance fill'd up his line,
 Then lack'd I matter; that enfeebled mine.

87

Farewell! thou art too dear for my possessing,
And like enough thou know'st thy estimate;
The charter of thy worth gives thee releasing;
My bonds in thee are all determinate. 4
For how do I hold thee but by thy granting?
And for that riches where is my deserving?
The cause of this fair gift in me is wanting,
And so my patent back again is swerving.
Thyself thou gavest, thy own worth then not
 knowing, 9
Or me, to whom thou gavest it, else mistaking;
So thy great gift, upon misprision growing,
Comes home again, on better judgement making.
 Thus have I had thee, as a dream doth flatter,
 In sleep a king, but waking no such matter.

88

When thou shalt be disposed to set me light,
And place my merit in the eye of scorn
Upon thy side against myself I'll fight,
And prove thee virtuous, though thou art for-
 sworn.
With mine own weakness being best acquainted,
Upon thy part I can set down a story 6
Of faults conceal'd, wherein I am attainted;
That thou in losing me shalt win much glory;
And I by this will be a gainer too;
For bending all my loving thoughts on thee,
The injuries that to myself I do, 11
Doing thee vantage, double-vantage me.

Such is my love, to thee I so belong,
That for thy right myself will bear all wrong.

89

Say that thou didst forsake me for some fault,
And I will comment upon that offence;
Speak of my lameness, and I straight will halt,
Against thy reasons making no defence.
Thou canst not, love, disgrace me half so ill,
To set a form upon desired change,   6
As I'll myself disgrace; knowing thy will,
I will acquaintance strangle and look strange;
Be absent from thy walks; and in my tongue
Thy sweet beloved name no more shall dwell,
Lest I, too much profane, should do it wrong,
And haply of our old acquaintance tell.   12
  For thee, against myself I'll vow debate,
  For I must ne'er love him whom thou dost hate.

90

Then hate me when thou wilt; if ever, now;
Now, while the world is bent my deeds to cross,
Join with the spite of fortune, make me bow,
And do not drop in for an after-loss;
Ah, do not, when my heart hath 'scaped this sorrow,   5
Come in the rearward of a conquered woe;
Give not a windy night a rainy morrow,
To linger out a purposed overthrow.
If thou wilt leave me, do not leave me last,
When other petty griefs have done their spite,
But in the onset come; so shall I taste   11
At first the very worst of fortune's might;
  And other strains of woe, which now seem woe,
  Compared with loss of thee will not seem so.

91

Some glory in their birth, some in their skill,
Some in their wealth, some in their body's force;
Some in their garments, though new-fangled ill;
Some in their hawks and hounds, some in their horse;
And every humour hath his adjunct pleasure,
Wherein it finds a joy above the rest;   6
But these particulars are not my measure;
All these I better in one general best.
Thy love is better than high birth to me,
Richer than wealth, prouder than garments' cost,
Of more delight than hawks or horses be;   11
And having thee, of all men's pride I boast;
  Wretched in this alone, that thou mayst take
  All this away and me most wretched make.

92

But do thy worst to steal thyself away,
For term of life thou art assured mine;
And life no longer than thy love will stay,
For it depends upon that love of thine.
Then need I not to fear the worst of wrongs,   5
When in the least of them my life hath end.
I see a better state to me belongs
Than that which on thy humour doth depend;
Thou canst not vex me with inconstant mind,
Since that my life on thy revolt doth lie.   10
O, what a happy title do I find,
Happy to have thy love, happy to die!
  But what's so blessed-fair that fears no blot?
  Thou mayst be false, and yet I know it not.

93

So shall I live, supposing thou art true,
Like a deceived husband; so love's face
May still seem love to me, though alter'd new;
Thy looks with me, thy heart in other place;
For there can live no hatred in thine eye,   5
Therefore in that I cannot know thy change.
In many's looks the false heart's history
Is writ in moods and frowns and wrinkles strange,
But heaven in thy creation did decree   9
That in thy face sweet love should ever dwell;
Whate'er thy thoughts or thy heart's workings be,
Thy looks should nothing thence but sweetness tell.
  How like Eve's apple doth thy beauty grow,
  If thy sweet virtue answer not thy show!

94

They that have power to hurt and will do none,
That do not do the thing they most do show,
Who, moving others, are themselves as stone,
Unmoved, cold, and to temptation slow;
They rightly do inherit heaven's graces   5
And husband nature's riches from expense;
They are the lords and owners of their faces,
Others but stewards of their excellence.
The summer's flower is to the summer sweet,
Though to itself it only live and die,   10
But if that flower with base infection meet,
The basest weed outbraves his dignity;
  For sweetest things turn sourest by their deeds;
  Lilies that fester smell far worse than weeds.

95

How sweet and lovely dost thou make the shame
Which, like a canker in the fragrant rose,
Doth spot the beauty of thy budding name!
O, in what sweets dost thou thy sins inclose!
That tongue that tells the story of thy days,   5
Making lascivious comments on thy sport,
Cannot dispraise but in a kind of praise;
Naming thy name blesses an ill report.
O, what a mansion have those vices got
Which for their habitation chose out thee,   10
Where beauty's veil doth cover every blot
And all things turn to fair that eyes can see!
  Take heed, dear heart, of this large privilege;
  The hardest knife ill used doth lose his edge.

96

Some say, thy fault is youth, some wantonness;
Some say, thy grace is youth and gentle sport;
Both grace and faults are loved of more and less;
Thou makest faults graces that to thee resort.
As on the finger of a throned queen   5
The basest jewel will be well esteem'd,
So are those errors that in thee are seen
To truths translated and for true things deem'd.
How many lambs might the stern wolf betray,
If like a lamb he could his looks translate!   10
How many gazers mightst thou lead away,
If thou wouldst use the strength of all thy state
  But do not so; I love thee in such sort,
  As thou being mine, mine is thy good report.

97

How like a winter hath my absence been
From thee, the pleasure of the fleeting year!
What freezings have I felt, what dark days seen!
What old December's bareness every where!   4

And yet this time 'removed was summer's time;
The teeming autumn, big with rich increase,
Bearing the wanton burthen of the prime,
Like widow'd wombs after their lord's decease;
Yet this abundant issue seem'd to me
But hope of orphans and unfather'd fruit; 10
For summer and his pleasures wait on thee,
And, thou away, the very birds are mute;
  Or, if they sing, 'tis with so dull a cheer
  That leaves look pale, dreading the winter's near.

98

From you have I been absent in the spring,
When proud-pied April, dress'd in all his trim,
Hath put a spirit of youth in every thing,
That heavy Saturn laugh'd and leap'd with him.
Yet nor the lays of birds, nor the sweet smell 5
Of different flowers in odour and in hue,
Could make me any summer's story tell,
Or from their proud lap pluck them where they grew;
Nor did I wonder at the lily's white,
Nor praise the deep vermillion in the rose; 10
They were but sweet, but figures of delight,
Drawn after you, you pattern of all those.
  Yet seem'd it winter still, and, you away,
  As with your shadow I with these did play.

99

The forward violet thus did I chide:
Sweet thief, whence didst thou steal thy sweet that smells,
If not from my love's breath? The purple pride
Which on thy soft cheek for complexion dwells
In my love's veins thou hast too grossly dyed.
The lily I condemned for thy hand, 6
And buds of marjoram had stol'n thy hair;
The roses fearfully on thorns did stand,
One blushing shame, another white despair;
A third, nor red nor white, had stol'n of both, 10
And to his robbery had annex'd thy breath;
But, for his theft, in pride of all his growth
A vengeful canker eat him up to death.
  More flowers I noted, yet I none could see
  But sweet or colour it had stol'n from thee.

100

Where art thou, Muse, that thou forget'st so long
To speak of that which gives thee all thy might?
Spend'st thou thy fury on some worthless song,
Darkening thy power to lend base subjects light?
Return, forgetful Muse, and straight redeem
In gentle numbers time so idly spent; 6
Sing to the ear that doth thy lays esteem
And gives thy pen both skill and argument.
Rise, resty Muse, my love's sweet face survey,
If Time have any wrinkle graven there; 10
If any, be a satire to decay,
And make Time's spoils despised every where.
  Give my love fame faster than Time wastes life;
  So thou prevent'st his scythe and crooked knife.

101

O truant Muse, what shall be thy amends
For thy neglect of truth in beauty dyed?
Both truth and beauty on my love depends;
So dost thou too, and therein dignified. 4

Make answer, Muse; wilt thou not haply say:
'Truth needs no colour, with his colour fix'd;
Beauty no pencil, beauty's truth to lay;
But best is best, if never intermix'd'?
Because he needs no praise, wilt thou be dumb?
Excuse not silence so, for 't lies in thee 10
To make him much outlive a gilded tomb
And to be praised of ages yet to be.
  Then do thy office, Muse; I teach thee how
  To make him seem long hence as he shows now.

102

My love is strengthen'd, though more weak in seeming;
I love not less, though less the show appear;
That love is merchandized whose rich esteeming
The owner's tongue doth publish every where.
Our love was new, and then but in the spring, 5
When I was wont to greet it with my lays;
As Philomel in summer's front doth sing,
And stops her pipe in growth of riper days;
Not that the summer is less pleasant now
Than when her mournful hymns did hush the night, 10
But that wild music burthens every bough,
And sweets grown common lose their dear delight.
  Therefore, like her, I sometime hold my tongue,
  Because I would not dull you with my song.

103

Alack, what poverty my Muse brings forth,
That having such a scope to show her pride,
The argument, all bare, is of more worth
Than when it hath my added praise beside!
O, blame me not, if I no more can write! 5
Look in your glass, and there appears a face
That over-goes my blunt invention quite,
Dulling my lines and doing me disgrace.
Were it not sinful then, striving to mend,
To mar the subject that before was well? 10
For to no other pass my verses tend
Than of your graces and your gifts to tell;
  And more, much more, than in my verse can sit,
  Your own glass shows you when you look in it.

104

To me, fair friend, you never can be old,
For as you were when first your eye I eyed,
Such seems your beauty still. Three winters cold
Have from the forests shook three summers' pride,
Three beauteous springs to yellow autumn turn'd
In process of the seasons have I seen, 6
Three April perfumes in three hot Junes burn'd,
Since first I saw you fresh, which yet are green.
Ah, yet doth beauty, like a dial-hand, 9
Steal from his figure, and no pace perceived;
So your sweet hue, which methinks still doth stand,
Hath motion, and mine eye may be deceived;
  For fear of which, hear this, thou age unbred;
  Ere you were born was beauty's summer dead.

105

Let not my love be call'd idolatry,
Nor my beloved as an idol show,
Since all alike my songs and praises be
To one, of one, still such, and ever so.

Kind is my love to-day, to-morrow kind, 5
Still constant in a wondrous excellence;
Therefore my verse to constancy confined,
One thing expressing, leaves out difference.
'Fair, kind, and true,' is all my argument,
'Fair, kind, and true,' varying to other words;
And in this change is my invention spent, 11
Three themes in one, which wondrous scope affords.
  'Fair, kind, and true,' have often lived alone,
  Which three till now never kept seat in one.

106

When in the chronicle of wasted time
I see descriptions of the fairest wights,
And beauty making beautiful old rhyme
In praise of ladies dead and lovely knights,
Then, in the blazon of sweet beauty's best, 5
Of hand, of foot, of lip, of eye, of brow,
I see their antique pen would have express'd
Even such a beauty as you master now.
So all their praises are but prophecies
Of this our time, all you prefiguring; 10
And, for they look'd but with divining eyes,
They had not skill enough your worth to sing;
  For we, which now behold these present days,
  Have eyes to wonder, but lack tongues to praise.

107

Not mine own fears, nor the prophetic soul
Of the wide world dreaming on things to come,
Can yet the lease of my true love control,
Supposed as forfeit to a confined doom.
The mortal moon hath her eclipse endured, 5
And the sad augurs mock their own presage;
Incertainties now crown themselves assured,
And peace proclaims olives of endless age.
Now with the drops of this most balmy time 9
My love looks fresh, and Death to me subscribes,
Since, spite of him, I'll live in this poor rhyme,
While he insults o'er dull and speechless tribes;
  And thou in this shalt find thy monument,
  When tyrants' crests and tombs of brass are spent.

108

What's in the brain, that ink may character,
Which hath not figured to thee my true spirit?
What's new to speak, what new to register,
That may express my love, or thy dear merit?
Nothing, sweet boy; but yet, like prayers divine, 6
I must each day say o'er the very same;
Counting no old thing old, thou mine, I thine,
Even as when first I hallow'd thy fair name.
So that eternal love in love's fresh case
Weighs not the dust and injury of age, 10
Nor gives to necessary wrinkles place,
But makes antiquity for aye his page;
  Finding the first conceit of love there bred,
  Where time and outward form would show it dead.

109

O, never say that I was false of heart,
Though absence seem'd my flame to qualify.
As easy might I from myself depart
As from my soul, which in thy breast doth lie;
That is my home of love; If I have ranged, 5
Like him that travels, I return again;
Just to the time, not with the time exchanged,
So that myself bring water for my stain.

Never believe, though in my nature reign'd
All frailties that besiege all kinds of blood, 10
That it could so preposterously be stain'd,
To leave for nothing all thy sum of good;
  For nothing this wide universe I call,
  Save thou, my rose; in it thou art my all.

110

Alas, 'tis true I have gone here and there,
And made myself a motley to the view,
Gored mine own thoughts, sold cheap what is most dear,
Made old offences of affections new;
Most true it is that I have look'd on truth 5
Askance and strangely; but, by all above,
These blenches gave my heart another youth,
And worse essays proved thee my best of love.
Now all is done, have what shall have no end;
Mine appetite I never more will grind 10
On newer proof, to try an older friend,
A god in love, to whom I am confined.
  Then give me welcome, next my heaven the best,
  Even to thy pure and most most loving breast.

111

O, for my sake do you with Fortune chide,
The guilty goddess of my harmful deeds,
That did not better for my life provide
Than public means which public manners breeds.
Thence comes it that my name receives a brand,
And almost thence my nature is subdued 6
To what it works in, like the dyer's hand;
Pity me then and wish I were renew'd;
Whilst, like a willing patient, I will drink
Potions of eisel 'gainst my strong infection; 10
No bitterness that I will bitter think,
Nor double penance, to correct correction.
  Pity me then, dear friend, and I assure ye
  Even that your pity is enough to cure me.

112

Your love and pity doth the impression fill
Which vulgar scandal stamp'd upon my brow;
For what care I who calls me well or ill,
So you o'er-green my bad, my good allow?
You are my all the world, and I must strive 5
To know my shames and praises from your tongue;
None else to me, nor I to none alive,
That my steel'd sense or changes right or wrong.
In so profound abysm I throw all care
Of others' voices, that my adder's sense 10
To critic and to flatterer stopped are.
Mark how with my neglect I do dispense:
  You are so strongly in my purpose bred
  That all the world besides methinks are dead.

113

Since I left you mine eye is in my mind,
And that which governs me to go about
Doth part his function and is partly blind,
Seems seeing, but effectually is out;
For it no form delivers to the heart 5
Of bird, of flower, or shape, which it doth latch;
Of his quick objects hath the mind no part,
Nor his own vision holds what it doth catch;

For if it see the rudest or gentlest sight,
The most sweet favour or deformed'st creature,
The mountain or the sea, the day or night, 11
The crow or dove, it shapes them to your feature;
  Incapable of more, replete with you,
  My most true mind thus maketh mine untrue.

114

Or whether doth my mind, being crown'd with
    you,
Drink up the monarch's plague, this flattery?
Or whether shall I say, mine eye saith true,
And that your love taught it this alchemy,
To make of monsters and things indigest 5
Such cherubins as your sweet self resemble,
Creating every bad a perfect best,
As fast as objects to his beams assemble?
O, 'tis the first; 'tis flattery in my seeing, 9
And my great mind most kingly drinks it up;
Mine eye well knows what with his gust is 'greeing,
And to his palate doth prepare the cup;
  If it be poison'd, 'tis the lesser sin
  That mine eye loves it and doth first begin.

115

Those lines that I before have writ do lie,
Even those that said I could not love you dearer;
Yet then my judgement knew no reason why
My most full flame should afterwards burn clearer.
But reckoning Time, whose million'd accidents 5
Creep in 'twixt vows, and change decrees of kings,
Tan sacred beauty, blunt the sharp'st intents,
Divert strong minds to the course of altering
    things;
Alas, why, fearing of Time's tyranny,
Might I not then say 'Now I love you best,' 10
When I was certain o'er incertainty,
Crowning the present, doubting of the rest?
  Love is a babe; then might I not say so,
  To give full growth to that which still doth
    grow?

116

Let me not to the marriage of true minds
Admit impediments. Love is not love
Which alters when it alteration finds,
Or bends with the remover to remove;
O, no! it is an ever-fixed mark, 5
That looks on tempests and is never shaken;
It is the star to every wandering bark,
Whose worth's unknown, although his height be
    taken.
Love's not Time's fool, though rosy lips and cheeks
Within his bending sickle's compass come; 10
Love alters not with his brief hours and weeks,
But bears it out even to the edge of doom.
  If this be error and upon me proved,
  I never writ, nor no man ever loved.

117

Accuse me thus: that I have scanted all
Wherein I should your great deserts repay,
Forgot upon your dearest love to call,
Whereto all bonds do tie me day by day; 4
That I have frequent been with unknown minds,
And given to time your own dear-purchased right;
That I have hoisted sail to all the winds
Which should transport me farthest from your
    sight.

Book both my wilfulness and errors down,
And on just proof surmise accumulate; 10
Bring me within the level of your frown,
But shoot not at me in your waken'd hate;
  Since my appeal says I did strive to prove
  The constancy and virtue of your love.

118

Like as, to make our appetites more keen,
With eager compounds we our palate urge;
As, to prevent our maladies unseen,
We sicken to shun sickness when we purge;
Even so, being full of your ne'er-cloying sweetness, 5
To bitter sauces did I frame my feeding;
And sick of welfare found a kind of meetness
To be diseased, ere that there was true needing.
Thus policy in love, to anticipate
The ills that were not, grew to faults assured,
And brought to medicine a healthful state, 11
Which, rank of goodness, would by ill be cured;
  But thence I learn, and find the lesson true,
  Drugs poison him that so fell sick of you.

119

What potions have I drunk of Siren tears,
Distill'd from limbecks foul as hell within,
Applying fears to hopes and hopes to fears,
Still losing when I saw myself to win! 4
What wretched errors hath my heart committed,
Whilst it hath thought itself so blessed never!
How have mine eyes out of their spheres been
    fitted,
In the distraction of this madding fever!
O benefit of ill! now I find true
That better is by evil still made better; 10
And ruin'd love, when it is built anew,
Grows fairer than at first, more strong, far greater.
  So I return rebuked to my content,
  And gained by ill thrice more than I have spent.

120

That you were once unkind befriends me now,
And for that sorrow which I then did feel
Needs must I under my transgression bow,
Unless my nerves were brass or hammer'd steel.
For if you were by my unkindness shaken, 5
As I by yours, you've pass'd a hell of time;
And I, a tyrant, have no leisure taken
To weigh how once I suffer'd in your crime.
O, that our night of woe might have remember'd
My deepest sense, how hard true sorrow hits, 10
And soon to you, as you to me, then tender'd
The humble salve which wounded bosoms fits!
  But that your trespass now becomes a fee;
  Mine ransoms yours, and yours must ransom
    me.

121

'Tis better to be vile than vile esteem'd,
When not to be receives reproach of being;
And the just pleasure lost, which is so deemed
Not by our feeling, but by others' seeing;
For why should others' false adulterate eyes 5
Give salutation to my sportive blood?
Or on my frailties why are frailer spies,
Which in their wills count bad what I think
    good?

No, I am that I am, and they that level
  At my abuses reckon up their own; 10
I may be straight, though they themselves be
    bevel;
By their rank thoughts my deeds must not be
    shown;
  Unless this general evil they maintain,
  All men are bad and in their badness reign.

122

Thy gift, thy tables, are within my brain
Full character'd with lasting memory,
Which shall above that idle rank remain,
Beyond all date, even to eternity;
Or, at the least, so long as brain and heart 5
Have faculty by nature to subsist;
Till each to razed oblivion yield his part
Of thee, thy record never can be miss'd.
That poor retention could not so much hold,
Nor need I tallies thy dear love to score; 10
Therefore to give them from me was I bold,
To trust those tables that receive thee more;
  To keep an adjunct to remember thee
  Were to import forgetfulness in me.

123

No, Time, thou shalt not boast that I do change;
Thy pyramids built up with newer might
To me are nothing novel, nothing strange;
They are but dressings of a former sight.
Our dates are brief, and therefore we admire
What thou dost foist upon us that is old; 6
And rather make them born to our desire
Than think that we before have heard them told.
Thy registers and thee I both defy,
Not wondering at the present nor the past, 10
For thy records and what we see doth lie,
Made more or less by thy continual haste.
  This I do vow, and this shall ever be,
  I will be true, despite thy scythe and thee.

124

If my dear love were but the child of state,
It might for Fortune's bastard be unfather'd,
As subject to Time's love or to Time's hate,
Weeds among weeds, or flowers with flowers
    gather'd.
No, it was builded far from accident; 5
It suffers not in smiling pomp, nor falls
Under the blow of thralled discontent,
Whereto th' inviting time our fashion calls;
It fears not policy, that heretic,
Which works on leases of short-number'd hours,
But all alone stands hugely politic, 11
That it nor grows with heat nor drowns with
    showers.
  To this I witness call the fools of time,
  Which die for goodness, who have lived for
    crime.

125

Were 't aught to me I bore the canopy,
With my extern the outward honouring,
Or laid great bases for eternity,
Which prove more short than waste or ruining?
Have I not seen dwellers on form and favour 5
Lose all, and more, by paying too much rent,
For compound sweet foregoing simple savour,
Pitiful thrivers, in their gazing spent?
No, let me be obsequious in thy heart,
And take thou my oblation, poor but free, 10
Which is not mix'd with seconds, knows no art
But mutual render, only me for thee.
  Hence, thou suborn'd informer! a true soul
  When most impeach'd stands least in thy con-
    trol.

126

O thou, my lovely boy, who in thy power
Dost hold Time's fickle glass, his sickle, hour;
Who hast by waning grown, and therein show'st
Thy lovers withering as thy sweet self grow'st;
If Nature, sovereign mistress over wrack, 5
As thou goest onwards, still will pluck thee back,
She keeps thee to this purpose, that her skill
May time disgrace and wretched minutes kill.
Yet fear her, O thou minion of her pleasure!
She may detain, but not still keep, her treasure;
Her audit, though delay'd, answer'd must be,
And her quietus is to render thee. 12

127

In the old age black was not counted fair,
Or if it were, it bore not beauty's name;
But now is black beauty's successive heir,
And beauty slander'd with a bastard shame; 4
For since each hand hath put on nature's power,
Fairing the foul with art's false borrow'd face,
Sweet beauty hath no name, no holy bower,
But is profaned, if not lives in disgrace.
Therefore my mistress' eyes are raven black,
Her eyes so suited, and they mourners seem
At such who, not born fair, no beauty lack, 11
Slandering creation with a false esteem;
  Yet so they mourn, becoming of their woe,
  That every tongue says beauty should look so.

128

How oft, when thou, my music, music play'st,
Upon that blessed wood whose motion sounds
With thy sweet fingers, when thou gently sway'st
The wiry concord that mine ear confounds,
Do I envy those jacks that nimble leap 5
To kiss the tender inward of thy hand,
Whilst my poor lips, which should that harvest
    reap,
At the wood's boldness by thee blushing stand!
To be so tickled, they would change their state
And situation with those dancing chips, 10
O'er whom thy fingers walk with gentle gait,
Making dead wood more blest than living lips.
  Since saucy jacks so happy are in this,
  Give them thy fingers, me thy lips to kiss.

129

The expense of spirit in a waste of shame
Is lust in action; and till action, lust
Is perjured, murderous, bloody, full of blame,
Savage, extreme, rude, cruel, not to trust;
Enjoy'd no sooner but despised straight; 5
Past reason hunted; and no sooner had,
Past reason hated, as a swallow'd bait,
On purpose laid to make the taker mad;
Mad in pursuit, and in possession so;
Had, having, and in quest to have, extreme;
A bliss in proof, and proved, a very woe; 11
Before, a joy proposed; behind, a dream.

All this the world well knows; yet none knows well
To shun the heaven that leads men to this hell.

130

My mistress' eyes are nothing like the sun;
Coral is far more red than her lips' red;
If snow be white, why then her breasts are dun;
If hairs be wires, black wires grow on her head.
I have seen roses damask'd red and white,   5
But no such roses see I in her cheeks;
And in some perfumes is there more delight
Than in the breath that from my mistress reeks.
I love to hear her speak, yet well I know
That music hath a far more pleasing sound;   10
I grant I never saw a goddess go,
My mistress, when she walks, treads on the ground;
And yet, by heaven, I think my love as rare
As any she belied with false compare.

131

Thou art as tyrannous, so as thou art,
As those whose beauties proudly make them cruel;
For well thou know'st to my dear doting heart
Thou art the fairest and most precious jewel.
Yet, in good faith, some say that thee behold,   5
Thy face hath not the power to make love groan;
To say they err I dare not be so bold,
Although I swear it to myself alone.
And to be sure that is not false I swear,
A thousand groans, but thinking on thy face,   10
One on another's neck, do witness bear
Thy black is fairest in my judgement's place.
In nothing art thou black save in thy deeds,
And thence this slander, as I think, proceeds.

132

Thine eyes I love, and they, as pitying me,
Knowing thy heart torments me with disdain,
Have put on black and loving mourners be,
Looking with pretty ruth upon my pain.
And truly not the morning sun of heaven   5
Better becomes the grey cheeks of the east,
Nor that full star that ushers in the even
Doth half that glory to the sober west,
As those two mourning eyes become thy face;
O, let it then as well beseem thy heart   10
To mourn for me, since mourning doth thee grace,
And suit thy pity like in every part.
Then will I swear beauty herself is black,
And all they foul that thy complexion lack.

133

Beshrew that heart that makes my heart to groan
For that deep wound it gives my friend and me!
Is't not enough to torture me alone,
But slave to slavery my sweet'st friend must be?
Me from myself thy cruel eye hath taken,   5
And my next self thou harder hast engrossed;
Of him, myself, and thee, I am forsaken;
A torment thrice threefold thus to be crossed.
Prison my heart in thy steel bosom's ward,
But then my friend's heart let my poor heart bail;   10
Whoe'er keeps me, let my heart be his guard;
Thou canst not then use rigour in my gaol;
And yet thou wilt; for I, being pent in thee,
Perforce am thine, and all that is in me.

134

So, now I have confess'd that he is thine
And I myself am mortgaged to thy will,
Myself I'll forfeit, so that other mine
Thou wilt restore, to be my comfort still;
But thou wilt not, nor he will not be free,   5
For thou art covetous and he is kind;
He learn'd but surety-like to write for me,
Under that bond that him as fast doth bind.
The statute of thy beauty thou wilt take,
Thou usurer, that put'st forth all to use,   10
And sue a friend came debtor for my sake;
So him I lose through my unkind abuse.
Him have I lost; thou hast both him and me;
He pays the whole, and yet am I not free.

135

Whoever hath her wish, thou hast thy 'Will,'
And 'Will' to boot, and 'Will' in overplus;
More than enough am I that vex thee still,
To thy sweet will making addition thus.
Wilt thou, whose will is large and spacious,   5
Not once vouchsafe to hide my will in thine?
Shall will in others seem right gracious,
And in my will no fair acceptance shine?
The sea, all water, yet receives rain still,
And in abundance addeth to his store;   10
So thou, being rich in 'Will,' add to thy 'Will'
One will of mine, to make thy large 'Will' more.
Let no unkind, no fair beseechers kill;
Think all but one, and me in that one 'Will.'

136

If thy soul check thee that I come so near,
Swear to thy blind soul that I was thy 'Will,'
And will, thy soul knows, is admitted there;
Thus far for love, my love-suit, sweet, fulfil.
'Will' will fulfil the treasure of thy love,   5
Ay, fill it full with wills, and my will one.
In things of great receipt with ease we prove
Among a number one is reckon'd none;
Then in the number let me pass untold,
Though in thy stores' account I one must be;   10
For nothing hold me, so it please thee hold
That nothing me, a something sweet to thee;
Make but my name thy love, and love that still,
And then thou lovest me, for my name is 'Will.'

137

Thou blind fool, Love, what dost thou to mine eyes,
That they behold, and see not what they see?
They know what beauty is, see where it lies,
Yet what the best is take the worst to be.
If eyes, corrupt by over-partial looks,   5
Be anchor'd in the bay where all men ride,
Why of eyes' falsehood hast thou forged hooks,
Whereto the judgement of my heart is tied?
Why should my heart think that a several plot
Which my heart knows the wide world's common place?   10
Or mine eyes seeing this, say this is not,
To put fair truth upon so foul a face?
In things right true my heart and eyes have erred,
And to this false plague are they now transferred.

138

When my love swears that she is made of truth,
I do believe her, though I know she lies,
That she might think me some untutor'd youth,
Unlearned in the world's false subtleties.
Thus vainly thinking that she thinks me young,
Although she knows my days are past the best,
Simply I credit her false-speaking tongue;   7
On both sides thus is simple truth suppressed.
But wherefore says she not she is unjust?
And wherefore say not I that I am old?   10
O, love's best habit is in seeming trust,
And age in love loves not to have years told;
  Therefore I lie with her and she with me,
  And in our faults by lies we flatter'd be.

139

O, call not me to justify the wrong
That thy unkindness lays upon my heart;
Wound me not with thine eye, but with thy tongue;
Use power with power, and slay me not by art.
Tell me thou lovest elsewhere; but in my sight,
Dear heart, forbear to glance thine eye aside;   6
What need'st thou wound with cunning, when thy might
Is more than my o'er-press'd defence can bide?
Let me excuse thee: ah, my love well knows
Her pretty looks have been mine enemies;   10
And therefore from my face she turns my foes,
That they elsewhere might dart their injuries;
  Yet do not so; but since I am near slain,
  Kill me outright with looks, and rid my pain.

140

Be wise as thou art cruel; do not press
My tongue-tied patience with too much disdain;
Lest sorrow lend me words, and words express
The manner of my pity-wanting pain.
If I might teach thee wit, better it were,   5
Though not to love, yet, love, to tell me so;
As testy sick men, when their deaths be near,
No news but health from their physicians know;
For, if I should despair, I should grow mad,
And in my madness might speak ill of thee;
Now this ill-wresting world is grown so bad,
Mad slanderers by mad ears believed be.   12
  That I may not be so, nor thou belied,
  Bear thine eyes straight, though thy proud heart go wide.

141

In faith, I do not love thee with mine eyes,
For they in thee a thousand errors note;
But 'tis my heart that loves what they despise,
Who, in despite of view, is pleased to dote;
Nor are mine ears with thy tongue's tune delighted;   5
Nor tender feeling, to base touches prone,
Nor taste, nor smell, desire to be invited
To any sensual feast with thee alone;
But my five wits nor my five senses can   9
Dissuade one foolish heart from serving thee,
Who leaves unsway'd the likeness of a man,
Thy proud heart's slave and vassal wretch to be;
  Only my plague thus far I count my gain,
  That she that makes me sin awards me pain.

142

Love is my sin, and thy dear virtue hate,
Hate of my sin, grounded on sinful loving;
O, but with mine compare thou thine own state,
And thou shalt find it merits not reproving;
Or, if it do, not from those lips of thine,   5
That have profaned their scarlet ornaments
And seal'd false bonds of love as oft as mine,
Robb'd others' beds' revenues of their rents.
Be it lawful I love thee, as thou lovest those
Whom thine eyes woo as mine importune thee;
Root pity in thy heart, that, when it grows,
Thy pity may deserve to pitied be.   12
  If thou dost seek to have what thou dost hide,
  By self-example mayst thou be denied!

143

Lo, as a careful housewife runs to catch
One of her feather'd creatures broke away,
Sets down her babe, and makes all swift dispatch
In pursuit of the thing she would have stay;
Whilst her neglected child holds her in chase,
Cries to catch her whose busy care is bent   6
To follow that which flies before her face,
Not prizing her poor infant's discontent;
So runn'st thou after that which flies from thee,
Whilst I thy babe chase thee afar behind;   10
But if thou catch thy hope, turn back to me,
And play the mother's part, kiss me, be kind;
  So will I pray that thou mayst have thy 'Will,'
  If thou turn back and my loud crying still.

144

Two loves I have of comfort and despair,
Which like two spirits do suggest me still;
The better angel is a man right fair,
The worser spirit a woman colour'd ill.
To win me soon to hell, my female evil   5
Tempteth my better angel from my side,
And would corrupt my saint to be a devil,
Wooing his purity with her foul pride.
And whether that my angel be turn'd fiend
Suspect I may, yet not directly tell;   10
But being both from me, both to each friend,
I guess one angel in another's hell;
  Yet this shall I ne'er know, but live in doubt,
  Till my bad angel fire my good one out.

145

Those lips that Love's own hand did make
Breathed forth the sound that said 'I hate,'
To me that languish'd for her sake;
But when she saw my woeful state,
Straight in her heart did mercy come,   5
Chiding that tongue that ever sweet
Was used in giving gentle doom;
And taught it thus anew to greet;
'I hate' she alter'd with an end,
That follow'd it as gentle day   10
Doth follow night, who, like a fiend,
From heaven to hell is flown away;
  'I hate' from hate away she threw,
  And saved my life, saying 'not you.'

146

Poor soul, the centre of my sinful earth,
My sinful earth these rebel powers that thee array,
Why dost thou pine within and suffer dearth,
Painting thy outward walls so costly gay?

Why so large cost, having so short a lease,   5
Dost thou upon thy fading mansion spend?
Shall worms, inheritors of this excess,
Eat up thy charge? is this thy body's end?
Then, soul, live thou upon thy servant's loss,
And let that pine to aggravate thy store;   10
Buy terms divine in selling hours of dross;
Within be fed, without be rich no more;
So shalt thou feed on Death, that feeds on men,
And Death once dead, there's no more dying
   then.

147
My love is as a fever, longing still
For that which longer nurseth the disease;
Feeding on that which doth preserve the ill,
The uncertain sickly appetite to please.
My reason, the physician to my love,   5
Angry that his prescriptions are not kept,
Hath left me, and I desperate now approve
Desire is death, which physic did except.
Past cure I am, now reason is past care,
And frantic-mad with evermore unrest;   10
My thoughts and my discourse as madmen's are,
At random from the truth vainly express'd;
  For I have sworn thee fair, and thought thee
    bright,
  Who art as black as hell, as dark as night.

148
O me, what eyes hath Love put in my head,
Which have no correspondence with true sight!
Or, if they have, where is my judgement fled,
That censures falsely what they see aright?
If that be fair whereon my false eyes dote,   5
What means the world to say it is not so?
If it be not, then love doth well denote
Love's eye is not so true as all men's; no,
How can it? O, how can Love's eye be true,
That is so vex'd with watching and with tears?
No marvel then, though I mistake my view;   11
The sun itself sees not till heaven clears.
  O cunning Love! with tears thou keep'st me
    blind,
  Lest eyes well-seeing thy foul faults should find.

149
Canst thou, O cruel! say I love thee not,
When I against myself with thee partake?
Do I not think on thee, when I forgot
Am of myself, all tyrant, for thy sake?
Who hateth thee that I do call my friend?   5
On whom frown'st thou that I do fawn upon?
Nay, if thou lour'st on me, do I not spend
Revenge upon myself with present moan?
What merit do I in myself respect,
That is so proud thy service to despise,   10
When all my best doth worship thy defect,
Commanded by the motion of thine eyes?
  But, love, hate on, for now I know thy mind;
  Those that can see thou lovest, and I am blind.

150
O, from what power hast thou this powerful might
With insufficiency my heart to sway?
To make me give the lie to my true sight,
And swear that brightness doth not grace the day?
Whence hast thou this becoming of things ill,
That in the very refuse of thy deeds   6
There is such strength and warrantise of skill,
That, in my mind, thy worst all best exceeds?

Who taught thee how to make me love thee more,
The more I hear and see just cause of hate?
O, though I love what others do abhor,   11
With others thou shouldst not abhor my state;
  If thy unworthiness raised love in me,
  More worthy I to be beloved of thee.

151
Love is too young to know what conscience is;
Yet who knows not conscience is born of love?
Then, gentle cheater, urge not my amiss,
Lest guilty of my faults thy sweet self prove;
For, thou betraying me, I do betray   5
My nobler part to my gross body's treason;
My soul doth tell my body that he may
Triumph in love; flesh stays no farther reason,
But rising at thy name doth point out thee
As his triumphant prize. Proud of this pride,
He is contented thy poor drudge to be,   11
To stand in thy affairs, fall by thy side.
  No want of conscience hold it that I call
  Her 'love' for whose dear love I rise and fall.

152
In loving thee thou know'st I am forsworn,
But thou art twice forsworn, to me love swearing;
In act thy bed-vow broke, and new faith torn,
In vowing new hate after new love bearing.   4
But why of two oaths' breach do I accuse thee,
When I break twenty? I am perjured most;
For all my vows are oaths but to misuse thee,
And all my honest faith in thee is lost;
For I have sworn deep oaths of thy deep kindness,
Oaths of thy love, thy truth, thy constancy;   10
And, to enlighten thee, gave eyes to blindness,
Or made them swear against the thing they see;
  For I have sworn thee fair; more perjured I,
  To swear against the truth so foul a lie!

153
Cupid laid by his brand and fell asleep;
A maid of Dian's this advantage found,
And his love-kindling fire did quickly steep
In a cold valley-fountain of that ground;
Which borrow'd from this holy fire of Love   5
A dateless, lively heat, still to endure,
And grew a seething bath, which yet men prove
Against strange maladies a sovereign cure.
But at my mistress' eye Love's brand new-fired,
The boy for trial needs would touch my breast;
I, sick withal, the help of bath desired,   11
And thither hied, a sad distemper'd guest,
  But found no cure; the bath for my help lies
  Where Cupid got new fire, my mistress' eyes.

154
The little Love-god lying once asleep
Laid by his side his heart-inflaming brand,
Whilst many nymphs that vow'd chaste life to
    keep
Came tripping by; but in her maiden hand
The fairest votary took up that fire   5
Which many legions of true hearts had warm'd;
And so the general of hot desire
Was sleeping by a virgin hand disarm'd.
This brand she quenched in a cool well by,
Which from Love's fire took heat perpetual,   10
Growing a bath and healthful remedy
For men diseased; but I, my mistress' thrall,
  Came there for cure, and this by that I prove,
  Love's fire heats water, water cools not love.

A LOVER'S COMPLAINT

From off a hill whose concave womb re-worded
A plaintful story from a sistering vale,
My spirits to attend this double voice accorded,
And down I laid to list the sad-tuned tale;
Ere long espied a fickle maid full pale, 5
Tearing of papers, breaking rings a-twain,
Storming her world with sorrow's wind and rain.

Upon her head a platted hive of straw,
Which fortified her visage from the sun,
Whereon the thought might think sometime it saw
The carcass of a beauty spent and done; 11
Time had not scythed all that youth begun,
Nor youth all quit; but, spite of heaven's fell rage,
Some beauty peep'd through lattice of scar'd age.

Oft did she heave her napkin to her eyne, 15
Which on it had conceited characters,
Laundering the silken figures in the brine
That season'd woe had pelleted in tears,
And often reading what contents it bears;
As often shrieking undistinguish'd woe, 20
In clamours of all size, both high and low.

Sometimes her levell'd eyes their carriage ride,
As they did battery to the spheres intend;
Sometime diverted their poor balls are tied 24
To the orbed earth; sometimes they do extend
Their view right on; anon their gazes lend
To every place at once, and nowhere fix'd
The mind and sight distractedly commix'd.

Her hair, nor loose nor tied in formal plat,
Proclaim'd in her a careless hand of pride; 30
For some, untuck'd, descended her sheaved hat,
Hanging her pale and pined cheek beside;
Some in her threaden fillet still did bide,
And, true to bondage, would not break from
 thence, 34
Though slackly braided in loose negligence.

A thousand favours from a maund she drew
Of amber, crystal, and of beaded jet,
Which one by one she in a river threw,
Upon whose weeping margent she was set;
Like usury, applying wet to wet, 40
Or monarch's hands that lets not bounty fall
Where want cries some, but where excess begs all.

Of folded schedules had she many a one,
Which she perused, sigh'd, tore, and gave the flood;
Crack'd many a ring of posied gold and bone,
Bidding them find their sepulchres in mud; 46
Found yet moe letters sadly penn'd in blood,
With sleided silk feat and affectedly
Enswathed, and seal'd to curious secrecy.

These often bathed she in her fluxive eyes, 50
And often kiss'd, and often 'gan to tear;
Cried, 'O false blood, thou register of lies,
What unapproved witness dost thou bear!
Ink would have seem'd more black and damned
 here!'
This said, in top of rage the lines she rents, 55
Big discontent so breaking their contents.

A reverend man that grazed his cattle nigh,—
Sometime a blusterer, that the ruffle knew
Of court, of city, and had let go by
The swiftest hours, observed as they flew,— 60
Towards this afflicted fancy fastly drew;
And, privileged by age, desires to know
In brief the grounds and motives of her woe.

So slides he down upon his grained bat,
And comely-distant sits he by her side; 65
When he again desires her, being sat,
Her grievance with his hearing to divide;
If that from him there may be aught applied
Which may her suffering ecstasy assuage,
'Tis promised in the charity of age. 70

'Father,' she says, 'though in me you behold
The injury of many a blasting hour,
Let it not tell your judgement I am old;
Not age, but sorrow, over me hath power;
I might as yet have been a spreading flower,
Fresh to myself, if I had self-applied 76
Love to myself, and to no love beside.

'But, woe is me! too early I attended
A youthful suit,—it was to gain my grace,—
Of one by nature's outwards so commended,
That maidens' eyes stuck over all his face; 81
Love lack'd a dwelling and made him her place;
And when in his fair parts she did abide,
She was new lodged and newly deified.

'His browny locks did hang in crooked curls;
And every light occasion of the wind 86
Upon his lips their silken parcels hurls.
What's sweet to do, to do will aptly find;
Each eye that saw him did enchant the mind;
For on his visage was in little drawn 90
What largeness thinks in Paradise was sawn.

'Small show of man was yet upon his chin;
His phœnix down began but to appear,
Like unshorn velvet, on that termless skin, 94
Whose bare out-bragg'd the web it seem'd to wear;
Yet showed his visage by that cost more dear;
And nice affections wavering stood in doubt
If best were as it was, or best without.

'His qualities were beauteous as his form, 99
For maiden-tongued he was, and thereof free;
Yet, if men moved him, was he such a storm
As oft 'twixt May and April is to see,
When winds breathe sweet, unruly though they be.
His rudeness so with his authorized youth
Did livery falseness in a pride of truth. 105

'Well could he ride, and often men would say,
"That horse his mettle from his rider takes;
Proud of subjection, noble by the sway,
What rounds, what bounds, what course, what stop he makes!"
And controversy hence a question takes, 110
Whether the horse by him became his deed,
Or he his manage by the well-doing steed.

'But quickly on this side the verdict went;
His real habitude gave life and grace
To appertainings and to ornament, 115
Accomplish'd in himself, not in his case;
All aids, themselves made fairer by their place,
Came for additions; yet their purposed trim
Pieced not his grace, but were all graced by him.

'So on the tip of his subduing tongue 120
All kind of arguments and question deep,
All replication prompt and reason strong,
For his advantage still did wake and sleep;
To make the weeper laugh, the laugher weep,
He had the dialect and different skill, 125
Catching all passions in his craft of will;

'That he did in the general bosom reign
Of young, of old, and sexes both enchanted,
To dwell with him in thoughts, or to remain 129
In personal duty, following where he haunted;
Consents bewitched, ere he desire, have granted,
And dialogued for him what he would say,
Ask'd their own wills and made their wills obey.

'Many there were that did his picture get, 134
To serve their eyes, and in it put their mind;
Like fools that in the imagination set
The goodly objects which abroad they find
Of lands and mansions, theirs in thought assign'd;
And labouring in moe pleasures to bestow them
Than the true gouty landlord which doth owe them; 140

'So many have, that never touch'd his hand,
Sweetly supposed them mistress of his heart.
My woeful self, that did in freedom stand,
And was my own fee-simple, not in part, 144
What with his art in youth, and youth in art,
Threw my affections in his charmed power,
Reserved the stalk and gave him all my flower.

'Yet did I not, as some my equals did,
Demand of him, nor being desired yielded;
Finding myself in honour so forbid, 150
With safest distance I mine honour shielded;
Experience for me many bulwarks builded
Of proofs new-bleeding, which remain'd the foil
Of this false jewel, and his amorous spoil.

'But, ah, who ever shunn'd by precedent 155
The destined ill she must herself assay?
Or forced examples, 'gainst her own content,

To put the by-past perils in her way?
Counsel may stop awhile what will not stay;
For when we rage, advice is often seen 160
By blunting us to make our wits more keen.

'Nor gives it satisfaction to our blood,
That we must curb it upon others' proof;
To be forbod the sweets that seem so good, 164
For fear of harms that preach in our behoof.
O appetite, from judgement stand aloof!
The one a palate hath that needs will taste,
Though Reason weep, and cry "It is thy last."

'For further I could say "This man's untrue,"
And knew the patterns of his foul beguiling; 170
Heard where his plants in others' orchards grew,
Saw how deceits were gilded in his smiling;
Knew vows were ever brokers to defiling;
Thought characters and words merely but art,
And bastards of his foul adulterate heart. 175

'And long upon these terms I held my city,
Till thus he 'gan besiege me: "Gentle maid,
Have of my suffering youth some feeling pity,
And be not of my holy vows afraid;
That's to ye sworn to none was ever said; 180
For feasts of love I have been call'd unto,
Till now did ne'er invite, nor never woo.

'"All my offences that abroad you see
Are errors of the blood, none of the mind;
Love made them not; with acture they may be,
Where neither party is nor true nor kind; 186
They sought their shame that so their shame did find;
And so much less of shame in me remains
By how much of me their reproach contains.

'"Among the many that mine eyes have seen,
Not one whose flame my heart so much as warmed,
Or my affection put to the smallest teen, 192
Or any of my leisures ever charmed;
Harm have I done to them, but ne'er was harmed;
Kept hearts in liveries, but mine own was free,
And reign'd, commanding in his monarchy. 195

'"Look here, what tributes wounded fancies sent me,
Of paled pearls and rubies red as blood;
Figuring that they their passions likewise lent me
Of grief and blushes, aptly understood 200
In bloodless white and the encrimson'd mood;
Effects of terror and dear modesty,
Encamp'd in hearts, but fighting outwardly.

'"And, lo, behold these talents of their hair,
With twisted metal amorously impleach'd, 205
I have received from many a several fair,
Their kind acceptance weepingly beseech'd,
With the annexions of fair gems enrich'd,
And deep-brain'd sonnets that did amplify 209
Each stone's dear nature, worth, and quality.

'"The diamond, why, 'twas beautiful and hard,
Whereto his invised properties did tend;
The deep-green emerald, in whose fresh regard
Weak sights their sickly radiance do amend;
The heaven-hued sapphire and the opal blend
With objects manifold; each several stone, 216
With wit well blazon'd, smiled or made some moan.

'" Lo, all these trophies of affections hot,
Of pensived and subdued desires the tender,
Nature hath charged me that I hoard them not,
But yield them up where I myself must render,
That is, to you, my origin and ender;   222
For these, of force, must your oblations be,
Since I their altar, you enpatron me.

'" O, then, advance of yours that phraseless hand,
Whose white weighs down the airy scale of praise;
Take all these similes to your own command,   227
Hallow'd with sighs that burning lungs did raise;
What me your minister, for you obeys,
Works under you; and to your audit comes
Their distract parcels in combined sums.   231

'" Lo, this device was sent me from a nun,
Or sister sanctified, of holiest note;
Which late her noble suit in court did shun,
Whose rarest havings made the blossoms dote;
For she was sought by spirits of richest coat,
But kept cold distance, and did thence remove,
To spend her living in eternal love.   238

'" But, O my sweet, what labour is't to leave
The thing we have not, mastering what not strives,
Playing the place which did no form receive, 241
Playing patient sports in unconstrained gyves?
She that her fame so to herself contrives,
The scars of battle 'scapeth by the flight,   244
And makes her absence valiant, not her might.

'" O, pardon me, in that my boast is true;
The accident which brought me to her eye
Upon the moment did her force subdue,
And now she would the caged cloister fly;
Religious love put out Religion's eye;   250
Not to be tempted, would she be immured,
And now, to tempt all, liberty procured.

'" How mighty then you are, O, hear me tell!
The broken bosoms that to me belong
Have emptied all their fountains in my well,
And mine I pour your ocean all among;   256
I strong o'er them, and you o'er me being strong,
Must for your victory so all congest,
As compound love to physic your cold breast.

'" My parts had power to charm a sacred nun,
Who disciplined, ay, dieted in grace,   261
Believed her eyes when they to assail begun,
All vows and consecrations giving place;
O most potential love! vow, bond, nor space,
In thee hath neither sting, knot, nor confine, 265
For thou art all, and all things else are thine.

'" When thou impressest, what are precepts worth
Of stale example? When thou wilt inflame,
How coldly those impediments stand forth
Of wealth, of filial fear, law, kindred, fame!
Love's arms are peace, 'gainst rule, 'gainst sense,
      'gainst shame;   271
And sweetens, in the suffering pangs it bears,
The aloes of all forces, shocks and fears.

'" Now all these hearts that do on mine depend,
Feeling it break, with bleeding groans they pine;
And supplicant their sighs to you extend,   276
To leave the battery that you make 'gainst mine,
Lending soft audience to my sweet design,
And credent soul to that strong-bonded oath
That shall prefer and undertake my troth."   280

' This said, his watery eyes he did dismount,
Whose sights till then were levell'd on my face;
Each cheek a river running from a fount   283
With brinish current downward flow'd apace;
O, how the channel to the stream gave grace!
Who glazed with crystal gate the glowing roses
That flame through water which their hue encloses.

' O father, what a hell of witchcraft lies
In the small orb of one particular tear!
But with the inundation of the eyes   290
What rocky heart to water will not wear?
What breast so cold that is not warmed here?
O cleft effect! cold modesty, hot wrath,
Both fire from hence and chill extincture hath.

' For, lo, his passion, but an art of craft, 295
Even there resolved my reason into tears;
There my white stole of chastity I daff'd,
Shook off my sober guards and civil fears;
Appear to him, as he to me appears,   299
All melting; though our drops this difference bore,
His poison'd me, and mine did him restore.

' In him a plenitude of subtle matter,
Applied to cautels, all strange forms receives,
Of burning blushes, or of weeping water,   304
Or swounding paleness; and he takes and leaves,
In either's aptness, as it best deceives,
To blush at speeches rank, to weep at woes,
Or to turn white and swound at tragic shows;

' That not a heart which in his level came
Could 'scape the hail of his all-hurting aim, 310
Showing fair nature is both kind and tame;
And, veil'd in them, did win whom he would maim;
Against the thing he sought he would exclaim;
When he most burn'd in heart-wish'd luxury,
He preach'd pure maid and praised cold chastity.

' Thus merely with the garment of a Grace   316
The naked and concealed fiend he cover'd;
That the unexperient gave the tempter place,
Which, like a cherubin, above them hover'd.
Who, young and simple, would not be so lover'd?
Ay me! I fell, and yet do question make   321
What I should do again for such a sake.

' O, that infected moisture of his eye,
O, that false fire which in his cheek so glow'd,
O, that forced thunder from his heart did fly, 325
O, that sad breath his spongy lungs bestow'd,
O, all that borrow'd motion seeming owed,
Would yet again betray the fore-betray'd,
And new pervert a reconciled maid!"

THE PASSIONATE PILGRIM

1

WHEN my love swears that she is made of truth,
I do believe her, though I know she lies,
That she might think me some untutor'd youth,
Unskilful in the world's false forgeries. 4
Thus vainly thinking that she thinks me young,
Although I know my years be past the best,
I smiling credit her false-speaking tongue,
Outfacing faults in love with love's ill rest.
But wherefore says my love that she is young?
And wherefore say not I that I am old? 10
O, love's best habit is a soothing tongue,
And age, in love, loves not to have years told,
Therefore I'll lie with love, and love with me,
Since that our faults in love thus smother'd be.

2

Two loves I have, of comfort and despair,
That like two spirits do suggest me still;
My better angel is a man right fair,
My worser spirit a woman colour'd ill.
To win me soon to hell, my female evil 5
Tempteth my better angel from my side,
And would corrupt my saint to be a devil,
Wooing his purity with her fair pride.
And whether that my angel be turn'd fiend,
Suspect I may, yet not directly tell; 10
For being both to me, both to each friend,
I guess one angel in another's hell;
  The truth I shall not know, but live in doubt,
  Till my bad angel fire my good one out.

3

Did not the heavenly rhetoric of thine eye,
'Gainst whom the world could not hold argument,
Persuade my heart to this false perjury?
Vows for thee broke deserve not punishment.
A woman I forswore; but I will prove, 5
Thou being a goddess, I forswore not thee;
My vow was earthly, thou a heavenly love;
Thy grace being gain'd cures all disgrace in me.
My vow was breath, and breath a vapour is;
Then, thou fair sun, that on this earth doth shine,
Exhale this vapour vow; in thee it is; 11
If broken, then it is no fault of mine.
  If by me broke, what fool is not so wise
  To break an oath, to win a paradise?

4

Sweet Cytherea, sitting by a brook
With young Adonis, lovely, fresh, and green,
Did court the lad with many a lovely look,
Such looks as none could look but beauty's queen.
She told him stories to delight his ear, 5
She show'd him favours to allure his eye;
To win his heart, she touch'd him here and there;
Touches so soft still conquer chastity.
But whether unripe years did want conceit,
Or he refused to take her figured proffer, 10
The tender nibbler would not touch the bait,
But smile and jest at every gentle offer;
  Then fell she on her back, fair queen, and toward;
  He rose and ran away; ah, fool too froward.

5

If love make me forsworn, how shall I swear to love?
O never faith could hold, if not to beauty vowed;
Though to myself forsworn, to thee I'll constant prove;
Those thoughts, to me like oaks, to thee like osiers bowed.
Study his bias leaves, and makes his book thine eyes, 5
Where all those pleasures live that art can comprehend.
If knowledge be the mark, to know thee shall suffice;
Well learned is that tongue that well can thee commend;
All ignorant that soul that sees thee without wonder;
Which is to me some praise, that I thy parts admire; 10
Thine eye Jove's lightning seems, thy voice his dreadful thunder,
Which, not to anger bent, is music and sweet fire.
  Celestial as thou art, O do not love that wrong,
  To sing heaven's praise with such an earthly tongue.

6

Scarce had the sun dried up the dewy morn,
And scarce the herd gone to the hedge for shade,
When Cytherea, all in love forlorn,
A longing tarriance for Adonis made
Under an osier growing by a brook, 5
A brook where Adon used to cool his spleen;
Hot was the day; she hotter that did look
For his approach, that often there had been.
Anon he comes, and throws his mantle by, 9
And stood stark naked on the brook's green brim;
The sun look'd on the world with glorious eye,
Yet not so wistly as this queen on him.
  He, spying her, bounced in, whereas he stood;
  'O Jove,' quoth she, 'why was not I a flood!'

7

Fair is my love, but not so fair as fickle,
Mild as a dove, but neither true nor trusty,
Brighter than glass and yet, as glass is, brittle,
Softer than wax and yet as iron rusty:
   A lily pale, with damask dye to grace her,   5
   None fairer, nor none falser to deface her.

Her lips to mine how often hath she joined,
Between each kiss her oaths of true love swearing!
How many tales to please me hath she coined,
Dreading my love, the loss thereof still fearing!
   Yet in the midst of all her pure protestings,
   Her faith, her oaths, her tears, and all were
      jestings.   12

She burn'd with love, as straw with fire flameth;
She burn'd out love, as soon as straw out-burneth;
She framed the love, and yet she foil'd the framing;
She bade love last, and yet she fell a-turning.   16
   Was this a lover, or a lecher whether?
   Bad in the best, though excellent in neither.

8

If music and sweet poetry agree,
As they must needs, the sister and the brother,
Then must the love be great 'twixt thee and me,
Because thou lovest the one and I the other.
Dowland to thee is dear, whose heavenly touch
Upon the lute doth ravish human sense;   6
Spenser to me, whose deep conceit is such
As passing all conceit needs no defence.
Thou lovest to hear the sweet melodious sound
That Phœbus' lute, the queen of music, makes;
And I in deep delight am chiefly drown'd   11
When as himself to singing he betakes.
   One god is god of both, as poets feign;
   One knight loves both, and both in thee remain.

9

Fair was the morn when the fair queen of love,
    *   *   *   *   *
Paler for sorrow than her milk-white dove,
For Adon's sake, a youngster proud and wild;
Her stand she takes upon a steep up-hill;   5
Anon Adonis comes with horn and hounds;
She, silly queen, with more than love's good will,
Forbade the boy he should not pass those grounds;
'Once,' quoth she, 'did I see a fair sweet youth
Here in these brakes deep-wounded with a boar,
Deep in the thigh, a spectacle of ruth!'   11
See, in my thigh,' quoth she, 'here was the sore.'
   She showed hers: he saw more wounds than one,
   And blushing fled, and left her all alone.

10

Sweet rose, fair flower, untimely pluck'd, soon
    vaded,
Pluck'd in the bud and vaded in the spring!
Bright orient pearl, alack, too timely shaded!
Fair creature, kill'd too soon by death's sharp
    sting!
Like a green plum that hangs upon a tree,   5
And falls through wind before the fall should be.

I weep for thee and yet no cause I have;
For why thou left'st me nothing in thy will;
And yet thou left'st me more than I did crave;
For why I craved nothing of thee still;   10

O yes, dear friend, I pardon crave of thee,
Thy discontent thou didst bequeath to me.

11

Venus, with young Adonis sitting by her
Under a myrtle shade, began to woo him;
She told the youngling how god Mars did try her,
And as he fell to her, so fell she to him.
'Even thus,' quoth she, 'the warlike god em-
    braced me,'   5
And then she clipp'd Adonis in her arms;
'Even thus,' quoth she, 'the warlike god unlaced
    me,'
As if the boy should use like loving charms;
'Even thus,' quoth she, 'he seized on my lips,'
And with her lips on his did act the seizure;   10
And as she fetched breath, away he skips,
And would not take her meaning nor her pleasure.
   Ah, that I had my lady at this bay,
   To kiss and clip me till I run away!

12

Crabbed age and youth cannot live together;
Youth is full of pleasance, age is full of care;
Youth like summer morn, age like winter wea-
    ther;
Youth like summer brave, age like winter bare.
Youth is full of sport, age's breath is short;   6
Youth is nimble, age is lame;
Youth is hot and bold, age is weak and cold;
Youth is wild, and age is tame.
Age, I do abhor thee; youth, I do adore thee;
O, my love, my love is young!   10
Age, I do defy thee; O, sweet shepherd, hie thee,
For methinks thou stay'st too long.

13

Beauty is but a vain and doubtful good;
A shining gloss that vadeth suddenly;
A flower that dies when first it 'gins to bud;
A brittle glass that's broken presently:
   A doubtful good, a gloss, a glass, a flower,   5
   Lost, vaded, broken, dead within an hour.

And as goods lost are seld or never found,
As vaded gloss no rubbing will refresh,
As flowers dead lie wither'd on the ground,
As broken glass no cement can redress,   10
   So beauty blemish'd once's for ever lost,
   In spite of physic, painting, pain, and cost.

14

Good-night, good rest. Ah, neither be my share;
She bade good night that kept my rest away;
And daff'd me to a cabin hang'd with care,
To descent on the doubts of my decay.
   'Farewell,' quoth she, 'and come again to-mor-
    row;'
   Fare well I could not, for I supp'd with sorrow.

Yet at my parting sweetly did she smile,
In scorn or friendship, nill I construe whether;
'T may be, she joy'd to jest at my exile,   9
'T may be, again to make me wander thither;
   'Wander,' a word for shadows like myself,
   As take the pain, but cannot pluck the pelf.

15

Lord, how mine eyes throw gazes to the east!
My heart doth charge the watch; the morning rise
Doth cite each moving sense from idle rest.
Not daring trust the office of mine eyes, 4
  While Philomela sits and sings, I sit and mark,
  And wish her lays were tuned like the lark;

For she doth welcome daylight with her ditty,
And drives away dark dreaming night;
The night so pack'd, I post unto my pretty; 9
Heart hath his hope and eyes their wished sight;
  Sorrow changed to solace, and solace mix'd with sorrow;
  For why, she sigh'd, and bade me come to-morrow.

Were I with her, the night would post too soon;
But now are minutes added to the hours; 14
To spite me now, each minute seems a moon;
Yet not for me, shine sun to succour flowers!
  Pack night, peep day; good day, of night now borrow;
  Short, night, to-night, and length thyself to-morrow.

16

It was a lording's daughter, the fairest one of three,
That liked of her master as well as well might be,
Till looking on an Englishman, the fair'st that eye could see,
  Her fancy fell a-turning.

Long was the combat doubtful that love with love did fight; 5
To leave the master loveless, or kill the gallant knight;
To put in practice either, alas, it was a spite
  Unto the silly damsel!

But one must be refused; more mickle was the pain
That nothing could be used to turn them both to gain, 10
For of the two the trusty knight was wounded with disdain;
  Alas, she could not help it!

Thus art with arms contending was victor of the day,
Which by a gift of learning did bear the maid away;
Then, lullaby, the learned man hath got the lady gay; 15
  For now my song is ended.

17

On a day, alack the day!
Love, whose month was ever May,
Spied a blossom passing fair,
Playing in the wanton air;
Through the velvet leaves the wind 5
All unseen 'gan passage find;
That the lover, sick to death,
Wish'd himself the heaven's breath.
'Air,' quoth he, 'thy cheeks may blow;
Air, would I might triumph so! 10
But, alas! my hand hath sworn
Ne'er to pluck thee from thy thorn;
Vow, alack! for youth unmeet;
Youth, so apt to pluck a sweet.

Thou for whom Jove would swear 15
Juno but an Ethiope were;
And deny himself for Jove,
Turning mortal for thy love.'

18

My flocks feed not,
My ewes breed not,
My rams speed not;
  All is amiss;
Love's denying, 5
Faith's defying,
Heart's renying
  Causer of this.
All my merry jigs are quite forgot,
All my lady's love is lost, God wot; 10
Where her faith was firmly fix'd in love,
There a nay is placed without remove.
One silly cross
Wrought all my loss;
  O frowning Fortune, cursed, fickle dame! 15
For now I see
Inconstancy
  More in women than in men remain.

In black mourn I,
All fears scorn I, 20
Love hath forlorn me,
  Living in thrall;
Heart is bleeding,
All help needing,
O cruel speeding, 25
  Fraughted with gall.
My shepherd's pipe can sound no deal;
My wether's bell rings doleful knell;
My curtal dog, that wont to have play'd,
Plays not at all, but seems afraid; 30
My sighs so deep
Procure to weep,
  In howling wise, to see my doleful plight.
How sighs resound
Through heartless ground, 35
  Like a thousand vanquish'd men in bloody fight!

Clear wells spring not,
Sweet birds sing not,
Green plants bring not
  Forth their dye; 40
Herds stand weeping,
Flocks all sleeping,
Nymphs back peeping
  Fearfully;
All our pleasure known to us poor swains, 45
All our merry meetings on the plains,
All our evening sport from us is fled,
All our love is lost, for Love is dead.
Farewell, sweet lass,
Thy like ne'er was 50
  For a sweet content, the cause of all my moan;
Poor Corydon
Must live alone;
  Other help for him I see that there is none.

19

When as thine eye hath chose the dame,
And stall'd the deer that thou shouldst strike,
Let reason rule things worthy blame,
  As well as fancy, partial wight;
Take counsel of some wiser head, 5
  Neither too young nor yet unwed.

And when thou comest thy tale to tell,
Smooth not thy tongue with filed talk,
Lest she some subtle practice smell,—
A cripple soon can find a halt;— 10
But plainly say thou lovest her well,
And set thy person forth to sell.

What though her frowning brows be bent,
Her cloudy looks will calm ere night;
And then too late she will repent 15
That thus dissembled her delight;
And twice desire, ere it be day,
That which with scorn she put away.

What though she strive to try her strength,
And ban and brawl and say thee nay, 20
Her feeble force will yield at length,
When craft hath taught her thus to say:
'Had women been so strong as men,
In faith, you had not had it then.'

And to her will frame all thy ways; 25
Spare not to spend, and chiefly there
Where thy desert may merit praise,
By ringing in thy lady's ear;
The strongest castle, tower and town,
The golden bullet beats it down. 30

Serve always with assured trust,
And in thy suit be humble true;
Unless thy lady prove unjust,
Press never thou to choose anew;
When time shall serve, be thou not slack 35
To proffer, though she put thee back.

The wiles and guiles that women work,
Dissembled with an outward show,
The tricks and toys that in them lurk,
The cock that treads them shall not know. 40
Have you not heard it said full oft,
A woman's nay doth stand for nought?

Think women still to strive with men,
To sin and never for to saint;
There is no heaven, by holy then, 45
When time with age shall them attaint.
Were kisses all the joys in bed,
One woman would another wed.

But, soft! enough,—too much, I fear,—
Lest that my mistress hear my song; 50
She will not stick to round me on th' ear,
To teach my tongue to be so long;
Yet will she blush, here be it said,
To hear her secrets so bewray'd.

20

Live with me, and be my love,
And we will all the pleasures prove
That hills and valleys, dales and fields,
And all the craggy mountains yields.

There will we sit upon the rocks, 5
And see the shepherds feed their flocks,
By shallow rivers, by whose falls
Melodious birds sing madrigals.

There will I make thee a bed of roses,
With a thousand fragrant posies, 10
A cap of flowers and a kirtle
Embroider'd all with leaves of myrtle.

A belt of straw and ivy buds,
With coral clasps and amber studs;
And if these pleasures may thee move, 15
Then live with me and be my love.

LOVE'S ANSWER.

If that the world and love were young,
And truth in every shepherd's tongue,
These pretty pleasures might me move
To live with thee and be thy love. 20

21

As it fell upon a day
In the merry month of May,
Sitting in a pleasant shade
Which a grove of myrtles made,
Beasts did leap and birds did sing, 5
Trees did grow and plants did spring;
Every thing did banish moan,
Save the nightingale alone;
She, poor bird, as all forlorn,
Lean'd her breast up-till a thorn, 10
And there sung the dolefull'st ditty,
That to hear it was great pity;
'Fie, fie, fie,' now would she cry;
'Tereu, tereu!' by and by;
That to hear her so complain, 15
Scarce I could from tears refrain;
For her griefs so lively shown
Made me think upon mine own.
Ah, thought I, thou mourn'st in vain!
None takes pity on thy pain; 20
Senseless trees they cannot hear thee;
Ruthless beasts they will not cheer thee;
King Pandion he is dead;
All thy friends are lapp'd in lead;
All thy fellow birds do sing, 25
Careless of thy sorrowing.
Even so, poor bird, like thee,
None alive will pity me.
Whilst as fickle Fortune smiled,
Thou and I were both beguiled. 30
Every one that flatters thee
Is no friend in misery.
Words are easy, like the wind;
Faithful friends are hard to find;
Every man will be thy friend 35
Whilst thou hast wherewith to spend;
But if store of crowns be scant,
No man will supply thy want.
If that one be prodigal,
Bountiful they will him call, 40
And with such-like flattering,
'Pity but he were a king;'
If he be addict to vice,
Quickly him they will entice;
If to women he be bent, 45
They have at commandment;
But if Fortune once do frown,
Then farewell his great renown;
They that fawn'd on him before
Use his company no more. 50

He that is thy friend indeed,
He will help thee in thy need;
If thou sorrow, he will weep;
If thou wake, he cannot sleep;

Thus of every grief in heart   55
He with thee doth bear a part.
These are certain signs to know
Faithful friend from flattering foe.

THE PHŒNIX AND TURTLE

LET the bird of loudest lay,
On the sole Arabian tree,
Herald sad and trumpet be,
To whose sound chaste wings obey.

But thou shrieking harbinger,   5
Foul precurrer of the fiend,
Augur of the fever's end,
To this troop come thou not near!

From this session interdict
Every fowl of tyrant wing,   10
Save the eagle, feather'd king;
Keep the obsequy so strict.

Let the priest in surplice white,
That defunctive music can,
Be the death-divining swan,   15
Lest the requiem lack his right.

And thou treble-dated crow,
That thy sable gender makest
With the breath thou givest and takest,
'Mongst our mourners shalt thou go.   20

Here the anthem doth commence:
Love and constancy is dead;
Phœnix and the turtle fled
In a mutual flame from hence.

So they loved, as love in twain   25
Had the essence but in one;
Two distincts, division none;
Number there in love was slain.

Hearts remote, yet not asunder;
Distance, and no space was seen   30
'Twixt the turtle and his queen;
But in them it were a wonder.

So between them love did shine,
That the turtle saw his right

Flaming in the phœnix' sight;   35
Either was the other's mine.

Property was thus appalled,
That the self was not the same;
Single nature's double name
Neither two nor one was called.   40

Reason, in itself confounded,
Saw division grow together,
To themselves yet either neither,
Simple were so well compounded;

That it cried, How true a twain   45
Seemeth this concordant one!
Love hath reason, reason none,
If what parts can so remain.

Whereupon it made this threne
To the phœnix and the dove,   50
Co-supremes and stars of love,
As chorus to their tragic scene.

THRENOS.

Beauty, truth, and rarity,
Grace in all simplicity,
Here enclosed in cinders lie.   55

Death is now the phœnix' nest;
And the turtle's loyal breast
To eternity doth rest,

Leaving no posterity;
'Twas not their infirmity,   60
It was married chastity.

Truth may seem, but cannot be
Beauty brag, but 'tis not she;
Truth and beauty buried be.

To this urn let those repair   65
That are either true or fair;
For these dead birds sigh a prayer.

THE END.

www.ingramcontent.com/pod-product-compliance
Lightning Source LLC
Chambersburg PA
CBHW020544300426
44111CB00008B/789